PRENTICE HALL

WORLD STUDIES

EASTERN HEMISPHERE

Geography • History • Culture

In association with DK

Discovery Channel School

PEARSON
Prentice Hall

Boston, Massachusetts
Upper Saddle River, New Jersey

Program Consultants

Heidi Hayes Jacobs

Heidi Hayes Jacobs has served as an education consultant to more than 1,000 schools across the nation and abroad. Dr. Jacobs serves as an adjunct professor in the Department of Curriculum on Teaching at Teachers College, Columbia University. She has written two best-selling books and numerous articles on curriculum reform. She received an M.A. from the University of Massachusetts, Amherst, and completed her doctoral work at Columbia University's Teachers College in 1981. The core of Dr. Jacobs's experience comes from her years teaching high school, middle school, and elementary school students. As an educational consultant, she works with K–12 schools and districts on curriculum reform and strategic planning.

Michal L. LeVasseur

Michal LeVasseur is the Executive Director of the National Council for Geography Education. She is an instructor in the College of Education at Jacksonville State University and works with the Alabama Geographic Alliance. Her undergraduate and graduate work were in the fields of anthropology (B.A.), geography (M.A.), and science education (Ph.D.). Dr. LeVasseur's specialization has moved increasingly into the area of geography education. Since 1996 she has served as the Director of the National Geographic Society's Summer Geography Workshops. As an educational consultant, she has worked with the National Geographic Society as well as with schools and organizations to develop programs and curricula for geography.

Senior Reading Consultants

Kate Kinsella

Kate Kinsella, Ed.D., is a faculty member in the Department of Secondary Education at San Francisco State University. A specialist in second-language acquisition and adolescent literacy, she teaches coursework addressing language and literacy development across the secondary curricula. Dr. Kinsella earned her M.A. in TESOL from San Francisco State University, and her Ed.D. in Second Language Acquisition from the University of San Francisco.

Kevin Feldman

Kevin Feldman, Ed.D., is the Director of Reading and Early Intervention with the Sonoma County Office of Education (SCOE) and an independent educational consultant. At the SCOE, he develops, organizes, and monitors programs related to K–12 literacy. Dr. Feldman has an M.A. from the University of California, Riverside in Special Education, Learning Disabilities and Instructional Design. He earned his Ed.D. in Curriculum and Instruction from the University of San Francisco.

Acknowledgments appear on page 888, which constitutes an extension of this copyright page.

Prentice Hall World Studies is published in collaboration with DK Designs, Dorling Kindersley Limited, 80 Strand, London WC2R ORL. A Penguin Company.

ISBN 0-13-181659-4
45678910 10 09 08 07 06

Cartography Consultant

DK Andrew Heritage

Andrew Heritage has been publishing atlases and maps for some 25 years. In 1991, he joined the leading illustrated nonfiction publisher Dorling Kindersley (DK) with the task of building an international atlas list from scratch. The DK atlas list now includes some 10 titles, which are constantly updated and appear in new editions either annually or every other year.

Academic Reviewers

Africa
Barbara B. Brown, Ph.D.
African Studies Center
Boston University
Boston, Massachusetts

Ancient World
Evelyn DeLong Mangie, Ph.D.
Department of History
University of South Florida
Tampa, Florida

Central Asia and the Middle East
Pamela G. Sayre
History Department,
Social Sciences Division
Henry Ford Community College
Dearborn, Michigan

East Asia
Huping Ling, Ph.D.
History Department
Truman State University
Kirksville, Missouri

Eastern Europe
Robert M. Jenkins
Center for Slavic, Eurasian and
East European Studies
University of North Carolina
Chapel Hill, North Carolina

Latin America
Dan La Botz
Professor, History Department
Miami University
Oxford, Ohio

Medieval Times
James M. Murray
History Department
University of Cincinnati
Cincinnati, Ohio

North Africa
Barbara E. Petzen
Center for Middle Eastern Studies
Harvard University
Cambridge, Massachusetts

Religion
Charles H. Lippy, Ph.D.
Department of Philosophy
and Religion
University of Tennessee
at Chattanooga
Chattanooga, Tennessee

Russia
Janet Vaillant
Davis Center for Russian
and Eurasian Studies
Harvard University
Cambridge, Massachusetts

South Asia
Robert J. Young
Professor Emeritus
History Department
West Chester University
West Chester, Pennsylvania

United States and Canada
Victoria Randlett
Geography Department
University of Nevada, Reno
Reno, Nevada

Western Europe
Ruth Mitchell-Pitts
Center for European Studies
University of North Carolina
at Chapel Hill
Chapel Hill, North Carolina

Reviewers

Sean Brennan
Brecksville-Broadview Heights
City School District
Broadview Heights, Ohio

Stephen Bullick
Mt. Lebanon School District
Pittsburgh, Pennsylvania

William R. Cranshaw, Ed.D.
Waycross Middle School
Waycross, Georgia

Dr. Louis P. De Angelo
Archdiocese of Philadelphia
Philadelphia, Pennsylvania

Paul Francis Durietz
Social Studies
Curriculum Coordinator
Woodland District #50
Gurnee, Illinois

Gail Dwyer
Dickerson Middle School,
Cobb County
Marietta, Georgia

Michal Howden
Social Studies Consultant
Zionsville, Indiana

Rosemary Kalloch
Springfield Public Schools
Springfield, Massachusetts

Deborah J. Miller
Office of Social Studies,
Detroit Public Schools
Detroit, Michigan

Steven P. Missal
Newark Public Schools
Newark, New Jersey

Catherine Fish Petersen (Retired)
East Islip School District
Islip Terrace, New York

Joe Wieczorek
Social Studies Consultant
Baltimore, Maryland

EASTERN HEMISPHERE

Develop Skills

Use these pages to develop your reading, writing, and geography skills.

Focus on Geography

Learn the basic tools and concepts of geography.

Build a Regional Background

Learn about the geography, history, and culture of Europe and Russia.

Focus on Countries

Create an understanding of the region by focusing on specific countries.

Build a Regional Background

Learn about the geography, history, and culture of Africa.

Focus on Countries

Create an understanding of Africa by focusing on specific countries.

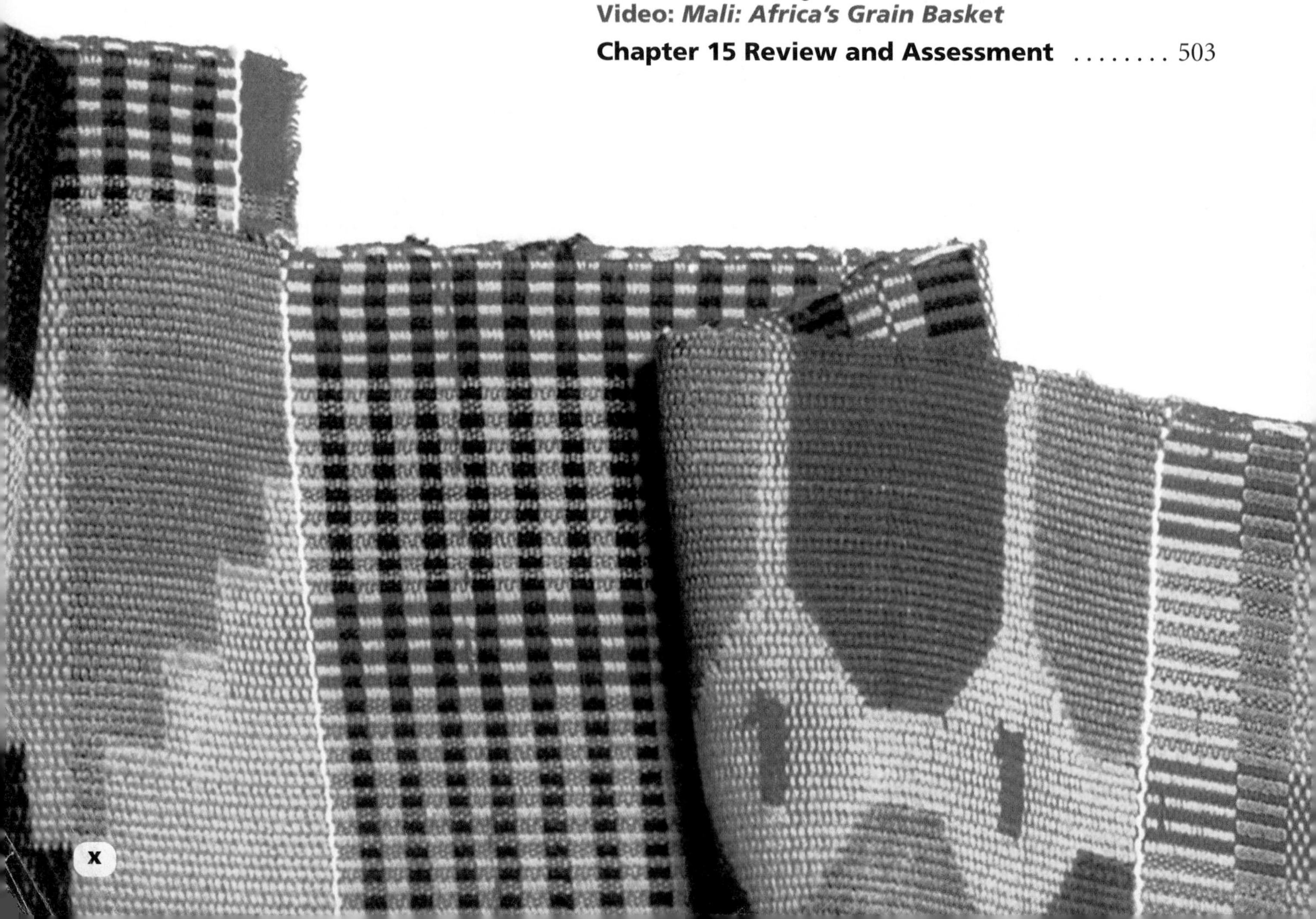

Build a Regional Background

Learn about the geography, history, and culture of Asia and the Pacific.

Focus on Countries

Create an understanding of Asia and the Pacific by focusing on specific countries.

- Learn map skills with the MapMaster Skills Handbook.
- Practice your skills with every map in this book.
- Interact with every map online and on CD-ROM.

Maps and illustrations created by DK help build your understanding of the world. The DK World Desk Reference Online keeps you up to date.

Discovery Channel School
Video/DVD

The World Studies Video Program takes you on field trips to study countries around the world.

The *World Studies* Interactive Textbook online and on CD-ROM uses interactive maps and other activities to help you learn.

Special Features

Read about Russia and all the countries that make up Europe.

COUNTRY DATABANK

Read about all the countries that make up Africa.

Read about all the countries that make up Asia and the Pacific.

Theme-based maps and charts provide a closer look at countries, regions, and provinces.

Links

See the fascinating links between social studies and other disciplines.

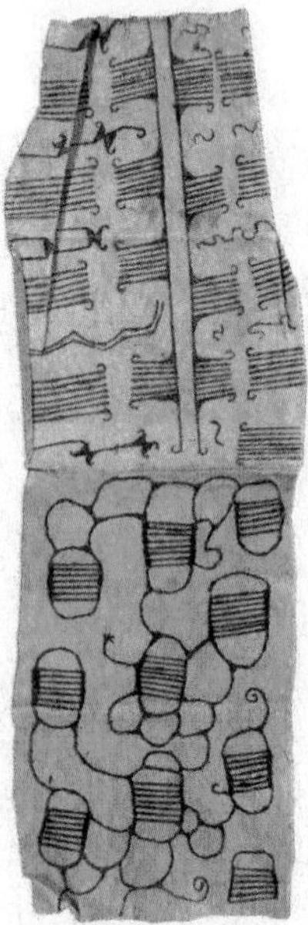

Eyewitness Technology

Detailed drawings show how technology shapes places and societies.

DIAGRAPHICS

Investigate geographic concepts using diagrams, maps, and photographs.

Skills for Life

Learn skills that you will use throughout your life.

Literature

Selections by noted authors bring social studies to life.

Target Reading Skills

Chapter-by-chapter reading skills help you read and understand social studies concepts.

Citizen Heroes

Meet people who have made a difference in their country.

Video/DVD

Explore the geography, history, and cultures of the countries of Europe, Africa, Asia, and the Pacific.

Maps and Charts

MAP MASTER™

Atlas

MAPMASTER™ Interactive

Go online to find an interactive of every MapMaster™ map in this book. Use the Web Code provided to gain direct access to these maps.

How to Use Web Codes:

1. **Go to www.PHSchool.com.**
2. Enter the Web Code.
3. Click Go!

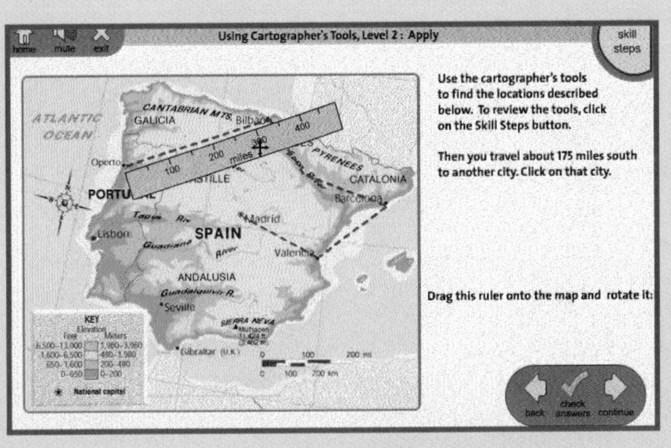

Charts, Graphs, and Tables

Building Geographic Literacy

Learning about a country often starts with finding it on a map. The MapMaster™ system in *World Studies* helps you develop map skills you will use throughout your life. These three steps can help you become a MapMaster!

The MAPMASTER™ System

1 Learn

You need to learn geography tools and concepts before you explore the world. Get started by using the MapMaster Skills Handbook to learn the skills you need for success.

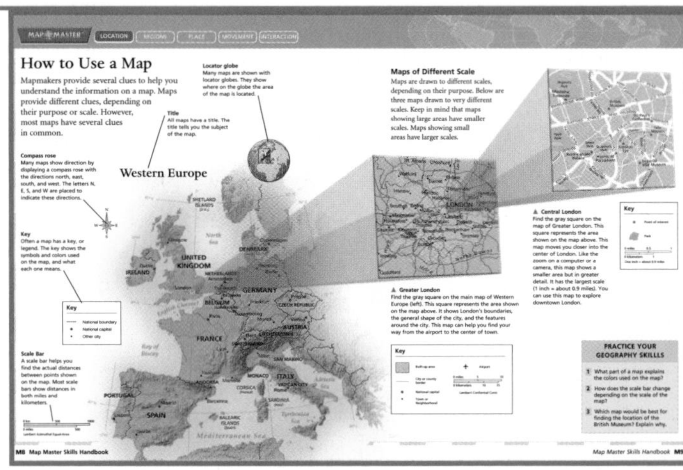

MAPMASTER™ Skills Activity

Location The Equator runs through parts of Latin America, but it is far from other parts of the region.
Locate Find the Equator on the map. Which climates are most common in Latin America, and how far is each climate region from the Equator?
Draw Conclusions How do climates change as you move away from the Equator?

Go Online
PHSchool.com Use Web Code **lfp-1142** for step-by-step **map skills practice.**

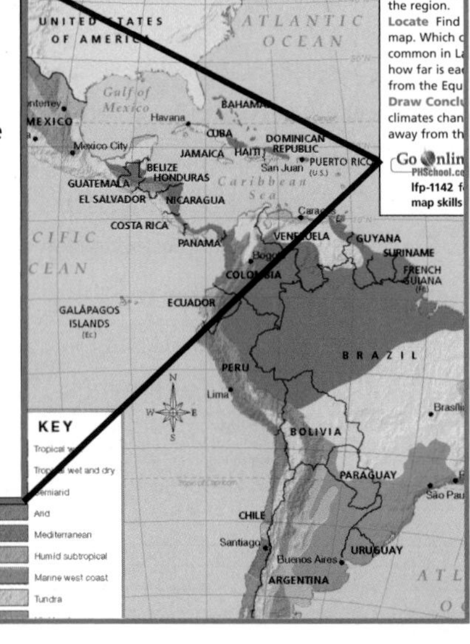

2 Practice

You need to practice and apply your geography skills frequently to be a MapMaster. The maps in *World Studies* give you the practice you need to develop geographic literacy.

3 Interact

Using maps is more than just finding places. Maps can teach you many things about a region, such as its climate, its vegetation, and the languages that the people who live there speak. Every MapMaster map is online at **PHSchool.com,** with interactive activities to help you learn the most from every map.

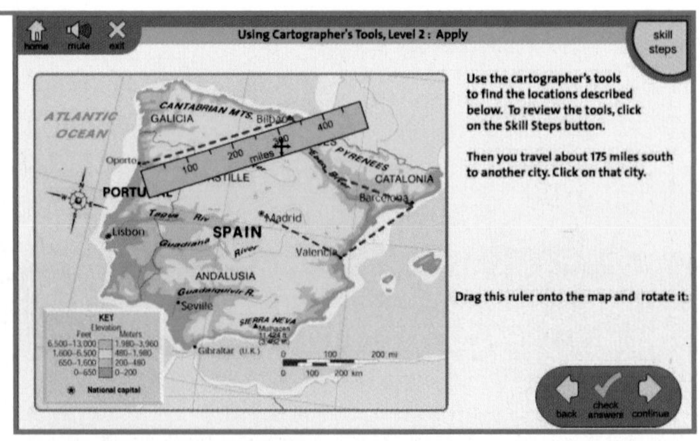

Learning With Technology

You will be making many exciting journeys across time and place in *World Studies*. Technology will help make what you learn come alive in your classroom.

World Studies Video Program

You are going to learn about many new people and places and thousands of years of history. The World Studies Video Program created by our partner, Discovery Channel School, will bring this new information to life. Look for the video reference in every chapter!

Discovery Channel School
Video
Learn about the geographic features of Africa.

For a complete list of features for this book, use Web Code **lfk-1000.**

For: An activity on Central Asia
Visit: PHSchool.com
Web Code: lcd-6203

Go Online at PHSchool.com

Use the Web Code in each Go Online box to access exciting information or activities at **PHSchool.com.**

How to Use the Web Code:

1. Go to **www.PHSchool.com.**
2. Enter the Web Code.
3. Click Go!

Interactive Textbook

The *World Studies* Interactive Textbook brings your textbook to life. Learn about the world, using interactive maps and other activities. Define and understand vocabulary words at the click of a mouse.

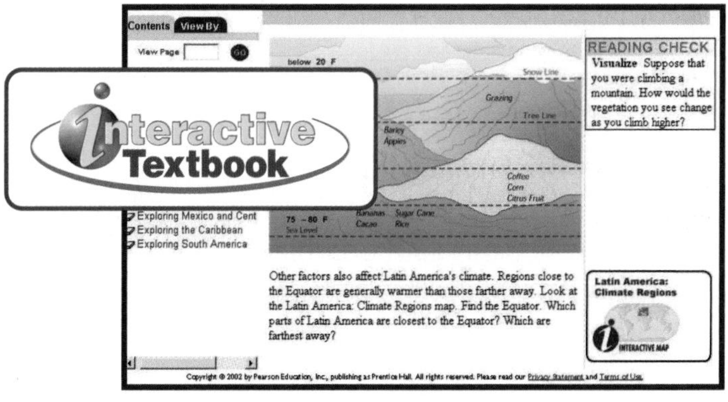

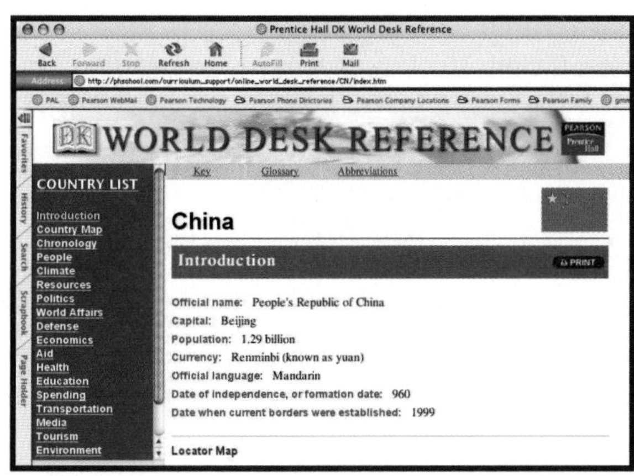

World Desk Reference Online

There are more than 190 countries in the world. To learn about them, you need the most up-to-date information and statistics. The **DK World Desk Reference Online** gives you instant access to the information you need to explore each country.

Reading Informational Texts

Reading a magazine, an Internet page, or a textbook is not the same as reading a novel. The purpose of reading nonfiction texts is to acquire new information. On page M18 you'll read about some Target Reading Skills that you'll have a chance to practice as you read this textbook. Here we'll focus on a few skills that will help you read nonfiction with a more critical eye.

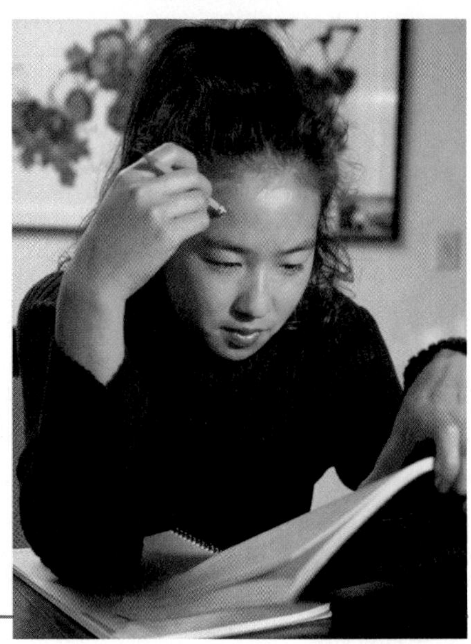

Analyze the Author's Purpose

Different types of materials are written with different purposes in mind. For example, a textbook is written to teach students information about a subject. The purpose of a technical manual is to teach someone how to use something, such as a computer. A newspaper editorial might be written to persuade the reader to accept a particular point of view. A writer's purpose influences how the material is presented. Sometimes an author states his or her purpose directly. More often, the purpose is only suggested, and you must use clues to identify the author's purpose.

Distinguish Between Facts and Opinions

It's important when reading informational texts to read actively and to distinguish between fact and opinion. A fact can be proven or disproven. An opinion cannot—it is someone's personal viewpoint or evaluation.

For example, the editorial pages in a newspaper offer opinions on topics that are currently in the news. You need to read newspaper editorials with an eye for bias and faulty logic. For example, the newspaper editorial at the right shows factual statements in blue and opinion statements in red. The underlined words are examples of highly charged words. They reveal bias on the part of the writer.

More than 5,000 people voted last week in favor of building a new shopping center, but the opposition won out. The margin of victory is irrelevant. Those radical voters who opposed the center are obviously self-serving elitists who do not care about anyone but themselves.

This month's unemployment figure for our area is 10 percent, which represents an increase of about 5 percent over the figure for this time last year. These figures mean unemployment is getting worse. But the people who voted against the mall probably do not care about creating new jobs.

Identify Evidence

Before you accept an author's conclusion, you need to make sure that the author has based the conclusion on enough evidence and on the right kind of evidence. An author may present a series of facts to support a claim, but the facts may not tell the whole story. For example, what evidence does the author of the newspaper editorial on the previous page provide to support his claim that the new shopping center would create more jobs? Is it possible that the shopping center might have put many small local businesses out of business, thus increasing unemployment rather than decreasing it?

Evaluate Credibility

Whenever you read informational texts, you need to assess the credibility of the author. This is especially true of sites you may visit on the Internet. All Internet sources are not equally reliable. Here are some questions to ask yourself when evaluating the credibility of a Web site.

- ❑ Is the Web site created by a respected organization, a discussion group, or an individual?
- ❑ Does the Web site creator include his or her name as well as credentials and the sources he or she used to write the material?
- ❑ Is the information on the site balanced or biased?
- ❑ Can you verify the information using two other sources?
- ❑ Is there a date telling when the Web site was created or last updated?

Writing for Social Studies

Writing is one of the most powerful communication tools you will ever use. You will use it to share your thoughts and ideas with others. Research shows that writing about what you read actually helps you learn new information and ideas. A systematic approach to writing—including prewriting, drafting, revising, and proofing—can help you write better, whether you're writing an essay or a research report.

Narrative Essays

Writing that tells a story about a personal experience

1 Select and Narrow Your Topic

A narrative is a story. In social studies, it might be a narrative essay about how an event affected you or your family.

2 Gather Details

Brainstorm a list of details you'd like to include in your narrative.

3 Write a First Draft

Start by writing a simple opening sentence that conveys the main idea of your essay. Continue by writing a colorful story that has interesting details. Write a conclusion that sums up the significance of the event or situation described in your essay.

4 Revise and Proofread

Check to make sure you have not begun too many sentences with the word *I*. Replace general words with more colorful ones.

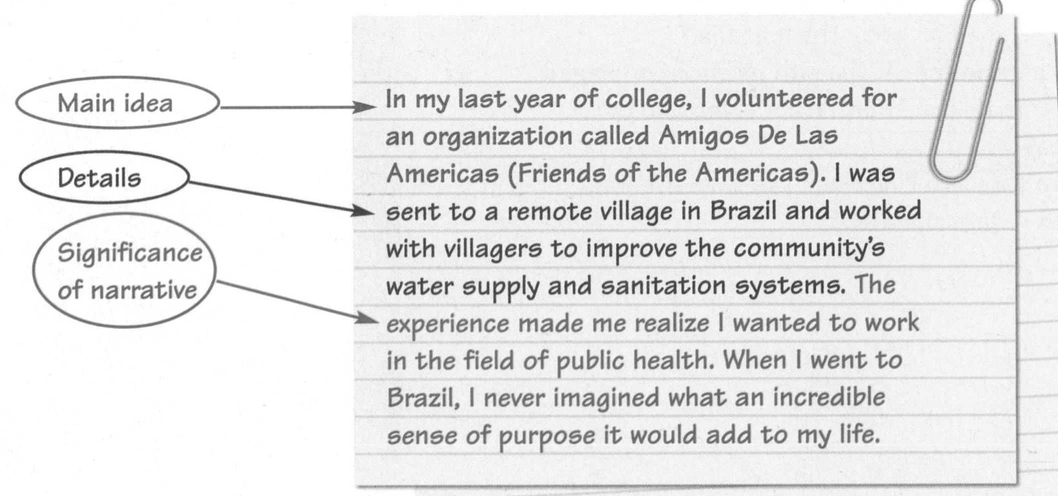

Main idea
Details
Significance of narrative
In my last year of college, I volunteered for an organization called Amigos De Las Americas (Friends of the Americas). I was sent to a remote village in Brazil and worked with villagers to improve the community's water supply and sanitation systems. The experience made me realize I wanted to work in the field of public health. When I went to Brazil, I never imagined what an incredible sense of purpose it would add to my life.

Persuasive Essays

Writing that supports an opinion or position

1 Select and Narrow Your Topic

Choose a topic that provokes an argument and has at least two sides. Choose a side. Decide which argument will appeal most to your audience and persuade them to understand your point of view.

2 Gather Evidence

Create a chart that states your position at the top and then lists the pros and cons for your position below, in two columns. Predict and address the strongest arguments against your stand.

3 Write a First Draft

Write a strong thesis statement that clearly states your position. Continue by presenting the strongest arguments in favor of your position and acknowledging and refuting opposing arguments.

4 Revise and Proofread

Check to make sure you have made a logical argument and that you have not oversimplified the argument.

Main Idea → It is vital to vote in elections.

Supporting (pro) argument → When people vote, they tell public officials how to run the government.

Opposing (con) argument → Not every proposal is carried out; however, politicians do their best to listen to what the majority of people want.

Transition words → Therefore, every vote is important.

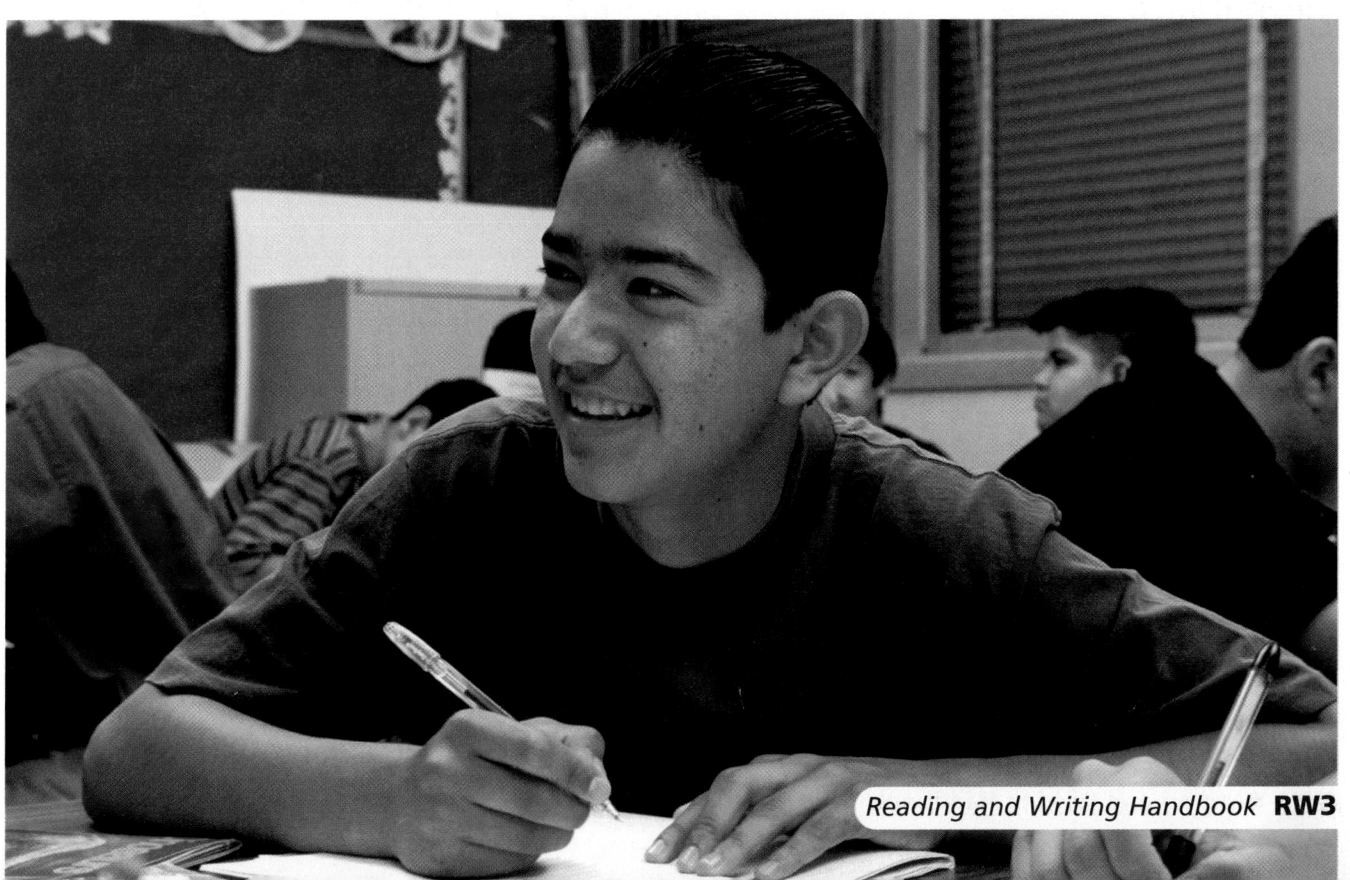

Expository Essays

Writing that explains a process, compares and contrasts, explains causes and effects, or explores solutions to a problem

1 Identify and Narrow Your Topic

Expository writing is writing that explains something in detail. It might explain the similarities and differences between two or more subjects (compare and contrast). It might explain how one event causes another (cause and effect). Or it might explain a problem and describe a solution.

2 Gather Evidence

Create a graphic organizer that identifies details to include in your essay.

Cause 1	Cause 2	Cause 3
Most people in the Mexican countryside work on farms.	The population in Mexico is growing at one of the highest rates in the world.	There is not enough farm work for so many people.

Effect
As a result, many rural families are moving from the countryside to live in Mexico City.

3 Write Your First Draft

Write a topic sentence and then organize the essay around your similarities and differences, causes and effects, or problem and solutions. Be sure to include convincing details, facts, and examples.

4 Revise and Proofread

Research Papers

Writing that presents research about a topic

1 Narrow Your Topic

Choose a topic you're interested in and make sure that it is not too broad. For example, instead of writing a report on Panama, write about the construction of the Panama Canal.

2 Acquire Information

Locate several sources of information about the topic from the library or the Internet. For each resource, create a source index card like the one at the right. Then take notes using an index card for each detail or subtopic. On the card, note which source the information was taken from. Use quotation marks when you copy the exact words from a source.

Source #1
McCullough, David. *The Path Between the Seas: The Creation of the Panama Canal, 1870-1914.* N.Y., Simon and Schuster, 1977.

3 Make an Outline

Use an outline to decide how to organize your report. Sort your index cards into the same order.

Outline
I. Introduction
II. Why the canal was built
III. How the canal was built
  A. Physical challenges
  B. Medical challenges
IV. Conclusion

Introduction

Building the Panama Canal

Ever since Christopher Columbus first explored the Isthmus of Panama, the Spanish had been looking for a water route through it. They wanted to be able to sail west from Spain to Asia without sailing around South America. However, it was not until 1914 that the dream became a reality.

Conclusion

It took eight years and more than 70,000 workers to build the Panama Canal. It remains one of the greatest engineering feats of modern times.

4 Write a First Draft

Write an introduction, a body, and a conclusion. Leave plenty of space between lines so you can go back and add details that you may have left out.

5 Revise and Proofread

Be sure to include transition words between sentences and paragraphs. Here are some examples:

To show a contrast—*however, although, despite.*

To point out a reason—*since, because, if.*

To signal a conclusion—*therefore, consequently, so, then.*

Evaluating Your Writing

Use this table to help you evaluate your writing.

	Excellent	Good	Acceptable	Unacceptable
Purpose	Achieves purpose—to inform, persuade, or provide historical interpretation—very well	Informs, persuades, or provides historical interpretation reasonably well	Reader cannot easily tell if the purpose is to inform, persuade, or provide historical interpretation	Purpose is not clear
Organization	Develops ideas in a very clear and logical way	Presents ideas in a reasonably well-organized way	Reader has difficulty following the organization	Lacks organization
Elaboration	Explains all ideas with facts and details	Explains most ideas with facts and details	Includes some supporting facts and details	Lacks supporting details
Use of Language	Uses excellent vocabulary and sentence structure with no errors in spelling, grammar, or punctuation	Uses good vocabulary and sentence structure with very few errors in spelling, grammar, or punctuation	Includes some errors in grammar, punctuation, and spelling	Includes many errors in grammar, punctuation, and spelling

CONTENTS

Use Web Code **lap-0000** for all of the maps in this handbook.

Five Themes of Geography

Studying the geography of the entire world is a huge task. You can make that task easier by using the five themes of geography: location, regions, place, movement, and human-environment interaction. The themes are tools you can use to organize information and to answer the where, why, and how of geography.

▲ **Location**
This museum in England has a line running through it. The line marks its location at 0° longitude.

LOCATION

1 Location answers the question, "Where is it?" You can think of the location of a continent or a country as its address. You might give an absolute location such as 22 South Lake Street or 40° N and 80° W. You might also use a relative address, telling where one place is by referring to another place. *Between school and the mall* and *eight miles east of Pleasant City* are examples of relative locations.

REGIONS

2 Regions are areas that share at least one common feature. Geographers divide the world into many types of regions. For example, countries, states, and cities are political regions. The people in any one of these places live under the same government. Other features, such as climate and culture, can be used to define regions. Therefore the same place can be found in more than one region. For example, the state of Hawaii is in the political region of the United States. Because it has a tropical climate, Hawaii is also part of a tropical climate region.

MOVEMENT

4 Movement answers the question, "How do people, goods, and ideas move from place to place?" Remember that what happens in one place often affects what happens in another. Use the theme of movement to help you trace the spread of goods, people, and ideas from one location to another.

PLACE

3 Place identifies the natural and human features that make one place different from every other place. You can identify a specific place by its landforms, climate, plants, animals, people, language, or culture. You might even think of place as a geographic signature. Use the signature to help you understand the natural and human features that make one place different from every other place.

INTERACTION

5 Human-environment interaction focuses on the relationship between people and the environment. As people live in an area, they often begin to make changes to it, usually to make their lives easier. For example, they might build a dam to control flooding during rainy seasons. Also, the environment can affect how people live, work, dress, travel, and communicate.

◀ **Interaction**
These Congolese women interact with their environment by gathering wood for cooking.

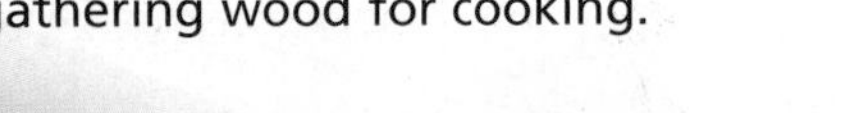

PRACTICE YOUR GEOGRAPHY SKILLS

1 Describe your town or city, using each of the five themes of geography.

2 Name at least one thing that comes into your town or city and one that goes out. How is each moved? Where does it come from? Where does it go?

Understanding Movements of Earth

The planet Earth is part of our solar system. Earth revolves around the sun in a nearly circular path called an orbit. A revolution, or one complete orbit around the sun, takes 365¼ days, or one year. As Earth orbits the sun, it also spins on its axis, an invisible line through the center of Earth from the North Pole to the South Pole. This movement is called a rotation.

▼ **Spring begins**
On March 20 or 21, the sun is directly overhead at the Equator. The Northern and Southern Hemispheres receive almost equal hours of sunlight and darkness.

How Night Changes Into Day

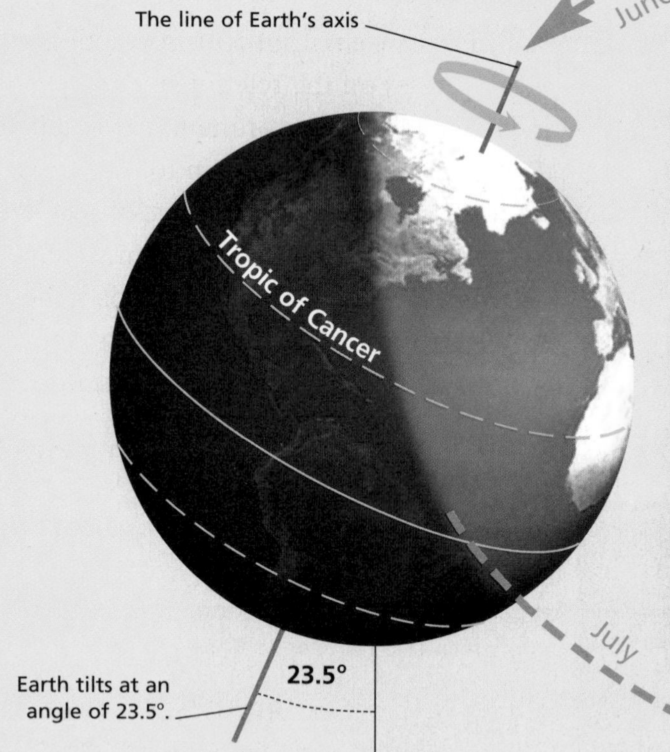

Earth takes about 24 hours to make one full rotation on its axis. As Earth rotates, it is daytime on the side facing the sun. It is night on the side away from the sun.

◀ **Summer begins**
On June 21 or 22, the sun is directly overhead at the Tropic of Cancer. The Northern Hemisphere receives the greatest number of sunlight hours.

The Seasons

Earth's axis is tilted at an angle. Because of this tilt, sunlight strikes different parts of Earth at different times in the year, creating seasons. The illustration below shows how the seasons are created in the Northern Hemisphere. In the Southern Hemisphere, the seasons are reversed.

PRACTICE YOUR GEOGRAPHY SKILLS

1. What causes the seasons in the Northern Hemisphere to be the opposite of those in the Southern Hemisphere?
2. During which two days of the year do the Northern Hemisphere and Southern Hemisphere have equal hours of daylight and darkness?

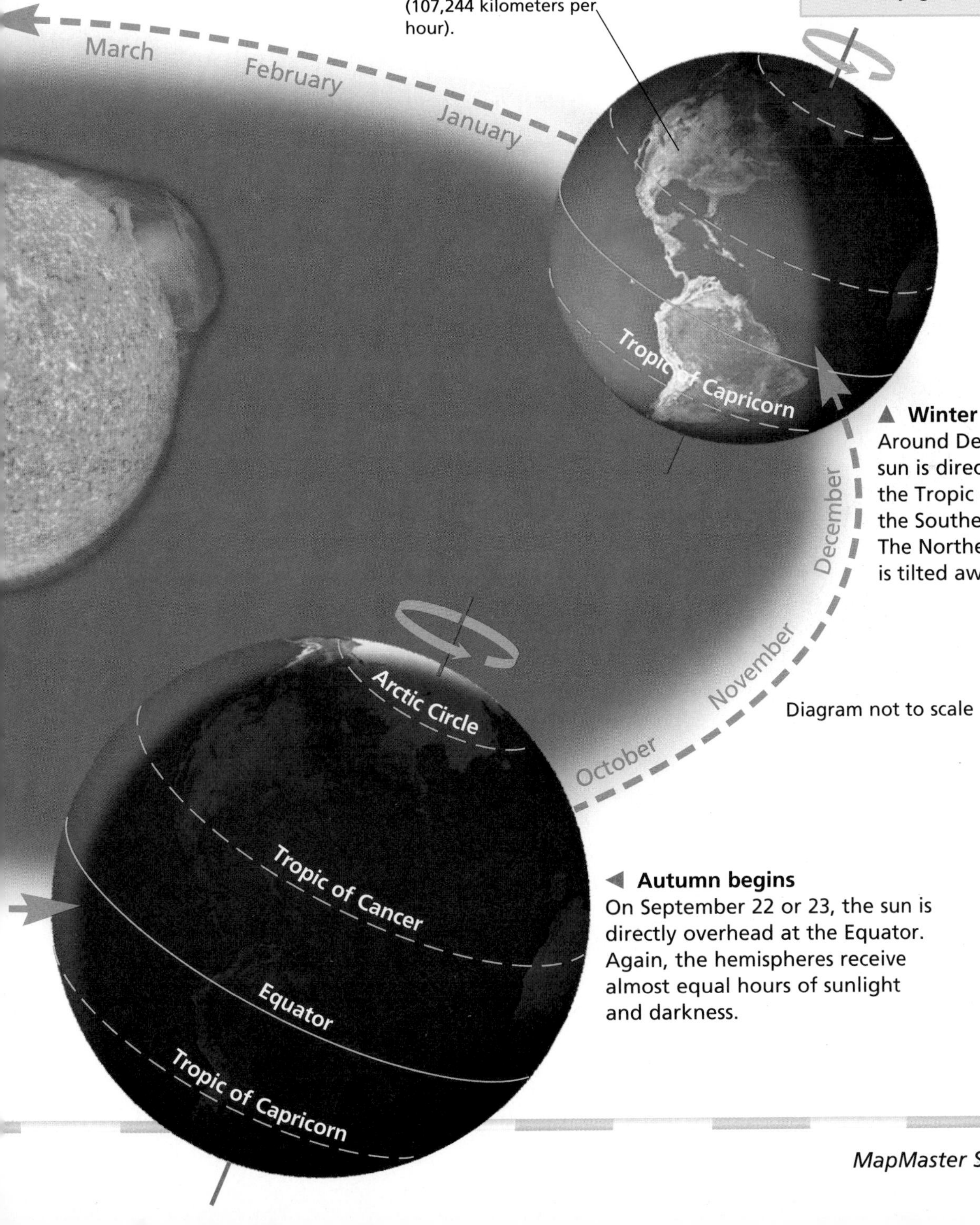

▲ **Winter begins**
Around December 21, the sun is directly overhead at the Tropic of Capricorn in the Southern Hemisphere. The Northern Hemisphere is tilted away from the sun.

◄ **Autumn begins**
On September 22 or 23, the sun is directly overhead at the Equator. Again, the hemispheres receive almost equal hours of sunlight and darkness.

Understanding Globes

A globe is a scale model of Earth. It shows the actual shapes, sizes, and locations of all Earth's landmasses and bodies of water. Features on the surface of Earth are drawn to scale on a globe. This means that a small unit of measure on the globe stands for a large unit of measure on Earth.

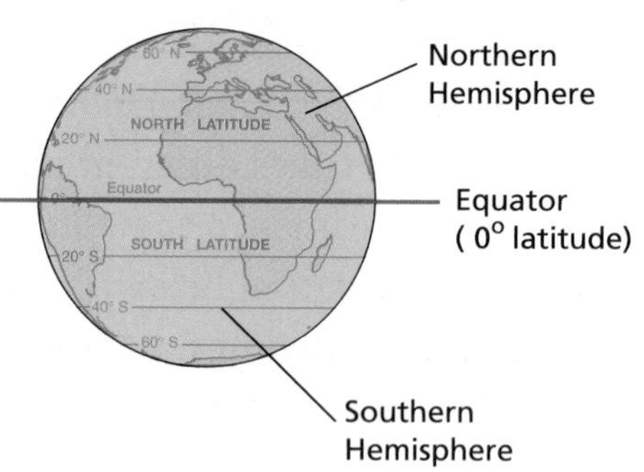

Parallels of Latitude

Geographers divide the globe along imaginary horizontal lines called parallels of latitude. One of these latitude lines is the Equator, located halfway between the North and South Poles. Parallels of latitude are measured in degrees (°). One degree of latitude represents a distance of about 69 miles (111 kilometers).

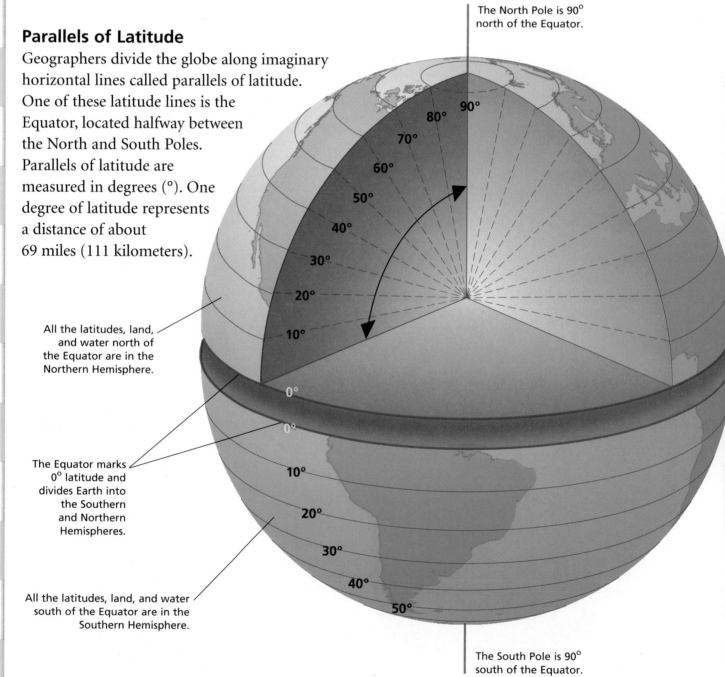

The North Pole is 90° north of the Equator.

All the latitudes, land, and water north of the Equator are in the Northern Hemisphere.

The Equator marks 0° latitude and divides Earth into the Southern and Northern Hemispheres.

All the latitudes, land, and water south of the Equator are in the Southern Hemisphere.

The South Pole is 90° south of the Equator.

Meridians of Longitude

Geographers also divide the globe along imaginary vertical lines called meridians of longitude, which are measured in degrees (°). The longitude line called the Prime Meridian runs from pole to pole through Greenwich, England. All meridians of longitude come together at the North and South Poles.

PRACTICE YOUR GEOGRAPHY SKILLS

1. Which continents lie completely in the Northern Hemisphere? In the Western Hemisphere?
2. Is there land or water at 20° S latitude and the Prime Meridian? At the Equator and 60° W longitude?

All the longitudes, land, and water west of the Prime Meridian are in the Western Hemisphere.

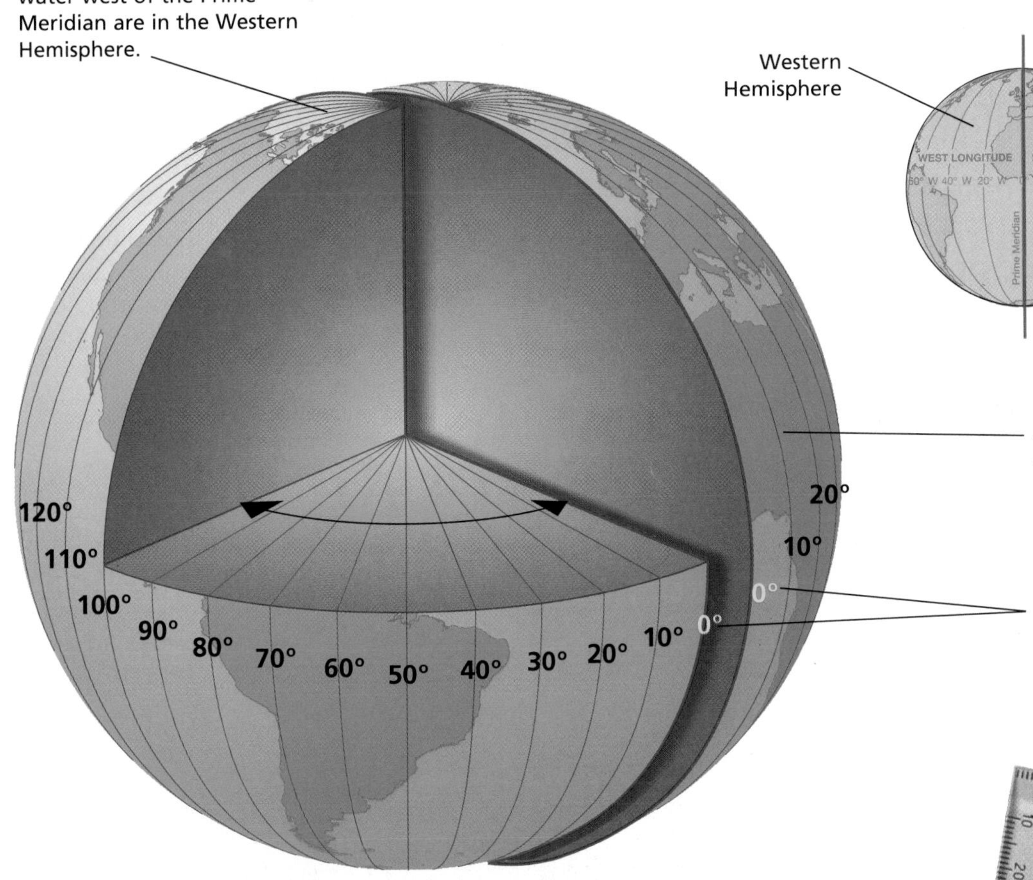

Western Hemisphere

WEST LONGITUDE
EAST LONGITUDE
60° W 40° W 20° W
20° E 40° E 60° E
Prime Meridian

Eastern Hemisphere

Prime Meridian (0° longitude)

All the longitudes, land, and water east of the Prime Meridian are in the Eastern Hemisphere.

The Prime Meridian marks 0° longitude and divides the globe into the Eastern and Western Hemispheres.

The Global Grid

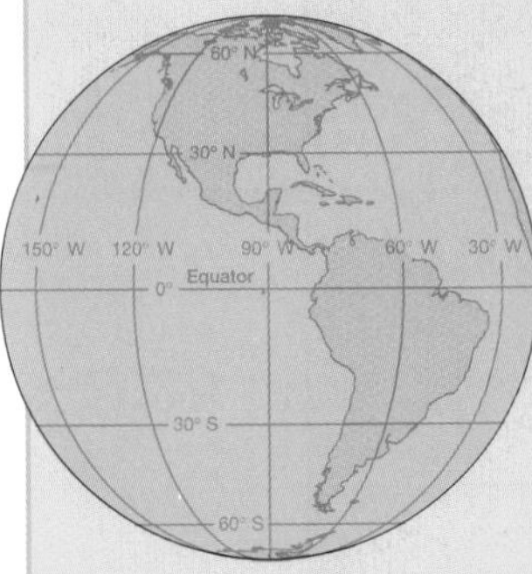

Together, the pattern of parallels of latitude and meridians of longitude is called the global grid. Using the lines of latitude and longitude, you can locate any place on Earth. For example, the location of 30° north latitude and 90° west longitude is usually written as 30° N, 90° W. Only one place on Earth has these coordinates—the city of New Orleans, in the state of Louisiana.

▲ **Compass**
Wherever you are on Earth, a compass can be used to show direction.

Map Projections

Maps are drawings that show regions on flat surfaces. Maps are easier to use and carry than globes, but they cannot show the correct size and shape of every feature on Earth's curved surface. They must shrink some places and stretch others. To make up for this distortion, mapmakers use different map projections. No one projection can accurately show the correct area, shape, distance, and direction for all of Earth's surface. Mapmakers use the projection that has the least distortion for the information they are presenting.

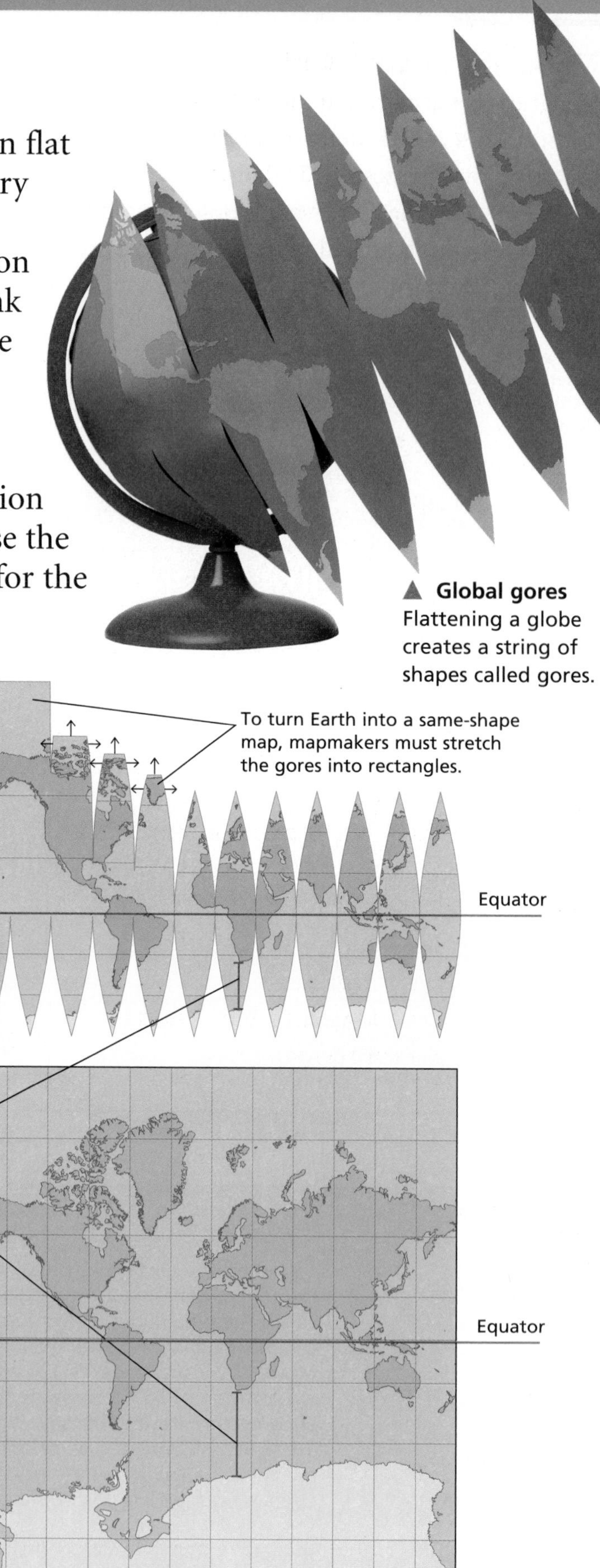

To turn Earth into a same-shape map, mapmakers must stretch the gores into rectangles.
Equator
Stretching the gores makes parts of Earth larger. This enlargement becomes greater toward the North and South Poles.
Equator

▲ **Global gores**
Flattening a globe creates a string of shapes called gores.

Same-Shape Maps

Map projections that accurately show the shapes of landmasses are called same-shape maps. However, these projections often greatly distort, or make less accurate, the size of landmasses as well as the distance between them. In the projection below, the northern and southern areas of the globe appear more stretched than the areas near the Equator.

Mercator projection ▶
One of the most common same-shape maps is the Mercator projection, named for the mapmaker who invented it. The Mercator projection accurately shows shape and direction, but it distorts distance and size. Because the projection shows true directions, ships' navigators use it to chart a straight-line course between two ports.

Equal-Area Maps

Map projections that show the correct size of landmasses are called equal-area maps. In order to show the correct size of landmasses, these maps usually distort shapes. The distortion is usually greater at the edges of the map and less at the center.

PRACTICE YOUR GEOGRAPHY SKILLS

1. What feature is distorted on an equal-area map?
2. Would you use a Mercator projection to find the exact distance between two locations? Tell why or why not.

To turn Earth's surface into an equal-area map, mapmakers have to squeeze each gore into an oval.

Equator

The tips of all the gores are then joined together. The points at which they join form the North and South Poles. The line of the Equator stays the same.

North Pole

Equator

South Pole

Robinson Maps

Many of the maps in this book use the Robinson projection, which is a compromise between the Mercator and equal-area projections. The Robinson projection gives a useful overall picture of the world. It keeps the size and shape relationships of most continents and oceans, but distorts the size of the polar regions.

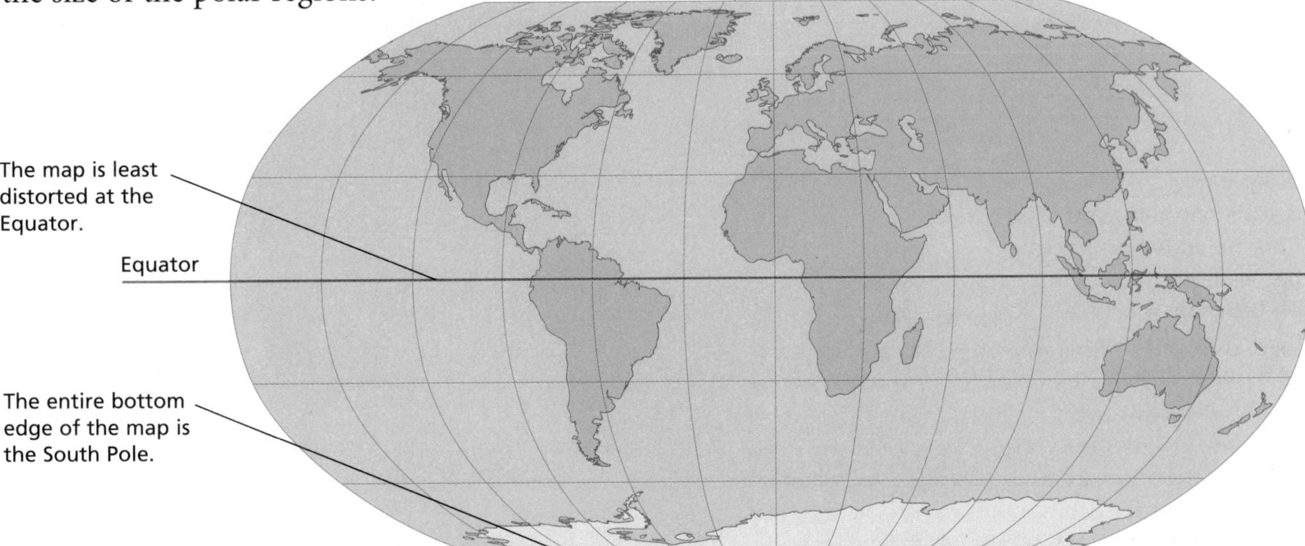
The entire top edge of the map is the North Pole.
The map is least distorted at the Equator.
Equator
The entire bottom edge of the map is the South Pole.

How to Use a Map

Mapmakers provide several clues to help you understand the information on a map. Maps provide different clues, depending on their purpose or scale. However, most maps have several clues in common.

Locator globe
Many maps are shown with locator globes. They show where on the globe the area of the map is located.

Title
All maps have a title. The title tells you the subject of the map.

Compass rose
Many maps show direction by displaying a compass rose with the directions north, east, south, and west. The letters N, E, S, and W are placed to indicate these directions.

Key
Often a map has a key, or legend. The key shows the symbols and colors used on the map, and what each one means.

Scale bar
A scale bar helps you find the actual distances between points shown on the map. Most scale bars show distances in both miles and kilometers.

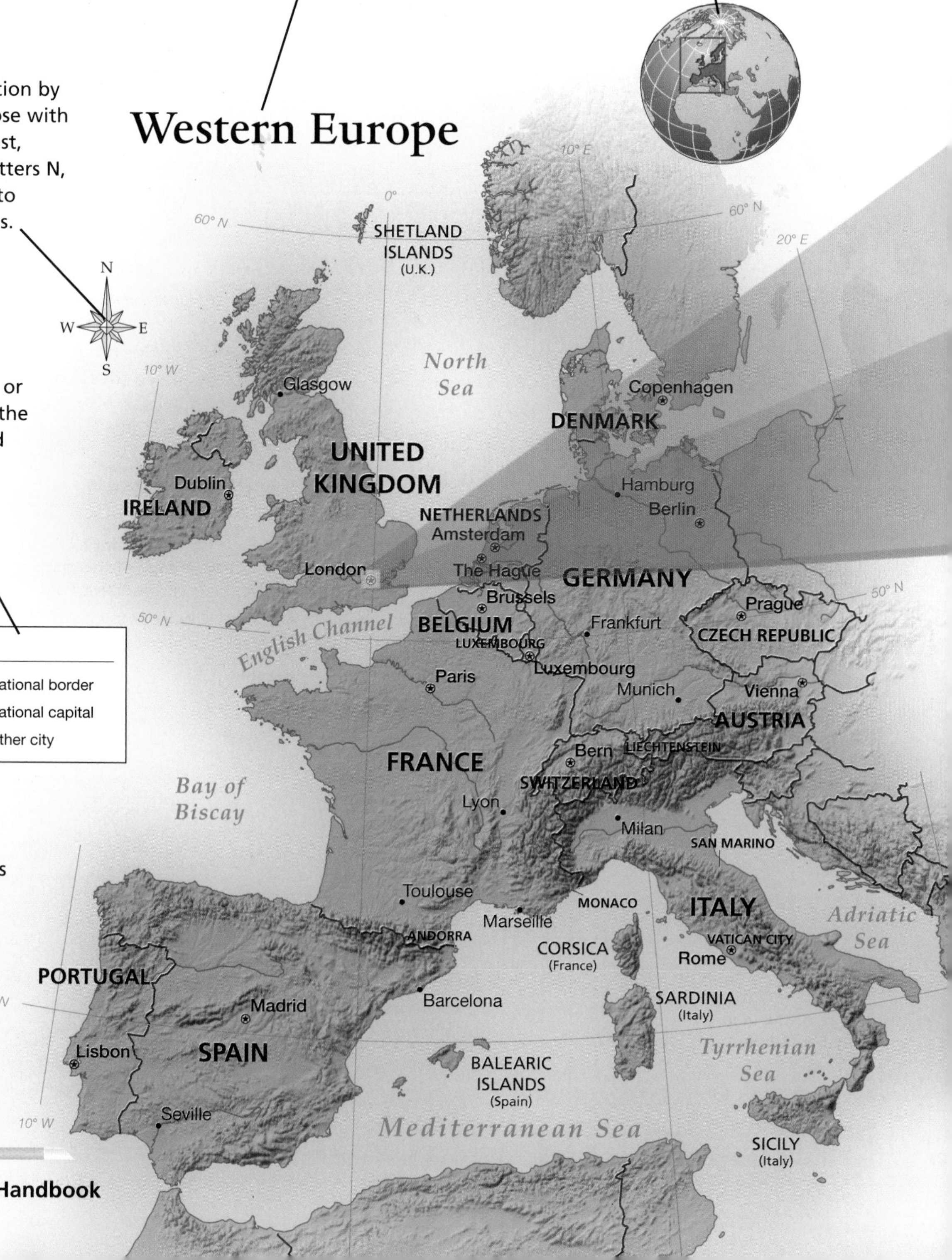

Maps of Different Scales

Maps are drawn to different scales, depending on their purpose. Here are three maps drawn to very different scales. Keep in mind that maps showing large areas have smaller scales. Maps showing small areas have larger scales.

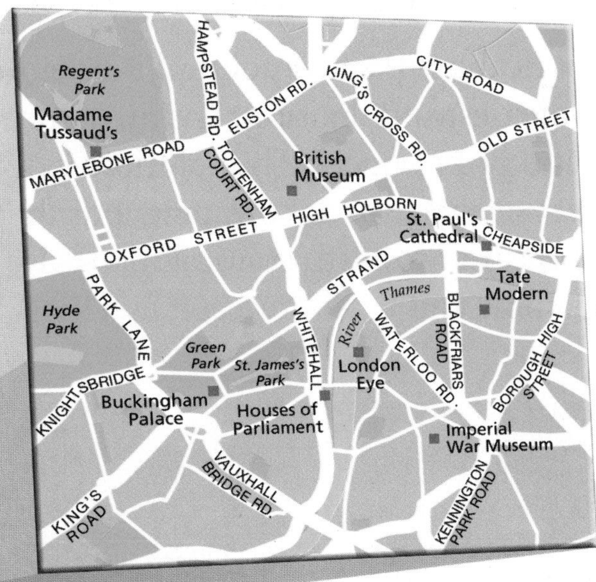

▲ Greater London

Find the gray square on the main map of Western Europe (left). This square represents the area shown on the map above. It shows London's boundaries, the general shape of the city, and the features around the city. This map can help you find your way from the airport to the center of town.

▲ Central London

Find the gray square on the map of Greater London. This square represents the area shown on the map above. This map moves you closer into the center of London. Like the zoom on a computer or a camera, this map shows a smaller area but in greater detail. It has the largest scale (1 inch represents about 0.9 mile). You can use this map to explore downtown London.

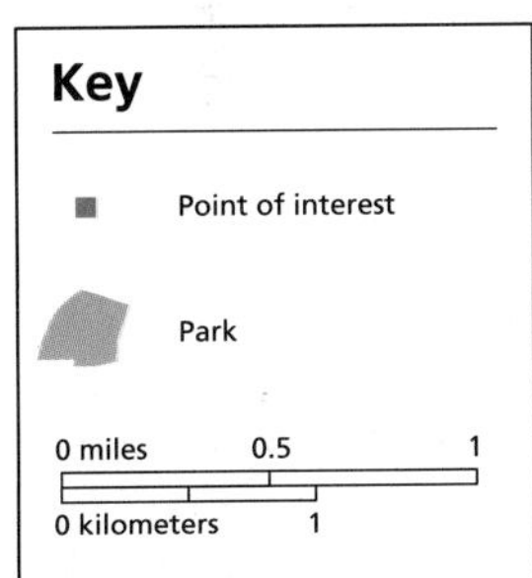

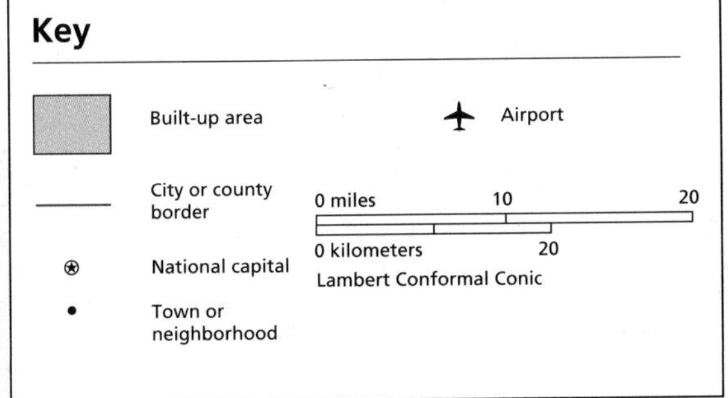

PRACTICE YOUR GEOGRAPHY SKILLS

1. What part of a map explains the colors used on the map?
2. How does the scale bar change depending on the scale of the map?
3. Which map would be best for finding the location of the British Museum? Explain why.

Political Maps

Political maps show political borders: continents, countries, and divisions within countries, such as states or provinces. The colors on political maps do not have any special meaning, but they make the map easier to read. Political maps also include symbols and labels for capitals, cities, and towns.

PRACTICE YOUR GEOGRAPHY SKILLS

1. What symbols show a national border, a national capital, and a city?
2. What is Angola's capital city?

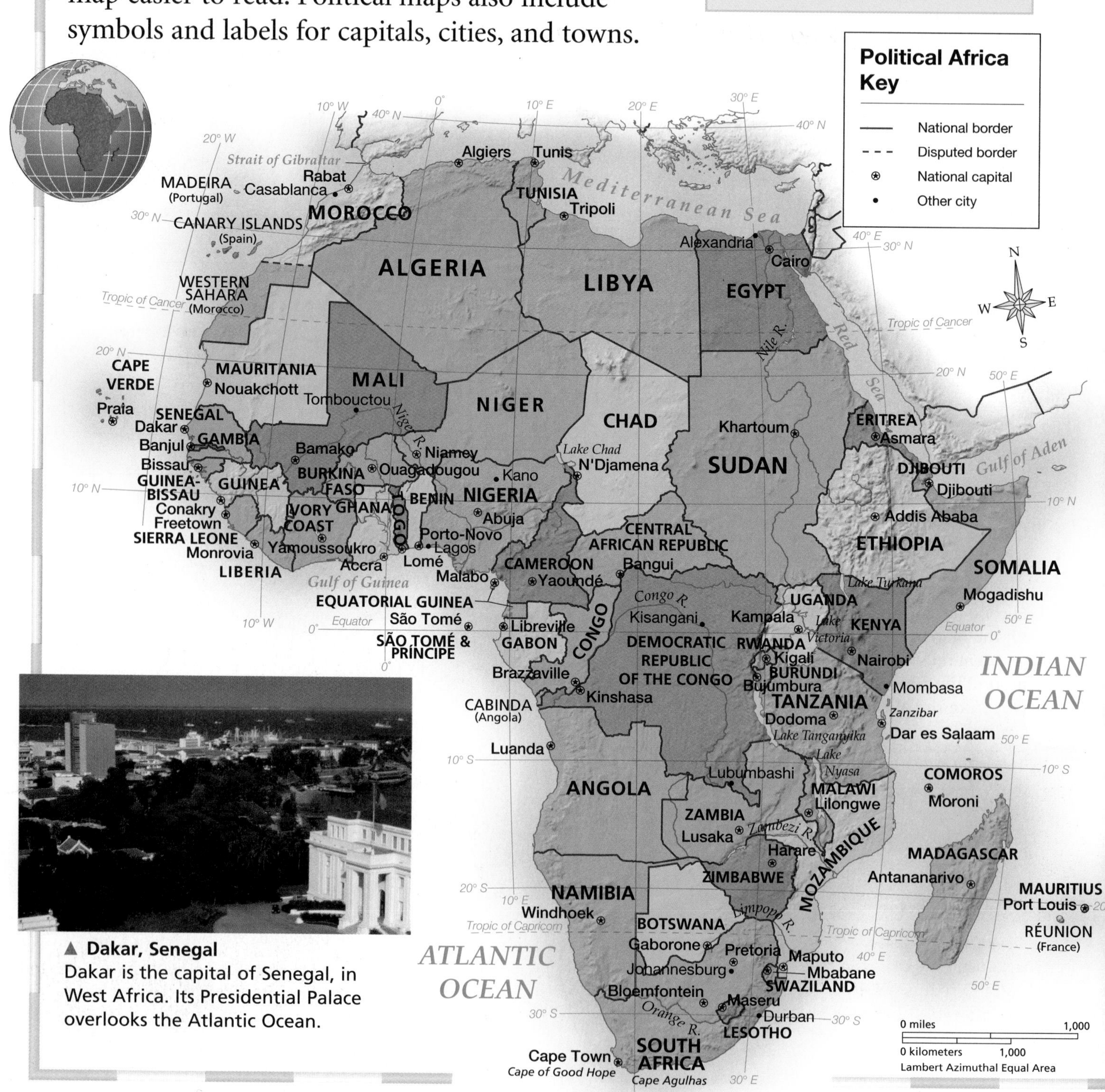

▲ **Dakar, Senegal**
Dakar is the capital of Senegal, in West Africa. Its Presidential Palace overlooks the Atlantic Ocean.

Physical Maps

Physical maps represent what a region looks like by showing its major physical features, such as hills and plains. Physical maps also often show elevation and relief. Elevation, indicated by colors, is the height of the land above sea level. Relief, indicated by shading, shows how sharply the land rises or falls.

PRACTICE YOUR GEOGRAPHY SKILLS

1. Which areas of Africa have the highest elevation?
2. How can you use relief to plan a hiking trip?

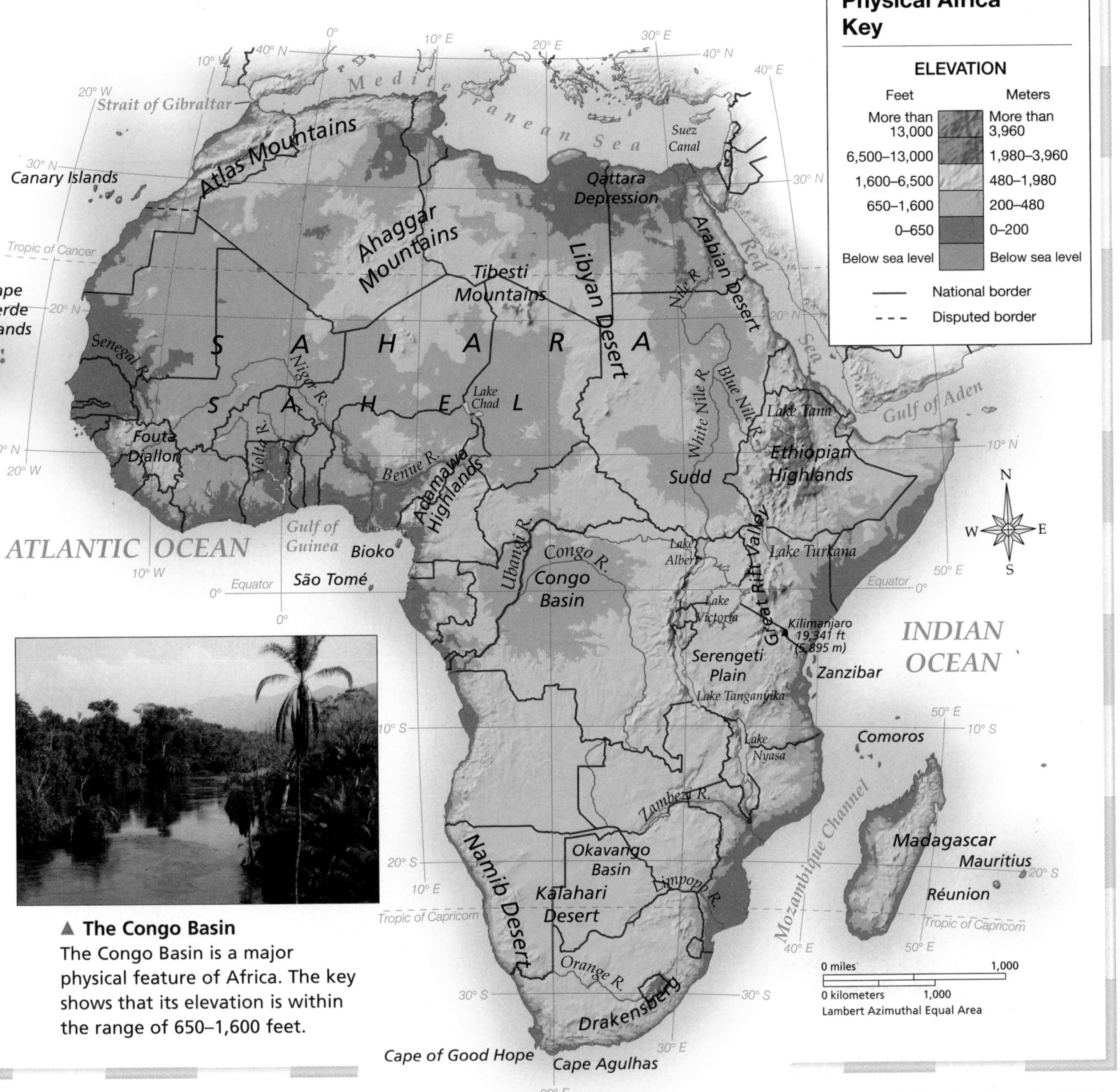

▲ **The Congo Basin**
The Congo Basin is a major physical feature of Africa. The key shows that its elevation is within the range of 650–1,600 feet.

Special-Purpose Maps: Climate

Unlike the boundary lines on a political map, the boundary lines on climate maps do not separate the land into exact divisions. For example, in this climate map of India, a tropical wet climate gradually changes to a tropical wet and dry climate.

PRACTICE YOUR GEOGRAPHY SKILLS

1. What part of a special-purpose map tells you what the colors on the map mean?
2. Where are arid regions located in India? Are there major cities in those regions?

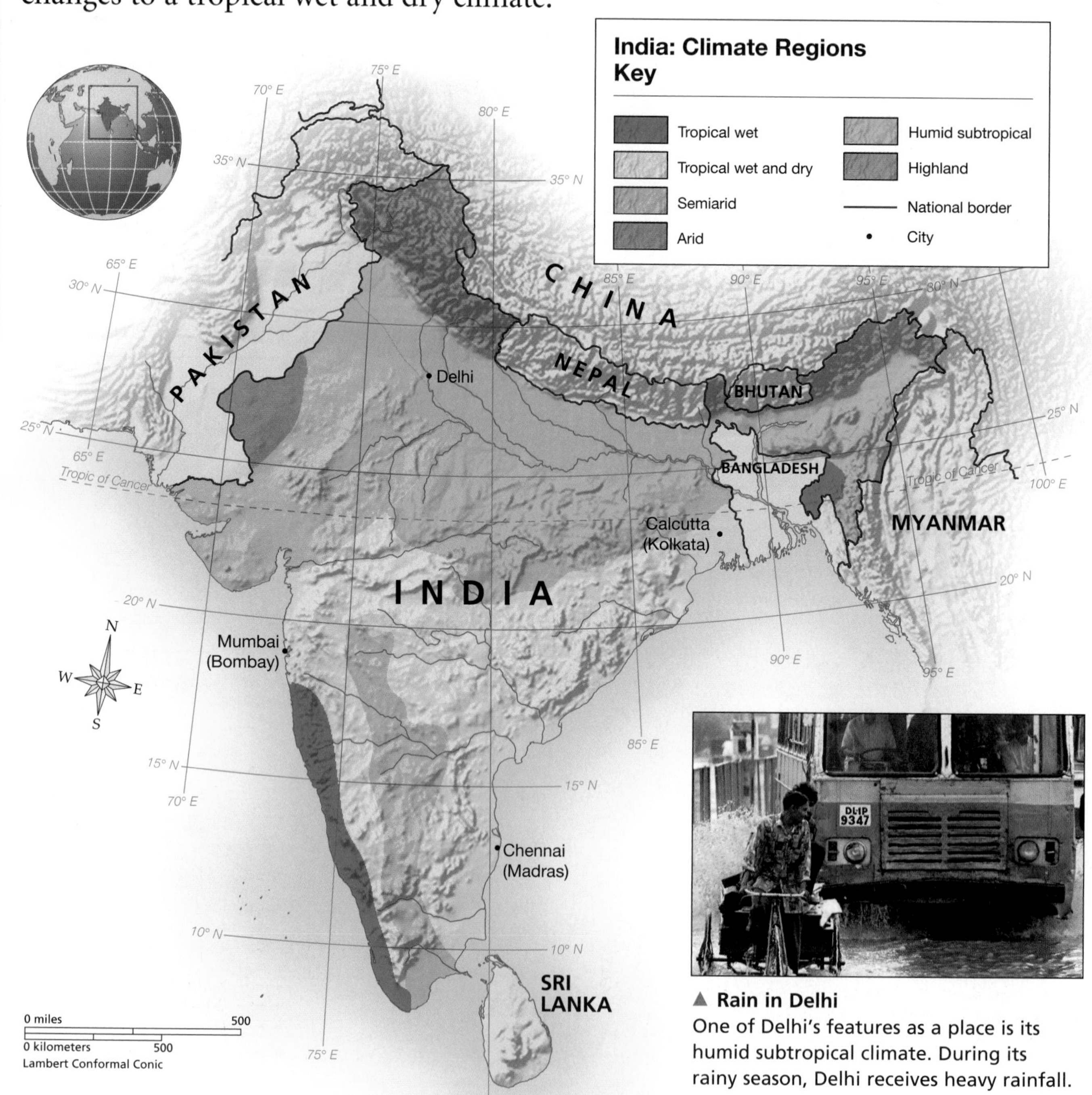

▲ **Rain in Delhi**
One of Delhi's features as a place is its humid subtropical climate. During its rainy season, Delhi receives heavy rainfall.

Special-Purpose Maps: Language

This map shows the official languages of India. An official language is the language used by the government. Even though a region has an official language, the people there may speak other languages as well. As in other special-purpose maps, the key explains how the different languages appear on the map.

PRACTICE YOUR GEOGRAPHY SKILLS

1. What color represents the Malayalam language on this map?
2. Where in India is Tamil the official language?

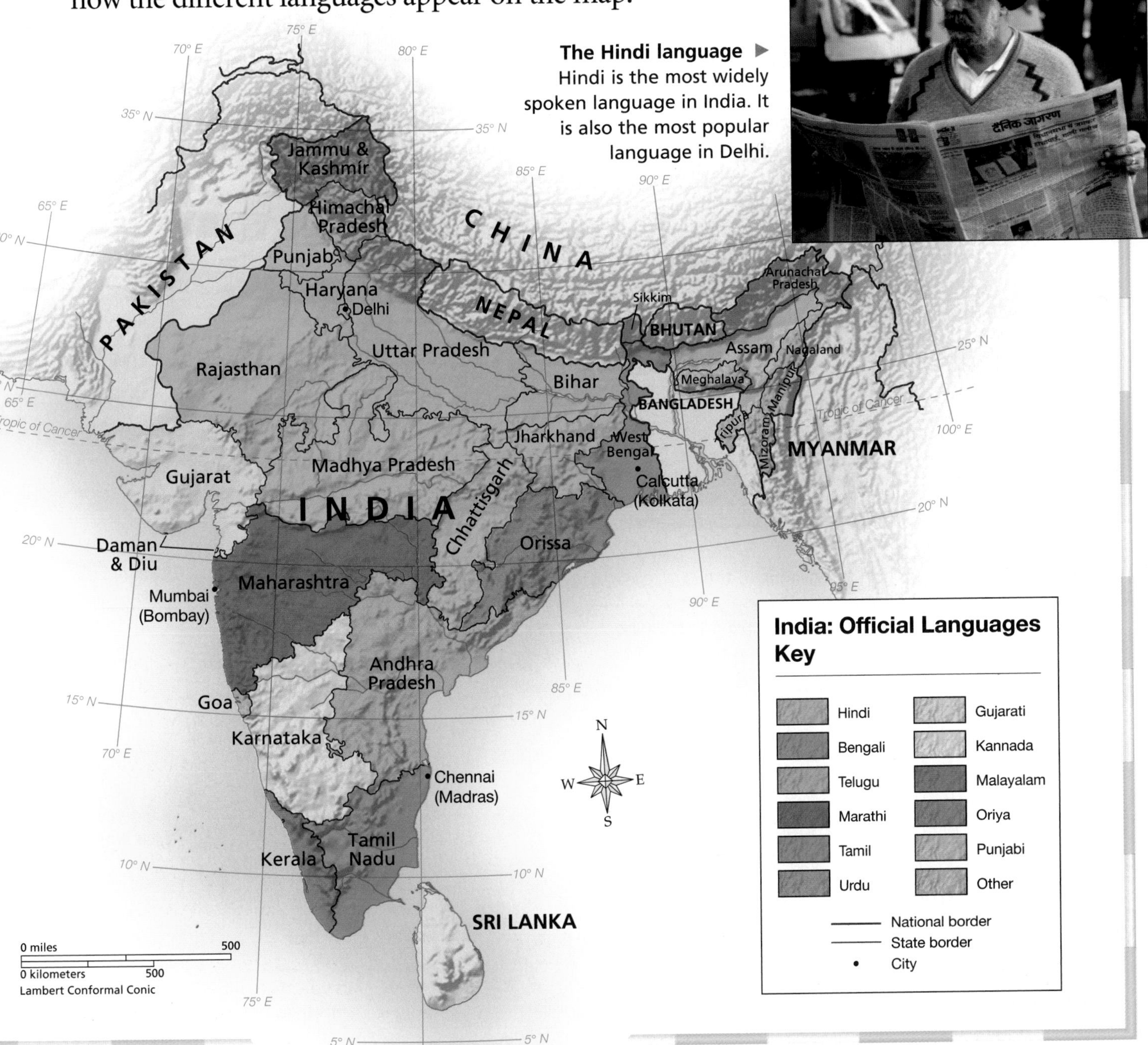

The Hindi language ▶ Hindi is the most widely spoken language in India. It is also the most popular language in Delhi.

Human Migration

Migration is an important part of the study of geography. Since the beginning of history, people have been on the move. As people move, they both shape and are shaped by their environments. Wherever people go, the culture they bring with them mixes with the cultures of the place in which they have settled.

Explorers arrive ▼
In 1492, Christopher Columbus set sail from Spain for the Americas with three ships. The ships shown here are replicas of those ships.

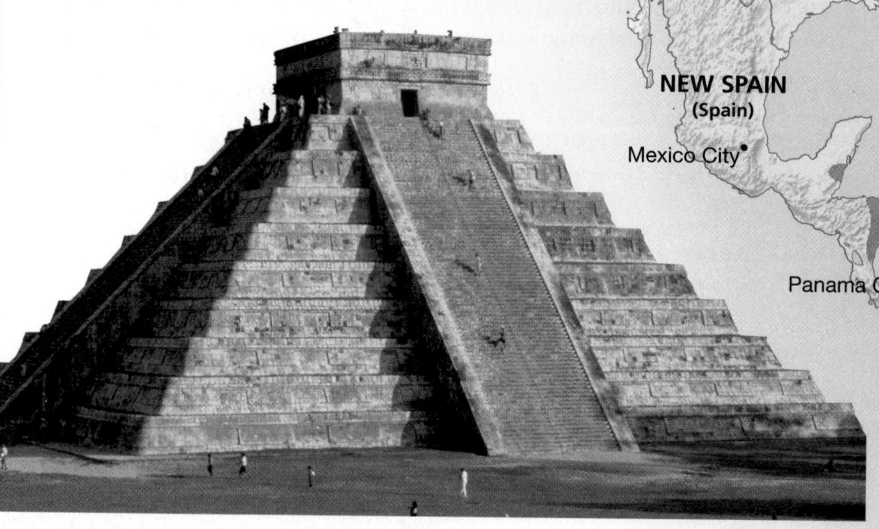

▲ **Native American pyramid**
When Europeans arrived in the Americas, the lands they found were not empty. Diverse groups of people with distinct cultures already lived there. The temple-topped pyramid shown above was built by Mayan Indians in Mexico, long before Columbus sailed.

ATLANTIC OCEAN
NEW SPAIN (Spain)
Mexico City
Caribbean Sea
Panama City
DUTCH GUIANA (Netherlands)
NEW GRENADA (Spain)
FRENCH GUIANA (France)
Amazon R.
PERU (Spain)
Lima
Cuzco
BRAZIL (Portugal)
Potosí
RIO DE LA PLATA (Spain)
Buenos Aires
Concepción
0 miles 1,000
0 kilometers 1,000
Wagner VII

Migration to the Americas, 1500–1800

A huge wave of migration from the Eastern Hemisphere began in the 1500s. European explorers in the Americas paved the way for hundreds of years of European settlement there. Forced migration from Africa started soon afterward, as Europeans began to import enslaved Africans to work in the Americas. The map to the right shows these migrations.

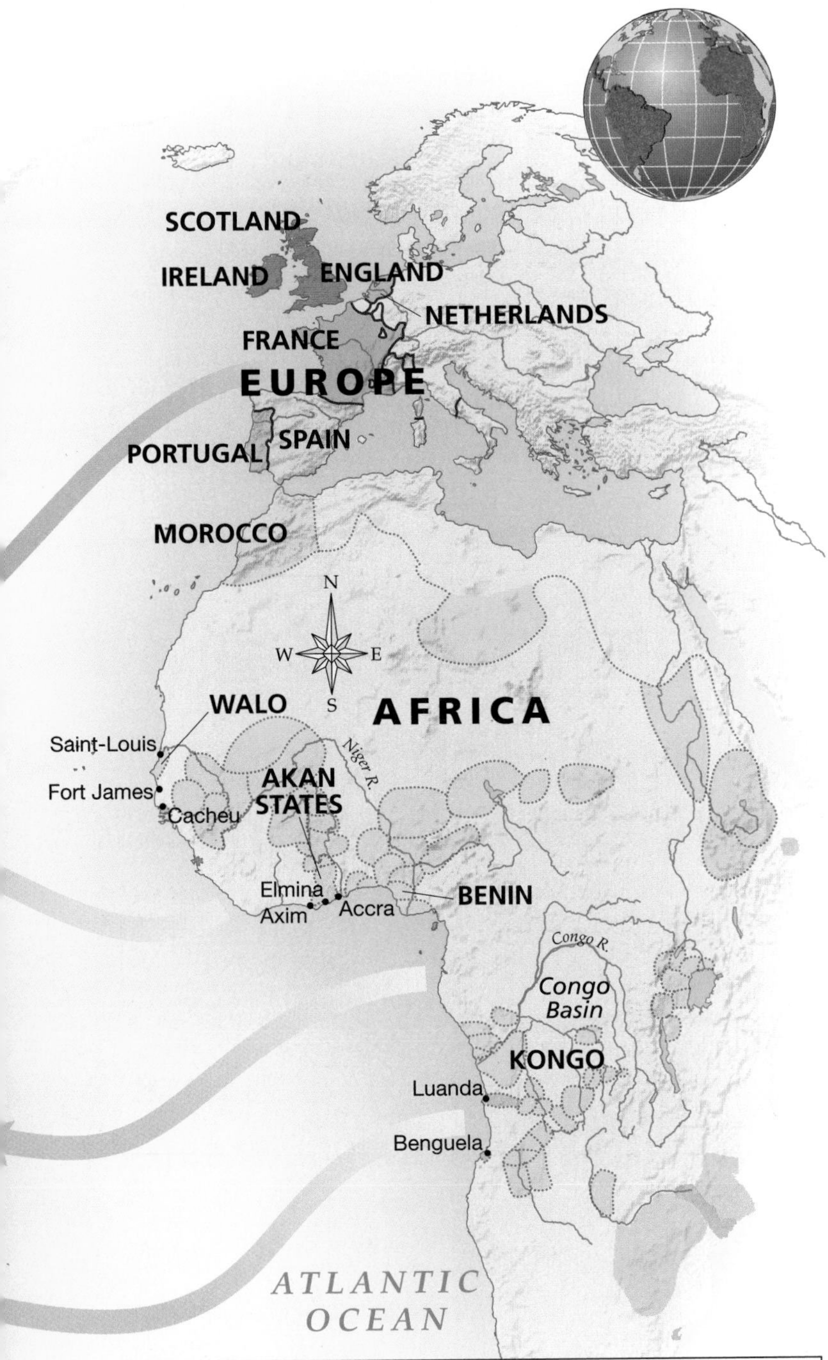

PRACTICE YOUR GEOGRAPHY SKILLS

1. Where did the Portuguese settle in the Americas?
2. Would you describe African migration at this time as a result of both push factors and pull factors? Explain why or why not.

SCOTLAND
IRELAND
ENGLAND
NETHERLANDS
FRANCE
EUROPE
PORTUGAL
SPAIN
MOROCCO
AFRICA
WALO
Saint-Louis
Fort James
Cacheu
AKAN STATES
Niger R.
Elmina
Axim
Accra
BENIN
Congo R.
Congo Basin
KONGO
Luanda
Benguela
ATLANTIC OCEAN

Migration to Latin America, 1500–1800

Key

 European migration

African migration

National or colonial border

Traditional African border

 African State

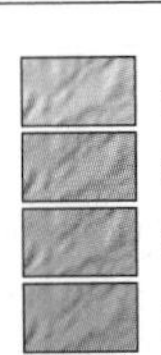 Spain and possessions

Portugal and possessions

Netherlands and possessions

France and possessions

England and possessions

"Push" and "Pull" Factors

Geographers describe a people's choice to migrate in terms of "push" factors and "pull" factors. Push factors are things in people's lives that push them to leave, such as poverty and political unrest. Pull factors are things in another country that pull people to move there, including better living conditions and hopes of better jobs.

▲ **Elmina, Ghana**
Elmina, in Ghana, is one of the many ports from which enslaved Africans were transported from Africa. Because slaves and gold were traded here, stretches of the western African coast were known as the Slave Coast and the Gold Coast.

World Land Use

People around the world have many different economic structures, or ways of making a living. Land-use maps are one way to learn about these structures. The ways that people use the land in each region tell us about the main ways that people in that region make a living.

World Land Use Key

- Nomadic herding
- Hunting and gathering
- Forestry
- Livestock raising
- Commercial farming
- Subsistence farming
- Manufacturing and trade
- Little or no activity
- National border
- Disputed border

▲ **Wheat farming in the United States**
Developed countries practice commercial farming rather than subsistence farming. Commercial farming is the production of food mainly for sale, either within the country or for export to other countries. Commercial farmers like these in Oregon often use heavy equipment to farm.

Levels of Development

Notice on the map key the term *subsistence farming*. This term means the production of food mainly for use by the farmer's own family. In less-developed countries, subsistence farming is often one of the main economic activities. In contrast, in developed countries there is little subsistence farming.

▲ **Growing barley in Ecuador**
These farmers in Ecuador use hand tools to harvest barley. They will use most of the crop they grow to feed themselves or their farm animals.

▲ **Growing rice in Vietnam**
Women in Vietnam plant rice in wet rice paddies, using the same planting methods their ancestors did.

PRACTICE YOUR GEOGRAPHY SKILLS

1. In what parts of the world is subsistence farming the main land use?
2. Locate where manufacturing and trade are the main land use. Are they found more often near areas of subsistence farming or areas of commercial farming? Why might this be so?

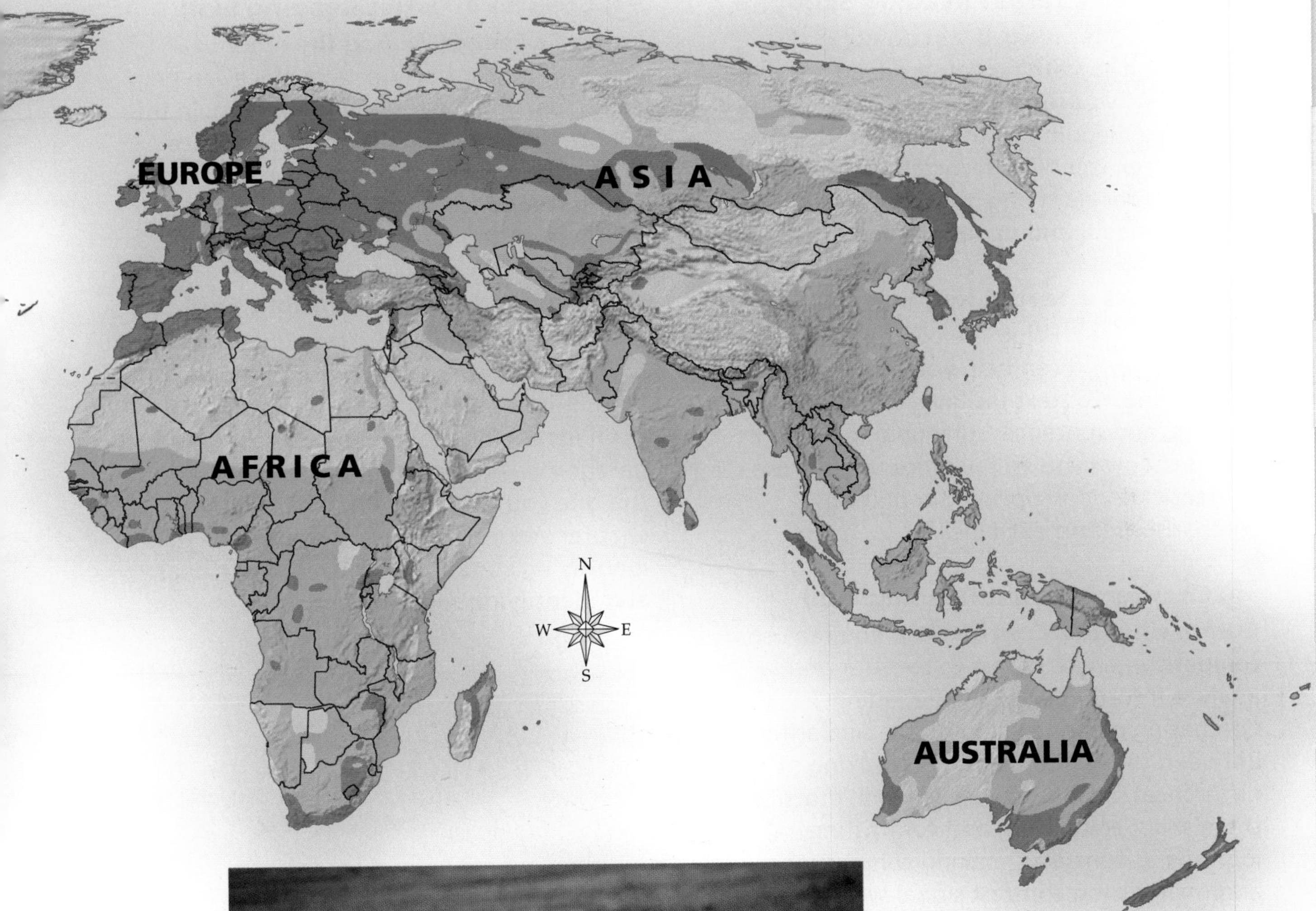

EUROPE
ASIA
AFRICA
AUSTRALIA
N
W
E
S

◀ **Herding cattle in Kenya**
Besides subsistence farming, nomadic herding is another economic activity in Africa. This man drives his cattle across the Kenyan grasslands.

Target Reading Skills

The Target Reading Skills introduced on this page will help you understand the words and ideas in this book and in other social studies reading you do. Each chapter in the Geography section focuses on one of these reading skills. Good readers develop a bank of reading strategies, or skills. Then they draw on the particular strategies that will help them understand the text they are reading.

Chapter 1 Target Reading Skill

Clarifying Meaning If you do not understand something you are reading right away, you can use several skills to help clarify the meaning of the word or idea. In this chapter you will practice these strategies for clarifying meaning: rereading, reading ahead, and paraphrasing.

Chapter 2 Target Reading Skill

Using Context Using the context of an unfamiliar word can help you understand its meaning. Context includes the words, phrases, and sentences surrounding a word. In this chapter you will practice using these context clues: descriptions, definitions, comparisons, and examples.

Chapter 3 Target Reading Skill

Comparing and Contrasting You can use comparison and contrast to sort out and analyze information you are reading. Comparing means examining the similarities between things. Contrasting is looking at differences. In this chapter you will practice these skills: comparing and contrasting, identifying contrasts, making comparisons, and recognizing contrast signal words.

Chapter 4 Target Reading Skill

Using Sequence Noting the order in which significant events take place can help you understand and remember them. In this chapter you will practice these sequence skills: sequencing, or finding the order of events, sequencing important changes, and recognizing sequence signal words.

Chapter 5 Target Reading Skill

Identifying the Main Idea Since you cannot remember every detail of what you read, it is important that you identify the main ideas. The main idea of a section or paragraph is the most important point and the one you want to remember. In this chapter you will practice these skills: identifying stated and implied main ideas and identifying supporting details.

FOUNDATIONS of GEOGRAPHY

Are you curious about our world? Do you want to know why winters are cold and summers are hot? Have you wondered why some people live and work in cities and others work on farms in the countryside? If you answered yes to any of these questions, you want to know more about geography.

Guiding Questions

The text, photographs, maps, and charts in this book will help you discover answers to these Guiding Questions.

1. **Geography** What are Earth's major physical features?
2. **History** How have people's ways of life changed over time?
3. **Culture** What is a culture?
4. **Government** What types of government exist in the world today?
5. **Economics** How do people use the world's natural resources?

Project Preview

You can also discover answers to the Guiding Questions by working on projects. Project possibilities are listed on page 136 of this book.

Investigate the Political World

There are more than 190 independent countries in the world. Some of those countries have dependencies, or areas outside of those countries that belong to them. Every land area where people live belongs to some country. The blue areas on maps in this book show the world's oceans, seas, and lakes. The other colors on this map show the areas of the world's countries and dependencies.

▲ **Denmark**
Denmark is one of the oldest continuously existing states. Christiansborg Palace is the seat of the Danish Parliament.

Use Web Code **lep-3020** for the **interactive maps** on these pages.

◀ **Niagara Falls**
The border between the United States and Canada runs through the falls. Both countries share its tourist and power-generating benefits.

LOCATION

1 Examine Country Borders

Governments have drawn the borders between countries. Some borders follow mountains or rivers. Others are straight lines. On the map, look at the United States and Canada. These are the large yellow and pink countries in North America. Parts of their borders are straight, but others are crooked. Why might this be? What might explain the location of other borders on this map?

The World: Political Key

—— National border
- - - Disputed border

PLACE

2 Analyze the Continents

Notice the six black labels on the world map. These labels name continents. Which continent's name is also the name of a country? You can see that some continents have more countries than others. Which continent is made up mostly of small countries?

▲ **Russia**
St. Basil's Cathedral was built in the 1500s in Moscow, the Russian capital. At that time, the Russian church had great political power.

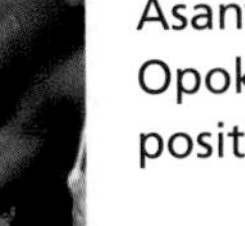

◀ **Ghana**
The traditional leader of the Ashanti people in Ghana is called the Asantehene. Otumfuo Opoku Ware II held this position for thirty years.

▲ **East Timor**
These people are celebrating the independence of East Timor, which became a nation in 2002.

Investigate the Physical World

People's lives are constantly shaped by their physical environment. The physical features of a place often determine where and how people live. Yet the physical world is always changing, too. Some changes come very slowly. For example, it took millions of years for Earth's crust to lift and form mountains. Other changes are fast and dramatic, such as when a volcano erupts or an earthquake hits.

▲ **Alaska**
Glaciers like this one at Portage, Alaska, have shaped the land for thousands of years.

PLACE

3 Infer From a Map

Notice the bumpy texture and brownish colors on the map. These indicate a mountainous landscape. Now find the continent of South America. Look for the Amazon Basin. What does the key tell you about its elevation? Notice the photograph of the Tigre River as it weaves through the basin. Describe that landscape. Now find the Andes on the map, and describe what you would expect to see there.

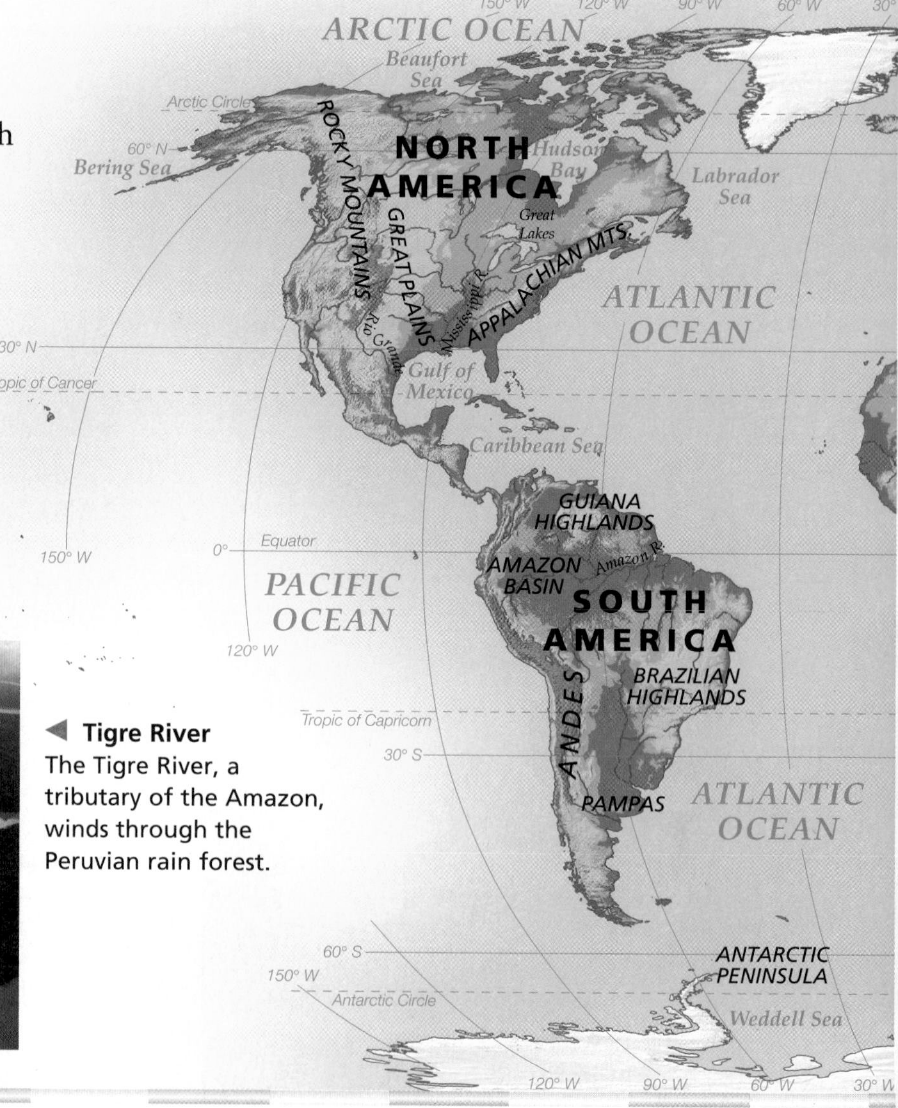

◀ **Tigre River**
The Tigre River, a tributary of the Amazon, winds through the Peruvian rain forest.

HUMAN-ENVIRONMENT INTERACTION

4 Examine Landforms as Barriers

Physical barriers can make movement between areas difficult. For example, take a look at the continents in the map below. Some of them are separated from one another by vast areas of water. Examine the elevation key. Look closely at the map's labels. What other physical landforms might have acted as barriers to movement?

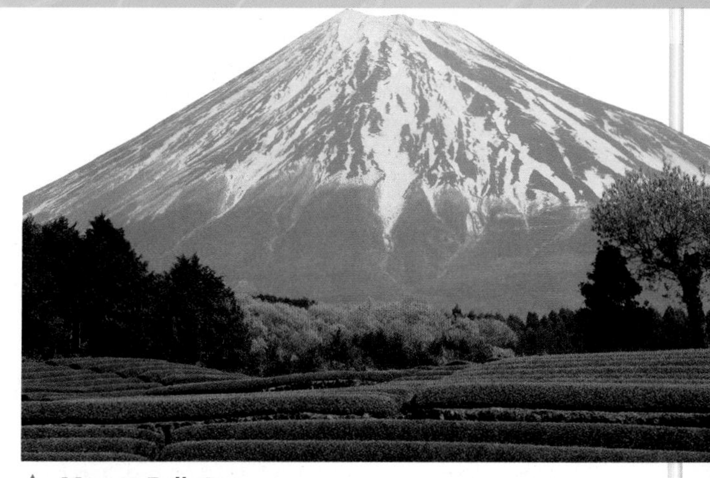

▲ **Mount Fuji, Japan**
Volcanoes such as this one have created islands along the rim of the Pacific Ocean.

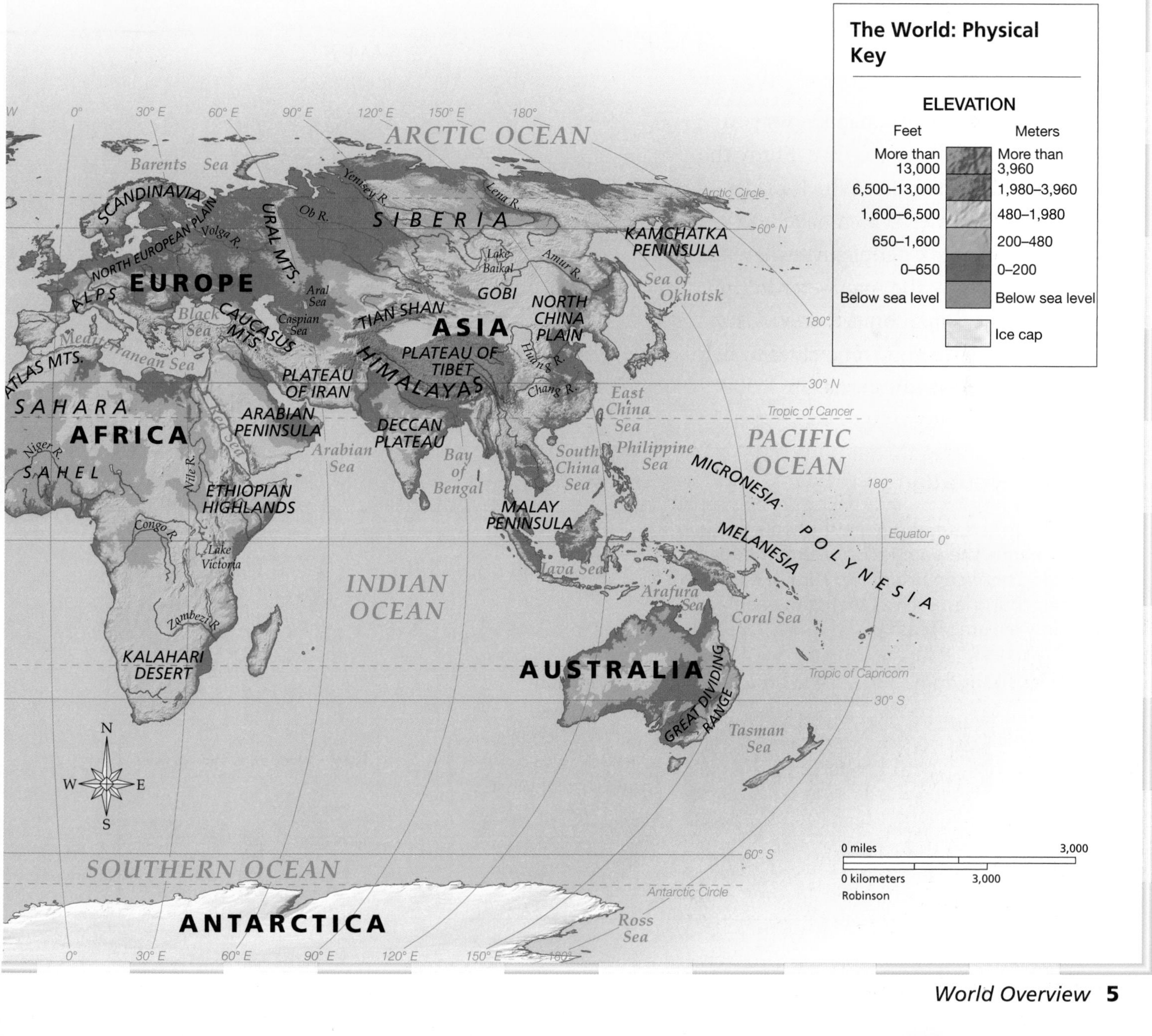

The World: Physical
Key

ELEVATION

Feet	Meters
More than 13,000	More than 3,960
6,500–13,000	1,980–3,960
1,600–6,500	480–1,980
650–1,600	200–480
0–650	0–200
Below sea level	Below sea level
Ice cap	

0 miles 3,000
0 kilometers 3,000
Robinson

Investigate Population

For thousands of years, the world's population grew slowly. In the past 200 years, however, health care, living conditions, and food production have greatly improved. This has led to a huge population burst. In 1800, the world's population numbered less than 1 billion people. Today, it is more than 6 billion, and growing quickly.

▲ **China**
A crowd of people walk through a park in the capital city of Beijing. China has the largest population of any country in the world.

REGIONS

5 Analyze Population Density

A population density map shows you where the world's people live. Study the world population map. Which places have many people? Which have few? Why do you think people live where they do? As you study the map, refer to the world physical map on the previous page. It may give you some clues to help you answer these questions.

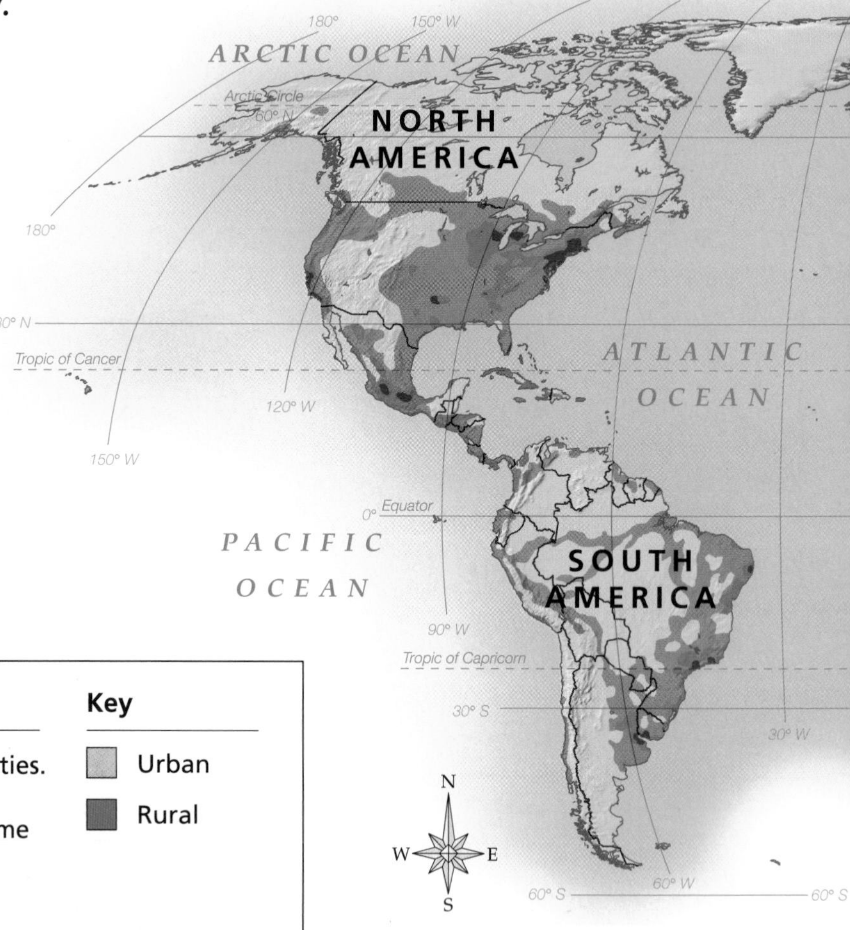

World Population

Key

Urban

Rural

In the United Kingdom, most people live in cities. In Panama, the population is almost equally divided between urban and rural areas. In some Asian countries, such as Vietnam, people live mainly in rural areas.

United Kingdom

10%

Panama

56%

44%

Vietnam

20%

80%

Source: Energy Information Administration

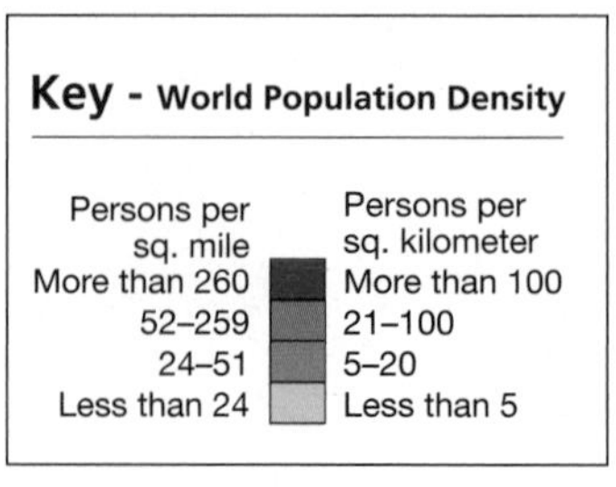

MOVEMENT

6 Compare Continents

When high population densities cover large areas, those areas have large populations. Look at the continents on the map. Which continent do you think has the largest population, based on the size of its areas of high population density? Which continent do you think has the lowest population? Compare North America and South America on the map. Which continent do you think has the larger population?

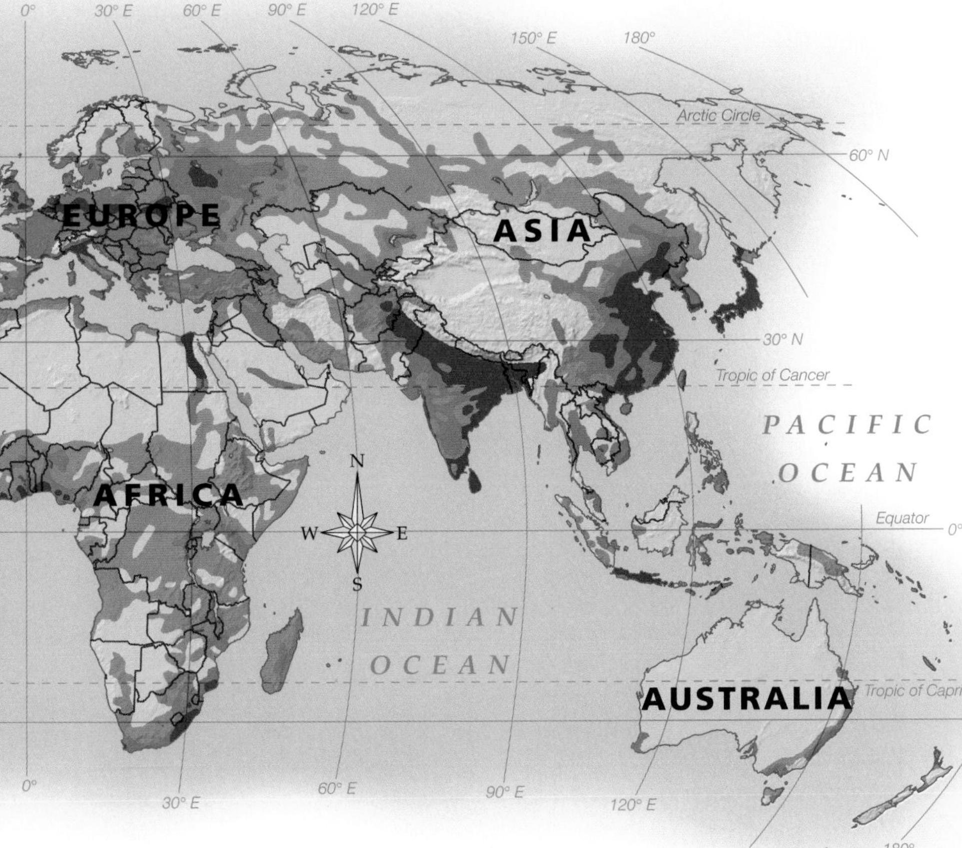

▲ **New Zealand**
The Whanganui River flows through a New Zealand national park. New Zealand has a low population density.

PRACTICE YOUR GEOGRAPHY SKILLS

1. In Asia there is a ring of dense population next to an area with low population. Look at the physical map of the world on pages 4 and 5. What landform may explain this difference?
2. Look at Northern Africa. Find the area of heavy population that forms a curving line on the map. How does the physical map on pages 4 and 5 explain this?

Monaco is the most densely populated European nation. ▶

Chapter 1 The World of Geography

Chapter Preview

This chapter will introduce you to the study of Earth, the planet where we live.

Target Reading Skill

Clarifying Meaning In this chapter you will focus on clarifying meaning by learning how to read ahead and how to paraphrase.

▶ **A satellite launched from the space shuttle *Discovery* orbits Earth.**

Section 1 The Five Themes of Geography

Prepare to Read

Objectives

In this section you will

1. Learn about the study of Earth.
2. Discover five ways to look at Earth.

Taking Notes

As you read the section, look for details about each of the five themes of geography. Copy the web diagram below and write down details related to each theme. Add ovals as needed for additional themes or details.

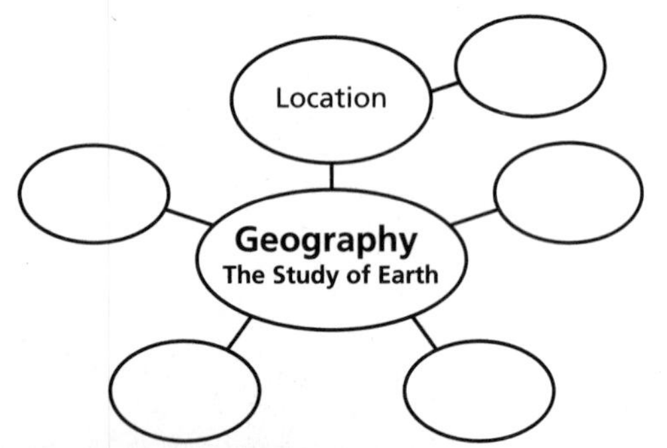

Target Reading Skill

Reread or Read Ahead If you do not understand a passage, reread it to look for connections among the words and sentences. Reading ahead can also help. Words and ideas may be clarified further on.

Key Terms

- **geography** (jee AHG ru fee) *n.* the study of Earth
- **cardinal directions** (KAHR duh nul duh REK shunz) *n.* the directions north, east, south, and west
- **latitude** (LAT uh tood) *n.* the distance north or south of Earth's Equator, in degrees
- **longitude** (LAHN juh tood) *n.* the distance east or west of the Prime Meridian, in degrees
- **hemisphere** (HEM ih sfeer) *n.* a half of Earth
- **parallel** (PA ruh lel) *n.* a line of latitude
- **meridian** (muh RID ee un) *n.* a line of longitude

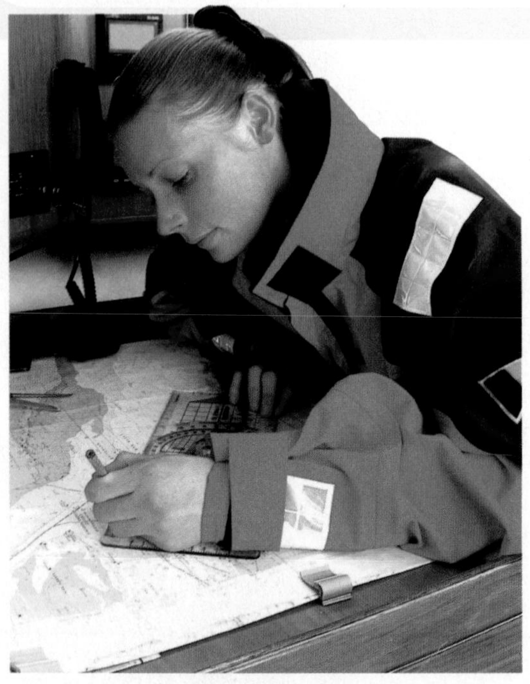

Geographers use maps and other tools to understand Earth.

The Study of Earth

Geography is the study of Earth, our home planet. Geographers try to answer two basic questions: Where are things located? and, Why are they there? To find answers to these questions, geographers consider Earth from many points of view.

✓ Reading Check **What questions do geographers try to answer?**

Five Ways to Look at Earth

Five themes can help you organize information about Earth and its people. These themes are location, regions, place, movement, and human-environment interaction. They can help you understand where things are located, and why they are there.

Location Geographers begin to study a place by finding where it is, or its location. Geographers use both cardinal and intermediate directions to describe location. The **cardinal directions** are north, east, south, and west. Intermediate directions lie between the cardinal directions. For example, northwest is halfway between north and west.

Geographers also use two special measurements of Earth to describe location. **Latitude** is the distance north or south of the Equator, measured in units called degrees. Degrees are units that measure angles. **Longitude** is the distance east or west of the Prime Meridian, measured in degrees.

Lines of latitude are east-west circles around the globe. All points on the circle have the same latitude. The line of latitude around the middle of the globe, at 0 degrees (0°) of latitude, is the Equator. Lines of longitude run north and south. The Prime Meridian is the line of longitude that marks 0° of longitude.

The Hemispheres

The Equator and the Prime Meridian both divide Earth in two. Each half of Earth is called a **hemisphere.** The Equator divides Earth into Northern and Southern hemispheres. The Prime Meridian divides Earth into Eastern and Western hemispheres.

The North Pole is 90° north of the Equator.

The Northern Hemisphere includes all lines of latitude north of the Equator.

The Southern Hemisphere contains all lines of latitude south of the Equator.

The Equator marks 0° latitude.

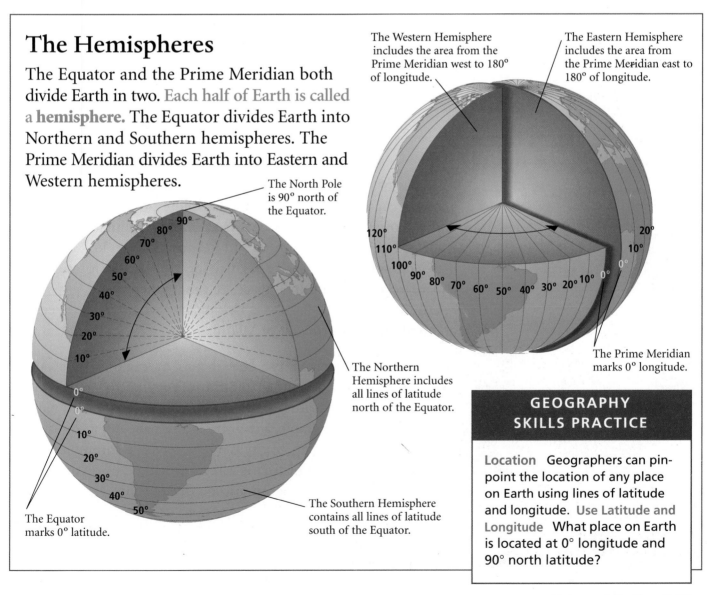

The Western Hemisphere includes the area from the Prime Meridian west to 180° of longitude.

The Eastern Hemisphere includes the area from the Prime Meridian east to 180° of longitude.

The Prime Meridian marks 0° longitude.

GEOGRAPHY SKILLS PRACTICE

Location Geographers can pinpoint the location of any place on Earth using lines of latitude and longitude. **Use Latitude and Longitude** What place on Earth is located at 0° longitude and 90° north latitude?

The Global Grid

Lines of longitude and latitude form a global grid. Geographers can identify the absolute location of any point on Earth by finding the latitude and longitude lines that intersect at that point. Lines of latitude are also called **parallels,** because they run east and west and are parallel to one another. This means that they never cross. Lines of longitude are also called **meridians.** Meridians run north and south, from the North Pole to the South Pole.

The North Pole has the greatest latitude north of the Equator.
The Equator, at 0° latitude, circles Earth midway between the North and South poles.
90° N
80° N
60° N
40° N
20° N
0°
20° S
40° S
60° S
80° S
90° S
60° W
40° W
20° W
0°
20° E
40° E
60° E
Equator
Prime Meridian
The Equator is the parallel around the middle of the globe.
A line of longitude
The Prime Meridian, at 0° longitude, runs through Greenwich, England.
The South Pole has the greatest latitude south of the Equator.

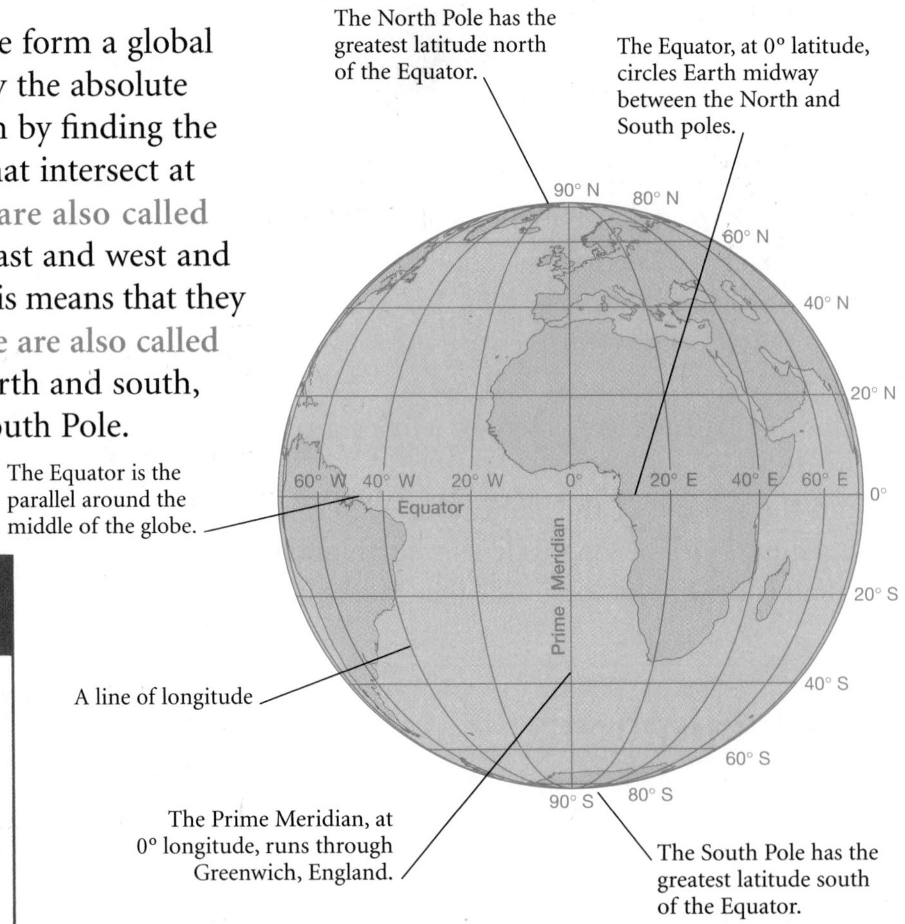

GEOGRAPHY SKILLS PRACTICE

Location Latitude and longitude are measured in degrees from imaginary lines on Earth's surface. **Compare and Contrast** From which line is latitude measured? Where do degrees of longitude start?

Lines of longitude and latitude form a global grid. This grid allows geographers to state the absolute location, or exact address, of any place on Earth. For example, Savannah, Georgia, is located at 32° north latitude and 81° west longitude.

Geographers also discuss relative location, or the location of a place relative to another place. A geographer might give the relative location of Tallahassee, Florida, by saying, "Tallahassee is about 400 miles northwest of Miami."

Target Skill **Read Ahead** Read ahead to see how physical features may define regions.

Regions Geographers use the theme of regions to group places that have something in common. A region has a unifying human or physical feature such as population, history, climate, or landforms. For example, a country is a region with a common national government, and a city is a region with a common local government. A school district is a region defined by a common school system. Land areas can also be divided into regions that share physical features, such as mountains or a dry climate. Physical regions of the western United States include the Rocky Mountains and the Mojave (mo HAH vee) Desert.

Place Geographers also study place. Place includes the human and physical features at a specific location. To describe physical features, you might say the climate is hot or cold. Or you might say that the land is hilly. To discuss human features, you might talk about how many people live in a place and the kinds of work they do. You might also describe their religions or the languages they speak.

Movement The theme of movement helps explain how people, goods, and ideas get from one place to another. For example, when people from other countries came to the United States, they brought traditional foods that enriched the American way of life. The theme of movement helps you understand such cultural changes. Movement helps you understand many other facts about the world. For example, radios and computers have helped music from the United States to spread and become popular around the world.

Human-Environment Interaction This theme explores how people affect their environment, or their natural surroundings, and how their environment affects them. Perhaps they have cut trails into the mountainside. Or they may have learned how to survive with little water.

Farmers in India
These women are using the wind to separate grain for flour from chaff, or husks. Farming is an example of human-environment interaction. **Infer** *Do you think that these farmers use much modern machinery?*

✓ Reading Check **What is the purpose of the five themes of geography?**

Section 1 Assessment

Key Terms
Review the key terms at the beginning of this section. Use each term in a sentence that explains its meaning.

Target Reading Skill
What did you learn about physical features and regions by reading ahead?

Comprehension and Critical Thinking
1. (a) **Recall** What do geographers study?
(b) **Explain** What basic questions guide geographers?
2. (a) **Explain** How can the five themes help geographers?
(b) **Predict** How might a geographer use the theme of movement to describe the area where you live?
3. (a) **Define** What does the theme of location cover?
(b) **Contrast** How would a description of your home town as a place be different from a description of your home town's location?

Writing Activity
Read the passage above on human-environment interaction. Then write a paragraph describing ways that people in your area interact with their natural environment.

For: An activity on the five themes of geography
Visit: PHSchool.com
Web Code: led-3101

Using Reliable Information

Would you seek medical advice from a plumber? Would you go to an encyclopedia to keep track of this season's basketball scores? Of course you wouldn't. Information is only as good as its source. To get reliable information, you have to go to an appropriate, trustworthy, and knowledgeable source.

Learn the Skill

Follow these steps to determine whether information is reliable.

1. **Find out the source of the information.** If it comes from a printed source, find out the name of the source, the author, and the date of publication. If it appeared on television, find out the name, date, and type of program (news, drama, or documentary). Do not accept information from Internet sites that do not give a date and an author.

2. **Find out if the information is recent enough for your purpose.** If you need current information, search for recent newspaper articles and up-to-date Web sites. Even if your topic is historic, researchers may have discovered new information about it. Seek the most current information.

3. **Find out if the information is accurate.** On certain topics, nearly all sources agree. For other topics, try to find information on which several respected sources agree. To be clear, you might say, "Several sources agree that" or "According to." If reliable sources disagree, you might note that disagreement in your writing.

4. **Look up the author's qualifications and methods.** When you check out an author's qualifications, always ask yourself whether he or she has a bias, or a one-sided view.

Is it Reliable?

To see if a source is reliable, ask

- What is the source?
- Is it recent enough?
- Is it accurate?
- Is the author qualified or biased?

Practice the Skill

Now use steps 1–4 to answer some questions about reliable information.

1. Where might you go to find information on the location of the capital of Japan? On the population of North Carolina? On the major industries of Cuba? On presidential election results in Russia?

2. Would a 20-year-old encyclopedia be a reliable source of information on active volcanoes in Hawaii? On the type of money used in Europe? On the longest river in the world? Explain your answers.

3. If you heard in a television documentary that most of the world's diamonds are mined in southern Africa, how could you check the accuracy of that statement?

4. Suppose you do an Internet search for information on the amount of beef produced in the United States last year. The search leads you to articles by three authors. Who would be the best source of information: an economist for the U.S. Department of Agriculture, the largest cattle rancher in Texas, or a leading university expert on beef production? Explain your answer.

Apply the Skill

If you had to research a report on the health of children in India, what kinds of sources would you search for reliable information? Name at least two sources, and explain why they would be reliable.

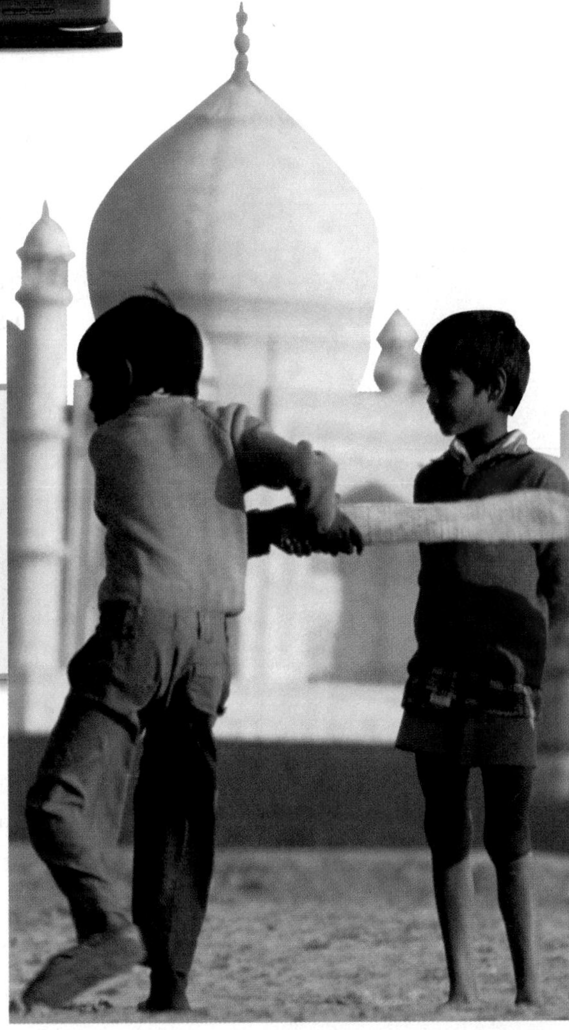

These boys are playing ball in front of the famed Taj Mahal, in India.

Section 2 The Geographer's Tools

Prepare to Read

Objectives

In this section you will

1. Find out how maps and globes show information about Earth's surface.
2. See how mapmakers show Earth's round surface on flat maps.
3. Learn how to read maps.

Taking Notes

As you read this section, look for details about each of the following map topics: comparing maps with globes, map projections, and parts of a map. Copy the outline below and write each detail under the correct topic.

I. Maps and globes
  A. Globes
  B.
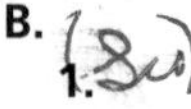
    1.
    2.
II. Projections
  A.

Target Reading Skill

Paraphrase When you paraphrase, you restate what you have read in your own words. For example, you could paraphrase the first paragraph after the heading Globes and Their Weaknesses this way:

"Mapmakers found that globes are the best way to show the shapes of continents, but at a different size."

As you read this section, paraphrase or restate the information after each red or blue heading.

Key Terms

- **scale** (skayl) *n.* relative size
- **distortion** (dih STAWR shun) *n.* loss of accuracy
- **geographic information systems** (jee uh GRAF ik in fur MAY shun SIS tumz) *n.* computer-based systems that provide information about locations
- **projection** (proh JEK shun) *n.* a way to map Earth on a flat surface
- **compass rose** (KUM pus rohz) *n.* a diagram of a compass showing direction
- **key** (kee) *n.* the section of a map that explains the symbols and colors on the map

A map can help you find directions.

Globes and Maps

As people explored Earth, they collected information about the shapes and sizes of islands, continents, and bodies of water. Map makers wanted to present this information accurately.

Globes and Their Weaknesses The best way was to put the information on a globe, or a model with the same round shape as Earth itself. By using an accurate shape for Earth, mapmakers could show the continents and oceans of Earth much as they really are. The only difference would be the **scale, or relative size.**

But there is a problem with globes. Try making a globe large enough to show the streets in your town. The globe might have to be larger than your school building. Imagine putting a globe that big in your pocket every morning! A globe just cannot be complete enough to be useful for finding directions and at the same time small enough to be convenient for everyday use.

Maps and Mapping People, therefore, use flat maps. Flat maps, however, present another problem. Earth is round. A map is flat. Can you flatten an orange peel without stretching or tearing it? There will be sections that are stretched or bent out of shape. The same thing happens when mapmakers create flat maps. It is impossible to show Earth on a flat surface without some **distortion,** or loss of accuracy. Something will look too large, too small, or out of place. Mapmakers have found ways to limit distortion of shape, size, distance, and direction.

Target Skill **Paraphrase** Paraphrase the paragraph at the left in 25 words or fewer.

Mapmakers rely on ground surveys, or measurements made on the ground, to make maps. They also use aerial photographs and satellite images.

Aerial Photographs and Satellite Images Aerial photographs are photographs of Earth's surface taken from the air. Satellite images are pictures of Earth's surface taken from a satellite in orbit. Both types of image are valuable sources of information for mapmakers because they provide current information about Earth's surface in great detail. But they are not useful for finding objects that are hidden, such as underground transit lines, or features such as streams that may be covered by vegetation. Also, like any map, flat aerial photographs and satellite images give a distorted view of Earth's surface.

Geographic Information Systems A **geographic information system,** or GIS, is a computer-based system that links information to locations. A GIS is useful not only to geographers but also to governments and businesses. A GIS connects information with places. For example, if a business needs to decide where to open an office, it can use a GIS to choose a location where it will reach the most customers. Military planners may use a GIS to improve their knowledge of the places where troops will operate. A GIS also may be used to produce maps.

✓ Reading Check **What are the advantages and disadvantages of each way of showing Earth's surface?**

Satellite Image of North and South America
This satellite view shows parts of North and South America. A storm system covers part of the southeastern United States. **Analyze Images** *How might this image pose problems as a source for making maps?*

Getting It All on the Map

In 1569, a mapmaker named Gerardus Mercator (juh RAHR dus mur KAY tur) created a flat map to help sailors navigate, or plan journeys, around the globe. To make his map flat and to keep his grid rectangular, Mercator expanded the area between lines of longitude near the poles. Mercator's map was very useful to sailors because it showed directions accurately, even though sizes and distances were distorted. More than 400 years later, nearly all seagoing navigators still use the Mercator **projection,** or method of mapping Earth on a flat surface.

The Mercator Projection Mercator maps make areas near the poles look bigger than they are. This is because on a globe, the lines of longitude meet at the poles. To keep lines of longitude straight up and down, Mercator had to stretch the spaces between them north and south of the Equator. Land near the Equator was about the right size, but land areas near the poles became much larger. For example, on Mercator's map, Greenland looks bigger than South America. Greenland is actually only about one eighth as big as South America. Geographers call a Mercator projection a conformal map. It shows correct shapes but not true distances or sizes. What other areas, besides Greenland, do you think might look larger than they should?

Making a Mercator Map

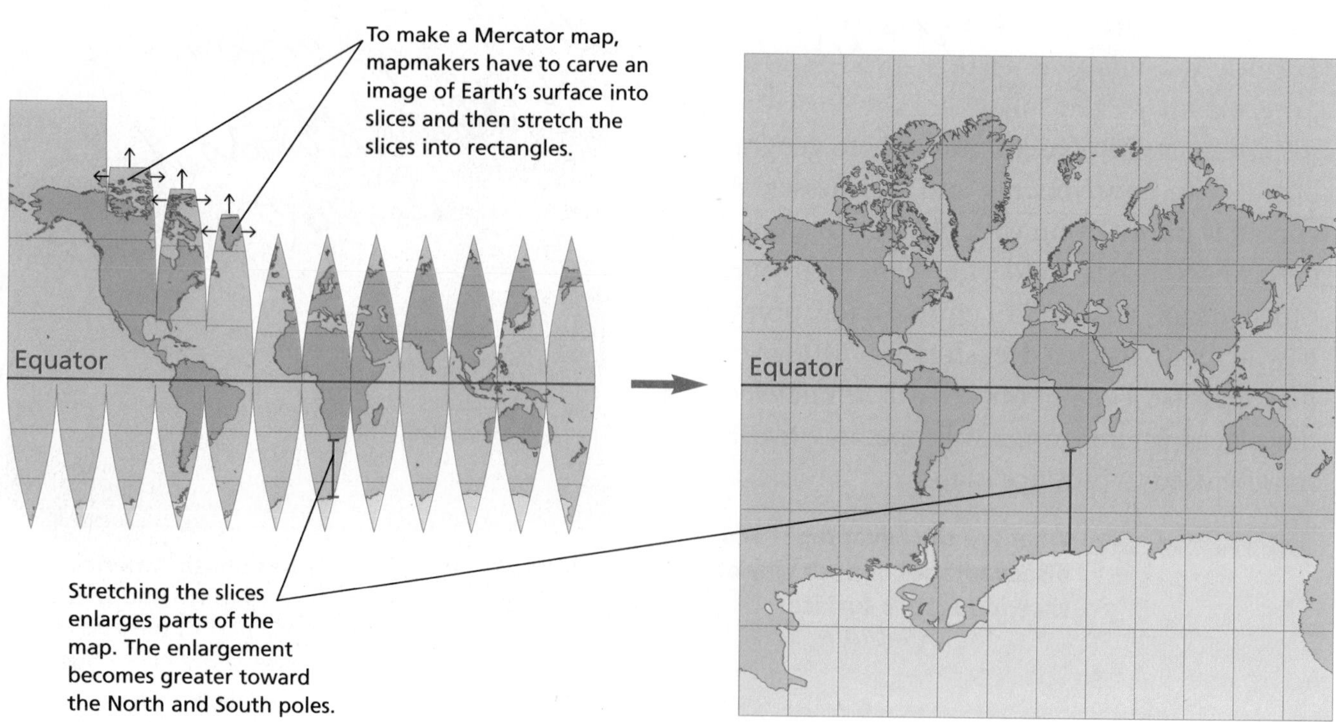

To make a Mercator map, mapmakers have to carve an image of Earth's surface into slices and then stretch the slices into rectangles.
Equator
Equator
Stretching the slices enlarges parts of the map. The enlargement becomes greater toward the North and South poles.

Equal-Area Projections An equal-area map shows the correct size of landmasses, but their shapes are altered. Lines that would be straight on Earth may be forced into curves to fit on the map's flat surface.

The Robinson Projection This projection is named for its designer, Arthur Robinson. Today, many geographers believe that the Robinson projection is the best world map available. It is used for most of the world maps in this book. This projection shows most distances, sizes, and shapes quite accurately. However, even a Robinson projection has distortions, especially in areas around the edges of the map.

Other Projections There are many other types of projections besides the ones shown here. Some are useful for showing small areas but not for showing the whole world. Others are good for specific purposes, such as planning a plane's flight route.

✓ Reading Check **What are the strengths and weaknesses of the Mercator, equal-area, and Robinson projections?**

Making an Equal-Area Map

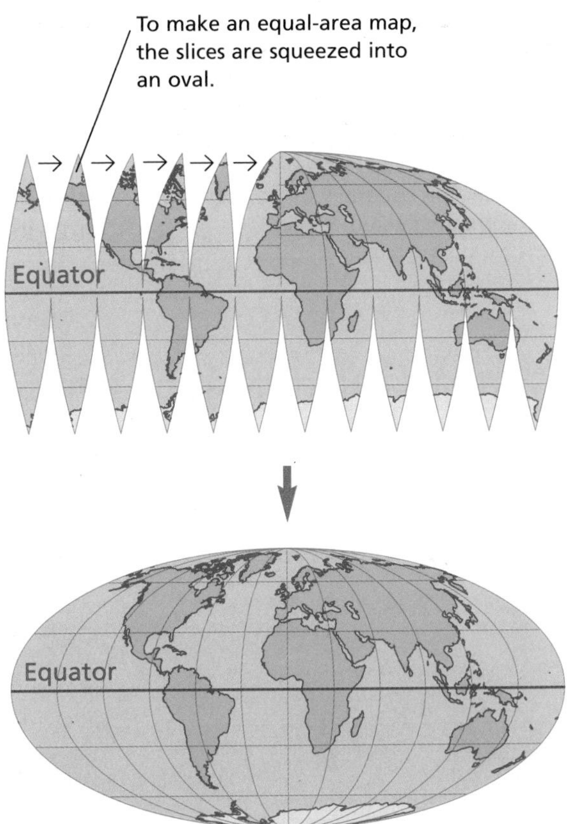
To make an equal-area map, the slices are squeezed into an oval.
Equator
Equator

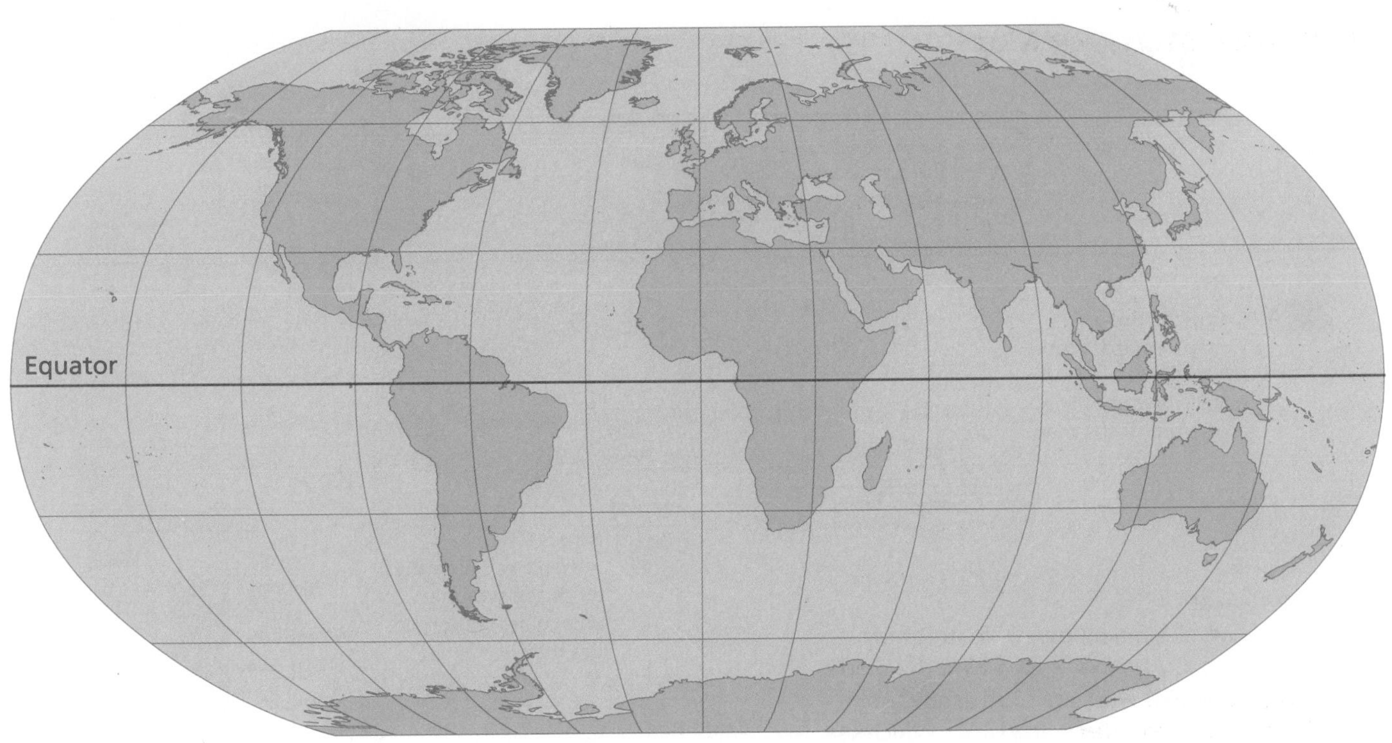
Equator

The World: Robinson Projection

Reading Maps

Look at the maps shown on these two pages. One is a physical map of the country of China. The other is a highway map of the state of Georgia. These maps cover completely different areas and show different kinds of information. Despite their differences, both maps have all of the basic parts that you will find on most maps. Knowing how to use these parts will help you to read and understand any kind of map.

Title
Most maps have a title near the top of the map. The title generally tells you the type of information and the area covered on the map.

Locator Globe
Maps may include a locator globe that shows on a globe the location of the area covered by the map.

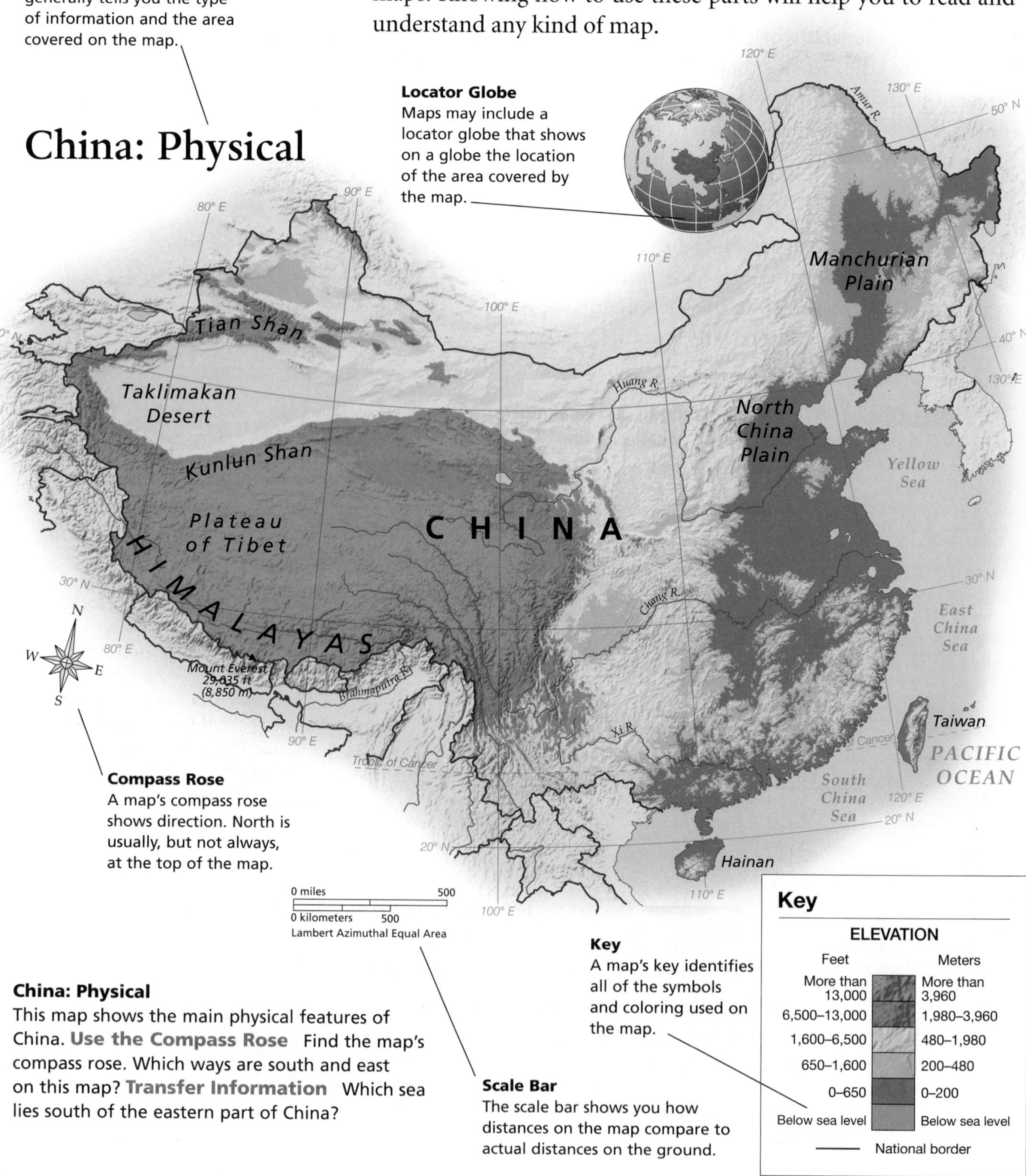

Compass Rose
A map's compass rose shows direction. North is usually, but not always, at the top of the map.

Key
A map's key identifies all of the symbols and coloring used on the map.

Scale Bar
The scale bar shows you how distances on the map compare to actual distances on the ground.

China: Physical
This map shows the main physical features of China. **Use the Compass Rose** Find the map's compass rose. Which ways are south and east on this map? **Transfer Information** Which sea lies south of the eastern part of China?

Georgia Highways

Georgia Highways
Notice that this map of Georgia has the same basic parts as the physical map of China: a title, a key, a locator globe, a compass rose, and a scale bar.
Use Scale *Using a ruler, measure the distance on the map between Atlanta and Macon. Then hold the ruler against the scale bar. How many miles is Atlanta from Macon?*

The Parts of a Map Both maps on these pages have what geographers call a **compass rose,** a diagram of a compass showing direction. If you want to find directions such as north, south, east, or west, just look for the map's compass rose.

Both maps also have a scale bar. The scale bar shows how distances on the map compare to actual distances on the land. Scales vary, depending on the map. If you compare the scale bar on the map of China to the bar on the map of Georgia, you will see that the map of China covers much greater distances on the ground even though the map is not much bigger.

On any map, the **key,** or legend, is the part of the map that explains the symbols and shading on the map. For example, the key on the highway map of Georgia shows the colored lines that stand for different kinds of highways. While some maps use symbols, other maps, like the physical map of China, use coloring to present information. The key shows which colors stand for which elevations.

✓ Reading Check **How do the different parts of a map help you to find information?**

MAP MASTER™ Skills Activity

Maps of Different Scale

Maps with different scales have different uses. Maps with a large scale, such as the map of Greater London, give a general picture of a large area. Maps with a smaller scale, such as the map of Central London, show more detail and are useful for finding landmarks.

Greater London

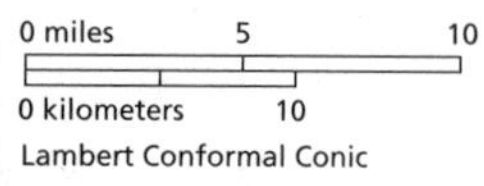

Key

- Built-up area
- City or county border
- National capital
- Town or neighborhood
- Airport

Central London

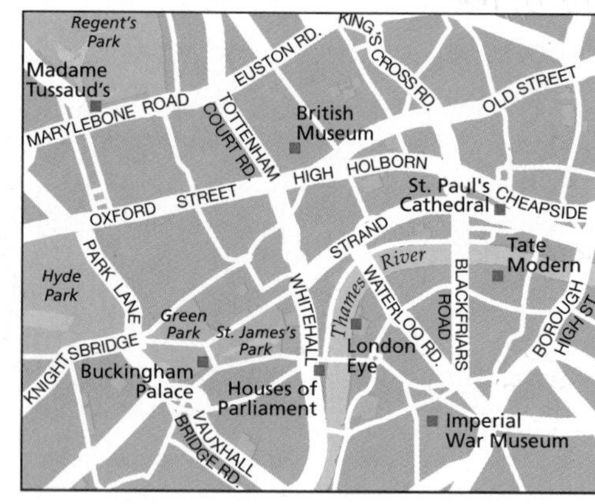

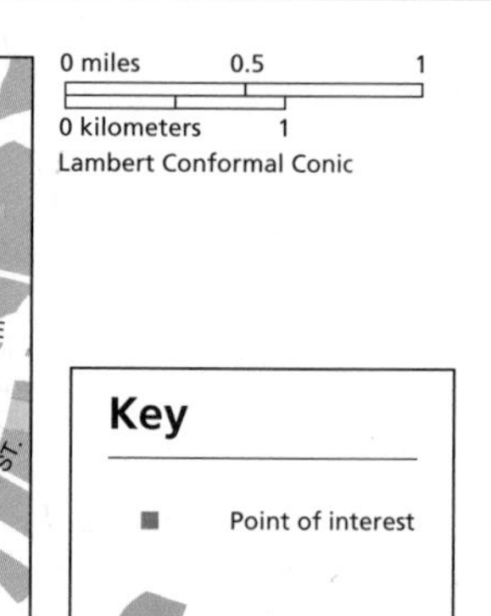

Two Maps of London
The map of Central London zooms in on the area inside the red box on the map of Greater London. **Analyze** Which map shows the city's size? Which shows tourist attractions?

Go Online
PHSchool.com Use Web Code **lep-3112** for step-by-step **map skills practice.**

Section 2 Assessment

Key Terms
Review the key terms at the beginning of this section. Use each term in a sentence that explains its meaning.

Target Reading Skill
Go back and find the paragraph under the heading The Mercator Projection. Paraphrase this paragraph, or rewrite it in your own words.

Comprehension and Critical Thinking
1. (a) Identify What information sources do mapmakers use?
(b) Evaluate What are the advantages and disadvantages of each information source?
(c) Predict To make a map of small streams in an area of thick vegetation, what source would a mapmaker most likely use?
2. (a) Recall What are the advantages and disadvantages of a Mercator projection and of an equal-area projection?
(b) Apply Information Which projection would you use to plan a voyage by ship in a straight line across an ocean?
3. (a) Define On a map, what are the key, title, compass rose, and scale bar?
(b) Synthesize Information If you made a map of places to shop in your area, what might you put in the map's key?

Writing Activity
Look at the physical map of China. Plan a route for a trip from its east coast to its western border. Using information from the map, describe the landscape that you will see along the way.

For: An activity on maps
Visit: PHSchool.com
Web Code: led-3102

Chapter 1 Review and Assessment

◆ Chapter Summary

Section 1: The Five Themes of Geography

- Geography is the study of Earth.
- Geographers can pinpoint any location on the surface of Earth using lines of latitude and longitude, which form an imaginary grid.
- There are five themes of geography—location, regions, place, movement, and human-environment interaction. They offer five ways to gather and understand information about places on Earth.

Section 2: The Geographer's Tools

- Maps can show more details of Earth's surface than globes, but showing Earth's round surface on flat maps causes distortion.
- Projections are different ways of showing Earth's round surface on a flat map.
- Parts of the map such as the key, compass rose, and scale bar can help you to find and understand information on any map.

Earth viewed from space

◆ Key Terms

Each of the statements below contains a key term from the chapter. If the statement is true, write *true*. If it is false, rewrite the statement to make it true.

1. The cardinal directions are north, east, south, and west.
2. Latitude is a measure of the distance north or south of Earth's Equator.
3. Longitude is a measure of the distance north or south of the Equator.
4. A hemisphere is a half of Earth.
5. A meridian is a line of latitude.
6. The scale is the part of the map that shows cardinal directions.
7. A projection is a way of mapping the flat surface of Earth onto a round globe.
8. The compass rose is the part of a map that shows symbols and their meanings.
9. The key is the part of the map that shows relative distances.

Review and Assessment (continued)

◆ Comprehension and Critical Thinking

10. **(a) List** What five themes can help you organize infomation about Earth?
(b) Categorize Under which theme would you discuss building a dam on a river in a desert?

11. **(a) Recall** How do geographers pinpoint the exact location of any place on Earth?
(b) Infer Why might it be useful to know the exact location of a place?

12. **(a) Identify** What unifying characteristics might be used to describe a region?
(b) Draw Conclusions Might a single place be part of more than one region? Explain.

13. **(a) Recall** What are the disadvantages of globes? What are the disadvantages of maps?
(b) Apply Information Which would be more helpful for studying the exact shapes of continents, a globe or a map?

14. **(a) Describe** What are the main features of the Mercator projection?
(b) Infer Why is the Mercator projection still used by navigators today?
(c) Generalize When might you want to use a projection other than the Mercator projection?

15. **(a) List** What are the basic parts that most maps have?
(b) Synthesize Information How can you use the parts of a new map to understand it?

◆ Skills Practice

Using Reliable Information In the Skills for Life activity in this chapter, you learned how to use reliable information. Review the steps for this skill. Then apply them to the text below. Suppose you found this text in a teen magazine. Decide whether you think the information is reliable. Write a sentence that explains why or why not.

"Japan is a very clean country. I spent a whole week in Japan. The buses and trains were very clean. I didn't go inside a Japanese home, but I bet they are very clean, too."

◆ Writing Activity: Geography

Write down the name of the place where you live. Below that name, list the five themes of geography. Next to each theme, describe how it applies to your city, town, or state.

MAP MASTER™ Skills Activity

The Globe

Place Location For each place listed below, write the letter from the map that shows its location.

1. Prime Meridian
2. Equator
3. North Pole
4. South Pole
5. Europe
6. Africa
7. South America
8. North America

Go Online PHSchool.com Use Web Code **lep-3113** for an **interactive map.**

Standardized Test Prep

Test-Taking Tips

Some questions on standardized tests ask you to make mental maps. Do the exercise in the box below. Then follow the tips to answer the sample question.

Draw a simple map of the world based on maps you have seen. Draw a rough shape for each landmass. Draw the Prime Meridian and the Equator across the map.

TIP Find the continents on your map. How is the world divided into hemispheres?

Pick the letter that best answers the question.

Which continent lies completely in both the Northern Hemisphere and the Western Hemisphere?

A Europe
B Greenland
C North America
D Australia

TIP Beware of careless errors. Read the question twice and think carefully about each answer choice.

Think It Through Australia is located completely in both the Southern Hemisphere and the Eastern Hemisphere. Europe is in the Northern Hemisphere but also mostly in the Eastern Hemisphere. Greenland is completely in both the Northern Hemisphere and the Western Hemisphere—as the question asks. But be careful! Greenland is not a continent. The answer is C.

Practice Questions

Use the tips above and other tips in this book to help you answer the following questions.

1. Which of the following is NOT a tool a geographer would use to study absolute location?
   A cardinal directions
   B climate
   C lines of latitude
   D degrees

2. What disadvantage do all flat maps share?
   A They have some sort of distortion.
   B They are hard to carry.
   C There are few sources to create them.
   D They can only show areas at a small scale.

3. A map with cities and colored lines marked with numbers is probably a type of
   A climate map.
   B road map.
   C physical map.
   D vegetation map.

Read the passage below and answer the question that follows.

This area is located in the United States, west of the Mississippi River. It is mainly hot and dry, with little rainfall, so people have built many dams there. Its landforms include rivers, canyons, and deserts.

4. Which of the five themes are used to describe this area?
   A location, movement, regions
   B movement, place, regions, human-environment interaction
   C regions, location, movement
   D location, place, human-environment interaction

Use Web Code **lea-3103** for a **Chapter 1 self-test.**

Chapter

2 Earth's Physical Geography

Chapter Preview

This chapter will introduce you to the physical geography of Earth, including the planet's structure, climate, and vegetation.

Target Reading Skill

Context In this chapter you will focus on using context to help you understand unfamiliar words. Context includes the words, phrases, and sentences surrounding a word.

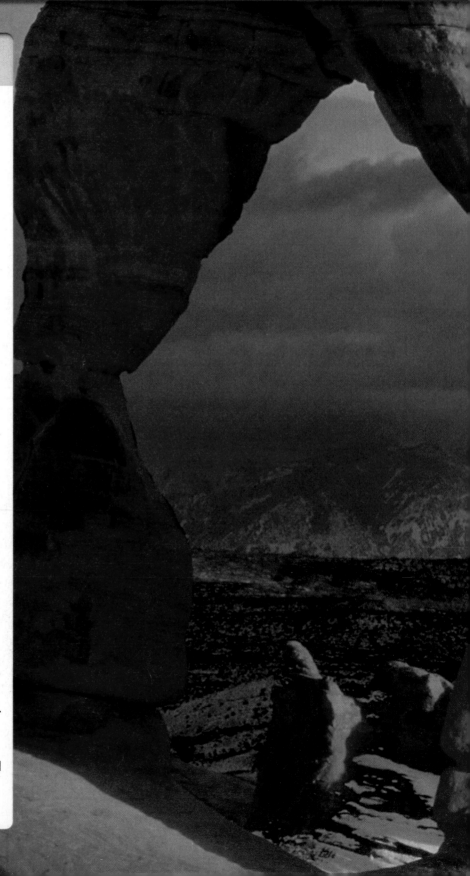

▶ **Delicate Arch in Arches National Park, Utah**

Section 1 Our Planet, Earth

Prepare to Read

Objectives

In this section you will

1. Learn about Earth's movement in relation to the sun.
2. Explore seasons and latitude.

Taking Notes

Copy the table below. As you read this section, fill in the table with information about the movements of Earth relative to the sun, days and nights, seasons, and latitude. Add more lines as you need them.

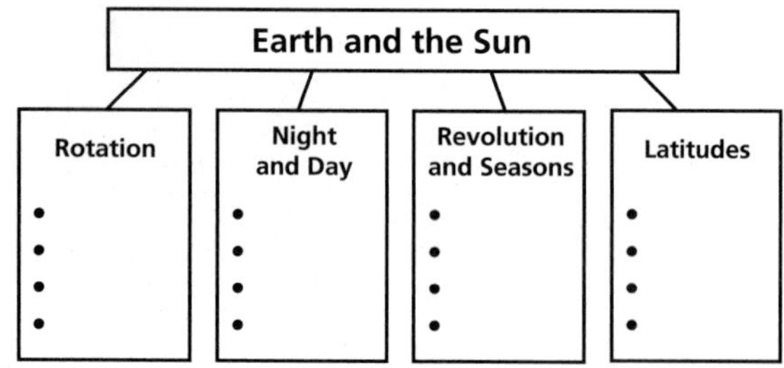

Target Reading Skill

Use Context Clues You can sometimes find the meaning of a word by using context—the words and sentences around that word. In some cases the context will describe the word. In this example, the phrase in italics describes a planet:

> A planet is a *large object that circles a star.*

As you read, look at the context for the word *galaxy* in the paragraph below. What do you think *galaxy* means?

Key Terms

- **orbit** (AWR bit) *n.* the path one body makes as it circles around another
- **revolution** (rev uh LOO shun) *n.* circular motion
- **axis** (AK sis) *n.* an imaginary line through Earth between the North and South poles, around which Earth turns
- **rotation** (roh TAY shun) *n.* a complete turn

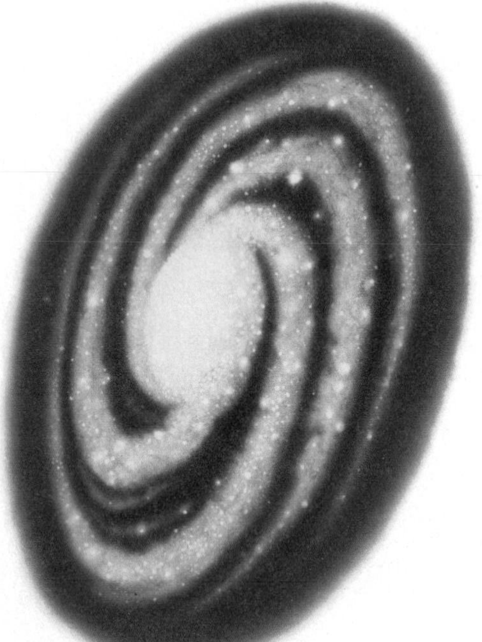
The Milky Way Galaxy

Earth and the Sun

Earth, the sun, the planets, and the stars in the sky are all part of a galaxy, or family of stars. Our galaxy is just one of the billions of galaxies in the universe. We call our galaxy the Milky Way because, in a dark night sky, away from city lights, its billions of stars look like a trail of spilled milk. Our sun is one of those stars. The sun is just a tiny speck compared to the rest of the Milky Way, but it is the center of everything for Earth and the other planets in the solar system. The solar system includes Earth, the other planets, and other objects that orbit the sun.

Even though the sun is about 93 million miles (150 million kilometers) away, it provides Earth with heat and light. Earth travels around the sun in a nearly circular **orbit,** which is the path one body makes as it circles around another. Earth takes 365¼ days, or one year, to complete one **revolution,** or circular motion, in its orbit around the sun.

Understanding Days and Nights As Earth circles the sun, it also spins in space. Earth turns around its **axis**—an imaginary line running through Earth between the North and South poles. Each complete turn, or **rotation,** takes about 24 hours. As Earth rotates, it is night on the side away from the sun. As Earth turns toward the sun, the sun appears to rise. When a side of Earth faces the sun, it is daytime. Then, as that side of Earth turns away from the sun, the sun appears to set.

Time Zones Earth rotates toward the east, so the day starts earlier in the east. The time difference is just a few seconds per mile. If every town had its own local time, it would be very confusing. So, governments have divided the world into standard time zones. Times in neighboring zones are one hour apart. There are also a few nonstandard time zones with times less than a full hour away from their neighbors.

✓ Reading Check **What is the connection between Earth's rotation and the change from day to night?**

Links to Math

Time Zones and Longitude
Earth's surface is divided into 360 degrees of longitude: 180 degrees east and west of the Prime Meridian. Since Earth rotates at a steady rate in about 24 hours, its 24 standard time zones are centered the same number of degrees of longitude apart. Can you find this number? (*Hint:* The number is 360° ÷ 24.)

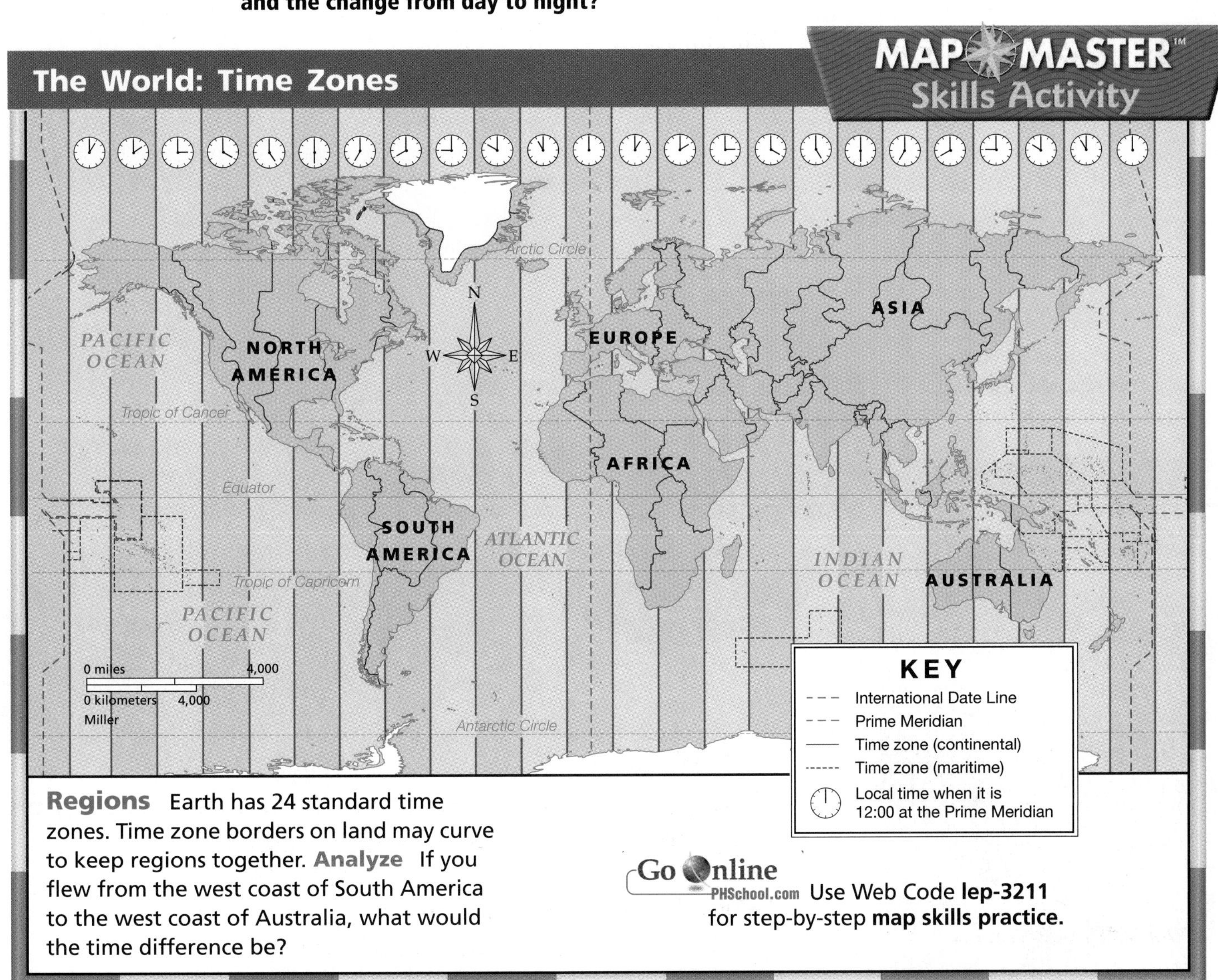

Regions Earth has 24 standard time zones. Time zone borders on land may curve to keep regions together. **Analyze** If you flew from the west coast of South America to the west coast of Australia, what would the time difference be?

Go Online PHSchool.com Use Web Code **lep-3211** for step-by-step **map skills practice.**

Seasons and Latitude

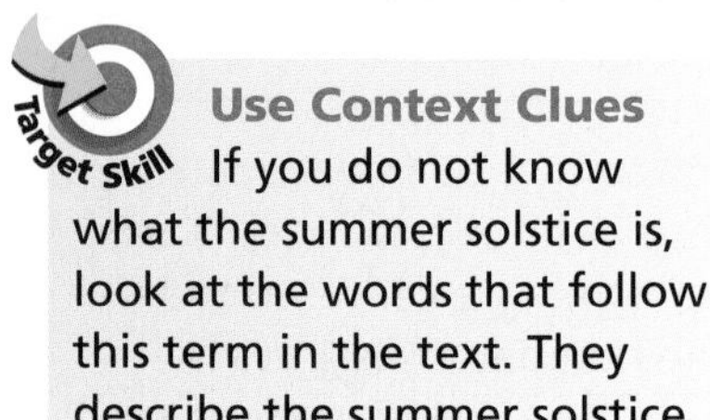

Use Context Clues If you do not know what the summer solstice is, look at the words that follow this term in the text. They describe the summer solstice.

The axis of Earth is tilted relative to its orbit. At different points in Earth's orbit, the Northern Hemisphere may tilt toward or away from the sun. At other points in the orbit, neither hemisphere tilts toward or away from the sun. The revolution of the tilted planet Earth causes seasons.

At the summer solstice, the Northern Hemisphere is tilted farthest toward the sun. Places in this hemisphere have longer daylight and more direct sunlight at the solstice than at other times of the year. This direct sunlight causes the heat of summer.

The Revolution of Earth

As Earth travels around the sun, the tilt of its axis causes our seasons. Each hemisphere shifts from the long days and direct sun of summer to the short days and indirect sun of winter, and then back again. This diagram shows seasons in the Northern Hemisphere.

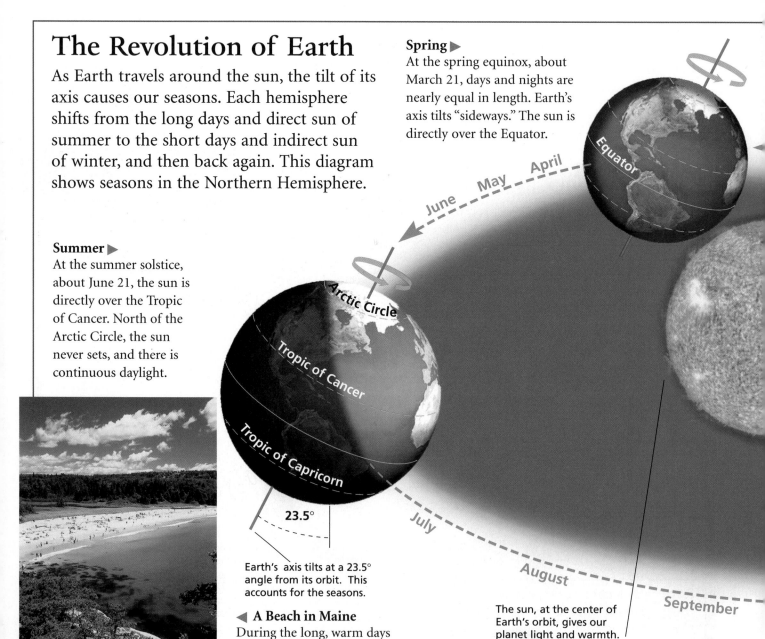

Spring ▶
At the spring equinox, about March 21, days and nights are nearly equal in length. Earth's axis tilts "sideways." The sun is directly over the Equator.

Summer ▶
At the summer solstice, about June 21, the sun is directly over the Tropic of Cancer. North of the Arctic Circle, the sun never sets, and there is continuous daylight.

Equator
April
May
June
Arctic Circle
Tropic of Cancer
Tropic of Capricorn
23.5°
July
August
September

Earth's axis tilts at a 23.5° angle from its orbit. This accounts for the seasons.

◀ A Beach in Maine
During the long, warm days of summer, green plants grow and people head for beaches.

The sun, at the center of Earth's orbit, gives our planet light and warmth.

Diagram not to scale

As Earth moves through its orbit, the Northern Hemisphere is tilted farther from the sun. Sunlight is less direct, and we have the chill of fall. When the Northern Hemisphere is tilted farthest from the sun at the winter solstice, days are short, the sun's rays reach us at a steep angle, and we have cold weather. Finally, Earth's revolution moves the Northern Hemisphere back toward the sun, and we have the warming trend of spring.

When the Northern Hemisphere is tilted toward the sun, the Southern Hemisphere is tilted away, and vice versa, so the seasons are reversed in the Southern Hemisphere.

▼ Winter
About December 21, at winter solstice, the sun is directly over the Tropic of Capricorn, and the area north of the Arctic Circle is in constant darkness.

◀ Fall
By about September 23, the sun is again directly over the Equator. Less direct sunlight in the Northern Hemisphere brings cooler temperatures.

▲ Winter in the Arctic
Iqaluit, Canada, is near the Arctic Circle. In winter, there is very little sun, and temperatures are bitterly cold.

GEOGRAPHY SKILLS PRACTICE

Regions Earth's tilt means that the seasons are different in the Northern and Southern hemispheres. **Compare and Contrast** When it is spring in the Northern Hemisphere, what is the season in the Southern Hemisphere?

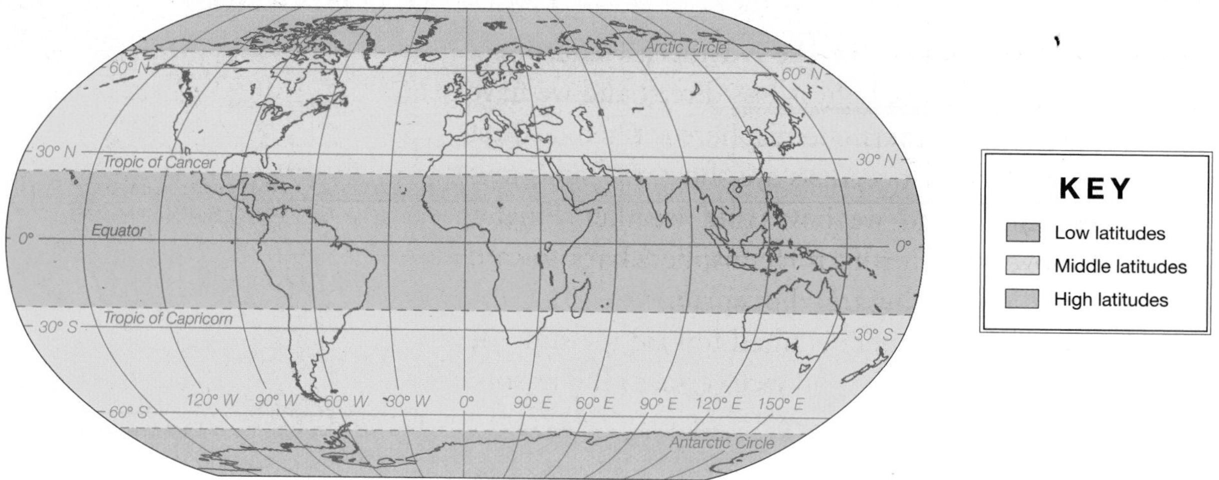

Zones of Latitude
The low latitudes, or tropics, are the single orange band around the Equator. The middle latitudes are the two yellow bands just to the north and south. The two green zones in the far north and south are the high latitudes, or polar zones.

Latitudes The areas between the Tropic of Cancer and the Tropic of Capricorn are called the low latitudes, or the tropics. The tropics have fairly direct sunlight and hot weather all year.

The areas above the Arctic Circle and below the Antarctic Circle are the high latitudes, or the polar zones. Though the polar zones may receive long hours of sunlight during the summer, the sun is never directly overhead. They are cool or very cold all year.

The areas between the high and low latitudes are the middle latitudes, or the temperate zones. In summer, these areas receive fairly direct sunlight. In winter, they get very indirect sunlight. So, the middle latitudes have marked seasons: a hot summer, a cold winter, and a moderate spring and fall.

✓ Reading Check **What is the relation between seasons and latitude?**

Section 1 Assessment

Key Terms
Review the key terms at the beginning of this section. Use each term in a sentence that explains its meaning.

Target Reading Skill
Find the phrase *winter solstice* on page 31. Use context to figure out its meaning. What do you think it means? What clues helped you find a meaning?

Comprehension and Critical Thinking
1. (a) Define What is the rotation of Earth?
(b) Synthesize Information How is Earth's rotation connected to the change from day to night?
2. (a) Identify On the time zone map on page 29, find the time zone where you live.
(b) Evaluate What is the time difference between your home and Greenwich, England?
(c) Analyze How is this time difference related to Earth's rotation?
3. (a) Recall What is Earth's tilt?
(b) Describe How does Earth's orbit affect its tilted hemispheres?
(c) Identify Cause and Effect How do Earth's tilt and orbit cause the seasons?

Writing Activity
Write a short passage for a younger child, explaining the movements of Earth.

For: An activity on our planet, Earth
Visit: PHSchool.com
Web Code: led-3201

Section 2 Forces Shaping Earth

Prepare to Read

Objectives

In this section you will

1. Learn about the planet Earth.
2. Explore the forces inside Earth.
3. Explore the forces on Earth's surface.

Taking Notes

As you read this section, look for details about Earth's structure, Earth's landforms, forces inside Earth, how continents move, and forces on Earth's surface. Copy the web diagram below, add more branches and ovals as needed, and write each detail in the correct oval.

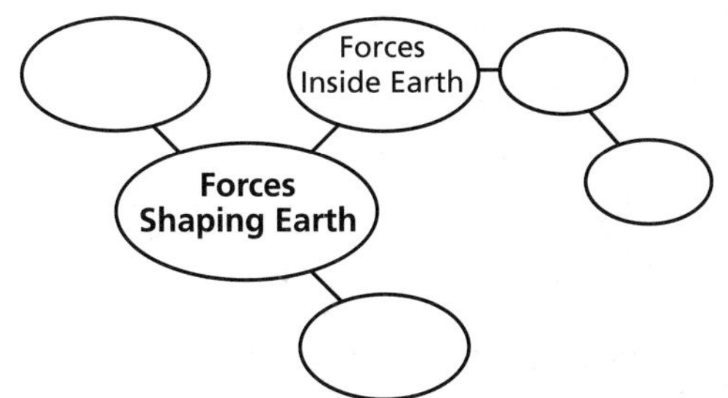

Target Reading Skill

Use Context Clues You can sometimes find the meaning of a word or phrase by using context. Sometimes the context will define or restate the word. In this example, the phrase in italics defines *continent*:

> A continent, or *one of Earth's large land areas . . .*

As you read, look at the context for the phrase *Ring of Fire* in the paragraph below. What do you think the phrase *Ring of Fire* means?

Key Terms

- **core** (kawr) *n.* the sphere of very hot metal at the center of Earth
- **mantle** (MAN tul) *n.* the thick layer around Earth's core
- **crust** (krust) *n.* the thin, rocky layer on Earth's surface
- **magma** (MAG muh) *n.* soft, nearly molten rock
- **plate** (playt) *n.* a huge block of Earth's crust
- **weathering** (WETH ur ing) *n.* a process that breaks rocks down into small pieces
- **erosion** (ee ROH zhun) *n.* the removal of small pieces of rock by water, ice, or wind

Understanding Earth

Around the rim of the Pacific Ocean is a string of volcanoes and earthquake belts called the "Ring of Fire." About 80 percent of the world's earthquakes and many of the world's active volcanoes occur in that ring. Earthquakes and volcanoes are two forces that shape and reshape Earth. They are one reason why Earth's surface constantly changes. They also provide clues about Earth's structure.

Hot rock from inside Earth flows into the Pacific Ocean to form new land in Hawaii.

What Is Earth Made Of? To understand the forces that shape Earth, you must study Earth's structure. A sphere of very hot metal at the center of Earth is called the **core.** The **mantle** is a thick, hot, rocky layer around the core. The thin layer of rocks and minerals that surrounds the mantle is called the **crust.** In effect, the crust floats on top of the mantle. The heat of the core and mantle helps shape Earth's crust. The surface of the crust includes Earth's land areas as well as the ocean floors.

Earth's Layers

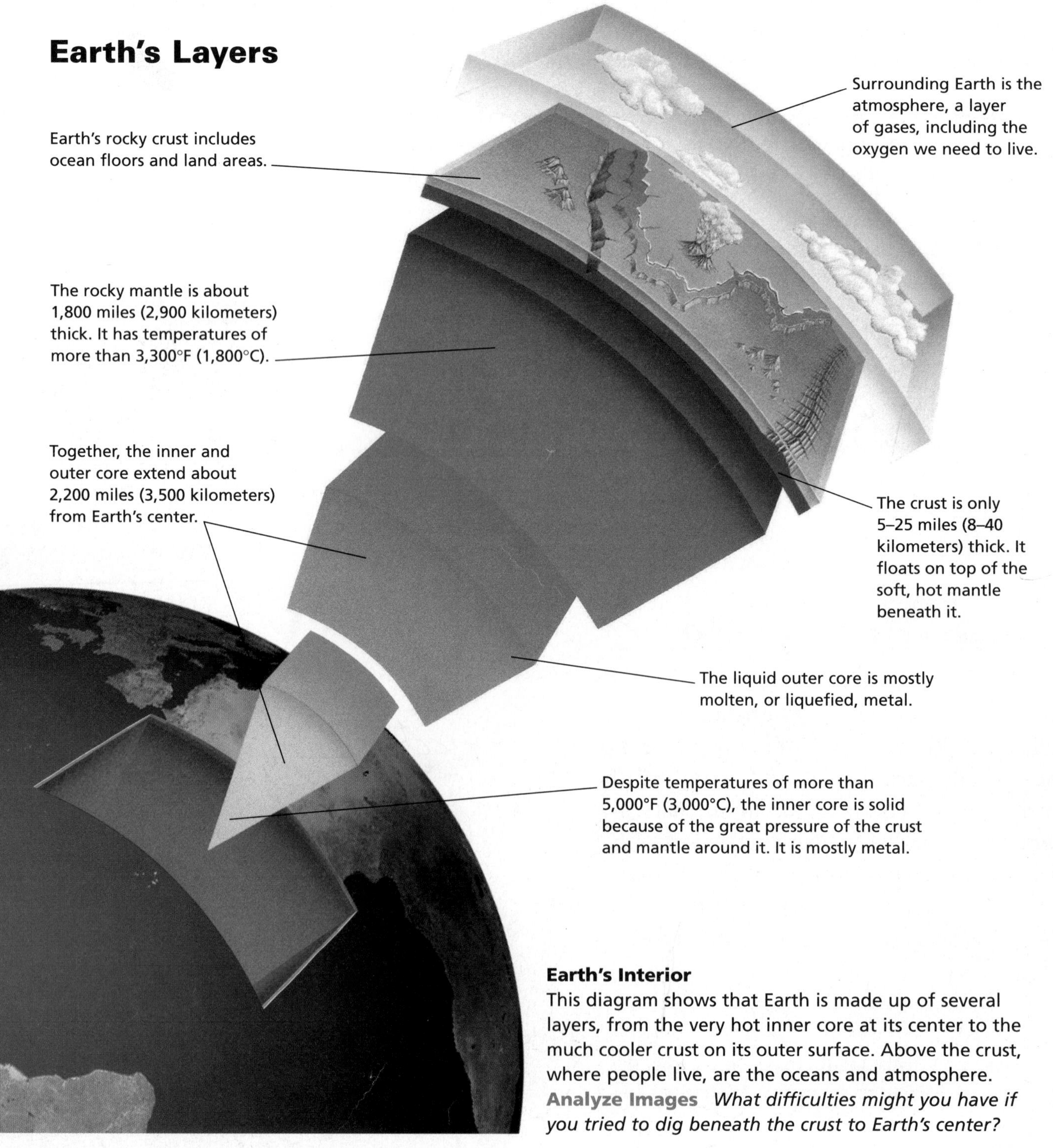

Earth's rocky crust includes ocean floors and land areas.
Surrounding Earth is the atmosphere, a layer of gases, including the oxygen we need to live.
The rocky mantle is about 1,800 miles (2,900 kilometers) thick. It has temperatures of more than 3,300°F (1,800°C).
Together, the inner and outer core extend about 2,200 miles (3,500 kilometers) from Earth's center.
The crust is only 5–25 miles (8–40 kilometers) thick. It floats on top of the soft, hot mantle beneath it.
The liquid outer core is mostly molten, or liquefied, metal.
Despite temperatures of more than 5,000°F (3,000°C), the inner core is solid because of the great pressure of the crust and mantle around it. It is mostly metal.

Earth's Interior
This diagram shows that Earth is made up of several layers, from the very hot inner core at its center to the much cooler crust on its outer surface. Above the crust, where people live, are the oceans and atmosphere.
Analyze Images *What difficulties might you have if you tried to dig beneath the crust to Earth's center?*

Water and Air Less than 30 percent of Earth's surface is land. Water covers more than 70 percent of Earth's surface in lakes, rivers, seas, and oceans. The oceans hold about 97 percent of Earth's water. This water is salty. Very little of Earth's water is fresh water, or water without salt. Most fresh water is frozen in ice sheets near the North and South poles. People can use only a small part of Earth's fresh water. This fresh water comes from lakes, rivers, and ground water, which are fed by rain.

Above Earth's surface is the atmosphere, a layer of gases a few miles thick. It provides life-giving oxygen to people and animals, and carbon dioxide to plants.

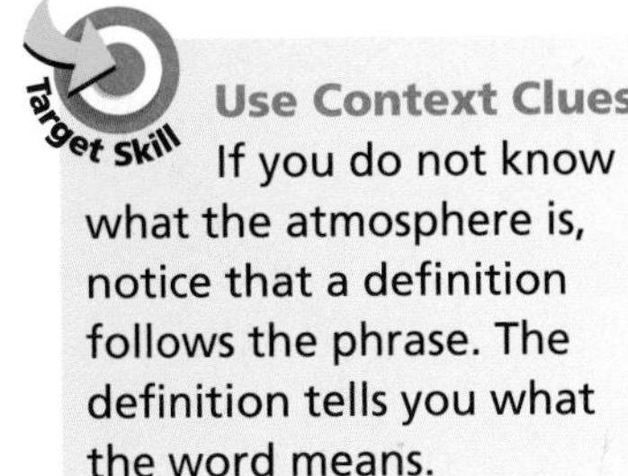

Use Context Clues If you do not know what the atmosphere is, notice that a definition follows the phrase. The definition tells you what the word means.

Landforms Many different landforms, or shapes and types of land, cover Earth's land surfaces. Mountains are landforms that rise more than 2,000 feet (610 meters) above sea level or the surrounding flatlands. They are wide at the bottom and rise steeply to a narrow peak or ridge. A volcano is a kind of mountain. Hills are landforms with rounded tops, which rise above the surrounding land but are lower and less steep than mountains. A plateau is a large, mostly flat area that rises above the surrounding land. At least one side of a plateau has a steep slope. Plains are large areas of flat or gently rolling land.

√ Reading Check **Which layer of Earth contains all of its landforms?**

Land and Water
Ice floes float near Alexander Island, off the coast of Antarctica. Salt water covers most of Earth's surface. Most fresh water is ice, frozen in polar regions such as Antarctica.
Analyze Images *What landforms can you see in this photograph?*

Forces Inside Earth

Heat deep inside Earth is constantly reshaping the planet's surface. The intense heat causes rock to rise toward the surface. Where streams of this soft, nearly molten rock called **magma** reach Earth's crust, they push up the crust to form volcanoes. Volcanoes spew molten rock, or lava, from inside Earth. Streams of magma may also push the crust apart along seams. Huge blocks of Earth's crust called **plates** are separated by these seams. Plates may include continents or parts of continents. Each plate also includes part of the ocean floor. Along seams, mainly beneath oceans, streams of magma rise from inside Earth. As the magma cools, it forms new crust and pushes the old crust away from the seams.

How Continents Move

Rising magma forms new crust along seams between Earth's plates. Beneath the surface, some scientists believe, magma moves like a conveyor belt. The belt drags the growing plates and the continents that they carry.

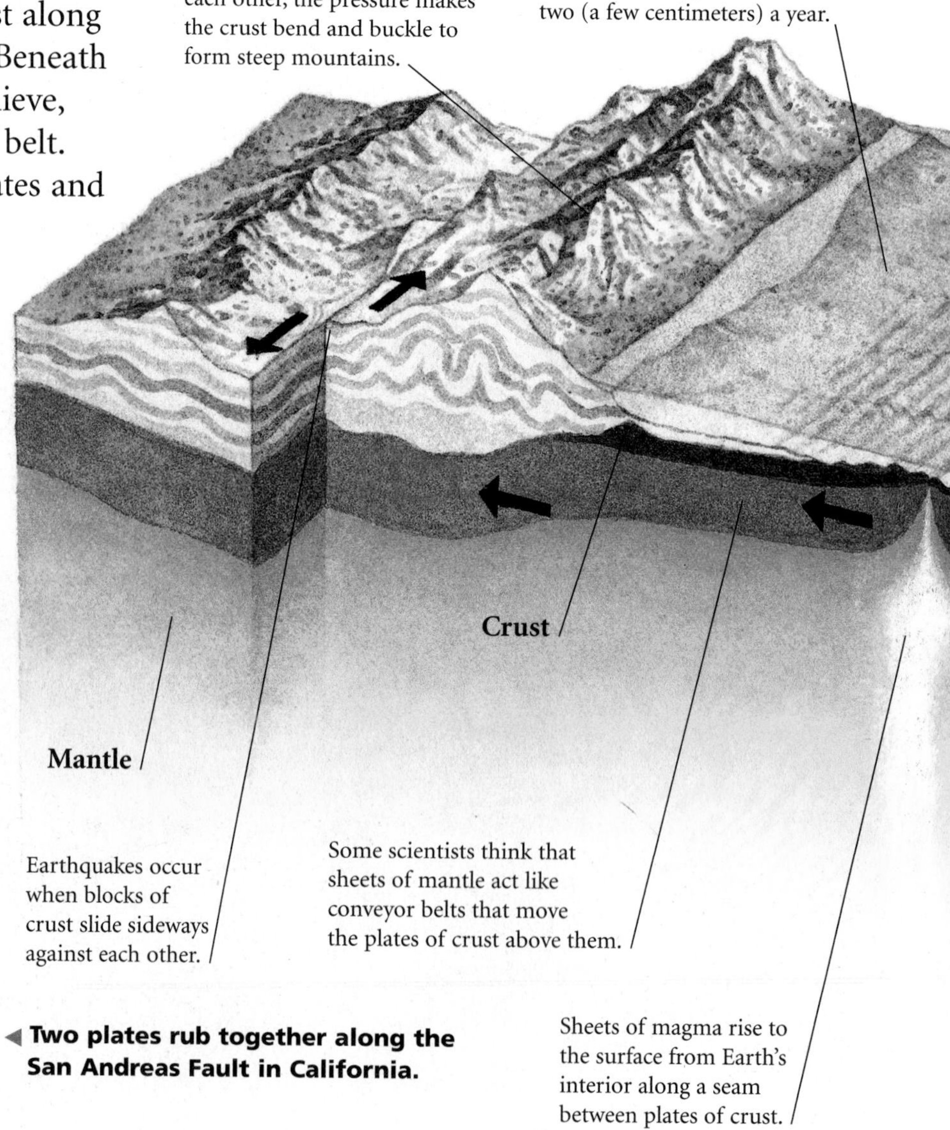
Where two plates push against each other, the pressure makes the crust bend and buckle to form steep mountains.
Plates move only an inch or two (a few centimeters) a year.
Crust
Mantle
Earthquakes occur when blocks of crust slide sideways against each other.
Some scientists think that sheets of mantle act like conveyor belts that move the plates of crust above them.
Sheets of magma rise to the surface from Earth's interior along a seam between plates of crust.

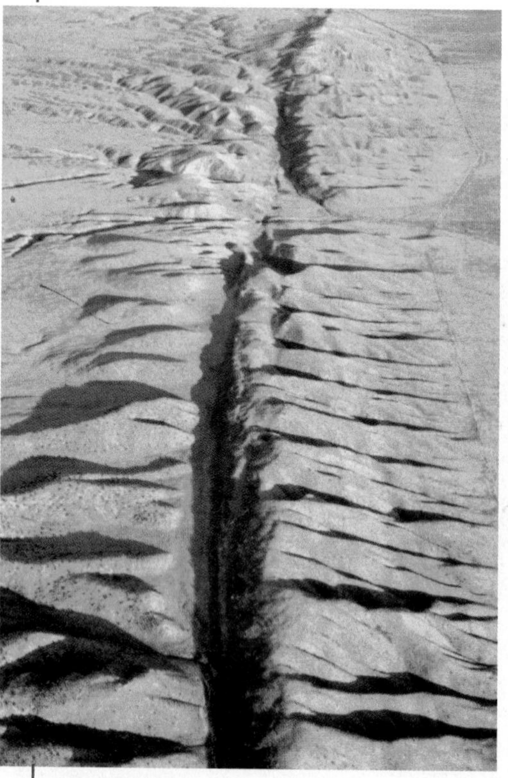

◀ **Two plates rub together along the San Andreas Fault in California.**

Volcanoes and Earthquakes Where a plate of ocean crust collides with a plate of continental crust, the ocean crust plunges underneath the continental plate and melts. Molten rock surges upward, exploding onto the surface through a volcano. The Ring of Fire surrounds the plates that make up the Pacific Ocean. Streams of magma also form volcanoes at places other than plate boundaries. Such volcanoes have shaped the Hawaiian Islands, which are far from a plate boundary.

When two plates push together, the crust cracks and splinters from the pressure. The cracks in Earth's crust are called faults. When blocks of crust rub against each other along faults, they release huge amounts of energy in the form of earthquakes.

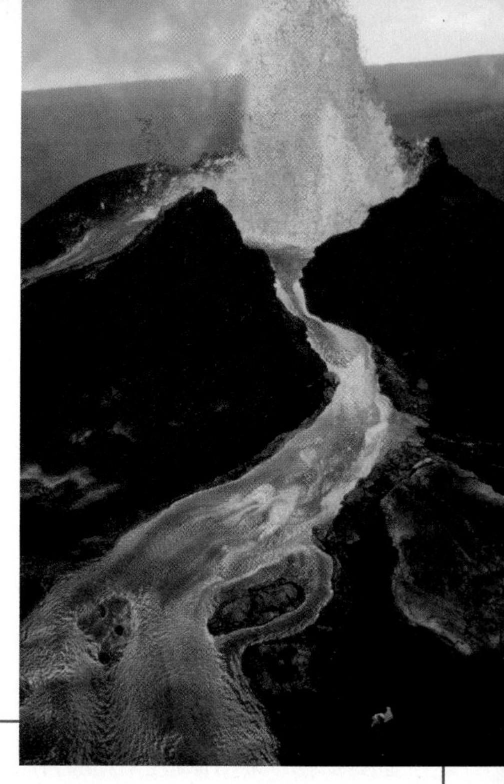

▲ **Molten rock pours from a volcano in Hawaii.**

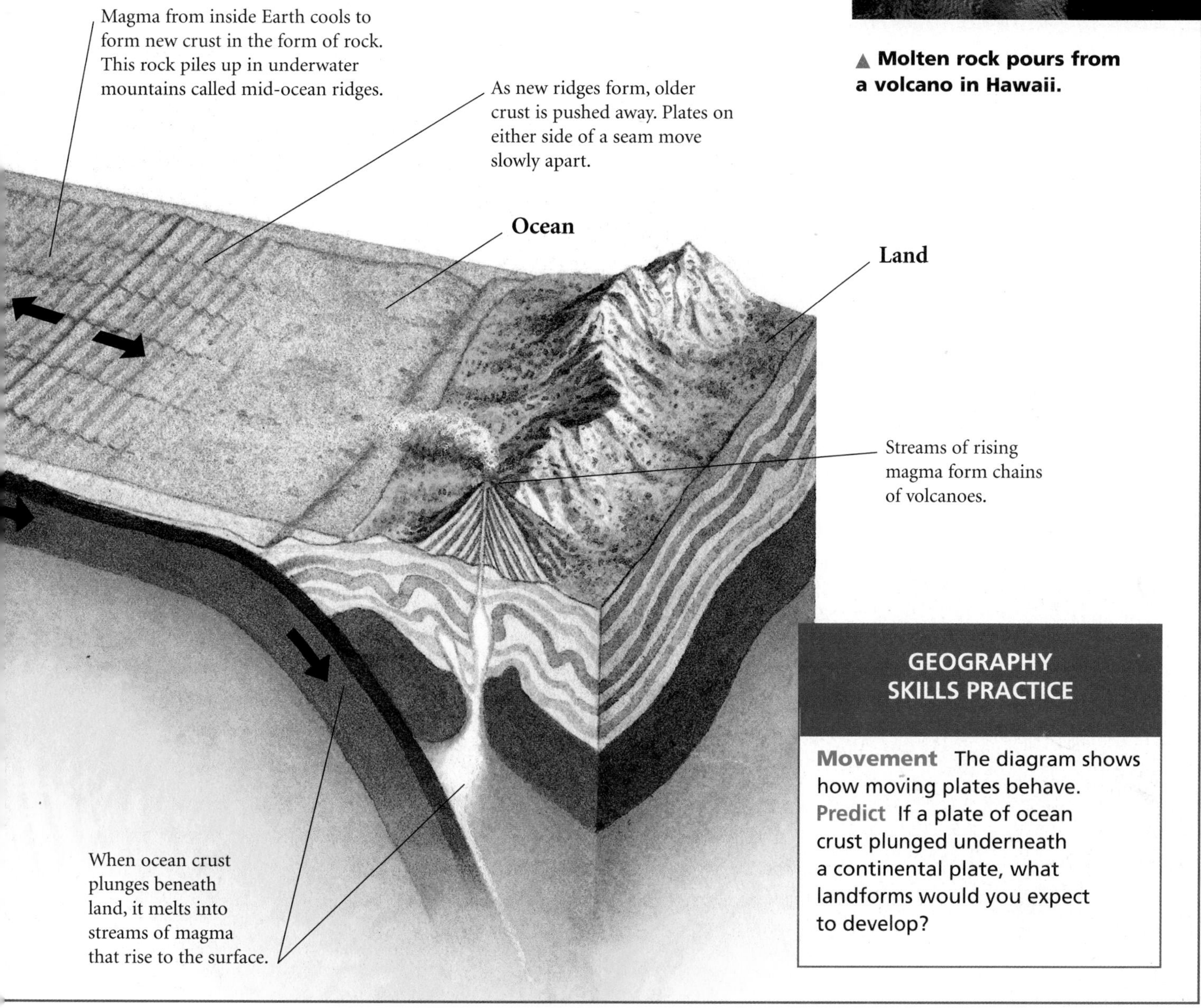

Magma from inside Earth cools to form new crust in the form of rock. This rock piles up in underwater mountains called mid-ocean ridges.

As new ridges form, older crust is pushed away. Plates on either side of a seam move slowly apart.

Ocean

Land

Streams of rising magma form chains of volcanoes.

When ocean crust plunges beneath land, it melts into streams of magma that rise to the surface.

GEOGRAPHY SKILLS PRACTICE

Movement The diagram shows how moving plates behave. **Predict** If a plate of ocean crust plunged underneath a continental plate, what landforms would you expect to develop?

A World of Moving Plates For hundreds of years, geographers wondered how Earth's landmasses took their present shapes and positions. When they looked at the globe, they thought they saw matching shapes in continents that are very far apart. Now that they know how forces inside Earth move continents, they know that those continents were once close together.

✓ Reading Check **How do continents move apart?**

Plate Movements

Plates Shifting Through Time
Most geographers believe that long ago Earth had only one huge continent. They call it Pangaea (pan JEE uh). About 200 million years ago, they conclude, plate movement began to split Pangaea apart. They think that these pieces came to form the continents that we know today. **Analyze** *According to these maps, which present-day continents were once joined together?*

Plates 250 million years ago

Plates 150 million years ago

Plates 75 million years ago

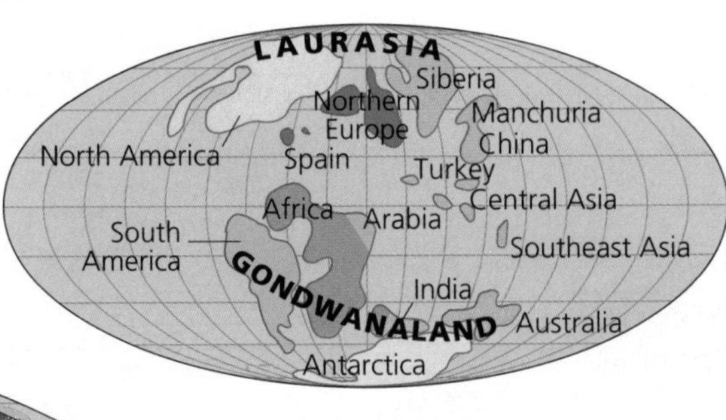

Present-Day Plates
The map below shows Earth's modern plates and plate edges. It also shows how the plates are moving. Earthquakes and volcanoes cluster along plate edges. **Identify** *Which plate is colliding with the North American Plate?*

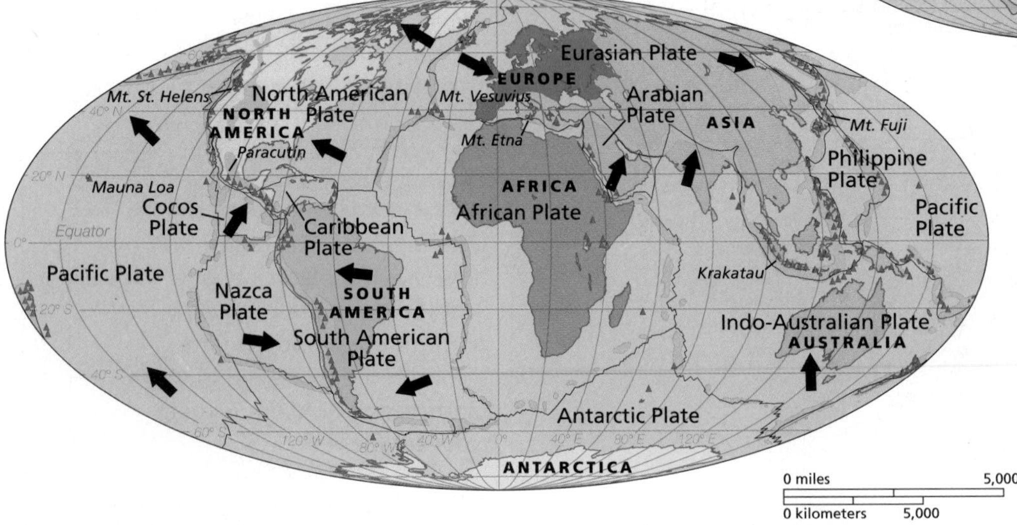

Forces on Earth's Surface

Forces inside Earth move plates apart, produce volcanoes, and slowly build up Earth's crust. Other forces slowly wear it down and reshape it. The forces that wear Earth down are not as dramatic as volcanoes, but over time they are just as effective.

Weathering is a process that breaks rocks down into tiny pieces. Water, ice, and living things like lichens on rocks all cause weathering. Weathering helps create soil, too. Tiny pieces of rock combine with decayed animal and plant material to form soil.

Once this breaking down has taken place, landforms are reshaped by **erosion,** or the removal of small pieces of rock by water, ice, or wind. Hundreds of millions of years ago, the Appalachian Mountains in the eastern United States were as high as the Rocky Mountains of the western United States now are. Rain, snow, and wind slowly wore them down into much lower peaks.

When water, ice, and wind remove material, they deposit it downstream or downwind to create new landforms. Plains are often made of material carried from upstream by rivers.

√ Reading Check **What landforms are products of weathering and erosion?**

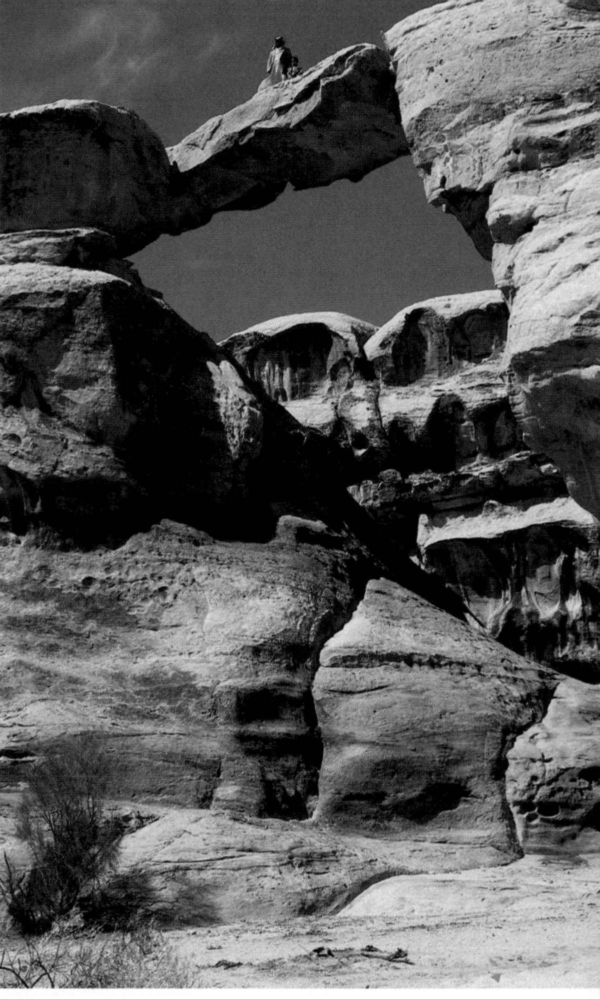

Weathering and erosion formed this natural sandstone bridge in Jordan.

Section 2 Assessment

Key Terms
Review the key terms at the beginning of this section. Use each term in a sentence that explains its meaning.

Target Reading Skill
Find the word *landforms* in the last paragraph of page 35. Use the context to find its meaning. What does it mean? What clues did you use to find its meaning?

Comprehension and Critical Thinking
1. (a) List What are Earth's three main layers?
(b) Synthesize Information How do those layers interact?
2. (a) Recall What forces inside Earth shape Earth's surface?
(b) Explain How do these forces explain the movement of the continents?
(c) Predict How might a continent split in two?
3. (a) Identify What forces cause weathering and erosion?
(b) Compare and Contrast How is erosion different from weathering?

Writing Activity
Think about the region where you live. Does it have steep mountains or volcanoes, rounded hills, or plains? Write a paragraph describing some of the natural forces that are slowly reshaping your region.

For: An activity on Pangaea
Visit: PHSchool.com
Web Code: led-3202

Section 3 Climate and Weather

Prepare to Read

Objectives

In this section you will

1. Learn about weather and climate.
2. Explore latitude, landforms, and precipitation.
3. Discover how oceans affect climate.

Taking Notes

As you read this section, look for topics related to climate and weather, such as landforms, precipitation, oceans, and storms. Copy the outline below and add headings as needed to show the relationships among these topics.

I. Weather
II. Climate
  A. Latitudes
  B.
    1.
    2.
III. Storms

Target Reading Skill

Use Context Clues You can sometimes learn the meaning of a word or phrase when the context gives a comparison. In this example, the word *cyclone* is compared to the phrase in italics.

A cyclone is like *a huge spiral escalator moving air upward.*

Key Terms

- **weather** (WETH ur) *n.* the condition of the air and sky from day to day
- **precipitation** (pree sip uh TAY shun) *n.* water that falls to the ground as rain, sleet, hail, or snow
- **temperature** (TEM pur uh chur) *n.* how hot or cold the air is
- **climate** (KLY mut) *n.* the average weather over many years
- **tropical cyclone** (TRAHP ih kul SY klohn) *n.* an intense wind and rain storm that forms over oceans in the tropics.

This Inuit woman and child are dressed for their cold climate.

Weather or Climate?

Every morning, most people check the weather before they get dressed. But in some parts of India, people have very serious reasons for watching the **weather,** or the condition of the air and sky from day to day. In parts of India, it rains only during one time of year. No one living there wants the rainy days to end too soon. That rain must fill the wells with enough fresh water to last for the entire year.

In India, people are concerned about **precipitation,** or water that falls to the ground as rain, sleet, hail, or snow. When you get dressed in the morning, you may want to know the **temperature,** or how hot or cold the air is. Weather is mainly measured by temperature and precipitation.

The **climate** of a place is the average weather over many years. Climate is not the same as weather. Weather is what people see from day to day. Climate is what usually happens from year to year.

✓ Reading Check **What is the difference between weather and climate?**

Why Climates Vary

Earth has many climates. Some climates are so hot that people rarely need to wear a sweater. In some cold climates, snow stays on the ground most of the year. And there are places on Earth where more than 30 feet (9 meters) of rain falls in a single year.

Climate depends on location. Places in the low latitudes, or tropics, have hot climates, because they get direct sunlight. Places in the high latitudes, or polar regions, have cold climates, because their sunlight is indirect.

Air and water spread heat around the globe as they move. Without wind and water, places in the tropics would overheat. Oceans gain and lose heat slowly, so they keep temperatures mild near coasts. Mountains can also affect climates.

✓ Reading Check **How does latitude affect temperature?**

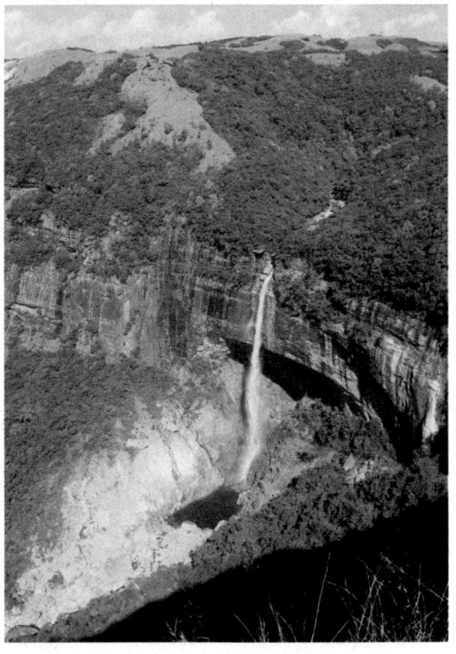

Cherrapunji, India, averages 37 feet (11 meters) of rain a year.

The Water Cycle

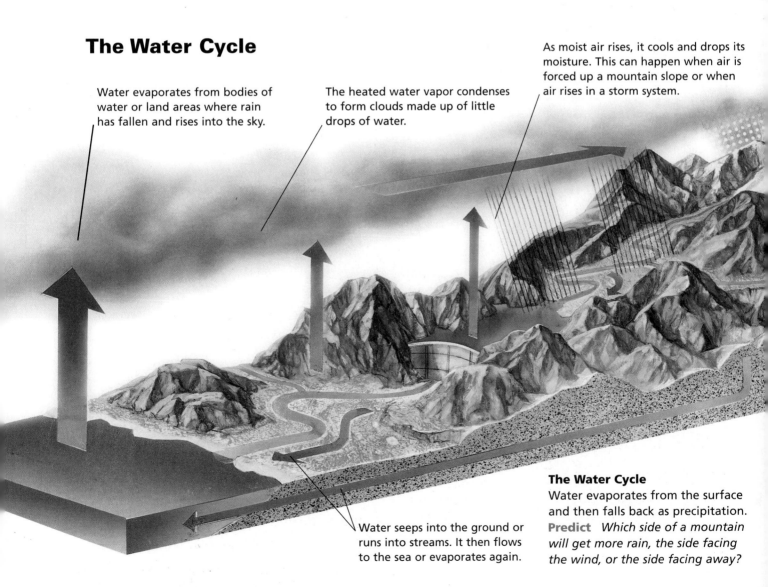

Water evaporates from bodies of water or land areas where rain has fallen and rises into the sky.

The heated water vapor condenses to form clouds made up of little drops of water.

As moist air rises, it cools and drops its moisture. This can happen when air is forced up a mountain slope or when air rises in a storm system.

Water seeps into the ground or runs into streams. It then flows to the sea or evaporates again.

The Water Cycle
Water evaporates from the surface and then falls back as precipitation. **Predict** *Which side of a mountain will get more rain, the side facing the wind, or the side facing away?*

Air Circulation and Wind

Winds and air currents move heat and moisture between different parts of Earth. These currents follow regular patterns related to latitude. The diagram below shows these circular patterns of air movement, which form a series of belts, or cells, that circle Earth.

A strong onshore wind blows in Miami Beach, Florida.

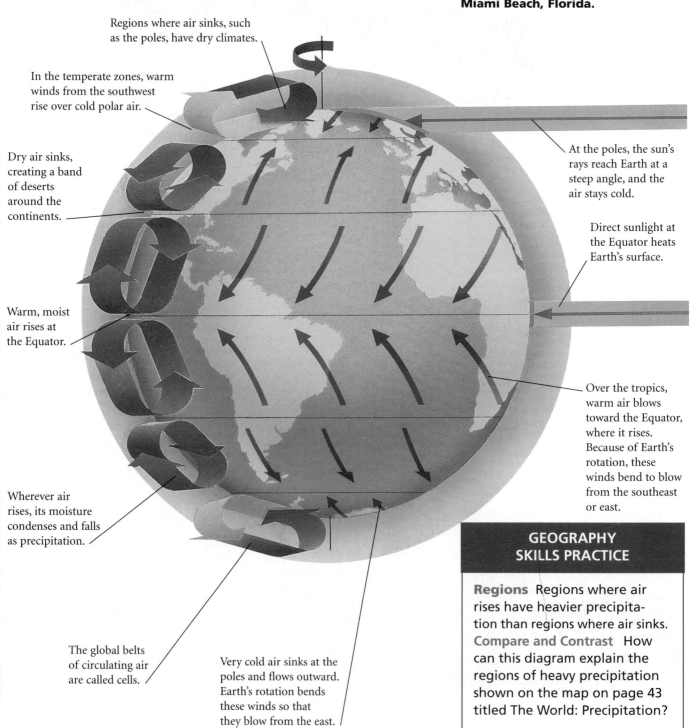

Regions where air sinks, such as the poles, have dry climates.

In the temperate zones, warm winds from the southwest rise over cold polar air.

Dry air sinks, creating a band of deserts around the continents.

Warm, moist air rises at the Equator.

Wherever air rises, its moisture condenses and falls as precipitation.

The global belts of circulating air are called cells.

Very cold air sinks at the poles and flows outward. Earth's rotation bends these winds so that they blow from the east.

At the poles, the sun's rays reach Earth at a steep angle, and the air stays cold.

Direct sunlight at the Equator heats Earth's surface.

Over the tropics, warm air blows toward the Equator, where it rises. Because of Earth's rotation, these winds bend to blow from the southeast or east.

GEOGRAPHY SKILLS PRACTICE

Regions Regions where air rises have heavier precipitation than regions where air sinks. **Compare and Contrast** How can this diagram explain the regions of heavy precipitation shown on the map on page 43 titled The World: Precipitation?

The World: Precipitation

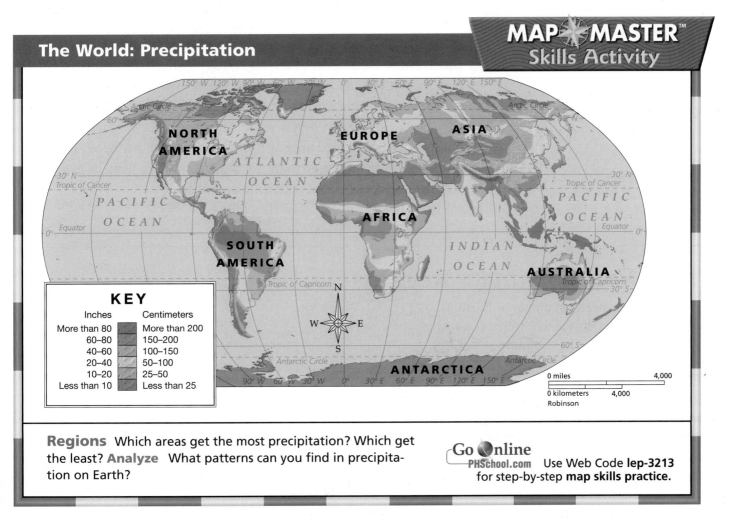

MAP MASTER™ Skills Activity

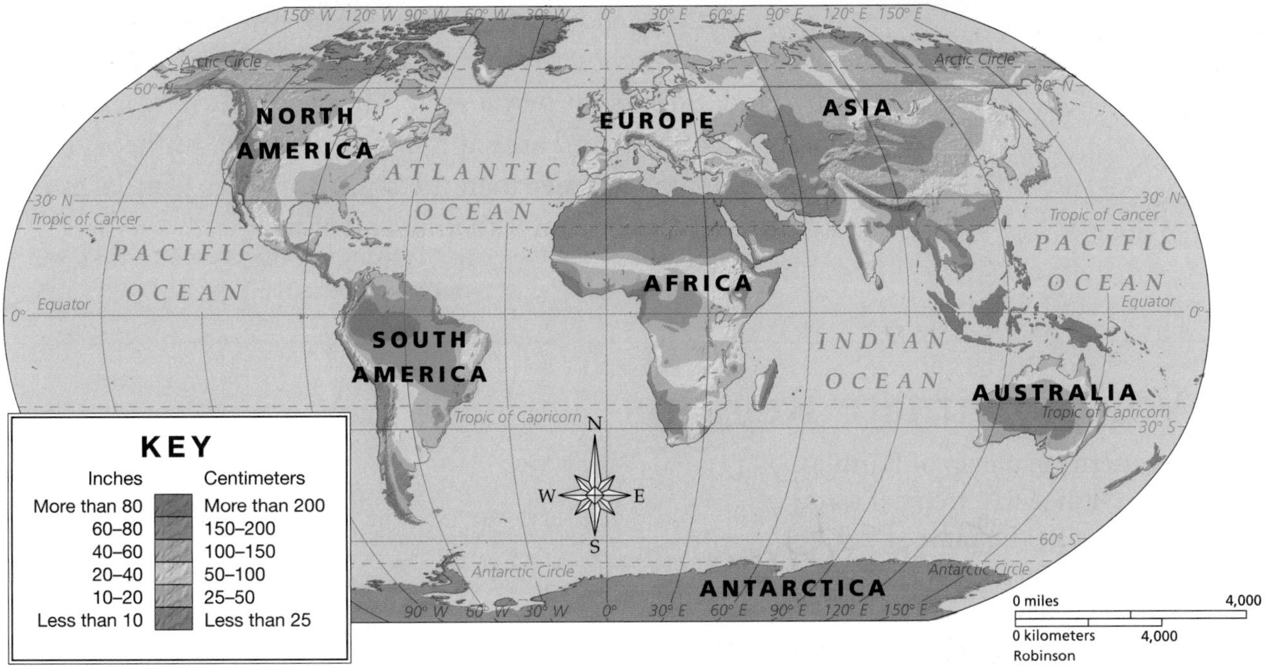

NORTH AMERICA
EUROPE
ASIA
AFRICA
SOUTH AMERICA
AUSTRALIA
ANTARCTICA
ATLANTIC OCEAN
PACIFIC OCEAN
INDIAN OCEAN

KEY

Inches	Centimeters
More than 80	More than 200
60–80	150–200
40–60	100–150
20–40	50–100
10–20	25–50
Less than 10	Less than 25

0 miles 4,000
0 kilometers 4,000
Robinson

Regions Which areas get the most precipitation? Which get the least? **Analyze** What patterns can you find in precipitation on Earth?

Go Online PHSchool.com Use Web Code **lep-3213** for step-by-step **map skills practice.**

Oceans and Climates

The oceans help distribute Earth's heat and shape climates. Global wind patterns help create ocean currents, which are like vast rivers in the oceans. Ocean currents move across great distances. Generally, warm water flows away from the Equator, while cold water moves toward the Equator.

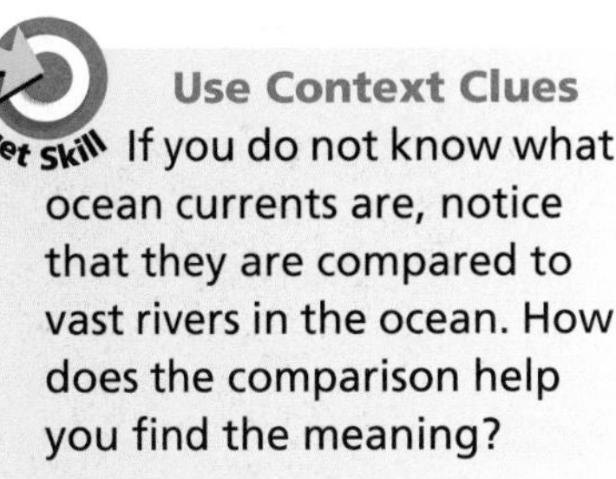

Target Skill **Use Context Clues** If you do not know what ocean currents are, notice that they are compared to vast rivers in the ocean. How does the comparison help you find the meaning?

Oceans and Currents In the Atlantic Ocean, the Gulf Stream, a warm current, travels northeast from the tropics. The Gulf Stream and the North Atlantic Current carry warm water all the way to western Europe. That warm water gives western Europe a milder climate than other regions at the same latitude.

The cold Peru Current moves north from Antarctica along the coast of South America. The city of Antofagasta (ahn toh fah GAHS tah) lies along that coast, in Chile. Even though Antofagasta is closer than Miami, Florida, is to the Equator, the average temperature in Antofagasta during the hottest month of summer is just 68°F (20°C).

The Ocean's Cooling and Warming Effects Bodies of water affect climate in other ways, too. Water takes longer to heat or cool than land. As the air and land heat up in summer, the water remains cooler. Wind blowing over the water cools the nearby land. So in summer, a region near an ocean or lake will be cooler than an inland area at the same latitude. In the winter, the water remains warmer than the land. So places near lakes or oceans are warmer in winter than inland areas.

The World: Climate Regions

You can see patterns in a map of Earth's climate regions. Notice that tropical wet climate regions hug the Equator on several continents. Farther from the Equator are arid and semiarid climate regions. Elsewhere, regions where the wind blows off the ocean have wetter climates than regions farther inland. Each climate region on this map is described more fully in the next section.

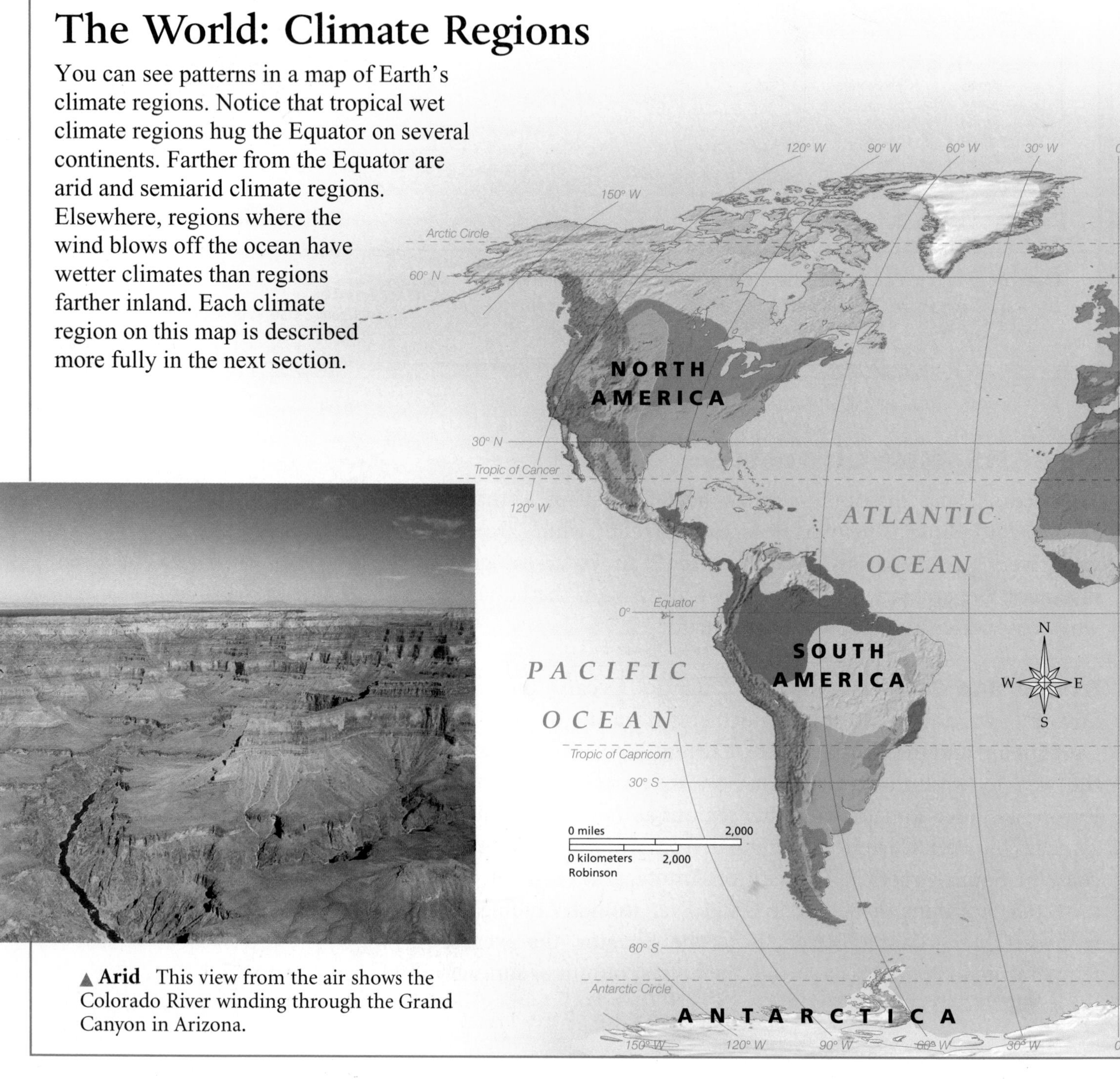

▲ **Arid** This view from the air shows the Colorado River winding through the Grand Canyon in Arizona.

Consider San Francisco, California, and St. Louis, Missouri. Both cities are near 38° north latitude. However, San Francisco borders the Pacific Ocean. In winter, the ocean is warmer than the air. The ocean keeps San Francisco much warmer than St. Louis in winter. In summer, the ocean is cooler than the air, so it keeps San Francisco cool.

✓ Reading Check **During the summer, are places near the ocean warmer or cooler than places inland?**

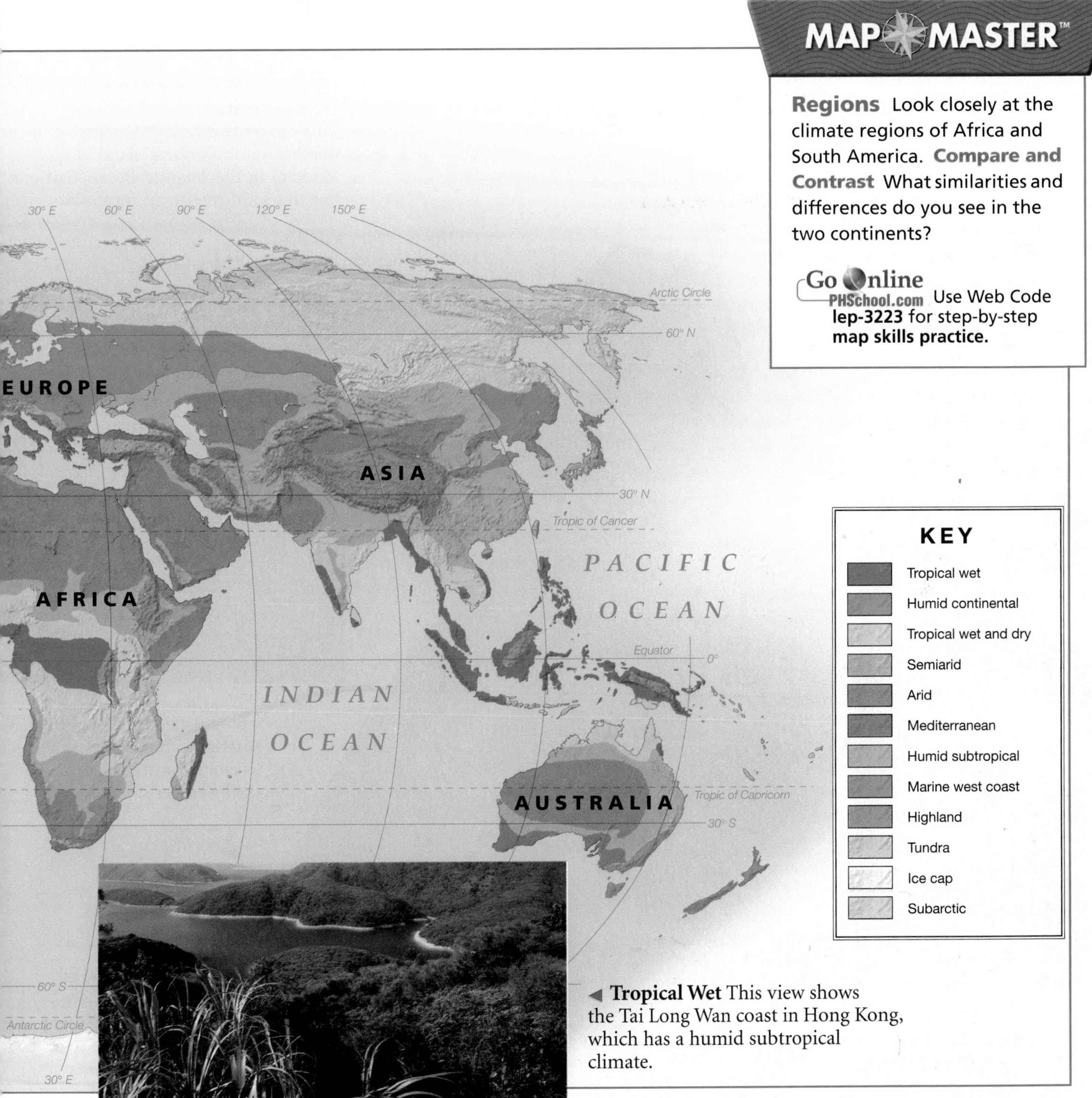

MAP MASTER™

Regions Look closely at the climate regions of Africa and South America. **Compare and Contrast** What similarities and differences do you see in the two continents?

Go Online PHSchool.com Use Web Code **lep-3223** for step-by-step **map skills practice.**

◀ **Tropical Wet** This view shows the Tai Long Wan coast in Hong Kong, which has a humid subtropical climate.

Weather Forecasting

Television weather forecasters rely on scientists and equipment from all over the world. Weather stations record local conditions. Satellites orbit overhead to photograph large weather systems. Weather balloons and radar provide still more data. The results, displayed on weather maps or presented in forecasts, can warn citizens of an approaching hurricane or simply remind people to carry an umbrella.

Weather station
This ranger is measuring rainfall at a weather station on the island of Madeira in the Atlantic Ocean. Stations like this send reports to forecasters.

Weather satellites
Scientists use satellites in space to record everything from wind patterns to the height of waves.

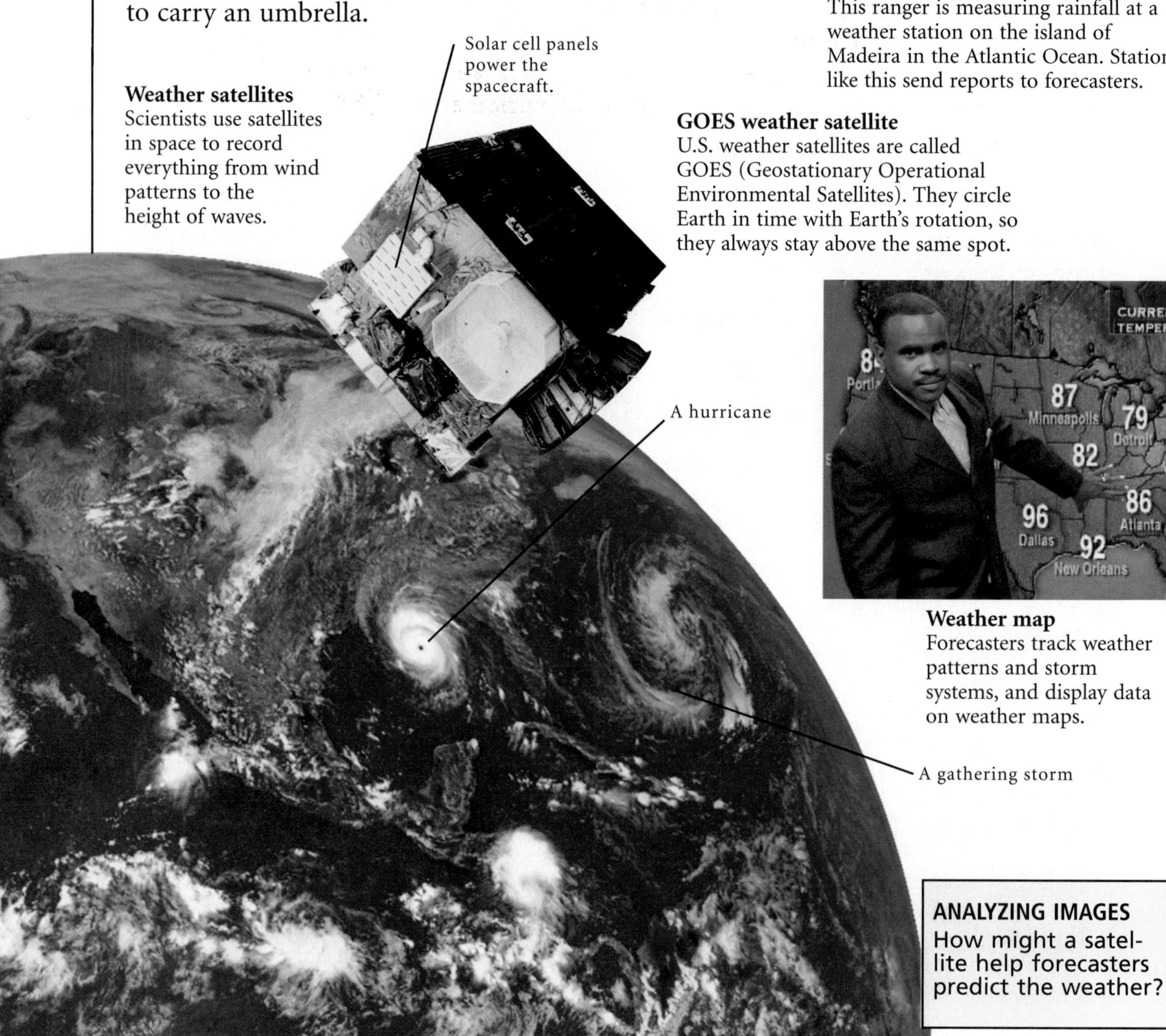

GOES weather satellite
U.S. weather satellites are called GOES (Geostationary Operational Environmental Satellites). They circle Earth in time with Earth's rotation, so they always stay above the same spot.

Weather map
Forecasters track weather patterns and storm systems, and display data on weather maps.

ANALYZING IMAGES
How might a satellite help forecasters predict the weather?

Raging Storms

Wind and water can make climates milder, but they also can create large and dangerous storms. **Tropical cyclones** are intense wind and rain storms that form over oceans in the tropics. Tropical cyclones that form over the Atlantic Ocean are called hurricanes. The winds near the center of a hurricane can reach speeds of more than 100 miles (160 kilometers) per hour. Hurricanes produce huge swells of water called storm surges, which flood over shorelines and can destroy buildings.

Hurricane Andrew
In 1992 Hurricane Andrew caused massive destruction and left 160,000 people homeless in south Florida. **Synthesizing Information** *Is a hurricane more likely on a tropical coast or in a polar region far from the ocean?*

Tornadoes are like funnels of wind that can reach 200 miles (320 kilometers) per hour. The winds and the low air pressure they create in their centers can wreck almost anything in their path. They can be just as dangerous as hurricanes, but they affect much smaller areas.

Other storms are less dangerous. In winter, blizzards dump huge amounts of snow on parts of North America. And severe rainstorms and thunderstorms strike the continent most often in spring and summer.

✓ Reading Check **Which storms cover larger areas, hurrricanes or tornadoes?**

Section 3 Assessment

Key Terms
Review the key terms at the beginning of this section. Use each term in a sentence that explains its meaning.

Target Reading Skill
Find the word *tornadoes* in the second paragraph on this page. Using the context, find out its meaning. What clues did you use to find its meaning?

Comprehension and Critical Thinking
1. (a) Identify What is climate?
(b) Explain How is climate different from weather?
(c) Analyze Are hurricanes an example of climate or of weather?
2. (a) Recall What kind of climate occurs in most places near the Equator?
(b) Contrast Why are climates near the poles different from climates near the Equator?
3. (a) Recall How do bodies of water affect temperatures?
(b) Predict A city in the interior of a continent has very cold winters. How would you expect winter temperatures to differ in a coastal city at the same latitude as the interior city?

Writing Activity
Write a paragraph describing your region's climate, or average weather. Are winters usually warm or cold? What can you say about summers? Do oceans affect your climate? How much precipitation does your region get? Is it mostly rain, or snow, or a mix?

Writing Tip Remember that every paragraph needs a main idea. Make a general statement about your climate in a topic sentence. Then add sentences with supporting details about your climate.

Using Climate Graphs

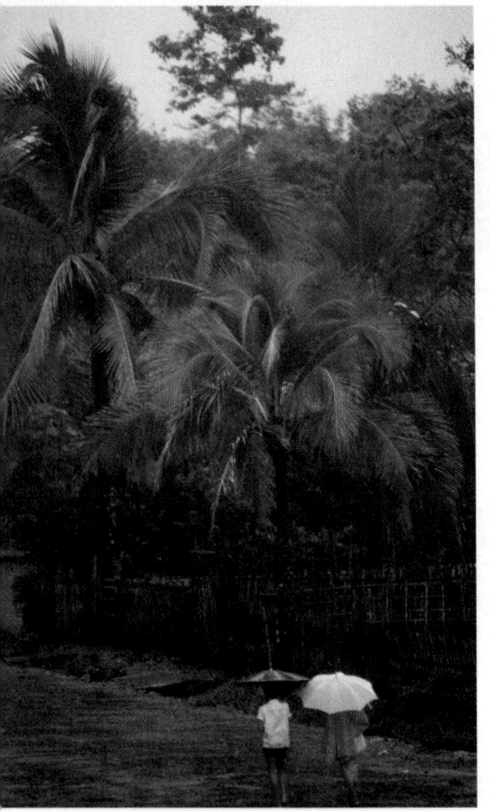

People in Menghai, China, walking in the rain

"Everybody talks about the weather, but nobody does anything about it," goes an old joke attributed to the humorist Mark Twain. It's still true, although today we track the weather so that we can predict and prepare for it. One way geographers track weather patterns is by making a climate graph. A climate graph usually presents information about average precipitation and average temperature. Often it shows a whole year of information, so you can see how conditions change with the seasons.

Learn the Skill

To read a climate graph, follow the steps below.

1. **Identify the elements of the graph.** A climate graph is actually two graphs in one: a line graph that shows temperature and a bar graph that shows rainfall. The scale on the left side goes with the line graph, and the scale on the right side goes with the bar graph. The scale along the bottom shows a time period.

2. **Study the line graph.** Notice changes in temperature from month to month and from season to season. Draw a conclusion about the temperature of the place.

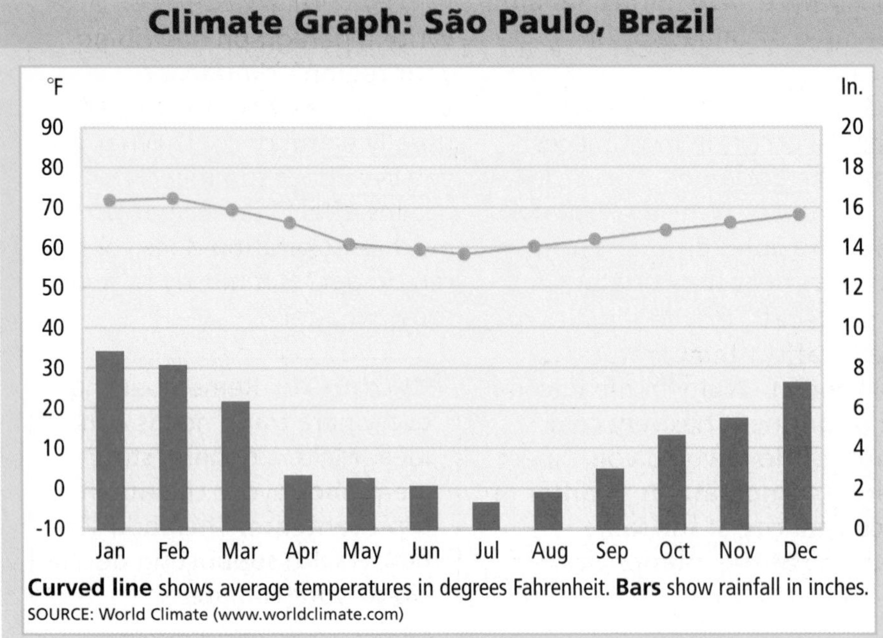

3. **Study the bar graph.** Again, notice changes for months and for seasons. Draw a conclusion about rainfall.

4. **Use your conclusions about both graphs to draw an overall conclusion about the climate of the location.** Does the location appear to have hot seasons and cold seasons? Or does it have a rainy season and a dry season? State your conclusion.

Practice the Skill

Look at the graph of São Paulo, Brazil, on page 48.

1. Read the labels on the sides and bottom of the graph. What do the numbers on the left side measure? What do the numbers on the right side measure? Look at the green bars. Which do they measure, temperature or rainfall? How do you know? Look at the line graph. What does it show? Now, look at the scale along the bottom of the graph. What period of time does it show?

2. Describe the shape of the line graph—is it generally flat, or does it go up and down? What and when is São Paulo's highest average temperature? Its lowest temperature? Do you think São Paulo has a hot season and a cold season? Write a conclusion about temperatures in the city.

3. What do the bars in the bar graph show? Are they generally the same height, or do they differ from month to month? What and when are São Paulo's highest and lowest average rainfall? Do you think São Paulo has a wet season and a dry season? Write a conclusion about rainfall in the city.

4. Using your conclusions about São Paulo's climate, write a summary that includes answers to these questions: What kind of seasons does the city have? Does the weather change much during the year?

Charleston, South Carolina

Month	Temperature (°Fahrenheit)	Precipitation (inches)
Jan	48.4	2.9
Feb	50.9	3.0
Mar	57.7	3.6
Apr	65.3	2.4
May	72.7	3.2
Jun	78.8	4.7
Jul	81.7	6.8
Aug	81.0	6.4
Sept	76.6	5.1
Oct	67.8	2.9
Nov	59.5	2.1
Dec	52.2	2.7

Apply the Skill

To make your own climate graph, draw a large square on graph paper. Divide the square into 10 horizontal rows and 12 vertical columns. Title your graph "Climate Graph of Charleston, South Carolina." Then label the left side of your graph using one colored pencil and the right side with a different colored pencil. Write the months of the year along the bottom. Using the temperature and precipitation information in the table above, plot your line graph. Draw the lines with the same colored pencils you used to make the labels for temperature and precipitation.

Section 4 How Climate Affects Vegetation

Prepare to Read

Objectives

In this section you will

1. Investigate the relationship between climate and vegetation.
2. Explore Earth's vegetation regions.
3. Study vertical climate zones.

Taking Notes

As you read, look for details about Earth's natural vegetation regions. Copy the chart below and list each type of climate in the first row of boxes. Add boxes as needed. In the box underneath each type of climate, list facts about each vegetation region that occurs in that type of climate.

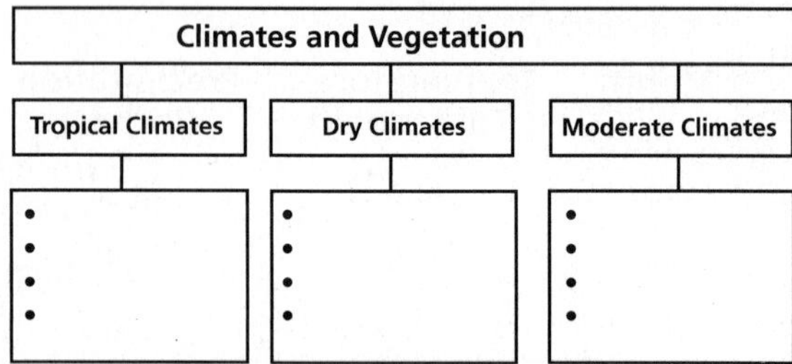

Target Reading Skill

Use Context Clues
You can sometimes learn the meaning of a word or phrase when the context gives examples. In the passage below, the meaning of the word *scrub* is given by the examples in italics.

> Scrub includes *bushes, small trees, and low, woody undergrowth.*

Key Terms

- **vegetation** (vej uh TAY shun) *n.* plants that grow in a region
- **tundra** (TUN druh) *n.* an area of cold climate and low-lying vegetation
- **canopy** (KAN uh pea) *n.* the layer formed by the uppermost branches of a rain forest
- **savanna** (suh VAN uh) *n.* a parklike combination of grasslands and scattered trees
- **desert scrub** (DEZ urt skrub) *n.* desert vegetation that needs little water
- **deciduous trees** (dee SIJ oo us treez) *n.* trees that lose their leaves seasonally
- **coniferous trees** (koh NIF ur us treez) *n.* trees that produce cones to carry seeds

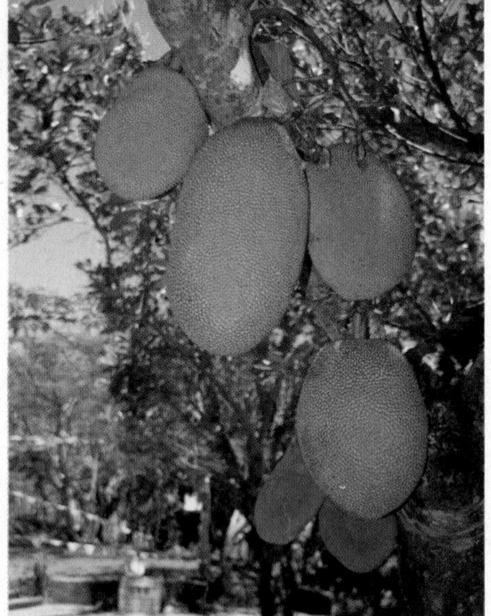

Jackfruit, an Asian fruit, grows huge in the tropical wet climate of Hainan Island, China.

Climate and Vegetation

There are five broad types of climate: tropical, dry, temperate marine, temperate continental, and polar. Each climate has its own types of natural **vegetation,** or plants that grow in a region. This is because different plants require different amounts of water and sunlight and different temperatures to survive. The map titled The World: Natural Vegetation, on page 53, shows the location of Earth's vegetation regions. If you compare this map with the map on pages 44 and 45 titled The World: Climate Regions, you will see that climate regions and vegetation regions often cover similar areas.

Tropical Climates In the tropics, there are two main climates. Both are hot. A tropical wet climate has year-round rainfall. Its typical vegetation is tropical rain forest. A tropical wet and dry climate has two seasons: a rainy season and a dry season. This climate supports grasslands and scattered trees.

Dry Climates Arid and semiarid climates have very hot summers and generally mild winters. They get very little rain. The driest arid climate regions have little or no vegetation. Others have plants that need little water. Semiarid climates get a little more rain. They support shrubs and grasses.

Temperate Marine Climates Temperate marine climates are found in the middle latitudes, usually near coastlines. There are three types: Mediterranean, marine west coast, and humid subtropical. The marine west coast and humid subtropical climates get plenty of rain. In the humid subtropical climate, the rain falls mainly in summer. Mediterranean climates get less rain, and it falls mainly in winter. All of the climates have mild winters. Mediterranean and humid subtropical climates generally have hot summers. With their heavy rainfall, marine west coast and humid subtropical climates support a variety of forests. The drier Mediterranean climates have their own vegetation, known as Mediterranean vegetation.

Temperate Continental Climates In a humid continental climate, summer temperatures are moderate to hot, but winters can be very cold. This climate supports grasslands and forests. Regions with subarctic climates are drier, with cool summers and cold winters. Most subarctic climate regions are forested.

Polar Climates The polar climates are cold all year-round. **The tundra** is an area, near the Arctic Circle, of cold climate and low-lying vegetation. The word *tundra* refers both to the vegetation and the climate, which has short, cool summers and long, very cold winters. Ice cap climates are bitterly cold all year. These areas are covered with ice. No vegetation can grow there.

√ Reading Check **Why are climate and vegetation related?**

Earth's Vegetation Regions

Geographers divide Earth into regions that share similar vegetation. A place's vegetation depends mainly on its climate, but also on other things, such as soil quality.

Links to Science

Plant Fossils In ancient rocks in Wyoming, scientists have found fossils of palm trees. Millions of years ago, sediments such as sand or ash buried the plants quickly. Over thousands of years, the sediment and plants within turned to rock. Scientists study fossils to learn about ancient climate and vegetation.

Polar bears crossing the tundra in Churchill, Manitoba, Canada

This tropical rain forest in Brazil supports dense vegetation.

Target Skill **Use Context Clues** If you do not know what Mediterranean vegetation is, consider the examples and other information given by the context. What does the context tell you about this vegetation?

- **Tropical Rain Forest** Because there is so much sunlight, heat, and rain, thousands of kinds of plants grow in a rain forest. Some trees rise 130 feet (40 meters) into the air. The dense, leafy layer formed by the uppermost branches of the rainforest is called the **canopy.** Other plants grow to lower heights in the shade beneath the canopy.
- **Tropical Savanna** In tropical areas with winter dry seasons or more limited rainfall, there is a parklike landscape of grasslands with scattered trees known as **savanna.**
- **Desert** In the driest parts of deserts, there may be no vegetation at all. Elsewhere, plants grow far apart. Their roots absorb scarce water before it evaporates in the heat.
- **Desert Scrub** Semiarid areas and deserts with a little more rain support **desert scrub,** or low desert vegetation that needs little water. Some plants flower only when it rains, so that seeds have a better chance to survive.
- **Mediterranean Vegetation** Mediterranean vegetation includes grasses, shrubs, and low trees. These plants must hold water from the winter rains to survive warm, dry summers.
- **Temperate Grassland** Vast grasslands straddle regions with semiarid and humid continental climates. The wetter grasslands, in humid continental climates, have a mix of tall grasses and other plants that is sometimes called prairie.
- **Deciduous Forest** Marine west coast, humid subtropical, and humid continental climates all support forests of **deciduous trees,** or trees that lose their leaves in the fall.
- **Coniferous and Mixed Forest** These same climates also support areas of coniferous and mixed forest. **Coniferous trees** are trees that produce cones to carry seeds. They generally have needles, not leaves. These features protect trees in drier climates. Mixed forests combine both coniferous and deciduous trees.
- **Tundra** The tundra is an area of cold climate and low-lying vegetation. Tundra vegetation includes mosses, grasses, and low shrubs that bloom during the brief, cool summers.
- **Highland** In highland regions, vegetation depends on elevation, since temperatures drop as elevation rises. Tropical forests may grow at low elevations, with grasslands and coniferous forests farther up. Still higher, tundra vegetation may grow.
- **Ice Cap and Pack Ice** Around the poles, thick ice caps form on land. Masses of ice called pack ice cover the sea. No vegetation can grow there.

✓ Reading Check **What types of vegetation grow in deserts?**

The World: Natural Vegetation

This map shows the natural vegetation regions of the world. The locations of these regions depend mainly on climate. Like the climates that support them, vegetation regions vary according to their distance from the Equator and the amount of precipitation they receive.

MAP MASTER™ Skills Activity

Location In which parts of Earth do you find tropical rain forests? **Compare and Contrast** Find tropical wet climates on the map in the previous section titled The World: Climate Regions. How do those locations compare with the locations of tropical rain forests?

Go Online PHSchool.com Use Web Code **lep-3214** for step-by-step **map skills practice.**

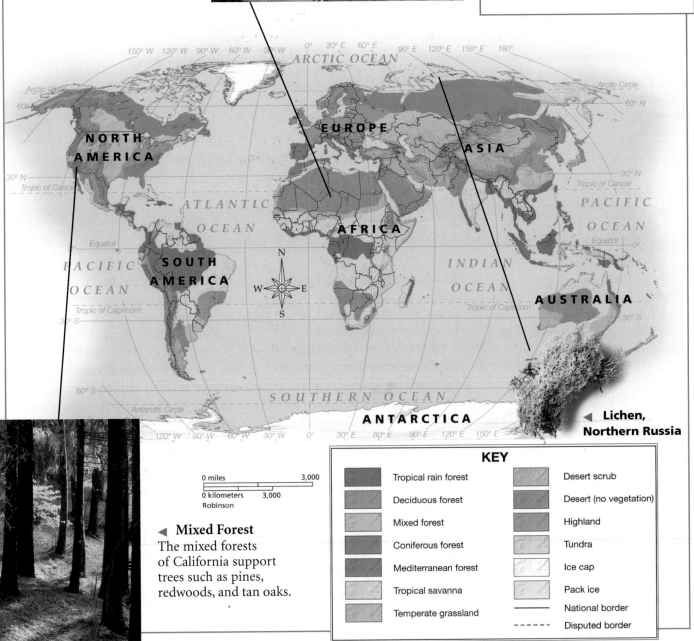

The Sahara ▶
The world's largest desert has vast sand dunes with little or no vegetation. This picture also shows an oasis, or a place in the desert where underground water allows trees or crops to grow.

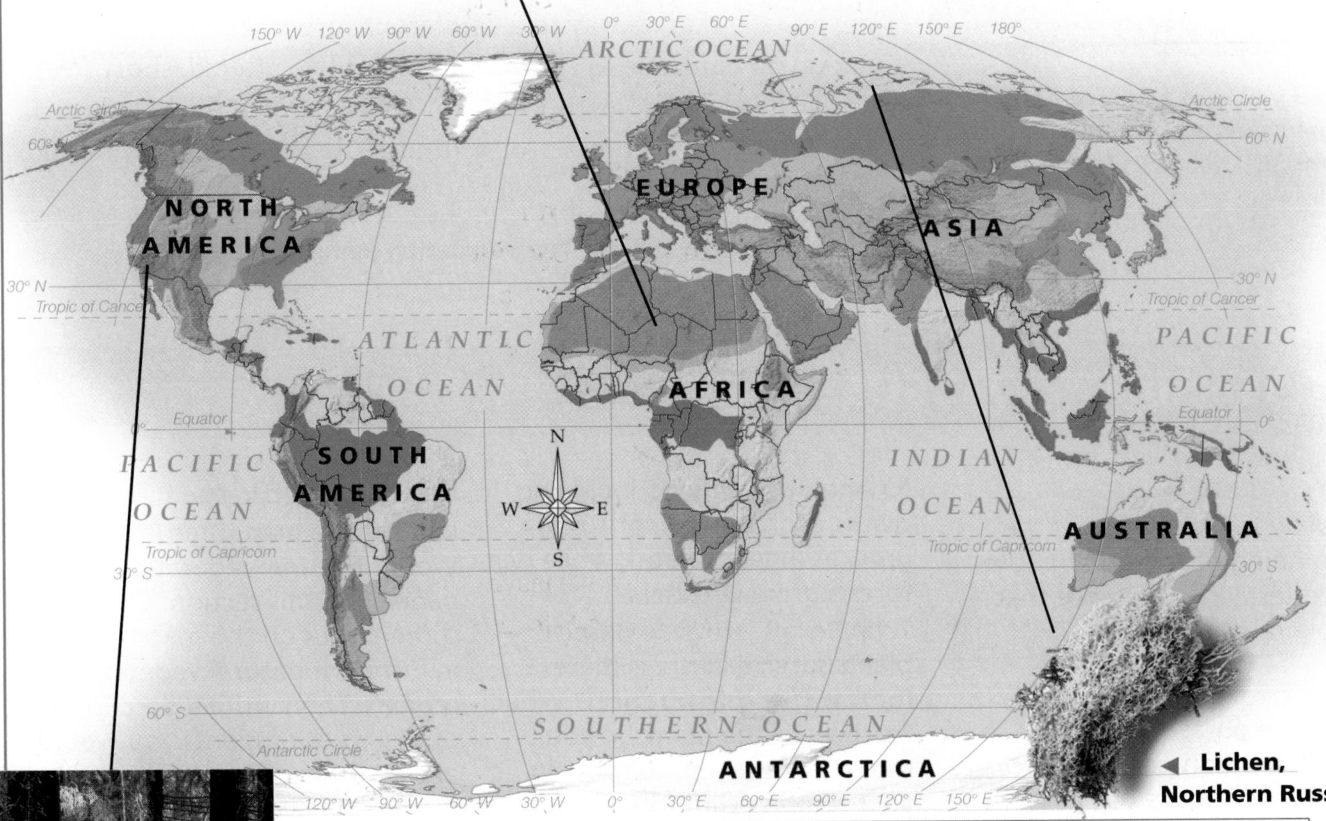

◀ Lichen, Northern Russia

KEY

- Tropical rain forest
- Deciduous forest
- Mixed forest
- Coniferous forest
- Mediterranean forest
- Tropical savanna
- Temperate grassland
- Desert scrub
- Desert (no vegetation)
- Highland
- Tundra
- Ice cap
- Pack ice
- National border
- Disputed border

0 miles 3,000
0 kilometers 3,000
Robinson

◀ Mixed Forest
The mixed forests of California support trees such as pines, redwoods, and tan oaks.

Forested valley at the foot of Machapuchare, a mountain in Nepal

Vertical Climate Zones

The climate at the top of Mount Everest, in southern Asia, is like Antarctica's. But Mount Everest is near the Tropic of Cancer, far from the South Pole. It is so cold at the top of the mountain because the air becomes cooler as elevation increases. Mountains have vertical climate zones, where the climate and vegetation depend on elevation.

In a tropical region, vegetation that needs a tropical climate will grow only near the bottom of a mountain. Farther up is vegetation that can grow in a temperate climate. Near the top is vegetation that can grow in a polar climate.

Picture yourself on a hike up a mountain in a temperate climate. Grassland surrounds the base of the mountain, and temperatures are warm. You begin to climb and soon enter an area with more precipitation and lower temperatures than below. The grassland gives way to a coniferous forest.

As you continue to climb, you find only scattered, short trees. Finally, it is too cold even for them. There are only the low shrubs, short grasses, and mosses of a tundra. At the mountain's peak, you find permanent ice, where no vegetation grows.

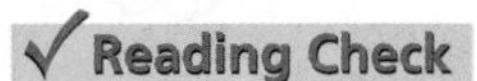
How does vegetation change with elevation?

Section 4 Assessment

Key Terms

Review the key terms at the beginning of this section. Use each term in a sentence that explains its meaning.

Target Reading Skill

Find the phrase *tundra vegetation* on page 52. Use context to figure out its meaning. What do you think it means? What clues helped you find the meaning?

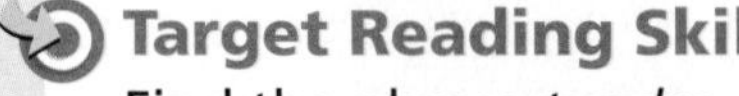

Comprehension and Critical Thinking

1. **(a) List** What are the five main types of climate?
(b) Evaluate How do differences in climate affect plant life?
(c) Analyze Why do low-lying plants, such as scrub or tundra, grow in some climates, while rich forests grow in others?
2. **(a) Recall** How do desert plants survive in dry climates?
(b) Transfer Information What features of the plants in your region allow them to grow in your region's climate?
3. **(a) Define** What is a vertical climate zone?
(b) Explain How do vertical climate zones affect vegetation on a mountain?
(c) Compare and Contrast Why is vegetation at the top of a tall mountain different from vegetation at the bottom?

Writing Activity

Look at the map titled The World: Natural Vegetation on page 53 in this section. Choose three places on the map that are in different natural vegetation regions. Then write a description of the types of plants you would expect to see if you visited each place you have chosen.

Writing Tip Since you are writing about three different types of natural vegetation, you may want to compare and contrast them. When you compare, you point out similarities. When you contrast, you focus on differences.

Chapter 2 Review and Assessment

◆ Chapter Summary

Section 1: Our Planet, Earth

- Earth's rotation on its axis changes day to night and night to day.
- The tilt of Earth's axis causes our seasons.

Section 2: Forces Shaping Earth

- Earth's three main layers are the crust, the mantle, and the core.
- Forces inside Earth move plates of crust to form mountains and volcanoes.
- Wind, water, and ice wear down and reshape Earth's surface.

Section 3: Climate and Weather

- Climate is the average weather in a region over a long period of time.
- Climate depends on latitude, landforms, and nearness to an ocean.
- Winds and ocean currents help spread Earth's warmth. They can also cause dangerous storms.

Section 4: How Climate Affects Vegetation

- Vegetation depends mainly on climate.
- Earth can be divided into several natural vegetation regions.
- Climate and vegetation change with elevation.

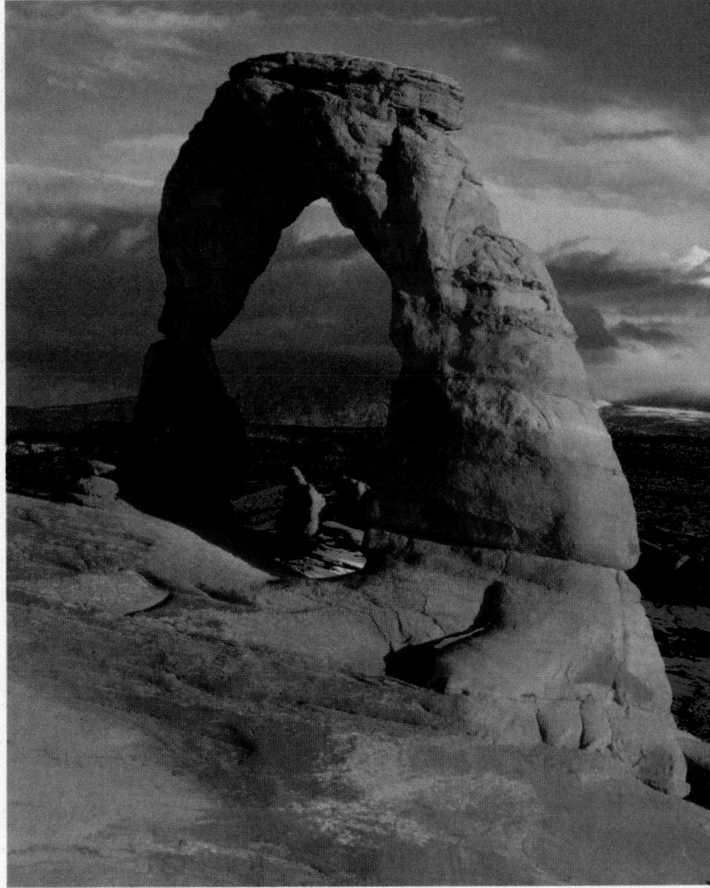

Delicate Arch, Utah

◆ Key Terms

Each of the statements below contains a key term from the chapter. If the statement is true, write *true*. If it is false, rewrite the statement to make it true.

1. Earth's movement around the sun is called rotation.
2. The mantle is a thick, rocky layer around Earth's core.
3. Earth's crust is at the center of the planet.
4. Magma is hot, flowing rock beneath Earth's surface.
5. The Appalachian Mountains have been worn down over time by erosion.
6. If you want to know how hot it will be tomorrow, you can look at a climate report.
7. Temperature measures how hot or how cold something is.
8. Vegetation is a term for the plants that grow in a region.
9. Deciduous forests grow in polar climates.

Review and Assessment (continued)

◆ Comprehension and Critical Thinking

10. **(a) Recall** How many standard time zones is Earth divided into?
(b) Analyze How are time differences related to the rotation of Earth?

11. **(a) Identify** As Earth moves around the sun, what event happens about June 21?
(b) Explain How does Earth's movement make summers hot and winters cold?
(c) Apply Information Why is Antarctica cold even in summer?

12. **(a) Recall** How much of Earth's water is fresh?
(b) Predict If Earth's climate became colder, how might the fresh water supply be affected?

13. **(a) Recall** What causes winds?
(b) Contrast What are some negative and positive effects of wind and water in the tropics?

14. **(a) Describe** How do oceans shape climate?
(b) Synthesize Information Why do some coastal cities in the tropics stay cool?

15. **(a) Describe** How does climate affect vegetation?
(b) Evaluate A tropical climate has year-round rainfall. Can forests grow there? Explain why or why not.

◆ Skills Practice

Using Special Geography Graphs Review the steps you learned in the Skills For Life activity in this chapter. Then look at the climate graph for Helsinki, Finland, below. After you have analyzed the graph, write a paragraph that summarizes Helsinki's climate.

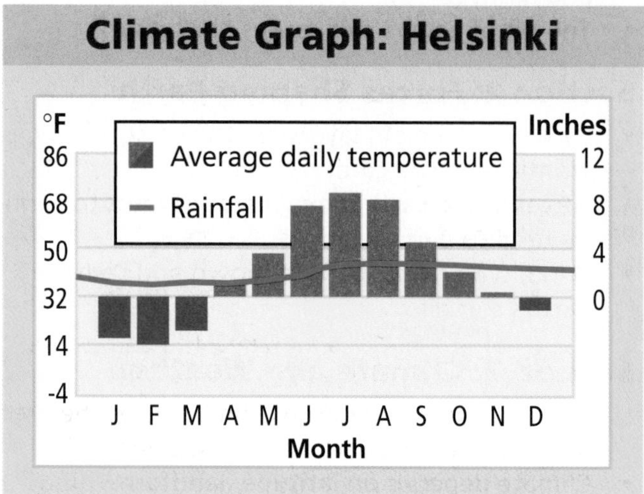

◆ Writing Activity: Science

Reread the descriptions of dry climates and of desert vegetation regions. Then design a plant that could live in these regions. Describe how it would get light, water, and nutrients.

MAP MASTER™ Skills Activity

Place Location For each place listed below, write the letter that marks its location on the map.

1. Atlantic Ocean
2. Arctic Ocean
3. Indian Ocean
4. Mediterranean Sea
5. Pacific Ocean
6. Southern Ocean

Go Online PHSchool.com Use Web Code **lep-3215** for step-by-step **map skills practice.**

Oceans and Seas

Standardized Test Prep

Test-Taking Tips

Some questions on standardized tests ask you to use map keys. Read the precipitation map key below. Then follow the tips to answer the sample question.

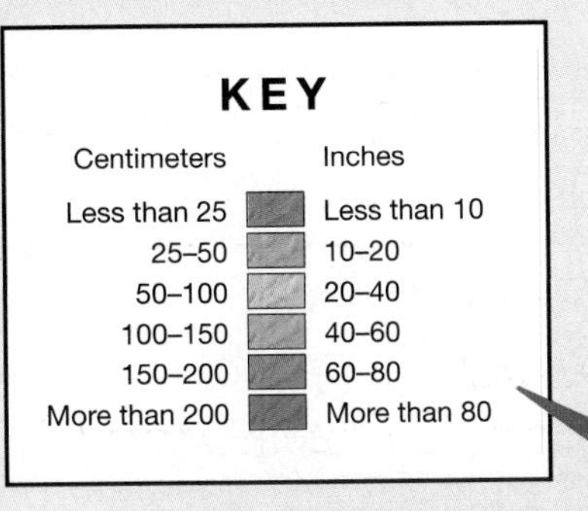

TIP On a map key, the colors line up with the data. To find information, read the numbers to the left or right of a given color.

Pick the letter that best answers the question.

On a precipitation map, the southern coastal states are colored dark green. According to the key at the left, how many inches of rain does this region get each year?

A 20–40
B 60–80
C 50–100
D 150–200

TIP To be sure you understand what the question is asking, restate it in your own words: *The color DARK GREEN on the map key stands for how many inches of rain each year?*

Think It Through The question asks about inches of rain, but the answers C and D show numbers from the centimeter column. The numbers 20–40 (answer A) are next to yellow, not dark green. The numbers 60–80 are next to dark green in the inches column. The answer is B.

Practice Questions

Use the tips above and other tips in this book to help you answer the following questions:

1. When the Northern Hemisphere has days and nights of equal length, it is
   A summer solstice.
   B spring equinox.
   C New Year's Day.
   D winter solstice.

2. Which of the following is NOT an example of a landform?
   A a mountain
   B a plateau
   C a plain
   D an atmosphere

3. In which vegetation region would you find a plant with shallow roots, meant to absorb water before it evaporates?
   A desert
   B deciduous forest
   C coniferous forest
   D tropical savanna

Study the following map key and answer the question that follows.

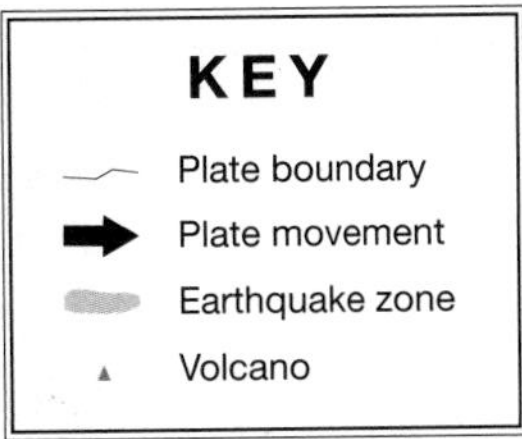

4. On a map with this key, you would find places where earthquakes happen by looking for
   A a brown area.
   B a red triangle.
   C a black arrow.
   D a black line.

Chapter 3

Earth's Human Geography

Chapter Preview

This chapter will introduce you to Earth's human geography, or the patterns of human activity on Earth.

Section 1
Population

Section 2
Migration

Section 3
Economic Systems

Section 4
Political Systems

Target Reading Skill

Comparison and Contrast In this chapter you will focus on the text structure by learning how to compare and contrast. Comparing and contrasting can help you to sort out and analyze information.

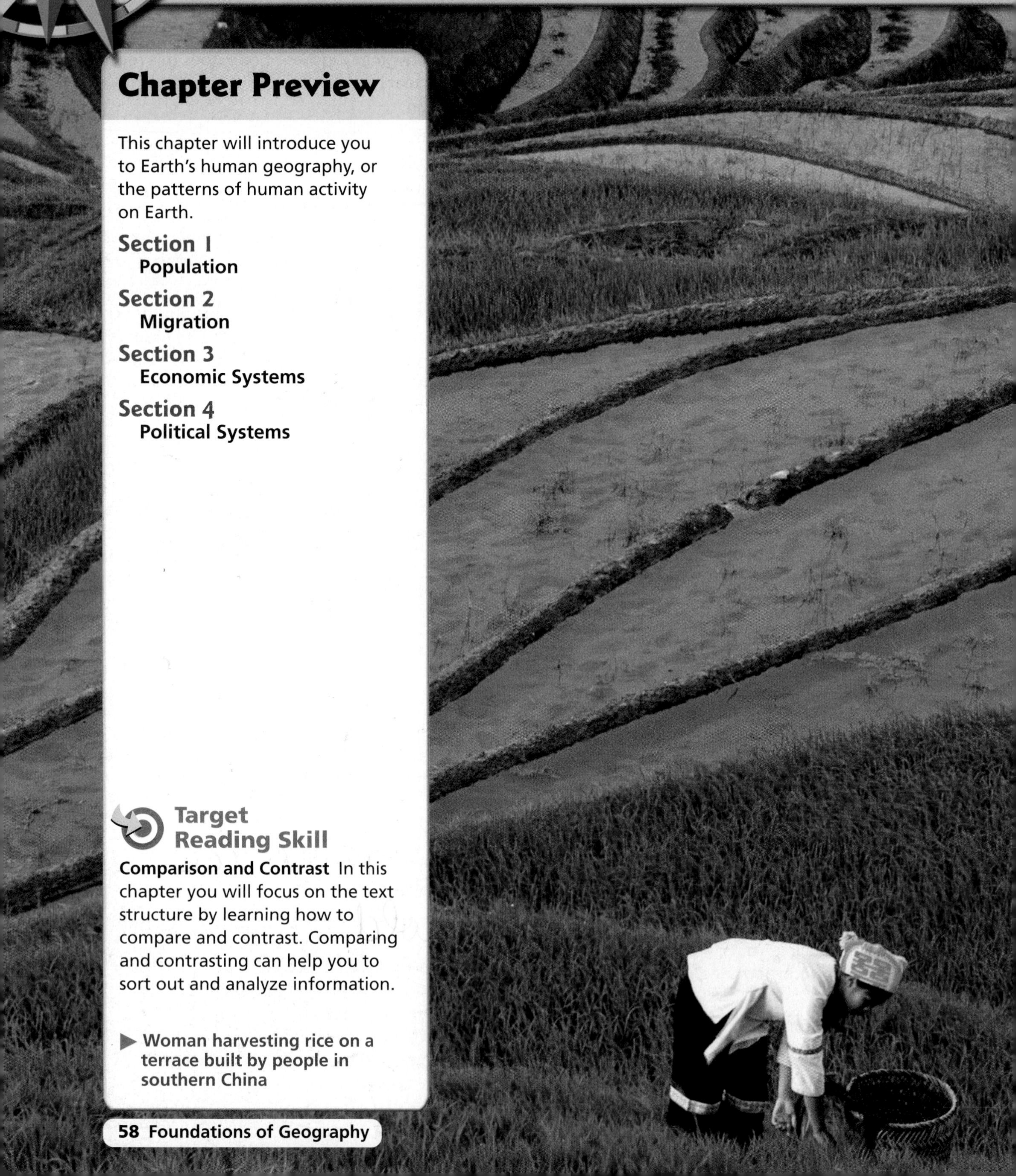

▶ **Woman harvesting rice on a terrace built by people in southern China**

Section 1 Population

Prepare to Read

Objectives

In this section you will
1. Learn about population distribution.
2. Explore population density.
3. Investigate population growth.

Taking Notes

Copy the concept web below. As you read this section, fill in the web with information about the causes and effects of population density and of population growth. Add more ovals as needed.

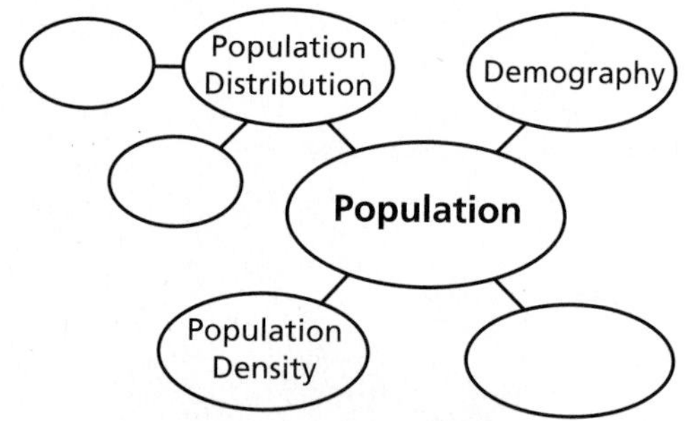

Target Reading Skill

Comparison and Contrast Comparing and contrasting can help you sort out information. When you compare, you examine the similarities between things. When you contrast, you look at the differences. As you read this section, compare and contrast population distribution and population density. Look for the similarities and differences between these two concepts.

Key Terms

- **population** (pahp yuh LAY shun) *n.* total number of people in an area
- **population distribution** (pahp yuh LAY shun dis trih BYOO shun) *n.* the way the population is spread out over an area
- **demography** (dih MAH gruh fee) *n.* the science that studies population distribution and change
- **population density** (pahp yuh LAY shun DEN suh tee) *n.* the average number of people per square mile or square kilometer
- **birthrate** (BURTH rayt) *n.* the number of live births each year per 1,000 people
- **death rate** (deth rayt) *n.* the number of deaths each year per 1,000 people

A crowded village on the Nile River near Aswan, Egypt

Population Distribution

The world's **population,** or total number of people, lives in uneven clusters on Earth's surface. Some places have many people. Other places are almost empty. **Population distribution** is the way the population is spread out over an area.

Demography is the science that tries to explain how populations change and why population distribution is uneven. Demographers study rates of birth, marriage, and death. And they ask why people move from one place to another.

Population and Places People usually don't move without a good reason. People may move because they can live better in a new place. Other times, people are forced to move, or they move because they cannot feed their families. However, as long as people can make a living where they are, they usually stay in that area. So, regions with large populations tend to keep them.

Population and History In the past, most people lived on farms where they grew their own food. They lived where the climate provided enough water and warm weather to support crops. Regions with a long history of farming, good soil, and plenty of water became crowded. These regions still have large populations. Most places too cold or too dry for farming still have small populations.

New Population Clusters However, after about 1800, improved transportation and new ways of making a living changed things. Railroads and steamships made it easier for people to move long distances, even across oceans. New jobs in factories and offices meant that more people were living in cities, where they could make a living without farming the land. Crowded cities grew in regions that once had few people, such as the United States, Australia, and northern Europe.

Villages in France have grown through centuries of farming.

✓ Reading Check **Why are some parts of the world more crowded than others?**

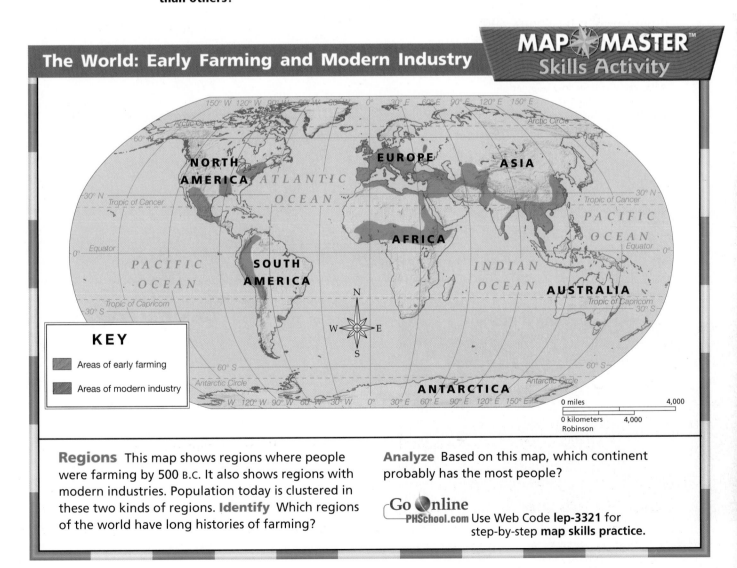

The World: Early Farming and Modern Industry

MAP MASTER™ Skills Activity

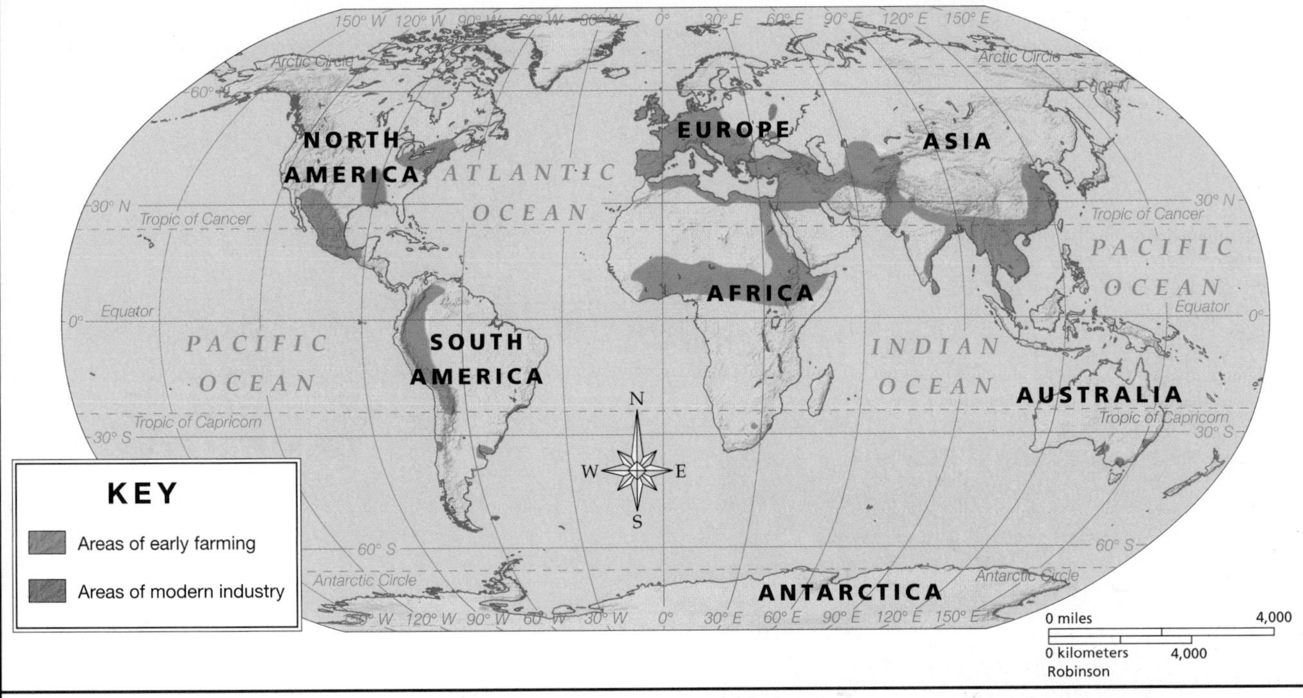

NORTH AMERICA
ATLANTIC OCEAN
EUROPE
ASIA
AFRICA
PACIFIC OCEAN
SOUTH AMERICA
INDIAN OCEAN
AUSTRALIA
ANTARCTICA
Arctic Circle
Tropic of Cancer
Equator
Tropic of Capricorn
Antarctic Circle

KEY
- Areas of early farming
- Areas of modern industry

0 miles 4,000
0 kilometers 4,000
Robinson

Regions This map shows regions where people were farming by 500 B.C. It also shows regions with modern industries. Population today is clustered in these two kinds of regions. **Identify** Which regions of the world have long histories of farming?

Analyze Based on this map, which continent probably has the most people?

Go Online PHSchool.com Use Web Code **lep-3321** for step-by-step **map skills practice.**

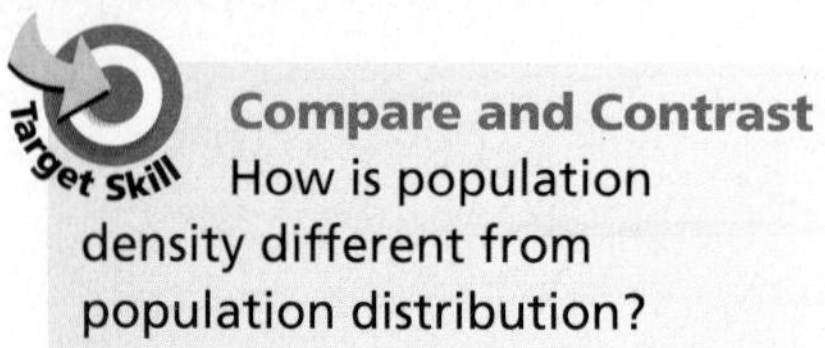

Compare and Contrast How is population density different from population distribution?

Population Density

How many people live in your neighborhood? How big is that neighborhood? If you take the population of an area and divide it by the size of that area in square miles or square kilometers, you can get a sense of how crowded or empty that area is. The average number of people per square mile or square kilometer is called **population density.**

Population distribution and population density both describe where people live. Population density differs from population distribution, however, because it gives an average number of people for an area. Population distribution gives actual numbers of people for an area.

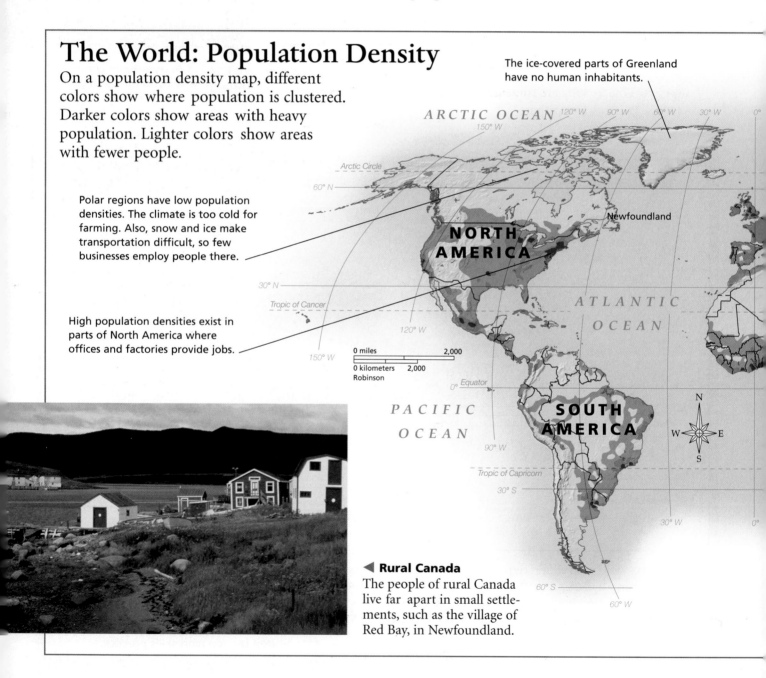

The World: Population Density

On a population density map, different colors show where population is clustered. Darker colors show areas with heavy population. Lighter colors show areas with fewer people.

The ice-covered parts of Greenland have no human inhabitants.

Polar regions have low population densities. The climate is too cold for farming. Also, snow and ice make transportation difficult, so few businesses employ people there.

High population densities exist in parts of North America where offices and factories provide jobs.

ARCTIC OCEAN

NORTH AMERICA

Newfoundland

ATLANTIC OCEAN

PACIFIC OCEAN

SOUTH AMERICA

Arctic Circle

Tropic of Cancer

Equator

Tropic of Capricorn

0 miles 2,000
0 kilometers 2,000
Robinson

◀ Rural Canada
The people of rural Canada live far apart in small settlements, such as the village of Red Bay, in Newfoundland.

Population density varies from one area to another. In a country with a high density, such as Japan, people are crowded together. Almost half of Japan's 127 million people live on only 17 percent of the land, or an area the size of West Virginia. In Tokyo, there is a population density of more than 25,000 people per square mile (9,664 per square kilometer). In contrast, Canada has a low overall population density. It has about 9 people per square mile (3 per square kilometer). Canada is bigger than the United States, but has only about one ninth as many people.

✓ **Reading Check** **Which has a higher population density, a city or an area in the countryside?**

MAP MASTER™ Skills Activity

Regions Population density is very high in some regions. Other regions, such as Greenland, have very few people. **Identify** Which regions have the highest population densities? **Compare** How do these areas compare with areas of industry or early farming on the map on page 61?

Go Online
PHSchool.com Use Web Code **lep-3331** for step-by-step **map skills practice.**

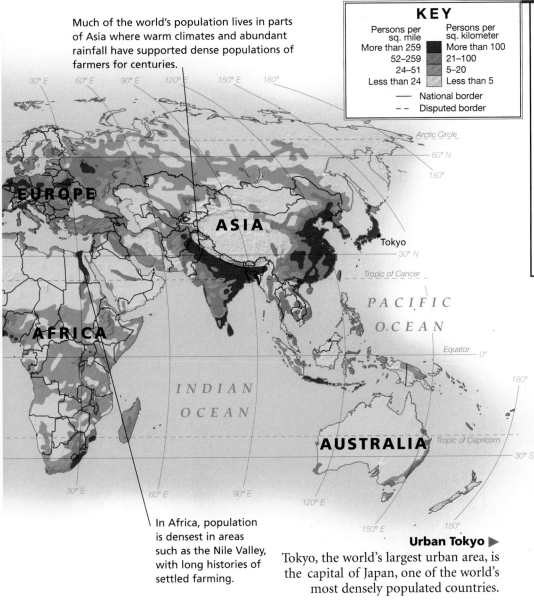

Much of the world's population lives in parts of Asia where warm climates and abundant rainfall have supported dense populations of farmers for centuries.

KEY

Persons per sq. mile	Persons per sq. kilometer
More than 259	More than 100
52–259	21–100
24–51	5–20
Less than 24	Less than 5

—— National border
- - Disputed border

EUROPE
ASIA
AFRICA
AUSTRALIA
PACIFIC OCEAN
INDIAN OCEAN
Tokyo
Arctic Circle
Tropic of Cancer
Equator 0°
Tropic of Capricorn
60° N
30° N
30° S
30° E
60° E
90° E
120° E
150° E
180°

In Africa, population is densest in areas such as the Nile Valley, with long histories of settled farming.

Urban Tokyo ▶
Tokyo, the world's largest urban area, is the capital of Japan, one of the world's most densely populated countries.

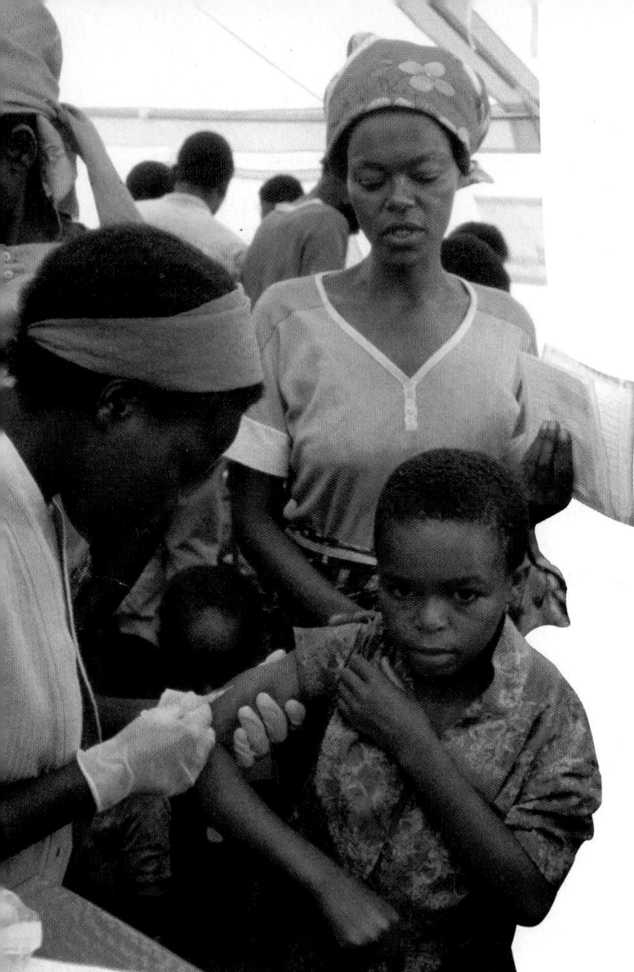

Modern Medicine
This Rwandan refugee is getting a measles vaccination in Tanzania. Modern medicine has lengthened lifespans worldwide.
Analyze *Does vaccination raise birthrates or lower death rates? Explain why.*

Population Growth

Suppose that all the years from A.D. 1 to A.D. 2000 took place in a single day. As the day began at midnight, there would be 300 million people in the world. Twelve hours later, at noon, there would be just 310 million people. By 8:24 P.M., the population would double to 600 million. It would double again by 10:05 P.M. to 1.2 billion. By 11:20, it would double again to 2.4 billion, and then double yet again by 11:48 to 4.8 billion, before reaching 6 billion as the day ended at midnight. As you can see, the world's population has grown very quickly in recent times. There are several reasons for this rapid growth.

Birthrates and Death Rates At different times in history, populations have grown at different rates. Demographers want to understand why. They know that population growth depends on the birthrate and the death rate. The **birthrate** is the number of live births each year per 1,000 people. The **death rate** is the number of deaths each year per 1,000 people.

For thousands of years, the world's population grew slowly. In those years, farmers worked without modern machinery. Food supplies often were scarce. People lived without clean water or waste removal. Many millions of people died of infectious diseases. As a result, although the birthrate was high, so was the death rate. The life expectancy, or the average number of years that people live, was short.

Graph Skills

If you subtract deaths from births, you get a country's rate of natural growth. When there are more deaths than births, the native-born population drops.
Identify Which of the countries shown here has the highest birthrate? **Compare** Where is the population growing faster, the United States or Zimbabwe?

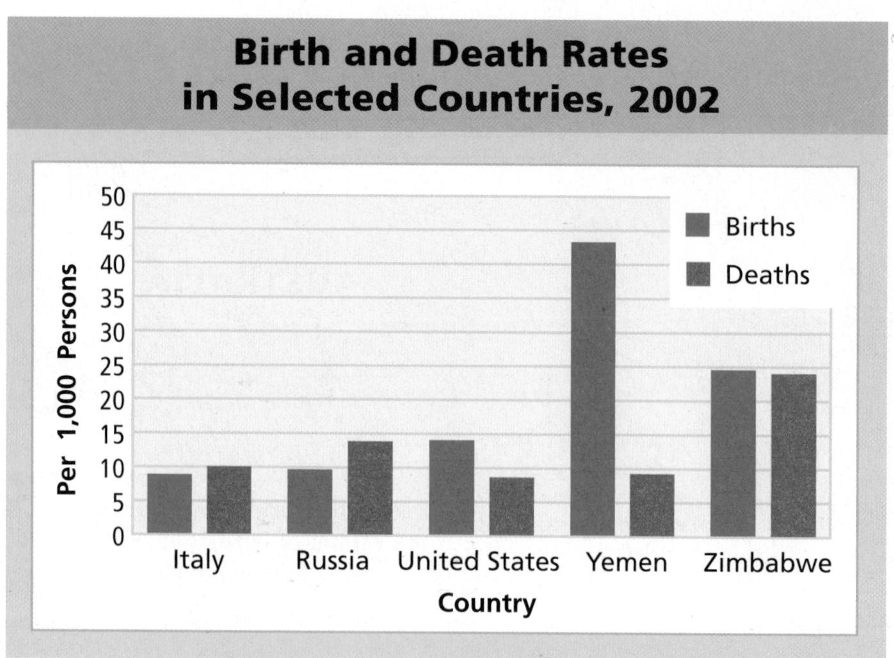

Reasons for Population Growth Today This all changed after the 1700s. Death rates dropped sharply. In some countries, birthrates increased. As a result, populations have grown very fast. In some countries, the population has doubled in less than 20 years. Meanwhile, people live longer than ever. In the United States, people born in 1900 could expect to live for 47 years. Today, they can expect to live for 77 years.

Scientific progress explains much of this change. First, new farming methods have increased the world's food supply. Scientists have improved important food crops and found new ways to protect crops against insects. Scientists have also found ways to raise crops with less water. These recent scientific improvements in agriculture are called the Green Revolution.

The second set of scientific advances has come in health and medicine. Scientists have convinced local governments to provide clean drinking water and sanitary waste removal. These measures sharply reduce disease. Researchers have also developed vaccines to prevent disease and antibiotics to fight infections. As a result, people live many more years.

Graph Skills

In recent centuries, population growth has soared. There are now 18 times as many people as there were 600 years ago. **Identify** Around what year did the world's population begin to rise rapidly? **Analyze a Graph** Looking at this graph, how can you tell that the world's population rose more quickly in recent years than in earlier centuries?

World Population Growth, 1200–2000

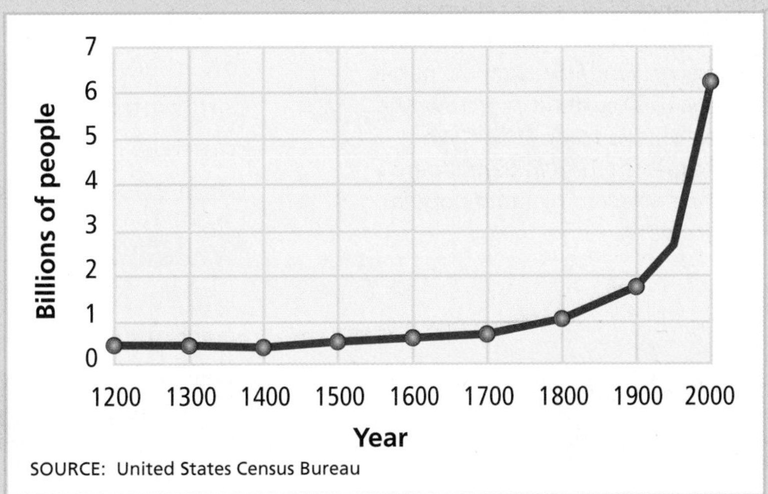

Due to a high birthrate and a low death rate, Yemen's population is skyrocketing.

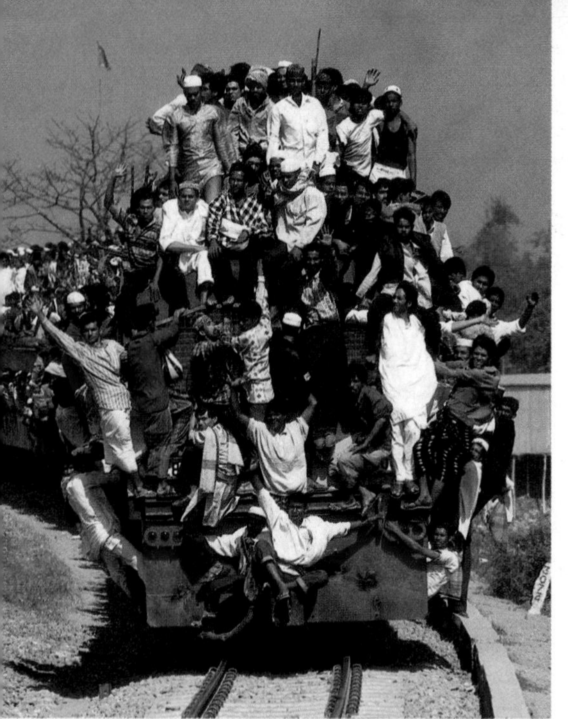

Overcrowding in Bangladesh
These Bangladeshis are returning from a festival. Bangladesh's population has grown faster than its public services. This results in overcrowding, as seen on this train. **Infer** *What other aspects of life in Bangladesh might be affected by rapid population growth?*

The Challenges of Population Growth Today, food supplies have increased and people live longer. Even so, people in many countries still face serious problems. Some nations, such as those in Southwest Asia, do not have enough fresh water. In parts of Asia and Africa, the population is growing faster than the food supply. Often, these countries do not have enough money to buy food elsewhere.

Population growth puts pressure on all aspects of life. The populations of many countries are increasing so fast that not everyone can find jobs. There are not enough schools to educate the growing number of children. Decent housing is scarce. Public services such as transportation and sanitation are inadequate.

Rapid population growth also affects the environment. For instance, forests in many countries are disappearing. People in poorer countries cut down the trees for wood and fuel. Clearing forests causes other problems. In a forest, tree roots hold soil in place, and forest soils soak up rain. With the forest gone, heavy rainfall may wash away the soil and cause dangerous floods. Demand for wood and fuel in wealthier countries also uses up the world's scarce resources. All of Earth's people must work to meet this challenge.

✓ Reading Check **Why have populations risen rapidly in recent times?**

Section 1 Assessment

Key Terms
Review the key terms at the beginning of this section. Use each term in a sentence that explains its meaning.

Target Reading Skill
How are population density and population distribution similar? How are they different?

Comprehension and Critical Thinking
1. **(a) Recall** In what parts of the world did most people live before modern times?
(b) Explain How does history help explain population distribution today?
(c) Contrast How is population distribution today different from the days before modern science was developed?

2. **(a) Define** What is population density?
(b) Transfer Information To figure out the population density of an area, what two pieces of information do you need?

3. **(a) Recall** How has population growth changed in 100 years?
(b) Explain What accounts for this change?
(c) Identify Cause and Effect What are the effects of this change in population growth?

Writing Activity
Suppose that you are a demographer studying the area where you live. How does population density vary across your area? Where is population growth taking place? Write a short description of your area's demography.

For: An activity on population
Visit: PHSchool.com
Web Code: led-3301

Section 2 Migration

Prepare to Read

Objectives

In this section you will

1. Learn about migration, or people's movement from one region to another.
2. Investigate urbanization, or people's movement to cities.

Taking Notes

Copy the chart below. As you read this section, fill in the chart with information about voluntary and involuntary migration and about urbanization.

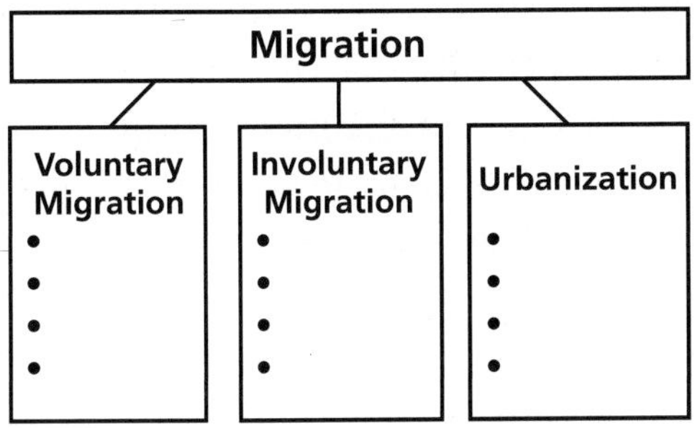

Target Reading Skill

Identify Contrasts
When you contrast two situations, you examine how they differ. Although both voluntary and involuntary migration involve the movement of people, the reasons for that movement differ. As you read, list the differences between voluntary and involuntary migration.

Key Terms

- **migration** (my GRAY shun) *n.* the movement of people from one place or region to another
- **immigrants** (IM uh grunts) *n.* people who move into one country from another
- **urbanization** (ur bun ih ZAY shun) *n.* the movement of people to cities, and the growth of cities
- **rural** (ROOR ul) *adj.* located in the countryside
- **urban** (UR bun) *adj.* located in cities and towns

Why People Migrate

For thousands of years, people have moved to new places. People's movement from one place or region to another is called **migration. Immigrants** are people who move into one country from another.

In the years from 1850 to 1930, more than 30 million Europeans moved to live in the United States. Since 1971, more than 4.5 million people have migrated here from Mexico, and more than 2.5 million have migrated from the Caribbean islands. Since 1971, Central America, the Philippines, China, and Vietnam have all lost more than 1 million immigrants to the United States. More than 800,000 immigrants have come from both South Korea and India.

During the late 1800s and early 1900s, millions of immigrants to the United States stopped at Ellis Island in New York Harbor.

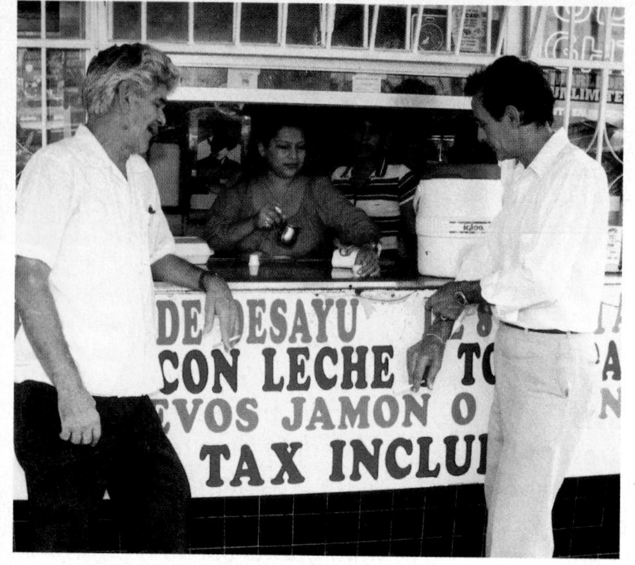

Cubans in Little Havana
These men ordering food at a cafe are part of a large community of Cuban immigrants in Miami, Florida. **Analyze Images** *What aspects of their life in Cuba have these immigrants preserved in their new home?*

Voluntary Migration in the Past Voluntary migration is the movement of people by their own choice. Today, most people move by their own choice. The push-pull theory says that people migrate because difficulties "push" them to leave. At the same time, the hope for a better life "pulls" people to a new country.

The push-pull theory helps to explain the great Irish migration in the 1840s and 1850s. In those years, 1.5 million people left Ireland for the United States. What pushed so many Irish people to come to America? In the 1840s, disease destroyed Ireland's main crop—potatoes. Hunger pushed people to migrate. Job opportunities pulled Irish families to the United States.

Voluntary Migration Today The same theory explains most migration today. The main sources of migration are countries where many people are poor and jobs are few. In some countries, such as Vietnam and Central American countries, wars have made life dangerous and difficult.

In China, Vietnam, and Cuba, governments limit people's freedom. These problems push people to leave. Meanwhile, the possibility of good jobs and political freedom pulls people to the United States and other well-off, democratic countries.

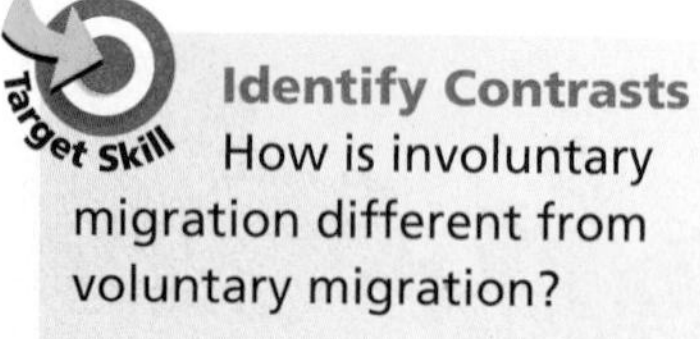

Identify Contrasts How is involuntary migration different from voluntary migration?

Involuntary Migration Sometimes people are forced to move. Because these people do not choose to move, their movement is known as involuntary migration. During the early 1800s, the British sent prisoners to Australia to serve their sentences. When their sentences were done, many stayed. War also forces people to migrate to escape death or serious danger.

The Transatlantic Slave Trade Perhaps the biggest involuntary migration in history was the transatlantic slave trade. From the 1500s to the 1800s, millions of Africans were enslaved and taken against their will to European colonies in North and South America. These Africans traveled under inhumane conditions across the Atlantic Ocean, chained inside ships for more than a month.

At first, their descendants in the United States lived mainly on the east coast. As cotton farming spread west, many enslaved African Americans were forced to migrate again, this time to new plantations in the Mississippi Valley and Texas.

✓ **Reading Check** **Why do people migrate?**

Migration in South Asia

At the end of British colonial rule in 1947, most of South Asia was divided along religious lines into two countries. India had a Hindu majority. Pakistan was mainly Muslim. Fearing religious discrimination or violence, Muslims from India and Hindus from Pakistan fled across the new borders. Many died when violence broke out during these massive migrations.

MAP MASTER™ Skills Activity

Movement This map shows migrations by South Asians. **Identify** Which countries did South Asia's largest migrations involve? **Contrast** How do the reasons for movement out of South Asia differ from the reasons for migration within the region?

Go Online PHSchool.com Use Web Code **lep-3312 for step-by-step map skills practice.**

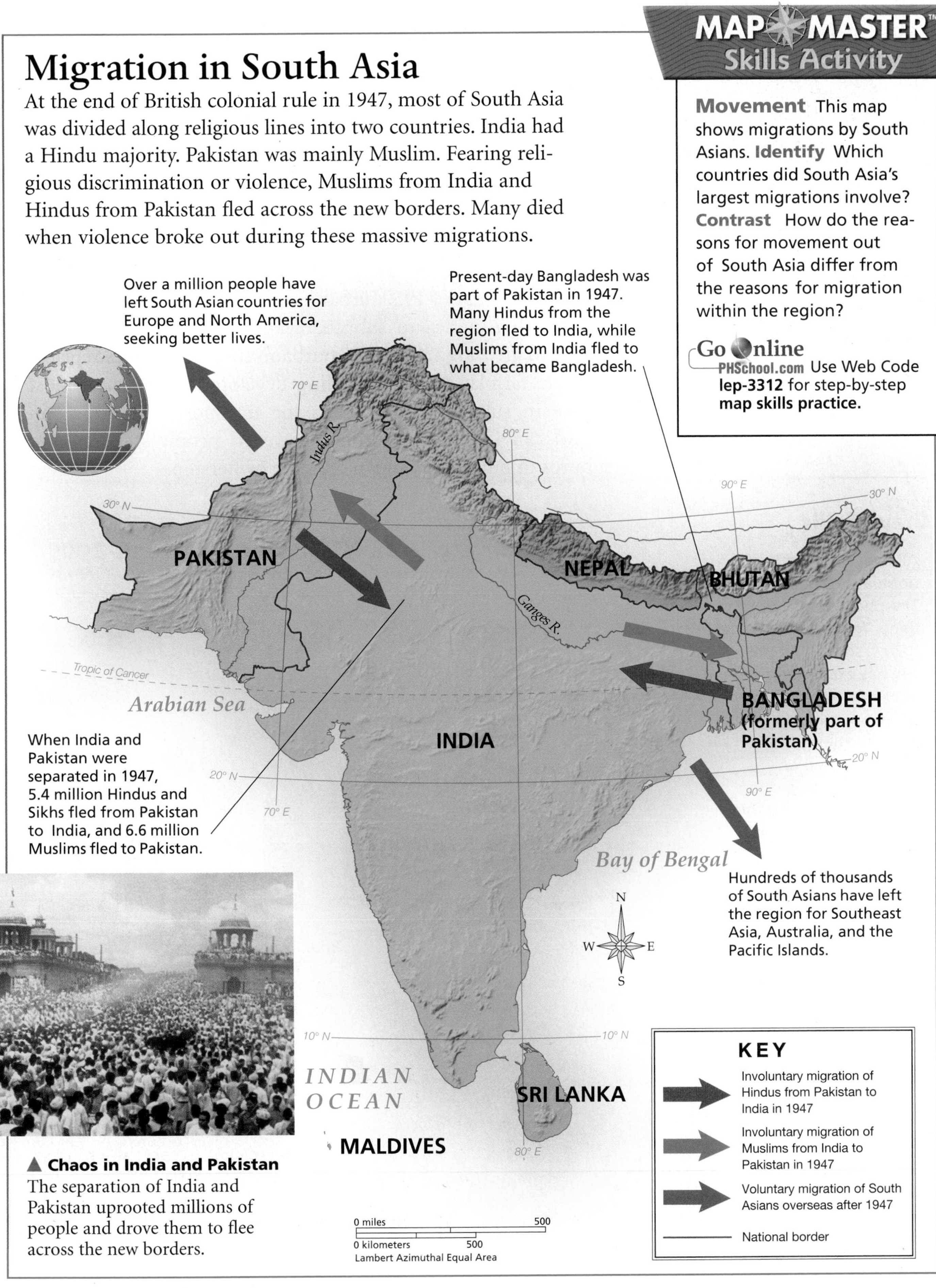

Over a million people have left South Asian countries for Europe and North America, seeking better lives.
Present-day Bangladesh was part of Pakistan in 1947. Many Hindus from the region fled to India, while Muslims from India fled to what became Bangladesh.
When India and Pakistan were separated in 1947, 5.4 million Hindus and Sikhs fled from Pakistan to India, and 6.6 million Muslims fled to Pakistan.
Hundreds of thousands of South Asians have left the region for Southeast Asia, Australia, and the Pacific Islands.
70° E
80° E
90° E
30° N
20° N
10° N
Indus R.
Ganges R.
Tropic of Cancer
PAKISTAN
NEPAL
BHUTAN
INDIA
BANGLADESH (formerly part of Pakistan)
SRI LANKA
MALDIVES
Arabian Sea
Bay of Bengal
INDIAN OCEAN
N
S
E
W
KEY
Involuntary migration of Hindus from Pakistan to India in 1947
Involuntary migration of Muslims from India to Pakistan in 1947
Voluntary migration of South Asians overseas after 1947
National border
0 miles 500
0 kilometers 500
Lambert Azimuthal Equal Area

▲ **Chaos in India and Pakistan**
The separation of India and Pakistan uprooted millions of people and drove them to flee across the new borders.

Discovery
CHANNEL
SCHOOL
Video
Learn more about migration.

Urbanization

Millions of people in many countries have migrated to cities from farms and small villages. In recent years, the population of some cities has grown tremendously. The movement of people to cities and the growth of cities is called **urbanization.**

Cities and Suburbs In Europe and North America, the growth of industry during the 1800s pulled people from the countryside to cities. They hoped for jobs in factories and offices. Since about 1950, urbanization has given way in Europe and North America to suburbanization, or the movement of people to growing suburbs. Suburbanization sometimes replaces valuable farmland with sprawling development. Because most people in suburbs rely on cars for transportation, suburban sprawl can increase pollution. However, people still move to suburbs to pursue the dream of home ownership.

Graph Skills

All over the world, city populations have soared. The photographs of Cape Town, South Africa, below, show how that city has expanded.
Identify What percent of the world's people lived in cities in 1800?
Predict Based on information from the graph, how do you think the world's rural and urban populations will compare in 2050?

World Urban and Rural Populations, 1800-2000

Percentage
100
90
80
70
60
50
40
30
20
10
0
1800 1960 1980 2000
Year
Urban
Rural

Cape Town, 1938

Modern Cape Town

Urbanization on Other Continents In Asia, Africa, and Latin America, people are still streaming from the countryside to growing cities. Indonesia is an example. In the past, most Indonesians lived in **rural** areas, or areas in the countryside. Recently, more and more Indonesians have moved to **urban** areas, or areas in cities and nearby towns. For example, in 1970, about 3.9 million people lived in Greater Jakarta, Indonesia's capital. By 2000, its population was about 11 million. Jakarta is not unique. Greater São Paulo, Brazil, grew from 8 million residents in 1970 to nearly 18 million residents in 2000.

The problem in cities like Jakarta and São Paulo is that too many people are moving to the city too fast. Cities cannot keep up. They cannot provide the housing, jobs, schools, hospitals, and other services that people need. Traffic jams and crowds often make getting around a struggle.

With so many daily problems, why do people flock to São Paulo and other big cities? As hard as life is in the cities, it can be even harder in the countryside, where there are few jobs and a shortage of land to farm. Most migrants to the city are seeking a better life for their families. They are looking for jobs, modern houses, and good schools. Above all, most want better lives for their children.

√ Reading Check **How is the population of urban areas changing in Africa, Asia, and Latin America?**

São Paulo, Brazil
São Paulo is Brazil's largest city.
Analyze Images *Do you think that this city has a high or a low population density?*

Section 2 Assessment

Key Terms

Review the key terms at the beginning of this section. Use each term in a sentence that explains its meaning.

Target Reading Skill

Contrast involuntary migration and voluntary migration. How are these two forms of migration different? List at least two differences between the two kinds of migration.

Comprehension and Critical Thinking

1. (a) Identify What are push factors and what are pull factors?
(b) Explain How do push factors and pull factors explain people's decision to migrate?
(c) Compare and Contrast Do push and pull factors account for involuntary migration? Explain why or why not.

2. (a) Recall What is urbanization?
(b) Identify Cause and Effect What are the causes and some of the effects of urbanization?

Writing Activity

Suppose that you are moving to the United States from one of the countries listed in the second paragraph on page 67. Write a paragraph describing your reasons for leaving that country and what attracts you to the United States.

For: An activity on migration
Visit: PHSchool.com
Web Code: led-3302

Analyzing and Interpreting Population Density Maps

Crowds gather in Amsterdam on Queen's Day, a national holiday in the Netherlands.

How dense is the population where you live? If you drew an imaginary five-mile square around your house and counted the number of people who lived within the square, would there be many residents, or few?

Population density is the average number of persons living within a certain area. You can find out how densely populated a place is by reading a population density map.

Learn the Skill

To read and interpret a population density map, follow these steps.

1. **Read the title and look at the map to get a general idea of what it shows.** The topic of the map could be population density, physical features, or some other subject.

2. **Read the key to understand how the map uses symbols and colors.** Each color represents a different population density range, as explained in the map key.

3. **Use the key to interpret the map.** Identify areas of various densities on the map. Some places average less than one person per square mile. In other places, thousands of people might be crammed into one square mile.

4. **Draw conclusions about what the map shows.** The history, geography, and cultural traditions of a place affect its population density. Draw on this information, plus what you read on the map, to make conclusions about why particular areas have a higher or a lower population density.

South Asia: Population Density

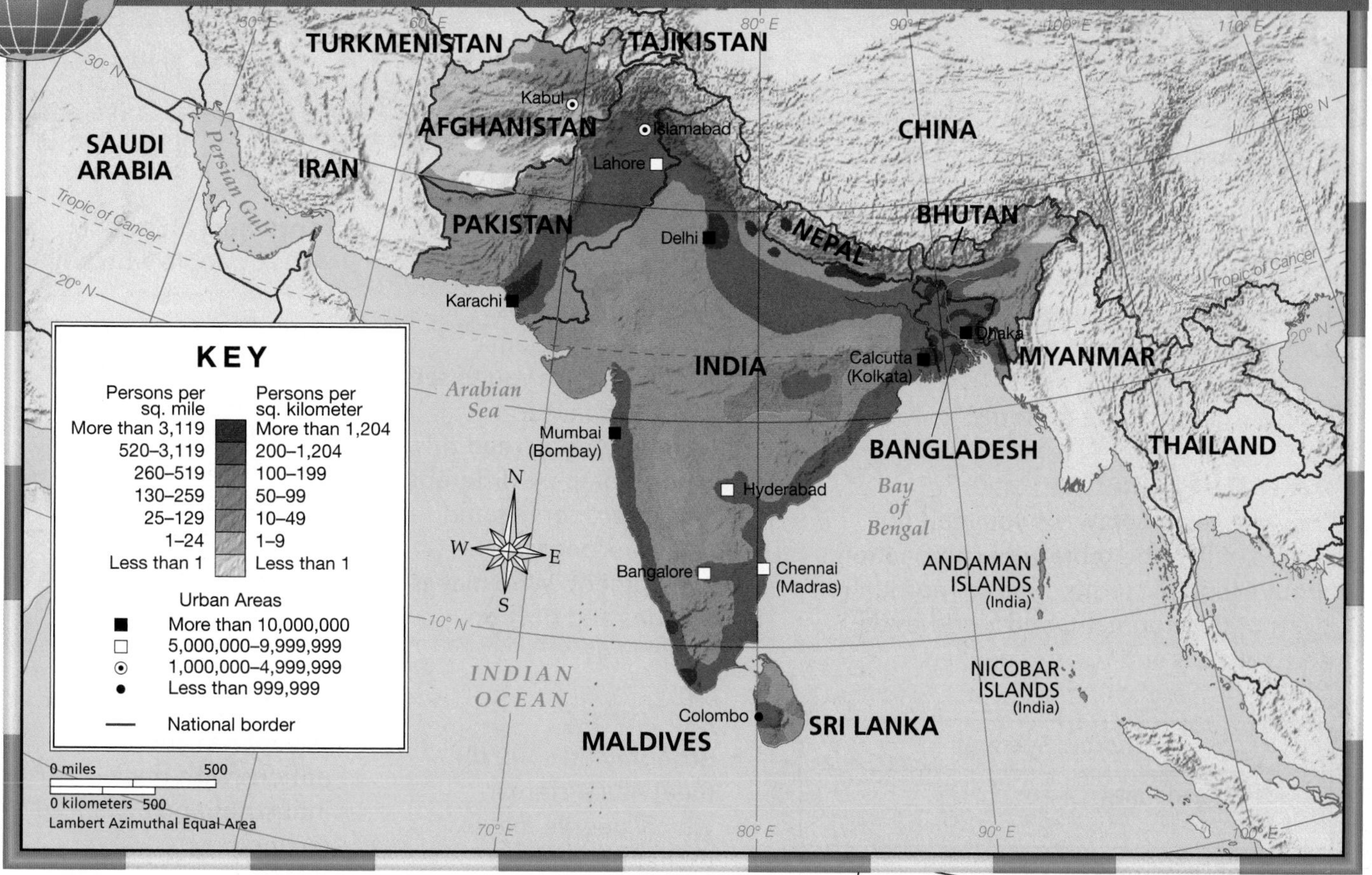

TURKMENISTAN
TAJIKISTAN
AFGHANISTAN
CHINA
SAUDI ARABIA
IRAN
PAKISTAN
NEPAL
BHUTAN
INDIA
MYANMAR
BANGLADESH
THAILAND
SRI LANKA
MALDIVES
ANDAMAN ISLANDS (India)
NICOBAR ISLANDS (India)
Persian Gulf
Arabian Sea
Bay of Bengal
INDIAN OCEAN
Tropic of Cancer
Kabul
Islamabad
Lahore
Delhi
Karachi
Dhaka
Calcutta (Kolkata)
Mumbai (Bombay)
Hyderabad
Bangalore
Chennai (Madras)
Colombo

KEY

Persons per sq. mile	Persons per sq. kilometer
More than 3,119	More than 1,204
520–3,119	200–1,204
260–519	100–199
130–259	50–99
25–129	10–49
1–24	1–9
Less than 1	Less than 1

Urban Areas
■ More than 10,000,000
□ 5,000,000–9,999,999
⊙ 1,000,000–4,999,999
• Less than 999,999
— National border

0 miles 500
0 kilometers 500
Lambert Azimuthal Equal Area

Practice the Skill

Use steps 1–4 to read and interpret the population density map above.

1. What is the topic of this map? Notice that the map has relief—that is, markings that indicate hills and mountains. It also has labels for cities and nations of South Asia.
2. Study the map key carefully. How many different colors are in the key? What color is used for the lowest population density? What color is used for the highest density?
3. Using the key, identify the areas of highest and lowest population densities in South Asia. Write a sentence or two that describes where the most and the fewest people are located.
4. Write a conclusion that makes a general statement about South Asia's population density and suggests possible reasons for the patterns shown on the map.

Apply the Skill

Now take a closer look at the map titled The World: Population Density on pages 62 and 63. Find the areas of greatest density. From what you already know and what you see on the map, what features do you think influence where people choose to live? Think about rivers and mountains as well as nearness to a coast or to the Equator.

Section 3 Economic Systems

Prepare to Read

Key Questions

In this section you will

1. Examine different kinds of economies.
2. Investigate levels of economic development.
3. Study global trade patterns.

Taking Notes

Copy the table below. As you read this section, fill in the table with information about economic terms, kinds of economies, levels of development, and world trade. Add columns and rows as needed.

Economic Systems	
Kinds of Economies	• •
Levels of Development	• •

Target Reading Skill

Make Comparisons
Comparing economic systems enables you to see what they have in common. As you read this section, compare different kinds of economies and levels of economic development. Who makes decisions and how do people live?

Key Terms

- **economy** (ih KAHN uh mee) *n.* a system in which people make, exchange, and use things that have value
- **producers** (pruh DOOS urz) *n.* owners and workers
- **consumers** (kun SOOM urz) *n.* people who buy and use products
- **capitalism** (KAP ut ul iz um) *n.* an economic system in which individuals own most businesses
- **communism** (KAHM yoo niz um) *n.* an economic system in which the central government owns factories, farms, and offices
- **developed nations** (dih VEL upt NAY shunz) *n.* nations with many industries and advanced technology
- **developing nations** (dih VEL up ing NAY shunz) *n.* nations with few industries and simple technology

Consumers choose produce at a market in Honolulu, Hawaii.

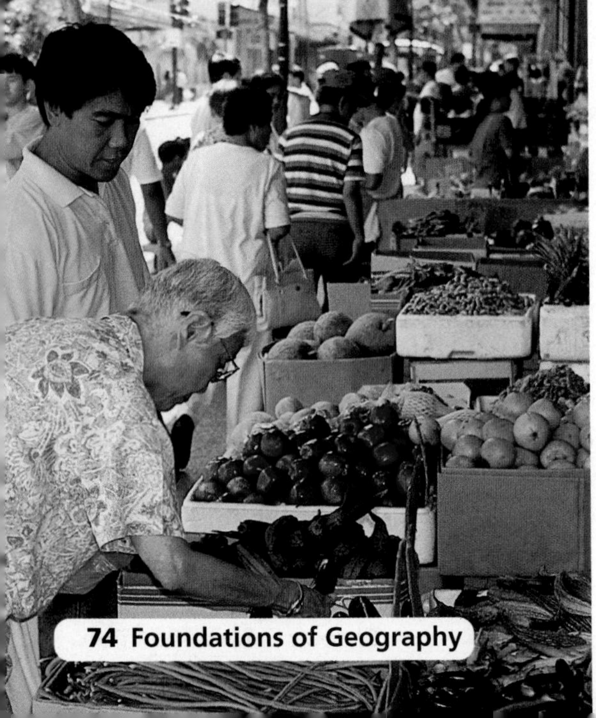

Different Kinds of Economies

An **economy** is a system in which people make, exchange, and use things that have value and that meet their wants or needs. Economies differ from one country to another. In any economy, owners and workers are **producers.** The things they sell are called products **Consumers** are people who buy and use products.

There are three basic economic questions: What will be produced? How will it be produced? And, for whom will it be produced? The answers to these questions depend on the economy.

Modern economies differ in who owns workplaces. The owners generally decide how products are produced. In some countries, most workplaces are privately owned. In others, the government owns most workplaces.

New York Stock Exchange Stocks are bought and sold on the busy trading floor of the New York Stock Exchange. **Draw Conclusions** *Would you expect to find a busy stock exchange in a communist economy? Explain why or why not.*

Private Ownership **Capitalism** is an economic system in which private individuals own most businesses. Capitalism is also called a free-market economy because producers compete freely for consumers' business.

In capitalism, people may save money in banks. Banks lend money to people and businesses in return for interest, or a percentage fee for the use of money. Banks also pay interest to savers. Under capitalism, people may directly invest in, or commit money to, a business. Owners of a business are also investors in that business.

Government Ownership **Communism** is an economic system in which the central government owns farms, factories, and offices. It controls the prices of goods and services, how much is produced, and how much workers are paid. The government decides where to invest resources. Today, only a few of the world's nations practice communism.

Mixed Ownership Hardly any nation has a "pure" economic system. For example, the United States has a capitalist economy. However, governments run schools, build and maintain roads, and provide other services. In communist countries, you may find a few small private businesses.

In some countries, the government may own some industries, while others belong to private owners. This system of mixed ownership is sometimes called a mixed economy.

√ Reading Check **What are the differences between capitalism and communism?**

Levels of Economic Development

Three hundred years ago, most people made their own clothes. Then came a great change. People invented machines to make goods. They found new sources of power to run the machines. Power-driven machines were a new technology, or way of putting knowledge to practical use. This change in the way people made goods was called the Industrial Revolution.

The Industrial Revolution created a new economic pattern. Nations with more industries and more advanced technology are considered **developed nations.** Because they are still developing economically, nations with fewer industries and simpler technology are considered **developing nations.** People live differently in developed and developing nations.

Target Skill **Make Comparisons** What do developed nations have in common with developing nations?

Developed Nations Only about one fifth of the world's people live in developed nations. These nations include the United States, Canada, Japan, and most European nations. People in these nations use goods made in factories. Businesses use advanced technologies to produce goods and services.

In developed nations, most people live in towns and cities. They work in offices and factories. Machines do most of the work. Most people have enough food and water. Most citizens can get an education and healthcare.

In developed nations, most food is grown by commercial farmers. These are farmers who grow crops mainly for sale rather than for their own needs. Commercial farms use modern technologies, so they need fewer workers than traditional farms.

Developed nations can have some problems. Unemployment is a challenge. Not everyone can find a job. Industry and cars can cause air, land, and water pollution. Developed nations are working to solve these problems.

Most of Thailand's subsistence farmers grow rice.

The World: Levels of Development

MAP MASTER™ Skills Activity

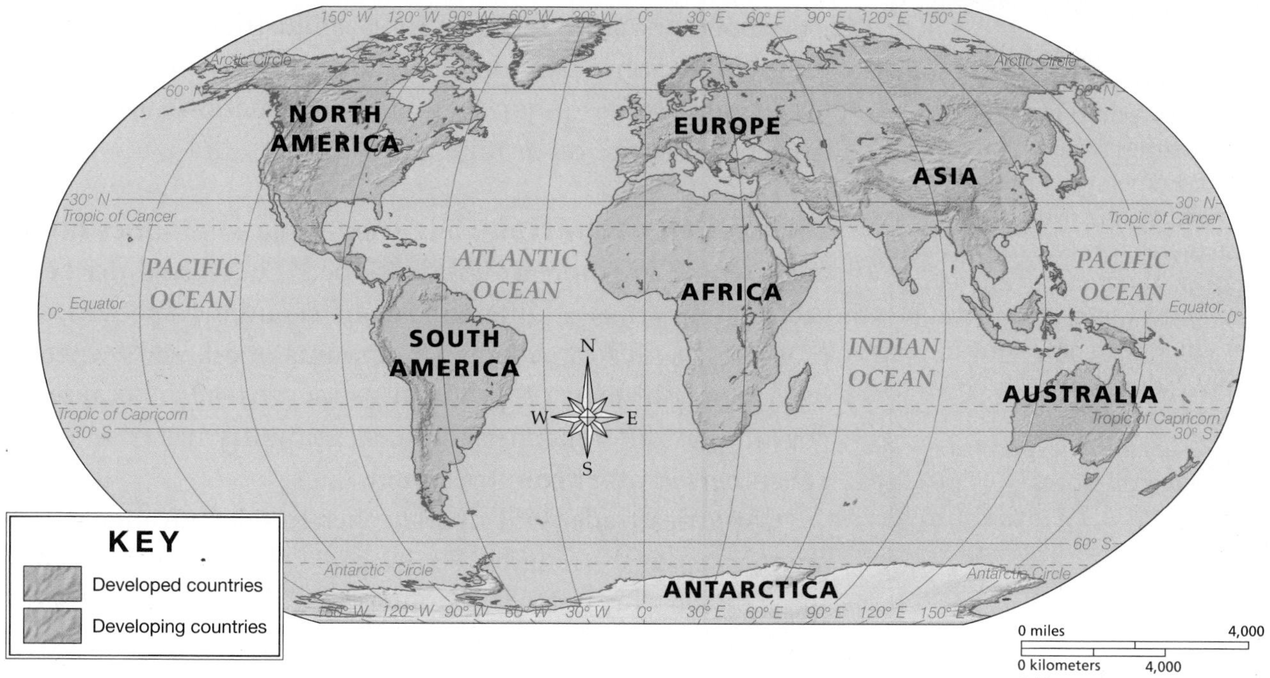

KEY
- Developed countries
- Developing countries

0 miles 4,000
0 kilometers 4,000
Robinson

Regions Most developed countries are in North America and Europe. Developing countries are mainly in South America, Africa, and Asia. **Identify** On which continents would you expect advanced industries, and farming that is mainly commercial?

Draw Inferences On which continents would you expect to find the most poor people?

Go Online PHSchool.com Use Web Code **lep-3321** for step-by-step **map skills practice.**

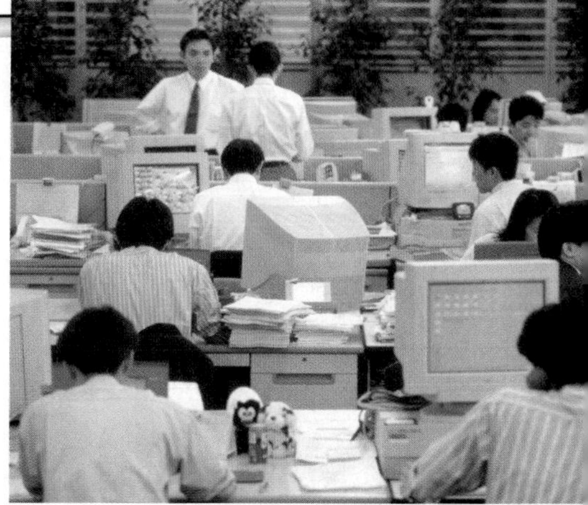

Many people in developed nations work in offices.

Developing Nations Not every economy is like that of the United States. Most of the people in the world live in developing nations, which are mainly in Africa, Asia, and Latin America.

Developing nations do not have great wealth. Many people are subsistence farmers, or farmers who raise food and animals mainly to feed their own families. Their farms have little or no machinery. People and animals do most of the work.

Many developing nations face great challenges. These include disease, food shortages, unsafe water, poor education and healthcare, and political unrest.

People in developing nations are confronting these challenges. Some nations, such as Saudi Arabia and South Africa, have grown richer by selling natural resources. Others, such as Thailand and China, have built successful industries. The more industrial developing nations are gradually becoming developed countries themselves.

✓ Reading Check **How do developed nations differ from developing nations?**

Links Across Time

The Silk Road
Long-distance trade is nothing new. Hundreds of years ago, merchants brought silks and other luxuries from China to ancient Rome along the Silk Road across Asia. However, those merchants had to load goods on the backs of animals or carry the goods themselves. They could take only lightweight, valuable goods. Today, ships, trains, and trucks can carry heavy and inexpensive goods long distances.

World Trade Patterns

Different countries have different economic strengths. Developed nations have strong industries with advanced technology. Some developing nations have low-cost industries. Other developing nations may grow plantation cash crops, or they may produce oil or minerals.

Different Specialties Countries' economies differ not only because they are more or less developed. They also differ because each country has a different set of economic specialties. For example, Saudi Arabia has vast amounts of oil, and Switzerland has a long history of producing fine watches. Because each country has different specialties, each country has products that consumers in other countries want.

Countries trade with one another to take advantage of one another's special strengths. For example, the United States makes some of the world's best computers. But the United States needs oil. Saudi Arabia has plenty of oil, but it needs computers. So Saudi Arabia sells oil to the United States, and the United States sells computers to Saudi Arabia.

How Does World Trade Work?

Country A produces more oil than it needs. It sells this oil so that it can buy computers and wheat.

Country B produces more wheat than it needs. It sells this wheat so that it can buy oil and computers.

Country C makes more computers than it needs. It sells computers so that it can buy wheat and oil.

How Trade Works
Countries sell what they have and what other countries want so that they can buy what they lack. **Predict** *Which country from the diagram would you expect to sell oil so that it can buy tea?*

Interdependence As world trade has grown, countries have grown interdependent, or dependent on one another. The United States depends on other countries for oil and inexpensive industrial goods. Meanwhile, other countries depend on the United States for computers and other products.

Developed nations tend to sell products made using advanced technologies. Developing nations tend to sell foods, natural resources such as oil, and simple industrial products. In return, they buy high-technology goods from developed countries.

Moving Goods
Much of the world's trade travels on container ships, like this one in Dubai, United Arab Emirates. These ships can carry huge loads across oceans. **Draw Conclusions** *How does technology make world trade easier?*

Some countries have formed trade alliances to reduce the costs of trade. For example, the United States, Canada, and Mexico belong to the North American Free Trade Area, or NAFTA. Most European countries belong to the European Union. Businesses may face increased competition from foreign competitors within these alliances, and workers may lose their jobs. However, businesses may benefit from increased sales in other countries. Consumers benefit from these alliances because they pay less for products from other countries.

✓ Reading Check **Why do countries trade with one another?**

Section 3 Assessment

Key Terms

Review the key terms at the beginning of this section. Use each term in a sentence that explains its meaning.

Target Reading Skill

What are two ways developed and developing countries are similar?

Comprehension and Critical Thinking

1. (a) Identify Who owns farms, factories, and offices in a communist economy?
(b) Compare and Contrast How is ownership different in a capitalist economy?

2. (a) Identify What is a country's level of development?
(b) Describe What are the main differences in level of development between countries?
(c) Predict What can we predict about a country's economy if we know its level of development?

3. (a) List What are two major trade alliances?
(b) Explain What is the main purpose of these alliances?
(c) Analyze What are some reasons why a country might want to join a trade alliance?

Writing Activity

Suppose you run a company, and you want to expand to another nation. Would you choose a capitalist or communist nation? A developed or developing nation? Would you choose a nation that belongs to a trade alliance? Write a letter to investors explaining your choice.

For: An activity on economic systems
Visit: PHSchool.com
Web Code: led-3303

Section 4 Political Systems

Prepare to Read

Objectives

In this section you will

1. Examine different types of states.
2. Investigate types of government.
3. Learn about alliances and international organizations.

Taking Notes

Copy the table below. As you read, fill the table with information about types of states, types of governments, and international organizations.

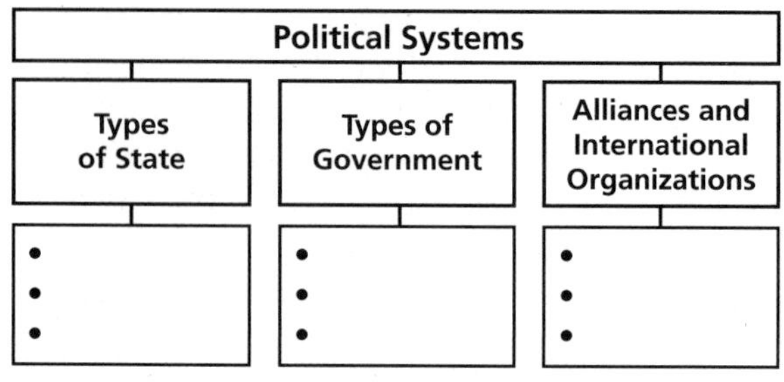

Target Reading Skill

Use Contrast Signal Words Signal words point out relationships among ideas or events. Certain words, such as *like* or *unlike,* can signal a comparison or contrast. As you read this section, notice the comparisons and contrasts among different types of states and governments. What signal words indicate the comparisons and contrasts?

Key Terms

- **government** (GUV urn munt) *n.* a body that makes and enforces laws
- **state** (stayt) *n.* a region that shares a government
- **dependency** (dee PEN dun see) *n.* a region that belongs to another state
- **nation-state** (NAY shun stayt) *n.* a state that is independent of other states
- **city-state** (SIH tee stayt) *n.* a small city-centered state
- **empire** (EM pyr) *n.* a state containing several countries
- **constitution** (kahn stuh TOO shun) *n.* a set of laws that define and often limit a government's power

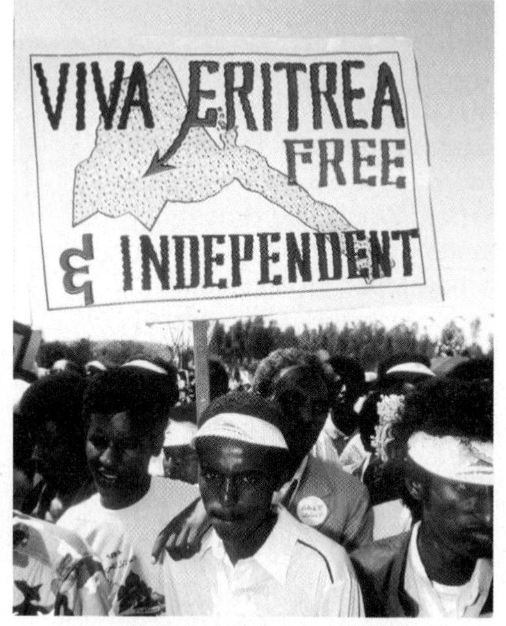

In 1994, Eritreans celebrated the first anniversary of their country's independence.

Types of States

Long ago, most people lived in small, traditional communities. All adults took part in group decisions. Some small communities still make decisions this way, but they are now part of larger units called nations. Nations are too large for everyone to take part in every decision. Still, nations have to protect people and resolve conflicts between individuals and social groups. In modern nations, these needs are met by **governments,** or organizations that set up and enforce laws.

You may remember that a region is an area united by a common feature. A **state** is a region that shares a government. You probably live in a state that is part of the United States. But the political units that we call "states" in the United States are just one kind of state. The entire United States can also be called a state. It is a region that shares a common government—the federal government.

Dependencies and Nation-States Some regions are **dependencies,** or regions that belong to another state. Others, like the United States, are **nation-states,** or states that are independent of other states. Each has a common body of laws. Nation-states are often simply called nations. Every place in the world where people live is part of a nation-state or dependency.

Most nation-states are large, but some are tiny. The smallest is Vatican City, which is surrounded by the city of Rome in Italy. Vatican City covers only about 109 acres (44 hectares)!

Use Contrast Signal Words

The first sentence in the paragraph at the left begins with the word *some*. The second sentence begins with *others*. These words signal that a contrast will be made. What contrast is being made?

How States Developed The first real states formed in Southwest Asia more than 5,000 years ago when early cities set up governments. Small city-centered states are called **city-states.** Later, military leaders conquered large areas and ruled them as **empires,** or states containing several countries.

After about 1500, European rulers founded the first true nation-states. European nations established dependencies all over the world. When those dependencies became independent, they formed new nation-states.

√ Reading Check **What is the difference between a government and a state?**

Vatican City
St. Peter's Basilica, shown below, is the seat of the pope. He leads the Roman Catholic Church and rules Vatican City. **Infer** *What must be true about Vatican City for it to be a nation-state?*

Kim Jong Il
Kim Jong Il, the dictator of North Korea, making a rare public appearance.
Analyze Images *What group in North Korea might be a source of power for Kim Jong Il?*

Types of Government

Each state has a government. There are many different kinds of government. Some governments are controlled by a single person or a small group of people. Others are controlled by all of the people.

Direct Democracy The earliest governments were simple. People lived in small groups. They practiced direct democracy, a form of government in which all adults take part in decisions. Many towns in New England today practice direct democracy. Decisions are made at town meetings where all adult residents can speak and vote.

Tribal Rule In time, communities banded together into larger tribal groups. Members of the tribe had a say in group decisions. But chiefs or elders usually made the final decision about what to do. Decisions were based upon the culture's customs and beliefs.

Absolute Monarchy Until about 200 years ago, one of the most common forms of government was absolute monarchy. In that system, a king or queen who inherits the throne by birth has complete control. Few absolute monarchies still exist today. Saudi Arabia and Brunei are two surviving absolute monarchies.

Dictatorship There are other countries today, however, where just one person rules. A leader who is not a king or queen but who has almost total power over an entire country is called a dictator. Dictatorship is rule by such a leader. Nations ruled by dictators include Cuba, Libya, and North Korea. Dictatorships differ from absolute monarchies because most dictators don't inherit power. Instead, they seize power. Dictators usually remain in power by using violence against their opponents. Dictators deny their people the right to make their own decisions.

Oligarchy Oligarchies are governments controlled by a small group of people. The group may be the leadership of a ruling political party. For example, China is an oligarchy controlled by the leadership of the Communist Party. There are other types of oligarchy. Myanmar, also called Burma, is run by a group of military officers. A group of religious leaders controls Iran. As in a dictatorship, ordinary people have little say in decisions.

Constitutional Monarchy Most monarchies today are constitutional monarchies, or governments in which the power of the king or queen is limited by law. The United Kingdom, the Netherlands, and Kuwait are examples. These nations have **constitutions,** or sets of laws that define and often limit the government's power. In a constitutional monarchy, the king or queen is often only a symbol of the country.

Queen Beatrix of the Netherlands heads a constitutional monarchy.

Representative Democracy Representative democracies are governments run by representatives that the people choose. Many constitutional monarchies are also representative democracies. In a representative democracy, the people indirectly hold power to govern and rule. They elect representatives who create laws. If the people do not like what a representative does, they can refuse to reelect that person. Citizens can also work to change laws they do not like. A constitution sets rules for elections, defines the rights of citizens, and limits the powers of the government. This system ensures that power is shared. The United States, Canada, and India are examples of representative democracies.

✓ Reading Check **What do absolute monarchies, dictatorships, and oligarchies have in common?**

Representative Democracy Members of the United States House of Representatives, shown below, are elected by the people of their districts. **Contrast** *How does a representative democracy differ from a direct democracy?*

International Organizations

Nations may make agreements to work together in an alliance. Members of an alliance are called allies. Alliances provide for nations to assist each other with defense. For example, members of the North Atlantic Treaty Organization (NATO) have agreed to defend any fellow member who is attacked.

The United Nations headquarters in New York, New York

Military bodies such as NATO are just one type of organization that is international, or involving more than one nation. Some international bodies are mainly economic in purpose. The European Union, for example, promotes economic unity among member nations in Europe.

The United Nations is an international organization meant to resolve disputes and promote peace. Almost all nations of the world belong to the United Nations. Every member has a vote in the General Assembly of the United Nations. But only the United Nations Security Council can make decisions over the use of force. The United States and four other permanent members have the power to prevent action in the Security Council.

The United Nations sponsors other international organizations with special purposes. For example, the Food and Agriculture Organization combats hunger worldwide. The United Nations Children's Fund (UNICEF) promotes the rights and well-being of children.

✓ Reading Check **What is the purpose of the United Nations?**

Section 4 Assessment

Key Terms

Review the key terms at the beginning of this section. Use each term in a sentence that explains its meaning.

Target Reading Skill

Reread the first paragraph on page 82. Which two main types of government are contrasted? Look for contrast signal words.

Comprehension and Critical Thinking

1. (a) Identify What were the earliest types of states?

(b) Compare and Contrast How did those early states differ from modern nation-states?

2. (a) List What are the main types of government?

(b) Categorize In which types of government do ordinary citizens take part in decisions?

3. (a) Define What is an alliance?

(b) Compare and Contrast What are the differences and similarities between alliances and other international organizations?

Writing Activity

Which type of government described in this section appeals most to you? Write a paragraph explaining your preference, and why it appeals to you.

Writing Tip When you write a paragraph, state the main idea in a topic sentence. In this case, the topic sentence will tell the type of government that you prefer. Other sentences should support the main idea with arguments.

Chapter 3

Review and Assessment

◆ Chapter Summary

Section 1: Population

- Where people live depends on factors such as climate, soil, and history.
- Population density measures the average number of people living in an area.
- Scientific progress has spurred population growth, which is straining Earth's resources.

Section 2: Migration

- People migrate to seek a better life, or, in some cases, because they have no other choice.
- Cities are growing rapidly in some regions.

Section 3: Economic Systems

- Economic systems may have private ownership of businesses, government ownership, or a mixture of both.
- Developed countries have more industry and technology than developing countries.
- Trade connects countries as buyers and sellers.

Section 4: Political Systems

- The world is divided into nation-states.
- States have governments that differ in the amount of power that citizens have.
- Nation-states may join together in alliances and international organizations.

Harvesting rice in China

◆ Key Terms

Each of the statements below contains a key term from the chapter. If the statement is true, write *true*. If it is false, rewrite the statement to make it true.

1. A country's population is the number of people who live there.
2. Population density measures the size of cities.
3. The movement of people from one region to another is migration.
4. Urbanization is the movement of people to cities.
5. An economy is a system of government.
6. Consumers are people who sell products.
7. Developing nations have few industries and simple technologies.
8. A government is a body that makes and enforces laws and resolves conflicts among its people.
9. A state is a system of government.

Chapter 3 Review and Assessment (continued)

◆ Comprehension and Critical Thinking

10. (a) Define What is population distribution?
(b) Explain What factors affect population distribution in a region?
(c) Compare and Contrast How are those factors different today than they were when most people were farmers?

11. (a) Identify How has the size of world populations changed in recent years?
(b) Identify Cause and Effect What difficulties have resulted from the change in the size of world populations?

12. (a) Define What is voluntary migration?
(b) Make Generalizations Why do people choose to migrate?

13. (a) Define What is capitalism?
(b) Contrast How does capitalism differ from communism?

14. (a) List What are some challenges faced by developing countries?
(b) Infer Why do developing countries face these challenges?

15. (a) Identify What are two types of democracy?
(b) Contrast How do democracies differ from other forms of government?

◆ Skills Practice

Using Population Density Maps In the Skills for Life activity in this chapter, you learned how to read a population density map using the map key.

Review the steps you followed to learn this skill. Then review the map on pages 62 and 63, titled The World: Population Density. Using the map key, describe what each color on the map represents and then list the most sparsely populated areas shown. Finally, draw conclusions about why these areas have such small populations.

◆ Writing Activity: Math

Suppose you are a demographer projecting population growth for three countries. Use the following information to create a population bar graph for each country:

	Birthrate	Death Rate
Country A	14.2	8.7
Country B	9.8	9.7
Country C	9.4	13.9

Then, write a brief paragraph explaining your graph. For each country, is the population increasing, decreasing, or stable? Explain why.

MAP MASTER™ Skills Activity

Place Location For each place listed below, write the letter from the map that shows its location.

1. Asia
2. Antarctica
3. Africa
4. South America
5. North America
6. Europe
7. Australia

Go Online PHSchool.com Use Web Code **lep-3215** for an **interactive map.**

Continents

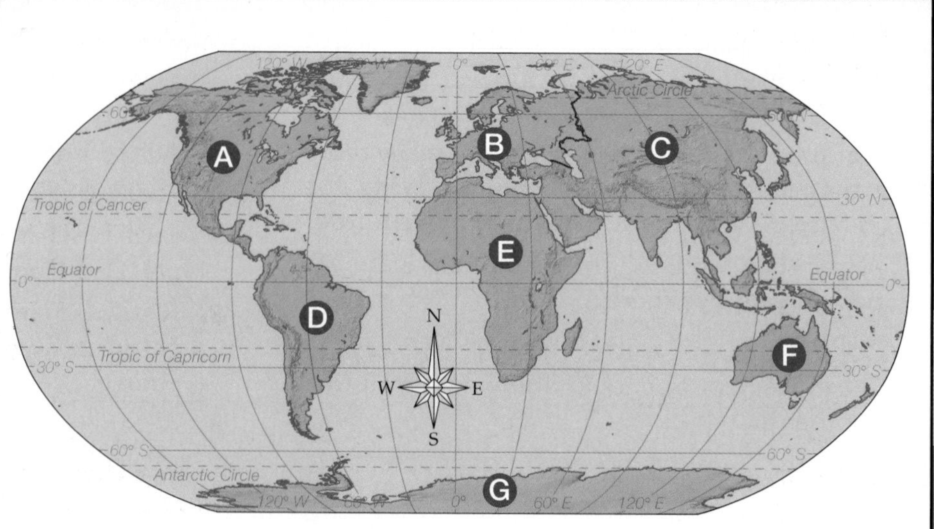

Standardized Test Prep

Test-Taking Tips

Some questions on standardized tests ask you to analyze a reading selection for a main idea. Read the passage in the box below. Then follow the tips to answer the sample question.

> This region has one of the highest population densities in the world. As many as 5,000 people per square mile live in parts of the region. There are good reasons for this heavy population density. The land is fertile. Though the desert is not far away, the river contains plenty of water for the people who live there.

TIP As you read each sentence, think about what main idea it supports.

Pick the letter that best answers the question.

Which sentence states this passage's main idea?

A ~~Demographers study human populations.~~
B Egypt's Nile River valley supports a large population.
C ~~People find ways to adapt to their environment.~~
D Many people live near the Mississippi River.

TIP Cross out answer choices that don't make sense. Then pick from the remaining choices the one that BEST answers the question.

Think It Through The passage does not mention demographers. So you can cross out answer A. You can also rule out C, because the passage does not discuss people adapting to their environment. Answers B and D both mention specific regions. Which region does the paragraph describe? The paragraph mentions a desert. There is no desert near the Mississippi River. So the answer is B.

Practice Questions

Use the tips above and other tips in this book to help you answer the following questions.

1. The number of people per square mile is a region's
   A population distribution.
   B population.
   C elevation.
   D population density.

2. People moving to a different region to seek better farming opportunities is an example of
   A trade.
   B voluntary migration.
   C involuntary migration.
   D urbanization.

3. In which of the following does the government own most workplaces?
   A capitalism
   B developing country
   C communism
   D developed country

Read the following passage, and answer the question that follows.

A constitutional monarch has little power. Under some constitutions, elected representatives have the law-making power instead of the monarch. In such cases, the government works much like other representative democracies.

4. What is the main idea of this passage?
   A An absolute monarch has great power.
   B Constitutions are always democratic.
   C A constitutional monarchy may also be a representative democracy.
   D A constitutional monarch cannot interfere with representative democracy.

Use Web Code **lea-3301** for a **Chapter 3 self-test.**

My Side of the Mountain

By Jean Craighead George

Prepare to Read

Background Information

Have you ever camped out overnight? Have you ever built a fire in order to keep warm? Suppose you had no electricity or your home had no heating system. How would you cope with the natural world without modern technology? Do you think that living closer to the natural world would change you in any significant way?

Sam Gribley is the fictional hero of the novel *My Side of the Mountain*. When he decided to live close to nature, he built a tree house in the Catskill Mountains of New York and then moved in with his only companion, Frightful, a falcon. This excerpt describes their first winter in the mountains.

Objectives

As you read this selection, you will

- Identify the skills Sam needed to survive alone in the wilderness.
- Discover how Sam came to understand the natural world.

I lived close to the weather. It is surprising how you watch it when you live in it. Not a cloud passed unnoticed, not a wind blew untested. I knew the moods of the storms, where they came from, their shapes and colors. When the sun shone, I took Frightful to the meadow and we slid down the mountain on my snapping-turtle-shell sled. She really didn't care much for this.

When the winds changed and the air smelled like snow, I would stay in my tree, because I had gotten lost in a blizzard one afternoon and had to hole up in a rock ledge until I could see where I was going. That day the winds were so strong I could not push against them, so I crawled under the ledge; for hours I wondered if I would be able to dig out when the storm blew on. Fortunately I only had to push through a foot of snow. However, that taught me to stay home when the air said "snow." Not that I

Fog-shrouded woodland in the Catskill Mountains, New York

was afraid of being caught far from home in a storm, for I could find food and shelter and make a fire anywhere, but I had become as attached to my hemlock house as a brooding bird to her nest. Caught out in the storms and weather, I had an urgent desire to return to my tree, even as The Baron Weasel returned to his den, and the deer to their copse. We all had our little "patch" in the wilderness. We all fought to return there.

I usually came home at night with the nuthatch that roosted in a nearby sapling. I knew I was late if I tapped the tree and he came out. Sometimes when the weather was icy and miserable, I would hear him high in the trees near the edge of the meadow, yanking and yanking and flicking his tail, and then I would see him wing to bed early. I considered him a pretty good barometer, and if he went to his tree early, I went to mine early too. When you don't have a newspaper or radio to give you weather bulletins, watch the birds and animals. They can tell when a storm is coming. I called the nuthatch "Barometer," and when he holed up, I holed up, lit my light, and sat by my fire whittling or learning new tunes on my reed whistle. I was now really into the teeth of winter, and quite fascinated by its activity. There is no such thing as a "still winter night." Not only are many animals running around in the breaking cold, but the trees cry out and limbs snap and fall, and the wind gets caught in a ravine and screams until it dies.

hemlock (HEM lahk) *n.* an evergreen tree with drooping branches and short needles
copse (kahps) *n.* a thicket of small trees or shrubs
yank (yangk) *v.* to give the call made by a nuthatch
barometer (buh RAHM uh tur) *n.* an instrument for forecasting changes in the weather; anything that indicates a change
whittle (WHIT ul) *v.* to cut or pare thin shavings from wood with a knife
teeth of winter (teeth uv WIN tur) *n.* the coldest, harshest time of winter

✓ Reading Check **What did Sam name the nuthatch? Explain why.**

About the Selection

My Side of the Mountain, by Jean Craighead George (New York: E. P. Dutton, 1959), includes sketches of Sam Gribley's adventures.

About the Author

Jean Craighead George (b. 1919) often went camping, climbed trees, and studied living things as she grew up. Ms. George has been writing about nature and its lessons since she was eight years old, and has written more than 80 books for young readers.

Review and Assessment

Comprehension and Critical Thinking

1. (a) **Identify** When the weather is bad, what is Sam's "urgent desire"?
(b) **Compare** To what does Sam compare this desire?
(c) **Interpret** What does Sam tell us about himself when he makes a comparison?

2. (a) **Recall** What are some of the clues Sam has about what the weather will be like?
(b) **Describe** What parts of the natural world does Sam seem to notice most?
(c) **Evaluate** Sometimes Sam talks about the wind and trees as if they were alive. Think about your relationship with nature. How is it like Sam's? How is it different?

Writing Activity

Make a list of sounds you hear only in winter. What are the tastes and smells that make you think of winter? List them. What are the sights of winter? Add them to your list. Then write an essay describing the place you most like to be in winter and explain why.

Chapter 4

Cultures of the World

Chapter Preview

This chapter will introduce you to the concept of culture, the things that make up culture, and the ways in which cultures change.

Target Reading Skill

Sequence In this chapter, you will focus on the text structure by identifying the order, or sequence, of events. Noting the sequence of events can help you understand and remember the events.

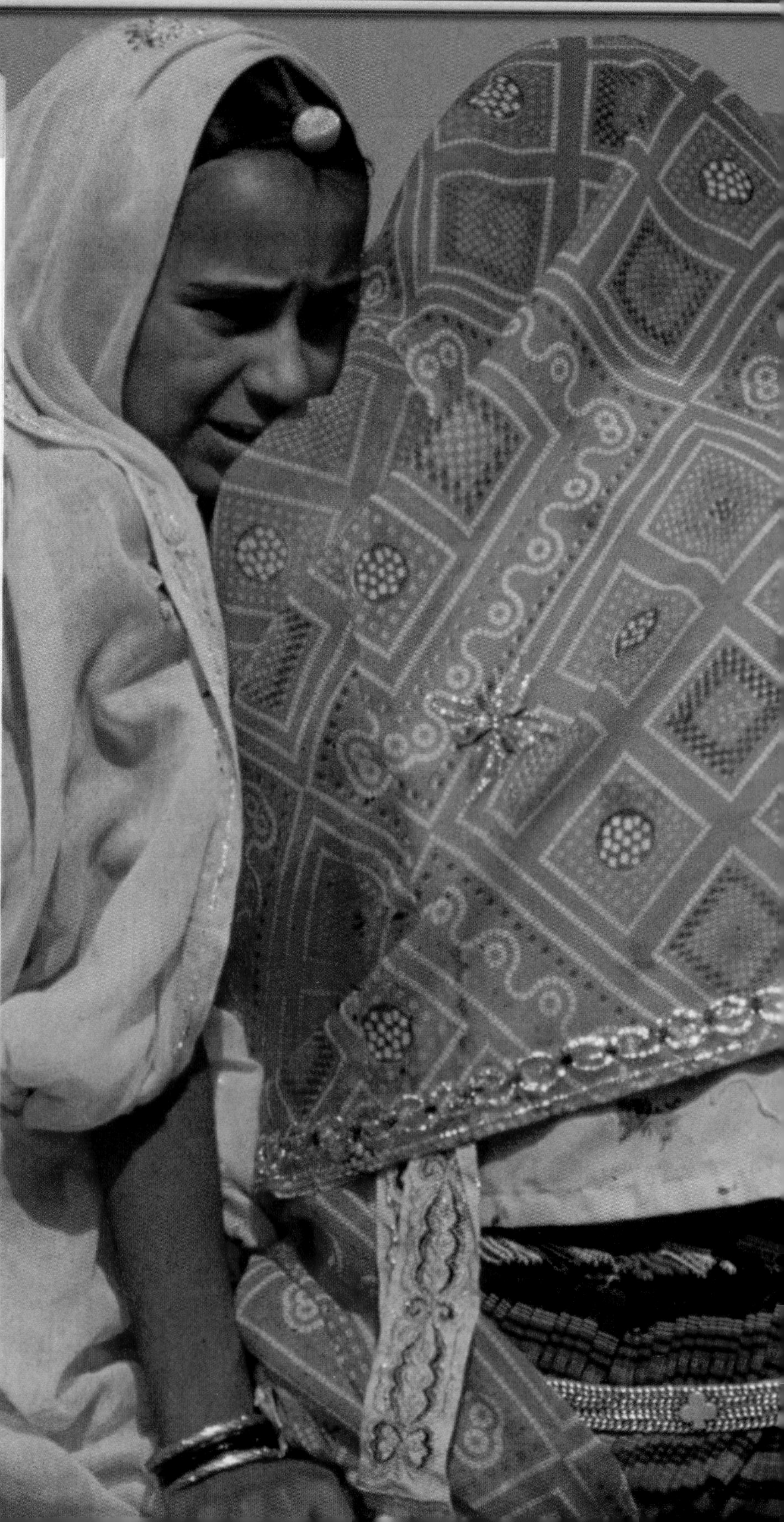

▶ Young women in traditional dress at a festival in Pushkar, India

Section 1

Understanding Culture

Prepare to Read

Objectives

In this section you will

1. Learn about culture.
2. Explore how culture has developed.

Taking Notes

Copy the concept web below. As you read this section, fill in the web with information about culture, its relation to the environment, and how it has developed. Add ovals as needed for concepts in the section.

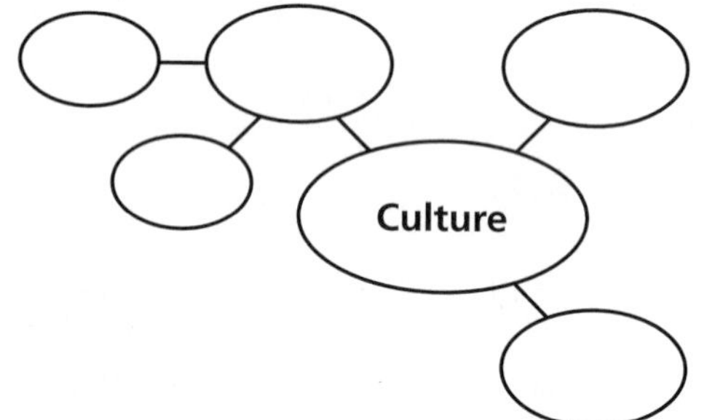

Target Reading Skill

Understand Sequence A sequence is the order in which a series of events occurs. Noting the sequence of important events can help you understand and remember the events. You can show the order of events by making a sequence chart. Write the first event, or thing that sets the other events in motion, in the first box. Then write each additional event in a box. Use arrows to show how one event leads to the next.

Key Terms

- **culture** (KUL chur) *n.* the way of life of a people, including their beliefs and practices
- **cultural landscape** (KUL chur ul LAND skayp) *n.* the parts of a people's environment that they have shaped and the technology they have used to shape it
- **civilization** (sih vuh luh ZAY shun) *n.* an advanced culture with cities and a system of writing
- **institution** (in stuh TOO shun) *n.* a custom or organization with social, educational, or religious purposes

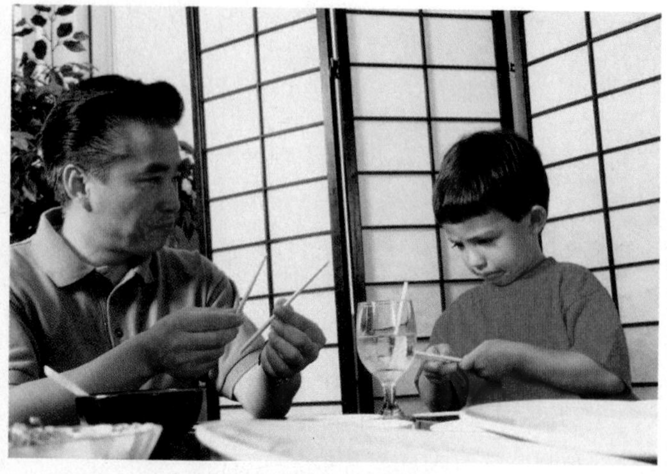

A grandfather in Japan teaching his grandson to use chopsticks

What Is Culture?

Culture is the way of life of a people, including their beliefs, customs, and practices. The language people speak and the way they dress are both parts of their culture. So are the work people do, what they do after work or school, and the ideas that influence them.

Elements of Culture Parents pass culture on to their children, generation after generation. Ideas and ways of doing things are called cultural traits. Over time, cultural traits may change.

Some elements of a culture are easy to see. They include material things, such as houses, television sets, food, and clothing. Sports and literature are visible elements of culture as well. Things you cannot see or touch are also part of culture. They include spiritual beliefs, government, and ideas about right and wrong. Finally, language is a very important part of culture.

People and Their Land Geographers study themes of culture, especially human activities related to the environment. The theme of human-environment interaction deals with these activities. Geographers want to know how the environment affects culture. For example, Japan is a nation of mountainous islands, with limited farmland. So the Japanese have turned to the sea. Fish and seaweed are popular foods in Japan.

However, environment does not dictate culture. Like Japan, Greece is a nation of mountainous islands and peninsulas surrounded by the sea. The Greeks eat some fish, but they have cleared mountainsides as well for use as pasture. Goats and sheep graze on the mountainsides and provide food for the Greeks.

Geographers are also interested in the effect people have on their environment. Often the effect is tied to a culture's technology, even if that technology is simple. For example, the Greeks have cleared their rugged land for pasture. The Japanese harvest seaweed.

A **cultural landscape** is the parts of a people's environment that they have shaped and the technology they have used to shape it. This varies from place to place. On hilly Bali (BAH lee), in Indonesia, farmers have carved terraces into hillsides. On the plains of northern India, farmers have laid out broad, flat fields.

✓ Reading Check **How are culture and environment related?**

Discovery
CHANNEL
SCHOOL
Video
Learn more about culture.

Balinese Terraces
A farmer on the island of Bali, in Indonesia, crosses terraced rice fields.
Analyze *How has Bali's environment affected its culture? How has Bali's culture affected its environment?*

The Development of Culture

Scientists think that early cultures had four major advances in technology. First was the invention of tools millions of years ago. Second and third were the control of fire and the beginning of agriculture. Fourth was the development of **civilizations,** or advanced cultures with cities and the use of writing.

Technology and Civilization For most of human existence, people were hunters and gatherers. While traveling from place to place, they collected wild plants, hunted game, and fished.

Later, people discovered how to grow crops. They tamed wild animals to help them with work or to raise for food. Over time, more and more people relied on farming for most of their food. Historians call this great change the Agricultural Revolution.

Agriculture provided a steady food supply. Agriculture let farmers grow more food than they needed. In parts of Asia and Africa, some people worked full time on crafts such as metal-working. They traded their products for food. People began to develop laws and government. To store information, they developed writing. These advances in culture produced the first true civilizations about 5,000 years ago.

Early civilizations developed new technologies, such as irrigation, that let people grow more crops. Over time, farming and civilization spread throughout the world.

The Development of Agricultural Technology

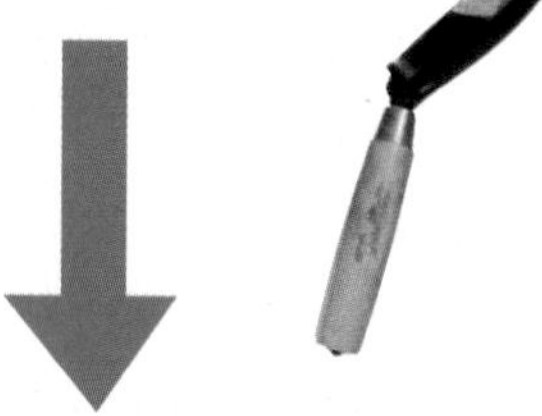

Sickle
The first farmers used hand-held sickles to harvest grain. The first sickles had stone blades. Later sickles, like the one shown here, had metal blades.

Horse-drawn reaper
By the late 1800s, farmers were using animal-powered machinery, such as this sail reaper, to harvest grain.

Combine harvester
Today, farmers harvest grain with large-scale, motorized machinery, such as this combine.

Tools for Harvesting When the Agricultural Revolution began, people used simple hand-powered tools. The Industrial Revolution later brought industrial tools to the fields. **Draw Conclusions** *How do you think the development of tools for harvesting affected the amount that each farmer could harvest?*

Then, about 200 years ago, people began to invent new technologies that used power-driven machinery. This change marked the beginning of the Industrial Revolution. It led to the growth of cities, science, and even more advanced technologies, such as computers and space flight.

Target Skill — Understand Sequence What important events led to the Industrial Revolution?

Development of Institutions Before the Agricultural Revolution, people had simple **institutions,** customs and organizations with social, educational, or religious purposes. These included extended families and simple political institutions, such as councils of elders.

As people gathered in larger groups and formed cities, they needed more complex institutions. People developed organized religions, with priests, ceremonies, and temples. Armies and governments appeared with states. Teachers started schools.

In the modern world, we have many different kinds of institutions, including museums, sports clubs, corporations, political parties, and universities. These institutions are important parts of our culture.

Oxford University, in Oxford, England, is more than 800 years old.

✓ **Reading Check** **What allowed civilizations to develop?**

Section 1 Assessment

Key Terms

Review the key terms at the beginning of this section. Use each term in a sentence that explains its meaning.

Target Reading Skill

Place the following events in the order in which they occurred: the development of civilization; the invention of tools; the development of industry; and the beginnings of agriculture.

Comprehension and Critical Thinking

1. **(a) Define** What is a cultural landscape?
(b) Explain What are the most important cultural traits that shape a people's cultural landscape?
(c) Identify Cause and Effect If two cultures occupy similar environments, why might their cultural landscapes still differ?
2. **(a) Identify** What was the Agricultural Revolution?
(b) Sequence What cultural advances followed the Agricultural Revolution?

Writing Activity

Think of all the ways that the culture of your region has shaped its landscape. Write a short paragraph describing your cultural landscape and the cultural traits that shaped it.

For: An activity on culture
Visit: PHSchool.com
Web Code: led-3401

Section 2
Culture and Society

Prepare to Read

Objectives
In this section you will
1. Learn how people are organized into groups.
2. Investigate language.
3. Explore the role of religion.

Taking Notes
Copy the outline below. As you read this section, fill in the outline with information about how society is organized, about language, and about religion. Add letters and numbers as needed.

I. How society is organized
  A. Social classes
  B.
    1.
    2.
II. Language
  A.

Target Reading Skill
Understand Sequence Noting the sequence of important changes can help you understand and remember the changes. You can show a sequence of changes by simply listing the changes in the order in which they occurred. As you read this section, list the sequence of the changes in people's ability to improve their status.

Key Terms
- **society** (suh SY uh tee) *n.* a group of people sharing a culture
- **social structure** (SOH shul STRUK chur) *n.* a pattern of organized relationships among groups of people within a society
- **social class** (SOH shul klas) *n.* a grouping of people based on rank or status
- **nuclear family** (NOO klee ur FAM uh lee) *n.* a mother, a father, and their children
- **extended family** (ek STEN did FAM uh lee) *n.* a family that includes several generations

A nuclear family in the United Kingdom

How Society Is Organized

Think about the people you see every day. Do you spend each day meeting random strangers? Or do you see the same family members, classmates, and teachers every day? Chances are, there is a pattern to your interactions.

A group of people sharing a culture is known as a **society.** Every society has a **social structure,** or a pattern of organized relationships among groups of people within the society. A society may be as small as a single community or as large as a nation or even a group of similar nations. Smaller groups within a society work together on particular tasks. Some groups work together to get food. Others protect the community. Still others educate children. Social structure helps people work together to meet one another's basic needs.

The family is the basic, most important social unit of any society. Families teach the customs and traditions of the culture to their children. Through their families, children learn how to dress, to be polite, to eat, and to play.

Social Classes Cultures also have another kind of social organization—**social classes,** or groupings of people based on rank or status. A person's status or position may come from his or her wealth, land, ancestors, or education. In some cultures in the past, it was often hard—or impossible—for people to move from one social class to another. Today, people in many societies can improve their status. They can obtain a good education, make more money, or marry someone of a higher class.

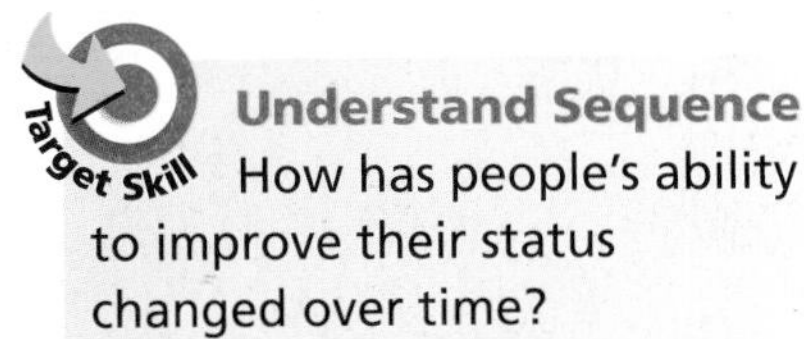

Understand Sequence How has people's ability to improve their status changed over time?

Kinds of Families Not all cultures define family in the same way. In some cultures, the basic unit is a **nuclear family,** or a mother, a father, and their children. This pattern is common in developed nations such as the United States, Australia, and Germany. The nuclear family gets its name from the word *nucleus*, which means "center."

Other cultures have **extended families,** or families that include several generations. In addition to a central nuclear family of parents and their sons or daughters, there are the wives or husbands of those sons or daughters. The family also includes grandchildren, or the children of those sons or daughters. In extended families, older people often help care for the children. They are respected for their knowledge and experience. Older family members pass on traditions. Extended families are less common than they used to be. As rural people move to cities, nuclear families are becoming more common.

✓ Reading Check **What is the basic social unit of societies?**

A Salvadoran-American Family
This family includes grandparents and more than one set of parents.
Infer *Is this a nuclear family or an extended family?*

A teacher using sign language with hearing-impaired students

Language

All cultures have language. In fact, language provides a basis for culture. People learn their cultures mainly through language. Most communication with others depends on language. Think how hard it would be if you had no way to say, "Meet me by the gate after school." How could you learn if you could not ask questions?

A culture's language reflects the things that are important in that culture. For example, English has words for Christian and Jewish concepts, such as *baptism* and *sabbath.* Some languages lack words for these concepts because their speakers are not Jewish or Christian. But those languages have words for concepts in their people's religions that have no English translation.

The World: Major Language Groups

This map shows the locations of the world's major language groups. Languages in each of these groups share a common ancestor, a language spoken long ago that gradually changed to become several related languages. For example, English and German are both Indo-European languages that share a common ancestor. Can you recognize the German words *Land, Mann,* and *Wagen?*

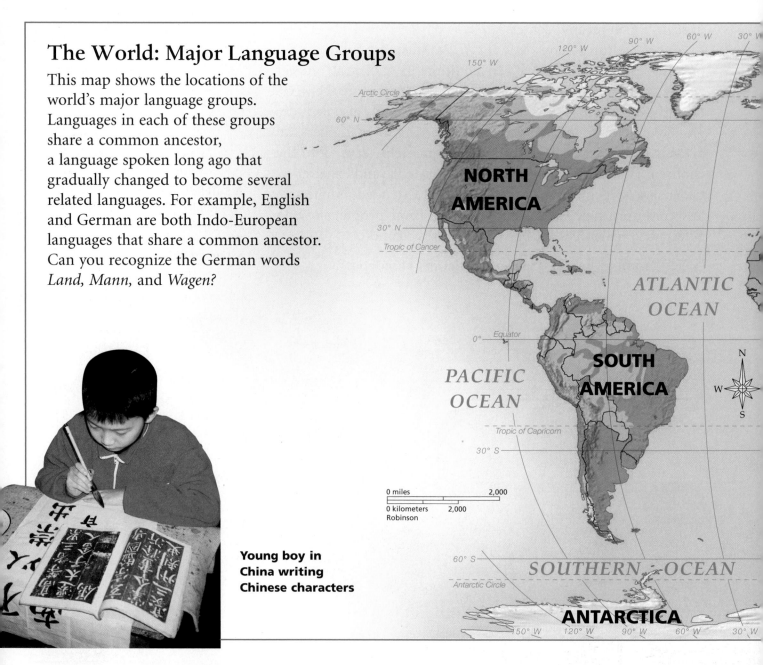

Young boy in China writing Chinese characters

In some countries, people speak more than one language. For example, Canada has two official languages, French and English. In the United States, you may usually hear English, but you can also hear Spanish, Chinese, Haitian Creole, and many other languages. India has 16 official languages, but people there speak more than 800 languages!

People who speak each language are culturally different in some ways from other people in their country who speak other languages. They may celebrate different festivals or have different customs for such things as dating or education. That is because each language preserves shared ideas and traditions.

✓ **Reading Check** **What is the relation between language and culture?**

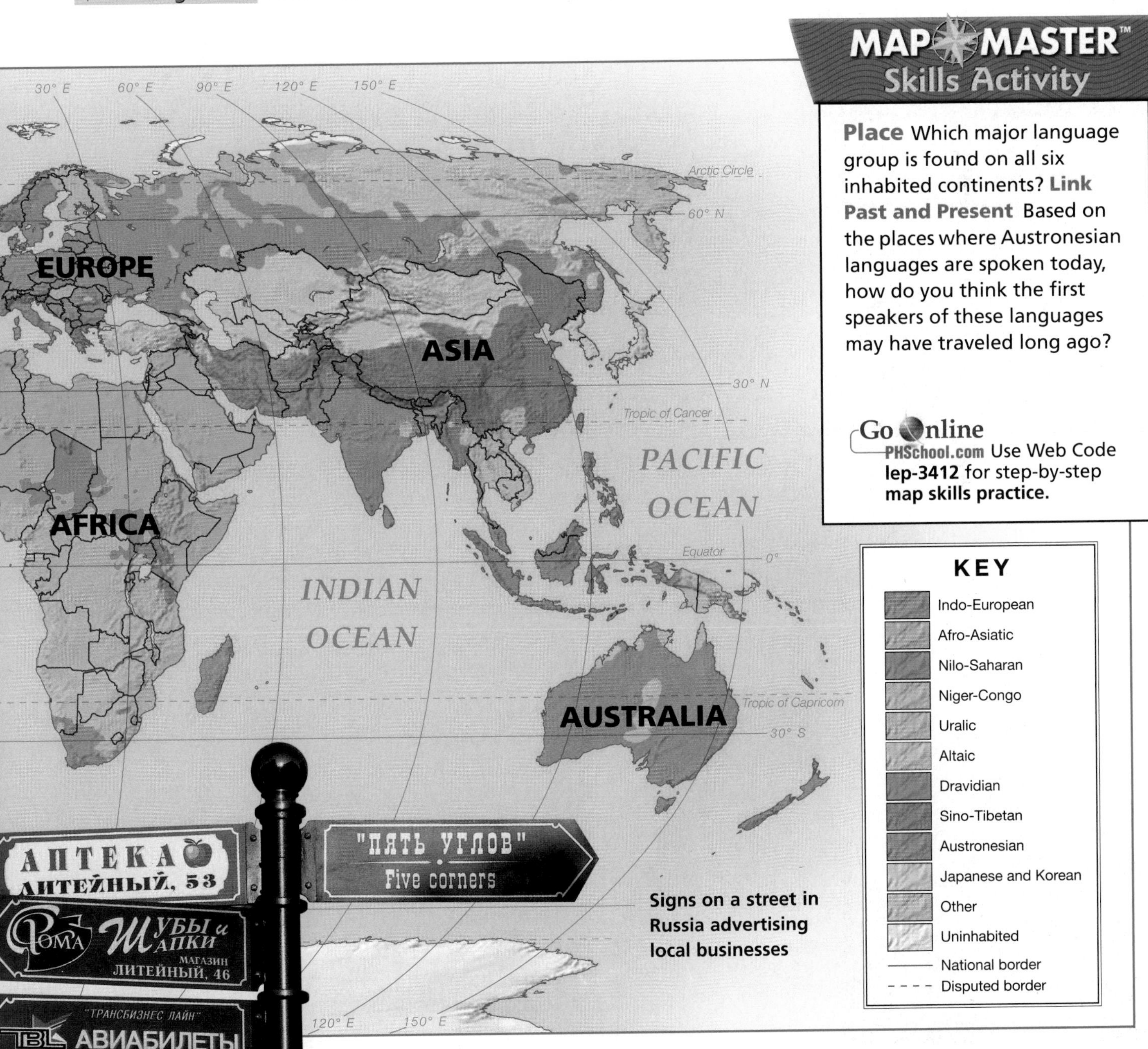

MAP MASTER™ Skills Activity

Place Which major language group is found on all six inhabited continents? **Link Past and Present** Based on the places where Austronesian languages are spoken today, how do you think the first speakers of these languages may have traveled long ago?

Go Online PHSchool.com Use Web Code **lep-3412 for step-by-step map skills practice.**

Signs on a street in Russia advertising local businesses

The World: Major Religions

The major religions of the world all began in Asia. India was the birthplace of Sikhism, Hinduism, and Buddhism, all of which later spread to other countries. The other great world religions had their start in Southwest Asia: first Judaism, then Christianity, and finally Islam. These religions also later spread to other parts of the world.

MAP MASTER™ Skills Activity

Place Which of the continents has the greatest variety of religions?
Draw Inferences Why do you think this is so?

Go Online
PHSchool.com Use Web Code **lep-3422** for step-by-step **map skills practice.**

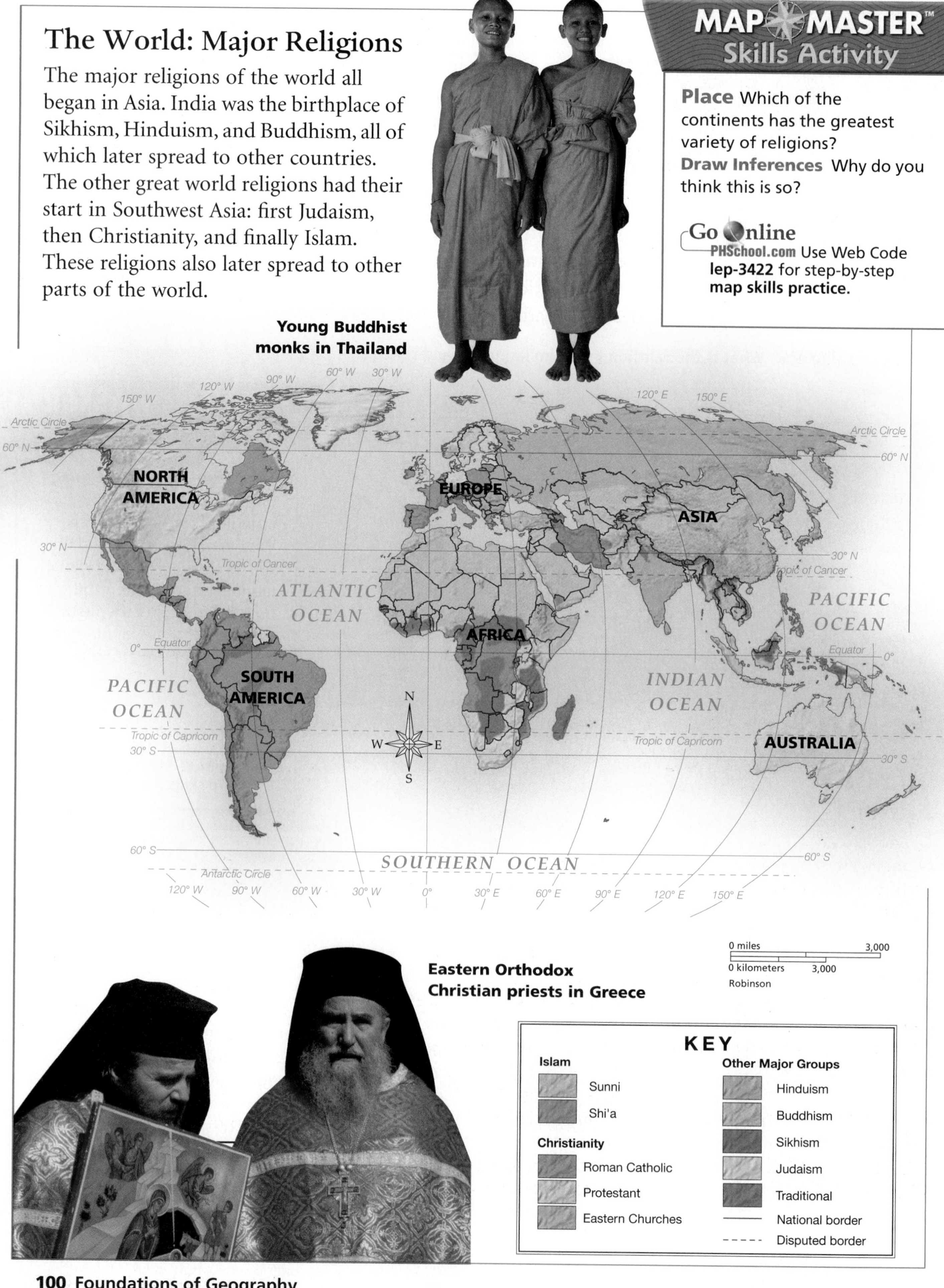

Young Buddhist monks in Thailand

Eastern Orthodox Christian priests in Greece

Religion

Religion is an important part of every culture. For example, most of the people of Saudi Arabia are Muslim. In some countries, such as the United States, people follow more than one religion. Beliefs and practices may differ among religions. However, religion remains important to many people.

Religion can help people make sense of the world. Religion can provide comfort and hope for people facing difficult times. And religion can help answer questions about the meaning and purpose of life. Religion also guides people in ethics, or standards of accepted behavior.

Religious beliefs vary. Members of some religions, such as Islam, Judaism, and Christianity, believe in one God. Members of other religions, such as Hinduism and traditional religions, believe in more than one god. But all religions have prayers and rituals. Every religion celebrates important places and times. And all religions expect people to treat one another well and to behave properly.

✓ Reading Check **Why is religion important to people?**

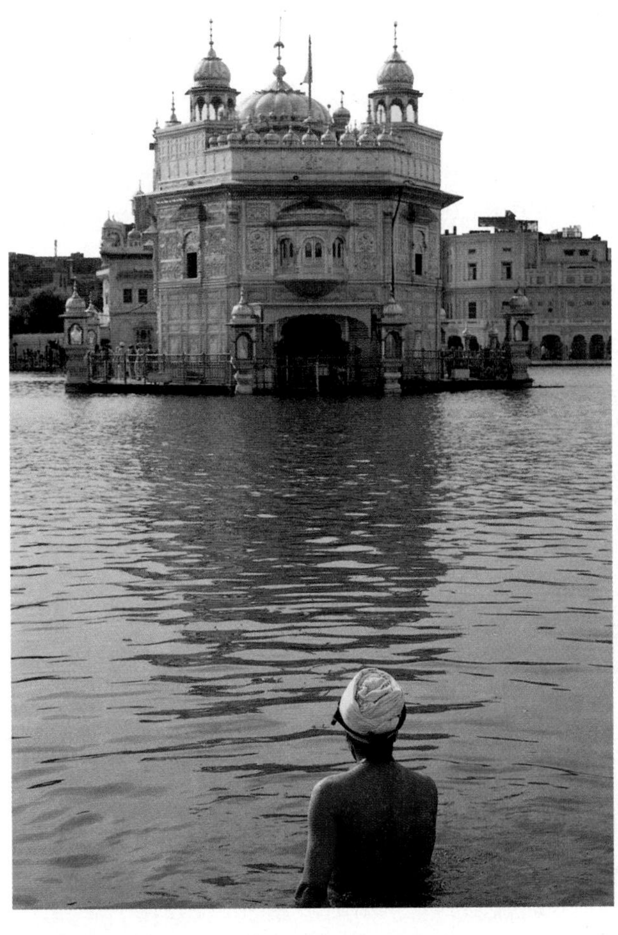

This temple, in Amritsar, India, is a holy place of Sikhism.

Section 2 Assessment

Key Terms

Review the key terms at the beginning of this section. Use each term in a sentence that explains its meaning.

Target Reading Skill

Place the following events in young people's lives in the correct sequence: learning their culture's language and learning their culture's beliefs.

Comprehension and Critical Thinking

1. (a) Identify What is the role of social structure in society?
(b) Explain What is the place of families in a social structure?
(c) Predict Would you expect the members of one family to fall within one social class or more than one?

2. (a) Recall How is language related to culture?
(b) Identify Cause and Effect Why do you think people who speak different languages tend to have different cultures?

3. (a) Identify What values do all religions share?
(b) Draw Conclusions How might those values help people of different religions overcome conflicts?

Writing Activity

In a journal entry, explore the ways in which family and language connect you to other people in your society.

Writing Tip When you write a journal entry, write about experiences from your own life. You may also express your own opinions and perspectives. For this exercise, think about which of your activities and interests involve family or the use of language.

Skills for Life

Making Valid Generalizations

A generalization is a broad conclusion. Some generalizations are valid—that is, they have value or worth—because they can be drawn reasonably from specific facts. Other generalizations are not valid, because they draw unreasonably broad conclusions and are not based on fact.

Many statements have clues that tell you they should be evaluated for validity. For example, statements with words such as *everybody* or *everyone* are very broad. They should always be evaluated. Is the statement "Everybody needs salt" a valid generalization? It is, because it is based on the scientifically proven fact that humans cannot survive without salt in our diet. However, generalizations such as "Everybody loves chocolate" are not valid. They draw unreasonably broad conclusions and cannot be proved.

You need to know how to evaluate a generalization to see if it is valid. You also have to know how to make a valid generalization yourself.

Testing for Validity

To find whether a generalization is valid, ask

- Are there enough facts—at least three in a short passage—to support the generalization?
- Do I know any other facts that support the generalization?
- Does the statement overgeneralize or stereotype a group of people? Words such as *all*, *always*, or *every* signal overgeneralization. Words such as *some*, *many*, *most*, and *often* help prevent a statement from being overgeneralized.

Learn the Skill

To make a valid generalization, follow these steps:

1. **Identify specific facts contained within a source of information.** Make sure you understand the topic that the facts support.
2. **State what the facts have in common, and look for patterns.** Do any of the facts fit together in a way that makes a point about a broad subject? Do data in a table or graph point toward a general statement?
3. **Make a generalization, or broad conclusion, about the facts.** Write your generalization as a complete sentence or a paragraph.
4. **Test the generalization and revise it if necessary.** You can test the validity of a generalization by using the guidelines in the box at the left.

Practice the Skill

Read the passage at the right describing three cultures, and then make a generalization about these cultures.

1. What is the topic of the text? List at least three specific facts that relate to that topic.
2. What do the facts you listed have in common? Do they suggest a general idea about the topic?
3. Make a generalization about the topic. Write it in a complete sentence. List three facts that support it.
4. Test your generalization to see if it is valid. If it is not valid, try rewriting it so that it is more limited. Be careful of exaggerated wording.

Apply the Skill

Turn to page 97 and read the paragraph under the heading Kinds of Families. Make as many generalizations as you can, and test them for their validity. Explain why each generalization is or is not valid.

The Maya thrived in present-day Mexico and Central America from about A.D. 300 to 900. Corn was their principal crop. They developed a sophisticated civilization, but they had abandoned their great cities by about A.D. 900. At about that time, the Hohokam people were growing corn and beans in what is now Arizona. The Hohokam left their settlements during the 1400s, possibly because of drought. Meanwhile, between about A.D. 900 and 1300, the Anasazi people lived to the northeast. They also grew corn. The Anasazi built multistory dwellings up against high cliff walls. Many families lived in these homes. During a drought in the late 1200s, the Anasazi abandoned some of their villages.

An extended Islamic family, spanning three generations, from the rural east coast of Malaysia

Section 3

Cultural Change

Prepare to Read

Objectives

In this section you will

1. Explore how cultures change.
2. Learn how ideas spread from one culture to another.

Taking Notes

Copy the concept web below. As you read this section, fill in the web with information about cultural change. Add ovals as needed for the concepts in the section.

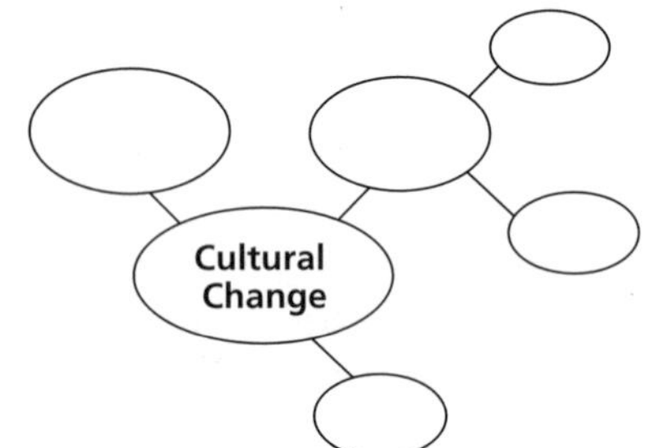

Target Reading Skill

Recognize Words That Signal Sequence
Signal words point out relationships among ideas or events. To help keep the order of events clear, look for words such as *first, later,* or *at that time* that signal the order in which the events took place.

Key Terms

- **cultural diffusion** (KUL chur ul dih FYOO zhun) *n.* the movement of customs and ideas
- **acculturation** (uh kul chur AY shun) *n.* the process of accepting new ideas and fitting them into a culture

Blue jeans and denim shirts have changed with the times.

How Cultures Change

All cultures change over time. The history of blue jeans is an example of cultural change. Some people think that blue jeans are typical American clothes. But many cultures contributed to them. Blue jeans were invented in the United States in the 1800s. They were marketed by Levi Strauss. Strauss was a German-born merchant who moved to California. He made the jeans with a cloth called denim. This may be a shortened form of *serge de Nîmes,* the name of a similar cloth from France.

At first, only Americans wore blue jeans, but they later became popular in other countries. In the 1980s, the Japanese and the French developed stonewashing. It made brand-new denim jeans look worn. Since then, designers from Asia, Europe, and America have promoted new styles, such as ripped and "dirty" denim. Today, jeans are popular all over the world. And the word *jeans* comes from an old French name for Genoa, an Italian city where a cloth similar to denim was first made. What could be more American than jeans?

Why Cultures Change Just as jeans have changed over time, so, too, has American culture. Cultures change all the time. Because culture is an entire way of life, a change in one part changes other parts. Changes in the natural environment, technology, and ideas all affect culture.

A teenager using a cell phone

New Technologies New technologies also change a culture. During the 1800s and early 1900s, the growth of industry and the spread of factories drew large numbers of Americans from the countryside to the nation's cities. Factories offered jobs to thousands of men, women, and children. Limited transportation meant that people had to live close to the factories. Cities grew larger as a result.

This all changed after the invention of the car in the late 1800s. Within a few years, advances in technology made cars more affordable. By 1920, many Americans had cars. People could live farther from their jobs and drive to work. Soon after, the idea of owning a house with a yard became more popular. The result has been the growth of sprawling suburbs since the mid-1900s and a new culture based on car travel.

A "bullet train" in Japan
Japanese engineers have developed new technologies that allow these trains to travel at speeds of more than 180 miles (300 kilometers) per hour. **Infer** *How might such high speeds affect how far away people can live from their work?*

How One Change Can Lead to Others Think of other ways technology has changed the culture of the United States. Radio and television brought entertainment and news into homes. Today instant information is part of our culture. Computers change how and where people work. Computers even help people live longer since doctors use computers to diagnose and treat patients. Radio, television, and computers add new words to our language, such as *broadcast, channel surfing,* and *hacker.* What other new words can you think of?

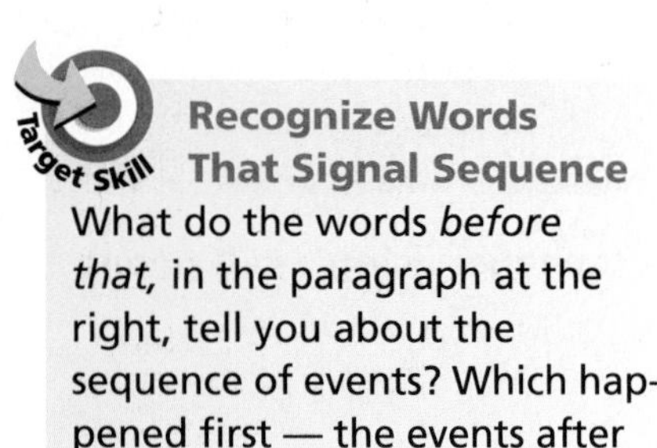

Recognize Words That Signal Sequence
What do the words *before that,* in the paragraph at the right, tell you about the sequence of events? Which happened first — the events after those words or the events in the preceding sentence?

Cultural Change Over Time Cultural change has been going on for a long time. Controlling fire helped early people survive in colder climates. When people started raising animals and growing crops, ways of life also changed. People began to work in the same fields year after year. Before that, they had roamed over a wider area looking for wild plant and animal foods.

√ Reading Check **How did the invention of cars change culture?**

How Ideas Spread

Advances in transportation technology, such as the airplane, make it easier for people to move all over the world. When they move, people bring new kinds of clothing and tools with them. They also bring ideas about such things as ways to prepare food, teach children, practice their religion, or govern themselves.

Ideas can travel to new places in other ways. People may obtain goods from another culture by trade and then learn to make those goods themselves. People may also learn from other cultures through written material. The movement of customs and ideas is called **cultural diffusion.**

A woman practicing yoga, a form of meditation that spread from Asia to Europe and North America

How Cultures Adopt New Ideas One example of cultural diffusion is the game of baseball. Baseball began as an American sport, but today it is played in countries all around the world. That is an example of cultural diffusion. The Japanese love baseball. However, they have changed the game to fit their culture. These changes are an example of **acculturation,** or the process of accepting new ideas and fitting them into a culture. Americans value competition. They focus on winning. A game of baseball does not end until one team wins. But in Japan, a game can end in a tie. The Japanese do not mind a tie game. In Japan, how well you play is more important than winning.

Communication Technology and the Speed of Change

What's the fastest way to get from your house to Japan? Would you use a jet plane? A phone call? The Internet? A fax? All these answers can be correct. The answer depends on whether you want to transport your body, your voice, a picture, or just words on a sheet of paper.

For thousands of years, cultures changed slowly. People and goods moved by foot or wagon or sailing ship, so ideas and technology also moved slowly. Recently, communication technology has increased the speed of change. Faxes and computers transport information almost instantly. Magazines and television shows can bring ideas and information from all over the world to any home. This rapid exchange of ideas speeds up cultural change.

Technology has brought many benefits. Computers let scientists share information about how to cure diseases. Telephones let us instantly talk to relatives thousands of miles away. In the Australian Outback, students your age use closed-circuit television and two-way radios to take part in class from their own homes.

Links to Technology

Digital Tunes Until recent years, music lovers had to lug around tapes or CDs. The invention of MP3s and MP3 players changed that. Fans can now download and store thousands of songs in MP3 format from the Internet. They no longer need bulky tapes and CDs.

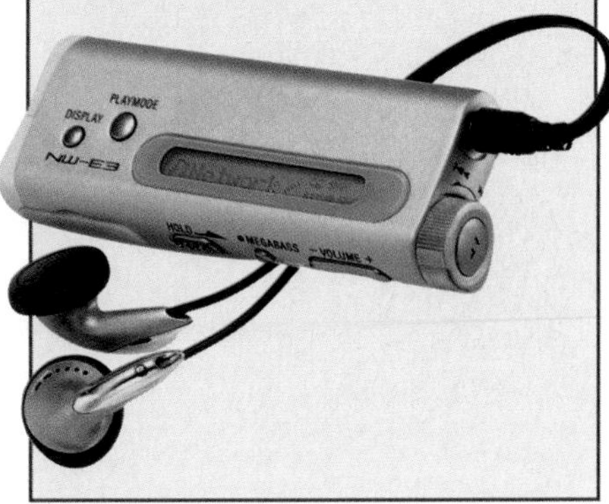

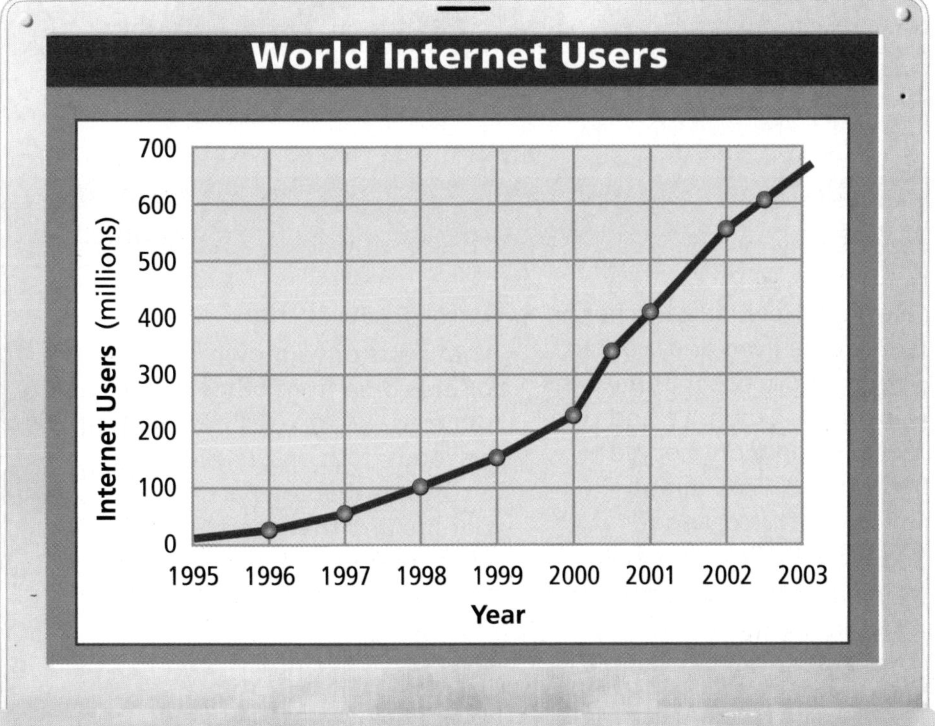

Graph Skills

Internet use grew rapidly after 1995. **Identify** What was the number of Internet users halfway through 2002? **Predict** Based on the trend shown in the graph, how do you think the number of Internet users has changed since 2002?

Defending Their Heritage
In 1988 Aborigines, descendants of Australia's original inhabitants, protested the 200th anniversary of the arrival of Europeans.
Analyze Images *What evidence do you see that the Aborigines' culture has changed over the past 200 years?*

Defending Traditions Change can help, but it can also hurt. If things change too fast, people may feel that their culture is threatened. Valuable traditions can disappear. Once traditional knowledge has been lost, it can never be regained. In many parts of the world, people are working to preserve, or save, their own cultures before it is too late. They do not want to lose what is valuable in their culture. They want to save the artistic traditions, the religious beliefs, and the wisdom that enriched the lives of past generations for the sake of future generations.

✓ Reading Check **How has technology affected the speed of cultural change?**

Section 3 Assessment

Key Terms
Review the key terms at the beginning of this section. Use each term in a sentence that explains its meaning.

Target Reading Skill
Review the second paragraph on page 107. Find the words that signal a sequence of events related to communication technologies.

Comprehension and Critical Thinking
1. (a) Describe What cultural changes in America followed the invention of cars?
(b) Explain How did cars change where people lived and worked?
(c) Predict Suppose that gasoline became more expensive and computers allowed more people to work at home. How might American culture change?
2. (a) List What are two main ways in which ideas travel from one culture to another?
(b) Describe Give an example of an idea that has passed from one culture to another.
(c) Compare and Contrast How has the spread of ideas changed with modern communication technologies?

Writing Activity
What parts of your own culture come from other countries? Make a list detailing the foods, fashions, music, or customs that are part of your life and that come from other countries.

For: An activity on cultural change
Visit: PHSchool.com
Web Code: led-3403

Chapter 4 Review and Assessment

◆ Chapter Summary

Section 1: Understanding Culture

- Culture is an entire way of life that is shaped by people's environment and that also shapes people's environment.
- Culture developed over time from simple technologies and institutions to more advanced technologies and institutions.

Section 2: Culture and Society

- A society is a group of people sharing a culture and held together by a social structure.
- Language expresses the basic concepts of a culture and transmits those concepts to young people.
- Religions help people make sense of the world. They are an important source of values for cultures and teach people to treat one another fairly.

Section 3: Cultural Change

- Changes in the environment or in technology lead to changes in culture.
- Ideas move among cultures through the movement of people, through trade, and through communication technologies.

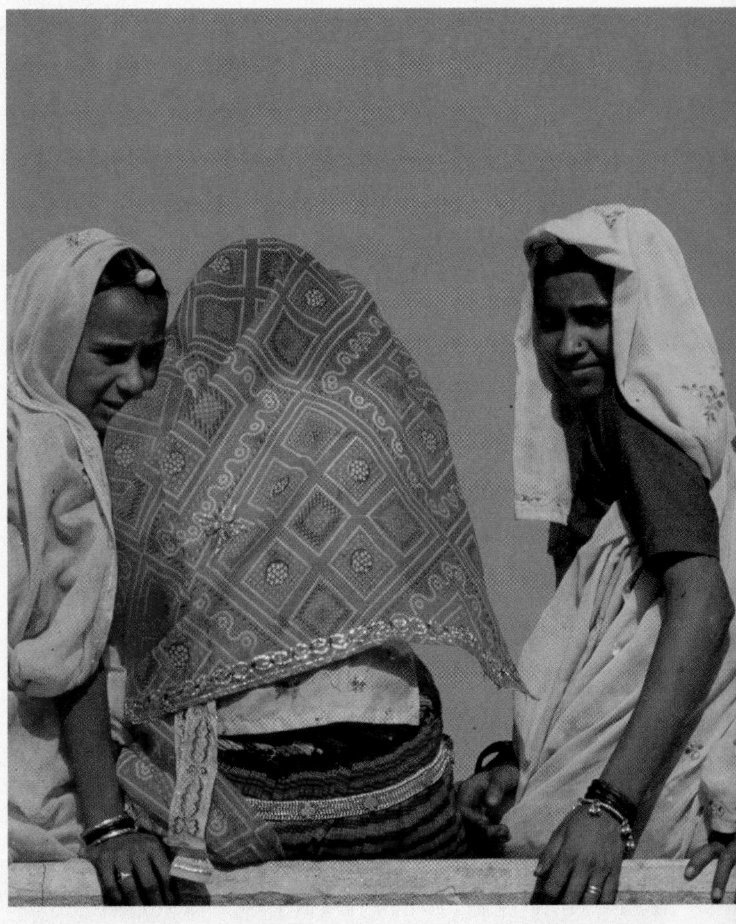

Traditional dress in India

◆ Key Terms

Each of the statements below contains a key term from the chapter. If the statement is true, write *true*. If it is false, rewrite the statement to make it true.

1. The culture of a people is their way of life, including their beliefs and customs.
2. A civilization is an organization with social, educational, or religious purposes.
3. An institution is an advanced culture with cities and the use of writing.
4. A society is a group of people sharing a culture.
5. A pattern of organized relationships among groups of people is a social structure.
6. An extended family consists of two parents and their children.
7. A nuclear family includes two grandparents, their children, and their grandchildren.
8. Cultural diffusion is the movement of customs or ideas from one culture to another.
9. Acculturation is an accumulation of several cultures in a single place.

Chapter 4 Review and Assessment (continued)

◆ Comprehension and Critical Thinking

10. (a) Describe What elements make up a culture?
(b) Apply Information Which of these elements might influence a people's environment, and how?

11. (a) Describe What was the Agricultural Revolution?
(b) Explain How did it affect population?
(c) Draw Conclusions How did it allow the growth of cities?

12. (a) Describe How does social class affect a person's status in society?
(b) Link Past and Present How has people's ability to improve their status changed?

13. (a) Recall Which major religions started in Asia?
(b) Infer What might explain their spread?

14. (a) Describe How did the development of industry and factories change culture?
(b) Compare and Contrast How do those changes compare with the ways technology has changed culture in your lifetime?

15. (a) List What technologies contribute to cultural change today?
(b) Draw Conclusions How have new technologies affected the rate of cultural change?

◆ Skills Practice

Making Valid Generalizations In the Skills for Life activity in this chapter, you learned to make generalizations. You also learned how to make sure that generalizations are valid, or justified, based on facts. You learned not to overgeneralize, or make claims that go beyond the facts.

Review the steps that you followed to learn this skill. Then reread the paragraphs on pages 94 and 95 under the heading Development of Culture. List several facts about the changes described there. Finally, use these facts to make a valid generalization about those changes.

◆ Writing Activity: Math

Look at the graph titled World Internet Users on page 107. Find the number of Internet users at the end of 1995 and the number of Internet users almost seven years later in mid-2002. How many more users were there in mid-2002 than in 1995? Based on this information, predict how many Internet users there will be in 2009, seven years after the latest date shown on this graph. Write a short paragraph describing your results and your prediction.

MAP MASTER™ Skills Activity

Place Location For each religion listed below, write the letter that marks its location on the map.

1. Buddhism
2. Eastern Christianity
3. Hinduism
4. Islam
5. Protestant Christianity
6. Roman Catholic Christianity
7. Traditional religions

Go Online PHSchool.com Use Web Code **lep-3414** for an **interactive map.**

World Religions

Arctic Circle
Tropic of Cancer
Equator
Tropic of Capricorn
Antarctic Circle
A B C D E F G
N S E W

Standardized Test Prep

Test-Taking Tips

Some questions on standardized tests ask you to supply information using prior knowledge. Analyze the web diagram below. Then follow the tips to answer the sample question.

TIP The title in the center circle describes all of the languages. Think about the word *Indo-European* and how it describes languages.

Pick the letter that best answers the question.

Another language that belongs on this web is

A ~~Mandarin Chinese.~~

B Swahili.

C ~~Japanese.~~

D Greek.

TIP Use your prior knowledge—what you know about history, geography, or government—to help you rule out choices.

Think It Through The word *Indo-European* describes languages of India and Europe. Therefore, you can rule out answers A and C because these languages do not come from India or Europe. That leaves Swahili and Greek. You may not be sure about where Swahili is spoken, but you probably know from prior reading that Greece (where people speak Greek) is in Europe. The correct answer is D.

Practice Questions

Use the tips above and other tips in this book to help you answer the following questions:

1. The Agricultural Revolution led
   A to a rebellion by farmers against taxes.
   B to widespread hunger.
   C to an increase in population.
   D people to begin using tools.

2. How does family structure change when countries become more developed?
   A People lose interest in their families.
   B Nuclear families become more common.
   C People move in with their grandparents, aunts, and uncles.
   D Extended families become more common.

3. Which of the following does NOT contribute to cultural change?
   A technological change
   B migration
   C tradition
   D television

Read the following passage, and answer the question that follows.

This country is the birthplace of three major religions. It is located on Earth's largest continent. Its neighbors include Bangladesh and Sri Lanka. The country has more than a billion inhabitants. Its people speak hundreds of different languages. Many people from this country have migrated overseas.

4. What country does the passage describe?
   A Israel
   B Mexico
   C India
   D China

Use Web Code **lea-3401** for a **Chapter 4 self-test.**

Chapter 5

Interacting With Our Environment

Chapter Preview

This chapter will introduce you to the ways in which people interact with their natural surroundings.

Section 1
Natural Resources

Section 2
Land Use

Section 3
People's Effect on the Environment

Target Reading Skill

Main Idea In this chapter you will construct meaning by identifying the main idea in a paragraph and the details that support it. Identifying a paragraph's main idea can help you remember what you have read.

▶ **Windmills capturing the wind's energy in Tehachapi Pass, California**

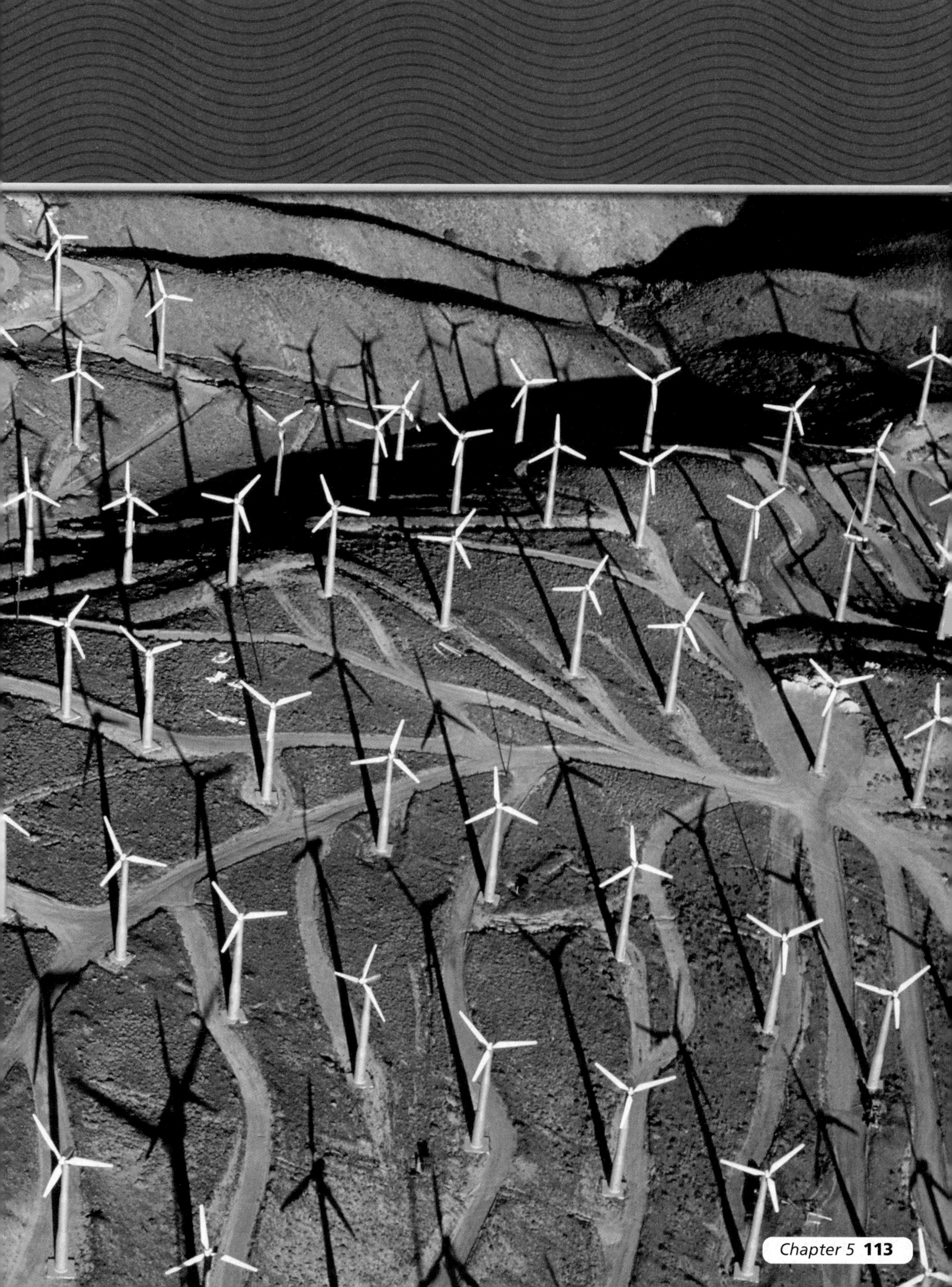

Section 1

Natural Resources

Prepare to Read

Objectives

In this section you will

1. Learn about natural resources.
2. Investigate energy.

Taking Notes

Copy the outline below. Add letters, numbers, and headings as needed. As you read this section, fill in the outline with information about natural resources and energy.

I. Natural resources
  A. Renewable resources
  B.
    1.
    2.
II. Energy
  A.

Target Reading Skill

Identify Main Ideas
Good readers identify the main idea in every written paragraph. The main idea is the most important point—the one that includes all of the other points. Sometimes this idea is stated directly. For example, in the first paragraph below, the first sentence states the paragraph's main idea. As you read, note the main idea of each paragraph.

Key Terms

- **natural resources** (NACH ur ul REE sawr siz) *n.* useful materials found in the environment
- **raw materials** (raw muh TIHR ee ulz) *n.* natural resources that must be worked to be useful
- **renewable resources** (rih NOO uh bul REE sawr siz) *n.* natural resources that can be replaced
- **nonrenewable resources** (nahn rih NOO uh bul REE sawr siz) *n.* natural resources that cannot be replaced

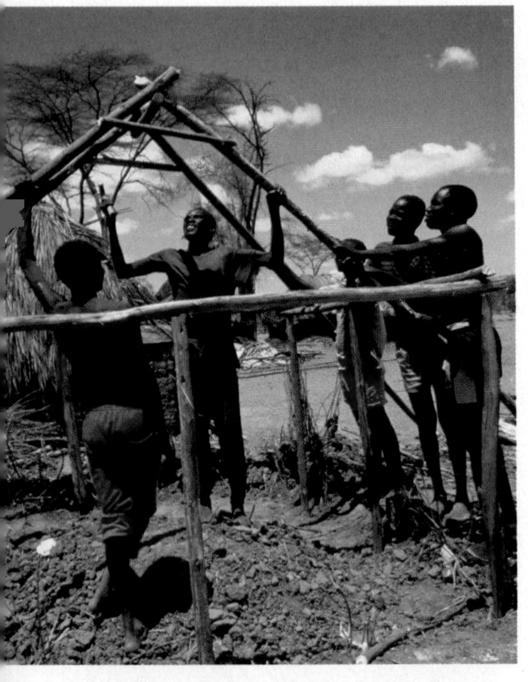

Men constructing a wooden hut in Kenya

What Are Natural Resources?

Everything that people use or consume is made with **natural resources,** or useful materials found in the environment. When people talk about natural resources, they usually mean such things as water, minerals, and vegetation.

All people need water, food, clothing, and shelter to survive. People drink water. People eat food that the soil produces. So do the animals that provide eggs, cheese, meat, and wool. Homes are made from wood, clay, and steel.

People can use some resources just as they are found in nature. Fresh water is one of these. But most resources must be changed before people can use them. Natural resources that must be worked to be useful are called **raw materials.** For example, people cannot just go out and cut down a tree if they want paper. Trees are the raw materials for paper and wood. To make paper, the wood must be soaked and broken up to create pulp. (Pulp is a kind of soup of wood fibers.) Machines collect the wet fibers on screens to form sheets of paper.

Renewable Resources The environment is filled with natural resources, but not all resources are alike. Geographers divide them into two main groups.

The first group is **renewable resources,** or resources that can be replaced. Some resources are replaced naturally because of the way Earth works. In the water cycle, water evaporates into the air and falls as rain, snow, hail, or sleet. This happens over and over again. Therefore, Earth has an unchanging amount of water. Other materials that go through natural cycles include nitrogen and carbon.

Some types of energy are also renewable resources. Using wind to make electricity will not use the wind up. Wind results from differences in the way the sun heats Earth. As long as the sun shines, there will always be more wind. Solar energy, or energy from the sun, is a renewable resource. No matter how much people use, there will always be more. Geothermal energy uses differences in heat between Earth's surface and its interior. This heat difference will not disappear in the foreseeable future.

Target Skill **Identify Main Ideas** Which sentence states the main idea of the paragraph at the left?

MAP MASTER™ Skills Activity

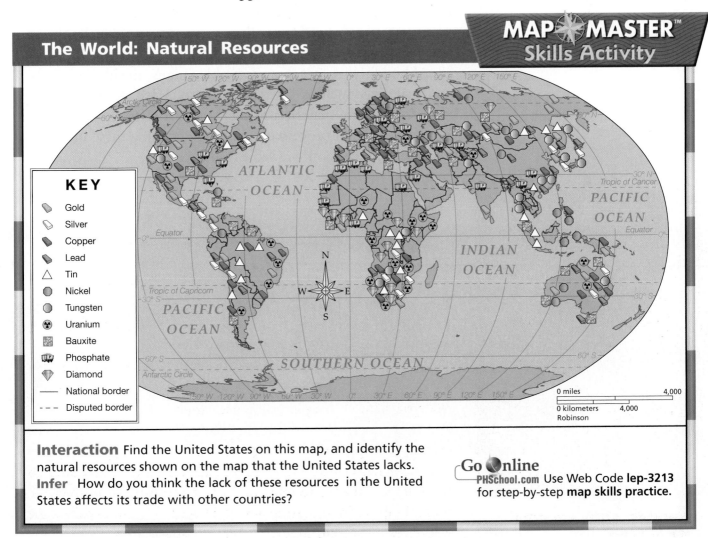

The World: Natural Resources

ATLANTIC OCEAN
PACIFIC OCEAN
INDIAN OCEAN
SOUTHERN OCEAN
Arctic Circle
Tropic of Cancer
Equator
Tropic of Capricorn
Antarctic Circle

KEY

- Gold
- Silver
- Copper
- Lead
- Tin
- Nickel
- Tungsten
- Uranium
- Bauxite
- Phosphate
- Diamond
- National border
- Disputed border

0 miles 4,000
0 kilometers 4,000
Robinson

Interaction Find the United States on this map, and identify the natural resources shown on the map that the United States lacks.
Infer How do you think the lack of these resources in the United States affects its trade with other countries?

Go Online
PHSchool.com Use Web Code **lep-3213** for step-by-step **map skills practice.**

Solar cells on the roof of a house in Felsberg, Germany

Living Resources Living things that provide natural resources, such as plants and animals, are also renewable resources. Like other resources, they must be properly managed so that people do not overuse them.

For example, a timber company may cut down all the trees in an area for use as wood. But the company may then plant new trees to replace the ones they cut. Even if they do not, seeds left in the ground will probably produce new trees. Every day, the people of the world eat many chickens and ears of corn. But farmers always make sure to grow more corn and chickens to replace what people eat. If people are careful, they can have a steady supply of these renewable living resources.

Nonrenewable Resources The second major group of resources is called **nonrenewable resources**, or resources that cannot be replaced. Most nonliving things, such as metal ores, most minerals, natural gas, and petroleum—or crude oil—are nonrenewable resources. If people keep mining minerals and burning fuels such as coal and oil, they will eventually run out. Therefore, people need to use these resources carefully. If they do run out, people will need to find substitutes for them.

Although they are nonrenewable, many metals, minerals, and materials such as plastics can be recycled. Recycling does not return these materials to their natural state. Still, they can be recovered and processed for reuse. Recycling these materials helps to conserve nonrenewable resources.

Fossil Fuels Most scientists think that coal, natural gas, and petroleum are fossil fuels, or fuels created over millions of years from the remains of prehistoric living things. If people continue using coal at today's rate, known supplies may run out in several hundred years. At current rates of use, known supplies of oil and natural gas may run out in less than 100 years.

If oil and natural gas are fossil fuels, they are renewable, since living things today will become fossil fuels in millions of years. But if these fuels take so long to develop, they are nonrenewable for our purposes.

✓ Reading Check **What is the difference between renewable and nonrenewable resources?**

Located on the border between Oregon and Washington, the Bonneville Dam produces hydroelectric power.

A Special Resource: Energy

Many natural resources are sources of energy. People use energy not only from fossil fuels, but also from the wind and the sun. Dams produce hydroelectric power by harnessing the power of falling water.

Energy is itself a resource that is needed to make use of other natural resources. Consider cotton. It takes energy to harvest cotton from a field, to spin the cotton into thread, and to weave it into fabric. Workers use energy to travel to a garment factory. It takes energy to sew a shirt with a sewing machine. It also takes energy to transport the shirt by ship and truck to a retail store. Finally, the consumer uses energy to bring the shirt home.

Strip Mining Coal
The machine below extracts coal from this exposed deposit in Banwen Pyrddin, Wales, United Kingdom. **Apply Information** *Do you think that coal is a recyclable, renewable, or nonrenewable resource?*

Pipes running across an oil field in Meyal, Pakistan

Energy "Have's" and "Have Not's" People in every country need energy. But energy resources are not evenly spread around the world. Certain areas are rich in energy resources. Others have very few.

Countries with many rivers, such as Canada and Norway, can use water energy to create electricity. Countries like Saudi Arabia and Mexico have huge amounts of oil that they sell to other countries. Countries like Japan and the United States do not produce as much energy as they use. These countries have to buy energy from other countries.

Meeting Energy Needs in the Future Over time, energy use worldwide has grown rapidly. Yet our supplies of fossil fuels may be limited. It seems likely that the world's people will need to find other sources of energy. Many possibilities exist.

Already, some countries, such as Denmark and Germany, are developing renewable energy sources such as wind and solar energy. Other sources of energy that will not run out are tidal energy, from the rise and fall of Earth's oceans, and geothermal energy, or energy from the heat of Earth's interior. Biomass, or plant material, is a renewable source of energy. These energy sources can reduce a country's need for imported oil.

Atomic energy uses radioactive materials, which are non-renewable but plentiful. Some people oppose atomic energy because radioactive materials can be dangerous. Others support it as a plentiful energy source that does not pollute the air.

Graph Skills

Some countries produce more oil than they use. These countries can sell their extra oil to other countries. Others consume more oil than they produce and have to buy it from other countries. **Identify** Which of the countries on this graph have to buy almost all of their oil? **Compare and Contrast** Which country buys the most oil?

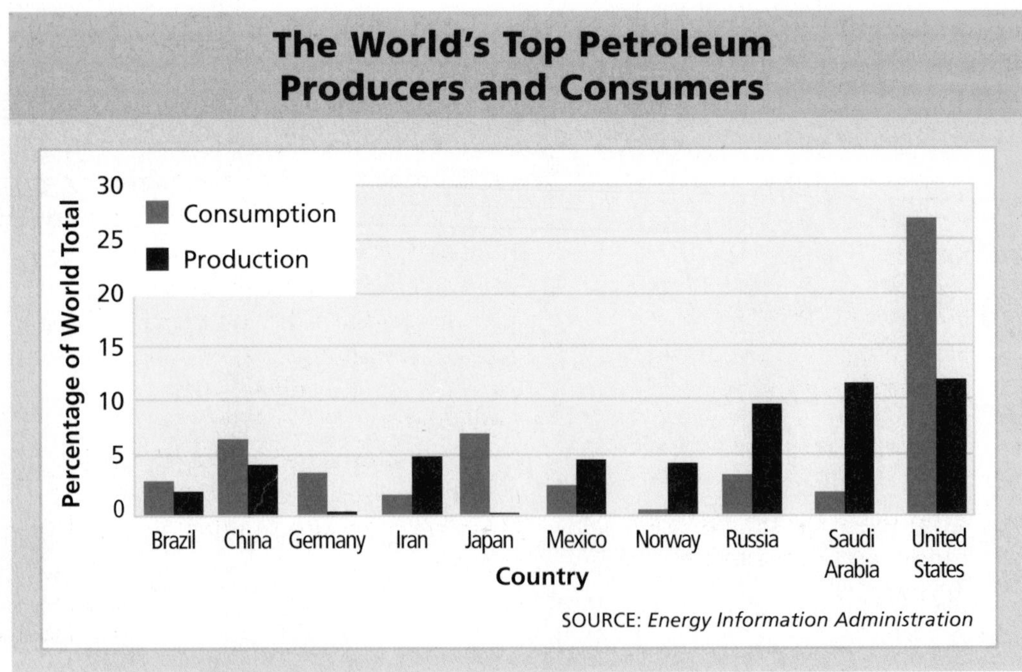

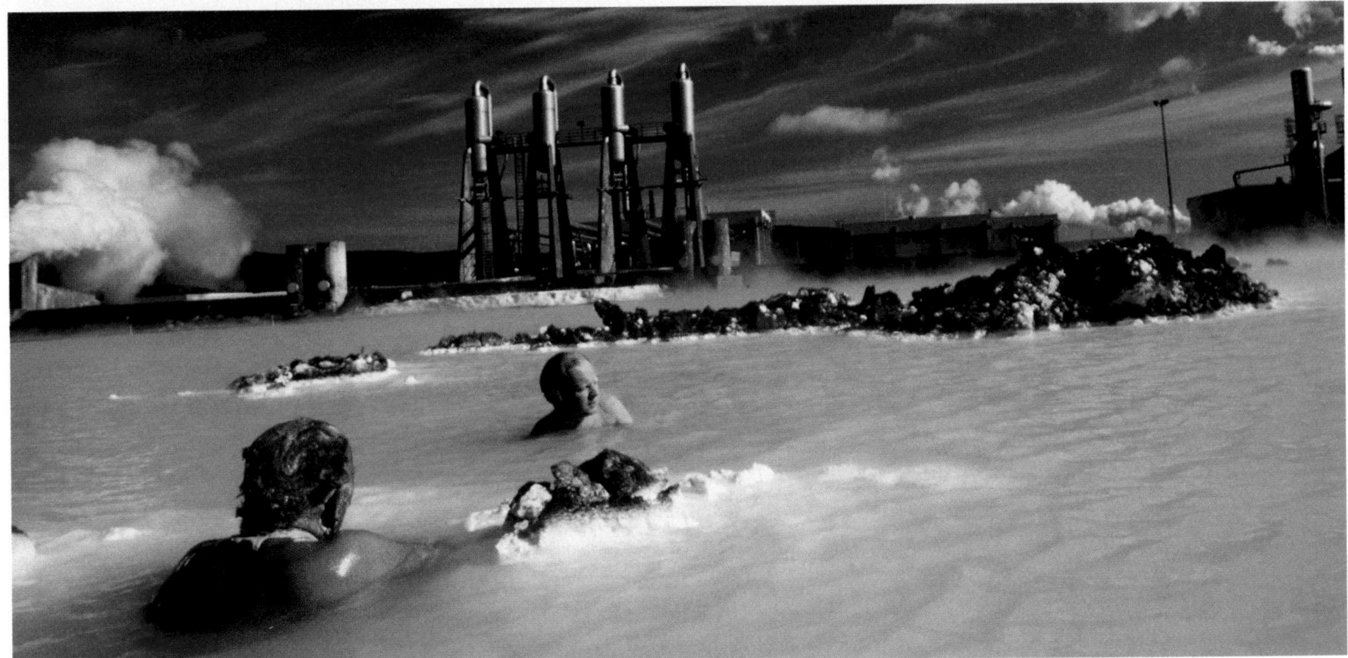

Geothermal power
In addition to producing energy, the geothermal power plant at Svartsengi, Iceland, heats the mineral-rich water of the Blue Lagoon. **Infer** *Are fossil fuels used to heat this pool?*

Fossil fuels will last longer if people use less energy. New technologies, such as hybrid cars, can reduce a country's need for imported oil by burning less gas per mile. Other technologies offer energy savings in heating and lighting buildings and in making new products. If people manage to use less energy, they will not need to buy as much from foreign countries. They will also have an easier time meeting their energy needs in the future.

✓ Reading Check **Why do some countries have to import energy?**

Section 1 Assessment

Key Terms
Review the key terms at the beginning of this section. Use each term in a sentence that explains its meaning.

Target Reading Skill
State the main idea of the paragraph on this page.

Comprehension and Critical Thinking
1. (a) Identify Why is wood considered a renewable resource?
(b) Apply Information What needs to happen after trees are cut in order for wood to remain a renewable resource?
2. (a) List Name some sources of energy other than fossil fuels.
(b) Categorize What do these energy sources have in common, and how do they differ from fossil fuels?
(c) Draw Conclusions Why might we need to use more of these energy sources in the future?

Writing Activity
Think about what you did this morning before you came to school. Write a journal entry describing the natural resources that you used and all of the ways that you used energy at home and on your way to school.

For: An activity on natural resources
Visit: PHSchool.com
Web Code: led-3501

Section 2
Land Use

Prepare to Read

Objectives

In this section you will

1. Study the relation between land use and culture.
2. Investigate the relation between land use and economic activity.
3. Explore changes in land use.

Taking Notes

Copy the concept web below. As you read the section, fill in the ovals with information about land use. Add ovals as needed.

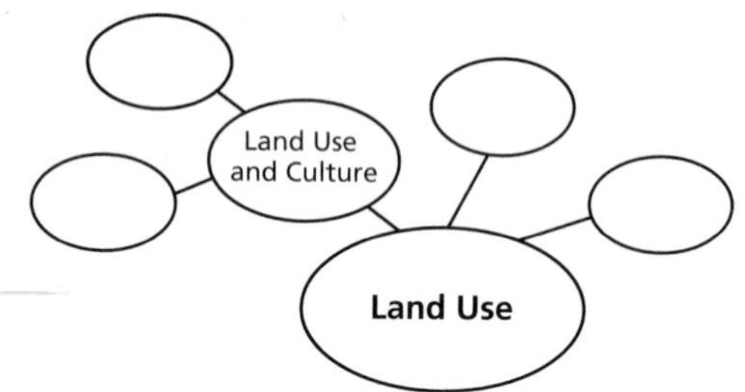

Target Reading Skill

Identify Supporting Details Sentences in a paragraph may provide details that support the main idea. These details may give examples or explanations. In the second paragraph on this page, this sentence states the main idea: "Even in similar environments, people may use land differently because they have different cultural traits." Note three details in the paragraph that explain this main idea.

Key Terms

- **environment** (en VY run munt) *n.* natural surroundings
- **manufacturing** (man yoo FAK chur ing) *n.* the large-scale production of goods by hand or by machine
- **colonization** (kayl uh nih ZAY shun) *n.* the movement of settlers and their culture to a new country
- **industrialization** (in dus tree ul ih ZAY shun) *n.* the growth of machine-powered production in an economy

A peanut farmer in Georgia inspecting his crop

Land Use and Culture

How people use the land depends on their culture. People may use their land differently because their cultures have developed in different **environments**, or natural surroundings. For example, the Inuit live in a cold, arctic climate. It is too cold to grow crops, so the Inuit use their land mainly for hunting wild animals, and they rely heavily on fishing. The Japanese live in a warmer, moister climate. Although much of Japan is too steep to farm, the Japanese use much of the remaining land for crops. Their main crop is rice, which grows well in the warm, moist climate of Japan.

Even in similar environments, however, people may use land differently because they have different cultural traits. For example, Georgia has a warm, moist climate like that of southern Japan. But Georgia does not produce much rice. Instead, Georgians raise chickens and grow crops such as peanuts. While the Japanese eat rice at nearly every meal, Americans eat more meat and peanut butter.

Cultures and Landscapes The examples of the Inuit and the Japanese show how people's environments help to shape their cultures. People's cultures, in turn, help shape the landscapes where they live. For example, in some parts of the Philippines, a culture of rice farming and a shortage of level land has led people to carve terraces into hillsides. Thousands of years ago, Western Europe was covered with forests. As farming cultures spread across that region, people cleared forests to use the land for farming. Today, most of Western Europe is open fields and pastures. Few forests remain.

Drip irrigation of grape vines in eastern Washington State

Land Use and Cultural Differences As the examples of Japan and Georgia show, however, similar environments do not necessarily produce similar cultures. People may respond differently to those environments, depending on their culture. For example, much of the western United States has a dry climate. Many crops need irrigation, or an artificial water supply. The Middle East also has climates too dry for most crops to grow without irrigation. However, the two regions have different cultures and different responses to this challenge. In the western United States, farmers use modern irrigation systems. For example, drip irrigation provides water to each plant through little pipes or tubes. Some Middle Eastern farmers use qanats, or brick irrrigation channels, to bring water to their crops. Both cultures face similar environments, but they interact with those environments differently.

✓ Reading Check **How is land use related to culture?**

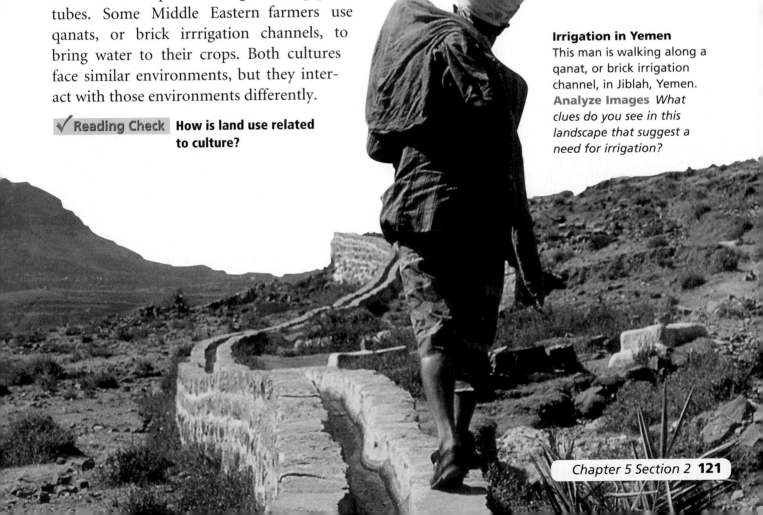

Irrigation in Yemen
This man is walking along a qanat, or brick irrigation channel, in Jiblah, Yemen. **Analyze Images** *What clues do you see in this landscape that suggest a need for irrigation?*

Land Use and Economic Activity

In some places, people use the land and its resources to make a living by farming, fishing, or mining. In other places, people work in factories, where they turn natural resources into finished products. In still other places, people sell or distribute products and make a living by providing services. These three ways of making a living correspond to three stages of economic activity. Geographers use stages of economic activity as a way to understand land use.

Target Skill **Identify Supporting Details**
Which details in the paragraph at the right give examples of first-level activities?

First-Level Activities In the first stage, people use land and resources directly to make products. They may hunt, cut wood, mine, or fish. They also may herd animals or raise crops. This is the first stage of activities. At this stage, people interact directly with the land or the sea. Most of the world's land is used for first-level activities. However, in developed countries such as the United States, only a small percentage of the people make a living at first-level activities.

Stages of Economic Activity

A series of economic activities connect a flock of sheep in a pasture to a wool sweater in a store. Sheep-raising, a first-level activity, makes it possible to manufacture woolen goods such as sweaters, a second-level activity. Manufacturing makes it possible to deliver sweaters to stores. Stores can then sell the sweaters. Delivery and sales are both third-level activities.

A flock of sheep being driven to a pasture in New Zealand

▲ **Farming, a first-level activity**
This farmer is shearing a sheep, or trimming away its wool. Raising and shearing sheep are first-level activities, or direct uses of natural resources.

Second-Level Activities At the second stage, people process the products of first-level activities. Most second-level activity is **manufacturing**, or the large-scale production of goods by hand or by machine. Manufacturing may turn a farmer's corn crop into cornflakes for your breakfast. Manufacturing, especially in urban areas, is an important land use in developed countries.

Third-Level Activities At the third stage, a person delivers boxes of cornflakes to your local grocery store. Third-level activities are also known as services. These activities do not produce goods. They may help sell goods. They often involve working directly for customers or for businesses. Many businesses offering services—doctors' offices, banks, automobile repair shops, shopping malls, and fast-food restaurants—are part of everyday living. Services are also clustered in urban areas, especially in developed countries.

✓ Reading Check **How is most of the world's land used?**

▲ **Manufacturing, a second-level activity**
Second-level activities process natural resources to make goods, such as the wool this worker is processing at a New Zealand mill.

GEOGRAPHY SKILLS PRACTICE

Human-Environment Interaction Each activity shown here occurs in a different part of New Zealand.
Apply Information Which activities occur in rural areas, and which activities are likely to occur in urban areas?

Retail sales, a third-level activity ▶
Selling manufactured goods, such as this sweater, in a store is a third-level activity. This woolen-goods store is in New Zealand.

Boston: A Changing Landscape

English colonists founded Boston, Massachusetts, on a narrow peninsula surrounded by water, marshes, and forest. The colonists cleared most of the forest for farmland. The colonists also built dams, piers, and retaining walls along the waterfront. By the 1800s, Boston's growing industries and growing population of workers faced a land shortage. Boston's solution was to drain marshes and to create new land by filling in areas of water. At first, Boston's people filled in around existing piers. Then, they filled in tidal ponds behind dams. Finally, they filled in whole bodies of open water.

MAP MASTER™ Skills Activity

Human-Environment Interaction Colonization and industrialization transformed Boston's landscape. **Identify** How much of the forest around Boston remained after colonization? **Compare and Contrast** How did Boston's land area change between colonial times and today?

Go Online PHSchool.com Use Web Code **lep-3312** for step-by-step **map skills practice.**

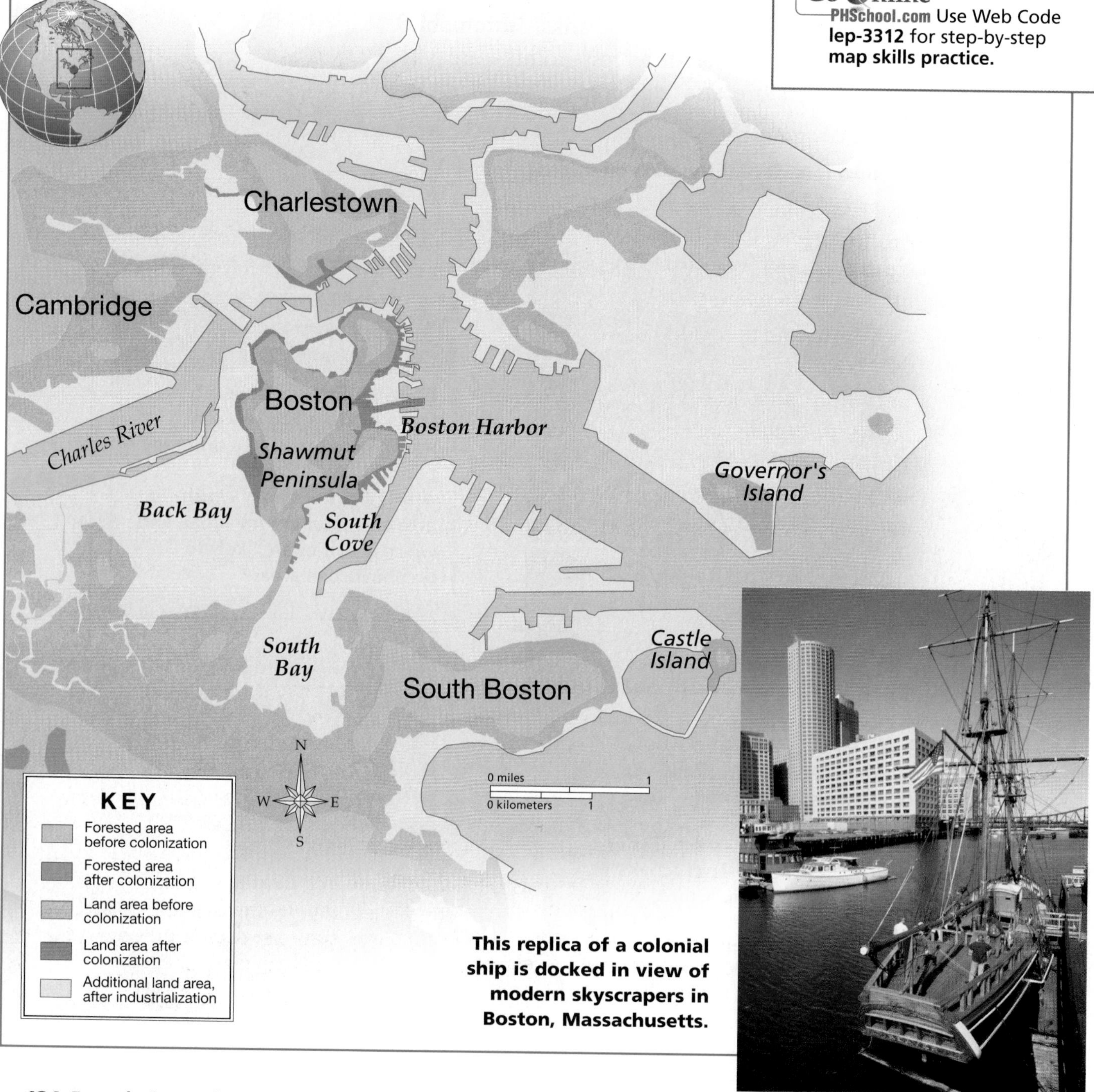

This replica of a colonial ship is docked in view of modern skyscrapers in Boston, Massachusetts.

Changes in Land Use

When a region undergoes **colonization,** or a movement of new settlers and their culture to a country, the newcomers may change that region's landscape to fit their cultural practices. For example, if farmers move to a region without farms, they will create farms. Similarly, as people find new ways of making a living, they start using the land in new ways, too.

Colonization Before European colonists came to Australia, there was no farming and no livestock raising. In North and South America before colonization, European crops such as wheat and grapes were unknown. So were livestock such as cows and chickens. When Europeans settled these continents, they cleared large areas for use as farmland and livestock pasture.

Industrialization and Sprawl Since the 1800s, the growth of machine-powered production, or **industrialization,** has changed landscapes in many countries. Cities have grown around industrial facilities worldwide. Since 1900, suburbs have spread out from cities in the United States and other developed countries to cover more and more land. The spread of cities and suburbs is known as sprawl.

✓ Reading Check **How did European colonization change landscapes in North and South America?**

Vineyards in Australia
Grapes did not grow in Australia before European colonists arrived. Now grapes thrive in Australia's Hunter Valley. **Infer** *What would have been different about this landscape before European colonization?*

Section 2 Assessment

Key Terms

Review the key terms at the beginning of this section. Use each term in a sentence that explains its meaning.

Target Reading Skill

State three details that explain the main idea of the second paragraph on page 120.

Comprehension and Critical Thinking

1. (a) Describe How have rice farmers in the Philippines transformed the landscape?
(b) Infer Why is the Philippines' farm landscape different from Western Europe's?

2. (a) Recall What are second-level activities?
(b) Categorize Name some examples of second-level activities.
(c) Compare and Contrast How do second-level activities differ from third-level activities?

3. (a) Recall What is industrialization?
(b) Identify Causes How is industrialization related to sprawl?

Writing Activity

Write a short encyclopedia article on land use around your hometown. Describe how culture has affected land use. Mention the different levels of economic activity around your town. Finally, give an example of a change in land use in or near your hometown.

Writing Tip Encyclopedia articles contain descriptions and statements of facts. Be careful not to express personal thoughts or opinions.

Making Predictions

The Oval Office, where leaders make predictions, is at the center of this photo of the White House.

When you watch an adventure movie, half the fun is in predicting what happens next. Decision makers, such as American presidents, make predictions, too, and their predictions guide their decisions. Good decision makers take actions that they predict will have good results. When you predict, you make an educated guess about the effects of a certain cause. The key word here is *educated.* Without knowledge, you can't predict—you just guess.

Learn the Skill

Follow these steps to make a good prediction.

1. **Identify a situation that has not been resolved.** As you read information, ask yourself questions, such as, "What will happen next? What effects will this situation produce?"
2. **Make a list of probable outcomes, or effects.** If possible, analyze examples of similar causes that have known effects.
3. **Make an educated guess about which outcome is most likely.** In order to make an *educated* guess, use information that you know or that you research.
4. **State your prediction.** In your prediction, explain why you think the cause will produce a particular effect, or outcome.

Practice the Skill

Read the text in the box at the right. Then predict the consequences of global struggles for water.

1. From what you have read about water supplies in Southwest Asia, identify a major issue that has not been resolved. State the problem as a question.

2. This chapter discusses problems in global oil supply. How are oil and water issues similar? What effects have resulted from world oil shortages? Study the graphic organizer below. It shows results that might occur when one country controls other countries' water.

3. Of the possible outcomes in the graphic organizer, which seems the most likely? Make an educated guess, using what you know about the oil issue.

4. Here's how your prediction might begin: "As the world's need for water grows, water-rich countries will probably ____________."

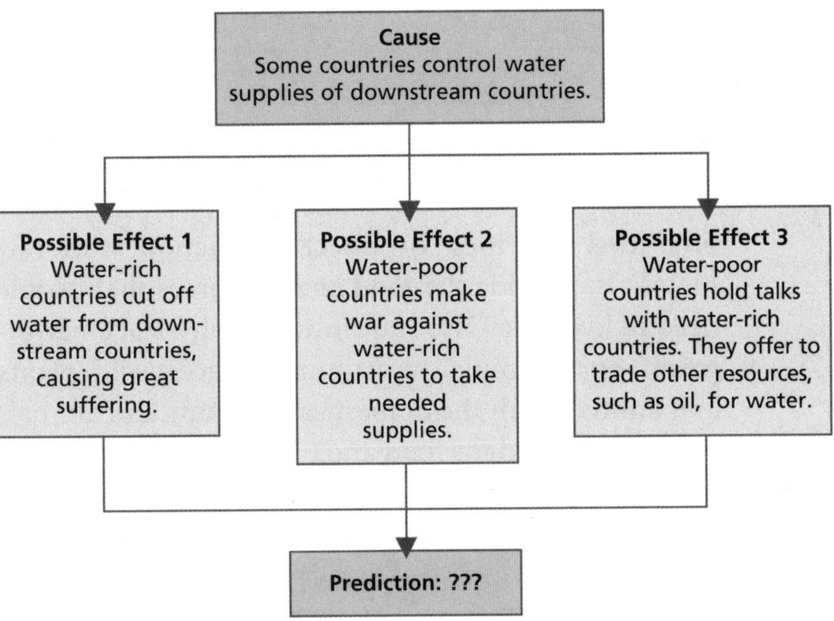

Cause
Some countries control water supplies of downstream countries.
Possible Effect 1
Water-rich countries cut off water from down-stream countries, causing great suffering.
Possible Effect 2
Water-poor countries make war against water-rich countries to take needed supplies.
Possible Effect 3
Water-poor countries hold talks with water-rich countries. They offer to trade other resources, such as oil, for water.
Prediction: ???

Apply the Skill

Study the graph on page 118. Note how much oil the United States consumes and produces. What do you learn from these facts? Make a prediction about what America might do when world oil supplies run low. Create a graphic organizer like the one on this page to help you make a prediction.

During the 1900s, oil-rich nations became wealthy and powerful by controlling world oil supplies. In the present century, water supplies may determine who is rich or poor. Much of the world's usable fresh water comes from rivers that flow through many countries. Nearly half the people in the world live in international river basins. Yet many of the countries that share rivers have no water treaties. Countries along these rivers build dams to store water for themselves. Nations downstream worry that they might run out of water. In Southwest Asia, Turkey controls sources of water flowing south into Syria and Iraq. A proposed system of 22 dams could allow Turkey to withhold water from its neighbors. Syria and Iraq have plentiful oil but not enough water.

Section 3 People's Effect on the Environment

Prepare to Read

Objectives

In this section you will

1. Investigate how first-level activities affect the environment.
2. Explore how second- and third-level activities affect the environment.

Taking Notes

Copy the table below. As you read this section, fill in the table with information about people's effect on the environment. Add rows to the table as needed.

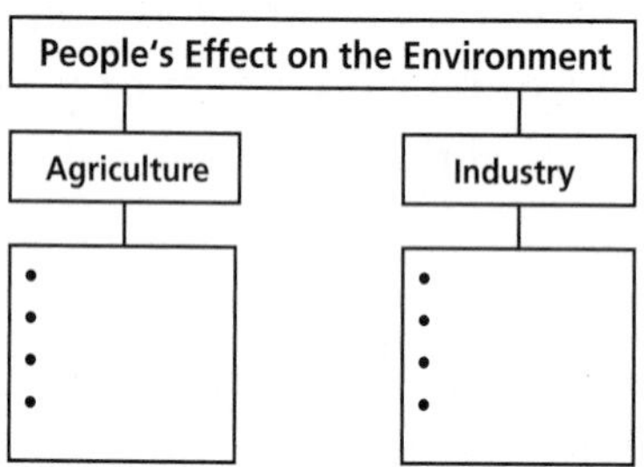

Target Reading Skill

Identify Implied Main Ideas Identifying main ideas can help you remember what you read. The details in a paragraph can add up to the main idea, even if it is not stated directly. For example, the details in the first paragraph below add up to this main idea: "While first-level activities are necessary for human survival, they also reshape the environment."

Key Terms

- **deforestation** (dee fawr uh STAY shun) *n.* a loss of forest cover in a region
- **biodiversity** (by oh duh VUR suh tee) *n.* a richness of different kinds of living things in a region
- **civil engineering** (SIV ul en juh NIHR ing) *n.* technology for building structures that alter the landscape, such as dams, roads, and bridges
- **pollution** (puh LOO shun) *n.* waste, usually man-made, that makes the air, water, or soil less clean

A rancher driving cattle in Manitoba, Canada

First-Level Activities

First-level activities, or direct interaction with raw materials, provide the food and resources that people need to live. They also transform the physical environment. For example, agriculture replaces wild plants and animals with the domesticated plants and animals that people need for food and other products.

Creating Farmland As countries have grown, they have met the challenge of feeding their people in different ways. The Great Plains of North America once supported wild grasses and buffalo. Today, farmers in that region grow corn and wheat and raise cattle. In the Netherlands, the people have drained lakes, bays, and marshes to create dry farmland. While creating new farmland destroyed wild grasslands and wetlands, the new land has fed millions.

Deforestation
Timber companies and farmers have cut down rain forests in Indonesia.
Apply Information *What are some of the advantages and disadvantages of cutting down forests?*

Environmental Challenges Agriculture, forestry, and fishing provide food and resources that people need to live. At the same time, they sometimes have harmful effects on the environment. For example, wood is needed to build houses. But cutting down too many trees can result in **deforestation,** or the loss of forest cover in a region. Cutting forests may result in the loss of more than trees and other plants. Animals that depend on the forest for survival may also suffer. Deforestation can lead to a loss of **biodiversity,** which is a richness of different kinds of living things. So timber companies face the challenge of harvesting needed wood while limiting damage to the environment.

Farmers often use fertilizers and other chemicals to grow more crops. This makes it possible to feed more people. But when rain washes these chemicals into streams, they sometimes harm fish and other water-dwelling creatures. Fish are a tasty and healthy food source. But if fishers catch too many, they may threaten the fishes' survival. Farmers and fishers face the challenge of feeding the world's people without harming important resources.

Finding a Balance The key is to find a balance. Around the world, governments, scientists, and business people are working to find ways of meeting our need for food and resources without harming the environment. One solution is planting tree farms for timber. When the trees are mature, they can be cut and new trees can be replanted without harming ancient forests. Farmers can grow crops using natural methods or use chemicals that will not damage waterways. Fishers can limit their catch of endangered fish and harvest fish that are more plentiful.

✓ Reading Check **How do people benefit when new farmland is created?**

Links to Math

Acres and Timber Yields
Tree farms, like the one below, in Newbury, England, are one way to fight deforestation. If these oak trees grow to yield 80,000 board feet of timber per acre (466 cubic meters per hectare), and the farm covers 300 acres (121 hectares), how much timber will the farm produce?

The Hybrid Car

Cars with gasoline engines are fast and can go long distances, but they pollute. Electric cars don't emit dangerous chemicals, but they can be driven only for a short distance before their batteries need to be recharged. The hybrid car combines the best features of gasoline and electric cars. It is fast and can go long distances, but it uses less gasoline and pollutes less. The hybrid car gets about 46 miles per gallon, while the conventional car of the same size gets about 33.

Traffic Jam
Today, traffic jams are common as drivers commute daily in and out of cities. Waiting in traffic jams wastes a lot of fuel and adds to air pollution.

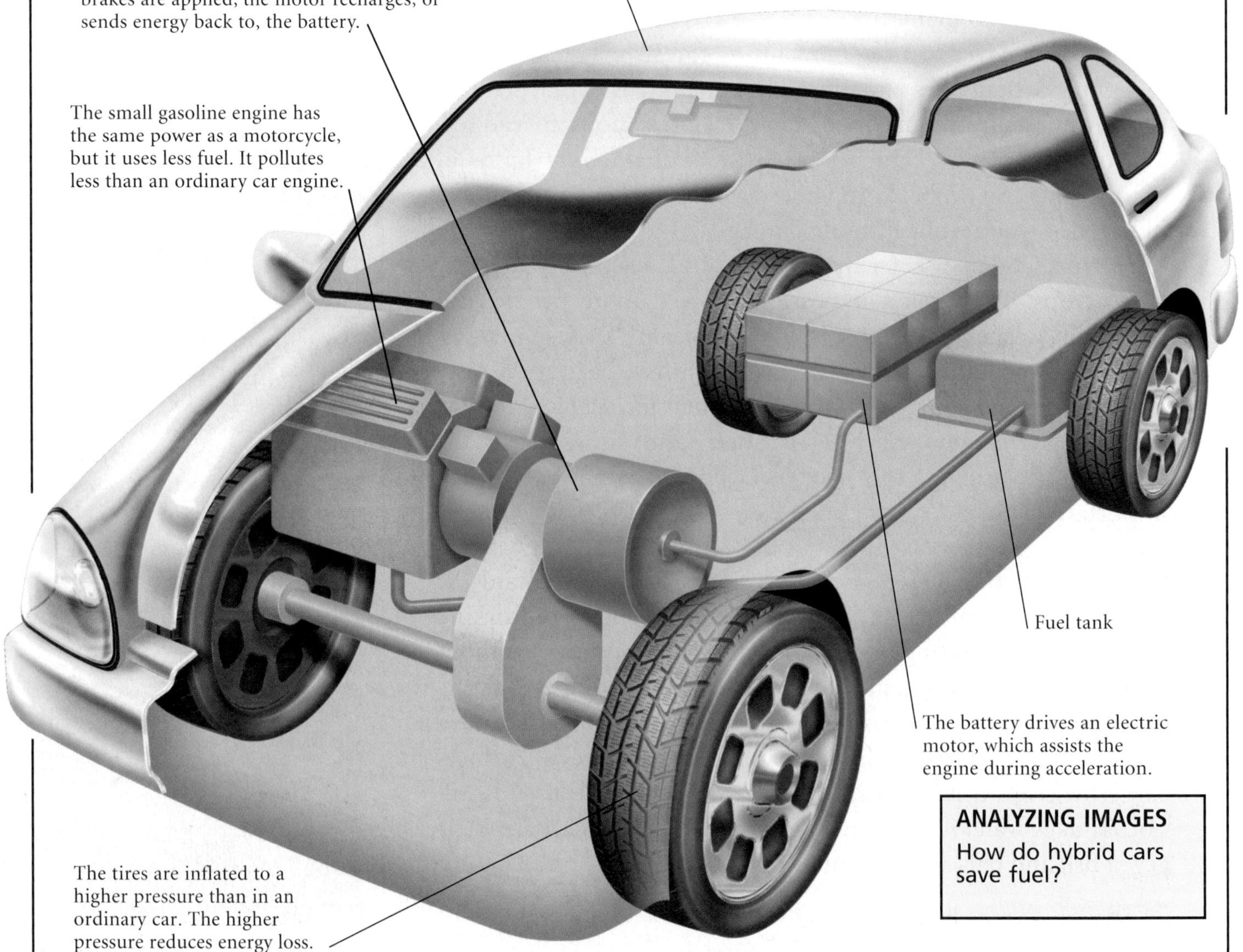

Hybrid cars are made of lightweight materials. It takes less fuel to move a lighter car.

The electric motor draws energy from the battery to accelerate the car. When the car's brakes are applied, the motor recharges, or sends energy back to, the battery.

The small gasoline engine has the same power as a motorcycle, but it uses less fuel. It pollutes less than an ordinary car engine.

Fuel tank

The battery drives an electric motor, which assists the engine during acceleration.

The tires are inflated to a higher pressure than in an ordinary car. The higher pressure reduces energy loss.

ANALYZING IMAGES
How do hybrid cars save fuel?

Second- and Third-Level Activities

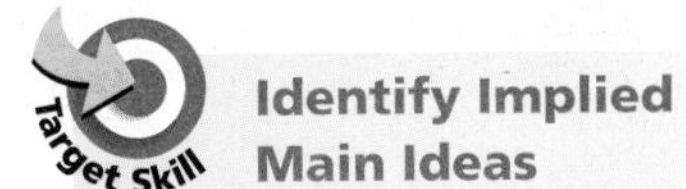

Identify Implied Main Ideas
In one sentence, state what all the details in the paragraph at the left are about.

Over the years, industry, or second-level activities, and services, or third-level activities, have transformed deserts, prairies, woodlands, and marshes. They have created our familiar urban landscapes of housing developments, offices, factories, railroads, and highways.

Providing Jobs, Reshaping the Environment Industrial and service activities provide most of the jobs in developed countries such as the United States. Those activities are the basis for the developed countries' prosperity. They are also the main land use in urban areas.

The main purpose of some of these activities is to change the environment. **Civil engineering** is technology for building structures that alter the landscape, such as dams, canals, roads, and bridges. Dams create reservoirs that cover large areas with water. They also provide water for farms and cities and protect areas downstream from flooding.

Other industrial and service activities have side effects on the environment. For example, shopping malls require large areas to be paved for parking. Industries use large amounts of resources and release industrial wastes into the environment. Service activities require the construction of roads, telephone lines, and power lines.

A Landscape Shaped by Industry The waterfront in Rotterdam, Netherlands, has been shaped to meet the needs of industry. **Analyze Images** *How might this landscape have been different before it was shaped by industry?*

Recycling
These seventh-grade students in Syracuse, New York, are sorting materials for recycling. **Apply Information** *What environmental problems does recycling help to solve?*

Environmental Challenges Industry is not the only source of **pollution,** waste that makes the air, soil, or water less clean. The trash that we throw away may pollute the soil, water, or air. Exhaust from cars and trucks is another source of air pollution. Many scientists believe that air pollution may cause higher temperatures or other changes in our climate.

Finding Solutions Working together, scientists, governments, businesses, and ordinary people can find solutions to these problems. One solution is to use more fuel-efficient vehicles, such as hybrid cars. Vehicles that burn less fuel create less air pollution. Renewable energy sources, such as solar power and wind power, can also reduce the need to burn fuels that pollute the air. In addition, reducing pollution may reduce the risk of harmful climate changes.

Many cities and counties in the United States have introduced waste recycling. Recycling reduces the amount of waste that local governments must burn or dump. It also saves natural resources. For example, when paper is recycled, fewer trees must be cut down to make new paper.

Finding solutions to environmental problems is one of the greatest challenges of our time. If we all work together, we can meet this challenge.

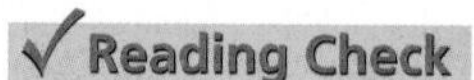
How do industrial activities affect the environment?

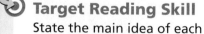

Section 3 Assessment

Key Terms
Review the key terms at the beginning of this section. Use each term in a sentence that explains its meaning.

Target Reading Skill
State the main idea of each paragraph on this page.

Comprehension and Critical Thinking
1. (a) Recall What are the causes of deforestation?
(b) Identify Cause and Effect How does deforestation threaten the environment?
2. (a) List List ways in which industrial and service activities transform landscapes.
(b) Categorize Which of these ways are common to both industrial and service activities?
(c) Analyze How are industrial activities different from service activities in their impact on the environment?

Writing Activity
Write a journal entry in which you discuss how your own activities today may have affected the environment.

For: An activity on the environment
Visit: PHSchool.com
Web Code: led-3503

Chapter 5 Review and Assessment

◆ Chapter Summary

Section 1: Natural Resources

- Almost everything that people use or consume is made with natural resources, which are either renewable or nonrenewable.
- Energy is a special resource needed for most economic activities, but some sources of energy are in limited supply, and some nations need to buy energy resources from others.

Section 2: Land Use

- How people use the land depends on their culture.
- Three levels of economic activity account for most land use.
- Land use changes when newcomers settle a region and as cultures change over time.

Section 3: People's Effect on the Environment

- First-level activities provide needed food and resources, but they reduce the land available for wild plants and animals.
- Second- and third-level activities provide jobs, but they can also pollute the environment.

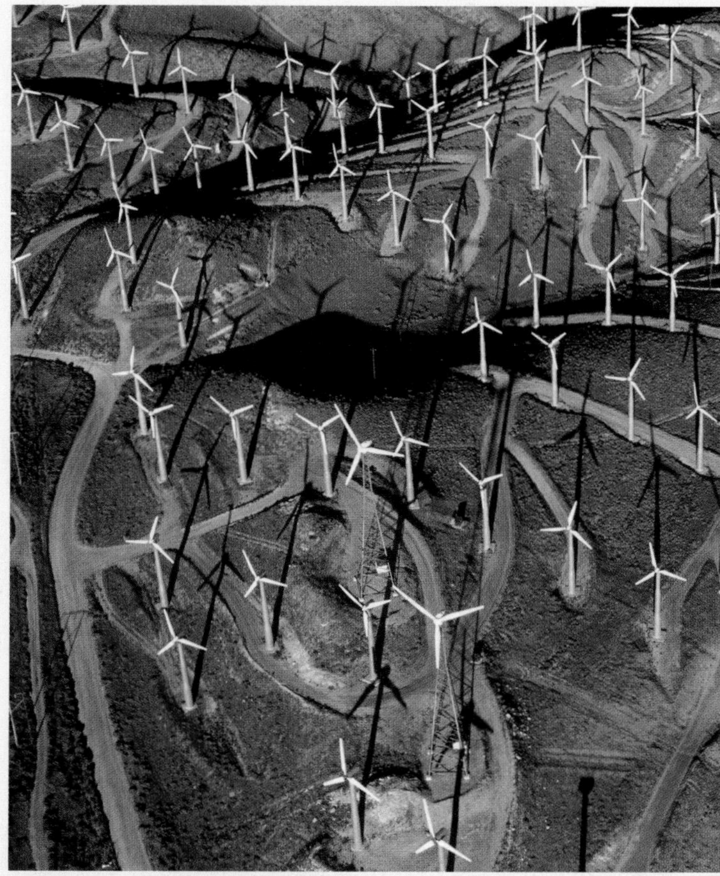

Windmills in California

◆ Key Terms

Each of the statements below contains a key term from the chapter. If the statement is true, write *true*. If it is false, rewrite the statement to make it true.

1. Raw materials are natural resources that can be used without reworking.
2. Renewable resources are natural resources that can be replaced.
3. Natural resources that cannot be replaced are called nonrenewable resources.
4. Our environment is our natural surroundings.
5. Manufacturing does not produce goods but involves working directly for customers.
6. Industrialization is the growth of manufacturing in an economy.
7. Deforestation is the planting of trees to replace forests cut down for timber.
8. Biodiversity is the loss of plant and animal life due to deforestation.
9. Pollution is waste, usually made by people, that makes air, soil, or water less clean.

Review and Assessment (continued)

◆ Comprehension and Critical Thinking

10. **(a) List** List at least three renewable resources.
(b) Explain Why is each of these resources renewable?
(c) Compare and Contrast How do renewable resources differ from nonrenewable resources?

11. **(a) Recall** Do all countries have adequate energy supplies?
(b) Analyze What energy sources are available to all countries?

12. **(a) Recall** Does culture affect land use?
(b) Predict What might happen to land use in a region if people with a different culture colonized it?

13. **(a) List** List three first-level activities.
(b) Compare and Contrast How do those activities differ from second- and third-level activities?

14. **(a) Describe** How can people obtain wood without cutting down wild forests?
(b) Predict How would leaving forests in place affect biodiversity?

15. **(a) Describe** What causes pollution?
(b) Infer How might companies and individuals reduce pollution?

◆ Skills Practice

Making Predictions In the Skills for Life activity on pages 126 and 127, you learned to make predictions. You also learned how to make sure that a prediction is an educated guess. That is, predictions should be based on information about the situation or about similar situations.

Review the steps that you followed to learn this skill. Then reread the paragraphs on pages 118 and 119 under the heading Meeting Energy Needs in the Future. List several facts about the issues described there. Finally, use these facts to make a prediction about how those issues might be resolved in the future.

◆ Writing Activity: Language Arts

Identify an environmental problem that interests you. Write a story about people solving the environmental problem. For your story, create characters with different roles in creating or solving the environmental problem. You should also create a plot for your story that describes how people come up with a solution to the problem and carry out that solution.

MAP MASTER™ Skills Activity

Place Location Refer to the map titled The World: Natural Resources on page 115. For each natural resource listed below, write the letter from the map at the right that shows its location.

1. Bauxite
2. Diamond
3. Nickel
4. Phosphates
5. Tungsten

Go Online PHSchool.com Use Web Code **lep-3514** for an **interactive map.**

Natural Resources

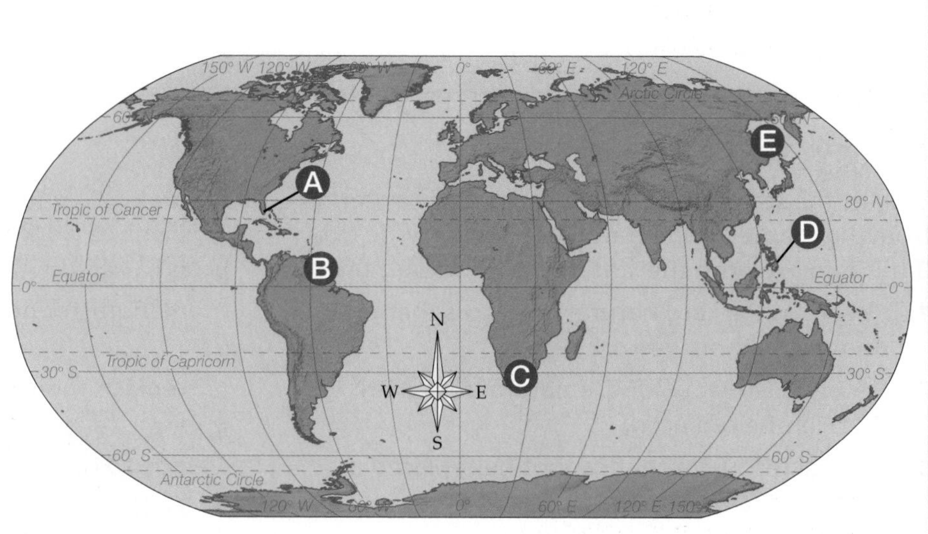

Standardized Test Prep

Test-Taking Tips

Some questions on standardized tests ask you to find a main idea by analyzing a reading selection. Read the passage below. Then follow the tips to answer the sample question.

Saudi Arabia, Mexico, Iraq, Venezuela, and Russia have large oil reserves. The United States and China are rich in coal and natural gas. Many Northern European countries have rivers with water energy to create electricity. By contrast, Japan has few energy sources.

TIP As you read the paragraph, try to identify its main idea, or most important point. Every sentence in a paragraph supports this main idea.

Pick the letter that best answers the question.

This paragraph describes which kind of resources?

A capital resources
B human resources
C natural resources
D entrepreneurial resources

TIP Look for key words in the question and in the answer choices that connect to the paragraph. In this case, the key word is *resources.*

Think It Through Start with the main idea of the paragraph: Different countries have different energy sources. What kind of resources are these energy sources: oil, coal, gas, and water? Energy is not a human resource. You may not know the words *entrepreneurial* or *capital*. But you probably recognize *natural resources* as useful materials found in the environment—such as oil, coal, gas, and water. The correct answer is C.

Practice Questions

Use the tips above and other tips in this book to help you answer the following questions:

1. Wind energy is a
   A fossil fuel.
   B raw material.
   C renewable resource.
   D nonrenewable resource.

2. When colonists settle in a new environment,
   A they will use land just as they did in their old environment.
   B the environment will not change.
   C they will adjust their previous land uses to the new environment.
   D they will give up all familiar land uses.

3. Which of the following environmental problems does paper recycling help solve?
   A deforestation
   B pollution
   C deforestation and pollution
   D neither deforestation nor pollution

Read the following passage and answer the question that follows.

Sierra Leone's economy produces raw materials and cash crops. The country's people mine diamonds, iron ore, and aluminum ore. People on the coast catch fish. Its farmers produce coffee, cocoa, rice, and palm oil. They also raise poultry and other livestock.

4. The passage's main idea refers to which type of activities?
   A first-level activities
   B second-level activities
   C third-level activities
   D financial activities

Use Web Code **lea-3501** for a **Chapter 5 self-test.**

Projects

Create your own projects to learn more about geography. At the beginning of this book, you were introduced to the **Guiding Questions** for studying the chapters and the special features. But you can also find answers to these questions by doing projects on your own or with a group. Use the questions to find topics you want to explore further. Then try the projects described on this page or create your own.

1. **Geography** What are Earth's major physical features?
2. **History** How have people's ways of life changed over time?
3. **Culture** What is a culture?
4. **Government** What types of government exist in the world today?
5. **Economics** How do people use the world's natural resources?

Project
Research a Country's Culture

Desktop Countries

What countries did your ancestors come from? Select one country and do some research on it. Interview someone, perhaps a relative from that country, or read about it. Find a recipe you can prepare to share with the class. Then make a desktop display about the country you have chosen. Write the name of the country on a card and put it on your desk. Add a drawing of the country's flag or map, or display a souvenir. On place cards, write several sentences about each object. Take turns visiting everyone's "desktop countries."

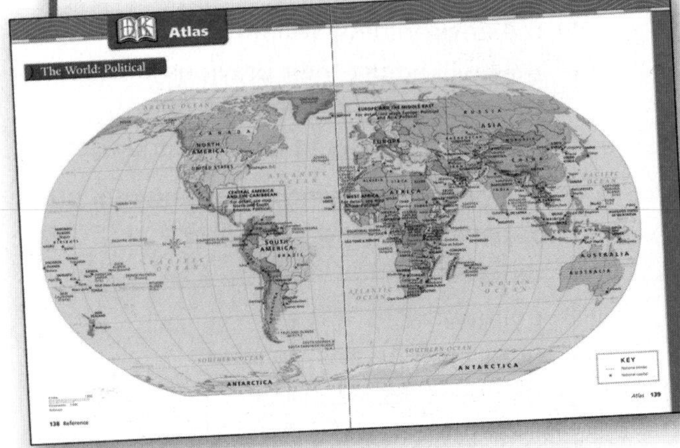

Project
Create a Physical Map

Focus on Part of the Whole

The world and its population are extremely varied. Choose a particular region or country. If you are working with a group, have each person choose a different country on a continent. Learn everything you can about the country's physical geography, the population, and the lifestyles of the people there. Use encyclopedias, almanacs, or other books.

Set up a display based on your research. Prepare a large map that includes important physical features of the land. Add captions that explain how the land's physical geography affects people's lives.

Target Reading Skills

The Target Reading Skills introduced on this page will help you understand the words and ideas in this book and in other social studies reading you do. Each chapter in the Europe and Russia section focuses on one of these reading skills. Good readers develop a bank of reading strategies, or skills. Then they draw on the particular strategies that will help them understand the text they are reading.

Chapter 6 Target Reading Skill

Using the Reading Process Previewing can help you understand and remember what you read. In this chapter you will practice using these previewing skills: setting a purpose for reading, predicting what the text will be about, and asking questions before you read.

Chapter 7 Target Reading Skill

Clarifying Meaning If you do not understand something you are reading right away, you can use several skills to help clarify the meaning of the word or idea. In this chapter you will practice these strategies for clarifying meaning: rereading, reading ahead, and paraphrasing.

Chapter 8 Target Reading Skill

Identifying the Main Idea Since you cannot remember every detail of what you read, it is important that you identify the main ideas. The main idea of a section or paragraph is the most important point and the one you want to remember. In this chapter you will practice these skills: identifying stated and implied main ideas and identifying supporting details.

Chapter 9 Target Reading Skill

Using Context Using the context of an unfamiliar word can help you understand its meaning. Context includes the words, phrases, and sentences surrounding a word. In this chapter you will practice using these context clues: descriptions, definitions, comparisons, and examples.

Chapter 10 Target Reading Skill

Comparing and Contrasting You can use comparison and contrast to sort out and analyze information you are reading. Comparing means examining the similarities between things. Contrasting is looking at differences. In this chapter you will practice these skills: comparing and contrasting, identifying contrasts, making comparisons, and recognizing contrast signal words.

EUROPE and RUSSIA

Europe and Russia lie on a gigantic landmass that stretches from the Atlantic Ocean to the Pacific. The countries of this region are as diverse as their geography, with distinctive cultures and societies. Ancient civilizations that developed in Europe still influence people around the world. Today, the region contains countries with histories that stretch back hundreds of years as well as countries that were formed just a decade or two ago.

Guiding Questions

The text, photographs, maps, and charts in this book will help you discover answers to these Guiding Questions.

1. **Geography** What are the main physical features of Europe and Russia?
2. **History** How have Europe and Russia been affected by their history?
3. **Culture** How have the people of Europe and Russia been shaped by their cultures?
4. **Government** What types of government have existed in Europe and Russia?
5. **Economics** How have Russian and European economies developed into what they are today?

Project Preview

You can also discover answers to the Guiding Questions by working on projects. Several project possibilities are listed on page 346 of this book.

Investigate Europe and Russia

Europe and Russia extend across more than half the world's longitudes, from Iceland in the west at about 25° W to easternmost Siberia at 175° E. Europe is a continent made up of many countries, while Russia is one country that actually lies on two continents—Europe and Asia. Together, Europe and Russia form a rich pattern of different cultures, histories, and languages.

▲ **Amsterdam, Netherlands**
Skating on one of the city's many frozen canals

LOCATION

1 Investigate Europe and Russia's Location

The location of an unfamiliar place can be described in relation to a familiar place. Use the map above to describe the location of Europe and Russia in relation to the United States. What ocean lies between Europe and the United States? If you were on the west coast of the United States, in what direction would you travel to get to the east coast of Russia? How close to the Equator are the two regions—Europe and Russia and the United States? How close are they to the Arctic Circle? Many people think the climates of Europe and the United States are similar. Look at the map, and explain why this might be so.

REGIONS

2 Estimate the Size of Europe and Russia

How big are Europe and Russia? To find out, compare the size of Europe and Russia together to that of the 48 states of the United States mainland. Now compare Europe alone to those states. Notice that Russia lies in two continents, Asia and Europe. The striped area shows the European part of Russia. The solid green area shows the Asian part of Russia.

Political Europe and Russia

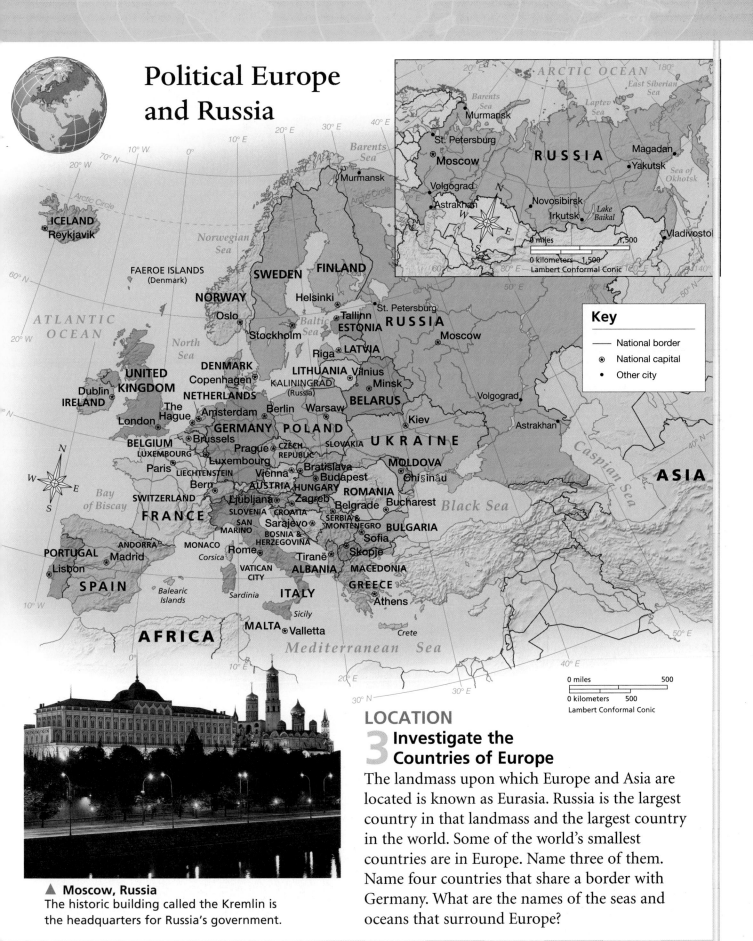

▲ **Moscow, Russia**
The historic building called the Kremlin is the headquarters for Russia's government.

LOCATION

3 Investigate the Countries of Europe

The landmass upon which Europe and Asia are located is known as Eurasia. Russia is the largest country in that landmass and the largest country in the world. Some of the world's smallest countries are in Europe. Name three of them. Name four countries that share a border with Germany. What are the names of the seas and oceans that surround Europe?

Physical Europe and Russia

The Matterhorn, Switzerland ▶
The Matterhorn is Switzerland's most famous mountain.

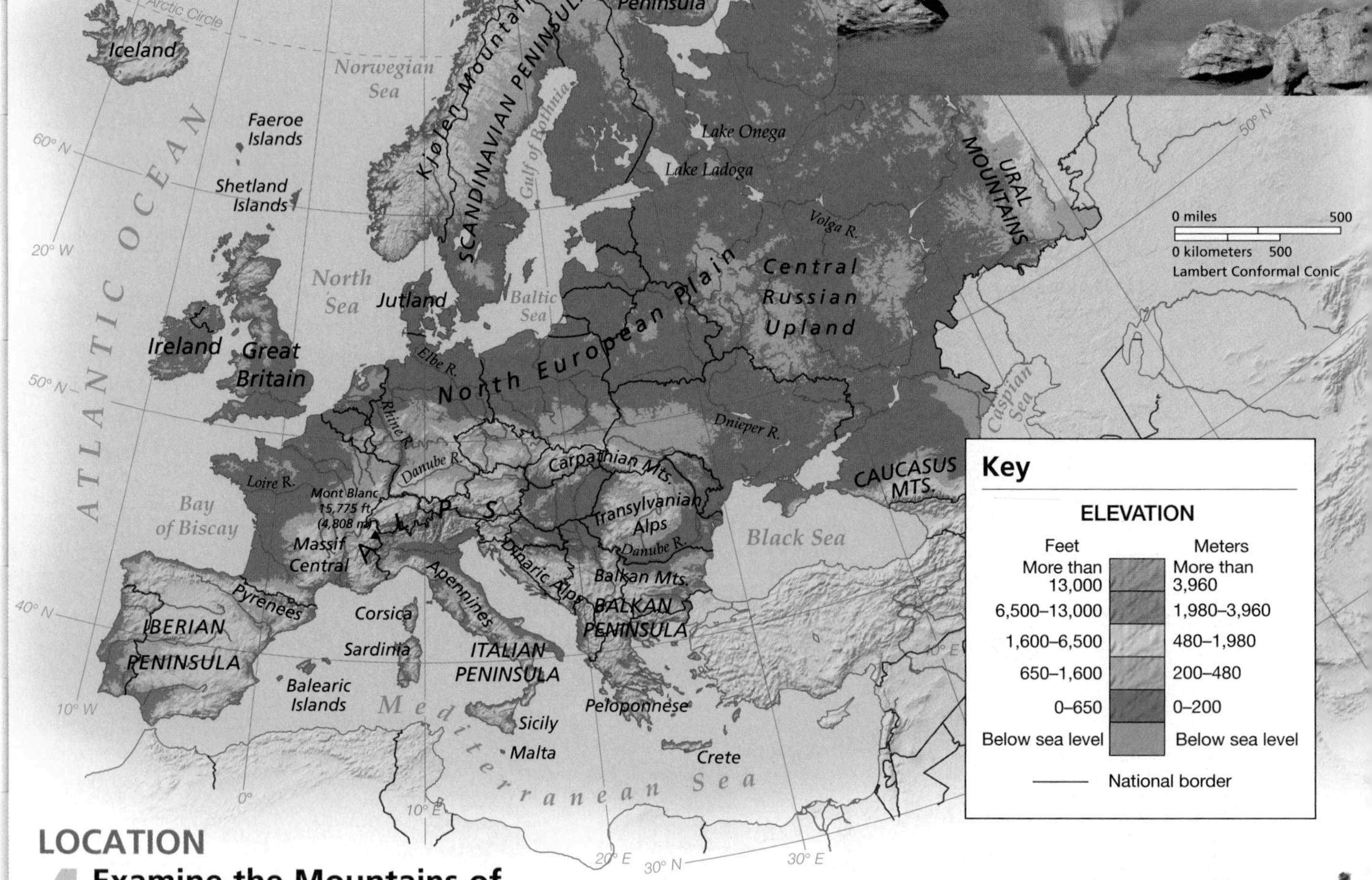

0 miles 500
0 kilometers 500
Lambert Conformal Conic

Key

ELEVATION

Feet	Meters
More than 13,000	More than 3,960
6,500–13,000	1,980–3,960
1,600–6,500	480–1,980
650–1,600	200–480
0–650	0–200
Below sea level	Below sea level

—— National border

LOCATION

4 Examine the Mountains of Europe and Russia

Several mountain ranges stretch through Central and Southern Europe, from the Bay of Biscay to the Caspian Sea. Find and name four of these mountain ranges. What mountain range separates France from Spain? Now locate Russia's Ural Mountains. Most of Russia lies in Asia, east of the Ural Mountains. Most Russians, however, live in the European part of Russia, west of the Ural Mountains.

Europe and Russia: Population Density

Population density describes how crowded a particular place is. Use the key below to determine what color on the map represents an area where many people live. What color represents an area where very few people live? Compare the parts of Europe where there are very few people with the parts of Europe where there are very many. How would you describe the population densities of the two regions?

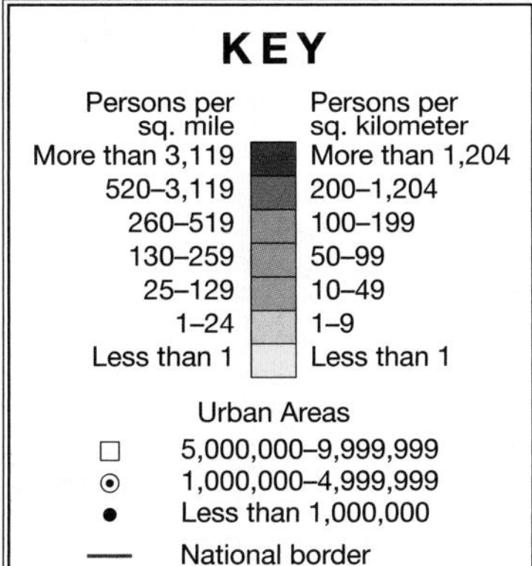
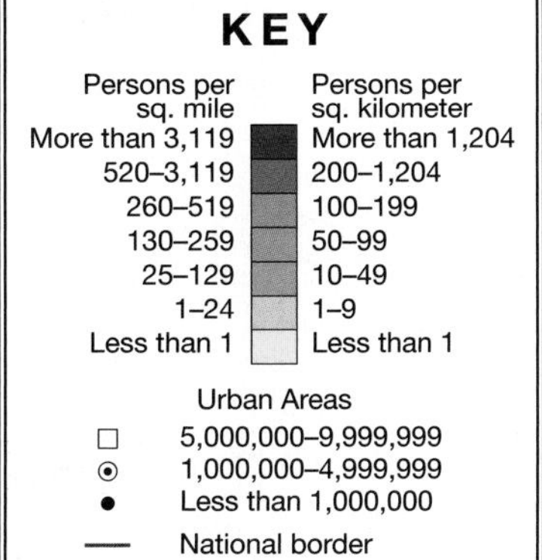

▼ **Norway**
Sami children on a snowmobile

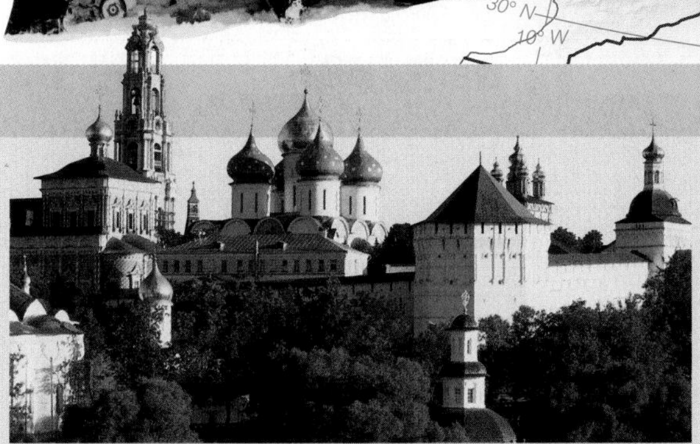

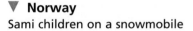

▲ **Sergivev Posad, Russia**
Trinity Monastery of St. Sergius

PRACTICE YOUR GEOGRAPHY SKILLS

1. You begin to explore Europe from its west coast. From Portugal you fly over the headwaters of the Danube and the Rhine rivers. In what direction are you flying?
2. You board a train in Moscow and travel east. When you get to the farthest point in Siberia, you have gone about one third of the way around the world. What mountain range did you cross?
3. You are going to drive from Warsaw to Moscow. In what direction will you travel?

Focus on Countries in Europe and Russia

Now that you've investigated the geography of Europe and Russia, take a closer look at some of the countries that make up this region. This map shows all of the countries of Europe and Russia. The 13 countries you will study in depth in the second half of this book appear in yellow on the map.

Go Online PHSchool.com Use Web Code **ldp-1000** for the **interactive maps** on these pages.

Key

- National border
- Countries with in-depth coverage
- Non-feature countries

ICELAND
ATLANTIC OCEAN
NORWAY
SWEDEN
North Sea
IRELAND
UNITED KINGDOM
NETHERLANDS
DENMARK
KALINING (Ru
BELGIUM
GERMANY
POLA
LUXEMBOURG
CZECH REPUBLIC
LIECHTENSTEIN
SLOVAK
SWITZERLAND
AUSTRIA
HUNGA
FRANCE
SLOVENIA
CROATIA
PORTUGAL
SPAIN
ANDORRA
SAN MARINO
BOSNIA & HERZEGOVINA
MONACO
ITALY
SERBI MONTENE
MACEDO
VATICAN CITY
ALBANIA
Mediterranean Sea
GRE
MALTA
Arctic Circle
70° N
60° N
50° N
40° N
20° W
10° W
0°
10° E
20° E

▲ **United Kingdom**
Britain once headed a great empire. Today, as a member of the United Nations, the United Kingdom plays an important role in world diplomacy.

Poland ►
Poland has undergone tremendous social, political, and economic changes since its communist government lost power in 1989. However, agriculture has remained an important part of the country's economy.

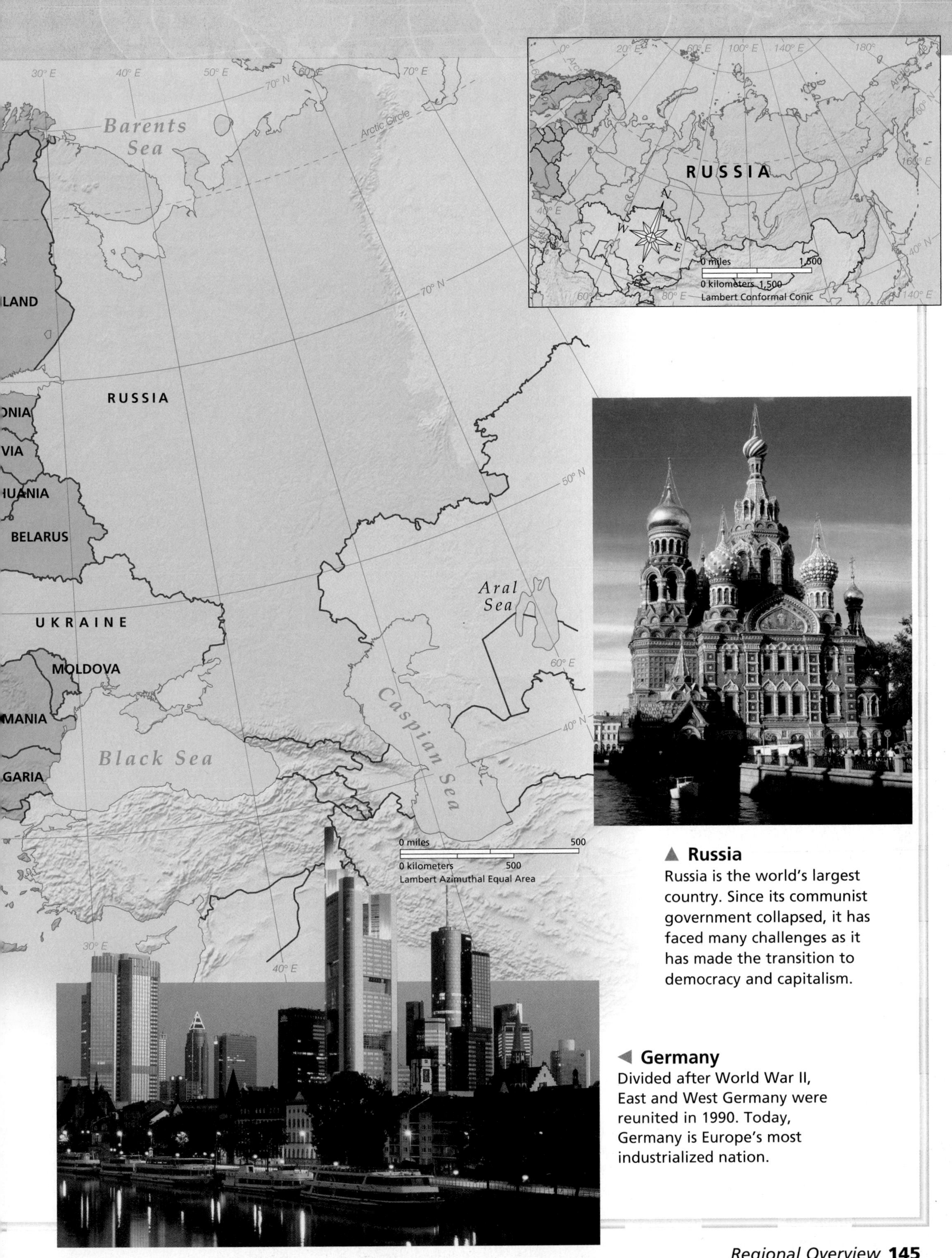

▲ Russia

Russia is the world's largest country. Since its communist government collapsed, it has faced many challenges as it has made the transition to democracy and capitalism.

◄ Germany

Divided after World War II, East and West Germany were reunited in 1990. Today, Germany is Europe's most industrialized nation.

Chapter 6

Europe and Russia: Physical Geography

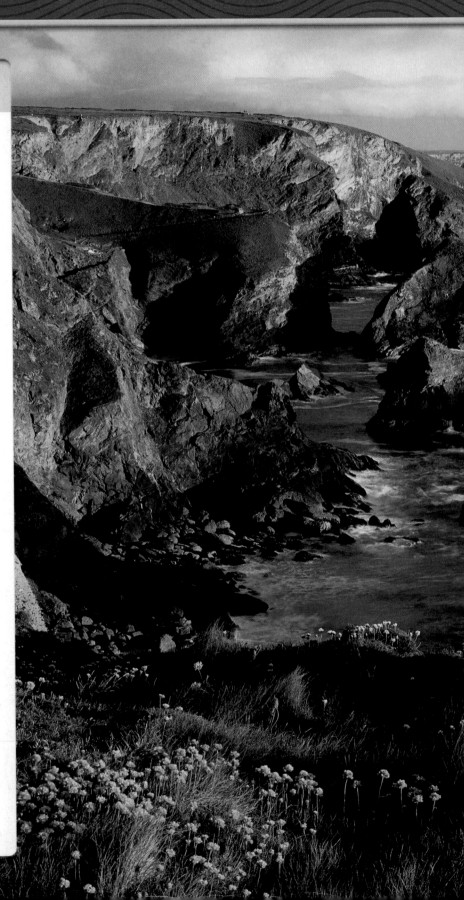

Chapter Preview

This chapter will introduce you to the geography of Europe and Russia and show how geography affects the people who live there.

Target Reading Skill

Reading Process In this chapter you will use previewing to help you understand and remember what you read.

▶ **Waves splash against the rocky coast of Cornwall in southern England.**

Europe and Russia: Climate Regions

MAP MASTER™ Skills Activity

Location The climates of Europe and Russia vary widely, from subtropical in Southern Europe to tundra in Russia. **Identify** Which climate is named after a major body of water in the region? **Contrast** Study the location of this climate. How do you think this climate differs from that of Northern Europe and Russia?

Go Online PHSchool.com Use Web Code **ldp-7111** for step-by-step **map skills practice.**

Section 1 Land and Water

Prepare to Read

Objectives

In this section you will

1. Learn about the size, location, and population of Europe and Russia.
2. Examine the major landforms of Europe and Russia.
3. Find out about the waterways of Europe and Russia.

Taking Notes

As you read this section, look for the main ideas about land and water. Copy the table below and record your findings in it.

Region	Landforms	Bodies of Water
Europe		
Russia		

Target Reading Skill

Set a Purpose for Reading When you set a purpose for reading, you give yourself a focus. Before you read this section, look at the headings, the maps, and the photographs to see what the section is about. Then set a purpose for reading the section. Your purpose might be to find out about the geography of Europe and Russia. As you read, use the Taking Notes table to help you achieve your purpose.

Key Terms

- **population density** (pahp yuh LAY shun DEN suh tee) *n.* the average number of people living in a square mile or a square kilometer
- **peninsula** (puh NIN suh luh) *n.* a land area nearly surrounded by water
- **plateau** (pla TOH) *n.* a large raised area of mostly level land bordered on one or more sides by steep slopes or cliffs
- **tributary** (TRIB yoo tehr ee) *n.* a river or stream that flows into a larger river
- **navigable** (NAV ih guh bul) *adj.* wide and deep enough for ships to travel through

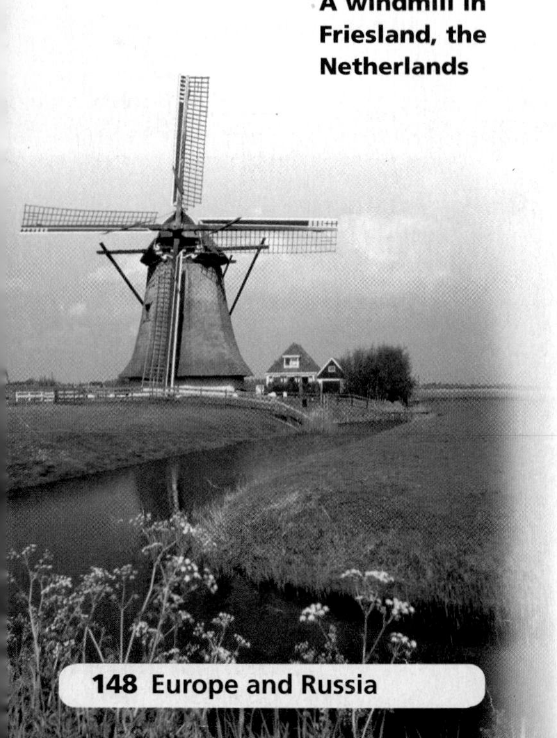

A windmill in Friesland, the Netherlands

If you cross a field in the Netherlands (NETH ur lundz), you could be walking where sea waves once roared. Water formerly covered more than two fifths of the country. Centuries ago, the people of the Netherlands began an effort to create land where there was water. They built long walls called dikes to hold back the water. They pumped the water into canals that empty into the North Sea. In this way, they created polders (POHL durz), or patches of new land.

The polders that lie below sea level are always filling with water. Netherlanders must continually pump them out. Keeping the polders dry is important. Like much of Europe, the country's many people must find living space on a small amount of land. The richest farmlands and some cities in the Netherlands are located on polders.

Size, Location, and Population

Europe and Russia are parts of Eurasia, the world's largest landmass. This landmass is made up of two continents, Europe and Asia. The country of Russia stretches over both continents. About one fourth of Russia is in Europe; the rest is in Asia. The Ural (YOOR ul) Mountains divide Europe from Asia.

Stretching North Trace a latitude line from the United States to Eurasia in the world political map in the Atlas. You will see that much of Europe and nearly all of Russia are farther north than is the United States. Berlin, the German capital, lies at about the same latitude as the southern tip of Canada's Hudson Bay.

A Small Continent With Many People Europe is a small continent. Only Australia is smaller. While Europe lacks size, it has 47 different countries. As you might guess, most of the countries are small. Many are the size of an average state in the United States. Russia, on the other hand, is the largest country in the world. It is almost twice the size of the United States.

Most of the countries of Europe have a much higher population density than other countries in the world. **Population density** is the average number of people living in a square mile or a square kilometer. The Netherlands has more than 1,236 people per square mile (477 people per sq kilometer). By comparison, the world average is about 106 people per square mile (42 people per sq kilometer). Russia, on the other hand, has a much lower population density—only about 22 people per square mile (9 people per sq kilometer).

✓ Reading Check **What is the largest landmass in the world?**

Rural Regions of Europe and Russia
The Ural Mountains, shown at the bottom, mark the dividing line between Europe and Russia. The inset photo shows a church situated in the highlands of northern Scotland. **Analyze Images** *Use clues from the photos to estimate the population densities of these two regions.*

Major Landforms

Study the shape of Europe on the map below. The continent of Europe forms a **peninsula** (puh NIN suh luh), or a body of land nearly surrounded by water. The European peninsula juts out into the Atlantic Ocean. Europe also has many smaller peninsulas with bays. These bays include harbors, or sheltered bodies of water where ships dock. Good harbors enabled Western European countries to become world leaders in the shipping industry.

Now find Russia on the political map of Asia in the Atlas. Notice how much of Russia lies on the Arctic Ocean. For most of the year, this body of water is frozen and cannot be used for shipping. Between Russia and the countries of Europe, however, there are no physical barriers. Movement between these two regions has always been easy.

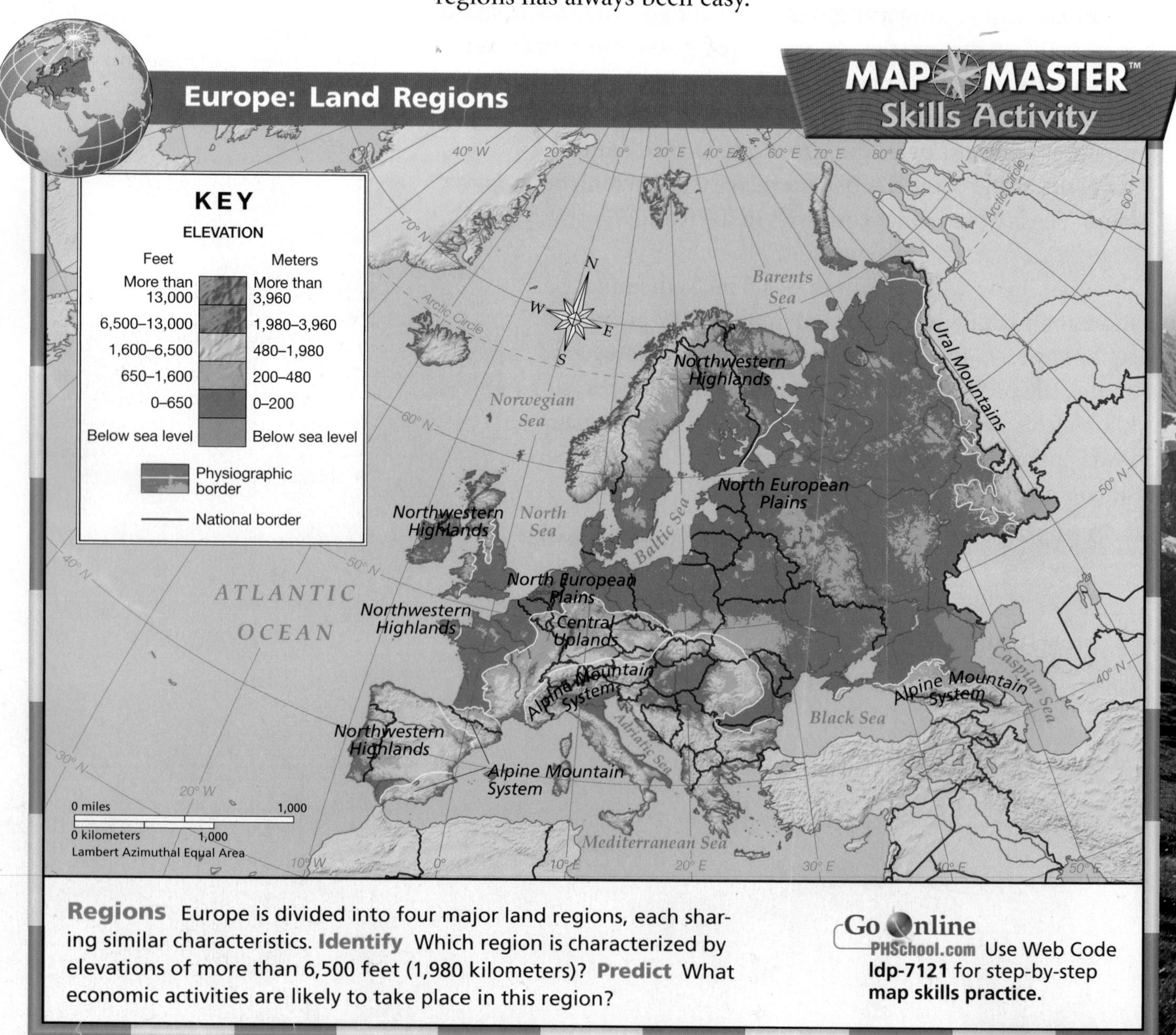

Regions Europe is divided into four major land regions, each sharing similar characteristics. **Identify** Which region is characterized by elevations of more than 6,500 feet (1,980 kilometers)? **Predict** What economic activities are likely to take place in this region?

Go Online PHSchool.com Use Web Code **ldp-7121** for step-by-step **map skills practice.**

Plains, Uplands, and Mountains of Europe Within the peninsula of Europe are four major land regions: the Northwestern Highlands, the North European Plain, the Central Uplands, and the Alpine Mountain System. Find these regions on the map on page 150.

The Northwestern Highlands stretch across the far north of Europe. It is a region of old mountains that have been worn down by wind and weather. Because they have steep slopes and thin soil, they are not good for farming, and few people live there. But the forests there support a successful timber industry. And people there raise goats and sheep, especially in Spain and Scotland.

Notice that the North European Plain covers more than half of Europe. These plains includes most of the European part of Russia and reach all the way to France. This region has the most productive farmland and the largest cities in Europe.

In the center of southern Europe are the Central Uplands. The Central Uplands are a region of highlands, made up of mountains and plateaus. **Plateaus** (pla TOHZ) are large raised areas of mostly level land bordered on one or more sides by steep slopes or cliffs. Most of the land there is rocky and not good for farming. But the uplands have other uses, including mining, industry, and tourism.

The mountains of the Alpine Mountain System stretch from France to the Balkan Peninsula. They include the Alps, the highest mountains in the system. Some families do small-scale farming in the mountain valleys and meadows of the Alps.

Discovery
CHANNEL
SCHOOL
Video
Learn about the geography of Europe and Russia.

Traveling in the Alps
A train carries people between alpine villages in southern Switzerland. The country has an extensive rail system. **Infer** *What geographical challenges does a nation like Switzerland face when building a rail system?*

Making a Living in Siberia
The nomadic Chukchi people make their living by herding reindeer in the uplands of northeastern Siberia. The name *Chukchi* means "rich in reindeer." **Infer** *Why does it make sense for the Chukchi to be nomadic—moving from place to place—rather than to live in fixed settlements?*

Plains, Uplands, and Mountains of Russia Europe and western Russia share the North European Plain. Russia's largest cities, Moscow (MAHS kow) and St. Petersburg, are in this region. Most of Russia's industries are there, too. More people live in this region than in any other part of Russia.

Where the plains end, the uplands begin. On the eastern border of the North European Plain, you will find the Ural Mountains. To the east of the Urals is the Asian part of Russia—a region known as Siberia (sy BIHR ee uh). This region makes up about 75 percent of Russian territory, but the climate is so harsh that only about 20 percent of Russia's people live there.

If you continue east into Siberia from the Ural Mountains, you will cross the largest plain in the world—the West Siberian Plain. This low, marshy plain covers more than one million square miles (2.59 million sq kilometers). More than half of it rises only 328 feet (100 meters) above sea level. Farther east is the Central Siberian Plateau, which slopes upward from the West Siberian Plain. If you travel still farther east, you will need to watch your step. The East Siberian Uplands include more than 20 active volcanoes among the rugged mountains and plateaus.

✓ Reading Check **Where are most of Russia's industries located?**

Waterways of Europe and Russia

Rivers and lakes provide the people who live in Europe and Russia with water and transportation.

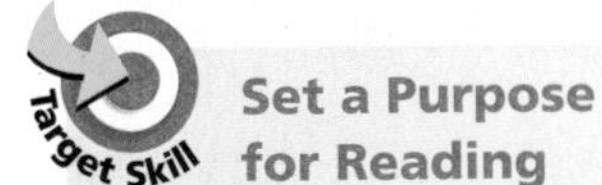

Set a Purpose for Reading
If your purpose is to learn about the geography of Europe and Russia, how do these paragraphs help you meet your goal?

Major Rivers High in the Alps in Switzerland (SWIT sur lund), melting glaciers create two streams that combine to form the Rhine River. Winding through forests and plains, the Rhine makes a journey of 865 miles (1,392 kilometers), from Switzerland to the Netherlands and the North Sea. The Rhine River is connected to the farthest reaches of Western Europe by canals and **tributaries** (TRIB yoo tehr eez). A tributary is a river or stream that flows into a larger river.

Another major waterway is the Danube (DAN yoob) River. The Danube is Europe's second-longest river. It begins in the Black Forest region of western Germany. It travels 1,770 miles (2,850 kilometers) to the Black Sea of southeastern Europe. Along the way, the Danube passes through nine countries.

The longest river in Europe is Russia's Volga (VOHL guh) River. It flows 2,291 miles (3,687 kilometers) through western Russia and empties into the Caspian (KASP ee un) Sea. Canals link the Volga and its tributaries to the Baltic Sea and other seas. Unfortunately, the Volga freezes along much of its length for three months of each year. During the winter months, it is not **navigable** (NAV ih guh bul), or clear enough for ships to travel through.

A Historical Waterway
The Rhine flows past old castles, mills, and factories along its course through Germany. Just as they did in ancient times, ships today use the river to transport goods. **Analyze Images** *What advantages would this location have given the people who settled here?*

A Seasonal Harbor
Ships wait in the harbor of Nizhay Novgorod, Russia, on the Volga River. **Analyze Images** *Is it likely that the river was navigable at the time the photo was taken?*

Lakes Though Europe is criss-crossed by rivers, it contains few lakes compared to other regions. Russia, in contrast, has a huge number of lakes, both large and small. The world's largest freshwater lake is found in Russia. Called Lake Baikal (by KAHL), it is located in southern Russia. Lake Baikal is nearly 400 miles long and has an average width of 30 miles. It is also the world's deepest lake, with some parts reaching 5,315 feet (1,620 meters). Lake Baikal contains about one fifth of Earth's fresh water and is home to hundreds of animal and plant species. In fact, the Russian word *baikal* means "rich lake."

✓ Reading Check **What is the longest river in Europe?**

Section 1 Assessment

Key Terms
Review the key terms at the beginning of this section. Use each term in a sentence that explains its meaning.

Target Reading Skill
How did having a purpose for reading help you understand important ideas in this section?

Comprehension and Critical Thinking
1. (a) Locate Which country is located on both the continents of Europe and Asia?
(b) Compare and Contrast How does the land size of Europe differ from the land size of Russia?
2. (a) Name What are the four major land regions of Europe?
(b) Identify What are the major land regions of Russia?
(c) Draw Conclusions How have physical features affected life in Europe and Russia?
3. (a) Explain Why is the Volga River in Russia not navigable year-round?
(b) Identify Effects How might Russia's industries be affected by ships not being able to travel on the rivers all year long?

Writing Activity
Write an entry in your journal describing what you learned about the landforms and waterways of Europe or Russia.

Writing Tip Remember that writing in a journal is writing you do for yourself. In a journal, you can let your ideas flow without stopping to correct your writing.

Section 2 Climate and Vegetation

Prepare to Read

Objectives

In this section you will

1. Find out about the wide range of climates in Europe and Russia.
2. Learn about the major climate regions of Europe and Russia.
3. Examine the natural vegetation regions of Europe and Russia.

Taking Notes

As you read this section, look for details about factors that affect climate and vegetation. Copy the flowchart below, and write each detail under the correct heading.

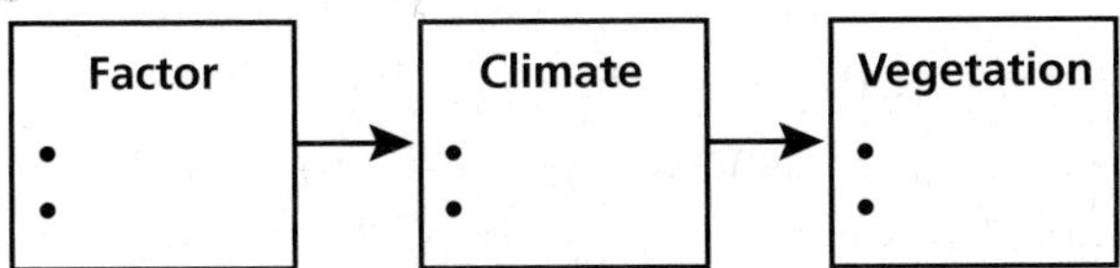

Target Reading Skill

Predict Making predictions about the text helps you set a purpose for reading and helps you remember what you read. Before you begin, preview the section by looking at the headings, photographs, charts, and maps. Then predict what the text might discuss about climate and vegetation. As you read this section, connect what you read to your prediction. If what you learn doesn't support your prediction, change your prediction.

Key Terms

- **rain shadow** (rayn SHAD oh) *n.* the area on the dry, sheltered side of a mountain, which receives little rainfall
- **steppes** (steps) *n.* the grasslands of fertile soil suitable for farming in Russia
- **tundra** (TUN druh) *n.* a cold, dry, treeless region covered with snow for most of the year
- **permafrost** (PUR muh frawst) *n.* a permanently frozen layer of ground below the top layer of soil

It is February in Barcelona (bahr suh LOH nuh), Spain. Twelve-year-old Pablo wakes up to the sun streaming through his bedroom window. It's another comfortable day, and the temperature is already 52°F (11°C). Pablo dresses quickly in jeans and a t-shirt and eats a breakfast of thick hot chocolate and *churros,* twisted loops of fried dough. He wants to go out and play soccer with his friends on this sunny Saturday morning.

At the very same moment, it is late afternoon in Irkutsk (ihr KOOTSK), a city in southern Siberia. Anya (AHN yuh) returns home from a day of cross-country skiing. She takes off her fur hat, gloves, boots, ski pants, and coat. The day has been sunny but cold, with an average temperature of −15°F (−26°C). Now Anya warms up with a dinner of *pelmeny* (PEL muh nee), chicken broth with meat-filled dumplings.

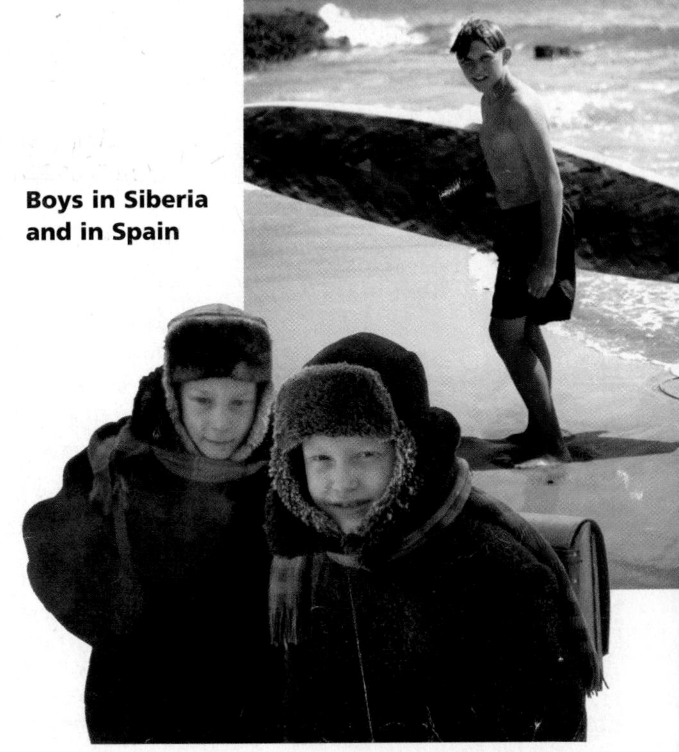

Boys in Siberia and in Spain

Achill Island, Ireland

A Wide Range of Climates

Barcelona, where Pablo lives, lies on the Mediterranean Sea. There, the summers are hot and dry, and the winters are mild. In Irkutsk, Anya's home, summers are short, and the winters are long and very cold. Temperatures in winter can drop to −50°F (−45°C). Snow covers the ground for about six months of the year.

How Oceans Affect Climate The two cities' distances from an ocean or a sea help explain their climate. Areas that are near an ocean or a sea have fairly mild weather year-round. Areas that are far from the ocean often have more extreme weather. Look at the map below and find the Gulf Stream. Notice that it becomes the North Atlantic Current as it crosses the Atlantic Ocean. This powerful ocean current carries warm water from the tropical waters of the Gulf of Mexico to northwestern Europe. It also warms winds blowing from the west across the Atlantic Ocean. The warm waters and winds bring mild weather to much of northwestern Europe.

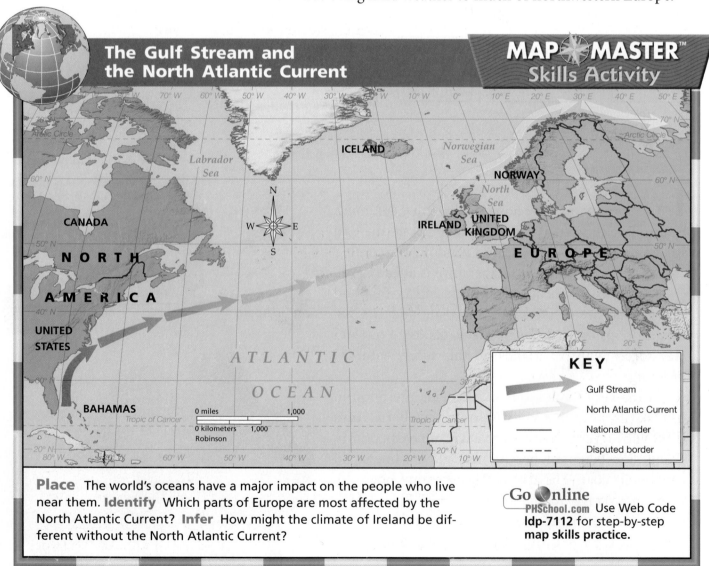

The Gulf Stream and the North Atlantic Current

MAP MASTER™ Skills Activity

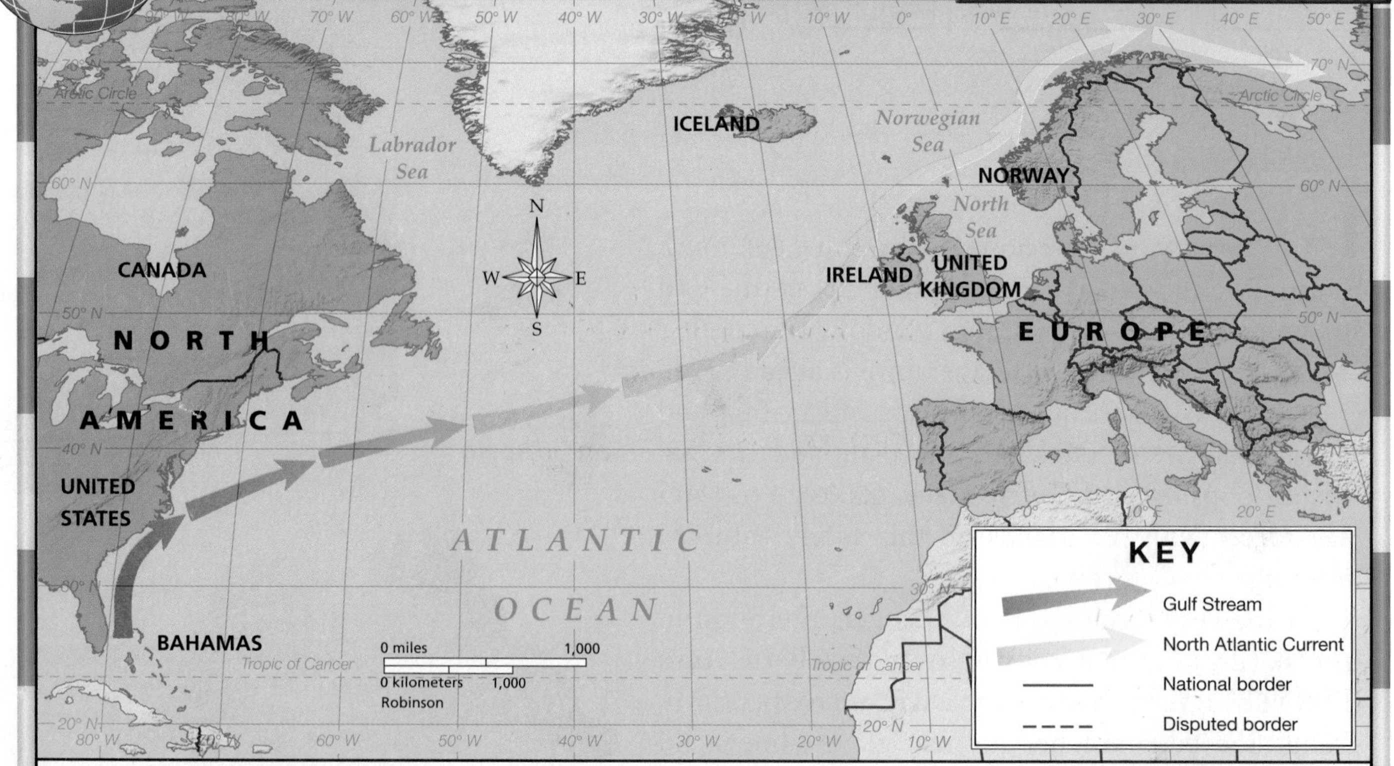

KEY

- Gulf Stream
- North Atlantic Current
- National border
- Disputed border

0 miles 1,000
0 kilometers 1,000
Robinson

Place The world's oceans have a major impact on the people who live near them. **Identify** Which parts of Europe are most affected by the North Atlantic Current? **Infer** How might the climate of Ireland be different without the North Atlantic Current?

Go Online PHSchool.com Use Web Code **ldp-7112 for step-by-step map skills practice.**

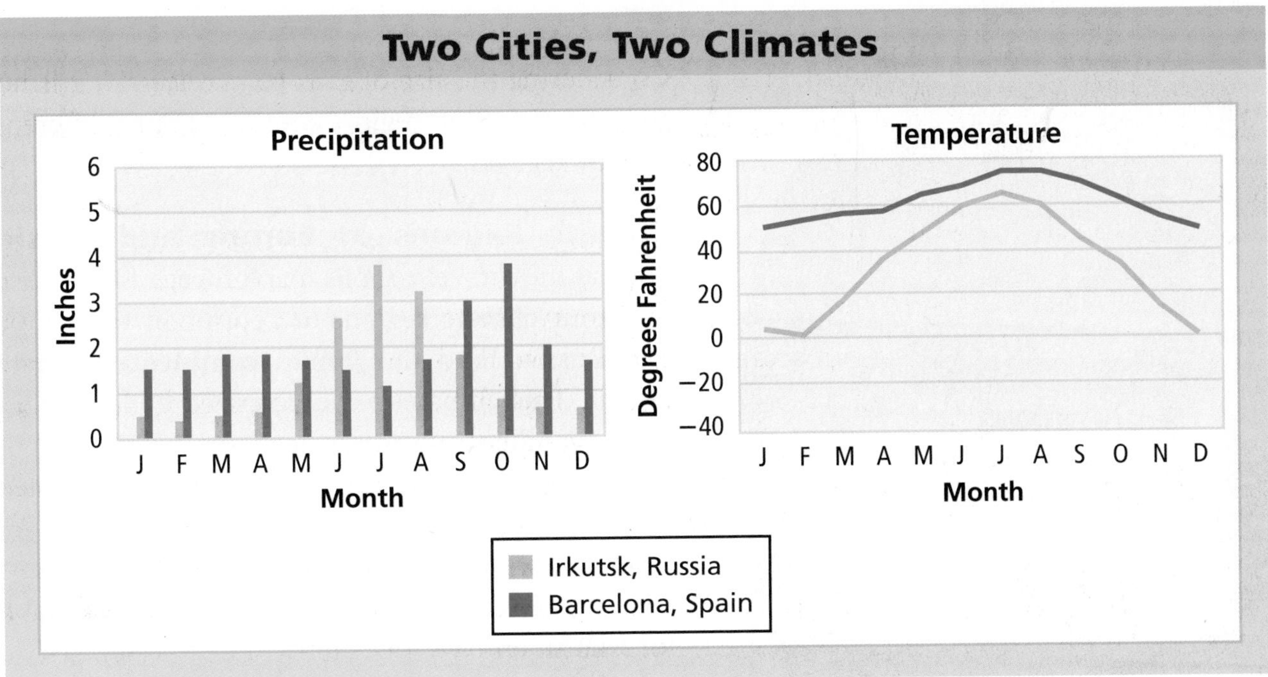

London, England, is farther north than any city in the continental United States, yet it has mild weather. How is this possible? The North Atlantic Current is the reason. But the most dramatic effect of the North Atlantic Current can be seen in northern Norway. Snow and ice cover most of this area in winter. Yet Norway's western coast is free of ice and snow all year. Snow melts almost as soon as it falls. Norway's ice-free ports have helped make its fishing industry one of the largest in Europe.

The ocean affects climate in other ways. Winds blowing across the ocean pick up a great deal of moisture. When these winds blow over land, they drop the moisture in the form of rain. Winds blowing from the west across the Atlantic bring a fairly wet climate to much of Western Europe.

Graph Skills

A city's climate is affected by its location and the geographical features that are located near it. **Identify** In how many months out of the year does Barcelona receive more precipitation than Irkutsk? **Draw Conclusions** What factors explain Irkutsk's low precipitation for most of the year?

How Mountains Affect Rainfall Mountains also affect the amount of rainfall in an area. In Europe, areas west of mountains receive heavy rainfall. These areas include parts of Great Britain, France, Germany, and Norway. Areas east of mountains have much lighter rainfall.

Why is this so? As winds rise up a mountain, they cool and drop their moisture. The air is dry by the time it reaches the other side of the mountain. Areas on the leeward side of a mountain, or the side away from the wind, are in a rain shadow. **A rain shadow** is an area on the dry, sheltered side of a mountain, which receives little rainfall.

✓ Reading Check **How do mountains affect the climates of Western Europe?**

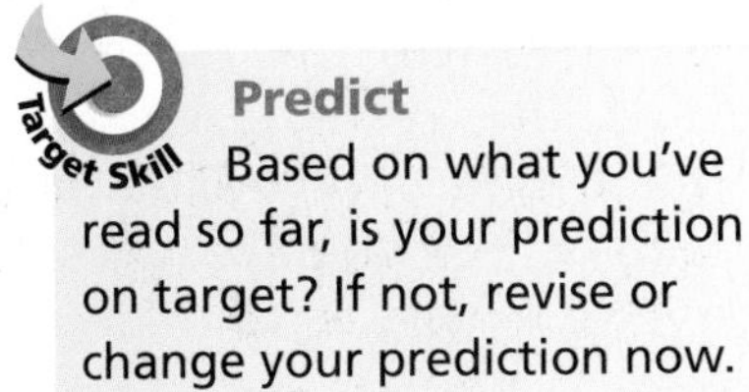

Predict Based on what you've read so far, is your prediction on target? If not, revise or change your prediction now.

Major Climate Regions

Considering the size of Europe and Russia, it is no surprise that this region contains many different climate regions.

Two Very Different Climates
Much of Russia has a tundra climate, as shown in the top photo of Siberia. In contrast, London, England (at bottom), enjoys a mild climate year-round. **Infer** *How might the population densities of the places in these photos differ?*

Climate Regions of Europe and Russia

Look at the climate regions map on page 147. Notice that four climate regions are common to Europe and Russia. Find the humid continental climate region. This climate is characterized by long, cold winters and hot summers.

Now find Irkutsk, Russia, on the map. It is located in a huge subarctic climate region. There summers are short, and winters are long and cold. You can see how cold it is all year by looking at the temperature graph for Irkutsk on page 157. Notice that this climate also stretches across northern Europe.

Europe and Russia share two other climate regions. The northernmost areas of Europe and Russia have an arctic climate. It is very cold in these areas. On the warmest days of the short summer, temperatures sometimes barely reach 60°F (14°C). In contrast, southeastern Europe and southwestern Russia have a semiarid climate region, with hot temperatures and little rainfall.

Moderate Climate Regions of Europe As you can see on the climate regions map, Europe has moderate climate regions that Russia does not have. For example, the marine west coast climate affects much of northwestern Europe, stretching from northern Spain to northern Norway. As you have read, winds and currents from the Atlantic Ocean keep this climate mild and rainy all year.

Another climate region surrounds the Mediterranean Sea. It is easy to remember the name of this type of climate—Mediterranean, just like the sea. Remember that Barcelona, Spain, is on the Mediterranean Sea. In the Mediterranean climate, summers are hot and dry. Winters are mild and rainy.

Finally, a band of humid subtropical climate is located in southern Europe. Warm temperatures and year-round rainfall characterize this climate.

√ Reading Check **What two climate regions are found in Europe but not Russia?**

Natural Vegetation Regions

The natural vegetation, or plant life, of Europe and Russia is as varied as the climate. Vegetation regions are related to climate regions. Vegetation in Europe and Russia varies from ice cap to desert. However, the main vegetation regions are forest, grassland, tundra, and Mediterranean. Compare the climate map on page 147 with the natural vegetation map below to see how the climate and vegetation regions overlap.

Forests of Europe and Russia The natural vegetation of much of Europe is forest. However, most of these forests have been cleared to make way for farms, factories, and cities. In northern Europe, you can still find large coniferous (koh NIF ur us) forests, which have evergreen trees with cones that carry and protect the seeds. Deciduous (dih SIJ oo us) forests, which contain trees that lose their leaves in fall, cover most of Western and Central Europe.

Russia is also heavily forested. One forest, called the taiga (TY guh), covers more than 4 million square miles (10 million square kilometers). Located in Siberia, it is the largest forest in the world.

Links Across The World

The Boreal Forest The boreal forest includes one third of all Earth's forests. The name comes from an ancient Greek god named Boreas, the god of the north wind. Russia's taiga makes up half of the boreal forest. The rest is located in the northern parts of Canada, Alaska, China, Mongolia, Scandinavia, and Scotland. Boreal forests play an important role in the environment, by filtering out carbon dioxide and other gases from the atmosphere.

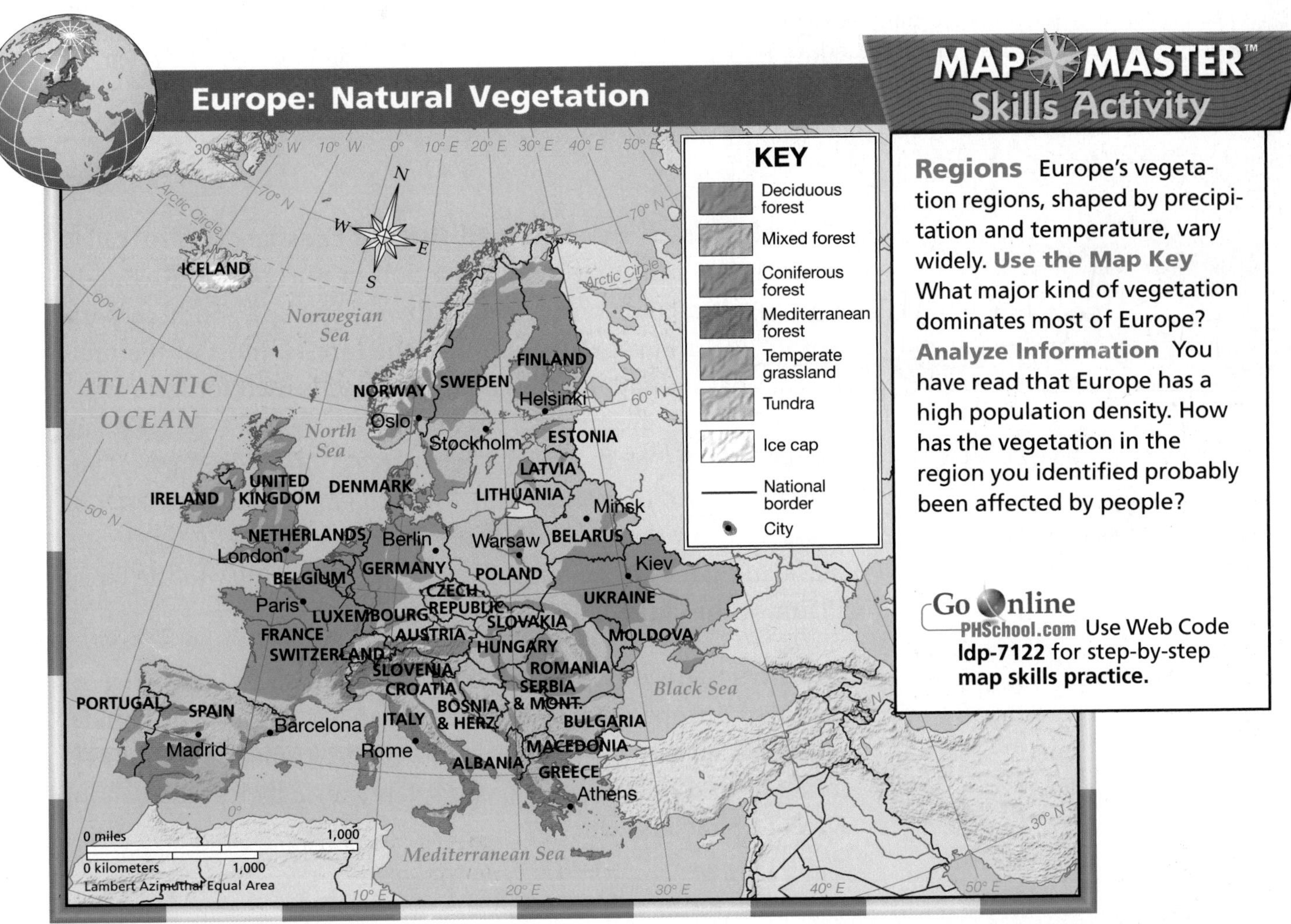

MAP MASTER™ Skills Activity

Regions Europe's vegetation regions, shaped by precipitation and temperature, vary widely. **Use the Map Key** What major kind of vegetation dominates most of Europe? **Analyze Information** You have read that Europe has a high population density. How has the vegetation in the region you identified probably been affected by people?

Go Online PHSchool.com Use Web Code **ldp-7122** for step-by-step **map skills practice.**

Russia: Natural Vegetation

Location Russia is located far from the Equator and the warm ocean currents that bring mild climates to most of Europe. **Use a Scale** How much of Russia's land is tundra? **Apply Information** Why are few major cities located in this region?

Go Online PHSchool.com Use Web Code **ldp-7132** for step-by-step **map skills practice.**

Grasslands of Europe and Russia Grasslands, also called prairies, are a major vegetation region in Europe and Russia. In Europe, grasslands once covered the central and southern parts of the North European Plain. Like the forests, most of the prairies have also disappeared. Today, the land is used for farming.

In Russia, the grasslands are called **steppes.** Steppes are located mainly in the southwestern parts of the country. They contain a mix of grasses and low-growing vegetation such as mosses. Below that vegetation, the soil of the steppes is fertile and black and good for farming. The steppes are similar to the Great Plains of the United States.

Mediterranean Regions of Europe Just as the area of southern Europe near the Mediterranean Sea has its own climate, it also has its own vegetation region. Mediterranean vegetation is a mix of trees, scrub, and smaller plants, usually less than about 8 feet (2.5 meters) tall.

Tundra of Europe and Russia Northern parts of Europe—including northern Scandinavia and Iceland—as well as northern Russia have a tundra vegetation region. **Tundra** is a cold, dry, treeless region that is covered with snow for most of the year. There winters last as long as nine months and the ground contains **permafrost,** a layer of permanently frozen ground below the top layer of soil. During the brief season when the top surface of the permafrost thaws, grasses, mosses, and other plant life grow quickly. Few people live in the tundra region.

✓ Reading Check **Where is the world's largest forest located?**

Flowers bloom during the short Siberian summer.

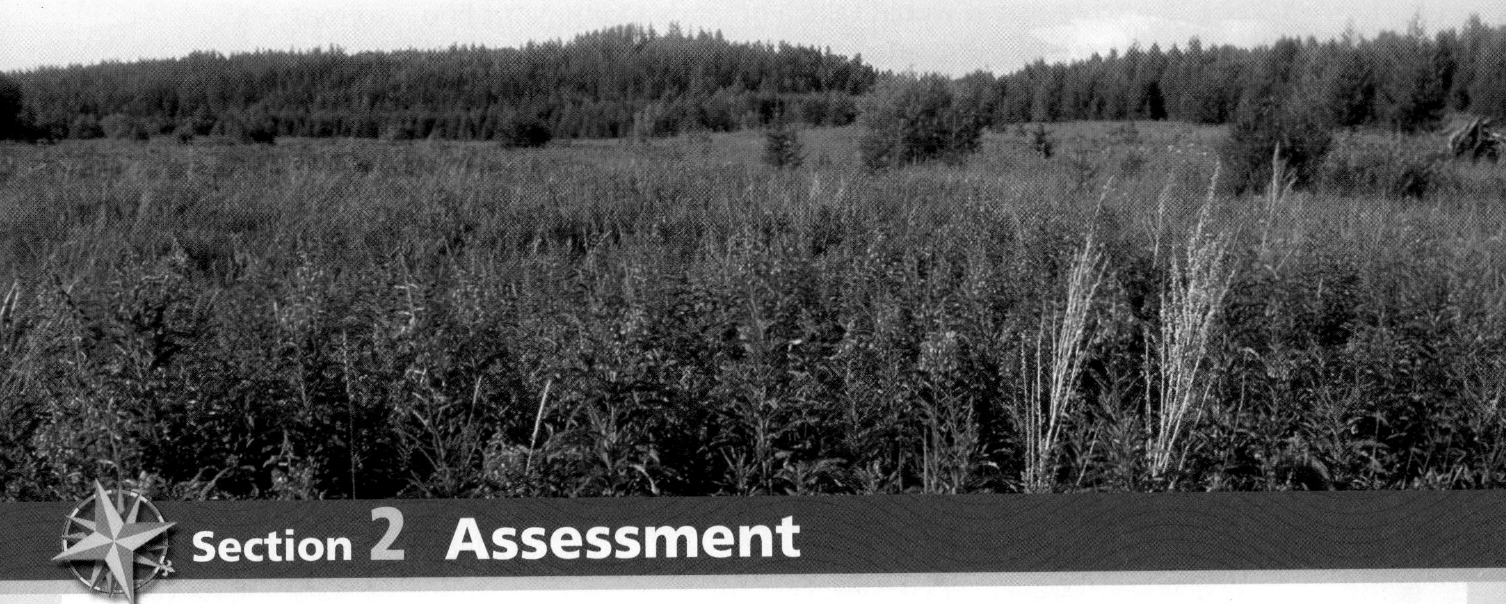

Section 2 Assessment

Key Terms

Review the key terms at the beginning of this section. Use each term in a sentence that explains its meaning.

Target Reading Skill

What did you predict about this section? How did your prediction guide your reading?

Comprehension and Critical Thinking

1. **(a) Describe** How do oceans affect climate?
(b) Identify Effects How does the North Atlantic Current affect northern Europe?

2. **(a) Recall** What are the major climate regions of Europe and Russia?
(b) Draw Conclusions Why are summers in Barcelona, Spain, hot and dry?

3. **(a) List** What are the natural vegetation regions of Europe and Russia?
(b) Summarize How are vegetation regions and climate regions related?
(c) Generalize What geographic features might lead someone to settle in Europe, rather than in Russia?

Writing Activity

Suppose you are planning a trip to one of the cities mentioned in this section. Decide what time of year you would want to go. Based on the climate of the city, make a list of the clothes that you would pack. Then write a brief paragraph explaining why you would pack the items on your list.

For: An activity about Ireland
Visit: PHSchool.com
Web Code: ldd-7101

Using a Precipitation Map

Suppose your teacher asks you to write a report that compares the physical geography of the United States to that of Russia. You know that both countries are huge. You also know that physical geography includes many different elements, such as climate, landforms, vegetation, and precipitation—moisture in the form of rain or snow. You realize it would take a great deal of time to find information in each of these categories for both countries.

One good way to find all the information you need is to look at a set of special-purpose maps. A special-purpose map shows information about a certain topic. A precipitation map, for example, shows the total amount of precipitation an area receives in a year. By looking at a world precipitation map, you can quickly compare the United States' precipitation with that of Russia.

Learn the Skill

Follow the steps below to learn how to use a precipitation map.

1. **Read the map title and look over the map to get a general idea of what it shows.** Notice that a precipitation map includes common map features, such as a title, key, scale, and labels.
2. **Read the key to understand how the map uses symbols, colors, and patterns.** A precipitation map often shows colors to represent different amounts of precipitation. Notice that the amounts are indicated in both inches and centimeters.
3. **Use the key to interpret the map.** Look on the map for the different colors shown in the key. Notice where areas with different amounts of precipitation are located on the map.
4. **Draw conclusions about what the map shows.** Information you discover when you analyze a precipitation map can help you draw conclusions about how precipitation affects people's lives.

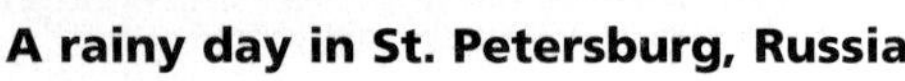
A rainy day in St. Petersburg, Russia

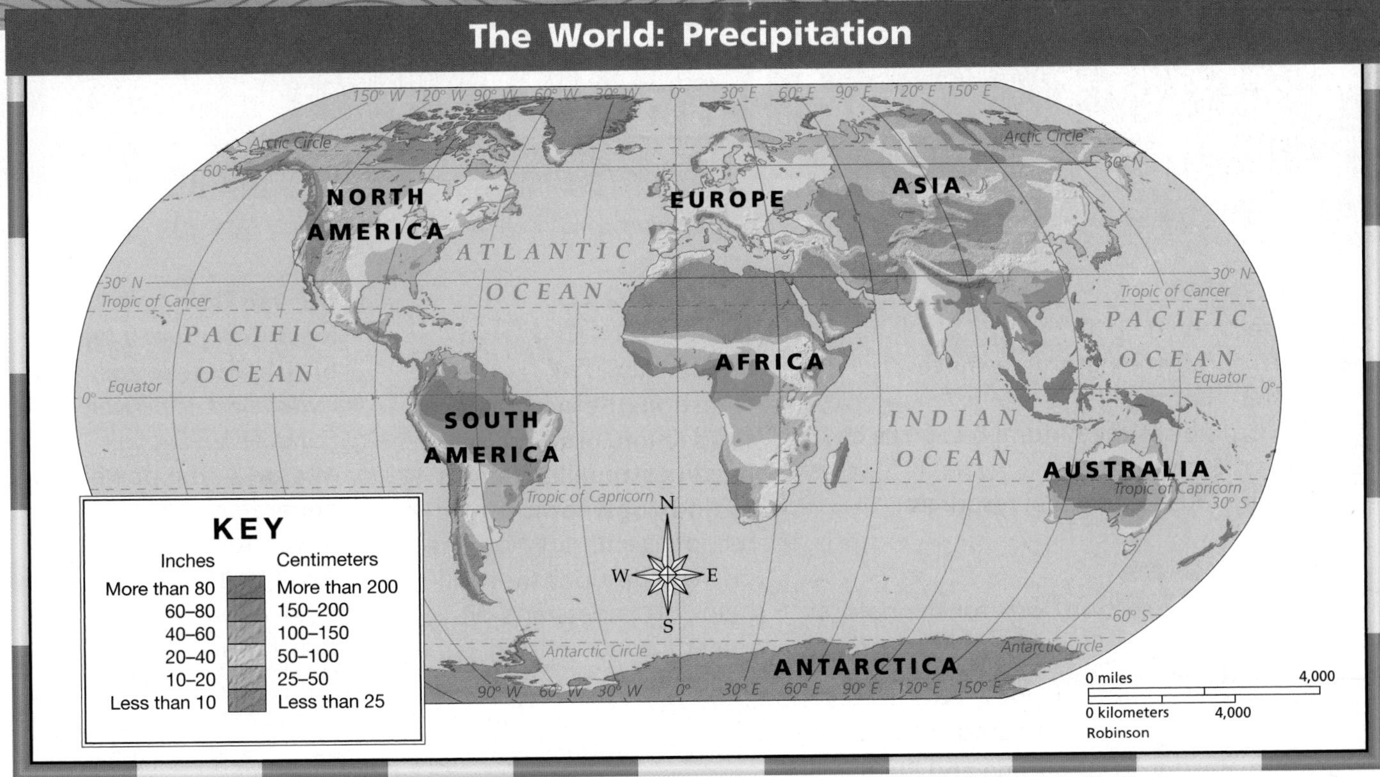

Practice the Skill

Use the precipitation map above to complete the following steps.

1. Become familiar with the map. What is the map's title? In general, what does it show?

2. Look at the key to see how different amounts of precipitation are shown. Familiarize yourself with the colors on the key.

3. Look for areas on the map with different amounts of precipitation. Because you want to compare the United States with Russia, find those two regions within the continents of North America, Asia, and Europe on the map. (If you need help finding the areas of the two countries, compare this map with the World: Political map in the Atlas).

4. Study the map. Use the information on it to compare precipitation in the United States and Russia. Which country has more variation in precipitation? Which country is generally dryer? Write a conclusion that summarizes your comparison.

Apply the Skill

Turn to Section 2 of Chapter 6 and look at the Europe: Natural Vegetation map on page 159. Use the steps of this skill to analyze and draw conclusions about this special-purpose map.

Section 3 Resources and Land Use

Prepare to Read

Objectives

In this section you will

1. Learn about the natural resources of Western Europe.
2. Find out about the natural resources of Eastern Europe.
3. Examine Russia's natural resources.

Taking Notes

As you read this section, look for the natural resources located in Europe and Russia. Copy the Venn diagram below, and record your findings in it.

Natural Resources of Europe and Russia

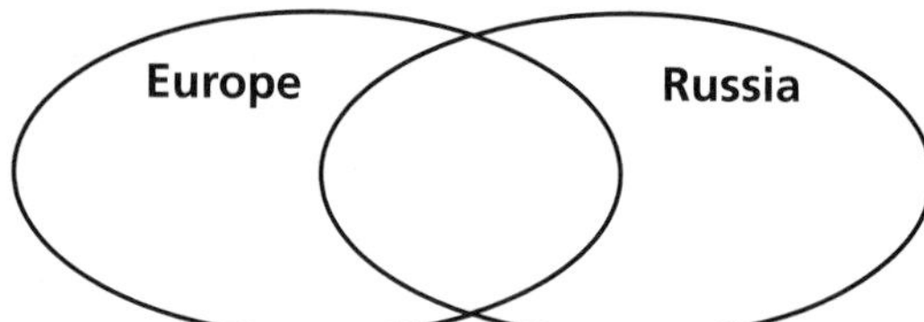

Target Reading Skill

Preview and Ask Questions Before you read this section, preview the headings and illustrations to find out what the section is about. Write one or two questions that will help you understand or remember something important in the section. Then read this section to answer your questions.

Key Terms

- **loess** (LOH es) *n.* a type of rich, dustlike soil
- **hydroelectric power** (hy droh ee LEK trik POW ur) *n.* the power generated by water-driven turbines
- **fossil fuel** (FAHS ul FYOO ul) *n.* a source of energy that forms from the remains of ancient plants and animals

A North Sea oil rig

How would you like to live and work on an ocean? Oil workers on the North Sea do just that. Their job is to pump oil from deep beneath the ocean floor. They work on a tower called an oil rig anchored over an oil field. Oil rig workers live and work as if they were on a ship. But they cannot seek the safety of a harbor when a big storm is stirring.

The North Sea, located between the United Kingdom and mainland northwestern Europe, sometimes has violent weather. Severe storms with winds of as much as 100 miles (160 kilometers) an hour are common. Waves as high as 90 feet (27 meters) batter oil rig platforms. Despite the harsh conditions, crews work around the clock to operate, inspect, and repair the rigs.

Making sure a rig operates properly is a very important job. The United Kingdom and other nations around the North Sea depend on oil and natural gas from the rigs.

Resources of Western Europe

Western Europe is a wealthy region and a world leader in economic development. Part of this wealth and success comes from Western Europe's rich and varied supply of natural resources. These natural resources include fertile soil, water, and fuels.

Fertile Soil Soil is one of Earth's most important natural resources because it is needed to grow food. Much of Western Europe is covered with rich, fertile soil, especially the region's broad river valleys.

Wind has helped create the fertile soil of the North European Plain. Over thousands of years, winds have deposited **loess** (LOH es), a type of rich, dustlike soil. This soil, combined with plentiful rain and moderate temperatures, provides for a long growing season. These conditions allow European farmers to produce abundant crops.

Tulips brighten the landscape at a flower farm in the Netherlands.

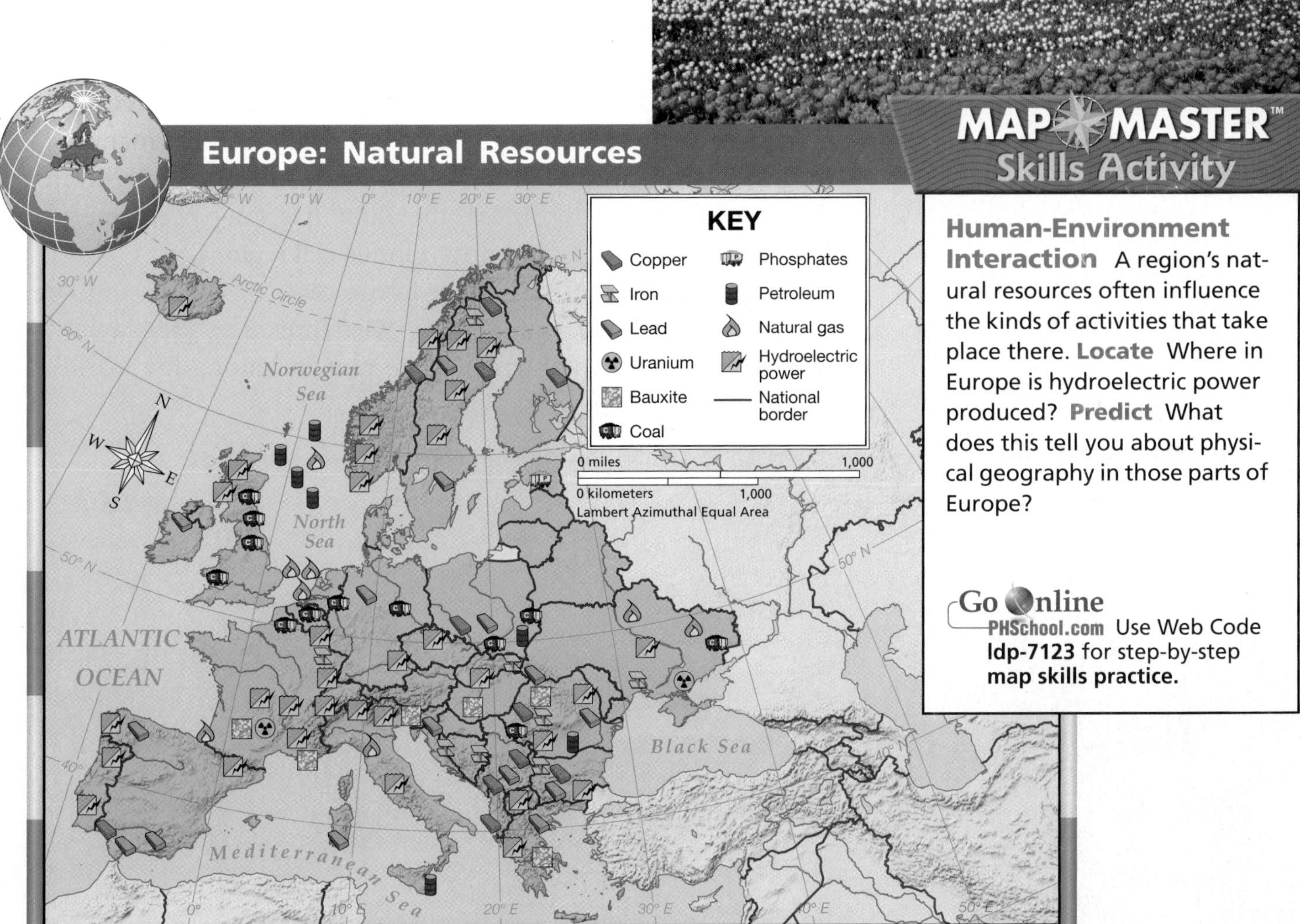

MAP MASTER™ Skills Activity

Human-Environment Interaction A region's natural resources often influence the kinds of activities that take place there. **Locate** Where in Europe is hydroelectric power produced? **Predict** What does this tell you about physical geography in those parts of Europe?

Go Online
PHSchool.com Use Web Code **ldp-7123** for step-by-step **map skills practice.**

Abundant Water Another important resource in Western Europe is water. People need water for drinking. Water nourishes crops. Water can also be used to produce electricity for industries and homes. To be used as a source of energy, water must flow very quickly. The force of water from a waterfall or a dam can be used to spin machines called turbines (TUR bynz). Spinning turbines generate, or create, electric power. Power generated by water-driven turbines is called **hydroelectric power** (hy droh ee LEK trik POW ur).

Many countries in Western Europe have favorable locations for the development of hydroelectric power. Some rivers that flow down through the mountains have been dammed to generate hydroelectric power. Norway gets almost all of its electric power from water. Hydroelectric power also keeps factories in Sweden, Switzerland, Austria, Spain, Scotland, and Portugal operating.

Fuel Deposits Like flowing water, fuel deposits are another source of energy for many industries. **Fossil fuels** are sources of energy that formed from the remains of ancient plants and animals. Fossil fuels include natural gas, oil, and coal.

Both the United Kingdom and Norway have large deposits of oil and natural gas. The United Kingdom also has large coal fields, as does Germany. The largest coal deposits in Germany are located in the Ruhr (ROOR), a region named for the Ruhr River. Because of its fuel resources, the Ruhr has long been one of Western Europe's most important industrial regions.

An abundance of coal and iron ore gave Western European industries a head start in the 1800s, when industries grew rapidly. Today, countries in Western Europe remain among the world's leading industrial powers.

✓ Reading Check **How is hydroelectric power generated?**

Producing hydroelectric power on the Tay River in Scotland

Resources of Eastern Europe

Now, shift your view from Western to Eastern Europe. Turn back to the map on page 165 showing Europe's natural resources. Notice that Eastern Europe has resources similar to those of Western Europe. Place a finger on the area around 50° N and 15° E. This is where Poland, the Czech (chek) Republic, and Germany come together. This area is called Silesia (sy LEE zhuh). Large deposits of coal there have helped to make Silesia a major industrial center.

Ukraine (yoo KRAYN), a large country in Eastern Europe, has coal deposits, too. It also has other fuel resources—especially oil and natural gas. However, the most important resource is probably its soil. The region's black earth is very fertile. Not surprisingly, farming is an extremely important activity in Ukraine.

Eastern Europe has fewer water resources than does Western Europe. However, the nations of the Balkan Peninsula produce a large amount of hydroelectric power.

√ Reading Check **What is Silesia, and where is it?**

Energy and Land Resources
The photo at the left shows miners on the job in a Silesian coal mine. Above, a Ukrainian woman harvests flowers to use in making perfume.
Compare and Contrast *What do mining and farming have in common? How are they different?*

Resources of Russia

Russia has a much greater supply of natural resources than does the United States. The United States has used its resources to become the richest nation on Earth. You might wonder why Russia has not done the same.

One answer is that Russia's harsh climate, huge size, and few navigable rivers have made it difficult to turn the country's resources into wealth. In addition, Russia has relatively few places that are suited for farming. Much of Russia lacks one or more of the key elements for farming: favorable climate, good soil, and plentiful water.

A tugboat pushes a barge loaded with logs along a Russian river.

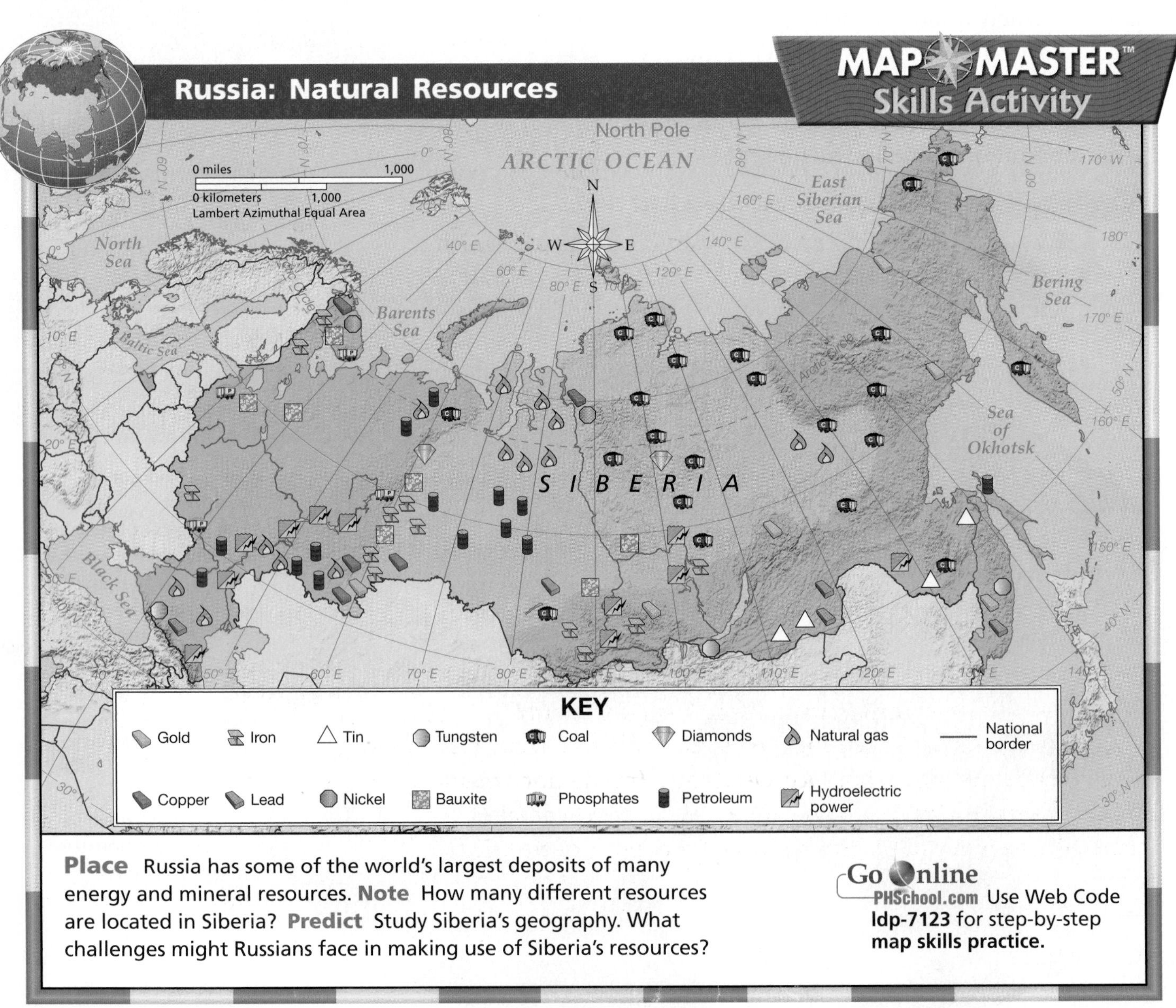

Place Russia has some of the world's largest deposits of many energy and mineral resources. **Note** How many different resources are located in Siberia? **Predict** Study Siberia's geography. What challenges might Russians face in making use of Siberia's resources?

Go Online
PHSchool.com Use Web Code **ldp-7123** for step-by-step **map skills practice.**

From Fossils to Fuel

1. Peat is made of partially decayed plant material.

2. Over millions of years, material built up over ancient peat deposits. The pressure of this material gradually changed the peat into brown coal.

3. Continuing pressure gradually turned brown coal into soft coal. Soft coal is the most common coal found on Earth. It is often used in industry.

Fossil Fuels and Minerals Russia has the largest reserves, or available supply, of natural gas in the world. It is also one of the world's five leading oil producers. Scientists estimate that the country has about one third of the world's coal reserves. In addition, Russia has huge deposits of minerals, including cobalt, chromium, copper, and gold.

Russia also has the world's largest reserves of iron ore, which is used to make steel. Many of these iron ore deposits are in the part of Russia that is on the continent of Europe. That is one reason why most of Russia's industry is west of the Ural Mountains. Fueled by its natural resources, Russian factories produce automobiles, cloth, machinery, computers, and chemicals.

Diagram Skills

A man in Ireland cuts pieces of peat from the ground. **Explain** If this peat stayed in the ground, how long would it take to turn into brown coal? **Apply Information** Explain why coal is a nonrenewable resource, using information from the diagram.

Forest, Fishing, and Energy Resources Russia has the world's largest forest reserves. Wood harvested from these forests is used to make paper and pulp, and it also supplies wood for houses and furniture.

Because of Russia's location on the Pacific Ocean, fish provide another abundant resource. Russians also fish the Black and Caspian seas, as well as the country's many inland lakes. The fishing industry is an important part of Russia's economy.

Finally, Russia has ample energy resources. It uses much of its fossil fuel resources to produce electricity. In addition, many Russian rivers are dammed to generate electricity in hydroelectric plants. Russia is one of the world's largest producers of electricity.

Preview and Ask Questions
Ask a question that will help you learn something important from this section. Then read the section, and answer your question.

Breaking Up Old Ships
When ships are no longer seaworthy, they are broken apart like this oil tanker in the harbor of Murmansk, Russia. Breaking up ships often causes environmental and health problems. **Infer** *What specific problems might breaking up an oil tanker cause?*

Challenges to Using Russia's Resources Most of Russia's deposits of oil, natural gas, and coal are located in Siberia. Three fourths of Russia's forests are located there, too. These forests contain half of the world's reserves of softwood timber. However, Siberia is far from the population and industrial centers of the country.

Russia's huge size presents a major challenge to transporting Siberian resources to areas where they are needed. Except for the Volga, Russia's rivers are not very useful for transportation. Siberia's rivers do not flow toward Russia's most important cities. Instead, they flow north into the Arctic Ocean. In spite of these problems and the bitter-cold winter weather, Russia has found ways to move resources from Siberia. Pipelines carry oil and natural gas, and railroads transport coal to European Russia.

Extracting Russia's resources has created a new challenge—protecting the environment. Some of the world's worst cases of pollution are found in Russia, especially Siberia. Nuclear waste has been dumped into rivers for 40 years. Air pollution from factories is very severe. Besides finding ways to develop its valuable resources, Russia must also consider how to restore polluted areas.

√ Reading Check **Where are most of Russia's oil, natural gas, and coal deposits located?**

Section 3 Assessment

Key Terms
Review the key terms at the beginning of this section. Use each term in a sentence that explains its meaning.

Target Reading Skill
Look at the list of questions you asked. Which ones helped you learn and remember something from this section?

Comprehension and Critical Thinking
1. (a) List Name Western Europe's major natural resources.
(b) Summarize How is water used as a natural resource in Western Europe?
2. (a) Recall Which important natural resources are located in Ukraine?
(b) Draw Conclusions Why is farming important to Ukraine?
3. (a) List Name Russia's major natural resources.
(b) Compare and Contrast How do Western Europe and Russia differ in their use of natural resources?
(c) Draw Conclusions Why is Russia not as wealthy as Western Europe?

Writing Activity
What do you think is the most important natural resource in Europe and Russia? What makes that resource so important? Write a paragraph explaining your choice. Be sure to include a main idea statement in your paragraph.

Writing Tip Before you begin writing, list all the natural resources discussed in the section. Then choose which you think is most important.

Chapter 6 Review and Assessment

◆ Chapter Summary

Section 1: Land and Water

- Europe and Russia are part of Eurasia, the world's largest landmass.
- Both Europe and Russia have plains, uplands, and mountains.
- Europe's major rivers are the Rhine and the Danube, and Russia's is the Volga.

Section 2: Climate and Vegetation

- Oceans and mountains both affect the climates of Europe and Russia.
- The climate regions of Europe and Russia range from Mediterranean to subarctic.
- The natural vegetation of Europe and Russia is as varied as its climate and includes forest, grassland, and tundra.

Ukraine

London

Section 3: Resources and Land Use

- The resources of Western Europe include fertile soil, water, and fossil fuels.
- Eastern Europe has resources similar to those of Western Europe, including coal, oil, and natural gas.
- Russia has abundant mineral, energy, and other resources, with the majority of these resources located in Siberia.

◆ Key Terms

Use each key term below in a sentence that shows the meaning of the term.

1. population density
2. navigable
3. peninsula
4. plateau
5. tributary
6. rain shadow
7. loess
8. tundra
9. permafrost
10. steppes
11. hydroelectric power
12. fossil fuel

Review and Assessment (continued)

◆ Comprehension and Critical Thinking

13. (a) **Identify** Which areas of Europe and Russia are the most densely populated?
 (b) **Summarize** What physical features encouraged people to settle in those areas?
14. (a) **Define** What are the European Central Uplands?
 (b) **List** Name two uses of these uplands.
 (c) **Contrast** How do the Central Uplands differ from the North European Plain?
15. (a) **Name** List two factors that affect the climates of Europe and Russia.
 (b) **Summarize** What effect do large bodies of water have on climate in Europe and Russia?
16. (a) **Describe** Explain what a Mediterranean climate is.
 (b) **Compare and Contrast** How is a Mediterranean climate similar to or different from a subarctic climate?
17. (a) **Identify** What are the major natural resources of Western Europe, of Eastern Europe, and of Russia?
 (b) **Predict** What factors might influence how well a river can be used to transport resources?
 (c) **Identify Cause and Effect** Why are Western Europe's natural resources more fully developed than Russia's natural resources?
18. (a) **List** Name three kinds of fossil fuels.
 (b) **Draw Conclusions** How does the development of natural resources affect the way that people live?

◆ Skills Practice

Using a Precipitation Map In the Skills for Life activity in this chapter, you learned how to use a precipitation map. The steps you followed to learn this skill can be applied to other kinds of special purpose maps.

Review the steps you used to learn the skill. Then turn to the map titled Europe: Natural Resources on page 165. Use the map title and key to read and interpret the map. Then write a conclusion about the information the map contains.

◆ Writing Activity: Geography

Suppose you are visiting a fourth-grade classroom. You have been asked to report to the students on Europe and Russia's geography. Write a brief report on this subject. To get started, write down the various kinds of landforms and bodies of water that are discussed in the chapter. Do the same for the human and natural resources of Europe and Russia. Then explain in your report how life is similar and difficult for the people who live in different regions of Europe and Russia.

MAP MASTER™ Skills Activity

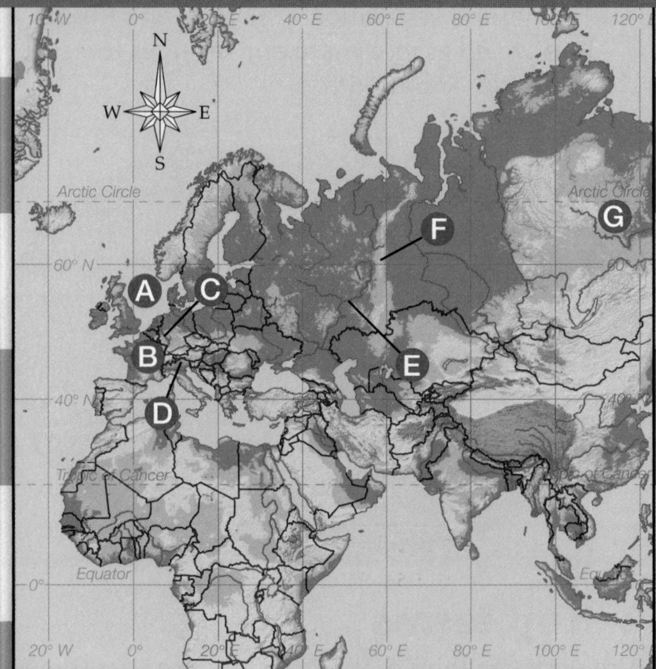

Place Location For each place listed below, write the letter from the map that shows its location.

1. France
2. Ural Mountains
3. Alps
4. Siberia
5. Rhine River
6. Volga River
7. North Sea

Go Online PHSchool.com Use Web Code **ldp-7183** for an **interactive map.**

Standardized Test Prep

Test-Taking Tips

Some questions on standardized tests ask you to make mental maps. Read the passage below. Then follow the tips to answer the sample question.

Ben is playing a trivia game. One of the geography questions asks, "Which mountain range divides Russia between two continents, Europe and Asia?" What is the correct answer?

Choose the letter that best answers the question.

A Kjolen Mountains

B Ural Mountains

~~**C** Pyrenees~~

~~**D** Alps~~

TIP Rule out choices that do not make sense. Then choose the best answer from the remaining choices.

Think It Through You can rule out the Alps and Pyrenees because both are inside Europe. Which sounds more familiar to you, the Ural Mountains or the Kjolen Mountains? The correct answer is an important range and is likely to be a name you have heard. As it turns out, the Kjolen Mountains are in Scandinavia—in northern Europe. The correct answer is B.

TIP Try to picture a physical map of Europe and Russia. Then try to place each of these mountain ranges on your mental map.

Practice Questions

Use the tips above and other tips in this book to help you answer the following questions.

1. Which Russian feature covers more than 4 million square miles (10 million square kilometers)?
   A grasslands **B** taiga
   C polders **D** tundra

2. Because of its location near the Mediterranean Sea, Barcelona's summers are
   A mild and wet.
   B cold and snowy.
   C hot and dry.
   D short and wet.

3. The climate of the northernmost areas of Europe and Russia is called
   A marine west coast.
   B Mediterranean.
   C humid continental.
   D arctic.

4. What is the location of Siberia relative to that of Spain?
   A northeast
   B southeast
   C northwest
   D west

5. The major vegetation region of Europe and Russia that is now mainly used for farming is
   A grasslands.
   B tundra.
   C taiga.
   D Mediterranean.

Use Web Code **lda-7101** for a **Chapter 6 self-test.**

Chapter 7

Europe and Russia: Shaped by History

Chapter Preview

This chapter presents the history of Europe and Russia and shows how that history affects the region to this day.

Target Reading Skill

Clarifying Meaning In this chapter you will focus on clarifying, or better understanding, the meaning of what you read.

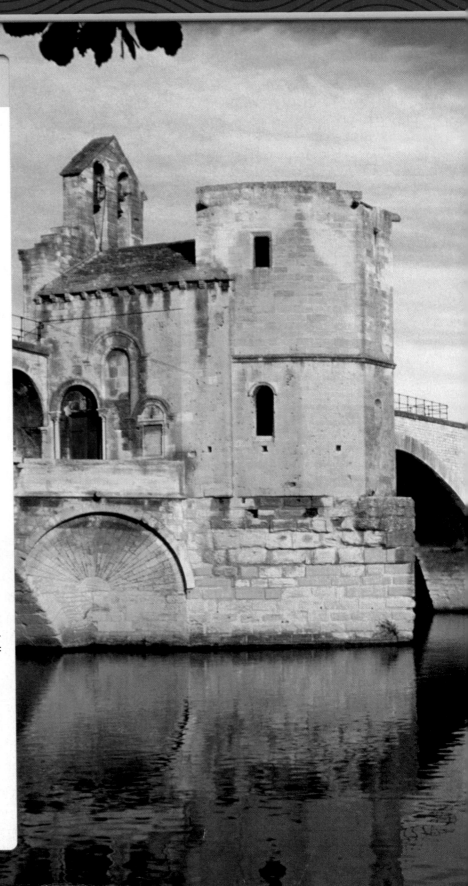

▶ A bridge built in the 1100s still spans the Rhone River in Avignon, France.

Europe About 1300

MAP MASTER™ Skills Activity

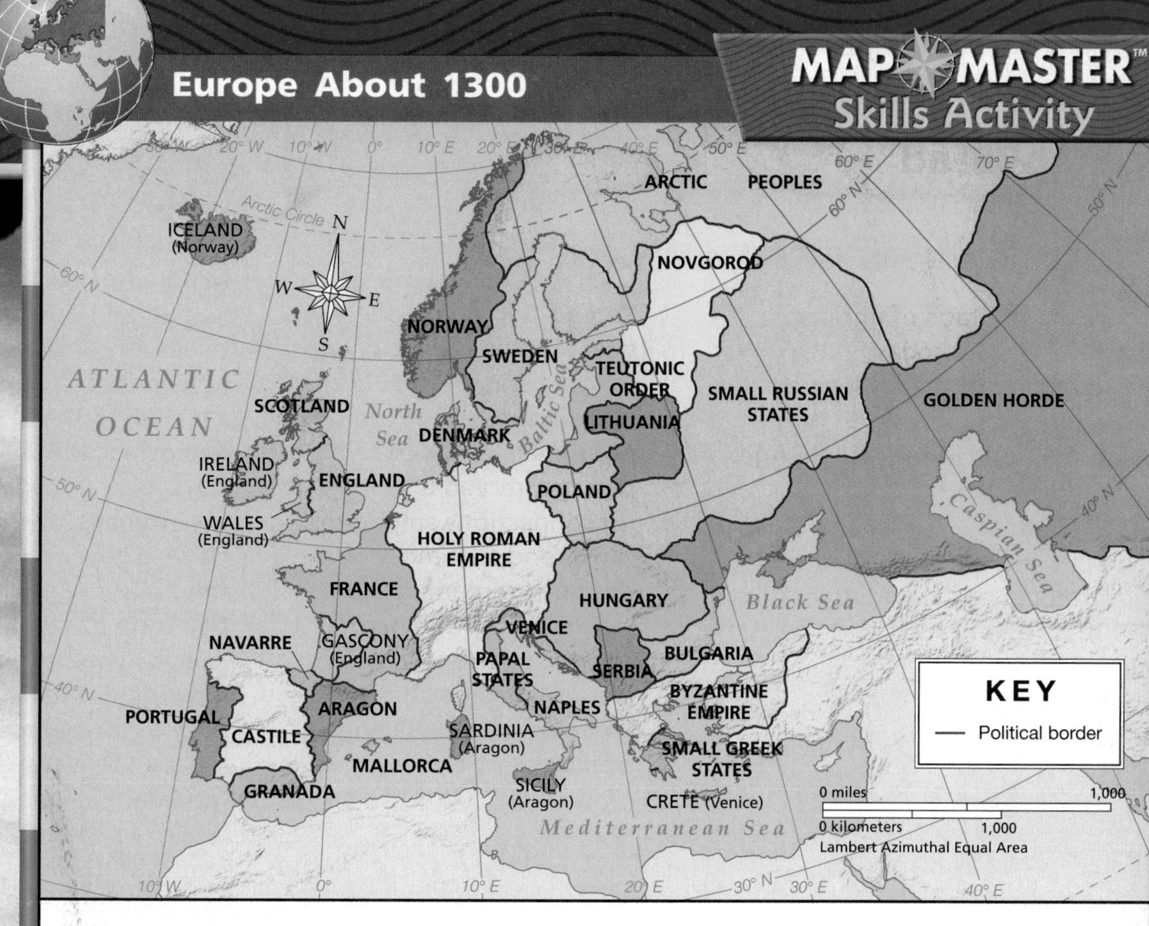

Place In 1300, Europe was divided into a number of states and kingdoms. **Compare and Contrast** Compare this map with the Europe: Political map in the Atlas. Which countries' political borders look similar in 1300 and today? Which are different? Which countries did not exist in 1300? **Analyze Information** How can physical geography help explain why some countries' borders have changed little?

Go Online PHSchool.com Use Web Code **ldp-7211** for step-by-step **map skills practice.**

Section I

From Ancient Greece to the Middle Ages

Prepare to Read

Objectives

In this section you will

1. Learn how the heritage of ancient Greece influences life today.
2. Discover the glory of the ancient Roman Empire.
3. Learn about Europe in the Middle Ages.

Taking Notes

As you read this section, look for information about ancient times and the Middle Ages. Copy the outline below and record your findings in it.

I. The Greek heritage
  A. Democracy
  B.
II.

Target Reading Skill

Reread Rereading is a strategy that can help you to understand words and ideas in the text. If you do not understand a certain passage, reread it to look for connections among the words and sentences. For example, rereading the second paragraph below can make it clear that marathons today are modeled after an event from ancient times.

Key Terms

- **Middle Ages** (MID ul AY juz) *n.* the time between the ancient and modern times, about A.D. 500–1500
- **democracy** (dih MAHK ruh see) *n.* a kind of government in which citizens govern themselves
- **city-state** (SIH tee stayt) *n.* a city with its own government that was both a city and an independent state
- **feudalism** (FYOOD ul iz um) *n.* a system in which land was owned by lords, but held by vassals in return for their loyalty

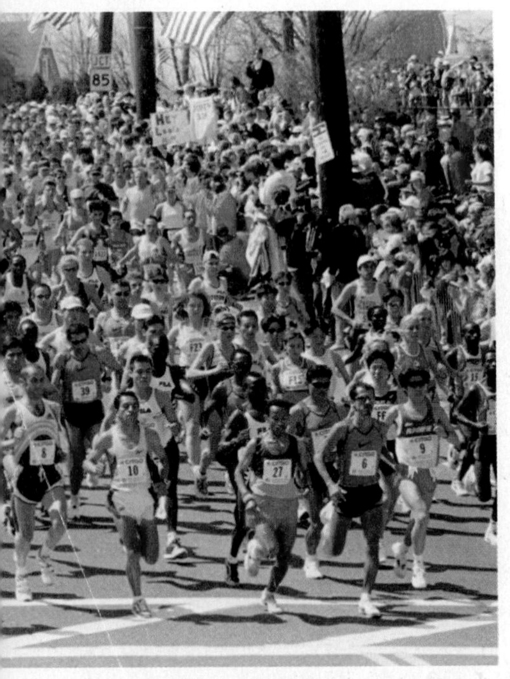

Runners beginning the Boston Marathon

Every April thousands of people from around the world gather in a small Massachusetts town. At noon, they begin a marathon race that requires great strength and willpower. The race ends in the city of Boston, some 26 miles (42 kilometers) away.

The Boston Marathon was inspired by an event that is said to have happened 2,500 years ago in the ancient Greek city of Athens. In 490 B.C., the people of Athens were at war with the Persians. The Athenians defeated the Persians at the Battle of Marathon. To announce their victory, an Athenian soldier named Pheidippides (fuh DIP ih deez) ran all the way to Athens, about 25 miles (40 kilometers) away. Pheidippides shouted, "Rejoice, we conquer!" as he entered the city. Then he died of exhaustion.

The Greeks loved the story, and people all over the world still run marathons. When they do, they show how history lives on. This chapter discusses three periods in the history of Europe and Russia—ancient times, modern times, and the **Middle Ages,** or the time between the ancient and modern times. We will see how the past affects the present in Europe and Russia.

The Greek Heritage

The Athenians and other ancient Greeks were Europe's first great philosophers, historians, poets, and writers. They invented new ideas about how the world worked and how people should live.

The Growth of Democracy One such idea was **democracy**, or a kind of government in which citizens, not a king or other ruler, govern themselves. In ancient times, Greece had more than a hundred **city-states**, or cities with their own governments that were both cities and independent states. The Greek city-states had several different kinds of government. Many of them were democracies.

One of the most famous democratic Greek city-states was Athens. Every citizen there voted on laws and government policies, or the methods and plans a government uses to do its work. Citizens were either elected or chosen at random for government positions.

Democracy was a fresh idea for the Greeks. However, it was not the same as the democracy we practice today. Most Greeks were not citizens. Only freeborn males whose fathers held Athenian citizenship were citizens of Athens. Women, slaves, freed slaves, non-Greeks, and people whose families came from other parts of Greece were not citizens. They could not vote. Still, the Greek idea that citizens should have a voice in their own government had a strong influence on people in later times.

The Golden Age of Athens Democracy reached its highest point in Athens from about 479 to 431 B.C., during Athens' "Golden Age." During that period, the arts, literature, and philosophy also flourished. The Greeks studied the nature of plants, animals, and the human body. In the process, they developed ways of thinking that still influence life today.

Chart Skills

Greek ideas that developed over two thousand years ago still influence societies around the world today. **Note** When were democratic ideals of government formed in Athens? **Apply Information** Which of these ideals can be seen in today's United States government?

The Legacy of the Greeks

Topic	Influence on Modern Society
Drama	Aristotle created the rules for drama in his work *The Poetics*. Today, playwrights and movie scriptwriters still use his ideas.
Architecture	Many modern building designs reflect the common Greek styles known as Ionic, Doric, and Corinthian.
Science	The ancient Greeks introduced many principles of modern medicine, physics, biology, and mathematics.
Politics	The democratic ideals of government by the people, trial by jury, and equality under the law were formed in Athens around 500 B.C.
History	Herodotus collected information from people who remembered the events of the Persian wars. This method of research set the standard for the way history is recorded today.

Empire of Alexander the Great

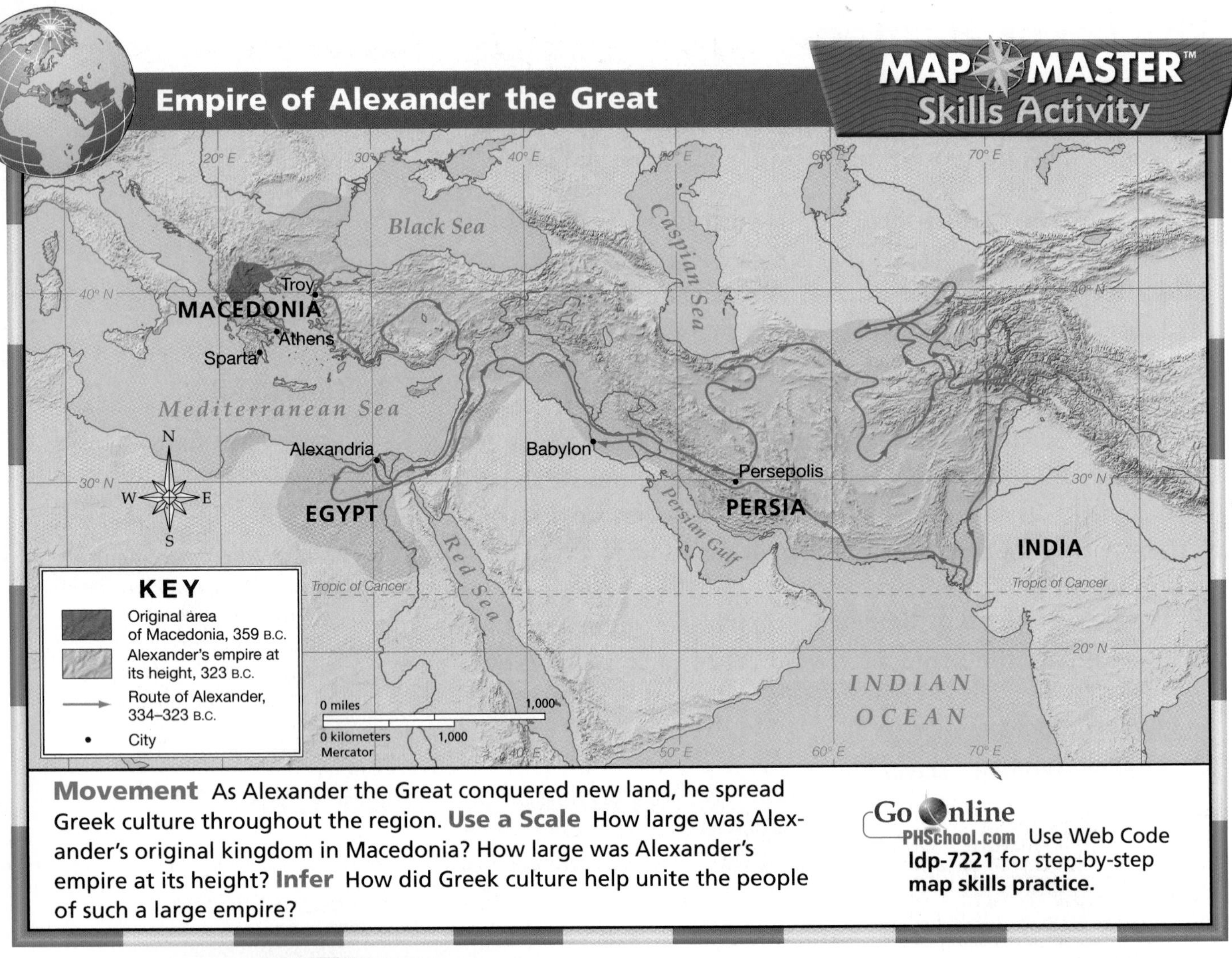

Movement As Alexander the Great conquered new land, he spread Greek culture throughout the region. **Use a Scale** How large was Alexander's original kingdom in Macedonia? How large was Alexander's empire at its height? **Infer** How did Greek culture help unite the people of such a large empire?

Go Online PHSchool.com Use Web Code **ldp-7221** for step-by-step **map skills practice.**

This ancient Italian mosaic shows Alexander the Great in battle.

The Spread of Greek Ideas A young man named Alexander, later called Alexander the Great, helped spread the ideas of the Greeks. At age 20, he became king of Macedonia (mas uh DOH nee uh) in northern Greece. But he was not satisfied with his small kingdom. In 334 B.C., Alexander set out to conquer the world. Within only ten years, he had conquered an empire almost as great in size as the United States is today. An empire is a collection of lands ruled by a single government. The map above shows Alexander's travels and the lands he conquered.

In all his new lands, Alexander established Greek cities, the Greek language, and Greek ideas. At the time of his death in 323 B.C., Greek culture linked the entire Mediterranean world. The people who next ruled the region, the Romans, also borrowed much from the Greeks.

✓ **Reading Check** **What is an empire?**

The Glory of Ancient Rome

Have you ever heard someone say, "All roads lead to Rome" or "Rome was not built in a day"? These expressions refer to the Roman Empire. At its peak, the Roman Empire covered a huge area, and Romans built magnificent cities and structures.

About 50,000 miles (80,500 kilometers) of hard-surfaced roads linked the cities of the Roman Empire. The Roman system of roads was one of the most outstanding transportation networks ever built. Constructed more than 2,000 years ago, many of these roads are still in use today.

Roman Art and Architecture
The Colosseum (above) held as many as 50,000 people for public events. The sculpture below is of Rome's first emperor, Augustus. **Conclude** *What does the art a society produces tell you about its culture and wealth?*

The Romans also built aqueducts, or canals that carried water to the cities from distant sources. Like Roman roads, some of these aqueducts are still in use.

The Pax Romana The Romans began building their empire soon after the death of Alexander the Great. The first emperor of Rome, Augustus, took control in 27 B.C. This began the *Pax Romana* (paks roh MAH nah), which means "Roman peace." It lasted for about 200 years. During the Pax Romana, Rome was the most powerful state in Europe and in the Mediterranean. With Rome in control, these regions remained stable.

Roman Law One of Rome's greatest gifts to the world was a system of written laws. Roman lawmakers were careful and organized. They did not rely on word of mouth to pass their laws from one generation to the next. Instead, they wrote the laws down. When a judge made a decision, he based it on written law. His decision was also put in writing to guide other judges. After a while, the law became so complex that it was difficult to learn. Various groups were appointed to gather the laws together into an organized system. Today, the legal system of almost every European country reflects the organization of ancient Roman law.

Roman laws protected all citizens. At first, citizens included only free people who lived in Rome. In time, the term came to include people all over the empire. Roman laws thus protected the rights of all citizens, not just the powerful and wealthy. Modern laws and government are based on this idea.

Christian Art
This mosaic of Jesus, at the right, decorates the dome of a monastery in Daphni, Greece. Symbols of Christianity—a cross and a fish—are shown below. Early Christians used the symbol of the fish because each letter in the Greek word for fish, *ichthys*, stood for a Christian phrase.
Analyze Information *Why might early Christians have depended on symbols to express their faith, rather than doing so openly?*

Beginnings of Christianity Roman emperors allowed a certain amount of religious freedom within the empire. Jews were allowed to practice their religion as long as they obeyed Roman law. For centuries, the Jewish people had believed that God would send them a messiah, or a savior, who would free them from outside rule. Many Jews were content to cooperate with the Romans, but others began resisting Roman rule. In present-day Israel, the Romans crushed their attempts to revolt.

In about A.D. 30 a spiritual leader, named Jesus of Nazareth, traveled and preached throughout the region. His followers believed that God was acting through him. They called him Jesus Christ. *Christ* meant "someone anointed, or a savior sent by God." After the Romans put Jesus to death for troublemaking, his followers began spreading his teachings. They eventually became known as Christians. At first, they were treated poorly by Roman emperors.

After three centuries, Christianity had become so strong that a Roman emperor, Constantine, became a Christian. He encouraged the spread of Christianity. It became the official religion of the Roman Empire. Many people who had suffered under Roman rule turned to the church for comfort at this time.

Target Skill
Reread
Reread the paragraphs under Beginnings of Christianity to understand the phrase "spiritual leader."

The Decline of Rome Over time, it grew more difficult to govern the huge Roman empire. Germanic invaders outside the empire grew strong and broke through Roman lines of defense. Sometimes they terrorized and looted Rome itself.

To fight the invaders, the empire needed more and more soldiers. The government raised taxes to pay for the warfare. This hurt the empire's economy. The empire had grown too large for one person to govern, so it was divided into two empires, one in the eastern Mediterranean and one in the west. The eastern empire remained strong. But the western one continued to weaken. In the 450s A.D., invaders attacked Rome itself. Finally in A.D. 476, invaders overthrew the Roman emperor, and the western Roman Empire collapsed.

✓ Reading Check **What was the Pax Romana?**

Europe in the Middle Ages

The collapse of the Roman Empire in western Europe led to a time of uncertainty and confusion. The legal system of the Roman Empire no longer protected people. The invading peoples did gradually settle down and establish kingdoms. But no kingdom was able to provide the unity and security that the Roman Empire had provided. Europe entered a long period of turmoil and warfare. Government, law, and trade broke down.

In such a time of chaos, people needed order and security. Eventually, a new structure of European society arose. It was based on a new political system and the Roman Catholic Church. The Roman Catholic Church was the name for the Christian church in the former western Roman Empire.

Details from books and calendars dating from the 1400s show farming scenes at medieval manors.

Feudalism To bring about order, people in western Europe needed a way to organize their society. The political system that developed is called **feudalism,** or a system in which land was owned by kinds of lords, but held by vassals in return for their loyalty. In each country, the king held the highest position. His greatest obligation was to provide security for his kingdom, which meant that he needed soldiers to build an army. Nobles provided the king with knights and foot soldiers. In exchange for knights and soldiers—as well as for the nobles' loyalty—the king, also called a lord, gave land to the nobles, also called vassals.

The noble landholders needed people to work their estates, or manors. They gave peasants the right to farm their land in exchange for the larger portion of the crops and any other income from the land. In exchange, they maintained order, enforced laws, and protected the peasants. This economic system is called manorialism. It provided a basis for the feudal political system.

Cathedral of Notre Dame
The Notre Dame cathedral in Paris, France, dates from the 1100s. It is one of the largest and most spectacular in the world. A carved figure from the roof of the cathedral is shown at the right. **Analyze Images** *What features from the cathedral do you think were meant to inspire awe in the people who worshipped there?*

The peasants who worked the land were called serfs. Serfs were not free people. They were bound to the land and could not leave without their lord's permission. But serfs were not slaves. They could not be sold away from the land.

Christianity Religious faith helped give people a sense of security and community during the Middle Ages. Most people's lives centered on the Roman Catholic Church. Religious ceremonies marked the major events in the calendar, as well as important events in the lives of individual members.

Wealthy nobles and kings donated large amounts of money for the construction of grand cathedrals, churches, and monasteries. In a world where most people's lives were marked by hardship and uncertainty, these grand buildings were awe-inspiring. They soared higher than any other buildings nearby. Their brilliant stained-glass windows taught religious stories to peasants who were unable to read.

Europe Begins to Change As the centuries passed, life in Europe changed. Trade increased. Towns offered excitement and opportunity to the merchants and other tradespeople who lived there. Towns grew into cities. By the A.D. 1400s, a new way of life centered around cities had begun to develop in Europe.

✓ Reading Check **How did serfs differ from slaves?**

Section 1 Assessment

Key Terms
Review the key terms at the beginning of this section. Use each term in a sentence that explains its meaning.

Target Reading Skill
What word or idea did you clarify by rereading certain passages?

Comprehension and Critical Thinking
1. **(a) Recall** What kind of government did ancient Athens have?
(b) Contrast How was the government of ancient Athens different from today's United States government?
2. **(a) List** What were the most important lasting ideas of the ancient Romans?
(b) Sequence Explain how the Roman Empire declined.
3. **(a) Name** Which institutions brought order and security to people in the Middle Ages?
(b) Summarize How did the feudal system work?
(c) Draw Conclusions Who benefited the most from feudalism? Explain.

Writing Activity
Suppose you are a Roman governor in Britain, far from your home and family in Rome. Write a journal entry describing the things you miss about Rome.

Writing Tip Remember to write your description in the first person, using the pronouns *I* or *we*. Use vivid words to describe Rome. You might write about things such as Rome's weather, art, and architecture.

Section 2 Renaissance and the Age of Revolution

Prepare to Read

Objectives

In this section you will

1. Discover what the Renaissance was like at its peak.
2. Examine the effects of increased trade and stronger rulers in the Renaissance.
3. Learn about revolutions in government and science in the 1600s and 1700s.

Taking Notes

As you read this section, look for details about the Renaissance and the Age of Revolution. Copy the chart below and record your findings in it.

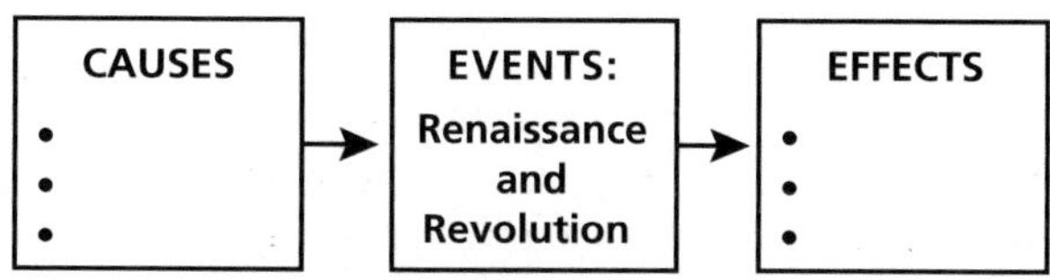

Target Reading Skill

Paraphrase When you pharaphrase, you restate what you have read in your own words. You could paraphrase the first two paragraphs of this section this way: "Marco Polo recorded his world travels in a book that influenced Christopher Columbus." As you read, paraphrase the information following each red or blue heading.

Key Terms

- **Renaissance** (REN uh sahns) *n.* a period of European history that included the rebirth of interest in learning and art
- **monarch** (MAHN urk) *n.* the ruler of a kingdom or empire, such as a king or a queen
- **revolution** (rev uh LOO shun) *n.* a far-reaching change
- **colony** (KAHL uh nee) *n.* a territory ruled by another nation

In about A.D. 1324 an elderly explorer named Marco Polo said before he died, "I have only told the half of what I saw!" Marco Polo indeed had an interesting life. For a time, he was a messenger of the great Mongol (MAHN gul) emperor Kublai Khan (KOO bly kahn), ruler of China. Polo also traveled across burning deserts and sailed south of the Equator. He visited the Spice Islands, which were the sources of the spices cinnamon, nutmeg, and cloves that Europeans valued. He earned great riches, only to be robbed on his way home to Italy.

Marco Polo and Kublai Khan

These stories were published in a book we know today as *The Travels of Marco Polo*. Two hundred years later, Marco Polo's book inspired Christopher Columbus, another explorer. When Columbus sailed west from Europe, he was searching for a new route to the rich lands Marco Polo had described: China, Japan, and India.

Glories of the Renaissance

Columbus's search for a new route to the riches of the East was only one example of the movement sweeping Europe. The changes began in Italy in the 1300s and spread over the continent. Traders bought and sold goods across the region. The rich grew even richer. They had the time to enjoy art and learning—and the money to support artists and scholars. This period is called the **Renaissance** (REN uh sahns), or the rebirth of interest in learning and art. The Renaissance reached its peak in the 1500s.

Looking to the Past In trying to understand the world around them, Renaissance thinkers re-examined, or looked at once again, the ideas of Greek and Roman thinkers. People learned again about the ancient world's great poetry, plays, ideas, buildings, and sculpture. What they learned changed them. Writers began writing fresh, powerful poetry. The wealthy built glorious new buildings and filled them with breathtaking paintings.

Humanism: A New View Recall that during the Middle Ages much of Europe was in chaos, and religion was a way to bring order to people's lives. Renaissance thinkers began to focus on improving this world rather than hoping for a better life after death. This new approach to knowledge was called humanism (HYOO muh niz um). Humanistic thinkers emphasized the importance of human nature and the abilities of human beings to change the world.

Humanism affected every part of Renaissance life. For example, in the early Middle Ages, statues had been carved as stiff symbols. In contrast, during the Renaissance period artists carved lifelike statues.

Works of Michelangelo
Michelangelo used themes from the Bible in many of his art works. Above is his sculpture of Moses. As an architect, Michelangelo worked on the dome of St. Peter's, the church of the Pope, in Rome. **Compare and Contrast** *Compare the photo of St. Peter's with that of Notre Dame on page 182. How are they alike? How are they different?*

An Important Renaissance Artist The Italian Michelangelo (my kul AN juh loh) was one such artist. Michelangelo was an accomplished painter, poet, architect, and sculptor. His lifelike statues were remarkably realistic and detailed. In some, you can see veins bulging in the hands. Or the drape of a cloak across the sculpted person looks so real that it appears to be made of cloth rather than of marble. Like other Renaissance artists, Michelangelo's work gave art a new importance. During the Renaissance, the role of art changed.

Art came to be seen as an important way to understand man, God, and nature. You can read about another important Renaissance figure, Leonardo da Vinci (lee uh NAHR doh duh VIN chee) in the box below.

Printing Spreads the Renaissance An important invention encouraged the spread of the Renaissance. Around 1450, the printing press was invented in Germany. Before printed books, books were made by carefully copying them by hand—a process that took a very long time. With the printing press, books could be made quickly.

Printed books made in large quantities could reach far more people than could books copied by hand. For that reason, the spread of printing had two important effects. First, it increased literacy, or the ability of people to read and write. Second, it allowed ideas of the Renaissance, written in books, to spread to large numbers of people. To understand the difference that the printing press made, consider this example. Before the printing press, there were a few thousand hand-copied books in Europe. Within 50 years after the printing press was invented, there were about 9 million books in Europe.

✓ Reading Check **What is literacy?**

Leonardo da Vinci: Renaissance Man

◀ Painting
Leonardo's *Mona Lisa* (1503–1506) is one of the most famous paintings in the world. The lady is believed to have been a merchant's wife. The style of her portrait and the misty background behind her continue to influence artists today.

Inventions ▶
Leonardo built machines of all kinds, but was especially interested in the possibility of human flight. He studied birds and drew imaginary flying machines. This helicopter-like machine, designed in 1487, was inspired by a child's toy.

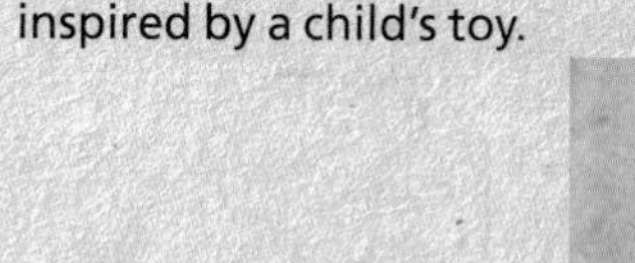

Science ▶
Leonardo studied the anatomy of the living and the dead to learn how the human body works. He often referred to his studies, like this one done in 1510, to make his paintings more realistic.

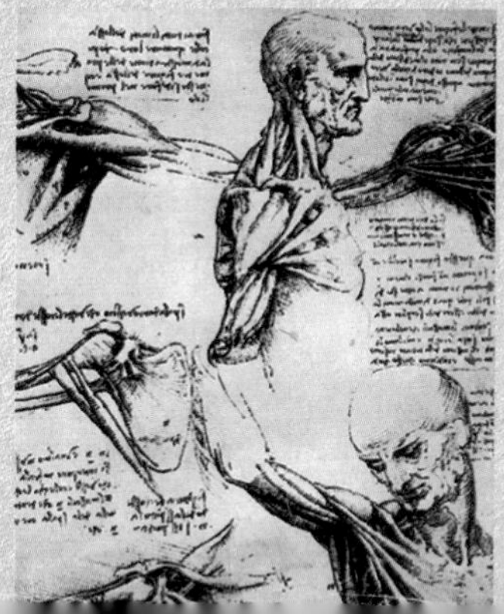

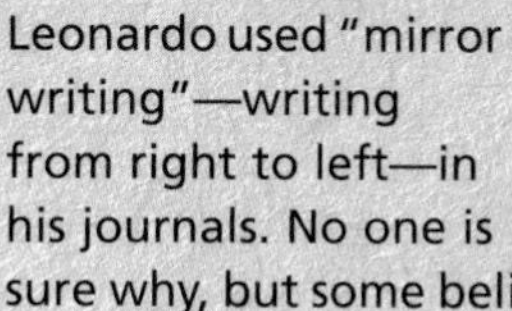

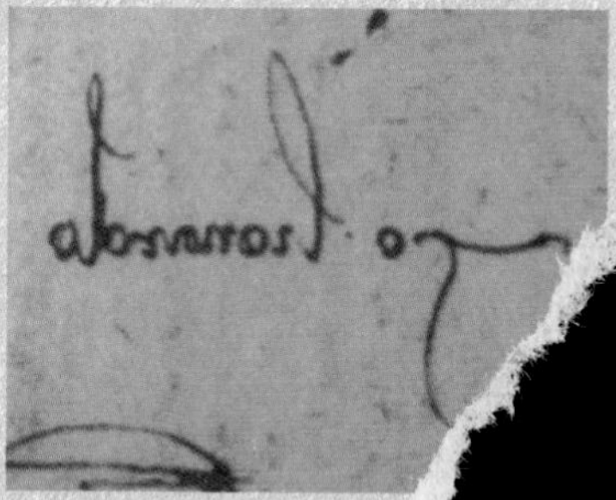

Mirror Writing ▶
Leonardo used "mirror writing"—writing from right to left—in his journals. No one is sure why, but some believe that because he wa
he found it easier to write from right to left
says "lo, Lionardo" or "I, Leonardo."

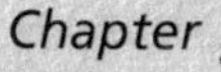

Diagram Skills

By the mid-1400s, European merchants like the one shown here sold a wide variety of goods, some from as far away as China. **Identify** What items in the diagram were made in Germany? **Analyze Information** What kinds of people most likely bought things from merchants such as this one? Why do you think so?

Woolen cloth came from the British Isles, while other kinds of cloth were made in France.
Dishes of various metals were made in present-day Germany.
Leather goods, such as shoes, came from towns in Spain.

More Trade, Stronger Rulers

During the Renaissance, traders began to travel more often outside of Europe. In the 1400s, Portuguese explorers traveled along the western coast of Africa. There they traded in gold, ivory, and slaves. This trade was very profitable. Some Portuguese traders traveled as far east as the Indian Ocean.

Then in 1492, a discovery brought even more possibilities for wealth. While searching for a shortcut to the Indian Ocean spice trade, Christopher Columbus landed in the Americas. He claimed the lands for Spain. Other Spanish explorers soon followed.

While Portugal grew rich from spices, Spain grew wealthy from American gold and silver. Other European countries grew envious. By the 1600s, France, England, and the Netherlands took a growing share of the riches to be gained from overseas trade and settlement.

The Effects of Trade Europeans raced to the Americas in search of wealth. Precious metals, such as gold and silver, and trade goods, such as fur and tobacco, poured into Europe. Much of the wealth went to European **monarchs** (MAHN urks), or rulers such as kings and queens. Some of it went to traders and merchants. These people formed a new social class. They became the middle class, the class between the privileged nobles and the lowly peasants or farmers. The taxes paid by prosperous merchants and traders made monarchs even wealthier. Soon, kings no longer needed the support of feudal lords. Feudalism declined, local lords grew weaker, and kings gained power.

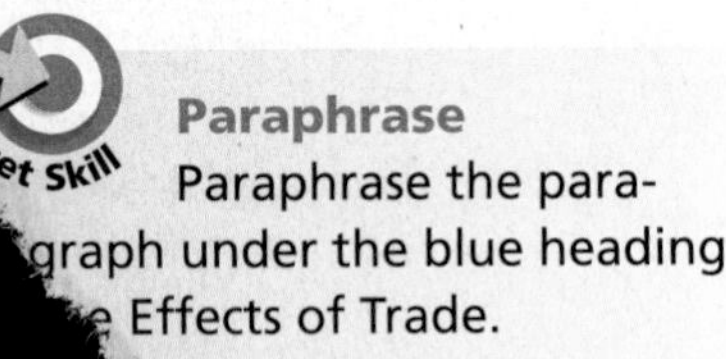

Paraphrase
Paraphrase the paragraph under the blue heading [...]e Effects of Trade.

The Age of Monarchs The period in European history from the 1600s to the 1700s can be called the Age of Monarchs. During this time, many European monarchs became absolute monarchs, meaning that they exercised great power over their subjects.

One such monarch was France's King Louis (LOO ee) XIV, who ruled from 1643 to 1715. One of Europe's most powerful kings, Louis XIV ruled at a time when France was a leading world power. Like other kings of his time, Louis was an absolute monarch; that is, he exercised complete power over his subjects. As he said, "I am the state." His wishes were law, and no one dared to disagree with him. Like other European monarchs, Louis believed that his power to rule came from God. To oppose him was the same as opposing God.

Louis used his power to make people pay heavy taxes. These taxes, in part, paid for his very expensive lifestyle. But Louis also wanted to make France strong. Other rulers wanted their countries to be strong as well. Over time, these monarchs made their countries stronger and more unified. As these changes took place, people began thinking again about government. Should the monarchs have such great power? What should the role of the government be?

✓ Reading Check **What is an absolute monarch?**

A Wealthy Monarch
Louis XIV, king of France, rides a horse in this painting from the mid-1600s. He built the palace of Versailles, shown below, to be his personal residence as well as the center of France's government. **Analyze Images** *How does Versailles reflect Louis XIV's lifestyle? What does it say about his vision of government?*

Citizen Heroes

Chemistry and Revolution

Antoine Laurent Lavoisier (1743–1794) is considered one of the founders of modern chemistry. He was the first scientist to recognize oxygen as an element, and he gave it its name. He was also an important public servant. He built workhouses, savings banks, and canals to improve the lives of people in his district.

During the French Revolution, people turned against Lavoisier and other people who were wealthy or had been part of the government. In 1793, Lavoisier was arrested and given an unfair trial. On May 8, 1794, he and 28 others were executed. Lavoisier is shown in this 1788 painting by Jacques-Louis David with his wife Marie-Anne, who helped her husband in his lab.

Revolutions in Government

The 1600s and 1700s are often called the Age of Revolution. A **revolution** is a far-reaching change. European thought, beliefs, and ways of life all changed. This period was the beginning of the modern age of science and democracy that we know today.

New Ideas in Government One sign of revolutionary change in Europe was that people began questioning their governments. People began to believe that kings should not have all the power. For example, in England, King Charles I refused to share power with Parliament (PAHR luh munt), the elected legislature. Following a civil war, he was put on trial and put to death. After this period in England's history, no ruler could again claim absolute power or ignore the law.

The American Revolution The idea that people should have a say in government spread to North America, where Great Britain had several colonies. A **colony** is a territory ruled by another nation, usually one far away. In 1776, 13 of the colonies rebelled against the British king because they felt that the laws applied to them were not fair. The colonists defeated the British and formed the independent nation of the United States.

In 1789, 13 years after the Americans declared their independence, a revolution occurred in France. In order to create a democracy, the French people used extreme violence to overthrow their government. They did this in the name of freedom, equality, and brotherhood. The French Revolution created chaos in France. It also inspired new, radical theories about political and economic change. Ideas born in the French Revolution continued to influence Europeans long after the revolution ended.

✓ Reading Check **What revolutions took place during the 1600s and 1700s?**

This painting captures the scene of angry colonists pulling down a statue of British King George III after declaring independence in 1776.

Revolutions in Science

For centuries, Europeans had based their view of the world on their religious faith. Scientists had studied nature to explain how the world fit with their religious beliefs. Slowly, scientists began to change their approach. Influenced by humanism and the Renaissance, scientists began to observe nature carefully and record only what they observed. Then they based their theories on facts instead of making the facts fit their religious beliefs. This change in outlook is called the Scientific Revolution.

The Scientific Method It is difficult to pinpoint the exact beginning of the Scientific Revolution. Yet many sources agree that it started at least in part with the work of a scientist named Copernicus (koh PUR nih kus), who lived during the Middle Ages. Before Copernicus, people believed that Earth was the center of the universe. Copernicus shocked the world by suggesting that the sun was the center of the universe, and that Earth moved around the sun. Over time, he was proved to be right. His theories sparked other scientists to look at the world in different ways.

Copernicus and other scientists needed new procedures to test their ideas. These procedures make up what is called the scientific method, in which ideas are tested with experiments and observations. Scientists will accept an idea only if it has been tested repeatedly. The chart on the right shows the steps of the scientific method. Using the scientific method, scientists made dramatic advances.

Other Scientific Developments Some of the greatest advances were in the fields of chemistry and medicine. Before the 1600s, chemistry as we know it today did not exist. Instead, the main idea of chemistry was that any metal could be turned into gold. A scientist named Robert Boyle changed that. Boyle's ideas about temperatures and the behavior of gases set the stage for modern chemistry.

New ideas in medicine came about at that same time. People made efforts to learn about the human body, both inside and out. An English doctor named William Harvey discovered how blood circulates inside the body. The Dutch inventor Antonie van Leeuwenhoek (ahn TOH ne van LAY vun hook) developed techniques for making lenses for microscopes. He used his microscopes to study small lifeforms, such as insects and bacteria.

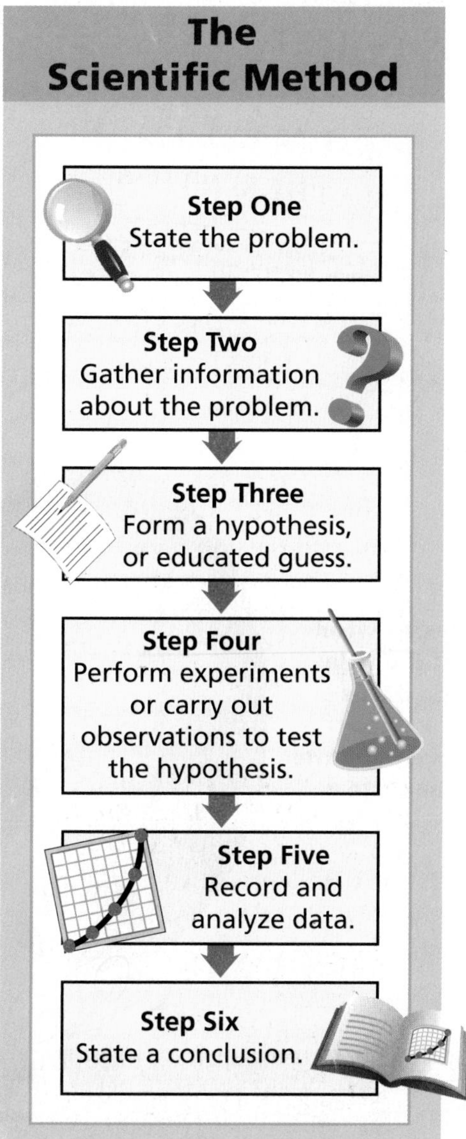

The Scientific Method
Step One
State the problem.
Step Two
Gather information about the problem.
Step Three
Form a hypothesis, or educated guess.
Step Four
Perform experiments or carry out observations to test the hypothesis.
Step Five
Record and analyze data.
Step Six
State a conclusion.

Diagram Skills

Though the scientific method is simple, it greatly changed the way science is done. **Explain** What is a hypothesis? How is it tested? **Apply Information** What was Copernicus's hypothesis about the universe?

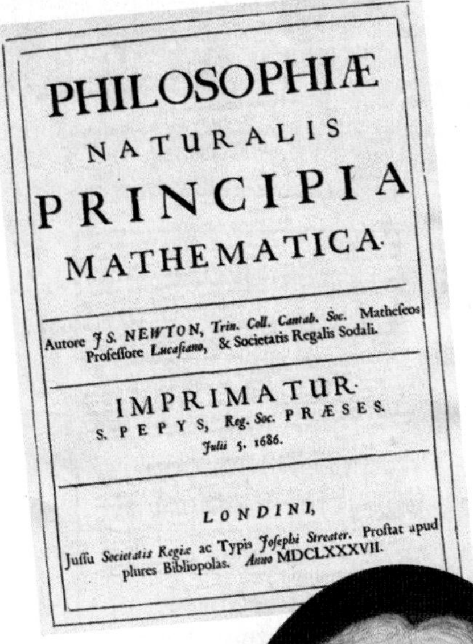

PHILOSOPHIÆ
NATURALIS
PRINCIPIA
MATHEMATICA.

Autore J. S. NEWTON, Trin. Coll. Cantab. Soc. Matheseos Professore Lucasiano, & Societatis Regalis Sodali.

IMPRIMATUR.
S. PEPYS, Reg. Soc. PRÆSES.
Julii 5. 1686.

LONDINI,
Jussu Societatis Regiæ ac Typis Josephi Streater. Prostat apud plures Bibliopolas. Anno MDCLXXXVII.

Isaac Newton and the title page of his book about gravity and the solar system

These and other developments led to a new way of thinking among scientists. With each new discovery, scientists began to see the universe as a giant machine. They believed this machine worked in a regular way, with set rules. They also believed that they could eventually learn everything about it.

Isaac Newton One of the greatest scientists of the Scientific Revolution was Isaac Newton. You may have heard a story about Newton, in which he saw an apple fall from a tree. He wondered if the force that pulled the apple to the ground was the same force that kept the moon in orbit around Earth.

To test this idea, Newton invented a new branch of mathematics called calculus (KAL kyoo lus). He had to invent calculus because the mathematics that existed at the time could not be used to explain his ideas. Using calculus and a few simple laws, Newton was able to demonstrate how the moon and planets move. Newton's laws and his mathematics are still used in science today.

By the end of the Age of Revolution, the nations of Europe were bustling with trade and bursting with new scientific ideas. Europe was about to begin a new kind of revolution. This time it would be an economic one.

✓ Reading Check **What did Isaac Newton invent?**

Section 2 Assessment

Key Terms

Review the key terms at the beginning of this section. Use each term in a sentence that explains its meaning.

Target Reading Skill

Paraphrase the text under the blue heading Isaac Newton above.

Comprehension and Critical Thinking

1. (a) **Define** What was the Renaissance?
(b) **Identify Causes** What invention helped spread the ideas of the Renaissance?

2. (a) **Recall** What was Christopher Columbus searching for when he landed in the Americas?
(b) **Identify Effects** How did Europeans' desire for wealth lead to voyages of exploration?

3. (a) **Explain** Why are the 1600s and 1700s called the Age of Revolution?
(b) **Summarize** How did the thinking of European scientists change during this period?
(c) **Make Inferences** How did humanism and advances in art help bring about changes in science?

Writing Activity

Marco Polo's writings excited readers and made them want to explore the places he had visited. Think about a place that you have visited. What makes it special? Describe in detail the features that you especially liked. Write about the place in a way that would make a reader want to go there.

For: An activity about Leonardo da Vinci
Visit: PHSchool.com
Web Code: ldd-7202

Section 3 Industrial Revolution and Nationalism

Prepare to Read

Objectives

In this section you will

1. Learn how the Industrial Revolution changed peoples' lives.
2. Examine how nationalism and war can be related.

Taking Notes

As you read this section, look for details about how life changed as a result of the Industrial Revolution. Copy the chart below and record your findings in it.

Changes During the Industrial Revolution		
Production • •	Society • •	Government • •

Target Reading Skill

Summarize You can better understand a text if you pause to restate the key points briefly in your own words. A good summary includes important events and details, notes the order in which the events occurred, and makes connections between the events or details. Because a summary leaves out less important details, it is shorter than the original text.

Key Terms

- **Industrial Revolution** (in DUS tree ul rev uh LOO shun) *n.* the life-changing period in the 1800s when products began to be made by machines in factories
- **textile** (TEKS tyl) *n.* a cloth product
- **imperialism** (im PIHR ee ul iz um) *n.* the political and economic control of one country by another
- **nationalism** (NASH uh nul iz um) *n.* pride in one's country
- **alliance** (uh LY uns) *n.* an agreement between countries to protect and defend each other

It was dawn. Thick, black smoke rose from the tall smokestack of the factory. The smoke and the roar of machines signaled that the factory workday had begun. Inside, women and children worked at rows of machines that wove cotton thread into cloth. Their work was dirty, noisy, and dangerous. The day before, a worker had severely injured his hand in a machine. Today, another worker stood in his place. Both were only 13 years old. But the machines kept going. Workers fed them thread for 12 hours every day—six days a week. Vacations did not exist, and there were few breaks.

Workers grind razors at a factory in Sheffield, England, in 1866.

Factories like this one could be found all across Europe in the early 1800s. They were a result of the **Industrial Revolution,** a life-changing period when goods changed from being made by hand to being made by machines in factories. Industrialization caused great suffering at first, but in time brought an easier way of life to people all over the world.

Improvements in Making Cloth For generations, people used spinning wheels like the one above to spin cloth. After the Industrial Revolution, huge machines called "spinning mules" in factories like the one at the right produced cloth cheaper and more quickly. **Evaluate Information** *How do you think the shift from using simple tools to complex machinery affected the average worker?*

The Industrial Revolution

Until the late 1700s, nearly all goods were made by hand. People made what they needed, or bought it from a craftsperson or at a store for a high price. The Industrial Revolution—a revolution in the way goods were made and in the ways people lived and worked—changed all that.

Changes in Production The first machines of the Industrial Revolution were invented in Great Britain to speed up the weaving of **textiles, or cloth products.** Large factories housed the machines. Factory work was very different from work done by hand. For example, a person weaving cloth would first spin the thread, then dye it, and then weave it. He or she might work on every step of the finished product. In contrast, in a factory each worker tended a specific machine, which performed a specific job over and over again. The machine worked much faster than a person could. This meant that goods could be made quickly and much more cheaply than they had been by hand.

This new factory system was improved by new inventions in machinery, transportation, and communication. Other new inventions also brought about improvements in agriculture. Food could be grown in larger quantities by fewer people, and transported quickly to supply factory workers in the cities.

Changes in Society Because Great Britain's factories were so successful, business people in other countries began to build factories. By 1900, factories produced many of the goods made in the United States and Western Europe.

The Industrial Revolution changed life in almost every way. Inventions created to fuel the Industrial Revolution were soon used in everyday life. Improved transportation meant that people could travel more quickly and often more cheaply. Better communications meant that people separated by long distances could talk to one another almost instantly.

Yet not all of the effects of the Industrial Revolution were positive. For hundreds of years, families had farmed the land. Now they moved to industrial centers to work in factories. Cities grew rapidly. People lived in cramped, dirty housing. Because of unclean and crowded conditions, diseases spread rapidly.

Factory work was also difficult. Factory owners took advantage of workers. Wages were low. Factory conditions were not safe. However, workers slowly began to form labor unions and to demand better working conditions. In the early 1900s, governments began passing laws to protect workers. Over time, conditions improved and wages rose. The Industrial Revolution helped give working people a greater voice in government. Many European nations became more democratic as a result.

Timeline Skills

Important inventions of the late 1700s and early 1800s had a major impact on industry and society. **Note** When was the spinning jenny invented? **Apply Information** Which inventions helped improve the process of making textiles?

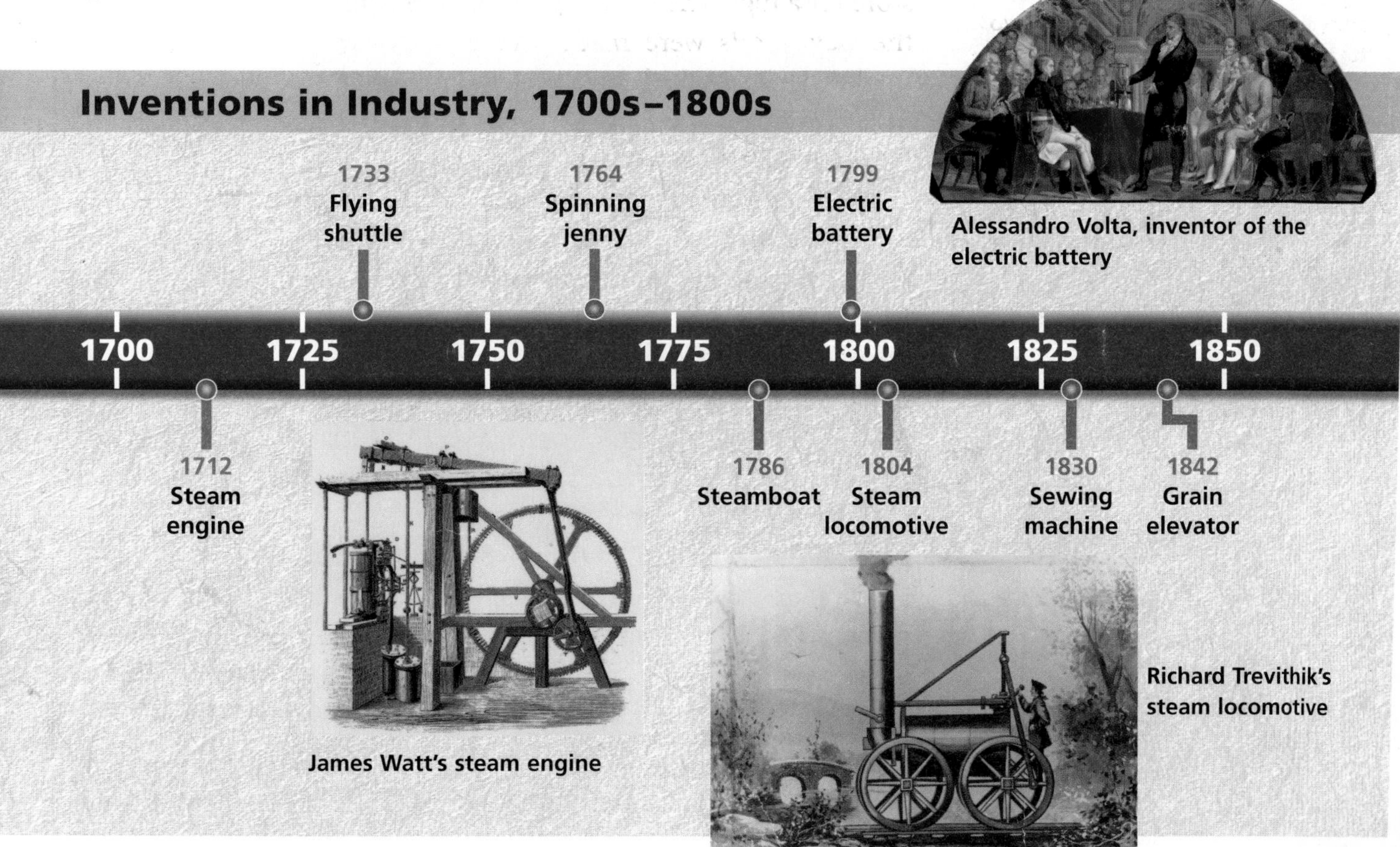

Alessandro Volta, inventor of the electric battery

James Watt's steam engine

Richard Trevithik's steam locomotive

Textile Mill

Weaving, or making cloth from threads or yarns, is one of the oldest crafts in the world. It was also the first to take advantage of the inventions that fed the Industrial Revolution. Water, and then steam, powered the first textile factories and their machines. In England, this new form of manufacturing produced goods for trade and export, and wealth and power for the nation.

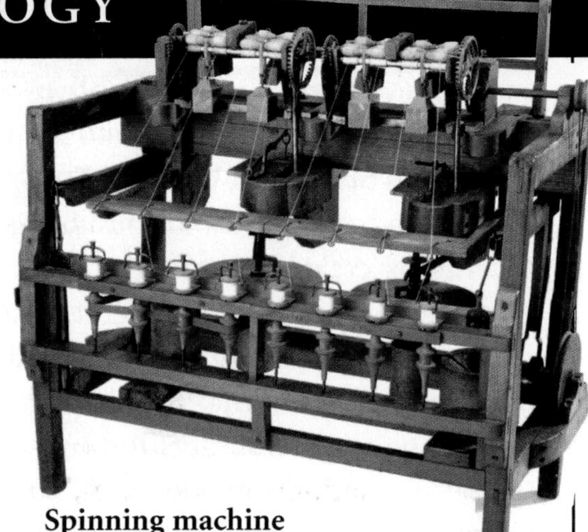

Spinning machine
A water-powered spinning machine (called a water frame) was invented by Sir Richard Arkwright.

Weaving loom

Some jobs were done by children.

The bell is used to signal the beginning and end of the workday, and the lunch break.

4 Belts, attached to pulleys, power the mill's many machines.

Spindles hold the cotton thread.

3 Gears transfer power to different parts of the mill.

1 Water flows under the mill, turning the wheel.

2 As the wheel turns, it spins the gears.

Water wheel
Flowing water turns the mill wheel, driving gears that cause the overhead shafts to turn. These shafts drive belts that power the machines.

ANALYZING IMAGES
Near what geographical feature must this textile mill have been located?

Changes in Government At the same time, though, European governments were becoming more aggressive abroad. Beginning in the 1600s, many European nations had followed the policy of **imperialism,** or taking over other countries and turning them into colonies. Colonies provided the raw materials, such as cotton, wood, and metals, that industry needed. Colonies also supplied markets for European goods. Finally, European countries hoped to spread their influence over people in those colonies by converting them to their own religions.

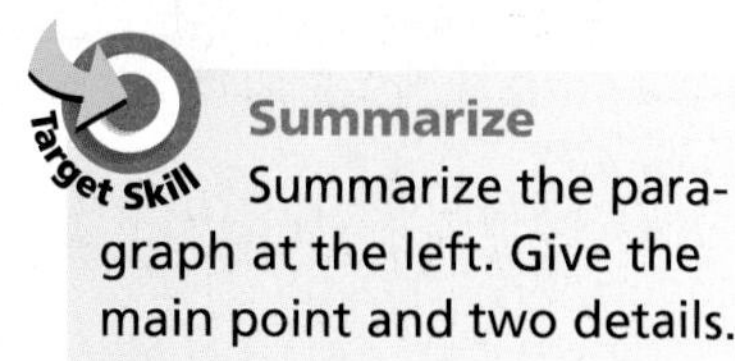

Summarize Summarize the paragraph at the left. Give the main point and two details.

The late 1800s are called the Age of Imperialism. During this time, the nations of Belgium, France, Italy, Spain, Portugal, Germany, and Great Britain colonized most of Africa. Some of these countries also took over much of Southeast Asia and many South Pacific islands. In time, struggles among the colonial powers would bring disaster to Europe.

✓ Reading Check **Why are the late 1800s called the Age of Imperialism?**

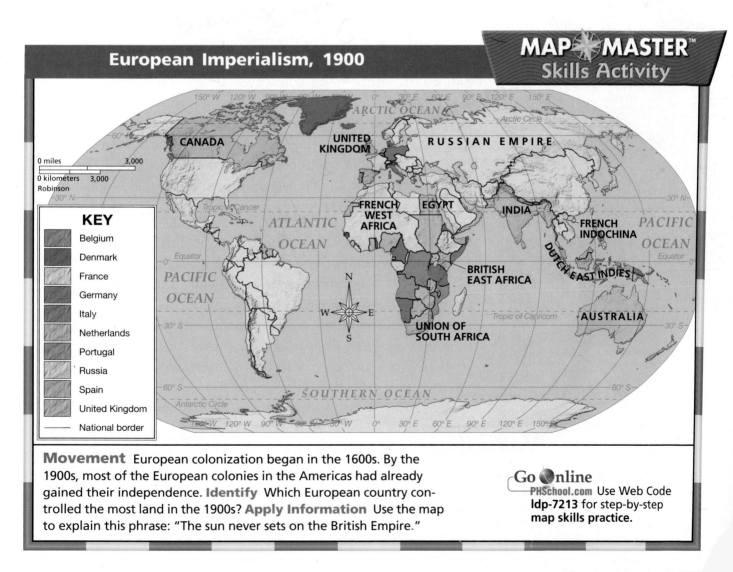

European Imperialism, 1900

MAP MASTER™ Skills Activity

KEY

- Belgium
- Denmark
- France
- Germany
- Italy
- Netherlands
- Portugal
- Russia
- Spain
- United Kingdom
- National border

Movement European colonization began in the 1600s. By the 1900s, most of the European colonies in the Americas had already gained their independence. **Identify** Which European country controlled the most land in the 1900s? **Apply Information** Use the map to explain this phrase: "The sun never sets on the British Empire."

Go Online PHSchool.com Use Web Code **ldp-7213 for step-by-step map skills practice.**

A Century of War and Nationalism

At the start of the 1900s, the people of Europe were filled with **nationalism,** or pride in their countries. Nationalism can be either a destructive or a constructive force, depending on what it leads people to do. It can make one nation harm another in an effort to get ahead. It can also prevent nations from working with one another. Then, hatred and warfare can erupt between countries. Between 1900 and 1950, destructive nationalism played a part in causing two world wars and the deaths of millions of people.

World War I During the early 1900s, European nations feared one another. Each nation was afraid another would invade, or try to take over, its territory. To protect themselves, nations made **alliances** (uh LY un sez), or agreements with one another. In such alliances, a nation promises to protect its friends if someone attacks them. Soon, Europe was divided into two major alliances. On one side were Germany, Austria-Hungary, and Turkey. On the other side were Great Britain, France, and Russia.

In 1914, fighting between the alliances broke out into what is now called World War I. Over the course of the war, most of the nations of Europe became involved. The United States—on the side of Great Britain, France, and Russia—also joined the war in 1917. The alliance of Germany, Austria-Hungary, and Turkey was defeated, but at an enormous cost. By the end of the war in 1918, more than 9 million soldiers had been killed. About 13 million civilians, or non-soldiers, had also died. Europe had lost almost an entire generation of young men.

During World War I, countries on both sides of the fight used posters to promote their causes.

World War II But the flame of nationalism still burned. In 1939, another war broke out. This war was called World War II. As in World War I, there were two alliances. On one side were the Axis Powers—Germany, Italy, and Japan. These countries sought to increase their national wealth and power by means of military conquest. They quickly captured most of Europe and parts of China and the South Pacific. Germany also attacked the Soviet Union.

The Allies—Great Britain, the Soviet Union, France, and China—opposed the Axis Powers. In 1941, the United States joined the Allies. More than 50 nations took part in this war, which was the most destructive ever fought. More people died, more property was damaged, and more money was spent than in any other war in history. The fighting finally ended in August of 1945. The Allies had won.

Two Paths Emerge in Europe After World War II, the Soviet Union and the United States emerged as the world's two superpowers. These nations had very different ideas about government and its role in society. Both nations used their ideas to influence people around the world.

After the war, much of Europe was in ruins. It was time to rebuild. The nations of Western Europe allied themselves with the United States. They also grew together as a region. With the shared values of peace and prosperity, they worked together to restore the economies and standards of living that had been shattered by war.

The nations of Eastern Europe, in contrast, took a different path. Many of the nations of Eastern Europe followed the example of the Soviet Union. Their economies failed to recover after the war, and their governments suspended many of their people's freedoms. You will read more about the Soviet Union and its influence on Eastern Europe in the next section.

Western and Eastern Europe remained divided, with very different governments and standards of living, until the 1990s. You will read about their recent history in Chapters 9 and 10.

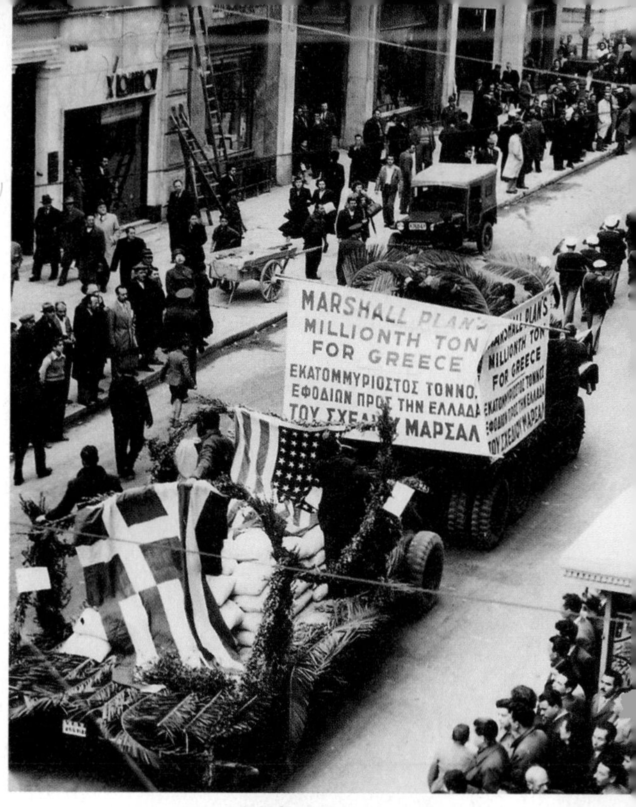

The United States led an effort called the Marshall Plan to rebuild the economies of Europe. In this photo, a parade in Greece celebrates the delivery of Marshall Plan food supplies.

✓ Reading Check **Which countries made up the Axis Powers? Which made up the Allies?**

Section 3 Assessment

Key Terms
Review the key terms at the beginning of this section. Use each term in a sentence that explains its meaning.

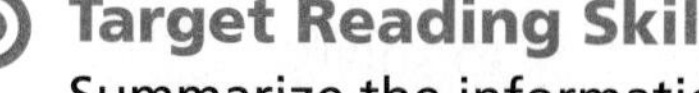

Target Reading Skill
Summarize the information in the paragraphs on this page.

Comprehension and Critical Thinking
1. **(a) Recall** Where did the Industrial Revolution begin?
(b) Find the Main Idea How did the Industrial Revolution change the way that goods were made?
(c) Identify Effects How did this change affect the lives of Europeans?
2. **(a) Describe** Give an example of destructive nationalism.
(b) Identify Cause and Effect How did nationalism help to cause World War I and World War II?
(c) Predict How might nationalism be used in the future as a creative force for peace?

Writing Activity
After World War II, colonies in Africa and Asia demanded their freedom. Suppose you were a citizen of a colony of one of the European nations. Write a paragraph explaining why you would want your country to be independent.

Writing Tip Use the following topic sentence to help you organize your thoughts: It is important for people to control their own destiny.

Problem Solving

In 1275, Marco Polo arrived at the court of Kublai Khan in China. The Mongol leader appointed Marco Polo governor of Yangchow, a busy Chinese city. After three years had passed, Marco Polo wanted to return to Venice. He had enemies within the court. The khan was getting older. Marco Polo worried that when the khan died, those enemies would have him killed. But the khan refused to let him return to Venice.

One year, a Mongol princess was promised as a bride to the Persian khan. Marco Polo proposed that he accompany the princess on the journey, to keep her safe. He knew that at the end of the trip he could escape to Venice. The khan agreed, and Marco Polo set out by sea with the princess and hundreds of men. The trip was dangerous, and most of the men died. But it might have been even more dangerous to go by land, because of robbers.

Marco Polo dressed in clothes worn by the Tatars, a nomadic tribe of eastern Asia

Solving a problem requires a range of skills. You must first state the problem clearly and identify the possible solutions. Then you must think about the likely outcome of each solution and choose the best option. In the passage above, Marco Polo identified and solved two problems.

Learn the Skill

Follow the steps below to learn how to solve problems.

1. **Identify the problem.** State the problem in a direct, complete, and accurate way. Your statement should contain facts, not opinions. The facts should be directly related to the problem.

2. **List possible solutions.** There may be more than one way to solve the problem. Identify all possible solutions.

3. **Review the possible solutions.** Identify the resources that would be needed to carry out each solution. Also identify consequences of each solution.

4. **Choose the best solution.** Decide which solution is the most effective, or the easiest to carry out. What will the likely outcome be?

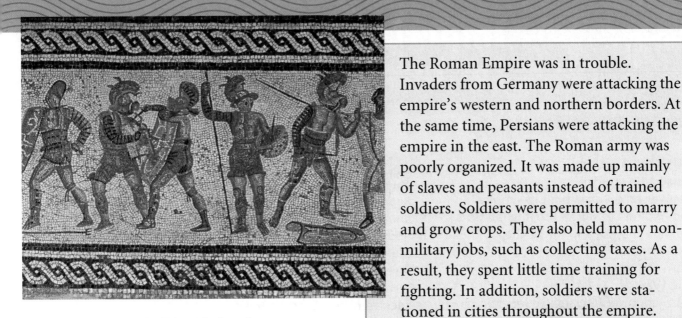

Mosaic of Roman gladiators in battle

The Roman Empire was in trouble. Invaders from Germany were attacking the empire's western and northern borders. At the same time, Persians were attacking the empire in the east. The Roman army was poorly organized. It was made up mainly of slaves and peasants instead of trained soldiers. Soldiers were permitted to marry and grow crops. They also held many non-military jobs, such as collecting taxes. As a result, they spent little time training for fighting. In addition, soldiers were stationed in cities throughout the empire. When attacks on the empire occurred, it was difficult to gather the soldiers together in one place for defense. Finally, the government had not kept the roads in repair, so travel was very difficult.

Practice the Skill

Read the passage above. Use the steps from Learn the Skill to identify the Roman Empire's problem and possible solutions.

1. Identify the Roman Empire's problem. State the problem in a clear sentence or two.
2. Identify possible solutions. Does the passage bring to mind any obvious solutions? Does it suggest any solutions that aren't as obvious?
3. Review the possible solutions. What kind of resources would each solution require? Think of what the possible outcome would be for each solution.
4. Identify the solution you think is best. Explain why you think it is the best one, and what its outcome would be.

Apply the Skill

Reread the passage titled Revolutions in Government on page 188. Then use the steps in this skill to identify the problem described in the passage, note its possible effects, and explain the solutions used.

Bronze statue of a Roman soldier

Section 4

Imperial Russia to the Soviet Union

Prepare to Read

Objectives

In this section you will

1. Discover how Russia built its empire.
2. Understand the fall of the Russian tsars.
3. Examine the rise and fall of the Soviet Union.
4. Learn the causes and effects of the Cold War.
5. Learn about the Russian Federation today.

Taking Notes

As you read this section, look for important dates in Russia's development as an empire. Copy the timeline below and record your findings on it.

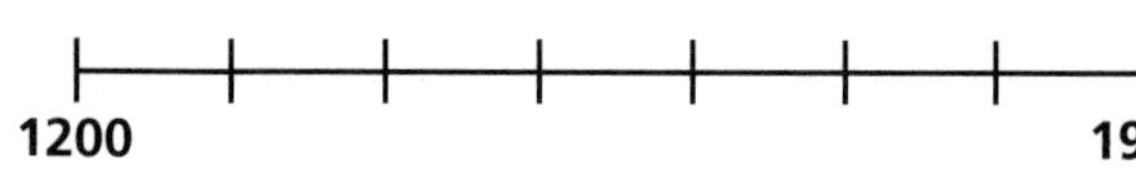

Target Reading Skill

Read Ahead Reading ahead can help you understand something you are not sure of in the text. If you do not understand a certain word or passage, keep reading. The word or idea may be clarified further on. For example, in the last paragraph below you may not be sure what is meant by the word *expansion*. As you read the section, that word will be clarified by the text.

Key Terms

- **westernization** (wes tur nuh ZAY shun) *n.* the adoption of western European culture
- **tsar** (zahr) *n.* a Russian emperor
- **revolutionary** (rev uh LOO shuh neh ree) *adj.* ideas that relate to or cause the overthrow of a government, or other great change
- **communism** (KAHM yoo niz um) *n.* a political system in which the central government owns farms, factories, and offices

Catherine the Great

The Russian court under Catherine the Great was dazzling. Catherine loved the arts, literature, philosophy, and French culture. She dreamed of creating a great nation, as glorious as France had been under Louis XIV.

Early in her rule, she made many efforts to improve the lives of the Russian people. She built schools and hospitals and gave people more religious freedom. She also became interested in ideas about liberty. Catherine did not bring freedom to all of her people, but she did make Russia a great empire. By the time of her death in 1796, she had expanded Russia southward to the Black Sea and westward into parts of Poland.

The history of Russia is a story with four themes: invasion and expansion, harsh treatment of the common people, slow **westernization,** or the process of becoming more like Western Europe, and autocratic (aw toh KRAT ik) government. An autocratic government is one in which one person has absolute power. As you read Russia's story, notice how these four themes appear again and again.

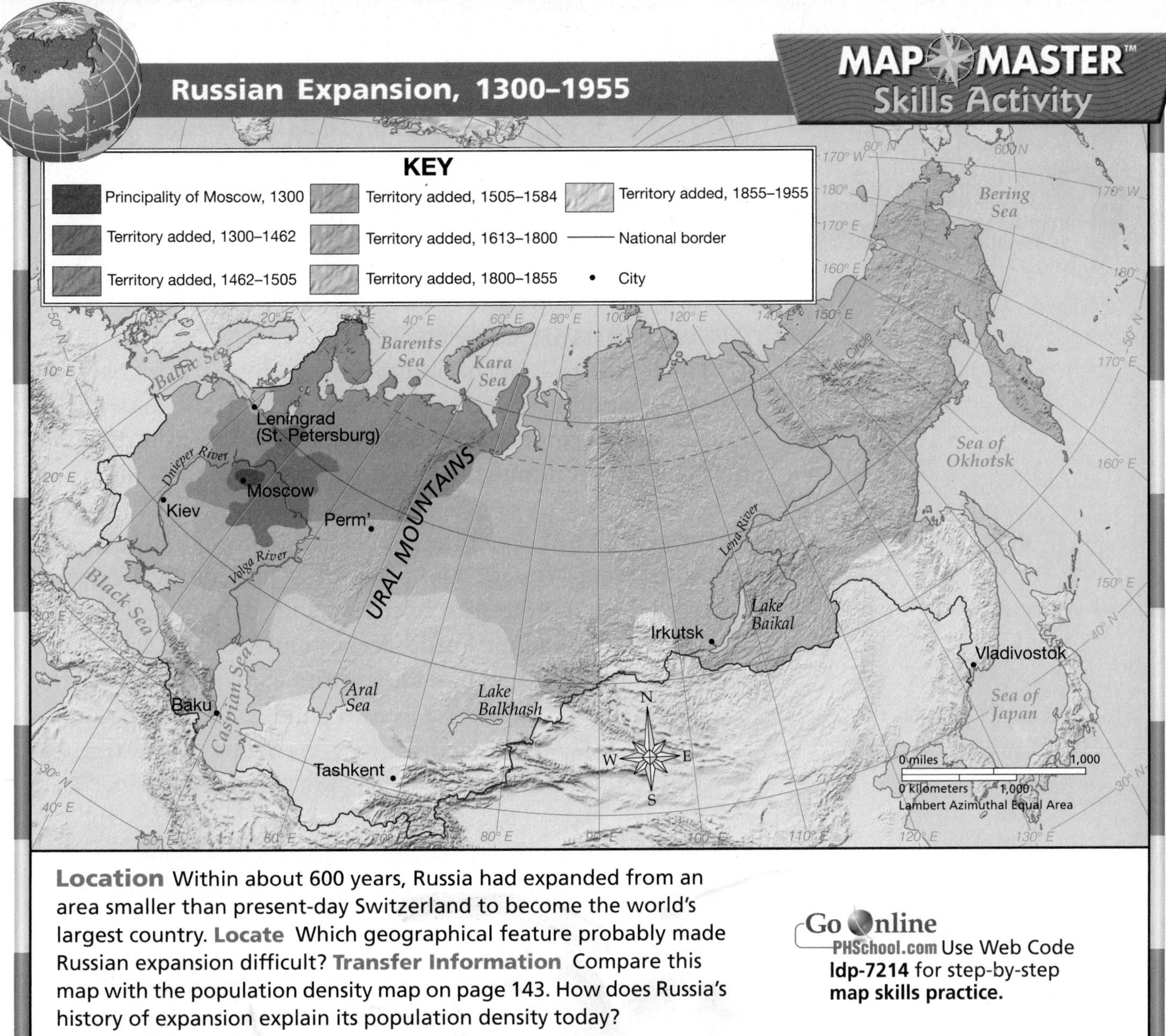

Location Within about 600 years, Russia had expanded from an area smaller than present-day Switzerland to become the world's largest country. **Locate** Which geographical feature probably made Russian expansion difficult? **Transfer Information** Compare this map with the population density map on page 143. How does Russia's history of expansion explain its population density today?

Go Online
PHSchool.com Use Web Code **ldp-7214** for step-by-step **map skills practice.**

Building a Vast Empire

Russia's story begins long before Catherine the Great. Many centuries before, various groups of people known as Slavs (slahvz) lived in small settlements. The Slavs lived in the region that eventually became the Russian Empire. In the 1200s, Mongol invaders from Asia swept in and conquered them.

The Rise of Moscow The prince of Moscow made clever agreements with the Mongols that helped him grow rich and powerful. By the 1330s, he had become the strongest ruler in the region. Slowly Moscow conquered surrounding territory. By the end of the 1400s, Moscow had freed itself entirely from Mongol rule. The map above shows how the small principality, or territory ruled by a prince, of Moscow grew into a huge country.

Discovery Channel
SCHOOL
Video
Learn how Peter the Great built St. Petersburg.

The Rise of the Tsars In the 1540s, Ivan IV became the leader of Moscow. He called himself **tsar** (zahr), or emperor. Ivan IV expanded Moscow's control of the territories to its south and east. He earned the name Ivan the Terrible for his cruelty both to those he conquered and to his own people.

After the death of Ivan the Terrible, Russia entered the Time of Troubles. During that period, the Russians endured about 20 years of civil wars and invasions by the Poles.

Finally, in 1613, Michael Romanov (ROH muh nawf) became tsar. During his reign, order was restored to Russia. The Romanovs continued expanding Russian territory throughout the 1600s and continued to rule Russia for more than 300 years.

Peter the Great Peter the Great came to power in 1689. Peter began bringing Western European ideas and culture to Russia. He hired foreign professors, scientists, and advisors, and encouraged Russians to adopt European customs. He also established new schools and reorganized his government and the army.

Peter believed that Russia needed good seaports to become a world power. He conquered land on the Baltic (BAWL tik) and Black seas, and moved the capital to St. Petersburg. Later tsars continued to expand Russian territory. Russia gained control over territories in present-day Poland, Turkey, China, and Sweden. With so many lands under its rule, Russia became an empire.

Invasion Being an empire did not mean that Russia was safe from invasion. A French army under Napoleon Bonaparte invaded Russia in 1812. Fierce fighting erupted as Napoleon's army approached Moscow. Napoleon's invasion plan, which did not take into account Russia's early winter, resulted in disastrous losses for the French. Of the 100,000 soldiers that reached Moscow, only about 10,000 survived.

√ Reading Check **Why did Peter the Great want to control land on the Baltic Sea?**

Napoleon's First View of Moscow
Napoleon and his troops approach Moscow in 1812 in this historical painting. **Analyze Images** *Which figure in the painting is Napoleon? How can you tell?*

The Last of the Tsars
A photo from the early 1900s shows Tsar Nicholas II with his family. **Compare and Contrast** *Describe the tsar and his family. How do you think their lives were different from those of poor Russians?*

The Fall of the Tsars

Russia had become a powerful empire, but the lives of most of its people had not improved. For hundreds of years, the tsar made all the important decisions. Below the tsar, Russian society was divided into two main groups. The first was a small number of landowners. The second group was a large number of very poor serfs. Tensions between the two groups began to rise.

Freeing of the Serfs In 1855, Alexander II became tsar. He soon freed the serfs and gave them their own land. He also gave towns more control over their own affairs. However, Alexander's son, Alexander III, reversed many of his father's reforms. Once again, the tsar ruled with absolute power.

Rumblings of Revolution In 1894, Nicholas II became tsar. He would be the last Russian tsar. Russia was badly beaten in a war with Japan in 1904 and 1905, and unrest grew among peasants, workers, and a small middle class. In 1905, thousands of workers in St. Petersburg marched to the tsar's Winter Palace. They wanted to appeal directly to the tsar for reforms. Troops stopped them and fired into the crowd, killing hundreds. This mass killing was known as Bloody Sunday.

Tsar Nicholas II was forced to agree to establish the Duma (DOO mah), a kind of congress. The people elected its members. In theory, the Duma shared power with the tsar. In fact, the Duma had very little power. Some progress toward reform was made, but many people wanted more.

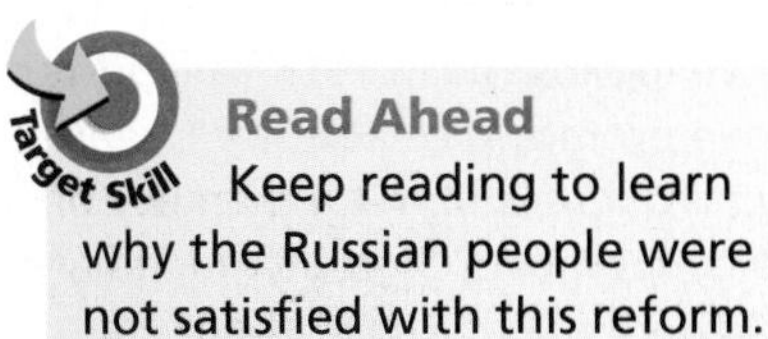

Read Ahead Keep reading to learn why the Russian people were not satisfied with this reform.

✓ Reading Check **What event is known as Bloody Sunday?**

Promoting Communism
At the top, Lenin gives a speech to a crowd in Moscow in 1918. The poster above promotes communism, reading, "You are still not a member of the cooperative? Sign up immediately!" **Synthesize** *What about communism might have appealed to poverty-stricken Russians?*

The Rise and Fall of the Soviet Union

On an afternoon in April 1917, a small group of Russians gathered at a German railroad station. Among them was a man named Vladimir Ulyanov, who was also called Lenin. Earlier, the Russian government had imprisoned Lenin for spreading ideas that they believed were **revolutionary,** or ideas that could cause the overthrow of a government. Later, the government gave him permission to leave Russia.

Now the Germans were taking Lenin back to Russia. The Germans made two rules. First, no member of Lenin's group could leave the train, and second, none of them could talk to any Germans during their journey. The Germans, like the Russians, knew that ideas could be more powerful than any army. At the time, Germany was at war with Russia and hoped that Lenin would cause changes in Russia. And he did.

The Russian Revolution To understand why the Germans helped Lenin, you need to go back to 1914. That year, Russia entered World War I against Germany. Millions of Russian soldiers were killed or wounded. At home, people suffered severe food and fuel shortages. By March 1917, the Russian people began rioting. Troops were sent to put down the uprising. They joined the rioters instead. Tsar Nicholas II was forced to give up his throne. The tsar and his family were held as prisoners, and were later killed by Lenin's followers. A weak government took over.

In November 1917, after his return to Russia, Lenin and his supporters pushed the weak government aside. Lenin knew that Russians wanted peace more than anything else. In March 1918, Russia signed an agreement with Germany and withdrew from World War I. Under Lenin's leadership, Russia also agreed to give up the Baltic republics, a large area of its territory that had been occupied by the Germans. This was just what the Germans had hoped for.

As the new leader of Russia, Lenin wanted to establish a communist government. **Communism** (KAHM yoo niz um) is a political system in which the central government owns farms, factories, and offices. No one person can own factories or land. Each person is supposed to work and share equally in the rewards of this work.

The idea of communism appealed greatly to many Russians. For hundreds of years, Russia's poor had suffered terrible hardships while the rich lived in luxury. Lenin promised that everyone would be equal and enjoy a better standard of living, but he broke that promise. Instead, the government took all power and most of the wealth for itself.

Building a Communist State The treaty with Germany ended the war, but peace still did not come to Russia. After the Communists came to power, there was a terrible civil war. On one side were Lenin's followers. On the other side were many groups who opposed them.

The Russian civil war lasted three years and cost millions of lives. Eventually, the Communists won. In 1922, Lenin created the Union of Soviet Socialist Republics (USSR), also called the Soviet Union. The Soviet Union was made up of Russia and several smaller republics under Russian control. It included most of the territory of the old Russian Empire. And as in the old empire, most of the people in the smaller republics were not Russian.

Lenin began turning the Soviet Union into a communist country. He jailed and even killed people who opposed him, calling them enemies of the revolution. Lenin died in 1924. Josef Stalin became the next leader. Under Stalin's form of Soviet communism, the government tried to control all aspects of citizens' lives.

Stalin's Dictatorship Josef Stalin was a dictator (DIK tayt ur), a leader who has absolute power. Stalin did not care about the suffering his decisions caused the Russian people. For example, he wanted to develop more industry in the Soviet Union. He knew that the increased number of factory workers would require great amounts of food. Therefore, Stalin forced the peasants to give their farm products to the government. Many peasants opposed the plan. As punishment, Stalin sent millions of peasants to prison camps in Siberia. Most died there. Stalin eventually succeeded in industrializing Russia. But all of the Soviet Union lived in terror of Stalin.

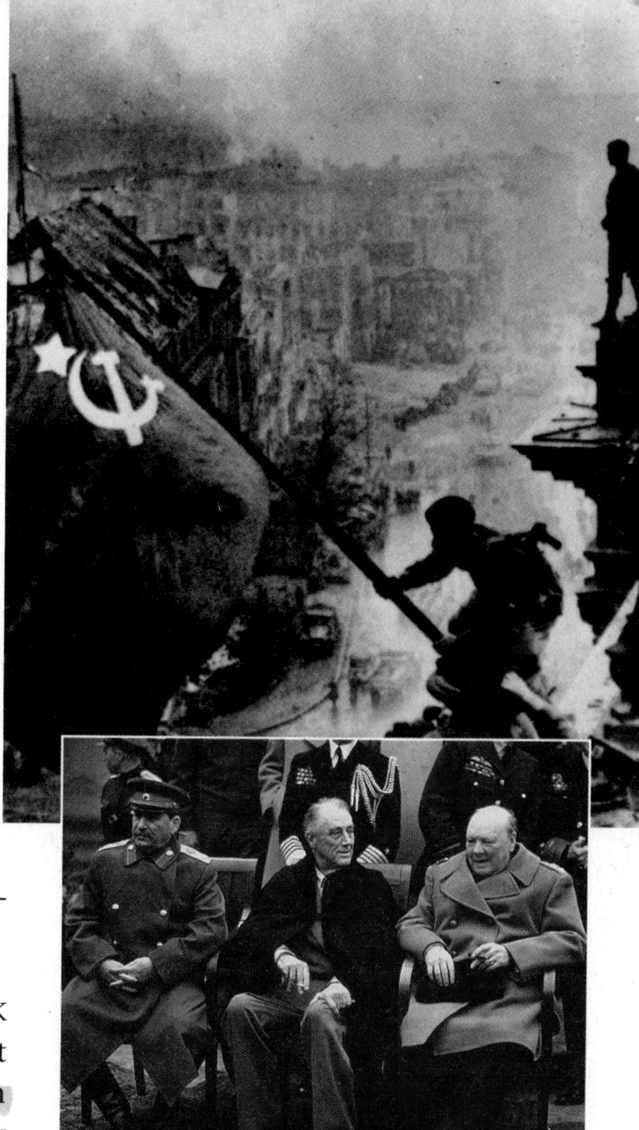

Ending World War II
In the photo at the top, a Russian soldier celebrates the Soviet victory in Berlin by raising the Soviet flag. Above, the leaders of the Soviet Union, the United States, and the United Kingdom meet to discuss their countries' roles in the post-war world. **Recognize Causes** *How did the Soviet Union's role in World War II help it become a world power?*

World War II Stalin signed an agreement with the Germans in 1939. It stated that the two countries would not go to war against each other. Despite the agreement, the Germans invaded the Soviet Union two years later. Three million German soldiers, with tanks and airplanes, advanced deep into the Soviet Union.

For a time, a German victory appeared likely. Many Soviet cities were destroyed. Millions of soldiers died or were captured. But the Soviet people fought bravely. By 1943, the Soviets had begun pushing the Germans out of Russia. Two years later, Soviet troops had captured Berlin, the capital of Germany.

✓ Reading Check **Why was Stalin called a dictator?**

A Nuclear Threat
By the 1980s, the superpowers had built enough powerful nuclear weapons to destroy the entire world. The top photo shows the explosion of a nuclear bomb. The bottom photo shows the universal yellow and black symbol of fallout shelters—underground rooms meant to protect people from fallout, or dangerous particles, after a nuclear explosion.
Sequence *What events led to the buildup of nuclear weapons by the Soviet Union and the United States?*

The Cold War

As you have read, after World War II the United States and the Soviet Union were so powerful that people called them superpowers. Relations between the superpowers became extremely tense. However, the two sides never fought each other. This time of tension without actual war is called the Cold War. It lasted roughly from 1945 until 1991, and shaped events within the two nations, and around the world.

Causes of the Cold War The first cause of the Cold War was the situation in Eastern Europe. During World War II the Soviet army moved westward to Berlin, freeing the Eastern European countries that the Germans had conquered. But after the war, the Soviet troops did not leave. They forced those countries to become communist. Trade and most contact with the West were cut off. British leader Winston Churchill said that it was as if an "iron curtain" had fallen across Eastern Europe, dividing the East from the West.

Second, the Soviets tried to expand their power beyond Eastern Europe. They encouraged rebels in other nations to turn to communism. The United States was determined to stop this. The superpowers often backed opposing sides in conflicts in Latin America, Asia, and Africa. They also built powerful nuclear (NOO klee ur) weapons to use against each other.

Collapse of an Empire The Soviet Union's economy grew weak during the Cold War. The government had invested most of its money in heavy industries and weapons. It did not produce enough basic consumer goods, such as food and clothing. Also, the government's central control of the economy was not working.

Almost all of the Soviet people had lost faith in the communist system by the early 1980s. They were still poor and no longer believed the government's promises. One Soviet leader responded. Mikhail Gorbachev (mee kah EEL GAWR buh chawf), who took power in 1985, made many changes in the Soviet system. He allowed more personal freedom. He also reduced the government's control of the economy.

When people who have lived under harsh rule are given a taste of freedom, they often want more. This happened across Eastern Europe and the Soviet Union by the late 1980s. Eastern European countries abandoned communism. The Soviet republics demanded their independence. Finally, at the end of 1991, the Soviet Union broke apart.

✓ **Reading Check** **What was the "Iron Curtain"?**

The Russian Federation

After the breakup of the Soviet Union, all of its republics became independent nations. The republic of Russia changed its name to the Russian Federation. A federation is a union of states or republics. In a federation, each member agrees to give certain powers to a central government. The Russian Federation includes Russians and peoples of many different ethnic groups. However, the Russian Federation is smaller in size than the old Soviet Union.

The Russian Federation has made efforts to build a free-market economy, or an economy in which producers compete freely for consumers' business. It sold its state-owned factories and businesses to private individuals. It has also tried to become more democratic. The transition away from a communist system has been difficult, however. Russia experienced economic chaos.

Russia also experienced conflicts among its ethnic groups. Many of these other peoples were tired of being ruled by Russians, who are the majority in Russia. The republic of Tatarstan, for example, negotiated with the Russians to have more rights. The republic of Chechnya (CHECH nee uh), however, has fought for its independence. Russia today faces many challenges to building a new way of life.

Russian president Vladimir Putin in 2000

✓ Reading Check **Why did the Russian Federation sell businesses to private individuals?**

Section 4 Assessment

Key Terms
Review the key terms at the beginning of this section. Use each term in a sentence that explains its meaning.

Target Reading Skill
What word or idea were you able to clarify by reading ahead?

Comprehension and Critical Thinking
1. (a) **Name** Who was the first Russian leader to begin westernization?
(b) **Draw Conclusions** Why did he encourage Russians to adopt western customs?
2. (a) **Define** What was the Russian Duma?
(b) **Identify Causes** Why did Tsar Nicholas II create the Duma?
3. (a) **Explain** Why had Lenin been imprisoned by the Russian government?
(b) **Sequence** How did Lenin become Russia's leader?
4. (a) **Define** What is a federation?
(b) **Summarize** How did the Russian Federation try to westernize its economy?

Writing Activity
Today, some people in Russia want to return to their lives under communist rule. Write a paragraph arguing either for or against returning to communism.

For: An activity about Leo Tolstoy
Visit: PHSchool.com
Web Code: ldd-7204

Section 5

The European Union

Prepare to Read

Objectives

In this section you will

1. Learn about the history of the European Union.
2. Understand the purpose of the European Union.
3. Examine the structure of the European Union.
4. Find out what the future holds for the European Union.

Taking Notes

As you read this section, look for details about the European Union. Copy the concept web below and record your findings in it.

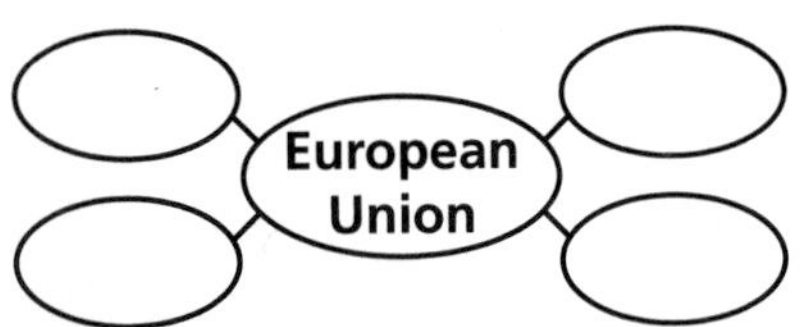

Target Reading Skill

Reread or Read Ahead
Both rereading and reading ahead can help you understand words and ideas in the text. If you do not understand a word or passage, use one or both of these techniques. In some cases, you may wish to read ahead first to see if the idea is clarified later on. If it is not, try going back and rereading the original passage.

Key Terms

- **euro** (YUR oh) *n.* the official currency of the European Union
- **single market** (SING ul MAHR ket) *n.* a system in which goods, services, and capital move freely, with no barriers
- **foreign minister** (FAWR in MIN is tur) *n.* a government official who is in charge of a nation's foreign affairs

Robert Schuman worked to repair war-torn Europe.

At the end of World War II, Europe lay in ruins. Many of the nations of Europe had been at war with one another for years. Europeans needed to work together to bring about peace, rebuild their nations, and strengthen their shattered economies.

A French government official named Robert Schuman had a plan. He wanted European nations to work together to control their coal and steel industries. He proposed a new organization called the European Coal and Steel Community (ECSC). Six nations—Belgium, France, Italy, Luxembourg, the Netherlands, and West Germany—joined the group in 1951.

Over time, this small group grew into a much larger group, with many more roles and responsibilities. Today, it is called the European Union (EU), and has 25 member states. Many additional countries are waiting to become members.

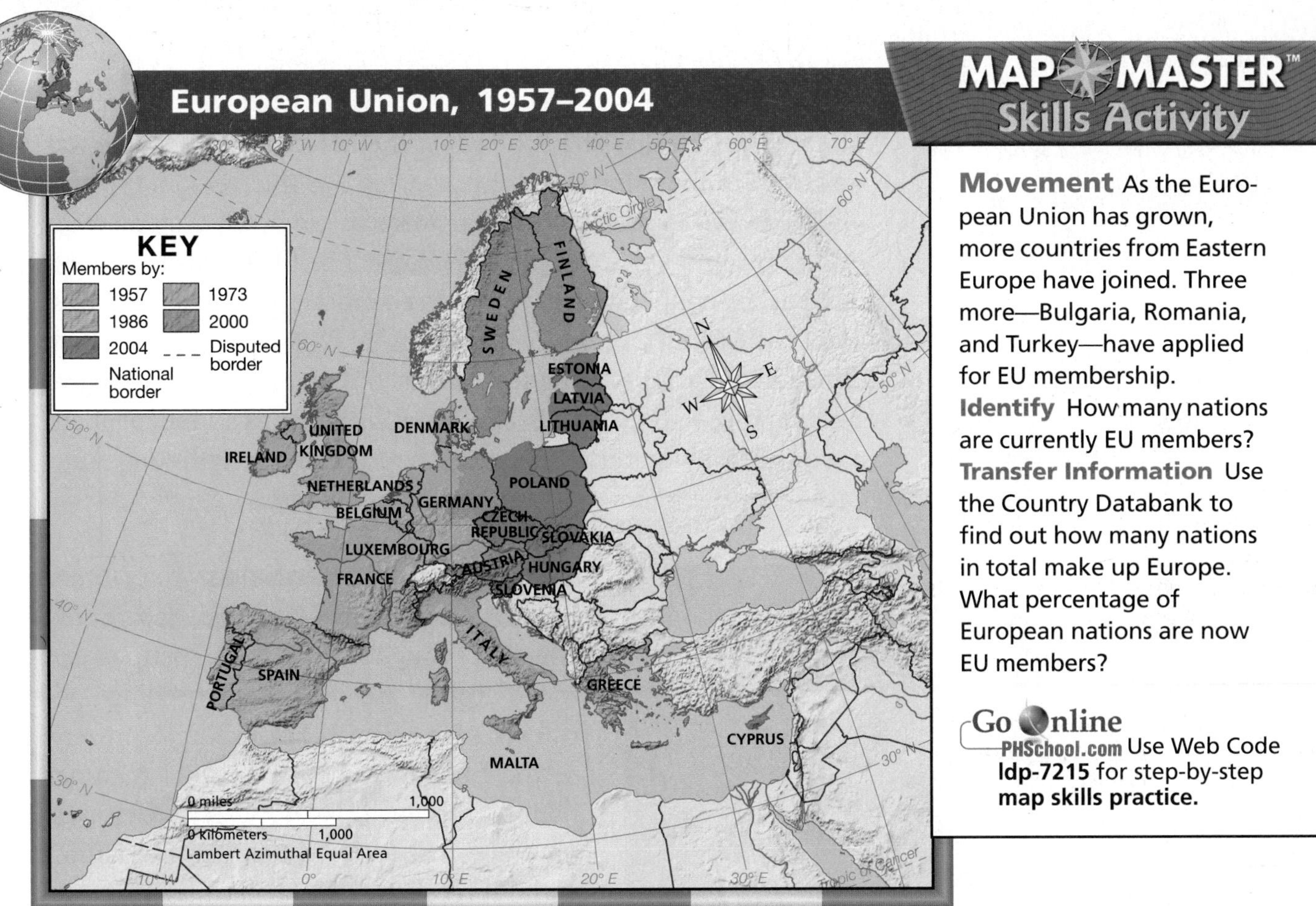

MAP MASTER™ Skills Activity

Movement As the European Union has grown, more countries from Eastern Europe have joined. Three more—Bulgaria, Romania, and Turkey—have applied for EU membership.
Identify How many nations are currently EU members?
Transfer Information Use the Country Databank to find out how many nations in total make up Europe. What percentage of European nations are now EU members?

Go Online
PHSchool.com Use Web Code **ldp-7215** for step-by-step **map skills practice.**

History of the European Union

The ECSC created the European Economic Community (EEC) in 1957. The EEC expanded the ECSC, giving it greater economic powers. It also added the power to make social policies.

Expanding Membership Throughout the 1970s and 1980s, more and more nations wanted to join the EEC. The United Kingdom, Ireland, and Denmark joined in 1973. Greece followed in 1981. Portugal and Spain joined in 1986. Soon, the member nations began working on a new plan for an even stronger union.

The EEC Becomes the EU In 1992 the member nations of the EEC signed the Maastricht (MAH strikt) Treaty. This treaty established the European Union. It also laid out the plan for EU nations to adopt a single currency, or money. The currency is called the **euro,** (YUR oh). By 2001, twelve countries had adopted the euro. Denmark, Sweden, and the United Kingdom chose not to adopt the euro.

At first, only businesses and financial markets used the euro. In 2002, most EU nations withdrew their own coins and paper bills from circulation and began using euros instead.

✓ Reading Check **What is the currency of the European Union?**

What Does the European Union Do?

The EU was created at a time when the memory of a terrible war was fresh in the minds of all Europeans. For that reason, the goal of the EU was to make future wars impossible by binding together the people and governments of Europe. The EU works to achieve that goal by cooperating to promote economic and social progress. Unlike the United States or Russia, the EU is not a federation of states. It is a group of individual countries that have agreed to give certain powers to the EU. Each EU nation remains an independent nation. But by working together, the EU has strength and influence that no individual nation could have alone.

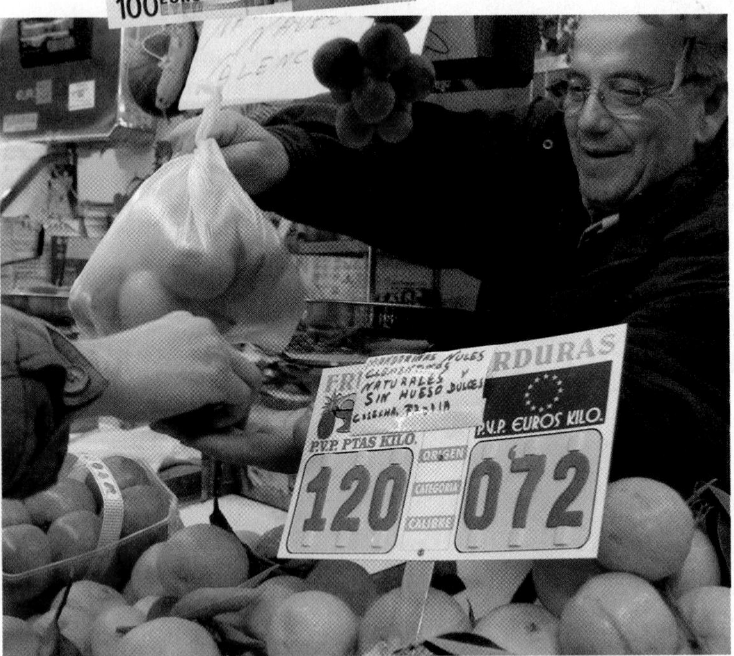

A Market With Two Currencies
A Spanish market lists prices in both euros (top) and pesetas, the old Spanish currency. Many European markets used both currencies before changing over completely to euros.
Generalize *What are some advantages of having just one currency throughout several countries?*

Common Social Policies The citizens of all EU member nations are considered equal. Throughout the EU, people can move around freely without needing special visas or permits. For example, citizens of the EU can travel to any EU member nation without a passport. They can even move permanently to another EU nation without receiving official permission.

EU member nations also establish common policies in areas such as education, the environment, and fighting crime. For example, EU nations have similar policies for combating poverty. EU nations also follow over 200 environmental guidelines set up by the EU.

Finally, the EU strives to protect European heritage and culture. European students are encouraged to learn foreign languages and study in other EU countries. The EU also sponsors cultural projects—such as theater, dance, and film—that are produced by EU member nations working together.

Common Economic Policies EU member nations can trade freely with one another without having to pay tariffs, or taxes, on international trade. In effect, the EU has a **single market,** or a system in which goods, services, and capital move freely, with no barriers. EU nations also cooperate to create jobs for citizens in all countries throughout the EU.

All EU member nations help plan and contribute to the EU's central budget. A special bank manages this budget, which pays for all of the EU's expenses.

Common Government and Foreign Policies

The EU has many different roles relating to government and foreign policy. It creates laws that govern its member nations. It also signs treaties with non-EU countries and organizations. Most of these treaties have to do with trade or industry. Finally, the EU oversees policies that have to do with crime and the national security of the region.

A court called the Court of Justice ensures that the EU's policies are applied fairly in every EU member nation. It settles any legal disputes between member nations, EU organizations, or EU citizens. The Court is made up of one judge from each EU member state.

A Seat of Government
The European Parliament is located in Strasbourg, France. **Infer** *What challenges might EU nations have faced in deciding on where to locate its parliament?*

Things the EU Does Not Handle Recall that all EU member nations still remain independent countries. Although EU member nations work together, they keep control over many of their countries' own policies. For example, each nation decides how best to handle its own healthcare, national defense, education, and housing policies. Still, member nations try to make policies that agree with the policies made by other member nations.

✓ Reading Check **What is the court that ensures EU policies are applied fairly?**

Structure of the European Union

The EU has three main policy-making institutions. These institutions are the European Parliament, the Council of the European Union, and the European Commission.

European Parliament The European Parliament passes the majority of the EU's laws. It is the only EU institution that meets and debates in public. It is elected by all the citizens of the EU and represents their interests.

The number of representatives to Parliament differs according to the size of each country. When the Parliament meets, the representatives are assembled by political party, not by nation.

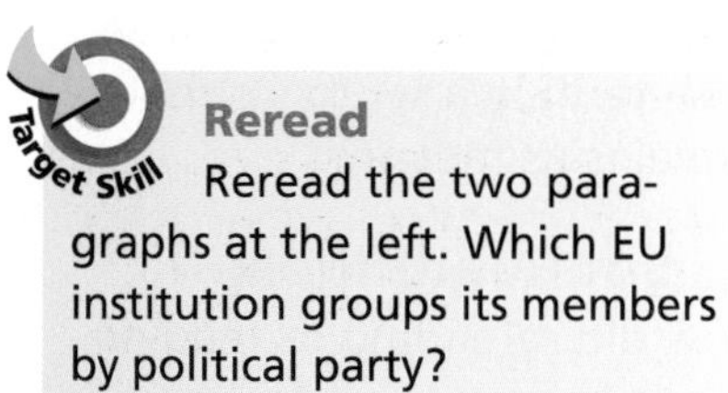

Reread
Reread the two paragraphs at the left. Which EU institution groups its members by political party?

Council of the European Union The Council of the European Union is made up of the foreign ministers from individual EU nations. A **foreign minister** is a government official who is in charge of a nation's foreign affairs, or relations with other nations. The Council represents the separate national interests of the member nations.

Members of the EU discuss energy resources with non-EU members.

Other EU Institutions The European Commission represents the interests of the whole EU community. It is made up of several different offices, each overseeing a certain area of policy. Each EU member nation sends representatives to the Commission. Other EU institutions perform services such as monitoring the EU's income and spending, advising on economic policy, and overseeing long-term investment.

✓ Reading Check **Which institution in the European Union represents each nation's national interests?**

Future of the European Union

In just over 50 years, the EU has enjoyed great success. It has brought peace and prosperity to almost 500 million Europeans.

The EU continues to expand. In 2004, ten nations from Eastern and Southern Europe joined. Three more countries have applied to join and are working to meet EU requirements. To join, new members must accept existing EU laws, values, and policies. The EU will continue to draw its strength from following its own rules and honoring its traditions. Its long-term goal is to bring all the democracies of Europe together. This process will be a careful and gradual one.

✓ Reading Check **What must a nation do to join the EU?**

Section 5 Assessment

Key Terms

Review the key terms at the beginning of this section. Use each term in a sentence that explains its meaning.

Target Reading Skill

How did rereading or reading ahead help your understanding?

Comprehension and Critical Thinking

1. **(a) Name** Which three nations in the EU did not adopt the euro?
(b) Infer Why might these countries not have wanted to adopt a single currency?

2. **(a) List** What are some examples of the EU's social policies?
(b) Analyze Information What do these policies tell you about how the EU views its citizens?

3. **(a) Recall** What are the EU's main policy institutions?
(b) Draw Conclusions Why do you think the representatives in Parliament are assembled by political group and not by nation?

4. **(a) Recall** What must new members of the EU accept before they can join the EU?
(b) Infer Why might some European countries not want to join the EU?

Writing Activity

Suppose that you are a citizen of a nation that is interested in joining the European Union. Write a letter to your local newspaper describing both the benefits and the disadvantages of joining.

Writing Tip A letter should begin with an overview sentence or two. After describing the benefits and disadvantages, end the letter with a closing statement.

Chapter 7 Review and Assessment

◆ Chapter Summary

Section 1: From Ancient Greece to the Middle Ages

- The first great philosophers, historians, and writers were the ancient Greeks.
- Ancient Romans created a system of written laws that are still in use today.
- In the Middle Ages, many people found order and security in feudalism and Christianity.

Section 2: Renaissance and the Age of Revolution

- The ideas, writing, and art of the ancient world later inspired Renaissance scholars and artists.
- Explorers began to travel beyond Europe in search of wealth.
- Revolutions in government and science changed European ways of life.

Section 3: Industrial Revolution and Nationalism

- The Industrial Revolution changed the way that goods were made and how people lived and worked.
- Workers began to demand better working conditions and a voice in government.
- Europe experienced a century of war and nationalism in the 1900s.

Section 4: Imperial Russia to the Soviet Union

- By the 1900s, Russia was a huge empire.
- Following the Russian Revolution, Vladimir Lenin came to power and a communist state was established.
- The Cold War was a time of great tension between the United States and Russia that lasted for nearly 50 years.
- After the collapse of the Soviet Union, the Russian Federation was formed.

Section 5: The European Union

- The European Union was officially created in 1992.
- The European Union works to achieve common security and economic goals.
- Three main institutions create European Union policy.
- The European Union continues to expand.

Euro bills and coins

◆ Key Terms

Match the vocabulary words with their correct definitions.

1. Industrial Revolution
2. euro
3. foreign minister
4. alliance
5. Renaissance
6. tsar

A a Russian emperor

B a government official who is in charge of relations with other nations

C the currency of the European Union

D the period of history when products began to be made by machines in factories

E a period of history that included the rebirth of interest in learning and art

F an agreement between countries to protect and defend each other

Review and Assessment (continued)

◆ Comprehension and Critical Thinking

7. **(a) List** Name two important ideas given to us by the ancient Greeks.
   (b) Synthesize How did Alexander the Great spread Greek ideas?
8. **(a) Recall** When did the Renaissance reach its peak?
   (b) Explain To what culture did Renaissance scholars and artists look for inspiration?
   (c) Contrast How did the art of the Renaissance differ from the art of the Middle Ages?
9. **(a) Name** In what ways did people suffer as a result of industrialization?
   (b) Draw Conclusions Why did labor unions begin to form during the Industrial Revolution?
   (c) Identify Effects How did changes in society during the Industrial Revolution lead to changes in government?
10. **(a) Explain** Why was there rioting in Russia in 1917?
    (b) Identify Effects How did Lenin use the power of ideas to persuade Russians to follow him?
11. **(a) Explain** How did Russia gain more territory and become an empire?
    (b) Summarize Why did the Russian people come to oppose the tsars?
    (c) Contrast How was Russia under the tsars different from the Soviet Union under communism?
12. **(a) Recall** What are the main goals of the European Union?
    (b) Analyze Why might EU member nations prefer to handle some issues, such as health-care, education, and housing policies, on their own?

◆ Skills Practice

Problem Solving In the Skills for Life activity in this chapter, you learned how to solve problems. Review the steps you followed to learn this skill. Then turn to the section titled Changes in Society on page 193 of this chapter. Identify the problem that factory workers faced. Then explain how the problem was solved.

◆ Writing Activity: Math

Rome's emperor Hadrian had a wall built from coast to coast across northern England, in order to defend his empire's land. The wall extends 73 miles (118 kilometers) from Wallsend in the east to Bowness in the west. There are many towers and gates along the wall. About every seven miles there is a fort. Calculate how long it would have taken an army to march the entire length of the wall, if their marching speed was three miles per hour. Write a paragraph explaining your opinion on whether a wall would work as a type of defense.

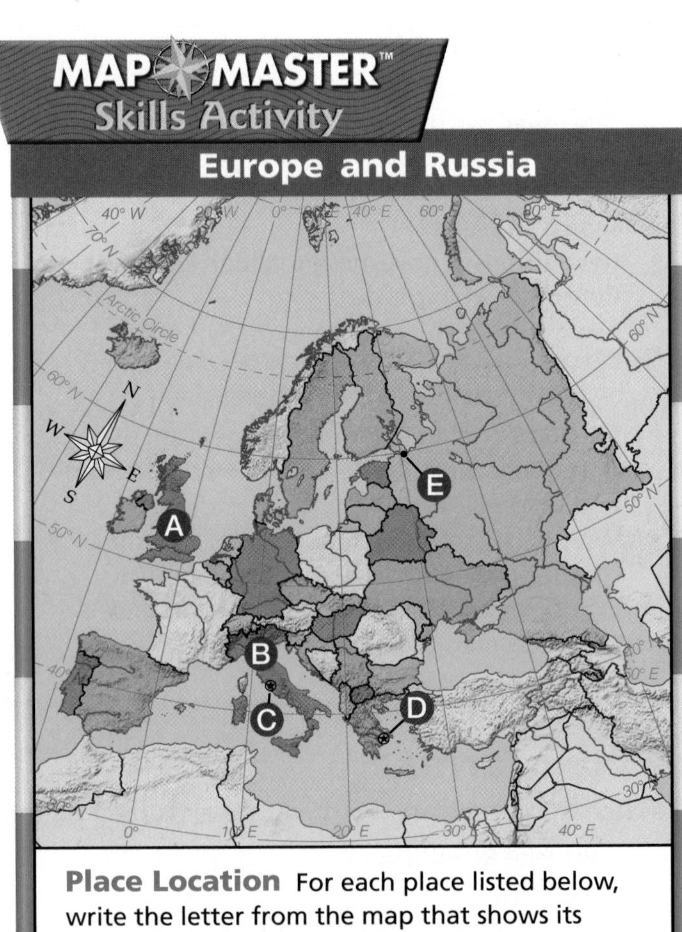

Place Location For each place listed below, write the letter from the map that shows its location. Use the maps in the Regional Overview to help you.

1. Athens
2. Rome
3. Italy
4. Great Britain
5. St. Petersburg

Go Online PHSchool.com Use Web Code **ldp-7225** for an **interactive map.**

Standardized Test Prep

Test-Taking Tips

Some questions on standardized tests ask you to find main ideas or topic sentences. Read the paragraph below. Then follow the tips to answer the sample question.

> **TIP** Some paragraphs have a topic sentence that states the main idea. All the other sentences in the paragraph support this point.

In 334 B.C., Alexander the Great set out from Greece to conquer the world. Within ten years, his empire extended from Egypt to northern India. He founded many new cities across these lands. Greek culture linked the whole Mediterranean world by the time of his death in 323 B.C.

Pick the letter that best answers the question.

Which topic sentence is missing from this paragraph?

A Alexander the Great was a great soldier, thinker, and artist.

B Alexander the Great was one of the world's greatest military minds.

C The accomplishments of Alexander the Great were enormous.

D Alexander's conquest spread Greek language, culture, and ideas.

> **TIP** Make sure that you read each answer choice carefully. Carelessness can easily cost points on a multiple-choice test.

Think It Through What is the main point of the paragraph? You can eliminate C because it is too general. Answer A may or may not be true, but even if it is true, it doesn't completely describe every sentence in the paragraph. That leaves B and D. Alexander was a great military mind, but the paragraph includes other accomplishments as well. The correct answer is D.

Practice Questions

Use the tips above and other tips in this book to help you answer the following questions.

1. In a feudal system, there is a special relationship between

   A knights and foot soldiers.

   B lords and vassals.

   C peasants and knights.

   D peasants and kings.

2. Which of the following would not be discussed under the topic sentence, Renaissance sculptors made powerful lifelike statues?

   A the work of Michelangelo

   B the importance of human beings to Renaissance artists

   C the role of printing in the Renaissance

   D the 1500 sculpture named *David*

3. After World War II, Eastern Europe was under the influence of which country?

   A the Soviet Union

   B France

   C Germany

   D the United States

4. What type of leader was Joseph Stalin?

   A president

   B tsar

   C prime minister

   D dictator

Use Web Code **lda-7201** for a **Chapter 7 self-test.**

From Pearl in the Egg

By Dorothy Van Woerkom

Prepare to Read

Background Information

In Europe in the Middle Ages, a typical day for a person your age was quite different than it is for you. For one thing, a child at that time was considered much closer to being an adult than is a child today. This is because people had shorter life expectancies. More people in those days died of diseases that today can be cured.

Pearl in the Egg was the name of a real girl who lived in the 1200s. Historians know little about her. Dorothy Van Woerkom has written a book of historical fiction about Pearl. Her descriptions of Pearl's life are based on what historians know about life in England in the 1200s. At that time, people in Europe were just beginning to use family names. Usually they gave themselves names that described their work or their families in some way.

In this part of Pearl's story, you will read about a typical day in her life.

Objectives

In this selection you will

1. Learn about the everyday life of a young serf in the Middle Ages.
2. Understand the importance of work on a feudal manor.

rushlight (RUSH lyt) *n.* a lamp made with grease and part of a rush, or swamp plant

dripping (DRIP ing) *n.* fat and juices drawn from cooking meat

serfs (surfs) *n.* peasant farmers who worked the land as the slaves of a wealthy landowner

Pearl set the bowl of cabbage soup down on the floor near the rushlight. She knelt beside the box of straw that was her father's bed. She wiped his forehead, listening to his heavy breathing.

"Please, Fa," she coaxed. She broke off a piece from a loaf of black bread and dipped it into the soup. She placed it on his lips, letting the soup trickle into his mouth. She ate the chunk of bread, and dipped another.

"I will be in the fields until the nooning," she said, "so you must try to eat a little now. See, I have put a bit of dripping in the soup."

She forced the warm, mild liquid down his throat until the bowl was half empty. She drank the rest herself, chewing hungrily on the lump of fat that the sick man had not been able to swallow.

Again she wiped his face, and then she blew out the light. She crossed the smooth dirt floor, and pulled a sack from a peg on the wall near the door as she left the hut. Outside, the sky was gray with the dawn. Ground fog swirled around her feet. The air smelled of ripening grain and moist earth.

From other huts of mud and timber, serfs hurried out into the early morning mist. Some, like Pearl, would spend the day in their own small holdings in the fields. It was the time for har-

A page from a French book dating from around 1460 shows people planting seeds.

vesting their crops, which would feed their families through the winter. Others, like Pearl's older brother, Gavin, had already left for work in the manor fields to bring in Sir Geoffrey's crops.

Sir Geoffrey was lord of the manor, which included his great stone house and all the land surrounding it. He owned this tiny village. He even owned most of the people in it. A few, like the baker, the miller, and the soapmaker, were freemen and free women. They worked for themselves and paid the lord taxes. For tax, Sir Geoffrey collected a portion of everything they produced. No one in the village had money.

But the serfs were not free. They could never leave the manor, or marry without the lord's permission. They could not fish in the streams or hunt in the forest. They owned only their mud huts and small gardens, called holdings, and an ox or cow, or a few geese or sheep. The serfs also paid taxes. Each year they gave Sir Geoffrey a portion of their crops. He took a share of their eggs; if a flock of sheep or geese increased, he took a share; and if a cow had a calf, he took that also. On certain days of the week each family had to send a man—and an ox if they had one—to help plow the lord's fields, harvest his crops, and do their work. Each woman had to weave one garment a year for the lord and his family.

The sun was up when Pearl reached the long furrows of her field, where the flat green bean pods weighed down their low bushes. She bent to see if the leaves were dry. Wet leaves would wither when she touched them.

furrows (FUR ohz) *n.* grooves in the earth made by a plow

The sun had dried them. Pearl began filling her sack, wondering how she could finish the harvest all by herself before the first frost. She had other plots to work as well.

Now that their father was ill, twelve-year-old Gavin was taking his place for three days each week in the manor fields. Sir Geoffrey would get his crops safely in! But if the frost came early, or if the only one left at home to work was an eleven-year-old like Pearl, that was of small matter to Sir Geoffrey.

Pearl stood up to rub her back. A serf's life was a hard life. Her father's was, and his father's before him. She sighed. Who could hope to change it?

Clotilde (kluh TILD)

Old Clotilde came swaying up the narrow path between her field and Pearl's. She waved her empty sack by way of greeting and squatted down among her plants.

"How be your Fa this morning?" she asked Pearl.

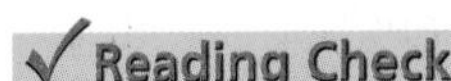

Why does Pearl work alone in her family's holdings?

A painting of nobles hunting illustrates this manuscript, created in 1515.

"He took some soup. But he wanders in his head. He thinks I am my mother, though she's been dead three summers now."

"Ah, and he'll join her soon, Big Rollin will." Clotilde's wrinkled face was nearly the same dirty gray as her cap. "They all do, soon as they take a mite of sickness. For the likes of us to stay alive, we must stay well! Get the priest for him! He won't plow these fields again."

Before Pearl could reply, the shrill blare of a hunting horn sounded across the meadow, followed by the baying of hounds on the trail of a wild boar. Startled to their feet, the serfs watched the terrified boar running in and out among the rows of crops.

"Run, lest you get trampled!" Clotilde screamed, dashing down the path toward the forest. The others followed her. Someone pulled Pearl along as she stumbled forward, blinded by angry tears, her fingers tightly gripping her sack.

The hounds came running in pursuit of the boar. Behind the hounds rode the hunting party of twenty horsemen, led by Sir Geoffrey. At the rear was another man Pearl recognized. Jack, one of Sir Geoffrey's bowmen, had come upon her one day as she scrounged for dead branches near the edge of the forest. He had baited her with cruel words, rudely ruffling her hair with the shaft end of an arrow.

bowmen (BOH mun) *n.* men with bows and arrows; archers

"Jack's my name. What's yours?" he had demanded, taking pleasure in her discomfort. For answer she had spat at him, and he had pressed the arrow's metal tip against her wrist until she'd dropped her bundle. Laughing, he had scattered the branches with his foot and grabbed her hair.

"Spit at me again, girl, and that will be the end of you!" Though his mouth had turned up in a grin, his eyes had been bright with anger. His fingers had tightened on the nape of her neck, bending her head back. She stared up at him, frightened, but defiant.

defiant (dee FY unt) *adj.* bold or resistant

"Perhaps you need a lesson in manners right now," he'd said, raising his other hand. He probably would have struck her, but for the rattle of a wagon and the tuneless whistle signaling someone's approach. He had let her go with a suddenness that had left her off balance, and had stalked away.

Shaken, Pearl had turned to see Sir Geoffrey's woodcutter driving out of the forest with a wagonload of wood for the manor house.

Now Pearl shuddered at the memory; but Jack was taking no notice of her. His eyes were on the boar and on his master. If the boar became maddened during the chase and turned on one of the hunters, Jack was ready with his arrows to put an end to the beast.

Over the meadow they galloped, and onto the fields. They churned up the soft earth, trampled down the precious bean plants, crushed the near-ripe ears of the barley and oats, tore up the tender pea vines. They chased the boar across the fields and back again, laughing at the sport.

When they had gone, Pearl ran back to her field. She crawled in the turned-up earth, searching for unbroken bean pods. The other serfs were doing the same.

"What is the matter with us?" she demanded of Clotilde, "Why do we stay silent, with spoiled crops all around us, just so Sir Geoffrey will have his sport?"

"Shish!" Clotilde warned, looking quickly around to see who might have heard. "Do you want a flogging for such bold words? Hold your tongue, as you see your elders do."

For the rest of the morning they worked in silence. At midday, Pearl picked up her half-filled sack. It should have been full by now. She glared fiercely across the meadow at the manor house, but she held her tongue.

Pearl returned home to find that her father had worsened. When she could not rouse him, she went for the priest.

About the Selection

Pearl in the Egg: A Tale of the Thirteenth Century, with illustrations by Joe Lasker, was published in 1980. Pearl in the Egg and Matil Makejoye, another character who appears in the book, were listed in the king's account books as minstrels in the court of King Edward I. The story of Pearl's life is fiction, but it is based on the life of real people in the 1200s.

flogging (FLAHG ing) *n.* a beating or whipping

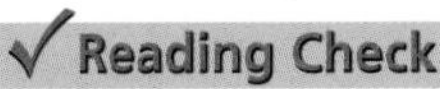

What stopped Jack from hitting Pearl?

Review and Assessment

Thinking About the Selection

1. (a) Recall What did the serfs use to pay their taxes?
(b) Explain Why did the serfs give Sir Geoffrey a portion of their crops every year?
(c) Infer The feudal system existed for more than 400 years. Why do you think it lasted for such a long time?

2. (a) Explain What did Clotilde mean when she said, "Do you want a flogging for such bold words?"
(b) Predict Based on what you know about Pearl, how do you think she might act the next time she sees the lord or one of his men?

Writing Activity

Write a Short Story

Write a preface to Pearl's story telling how she received the name Pearl in the Egg. Or write a short story in which Pearl awakens in 2005. She is still 11 years old, and her father is still ill. Describe her reaction to today's world.

About the Author

Dorothy Van Woerkom (b. 1924) was born in Buffalo, New York. She was an elementary school teacher before becoming a writer. She is most noted for her folktale translations and her religious stories. She often rewrites folktales, sometimes changing the characters' names and the settings, but keeping the plot.

Chapter 8

Cultures of Europe and Russia

Chapter Preview

This chapter will introduce you to the cultures of Europe and Russia.

Section 1
The Cultures of Western Europe

Section 2
The Cultures of Eastern Europe

Section 3
The Cultures of the Russian Federation

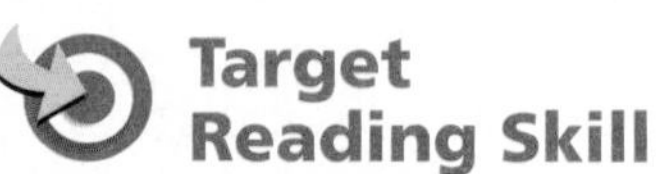

Target Reading Skill

Identify Main Ideas In this chapter you will focus on finding and remembering the main idea, or the most important point, of sections and paragraphs.

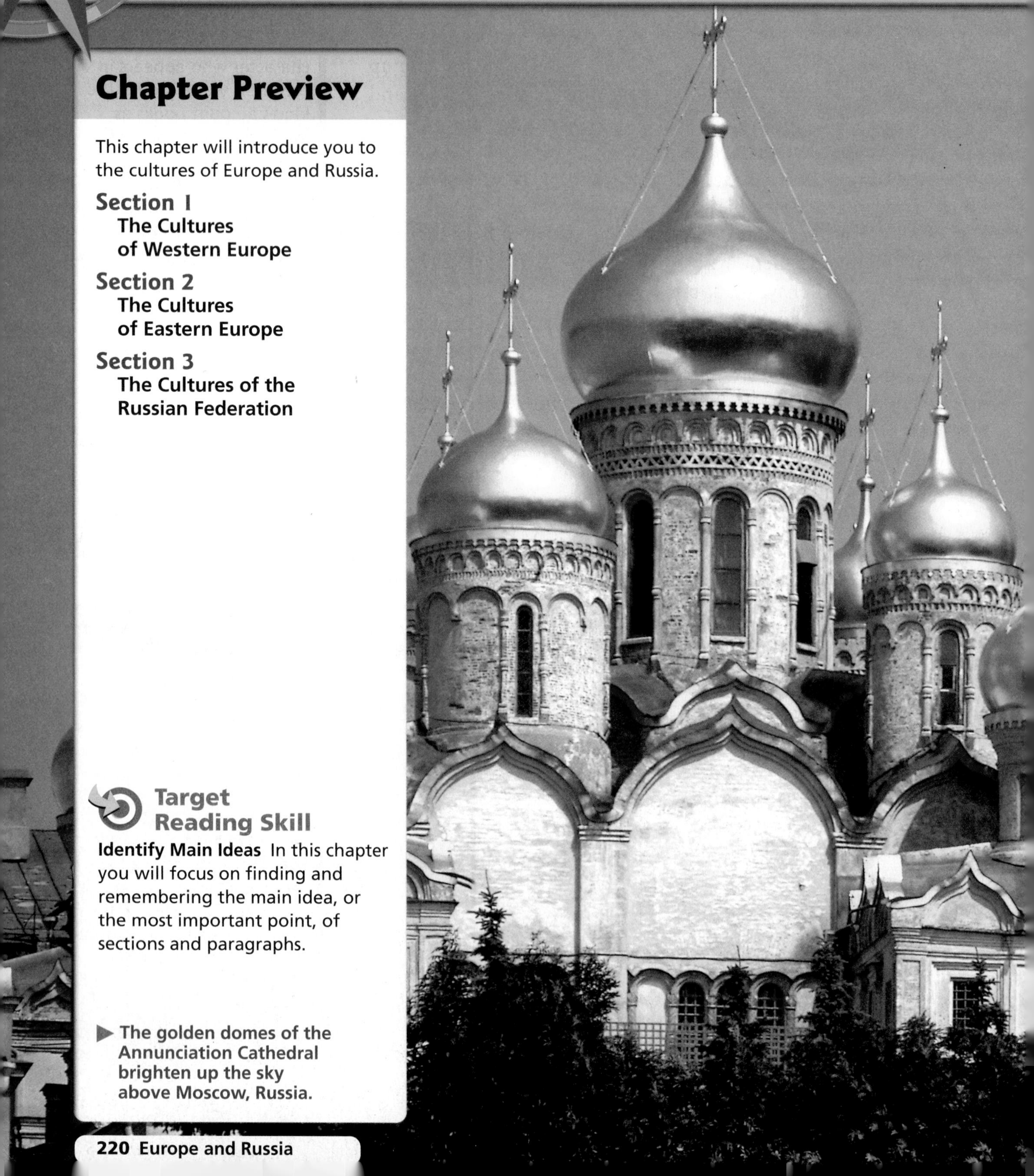

▶ **The golden domes of the Annunciation Cathedral brighten up the sky above Moscow, Russia.**

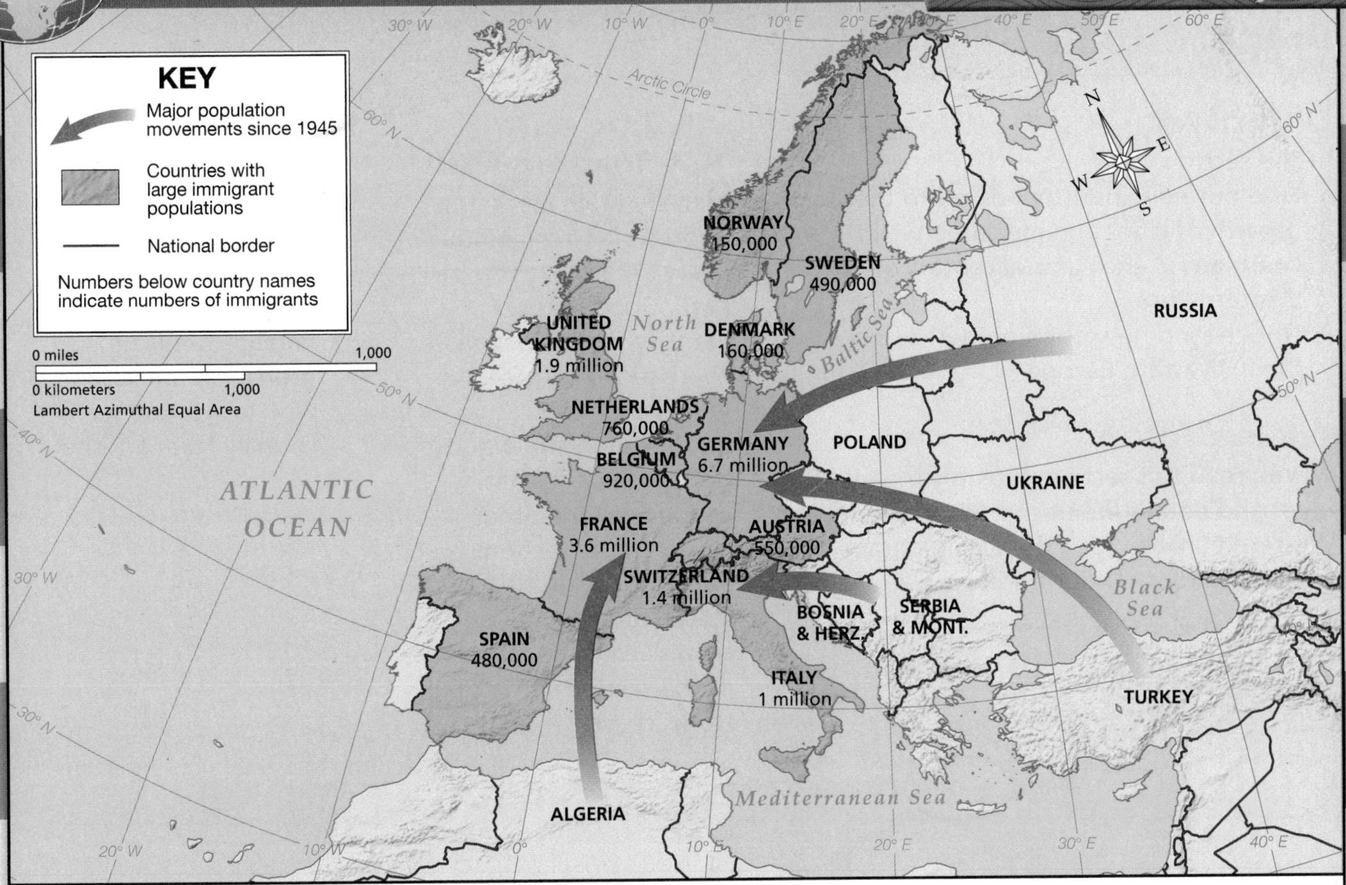

Migration to Western Europe

MAP MASTER™ Skills Activity

KEY
Major population movements since 1945
Countries with large immigrant populations
National border
Numbers below country names indicate numbers of immigrants
0 miles 1,000
0 kilometers 1,000
Lambert Azimuthal Equal Area
Arctic Circle
ATLANTIC OCEAN
North Sea
Baltic Sea
Black Sea
Mediterranean Sea
NORWAY 150,000
SWEDEN 490,000
DENMARK 160,000
UNITED KINGDOM 1.9 million
NETHERLANDS 760,000
BELGIUM 920,000
GERMANY 6.7 million
POLAND
RUSSIA
UKRAINE
FRANCE 3.6 million
AUSTRIA 550,000
SWITZERLAND 1.4 million
BOSNIA & HERZ.
SERBIA & MONT.
SPAIN 480,000
ITALY 1 million
TURKEY
ALGERIA
30° W
20° W
10° W
0°
10° E
20° E
30° E
40° E
50° E
60° E
60° N
50° N
40° N
30° N

Movement Every year, the countries of Western Europe attract large numbers of immigrants. **Identify** How many immigrants have come to France from Algeria? **Predict** As more countries from Eastern Europe join the EU, how might that affect immigration to Western Europe?

Go Online
PHSchool.com Use Web Code **ldp-7311** for step-by-step **map skills practice.**

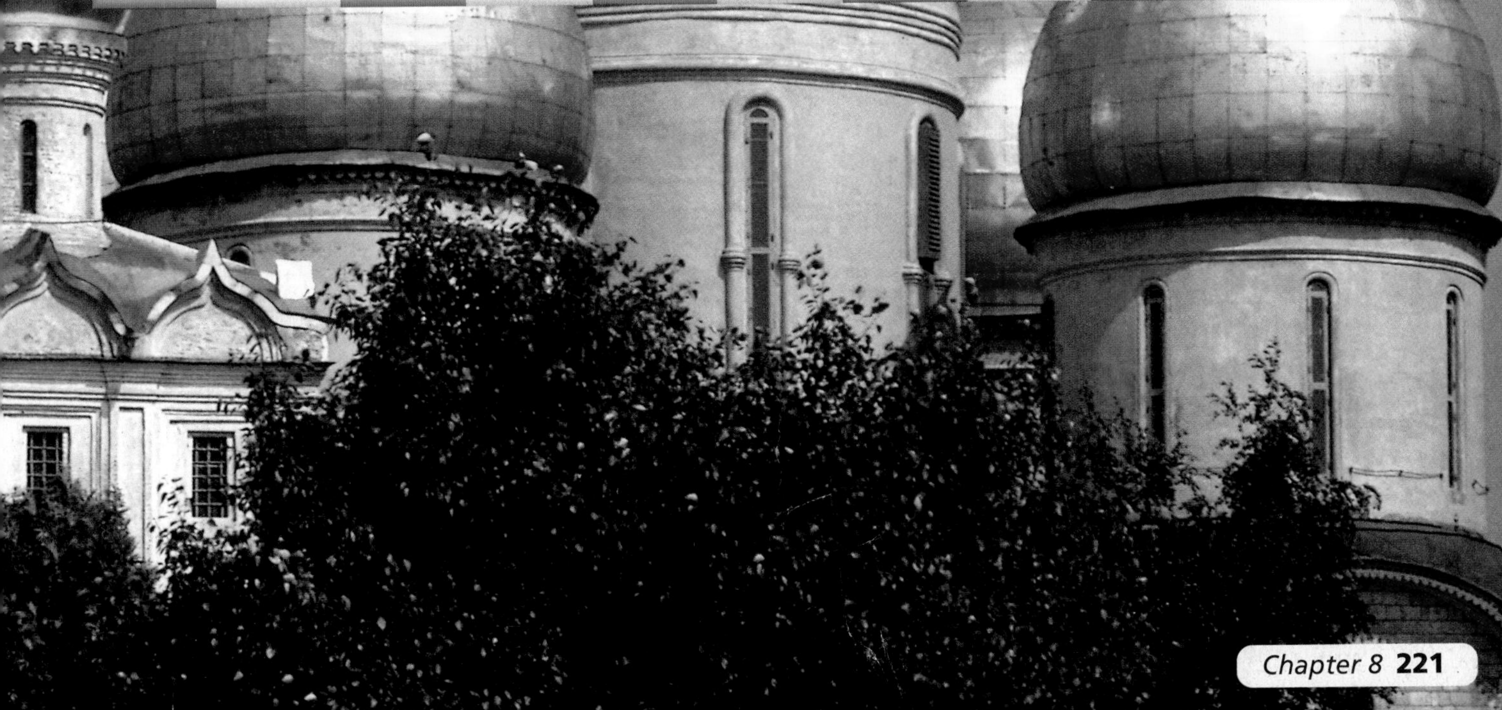

Section 1

The Cultures of Western Europe

Prepare to Read

Objectives

In this section you will

1. Find out how industry has led to the growth of cities and increased wealth.
2. Learn about the cultural centers of Western Europe.
3. Understand how open borders affect life in Western Europe.

Taking Notes

As you read this section, look for the main ideas and details about the cultures of Western Europe. Copy the web diagram below and record your findings in it.

Target Reading Skill

Identify Main Ideas It is impossible to remember every detail that you read. Good readers identify the main idea in every section. The main idea is the most important or the biggest point—the one that includes all the other points in the section. Sometimes this idea is stated directly. As you read, record the main ideas of this section in the Taking Notes chart.

Key Terms

- **urbanization** (ur bun ih ZAY shun) *n.* the movement of populations toward cities
- **immigrant** (IM uh grunt) *n.* a person who moves to one country from another

A high-speed train travels across Europe.

As the train speeds down the track, the passengers hear hardly a whisper. As the passengers sit in their comfortable seats, they can look out the window at the highway next to the railroad. They know that the cars are traveling at least 60 miles (96 kilometers) per hour, but the cars seem to be moving backward. That's because the train is traveling three times faster than the cars—about 180 miles (289 kilometers) per hour.

Would you like to take a trip like that? You can if you go to France, which has some of the world's fastest trains. Great Britain also has speedy rail travel. Some British trains reach speeds of 140 miles (225 kilometers) per hour. In Western Europe, high-speed trains have made travel between countries easy and fast. Someone in a European country can be in another country in hours. Such easy movement through Western Europe affects the entire culture of the region.

Growth of Industry

Most Western European countries are prosperous, or wealthy. This prosperity is based on strong economies. The economies of Western Europe have grown because of productive industries and high-quality services.

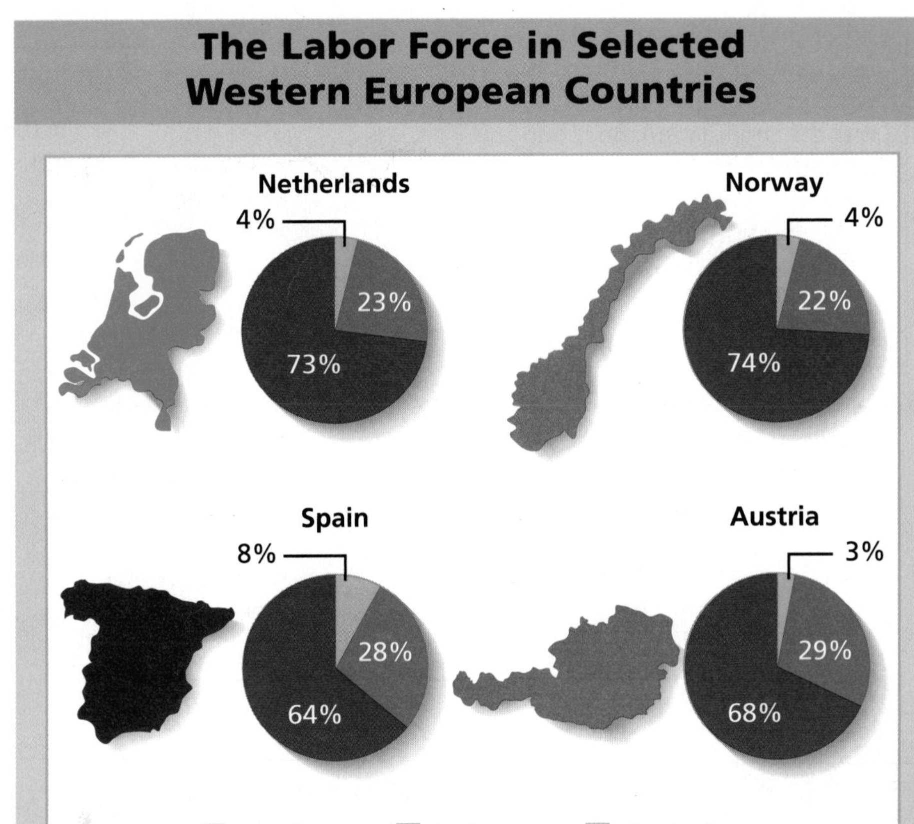

Agricultural Revolution The Industrial Revolution of the late 1700s sped up the development of industry in Western Europe. Before the Industrial Revolution, most people worked on farms. They could grow little beyond their basic food needs. There were few machines to help them do their work. Over time, new and better farm machines were able to do tasks that once required many workers. Farmers also learned ways to improve soil quality and fight insects. With these advances, farms could produce more and better crops with fewer laborers.

This revolution in farming, called the Agricultural Revolution, took place around the same time as the Industrial Revolution. Thus, as the need for farm workers declined, the need for industrial workers grew. Many people began moving to cities, where factories were located.

Diagram Skills

The economies of most Western European countries today are based on service industries. **Identify** Which country has the second-highest percentage of its labor force in services? **Apply Information** Recall the description of this country's geography in Chapter 6. Use this information to explain why its economy depends on services.

The Growth of Cities **Urbanization** (ur bun ih ZAY shun), or the movement of populations toward cities, was a trend throughout the 1800s and 1900s. Following World War II, it increased rapidly. The United States provided billions of dollars to help Western Europe recover from the war. With this help, the region's industries came back stronger than ever. And even more people left rural areas to work in cities.

Today, the majority of Western Europeans have a comfortable life. They earn good wages working in factories or in service industries such as banking and food service.

✓ Reading Check **What was the Agricultural Revolution?**

MAP MASTER™ Skills Activity

Place Though more than 50 languages are spoken in Western Europe, many of these languages are related. **Locate** Where are languages other than Indo-European languages spoken? **Infer** For what geographical feature was the Uralic language group named?

Go Online PHSchool.com Use Web Code **ldp-7321 for step-by-step map skills practice.**

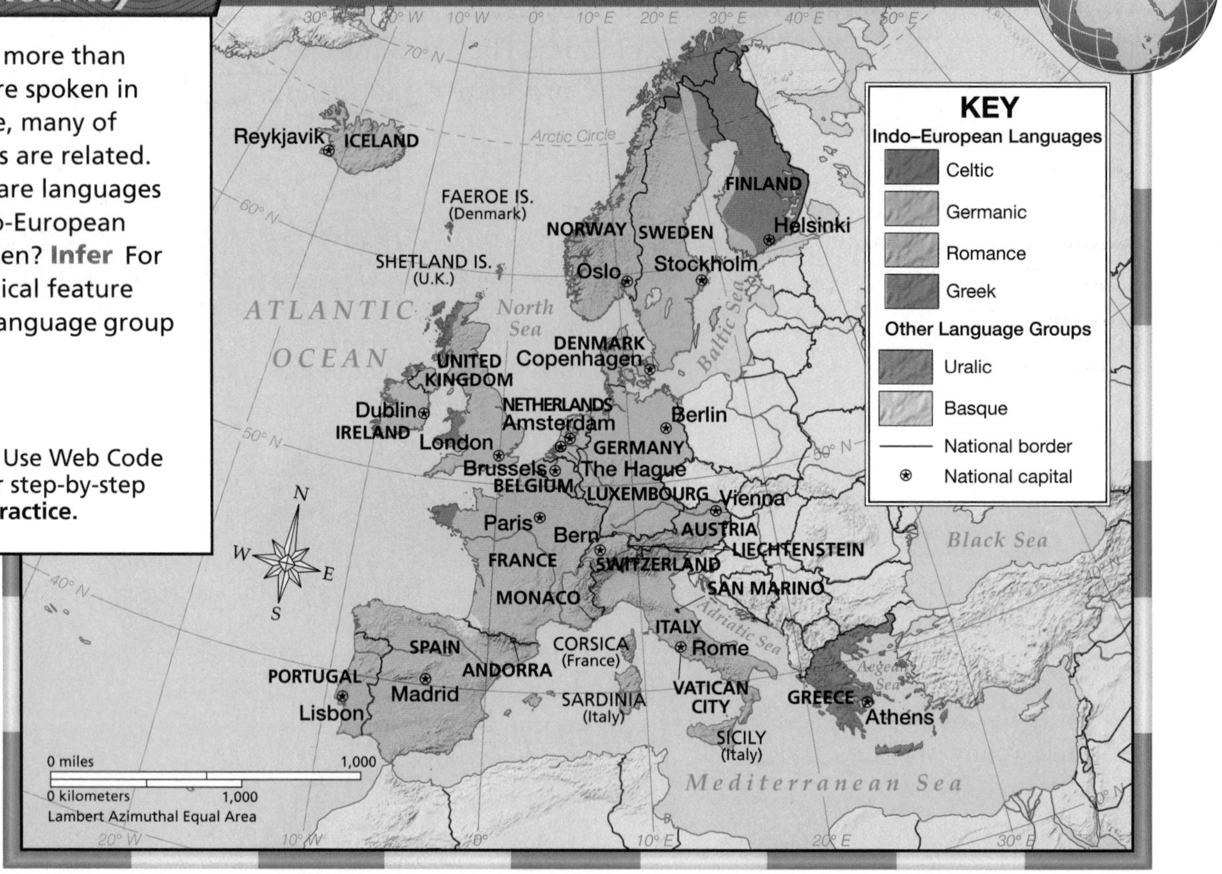

Western Europe: Languages

KEY

Indo–European Languages
- Celtic
- Germanic
- Romance
- Greek

Other Language Groups
- Uralic
- Basque

National border
National capital

0 miles 1,000
0 kilometers 1,000
Lambert Azimuthal Equal Area

Centers of Culture

It is difficult to travel far in Europe without coming across a city. People travel from small towns and villages to cities to find jobs. Some people go to cities to attend school. People also travel to cities to enjoy cultural attractions. These include museums, concerts, restaurants, nightclubs, theaters, and stores.

A modern entrance was added to the over-400-year-old Louvre Museum in Paris, France.

The Old and the New Most Western European cities are a mix of the old and the new. Both public buildings and houses from the Middle Ages are a common sight. They stand next to modern apartments and office buildings. Cars and buses drive along cobblestone streets once used by horse-drawn carriages. Monuments honor leaders who lived hundreds of years ago. Market plazas dating back to medieval times still thrive today.

Vibrant Cities Each city in Western Europe is different from every other city. However, they all share certain characteristics. The majority of Western Europeans live and work in cities. Cities are also the centers of Western European culture.

Let's take a look at some Western European capital cities. Paris, the capital of France, attracts scholars, writers, and artists from all over the world. England's capital, London, is known for its important financial center as well as for its grand historic buildings and lovely parks. The Spanish capital city of Madrid (muh DRID) is known as a place with a vibrant street life, a place where people meet on cafe terraces to relax outdoors after work. As publishing capital of the Spanish-speaking world, it is also an important literary city. The German capital, Berlin, is always full of activity and attracts many visitors to its theaters and museums.

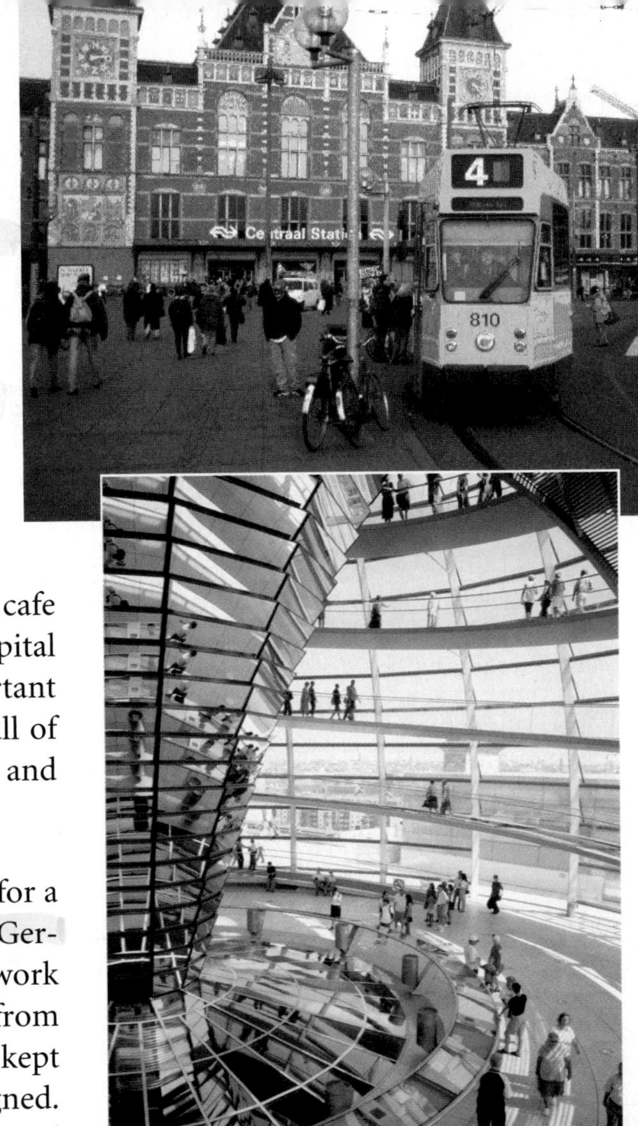

European City Scenes
A trolley passes by historical buildings in Amsterdam, the Netherlands, in the top photo. The photo above shows Germany's Parliament building, called the Reichstag, in Berlin. It was built in 1995 after the country was reunified. **Infer** *Why do you think the German government chose a modern style of architecture for its new Parliament building?*

Work and Leisure Let's focus on life in Germany for a moment. Most visitors to Germany think that the Germans are efficient. In other words, Germans do their work without waste or extra effort. Visitors get this idea from what they see. German cities, streets, and buses are kept clean. Hotels are well run. German cars are well designed. Travel is swift on an excellent system of highways. Travel is equally fast on high-speed trains.

But life in Germany is not all hard work and fast-paced activity. Many workers enjoy as much as six weeks of vacation each year. Skiing, hiking, and camping are popular recreational activities throughout the country's mountains and highlands. The country's many rivers, as well as the North and Baltic seas, are good for swimming and boating. Those who prefer city life enjoy the museums, concerts, and plays. Life is similar in countries throughout Western Europe.

The European Union and the Arts One of the goals of the European Union is to support Europe's cultural community. Although different from one another geographically and politically, European nations often share a common history and cultural heritage. They all belong to the European community. The EU organizes concerts, cultural events, exhibits, and conferences to bring Europeans together. The EU's goal is to respect individual cultures, while encouraging cooperation among them.

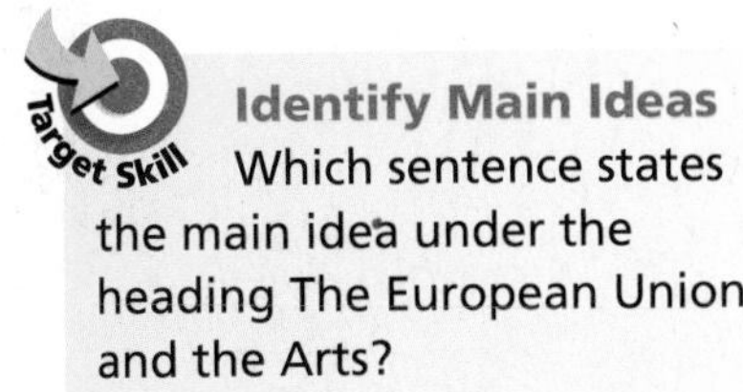

Identify Main Ideas Which sentence states the main idea under the heading The European Union and the Arts?

Links Across Time

Immigrants in the United Kingdom The United Kingdom's immigrant population today reflects its history as a world power. In 2001, nine of the ten countries from which the most immigrants came—including Ireland, Pakistan, Somalia, India, and Nigeria—were once under British rule. In the future, the UK's immigration patterns are expected to change. As more countries from Eastern and Central Europe join the EU, large numbers of people from those regions are expected to immigrate to the UK and other Western European countries.

To achieve that goal, the EU finances programs that help cultural development and encourage cultural exchange. One of the programs that the EU funds is the DEBORA (Digital Access to Books of the Renaissance) project. It gives Internet users access to documents from the Renaissance. The books and materials dating from the 1500s are stored in libraries throughout Europe. However, access to these collections is often limited. With the EU's support, Internet technology now makes viewing the collections possible.The EU helps museums, libraries, and other cultural institutions make these collections accessible to more people. By doing so, it helps connect people to their cultural heritage.

Changing Immigration Patterns Although life in Western Europe is good now, it was not always so. In the 1800s and early 1900s, millions of Western Europeans left Europe. Most went to the United States, Canada, and South America. They left in search of more opportunities and better lives.

Since World War II, patterns of human movement have been reversed. Large numbers of people stopped leaving Western Europe. Industry continued to expand in the postwar years and more workers were needed. As a result, people from other countries began moving to Western Europe.

Today's Immigrants Today, about 6 percent of workers in Western Europe are **immigrants** (IM uh grunts), or people who move to one country from another. Most of the immigrants in Western Europe are from Eastern Europe, North Africa, South Asia, and the Middle East. The four largest countries in the European Union—France, Germany, Italy, and the United Kingdom—all have large immigrant populations.

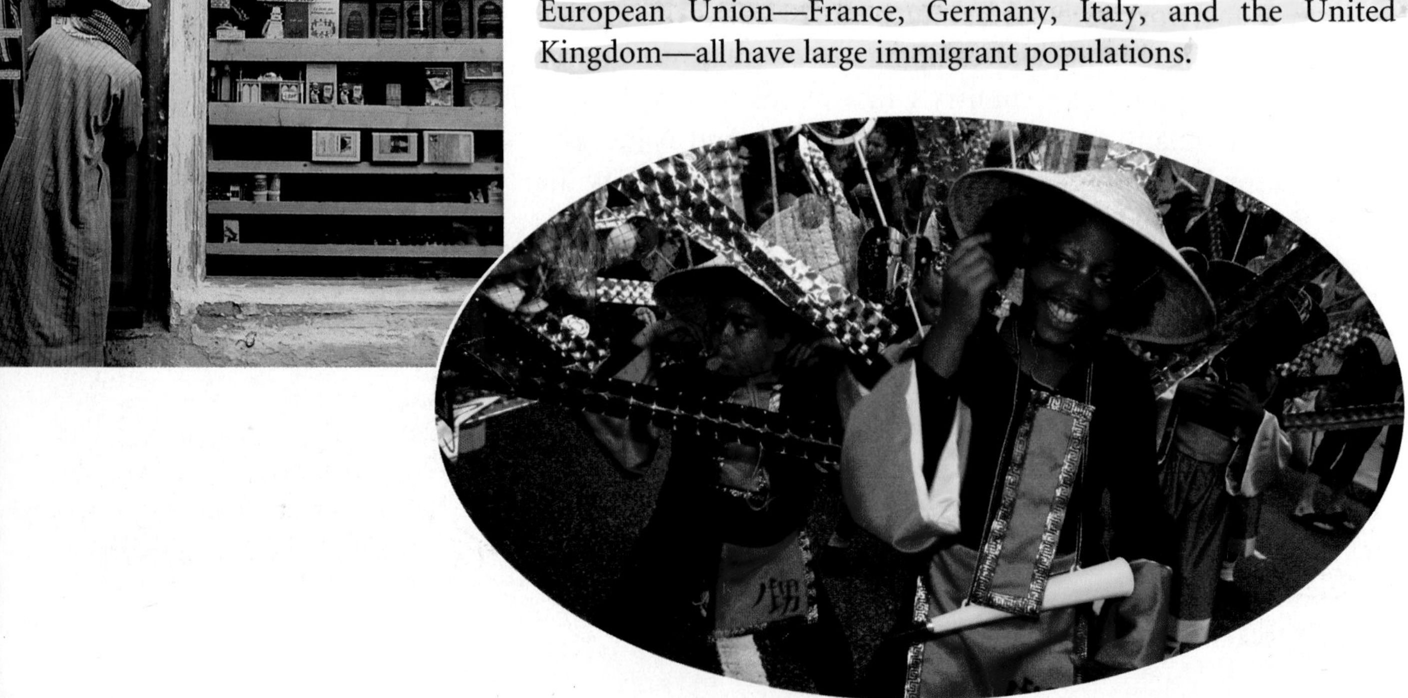

More than 4 million immigrants live in France, making up 6 percent of the total population. Algerians make up the largest group of immigrants in the country. In 2000, the number of immigrants in Germany accounted for nearly 9 percent of its total population, or more than 7 million people. The majority of Germany's immigrants are citizens from Turkey and the former Yugoslavia, with smaller numbers of other Europeans and Asians.

About 2 percent of Italy's population is foreign-born, with Moroccans and Albanians being the largest groups. Increasing numbers of immigrants are also arriving in Italy from South America and China. Most of the United Kingdom's 2 million immigrants come from Ireland, India, and Central and Eastern Europe. They make up about 3 percent of the country's population.

Discovery Channel School
Video
Learn how soccer brings Europeans together.

Blending Cultures Immigrants do not leave their cultures behind when they leave their homelands. They bring their languages, religious beliefs, values, and customs to their new homes. But most immigrants make changes in their ways of life. They may change the way they dress. They may try new foods and discover new ways of cooking. Most immigrants learn the language of their new country.

In many ways, immigration has changed the cultures of Western Europe. In countries like the United Kingdom and France, people from many different backgrounds live and work together. They learn about one another's ways of life. In the process, the cultures blend and change. In this way, many Western European countries have become multicultural.

✓ Reading Check **What does the European Union hope to gain by supporting the arts?**

Faces of Western European Immigration
The photos from left to right show Africans in France, Caribbean Islanders in the UK, a Turkish woman in Germany, and a South American in Italy. All are immigrants.
Analyze Images *Identify some cultural traditions that these people have brought with them.*

Goods are transferred from a train to a truck in Munich-Reim, Germany.

Open Borders

You read that on a high-speed train, travelers can go from one country to another in a matter of hours. Ideas, goods, and raw materials can travel quickly as well. In addition to the closeness of the countries and the good train service, Western Europe is becoming more prosperous because goods and people can now flow freely across its borders.

Adding to the ease of movement across the borders is the use of a single European currency, the euro, which you read about in Chapter 7. Think about how different it was when a traveler had to stop at every country's border to show a passport and to change money to the local currency. Since 2002, the euro has replaced old currencies such as the French franc, the German mark, and the Italian lira.

Adopting the euro is one step in a series of efforts to move Europe toward both economic and political unity. Even the colorful design of the euro coins and bills reflects this effort. They do not have any famous people on them. Instead, they symbolize European unity by featuring a map of Europe, flags of the EU member nations, and bridges, gateways, and windows. The open exchange of ideas, goods, and money is an outcome of the European Union and has helped Western Europe thrive.

Which factors have created a prosperous Western Europe?

Section 1 Assessment

Key Terms
Review the key terms at the beginning of this section. Use each term in a sentence that explains its meaning.

Target Reading Skill
State the main ideas in Section 1.

Comprehension and Critical Thinking
1. **(a) Recall** What is Western Europe's prosperity based on?
(b) Identify Effects How has the growth of industry affected cities in Western Europe?
2. **(a) List** Which four Western European countries have large immigrant populations?
(b) Summarize How have immigrants changed the cultures of Western Europe?
3. **(a) Explain** Why is it easy to travel among Western European countries?
(b) Make Generalizations How would life be different for travelers in Western Europe if borders were not open?

Writing Activity
Write down two facts about Western Europe that you were surprised to learn. How has this new information changed the way you think about Western Europe or its people?

For: An activity on the European Union
Visit: PHSchool.com
Web Code: ldd-7301

Section 2 The Cultures of Eastern Europe

Prepare to Read

Objectives

In this section you will

1. Learn about the different ethnic groups in Eastern Europe.
2. Understand the impact of foreign domination on the region.
3. Find out about ethnic conflict in Eastern Europe.
4. Learn about Eastern Europe's cultural centers.

Taking Notes

As you read, create an outline of this section. The outline below has been started for you.

I. Eastern Europe's ethnic groups
  A. Slavic heritage
    1.
    2.
  B. Non-Slavic groups
II.

Target Reading Skill

Identify Supporting Details The main idea of a section is supported by details that explain or develop the main idea with reasons or examples. The main idea of the section titled Eastern Europe's Ethnic Groups is stated in the first sentence of the first paragraph under the heading Slavic Cultures. As you read, note the details following each of the blue headings that tell more about the cultures of Eastern Europe.

Key Terms

- **migration** (my GRAY shun) *n.* movement from place to place
- **ethnic group** (ETH nik groop) *n.* a group of people who share the same ancestors, culture, language, or religion
- **dialect** (DY uh lekt) *n.* a version of a language found only in a certain region

If you look at a map of Europe as it was one hundred years ago, you may notice something odd. Many of today's Eastern European countries are missing. Until 1918, three large empires ruled most of this region.

Eastern Europe formed a crossroads between east and west. To the east lay the Russian and Ottoman empires. To the west lay Germany and Austria. There were few mountains or other natural barriers to keep invaders out of Eastern Europe. For example, Russia, Prussia, and Austria moved into Poland and divided it among themselves in 1795. Poland did not become independent again until the end of World War I in 1918.

Movement throughout much of Eastern Europe has always been easy. For thousands of years, various groups have entered or crossed this region. This movement from place to place, called **migration** (my GRAY shun), is still happening today.

An Ottoman Empire map from the 1800s

MAP MASTER™ Skills Activity

Regions Slavic languages, such as Czech, Polish, and Russian, are the most widely spoken languages in Eastern Europe. **Identify** Where are Turkic languages spoken? **Transfer Information** Notice the non-subject areas of the map. Where do you think Turkic languages originated?

Go Online
PHSchool.com Use Web Code **ldp-7312** for step-by-step **map skills practice.**

A Roma family

There are many reasons for the frequent migration that has occurred in Eastern Europe. Throughout history, people moved in search of good farmland or plentiful natural resources. Sometimes people moved to escape enemies. People have also fled places where their religious or political beliefs put them in danger. And they have often moved in search of a better life.

Eastern Europe's Ethnic Groups

One of the groups that migrated across Eastern Europe long ago was the Slavs (slahvz). These people first lived in present-day Poland, Slovakia (sloh VAH kee uh), and Ukraine. By the 700s, the Slavs had spread south to Greece, west to the Alps, north to the Baltic Sea, and east into Russia.

Slavic Cultures Today, descendants of Slavs make up most of Eastern Europe's ethnic groups. An **ethnic group** is a group of people with a shared culture, language, or religion that sets them apart from their neighbors. Two thousand years ago, there was a single Slavic language. As the Slavs separated and moved to different areas, different Slavic languages developed. Today, about ten Slavic languages are spoken in Eastern Europe. These include Czech, Polish, and Russian.

Some countries in Eastern Europe are almost entirely Slavic-speaking. These countries include Poland, Croatia (kroh AY shuh), Slovenia (sloh VEE nee uh), and the Czech Republic.

However, even two people who speak the same Slavic language may not speak the same dialect. A **dialect** (DY uh lekt) is a version of a language that can be found only in a certain region.

There are also major religious differences among descendants of Slavs. Most follow the Eastern Orthodox faith or Roman Catholicism. Others may be Protestant or Muslim.

Identify Supporting Details
What details in these paragraphs give examples of Slavic languages?

Other Ethnic Groups Many other ethnic groups live in Eastern Europe as well. About 90 percent of the people of Hungary belong to an ethnic group called the Magyars (MAG yahrz). In Romania, most people are Romanians. Similarly, in Albania, most people are Albanian. Roma, sometimes called Gypsies, and Germans live in several of the countries of Eastern Europe.

✓ Reading Check **Name three Slavic languages that are spoken in Eastern Europe.**

Worshiping in Different Ways
Below, hundreds of Muslims pray at a mosque in Bosnia. At the left, women participate in a religious ceremony in an Eastern Orthodox church in Macedonia.
Synthesize *Though these Eastern Europeans practice different religions, what other cultural traditions might they share?*

MAP MASTER™ Skills Activity

Regions This book uses the term *Eastern Europe* to describe the region including the former Yugoslavia and the nations dominated by the Soviet Union after World War II.
Identify Which nation is physically in the eastern half of Europe, but is not part of what we call Eastern Europe?
Apply Information Why is this country not considered part of Eastern Europe?

Go Online PHSchool.com Use Web Code **ldp-7322** for step-by-step **map skills practice.**

Eastern Europe: Political

Foreign Domination

As you read at the beginning of this section, Eastern Europe is a region with a history of foreign domination. As you read in Chapter 7, most of Eastern Europe came under Soviet control following World War II. Communist leaders, influenced by the Soviet Union, led the governments of most Eastern European countries.

As in the Soviet Union, the Communists tried to control almost every aspect of people's lives. They took private land, and punished people for criticizing the government. They discouraged traditional expressions of culture such as religion. However, they did not succeed in destroying Eastern European culture. Instead, the cultural traditions you have read about brought people together. In Poland, for example, the Roman Catholic faith unified people in opposition to the Soviets. In Ukraine, people continued to speak Ukrainian even though Russian was the official language.

✓ Reading Check **What country influenced Eastern Europe's leaders?**

Ethnic Conflict

Eastern Europe's long history of migration and foreign domination have made it an ethnically diverse region. At times, that diversity has brought ethnic conflict. Ethnic conflict in the region has been resolved both peacefully and violently.

Czechs and Slovaks: A Peaceful Division Czechoslovakia (chek uh sloh VAH kee uh) had two main ethnic groups. The Czechs lived mostly in the western regions of Bohemia and Moravia. The Slovaks lived mostly in the eastern region of Slovakia. Hungarians, Ukrainians, Germans, and Poles lived in both areas.

Czechoslovakia was taken over by Communists, heavily influenced by the Soviet Union, after World War II. From the 1960s to the 1980s, students and writers formed groups protesting communism and calling for a return to democracy. Vaclav Havel, a playwright, explained his reasons for staying in Czechoslovakia.

> **"I am Czech. . . . This is my language, this is my home. I don't feel myself to be patriotic, because I don't feel that to be Czech is to be something more than French, English, or European, or anybody else. . . . I try to do something for my country because I live here."**
>
> —*Vaclav Havel*

Such protests helped end communism in Czechoslovakia. However, Czechs and the Slovaks disagreed about how to run the newly democratic country. In 1993, they agreed to peacefully separate into two countries—the Czech Republic and Slovakia.

Yugoslavia: A Violent Division Unlike in Czechoslovakia, ethnic differences in the former country of Yugoslavia (yoo goh SLAH vee uh) led to violence and the breakup of the country. You will read more about this conflict in Chapter 10.

√ Reading Check **Who is Vaclav Havel?**

The Velvet Revolution
Crowds celebrate Czechoslovakia's transition to a democratic government, which took place in a peaceful movement called the Velvet Revolution. Playwright Vaclav Havel, shown below, became the country's first president. **Infer** *Why was Czechoslovakia's change in government called the "Velvet Revolution"?*

Prague: A Historic City
Prague's buildings are a rich mix of architectural styles, including Renaissance, Gothic, and modern. Many of Prague's historic buildings house art collections. **Apply Information** *What role do you think tourism plays in the economy of the Czech Republic?*

European Centers of Culture

As in Western Europe, Eastern Europe's cities are important centers of life and culture throughout the region. These cities have thrived particularly since the fall of communist governments in the region in the 1980s.

Prague: A City Rich in Culture Prague (prahg) is the capital of the Czech Republic. Though people settled in the region thousands of years ago, the city first developed in the A.D. 800s. The Vltava (VUL tuh vuh) River winds its way through the city. Prague Castle, built in the late 800s, sits high on a hill overlooking the city. Houses dating back hundreds of years line the narrow streets of the historic city center.

Prague has always been an important center of culture. Antonín Dvorák (AHN toh nin DVAWR zhahk) and several other famous Czech composers lived in Prague. Today, their music is performed every year at a spring music festival in the city. The composer Wolfgang Mozart, an Austrian, also lived and wrote some of his famous pieces in Prague.

Prague is well known for its many theaters. It is also an important center for art, with its many museums and galleries.

Budapest: Queen of the Danube Budapest (BOO duh pest) is Hungary's capital and its largest city. The Danube River runs through the city and separates it into two regions, Buda and Pest. These two regions, once separate cities, were joined together in 1873. Budapest got the nickname "Queen of the Danube" because of the beauty of the Danube and the hills surrounding the city.

Hungarian composers Béla Bartók (seated at left) and Zoltán Kodály (seated at right), with other Hungarian musicians, in the early 1900s

The history of Budapest stretches back to pre-Roman times. Ruins of Roman houses and baths can still be seen in Budapest. Today, it is a bustling capital city where more than one fifth of all Hungarians live. Unlike many Eastern European cities, Budapest remained a thriving cultural center even during communist times. This was because Hungary had stronger ties to Western Europe than other Eastern European countries had.

Like Prague, Budapest has produced famous composers such as Béla Bartók (BAY lah BAHR tawk) and Franz Liszt (frahntsz list). It is also an important center of art, theater, and scientific research.

 ✓ Reading Check **What is the capital of the Czech Republic?**

Section 2 Assessment

Key Terms
Review the key terms at the beginning of this section. Use each term in a sentence that explains its meaning.

Target Reading Skill
State the details that support the main idea on page 233.

Comprehension and Critical Thinking
1. (a) Locate Where did Slavs first live in Europe?
(b) Generalize What are some differences among Slavic groups?
(c) Summarize How did Poles use their culture to oppose the Soviet Union?
2. (a) Note Give an example of an Eastern European ethnic conflict that was solved peacefully.
(b) Conclude Why were the groups in this conflict able to come to an agreement without violence?
3. (a) Identify Name two important Eastern European cities that are centers of culture.
(b) Predict How might EU membership affect life in these two cities?

Writing Activity
Write a paragraph about ethnic diversity in Eastern Europe. In your paragraph, explain how ethnic diversity can enrich a country's culture and how it can create challenges as well.

Writing Tip Begin your paragraph with a topic sentence that states your main idea. Be sure to include examples that support your main idea.

Supporting a Position

Mr. St. Jean's debate class was discussing immigration. Mr. St. Jean had chosen that topic because he knew people had strong—and often opposing—opinions about the subject. For example, he pointed out that some people believe that when a country's economy is not doing well, immigration should be limited. They reason that immigrants might take jobs from people who have lived in the country for many years. Mr. St. Jean asked his class to think about this issue. Should countries limit immigration? And if so, what should the limits be?

Asiya thought about her own family. They had emigrated from Algeria to France. Her mother worked in a restaurant, and her father worked in a library. She did not think her parents had taken jobs from any French people. And if they had stayed in Algeria, they would not have had as good a life as they had in France. She decided to argue in favor of immigration.

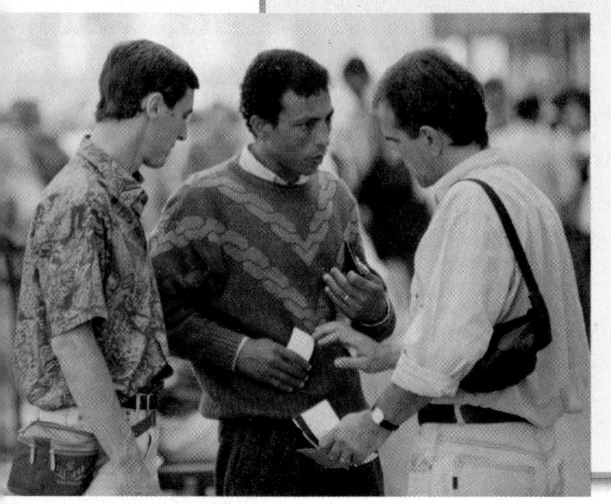

A French police officer checks an immigrant's passport.

When you support a position, you present the reasoning and the evidence that back up your opinion or statement.

Learn the Skill

To learn how to support a position, follow the steps below:

1. **Write a statement that summarizes the position you want to support.** In general, a position is a broadly stated opinion that can be supported with facts. For her position statement, Asiya wrote, *Countries should not limit immigration.*
2. **Identify at least three reasons that support your position.** You may want to make notes or create a chart. Add as many details as you can to strengthen your argument. Use examples.
3. **Support each reason with accurate evidence.** Use reliable sources to strengthen your argument.
4. **Organize your reasons and supporting evidence.** Explain the connections between pieces of information, such as cause and effect.
5. **Add a reasoned conclusion.** Your conclusion should restate your position and summarize your reasons for it.

Practice the Skill

Reread the passages about immigration and culture on pages 226–227. Then decide what *your* position is about immigration. Use the steps in Learn the Skill to support your position.

1. Prepare to write a statement summarizing your position by first jotting down your ideas about immigration. Think about these questions as you decide on your position: Why do people emigrate? Why do some countries welcome immigrants? Why do other countries sharply limit immigration? How do immigrants affect the countries they move to? Now choose a position, and write a statement that summarizes it.

2. Add at least three reasons to explain why you hold your position. Clarify your reasons with examples or other details.

3. Research your position using reliable sources. Add additional reasons, details, and examples.

4. Review the information you have gathered and organize it in order to strengthen your argument. Does one reason lead to another?

5. Summarize your position about immigration in a one-sentence conclusion.

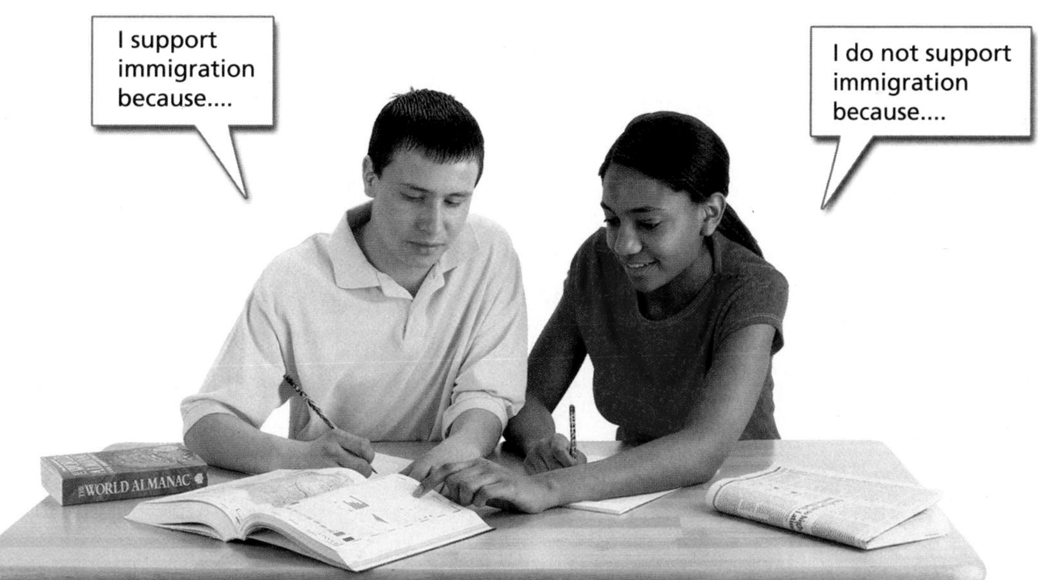

I support immigration because....
I do not support immigration because....
WORLD ALMANAC

Apply the Skill

Reread the passage titled Growth of Industry on page 223. Use the steps you have learned in this lesson to identify and support a position on whether the trend toward urbanization in Europe is a positive or a negative thing.

Section 3

The Cultures of the Russian Federation

Prepare to Read

Objectives

In this section you will

1. Learn about Russia's ethnic groups.
2. Find out about Russia's culture and its educational system.

Taking Notes

As you read this section, look for information about how cultural expression differed in the Soviet Union and Russia. Copy the table below and record your findings in it.

Cultural Expression	
Soviet Union	**Russia**
•	•
•	•
•	•
•	•

Target Reading Skill

Identify Main Ideas Identifying main ideas can help you remember what you read. Sometimes the main idea is not stated directly. To find the main idea, add up all the details in the paragraphs and then state the main idea in your own words. Carefully read the details in the two paragraphs below. Then state the main idea of that section.

Key Terms

- **heritage** (HEHR uh tij) *n.* the customs and practices passed from one generation to the next
- **propaganda** (prahp uh GAN duh) *n.* the spread of ideas designed to support a cause or hurt an opposing cause

Moscow's St. Basil's Cathedral was built in the 1500s.

For many years, Russians passing the Church of Saints Cosmas and Damian in Moscow never heard a choir. They never saw a bride and groom leave the church. They never heard religious services. The only sound they heard was the hum of machines printing government documents. The government of the Soviet Union owned the church and used it as a printing shop. In the Soviet Union, the government tried to prevent people from practicing religion.

In 1991, the Soviet Union collapsed. Two years later, Russians who had never given up their faith took back their church. Now the Church of Saints Cosmas and Damian is filled with people singing songs of worship. In recent years, hundreds of other churches in Moscow have reopened their doors. The same return to religion can be seen in places of worship across all of Russia.

Russia's Ethnic Groups

The Russian Orthodox religion is a branch of Christianity closely related to the Eastern Orthodox Church. It has been a powerful bond among many Russians for hundreds of years. It is part of the Russian **heritage** (HEHR uh tij), or the customs and practices that are passed from one generation to the next.

Russia's ethnic culture is another part of the Russian heritage. More than 80 percent of Russian citizens belong to the ethnic group of Russian Slavs. These people generally speak the Russian language. Most of them live in the western parts of the Russian Federation. However, Russia is also home to many non-Russian ethnic groups.

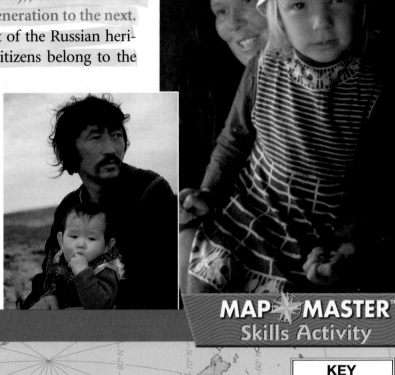

Both of the families at the right live in Siberia.

Place Altaic languages, originating in Asia, are spoken in Russia today along with Indo-European and other languages. **Locate** In what parts of Russia are Asian languages spoken? **Analyze Information** How has Russia's location on two continents shaped its culture?

Go Online PHSchool.com Use Web Code **ldp-7313 for step-by-step map skills practice.**

Buddhism in Russia
A Buddhist monastery in southern Siberia reflects the Tibetan heritage of the people who live there.
Compare and Contrast *Compare this photo with the ones on page 231. Besides religion, what other cultural differences might there be among the three groups?*

Other Ethnic Groups More than 60 non-Russian ethnic groups live in Russia. Most of them live far from the heavily populated western areas. People speaking languages related to Finnish and Turkish live near the Ural and Caucasus (KAW kuh sus) mountains. Armenians and Mongolians live along Russia's southern edges. The Yakuts (yah KOOTS) live in small areas of Siberia. These groups speak languages other than Russian.

They also follow different religions. Muslims make up Russia's second-largest religious group, after Russian Orthodox. Many followers of Buddhism (BOOD iz um) live near Russia's border with China.

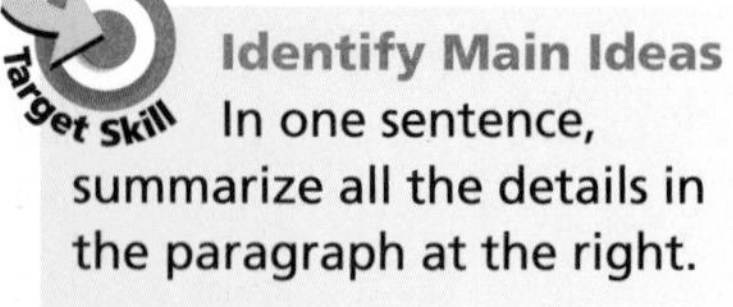

Identify Main Ideas In one sentence, summarize all the details in the paragraph at the right.

Ethnic Majorities Recall that the Soviet Union was made up of many republics. Each Soviet republic was the homeland of a large ethnic group. When the Soviet Union came apart, the non-Russian republics broke away and formed their own countries. For example, Armenia is a former Soviet republic with a majority of ethnic Armenians. It gained its independence in 1991.

Other ethnic groups remained part of Russia, sometimes unwillingly. Many of them have called for more rights to rule themselves. Some have even called for independence. These efforts have brought much ethnic tension. Yet despite this great tension, fighting has broken out only between Russia and one other ethnic group—the Chechens. You will read about their independence movement, and the Russian government's repression of it, in Chapter 10.

The government of the Russian Federation has tried to keep the country unified. It has given many ethnic groups the right to rule themselves. However, it must work hard to turn the nation's ethnic diversity into an asset, rather than a source of conflict.

√ Reading Check **What is Russia's largest religious group?**

The Space Age Begins

When the Soviet Union launched the first artificial satellite on October 4, 1957, it took the world by surprise. Less than four years later, the Soviet Union shocked the world again by sending the first human being into space. On April 12, 1961, twenty-seven-year-old Cosmonaut Yuri Gagarin spent one hour and 48 minutes in space. Gagarin completed a single orbit in the spacecraft *Vostok I*, before returning to Earth.

Yuri Gagarin
Yuri Gagarin completed two years of secret training before the flight.

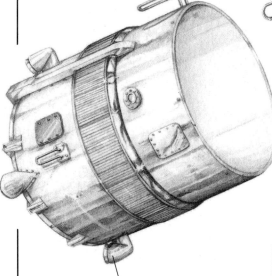

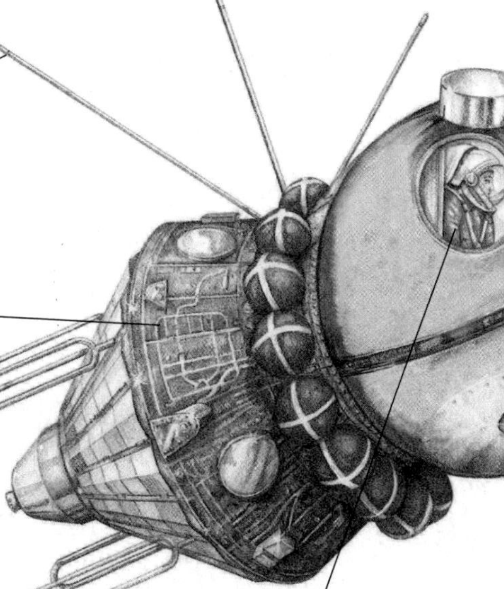

Antennas allowed Gagarin to communicate with Soviet scientists at home.
The spacecraft's instruments and main engine were located in this section, which separated from the capsule before landing.
Gagarin was just a passenger in the capsule. He could not control the spacecraft.
Four jets at the base of this section helped turn and tilt the spacecraft as it headed for orbit.

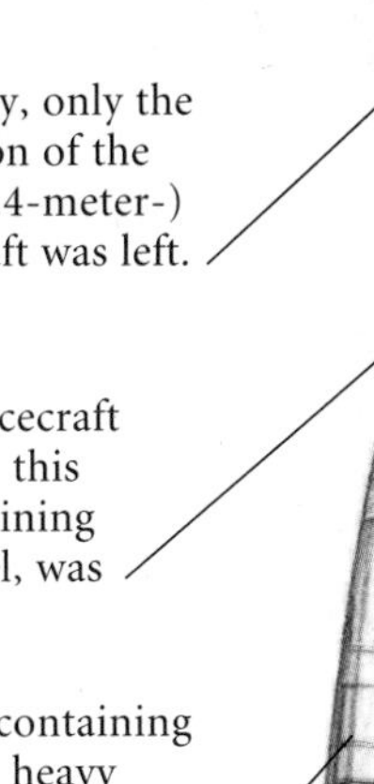

Upon re-entry, only the capsule section of the 14.4-foot- (4.4-meter-) long spacecraft was left.
When the spacecraft reached orbit, this section, containing additional fuel, was released.
This section, containing fuel to lift the heavy spacecraft, was released within two minutes after liftoff.

Blasting off
Vostok I takes off with Yuri Gagarin on board. After 15 minutes, Gagarin reported, "The flight is proceeding normally. I feel well."

ANALYZING IMAGES
In which section of *Vostok I* did the cosmonaut sit?

Elaborately decorated Fabergé eggs like this one were made in St. Petersburg in the late 1800s.

Russian Culture and Education

Russia has produced many great artists. Russia's artistic heritage includes outstanding architecture, fine paintings, great plays, and intricate art objects like Fabergé (FAB ur zhay) eggs.

Russian Artists The novelist Leo Tolstoy (TOHL stoy) wrote powerful stories of life in Russia in the 1800s. Peter Tchaikovsky (chy KAWF skee) composed moving classical music. Russian painters, such as Wassily Kandinsky (VAS uh lee kan DIN skee), were leaders in the modern art movement in the early 1900s. Creating works of art has been a tradition among Russians.

Under Soviet communism, the creation of new works of art nearly came to a halt. The Soviet government believed that the purpose of art was to serve political goals. The government only approved art that supported its propaganda campaigns. **Propaganda** is the spread of ideas designed to support some cause or to hurt an opposing cause.

The Soviet Union broke apart in 1991. With the collapse of Soviet communism, the Russian people eagerly returned to their artistic traditions. Creating new works was once again possible.

Artistic Traditions in Russia

Painting ▲
Russian painter Wassily Kandinsky (1866–1944), above, was an influential abstract artist. Abstract artists do not try to depict things the way that they appear to the eye. His style ranged from pure bursts of color to exact geometric shapes.

Cinema ▶
Motion pictures came to Russia in 1896. The cinema was extremely popular there before the 1917 revolution and during World War I. After the revolution, Soviet leaders used the cinema to spread communist ideas. The golden age of Russian cinema was the 1920s, although filmmaking techniques continued to develop under Stalin.

A 1929 Russian movie poster

Tolstoy and Chekhov in 1901

◀ Literature
Russian literature is rich and varied, from the short stories of Nikolay Gogol to the novels of Leo Tolstoy and the plays of Anton Chekhov. Often writing in a harsh political environment, Russian authors have influenced writers all over the world with their wit, expressiveness, and insight into the human mind.

St. Petersburg: A Cultural Symbol The second-largest city and the largest seaport in Russia, the city of St. Petersburg lies on the Gulf of Finland and is an important center of Russian culture. Visitors to the city can clearly see the mixture of Russian and other European cultures. St. Petersburg was founded by Peter the Great in 1703. His goal was to create a Russian city as beautiful as any Western European city. He employed Western architects to design the city. St. Petersburg was the capital of Russia for more than 200 years before it was renamed Leningrad in 1924. In September 1991, its name was changed back to St. Petersburg.

Because of its grand architecture and many canals, St. Petersburg was once called Venice of the North. The Neva (NEE vuh) River winds gracefully through the city. Along the river's banks are palaces and public buildings hundreds of years old. St. Petersburg's grandest sight, the Winter Palace, is on the Neva. The palace has more than 1,000 rooms and was the winter home of Russia's tsars. Part of the palace is now the Hermitage (HUR muh tij) Museum. Built in 1764, it houses one of the world's finest art collections of Russian, Asian, and European art.

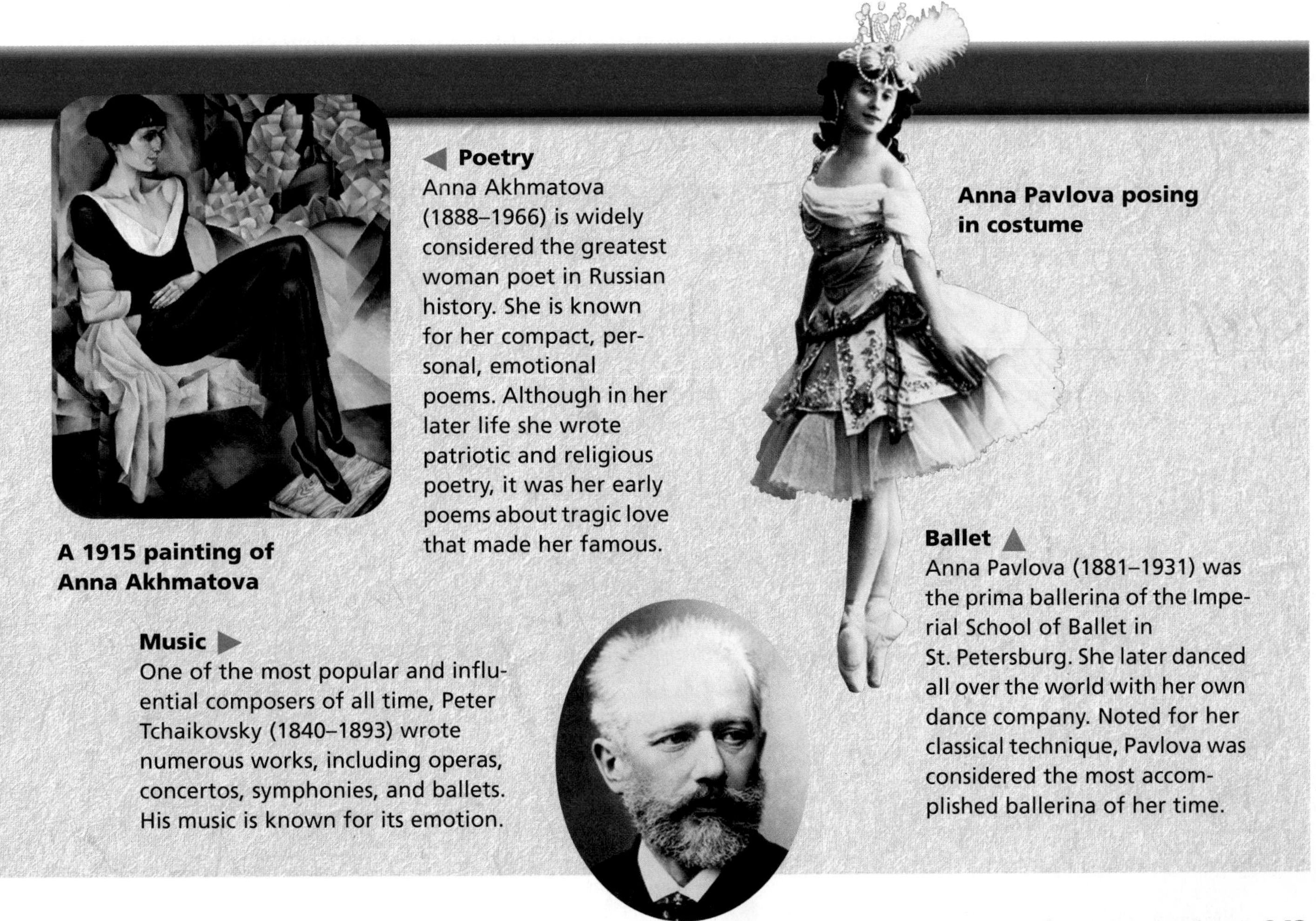

A 1915 painting of Anna Akhmatova

◀ **Poetry**
Anna Akhmatova (1888–1966) is widely considered the greatest woman poet in Russian history. She is known for her compact, personal, emotional poems. Although in her later life she wrote patriotic and religious poetry, it was her early poems about tragic love that made her famous.

Anna Pavlova posing in costume

Ballet ▲
Anna Pavlova (1881–1931) was the prima ballerina of the Imperial School of Ballet in St. Petersburg. She later danced all over the world with her own dance company. Noted for her classical technique, Pavlova was considered the most accomplished ballerina of her time.

Music ▶
One of the most popular and influential composers of all time, Peter Tchaikovsky (1840–1893) wrote numerous works, including operas, concertos, symphonies, and ballets. His music is known for its emotion.

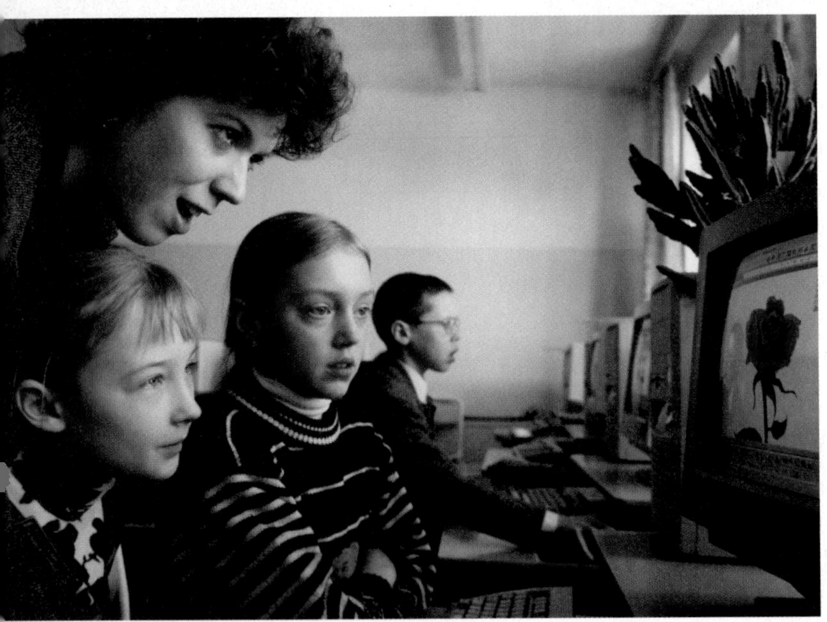

Children learning computer skills in a Russian school

Russia's Educational System One of the strengths of the Soviet Union was its free public education system. Under that system, the number of Russians who could read and write rose from about 40 percent to nearly 100 percent. Higher education was also free for Soviet citizens.

The Russian Federation continued free public schooling for children between ages 6 and 17. When students finish ninth grade, they can choose to continue their education in a secondary school or a vocational school. Secondary schools emphasize academic subjects such as mathematics and science, while the vocational schools prepare students for careers in industry and agriculture. Schools are updating their old courses of study, which used to emphasize only one official point of view.

These changes show that Russia is trying to recover the riches of its past even as it prepares for a new future. Religion and art, two important parts of Russia's cultural heritage, can now be freely expressed. And Russia's young people, unlike their parents, can grow up deciding their future for themselves.

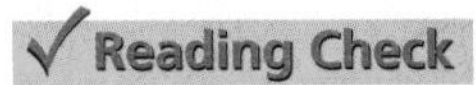

Who founded the city of St. Petersburg?

Section 3 Assessment

Key Terms

Review the key terms at the beginning of this section. Use each term in a sentence that explains its meaning.

Target Reading Skill

State the main ideas in Section 3.

Comprehension and Critical Thinking

1. (a) Recall What is Russia's major ethnic group?
(b) Identify Point of View Why do some ethnic groups in Russia seek independence?
(c) Draw Conclusions How has Russia's ethnic mix created challenges for the new Russian government?
2. (a) List Give some examples of the ways in which Russians are reconnecting with their past.
(b) Identify Effects How have political changes in Russia led to changes in education?
(c) Predict How might the lives of young people in Russia today be different from those of their parents' generation?

Writing Activity

Suppose that you are visiting St. Petersburg. Write a postcard to your family describing the works of art, architecture, and other expressions of Russian culture that you have seen.

For: An activity on Russian cities
Visit: PHSchool.com
Web Code: ldd-7303

Chapter 8

Review and Assessment

Celebrating Carnival in London

Chapter Summary

Section 1: The Cultures of Western Europe

- Industry has made many Western European countries wealthy.
- Western European cities are the cultural centers of their countries.
- Goods, materials, and ideas can travel easily and quickly across Western Europe.

Section 2: The Cultures of Eastern Europe

- Long ago, many ethnic groups migrated across Eastern Europe.
- Under foreign domination, some expressions of Eastern European culture were discouraged.
- Ethnic conflict has influenced the modern history of Eastern Europe.
- Prague and Budapest are important cultural centers of Eastern Europe.

Section 3: The Cultures of the Russian Federation

- Russia has more than 60 different ethnic groups.
- Russia has a rich cultural heritage.

A Fabergé egg from Russia

Key Terms

Each of the statements below contains a key term from the chapter. If the statement is true, write *true*. If it is false, change the term to make it true.

1. A tariff is a different version of a language.
2. Propaganda is the spread of ideas designed to support a cause.
3. Someone who moves to one country from another is an immigrant.
4. People in the same ethnic group share the same ancestors, culture, or religion.
5. Heritage is the customs and practices passed from one generation to the next.
6. Diversification is the movement of populations toward cities and the resulting city growth.
7. Migration is a movement from place to place.

Review and Assessment (continued)

◆ Comprehension and Critical Thinking

8. (a) **List** Name three cities in Western Europe.
   (b) **Summarize** What features make cities in Western Europe centers of culture?
9. (a) **Explain** What does the concept of open borders mean?
   (b) **Infer** Why do Western Europeans generally have a higher standard of living than do Eastern Europeans?
10. (a) **Identify** Who were the Slavs?
    (b) **Synthesize** How does Slavic culture live on in Eastern Europe today?
11. (a) **Recall** Name two of Czechoslovakia's ethnic groups.
    (b) **Compare and Contrast** How was the breakup of Czechoslovakia different from the breakup of Yugoslavia?
    (c) **Draw Conclusions** Why was Czechoslovakia able to break up peacefully?
12. (a) **Note** About how many ethnic groups live in Russia?
    (b) **Analyze** How have non-Russian ethnic groups reacted to recent changes in Russia?
13. (a) **Recall** When did the Soviet Union break apart?
    (b) **Find Main Ideas** How has life changed for the Russian people since the collapse of the Soviet Union?
    (c) **Predict** What might the future hold for the Russian people?

◆ Skills Practice

Supporting a Position In the Skills for Life activity in this chapter, you learned how to support a position. Review the steps you followed to learn this skill. Then turn to the section titled Ethnic Majorities on page 240. Read about Russia's republics. Decide whether you support or oppose independence for Russia's republics and then support your position.

◆ Writing Activity: Language Arts

Suppose you had friends who were visiting Europe and Russia for the first time. What information would you want to share with them? Create a brief travel guide that your friends could use to plan their trip. Mention interesting places and activities, and provide background information on the cultures of the people they will meet.

MAP MASTER™ Skills Activity

Place Location For each place listed below, write the letter from the map that shows its location.

1. France
2. Ukraine
3. Russia
4. Germany
5. Slovakia
6. St. Petersburg

Go Online PHSchool.com Use Web Code **ldp-7363** for an **interactive map.**

Europe and Russia

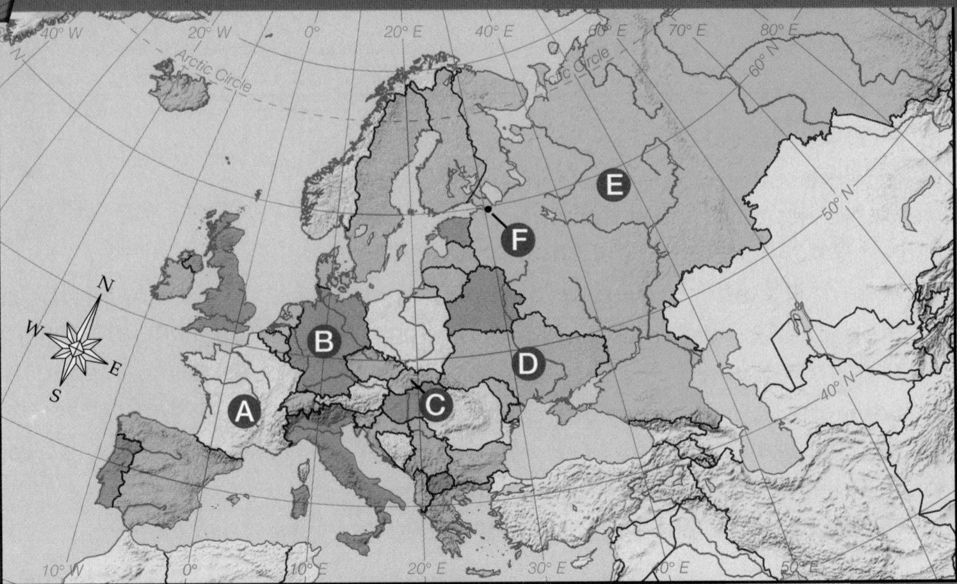

Standardized Test Prep

Test-Taking Tips

Some questions on standardized tests ask you to analyze graphic organizers. Study the concept web below. Then follow the tips to answer the sample question at the right.

TIP Preview the question. Keep it in mind as you study the information in the web.

Pick the letter that best answers the question.
Another name that belongs on this web is

- **A** Peter the Great.
- **B** Tsar Nicholas II.
- **C** Pablo Picasso.
- **D** Peter Tchaikovsky.

TIP Be sure that you read all four options. If you don't read each one, you can't be certain that you've found the best choice.

Think It Through What other name belongs in the web? The center of the web says Russian Artists—meaning painters, writers, musicians, dancers, and so on. You can rule out A and B, because both are political figures in Russian history. That leaves C and D. You may know that Picasso is Spanish. That leaves Tchaikovsky, answer D.

Practice Questions

Use the tips above and other tips in this book to help you answer the following questions.

1. Advances in farming about 200 years ago led to
   - **A** the Velvet Revolution.
   - **B** increased immigration.
   - **C** the growth of cities.
   - **D** open borders in Western Europe.
2. Which group's descendants make up most of Eastern Europe's ethnic groups?
   - **A** the Romanians
   - **B** the Albanians
   - **C** the Russians
   - **D** the Slavs
3. More than 80 percent of Russian citizens belong to this ethnic group.
   - **A** Russian Slavs
   - **B** Mongolians
   - **C** Yakuts
   - **D** Buddhists

Study the concept web and answer the question that follows.

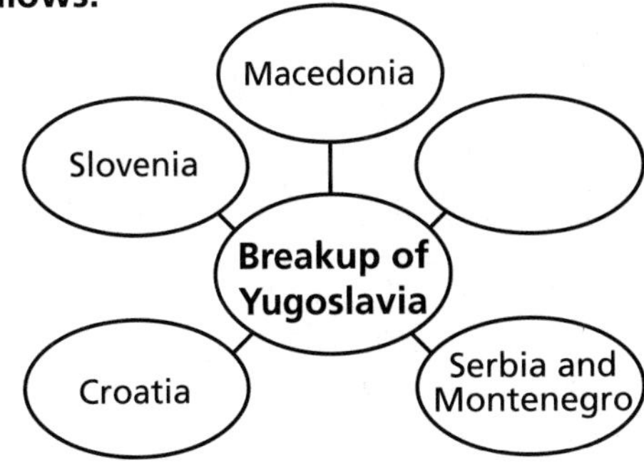

4. What other country belongs on the web?
   - **A** Russia
   - **B** Bosnia and Herzegovina
   - **C** Austria
   - **D** Romania

Use Web Code **lda-7303** for a **Chapter 8 self-test.**

Chapter 9

Western Europe

Chapter Preview

This chapter focuses on key countries in Western Europe: the United Kingdom, France, Sweden, Italy, and Germany.

Country Databank

The Country Databank provides data and descriptions of each of the countries in Western Europe.

Target Reading Skill

Using Context In this chapter you will focus on using context to help you understand unfamiliar words. Context includes the words, phrases, and sentences surrounding the word.

▶ **Boats on one of the many canals in Venice, Italy**

Place Western Europe stretches from just north of Africa to the Arctic Circle, and from the Atlantic Ocean to the Mediterranean Sea. **Identify** Which countries lie partly within the Arctic Circle? **Apply Information** How do the climates of these countries differ from those countries that border the Mediterranean Sea?

Go Online
PHSchool.com Use Web Code **ldp-7411** for step-by-step **map skills practice.**

Introducing Western Europe

Guide for Reading

This section provides an introduction to the 24 countries of Western Europe.

- Look at the map on the previous page and then read the paragraphs to learn about each nation.
- Analyze the data to compare the countries.
- What characteristics do most of these countries share?
- What are some key differences among the countries?

Viewing the Video Overview

View the World Studies Video Overview to learn more about each of the countries. As you watch, answer these questions:

- What are the four major geographic regions of Western Europe?
- What are the major bodies of water and why are they important?

Discovery
CHANNEL
SCHOOL
Video
Explore the geography of Western Europe.

Andorra

Capital	Andorra la Vella
Land Area	181 sq mi; 468 sq km
Population	68,403
Ethnic Group(s)	Spanish, Andorran, French, Portuguese
Religion(s)	Roman Catholic
Government	parliamentary democracy
Currency	euro
Leading Exports	tobacco products, furniture
Language(s)	Catalan (official), Spanish, French, Portuguese

The small country of Andorra (an DAWR uh) lies high in the eastern Pyrenees mountain range between France and Spain. France and Spain together ruled Andorra from the 1200s until the first full elections were held in 1993. Today, a 28-member legislature governs the country. Andorra's main source of income is its tourist industry. Most tourists come from France, Italy, or Spain to shop in the tax-free stores or to ski. Andorra's wealthiest citizens are its hotel owners.

The town of Andorra la Vella, Andorra

Austria

Capital	Vienna
Land Area	31,945 sq mi; 82,738 sq km
Population	8.2 million
Ethnic Group(s)	German, Croatian, Slovene, Hungarian, Czech, Slovak, Roma
Religion(s)	Roman Catholic, Protestant, Muslim, Jewish
Government	federal republic
Currency	euro
Leading Exports	machinery and equipment, motor vehicles and parts, paper and paperboard, metal goods, chemicals, iron and steel, textiles, foodstuffs
Language(s)	German (official), Croatian, Slovenian

Austria (AWS tree uh) borders several countries including the Czech Republic, Germany, Hungary, Italy, and Slovenia. In 1273, Austria came under the control of the Hapsburg Empire. Present-day Austria was established in 1918 after the fall of the Austro-Hungarian Empire during World War I. In 1938, Germany took control of Austria. Austria regained full independence 17 years later, in 1955. Having few natural resources, Austria imports large amounts of fossil fuels and energy from Russia.

A poster for the 1924 Commercial Fair in Brussels, Belgium

Belgium

Capital	Brussels
Land Area	11,672 sq mi; 30,230 sq km
Population	10.3 million
Ethnic Group(s)	Fleming, Walloon
Religion(s)	Roman Catholic, Protestant
Government	federal parliamentary democracy under a constitutional monarch
Currency	euro
Leading Exports	machinery and equipment, chemicals, diamonds, metals and metal products
Language(s)	Dutch (official), French (official), German (official)

Belgium (BEL jum) is a small country bordered by Germany, France, Luxembourg, and the Netherlands. It only takes about four hours to cross Belgium by car or by train. Belgium is one of the most densely populated countries in Europe. More than 95 percent of its citizens live in cities. The city of Antwerp is Belgium's main commercial center and Europe's second-largest port. Antwerp is important because Belgium has few natural resources and depends on the export of goods and services from other countries.

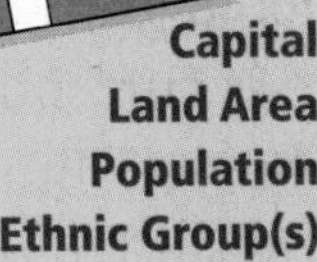

Denmark

Capital	Copenhagen
Land Area	16,368 sq mi; 42,394 sq km
Population	5.4 million
Ethnic Group(s)	Scandinavian, Inuit, Faeroe, Southwest Asian, Central Asian
Religion(s)	Protestant, Roman Catholic, Muslim
Government	constitutional monarchy
Currency	Danish krone
Leading Exports	machinery and instruments, meat and meat products, dairy products, fish, chemicals, furniture, ships, windmills
Language(s)	Danish (official)

Denmark (DEN mahrk) is the southernmost country in the region of northern Europe known as Scandinavia (skan duh NAY vee uh). Denmark contains many hundreds of islands, including self-governing Greenland. Greenland, located in the North Atlantic Ocean, is the world's largest island. Denmark itself is one of the flattest countries in the world. More than 65 percent of its land is used to raise crops. The North Atlantic current creates a damp but usually mild climate. These conditions help to make the region's farming profitable.

Introducing Western Europe

A brown bear in Lappi, Finland

Finland

Capital	Helsinki
Land Area	11,610 sq mi; 305,470 sq km
Population	5.2 million
Ethnic Group(s)	Finnish, Swedish, Sami, Roma, Tartar
Religion(s)	Protestant, Russian Orthodox
Government	republic
Currency	euro
Leading Exports	machinery and equipment, chemicals, metals, timber, paper, pulp
Language(s)	Finnish (official), Swedish (official), Sami

Bordered by Norway, Sweden, and Russia, Finland (FIN lund) is a low-lying country that can be divided into three geographic zones. There is a low-lying coastal strip in the south and west, where most of the cities are located. The interior of Finland is made up of vast forests and woodlands. This area also contains more than 60,000 lakes. Finland's third region is thinly wooded or barren and lies north of the Arctic Circle. The climate is extreme there. Temperatures fall well below zero degrees Fahrenheit during the six-month winter.

France

Capital	Paris
Land Area	210,668 sq mi; 545,630 sq km
Population	59.8 million
Ethnic Group(s)	French, North African, German, Breton, Basque
Religion(s)	Roman Catholic, Protestant, Jewish, Muslim
Government	republic
Currency	euro
Leading Exports	machinery and transportation equipment, aircraft, plastics, chemicals, pharmaceutical products, iron and steel, beverages
Language(s)	French (official), Provençal, German, Breton, Catalan, Basque

Located between the English Channel and the Mediterranean Sea, France (frans) is bordered by Italy, Switzerland, Germany, Belgium, and Spain. France has a long history of wars, invasions, and foreign occupations. Though it suffered great damage during both world wars, France is currently an economic leader among the nations of Europe. France helped to establish the European Union. It is the fourth-largest exporter in the world. Paris, the capital, is considered to be one of the world's great cultural centers.

Germany

Capital	Berlin
Land Area	134,835 sq mi; 349,223 sq km
Population	83 million
Ethnic Group(s)	German, Turkish, Southeast Asian
Religion(s)	Protestant, Roman Catholic, Muslim
Government	federal republic
Currency	euro
Leading Exports	machinery, vehicles, chemicals, metals and manufactured goods, foodstuffs, textiles
Language(s)	German (official), Turkish

Germany (JUR muh nee) is located in Central Europe, with coastlines on the Baltic and North seas. It is bordered by nine countries, including France, Poland, and Austria. Germany was divided into two countries from 1949 to 1990. Today the country faces problems such as unemployment and an aging population. Germans are also still working to rebuild the former East Germany. However, Germany, an EU member, is now an economic leader. It is the second-largest exporter in the world. Germany's economy—based mainly on services and industry—is Europe's largest.

Greece

Capital	Athens
Land Area	50,502 sq mi; 130,800 sq km
Population	10.6 million
Ethnic Group(s)	Greek
Religion(s)	Eastern Orthodox, Muslim
Government	parliamentary republic
Currency	euro
Leading Exports	food and beverages, manufactured goods, petroleum products, chemicals, textiles
Language(s)	Greek (official), Turkish, Macedonian, Albanian

Greece (grees) is located in southern Europe. It is made up of the southern tip of the Balkan Peninsula and more than 2,000 islands. It is surrounded by the Aegean, Ionian, and Mediterranean seas. Greece's landscape is dominated by mountains and coastlines. Greece is famous for its ancient culture, which influenced the development of the modern world. Today, Greece is a member of the EU. However, it has one of the weakest economies in that organization. Efforts to strengthen the Greek economy have been slowed by government policies and conflicts with Greece's neighbors.

Iceland

Capital	Reykjavík
Land Area	38,707 sq mi; 100,250 sq km
Population	279,384
Ethnic Group(s)	Norse, Celtic
Religion(s)	Protestant, Roman Catholic
Government	constitutional republic
Currency	Icelandic króna
Leading Exports	fish and fish products, animal products, aluminum, diatomite, ferrosilicon
Language(s)	Icelandic (official)

Iceland (EYES lund) is an island in northern Europe, between the Greenland Sea and the North Atlantic Ocean. Located just south of the Arctic Circle, Iceland's climate is generally cold. However, the warm waters of the Gulf Stream keep its ports ice-free in the winter. Iceland's varied landscape includes volcanoes, glaciers, fjords, and hot springs. More than half the population of Iceland lives in or near Reykjavík, the capital city. Fishing is the country's largest industry. The people of Iceland enjoy a high standard of living and a strong economy.

Introducing Western Europe

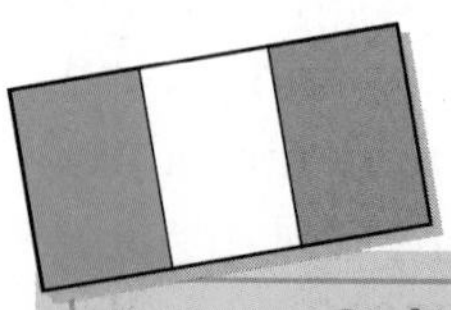

Ireland

Capital	Dublin
Land Area	26,598 sq mi; 68,890 sq km
Population	3.9 million
Ethnic Group(s)	Celtic, English
Religion(s)	Roman Catholic, Protestant
Government	republic
Currency	euro
Leading Exports	machinery and equipment, computers, chemicals, pharmaceuticals live animals, animal products
Language(s)	Irish Gaelic (official), English (official)

Ireland (EYER lund) is located in the North Atlantic Ocean off the west coast of Britain. It is an independent republic that occupies most of the island of Ireland. About one sixth of the island is Northern Ireland, which is part of the United Kingdom. Despite decades of violent conflict with Northern Ireland, Ireland's economy has grown at a remarkable rate in recent years. Its low taxes have brought in businesses from around the world. It is a member of the European Union and helped launch the euro currency. Often called the Emerald Isle, Ireland is known for its rolling green hills and mild, damp climate.

Italy

Capital	Rome
Land Area	113,521 sq mi; 294,020 sq km
Population	57.7 million
Ethnic Group(s)	Italian, Sardinian
Religion(s)	Roman Catholic
Government	republic
Currency	euro
Leading Exports	fruits, vegetables, grapes, potatoes, sugar beets, soybeans, grain, olives, beef, dairy products, fish
Language(s)	Italian (official), German, French, Rhaeto-Romanic, Sardinian

Italy (IT ul ee) is a peninsula in southern Europe. It lies in the Mediterranean Sea northeast of Tunisia. Italy also includes Sicily, Sardinia, and several other islands. Italy has a long and influential history. As the center of the Roman Empire, it was once a world leader. A system of law developed in Rome more than 2,000 years ago still influences law and citizenship in many countries today. Modern Italy became a democratic republic in 1946. Italy, a founding member of the European Union, has a strong economy based largely on manufacturing and industry.

Liechtenstein

Capital	Vaduz
Land Area	62 sq mi; 160 sq km
Population	32,842
Ethnic Group(s)	Alemannic, Italian, Southwest Asian
Religion(s)	Roman Catholic, Protestant
Government	hereditary constitutional monarchy
Currency	Swiss franc
Leading Exports	small specialty machinery, dental products, stamps, hardware, pottery
Language(s)	German (official), Alemannic dialect, Italian

Liechtenstein (LIK tun styn) is a small country in the Alps of central Europe, between Austria and Switzerland. Despite its small size, Liechtenstein has a strong free-enterprise economy and a high standard of living. It has a low tax rate, which attracts businesses from other countries. It also has many banks, with laws that protect international investors. Liechtenstein is closely tied to Switzerland, which provides the smaller country's defense. Liechtenstein uses Switzerland's franc as its national currency. Tourists visit Liechtenstein to ski, climb, and hike in the mountains.

A 1900 poster for railroad travel in Luxembourg

Luxembourg

Capital	Luxembourg-Ville
Land Area	998 sq mi; 2,586 sq km
Population	448,569
Ethnic Group(s)	Celtic, French, German, Portuguese, Italian, Slavic
Religion(s)	Roman Catholic, Protestant, Jewish, Muslim
Government	constitutional monarchy
Currency	euro
Leading Exports	machinery and equipment, steel products, chemicals, rubber products, glass
Language(s)	French (official), German (official), Luxembourgish (official)

Luxembourg (LUK sum burg) is bordered by France, Germany, and Belgium. Luxembourg became wealthy from steel production before World War II and today is a financial center. Its capital city has more banks than any other city in the world. Luxembourg is also the home of important EU organizations. The people of Luxembourg enjoy high income, low unemployment, and few social problems. More than 90 percent of the population lives in cities. Tourists visit Luxembourg to see its forests, mountains, and historic castles.

Malta

Capital	Valletta
Land Area	122 sq mi; 316 sq km
Population	397,499
Ethnic Group(s)	Maltese
Religion(s)	Roman Catholic
Government	republic
Currency	Maltese lira
Leading Exports	machinery and transport equipment, manufactured goods
Language(s)	Maltese (official), English (official)

Malta (MAWL tuh) is a group of islands south of Italy in the Mediterranean Sea. Only three islands of this rocky archipelago are inhabited. Malta fell under British rule in 1814, and the United Kingdom defended Malta through World War I and World War II. In 1964, Malta gained its independence and ten years later became a republic. Since that time, Malta has become an important transportation port, financial center, and tourist destination. Economically, it depends on trade with other countries, manufacturing, and tourism. Malta has recently joined the European Union.

Monaco

Capital	Monaco
Land Area	0.75 sq mi; 1.95 sq km
Population	31,987
Ethnic Group(s)	French, Monégasque, Italian
Religion(s)	Roman Catholic
Government	constitutional monarchy
Currency	euro
Leading Exports	no information available
Language(s)	French (official), Italian, Monégasque, English

Monaco (MAHN uh koh) is located on the southeastern coast of France, bordering the Mediterranean Sea. In the late 1800s, Monaco was linked to France with a railroad. This event brought tourists and money to the small country. Since that time, Monaco has grown into a popular vacation destination for tourists seeking beautiful scenery, a pleasant climate, and shopping. The government is focused on developing other services and industries as well. Monaco has no income tax and low business taxes. However, the cost of living is high.

Introducing Western Europe

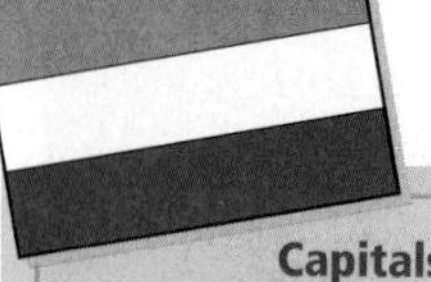

The Netherlands

Capitals	Amsterdam and The Hague
Land Area	13,082 sq mi; 33,883 sq km
Population	16.1 million
Ethnic Group(s)	Dutch, Southwest Asian, North African, Southeast Asian, South American, West Indian
Religion(s)	Roman Catholic, Protestant, Muslim
Government	constitutional monarchy
Currency	euro
Leading Exports	machinery and equipment, chemicals, fuels, foodstuffs
Language(s)	Dutch (official), Frisian

The Netherlands (NETH ur lundz) is located in northwest Europe between Belgium and Germany, bordering the North Sea. The country is also known by the name *Holland*. The Netherlands suffered through German invasion and occupation during World War II. Very active in international politics, the nation helped to form both NATO and the European Union. Stable relationships with other industrial countries help to keep its economy strong and growing. The Netherlands also serves as an important transportation center in Europe—particularly Rotterdam, on the Mans River.

Norway

Capital	Oslo
Land Area	118,865 sq mi; 307,860 sq km
Population	4.5 million
Ethnic Group(s)	Norwegian, Sami
Religion(s)	Protestant, Roman Catholic
Government	constitutional monarchy
Currency	Norwegian krone
Leading Exports	petroleum and petroleum products, machinery and equipment, metals, chemicals, ships, fish
Language(s)	Norwegian (official), Sami

Norway (NAWR way) is located in northern Europe west of Sweden. In 995, Norway's king converted to Christianity. He also ended two hundred years of Viking raids. In 1397, the nation became part of Denmark, and it remained so for more than four hundred years. The following two hundred years saw Norway gain independence, fall under Swedish rule, gain its independence again, fall under German rule, and regain its independence a third time, in 1945. In the 1960s, the discovery of oil and gas strengthened the Norwegian economy. Like Sweden, Norway has a mix of modern capitalism with many social welfare benefits, and has a very high standard of living. Norway has decided not to join the European Union.

A Sami man trains a reindeer to pull a sleigh.

Portugal

Capital	Lisbon
Land Area	35,502 sq mi; 91,951 sq km
Population	10.1 million
Ethnic Group(s)	Portuguese, African
Religion(s)	Roman Catholic, Protestant
Government	parliamentary democracy
Currency	euro
Leading Exports	clothing and footwear, machinery, chemicals, cork and paper products, hides
Language(s)	Portuguese (official)

Portugal (PAWR chuh gul) is located in southwestern Europe. It is west of Spain, bordered by the North Atlantic Ocean. Though Portugal is a fairly small country, it has played a major role in world history. From the 1400s to the 1600s, Portugal dominated the world sea trade. Portuguese explorers sailed the world, seeking wealth and colonies. They established colonies throughout the Americas and in Africa, some of which they ruled into the 1900s. Portugal became part of the European Union in 1986. Since then, the Portuguese economy has grown stronger, but a poor educational system is hindering greater growth.

San Marino

Capital	San Marino
Land Area	23.6 sq mi; 61.2 sq km
Population	27,730
Ethnic Group(s)	Sammarinese, Italian
Religion(s)	Roman Catholic
Government	independent republic
Currency	euro
Leading Exports	building stone, lime, wood, chestnuts, wheat, baked goods, hides, ceramics
Language(s)	Italian (official)

San Marino (sahn mah REE noh) is located in southern Europe, in the Italian Apennine Mountains. It is completely surrounded by the nation of Italy. San Marino is the third-smallest country in Europe and claims to be the world's oldest republic. It has remained independent since around A.D. 300. San Marino's political and social trends are similar to those of Italy. The tourist industry is extremely important to San Marino. Other industries include banking, clothing, electronics, ceramics, and cheese-making. San Marino enjoys a standard of living similar to the wealthiest areas of Italy.

Spain

Capital	Madrid
Land Area	192,873 sq mi; 499,542 sq km
Population	40.1 million
Ethnic Group(s)	Castilian Spanish, Catalan, Galician, Basque, Roma
Religion(s)	Roman Catholic
Government	parliamentary monarchy
Currency	euro
Leading Exports	machinery, motor vehicles, foodstuffs, other consumer goods
Language(s)	Spanish (official), Galician (official), Catalan (official), Basque (official)

Spain (spayn) is located in southwestern Europe between Portugal and France. It has coasts on the North Atlantic Ocean, the Mediterranean Sea, and the Bay of Biscay. Spain was a powerful world empire in the 1500s and 1600s. However, Spain's economy did not industrialize as quickly in later centuries as did other Western European countries such as Britain, Germany, and France. Spain was neutral during World War I and World War II but suffered through its own civil war in the 1930s. Spain joined the EU in 1986, and was among the first countries to begin using the euro currency. The country's economy is generally strong, though high unemployment continues to be a problem.

Introducing Western Europe

Sweden

Capital	Stockholm
Land Area	158,662 sq mi; 410,934 sq km
Population	8.9 million
Ethnic Group(s)	Swedish, Finnish, Sami
Religion(s)	Protestant, Roman Catholic, Muslim, Jewish, Buddhist
Government	constitutional monarchy
Currency	Swedish krona
Leading Exports	machinery, motor vehicles, paper products, pulp and wood, iron and steel products, chemicals
Language(s)	Swedish (official), Finnish, Sami

Sweden (SWEED un) is located in northern Europe between Norway and Finland, bordering the Baltic Sea and the Gulf of Bothnia. Sweden has a high standard of living, with a mixture of modern capitalism and broad social welfare benefits. The nation joined the EU in 1995 but has not accepted the euro as its own currency. Beginning in the 1990s, Sweden faced high unemployment and other economic problems. However, with a population of skilled workers, rich resources, and a modern transportation system, Sweden's economy is still relatively strong. Sweden is one of the world's leaders in equal rights for women.

Swedish soccer player Malin Moestroem in 2003

Switzerland

Capital	Bern
Land Area	15,355 sq mi; 39,770 sq km
Population	7.3 million
Ethnic Group(s)	German, French, Italian, Romansch
Religion(s)	Roman Catholic, Protestant
Government	federal republic
Currency	Swiss franc
Leading Exports	machinery, chemicals, metals, watches, agricultural products
Language(s)	French (official), German (official), Italian (official), Swiss German, Romansch

Switzerland (SWIT sur lund) is located between France and Italy. It is the source of all four of the region's major river systems: the Po, the Rhine, the Rhône, and the Inn-Danube. Politically, Switzerland is famous for its neutrality. Switzerland is also economically neutral and has so far remained outside the European Union. Switzerland does, however, participate in international organizations, including the UN. This small, landlocked Alpine country has one of the strongest market economies in Europe. It is a center of international finance.

United Kingdom

Capital	London
Land Area	93,278 sq mi; 241,590 sq km
Population	59.8 million
Ethnic Group(s)	English, Scottish, Irish, Welsh, Ulster, West Indian, South Asian
Religion(s)	Protestant, Roman Catholic, Muslim
Government	constitutional monarchy
Currency	pound sterling
Leading Exports	manufactured goods, fuels, chemicals, food, beverages, tobacco
Language(s)	English (official), Welsh (official), Scottish Gaelic, Irish Gaelic

The United Kingdom (yoo NYT id KING dum) is made up of several islands lying northwest of France, between the North Atlantic Ocean and the North Sea. In the 1800s, the United Kingdom was an expanding empire with great industrial and military strength. However, World War I and World War II seriously weakened the nation. In the following decades, the United Kingdom withdrew from its colonies around the world. It then rebuilt itself into a modern world power. The United Kingdom is a founding member of NATO and one of the five permanent members of the UN Security Council. It is also a member of the European Union, although the British have not accepted the euro.

Vatican City

Capital	Vatican City
Land Area	0.17 sq mi; 0.44 sq km
Population	900
Ethnic Group(s)	Italian, Swiss, Polish
Religion(s)	Roman Catholic
Government	ecclesiastical
Currency	euro
Leading Exports	none
Language(s)	Latin (official), Italian (official)

Vatican City (VAT ih kun SIH tee), also known as the Holy See, is an enclave of Rome. This means it is entirely surrounded by Italy's capital city. The Vatican is the world's smallest independent state. It is the home of the pope, who is the leader of the Roman Catholic Church. The pope is also the head of the Vatican City government. The Vatican's unique economy is supported by donations from Roman Catholics around the world. It also earns income from investments and tourism.

SOURCES: DK World Desk Reference Online; CIA World Factbook Online, 2002; *The World Almanac,* 2003

Assessment

Comprehension and Critical Thinking

1. Compare and Contrast Which countries in the region are the largest and the smallest?
2. Make Generalizations What are some characteristics that many of the region's countries share?
3. Infer Which countries do not have any exports? Why might this be so?
4. Categorize What kinds of exports do many of the countries of Western Europe rely on?
5. Make a Circle Graph The total population of Western Europe is about 392 million. Find the Western European country with the largest population. Make a circle graph that shows this country's population as a percent of the population of Western Europe as a whole.

Keeping Current

Access the **DK World Desk Reference Online** at **PHSchool.com** for up-to-date information about the 24 countries in this region.

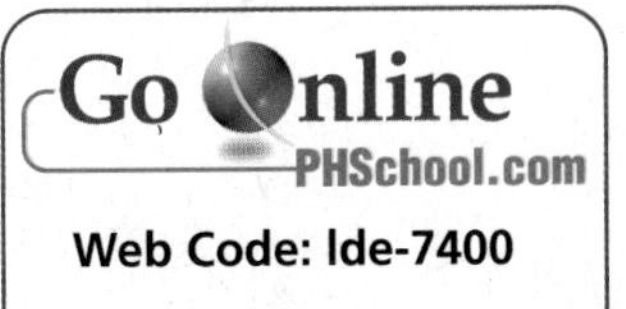

Web Code: lde-7400

Section 1

The United Kingdom

Democracy and Monarchy

Prepare to Read

Objectives

In this section you will

1. Examine the regions that make up the United Kingdom.
2. Learn about the United Kingdom's democratic heritage.
3. Find out how the United Kingdom combines democracy and monarchy.
4. Understand why trade is important to the United Kingdom.

Taking Notes

As you read this section, look for important events that have taken place in British history. Copy the table below, and write each event in the correct time period.

Events in British History			
1500s	1700s	1800s	1900s

Target Reading Skill

Use Context Clues When reading, you may come across a word that is used in an unfamiliar way. Look for clues in the context—the surrounding words, sentences, and paragraphs—to help you understand the meaning. Sometimes the context will define the word. In the first paragraph below, for example, you know the words *crown* and *jewels,* but may not know what the term *crown jewels* means. The context of the second paragraph helps explain this term.

Key Terms

- **Parliament** (PAHR luh munt) *n.* the lawmaking body of the United Kingdom
- **representative** (rep ruh ZEN tuh tiv) *n.* a person who represents, or speaks for, a group of people
- **constitution** (kahn stuh TOO shun) *n.* a set of laws that describes how a government works
- **constitutional monarchy** (kahn stuh TOO shuh nul MAHN ur kee) *n.* a government in which a monarch is the head of state but has limited powers

A Beefeater in front of the Tower of London

The line of tourists seems to go on forever. People in the line are speaking English, French, Arabic, and Japanese. In all of these languages, the tourists are talking about the same thing: the British crown jewels.

The jewels are kept under guard in the Tower of London. The priceless collection includes crowns worn by the kings and queens of England. After a long wait, the tourists finally reach the amazing jewels. Their eyes widen at the sight of huge diamonds, bright-red rubies, and cool-blue sapphires.

British history can be felt everywhere in and around the Tower of London. Near the Tower, rebellious nobles met their deaths on the executioner's block. Young King Edward V and his brother were most likely murdered in the Tower of London. The Tower is watched over by guards called Beefeaters. No one knows for sure where this name came from. But Beefeaters in their colorful red uniforms have guarded the Tower for hundreds of years.

Regions of the United Kingdom

You may have heard people use different names for the nation located on the British Isles: England, Great Britain, and the United Kingdom. Each name has a specific meaning.

England England is a region within the United Kingdom. Find England on the map below. About two thousand years ago, Romans ruled over present-day England. After the Roman Empire fell, many small kingdoms arose. Over time, one of these kingdoms, Wessex, grew stronger than the others. By conquering other kingdoms, Wessex unified England into a single nation by the 800s.

Great Britain England grew in power and strength. Soon, it began to exert power over its neighbors, including Wales and Scotland. Wales officially became part of the English nation in the 1500s. By the early 1700s, England and Scotland had joined together. Now all of the nations on the island of Great Britain were united. The name of the nation changed to Great Britain.

Hadrian's Wall, built in about A.D.122 by the Roman emperor Hadrian, marked the northern boundary of the Roman Empire. It still stands today in northern England.

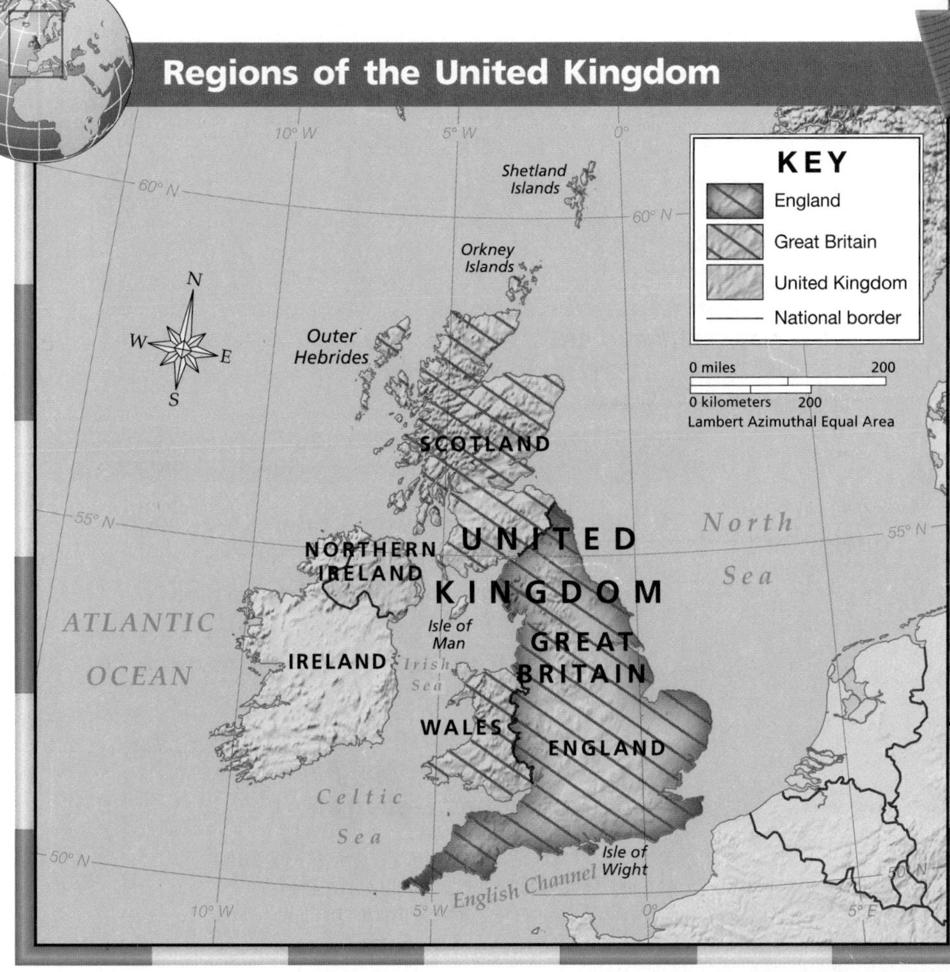

MAP MASTER™ Skills Activity

Regions The United Kingdom is a single nation made up of several smaller regions. **Identify** Which three regions do the islands called the Outer Hebrides belong to? **Compare and Contrast** How does the political structure of the United Kingdom compare to that of the United States?

Go Online PHSchool.com Use Web Code **ldp-7421** for step-by-step map skills practice.

Focus on Economics

United Kingdom

The United Kingdom has few mineral resources. Yet it has more energy resources—including coal, natural gas, and petroleum—than any other EU member. In the early 2000s, it was among the world's top ten oil producers. From about the mid-1970s on, the United Kingdom has produced enough fuel to export it to other countries. The United Kingdom also uses its energy resources to run the factories that produce manufactured goods, the country's most important export. Study the map and graphs to learn more about the United Kingdom's economy.

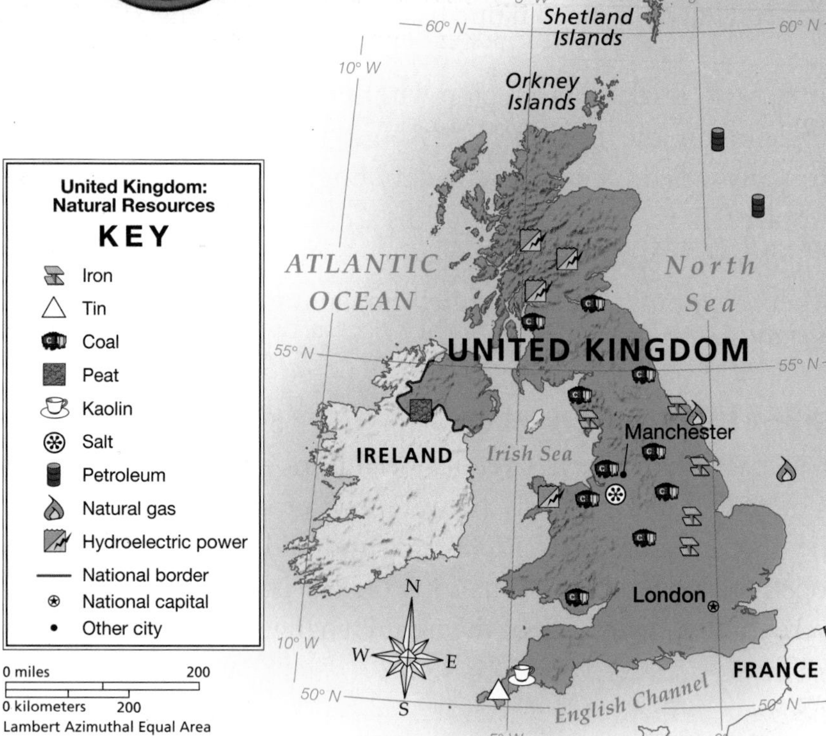

Leading Exports

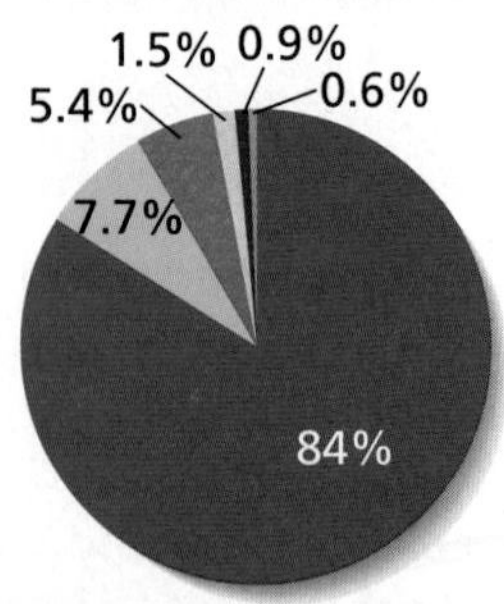

Leading Imports

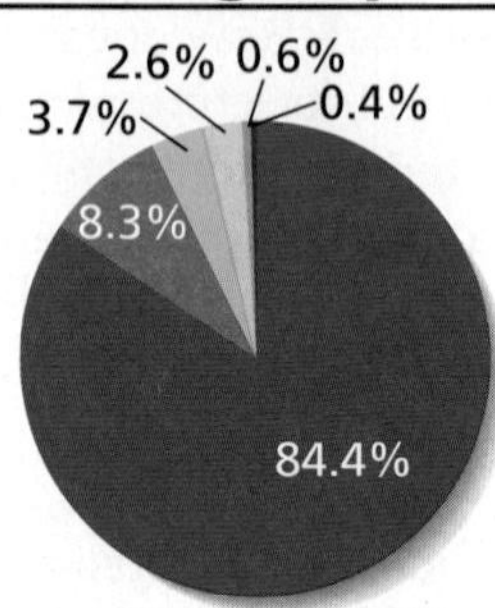

- Manufactured goods
- Oil
- Food, beverages, and tobacco
- Raw materials
- Non-oil fuels
- Other

Note: Numbers may not equal 100% due to rounding.
SOURCE: U.K. Office for National Statistics, 2002

Fossil Fuel Production, 1972–2001

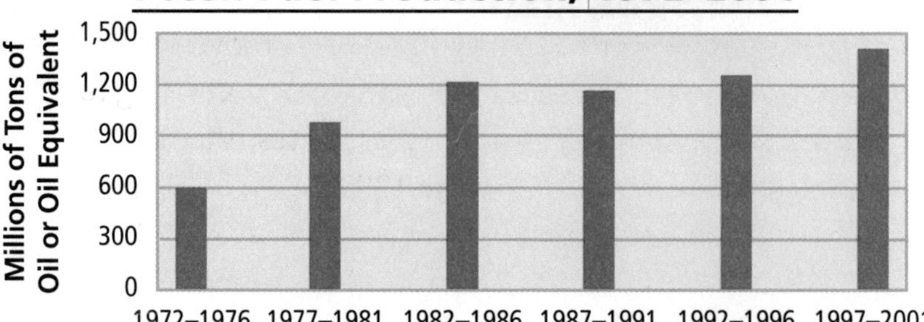

SOURCE: U.K. Office for National Statistics, 2002

Map and Chart Skills

1. **Identify** Where is the United Kingdom's petroleum located?
2. **Locate** Compare the United Kingdom's exports and imports. Which products are the only ones that the country exports more of than it imports?
3. **Synthesize Information** How does the information in the bar graph explain the answer to the question above?

Use Web Code **lde-7401** for **DK World Desk Reference Online.**

United Kingdom In 1801, Great Britain officially brought Ireland under its control with a law called the Act of Union. The name of the nation changed to the United Kingdom of Great Britain and Ireland. In the 1920s, the southern part of Ireland became an independent nation. The rest of the island, Northern Ireland, has remained part of the United Kingdom. However, some Northern Irish groups seek to break away from Great Britain and join Ireland.

Target Skill **Use Context Clues** How do the sentences in this paragraph explain what an *Act of Union* is?

Today, the full name of this nation is the United Kingdom of Great Britain and Northern Ireland. Most people use the shortened form of the name, United Kingdom, or UK. Within the United Kingdom are four regions: England, Scotland, Wales, and Northern Ireland. Each region continues to have its own culture, traditions, and customs. The British government unifies them all.

√ Reading Check **Which regions make up Great Britain?**

A Democratic Heritage

Today, the United Kingdom is headed by Queen Elizabeth II. As the country's monarch, she is a symbol of Britain's past and its customs. The United Kingdom also has a strong democratic government. The roots of British democracy go back many centuries.

The Magna Carta During the Middle Ages, kings needed large sums of money for major undertakings, such as going to war. If they did not have the money themselves, they asked the nobles to provide the funds. In the 1200s, the nobles used the influence their money gave them to limit the power of the king. In 1215, a group of nobles required King John to sign a document called the Magna Carta, or "Great Charter." The Magna Carta required the king to obey the laws of the land.

Links Across Time

The Magna Carta King John signed the Magna Carta in 1215 in a meadow called Runnymede, beside the River Thames in southeastern England. The Magna Carta holds an important place in history because it was the first written document that limited the power of a monarch. Hundreds of years later, British colonists in the Americas used the Magna Carta to support their fight for more rights. The document itself was written in Latin, which was the language of formal documents at that time. Four copies of the original charter still exist today in England, including the one shown at the right. Two are held in the British Library, while the other two are stored in the archives of the cathedrals at Lincoln and Salisbury.

Parliament In time, the group of nobles became known as the Parliament. **Parliament** is the legislature, or lawmaking body, of the United Kingdom. This word comes from the French word *parler* (PAHR lay), which means "to talk." Parliament is the place where officials discuss laws and other government business. Parliament changed over time. It later came to include common people as well as nobles. As it became more responsive to the needs of the people, it also gained more power. It helped decide the kinds of taxes paid by citizens. People elected from each region of the country served as representatives in the Parliament. A **representative** represents, or speaks for, a group of people.

The modern Parliament is made up of the House of Lords and the House of Commons. Members of the House of Lords are not elected. They are high-ranking clergy and judges or people who have distinguished themselves in public life. Their power has become limited over the years. In contrast, members of the House of Commons are elected. They govern the nation.

✓ Reading Check **What was the purpose of the Magna Carta?**

Parliament, Past and Present
Below, an illustration shows King Edward I before the Parliament in the late 1200s. At the bottom, Queen Elizabeth II attends a session of Parliament in 1995. **Compare** *Compare the two images. What traditions has Parliament kept throughout its history?*

A Changing Monarchy

Today, the monarchy serves as an important symbol of Britain's past. It also helps to unify the British people. The British honor the monarchy in many ways. When the queen is in London, a royal flag is flown over her home at Buckingham (BUK ing um) Palace. A ceremony called the changing of the guard takes place there every day. Trumpets blare and guardsmen march back and forth at the palace gate.

A Constitutional Monarchy While Parliament gained power, the power of British monarchs lessened. They no longer make laws or collect taxes. The United Kingdom is now governed by a constitution. A **constitution** is a set of laws that describes how a government works. Some nations have one written document that serves as a constitution, such as the Constitution of the United States. The British constitution is different. It is not one written document. Instead, the British constitution is made up of laws passed by Parliament, important court decisions, and certain legal practices. Parliament can change it as necessary. One of the greatest strengths of the United Kingdom's government is its ability to adopt modern ideas while keeping old ideas that still work.

The British government is a **constitutional monarchy,** or a government in which the power of kings and queens is limited. In a constitutional monarchy, kings and queens must obey the laws. And in the United Kingdom, the laws are made by Parliament, not by the monarch. This is very different from an absolute monarchy. An absolute monarch makes all the laws and has the power to ignore them as he or she chooses.

Devolution Until the late 1990s, Parliament made the laws for the entire nation. It even made specific laws for each of the country's regions—laws that affected only England, Scotland, Wales, or Northern Ireland. By the end of the 1990s, the national Parliament turned over some of its lawmaking powers to regional assemblies. Now, the Scottish Parliament makes certain laws that apply only to Scotland. The Welsh Assembly makes laws for Wales, and the Northern Ireland Assembly makes laws for Northern Ireland. Only England does not have a regional assembly. Its laws are still made by the national Parliament. The process of moving lawmaking power from the national level to the regional level is called devolution.

✓ **Reading Check** **What is devolution?**

Links Across The World

The Brightest Jewel Rare spices, silks, and other riches attracted the British East India Company to India in the 1600s. The company established trading outposts in India, with the goal of making huge profits. Over time, the company's goals changed. It gained great political power, and called for social change such as ending India's system of discrimination against people of lower class. In 1858, the British government took over the company, and officially turned India into a colony. Many people called India the "brightest jewel" in the British "crown" of colonies. The coat of arms shown here was a symbol of the British East India Company.

Regional Seats of Government
At the left, Queen Elizabeth II opens the Scottish Parliament in 1999—Scotland's first parliament in nearly 300 years. Northern Ireland's Assembly building is shown below. **Apply Information** *In what ways does allowing more power to regional lawmakers strengthen the United Kingdom's government?*

A Far-Flung Empire
The postcard below shows several of the British Empire's colonies in 1919. At the right, Lord Curzon, the British monarch's deputy in India, poses with an Indian prince in 1907. **Analyze Images** *Read the words and phrases on the postcard. What kind of image of the British Empire is the postcard trying to convey?*

The Importance of Trade

As an island nation, the United Kingdom has limited natural resources. It must trade with other nations for resources. For that reason, trade has been important throughout the United Kingdom's history.

The British Empire In the 1500s, trade enabled the British to begin building a large empire. The British Empire grew to include colonies in British-ruled areas on six continents. Its empire was so vast that one could say in the 1800s, "The sun never sets on the British Empire." Recall that 13 of today's United States used to be British colonies. The American and other colonies provided British factories with raw materials. They also provided markets to sell the goods made in British factories. Its many colonies helped the United Kingdom become a world economic power.

But that changed in the 1900s. Fighting World War I and World War II weakened the United Kingdom. In the years after World War II, most of the colonies within the British Empire began seeking independence. The British Empire rapidly came to an end. It had turned over most of its colonies by the mid-1960s. The last colony, Hong Kong, was returned to China in 1997. However, the United Kingdom continues to trade with its former colonies.

Discovery
CHANNEL
SCHOOL
Video
Learn about the suburbs of Great Britain.

A European Union Member The United Kingdom has many strong industries, or businesses. For example, it has good supplies of fossil fuels—especially oil from deposits beneath the North Sea. It also continues to export many manufactured goods, such as clothing and electronic products. However, the United Kingdom is not as strong a world power as it once was.

The United Kingdom no longer relies on its colonies to boost its economy. In 1973, the United Kingdom joined the European Union. As you have read, the EU is a group of nations that promotes trade and other forms of cooperation among its members.

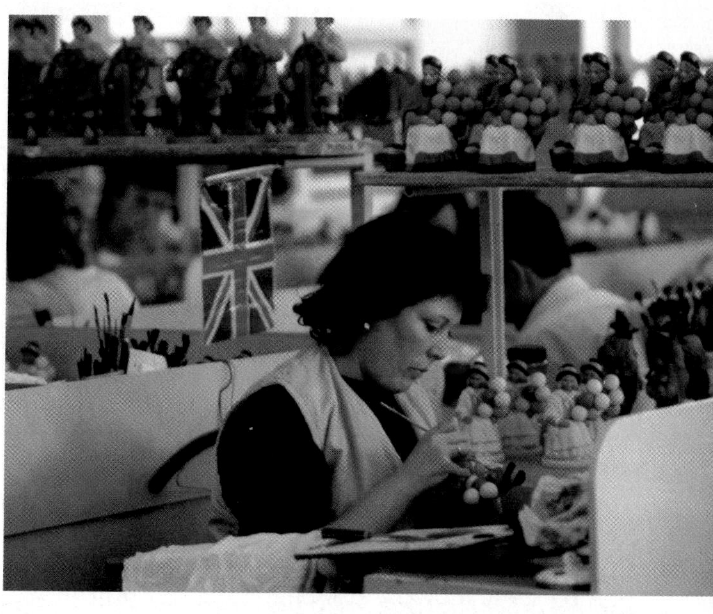
A woman paints figures by hand at a British company that exports tableware and gifts.

The United Kingdom today is a leading member of the EU. Its experience in such areas as shipping and finance has strengthened the EU in global trade. In turn, easier access to European markets has helped replace the trade the United Kingdom lost when its empire broke apart. With new links to the resources and markets of other European countries, the British look forward to a bright economic future.

✓ Reading Check **In what ways did the United Kingdom rely on its colonies?**

Section 1 Assessment

Key Terms
Review the key terms at the beginning of this section. Use each term in a sentence that explains its meaning.

Target Reading Skill
Find the phrase *common people* on page 264. How do the other words in the same sentence explain its meaning?

Comprehension and Critical Thinking
1. (a) Explain What is the difference between the terms *Great Britain* and *United Kingdom*?
(b) Sequence List four events, in order, that led to the formation of the United Kingdom.
2. (a) Name What are the two houses of the British Parliament?
(b) Contrast How do the two houses of Parliament differ?
3. (a) Recall What kind of government does the United Kingdom have?
(b) Contrast How does the British constitution differ from that of the United States?
4. (a) Note What factor led the British to build a large empire?
(b) Draw Conclusions How did the United Kingdom remain strong after losing its colonies?

Writing Activity
Suppose that you are a British tour guide operator. You tell an American tourist that you are from three places: England, Great Britain, and the United Kingdom. Write a paragraph that explains to the tourist how this can be so.

For: An activity on the British Empire
Visit: PHSchool.com
Web Code: ldd-7401

Section 2 France
Cultural Heritage and Diversity

Prepare to Read

Objectives
In this section you will
1. Find out why the French take pride in their traditional culture.
2. Learn about growing cultural diversity in France.

Taking Notes
As you read this section, look for details about French culture, including recent influences on it. Copy the chart below, and record your findings in it.

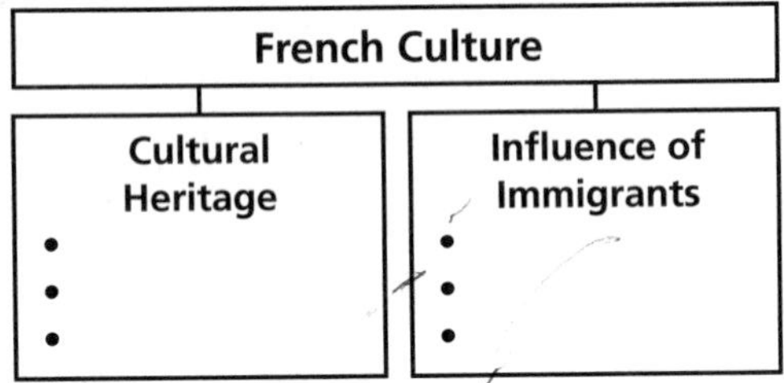

Target Reading Skill
Use Context Clues
Context, the words and phrases surrounding a word, can help you understand a new word. In this example, the phrase in italics helps explain what Impressionism is: French Impressionist artists such as Claude Monet developed *new techniques to paint light and shadow.*

Key Term
- **philosophy** (fil LAHS uh fee) *n.* a system of ideas and beliefs

In 1998, the words "world champions" were projected onto France's Arc de Triomphe.

It's July of 1998 in Paris, France. Hundreds of thousands of people crowd onto the Champs Elysées (shawnz eh lee ZAY), one of the most fashionable streets in the world. The sidewalks are packed. Some people have even climbed to the tops of lampposts or newspaper stands for a better view. They're all here for a huge celebration. The French soccer team has just won the World Cup championship for the first time ever.

Fans are waving French flags. Others have their faces painted in the colors of the French flag—red, white, and blue. But in the crowd, many fans are waving the Algerian flag and chanting, "Zizou! Zizou!" They are calling for Zinedine Zidane, the midfielder who scored two of the goals in the winning game. Like many of the team's players, Zidane, of Algerian descent, is the son of immigrants.

This victory celebration is symbolic of a new France—a France that is fiercely proud of its culture and is increasingly diverse.

Pride in French Culture

French people generally take great pride in their culture—for good reason. Over centuries, the French have made many important contributions to art, religion, music, literature, and philosophy. A **philosophy** is a system of ideas and beliefs. Many French people are committed to preserving their traditional French culture.

The French Language Some people want to prevent the French language from changing too much. An organization called the French Academy determines which words are officially accepted as part of the French language. Since 1635, it has published dictionaries explaining the usage of these words. The Academy is one example of how the French strive to preserve their culture.

Enduring Philosophies Many important philosophies originated in France. Some of these philosophies had to do with government, and they had a great influence on many other nations. For example, the idea that government should be divided into three branches comes from a French philosopher named Baron de Montesquieu (MAHN tus kyoo). A Swiss philosopher living in France named Jean-Jacques Rousseau (zhahn zhahk roo SOH) developed the idea that no laws are binding unless the people have agreed to them. These ideas helped shape the United States Constitution.

Achievements in the Arts French painters are world-famous for their achievements. For example, Eugène Delacroix (ooh ZHEHN deh la KWAH) painted works full of intense emotion and rich color in the early 1800s. Impressionist artists such as Claude Monet (moh NAY) developed new techniques for painting light and shadow.

French composers have written beautiful works of classical music. Claude Debussy (deh boo SEE), for example, composed music in the late 1800s and early 1900s. His work was influenced by artists such as Monet. In turn, Debussy influenced other composers.

French literature is world-famous. For example, Alexandre Dumas (doo MAH) wrote novels in the 1800s. Even today, many of his novels are read by people around the world and have been made into movies.

French Cultural Milestones

1637 René Descartes publishes *Discourse on Method*, one of the world's most important works in philosophy.

1664 Molière, considered to be France's greatest comic playwright, writes his masterpiece, *Tartuffe*.

1751 Denis Diderot publishes an important encyclopedia of science and philosophy that reflects the ideals of the Scientific Revolution.

1790 Marie Louise Élisabeth Vigée-Lebrun, one of France's most successful woman painters, paints her self-portrait.

1830s A French artist and a French inventor together develop the first methods for making photographs.

1899 Claude Monet paints *The Water-Lily Pond*, an important Impressionist painting.

1908 Auguste Rodin, considered to be France's finest sculptor, creates *The Cathedral*.

1939 Film director Jean Renoir produces his masterpiece *The Rules of the Game*, which influences cinema around the world.

1957 Writer Albert Camus, who wrote about human emotion in the post–World War II world, wins the Nobel Prize in Literature.

Diagram Skills

The French have made major contributions to the world's art, literature, cinema, and philosophy. **Identify** Which event had an influence on cinema around the world? **Identify Causes** What earlier event in this diagram paved the way for this event?

The Eiffel Tower
Paris's Eiffel Tower was built in 1889 to celebrate the French Revolution. The 984-foot- (300-meter-) tall tower was the tallest structure in the world until 1930. **Infer** *What feelings about the French Revolution might this tower bring about in French people?*

Innovative Architecture French architects have created magnificent buildings. In the 1100s, a style of art and architecture called Gothic developed in and around Paris. Gothic architecture is characterized by high ceilings, thin walls, and the use of columns and arches. French architects built stunning Gothic-style medieval cathedrals, like the Cathedral of Notre Dame (noh truh DAHM). Built in the 1200s in Paris, Notre Dame is one of Europe's most famous cathedrals. It has a number of huge stained-glass windows, one of which is 42 feet (13 meters) in diameter.

In later years, French architects designed other important buildings. For example, work on the Louvre (LOO vruh) Museum was begun during the Renaissance. At first, the Louvre was a royal palace. Over time, many of France's monarchs added to the original building. As they collected great works of art, they housed them in different parts of the Louvre. By the late 1700s, monarchs no longer used the Louvre as a palace, and it became a national museum.

French architects today continue to design great buildings, such as the national library that opened in 1998. This library is made up of four glass skyscrapers surrounding an open square. Though the building is new and modern, the collection it holds is one of the oldest in the world.

Links to Economics

The Department Store In 1852, a French merchant named Aristide Boucicaut (BOO sih koh) took over the Bon Marché, a fabric shop in Paris. By 1914, he had transformed it into the world's first single department store. The department store allowed people, mainly women, to choose from a variety of ready-made clothing and household items in one attractive store. Before this, people went to individuals who specialized in making or selling one type of product. The department store also introduced innovations such as advertising, fixed prices on goods, and a system of returns or exchanges. Department stores were also introduced in the late 1800s in the United States and England.

The Bon Marché, in an engraving made around 1880

New Styles in Fashion For centuries, many people looked to France for the latest styles. Russian aristocrats of the 1700s followed French fashion and used French manners. They even spoke French. Wealthy British and American women traveled to Paris in the 1800s to have their clothes made. Less wealthy women admired French fashions in magazines. They often had their local seamstresses make copies of French originals.

French fashion continued to set trends in the 1900s. For example, a French fashion designer named Christian Dior (dee AWR) created a "New Look" in 1947. His designs featured narrow shoulders and long, full skirts. His fashions became popular all over the world.

Paris continues to be one of the most important centers of the fashion industry. Each year, people come from countries around the world to see the latest fashions from French designers.

Fine Food French cooking has long been one of the most respected styles of cooking in the world. In about 1805, a French pastry chef named Marie-Antoine Carême (muh REE ahn TWAHN kuh REM) delighted the rich and powerful people of France with his desserts. Some of his cakes looked like buildings or monuments. His puddings looked like birds or flowers.

In 1833, Carême wrote a book on the art of French cooking. His book was similar to the dictionaries of the French Academy. It set strict standards of excellence for cooking. Today, many of the world's best chefs are trained in France.

Discovery
CHANNEL
SCHOOL
Video
Learn about Napoleon Bonaparte.

✓ Reading Check **Name two examples of the influence of French culture on the rest of the world.**

COUNTRY PROFILE Focus on Economics

France

Like most developed countries, France's economy is increasingly based on services. Agriculture, however, is still very important to the nation's economy. France is the leading agricultural exporter among EU nations. Agricultural products, mainly cereals such as wheat and corn, make up about 16 percent of France's total exports. Use the data on this page to learn more about France's land use and economy.

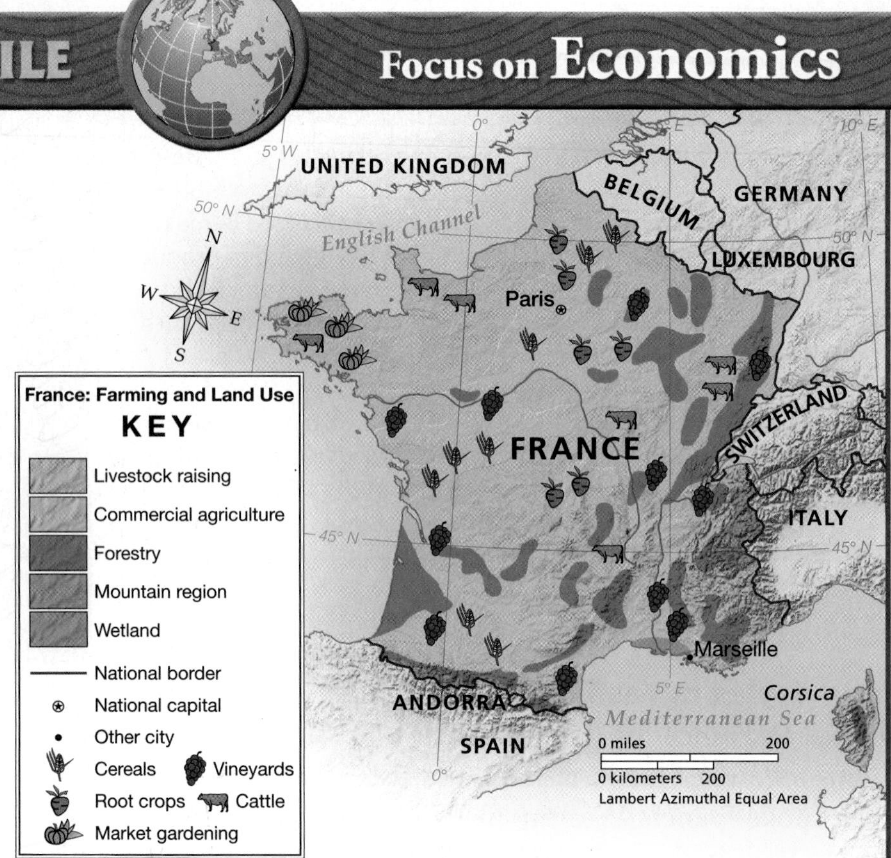

Export Partners

Export Destination	Percent of France's Exports
European Union	
Germany	15
United Kingdom	10
Spain	9
Italy	9
Belgium	7
United States	8
Other	42

SOURCE: CIA World Factbook Online, 2003

Labor Force by Occupation

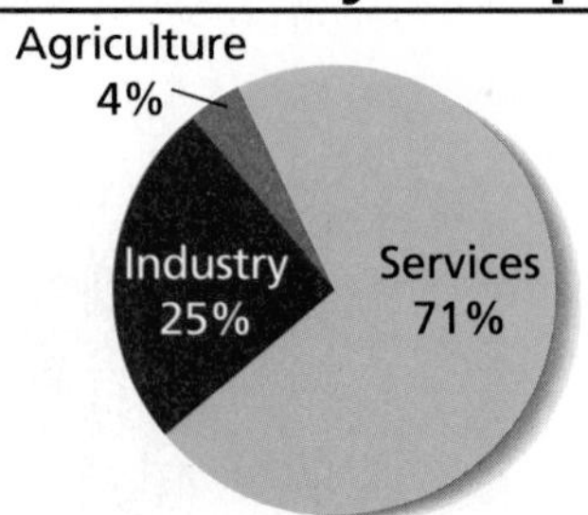

SOURCE: CIA World Factbook Online, 2003

Land Use

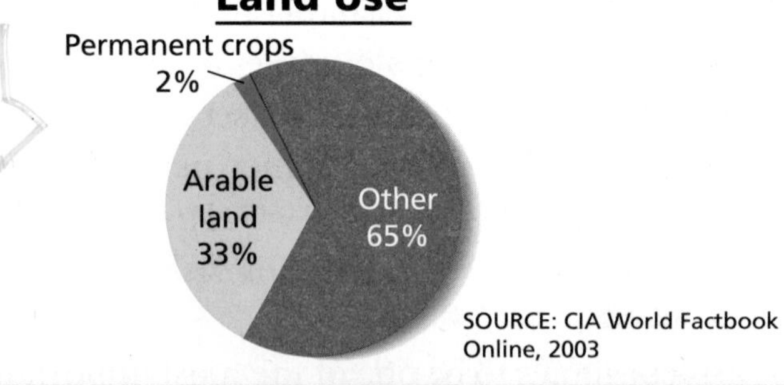

SOURCE: CIA World Factbook Online, 2003

Map and Chart Skills

1. **Note** How much of France's land can be used to grow crops? Where is this land located?
2. **Infer** Compare the percentage of France's arable land and cropland with the percentage of France's labor force in agriculture. From this information, what can you infer about how many laborers are needed to carry out modern agriculture?
3. **Transfer Information** What is the total percentage of France's exports to EU countries? What does this tell you about the importance of the EU to France's economy?

Use Web Code **lde-7412** for **DK World Desk Reference Online.**

Diversity in France

Many French citizens believe French culture is both unique and valuable. Yet life in France is changing. The cultures of other nations are influencing French culture more and more.

The French language, for example, has picked up words from other languages. French has borrowed words from English, such as *weekend, barbecue, laser*, and *cross-country*. It has borrowed German words, such as *Bretzel* (pretzel) and *Knödel* (dumpling). French also includes words from languages such as Italian, Malaysian, Turkish, and Hindi. These words are a sign of France's ties with many other nations.

Cultural influences from other nations come from many different sources, such as film, television, and radio. Another source is immigration.

Influences on French Culture
At the top, Indian immigrants celebrate a Hindu festival. Above, a cable advertisement on a bus uses both French and English words.
Identify Effects *How might increasing immigration continue to affect the French language?*

A History of Immigration From the mid-1800s on, France was especially welcoming to immigrants. In fact, between 1850 and about 1940, over 7 million immigrants entered France. In the late 1800s and early 1900s, these immigrants were from European countries such as Poland, Italy, Spain, Belgium, and Switzerland. Because these immigrants came from cultures similar to that of France, they quickly and easily adopted French culture.

A Political Protest
Muslim women protest a French law proposed in 2004 to ban students from wearing headscarves, Jewish caps, or other religious symbols in school. The women are holding a French flag. **Evaluate Information** *What point are the women making by displaying a French flag?*

After World War II France had a shortage of workers, because repeated wars had resulted in many deaths and a lowered birth rate. The French government began to encourage people from other countries to immigrate to France. By the 1950s, the largest group of immigrants came from Algeria, a French colony in North Africa. In the past few decades, many immigrants have arrived from northern and southern Africa, as well as Southeast Asia.

Rising Tensions After World War II, Algerians and other immigrants helped rebuild France's economy. They took jobs that French employers found hard to fill. The French government assumed that these immigrants would work in France temporarily and then return home. Instead, many North African immigrants decided to make France their permanent home. Large numbers of immigrants along with their families moved to France in the 1970s, a time when the French economy was weak. Tension began to build between native-born French citizens and recent immigrants.

Target Skill **Use Context Clues** In this paragraph, the contrast word *instead* gives you a clue to the meaning of the word *temporarily.*

Some native French people had questions about the immigrants. Would they take jobs away from people already in France? Would the immigrants adopt French culture, or would they try to change it? Unlike earlier European immigrants, these recent immigrants often came from very different cultures. As they thought about these questions, some French people felt threatened by the immigrants. In the 1970s, the French government began to limit immigration.

Immigrants' Influences Today the debate over immigration continues. Immigrants from Algeria, Morocco, and Tunisia bring African and Arab cultures with them. Their food, dress, and music are quite different from those of traditional French culture. The same is true of immigrants from Asia and other regions. The influence of all these groups can be seen especially in the big cities. In Paris and in many other large cities in France, it is common to hear people speaking languages other than French. Every year, there are more and more restaurants and stores that sell foreign food.

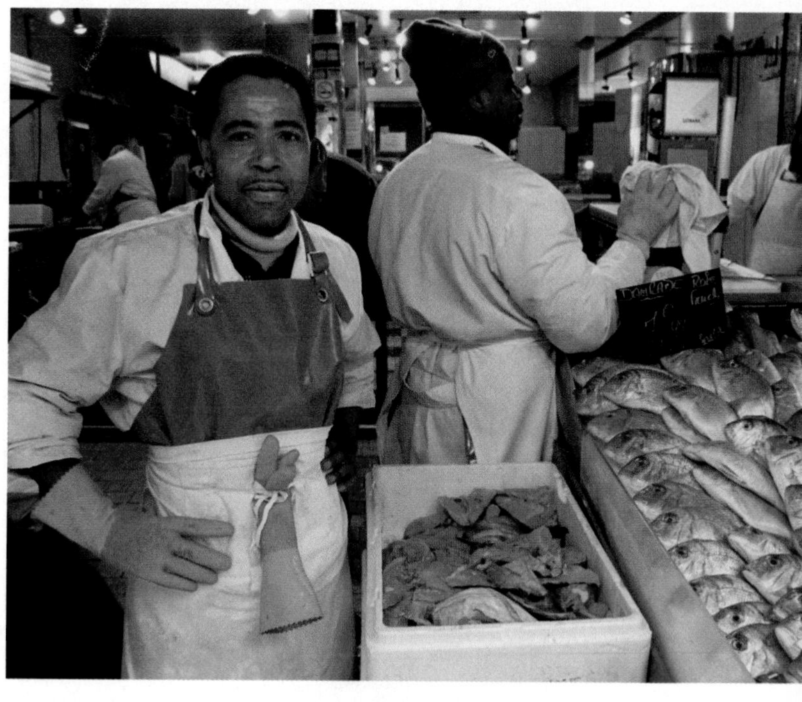

An African immigrant selling fresh fish

France has always been a diverse society. But unlike in the past, recent immigrants have arrived from countries with very different cultures from that of France. France and its people are making adjustments. Many French people were shocked when a politician who promoted an anti-immigrant message won significant popular support in the 2002 presidential election. But most people have come to value the benefits of a diverse population.

✓ Reading Check **How are France's immigrants different from those of the past?**

Section 2 Assessment

Key Terms

Review the key terms at the beginning of this section. Use each term in a sentence that explains its meaning.

Target Reading Skill

Find the word *aristocrats* on page 271. What clues in that paragraph helped you figure out its meaning?

Comprehension and Critical Thinking

1. (a) List Name two French cultural contributions to the arts.
(b) Explain What were Montesquieu's and Rousseau's philosophies about government?
(c) Synthesize How did these philosophies influence the United States?

2. (a) Recall Why did the French government encourage immigration following World War II?
(b) Summarize Why did tensions arise between native-born French citizens and immigrants to France in the 1970s?
(c) Identify Effects When immigrants move to a new country, how do they change a country for better or worse?

Writing Activity

Suppose that you are a television reporter covering a story on French culture. You interview an elderly woman for your report. What questions might you ask her to determine how French culture has changed and how it has stayed the same over the past few decades?

Writing Tip Use the blue headings in this section to help you decide on topics. Reread the text under the headings to get ideas for your questions.

Section 3

Sweden

A Welfare State

Prepare to Read

Objectives

In this section you will

1. Learn about Sweden's welfare state.
2. Find out how Sweden became a welfare state.
3. Examine possible solutions to Sweden's economic problems.

Taking Notes

As you read this section, look for details about Sweden's welfare state. Copy the table below and record your findings in it.

Sweden's Welfare State	
Benefits	**Economic Challenges**
• • •	• • •

Target Reading Skill

Use Context Clues

Remember that a word that looks familiar to you may have a different meaning in the context of the text you are reading. For example, you have probably heard of the word *welfare*. As you read the text under the red heading A Welfare State, you will learn that the word has a different meaning than the one you have thought of. The last sentence of the first paragraph under A Welfare State makes that difference clear.

Key Terms

- **welfare state** (WEL fayr stayt) *n.* a country in which many services and benefits are paid for by the government
- **national debt** (NASH uh nul det) *n.* the amount of money a government owes

A baby being examined by a doctor in Sweden

A young Swedish couple is expecting a new baby any day now. Excited, they decorate the baby's room and talk about how they will raise her. They even joke about where she will go to college and what career she might choose when she grows up.

Like all new parents, they have many hopes and plans for their baby. They have concerns, too—concerns about her health and well-being. But they feel confident about certain things. For example, both parents will have paid time off from work to care for the baby. The baby will also receive excellent health care, child care, and schooling—all for free or at a very low cost. To understand why the government provides these services, you need to understand the nature of Sweden's society.

A Welfare State

Sweden is a welfare state. In a **welfare state,** the government provides many services and benefits either for free or for a very low cost. These services and benefits include medical care, paid time off from work, and child care. A welfare system means something very different in Sweden than it does in the United States. The American welfare system helps people who are in great need—people who cannot afford medical care or food. The Swedish system helps everyone.

A Cradle-to-Grave System Sweden has a "cradle-to-grave" welfare system. That means that the system provides basic services for all people at every stage of life. When a child is born, the government pays for parents to stay home from work for as long as 15 months. The state then provides child care at a reduced cost, so that parents can work or continue their education. The government pays the costs of schooling, including books and lunches for all students. College education is also paid for everyone. And every Swedish citizen—child or adult—has access to free or inexpensive health care.

As part of the government benefits program, all workers receive five weeks paid vacation. Most workers generally take their vacation at the same time during the summer. That is because in the summer, the nights in this far-northern country are very short. It is daylight for most of the day.

Swedish people are allowed more paid sick days than the workers of any other European nation. Some of the money to pay for this leave comes from the government. And when Swedish workers retire, they receive a monthly payment from the government. This payment nearly equals the pay they received when they were working.

Daily Life in Sweden
Sweden's government funds this day care center (below) and senior citizen community center (bottom left). Both are located in Stockholm, Sweden's capital. **Summarize** *What other benefits do Swedes receive from the government?*

COUNTRY PROFILE

Focus on **Geography**

Sweden

Sweden is located far to the north, with about a fifth of its land within the Arctic Circle. Because of its great length from north to south, its climate varies greatly. The northern interior receives heavy snowfall and is cold for months, while in the southern regions temperatures are moderate, and the coastal waters do not freeze. The country is heavily forested, especially in the northern part of the country. Study the map and the charts to learn how Sweden's geography shapes the lives of its people.

Sweden: Natural Vegetation

KEY

- Deciduous forest
- Mixed forest
- Coniferous forest
- Highland (vegetation varying with elevation)
- Tundra
- National border
- National capital
- Other city

SWEDEN, NORWAY, FINLAND, DENMARK, Norwegian Sea, North Sea, Gulf of Bothnia, Baltic Sea, Arctic Circle, Uppsala, Stockholm, Linköping, Göteborg, Malmö

0 miles 300
0 kilometers 300
Lambert Azimuthal Equal Area

Largest Cities

City	Population (2002)
Stockholm	
Göteborg	
Malmö	
Uppsala	
Linköping	

SOURCE: Statistics Sweden

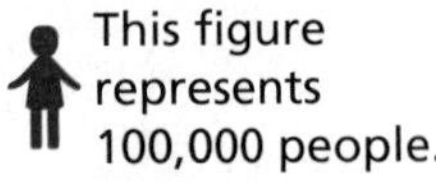
This figure represents 100,000 people.

Sweden's Weather

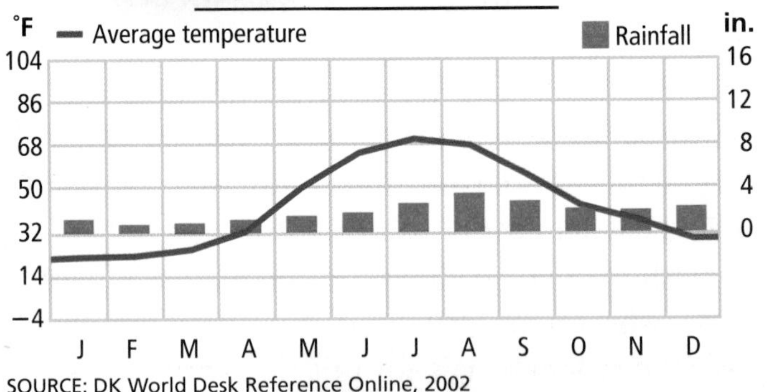

SOURCE: DK World Desk Reference Online, 2002

Urban and Rural Population

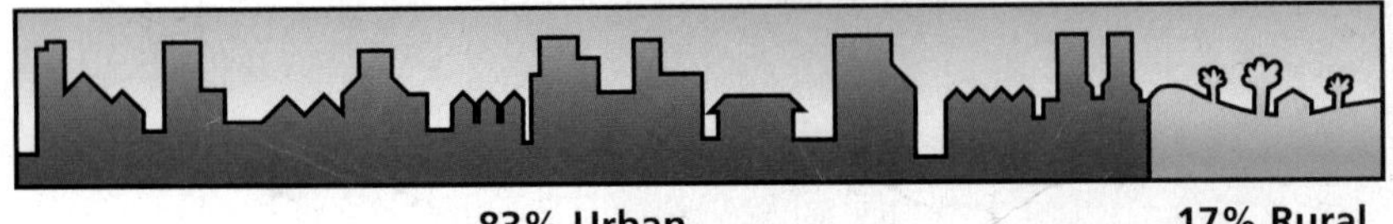

83% Urban

17% Rural

Map and Chart Skills

1. **Locate** Where are Sweden's five largest cities located?
2. **Contrast** How is the vegetation of that area different from that of the regions with no large cities?
3. **Synthesize Information** What factors might explain the location of the majority of Sweden's population?

Use Web Code **lde-7413** for **DK World Desk Reference Online.**

High Taxes Swedish people believe that welfare benefits are very important. They are willing to pay the highest taxes in Europe in order to have these benefits. Swedes pay as much as 60 percent of their income in taxes. Food is taxed at 12 percent. Clothing and other goods are taxed at 25 percent. But in exchange for these high taxes, all Swedes have financial security. Whether they are rich or poor, they know that their children will get a good education. Medical costs are low. Rents are affordable.

Discovery CHANNEL SCHOOL Video
Learn the importance of Swedish forests.

✓ Reading Check **What is a "cradle-to-grave" system?**

Building a Welfare State

As it has been for hundreds of years, Sweden is a monarchy. Yet the government has changed greatly throughout Sweden's history.

Sweden's History The history of Sweden begins with the Vikings—an early sailing people from Scandinavia who colonized many parts of Europe. Beginning in about the 900s, Sweden was ruled by a series of kingdoms. In the 1600s, Sweden emerged as a great power in northern Europe. From its capital city, Stockholm, Sweden ruled a thriving empire. However, the country's strength declined in the 1700s after Sweden lost a war with Russia. Sweden remained neutral in both world wars.

Like the monarchy in the United Kingdom, Sweden's monarchy changed over time. The monarch slowly gave more and more power to the people, represented in a parliament. And political parties arose to represent the people and bring about change in government. Today Sweden is a constitutional monarchy. The monarch is the ceremonial leader, but parliament makes the laws.

A 2002 photo shows the current Swedish monarch, King Carl Gustaf XVI, with other members of the royal family.

Target Skill

Use Context Clues Use the contrast word *but* and the sentence before it to figure out what the word *lagged* means.

Meeting Economic Challenges Economic problems led to the rise of Sweden's modern welfare state. By the late 1800s, industry had grown in the United States and most of Europe. But Sweden lagged far behind. There were few factories or railroad lines or even good roads. Farming methods had not changed much since the Middle Ages. Many people were very poor. By the end of the 1800s, about 1.5 million Swedes had left the country in search of a better life. Most of them settled in the midwestern states of the United States, such as Minnesota and Wisconsin.

In 1932, a political party called the Social Democrats came to power. The Social Democrats promised a better life for Swedes. Over the next few decades, the party made Sweden into a welfare state. At the same time, Sweden became an industrial country, and its economy grew stronger. Today the Social Democrats are still the country's largest political party.

✓ Reading Check **Which political party created Sweden's welfare state?**

Problems and Solutions

Sweden's welfare state has served as a model for government throughout Europe. Still, the system has its problems. Everyone in Sweden receives benefits, but the government has faced challenges in providing those benefits.

Sweden's Troubles For decades, Sweden was able to offer its citizens very generous benefits, no matter how poorly the economy performed. But that changed in the late 1980s. People bought fewer items because of the high taxes on groceries, clothing, and other goods. Thus, there was less spending to boost the economy. Sweden's companies were less productive than companies in other nations. Long vacations meant that workers spent less time on the job. Sweden's economic growth stalled.

The benefits of the welfare system continued to be very important to Swedish citizens. To continue paying these benefits, the government had to borrow money. Soon, the **national debt,** or the amount of money their government owed, began to grow. The government increased taxes and cut some spending to try controlling the debt. But paying down the national debt remains a challenge.

Chart Skills

Sales tax is a tax on goods and services. This chart shows the rate, or percent, of sales tax in various Western European countries and two American states. **Compare** How does Sweden's sales tax compare to those of the other European countries shown? To the states shown? **Generalize** Do you think governments with very low taxes generally provide many or few social services? Why do you think so?

Sales Tax Rates in Western Europe and the United States

Country or State	Standard Rate (%)
France	19.6
Germany	16.0
Sweden	25.0
United Kingdom	17.5
United States: Florida	6.0
United States: New York	4.25

A Graying Population Sweden has 1.5 million retired people out of a population of about 9 million. This means that about one out of six people is retired. That is the highest proportion of retired people in the world. Sweden's aging population presents many challenges for the nation. Elderly people often need increased health care and medicines. Many elderly people who cannot take care of themselves must be cared for by other people.

Yet an aging population presents an even greater problem. As you have read, Swedes receive many benefits, such as low medical costs and low rents. The money for these benefits comes from the paychecks of Swedish workers, who pay high taxes on their salaries. In an aging population, there are fewer workers, because so many people are retired. As a result, there is less tax money to pay for benefits.

Over time, the money received from taxes is not enough to pay for the extra care needed by an elderly population. Some studies say that unless Sweden's government reforms its welfare benefits, there will not be any money left by 2015. Raising taxes even higher to cover the high costs of benefits has been proposed, but it is not a popular idea.

Government Solutions Sweden's government is looking for ways to solve these problems. One solution would be for the government to reduce benefits and spend less money. The government made many attempts to reduce benefits in the 1990s. It reduced the payments for sickness benefits. It also required workers to save more of their own money for retirement. But these reforms angered Swedish voters, who voted against their leaders in two major elections.

Links to Science

Sun at Midnight It is midnight in northern Sweden, and some friends are playing volleyball outside. How is this so? From about March 20 to September 23 in the most northern arctic regions, the sun can be seen on the horizon 24 hours a day. This is because the northern hemisphere is tilted directly toward the sun at this time. In northern Sweden, the sun never sets for a few days around June 21. The Swedes celebrate this time as Midsummer's Eve, with dancing (below), food, and music.

A woman assembles parts at a car factory in Göteborg, Sweden.

Business Solutions Another solution would be for businesses to earn more, giving more money to the government in the form of taxes. One way for businesses to grow is to take better advantage of Sweden's natural resources. Sweden has high-grade iron ore and produces enough steel for itself and for export. Hydroelectric turbines run by Sweden's fast rivers and many waterfalls produce half of Sweden's electricity. Sweden's vast forests support the timber industry, which supplies Sweden's needs as well as those of other countries.

Even with these ample resources, Swedish companies have had trouble competing with firms in other countries. Most Swedish products are of high quality. But the Swedes have not been able to make them as quickly and cheaply as other countries. Some companies have found a solution to this problem. Swedish automakers, for example, have followed the example of American companies. Using the methods of American auto factories, the Swedes can now make a car in about 40 hours. It used to take them about 100 hours.

Improving the economy means changing the ways that things are done in Sweden. The welfare system is very important to Swedes. However, they need to find better ways of paying for it. That is the greatest challenge facing Sweden today.

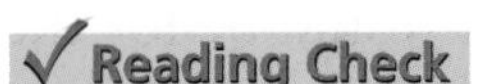

What natural resources could help the Swedish economy?

Section 3 Assessment

Key Terms

Review the key terms at the beginning of this section. Use each term in a sentence that explains its meaning.

Target Reading Skill

Find the word *vast* in the first paragraph on this page. How does its context explain its meaning?

Comprehension and Critical Thinking

1. (a) Describe What benefits do Swedish citizens receive?
(b) Identify Frame of Reference Why are some Swedes willing to pay such high taxes?
2. (a) Explain Why did many Swedes leave their country in the late 1800s?
(b) Identify Effects What effect did industrialization have on Sweden's economy?
3. (a) Explain Why did the Swedish economy stall in the late 1980s?
(b) Apply Information How could the government and businesses work together to solve Sweden's financial problems?

Writing Activity

Consider that in the United States, most people pay 20 to 30 percent of their income in taxes, compared to about 60 percent in Sweden. What lessons do you think the two countries might learn from each other? Write a paragraph summarizing your thoughts.

For: An activity on the Vikings
Visit: PHSchool.com
Web Code: ldd-7403

Section 4

Italy

Northern and Southern Divisions

Prepare to Read

Objectives

In this section you will

1. Discover that there is another country within Italy called Vatican City.
2. Understand why there are divisions between northern and southern Italy.

Taking Notes

As you read this section, look for ways that life is similar and different in northern and southern Italy. Copy the Venn diagram below and record your findings in it.

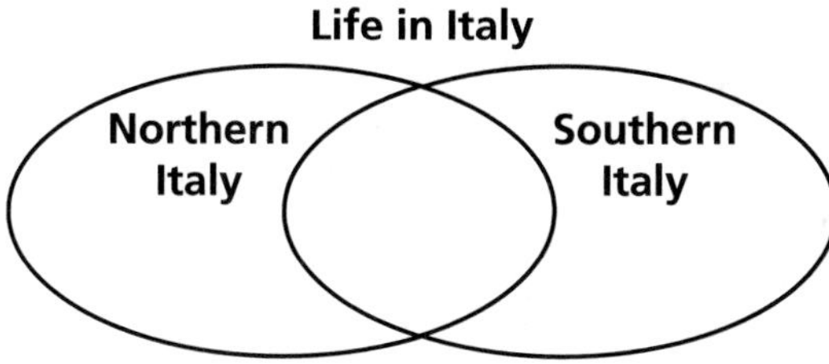

Target Reading Skill

Use Context Clues To make sure you have correctly determined the meaning of an unfamiliar word by looking at its context, look at the word itself for clues. For example, examine the word *guidance* in the first paragraph below. The sentence in which the word appears tells you that it has something to do with the leader. To double check, look at the word itself. What verb sounds like *guidance*?

Key Terms

- **basilica** (buh SIL ih kuh) *n.* a Roman Catholic church that has special, high status because of its age or history
- **manufacturing** (man yoo FAK chur ing) *n.* the process of turning raw materials into finished products
- **land reform** (land ree FAWRM) *n.* the process of dividing large properties into smaller ones

Can you solve this riddle? A magazine photographer spent about a year exploring a certain country, yet the country is so tiny that he was able to walk around it in 40 minutes. Its population is only about 1,000. But about one billion people look to its leader for guidance. What is the country?

The tiny country is called Vatican City (VAT ih kun SIH tee). It is the world headquarters of the Roman Catholic Church. The pope is its leader. Every day, Roman Catholics all over the world look to him for leadership. Politically, Vatican City is not part of Italy. Yet it holds an important place in the culture of all Italians.

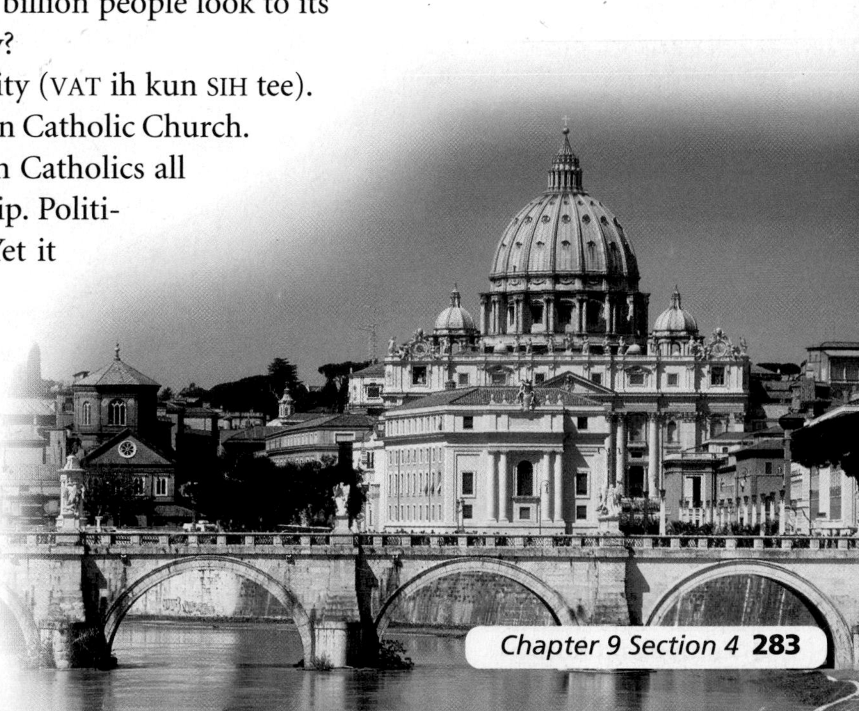

St. Peter's Basilica rises above Vatican City.

A Unifying Force

Vatican City is also known as the Vatican. It is a country within a country. Located within Rome, the capital of Italy, the Vatican is an independent city-state. The Vatican has its own banks and its own money, although you can also use euros there. It is a member of the United Nations. It also has its own police force, radio station, newspaper, and fire department.

Vatican City symbolizes the Roman Catholic Church that unites most Italians. Every day, Catholics and non-Catholics stream into this little country. Most visitors come to see St. Peter's Basilica. A **basilica** is a Roman Catholic church that has a special, high status because of its age or history. The Vatican's palace and art museums are also popular attractions. These museums have priceless collections of religious art, as well as artwork from ancient Greece and Rome.

Target Skill **Use Context Clues** If you do not know what *priceless* means, look in the surrounding words and phrases for context clues.

The Sistine (SIS teen) Chapel, located inside the Vatican, contains many famous paintings, sculptures, and other works of art. Tourists crowd into this chapel, but there is nearly perfect silence inside. No one is allowed to speak above a whisper. Everyone leans back to see the religious scenes painted on the ceiling. The artist Michelangelo painted the ceiling in the 1500s. It is the most famous ceiling in the world.

✓ Reading Check **What is the Vatican?**

A View Inside St. Peter's
Tourists gaze in awe at the art decorating St. Peter's Basilica, including these sculptures by the Italian Renaissance artist Bernini. **Apply Information** *How was the Vatican influenced by the Renaissance?*

Italy

Historically, Italy's location on the Mediterranean Sea made it an important agricultural center and a crossroads of world trade. Today, Italy's economy is shifting toward services, and its main trade partners are other EU members. The "two Italies"—northern and southern—continue to have unequal economies. Use the data on this page to learn more about the economy of Italy.

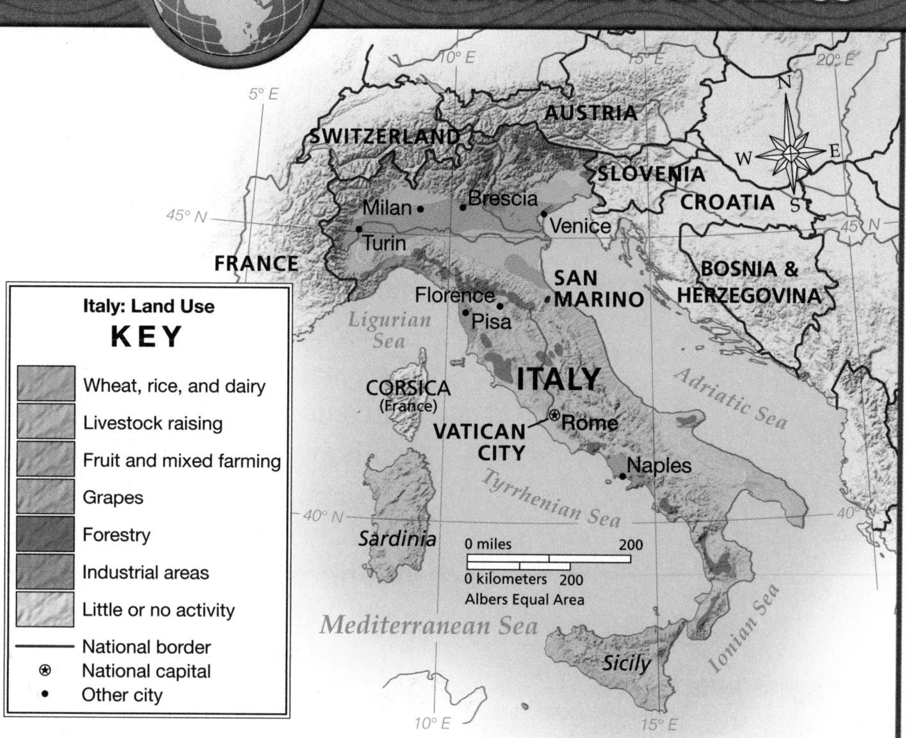

Economic Output per Person, 2001

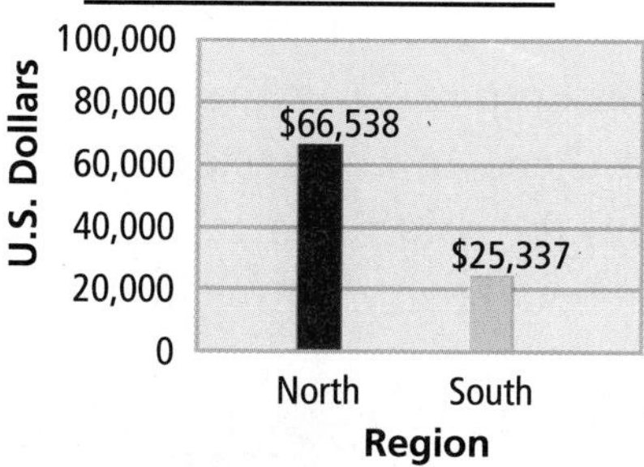

SOURCES: The European Commission; The World Bank Group

Structure of Italy's Economy

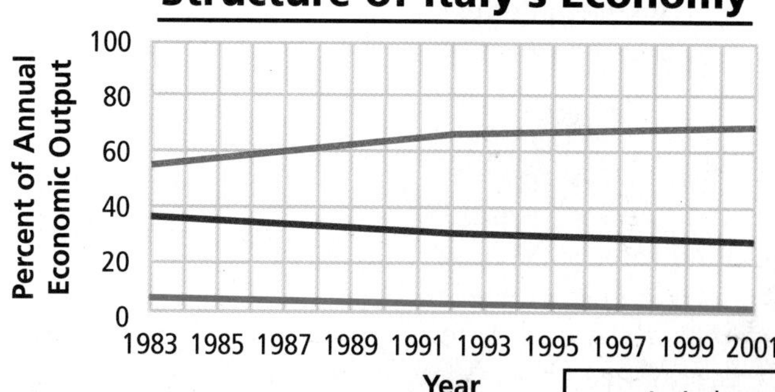

SOURCE: The World Bank Group

Trade, 2001

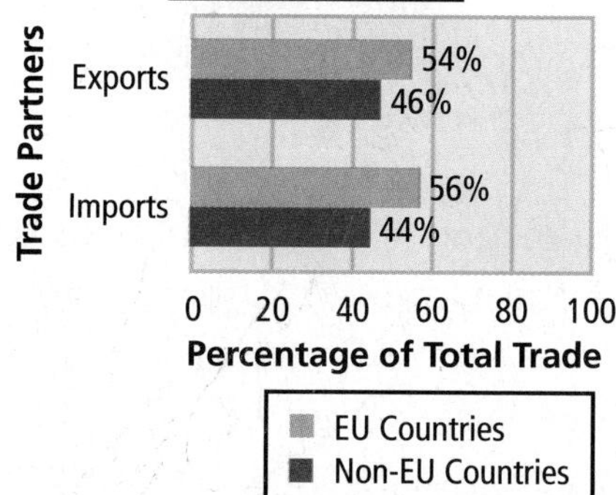

SOURCE: Italy in Figures

Map and Chart Skills

1. **Identify** Where is most of Italy's industry?
2. **Compare and Contrast** How does northern Italy's economic output per person compare to that of southern Italy?
3. **Predict** What changes might southern Italy need to make to its economy in order to catch up with the economy of northern Italy?

Use Web Code **lde-7414** for **DK World Desk Reference Online.**

Discovery CHANNEL SCHOOL Video
Learn about life in ancient Rome.

Divisions Between North and South

Roman Catholicism, with its base in the Vatican, unites about one billion people around the world. It also unites most Italians. Not every Italian is a Catholic, but Italy's history is closely tied to the history of Catholicism. Other things also bring Italians together. Most people living in Italy are ethnic Italians. There are few ethnic minorities. Strong family ties are common among Italians. Even a love of soccer unites many Italians.

Despite these things that many Italians have in common, there are many differences among Italians. Some of the major differences are regional. Italians in the north and Italians in the south live, work, and even practice Roman Catholicism in different ways.

A Divided History For hundreds of years, there was no single, unified Italy. What we now call Italy was once the center of the Roman Empire. Around 2,000 years ago, the Roman Empire stretched across Europe and into northern Africa. When the Roman Empire broke up, Italy itself was divided into many separate city-states, territories, and small kingdoms. The people in these areas had different governments and spoke different languages.

Over time, a regional pattern emerged. Northern Italy was influenced by invaders from Western Europe, who came by land after the breakup of the Roman Empire. Over time, their culture shaped the peoples who lived there. In contrast, southern Italy was colonized by invaders from the south and east, who arrived by way of the Mediterranean Sea. Their culture influenced the region of southern Italy.

The two regions also developed differently in terms of government and economy. In northern Italy, city-states became bustling cities. In modern times, this region became a center of industry. In contrast, in southern Italy, feudal kingdoms dominated, with large numbers of peasants working the land. As a result, southern Italy has always been heavily agricultural.

Italy Unites In the late 1800s, the regions of Italy were united into one nation. A standard form of the Italian language was introduced to help unify the people. After hundreds of years of a divided history, it was not always easy for Italians to identify themselves with this new nation. Even today, there are strong differences between life in the north and in the south.

Links Across Time

The Risorgimento: "Rising Again" The Risorgimento was a movement in the 1800s that inspired the Italian people to unite as one nation. Poets and philosophers used words and ideas to create a sense of nationalism. Today, Italian school children learn about and celebrate the movement. Cities have streets and squares that bear the names of many of the Risorgimento's heroes. Giuseppe Garibaldi (right) was one of the Risorgimento's leaders and is today considered an Italian patriot.

Cars being assembled at the Ferrari factory in Maranello, Italy

Life in the North Milan (mih LAN) is typical of northern Italy. Abundant minerals, fast rivers, and a well-developed economy have brought wealth to the region. Many international businesses are located there. Northern Italy is much more prosperous than southern Italy.

The cities of Milan, Turin, and Genoa are home to most of Italy's manufacturing industries. **Manufacturing** is the process of turning raw materials into finished products. Milan's factories produce cars, planes, leather goods, and plastics.

Milan has a more stylish side, too. Every season, people interested in fashion crowd into Milan to see the new collections from clothing designers. Milan is now second only to Paris as a fashion capital.

Like many European cities, Milan is a mix of the old and the new. In a 400-year-old palace, you can see one of the oldest public libraries in Europe. Millions of dollars have been spent to keep it in good condition. Less than a mile away, you can drive past modern steel and glass office buildings.

Life in the South Southern Italy is very different from Milan. Southern Italy is mostly agricultural. Fertile areas near the coast receive enough rainfall to grow abundant crops. Olives, tomatoes, fruits, and other crops grow there. Inland, farmers have difficulty making a living because of the thin soil and dry climate.

Locorotondo (loh koh roh TOHN doh) is a small town located in the southernmost part of Italy. It is on the "heel" of the Italian "boot." Most people in Locorotondo make a living by farming. They grow wheat, olives, and fruits there. Fishing is also an important business for people there.

Most people in southern Italy follow a more traditional way of life. Many people in southern Italy talk about northern Italy as if it were another country. There are fewer large cities in southern Italy. The high fashions of Milan and the busy city of Turin seem very far away.

Making Cheese
These men use traditional methods to make cheese. **Contrast** *How does this work differ from that performed by the men in the photo at the top of this page?*

Religion in the Two Italies The Roman Catholic Church provides a focus particularly for southern Italians. Today, in the small towns of the south, life is organized around the larger family of the Church and the smaller family in the home. In the north, these ties may not be as strong.

Many religious events are celebrated in the streets of southern towns. Every year, the Feast of Corpus Christi, a Catholic religious festival, takes place several weeks after Easter. In this festival, women hang their wedding clothes over their balconies and place flowers on them. Additional displays are set up on the streets around town. People walk together around the town, from church to church and from display to display.

Economics and the Two Italies After World War II, Italy's economy boomed. Because most of its large cities and industrial centers are located in the north, northern Italy boomed, too. Meanwhile, the agriculture-based economy of southern Italy failed to thrive. Southern Italians moved to the north in large numbers to find jobs.

Italy's government took measures to help the south catch up with the north. First, it introduced land reform. **Land reform** is a process of dividing large properties into smaller ones. Governments sponsor land reform so that more people can own land. Italy's government hoped that land reform would increase agricultural production. The government also modernized the southern region by building roads and new irrigation systems.

A Coastal Scene
The town of Positano clings to a steep cliff on the edge of the ocean in southern Italy. **Analyze Images** *What evidence do you see in the photo of the importance of religion to southern Italians?*

These measures increased agricultural output in the south. Still, southern Italy today lags behind northern Italy. Unemployment in southern Italy is higher than elsewhere in the country. And many southern Italians still move north, particularly to the cities of Rome and Milan. There, they seek jobs and a better standard of living.

Politics and the Two Italies Northern and southern Italy are so different that some Italians have urged northern Italy to become a separate country. Throughout the 1990s, a party called the Northern League called for northern Italy to secede, or leave the rest of Italy to form its own country. In 1996, the party won 10 percent of the vote in a national election.

However, in recent elections, the Northern League has not done so well. For most Italians, no matter how much they differ, they will never lose their strong Italian identity. Religion and family will probably keep the people of Italy unified for many years to come.

✓ Reading Check **Why do some Northern Italians support the Northern League?**

Links to Art

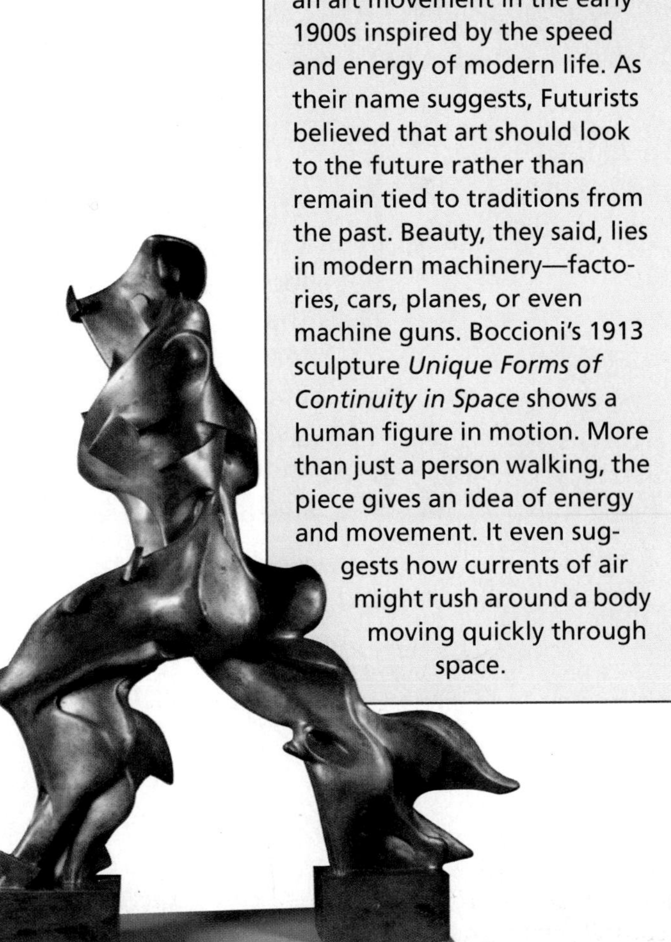

Futurism Italian Futurism was an art movement in the early 1900s inspired by the speed and energy of modern life. As their name suggests, Futurists believed that art should look to the future rather than remain tied to traditions from the past. Beauty, they said, lies in modern machinery—factories, cars, planes, or even machine guns. Boccioni's 1913 sculpture *Unique Forms of Continuity in Space* shows a human figure in motion. More than just a person walking, the piece gives an idea of energy and movement. It even suggests how currents of air might rush around a body moving quickly through space.

Section 4 Assessment

Key Terms

Review the key terms listed at the beginning of this section. Use each term in a sentence that explains its meaning.

Target Reading Skill

Use context clues to explain the meaning of the word *secede* in the second paragraph on this page.

Comprehension and Critical Thinking

1. **(a) Locate** Where is Vatican City?
(b) Summarize How does the Vatican operate as a city-state?
(c) Synthesize Information How does the Roman Catholic religion unite Italians?

2. **(a) List** Name three differences between life in northern Italy and life in southern Italy.
(b) Sequence How did regional differences emerge in Italy over time?
(c) Make Generalizations Do you think Italy's government should continue to introduce reforms to make northern Italy and southern Italy equal? Explain why or why not.

Writing Activity

Write a letter as if you are an Italian writing to a relative about life in either northern or southern Italy. Write details about your life, including what you do for fun, what kinds of work your parents do, and so on.

Writing Tip Be sure to include a greeting, a closing, and a signature in your letter. Also decide on the age, gender, and personality of the person writing the letter.

Using Visual Information to Write a Paragraph

Jerry had to write a report on Rome's Vatican City. He was surprised to discover that Vatican City is a country. He had thought that it was only a religious center in Italy. To write his report, Jerry looked at different charts, graphs, maps, and diagrams. He found that the Vatican has been a country since 1929. From a chart, Jerry learned that the Vatican is about 109 acres (44 hectares) in area. Looking at a diagram, he saw that it is surrounded by a wall with gates that can be locked at night. Its population is fewer than a thousand people. The number of tourists who visit the Vatican each day is far greater than the number of its residents.

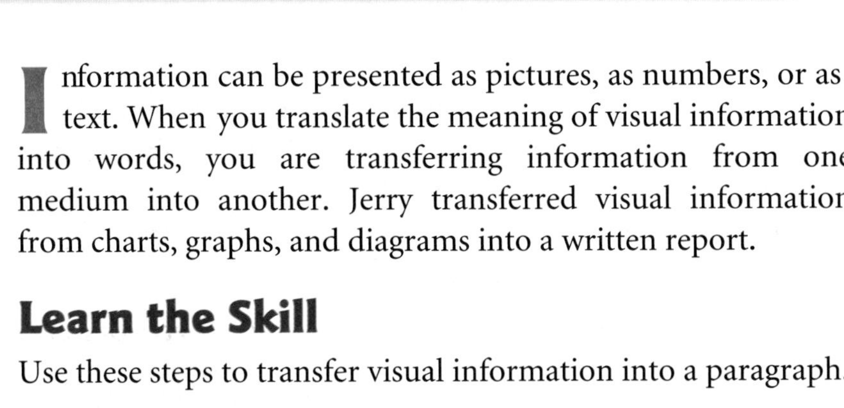

St. Peter's Basilica

Information can be presented as pictures, as numbers, or as text. When you translate the meaning of visual information into words, you are transferring information from one medium into another. Jerry transferred visual information from charts, graphs, and diagrams into a written report.

Learn the Skill

Use these steps to transfer visual information into a paragraph.

1. **Identify the topic of the chart, diagram, or graph by reading the title.** Then look at it to get a general idea of its purpose.

2. **Identify the key pieces of information.** Read headings and other key pieces of information carefully. The headings are usually set off in some way. If you are using a chart or a table, look for similarities and differences among the types of information in the columns.

3. **Analyze the meaning of the information.** Write down several conclusions that can be drawn from the information you have put together.

4. **Rewrite the key pieces of information and your conclusions in a clear paragraph.**

Practice the Skill

Use the steps in Learn the Skill to translate the information in the table into a paragraph.

ITALY: POPULATION STATISTICS		
	1990	2003 (Estimated)
Population	57,664,405	57,998,353
Birth Rate	10 births per 1,000 population	9 births per 1,000 population
Death Rate	9 deaths per 1,000 population	10 deaths per 1,000 population
Fertility Rate	1.4 children born per woman	1.3 children born per woman
Life Expectancy	74, male; 81, female	76, male; 83, female

1. What is the title of the table? What does it tell you about the subject of the table?
2. What are the important headings in the table? Do they indicate key pieces of information? Note the information that is compared and contrasted in the table. How are all the statistics shown on this table related? In what ways are the two sets of numbers similar and different? Which categories have changed over time? Why do you think they have changed?
3. Analyze the meaning of the facts you have learned. What conclusions can you draw? For example, how might the change in the birth rate have affected Italy's population? How might the change in the death rate have affected Italy's population? Is the population getting older or younger? In what ways might the changes in Italy's population affect life in Italy in the future? Consider jobs, school, family life, health care, and so on.
4. Write a paragraph that contains the major pieces of information you have learned. Include the conclusions you have drawn.

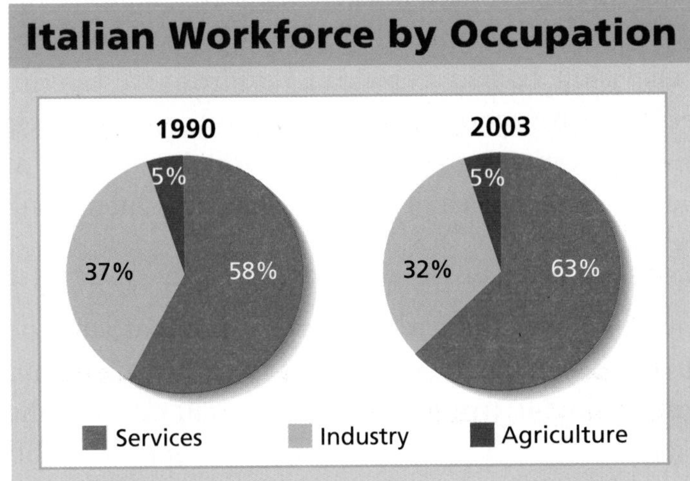

Apply the Skill

Compare the circle graphs. Then use the steps above to write a short paragraph. Include key facts from the graphs, explaining what has changed from 1990 to 2003. Note that agriculture has remained the same. Why do you think that is so? Look at the two graphs and draw some conclusions about how these changes might have affected the country.

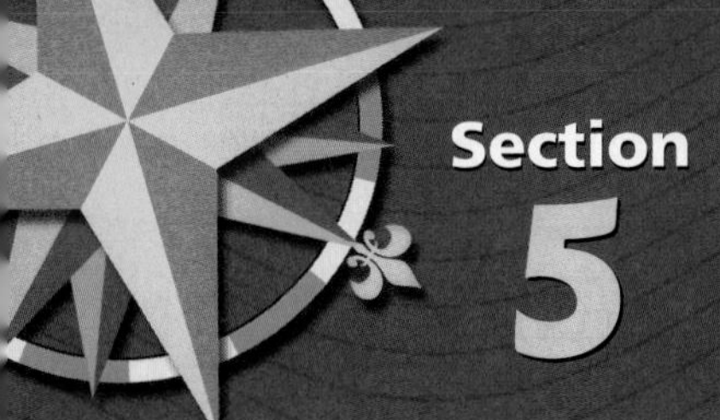

Section 5

Germany
A Unified Nation

Prepare to Read

Objectives
In this section you will
1. Learn about Germany's past.
2. Find out how Germany became reunited.

Taking Notes
As you read this section, look for the events that caused Germany to be divided and later reunited. Copy the flowchart below and record your findings in it.

1918: Germany loses World War I.
1933:

Target Reading Skill
Use Context Clues When you first encounter an unfamiliar word, jot down some ideas about its meaning. As you read and reread the paragraphs that provide its context, adjust the word's definition until you are certain of it. For example, find the word *desperate* in the first paragraph on the next page. You may need to read several paragraphs before you can be certain of its meaning.

Key Terms
- **Holocaust** (HAHL uh kawst) *n.* the mass murder of six million Jews
- **reunification** (ree yoo nih fih KAY shun) *n.* the process of becoming unified again
- **standard of living** (STAN durd uv LIV ing) *n.* the level of comfort in terms of the goods and services that people have

A guard stands watch while East Berlin workmen add blocks to the Berlin Wall in October, 1961.

In 1961, Conrad Schumann, a 19-year-old policeman, stood guard at a barbed-wire fence in East Berlin. His job was to shoot anyone who tried to get across the fence. East Berlin was part of communist East Germany. The fence was built to prevent East Berliners from escaping to West Berlin, where they could reach democratic West Germany.

To Schumann, the fence was a terrible thing. He could see the buildings of West Berlin on the other side. They seemed very beautiful. On television, he had seen a program from West Berlin that showed people dancing to Western music and speaking their views freely. In East Germany, the government did not approve of Western music and free speech. The stores had few interesting things to buy.

Schumann thought about all these things. Then he made a decision and jumped over the barbed wire. A moment later, he was on the other side—in the freedom of the West. Just a few days after Schumann jumped to freedom, a concrete wall replaced the barbed-wire fence. The Berlin Wall separated families and friends. On one side of it, communism ruled. On the other side, the people did. What were the effects of a divided Germany?

Germany's Past

To understand the importance of the Berlin Wall, you need to understand part of Germany's past. Germany lost World War I in 1918. The German government had to pay billions of dollars as punishment for attacking other countries. In the early 1920s, the German economy collapsed. Prices soared. Germans became desperate.

Hitler and World War II When World War I began, Adolf Hitler (AD awlf HIT lur) was a 25-year-old Austrian soldier in the German army. When Germany lost the war, he promised himself that Germany would never suffer such a defeat again. Hitler became deeply involved in politics. In speech after speech, he promised to make Germany great again. By 1933, this former soldier had become dictator of Germany.

Hitler blamed Germany's economic problems on Jews. He spread hateful theories about Jews, Roma, and other ethnic groups in Germany. He claimed that they were inferior to other Germans. He claimed that Germans were a superior ethnic group—and that they should rule Europe.

Adolf Hitler salutes a crowd of people in 1934.

Divided Berlin

KEY
Berlin Wall
City border
Airport

0 miles 10
0 kilometers 10
Transverse Mercator

5° E 10° E 15° E 55° N 50° N
Berlin
EAST GERMANY
WEST GERMANY

N S W E
East Berlin
West Berlin
Tegel Airport
Reichstag
Brandenburg Gate
Gatow Airport
Tempelhof Airport
Havel River
Spree River
Schönefeld Airport

MAP MASTER™ Skills Activity

Location Though Berlin was divided into eastern and western halves, the entire city itself lay within the country of East Germany. **Locate** Which half of the city contained three airports? **Identify Point of View** How might Germans living in West Berlin have felt being surrounded by a communist nation?

Go Online **PHSchool.com** Use Web Code **ldp-7415** for step-by-step **map skills practice.**

COUNTRY PROFILE

Focus on History

Germany

Germany has a long, complex history. At the time of the Roman Empire, various Germanic tribes lived all across Central Europe and into Scandinavia. Present-day Germany developed in the late 1800s out of a patchwork of kingdoms and small states. Just a few decades later, the country dramatically altered its history by fighting a global war. Use the data on this page to learn about modern Germany's history.

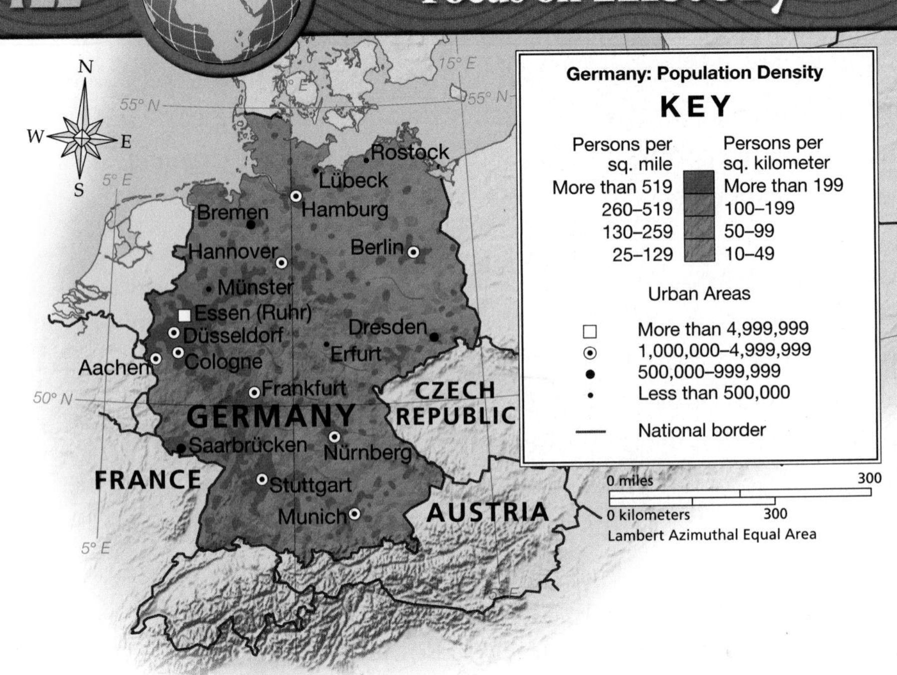

Germany Since 1914

- 1900
- **1914–1918** Germany is defeated in World War I; loses land, colonies, and wealth.
- 1920
- **1920s** Germany faces severe economic challenges.
- **1933** Adolf Hitler and Nazi Party take political control.
- **1935** Nuremberg Laws legalize the persecution of Jews.
- 1940
- **1939–1945** Germany fights in World War II; is defeated by Allies.
- **1949** Germany divides into communist East Germany and democratic West Germany.
- 1960
- **1961** Berlin Wall is built.
- 1980
- **1989** Berlin Wall falls.
- **1990** East Germany and West Germany reunite; Helmut Kohl is elected chancellor.
- **1998** Gerhard Schröder becomes chancellor.
- 2000
- **2002** Schröder is re-elected; Germany adopts euro as its currency.

SOURCE: DK World Desk Reference Online, 2002

A World War I gas mask

German Capital Cities

Years	German Region	Region's Capital
1871–1918	German Empire	Berlin
1919–1949	Germany	Berlin
1949–1990	East Germany	East Berlin
1949–1990	West Germany	Bonn
1990–1999	Germany	Bonn
1999–present	Germany	Berlin

SOURCE: Encyclopedia Britannica Online

Map and Chart Skills

1. **Note** What was the capital of West Germany from 1949 to 1990?
2. **Explain** Why did Germany have two different capitals during the years 1949–1990?
3. **Predict** How might the population density of eastern Germany change as long as Berlin remains the capital?

Use Web Code **lde-7415** for **DK World Desk Reference Online.**

Freedom From Concentration Camps

Soviet soldiers free Holocaust survivors from an Austrian concentration camp in 1945. **Synthesize** *How might images like this one have helped Europeans' resolve to avoid another world war?*

Many people did not believe Hitler's ideas. But Hitler was deadly serious. He ordered attacks on neighboring countries and forced them to submit to German rule. His actions led to the start of World War II in 1939. Great Britain, the Soviet Union, and finally the United States joined other nations to stop the Germans.

By the end of the war, Europe was in ruins. People around the world learned that the Germans had forced countless Jews, Roma, Slavs, and others into brutal concentration camps. Millions of people were murdered in these camps. The majority of them were Jews. This horrible mass murder of six million Jews is called the **Holocaust** (HAH luh kawst).

A Divided Capital At the end of the war, the victors divided up Germany. The Americans, British, and French joined their sections together to create the Federal Republic of Germany. This democratic country was also known as West Germany. The Soviet Union created a communist system in the German Democratic Republic, or East Germany.

The city of Berlin was in East Germany. But the western half of the city, called West Berlin, became part of democratic West Germany. The western half of Berlin was turned into an island of democracy in the middle of communism. The Berlin Wall separated the two halves of Berlin. It also stood as a symbol of a divided world.

Berlin had once been the capital of all of Germany. But now Germany was divided. The city of Bonn became the new capital of West Germany. East Berlin was the capital of East Germany.

Citizen Heroes

Raoul Wallenberg

Raoul Wallenberg (rah OOL WAHL un burg) came from a wealthy Swedish family of bankers and diplomats. Wallenberg studied architecture in the United States. But in 1944, with World War II raging, he persuaded the Swedish government to send him to Hungary as a diplomat. In Hungary, Wallenberg used Sweden's status as a neutral nation to create "safe houses" for Hungarian Jews. Wallenberg's safe houses sheltered several thousand Hungarian Jews and ultimately saved their lives. Wallenberg's efforts put his own life at great risk. In 1945, he was mistakenly arrested as a spy by Soviet troops in Hungary. Wallenberg died in a Soviet prison.

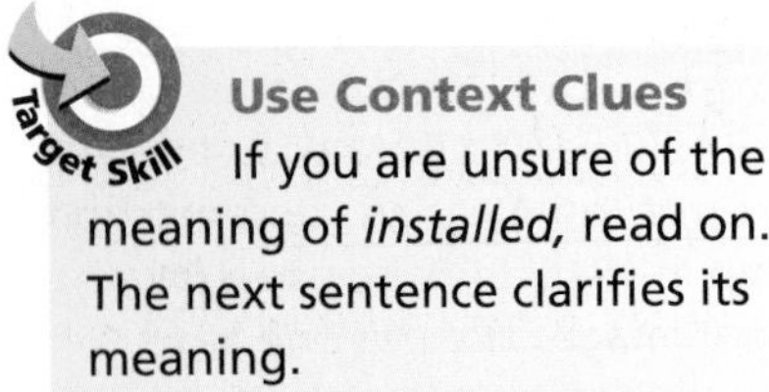

Use Context Clues If you are unsure of the meaning of *installed,* read on. The next sentence clarifies its meaning.

The Cold War During the Cold War, the United States and Western Europe became partners. These countries had democratic governments and were opposed to communism. Eastern European countries had communist governments that had been installed by the Soviet Union. Soviet troops stayed in Eastern Europe to make sure that these countries remained communist.

Think about the effects of the Cold War on European countries. Recall that these countries are small and close together. Cold War borders separated families and friends. Even some who had managed to escape to the West suffered. They could no longer see the relatives they had left behind.

East Germans led far different lives from West Germans. The communist government required people to obey without asking questions. It even encouraged people to spy on family members and neighbors. Children were taught to respect only those things that promoted communism. Western movies, music, and magazines were seen as harmful influences.

While Eastern German border guards look on, a protestor hammers against the Berlin Wall in November, 1989.

The Communists Weaken In time, communist rule started to change. The East German economy fell far behind the West German economy. The average West German had a much more comfortable life than the average East German had. Many East Germans wanted to go to the West, but the East German government did not let them.

In the late 1980s, changes in the Soviet Union weakened the East German government. It became clear that the Soviets would no longer use force to protect communism in Eastern Europe. Fear of the Soviets had helped keep the East German government in power. Now this fear was gone, and the people were ready for change.

Some East Germans began to escape to West Germany by way of Hungary, Czechoslovakia, and Poland. Others began protesting in the streets. To stop the protests, the East German government softened its rules. It announced that under certain conditions, East Germans could visit West Germany.

The East German Government Falls Many people misunderstood the announcement. They thought that the government was opening the Berlin Wall permanently. On November 9, 1989, huge crowds of people demanded to cross into West Berlin. The border guards let them.

Thousands of East Berliners crossed into West Berlin that night. People climbed on top of the wall. They danced and celebrated their new freedom. They also began to destroy the wall, taking it apart piece by piece. The hated wall that had separated them for so long was now gone.

The destruction of the Berlin Wall was the beginning of the end for the East German government. People continued protesting against the government. They wanted more democracy. They wanted Germany to be united again. Less than a year later, the governments of East Germany and West Germany united. Germany had become a single country again.

✓ Reading Check **How was Germany divided after World War II?**

Germany Reunited

Most Germans were thrilled about the fall of the Berlin Wall. Despite having been separate countries for about 50 years, the cultures of East Germany and West Germany had remained similar in many ways. People in both East Germany and West Germany spoke the same language and ate the same foods. They knew the same German composers, writers, and painters. Still, **reunification** (ree yoo nih fih KAY shun), or the process of becoming unified again, would not be easy.

Changing East Germany The East German economy was very weak. Germans in the west had to spend huge amounts of money to improve the economy in the east. The government sold the state-owned factories of East Germany to private companies. They modernized factories and businesses. They cleaned up toxic waste sites. They began producing more consumer goods, such as televisions and cars. This process was very expensive.

East Germans had some concerns about life after communism. For example, in communist East Germany, people had had guaranteed jobs. There were no such guarantees under the democratic system of West Germany. Even today, there are many more people in the east without jobs than there are in the west. Even so, Germans in the east now enjoy a much better standard of living than they did under communism. A **standard of living** is the level of comfort in terms of the goods and services that people have.

Links to Science

Albert Einstein German-born scientist Albert Einstein (below) was teaching physics at the University of Berlin when World War I broke out. He was also developing the important scientific theories that would make him world famous. Einstein was strongly opposed to the war. When Hitler rose to power, Einstein gave up his German citizenship and emigrated to the United States. When scientists began to investigate ways to create the atomic bomb in the 1930s, Einstein urged U.S. President Roosevelt to develop the bomb first, before Germany could. Yet Einstein was still opposed to war and spent the last years of his life promoting peace.

Learn about the history of the Berlin Wall.

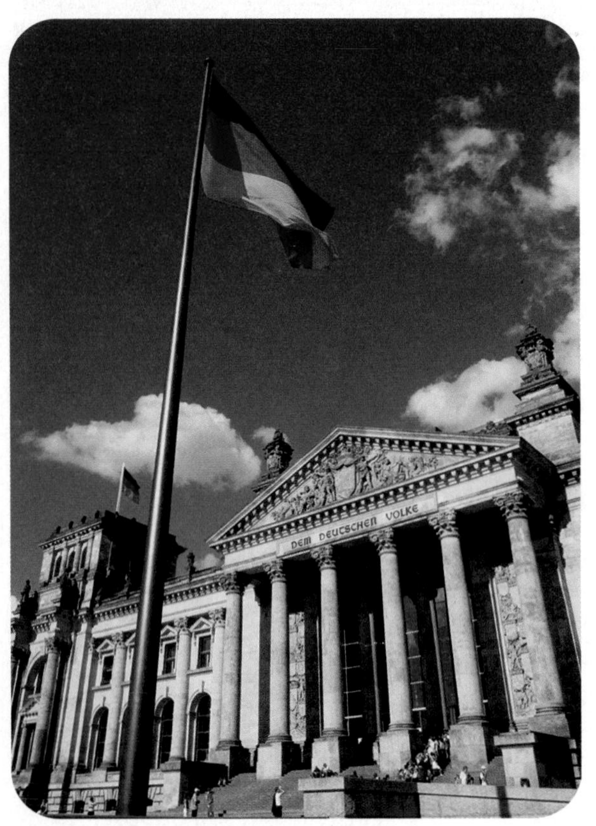

The German flag flies in front of the Reichstag, Germany's parliament building.

Moving Forward When Germany reunited, the German legislature decided Berlin would be the nation's capital once more. By 1999, most government offices had been moved back to Berlin from Bonn.

The cost of moving the capital was enormous. It led to budget cuts and the elimination of many public-service jobs. Still, Germans believed that the move benefited the "new Germany." Berlin's central location, they said, would aid reunification by linking Germans in the east with Germans in the west.

Reunification has been a huge undertaking. It has been difficult and expensive to merge two countries into one unified nation. Even so, Germany remains strong. Despite the high cost of reunification, Germany still has one of the world's strongest economies. It is also a powerful member of the European Union. As the European Union adds new members from Eastern Europe, Germany's central location will be to its advantage. Finally, because Germany was divided for only about 50 years, its people remember their shared history and culture. They will build on this common heritage as they move forward.

✓ Reading Check **Why was Berlin chosen as the reunified nation's capital?**

Section 5 Assessment

Key Terms
Review the key terms listed at the beginning of this section. Use each term in a sentence that explains its meaning.

Target Reading Skill
Find the word *elimination* at the top of this page. How do the surrounding phrases help explain it?

Comprehension and Critical Thinking
1. (a) Explain What was Germany's punishment for its role in World War I?
(b) Identify Effects How did that punishment lead to the rise of Adolf Hitler and the beginning of World War II?
(c) Sequence Describe the events that led to the division of Germany.
2. (a) Recall How did most Germans feel about the fall of the Berlin Wall?
(b) Sequence Describe the events that led to the reunification of Germany.
(c) Identify Effects How has the reunification of Germany affected life in the former East Germany?

Writing Activity
Write a journal entry from the point of view of an East Berliner. Describe the night the Berlin Wall was torn down. How did you feel? Whom and what did you want to see?

Writing Tip Before you write, decide what your age will be. If you are a young East Berliner, write as if you have never lived without the wall. If you are older, write as if you have experienced life both with and without the wall.

Chapter 9 Review and Assessment

◆ Chapter Summary

Section 1: The United Kingdom

- There are four regions within the United Kingdom: England, Scotland, Wales, and Northern Ireland.
- The Magna Carta and Parliament played important roles in the development of British democracy.
- The United Kingdom is a constitutional monarchy.
- Trade is important to the United Kingdom because it is an island with limited natural resources.

Section 2: France

- France has made important contributions to art, philosophy, architecture, fashion, and cooking.
- France is becoming more culturally diverse.

Boccioni's *Unique Forms of Continuity in Space* (1913)

Section 3: Sweden

- Sweden is a welfare state that provides many services to its citizens.
- Sweden became an industrialized country in the early 1900s.
- In order to continue providing benefits to everyone, the Swedish government needs to find better ways of paying for them.

Section 4: Italy

- Vatican City is an important city-state within Rome, Italy.
- Many Italians have close ties to the Roman Catholic Church.
- Life in northern Italy differs in many ways from life in southern Italy.

Section 5: Germany

- The Berlin Wall divided communist East Germany from democratic West Germany.
- After the fall of the Berlin Wall, the governments of East and West Germany reunited.

◆ Key Terms

Complete each sentence with a key term from the list.

Parliament
standard of living
land reform
philosophy
national debt
reunification
welfare state
constitutional monarchy

1. A _____ is a system of ideas or beliefs.
2. _____ is the lawmaking body of the United Kingdom.
3. A _____ is the level of comfort in terms of the goods and services that people have.
4. A _____ is a government in which a monarch is the head of state but has limited powers.
5. The process of dividing large properties into smaller ones is called _____.
6. In a _____, the government provides many services and benefits free or at a low cost.
7. _____ is the amount of money a government owes.
8. The process of becoming unified again is called _____.

Chapter 

Review and Assessment (continued)

◆ Comprehension and Critical Thinking

9. (a) **Explain** What is the role of the British monarch?
   (b) **Draw Conclusions** Why does Britain remain a monarchy even though the monarch now has little power?
   (c) **Predict** Do you think the United Kingdom will continue to have a monarch in the future? Explain why or why not.

10. (a) **Explain** What is the French Academy?
    (b) **Infer** Why do foreign words enter the French language even though the French Academy tries to limit them?

11. (a) **Explain** What benefits does Sweden's welfare system provide?
    (b) **Summarize** What problems does Sweden face today?
    (c) **Predict** How might Sweden solve some of its economic problems?

12. (a) **Identify** What is the political status of Vatican City?
    (b) **List** Which things do most Italians have in common?
    (c) **Compare and Contrast** How is life in northern Italy different from life in southern Italy?

13. (a) **Recall** How was Germany divided?
    (b) **Explain** Why was Germany reunified?
    (c) **Summarize** What challenges has reunification brought to Germany?

14. (a) **List** Name two things that the East German government did not allow.
    (b) **Compare and Contrast** Compare personal freedom in East Germany and West Germany during the Cold War.

◆ Skills Practice

In the Skills for Life activity in this chapter, you learned how to use visual information to write a paragraph. Review the steps you followed to learn this skill. Then turn to the Country Profile on page 294. Use the data on this page to write a paragraph titled A History of Germany Since World War I.

◆ Writing Activity: Government

You read about Germany's division after World War II. Recall that some Italians today are in favor of dividing Italy. Write a paragraph comparing Germany's situation after World War II with Italy's situation today.

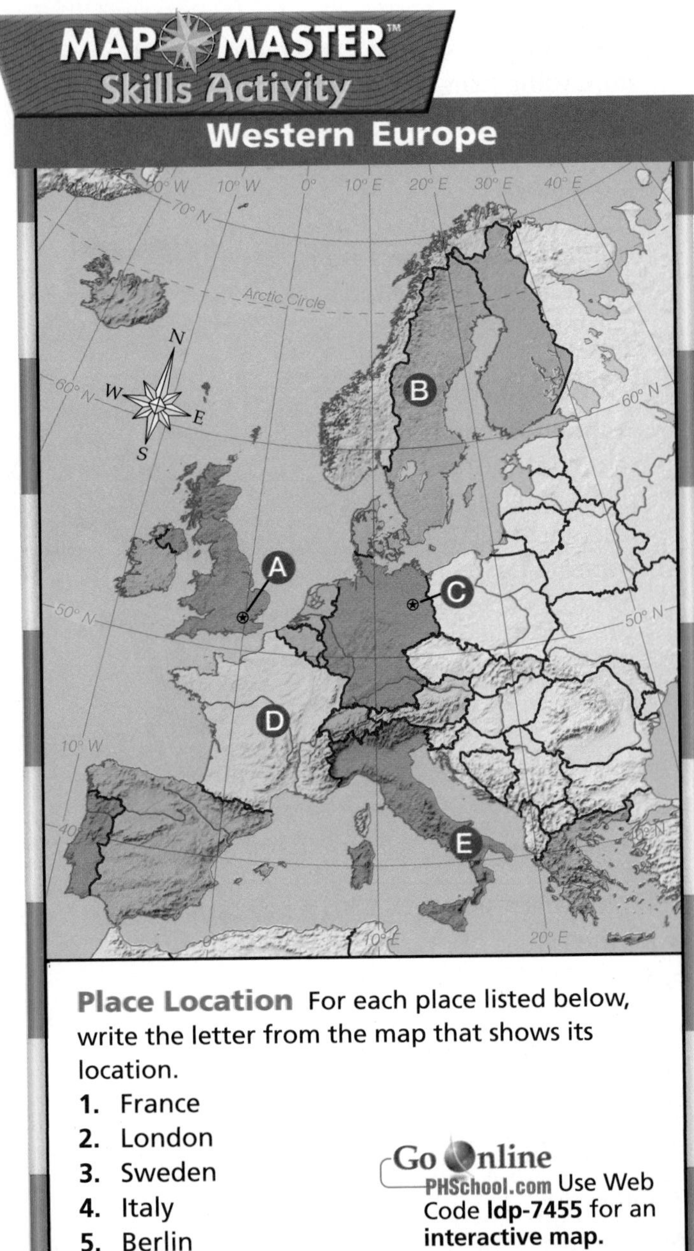

Place Location For each place listed below, write the letter from the map that shows its location.

1. France
2. London
3. Sweden
4. Italy
5. Berlin

Go Online PHSchool.com Use Web Code **ldp-7455** for an **interactive map.**

Standardized Test Prep

Test-Taking Tips

Some questions on standardized tests ask you to analyze a point of view. Read the passage below. Then follow the tips to answer the sample question.

> On November 9, 1989, crowds began to tear down the Berlin Wall, block by block. People helped each other over the wall to the other side. Someone watching from a window nearby said, "Today they are happy. But will they still be cheering when they realize that they no longer have the promise of either a job or food to eat?"

Choose the letter that best answers the question.

Who might have made this statement?

A an old East German who wants to have his son visit from West Germany

B a young East German who dreams of finding a job in West Germany

C an East German communist with a job running a state business

D a West German whose parents live in East Germany

TIP Be sure that you understand the question: Who might have said the words that begin, *Today they are happy. But will they still be cheering . . .?*

Think It Through

The person who made this statement is not happy that the wall is coming down. He or she wonders whether the people tearing it down will still be cheering about it in the future. Who would not be happy about the wall coming down? You can eliminate A and D because both people have families that will be reunited with the wall torn down. You can also rule out B because that person will now be able to go to West Germany to look for work. The correct answer is C.

TIP Use good reasoning to help you choose an answer that makes sense.

Practice Questions

Use the tips above and other tips in this book to help you answer the following questions.

1. What historical document first limited the power of the British king?
   - **A** the Magna Carta
   - **B** Parliament
   - **C** the British constitution
   - **D** the Northern League

2. Which style of architecture began in the region of Paris hundreds of years ago?
   - **A** Renaissance
   - **B** French Academic
   - **C** Gothic
   - **D** classical

3. What happened when the Roman Empire broke up?
   - **A** The nation of Italy was formed.
   - **B** It broke into a number of kingdoms, city-states, and territories.
   - **C** Italy became part of the United Kingdom.
   - **D** The Italian language became standardized.

4. When was Germany divided into two countries?
   - **A** at the end of the Cold War
   - **B** at the end of World War I
   - **C** during the Cold War
   - **D** at the end of World War II

Use Web Code **lda-7405** for a **Chapter 9 self-test.**

Chapter 10

Eastern Europe and Russia

Chapter Preview

This chapter focuses on Poland, five Balkan nations, Ukraine, and Russia.

Country Databank

The Country Databank provides data and descriptions of Russia and each of the countries in Eastern Europe.

Target Reading Skill

Comparing and Contrasting In this chapter you will focus on comparison and contrast to help you sort out and analyze information.

▶ Harvesting lavender on a hillside in Croatia

Eastern Europe and Russia: Political

MAP MASTER™ Skills Activity

Regions For many years following World War II, the Soviet Union dominated many of the countries of Eastern Europe. **Identify** Which countries border Russia? **Analyze Information** How did the size and location of these countries make them more open to Soviet domination?

Go Online PHSchool.com Use Web Code **ldp-7511** for step-by-step **map skills practice.**

Introducing Eastern Europe and Russia

Guide for Reading

This section provides an introduction to Russia and the 18 countries of Eastern Europe.

- Look at the map on the previous page and then read the paragraphs to learn about each nation.
- Analyze the data to compare the countries.
- What characteristics do most of these countries share?
- What are some key differences among the countries?

Viewing the Video Overview

View the World Studies Video Overview to learn more about each of the countries. As you watch, answer these questions:

- What are the major land regions in Eastern Europe?
- How is the terrain both different from and similar to that in Western Europe?

Discovery CHANNEL SCHOOL
Video
Explore the geography of Eastern Europe and Russia.

Albania

Capital	Tirana
Land Area	10,578 sq mi; 27,398 sq km
Population	3.5 million
Ethnic Group(s)	Albanian, Greek
Religion(s)	Muslim, Eastern Orthodox, Roman Catholic
Government	emerging democracy
Currency	lek
Leading Exports	textiles and footwear, asphalt, metals and metallic ores, crude oil, vegetables, fruits, tobacco
Language(s)	Albanian (official), Greek

Albania (al BAY nee uh) is located in southeastern Europe on the Adriatic and Ionian Seas. It is bordered by Serbia and Montenegro, Macedonia, and Greece. Albania became a communist state during World War II. In the early 1990s, the country tried to establish democracy. But government instability, high unemployment rates, and violence have prevented Albania from achieving that goal. Economically, the country is poor and struggling. Today, the country depends on aid from other countries to survive. However, the Albanians are slowly creating an open-market economy.

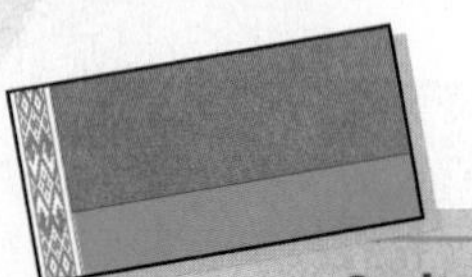

Belarus

Capital	Minsk
Land Area	80,154 sq mi; 207,600 sq km
Population	10.3 million
Ethnic Group(s)	Belarusian, Russian, Polish, Ukrainian
Religion(s)	Eastern Orthodox, Roman Catholic, Protestant, Muslim, Jewish
Government	republic
Currency	Belarusian ruble
Leading Exports	machinery and equipment, mineral products, chemicals, textiles, foodstuffs, metals
Language(s)	Belarusian (official), Russian (official)

Belarus (bay luh ROOS) is located between Poland and Russia. It was a Soviet republic for seven decades until its independence in 1991. Unlike many other former Soviet republics, Belarus has remained politically close to Russia. Russia also supplies Belarus with resources, as the country has few natural resources of its own. Belarus does have the potential, however, to develop its agriculture and forestry industries. Belarus faces major health and environmental problems caused by the 1986 Chernobyl explosion in neighboring Ukraine.

Bosnia and Herzegovina

Capital	Sarajevo
Land Area	19,741 sq mi; 51,129 sq km
Population	4.0 million
Ethnic Group(s)	Serb, Bosniak, Croat
Religion(s)	Muslim, Eastern Orthodox, Roman Catholic, Protestant
Government	emerging federal democratic republic
Currency	marka
Leading Exports	miscellaneous manufactured goods, raw materials
Language(s)	Serbo-Croat (official)

Bosnia and Herzegovina (BAHZ nee uh and hurt suh goh VEE nuh) is located on the Adriatic Sea in southeastern Europe, between Croatia and Serbia and Montenegro. Bosnia and Herzegovina declared independence from Yugoslavia in 1992. However, conflict among Serbs, Bosniaks, and Croats drew the country immediately into civil war. Peace was reached in 1995 with the help of NATO. Today, Bosnia and Herzegovina is struggling to recover from the years of war. Because of its natural resources, it has the potential to develop a thriving economy.

Bulgaria

Capital	Sofía
Land Area	42,683 sq mi; 110,550 sq km
Population	7.6 million
Ethnic Group(s)	Bulgarian, Southwest Asian, Roma, Macedonian, Armenian, Tartar, Circassian
Religion(s)	Eastern Orthodox, Muslim, Roman Catholic, Jewish
Government	parliamentary democracy
Currency	lev
Leading Exports	clothing, footwear, iron and steel, machinery and equipment, fuels
Language(s)	Bulgarian (official), Turkish, Macedonian, Romany

Bulgaria (bul GEHR ee uh) is located in southeastern Europe between Romania and Greece, bordering the Black Sea. The first Bulgarian state was created in the 600s when a central Asian Turkic tribe merged with the Slavic people of the region. Bulgaria was ruled by the Ottoman Empire for hundreds of years. The country regained its independence in 1878 but fell under communist rule after World War II. In 1990 the first open elections were held. Since then, the country has continued to develop a democratic political system with a free-market economy. Bulgaria is a member of NATO and has taken the first steps to becoming part of the EU.

Croatia

Capital	Zagreb
Land Area	21,781 sq mi; 56,414 sq km
Population	4.4 million
Ethnic Group(s)	Croat, Serb, Bosniak, Hungarian, Slovene, Czech, Albanian, Montenegrin, Roma
Religion(s)	Roman Catholic, Eastern Orthodox, Muslim
Government	presidential-parliamentary democracy
Currency	kuna
Leading Exports	transport equipment, textiles, chemicals, foodstuffs, fuels
Language(s)	Croation (official)

Croatia (kroh AY shuh) is located in southeastern Europe between Slovenia and Bosnia and Herzegovina. It borders the Adriatic Sea. Croatia was formerly part of the nation called Yugoslavia. Croatia declared its independence in 1991, but Serbian armies remained and fought on Croatian land for several years afterward. Economically, the country is struggling to recover from costly war damage and a high unemployment rate. The EU has spent over $1 billion in aid to help Croatia rebuild. The nation has rich fishing resources in the Adriatic Sea.

Introducing Eastern Europe and Russia

Czech Republic

Capital	Prague
Land Area	29,836 sq mi; 78,276 sq km
Population	10.3 million
Ethnic Group(s)	Czech, Moravian, Slovak, Polish, German, Silesian
Religion(s)	Roman Catholic, Protestant, Eastern Orthodox
Government	parliamentary democracy
Currency	Czech koruna
Leading Exports	machinery and transportation equipment, intermediate manufactured goods, chemicals, raw materials, fuel
Language(s)	Czech (official), Slovak, Hungarian

The Czech Republic (chek rih PUB lik) is a landlocked nation surrounded by Germany, Slovakia, Austria, and Poland. In 1918, the Slovaks joined with the Czechs to form Czechoslovakia. Czechoslovakia fell under Soviet rule after World War II but gained back its freedom in 1989. In 1993, the Czechs and the Slovaks peacefully separated into two nations, the Czech Republic and Slovakia. The Czech Republic has become one of the most stable and successful countries of those dominated by the Soviet Union during the Cold War. It has strong industries, mineral resources, and a thriving tourist industry. The Czech Republic has become a member of NATO and the EU.

Estonia

Capital	Tallinn
Land Area	16,684 sq mi; 43,211 sq km
Population	1.4 million
Ethnic Group(s)	Estonian, Russian, Ukrainian, Belarusian, Finnish
Religion(s)	Protestant, Eastern Orthodox, Jewish
Government	parliamentary republic
Currency	kroon
Leading Exports	machinery and equipment, wood products, textiles, food products, metals, chemical products
Language(s)	Estonian (official), Russian

Estonia (es TOH nee uh) borders the Baltic Sea, Latvia, and Russia. It is actually a small peninsula, and includes more than 1500 small islands. For centuries, foreign powers controlled the region. But in 1918, Estonia gained its independence. Like several other eastern European states, it was taken over by the Soviet Union in 1940 and regained its independence in 1991. Since then, Estonia has adopted political and economic ideas from Western Europe. Its three major trading partners are Finland, Sweden, and Germany. The country has joined the EU and NATO.

A hawk moth in Viidumae Nature Reserve, Estonia

Hungary

Capital	Budapest
Land Area	35,652 sq mi; 92,340 sq km
Population	10.1 million
Ethnic Group(s)	Hungarian, Roma, German, Serb, Slovak, Romanian
Religion(s)	Roman Catholic, Protestant
Government	parliamentary democracy
Currency	forint
Leading Exports	machinery and equipment, other manufactured goods, food products, raw materials, fuels and electricity
Language(s)	Hungarian (official)

Hungary (HUNG guh ree) is landlocked among Austria, Romania, and five other countries in central Europe. For hundreds of years the nation was part of the Austro-Hungarian Empire. After World War II, the country came under communist rule. In the late 1960s, Hungary took some steps away from a government-controlled economy. But real reforms came in 1990 with the first open elections and a free-market economy. Since then, Hungary has had strong economic growth, and has become a member of both NATO and the EU. Hungary's capital, Budapest, has long been a cultural center of the region.

Latvia

Capital	Riga
Land Area	24,552 sq mi; 63,589 sq km
Population	2.4 million
Ethnic Group(s)	Latvian, Russian, Belarusian, Ukrainian, Polish, Lithuanian
Religion(s)	Protestant, Roman Catholic, Eastern Orthodox
Government	parliamentary democracy
Currency	lat
Leading Exports	wood and wood products, machinery and equipment, metals, textiles, foodstuffs
Language(s)	Latvian (official), Russian

Located between Estonia and Lithuania, Latvia (LAT vee uh) sits on the eastern coast of the Baltic Sea. The entire country lies on a flat, low plain. Its climate is temperate, with cool summers and cold winters. Between World War I and World War II, Latvia enjoyed a period of independence, but in 1940 it was taken over by the Soviet Union. Along with many other Soviet republics, it declared its independence in 1991. Since then it has adopted many of the political and economic ideas of Western Europe. After a Russian economic crisis in 1998, Latvia further decreased is dependence on Russia. It has joined the EU and NATO.

Lithuania

Capital	Vilnius
Land Area	25,174 sq mi; 65,200 sq km
Population	3.6 million
Ethnic Group(s)	Lithuanian, Russian, Polish, Belarusian
Religion(s)	Roman Catholic, Protestant, Russian Orthodox, Muslim, Jewish
Government	parliamentary democracy
Currency	litas
Leading Exports	mineral products, textiles and clothing, machinery and equipment, chemicals, wood and wood products, foodstuffs
Language(s)	Lithuanian (official), Russian

Lithuania (lith oo AY nee uh) is located between Latvia and Poland and borders the Baltic Sea. It was an independent state before World War II, but the Soviet Union claimed it in 1940. Lithuania was the first Soviet republic to declare independence in 1990. Since independence, the Lithuanians have taken steps toward establishing a free-market economy and privatizing businesses. Most of Lithuania's income is from services and agriculture. However, it has few natural resources and is one of the poorer nations in the region. Lithuania has joined the EU and NATO.

Introducing Eastern Europe and Russia

Macedonia

Capital	Skopje
Land Area	9,597 sq mi; 24,856 sq km
Population	2.1 million
Ethnic Group(s)	Macedonian, Albanian, Southwest Asian, Serb, Roma
Religion(s)	Eastern Orthodox, Muslim
Government	emerging democracy
Currency	Macedonian denar
Leading Exports	food, beverages, tobacco, miscellaneous manufactured goods, iron and steel
Language(s)	Macedonian (official), Albanian (official), Serbo-Croat

Macedonia (mas uh DOH nee uh) is located in southeastern Europe north of Greece. It gained its independence from Yugoslavia in 1991. Macedonia is the poorest of the countries that used to make up Yugoslavia. The nation has a weak economy, and one third of its labor force is unemployed. Macedonia faces ethnic conflict and government instability. It has also faced political conflict with its neighbor, Greece. Because Macedonia is the name of a region in northern Greece, Greece opposed the country's choice of name. However, a treaty signed in 1995 settled the dispute.

A woman spins wool into yarn in her home in Moldova, 1995.

Moldova

Capital	Chisinau
Land Area	12,885 sq mi; 33,371 sq km
Population	4.4 million
Ethnic Group(s)	Moldovan, Ukrainian, Russian, Bulgarian, Gagauz
Religion(s)	Eastern Orthodox, Jewish
Government	republic
Currency	Moldovan leu
Leading Exports	foodstuffs, textiles and footwear, machinery
Language(s)	Moldovan (official), Romanian, Russian

Moldova (mohl DOH vuh) is located between Romania and Ukraine. Before World War II, Moldova was ruled by Romania. It became part of the Soviet Union after World War II and gained its independence in 1991. With few minerals and energy sources, Moldova's economy is based mostly on farming. One of the poorest nations in Europe, it recently saw an improvement in its economy due to some free-market reforms. However, in 2001 Moldova became the first former Soviet state to elect a communist president. Consequently, fewer free-market reforms are expected in the future.

Poland

Capital	Warsaw
Land Area	117,554 sq mi; 304,465 sq km
Population	38.6 million
Ethnic Group(s)	Polish, German, Ukrainian, Belarusian
Religion(s)	Roman Catholic, Eastern Orthodox
Government	republic
Currency	zloty
Leading Exports	machinery and transport equipment, intermediate manufactured goods, miscellaneous manufactured goods, food and live animals
Language(s)	Polish (official)

Polish postage stamps

Poland (POH lund) is located in central Europe between Germany and Ukraine. Poland was taken over by Germany and the Soviet Union during World War II. Following the war, Poland was dominated by the Soviet Union. Since the fall of the Soviet Union, Poland has changed successfully from a government-controlled economy to an open economy, and has entered the EU and NATO. Poland has an almost homogeneous population, and the vast majority of Poles are Roman Catholic.

Romania

Capital	Bucharest
Land Area	88,934 sq mi; 230,340 sq km
Population	22.3 million
Ethnic Group(s)	Romanian, Hungarian, Roma, Ukrainian, German, Russian
Religion(s)	Eastern Orthodox, Protestant, Roman Catholic
Government	republic
Currency	Romanian leu
Leading Exports	textiles and footwear, metals and metal products, machinery and equipment, minerals and fuels
Language(s)	Romanian (official), Hungarian, German, Romany

Romania (roh MAY nee uh) is located in southeastern Europe between Ukraine and Bulgaria, bordering the Black Sea. Following World War II, Romania was occupied by the Soviet Union. It became a communist republic in 1947. A single harsh dictator ruled Romania from 1965 to 1989. In the late 1990s, the country became a limited democracy. Today, the country still struggles with widespread poverty and government instability. Romania would like to become part of the EU, but must achieve more political and economic reforms before it can apply.

Russian Federation

Capital	Moscow
Land Area	6,592,100 sq mi; 16,995,800 sq km
Population	145 million
Ethnic Group(s)	Russian, Tatar, Ukrainian, Chuvash, Bashkir, Belarusian, Moldavian
Religion(s)	Russian Orthodox, Muslim, Jewish
Government	federation
Currency	Russian ruble
Leading Exports	petroleum and petroleum products, natural gas, wood and wood products, metals, chemicals
Language(s)	Russian (official), Tatar, Ukrainian, Chuvash, and others

Russia (RUSH uh), the world's largest country, is located in northern Asia between Ukraine and China, bordering the Arctic and North Pacific Oceans. The region west of the Ural Mountains is considered part of Europe. Throughout most of its history, Russia was ruled by royal families. The last royal dynasty was overthrown in 1917. The world's first communist government, the Soviet Union, was formed after World War I and ruled for decades. In 1991, the USSR split into 15 independent nations. Today, Russians are moving toward a more democratic political system and a free-market economy.

Introducing Eastern Europe and Russia

Serbia and Montenegro

Capital	Belgrade
Land Area	39,435 sq mi; 102,136 sq km
Population	10.7 million
Ethnic Group(s)	Serb, Albanian, Montenegrin, Hungarian
Religion(s)	Eastern Orthodox, Muslim, Roman Catholic
Government	republic
Currency	dinar and euro
Leading Exports	manufactured goods, food and live animals, raw materials
Language(s)	Serbo-Croat (official), Albanian, Hungarian

Serbia and Montenegro (SUR bee uh and mahnt uh NEE groh) are located in southeastern Europe between Croatia and Romania, bordering the Adriatic Sea. These two republics were once part of Yugoslavia. They experienced years of ethnic conflict and civil war after Yugoslavia broke up. Serbia's violence against ethnic Albanians in Kosovo caused NATO troops to invade the region in 1999 to restore peace. In 2003, Serbia and Montenegro agreed to become a loose partnership of two states. Both republics are currently focused on rebuilding their troubled economies and recovering from years of war.

Slovakia

Capital	Bratislava
Land Area	18,842 sq mi; 48,800 sq km
Population	5.4 million
Ethnic Group(s)	Slovak, Hungarian, Roma, Czech, Moravian, Silesian, Ruthenian, Ukrainian, German, Polish
Religion(s)	Roman Catholic, Protestant, Eastern Orthodox
Government	parliamentary democracy
Currency	Slovak koruna
Leading Exports	machinery and transport equipment, manufactured goods, chemicals
Language(s)	Slovak (official), Hungarian, Czech

Slovakia (sloh VAH kee uh) is located in Central Europe between the Czech Republic and Ukraine. In 1918, the Slovaks joined with the Czechs to form Czechoslovakia. Czechoslovakia fell under Soviet domination after World War II but gained back its freedom in 1989. In 1993, the Slovaks and the Czechs peacefully separated into two democratic nations, Slovakia and the Czech Republic. Slovakia has a stable economy and has joined the EU and NATO.

An Eastern Orthodox Church in Montenegro

Slovenia

Capital	Ljubljana
Land Area	7,780 sq mi; 20,151 sq km
Population	1.9 million
Ethnic Group(s)	Slovene, Croat, Serb, Bosniak, Yugoslav, Hungarian
Religion(s)	Roman Catholic, Protestant, Muslim
Government	parliamentary democratic republic
Currency	tolar
Leading Exports	manufactured goods, machinery and transport equipment, chemicals, food
Language(s)	Slovene (official), Serbo-Croat

Slovenia (sloh VEE nee uh) is located in Central Europe between Austria and Croatia, bordering the Adriatic Sea. The Slovene lands were once part of Austria and the Holy Roman Empire. In the mid-1900s, they became part of Yugoslavia. Since independence in 1991, Slovenia has become a stable democracy with a strong economy and a good relationship with Western Europe. Slovenia has joined the EU and NATO. The country has Eastern Europe's highest standard of living.

Ukraine

Capital	Kiev
Land Area	233,090 sq mi; 603,700 sq km
Population	48.4 million
Ethnic Group(s)	Ukrainian, Russian, Belarusian, Moldovan, Crimea Tartar, Bulgarian, Hungarian, Romanian, Polish
Religion(s)	Eastern Orthodox, Jewish
Government	republic
Currency	hryvnia
Leading Exports	ferrous and nonferrous metals, fuel and petroleum products, machinery and transport equipment, food products
Language(s)	Ukrainian (official), Russian, Tartar

Ukraine (yoo KRAYN) is located between Poland and Russia, bordering the Black Sea. During the 900s and 1000s, Ukraine was the center of the largest and most powerful state in Europe. However, since that time, the region has suffered invasions, occupations, and rebellions. Millions of Ukrainians died under Soviet occupation in the 1920s and 1930s and millions more during World War II. Although Ukraine gained independence from the Soviet Union in 1991, many of its leaders have been slow to encourage political or economic reforms.

SOURCES: CIA World Factbook Online 2002; DK World Desk Reference Online; *The World Almanac*, 2003

Assessment

Comprehension and Critical Thinking

1. **Compare and Contrast** Compare the physical size and the population of Ukraine to those of Macedonia.
2. **Make Generalizations** Identify the five countries that were once part of Yugoslavia. What are some characteristics that they share?
3. **Categorize** Which religions do most people in the region practice?
4. **Draw Conclusions** The governments of some of these countries are listed as "emerging," or developing democracies. Read about these countries' histories. Why might it be difficult for them to establish democratic governments?
5. **Make a Bar Graph** Create a bar graph that shows the populations of the countries in the region.

Keeping Current

Access the **DK World Desk Reference Online** at **PHSchool.com** for up-to-date information about the 19 countries in this region.

Web Code: lde-7500

Section 1

Poland

Preserving Tradition Amidst Change

Prepare to Read

Objectives

In this section you will

1. Find out about Polish traditions.
2. Learn about economic changes that have taken place in Poland since the collapse of communism.
3. Understand the future challenges that Poland faces.

Taking Notes

As you read, create an outline of this section. The outline below has been started for you.

I. Tradition in Poland
  A. Catholicism
  B.
    1.
    2.
II.

Target Reading Skill

Compare and Contrast
When you compare, you look for the similarities between things. When you contrast, you look at the differences. Comparing and contrasting can help you sort out and analyze information. As you read this section, look for similarities and differences in Polish life during and after Soviet domination.

Key Terms

- **shrine** (shryn) *n.* a holy place
- **capitalism** (KAP ut ul iz um) *n.* an economic system in which businesses are privately owned
- **entrepreneur** (ahn truh pruh NOOR) *n.* a person who develops original ideas in order to start new businesses

Dancers at a traditional festival in Mazuka, Poland

In June of 2003, Polish citizens celebrated an event that could not possibly have occurred just two decades earlier. Poland had voted to join the European Union. It was an exciting event for a nation that at one time did not even appear on maps of Europe.

Poland has had a difficult history. In medieval times, it was the largest state in Europe. But by the late 1700s, it had been divided up among its stronger neighbors. For the next two hundred years, Polish territory changed hands many times. Controlled at different times by Russia, Germany, and Austria, Poland became free again at the end of World War I. But after World War II, the Polish government fell under the influence of the Soviet Union. For several decades, Poles lived under a harsh communist government. Poles regained their freedom when that government fell in 1989. Poland then began a long process of reform and rebuilding.

Tradition in Poland

Poland has experienced great change in its long history. Borders have shifted. Rulers have come and gone. Economic systems have changed. But many parts of Polish life have remained the same.

Catholicism in Poland Catholicism has been at the center of Polish tradition for centuries. The communist government tried to discourage Catholicism, but it could not change the devotion many Poles have for the Roman Catholic Church.

Today, about 95 percent of Poles are still Catholic. Poles have their own way of observing Catholic holidays and their own way of prayer. Polish Catholics felt tremendous pride in 1978, when a Pole was selected as pope of the Catholic Church. Pope John Paul II quickly became the most widely traveled Catholic leader in history. He also made the world more aware of Poland and its struggle under communism.

In 1979, the pope visited Poland. About one million joyful and enthusiastic Poles gathered to see him. Mothers held babies over their heads for the pope's blessing. The crowd sang hymns and threw flowers toward the stage on which he sat. For most of these people, the pope stood for traditional Poland.

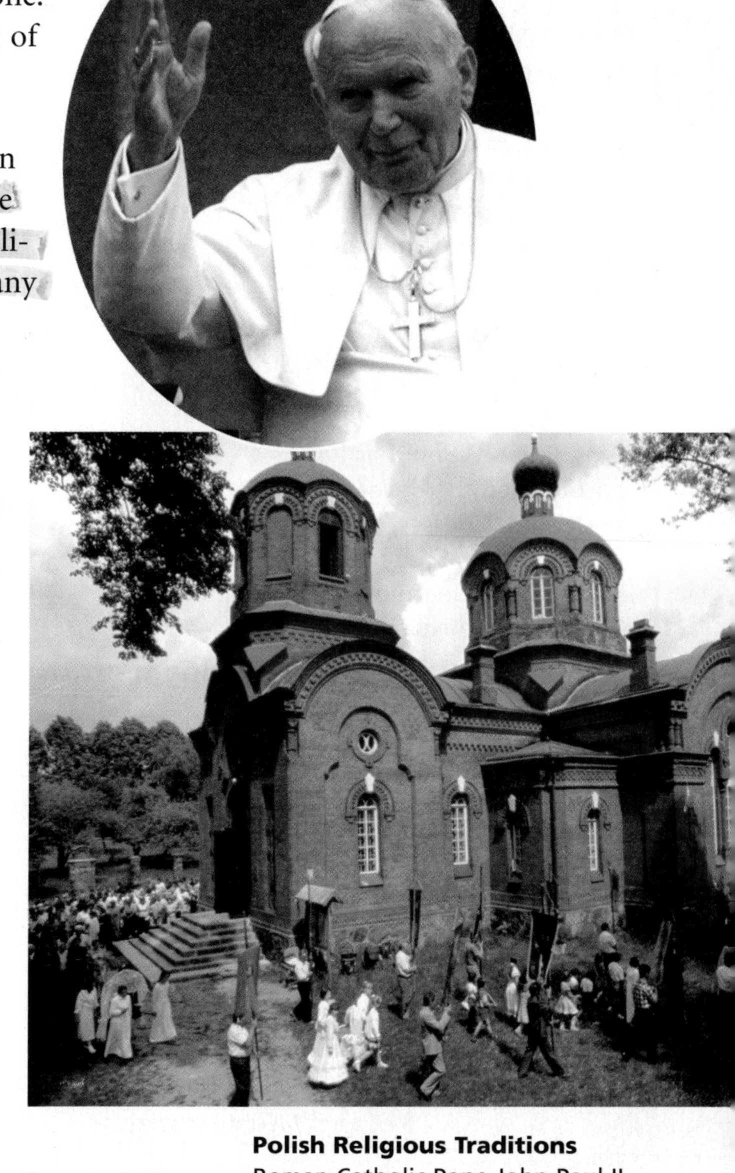

Polish Religious Traditions
Roman Catholic Pope John Paul II, at the top, waves to crowds in his hometown of Wadowice (vah duh VEET seh). Above, Eastern Orthodox worshipers take part in a festival in Bialowieza. **Apply Information** *What role does religion play in the lives of most Poles?*

Orthodoxy in Poland However, not all Poles are Catholic. A minority of Poles are Polish Orthodox. An example of Polish Orthodox religious life can be seen in northeastern Poland, near the forest of Bialowieza (byah woh VYEH zhah). Not far from the forest is the holy hill of Grabarka, with an Orthodox church at the top. In mid-August, visitors climb this hill to visit the church. Each visitor plants a cross in the earth. Among the trees on the hillside are hundreds of crosses. Some are as tall as trees, and others as tiny as flowers. You can see such Orthodox shrines, or holy places, all over Poland.

Judaism in Poland A small minority of Poles are Jewish. Today, Poland's Jewish population numbers only in the thousands. However, more than 3 million Jews used to live in Poland. During the Holocaust, about 85 percent of Polish Jews were killed by the German government.

COUNTRY PROFILE Focus on Government

Poland

A few powerful people had run Poland's communist government. In contrast, as a republic, Poland has a three-branch form of government similar to that of the United States. Poland's economy has also changed. Under communism, the government took control of most privately owned businesses and industries. Poland's republic has encouraged the development of small businesses, as well as foreign trade. Study the map and charts to learn more about Poland's government.

Employment by Sector and Ownership

1989

Sector	Privately Owned	Government Owned
Agriculture	79%	21%
Industry	15%	85%
Construction	27%	73%
Transport	6%	94%
Trade	8%	92%

2001

Sector	Privately Owned	Government Owned
Agriculture	99%	1%
Industry	77%	23%
Construction	94%	6%
Transport	48%	52%
Trade	98%	2%

SOURCES: Glowny Urzad Statystyczny (GUS), Rocznik Statystyczny

Poland's Government

Executive Branch	Legislative Branch	Judicial Branch
President Elected by the people for a five-year term	**National Assembly** Made up of two houses, the Sejm and the Senate	**Supreme Court** Judges appointed by the president for life
Prime Minister Appointed by the president, and confirmed by the Sejm	**Sejm** Includes 460 members, who are elected to four-year terms	**Constitutional Tribunal** Judges appointed by the Sejm for nine-year terms
Council of Ministers Appointed by the President, and approved by the Sejm	**Senate** Includes 100 members, who are elected to four-year terms	

SOURCE: CIA World Factbook Online, 2003

Map and Chart Skills

1. **Locate** Around which Polish cities are the manufacturing industries and trade centered?
2. **Compare** How did the percentage of people employed in privately owned industries change from 1989 to 2001?
3. **Apply Information** How does Poland's government compare to that of the United States?

Use Web Code **lde-7501** for **DK World Desk Reference Online.**

The Polish Language The language of the Poles has stood the test of time. In the past, some foreign rulers banned the use of Polish in schools and in the government. Although the communists did not ban Polish, they did force Polish schoolchildren to learn Russian, the official language of the Soviet Union.

Today, Polish is spoken by the majority of the population. The Polish language is a cultural tie that unites Poles, giving them pride in their unique heritage. As a Slavic language, it also links the nation to other Slavic nations in Eastern Europe.

Discovery CHANNEL SCHOOL Video
Learn about life for Jews in Poland.

✓ Reading Check **What religion do most Poles belong to?**

Great Economic Changes

Communism ended in Poland in 1989. After that, Poland underwent rapid change. The greatest of these changes occurred in Poland's economy.

Capitalism Poland has been very successful in making the change from communism to capitalism. **Capitalism** is an economic system in which businesses are privately owned. Most former communist countries made this change gradually. Poland changed almost overnight. On January 1, 1990, Polish leaders made a number of changes. They ended the government's control over prices. They also froze taxes and wages. A year later, Poland set up a stock market. Although these were dramatic changes, they helped Poland successfully make the difficult transition to capitalism.

Links to Government

Poland's Solidarity Movement In the 1980s, a radical group formed in Poland. This was a labor union—a group of people seeking workers' rights—called Solidarity. This group was radical because it was the first independent labor union to form in a Soviet-dominated country. Solidarity was formed to protest rising food prices. It organized strikes and demonstrations such as the 1987 march shown in the photo at the left. Solidarity's first leader was an electrician named Lech Walesa. Under Walesa, Solidarity began openly criticizing the communist government, and helped bring about its downfall. Lech Walesa served as president of Poland from 1990 to 1995. Solidarity is still a political party in Poland today.

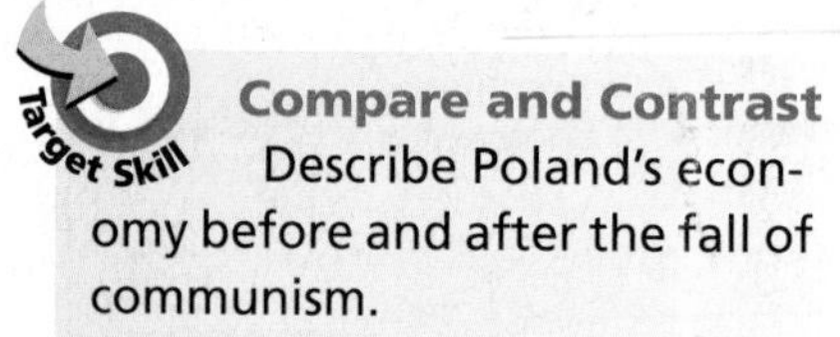

Compare and Contrast Describe Poland's economy before and after the fall of communism.

Foreign Investment With the collapse of the communist government, many foreigners began to invest their money in Poland. By 2001, Poland had brought in more foreign investment than had any other Central European country. Foreign investment has greatly strengthened the Polish economy.

Privatization A growth in the number of private businesses has also helped Poland's economy. With the end of communist rule, Poles were free to find new ways of making money. Small businesses soon blossomed in Poland's cities. At first, traders set up booths on the streets. They sold everything they could find, from American blue jeans to old Soviet army uniforms.

Slowly but surely, some traders earned enough money to take over stores that the government had once owned. Now, more than two million businesses are run by entrepreneurs (ahn truh pruh NOORZ). An **entrepreneur** is a person who develops original ideas in order to start new businesses.

Polish industries have also been slowly privatized over the last few years. Poland's most important private industries are food, energy, and mining.

Consumer Goods Poles now have access to more consumer goods than they did under communism. Only half of the homes in Poland had televisions in 1989. Now, almost every home has one. On the streets of cities such as Warsaw, Poland's capital, many people use mobile phones and wear the latest fashions. For these people, the new way of life is good.

Chart Skills

Life expectancy and per capita GDP, or the economic output per person, are two factors used to measure a country's standard of living. **Compare** Which Eastern European country has the highest standard of living? **Generalize** Germany is shown as an example of a Western European country. How do standards of living in Western Europe compare to those in Eastern Europe?

Standard of Living Comparison for Selected European Countries

Country	Per Capita GDP	Life Expectancy	
		Male	Female
Bulgaria	$6,600	68.3	75.6
Czech Republic	$15,300	71.7	78.9
Hungary	$13,300	67.8	76.8
Poland	$9,500	69.8	78.3
Slovenia	$18,000	71.7	79.6
Germany (Western Europe)	$26,600	75.5	81.6

Changes in Farm Life Unlike many businesses, most farms under communism had remained privately owned. Still, the change to a capitalist economy was harder on farmers than on most other Poles. Under communism, the government always bought produce and meat from farmers, providing them with a reliable income. The government also made sure that prices for farm produce stayed high. After communism, prices dropped, and sales were no longer guaranteed. Farmers learned to be innovative, or creative, to survive.

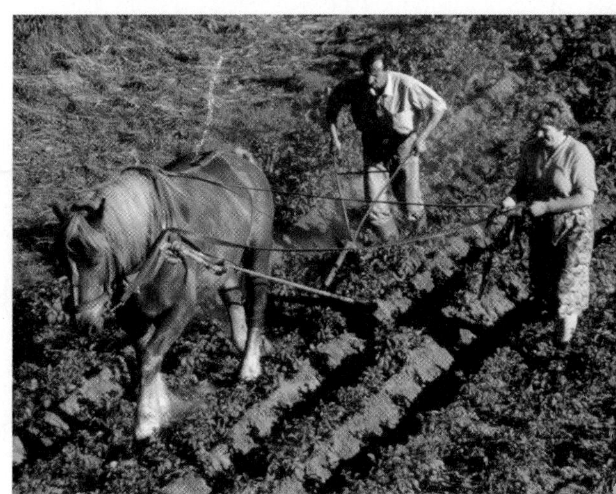

A Polish husband and wife use a draft horse to plow a field in Bialowieza.

Some farmers now take on part-time jobs to make extra money. Others invite paying guests from the city to stay on their farms for rural vacations. Some farmers produce organic vegetables, fruits, and meats, which they can sell at higher prices than other farmers' products.

Farmers who cannot find other sources of income often struggle to make a living. Most farms in Poland are small. Many farmers only own about 5 to 12 acres (2 to 5 hectares) of land, which may not produce enough money to live on.

✓ Reading Check **Why did farmers have a steady income under communism?**

Future Challenges

Poland has made the change from communism to capitalism with speed and success. It has the strength to compete with other nations as part of the EU. However, the Polish people still face many challenges.

Kraków—A Cultural Treasure
Kraków is Poland's third-largest city. It is also a cultural center with historic architecture, an excellent university, and a marketplace that has existed since the 1200s. **Infer** *How have cities such as Kraków changed since the fall of communism in Poland?*

Bringing Back the Forests
People on a tree farm plant young trees. Once the trees have grown larger, they will be transplanted to regions that were deforested during the communist years. **Conclude** *How can renewed forests strengthen Poland's economy?*

Pollution During the communist era, coal-mining and steel production in southern Poland caused terrible pollution. This pollution destroyed much of the forests in southern Poland and increased rates of diseases, such as cancer.

After the communists left power, Polish leaders began to repair some of the damage to the environment. Old polluting factories were closed. Other factories invested in equipment to reduce pollution. The use of unleaded gasoline reduced the pollutants coming from cars. By 2003, Poland had reduced many forms of pollution by 50 percent.

Unemployment Poland faces other challenges, such as a high unemployment rate. Under communism, people were guaranteed jobs. In the current capitalist system, there is no such guarantee. Many Poles emigrate to other places in Europe to find work. In fact, about one out three Poles today lives outside of Poland. Other Poles hope that membership in the EU will bring more long-term investment into Poland, creating more jobs.

Poles will have to find ways to deal with such challenges, but they are ready to do whatever is needed. For the first time in many years, their future is in their own hands.

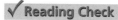

✓ Reading Check **How did Poland reduce its air pollution?**

Section 1 Assessment

Key Terms
Review the key terms at the beginning of this section. Use each term in a sentence that explains its meaning.

Target Reading Skill
How is farm life in Poland the same as and different from the way it was under communism?

Comprehension and Critical Thinking
1. (a) **Identify** What parts of Polish life did not change under communism?
(b) **Analyze Information** Why did the communist government force Polish schoolchildren to learn Russian?
2. (a) **Explain** What measures did Poland's leaders take to convert the economy to capitalism?
(b) **Identify Point of View** How might many Polish farmers view the transition to capitalism?
3. (a) **Recall** What major challenges does Poland still face?
(b) **Predict** What further changes might membership in the EU bring to Poland?

Writing Activity
Suppose you are a journalist in Poland today. You interview two Poles—a young entrepreneur in Warsaw and an elderly farmer in the countryside. Write a dialogue that gives their views on how capitalism has changed the country.

Writing Tip Be sure to use appropriate language for each of the two people. Also, consider what is important to people of different ages before you begin writing.

Section 2

Five Balkan Nations

A Region Tries to Rebuild

Prepare to Read

Objectives

In this section you will

1. Identify the groups of people who live in the Balkans.
2. Understand how Yugoslavia was created and how it broke up.
3. Identify issues that these Balkan nations face in the future.

Taking Notes

As you read this section, look for important events in the history of these five Balkan nations. Copy the timeline below and record the events in the proper places on it.

1918

Target Reading Skill

Make Comparisons
Comparing two or more situations enables you to see how they are alike. This section is about five countries with similar situations. As you read this section, compare the five nations by considering their histories, economies, cultures, and challenges.

Key Terms

- **civil war** (sih vul wawr) *n.* a war between groups of people within the same nation
- **secede** (sih SEED) *v.* to leave a group, especially a political group or a nation
- **embargo** (em BAHR goh) *n.* a ban on trade
- **economic sanctions** (ek uh NAHM ik SANGK shunz) *n.* actions to limit trade with nations that have violated international laws

In January 1984, the people of the city of Sarajevo (sa ruh YAY voh) were filled with anticipation. They had proudly won the right to host the 1984 Winter Olympics. To prepare for the games, they had built new hotels and restaurants. They had carved ski-racing trails into the mountains and built ski lifts. New bobsled runs and an elegant skating complex awaited the athletes. A shiny new Olympic Village waited to welcome athletes and visitors to the Games.

Ten years later, most of these facilities lay in ruins. So did much of Sarajevo. How could this have happened? The answer is **civil war,** or a war between groups of people within the same nation. Civil war broke up the nation of Yugoslavia and shattered the grand city.

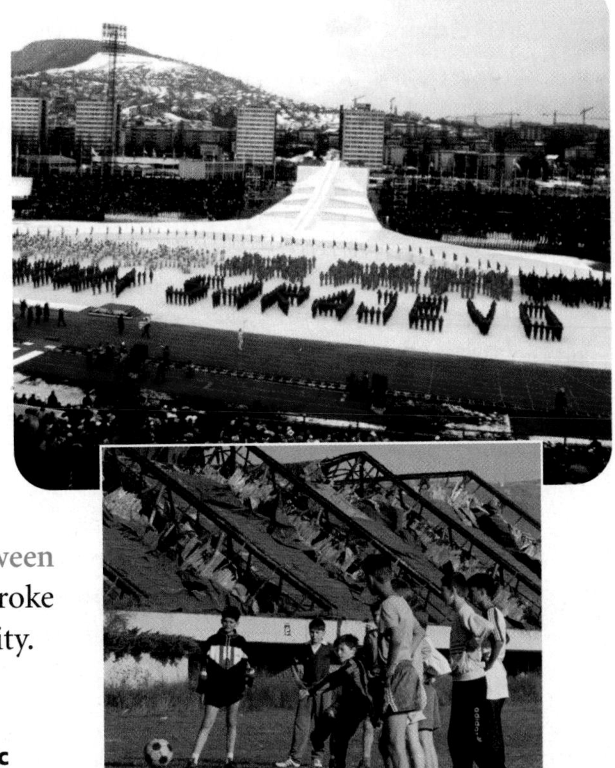

Scenes of Sarajevo's Olympic Village before and after the war

COUNTRY PROFILE Focus on Culture

Five Balkan Nations

Ethnic diversity is one of the most enduring characteristics of the Balkans. In ancient times, the region was occupied by different tribes who often fought among themselves. The arrival of Christianity and then Islam brought more diversity and more ethnic and political differences to the region. Political unrest still continues in modern times. The Balkans occupy an area slightly smaller than the state of Texas. As you study the map and the table, think about what challenges great diversity might present to a small region.

Peoples of Five Balkan Nations

Ethnic Group	Population (millions)	Main Homeland(s)	Language	Main Religion
Croats	5.0	Croatia, Bosnia & Herz.	Serbo-Croat	Roman Catholicism
Serbs	8.4	Serbia & Mont., Bosnia & Herz.	Serbo-Croat	Eastern Orthodox
Slovenes	1.7	Slovenia	Slovenian	Roman Catholicism
Bosniaks	2.0	Bosnia & Herz.	Serbo-Croat	Islam
Montenegrins	0.5	Serbia & Mont.	Serbo-Croat	Eastern Orthodox
Macedonians	1.3	Macedonia	Macedonian	Eastern Orthodox
Albanians	2.3	Serbia & Mont., Macedonia	Albanian	Islam
Hungarians	0.4	Serbia & Mont.	Hungarian	Roman Catholicism
Turks	0.3	Serbia & Mont., Macedonia	Turkish	Islam
Romany	0.2	Serbia & Mont., Macedonia	Romany	Various beliefs

SOURCES: Ethnologue; CIA World Factbook Online, 2003

Map and Chart Skills

1. **Identify** Which ethnic groups live in Serbia and Montenegro?
2. **Analyze Information** Which religion do most people in the region practice? What language is spoken by the most people?
3. **Apply Information** How do the data help explain today's political unrest in the region?

Use Web Code **lde-7502** for **DK World Desk Reference Online.**

Land of Many Peoples

Faces of the Balkans
Both of the photos above show children of various ethnic groups. The upper photo is from Macedonia, while the lower photo is from Croatia. **Apply Information** *Though these children all live on the Balkan Peninsula, what cultural differences might there be among them?*

The Balkan Peninsula—also known as the Balkans—is located in southeastern Europe. The Balkans include Serbia and Montenegro, Bosnia and Herzegovina, Macedonia, Croatia, Slovenia, Albania, Romania, Bulgaria, Greece, and European Turkey. This section discusses the first five of these countries, which used to make up the nation of Yugoslavia.

The largest ethnic groups in these five Balkan countries are the Serbs and the Croats (KROH atz), who speak Serbo-Croatian, a Slavic language. Montenegrins (mahnt uh NEE grinz) and Bosniaks, two smaller groups, also speak Serbo-Croatian. Slovenes and Macedonians (mas uh DOH nee unz) speak related Slavic languages.

Although these groups speak related languages, there are important cultural differences among them. For example, both Serbs and Croats speak Serbo-Croatian, but they use different alphabets to write the language.

Religion may be the most important difference, since it separates groups that speak the same language. Most Serbs, Montenegrins, and Macedonians belong to the Eastern Orthodox Church. Croats and Slovenes are mainly Roman Catholic. Bosniaks are mainly Muslim.

In these five countries, there are also groups that speak non-Slavic languages. These groups include Albanians, Hungarians, Roma, and Turks. The Albanians and Turks are mainly Muslim. The Hungarians are mostly Roman Catholic. The Roma have their own unique customs and religious beliefs.

✓ Reading Check **What are the largest ethnic groups in the Balkans?**

The Creation of Yugoslavia

For hundreds of years, the Ottoman Empire, based in Turkey, ruled much of the Balkans. Beginning in the late 1800s, several kingdoms within the empire attempted to form their own states. Sometimes they were supported in their efforts by Russia or western nations, who hoped to gain influence in the region. But none of these groups was successful until World War I ended, and the Ottoman Empire broke up.

A New Nation Is Formed Yugoslavia was the first new Balkan nation to emerge from the old Ottoman Empire. Formed in 1918, the new nation joined together many ethnic and religious groups. From the beginning, these groups disagreed about how the government should be structured.

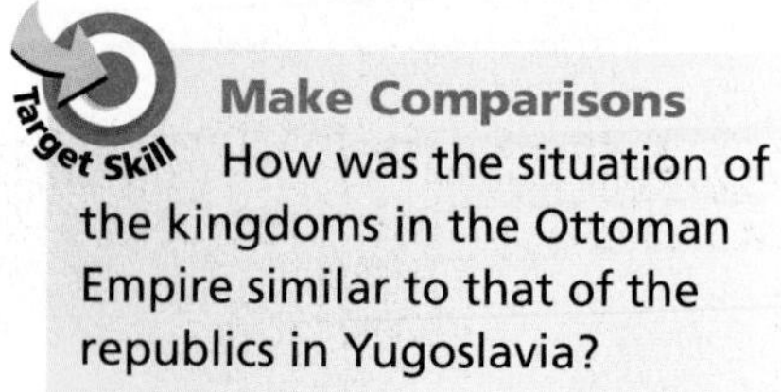

Make Comparisons How was the situation of the kingdoms in the Ottoman Empire similar to that of the republics in Yugoslavia?

Though one nation, Yugoslavia was divided into smaller units called republics. These republics included Serbia, Montenegro, Croatia, Bosnia and Herzegovina, Slovenia, and Macedonia. In each of those republics, one ethnic group held the majority. Yugoslavia's largest republic was Serbia, peopled by Serbs. This republic held the most power, and ran the national government. Other republics, in which Serbs were not the majority, did not always support the government. Resentment against the government grew, along with ethnic conflict among peoples.

The Communist Era During World War II, Germany and Italy occupied Yugoslavia. Josip Broz Tito led the Yugoslav fight against Germany. When the war ended in 1945, Tito became head of the government and changed Yugoslavia into a communist state. Yugoslavia became a firm ally and trade partner of the Soviet Union.

At first, Tito modeled his government after that of the Soviet Union. After a few years, however, he wanted to develop his own government and economic policies. For example, he wanted to maintain trading relations with Western countries in order to strengthen Yugoslavia's economy. This put him in conflict with the Soviet dictator, Joseph Stalin, who broke many ties with Yugoslavia in 1948.

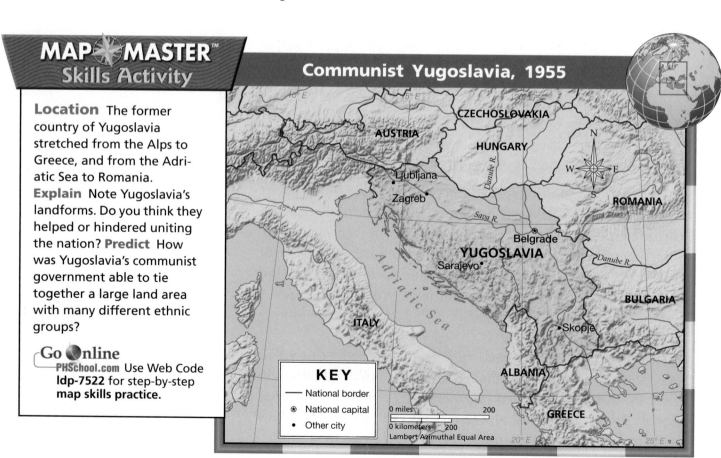

MAP MASTER™ Skills Activity

Location The former country of Yugoslavia stretched from the Alps to Greece, and from the Adriatic Sea to Romania. **Explain** Note Yugoslavia's landforms. Do you think they helped or hindered uniting the nation? **Predict** How was Yugoslavia's communist government able to tie together a large land area with many different ethnic groups?

Go Online PHSchool.com Use Web Code **ldp-7522** for step-by-step **map skills practice.**

Communist Yugoslavia, 1955

CZECHOSLOVAKIA
AUSTRIA
HUNGARY
ROMANIA
YUGOSLAVIA
BULGARIA
ITALY
ALBANIA
GREECE
Ljubljana
Zagreb
Belgrade
Sarajevo
Skopje
Danube R.
Sava R.
Adriatic Sea

KEY
National border
National capital
Other city

0 miles 200
0 kilometers 200
Lambert Azimuthal Equal Area

Tito continued to rule Yugoslavia according to communist principles, but he also had good relations with anti-communist nations. For several years, the economy under Tito grew strongly. Tito's strong government also unified Yugoslavia by reducing tensions among ethnic groups. During Tito's time, people began to identify themselves as citizens of a united Yugoslavia.

Yugoslavia Begins to Splinter After Tito's death in 1980, politicians from various ethnic groups struggled for power. They encouraged their followers to once again identify strongly with their own ethnic group. People began to think of themselves less and less as citizens of Yugoslavia.

✓ Reading Check **What event caused Yugoslavia to splinter?**

Yugoslavia Breaks Up

Yugoslavia's problems continued to worsen through the 1980s. In 1989, communism began to crumble in Eastern Europe. Yugoslavia had an unstable government and economy. Many people blamed the Serbs, who still held most of the power in the government. Some republics wanted to govern themselves. In some cases, political change happened almost peacefully. In others, bitter civil wars erupted.

Slovenia and Croatia In 1990, Slovenes and Croats began to pull away from Yugoslavia. That year, the leaders of Slovenia issued a new constitution in which they said they had the right to **secede** from, or leave, the state of Yugoslavia. Meanwhile, the Yugoslav army threatened to take territory from the republic of Croatia. This alarmed Slovenes and Croats, but also strengthened their desire for independence.

A Croat was elected the new president of Yugoslavia in May 1991. However, Serbia refused to accept the new president. This was the last straw for Slovenia and Croatia. Both republics declared their independence. Serb forces briefly tried to prevent Slovenia from seceding. But soon Serbia recognized the country's independence.

In contrast, war erupted in Croatia. The Serbs attacked Croatian cities. They used terror to drive out the people. This led the United Nations to become involved. In an effort to restore peace, the UN sent peacekeepers to the area and imposed an embargo against Serbia and Montenegro. An **embargo** is a ban on trade. But peace could not be reached until conflict in neighboring Bosnia and Herzegovina was settled.

Links Across

The World

The UN and NATO When World War II ended, many people feared the outbreak of another world war. To help prevent this, several international groups were formed. The United Nations, whose flag is shown below, is an international group founded in 1945. Its member countries work together to bring about peace and cooperation. The UN has 191 member countries, and its headquarters is located in New York City. NATO, or the North Atlantic Treaty Organization, is a group of nations formed in 1949. Its purpose is to provide its members with defense in case of attack.

Discovery
CHANNEL
SCHOOL
Video
Learn about the rebuilding of Kosovo.

Bosnia and Herzegovina Tensions among different ethnic groups led to a long and bitter war in Bosnia and Herzegovina, beginning in 1992. People on all sides were mistreated by their enemies. Many people were killed. Some were forced to move away from where they had lived peacefully for years, simply because they were Serbs or Croats.

As you have read, during the war much of Sarajevo, the capital of Bosnia and Herzegovina, was destroyed. Homes and schools were bombed. People were shot as they tried to go about their daily business. Serb armies cut Sarajevo off from the rest of the world. People ran out of food and other necessities.

In 1993, the United Nations began sending troops and supplies to the city. In 1995, NATO forces joined the fighting. Finally, peace talks took place. In 1995, the United States played a key role in getting the Serbs, Croats, and Bosniaks to sign a peace treaty in Dayton, Ohio.

Serbia: Crisis in Kosovo Conflict also broke out in the Serbian province of Kosovo. The population of Kosovo is about 90 percent Albanian. In the old Yugoslavia, Albanians in Kosovo were autonomous, or able to make many decisions for themselves. That situation changed dramatically.

In 1989, Yugoslavian President Slobodan Milosevic (SLOH boh dawn mih LOH suh vich) wanted to increase Serbia's power. He took away Kosovo's freedoms. Tensions between Serbs and Albanians in Kosovo increased, and many Albanians began rebelling against Serbian rule. In the late 1990s, Milosevic tried to end the uprising. Serb forces attacked Albanians in Kosovo. They destroyed homes and villages, forcing thousands of Albanians to become refugees.

These attacks prompted western nations to ask NATO to intervene. A peace agreement was signed in June 1999. Serb forces withdrew from Kosovo, and NATO troops took their place to keep the peace. Many of the Albanian refugees returned to Kosovo.

Peace Rally in Sarajevo
Before war broke out in 1992, people in Bosnia and Herzegovina held a peace rally. Some of them displayed a picture of Tito. **Infer** *Why might people have used images of Tito to support their drive for peace?*

Macedonia Macedonia declared its independence from Yugoslavia in 1991. From the beginning, ethnic conflict was a problem in the new country. Tensions existed between ethnic Macedonians and ethnic Albanians, who make up a large minority of the population.

Albanians began demanding a number of reforms. The call for reform erupted into violence in 2001. Clashes between ethnic Albanians and the Macedonian military lasted seven months. This prompted fears of another war in the Balkans. A peace agreement was reached after the involvement of NATO.

Soon, Macedonia adopted a new constitution. It made Albanian an official language of the nation. It increased Albanians' access to government jobs. Most important, it removed language in the constitution that had made Albanians second-class citizens.

Ethnic Albanians in Macedonia demand more rights in 2004.

✓ Reading Check **To which ethnic group do most of the people of Kosovo belong?**

Yugoslavia Today

SLOVAKIA
AUSTRIA
HUNGARY
SLOVENIA
Ljubljana
Zagreb
CROATIA
ROMANIA
BOSNIA & HERZEGOVINA
Belgrade
Sarajevo
SERBIA & MONTENEGRO
BULGARIA
Skopje
MACEDONIA
ALBANIA
ITALY
GREECE
Adriatic Sea
Danube R.
Sava R.
15° E
20° E
25° E
45° N
40° N
N
S
E
W

KEY
— National border
⊛ National capital

0 miles 200
0 kilometers 200
Lambert Azimuthal Equal Area

MAP MASTER™ Skills Activity

Regions Five separate countries occupy the lands that once made up Yugoslavia.
Identify Which of these countries is the largest today?
Apply Information What does the size of this country tell you about its importance when it was still part of Yugoslavia?

Go Online
PHSchool.com Use Web Code **ldp-7532** for step-by-step **map skills practice.**

Business has picked up at markets like this one in Slovenia.

The Region's Future

Although peace treaties were signed and several republics in the region gained independence, trouble did not end. Tensions between different ethnic groups still existed. The United States and Europe held Slobodan Milosevic responsible for the violence that had occurred in the region. To show their disapproval, they placed economic sanctions on Yugoslavia. **Economic sanctions** are actions to limit trade with nations that have violated international laws.

In 2000, Yugoslavia held new presidential elections. Milosevic was defeated, and then arrested by the new government. He was put on trial for war crimes by the court of the United Nations. The United States and European nations promised to lift the sanctions against Yugoslavia. In 2003, the two remaining republics of Yugoslavia—Serbia and Montenegro—decided they would no longer call themselves Yugoslavia. Today, the country is known as Serbia and Montenegro. However, many people in Montenegro want to be independent of Serbia.

What lies ahead for these nations in the Balkans? The destruction that occurred in the 1990s has left the region's population of more than 50 million with deep economic problems. These countries hope to move toward peace and stability, but they will have to overcome a history of ethnic conflict and war.

✓ Reading Check **What problems face people of the Balkans today?**

Section 2 Assessment

Key Terms
Review the key terms at the beginning of this section. Use each term in a sentence that explains its meaning.

Target Reading Skill
Compare the histories of these five nations.

Comprehension and Critical Thinking
1. (a) List Which five Balkan nations used to make up the country of Yugoslavia?
(b) Contrast What differences exist among the people of these five nations today?
2. (a) Note Which foreign power ruled the Balkans for hundreds of years?
(b) Sequence When was Yugoslavia created? When did its government turn to communism?
(c) Synthesize Information How did the collapse of communism affect Yugoslavia?
3. (a) Identify Who did the United States and European nations hold responsible for the violence in the Balkans?
(b) Identify Effects How did these nations show their disapproval of Yugoslavia's president?

Writing Activity
Choose one of the Balkan nations discussed in this section. What do you think is the most important challenge facing this nation in the future? Write a paragraph that explains why.

For: An activity on the Dayton peace accord
Visit: PHSchool.com
Web Code: ldd-7502

Section 3 Ukraine
Independence and Beyond

Prepare to Read

Objectives
In this section you will
1. Understand how Ukraine's history has been shaped by foreign rule.
2. Explain the major issues that Ukrainians have faced since independence.
3. Describe life in Ukraine today.

Taking Notes
As you read this section, look for ways in which the natural resources of Ukraine have shaped its history. Copy the flowchart below and record your findings in it.

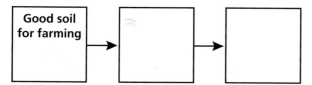

Target Reading Skill
Compare and Contrast One way to understand a nation's history is to compare and contrast different times in its history. When you compare, you look at similarities between things. When you contrast, you look at differences. As you read this section, compare and contrast life in Ukraine before and after independence.

Key Terms
- **chernozem** (CHEHR nuh zem) *n.* rich, black soil
- **collective** (kuh LEK tiv) *n.* a huge government-controlled farm

How many people, linked hand-to-hand, would it take to cover 300 miles (483 kilometers)? The people of Ukraine can tell you, because they did it in 1990. It took about 500,000 Ukrainians to make a human chain that long. It stretched from Kiev, Ukraine's capital, to the city of L'viv (luh VEEF). The chain was a symbol of protest against the Soviet Union's control of Ukraine. It also showed that Ukrainians know how to work together to solve their problems. Today, the people of Ukraine are enjoying their independence and are working hard for a better future.

Ukrainians form a human chain.

COUNTRY PROFILE

Focus on Economics

Ukraine

When Ukraine became independent in 1991, it faced economic hardship. The Soviet Union had controlled Ukraine's economy. Ukraine's new leaders had no experience with capitalism, and the country had no free markets for its products. After a slow, painful transition, Ukraine's economy began to strengthen. Still, Ukraine's economy relies heavily on Russia as a trade partner. Study the map and graphs to learn more about Ukraine's economy today.

Structure of the Economy, 2002

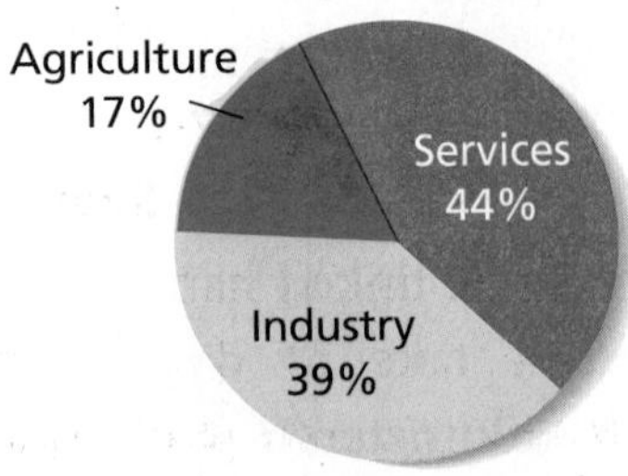

SOURCE: The World Bank Group

Leading Export Partners

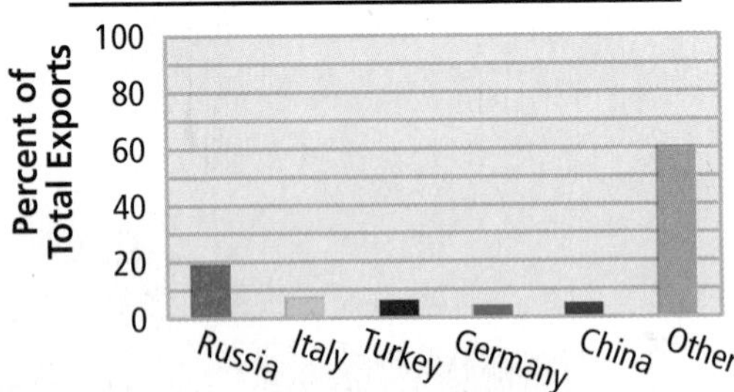

SOURCE: CIA World Factbook Online, 2003

Leading Import Partners

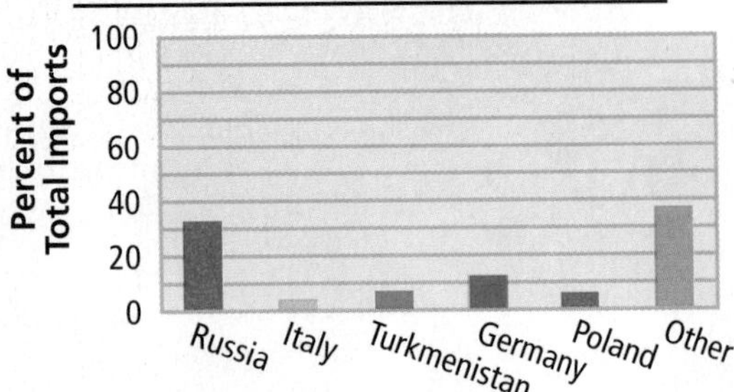

SOURCE: CIA World Factbook Online, 2003

Map and Chart Skills

1. **Locate** In what regions of Ukraine is land used for forestry?
2. **Synthesize Information** In 2002, what percentage of Ukraine's economy did agriculture make up? How much of Ukraine's land is used for this purpose?
3. **Make Inferences** Why do you think Ukraine exchanges more exports and imports with Russia than with its other trade partners?

Use Web Code **lde-7503** for **DK World Desk Reference Online.**

A History of Occupation

For hundreds of years, Ukraine was ruled by its more powerful neighbors. You can see how this happened if you look at Ukraine's location on the map on page 303. This huge land lies between Russia and the other nations of Europe. In fact, the name Ukraine means "borderland." Look at the political map of Eastern Europe and Russia at the beginning of this chapter. Notice that to the west of Ukraine are Poland, Slovakia, and Hungary. To the east of Ukraine is Russia. The map makes it easy to see why Ukraine has been open to invasion by its neighbors.

Location has been only part of the problem. The other problem has been Ukraine's vast natural resources. These resources have attracted invaders. At one time or another, Poland, Czechoslovakia, and Romania have occupied areas of Ukraine. During World War II, the German army invaded Ukraine to gain access to its natural resources. Russia has been the most difficult neighbor of all, however. Russia, and later the Soviet Union, ruled Ukraine between the late 1700s and 1991.

Supplying the Soviets Under Soviet rule, Ukrainian industries grew. In time, factories in Ukraine were making nearly 20 percent of the Soviet Union's goods. Ukraine produced much of the equipment for the Soviet armed forces. And Ukrainian mines supplied much of the iron ore, coal, and other minerals for Soviet industries.

The Soviets used other Ukrainian resources as well. Ships used Ukraine's ports on the Black Sea to bring goods into and out of the Soviet Union. Several of Ukraine's rivers reach like highways into other countries. The Soviets made use of these rivers to ship goods.

Because Ukraine was one of Europe's largest grain-producing regions, it became known as the breadbasket of Europe. Why is Ukraine's farmland so productive? More than half of the country is covered by a rich, black soil called **chernozem** (CHEHR nuh zem). When the Soviet Union took control of Ukraine in 1922, Ukrainian farmers were forced to supply the rest of the Soviet Union with food. By the end of the 1980s, they were producing one fourth of the grain and meat consumed by the Soviet Union.

1854 An illustration shows the port of Odessa when Ukraine was part of the Russian Empire.

1941 Ukrainian villagers report to soldiers of the German forces that occupied Ukraine during World War II.

1947 Farmers work on a collective farm during the Soviet rule of Ukraine.

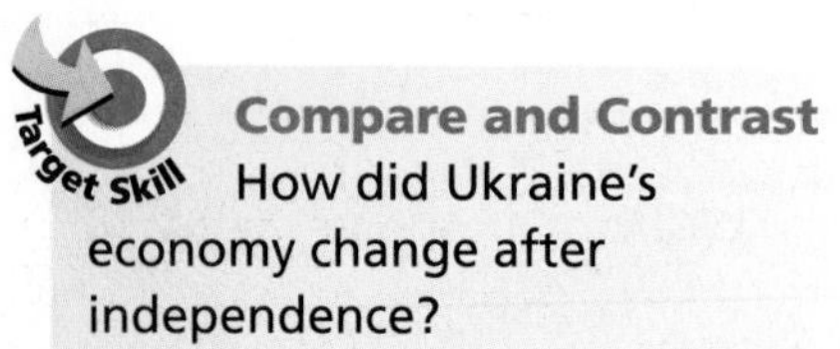

Compare and Contrast How did Ukraine's economy change after independence?

Collectives Bring Starvation To produce all of this grain and meat, Soviet rulers took land away from farmers and created huge government-controlled farms called **collectives.** Most farmers were forced to become workers on these collectives. Other farmers were sent to cities to work in the new factories. All the crops from the collectives went to the government. The people who worked the land were allowed to keep very little of the food they grew. As a result, millions of Ukrainians died of hunger in the 1930s. Over the years, however, life improved on the farms.

√ Reading Check **For what purpose did the Soviets use Ukraine's ports and rivers?**

Odessa—A Thriving Seaport
In the 1800s and 1900s, huge quantities of grain were shipped from Odessa to Russia and later the Soviet Union. Today, the city is a major port and a center of Ukrainian industry. **Compare and Contrast** *Compare this photo with the illustration of Odessa on page 329. What similarities and differences do you see?*

Independence Brings Challenges

In 1991, Ukraine won its independence from the Soviet Union. After centuries of foreign rule, the new country now had to decide many important issues for itself.

Building an Independent Economy One of the first issues Ukrainians had to decide was how to build up their economy. Like people in other former Soviet republics, Ukrainians had to learn how to start new businesses. They also needed to learn how to make consumer goods and keep prices under control. Finally, they had to improve their agricultural production by breaking up the inefficient collective farm system put in place by the Soviets.

Choosing a Language Ukrainians also had to restore their culture. Under Soviet rule, the official language of Ukraine was Russian. Books and newspapers were published only in Russian, and schools used Russian textbooks. As a result, many Ukrainians speak only Russian, especially in the cities and in the eastern part of the nation. Russian is also the language of ethnic Russians, who make up about one fifth of the population. The Ukrainian language is widely spoken only in rural areas and in the western part of the nation.

With independence, Ukrainian was made the official language. Many of the people of Ukraine believe that speaking Ukrainian could tie the country together and free Ukraine from its Soviet past. Elementary and secondary schools have begun using Ukrainian, though Russian is also still used in high schools. Most Ukrainians are pleased about the change. One teacher said, "Language is the anchor of our independence."

A Ukrainian Classroom
Elementary school students sit in class on their first day of school.
Analyze Images *Besides language, what other cultural traditions are important to Ukrainians?*

Discovery
CHANNEL
SCHOOL
Video
Learn about the
after-effects of Chernobyl.

Recovering From Chernobyl Ukraine is still recovering from a terrible event that occurred during the Soviet period. It became one of the most difficult issues Ukraine has had to face since it gained independence.

Under Soviet rule, Ukrainians built five nuclear power plants. These supply about one third of the country's electricity. The Chernobyl (chehr NOH bul) nuclear plant is located 65 miles (105 kilometers) from the city of Kiev. In 1986, an explosion caused by carelessness rocked the Chernobyl plant. Radioactive materials filled the air. Some people died within days or weeks. Others developed serious health problems that killed them slowly or left them suffering. More than 100,000 people had to be moved out of the area. It was no longer safe to live there. In later years, traces of the dangerous materials released at Chernobyl were found all over the world.

Even today, much of Ukraine's soil and water are still poisoned. More than 32,000 square miles of farmland are contaminated. Some towns and farms remain abandoned. With the help of other nations, the Ukrainians are cleaning up the dangerous materials around Chernobyl, but it may take as long as a hundred years to repair the damage.

✓ Reading Check **What are the far-reaching effects of Chernobyl?**

Links to Science

Creating Nuclear Power
Nuclear power is produced from a metal called uranium. The central part of an atom is called the nucleus. To create energy, the uranium nucleus is split in a process called nuclear fission. This splitting releases heat, which turns water into steam. The steam turns large machines called generators, which produce electricity. When nuclear power is made, radioactive waste is produced. The waste must be carefully stored, because radioactive materials are dangerous to people. If the process of making nuclear power is not tightly controlled, too much heat can destroy the reactor and the entire building that contains it, as happened at Chernobyl. Then radioactive materials can escape into the air. The photo at the right shows a town near Chernobyl after the explosion.

Life in Ukraine

Independence has brought changes to life in Ukraine. For example, the Kreshchatik (kresh CHAH tik), the main street in Kiev, is often jammed with people. Along this street are many parks, stores, and restaurants. People sell ice cream and pyrohy (pih ROH hee), dumplings filled with vegetables, cheese, or fruit. Newsstands are filled with magazines and newspapers, many of which have been published only since independence. At local markets, farmers sell cheese or produce from their own farms.

Other Ukrainian cities are also alive with the new spirit of freedom. East of Kiev is the city of Kharkiv. Located near huge reserves of iron ore and coal, it is the busiest industrial center in the nation. But Kharkiv is not all work. It is also a vibrant cultural area, where people can attend plays or concerts.

Ukraine is in the early stages of an exciting time in its history. The people have always wanted freedom, and now they have it in their grasp. They know that independence is not easy. But with the land's great resources and the people's ability to work together, the Ukrainians have the ability to make independence succeed.

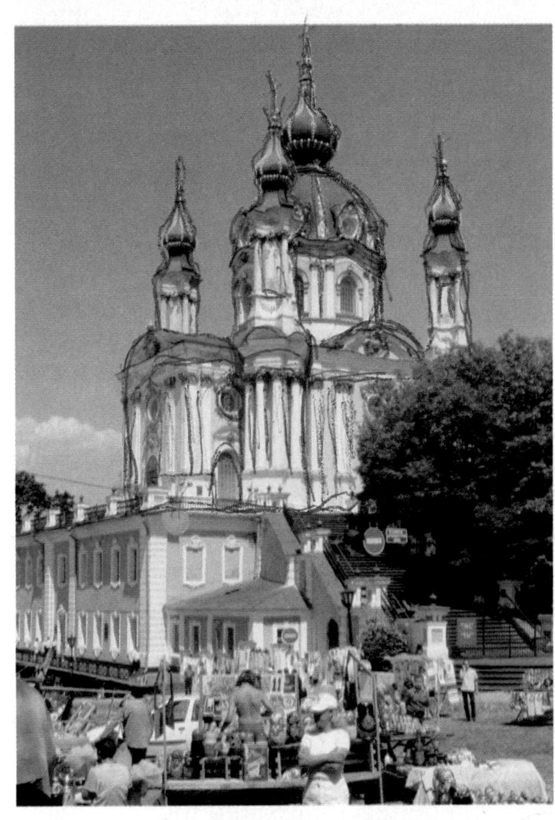

Vendors sell souvenirs in front of a Roman Catholic church in Kiev.

✓ Reading Check **What is Ukraine's busiest industrial center?**

Section 3 Assessment

Key Terms

Review the key terms at the beginning of this section. Use each term in a sentence that explains its meaning.

Target Reading Skill

Describe education in Ukraine before and after independence.

Comprehension and Critical Thinking

1. (a) Identify Who controlled Ukraine until 1991?
(b) Find the Main Idea What uses were made of Ukraine's resources?

(c) Predict Now that Ukraine is not supplying another country with its resources, how might that affect its economy?

2. (a) Explain What issues faced Ukraine after independence?
(b) Identify Point of View How might ethnic Russians have reacted when Ukrainian was made the official language?

3. (a) Describe What changes has independence brought to Ukrainian life?
(b) Contrast How was life different in Ukraine before independence?

Writing Activity

Suppose you are a newspaper writer in Ukraine in 1991. Write a short article that describes the views of the people as they start life in an independent country. Be sure to include the views of both Ukrainians and ethnic Russians.

For: An activity on Chernobyl
Visit: PHSchool.com
Web Code: ldd-7503

Skills for Life

Identifying Frame of Reference

Before Poland joined the European Union, Poles strongly debated the subject. According to 48-year-old Polish farmer Lech Lebedzki, ". . . both of my hands were raised, ready to vote for [it]. . . ." But after hearing that as part of the EU Polish farmers would not receive as much support from the government, he changed his mind. "It's a stab in the back. . . . I will vote against it."

Lebedzki's job as a farmer gave him a certain frame of reference, which influenced his view on EU membership. When you identify a person's frame of reference, you can better understand the influences that shaped his or her position. Writers, for example, may leave information out of an article on purpose to give a stronger argument for their point of view. They may only present one side of the story. Understanding a writer's frame of reference can help you decide whether the writer is a reliable source.

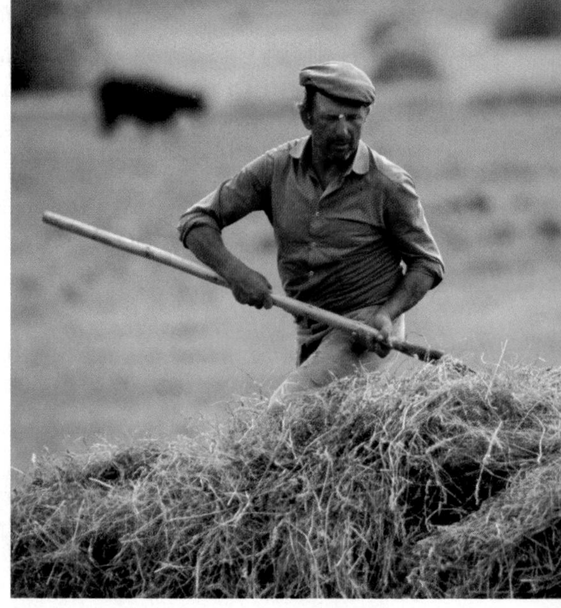

A Polish farmer

Learn the Skill

To identify frame of reference, use the following steps:

1. **Determine the issue.** Read through the passage quickly. What is the main idea?

2. **Look carefully at who the writer is.** What qualifications, if any, does he or she bring to the topic of the passage?

3. **Identify the position taken by the writer.** Look for direct statements of the writer's position. Look also for any emotional language that may give clues to the writer's views. What is the tone, or overall feeling, of the passage? Think about why the writer feels he or she has to write.

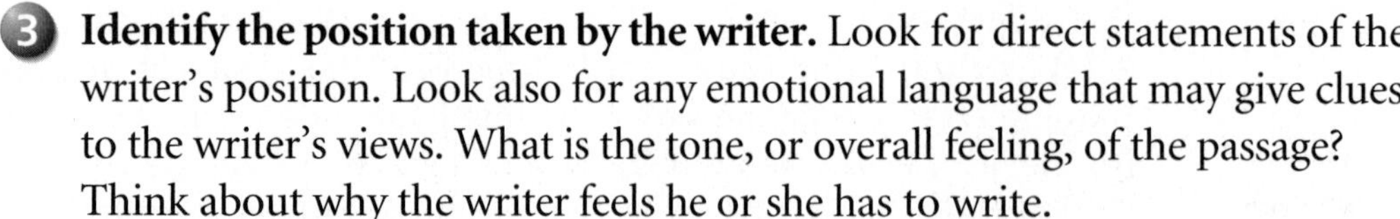

4. **Note how the writer's frame of reference may have influenced his or her position on the issue.** Look for connections between who the writer is, the language he or she uses, and the writer's stated position.

5. **Draw a conclusion identifying the writer's position and his or her frame of reference.** Decide whether the writer is giving a reliable picture of the situation.

Practice the Skill

Use the steps in Learn the Skill to identify frame of reference in the passage at the right.

1. Read through the passage to identify the issue. What main idea does the writer develop in the passage?
2. Look at who the writer is. What qualifications does the writer have that enables her to write the article? Does she have any experience that helps her write the article?
3. What is the writer's position? What is the tone of the passage? Can you find any emotional language in the passage?
4. How might the writer's age affect her viewpoint? Why might her opinion be different from the one expressed by the Polish farmer at the beginning of the previous page?
5. Write a short paragraph explaining the writer's frame of reference.

Over the months Poland's youth gradually became aware that the issue [of joining the EU] was important to us, because it is we, not our parents, who are going to spend much of our lives in the enlarged EU. Through referenda [votes] and debates in our high schools and universities, we demanded that our voice be heard by those who were longer in the tooth [older]—even though our opinions had no legal value.

—Joanna Margueritte, a young Polish woman

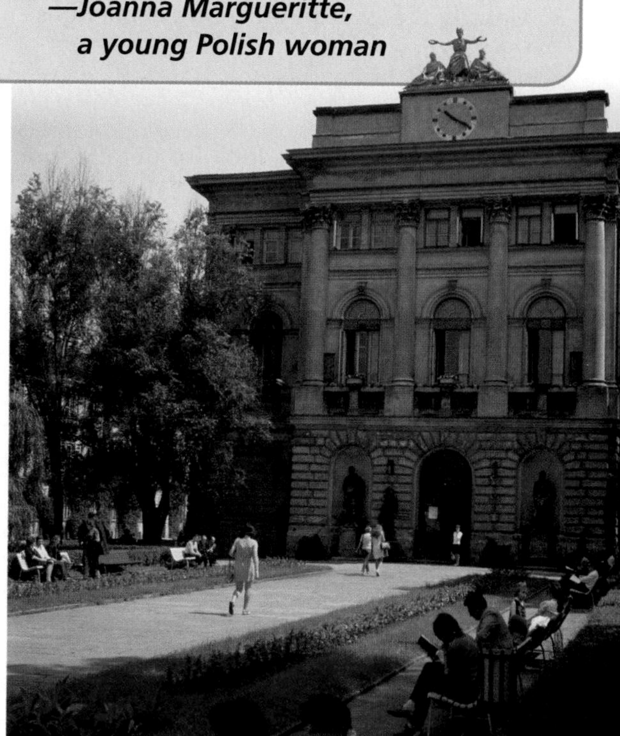

The University of Warsaw

Agricultural production in Poland is now lower than it's been in any time in the last 50 years. . . . The reason is that the European Union and America and other countries have turned Poland into a dumping ground for overproduction. If we are not treated as equals, if the European Union tries to exploit us . . . we will start a propaganda war and make sure that Poles vote No in the referendum. . . .

—Andrzej Lepper, leader of the Self Defence Alliance, a Polish political party

Apply the Skill

Read the passage at the left. Use the steps above to identify the frame of reference of the writer. Then compare this writer's views with those of the writer at the top of this page. How does the tone differ? How would you compare the writers' purposes? Which of these writers do you think is presenting a more reliable picture of the situation?

Section 4 Russia

A Huge Country Takes a New Path

Prepare to Read

Objectives

In this section you will

1. Investigate the changes that capitalism has brought to Russia.
2. Understand the cultural traditions that have endured throughout Russia.
3. Identify the issues that create challenges for Russians.

Taking Notes

As you read the section, look for details about the changes in Russia since the fall of Soviet communism. Copy the flowchart below and write each detail under the correct heading.

Life After Communism

Moscow	Siberia
•	•
•	•
•	•

Target Reading Skill

Identify Contrasts When you contrast two regions, you examine how they are different. In this section you will read about two regions in Russia—Moscow and Siberia. As you read, list the differences between these two regions and ways people live in them.

Key Terms

- **investor** (in VES tur) *n.* someone who spends money on improving a business in the hope of making more money
- **inflation** (in FLAY shun) *n.* an increase in the general level of prices when the amount of goods and services remains the same.

Open-air markets like this one in Perm are a more common sight since the fall of communism.

In 1991, Yura and Tanya Tabak lived in a tiny one-bedroom apartment in Moscow. Soviet communism had ended. Yura had more freedom to pursue his interest in religious studies. Yet life was difficult for the couple. Their wallpaper was peeling off the walls, and their plumbing didn't always work.

In 2002, the Tabaks had a large, bright apartment filled with goods such as a new television. They had even sent their daughter abroad to study. Yura said, "Sometimes I wake up in the morning and want to pinch myself. . . . Are these things really available to us?"

Yet like many Russians, the Tabaks fear what would happen if one of them were to become ill. Medical care used to be free. Now it is expensive and hard to get. Corruption in business and government is widespread, and the economy is unstable. In Russia, many things have changed—but life is still difficult for most Russians.

Emerging Capitalism

When the Soviet Union dissolved in 1991, the new Russian Federation—the world's largest country—had to find a new identity for itself. The nation had no experience of democracy, or any laws that supported it. Russian leaders often fought for power within the new government. The new country also struggled to make the transition from communism to a free-market economy.

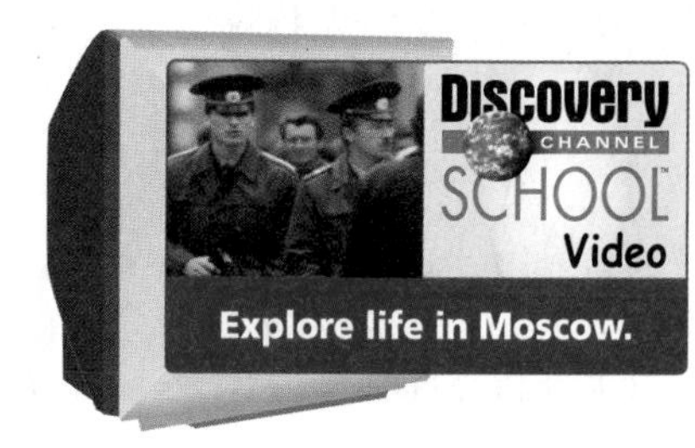

Moscow, Russia's Capital Moscow is the capital of Russia and the center of its economic activities. It has a population of more than 9 million people. When the Soviet Union first collapsed, business in Moscow boomed. Investors came from many different countries to make money in Moscow. An **investor** is someone who spends money on improving a business in the hope of making more money if the business succeeds.

Some investors became very wealthy. When the first American fast-food chain in Russia opened in Moscow, people lined up in the streets to eat there. The restaurant served 30,000 people on the first day. Ikea, a Swedish furniture store, opened a 250-store mall in Moscow. Russian investors opened 24-hour supermarkets and high-tech companies.

Economic success has not come equally to all Russians. Some Russians have become wealthy because they have influence within the government. For example, a former Soviet official started Russia's largest oil and gas company, Gazprom (GAHS prahm), which is hugely profitable. Other Russians have gained their wealth through corruption.

Investment in Moscow
Russia's biggest department store (at the left), built over a hundred years ago in a traditional style, bustles with people and new stores. The modern International Business Center (above) was built in 2001.
Analyze Images *Describe the scene in the department store. Would the scene have been different during Soviet times?*

Widespread Corruption Average Russians have been working hard since the collapse of the Soviet government. Many have opened small businesses or factories. Like the Tabaks, more Russians today can afford to fix up their apartments, buy expensive goods, and travel abroad. Yet most Russians still face challenges in their daily lives. Salaries are still low for Russian workers. About 25 percent of all Russians live in poverty.

Corruption is one reason that many Russians have not been able to improve their situations. Criminal gangs often force honest people who own businesses to pay them money. The Russians who own or work in these businesses therefore cannot keep all the money they earn. Laws meant to protect people are often not enforced.

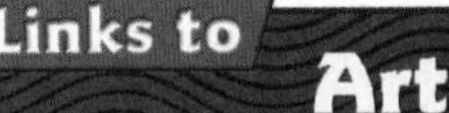

Moscow's "Underground Palaces" When work on Moscow's subway began in the 1930s, its planners wanted to build more than a comfortable, useful mode of transportation. They also wanted to surround the subway riders with beauty. Architects created palace-like subway stations using more than 20 kinds of marble and other different colored stones. The Kievskaya station, shown below, includes domed ceilings hand-painted by famous artists. Others contain stained-glass windows, murals, and statues. Light reflects off of the colored walls of many stations, filling the halls and brightening the day of many passengers.

Economic and Health Problems Average Russians also suffer when the economy does not thrive. In the 1990s, large numbers of Russians lost their life savings when banks failed and inflation rose to high levels. **Inflation** is an increase in the general level of prices at a time when the amount of goods and services remains the same. The economy slowly recovered. But some Russians are still working to regain the money they lost years ago.

Finally, as you have read, Russians have major concerns about health care. Life expectancy in Russia is very low for a developed country—just 62 years for men. Hospitals often contain outdated equipment. In some hospitals, patients have to bring their own sheets. Russia's wealthy people can afford better care, but ordinary Russians cannot.

COUNTRY PROFILE **Focus on Geography**

Russia

As the world's largest country in area, Russia spreads across nearly 180° of latitude. Because of its vast size, the country is divided into eleven separate time zones. While the climate varies from place to place, the summers are generally mild and the winters chilly to bitterly cold. Russia is home to many different landforms, from arctic deserts and tundra to forests, plains, and mountains. Study the map and tables to learn more about Russia's geography.

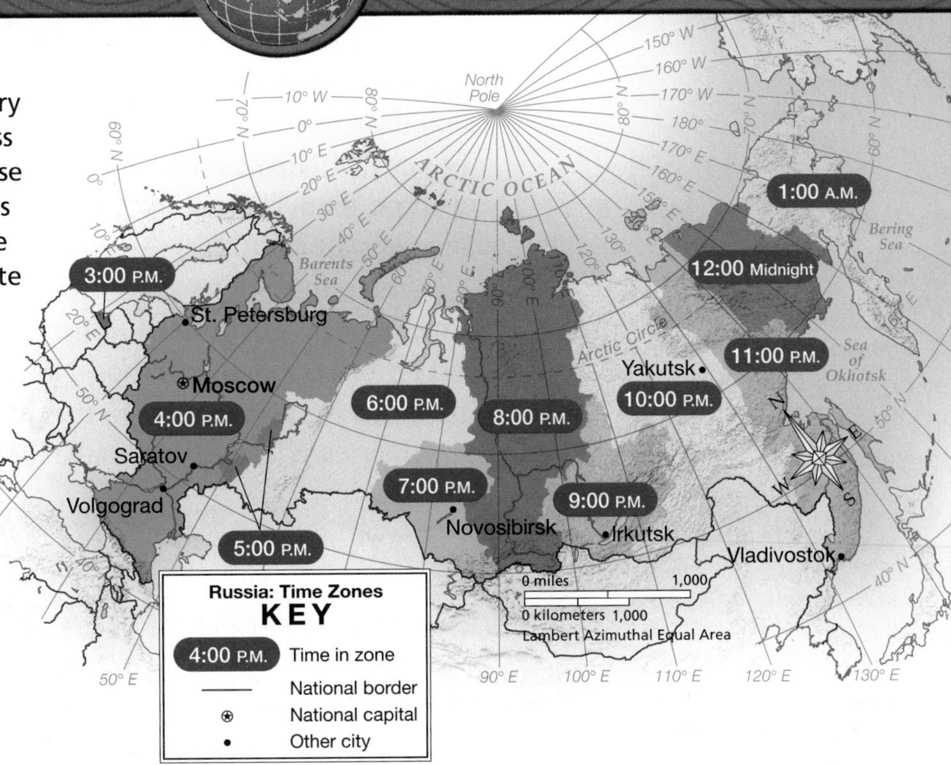

European Railroads by Length

Country	Total Mileage
Russia	
Germany	
France	
Italy	
Spain	
Romania	

This symbol represents 5,000 miles of railroad track.

SOURCE: *DK World Desk Reference*, 2002

World's Largest Countries

Country	Land Area
Russia	6,562,110 sq mi; 16,995,790 sq km
China	3,600,944 sq mi; 9,326,406 sq km
Canada	3,560,234 sq mi; 9,220,968 sq km
United States	3,536,292 sq mi; 9,158,958 sq km
Brazil	3,265,074 sq mi; 8,456,506 sq km

SOURCE: *The World Almanac*, 2004

Map and Chart Skills

1. **Identify** What time is it in Yakutsk when it is noon in Moscow?
2. **Compare** How does Russia's land area compare to that of the United States?
3. **Analyze Information** Why do you think there are so many more miles of railroad track in Russia than in other European countries?

Use Web Code **lde-7504** for **DK World Desk Reference Online.**

Changes in Siberia Siberia is a region with rich reserves of coal, gold, iron, oil, and natural gas. During the Soviet years, the government built factories, set up mining operations, and built the Trans-Siberian railroad to carry out materials. Although much of Siberia is rural, large cities developed there over time. In fact, four of the ten largest Russian cities are located in Siberia. The city of Novosibirsk (NOH vuh sih BIHRSK) has a population of more than 1.3 million people. Outside of the cities, much of Siberia is agricultural.

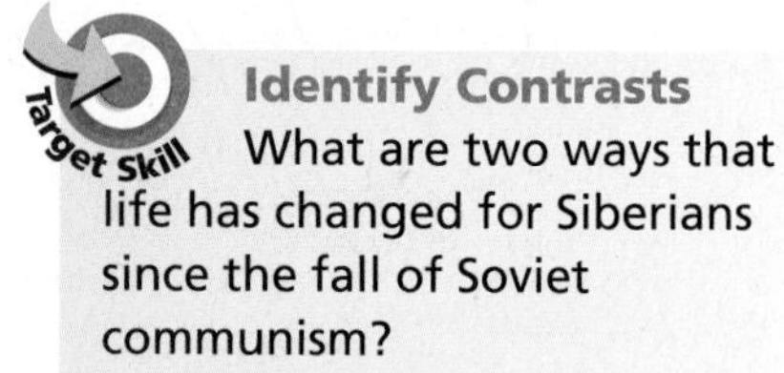

Identify Contrasts What are two ways that life has changed for Siberians since the fall of Soviet communism?

Under the Soviet communist system, factory workers and miners were guaranteed jobs, and farmers were guaranteed certain prices for their crops. Now Siberians worry about losing their jobs or their farms. On the other hand, Siberians are able to buy their own homes and make their own decisions.

√ Reading Check **Why are Siberians worried about jobs?**

Cultural Traditions Continue

The collapse of Soviet communism brought major changes to the lives of many Russians. But traditional Russian ways endure.

Life in Moscow As it was in Soviet times, Moscow is still the cultural center of the nation. Art, theater, and dance thrive there. The Bolshoi (BOHL shoy) Ballet is based in Moscow. Dancers from this famous Russian school of ballet have performed around the world. And traveling performers, such as folk dancers from northern Russia, come to Moscow.

On Moscow's streets street vendors sell traditional Russian crafts next to vendors selling electronic goods from China. On very cold winter days, some people in Moscow go to the parks to celebrate an old tradition: picnicking in the snow.

Russian Teenagers
Teenagers walk across the square in front of St. Basil's Cathedral in Moscow. **Generalize** *How might teenagers' lives have been the same and different before and after the fall of Soviet communism?*

Life in Rural Siberian Villages Much of Siberia's vast expanse is rural. Few people live in these areas, where change comes slowly. Many homes have no running water. Water has to be hauled from wells. Sometimes the wells freeze in the winter. Then people have to drink and cook with melted snow.

Despite problems like these, Siberians have adapted to life in their frigid climate. Farmers work overtime to harvest crops before the frost. Before winter comes, they start collecting nuts and honey. In winter, some families hang huge pieces of meat from their porches. Temperatures in winter are so cold that the meat freezes solid and does not spoil.

During winter, women wearing many layers of clothing leave their log houses to fetch firewood. Inside the log houses, large stoves are used for both cooking and heating. When the nights become bitterly cold, the family may spread a straw mat on top of the still-warm stove and sleep there to stay warm.

A Nenets mother and child in a reindeer-skin tent in Siberia

✓ Reading Check **What are some cultural traditions in Moscow?**

Uniting a Vast Nation

Russia is a vast country, covering more than 6 million square miles (17 million square kilometers). Russia has more than 144 million people. The majority of these people are ethnic Russians. However, the nation also includes many different ethnic groups who speak different languages and practice different religions. How can a country with so much land, so many different ethnic groups, and a struggling economy stay united?

War in Chechnya You have read that some Russian republics populated by ethnic minorities have grown tired of Russian rule. One such republic, located in southwestern Russia, is called Chechnya (CHECH nee uh). The people who live in this oil-rich republic are mainly Muslims. In 1991, Chechnya declared its independence from Russia. To prevent the republic from seceding, Russia sent troops into the Chechen capital. For several years during the 1990s, Russian and Chechen troops fought bitterly over the status of the republic. Tens of thousands of people were killed in the struggle. Hundreds of thousands were forced to flee their homes. Although Chechnya remains part of Russia today, conflict still goes on there.

Chechen refugees make a temporary home in a train car.

Economic Problems Remain In the early 2000s, Russia's economy shows signs of strengthening. Yet serious economic problems remain. Even one of the country's most important assets—its natural resources—presents problems. For example, Russia has enormous deposits of oil, natural gas, and metals. But Russia depends too heavily on sales of these materials, rather than on creating new jobs. If world prices are low, then Russia's economy suffers.

Corruption is still a problem throughout the country. Laws are still not usually enforced. And banks have never fully recovered from the failures in the 1990s. For these reasons, many Russians distrust the government.

However, Russia is still a powerful nation with many important assets. Besides its natural resources, it has a talented workforce of scientists and engineers. If the country can continue to improve its economy and resolve some of its ethnic tensions, its future should be bright.

The Russian Dacha
Country homes called *dachas*, like the one below, were first built by Peter the Great and given to wealthy nobles. In Soviet times, they were usually given to Communist Party officials. **Infer** *Do you think average Russians are able to buy dachas today? Explain why or why not.*

✓ **Reading Check** **Why is Russia's dependence on its natural resources a problem?**

Section 4 Assessment

Key Terms

Review the key terms at the beginning of this section. Use each term in a sentence that explains its meaning.

Target Reading Skill

Contrast the situation in Chechnya before and after the fall of the Soviet Union.

Comprehension and Critical Thinking

1. **(a) Explain** Why have average Russians had difficulty running their own businesses?
(b) Draw Conclusions How has the change to a free-market economy both helped and harmed ordinary Russians?
2. **(a) Describe** What cultural traditions have endured throughout Russia?
(b) Contrast How does life in rural Siberia differ from life in Moscow?
3. **(a) Recall** Which Russian republic declared its independence in 1991?
(b) Infer Why did Russia go to war to prevent that republic from seceding?

Writing Activity

Do you live in a city, a small town, or the countryside? Write a paragraph comparing your life with the lives of Russians in one of the places described in this section.

Writing Tip Before you begin, list details about Russian life in the place you have chosen. For each detail, record a detail about your own life that relates to that topic.

Chapter 10 Review and Assessment

◆ Chapter Summary

Section 1: Poland

- Despite years of foreign rule, cultural traditions and language have endured in Polish life.
- In 1990, Poland's communist-based economy shifted to capitalism.
- Poland must still overcome environmental problems and unemployment.

Section 2: Five Balkan Nations

- The Balkans is a diverse region of many ethnic groups, religions, and languages.
- Yugoslavia had a troubled history of ethnic conflict from its beginning.
- The countries created upon the breakup of Yugoslavia have faced their own problems of ethnic conflict and political instability.

Section 3: Ukraine

- Ukraine has a long history of occupation by foreign powers.
- Since independence from the Soviet Union, Ukraine has had to face economic and environmental challenges.
- Life in Ukraine is changing as the country embraces its independence.

Section 4: Russia

- Since the fall of the Soviet government, the transition to capitalism has brought some benefits, but also many economic challenges.
- Many cultural traditions have endured throughout Russia.
- Russia's huge size, ethnic diversity, and economic problems have presented challenges to preserving national unity.

◆ Key Terms

Each of the statements below contains a key term from the chapter. If the statement is true, write *true*. If it is false, replace the term to make it true.

1. In the Eastern Orthodox religion, a **shrine** is a holy place where visitors often plant crosses.
2. An **investor** is a person who spends money to make more money.
3. Slovenia and Croatia **seceded** from Yugoslavia in 1990.
4. **Capitalism** is an economic system in which the government owns the businesses.
5. More than half of Ukraine is covered with a thick, black soil called **collectives.**
6. After Yugoslavia broke apart, **entrepreneurs** erupted in Bosnia and Herzegovina.

Chapter 

Review and Assessment (continued)

◆ Comprehension and Critical Thinking

7. **(a) Identify** What religion do most Poles belong to?
   (b) Synthesize Information How has religious belief strengthened the pride Poles feel for their country?
8. **(a) Name** What group of people in Poland has found it hardest to manage the transition to capitalism?
   (b) Analyze Information In what ways did communism help Polish farmers?
   (c) Identify Effects What are Polish farmers doing to make extra money?
9. **(a) List** Which five Balkan nations share a Slavic heritage?
   (b) Contrast Discuss the differences among the peoples of these nations.
   (c) Summarize How did these differences lead to the breakup of Yugoslavia?
10. **(a) Recall** What problems are faced by all the nations created by Yugoslavia's breakup?
    (b) Identify Cause and Effect Why were UN and NATO forces sent to the Balkans several times?
11. **(a) Note** What are the natural resources of Ukraine?
    (b) Identify the Main Idea How have these resources affected Ukraine's history?
12. **(a) Describe** What changes did the transition to capitalism bring to Russia?
    (b) Evaluate Information How has capitalism both helped and hurt average Russians?

◆ Skills Practice

Identifying Frame of Reference In the Skills for Life activity in this chapter, you learned how to identify frame of reference. Review the steps you followed to learn this skill. Then reread the quotation by Vaclav Havel on page 233. Identify the writer's tone and qualifications for his position. Then use this information to write a paragraph that explains his frame of reference.

◆ Writing Activity: Science

Suppose you are a writer for a science magazine. Your assignment is to write an article about environmental problems in Eastern Europe. Write a short article about the causes and effects of pollution in Poland, or of the Chernobyl accident in Ukraine.

MAP MASTER™ Skills Activity

Place Location For each place listed below, write the letter from the map that shows its location.

1. Ukraine
2. Kiev
3. Sarajevo
4. Bosnia and Herzegovina
5. Serbia and Montenegro

Go Online PHSchool.com Use Web Code **ldp-7514** for an **interactive map.**

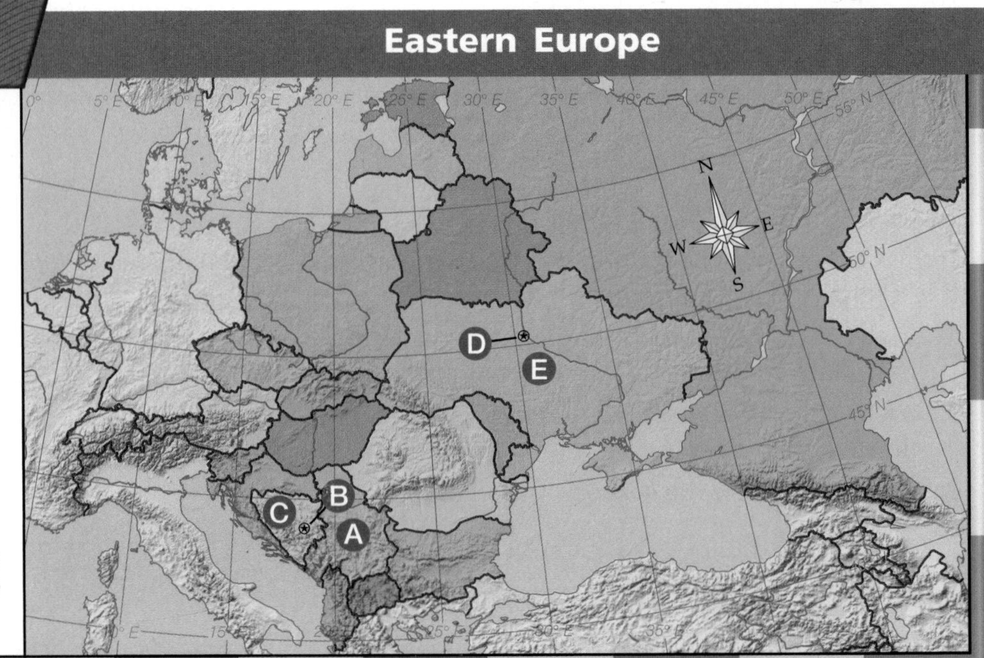

Standardized Test Prep

Test-Taking Tips

Some questions on standardized tests ask you to analyze graphic organizers. Study the table below. Then follow the tips to answer the sample question.

Five Balkan Nations: Ethnic Groups	
Macedonia	Macedonian (67%) Albanian (23%)
Croatia	Croat (90%) Serb (5%)
Bosnia and Herzegovina	Bosniak (48%) Serb (37%)
Serbia and Montenegro	Serb (63%) Albanian (17%)
Slovenia	Slovene (88%) Croat (3%)

TIP Use what you know about history and geography to help you answer the question.

What is the subject of this chart?

A major ethnic groups of countries that make up Eastern Europe

B major ethnic groups of countries that made up the former Soviet Union

C major ethnic groups of countries that were formed after Yugoslavia broke up

D major ethnic groups of countries that were formed at the end of World War II

TIP Try to answer the question before you look at the answer choices.

Think It Through Each of the names in bold print is a country; to the right of each country is its ethnic makeup. You can eliminate A and B. Eastern Europe includes more than these five countries, and the Soviet Union did not include these countries. You may not know which countries were formed after World War II, but you have probably heard most of these five countries mentioned in reference to Yugoslavia. The answer is C.

Practice Questions

Use the tips above and other tips in this book to help you answer the following questions.

1. Which of the following is NOT an important Polish tradition?
   A communism
   B Polish Orthodoxy
   C Roman Catholicism
   D the Polish language

2. In which country is the republic of Kosovo located?
   A Macedonia
   B Croatia
   C Bosnia and Herzegovina
   D Serbia and Montenegro

3. What led to the growth of towns and cities in Siberia?
   A the collapse of Soviet communism
   B the Trans-Siberian Railroad
   C the transition to capitalism
   D migration from Europe

Use the table below to answer Question 4. Choose the letter of the best answer to the question.

Ukrainian Resources	
Resource	**Use by Soviet Union**
Farmland	Grain, meat
Minerals	Iron ore, coal for industries
	Shipping of goods to and from Soviet Union

4. Which answer would best fit in the blank space on the table?
   A Collectives
   B Seaports and rivers
   C Mines
   D Factories

Use Web Code **lda-7504** for a **Chapter 10 self-test.**

Projects

Create your own projects to learn more about Europe and Russia. At the beginning of this book, you were introduced to the **Guiding Questions** for studying the chapters and the special features. You can also find answers to these questions by doing projects on your own or with a group. Use the questions to find topics you want to explore further. Then try the projects described on this page or create your own.

1. **Geography** What are the main physical features of Europe and Russia?
2. **History** How have Europe and Russia been affected by their history?
3. **Culture** How have the people of Europe and Russia been shaped by their cultures?
4. **Government** What types of government have existed in Europe and Russia?
5. **Economics** How have Russian and European economies developed into what they are today?

Project

CREATE A DISPLAY

Folklore Corner

Create a library of folk and fairy tales from countries throughout Europe. As you read about a country in this book, find a traditional tale from that country. Think about how the stories reflect the country's culture. With your classmates, build a Folklore Corner in your classroom. Create a display of books of folk tales. Include objects, drawings, and photographs that represent the culture in these tales. Label each tale with its country of origin.

Project

WRITE A PROPOSAL

Olympic Cities

Plan an Olympic season in a European city. As you read this book, keep track of cities that you find interesting. Research them at the library or on the Internet. After you have gathered your information, choose a city that you think would be a good host of either the summer or winter Olympics. Write a proposal to Olympic officials, explaining what the city has to offer to the Olympics. Include maps or pictures of your city with your proposal.

Target Reading Skills

The Target Reading Skills introduced on this page will help you understand the words and ideas in this book and in other social studies reading you do. Each chapter in the Africa section focuses on one of these reading skills. Good readers develop a bank of reading strategies, or skills. Then they draw on the particular strategies that will help them understand the text they are reading.

Chapter 11 Target Reading Skill

Clarifying Meaning If you do not understand something you are reading right away, you can use several skills to clarify the meaning of the word or idea. In this chapter you will practice these strategies: rereading, paraphrasing, and summarizing.

Chapter 12 Target Reading Skill

Using the Reading Process Previewing can help you understand and remember what you read. In this chapter you will practice these skills: setting a purpose for reading, predicting, asking questions, and using prior knowledge.

Chapter 13 Target Reading Skill

Comparing and Contrasting You can use comparison and contrast to sort out and analyze information you are reading. In this chapter you will practice these skills: making comparisons, identifying contrasts, and using signal words.

Chapter 14 Target Reading Skill

Using Cause and Effect Recognizing cause and effect will help you understand relationships among the situations and events you are reading about. In this chapter you will practice these skills: recognizing causes and effects and using signal words.

Chapter 15 Target Reading Skill

Identifying the Main Idea Since you cannot remember every detail of what you read, it is important to identify the main ideas. In this chapter you will practice these skills: identifying main ideas, identifying implied main ideas, and identifying supporting details.

Chapter 16 Target Reading Skill

Using Context Using the context of an unfamiliar word can help you understand its meaning. Context includes the words, phrases, and sentences surrounding a word. In this chapter you will practice these skills: using context clues and interpreting nonliteral meanings.

Chapter 17 Target Reading Skill

Using Sequence Identifying the sequence, or order, of important events can help you understand and remember the events. In this chapter you will practice these skills: understanding sequence and recognizing words that signal sequence.

AFRICA

The name *Africa* may have come from the Latin word *aprica,* which means "sunny." In much of Africa, the sun does shine brightly. Each morning, the African sunrise awakens one eighth of the world's population, in more than fifty different countries. In the chapters that follow, you will spend the day with some of these people.

Guiding Questions

The text, photographs, maps, and charts in this book will help you discover answers to these Guiding Questions.

1. **Geography** What are the main physical features of Africa?
2. **History** How have historical events affected the cultures and nations of Africa?
3. **Culture** What features help define different African cultures?
4. **Government** What factors led to the development of different governments across Africa?
5. **Economics** What factors influence the ways in which Africans make a living?

Project Preview

You can also discover answers to the Guiding Questions by working on projects. Several project possibilities are listed on page 564 of this book.

Investigate Africa

Africa is the second-largest continent in the world after Asia. Africa's climate and physical geography are diverse, ranging from flat, arid deserts to tropical wet rain forests and high mountains. Africa also has a wide range of peoples with their own distinctive languages and cultures. It is a continent potentially rich in natural resources.

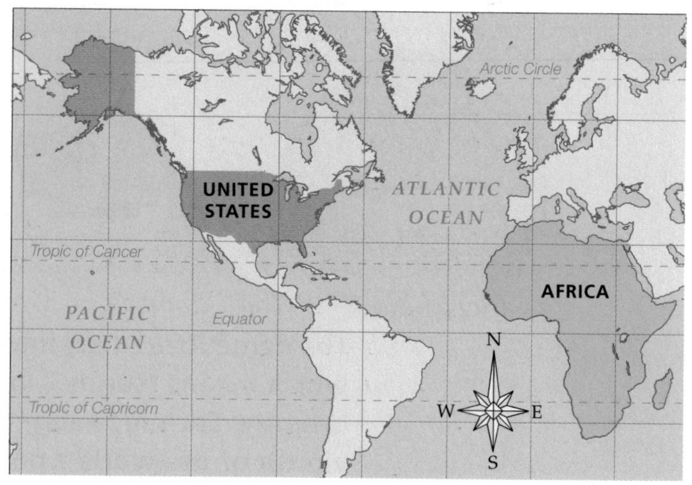

▲ **Tanzania**
The vast, flat grasslands of the savannas support a diverse population of animals.

LOCATION

1 Explore Africa's Location

How would you describe Africa's location? One way would be to compare where it is to where the United States is. What ocean lies between Africa and the United States? Find the Equator. What do you know about the climate of countries near the Equator? How do you think the climates of the United States might differ from the climates of Africa?

REGIONS

2 Estimate the Size of Africa

The United States is 3,500,000 square miles (9,064,958 square kilometers) in land area. How does Africa's size compare to that of the continental United States (all states except Alaska and Hawaii)? Measure mainland Africa at its widest point from east to west. Measure Africa from north to south. Now measure the United States the same way. How do they compare? Estimate Africa's area in square miles.

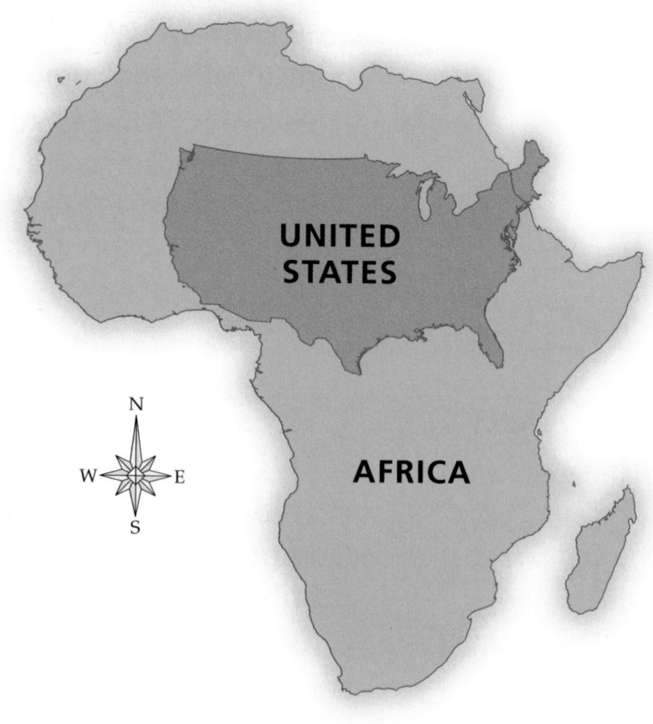

Political Africa

LOCATION

3 Predict How Location Affects Economics

When a country does not border any large body of water, it is described as being landlocked. Make a list of the African countries that are landlocked. Think about how being landlocked might limit the ability of a country to trade with other countries. How might being landlocked affect the economy of a country? How might landlocked countries trade in other ways?

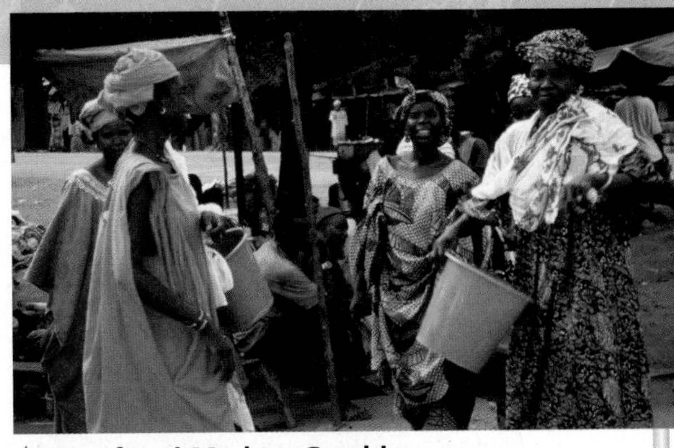

▲ **Farafenni Market, Gambia**
This thriving street market is an important part of the local economy. Farmers sell their produce at such local markets, benefiting themselves and the community.

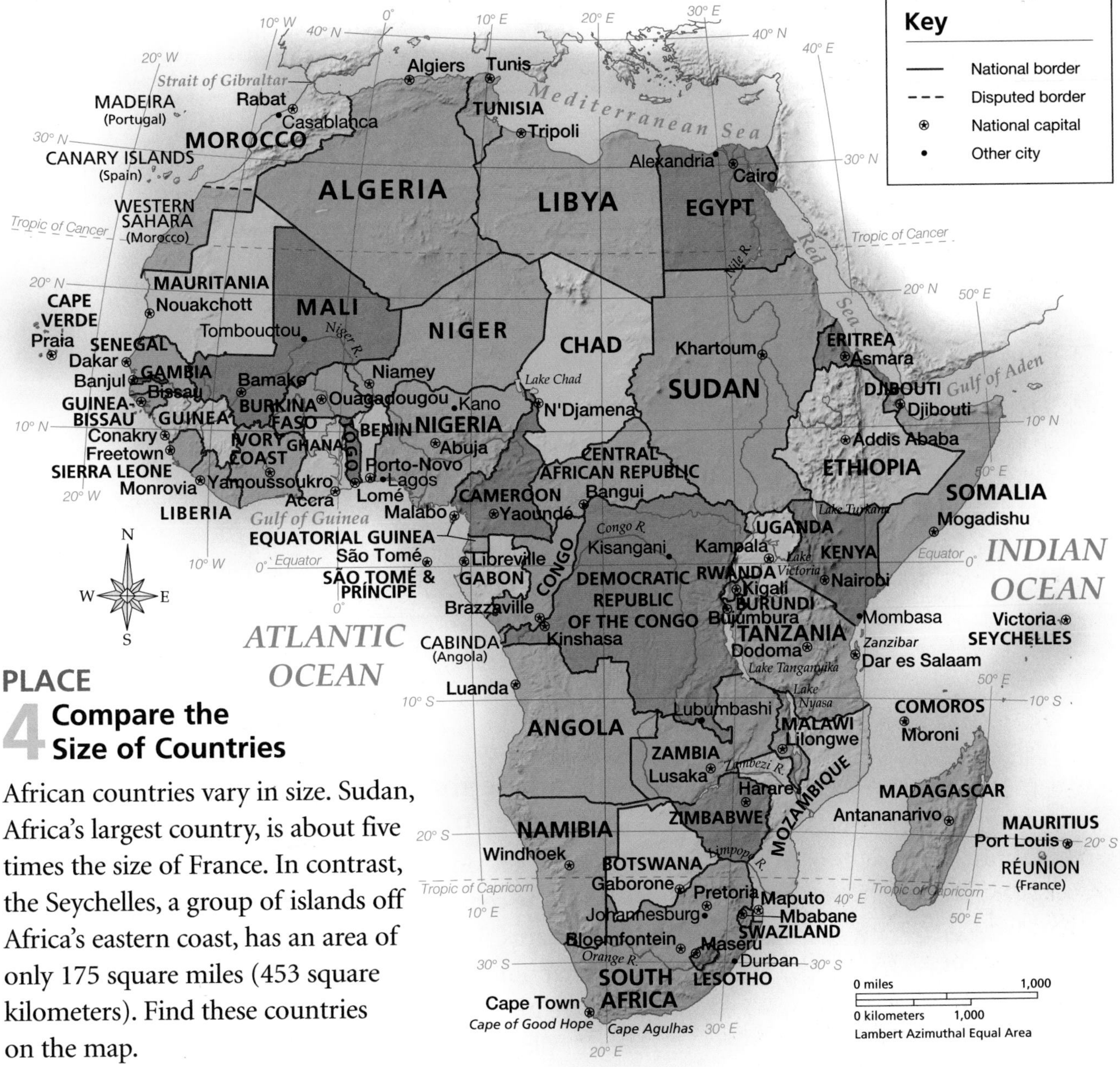

PLACE

4 Compare the Size of Countries

African countries vary in size. Sudan, Africa's largest country, is about five times the size of France. In contrast, the Seychelles, a group of islands off Africa's eastern coast, has an area of only 175 square miles (453 square kilometers). Find these countries on the map.

Physical Africa

Strait of Gibraltar
Mediterranean Sea
Atlas Mountains
Canary Islands
Tropic of Cancer
Cape Verde Islands
Ahaggar Mountains
Tibesti Mountains
Libyan Desert
Qattara Depression
Suez Canal
Arabian Desert
Red Sea
Nile R.
S A H A R A
S A H E L
Senegal R.
Niger R.
Lake Chad
Fouta Djallon
Volta R.
Benue R.
Adamawa Highlands
White Nile R.
Blue Nile R.
Lake Tana
Gulf of Aden
Ethiopian Highlands
Sudd
ATLANTIC OCEAN
Gulf of Guinea
Bioko
São Tomé
Equator
Ubangi R.
Congo R.
Congo Basin
Lake Albert
Lake Turkana
Great Rift Valley
Lake Victoria
Kilimanjaro 19,341 ft (5,895 m)
Serengeti Plain
INDIAN OCEAN
Zanzibar
Seychelles
Lake Tanganyika
Lake Nyasa
Comoros
Zambezi R.
Mozambique Channel
Madagascar
Mauritius
Réunion
Namib Desert
Okavango Basin
Kalahari Desert
Limpopo R.
Tropic of Capricorn
Orange R.
Drakensberg
Cape of Good Hope
Cape Agulhas

Key

ELEVATION Feet	Meters
More than 13,000	More than 3,960
6,500–13,000	1,980–3,960
1,600–6,500	480–1,980
650–1,600	200–480
0–650	0–200
Below sea level	Below sea level

—— National border
- - - Disputed border

0 miles 1,000
0 kilometers 1,000
Lambert Azimuthal Equal Area

▲ **Atlas Mountains**
The Berber people make their home in North Africa's Atlas Mountains.

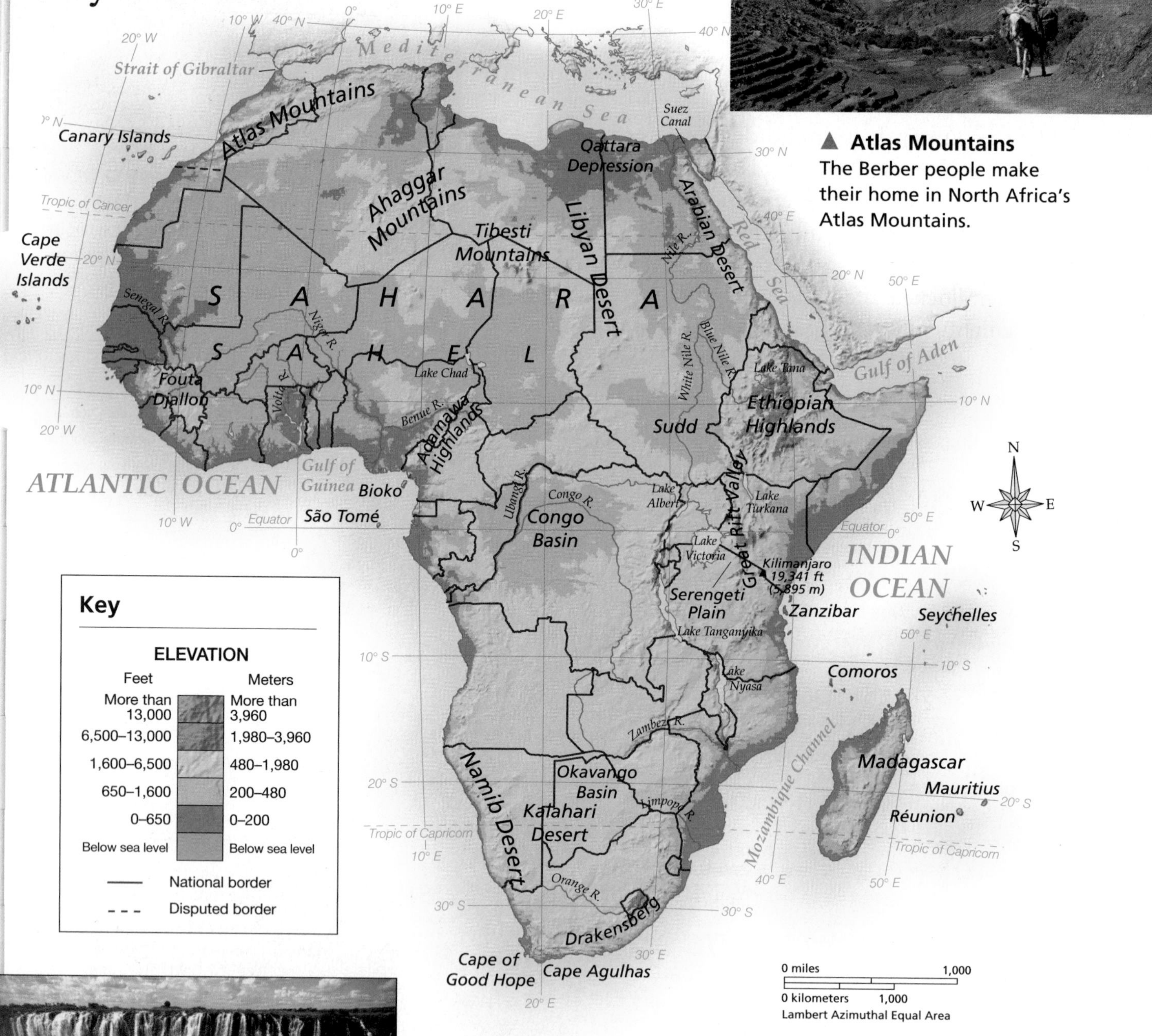

▲ **Victoria Falls**
The Zambezi River tumbles over Victoria Falls between Zambia and Zimbabwe in Southern Africa.

PLACE

5 Examine the Physical Features of Africa

Check the key on the physical map and you will see that some of the coastline of Africa has narrow strips of low plains. The interior is a flat plateau covered by the Sahara in the north. On the coast of Southern Africa there are many steep cliffs. Find other places where the interior plateau comes close to the ocean.

Africa: Land Use

Mediterranean Sea
Red Sea
Tropic of Cancer
Tropic of Capricorn
Equator
ATLANTIC OCEAN
INDIAN OCEAN
40° N
20° N
0°
20° S
20° W
20° E
40° E
N
S
E
W
Key
Nomadic herding
Livestock raising
Commercial farming
Subsistence farming
Manufacturing and trade
Little or no activity
National border
Disputed border
0 miles 1,500
0 kilometers 1,500
Lambert Azimuthal Equal Area

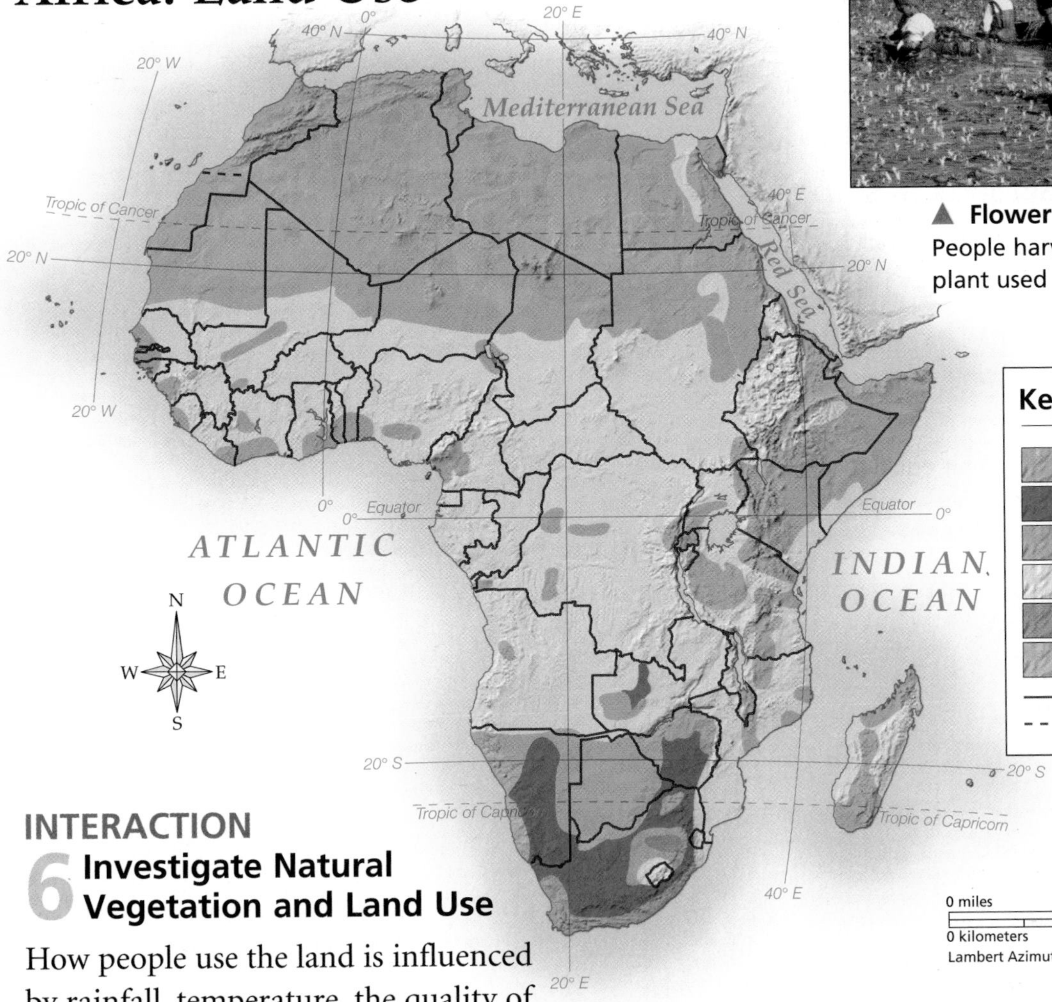

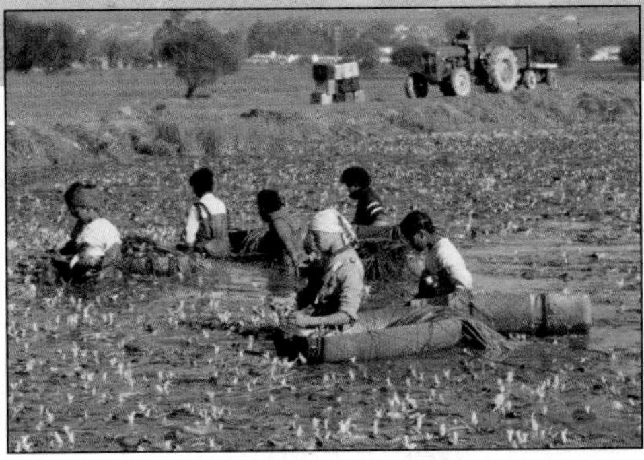

▲ **Flower farming, South Africa** People harvest "water flowers," a plant used in traditional cooking.

INTERACTION

6 Investigate Natural Vegetation and Land Use

How people use the land is influenced by rainfall, temperature, the quality of the soil, landforms, politics, and many other factors. Along the Mediterranean coast, moisture from the sea makes some agriculture possible. In the vast Sahara, most people live as nomadic herders. Where on the continent is livestock raised?

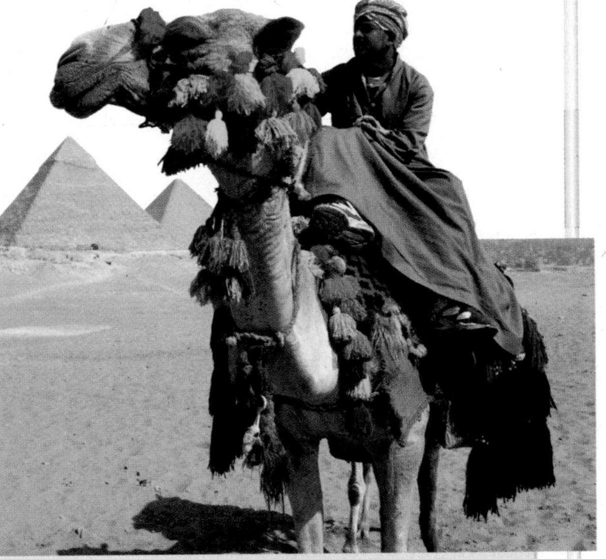

▲ **Camels are still used as a means of transportation in parts of Egypt.**

PRACTICE YOUR GEOGRAPHY SKILLS

1. You are in Egypt. A river meets the sea near the country's capital. What is the name of the river?
2. Flying east from the mouth of the Zambezi River, you come to an island. What is its name, and how is land used there?
3. Now you are traveling west by ship toward the southern tip of Africa. You stop at a port near the Tropic of Capricorn. What country are you in?

Focus on Countries in Africa

Now that you've investigated the geography of Africa, take a closer look at some of the countries that make up this continent. The map shows all of the countries of Africa. The ten countries you will study in depth in the second half of this book are shown in yellow on the map.

Go Online PHSchool.com Use Web Code **lap-5020** for the **interactive maps** on these pages.

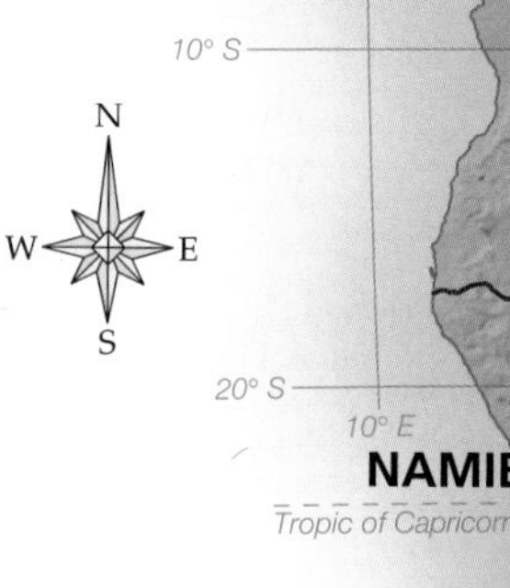

▲ **Nigeria**
The Hausa-Fulani, Igbo, Yoruba, and a number of other, smaller ethnic groups make up Nigeria, where more than 200 languages are spoken. Nigeria is a major oil-producing country.

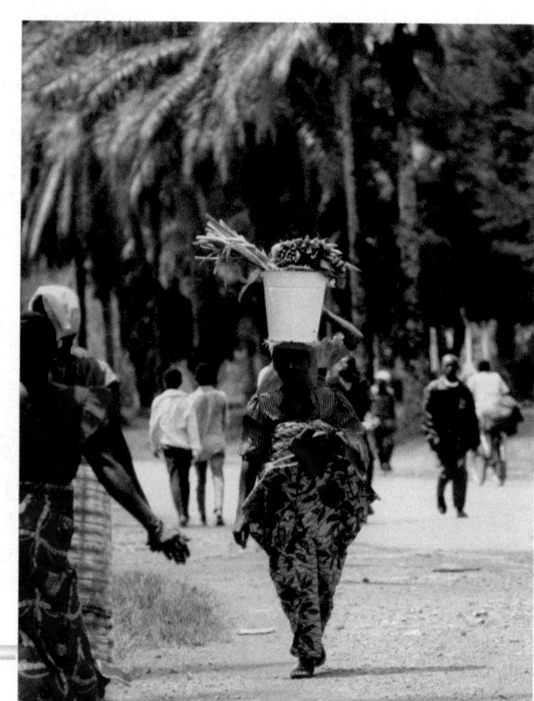

Democratic Republic of the Congo ▶
The Democratic Republic of the Congo is Africa's third-largest country. It is rich in minerals including diamonds, petroleum, cobalt, and copper.

◀ **Egypt**
Almost all of the people of Egypt live in the fertile valley of the Nile. The vast desert on either side of this river is almost completely unpopulated.

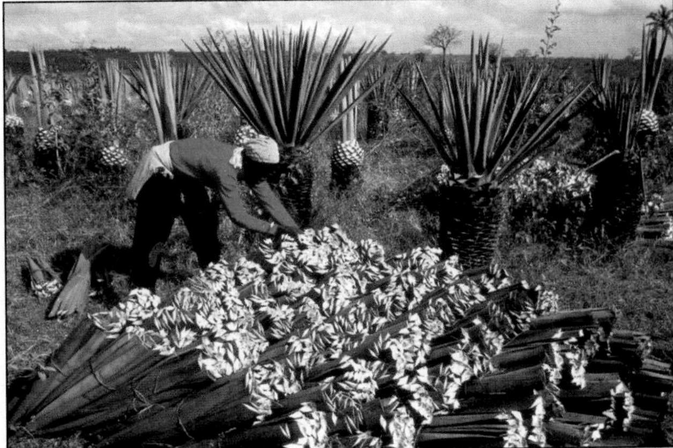

▲ **Kenya**
Two thirds of Kenya's people live in the countryside. Many Kenyan women raise cash crops or work on plantations, while the men work in the cities.

▲ **South Africa**
South Africa, at Africa's southern tip, is bordered by oceans on three sides. It is a resource-rich country with a strong economy.

Africa: Physical Geography

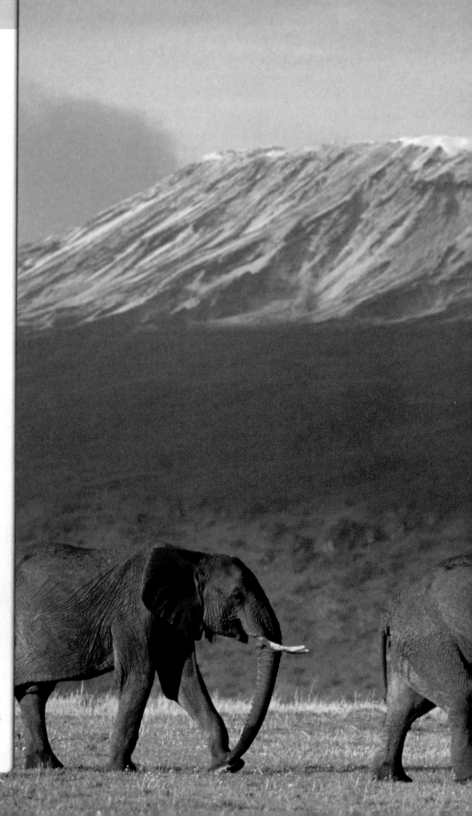

Chapter Preview

This chapter will introduce you to the geography of Africa and show you how geography affects the people of the continent.

Section 1
Land and Water

Section 2
Climate and Vegetation

Section 3
Resources and Land Use

Target Reading Skill

Clarifying Meaning In this chapter you will focus on clarifying, or better understanding, the meaning of what you read. Rereading, paraphrasing, and summarizing can help you better understand sentences and passages.

▶ **Elephants walk across the plains below Africa's tallest mountain, Mount Kilimanjaro.**

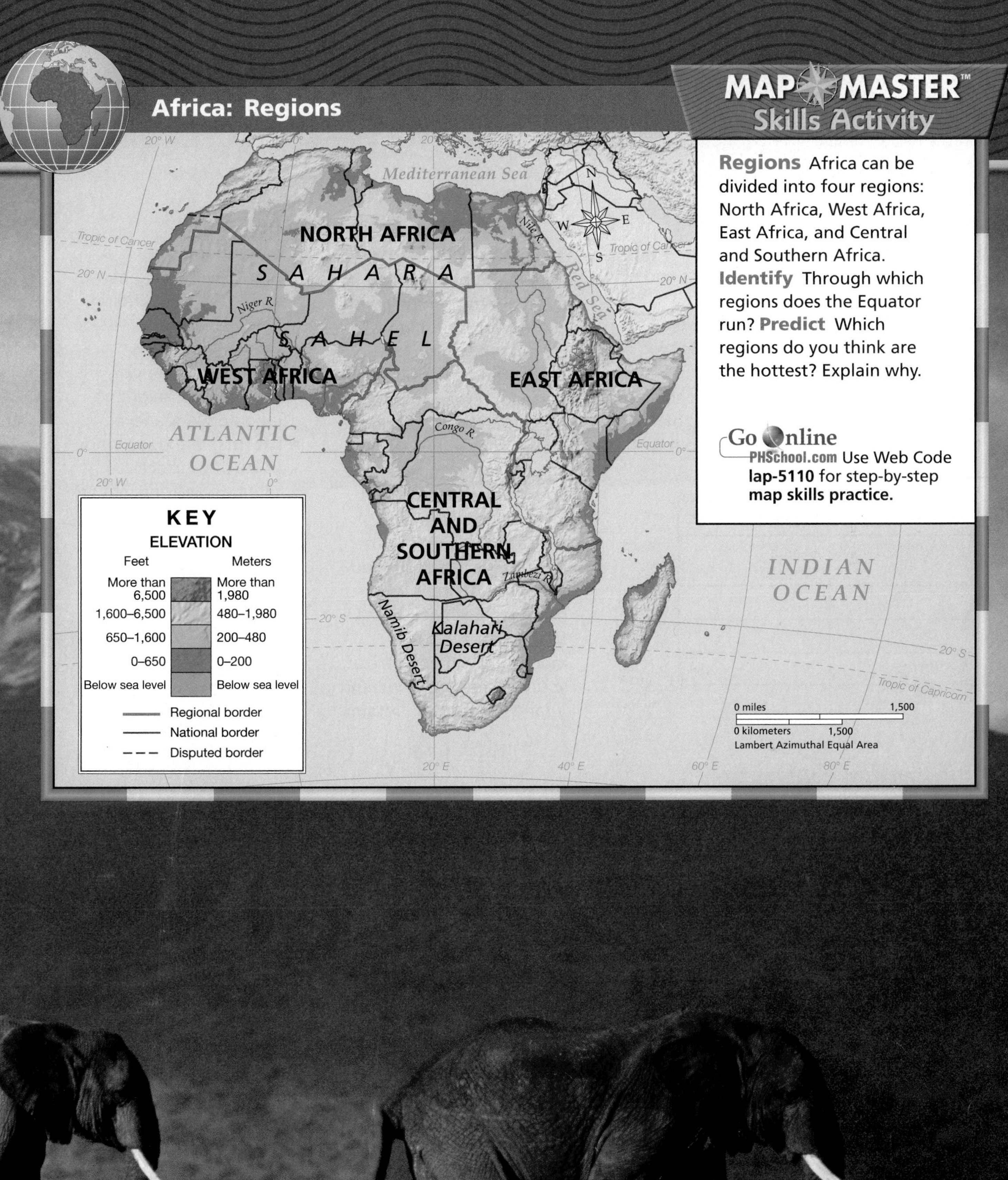

MAP MASTER™ Skills Activity

Regions Africa can be divided into four regions: North Africa, West Africa, East Africa, and Central and Southern Africa. **Identify** Through which regions does the Equator run? **Predict** Which regions do you think are the hottest? Explain why.

Go Online
PHSchool.com Use Web Code **lap-5110** for step-by-step **map skills practice.**

Section 1 Land and Water

Prepare to Read

Objectives

In this section you will

1. Learn about Africa's four regions and its major landforms.
2. Find out about Africa's major rivers.

Taking Notes

As you read, look for details about the land and waterways of the four regions of Africa. Copy the table below, and use it to record your findings.

Region of Africa	Physical Features
North	• Land: • Water:

Target Reading Skill

Reread Rereading is a strategy that can help you clarify words and ideas in the text. If you do not understand a certain passage, reread it to look for connections among the words and sentences.

In the following example, you may not know what *level* means. "Much of Africa is made up of raised, mostly level areas of land. Not all of Africa is level, however. Each of Africa's four regions has mountains." If you reread, you will see that level land is land without mountains.

Key Terms

- **plateau** (pla TOH) *n.* a large, level area that rises above the surrounding land; has at least one side with a steep slope
- **elevation** (el uh VAY shun) *n.* the height of land above sea level
- **rift** (rift) *n.* a deep crack in Earth's surface
- **tributary** (TRIB yoo tehr ee) *n.* a river or stream that flows into a larger river
- **fertile** (FUR tul) *adj.* rich in the substances plants need to grow well

Dinosaurs like this allosaurus once lived in Africa.

Scientists believe that more than 200 million years ago, dinosaurs were able to walk from Africa to South America. They could do that because Africa and South America were connected then. Turn to page 818 of the Atlas. Find Africa on the map titled The World: Physical. As you can see, it would be impossible to walk from Africa to South America today.

How did Africa and South America become separated? At least 65 million years ago, forces on our planet's surface caused South America and Africa to move apart, forming the southern part of the Atlantic Ocean. In the process, Africa became the second-largest continent on Earth. To learn more about this vast continent, first examine the geography of Africa's regions.

Africa's Regions and Landforms

Africa includes more than 50 countries. This large continent can be divided into four regions: North Africa, West Africa, East Africa, and Central and Southern Africa. Each region contains several different climates and landforms. Turn to the map on page 357 titled Africa: Regions to see the physical features of the four regions.

Discovery
CHANNEL
SCHOOL
Video
Learn about the geographic features of Africa.

The Four Regions The region of North Africa is marked in places by rocky mountains. It is also home to seemingly endless stretches of the world's largest desert, the Sahara (suh HA ruh). West Africa, the continent's most populated region, consists mostly of grassland. The soil in the grassland is good for farming. The region of East Africa has many mountains and a few **plateaus,** which are large, raised areas of mostly level land. Grasslands and hills are also found there. Much of Central and Southern Africa is flat or rolling grassland. The region also has thick rain forests, mountains, and swamps. The Namib (NAH mib) Desert and the Kalahari (kah luh HAH ree) Desert are in Southern Africa.

The Plateau Continent Africa is often called the plateau continent because much of the continent is made up of raised, mostly level areas of land that drop off sharply near the sea. Much of this land has a high **elevation,** or height above sea level.

Mountains Not all of Africa is level, however. All of Africa's four regions have mountains. The highest are in East Africa. Mount Kilimanjaro in Tanzania is Africa's tallest mountain. It rises to a height of 19,341 feet (5,895 meters).

Rising Up From Flat Land
The Kassala Mountains in the East African country of Sudan rise up from flat land that the people farm. **Analyze Images** *Do these mountains prevent people from farming the land?*

MAP MASTER™ Skills Activity

Place The steep walls of the Great Rift Valley open out into a valley that can be 30 to 40 miles (50 to 65 kilometers) wide.

Locate Name the northernmost country and the southernmost country through which the Great Rift Valley runs.

Analyze Information What effects do you think the Great Rift Valley has on communication and travel between countries on either side of the valley?

Go Online PHSchool.com Use Web Code **lap-5111** for step-by-step **map skills practice.**

The Great Rift Valley

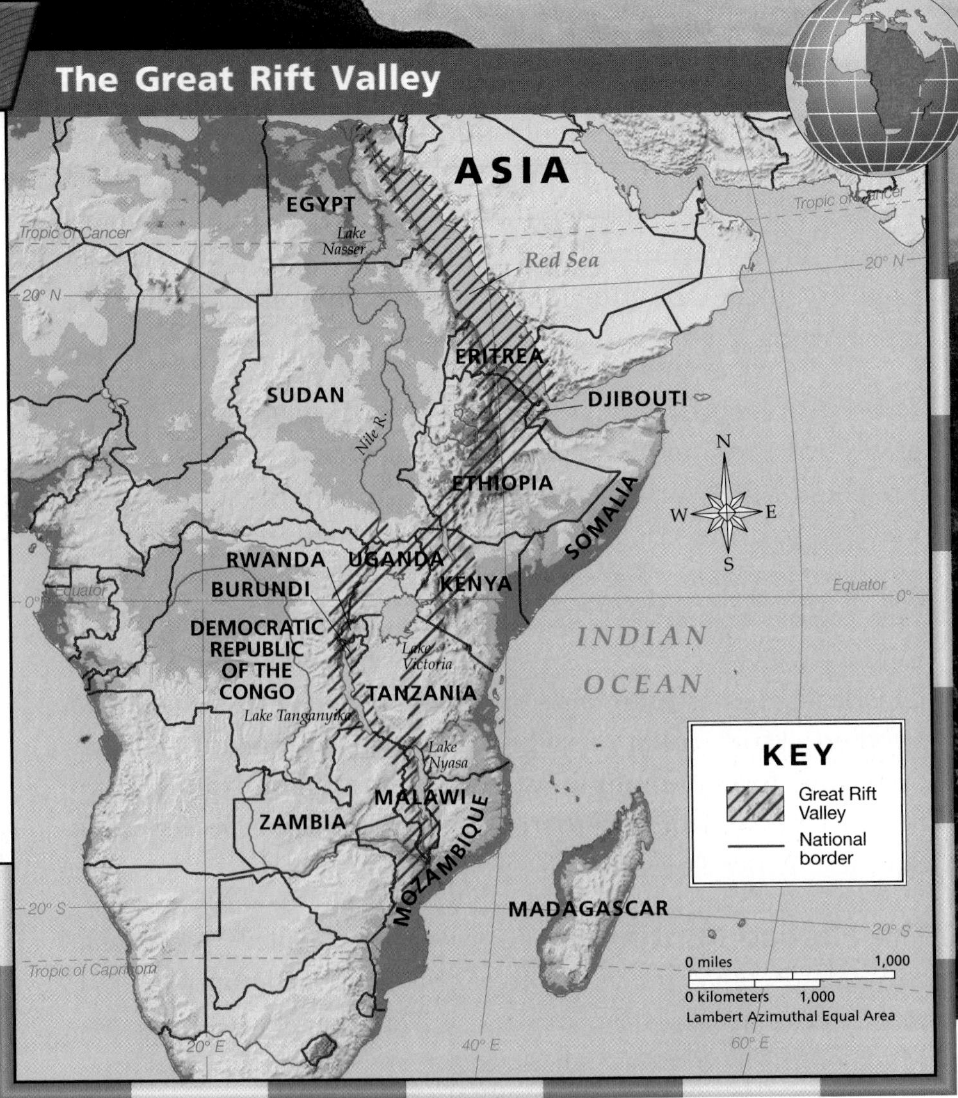

Coastal Plains Edge the Continent There is a strip of coastal plain that runs along much of Africa's coast. This land is dry and sandy in some places and marshy and moist in other places. Turn to the political map of Africa on page 351 of the Regional Overview. Find the West African country of Ghana (GAH nuh). The western edge of the coastal strip in Ghana is only about 5 miles (8 kilometers) wide. There, the coastal strip ends in a long, steep slope that rises to a plateau.

The Great Rift Valley Mount Kilimanjaro, Africa's highest peak, is located in East Africa on the edge of the Great Rift Valley. This valley was formed millions of years ago, when the continents pulled apart and left a **rift,** or deep trench. The rift that cuts through East Africa is 4,000 miles (6,400 kilometers) long. Most of Africa's major lakes are located in or near the Great Rift Valley.

✓ Reading Check **Why is Africa called the plateau continent?**

The Great Rift Valley

Africa's Rivers

Four large rivers carry water from the mountains of Africa's plateaus to the sea. They are the Nile (nyl), the Congo (KAHNG goh), the Zambezi (zam BEE zee), and the Niger (NY jur). Turn to page 352 and find these rivers on the physical map of Africa. Sections of these four rivers may be used for travel. But the rivers are broken in places by large waterfalls or steep rapids. These obstacles make it impossible for ships to sail the whole way between Africa's interior and the sea.

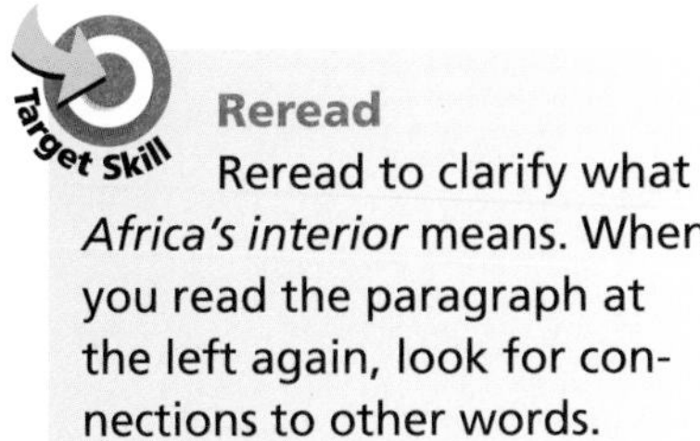

Reread
Reread to clarify what *Africa's interior* means. When you read the paragraph at the left again, look for connections to other words.

The Nile River The Nile is the longest river in the world. Its length, more than 4,000 miles (6,400 kilometers), is almost twice the length of the Mississippi River. The White Nile in Sudan and the Blue Nile in the highlands of Ethiopia are tributaries of the Nile. **Tributaries** are rivers and streams that flow into a larger river. After the White Nile and Blue Nile combine to form the Nile, the river flows north into the Mediterranean Sea.

Farming on the Banks
Farmers planted the crops shown above near the banks of the Nile River. **Summarize** *What are the benefits of farming near a river?*

Farming Along the Nile People have farmed the land surrounding the Nile for thousands of years. At one time, the Nile flooded its banks regularly. Farmers planted their crops to match the flood cycle of the river. The floods provided water for the crops and left behind a layer of silt, tiny bits of rock and dirt carried downstream by the river. Silt helps make soil **fertile,** or rich in the substances that plants need to grow well.

In the 1960s, Egypt's government built the Aswan High Dam to control the flooding of the Nile. As the water backed up behind the dam, Lake Nasser was created. Waters from the lake are channeled to water crops that grow in the desert. Water rushing through the dam produces electricity. Since the dam was built, the Nile no longer floods the land.

The Congo River The Congo River flows through the rain forests of the Central African countries of the Congo and the Democratic Republic of the Congo. At 2,900 miles (4,677 kilometers), the Congo River is Africa's second-longest river. It is fed by hundreds of tributaries. Many farmers in this region grow yams and cassava (kuh SAH vuh), a starchy plant that is a bit like a potato. They also catch many different types of fish in the Congo River.

Links to Science

A River Without a Delta
A delta is a plain that forms at the mouth of a river. The Congo River's current is so strong that it does not form a delta. Instead, the river has cut a deep, wide canyon beneath the sea for a distance of about 125 miles (200 kilometers).

The Niger River The third-longest river in Africa, the Niger, begins its journey in Guinea (GIH nee). For 2,600 miles (4,180 kilometers), the river flows north and then bends south. It provides water for farms in the river valley. Many people make their living fishing in the river.

The Zambezi River Africa's fourth-longest river, the Zambezi, is in Southern Africa. It runs through or forms the border of six countries: Angola (ang GOH luh), Zambia (ZAM bee uh), Namibia (nuh MIB ee uh), Botswana (baht SWAH nuh), Zimbabwe (zim BAHB way), and Mozambique (moh zum BEEK). The river is 2,200 miles (3,540 kilometers) long, but boats can travel only on about 460 miles (740 kilometers) of it because of its waterfalls and rapids.

People have used the Zambezi's strong current to produce electricity. About halfway to its outlet in the Indian Ocean, the Zambezi plunges into a canyon, creating the spectacular waterfall known as Victoria Falls. Tourists from around the world visit these falls. People can sometimes see the mist and spray of Victoria Falls from as far away as 40 miles (65 kilometers).

√ Reading Check **What effect has the Aswan High Dam had on Egypt and on the waters of the Nile?**

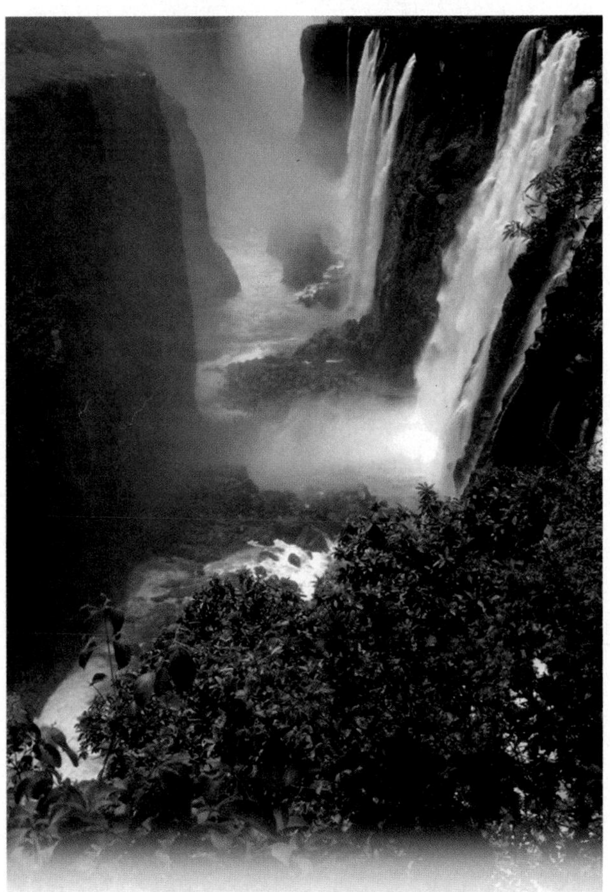

Victoria Falls is located on the border between Zambia and Zimbabwe.

Section 1 Assessment

Key Terms
Review the key terms at the beginning of this section. Use each term in a sentence that explains its meaning.

Target Reading Skill
Name a word or an idea that you were able to clarify on your own by rereading. Explain it in your own words.

Comprehension and Critical Thinking
1. **(a) Identify** Name the four regions of Africa.
(b) Compare What physical features do all of the regions have in common?
(c) Draw Conclusions Why might West Africa be the continent's most populated region?
2. **(a) Describe** Describe the course traveled by each of Africa's major rivers.
(b) Identify Effects How do Africa's four major rivers affect the lives of its people?
(c) Draw Inferences How did farming on the Nile change after the Aswan High Dam was built?

Writing Activity
List several landforms and rivers in Africa that you would like to visit. Explain why you would like to visit them and what you would do on your trip.

Writing Tip Use vivid details to describe your trip. These will help support your explanation of the reasons you chose the landforms you did.

Section 2 Climate and Vegetation

Prepare to Read

Objectives

In this section you will

1. Discover the factors that influence Africa's climate.
2. Learn the characteristics of each of Africa's vegetation regions.
3. Find out how climate can affect the health of people in Africa.

Taking Notes

Copy the outline below. As you read, find details about Africa's climate and vegetation, and record them in your outline.

I. Africa's climate factors
  A. Distance from the Equator
    1.
    2.
  B.
II. Vegetation regions

Target Reading Skill

Paraphrase Paraphrasing can help you understand what you read. You paraphrase by restating what you have read in your own words.

For example, you could paraphrase the first paragraph on page 368 this way: "Africa has different kinds of vegetation in different parts of the continent. It has rain forests, savannas, and deserts."

As you read this section, paraphrase, or restate, the information following each red or blue heading.

Key Terms

- **irrigate** (IHR uh gayt) *v.* to supply with water through a ditch, pipe, channel, or sprinkler
- **drought** (drowt) *n.* a long period of little or no rain
- **oasis** (oh AY sis) *n.* a fertile place in a desert where there is water and vegetation
- **savanna** (suh VAN uh) *n.* a region of tall grasses with scattered trees
- **nomad** (NOH mad) *n.* a person who has no permanent, settled home and who instead moves from place to place

A home in a forest region of Uganda

If you were to travel throughout Africa, you would experience many different climates. Deserts would feel hot and dry. The highlands would feel cool and moist. In some places close to the Equator, hot weather and rainfall would occur throughout the year.

Africa's vegetation is as diverse as its climate. Forest regions are filled with trees and a great variety of plant life. Grasslands are dotted with low trees and scrub bushes. Low mountain areas support plant life, while the highest mountains are covered with snow and ice. A region's climate has a great influence on its vegetation. But what influences climate?

What Influences Climate?

Although people sometimes think of Africa as a hot place, not all parts of it are hot. That is because there are several geographic factors that influence climate. Some key factors are distance from the Equator and elevation. Nearness to large bodies of water and major landforms also affects climate.

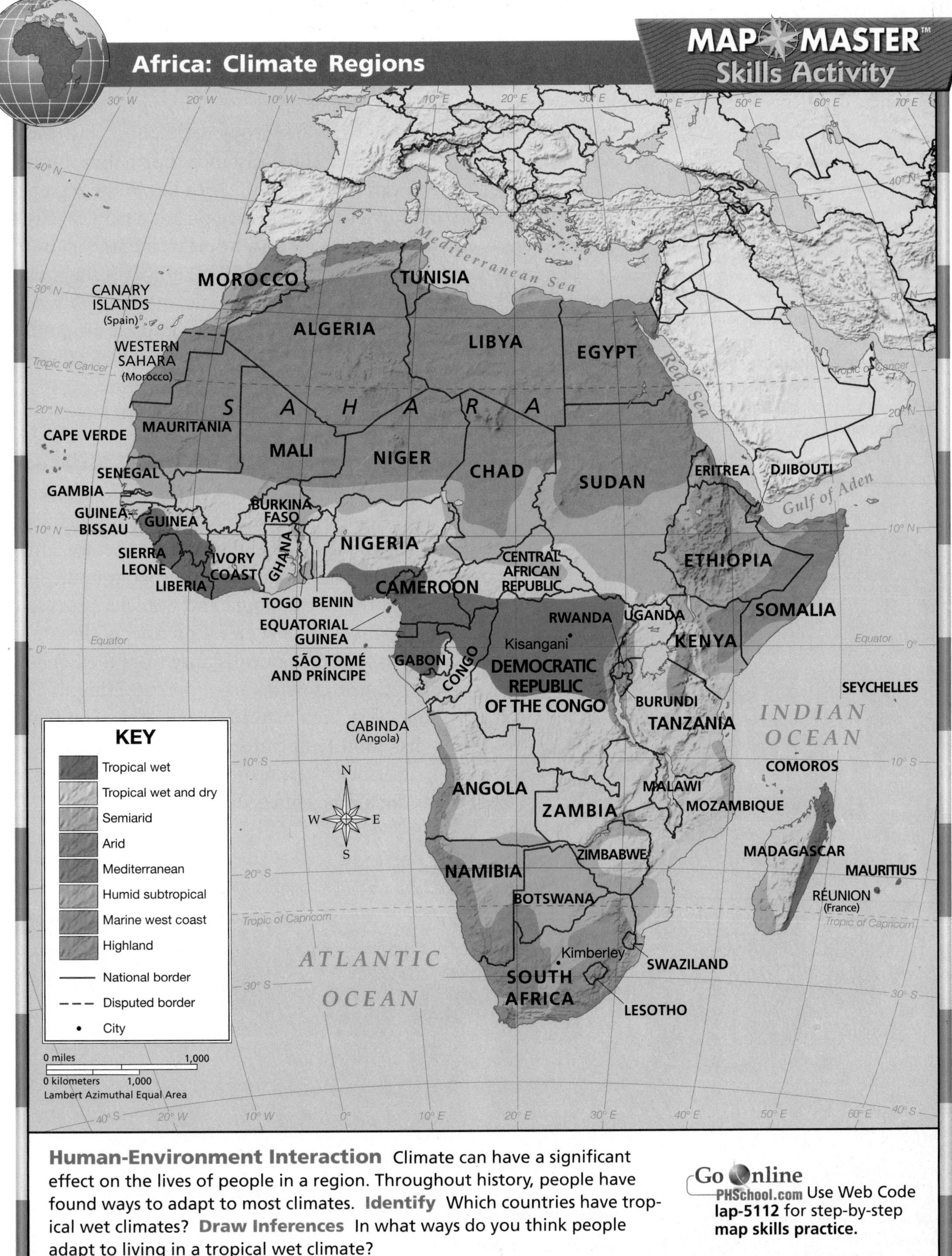

Human-Environment Interaction Climate can have a significant effect on the lives of people in a region. Throughout history, people have found ways to adapt to most climates. **Identify** Which countries have tropical wet climates? **Draw Inferences** In what ways do you think people adapt to living in a tropical wet climate?

Go Online PHSchool.com Use Web Code **lap-5112 for step-by-step map skills practice.**

Distance From the Equator Look at the map on page 365 titled Africa: Climate Regions. Notice that the Equator runs through the midsection of the continent. Regions near the Equator are usually hot. Now find the Tropic of Cancer and the Tropic of Capricorn, which are equal distances north and south of the Equator. As you can see, much of Africa lies in the region between these two lines of latitude. This region has a tropical climate. Therefore, much of Africa lies in a tropical climate region.

The location of a place in relation to the Equator influences more than the place's climate—it also influences the place's seasons. North of the Equator, winter and summer occur at the same time as they do in the United States and the rest of the Northern Hemisphere. South of the Equator, the seasons are reversed. For example, July in South Africa is the middle of winter.

Home to Many Animals
The open grasslands of Tanzania's Tarangire National Park are home to many thousands of large animals. Elephants may be seen in herds of 500 or more at a time. **Infer** *Given that animals thrive in this environment, do you think it has a mild or a harsh climate?*

The Role of Elevation Recall that elevation is the height of land above sea level. The higher the elevation, the cooler a place tends to be. For example, Mount Kilimanjaro, Africa's highest peak, is located close to the Equator. Yet ice and snow blanket the peak of Kilimanjaro year-round.

The countries of Ethiopia and Somalia provide another example of how elevation affects climate. They are about the same distance from the Equator, yet their climates are different. Ethiopia is on a very high plateau. Much of the country has mild temperatures and abundant rain. Farmers there grow a wide range of crops, including coffee, dates, and cereals.

Because Ethiopia usually gets plenty of rain, many farmers there do not irrigate their crops. To **irrigate** is to supply with water through a ditch, pipe, channel, or sprinkler. Even so, the country sometimes goes through a **drought** (drowt), or a long period of little or no rain. With little water, crops and livestock are harder to raise, and food becomes scarce. Ethiopia has suffered severe droughts several times since the 1980s.

Somalia is at a much lower elevation than Ethiopia is. The Somalian climate is hot and dry. Farming is possible only near a river or in or near an oasis, where crops can be irrigated. An **oasis** is a fertile place in a desert, with water and vegetation. Fresh underground water can support life in a region that gets little rain.

Unpredictable Rainfall Rainfall varies greatly from one region of Africa to another. Along parts of the west coast, winds carry moisture from the warm ocean over the land. Rainfall there averages more than 100 inches (250 centimeters) per year. Compare that with your own height. Forty inches (100 centimeters) of rain might fall during June alone. But in parts of the Sahara in the north and the Namib Desert in the south, rain may not fall at all for several years in a row.

Farmers who live in dry regions can never be sure whether there will be enough rain for their crops. Some farmers choose to plant a variety of crops, each needing a different amount of rainfall. These farmers hope they will have at least one successful crop.

✓ Reading Check **How does elevation affect the climate of regions in Africa?**

Graph Skills

The city of Kimberley is located in a desert region, while the city of Kisangani is located in a tropical region. **Identify** Which city has higher temperatures throughout the year? Which city gets more total rainfall in a year? **Synthesize Information** How does location help explain the differences in temperature and in rainfall?

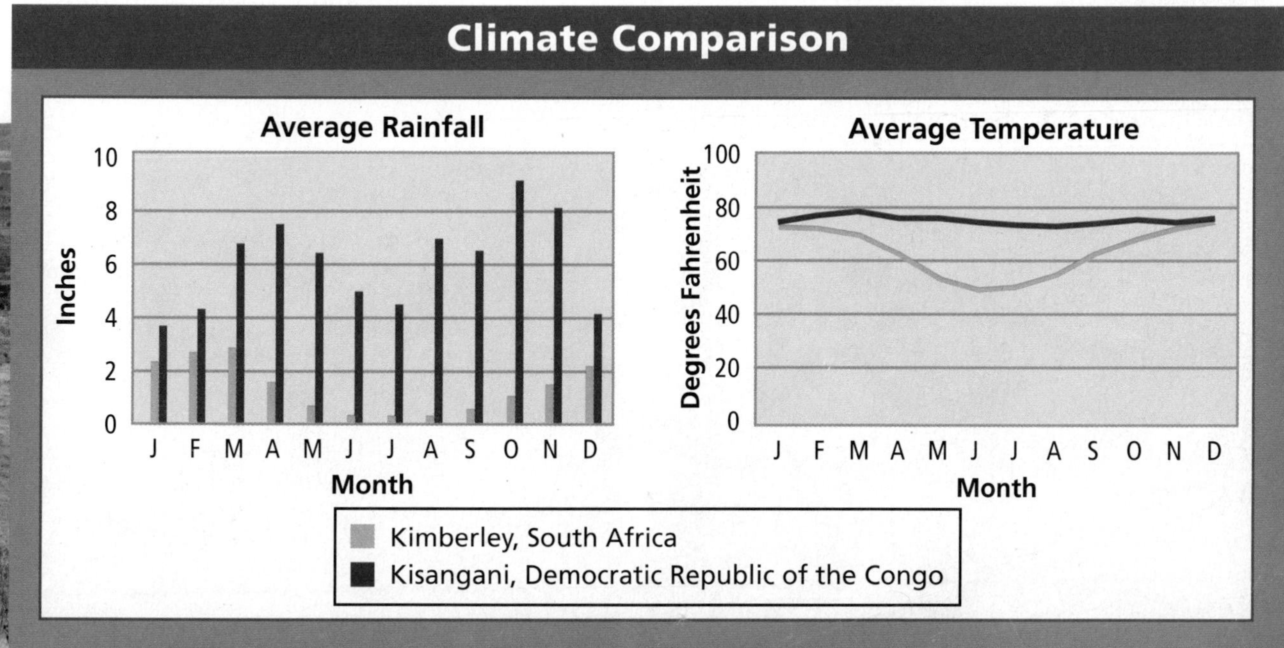

Vegetation Regions of Africa

Africa's vegetation varies across the land. Near the Equator, there are rain forests. North and south of the rain forests lie **savanna,** a region of tall grasses with scattered trees. Beyond the savanna, many parts of northern Africa, as well as the southwestern coast of the continent, are covered in desert.

Tropical Rain Forests Tropical rain forests are regions where rain falls often throughout the year. Rain forests exist in parts of West and Central Africa, covering close to 20 percent of the continent. Rain forests are well known for supporting a great number and variety of life forms. Forest moisture provides a rich environment of trees and plants that supports animals such as gorillas and chimpanzees.

People in rain forest regions live in towns, cities, or on farms built on cleared land. Cacao (kuh KAY oh), the plant from which chocolate is made, and cassava grow well in these regions. People also fish, hunt, and harvest timber in the rain forests. However, logging threatens these forests and the many species that live in them.

Tropical Savannas The most common vegetation in Africa is tropical savanna. Tall grasses, thorny bushes, and scattered trees grow in the savanna region. It is also home to large herd animals such as lions, elephants, and zebras. Tropical savannas cover more of Africa than any other type of vegetation.

The savanna has two seasons: dry and wet. During the dry season, farming is impossible. Trees lose their leaves and rivers run dry. Farmers use this time to trade, build houses, and visit friends. In the wet season, the land turns green and farmers plant crops.

World's Largest Desert
The Sahara is famous for sand dunes like the ones shown below. However, most of the Sahara is rock plateau or gravel. Mountains exist there as well.
Apply Information *Do you think the Sahara is an easy place for people and animals to live?*

Deserts in Africa Beyond the savanna lie the deserts. The immense Sahara extends across most of North Africa. This desert covers almost as much land as the entire United States. A journalist traveling in the Sahara described what she saw:

> **"[H]orizon-to-horizon vistas [views] of sand in a palette of colors, luxurious arches of palm trees swaying in the wind . . . heaving mountains of rough stone unbroken by the slightest sign of vegetation, vast expanses of sand obscured [hidden] by a veil of dust."**
>
> —*Christine Negroni,* The New York Times

The southern edge of the Sahara meets the savanna in a region called the Sahel (sah HEL), which is the Arabic word for "shore" or "border." The Sahel is very hot and dry. Each year it receives only 4 to 8 inches (10 to 20 centimeters) of rain. Small shrubs, grass, and some trees grow there.

The Namib and Kalahari deserts reach across Namibia and Botswana in Southern Africa. Large parts of the Kalahari are covered in scrub and small bushes, while the smaller Namib has more sand dunes.

The fennec fox, the world's smallest fox, lives in the Sahara.

The Sahara and the Sahel

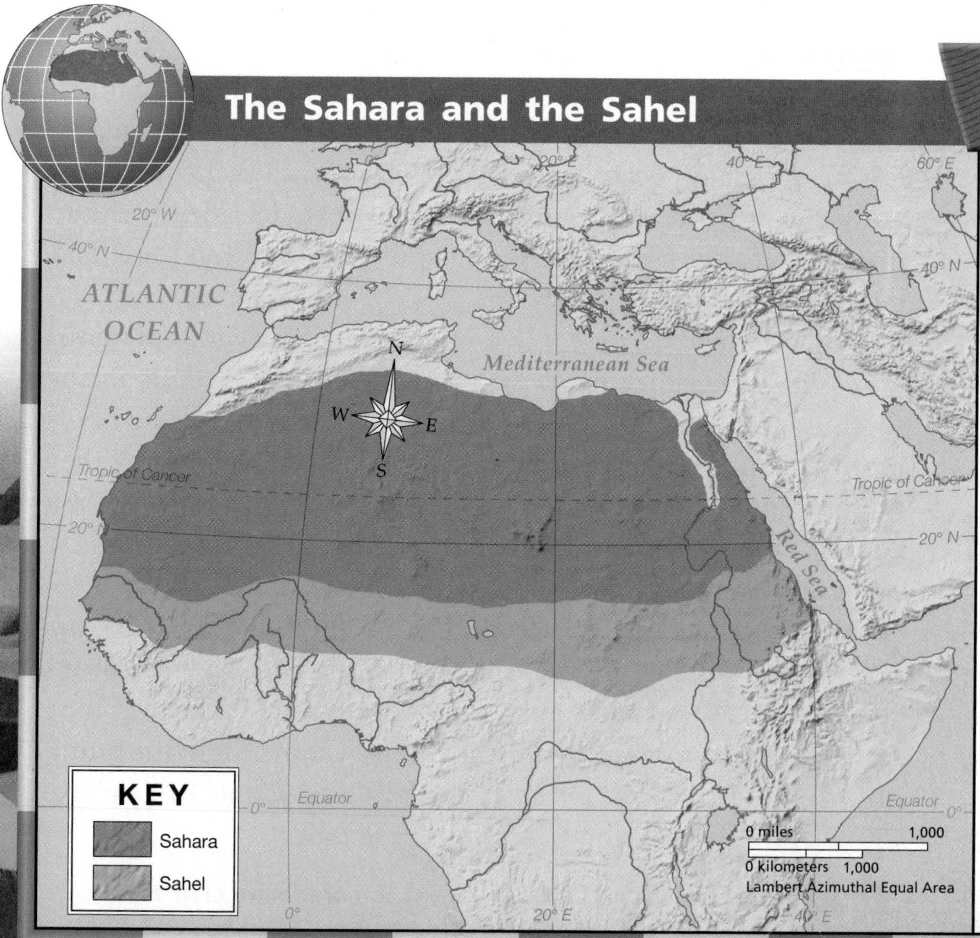

ATLANTIC OCEAN

Mediterranean Sea

Red Sea

Tropic of Cancer

Equator

KEY

Sahara

Sahel

0 miles 1,000

0 kilometers 1,000

Lambert Azimuthal Equal Area

MAP MASTER™ Skills Activity

Regions Unlike the Sahara, the Sahel does receive some rain. However, rain falls in the Sahel only during the summer months. **Locate** In what direction does the Sahel lie in relation to the Sahara? **Analyze Information** How does this location help explain why the Sahel gets more rain than the Sahara does?

Go Online
PHSchool.com Use Web Code **lap-5122** for step-by-step **map skills practice.**

A desert nomad traveling through the Sahara with his camel

Desert Living Few people live in Africa's deserts. Most of those who do are **nomads,** or people who have no permanent, settled home. Nomads move around to various places, often following the same route each year, to make their living. Most nomads are herders who also take part in trade. They travel to places where they know they can find water and food for their herds of goats, camels, or sheep.

Some nomadic herders live mainly in Africa's mountainous areas. In spring, they leave their winter grazing grounds in the foothills and head up into the mountains. Other nomadic herders live mainly in the flat desert areas. During the dry season, they set up tents near oases (oh AY seez). When the rainy season comes, they move their goats and camels to pastures that are better for grazing.

Desert nomads have herded camels for hundreds of years because the animals are well suited to desert life. They are large, strong animals that can transport goods on their backs over long distances. In addition, when a camel eats, it stores fat in the hump on its back. If no food or water is available, a camel can survive for several days by using the stored fat as food.

√ Reading Check **What kinds of vegetation are found in Africa's savanna regions?**

Links Across The World

The Oldest Sunscreen In the United States, people often wear sunscreen to protect their skin from sunburn. But in vast desert regions like the Sahara, sunscreen is unknown. Desert nomads hide their skin from the sun by wearing long, loose robes that cover them from head to toe.

Climate and Health

The climate people live in can affect their health. Throughout Africa, there are regions that present health risks to livestock and people. In rain forest regions, the moist environment is home to many disease-carrying insects. Even in the drier grasslands, disease and illness take their toll.

Paraphrase Use your own words to paraphrase the paragraph at the left. What would be a good way to restate *take their toll*? In your own words, you might say "disease and illness cause serious problems."

Sleeping Sickness Nearly one fifth of Africa is home to the tsetse (TSET see) fly, a pest that makes raising cattle almost impossible. A tsetse bite can kill cattle and can cause a disease called sleeping sickness in humans. African researchers, together with cattle herders, have worked to find ways to control the spread of the tsetse fly. Cattle herders in Kenya are setting traps for flies. Herders in the country of Uganda catch flies by sewing into tents netting that contains poison.

Malaria Another disease, malaria (muh LEHR ee uh), is spread to humans by the bite of an infected mosquito. Mosquitoes thrive in warm, moist climates and breed in swamps, ponds, and pools of standing water. These conditions make malaria a particular problem in parts of Africa south of the Sahara. Researchers continue to look for ways of fighting the spread of malaria. Protective clothing and insecticide can help prevent infection.

✓ Reading Check **What is being done to control the spread of the tsetse fly?**

Section 2 Assessment

Key Terms
Review the key terms at the beginning of this section. Use each term in a sentence that explains its meaning.

Target Reading Skill
Read the paragraphs under Desert Living on page 370. Then, paraphrase the paragraphs in 25 words or fewer.

Comprehension and Critical Thinking
1. (a) **Identify** Name three factors that influence climate.
(b) **Summarize** Give an example of how one of these factors can influence the climate of an area.
2. (a) **Name** Identify the types of vegetation found in each of Africa's four regions.
(b) **Identify Effects** How do climate and vegetation affect the ways Africans make a living?
3. (a) **Recall** What health risks do people and animals in different climate regions of Africa face?
(b) **Draw Conclusions** In which of Africa's climate regions do you think you would be least likely to contract malaria?

Writing Activity
Choose a region of Africa that you would like to live in or visit. Write a short essay about the climate and vegetation. Include several reasons why the region is of interest to you.

For: An activity on vegetation in Africa
Visit: PHSchool.com
Web Code: lad-5102

Interpreting Diagrams

Africa makes up about one fifth of all the land on Earth. It is a plateau continent with sloping coastal plains, a broad central basin, towering mountains, and a deep rift, or crack, in Earth's surface. If you drove across the widest stretch of Africa, going 65 miles (105 kilometers) per hour and not stopping for gas or sleep, the trip would take about three full days.

An effective way to learn about Africa's landforms is by looking at a cross-sectional diagram. A cross section is what you would see if you sliced through the continent from its highest point to its lowest point and looked at it from the side.

Learn the Skill

To interpret information in any type of diagram, including a cross-sectional diagram, follow the steps below.

1. **Study the diagram.** Notice the various parts of the diagram. What can you learn from the title? What details are shown?
2. **Read the labels.** Notice the lines that lead from each label to the cross section. Make sure you understand what all the labels refer to.
3. **Summarize the information in the diagram.** Describe what you learned from studying the diagram and its labels.

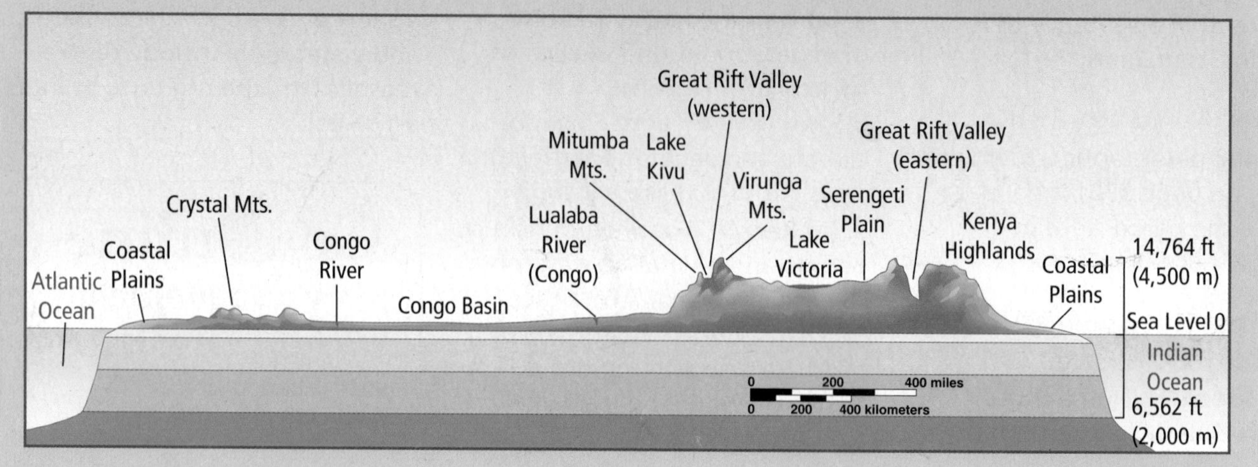

Practice the Skill

Study the cross section of Africa on page 372. Use the steps below to interpret the diagram and learn about Africa's landforms.

1. Look at the diagram. What information can you learn from the title? What kinds of landforms are shown?
2. Examine the labels. Name the mountain ranges and bodies of water shown in the diagram. Identify the elevation of at least three features in the diagram.
3. Write a sentence or two describing the ways in which the elevation of Africa changes as you travel from the Atlantic Ocean to the Indian Ocean.

Apply the Skill

Study the diagram of Earth's movements on pages M2–M3 of the MapMaster Skills Handbook. In a sentence or two, summarize the information given in the diagram.

The Virunga Mountains of East Africa

Section 3 Resources and Land Use

Prepare to Read

Objectives

In this section you will

1. Discover the ways in which Africans make use of their agricultural resources.
2. Learn about the mineral and energy resources found in Africa.
3. Find out what African countries are doing to improve their economic health.

Taking Notes

As you read, look for details about Africa's natural resources. Copy the chart below, and use it to record your findings.

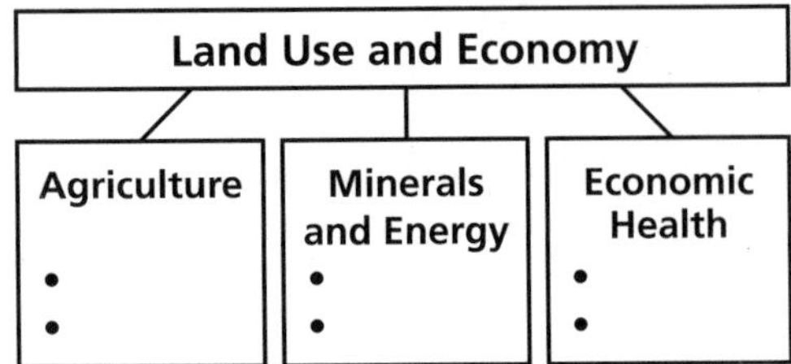

Target Reading Skill

Summarize When you summarize, you review what you have read so far. Then you state the main points in the correct order. Summarizing what you read is a good technique to help you comprehend and study. As you read, pause occasionally to summarize what you have read.

Key Terms

- **subsistence farming** (sub SIS tuns FAHR ming) *n.* raising just enough crops to support one's family
- **cash crop** (kash krahp) *n.* a crop that is raised for sale
- **economy** (ih KAHN uh mee) *n.* a system for producing, distributing, consuming, and owning goods and services
- **diversify** (duh VUR suh fy) *v.* to add variety to; to expand a country's economy by increasing the variety of goods produced

Cacao beans (inset photo) grow on trees as shown below.

"Here, in this load, I bear the seeds of a wonderful tree which, if cultivated in this land, will bless its sons everlastingly with wealth, and people far and near with health. These are the seeds of the cacao tree which I have brought with me from across the sea. . . . Would you, therefore, be kind enough to grant me a mere acre of land in this neighborhood to try my luck, and yours, and that of this country as a whole?"

—*from the play* Cocoa Comes to Mampong *by Michael Francis Dei-Anang*

In the excerpt above, the character Tete Quarshie (TEH tay KWAWR shee) asks for land on which to plant cacao trees in Ghana. These trees, from which cocoa and chocolate are made, originally grew only in Central and South America. As Americans, Europeans, and Africans began to trade with one another, they found that cacao trees could grow in West Africa. In the play, the people grant Tete Quarshie the land, who then raises the first crop of cacao beans in Ghana. Cacao is now one of Africa's many agricultural resources.

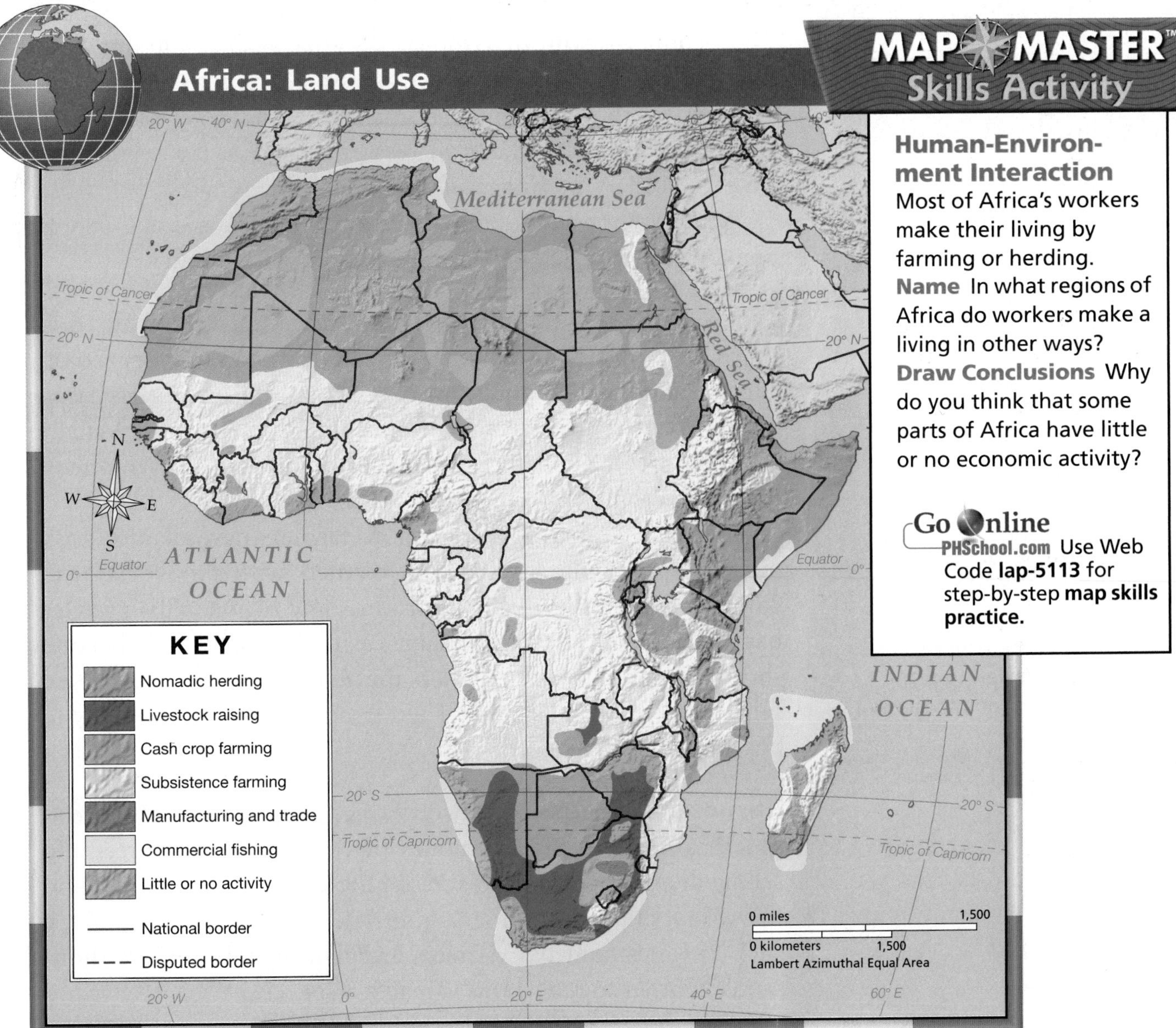

MAP MASTER™ Skills Activity

Human-Environment Interaction Most of Africa's workers make their living by farming or herding.
Name In what regions of Africa do workers make a living in other ways?
Draw Conclusions Why do you think that some parts of Africa have little or no economic activity?

Go Online PHSchool.com Use Web Code **lap-5113** for step-by-step **map skills practice.**

Agricultural Resources

Most Africans are farmers. Some of these farmers live in areas with fertile soil and much rain. But most live on land that is extremely difficult or impossible to farm because of poor soil or too little rain.

Farming to Live On the map above, you can see how much of Africa's land is used for **subsistence farming,** or raising just enough crops to support one's family. Subsistence farmers may sell or trade a few crops for other items they need.

In North African countries such as Morocco, subsistence farmers raise barley and wheat. They also irrigate fields to grow fruits and vegetables. Farms at Saharan oases in Egypt produce dates and small crops of barley and wheat.

In countries with dry tropical savanna, such as Burkina Faso (bur KEE nuh FAH soh) and Niger, subsistence farmers grow grains. In regions with more rainfall, farmers also grow vegetables, fruits, and root crops such as yams and cassava. Tapioca (tap ee OH kuh), which is used in the United States to make pudding, is made from cassava. In West Africa, corn and rice are important crops. People in many of Africa's cultures fish or raise goats or poultry.

Crops for Sale In all regions of Africa, farmers grow **cash crops,** or crops that are raised for sale. Farmers in Ivory Coast, Ghana, and Cameroon grow cash crops of coffee and cacao beans. Farmers in Kenya, Tanzania (tan zuh NEE uh), Malawi (MAH lah wee), Zimbabwe, and Mozambique grow tea as one of their cash crops.

Target Skill **Summarize** To summarize the paragraph at the right, first state the main points. An important point is that more African farmers have started to plant cash crops. Which point follows that one?

In recent years, more and more farmers have planted cash crops. As a result, less land is planted with crops that can completely meet a family's needs. In some regions, this practice has led to food shortages when cash crops have failed. Food shortages can also occur when the market prices of coffee or other cash crops fall steeply. Then families receive less money to buy the things they need.

Harvesting Trees Hardwood trees grow in all four regions of Africa. People can earn money by cutting down the trees and selling them. Thousands of acres of these trees have been cut and the wood shipped to other countries. A number of countries, such as Kenya and Ivory Coast, are planting trees by the thousands in order to renew this valuable resource.

√ Reading Check **What are some of the crops grown in Africa, and where are they grown?**

Replanting the Forest
Thousands of Kenyan women have responded to the cutting down of trees in their country. Like the women shown here, they have prepared millions of young trees for local families to plant. **Predict** *How easy do you think it will be for people in Kenya to replace all the cut trees?*

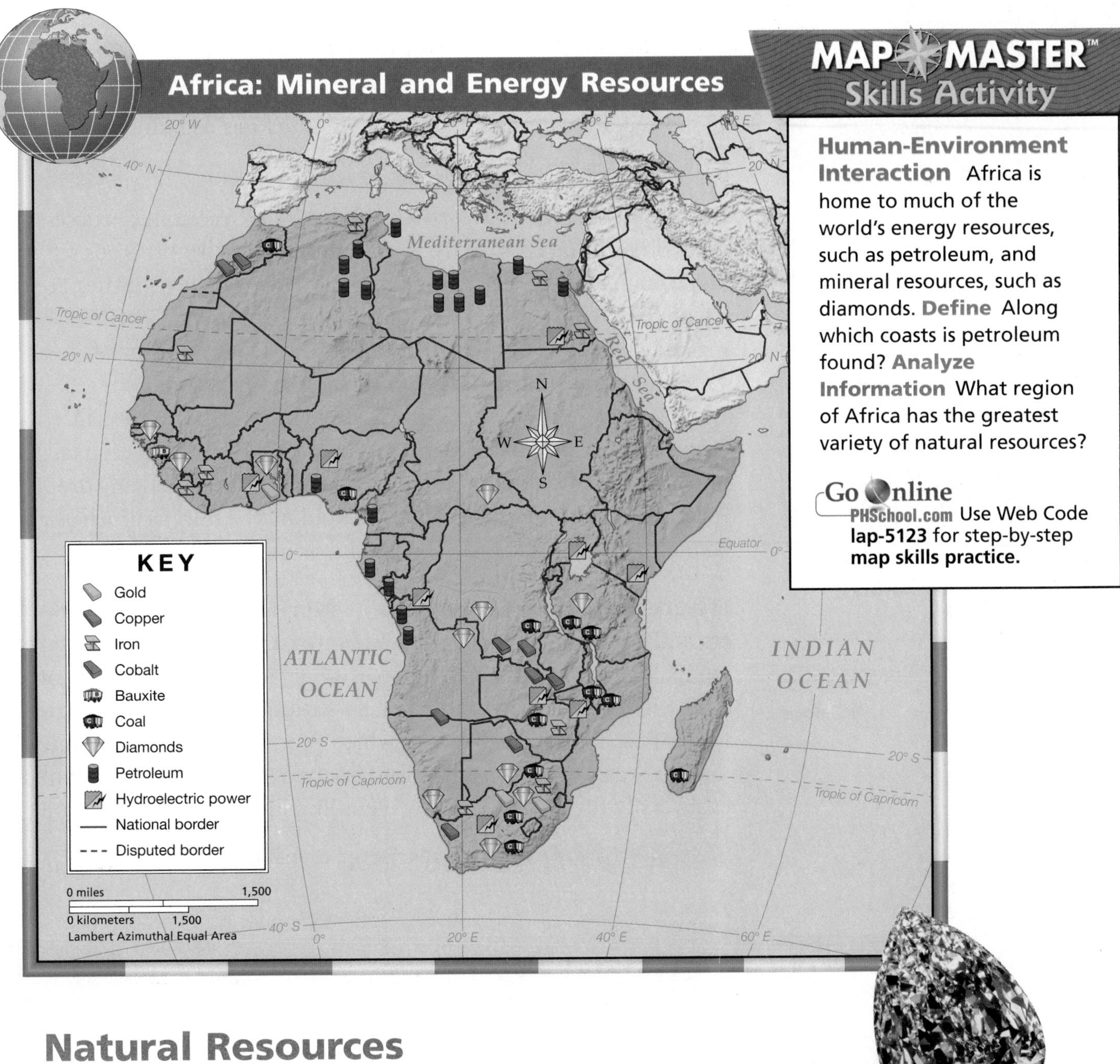

MAP MASTER™ Skills Activity

Human-Environment Interaction Africa is home to much of the world's energy resources, such as petroleum, and mineral resources, such as diamonds. **Define** Along which coasts is petroleum found? **Analyze Information** What region of Africa has the greatest variety of natural resources?

Go Online PHSchool.com Use Web Code **lap-5123** for step-by-step **map skills practice.**

Natural Resources

Each African country has its own economy. An **economy** is a system for producing, distributing, consuming, and owning goods and services. You have read that farming is an important part of many African economies. The same is true of mining. Look at the map above. Notice how many countries conduct mining operations.

Parts of Africa are rich in mineral resources. Some African countries have large amounts of petroleum, which is used to make oil and gasoline. Major oil producers include Libya and Algeria in North Africa, and Nigeria, Cameroon, Gabon, and Angola along the west coast of Africa. Ghana is a leading exporter of gold. Other mineral resources from Africa include copper, silver, uranium, titanium, and diamonds.

Diamonds that have just been mined (bottom photo) are not nearly as dazzling as ones that have been cut (top photo).

✓ **Reading Check** **How is petroleum used?**

A man assembling electronic equipment in Johannesburg, South Africa

Improving Economic Health

As you have read, most of Africa's workers are farmers. When an economy of a nation is dependent on one kind of industry, such as farming, it is called a specialized economy.

Strengthening Economies In Africa, economic success relies on farming regions receiving enough rainfall, and crops selling at high enough prices. For that reason, African countries are trying to diversify (duh VUR suh fy) their economies. To **diversify** means to add variety. These countries are working to produce a variety of crops, raw materials, and manufactured goods.

In general, a diverse economy is more flexible than a specialized economy is. For example, suppose a country's major cash crop fails or world prices for one of its major mineral exports suddenly drop. A country with a diverse economy would not be hurt as much as a country that depends only on farming or mining.

Where Does the Money Go? Mining requires many workers and costly equipment. Throughout much of Africa, foreign companies mine African resources and take the profits out of Africa. This system does little to help African economies. In addition, Africa has few factories in which products from its own raw materials can be made. Therefore, many African countries want to diversify their economies by including manufacturing.

√ Reading Check **What is a specialized economy?**

Section 3 Assessment

Key Terms

Review the key terms at the beginning of this section. Use each term in a sentence that explains its meaning.

Target Reading Skill

Reread the paragraphs under Improving Economic Health. Then write a summary of them. Include at least two main points.

Comprehension and Critical Thinking

1. (a) **Recall** What makes most land Africans live on hard to farm?
(b) Compare and Contrast Compare subsistence farming with farming to raise cash crops. How are they similar? How are they different?
2. (a) **Identify** What are some of the important natural resources found in Africa?
(b) Draw Conclusions What do you think happens to most of Africa's mineral resources after they are mined?
3. (a) **Recall** What kind of work is done by most Africans?
(b) Predict In what ways could African countries benefit from diversifying their economies?

Writing Activity

List some of Africa's natural resources that you and your family use. Which resource would you miss most if you did not have it? Write a paragraph explaining why.

For: An activity on natural resources in Africa
Visit: PHSchool.com
Web Code: lad-5103

Review and Assessment

◆ Chapter Summary

Section 1: Land and Water

- Africa can be divided into four regions: North, West, East, and Central and Southern. Africa's major landforms include plateaus, mountains, coastal plains, and a rift valley.
- Africa's four major rivers are the Nile, the Congo, the Zambezi, and the Niger.

Section 2: Climate and Vegetation

- Distance from the Equator and elevation are both factors that influence climate.
- Africa's vegetation regions include tropical rain forests, tropical savannas, and deserts.
- Disease-carrying insects thrive in some of Africa's climate regions, threatening the health of the people who live there.

Section 3: Resources and Land Use

- Africa's agricultural resources are used for subsistence farming and cash crops.
- Natural resources, such as minerals, are an important part of African economies.
- African countries are working to improve their economic health by diversifying their specialized economies.

Kassala Mountains, Sudan

◆ Key Terms

Choose the key term from the list that best completes each sentence.

1. _____ is the height of land above sea level.
2. A(n) _____ is a deep crack in the surface of Earth.
3. A(n) _____ flows into a river.
4. People who practice _____ raise just enough crops to support their families.
5. A(n) _____ is a region of tall grasses with scattered trees.
6. In areas that receive plenty of rain, many farmers do not need to _____ their crops.
7. A nomad traveling through the Sahara would probably visit a(n) _____ for water.
8. A(n) _____ is a system for producing, distributing, consuming, and owning goods and services.
9. To _____ is to add variety.
10. A period of little or no rainfall is a(n) _____.

Key Terms
plateau
elevation
drought
rift
fertile
tributary
irrigate
oasis
savanna
nomad
subsistence farming
cash crop
economy
diversify

Chapter 11 Review and Assessment (continued)

◆ Comprehension and Critical Thinking

11. **(a) Describe** Describe the physical features of each of the major rivers in Africa.
(b) Identify Cause and Effect How did the regular flooding of the Nile in the past affect farmers in the Nile Valley? How did the building of the Aswan High Dam change life for farmers?

12. **(a) Recall** What do elevation and distance from the Equator have to do with climate?
(b) Explain Why are some parts of Africa cold even though they are near the Equator?
(c) Compare and Contrast Compare the climates of Ethiopia and Somalia. Explain why their climates are similar or different.

13. **(a) Locate** Where in Africa can you find tropical savannas? Tropical rain forests? Deserts?
(b) Describe What characterizes the climate and plant life of each vegetation region?
(c) Apply Information Choose one of these regions and describe how the people who live there adapt to their environment. Give examples.

14. **(a) Name** List three cash crops raised in Africa.
(b) Identify Causes Why is there little or no farming in much of North Africa and parts of Southern Africa?
(c) Summarize Why and in what ways are many African nations trying to strengthen and diversify their economies?

◆ Skills Practice

Interpreting Diagrams You have learned how to interpret diagrams in this chapter's Skills for Life activity. You have also learned how to summarize information found in diagrams.

Review the steps you followed to learn this skill. Then turn to the diagram of Earth's longitude on page M5 of the MapMaster Skills Handbook. Identify and summarize the main ideas in the diagram.

◆ Writing Activity: Math

Make a bar graph that shows the lengths of rivers in Africa. Include the four rivers mentioned in the chapter as well as at least three others that you research on your own. Then write a short paragraph comparing the lengths of the various rivers.

MAP MASTER™ Skills Activity

Place Location For each place listed, write the letter from the map that shows its location.

1. Nile River
2. Congo River
3. Sahara
4. Namib Desert
5. Zambezi River
6. Kalahari Desert
7. Niger River
8. Great Rift Valley

Go Online PHSchool.com Use Web Code **lap-5120** for an **interactive map.**

Africa

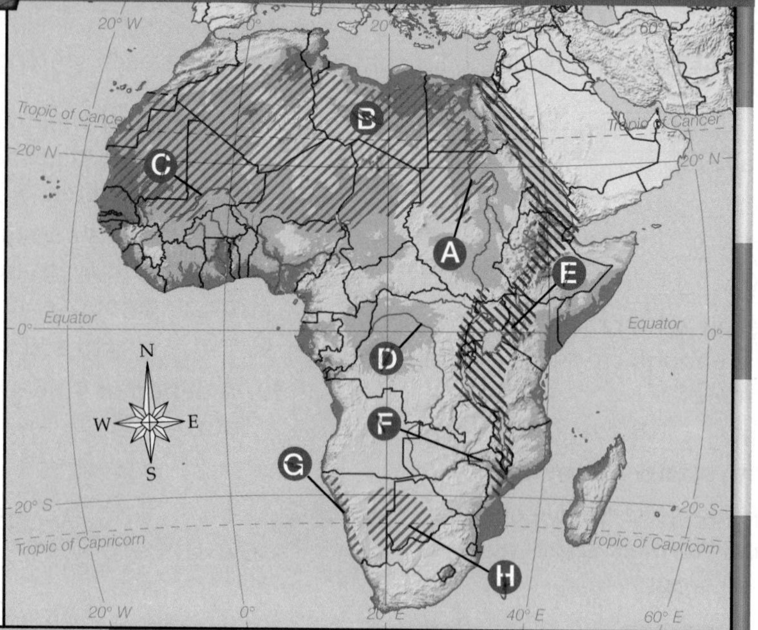

Standardized Test Prep

Test-Taking Tips

Some questions on standardized tests ask you to analyze parts of maps. Study the map key below. Then follow the tips to answer the sample question.

KEY

- Nomadic herding
- Livestock raising
- Commercial farming
- Subsistence farming
- Manufacturing and trade
- Little or no activity

TIP On a map key, the color column lines up with the data in the information column. To find the information you need, move from a given color to the data on the right.

Pick the letter that best answers the question.

On a land-use map, Angola is colored mostly yellow with a small amount of light green. Using the key at the left, you can determine that the people of Angola

A make a great deal of money.

B use the land mainly to support themselves.

C export many products.

D use their land in many different ways.

TIP Restate the question in your own words to make sure you understand it: *What conclusion can you draw from the map key about the people of Angola and their land?*

Think It Through Yellow on the map stands for subsistence farming. Light green stands for commercial farming. Subsistence farmers grow just enough food to feed and support their families. Since most of Angola is colored yellow, you can rule out A and D. Commercial farmers may raise their crops for export. However, since most of Angola is yellow, you can rule out C also. The correct answer is B.

Practice Questions

Use the tips above and other tips in this book to help you answer the following questions.

1. Most of North Africa is along the border of the
   A Mediterranean Sea.
   B Indian Ocean.
   C Atlantic Ocean.
   D Red Sea.

2. Areas that are higher in elevation
   A tend to be closer to the Equator.
   B tend to be cooler than places lower in elevation.
   C have very mild climates.
   D have little or no rainfall.

3. African economies
   A are based largely on manufacturing.
   B could benefit from increased diversification.
   C rely solely on exports.
   D are usually dependent on a wide variety of industries.

Study the map key below, and then answer the question that follows.

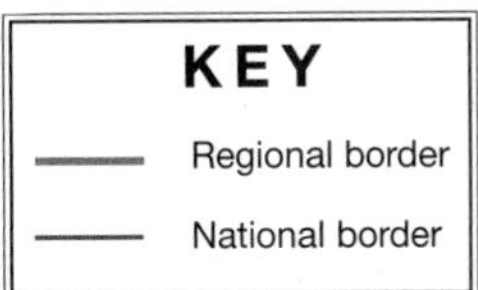

4. The boundaries of Egypt are marked by black and red lines. Using the key, you can conclude that
   A Egypt is part of two regions of Africa.
   B Egypt borders other nations of Africa but not other regions.
   C Egypt borders other regions of Africa but not other nations.
   D Egypt borders other regions and nations.

Use Web Code **laa-5100** for **Chapter 11 self-test.**

Chapter 12

Africa: Shaped by Its History

Chapter Preview

This chapter will introduce you to the history of Africa and help you understand how historical events have affected people throughout the region.

Target Reading Skill

Reading Process In this chapter you will focus on processes that help you understand and remember what you read. Setting a purpose, predicting, asking questions, and using prior knowledge are all processes that will help you learn as you read.

▶ **This ancient Egyptian mural, painted on an interior wall of a tomb, is more than 3,000 years old.**

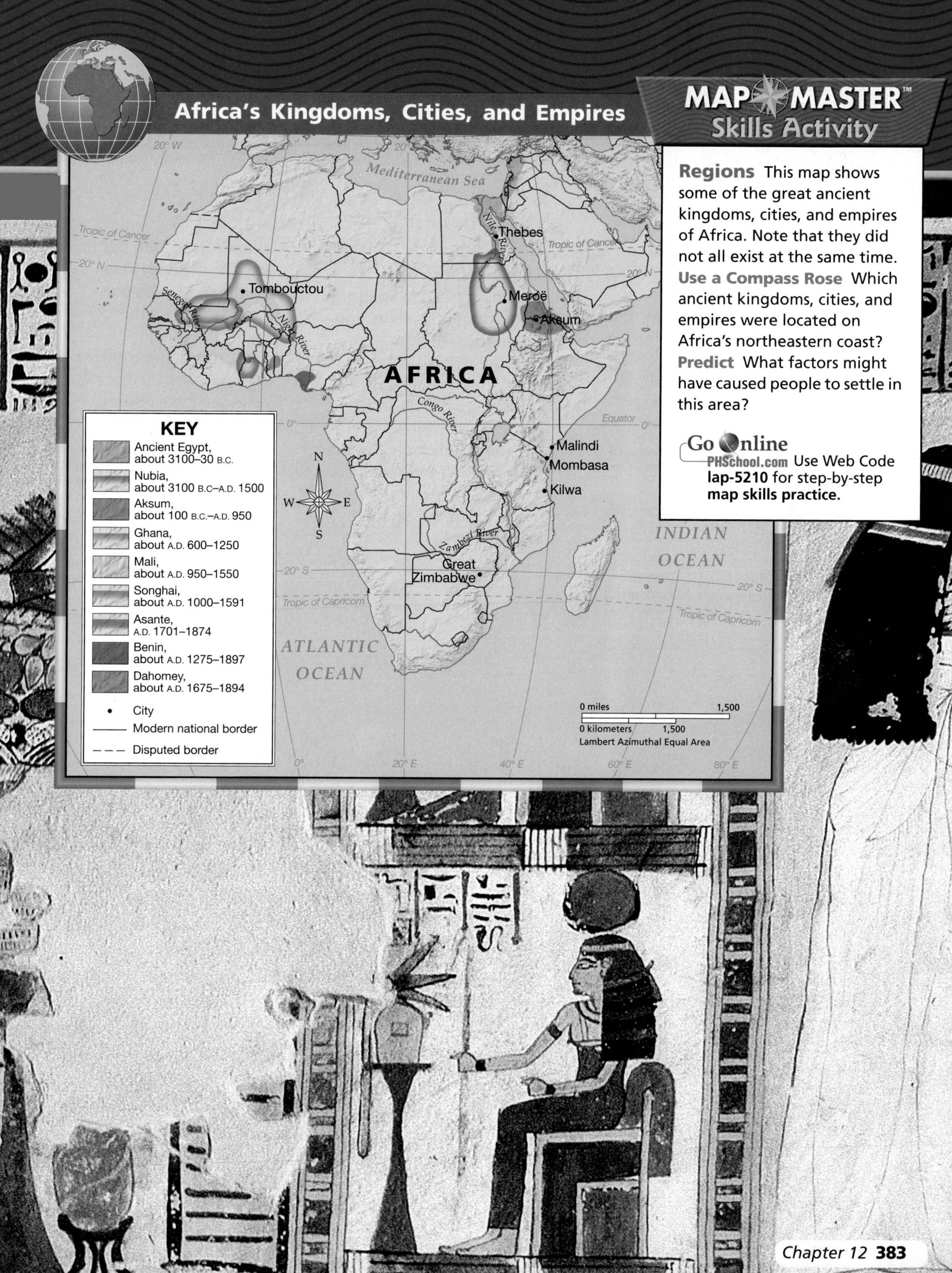

MAP MASTER™ Skills Activity

Regions This map shows some of the great ancient kingdoms, cities, and empires of Africa. Note that they did not all exist at the same time.
Use a Compass Rose Which ancient kingdoms, cities, and empires were located on Africa's northeastern coast?
Predict What factors might have caused people to settle in this area?

Go Online PHSchool.com Use Web Code **lap-5210** for step-by-step **map skills practice.**

Section 1 African Beginnings

Prepare to Read

Objectives

In this section you will

1. Examine the ways in which the survival skills of early Africans changed over time.
2. Find out about early civilizations that arose along the Nile River.
3. Learn about the Bantu migrations.

Taking Notes

As you read, look for details about Africa's first people. Copy the chart below, and use it to record your findings.

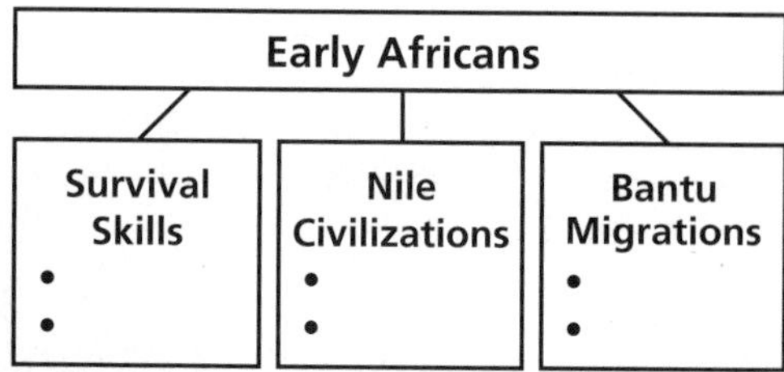

Target Reading Skill

Set a Purpose for Reading When you set a purpose for reading, you give yourself a focus. Before you read this section, look at the headings and illustrations to see what the section is about. Then set a purpose for reading this section. Your purpose might be to learn about the people who lived in Africa long ago. Finally, read to meet your purpose.

Key Terms

- **domesticate** (duh MES tih kayt) *v.* to adapt wild plants or animals and breed them for human use
- **civilization** (sih vuh luh ZAY shun) *n.* a society that has cities, a central government, and social classes and that usually has writing, art, and architecture
- **migrate** (MY grayt) *v.* to move from one place to settle in another
- **ethnic group** (ETH nik groop) *n.* a group of people who share the same ancestors, culture, language, or religion

Today, the dry sands and rocks of the Sahara cover most of North Africa. But 10,000 years ago, this large area held enough water to support many people and animals. Scientists think Africa's first farmers lived in the Sahara. Ancient paintings on cliffs and cave walls tell their story.

The history of humans in Africa goes back even further in time than the history of farmers in the Sahara. Scientists believe that our early human ancestors lived in East Africa at least 2 million years ago. Today, scientists study the stone tools and bones that these ancestors left behind. By doing so, they learn about the ways our early human ancestors found to survive.

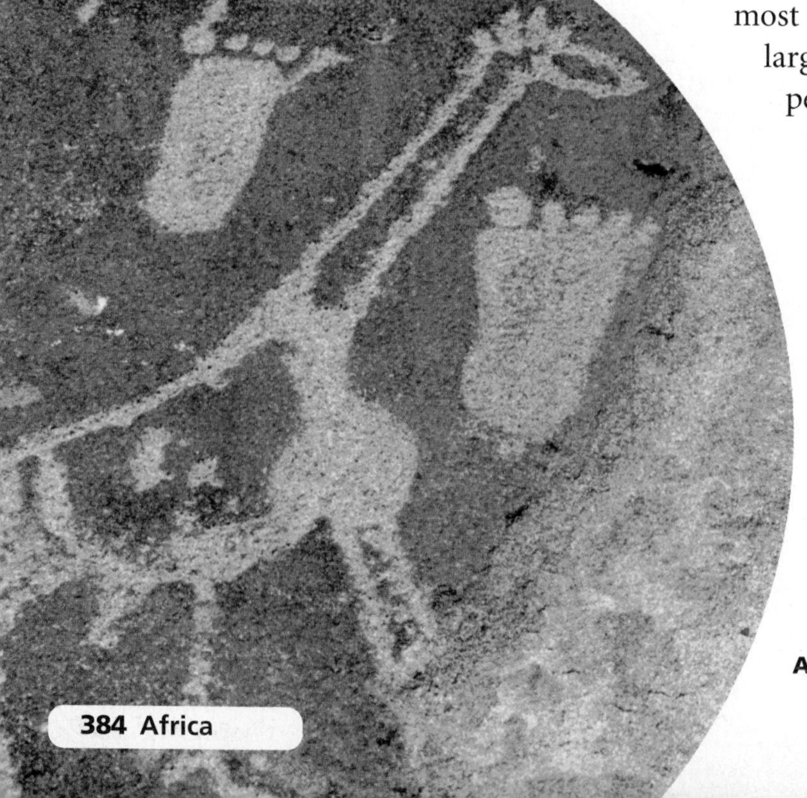

Ancient cave painting from Namibia

Changing Survival Skills

What skills did our early human ancestors need to survive? Like people today, they needed to find food, water, and shelter to live. Survival skills changed and developed over the course of many thousands of years.

Hunting and Gathering Our early human ancestors were hunter-gatherers. A hunter-gatherer is someone who hunts animals and gathers food in the wild to survive. Hunter-gatherers hunted animals to use the meat for food and the hides and fur for clothing and shelter. They ate foods such as fruits, nuts, and roots. They made tools out of wood, animal bones, and eventually stone. The first use of stone tools marks the beginning of a time period scientists call the Stone Age.

The stone tools made by our early human ancestors worked very well. The scientist Louis Leakey found some of the first evidence of human ancestors in East Africa. He also taught himself how to make and use their tools. Using a two-inch, 25,000-year-old stone knife, Leakey could skin and cut up a gazelle in just 20 minutes.

Studying Early Human Ancestors This stone tool (above) was made by one of our early human ancestors. For more than 30 years, Louis Leakey studied finds like this one at Olduvai Gorge (left) in Tanzania. His family (below) also studied them. **Analyze Images** *Do you find it easy or hard to tell this stone tool from an ordinary stone?*

Set a Purpose What purpose did you set for the section? Has the text you have read so far helped you toward achieving this purpose? If not, set a new purpose for the rest of the section.

Farming and Herding Between 10,000 and 6,000 years ago, some hunter-gatherers began to farm and to herd animals. As you read earlier, farming in Africa probably began in North Africa, when the area that is now the Sahara offered more water than is available there today. The first farmers probably planted wild grains such as barley. At first, gatherers just protected the areas where these grains grew best. Then they began to save some seeds to plant for the next year's crop.

Later, people began to **domesticate** plants, or adapt them for their own use. They threw away seeds from weaker plants and saved seeds from stronger ones. People also domesticated certain wild animals by taming and breeding them.

Early Settlements Domesticating plants and animals meant people could have better control over their food supply. They did not have to travel to places where grains were already growing. Instead, they planted the crops they wanted. As a result, they could settle in one place. Most early farmers settled on fertile land near a water supply. Some communities produced a food surplus, or more than what was needed. Surpluses allowed some people in the community to do work other than farming.

√ Reading Check **What was the Stone Age?**

African Farmers Today
In African communities that practice agriculture today, women play a variety of roles. Here, Central African women carry firewood to their homes. **Predict** *What activities are essential to a successful agricultural community?*

Civilizations on the Nile

Over a period of hundreds of thousands of years, some Stone Age groups became civilizations. A **civilization** is a society with cities, a government, and social classes. A social class is a group that is made up of people with similar backgrounds, wealth, and ways of living. Social classes form when people do different jobs. The types of jobs people do determine whether they are rich, poor, or in the middle. Civilizations also usually have architecture, writing, and art. A few thousand years ago, two important African civilizations—Egypt and Nubia—arose along the Nile River.

Egypt Each summer, the Nile River used to flood its banks. The flooding waters would cover the ground with a layer of fertile silt that was ideal for farming because it enriched the soil. Around 5000 B.C., people began farming along the river's banks. They settled in scattered villages. Over many years, these villages grew into the civilization of ancient Egypt.

Ancient Egypt was ruled by kings and queens. The kings of Egypt were called pharaohs (FEHR ohz). The people believed that their pharaohs were also gods. When kings and queens died, they were buried in tombs. Some of the tombs were built as large pyramids. People painted murals and picture-writing symbols called hieroglyphs (HY ur oh glifs) on the inner walls of the tombs. The ancient Egyptians became skilled in papermaking, architecture, medicine, and astronomy.

Nubia In about 6000 B.C., settled hunting and fishing communities began to arise along the Nile south of Egypt. About 1,000 years later, these communities began farming. This area was called Nubia. Scientists believe the formation of Nubian kingdoms may have started around 3100 B.C.

One of the greatest Nubian kingdoms was centered in the city of Napata. Around 724 B.C., the Nubians of Napata conquered Egypt. Nubians ruled Egypt for about 60 years. A later Nubian kingdom was based farther south, in the city of Meroë (MEHR oh ee). Meroë began to weaken in the A.D. 200s. It was finally conquered in A.D. 350 by invading forces from the Ethiopian kingdom of Aksum (AHK soom).

Leftover From Ancient Times
The Nubian mural (top) was painted inside a tomb more than 3,000 years ago. The pair of Egyptian leather sandals (above), which are similar to the ones shown in the mural, are more than 5,000 years old. **Infer** *What kind of information can objects like these teach us about ancient civilizations?*

✓ Reading Check **What are social classes, and how are they formed?**

MAP MASTER™ Skills Activity

Movement The Bantu migrations were some of the largest movements of people in history. As a result, millions of Africans today speak Bantu languages. **Identify** Where did the Bantu migrations begin? **Analyze Information** Notice that the arrows on the map change color to show time passing. Which place did the migrations reach first, Lake Tanganyika or the Orange River?

Go Online PHSchool.com Use Web Code **lap-5211** for step-by-step **map skills practice.**

Routes of the Bantu Migrations

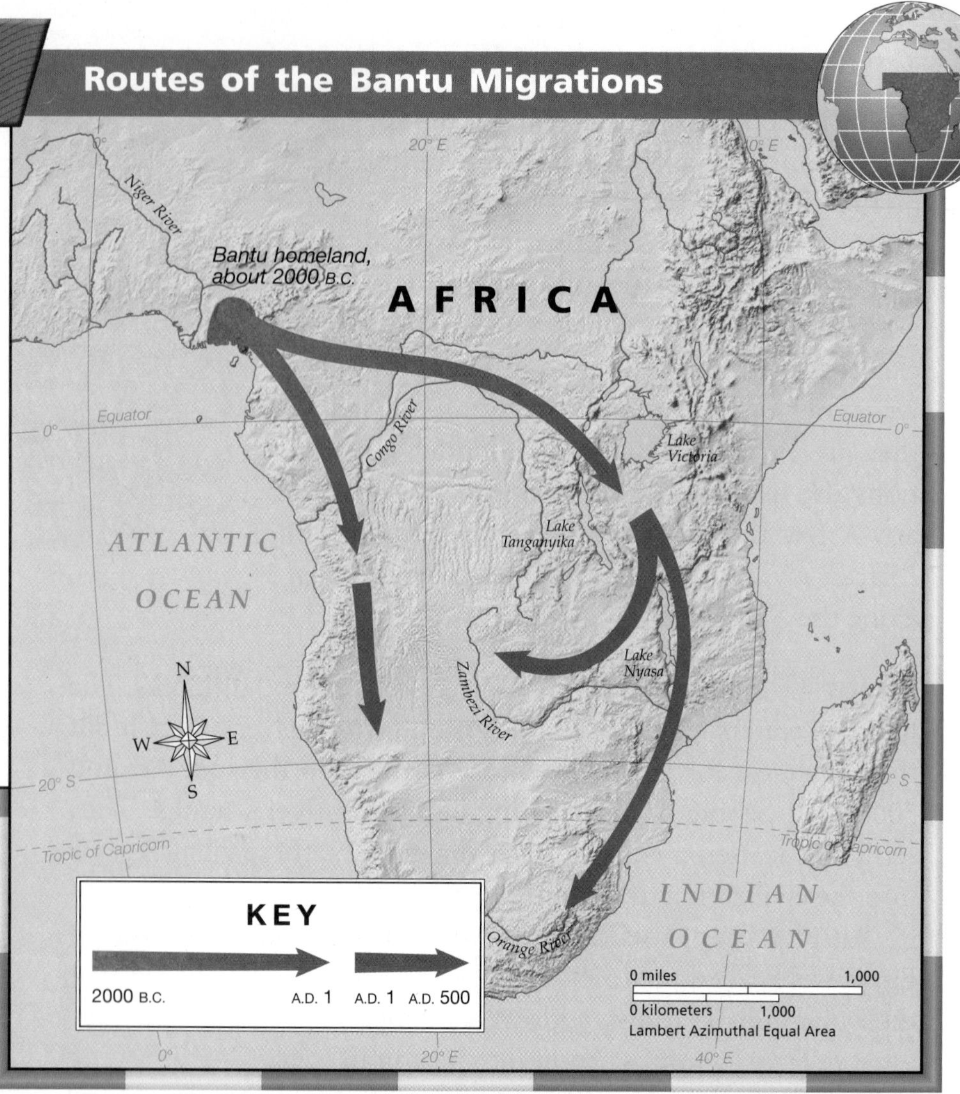

The Bantu Migrations

About 4,000 years ago, people in Africa began one of the largest migrations that has ever taken place. To **migrate** is to move from one place to resettle in another. Around that time, a group of people who spoke Bantu (BAN too) languages began to migrate out of the region that today forms the border between Nigeria and Cameroon.

Why Migrate? No one knows for certain why the migrations began. Some experts believe that a new ability to grow certain crops in the tropical rain forest made the migrations possible. For example, yams and oil palms became a larger part of people's diet. Then increased food supplies may have led to overpopulation, or overcrowding of people living in one area. As a result, Bantu-speaking farmers migrated, perhaps looking for new land to farm. Over hundreds of years, settlements of Bantu speakers spread across Central and Southern Africa.

Bantus Spread Their Language People had been living in most parts of Africa before the Bantu speakers arrived. As the Bantu-speaking farmers settled, their language became the one that most people spoke. Not everyone agrees on how the Bantu languages spread. People who investigate the migrations have found evidence of various routes Bantu speakers took across Africa. By studying cultural clues and modern African languages, experts may eventually understand how many people followed each route and when.

Language and Ethnic Groups Today, people in Central and Southern Africa belong to hundreds of **ethnic groups**, or groups that share languages, religions, family ties, and customs. People in an ethnic group share an identity separate from others. Most often, this identity is based on a shared history or culture. An ethnic group may also share a distinct language. Most of the ethnic groups living in Central and Southern Africa today are Bantu speakers. In fact, more than 200 million people in the region speak one of the many Bantu languages. The most widely spoken of these languages include Zulu, Xhosa (KOH sah), Shona, and Swahili.

✓ Reading Check **How many people in Central and Southern Africa speak Bantu languages today?**

Links Across The World

Ethnic Groups Ethnic groups can be found around the world. French Canadians are a major ethnic group in Canada. Hispanics, African Americans, and Irish Americans are just a few of the many ethnic groups found in the United States. Below, members of various ethnic groups gather in Paris, France.

Section 1 Assessment

Key Terms

Review the key terms at the beginning of this section. Use each term in a sentence that explains its meaning.

Target Reading Skill

How did having a purpose help you understand the important ideas in this section?

Comprehension and Critical Thinking

1. (a) **Locate** Where in Africa did farming most likely begin?
(b) **Identify Causes** Why did people give up hunting and gathering for farming and herding?
(c) **Identify Effects** What effects did farming have on people?
2. (a) **Recall** What were some characteristics of the civilizations that arose along the Nile River?
(b) **Predict** How might the Egyptian and Nubian civilizations have been affected if the Nile River did not regularly flood its banks?
3. (a) **Identify** What were the Bantu migrations?
(b) **Draw Conclusions** How do you think the Bantu-speaking farmers adapted to different environments during the hundreds of years of migrations?

Writing Activity

Make a poster that illustrates, step by step, an important idea from this section. For example, your poster could show how scientists learn about early people or how languages spread from one part of Africa to another.

For: An activity on early human ancestors in Africa
Visit: PHSchool.com
Web Code: lad-5201

Section 2

Kingdoms, City-States, and Empires

Prepare to Read

Objectives

In this section you will

1. Learn how trade affected the development of early East African civilizations.
2. Examine the forces that shaped the history of the North African trading powers.
3. Find out how West African kingdoms gained wealth and power.

Taking Notes

As you read, look for details about important African kingdoms and city-states. Copy the table below, and use it to record your notes.

Early African Civilizations		
Kingdom or City-State	Location	Historical Events

Target Reading Skill

Predict Making predictions before you read helps you set a purpose for reading and remember what you read. First, preview the section by looking at the headings. Then note illustrations or anything else that stands out. Finally, predict what might be discussed in the text. For example, after previewing this section, you might predict that the text will explain the history of trade in Africa. As you read, compare what you read to your prediction.

Key Terms

- **Swahili** (swah HEE lee) *n.* a Bantu language spoken in much of East Africa; also an ethnic group
- **city-state** (SIH tee stayt) *n.* a city that is also an independent state, with its own traditions, government, and laws
- **pilgrimage** (PIL gruh mij) *n.* a religious journey
- **Tombouctou** (tohm book TOO) *n.* a city in Mali near the Niger River; also spelled *Timbuktu*

Aksum was the first African kingdom to make coins for trade.

In the decades before A.D. 100, a Greek writer made a list of goods for sale in the markets of Adulis, East Africa. The list included the following:

> **"Cloth made in Egypt . . . many articles of flint glass . . . and brass, which is used for ornament and in cut pieces instead of coin; sheets of soft copper, used for cooking utensils and cut up for bracelets and anklets for the women; iron, which is made into spears used against the elephants and other wild beasts, and in their wars."**
>
> —*anonymous Greek trader*

Adulis was a bustling trade center along the Red Sea. It was also the main port of the wealthy and powerful kingdom of Aksum.

East African Trading Civilizations

Early East African civilizations grew strong from trade. Turn to the map titled Africa: Regions on page 357. Notice that the boundaries of East Africa include the Red Sea and the Indian Ocean. East Africa's early trading civilizations developed on or near a coastline, providing access to important markets in Arabia, India, and East Asia.

Aksum The kingdom of Aksum was located in East Africa, where the present-day countries of Ethiopia and Eritrea lie. Around 1000 B.C., African and Arab traders began settling along the west coast of the Red Sea. They were the ancestors of the people of Aksum. Over time, Aksum came to control trade in the Red Sea area. By the A.D. 200s, the kingdom controlled a trade network that stretched from the Mediterranean Sea to India.

Ideas, as well as goods, traveled along trade routes. In the A.D. 300s, many people in Aksum became Christian as news about the religion spread. Aksum became a center of the early Ethiopian Christian Church. During the A.D. 600s, Aksum began to decline as Arabs took control of much of the region's trade.

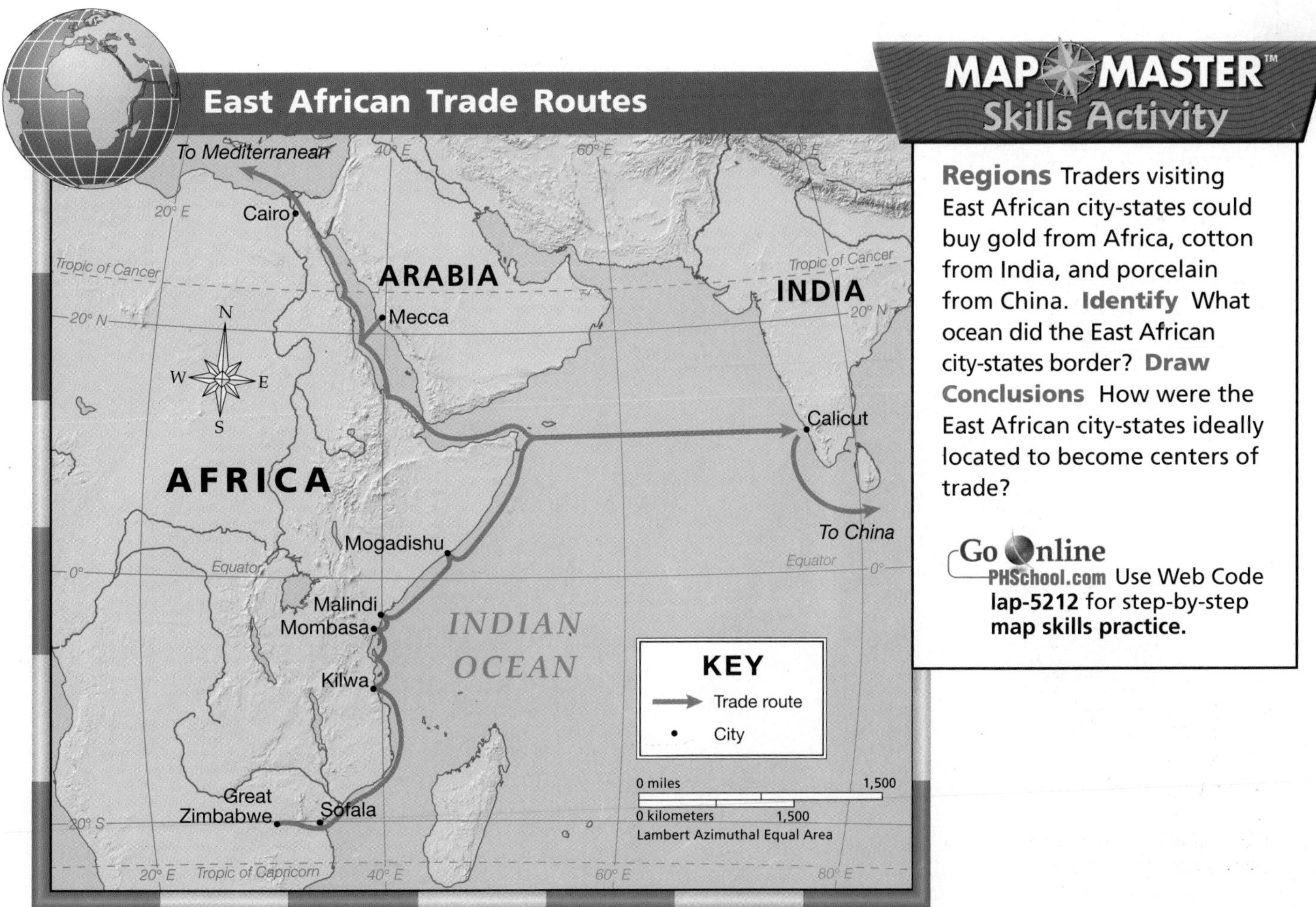

MAP MASTER Skills Activity

Regions Traders visiting East African city-states could buy gold from Africa, cotton from India, and porcelain from China. **Identify** What ocean did the East African city-states border? **Draw Conclusions** How were the East African city-states ideally located to become centers of trade?

Go Online PHSchool.com Use Web Code **lap-5212** for step-by-step **map skills practice.**

Cities of Trade Around the time that Aksum declined, trading cities arose along East Africa's coast. Traders from these cities used seasonal winds to sail northeast to India and China. The traders carried animal skins, ivory, and gold and other metals. When the winds changed direction, the traders sailed back. They brought many goods, including cotton, silk, and porcelain.

Trade affected the culture of coastal East Africa. Some of the traders who visited the area or settled in it were Muslim. They introduced the religion of Islam to East Africa. As well, a new language, called Swahili (swah HEE lee), developed in the area. **Swahili** is a Bantu language that includes some Arab words. Today, it is the most widely spoken Bantu language in Africa.

Rise of City-States Some East African trading cities grew into powerful city-states. A **city-state** is a city that has its own traditions, government, and laws. It is both a city and an independent state. City-states often control much of the surrounding land. Among the greatest of the East African city-states were Malindi (muh LIN dee), Mombasa (mahm BAH suh), Great Zimbabwe (grayt zim BAHB way), and Kilwa (KEEL wah).

Origins of Ivory
Ivory comes from elephant tusks such as the one the men below are holding. Although it is no longer legal to trade ivory, a monument (bottom) in Mombasa, Kenya, commemorates the role ivory played in African trade. **Draw Conclusions** *Why do you think it is no longer legal to trade ivory?*

Kilwa Ibn Battutah (IB un bat TOO tah) was a Muslim from North Africa who became famous for traveling to and writing about many countries. He visited Kilwa in 1331. He had seen great cities in China, India, and West Africa. Ibn Battutah wrote that Kilwa was "one of the most beautiful and best-constructed towns in the world." In Kilwa, people lived in three- and four-story houses made of stone and sea coral.

Kilwa and other East African city-states grew rich from trade and taxes. Traders had to pay huge taxes on goods they brought into the city. "Any merchant who wished to enter the city paid for every five hundred pieces of cloth, no matter what the quality, one gold [piece] as entrance duty," reported one visitor. "After this, the king took two thirds of all the merchandise, leaving the trader one third."

In the early 1500s, Kilwa and the other East African city-states were conquered and destroyed by the European country of Portugal. The Portuguese wanted to build their own trading empire.

Many tall walls of Great Zimbabwe still stand today.

Southern and East African Trade Ties Inland and south from the East African city-states, another great trading civilization developed. Great Zimbabwe was located near the bend of the Limpopo (lim POH poh) River in Southern Africa. It was connected to the trade civilizations of East Africa through a trade network that extended to the coast of the Indian Ocean. Great Zimbabwe reached the peak of its power in about the year 1300. At one time, thousands of people lived in the gigantic stone buildings that covered the area. Today, ruins of Great Zimbabwe remain, including city walls, a fortress, and homes.

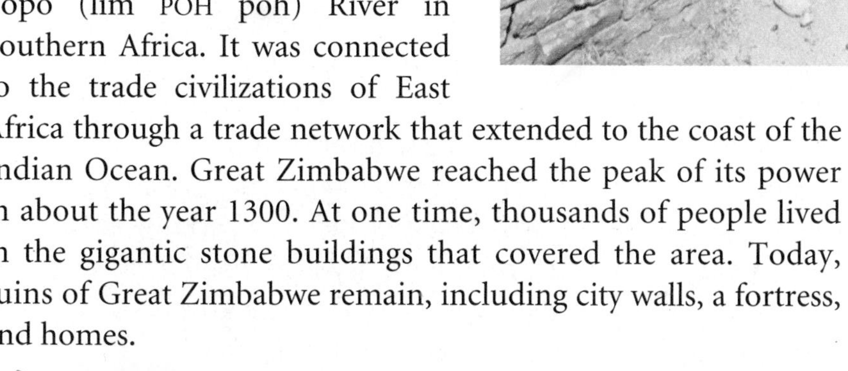

√ Reading Check **What kinds of goods traveled to and from East Africa's trading cities?**

Target Skill

Predict Is the text saying what you predicted it would? If not, look over the headings and illustrations again, and then revise your prediction.

North African Trading Powers

North Africa's history was shaped in part by its location. The region's major boundaries are the Sahara and the Mediterranean Sea. Its long Mediterranean coastline attracted sea traders. As early as 1000 B.C., ships from Phoenicia (fuh NISH uh) began searching the North African coast for ports that would connect them to Africa's riches. Phoenicia included present-day Lebanon and parts of Syria and Israel.

The Rise and Fall of Carthage By 800 B.C., the Phoenicians had established the city of Carthage (KAHR thij) as a trading post in present-day Tunisia. In time, Carthage became a powerful city-state that controlled the coast of North Africa. Carthage grew rich from the trade of textiles, metals, slaves, and food products. Possibly the wealthiest city in the world at the time, Carthage maintained control over Mediterranean trade from the late 500s B.C. through the 200s B.C. However, wars with the Roman Republic weakened the Carthaginians. In 146 B.C., Carthage fell to the Roman Empire, and the city was destroyed.

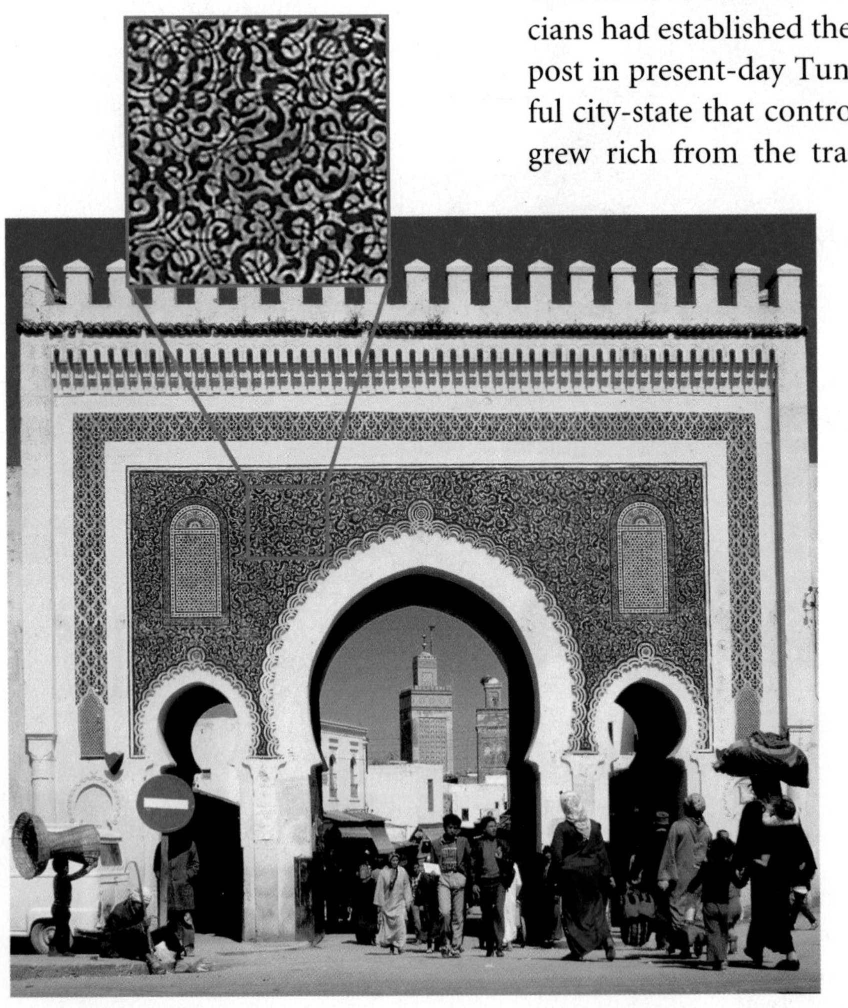

Islam and Art
As Islam spread into North Africa, so did Islamic art styles. The gate shown above, which leads into the city of Fès, Morocco, is Islamic in design.
Analyze Images *How would you describe Islamic art from looking at this gate?*

Roman and Islamic Influences Under Roman rule, cities grew up in areas that are parts of present-day Morocco, northern Algeria, and Tunisia. Christianity also spread to North African cities. The Romans built thousands of miles of roads throughout the territory, and North Africa's ports flourished.

After the Roman Empire fell in A.D. 476, invading forces competed for control of parts of North Africa. During the A.D. 600s, Arabs took control of Egypt and began to invade areas to the west of it. Thus began a long period of Arab control of North Africa. With Arab rule came the spread of Islam, the major religion of the Arabs. Soon many North Africans became Muslim. Then through trade, North Africa's Muslims helped spread Islam to people in West Africa, many of whom also accepted the religion.

✓ Reading Check **Why did the Phoenicians establish Carthage?**

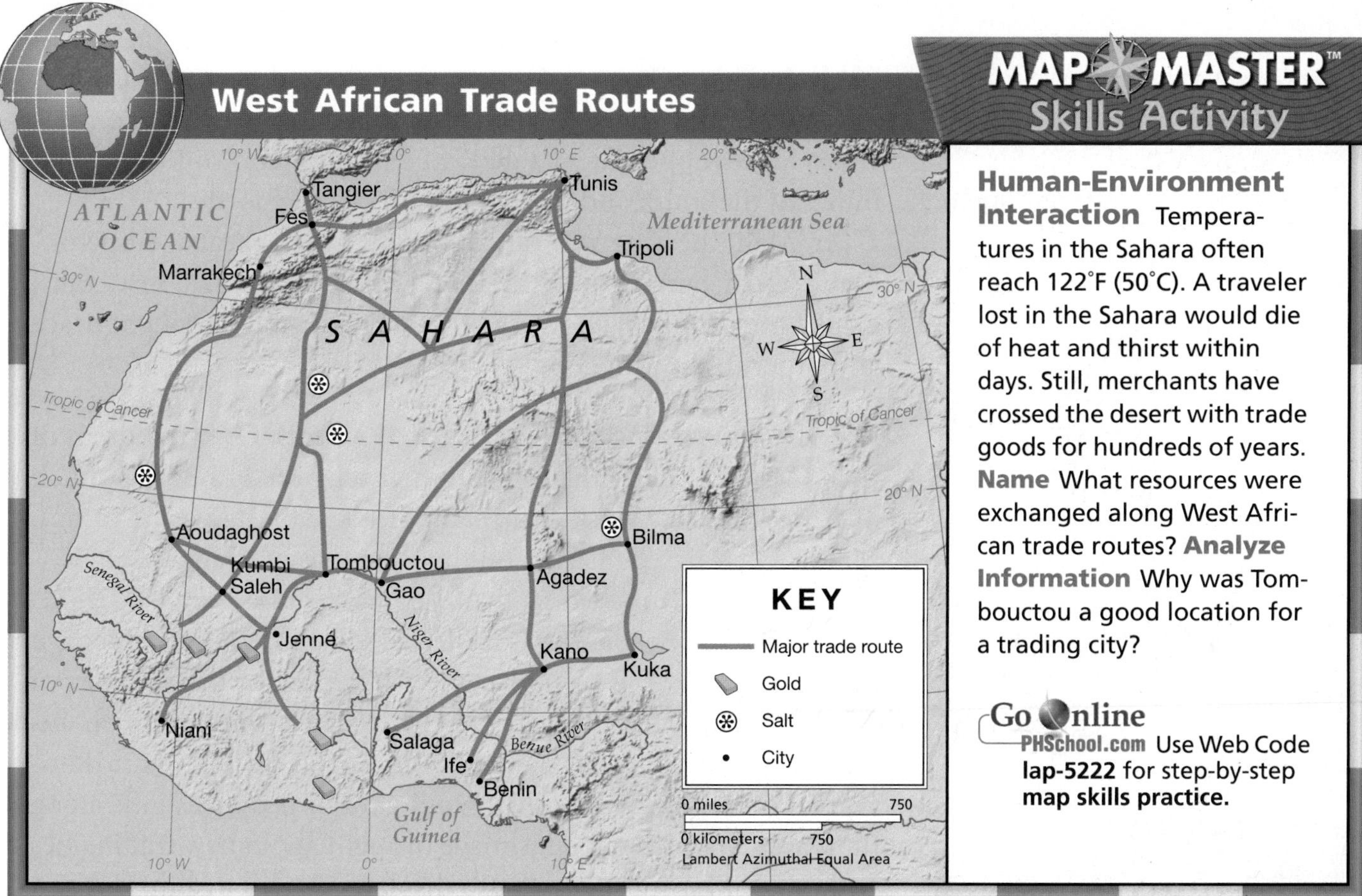

MAP MASTER™ Skills Activity

Human-Environment Interaction Temperatures in the Sahara often reach 122°F (50°C). A traveler lost in the Sahara would die of heat and thirst within days. Still, merchants have crossed the desert with trade goods for hundreds of years. **Name** What resources were exchanged along West African trade routes? **Analyze Information** Why was Tombouctou a good location for a trading city?

Go Online PHSchool.com Use Web Code **lap-5222** for step-by-step **map skills practice.**

West African Kingdoms

Around the time that East and North African city-states were developing, great trading kingdoms arose on the west side of the continent. The power of the West African kingdoms was based on the trade of salt and gold. People need salt to survive, especially in areas with hot climates such as West Africa. But there were no local sources of salt in the region. However, West Africa had plenty of gold. In North Africa, the opposite was true. There was salt, but no gold.

A brisk trade between North Africa and West Africa quickly grew. Control of this trade brought power and riches to three West African kingdoms: Ghana (GAH nuh), Mali (MAH lee), and Songhai (SAWNG hy). Forest kingdoms such as Benin (beh NEEN) also grew wealthy from trade.

Ghana You can see on the map titled Africa's Kingdoms, Cities, and Empires on page 383 that the kingdom of Ghana was located between the Senegal and Niger rivers. From that location Ghana controlled much of the trade across West Africa. Ghana's kings grew rich from the taxes they charged on the salt, gold, and other goods that flowed through their land. The flow of gold was so great that Arab writers called Ghana "land of gold."

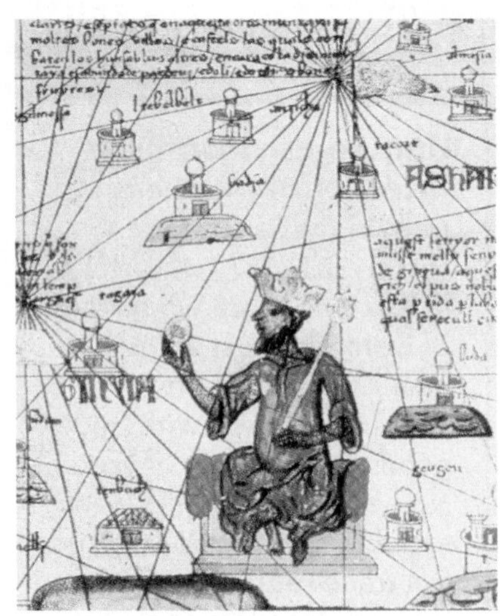

Mansa Musa was so famous that he was portrayed on a Spanish map of the world from the 1300s.

Mali In time, Ghana lost control of its trade routes to a new power, the kingdom of Mali. This kingdom arose in the mid-1200s in the upper Niger valley. Mali's kings controlled the gold mines of the south and the salt supplies of the north.

In Mali, the king was called *Mansa,* which means "emperor." Mali's most famous king, Mansa Musa (MAHN sah MOO sah), gained the throne in about 1312. His 20-year reign brought peace and order to the kingdom.

Mansa Musa and the Spread of Islam Over hundreds of years, Muslim traders had spread their religion, Islam, into much of Africa. Mansa Musa and many of his subjects were Muslim. Mansa Musa based his laws on the teachings of Islam.

In 1324, Mansa Musa made a **pilgrimage,** or a religious journey, to the Arabian city of Mecca. Muslims consider Mecca a holy place. It is the birthplace of Muhammad, the founder of Islam. Mansa Musa brought 60,000 people with him on his pilgrimage. Each of 80 camels carried 300 pounds (136 kilograms) of gold, which Mansa Musa gave to people as gifts along the way. Mansa Musa's pilgrimage brought about new trading ties with other Muslim states. It also displayed Mali's wealth. Hearing the reports, Europe's rulers eagerly began to buy Mali's gold.

Songhai After Mansa Musa's death in about 1332, the Songhai empire became West Africa's most powerful kingdom. Songhai's rulers controlled important trade routes and wealthy cities. The wealthiest Songhai trading city was **Tombouctou** (tohm book TOO), an important caravan stop located along the Niger River. People considered Tombouctou a great Muslim learning center.

Links Across The World

The Spread of Islam In the A.D. 600s, Islam began to spread west from Arabia through Southwest Asia and North Africa. Later, it reached West Africa. Islam also spread east—to Central Asia, India, Pakistan, Bangladesh, and Indonesia. About one billion people around the world practice Islam today. On some days, millions of Muslims visit the holy site of Mecca, as shown below.

> "Salt comes from the north, gold from the south, and silver from the city of white men. But the word of God and the treasures of wisdom are only to be found in Tombouctou."
>
> —*West African proverb*

Invaders from North Africa defeated Songhai in 1591. However, Songhai people still live near the Niger River, and Islam remains important in the region.

Forest Kingdoms Songhai traded with kingdoms located to the south in the forested region of West Africa. One such kingdom, Benin, arose in the late 1200s. Trade in ivory, palm oil, and pepper made the kingdom of Benin wealthy. Benin's artisans worked in ivory, bronze, brass, and wood in a distinctive style. They created some of the finest sculptures and carvings of the time.

Because it was located on the coast, Benin also traded with other African kingdoms as well as with Europeans arriving by sea. In the 1500s, Europeans began to trade guns for slaves from coastal forest kingdoms such as Benin, Asante (uh SAHN tee), and Dahomey (duh HOH mee). Many African Americans are descendants of enslaved people from those kingdoms.

Bronze sculpture from the forest kingdom of Owo

✓ Reading Check **Who was Mansa Musa?**

Section 2 Assessment

Key Terms

Review the key terms at the beginning of this section. Use each term in a sentence that explains its meaning.

Target Reading Skill

What did you predict about this section? Did your prediction help you remember what you read?

Comprehension and Critical Thinking

1. (a) Name Identify two city-states that were important to East African trade.

(b) Identify Effects How did trade affect the coastal culture of East Africa?

(c) Analyze Information Why do you think East African traders had to pay taxes for the right to bring goods into Kilwa?

2. (a) Identify Sequence What forces influenced North Africa throughout its history?

(b) Analyze Information How did Islam become a major religion in North Africa?

3. (a) Describe How did location affect the various kingdoms of West Africa?

(b) Draw Conclusions How did Ghana, Mali, and Songhai become wealthy from gold and salt?

Writing Activity

Suppose you are a traveler visiting one of Africa's ancient kingdoms or city-states during the time that it thrived. Write a short letter home about some of the things that you see and the people that you meet. Explain what your favorite part of the visit has been.

For: An activity on the empire of Ghana
Visit: PHSchool.com
Web Code: lad-5202

Section 3

European Conquest of Africa

Prepare to Read

Objectives

In this section you will

1. Discover what motivated Europeans to explore the African coast.
2. Find out how the Atlantic slave trade developed in the 1500s.
3. Learn how Europeans colonized regions of Africa.

Taking Notes

As you read, find important details about the European conquest of Africa. Copy the flowchart below, and use it to record your findings.

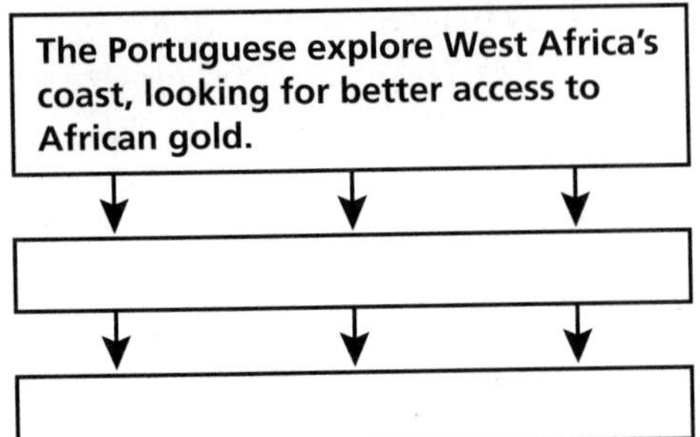

The Portuguese explore West Africa's coast, looking for better access to African gold.

Target Reading Skill

Ask Questions Before you read this section, preview the headings and illustrations to see what the section is about. Write one question that will help you understand or remember something important in the section. For example, you could write this question: "Why did Europeans originally go to Africa?" Then read to answer your question.

Key Terms

- **Cape of Good Hope** (kayp uv good hohp) *n.* a former province of the Republic of South Africa; the point of land at the southern end of Cape Peninsula, South Africa
- **plantation** (plan TAY shun) *n.* a large farm where cash crops are grown
- **Olaudah Equiano** (oh LOW duh ek wee AHN oh) *n.* an antislavery activist who wrote an account of his enslavement
- **colonize** (KAHL uh nyz) *v.* to settle in an area and take control of its government

Many Africans stayed in cells like this one at Gorée.

On the island of Gorée (goh RAY), off the coast of the West African country of Senegal, stands a museum called the House of Slaves. It honors the millions of Africans who were enslaved and then shipped across the Atlantic Ocean. Many Africans passed through the building that now houses the museum. Their last view of Africa was an opening called "The Door of No Return." Beyond it lay the ocean and the slave ships bound for the Americas.

The Atlantic slave trade began in the 1500s and continued through the late 1800s. But contact between Europeans and Africans began long before that. In North Africa, Europeans traded for gold from the empires of Ghana and Mali. Why do you think Europeans' first contacts with Africans took place in North Africa?

Europeans on the Coast

After 1500, Europe's relationship with Africa changed. It had begun as trade between equals. But it turned into the enslavement and forced migration of millions of Africans. The African slave trade eventually ended in the 1800s. Afterward, Europeans became more interested in Africa's natural resources. By 1900, European countries had divided Africa among themselves.

Portuguese Exploration In the mid-1400s, the Portuguese began sailing along the West African coast in search of gold. For centuries, gold from West Africa had been transported across the Sahara to North African ports. It was then shipped across the Mediterranean to arrive at European markets. But the Portuguese and other Europeans wanted to trade directly for West African gold and ivory, instead of dealing with North African merchants. They also wanted to trade with Asia.

Many inventions helped the Portuguese explore Africa's coast. The Portuguese used a lateen sail, a triangle-shaped sail designed in North Africa. The lateen sail allowed ships to sail against the wind as well as with it. And better instruments, such as the astrolabe (AS troh layb), helped sailors navigate at sea. With these improvements, Portuguese sailors became the first Europeans to travel south along Africa's coasts.

A Change in Trade Relations At first, Africans and Europeans traded with one another as equals. Africans traded gold, cotton, ivory, skins, metal objects, and pepper. In return, Europeans traded copper, brass, and clothing. Europeans also introduced corn, cassava, and yams from the Americas. These plants became food crops in Africa. Africans in turn introduced Europeans to okra, watermelon, and the best type of rice for growing in the Americas.

Over time, however, the trade relationship changed. In 1498, three Portuguese ships rounded the tip of Southern Africa and sailed north along Africa's east coast. The wealth of the East African city-states amazed the Portuguese. More Portuguese ships followed—not to trade but to seize the riches of the city-states. Portugal controlled the wealth of East Africa's coast until well into the 1600s.

Portuguese Ship, African Sails
This illustration shows a typical Portuguese sailing ship of the 1300s, called a caravel. It used lateen sails.
Synthesize *How does this ship show that Europeans adopted elements of African culture?*

Europeans in Africa

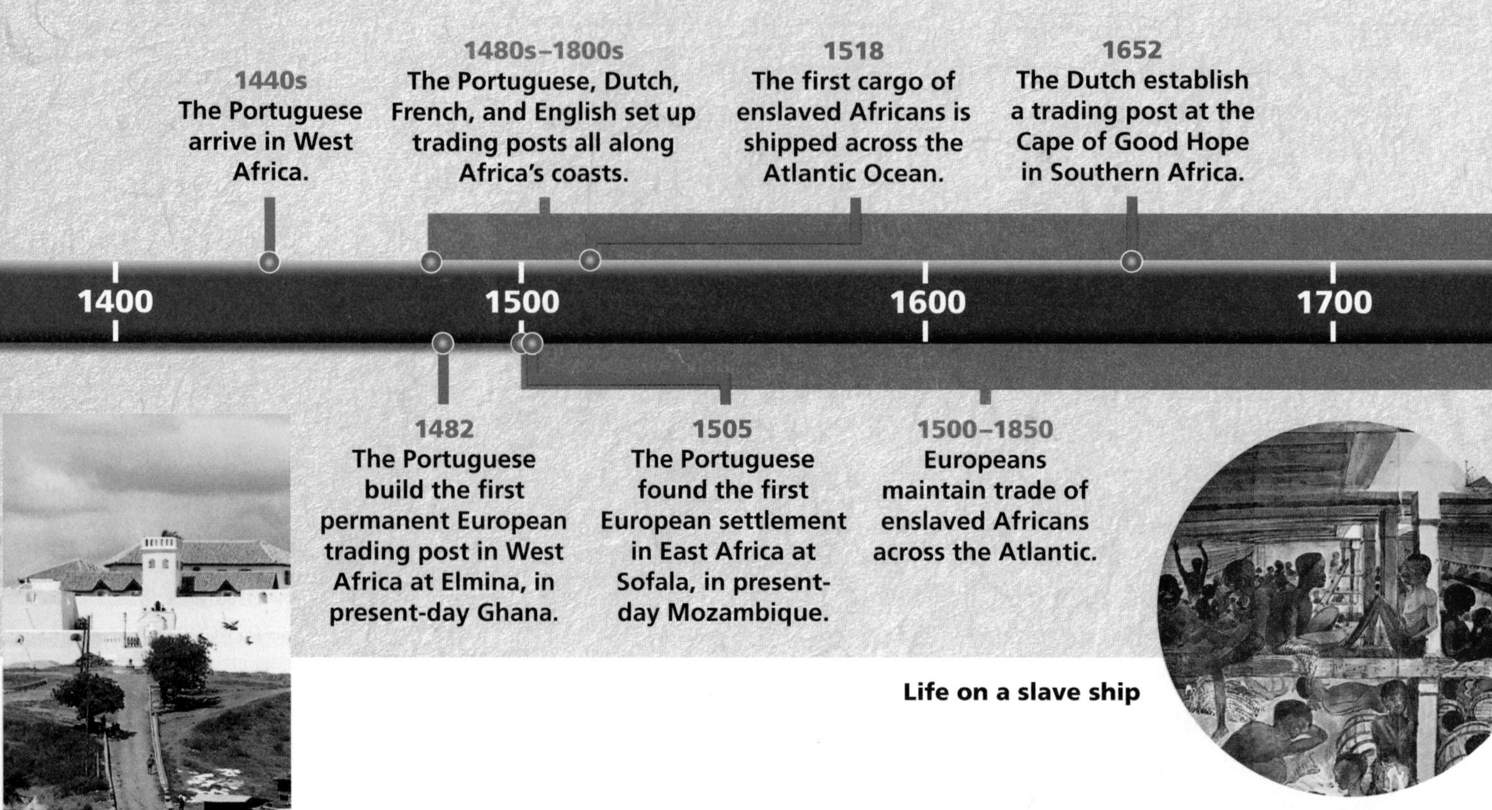

1440s
The Portuguese arrive in West Africa.
1480s–1800s
The Portuguese, Dutch, French, and English set up trading posts all along Africa's coasts.
1518
The first cargo of enslaved Africans is shipped across the Atlantic Ocean.
1652
The Dutch establish a trading post at the Cape of Good Hope in Southern Africa.
1400
1500
1600
1700
1482
The Portuguese build the first permanent European trading post in West Africa at Elmina, in present-day Ghana.
1505
The Portuguese found the first European settlement in East Africa at Sofala, in present-day Mozambique.
1500–1850
Europeans maintain trade of enslaved Africans across the Atlantic.

Life on a slave ship

Trading post at Elmina

European Trade Spreads The Dutch, French, and English soon followed the Portuguese. They set up trading posts along Africa's coasts, where sailors could get supplies. The Dutch built a trading post on the **Cape of Good Hope,** a point of land at Africa's southern tip. Soon, settlers arrived. They moved inland, building homes and farms.

As Europeans spread out, sometimes by force, their relations with Africans worsened. But it was the growing trade in enslaved Africans that poisoned future relations between Africans and Europeans the most.

√ Reading Check **What advantages allowed the Portuguese to be the first Europeans to trade directly with West Africans?**

The Atlantic Slave Trade

Before the 1500s, slavery was common in some parts of Africa. There, enslaved people became the property of their owners and were forced to work for them. Slaves could win their freedom after a few years. Some became important citizens among the people who had enslaved them. Slaves could even be bought out of slavery by their own people.

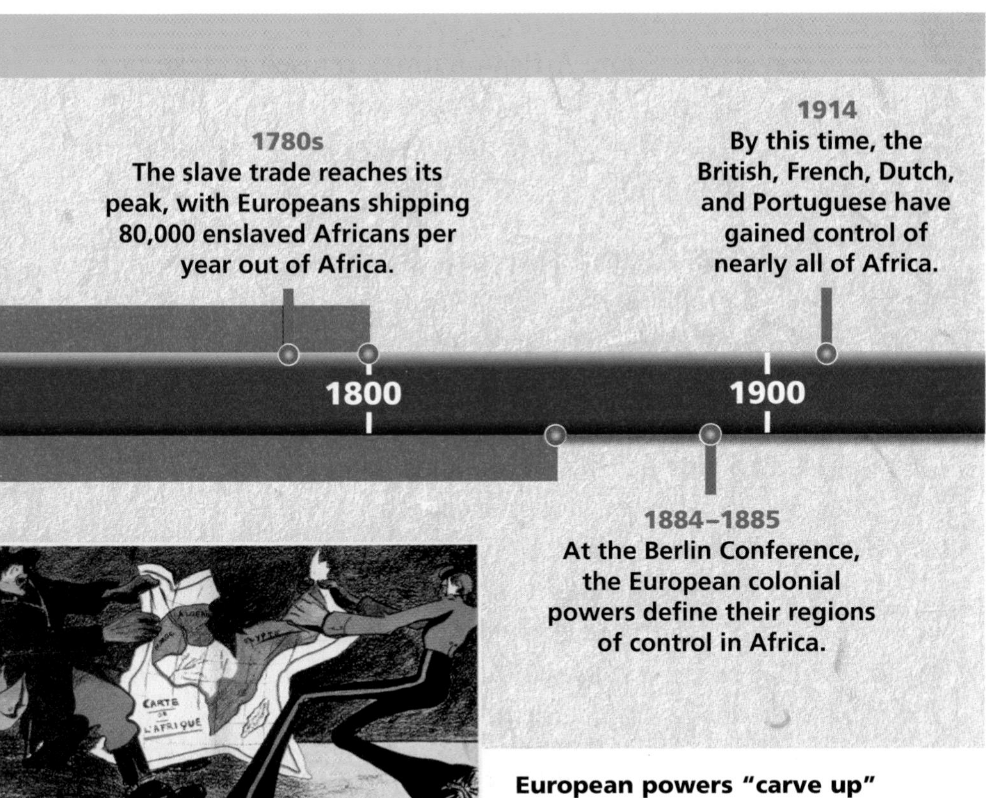

1780s
The slave trade reaches its peak, with Europeans shipping 80,000 enslaved Africans per year out of Africa.
1914
By this time, the British, French, Dutch, and Portuguese have gained control of nearly all of Africa.
1800
1900
1884–1885
At the Berlin Conference, the European colonial powers define their regions of control in Africa.
CARTE DE L'AFRIQUE

European powers "carve up" Africa.

Timeline Skills

Over the course of 500 years, Europeans had a strong influence on Africa. **Note** When did Europeans establish their first trading post in Africa? **Identify Effects** What were the effects of European trade interests on Africa?

Then the European powers began to establish colonies in North, South, and Central America, as well as the Caribbean. The Europeans practiced a different type of slavery in the Americas. They treated the enslaved Africans as property that they shipped across the Atlantic to the Americas. The Europeans rarely freed their slaves. When the African slave trade ended in the mid-1800s, millions of Africans had been taken from their homelands, most never to return.

The Demand for Slaves European settlers in the Americas needed workers for their mines and plantations. A **plantation** is a large farm where cash crops are grown. Instead of paying plantation workers, the settlers preferred to use enslaved laborers. At first the settlers enslaved Native Americans. But many Native Americans became sick and died from diseases or brutal working conditions. Others ran away.

Therefore the European settlers decided to enslave Africans instead. The settlers knew Africans were skilled farmers, miners, and metal workers. They also thought Africans would easily adapt to the climate of the American tropics, which is similar to that of Africa. And since Africans would be in unfamiliar territory, they would not be able to escape easily.

Discovery
CHANNEL
SCHOOL
Video
Learn what the African slave trade was like.

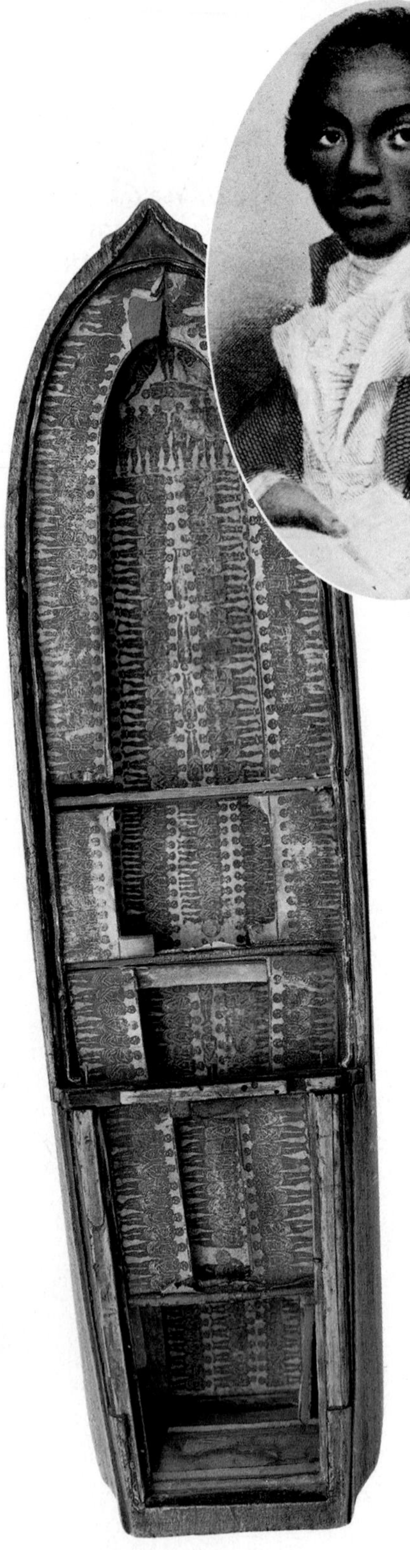

The Trials of Slavery
Olaudah Equiano (top right) was a slave who bought his own freedom. He traveled to America in cramped quarters on a slave ship similar to this model (above). **Analyze Images** *Do you think it would have been bearable to live on a ship like this one?*

The Slave Trade Begins By the 1600s, Portuguese traders were exchanging goods, such as guns, for African slaves. Some African nations refused to take part. But others sold people they captured during battles. By 1780, about 80,000 African slaves were being shipped across the Atlantic each year.

The Horrors of Slavery Captured Africans were often branded with hot irons to identify them as slaves. On the journey across the Atlantic, captives lay side by side on filthy shelves stacked from floor to ceiling. They received little food or water. As many as 20 percent of the slaves died during each crossing. To make up for these losses, ships' captains packed in even more people.

Olaudah Equiano (oh LOW duh ek wee AHN oh) was a slave who bought his own freedom and then fought against slavery. Equiano had been captured and sold at a slave auction in 1756, at about age 11. He felt sure he would die. In a book he later wrote about his experience, Equiano explained,

> **"[W]hen I looked around the ship and saw a large furnace of copper boiling and a multitude of black people of every description chained together . . . I no longer doubted of my fate."**
>
> —The Interesting Narrative of the Life of Olaudah Equiano, or Gustavus Vassa, the African, *by Olaudah Equiano*

Equiano proved luckier than most African slaves. In time, he was able to buy his freedom. For most enslaved people, freedom was little more than a distant dream.

The Effects of Slavery on Africa Some native Africans grew wealthy from the slave trade. Overall, however, the slave trade was a disaster for Africa. West Africa lost much of its population. Robbed of skilled workers, and with many families torn apart, many African societies broke down.

✓ Reading Check **What fueled the European demand for slaves?**

Europeans Colonize Africa

In the mid-1800s, the African slave trade ended. Europeans then began to raid Africa's interior for its natural resources. They wanted the resources to run factories that were springing up all across Europe. They also viewed Africa as a place to build empires. Many Africans fiercely resisted European conquest. But their old guns proved no match for modern European weapons.

Africa: European Rule

MAP MASTER™ Skills Activity

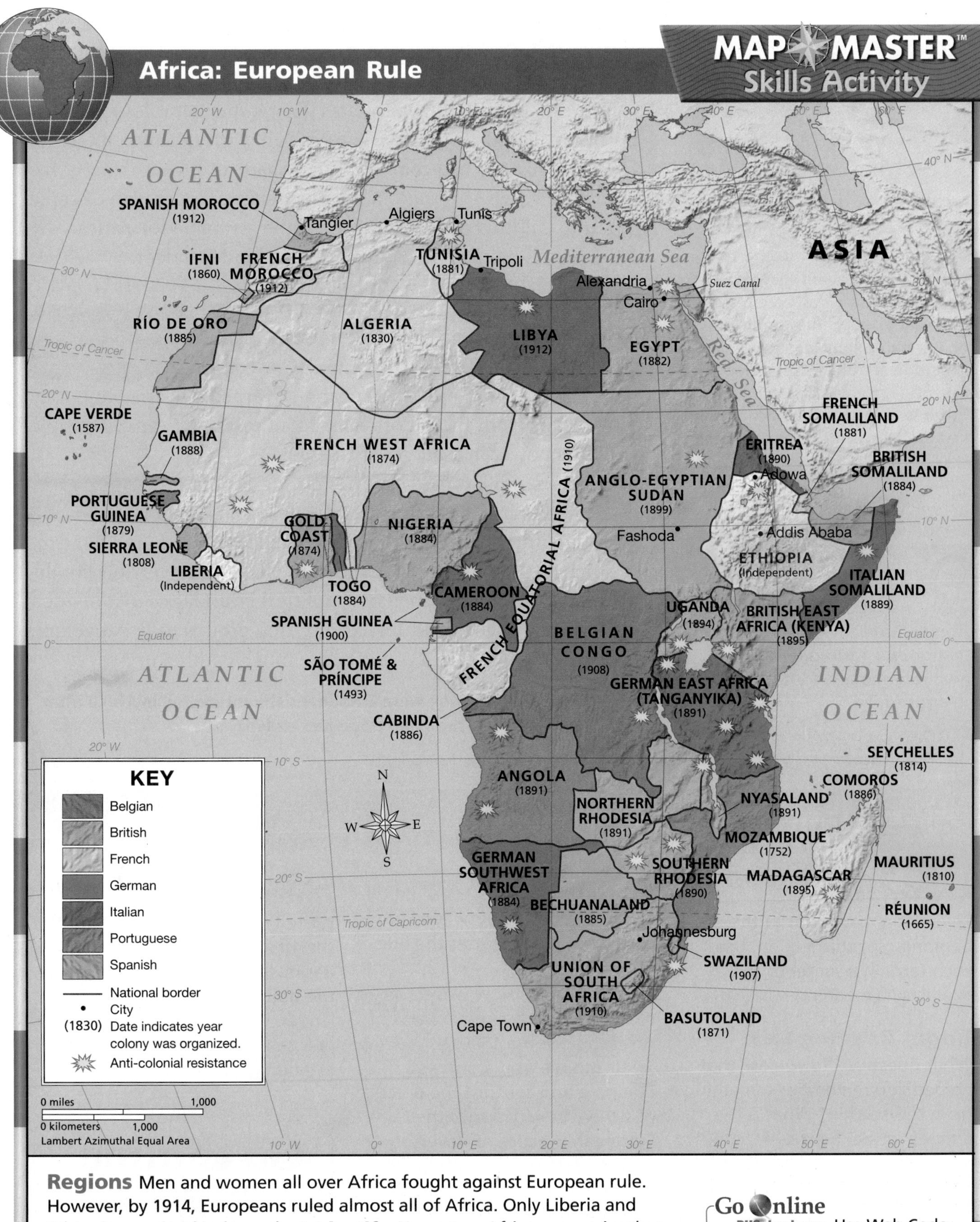

Regions Men and women all over Africa fought against European rule. However, by 1914, Europeans ruled almost all of Africa. Only Liberia and Ethiopia remained independent. **Identify** Name two African countries that were not yet ruled by Europeans in 1900. **Draw Conclusions** Why do you think most of the regions that resisted colonization were near the coasts?

Go Online PHSchool.com Use Web Code **lap-5213** for step-by-step **map skills practice.**

How Stamps Reveal History
These postage stamps were printed in the early 1900s. They are from the German colony in present-day Cameroon and the British colony in present-day Kenya, Uganda, and Tanzania. **Infer** *Did Europeans view their colonies as African or European?*

The Scramble for Africa European nations competed with one another to gain African territory. But they did not want this competition to lead to war. In 1884, leaders of several European countries met in Berlin, Germany. There, they set rules for which European countries could claim which African land. By 1900, European nations had colonized many parts of Africa. To **colonize** means to settle an area and take control of its government. People began to call this rush for territory "the scramble for Africa." By 1914, only Ethiopia and Liberia remained independent.

Effects of European Control on Africa Not all the European countries ruled their colonies the same way. The Belgian government directly ran the Belgian Congo (now the Democratic Republic of the Congo). Africans governed Nigeria, but they took orders from British officials. In all cases, the African people had little power in their governments.

The scramble for Africa caused long-lasting problems. Europeans had gained power in part by encouraging rivalries among African ethnic groups. Europeans also took the best land to farm. In some areas, they forced Africans to labor under terrible conditions. Europeans also drew new political boundaries that divided some ethnic groups and forced differing groups to live together. Later, these boundaries would cause much conflict in Africa.

Target Skill **Ask Questions** Ask yourself why the competition among European nations for African territory was referred to as "the scramble for Africa."

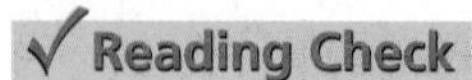

✓ Reading Check **Why were Europeans still interested in Africa after the slave trade had ended?**

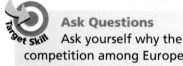

Section 3 Assessment

Key Terms
Review the key terms at the beginning of this section. Use each term in a sentence that explains its meaning.

Target Reading Skill
What question did you ask that helped you remember something from this section? What is the answer to the question?

Comprehension and Critical Thinking
1. **(a) Recall** What region of Africa did most Europeans trade with before the mid-1400s?
(b) Identify Causes How did the trade relationship between Europe and Africa change after the late 1400s?
2. **(a) Describe** How was slavery traditionally practiced in parts of Africa before the 1500s?
(b) Compare and Contrast Compare and contrast the practice of slavery in Africa with the European practice of slavery.
3. **(a) Recall** In what different ways did the Europeans govern their African colonies?
(b) Identify Sequence How did relations between Africa and Europe change over time?

Writing Activity
Write two brief editorials about the 1884 European conference in Berlin. Write one editorial from the point of view of an African leader. Write the other from the point of view of a European leader attending the conference.

For: An activity on the Boers
Visit: PHSchool.com
Web Code: lad-5203

Section 4 Independence and Its Challenges

Prepare to Read

Objectives

In this section you will

1. Learn about the growth of nationalism in Africa.
2. Find out about the effects of World War II on Africa and on the growing independence movement.
3. Examine the different challenges faced by African nations on their paths to independence.

Taking Notes

As you read, find details on the causes and effects of the African movement for independence. Copy the flowchart below, and use it to record your findings.

Target Reading Skill

Use Prior Knowledge Prior knowledge is what you already know about a topic before you begin to read. Building on what you already know can give you a head start on learning new information.

Before you begin to read, page through your reading assignment, looking at the headings and illustrations to spark your memory. Write down what you know about a certain topic, such as World War II. As you read, connect what you learn to what you already know.

Key Terms

- **nationalism** (NASH uh nul iz um) *n.* a feeling of pride in one's homeland; a group's identity as members of a nation
- **Pan-Africanism** (pan AF rih kun iz um) *n.* the belief that all Africans should work together for their rights and freedoms
- **boycott** (BOY kaht) *n.* a refusal to buy or use certain products or services
- **democracy** (dih MAHK ruh see) *n.* a government in which citizens exercise power through elected representatives

On April 18, 1980, the people of Rhodesia took to the streets. They had recently elected Robert Mugabe (muh GAH bee) prime minister in Rhodesia's first free election. People waited excitedly through the evening. Then, at midnight, the British flag came down for the last time. At that moment, the British colony of Rhodesia became the independent country of Zimbabwe.

The fight for independence had been difficult and sometimes violent. Now, Prime Minister Mugabe asked all the people to work together. They would have to build a new nation. Zimbabwe was one of the last African countries to win independence. But the movement for freedom there had begun many years before.

People in Zimbabwe celebrate the country's independence.

The Growth of Nationalism

A Lasting Legacy
Some 80 years after it was founded, the African National Congress achieved its goal of equal rights for all South Africans with Nelson Mandela (below) as its leader. People cheer for Mandela during South Africa's 1994 presidential campaign (bottom). **Evaluate** *Based on this information, would you say that nationalism stayed strong in South Africa during the 1900s?*

After "the scramble for Africa," many Africans dreamed of independence. In 1897, Mankayi Sontanga (mun KY ee sun TAHN guh) put this dream to music. His song, called "Bless, O Lord, Our Land of Africa," expressed the growing nationalism of Africans. **Nationalism** is a feeling of pride in one's homeland.

Political Parties and Nationalism Most European colonial rulers did not view Africans as their equals. For that reason, many African leaders knew they would have to work hard at developing pride in being African. The colonial powers had drawn political borders that combined many nations and ethnic groups. Some of these groups were old rivals. African leaders saw that to end colonial rule, they would have to build a spirit of unity.

Nationalism grew during the early 1900s. In 1912, Africans in South Africa formed a political party called the South African Native National Congress. (Today this party is the African National Congress, or the ANC.) Party members protested laws that limited the rights of black South Africans. In 1920, African lawyers in British West Africa formed the National Congress of British West Africa. This group also worked to gain rights for Africans, including the right to vote.

Pan-Africanism In the 1920s, Africans formed a movement based on **Pan-Africanism,** the belief that all Africans should work together for their rights and freedoms. This movement stressed unity and cooperation among all Africans, whether they lived in Africa or not. Their slogan was "Africa for Africans." The movement won many supporters.

One of the greatest leaders of the Pan-African movement was Léopold Senghor (lay oh POHLD sahn GAWR) of Senegal. Senghor was a poet and a political leader. He encouraged Africans to study their traditions and be proud of their culture. Senegal became independent in 1960, with Senghor as its first president.

√ Reading Check **Name two African political parties. What work did these parties do?**

Africa and World War II

A major boost to African independence came unexpectedly in the 1930s and 1940s, when World War II unfolded. The war would inspire many people throughout Africa to seek freedom for their own nations.

These men from Ghana fought in the British Army during World War II.

The Invasion of North Africa During World War II, Great Britain, France, and the United States formed a group called the Allies. Together, the Allies fought the armies of Germany, Italy, and Japan, which were invading much of the world. German and Italian forces invaded North Africa, much of which was under British or French colonial control. Italian forces also invaded Ethiopia.

Some African nations played a major role in supporting the Allies. Countries such as Liberia and the Belgian Congo supplied the Allies with rubber and other needed resources. Allied planes were allowed to use African airfields to move supplies into Asia. Many thousands of African soldiers fought and died to help free Europe from conquest. About 170,000 soldiers from West Africa and 280,000 soldiers from East Africa and Southern Africa served in the British Army.

An Inspirational Victory Africans came home victorious. After the sacrifices they made, however, they wanted their own freedom. One soldier said, "We have been told what we fought for. That is 'freedom.' We want freedom, nothing but freedom."

√ Reading Check **What parts of Africa were invaded during World War II?**

Africa: Independence

MAP MASTER™ Skills Activity

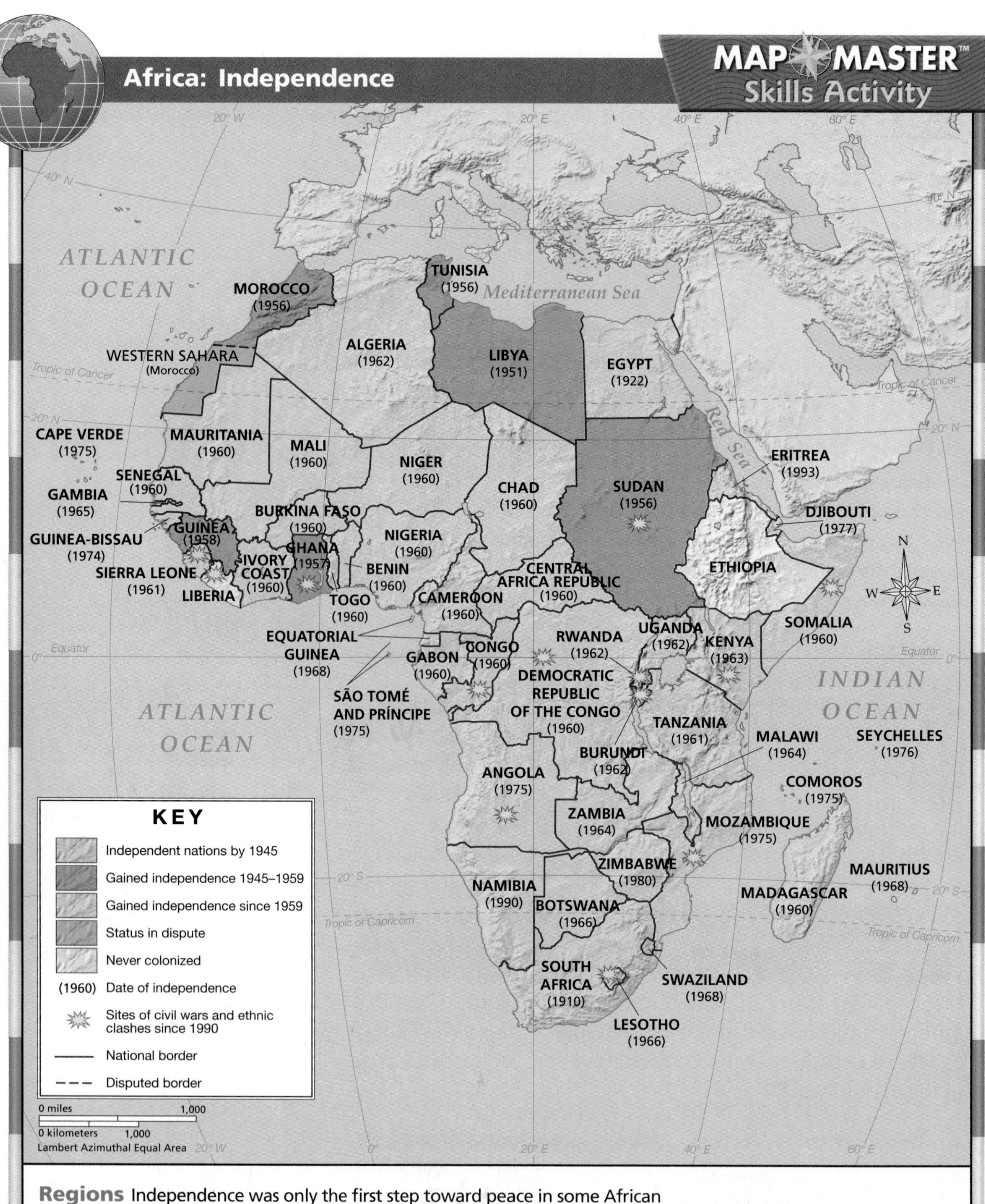

Regions Independence was only the first step toward peace in some African countries. Some countries have suffered through major civil wars since independence. **Identify** During what period of time did the most African countries gain independence? **Analyze Information** Why do you think there was an increase in the number of countries that became independent after a certain time?

Go Online PHSchool.com Use Web Code **lap-5214** for step-by-step **map skills practice.**

Different Paths to Independence

World War II did not only inspire Africans to win their freedom. The war also weakened the economies of colonial powers such as France and Great Britain. Colonialism was about to come to an end in Africa.

Winds of Change Public opinion began to turn against the practice of colonialism as well. Many people in Britain felt they could no longer afford a colonial empire. Even the United States and the Soviet Union—Britain's allies during the war—began to speak out against colonialism.

British leader Harold Macmillan realized that Britain would not be able to keep its African colonies. "The winds of change are blowing across Africa," he said. As more and more Africans demanded freedom, European countries began to give up their African colonies. Some colonial powers gave up their colonies peacefully, while others fought to maintain control. Ghana was granted its independence from Britain. But Algeria, a French colony, had to fight for its freedom.

Independence Across Africa
Women in Mauritius in 1965 hold up signs asking for independence from Britain (bottom). Prince Philip of Britain and Prime Minister Jomo Kenyatta of Kenya shake hands at an independence ceremony in 1963 (below). **Predict** *Do you think Mauritius and Kenya gained independence peacefully or through fighting?*

From Gold Coast to Ghana In the Gold Coast colony, Kwame Nkrumah (KWAH mee un KROO muh) organized protests against British rule in the early 1950s. The protests were peaceful strikes and boycotts. In a **boycott,** people refuse to buy or use certain products or services. The British jailed Nkrumah several times for his actions, but the protests continued. In 1957, the people achieved their goal: independence. The new country took on the name Ghana, and Nkrumah became its president.

War in Algeria The French people who had settled in Algeria thought of it as more than a colony. To them, it was part of France. Algerians disagreed. They were willing to fight for the right to govern themselves. A bloody war began in Algeria in 1954. The eight-year struggle cost the lives of 100,000 Algerians and 10,000 French. But by 1962, the Algerians had won.

Challenges of Independence The new leaders of Africa had spent many years working for independence. But the colonial powers had rarely allowed Africans to gain experience in government. After agreeing to independence, the colonial powers did little to prepare the new leaders to govern. As a result, many new governments in Africa were unstable.

The Right to Vote
A key part of democracy is allowing all citizens to vote. An elderly woman casts her vote in an election in Mali (below). Voters line up for miles to cast votes in South Africa's first democratic elections in 1994 (bottom).
Apply Information *Why do you think South Africans were willing to walk miles in order to cast a vote?*

In some African countries, African military leaders took control of the government by force. Military governments do not always govern fairly. The people often have few rights. Further, citizens may be jailed if they protest. But military governments have held together some African countries that otherwise might have been torn apart by war.

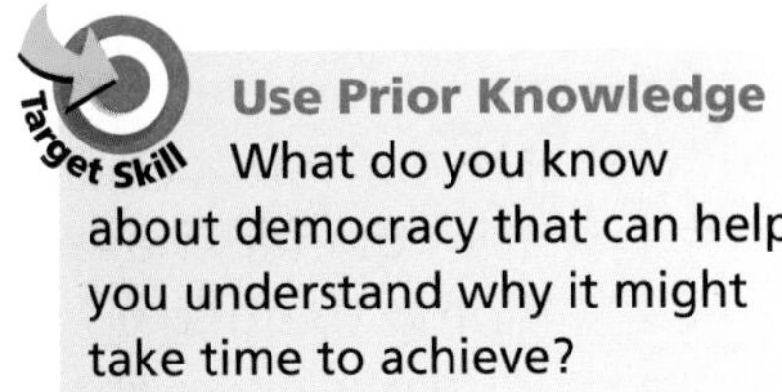

Use Prior Knowledge What do you know about democracy that can help you understand why it might take time to achieve?

Building Democracy In many parts of Africa, there is a long history of democracy. A **democracy** is a government in which citizens exercise power through elected representatives. In a democracy, citizens influence governmental decisions. Some countries have made traditional ways a part of governing. For example, in Botswana, lively political debates take place in "freedom squares." These outdoor meetings are like the traditional kgotla (GOHT lah), in which people talk with their leaders.

Most African countries are less than 50 years old. In contrast, the stable, democratic country of the United States is more than 200 years old. Many Africans feel that building stable countries will take time. As one leader said, "Let Africa be given the time to develop its own system of democracy."

✓ Reading Check **How did Algeria gain independence?**

Section 4 Assessment

Key Terms

Review the key terms at the beginning of this section. Use each term in a sentence that explains its meaning.

Target Reading Skill

Look back at what you wrote down about what you already knew. How did what you learned relate to what you already knew?

Comprehension and Critical Thinking

1. **(a) Recall** How did Africans respond to years of colonial rule?
(b) Infer Why did African leaders encourage people to feel pride about being African?
2. **(a) Describe** What was Africa's role in World War II?
(b) Identify Effects How did World War II boost the independence movement in Africa?
3. **(a) Identify Causes** What pressures forced European countries to give up their colonies?
(b) Compare and Contrast How was Ghana's road to independence similar to that of Algeria? How was it different?

Writing Activity

Use a book, an encyclopedia, or the Internet to research an African country that won its independence after 1950. Write a headline and a short newspaper article that might have appeared on the day that country became independent.

Writing Tip Be sure to write a good headline for your newspaper article. The headline should identify the main point of the article. It should also be catchy so that the reader wants to read on.

Skills for Life Sequencing

Mr. DeNoto's class had just finished reading about the ways African countries gained independence. Then the class formed groups. Each group was going to build a float to celebrate the independence of an African country.

"Let's make the flag first," said Tamika.

"No, no, we need to build the float frame first," cried Ari.

"Well, I don't see how we can do anything until we buy the materials we need!" complained Sarah.

Mr. DeNoto held up a hand to quiet the class. "Building a float is complicated. The first thing you have to do is make a plan," he said. "Otherwise, you might cover the same ground more than once. You might even forget an important step. Adam, why don't you come up to the board and be our scribe? We're going to make a flowchart to help us plan."

A flowchart shows sequence, or the order in which actions or events happen. Understanding sequence can help you plan an activity or remember what you have read. A flowchart usually uses arrows to show which step or event happens when. A diagram such as a timeline uses dates to show the order of events.

Learn the Skill

Use these steps when you read a diagram for sequence.

1. **Read the title first.** The title will help you understand what the diagram is about. Mr. DeNoto's class titled its flowchart Building a Float. From the title, you know that the flowchart shows how the class plans to build a float.

2. **Find clues that show the order of events.** On a flowchart, the arrows tell you the order in which you should read the chart. Find the beginning and start there. Mr. DeNoto's class decided that their first step would be "Choose a country."

3. **Read the diagram carefully for connections.** Think about how one step leads to the next step. What are the connections? If there are no illustrations, try imagining each step in your head to help you understand the sequence.

Practice the Skill

Follow the steps below to read the flowchart about Ghana.

1. Read the title. What does it tell you the flowchart will be about?
2. Find the beginning of the chart and identify the first step. Start there and follow the arrows through each step.
3. Now reread the flowchart and answer these questions: (a) What is the first step on the flowchart? (b) What step leads to Nkrumah being jailed? (c) What step comes after Nkrumah being jailed? (d) What is the final result of the Gold Coast colony's struggle for independence?

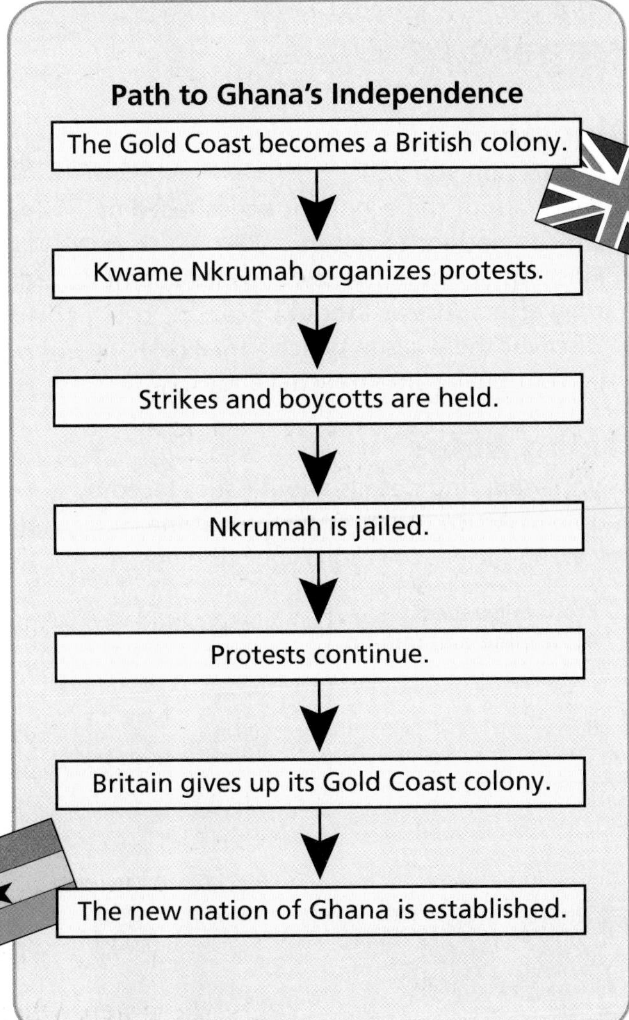

Path to Ghana's Independence
The Gold Coast becomes a British colony.
Kwame Nkrumah organizes protests.
Strikes and boycotts are held.
Nkrumah is jailed.
Protests continue.
Britain gives up its Gold Coast colony.
The new nation of Ghana is established.

After Ghana was established, its government created this coat of arms to represent the nation.

Apply the Skill

Turn to pages 400–401 and study the timeline. Use the steps in this skill to understand what events are shown on the timeline as well as what the sequence of events was.

Section 5 Issues for Africa Today

Prepare to Read

Objectives

In this section you will

1. Learn about the economic issues faced by African nations today.
2. Find out about major social issues and how they affect Africans today.
3. Discover the ways in which Africa is facing current environmental challenges.

Taking Notes

As you read, find details about issues faced by people in Africa today. Copy the outline below, and use it to record your findings.

I. Economic issues
  A. Farming and mining
    1.
    2.
  B.
II.

Target Reading Skill

Predict As you have learned, making predictions before you read helps you set a purpose for reading and helps you remember what you read.

Before you read this section, think about what you know about Africa's history. Then predict some issues the region might face today. As you read, connect what you read to your prediction. If what you learn doesn't support your prediction, revise the prediction.

Key Terms

- **commercial farming** (kuh MUR shul FAHR ming) *n.* the large-scale production of crops for sale
- **hybrid** (HY brid) *n.* a plant that is created by breeding different types of the same plant
- **literate** (LIT ur it) *adj.* able to read and write
- **life expectancy** (lyf ek SPEK tun see) *n.* the average length of time a person can expect to live

A young man digs an irrigation ditch in Niger.

In the past, nothing grew during the dry season in the Sahel. Farmers had to travel to cities to find work. Now, the West African country of Niger has a new irrigation program for its part of the Sahel. Irrigation allows farmers to grow a second crop during the dry season, in addition to their usual crop in the wet season. One farmer says that raising two crops a year means he can stay on village land.

> **"Dry-season crops are such a normal practice now that everyone grows them. Before, each year after the harvest, I went to the city to look for work. But today, with the dry-season crops, I have work in the village. Truly it is a good thing."**
>
> *—Adamou Sani, farmer*

Niger's irrigation program is one way Africans are improving their lives. Africans are also finding ways to meet economic, social, and environmental challenges.

Economic Issues

The colonial powers saw Africa as a source of raw materials and a market for their own manufactured goods. They did little to build factories in Africa. Today, African countries still have little manufacturing. Most economies are based on farming and mining.

Farming Farming is the most important economic activity in Africa. About 60 percent of workers are farmers. And more than half of the goods that African countries sell overseas are farm goods. Africans practice two kinds of farming—subsistence farming and commercial farming. Recall that subsistence farmers work small plots of land. They try to raise as much food as their families need. **Commercial farming** is the large-scale production of cash crops for sale. In Africa, commercial farmers grow cash crops such as coffee, cacao, and bananas.

Mining Many African nations have rich mineral resources. They export minerals to other countries. Nigeria has oil and coal. The Democratic Republic of the Congo and Zambia have copper, while South Africa has gold and diamonds.

Farming for Food or for Profit? A man bicycles through a banana farm in Ivory Coast (bottom). A woman picks coffee in Zambia (below). **Analyze Information** *Do you think the farms shown are commercial or subsistence farms? Explain why.*

South African Gold Mine

In South Africa's deep-level gold mines, miners work as far down as two miles (3.2 kilometers) underground. The mines run 24 hours a day. Because it is so hot at that depth, deep-level mining requires ventilation and cooling. In addition to tunnels, there are shafts, elevators to lift the ore to the surface, and surface processing plants. South Africa produces almost half of the world's gold.

Working in the Mines
Miners like this man train for their jobs by stepping up and down on blocks for hours in a very hot room.

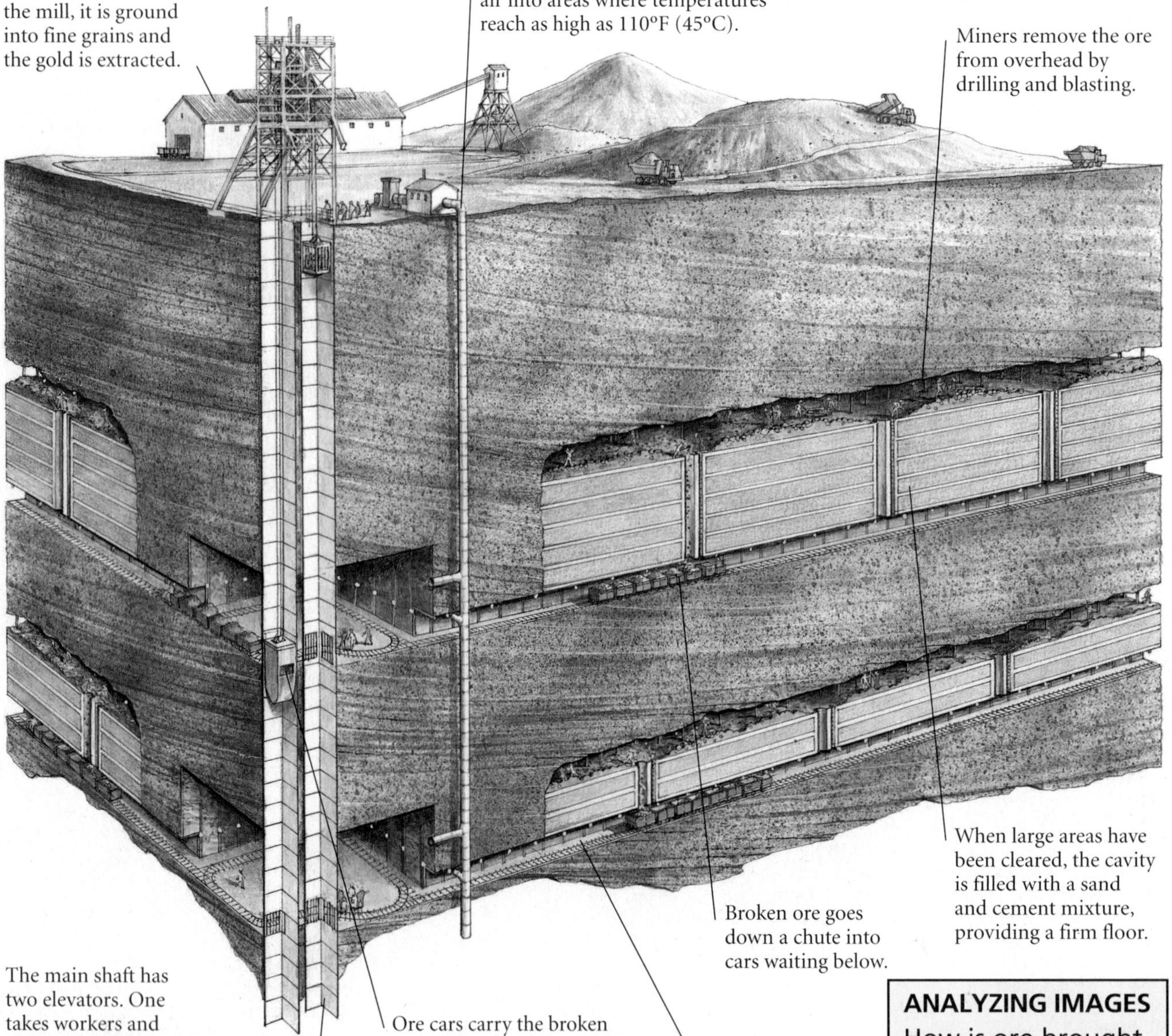

When the ore reaches the mill, it is ground into fine grains and the gold is extracted.

The ventilation shaft brings fresh air into areas where temperatures reach as high as 110°F (45°C).

Miners remove the ore from overhead by drilling and blasting.

When large areas have been cleared, the cavity is filled with a sand and cement mixture, providing a firm floor.

Broken ore goes down a chute into cars waiting below.

The main shaft has two elevators. One takes workers and supplies into the mine, and the other takes the broken ore up to the surface for processing. The shaft works on a continuous, automated system.

Ore cars carry the broken ore to a loading area, where it is loaded into huge containers called skips. The skips travel up the elevator.

Cars run on tracks at each level of the mine.

ANALYZING IMAGES
How is ore brought from the deep mines to the mill?

Economic Challenges About 75 percent of African countries have specialized economies—they depend on exporting one or two products. Gambia depends on peanuts, while Zambia relies on the export of copper. As a result, African economies are especially sensitive to the rise and fall of world prices. A fall in prices hurts economies that depend on the sale of one crop or mineral.

African countries are now trying to reduce their dependence on one export by diversifying their economies. For example, Senegal became independent in 1960. At that time, more than 70 percent of Senegal's people worked in the peanut industry. Today, Senegal has other major export industries, such as fishing, fish processing, and mining. Peanuts now account for only a small percent of the money Senegal earns from exports.

Target Skill **Predict** Based on what you know about specialized economies, predict whether more African countries are likely to change their economies.

Farming Improvements African nations face another economic problem—how to feed a growing population. Several governments are trying to help farmers increase the size of their crops. One method they use is to develop hybrid plants. A **hybrid** is a plant created by breeding different types of the same plant. The goal is that the best qualities of each type of plant will show up in the hybrid. Since the late 1990s, West Africans have been planting hybrid rice that combines the best aspects of African and Asian rices. As a result, these farmers have been able to produce more rice.

✓ Reading Check **Which two activities do most African economies depend upon?**

Expanding Economies
Today, fish markets like the ones below are helping Senegal's economy succeed. Fish products have become Senegal's major export.
Generalize *What advantages do you think the fish industry offers to a country with a specialized economy?*

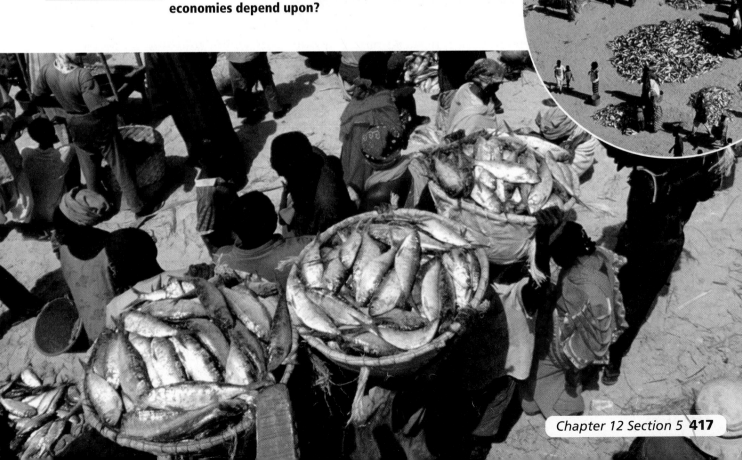

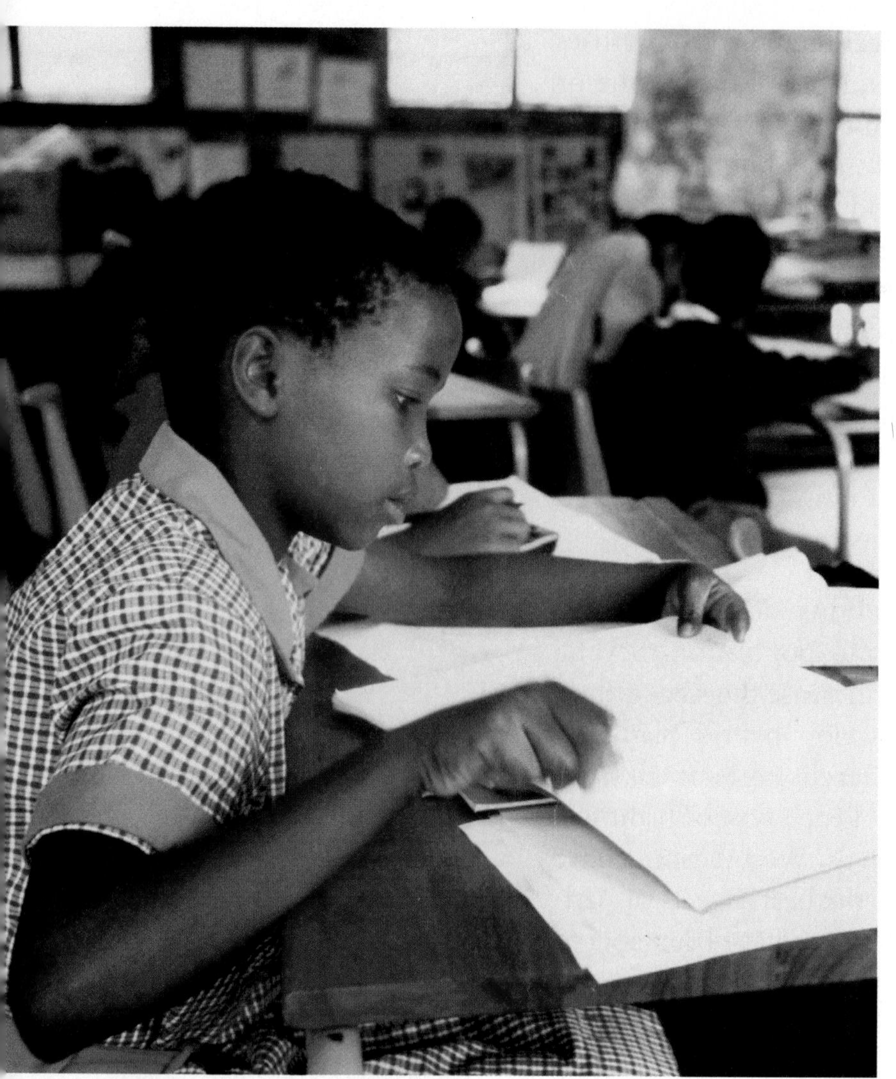

A South African girl focuses on her schoolwork.

Social Issues

In addition to making economic improvements, African nations also must provide social services to their growing populations. Many Africans need better access to education and health care.

Education African children must often contribute to their family's income by working on family farms or by selling goods in the market. When girls and boys go to school, families sacrifice. But most Africans are willing to make this sacrifice because they know education can improve their children's lives.

It has long been a tradition in Africa for communities to actively support their schools. If needed, people will construct new schools. For example, parents in South Africa have often helped to build new schools when the government could not do it alone. Even so, many of the schools are overcrowded, so students must take turns attending classes.

The headmaster at one such school said that students "who couldn't cram into the desks knelt on the floor or stood on their toes so as not to miss a word the teacher was saying." African students are often expected to help keep their school and its grounds clean. The students might do this by sweeping the floors or disposing of the trash.

Reading and Writing The number of Africans who are literate varies from country to country. Being **literate** means being able to read and write. In all African countries, more people have learned to read and write since independence. When Mozambique gained independence from Portugal in 1975, less than 7 percent of its people were literate. Today, about 48 percent of the people in Mozambique are literate. In Tanzania, progress with literacy has been even more dramatic. When the country gained independence from Britain in 1961, only 15 percent of Tanzania's people were literate. Today, about 78 percent of Tanzanians can read and write.

Health Another social issue that differs from country to country in Africa is **life expectancy**—the average length of time a person can expect to live. In Morocco, life expectancy is between 67 and 72 years. In Southern Africa, however, the average life expectancy is less than 50 years. In the Southern African country of Botswana, people only live an average of 32 years.

The main reason for low life expectancy in Africa is childhood disease. There are many diseases for which children have low resistance. For example, insects spread diseases such as malaria. Unclean drinking water and living conditions help spread other diseases. The virus called HIV causes AIDS. Millions of African children have been born with HIV, and millions more adults have died of AIDS before age 50.

Preventing Disease Although the problem of AIDS exists around the world, it is worst in Southern Africa. One reason is that many Southern Africans who are poor cannot afford drugs that might help them. Also, many people have not had access to education, so they have not learned how to prevent the disease. African governments are working with groups such as the World Health Organization to prevent and treat health problems. Some progress has been made. For example, individuals and organizations in Uganda have worked hard to reduce the number of HIV infections there. Because of its success, Uganda may serve as a model for preventing and controlling HIV in other countries.

✓ Reading Check **What is the main reason for low life expectancy in Africa?**

Health Concerns in Africa
Children surround a health worker at a clinic in Gambia as she writes down information about their health.
Predict *In what ways do you think the health worker can help this community?*

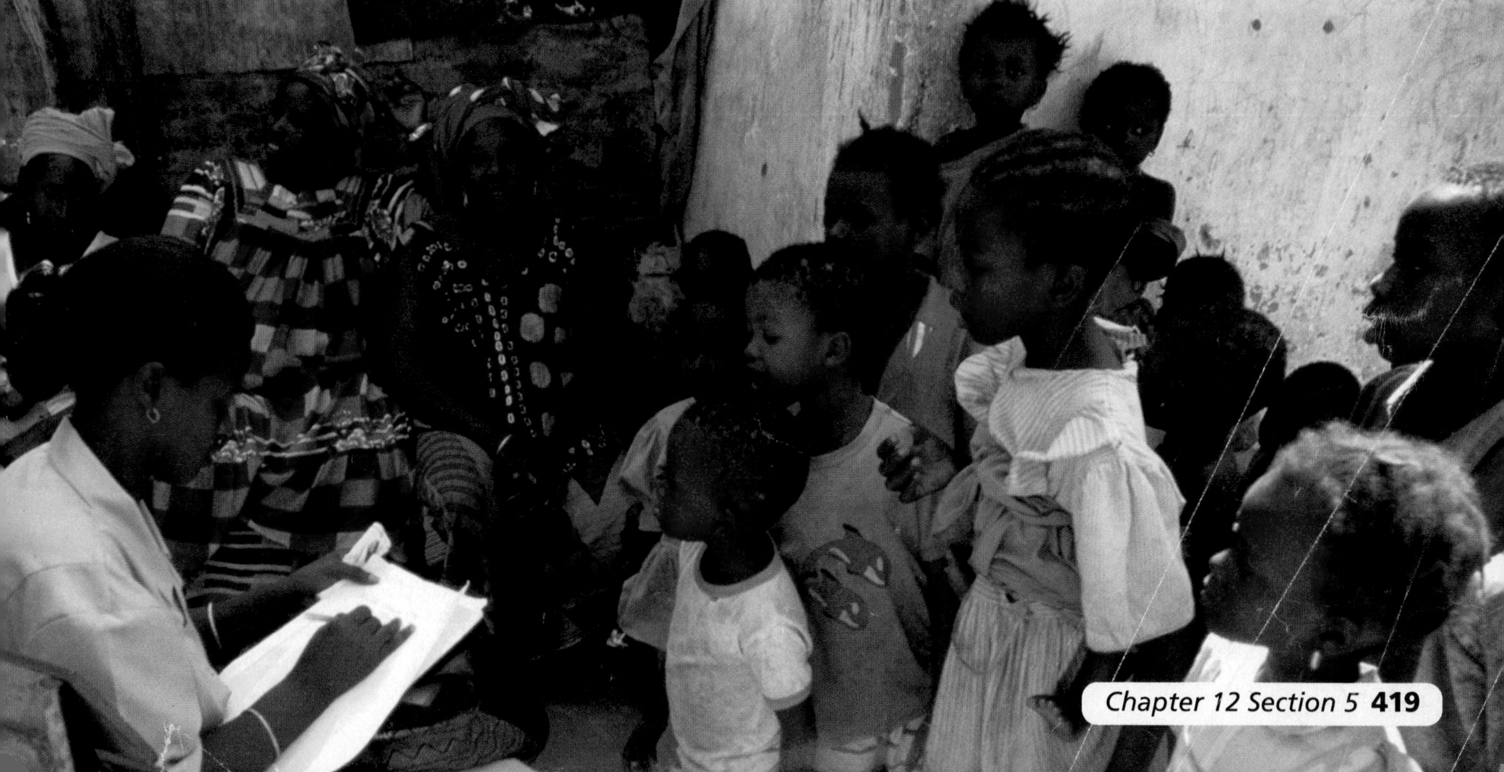

Men plant trees in Madagascar to help prevent erosion.

The Environment

Like other countries around the world, the countries of Africa face a number of environmental challenges. About two thirds of Africa is desert or dry land. High-quality farmland is scarce, and rainfall may vary greatly over the year. These environmental factors make farming especially challenging in parts of Africa.

Soil Problems People in Africa's rural areas often struggle to make a living. Much of the land in Africa is poor for farming. People thus need great areas of land to raise enough crops to support their families. They may cut down trees to use or sell the wood and to clear land for farming. With no cover from trees, soil is exposed to wind and rain. The soil then erodes, or wears away. Soil erosion reduces the amount of land on which food can grow. Without enough farmland, many Africans face starvation.

Solutions From Science Improvements in science can help feed Africans and protect Africa's environment. Irrigation projects, hybrids, and plants that hold water in the ground have all increased crop harvests. To fight soil erosion, Nigerian farmers now plant traditional crops like yams in long rows. Between the rows they plant trees that hold the soil in place. African nations still face many challenges, but they are trying to meet these challenges by using their resources and improving education.

✓ Reading Check **How have Nigerian farmers fought soil erosion?**

Section 5 Assessment

Key Terms

Review the key terms at the beginning of this section. Use each term in a sentence that explains its meaning.

Target Reading Skill

What did you predict about this section? How did your prediction guide your reading?

Comprehension and Critical Thinking

1. (a) Recall Do many African nations today have specialized economies?

(b) Draw Conclusions Why are African nations trying to diversify their economies?

2. (a) Identify What social issues are people facing in Africa today?

(b) Infer Literacy rates in most African countries have increased since independence. Education has also improved. From these facts, what can you infer that people value in Africa?

3. (a) Name Give an example of an environmental challenge African nations face today.

(b) Analyze How is that challenge being addressed?

Writing Activity

Suppose you are the economic advisor to the president of an African country. Write a brief report on some steps the president might take to improve the economy.

For: An activity on environmental issues in Africa
Visit: PHSchool.com
Web Code: lad-5205

Chapter 12 Review and Assessment

◆ Chapter Summary

Section 1: African Beginnings

- Our ancestors were originally hunters and gatherers and became herders and farmers.
- The early African civilizations of Egypt and Nubia arose along the Nile River.
- When Bantu-speaking farmers migrated, Bantu languages spread throughout much of Africa.

Bronze head

Section 2: Kingdoms, City-States, and Empires

- Along East Africa's coast, civilizations grew strong from trade.
- North Africa was shaped by the Carthaginians, the Romans, and the Arabs.
- West African kingdoms grew rich from trade with North Africa.

Section 3: European Conquest of Africa

- Europeans explored Africa's coast to expand their trade ties beyond North Africa.
- Europeans expanded their trade with Africa to include slaves, whom they sent to work on plantations in the Americas.
- European countries claimed African lands for themselves, which had lasting effects on Africa.

Section 4: Independence and Its Challenges

- Fueled by increased feelings of African nationalism, African political parties and leaders worked for the rights of Africans.
- Africans who fought in World War II returned home seeking freedom and independence for their own countries.
- After World War II, African nations gradually gained independence from colonial powers.

Section 5: Issues for Africa Today

- To increase economic stability, African countries are trying to diversify their economies.
- Africans today are working to increase literacy rates and life expectancy.
- Africans are trying to address environmental issues, such as soil erosion, through the help of science, education, and the sensible use of land and other resources.

South Africa

◆ Reviewing Key Terms

Use each key term below in a sentence that shows the meaning of the term.

1. domesticate
2. civilization
3. migrate
4. ethnic group
5. city-state
6. pilgrimage
7. plantation
8. colonize
9. nationalism
10. Pan-Africanism
11. boycott
12. democracy
13. commercial farming
14. hybrid
15. literate
16. life expectancy

Chapter 12 Review and Assessment (continued)

◆ Comprehension and Critical Thinking

17. (a) List Identify some of the skills early Africans used to survive.
(b) Draw Conclusions How did the onset of farming affect early civilizations in Africa?

18. (a) Name Identify an ancient trading civilization from each of the following areas: East Africa, North Africa, and West Africa.
(b) Explain Why was trade important to ancient African civilizations?
(c) Analyze Information What was the relationship between trade and the spread of Islam in Africa?

19. (a) Recall How did the relationship between Europeans and Africans begin?
(b) Identify Sequence How did the relationship between Europeans and Africans change over time?
(c) Identify Effects Describe the effects of the Atlantic slave trade on Africa.

20. (a) Define What is meant by the phrase "the scramble for Africa"?
(b) Describe What challenges have African nations faced since independence?
(c) Make Inferences In what ways did colonial rule cause problems for African countries after independence?

21. (a) Identify What economic, social, and environmental issues challenge Africans today?
(b) Explain How are Africans working to improve their economies and social conditions?

◆ Skills Practice

Sequencing In the Skills for Life activity in this chapter, you learned how to show sequence. Review the steps you followed to learn this skill. Then make a timeline of key events in this chapter.

◆ Writing Activity: Language Arts

In the 1800s, many people in the United States spoke out against slavery. They were called abolitionists because they wanted to abolish, or put an end to, slavery. Using what you have learned about the slave trade, write a speech that could be used by an abolitionist to help end slavery.

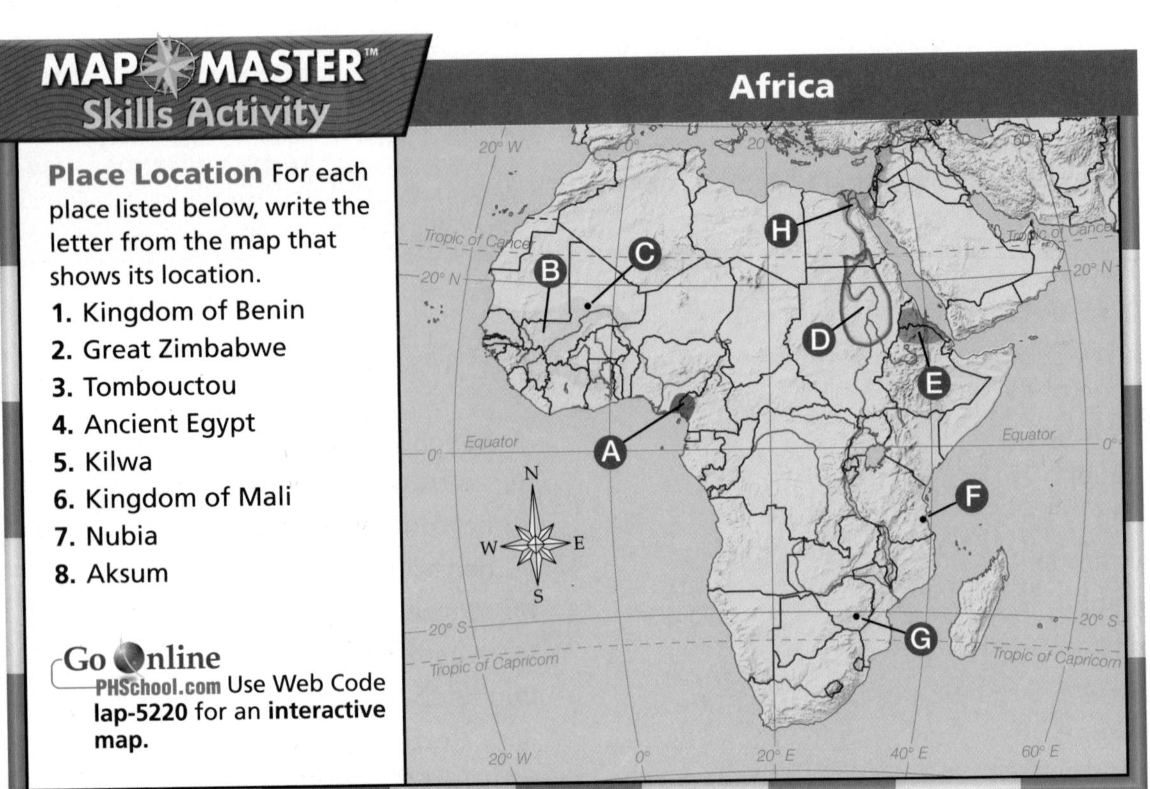

MAP MASTER™ Skills Activity

Place Location For each place listed below, write the letter from the map that shows its location.

1. Kingdom of Benin
2. Great Zimbabwe
3. Tombouctou
4. Ancient Egypt
5. Kilwa
6. Kingdom of Mali
7. Nubia
8. Aksum

Go Online PHSchool.com Use Web Code **lap-5220** for an **interactive map.**

Standardized Test Prep

Test-Taking Tips

Some questions on standardized tests ask you to analyze a reading selection. Study the passage below. Then follow the tips to answer the sample question.

In A.D. 1312, Mansa Musa became emperor of Mali. As emperor, he controlled huge supplies of gold and salt. Mansa Musa brought laws based on Islam to his land. Mali became a safe place to live and travel. The emperor also promoted trade with North Africa. His fame spread to Europe.

TIP Try to identify the main idea, or most important point, in the paragraph. Every sentence in a paragraph helps to support this idea.

Pick the letter that best answers the question.

From this paragraph, it is clear that Mansa Musa

A ~~became too powerful for the good of his people.~~

B ~~was the most powerful ruler in the world at that time.~~

C brought order and prosperity to his land.

D traveled to Europe to promote trade.

TIP Cross out answer choices that don't make sense. Then choose the BEST answer from the remaining choices.

Think It Through You can rule out A and B. Mansa Musa was powerful, but the paragraph doesn't suggest that he was too powerful or that he was the world's most powerful ruler. That leaves C and D. It is true that Mansa Musa's travels promoted trade, but the paragraph doesn't mention a trip to Europe. The correct answer is C.

Practice Questions

Use the tips above and other tips in this book to help you answer the following questions.

1. An early civilization formed in which area along the Nile River?
   A Mali
   B Ghana
   C Nubia
   D Great Zimbabwe

2. During the time of the Atlantic slave trade,
   A Europeans traded weapons for African slaves.
   B slaves in the European colonies usually won their freedom after a few years.
   C almost all slaves survived the voyage across the Atlantic.
   D Africans did not profit from slavery.

3. What was the goal of the Pan-African movement?
   A bringing all Africans together in one nation
   B bringing all Africans living around the world together to work for their rights and freedoms
   C bringing only Africans living in Africa together to work for their rights and freedoms
   D bringing all Africans living outside of Africa back to Africa

Read the passage below, and then answer the question that follows.

European countries competed with one another to gain African territory. Instead of going to war over territory, they set rules for how they could claim African land. By 1900, European nations had colonized many parts of Africa.

4. What can you conclude from this passage about the colonization of Africa?
   A Africans did not resist colonization.
   B Africa was colonized sometime after 1900.
   C European nations believed they could benefit from controlling Africa's resources.
   D European nations were not good at fighting wars with one another.

Use Web Code **laa-5200** for **Chapter 12 self-test.**

Chapter

13 Cultures of Africa

Chapter Preview

This chapter will introduce you to the cultures of Africa and help you understand what the lives of the people in the region are like.

Target Reading Skill

Comparison and Contrast In this chapter you will focus on comparing and contrasting ideas to help you understand the text that you read. Making comparisons, identifying contrasts, and using signal words are all ways for you to learn as you read.

▶ A dancer leaps through the air to the rhythm of the drums at a performance in Burundi.

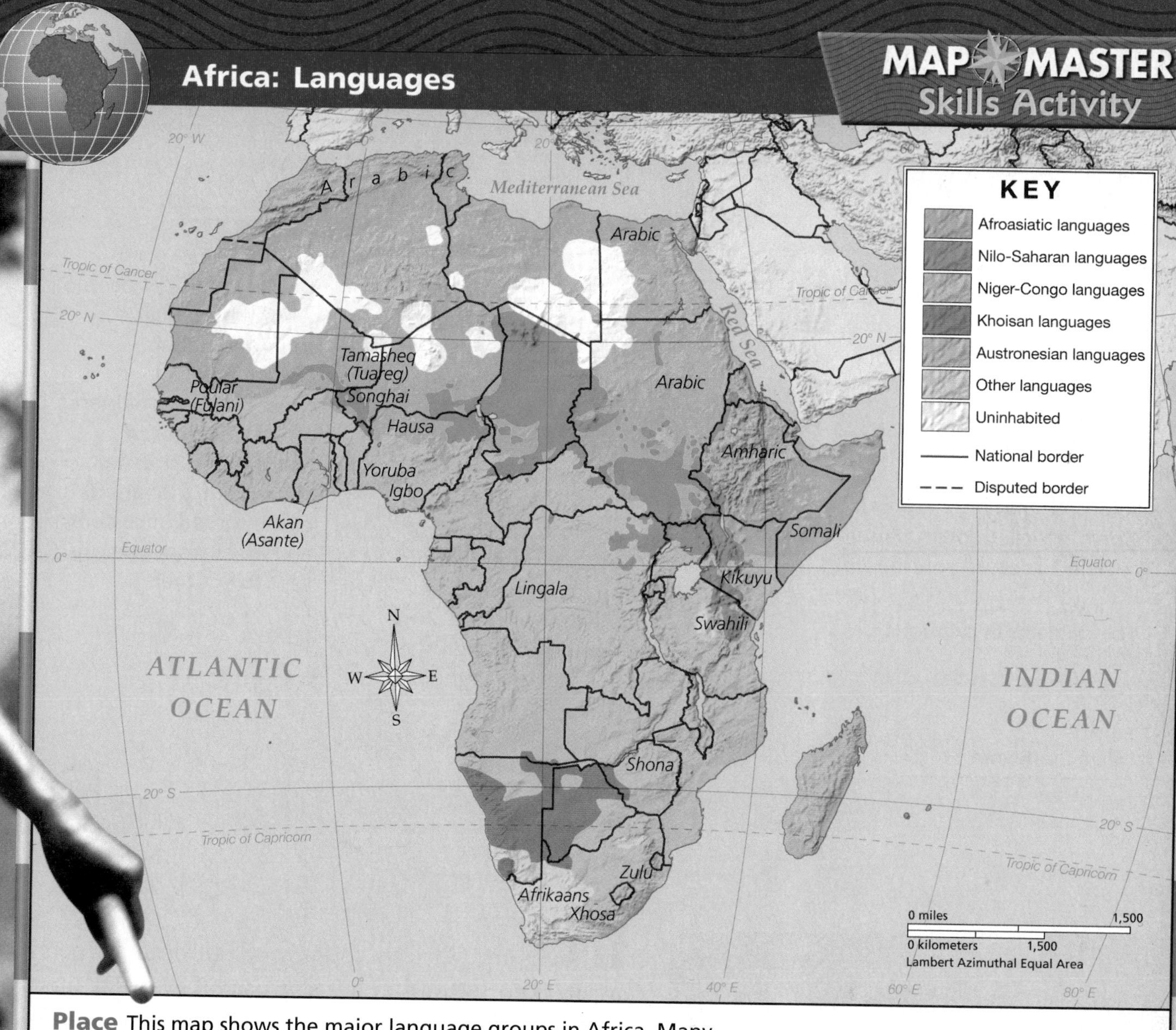

Place This map shows the major language groups in Africa. Many individual languages exist within each group. In all, more than 1,500 languages are spoken in Africa. **Identify** Name the two African language groups that are the largest. **Draw Conclusions** Why do you think large numbers of people who live near one another tend to speak languages from the same language group?

Go Online
PHSchool.com Use Web Code **lap-5310** for step-by-step **map skills practice.**

Section 1 The Cultures of North Africa

Prepare to Read

Objectives

In this section you will

1. Learn about the elements of culture.
2. Discover how Islam influences life in North Africa.
3. Find out about cultural change in North Africa.

Taking Notes

As you read, find details about the cultures of North Africa. Copy the outline below, and use it to record your findings.

I. The elements of culture
  A.
    1.
    2.
  B.
II. Islamic influence

Target Reading Skill

Make Comparisons Making comparisons between groups or situations can help you see what they have in common. As you read this section, compare the ways of life of different peoples in North Africa. Look for similarities among ethnic groups, among people who live in different locations, or among other groups that are logical to compare.

Key Terms

- **culture** (KUL chur) *n.* the way of life of people who share similar customs and beliefs
- **Quran** (koo RAHN) *n.* the sacred book of Islam; also spelled *Koran*
- **cultural diffusion** (KUL chur ul dih FYOO zhun) *n.* the spread of customs and ideas from one culture to another

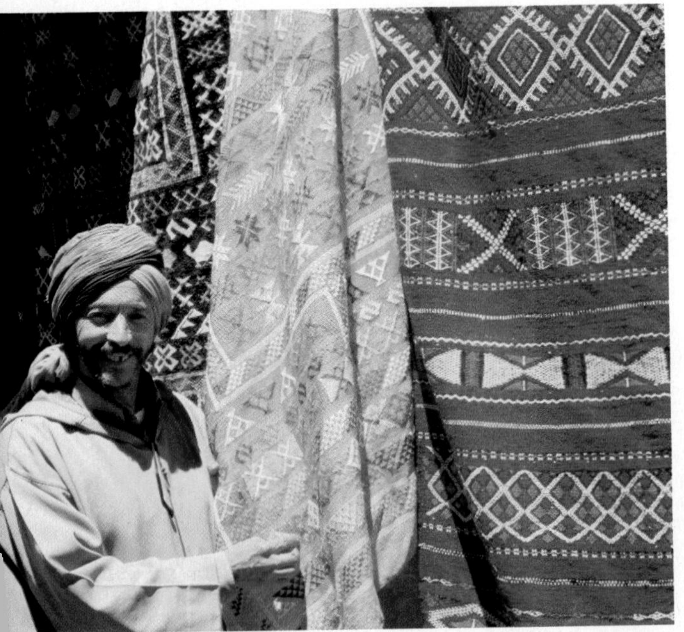

A carpet salesman in Marrakech

In the North African country of Morocco, carpets are an export. But they are also part of everyday life. In some Moroccan homes, carpets serve as more than just floor coverings. People may use them as places to sit and to sleep. People also use special carpets as prayer mats.

Suppose your family lives in the Moroccan city of Marrakech (ma ruh KESH). A typical day might unfold in the following way. After breakfast, your mother spends the day weaving carpets. She learned this skill from her mother, who learned it from her mother. Her workday ends at sunset, when she hears the crier who calls out from the nearby mosque (mahsk), the Muslim house of worship. When she hears the call, your mother joins many others in reciting this prayer in Arabic: "There is no god but God, and Muhammad is His messenger."

The Elements of Culture

The way of life you just read about is different in some ways from yours. In other words, Morocco's culture is somewhat different from yours. **Culture** is the way of life of a group of people who share similar customs and beliefs.

What Defines Culture? Culture has many elements. Culture includes food, clothing, homes, jobs, and language. It also includes things that are not so easy to see, such as how people view their world and what their beliefs are. These views and beliefs shape the way people behave. In Morocco, for example, many people take time from their activities to pray several times each day.

Shared Elements Different cultures may have elements in common. People in different places sometimes share the same language, although they may speak different dialects, or versions of that language. Similarly, cultures sometimes share the same religion, although people may practice it in different ways.

Some shared elements of culture are easy to notice. People of different cultures might wear similar clothing or live in similar housing. In many rural villages in Morocco, for example, houses are made of thick adobe (uh DOH bee), a type of brick made from sun-dried clay. Far from Morocco, in Mexico and in the southwestern United States, many people in rural areas also live in adobe houses.

✓ Reading Check **Name some cultural elements that are easy to see.**

Links to Science

Building With Adobe
Adobe bricks are made of clay and plant fibers. The fibers strengthen the bricks and keep them from crumbling. Techniques for making adobe first spread around the globe with the Arabs. Later, the Spanish introduced these techniques to present-day Mexico and the southwestern United States.

Adobe is a good building material because it acts as an insulator, a material that helps keep outside heat from traveling inside. This insulating quality is especially important in hot climates, such as Morocco's (below).

Religion and Culture in North Africa

The peoples of North Africa are spread out over a large area that includes the following countries: Egypt, Libya, Tunisia, Algeria, and Morocco. North Africans have many different backgrounds and ways of life. The Arabic language helps unify the different peoples of North Africa. So does Islam.

Muslim Beliefs Religion is an important part of North African culture. More than 95 percent of North Africans are Muslims. Muslims believe in God, whom they call by the Arabic word *Allah* (AL uh). The founder of Islam was a man named Muhammad. Muslims believe that Muhammad was a prophet, or a religious teacher who speaks for God or a god. In Islam, Jesus and the prophets of the Hebrew Bible, or Christian Old Testament, are also believed to be God's messengers. However, Muhammad is considered God's final messenger.

The sacred book of Islam is called the **Quran** (koo RAHN). Muslims consider the Quran to be the word of God. They believe that God revealed the verses of the Quran to the prophet Muhammad. Like the Hebrew and Christian Bibles, the Quran contains many kinds of writing, including stories, promises, and instructions. The Quran teaches about God, and it also provides a guide to living. The Quran forbids lying, stealing, and murder. It also prohibits gambling, eating pork, and drinking alcohol.

Chart Skills

Muslims call Muhammad's most essential teachings the Five Pillars of Islam. These pillars are duties that all Muslims are expected to follow, such as praying daily, as shown above. **Define** What are alms? **Infer** Why do you think Muhammad wanted Muslims to regularly declare their belief in God?

The Five Pillars of Islam

Pillar	Description
Declaration of Faith	Muslims must regularly declare the belief that there is only one God and Muhammad is God's messenger.
Prayer	Muslims must pray five times each day, facing in the direction of the holy city of Mecca.
Almsgiving	Muslims must give alms, or money that goes to the needy.
Fasting	Muslims must fast during daylight hours in the month of Ramadan.
Pilgrimage	Muslims must make a pilgrimage to Mecca at least one time in their lives if they are able.

Islam and Law The Islamic system of law is based on the Quran. Islamic law governs many aspects of life, including family life, business practices, banking, and government. Because so many North Africans are Muslims, Islamic law influences the cultures of the region.

Ethnic Groups of North Africa Most North Africans are Arabs. Because the Arab influence is so strong, North Africa is sometimes seen as a part (the western end) of the Arab world. But the region has other ethnic groups besides the Arabs. The largest of these groups is the Berbers, who live mainly in Algeria and Morocco. Most Berbers speak both Berber and Arabic, and almost all are Muslim.

Many Berbers live in cities, while others live in small villages in rugged mountain areas. They make their living by herding and farming. The Tuareg (TWAH reg) are a group of Berbers who live in the Sahara, the enormous desert that stretches across the southern part of North Africa. The Tuareg herd camels, goats, and other livestock and also engage in long-distance trade.

Traditional and Modern Lifestyles In parts of rural North Africa, some people live traditionally, or in ways similar to those of their parents and grandparents. But traditional and modern ways of life mix in towns and large cities such as Cairo (KY roh), in Egypt, and Tunis (TOO nis), in Tunisia.

Some city people work at traditional crafts such as carpet weaving. Others work as architects, scientists, bus drivers, or bankers. Some sell baskets in outdoor markets. Others sell television sets, books, and other items in modern stores. The peoples of North Africa may live vastly different lives, yet Islam helps form a common bond of culture among them.

✓ Reading Check **What are the two largest ethnic groups of North Africa?**

Mixing Old and New
As is traditional for Muslim women, these Moroccan girls are wearing head scarves. At the same time, one is using a cell phone. **Analyze Images** *Do you think these girls would say it is easy or difficult to blend old and new ways?*

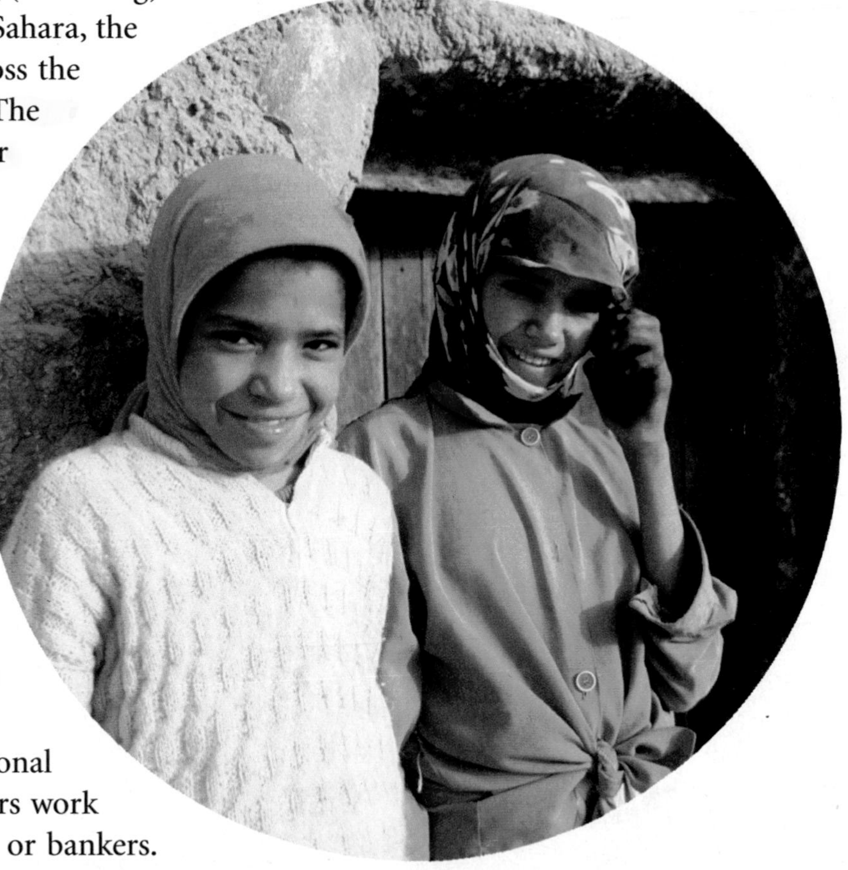

Target Skill

Make Comparisons
The people who live in North Africa's cities practice a variety of lifestyles. What element of culture do they have in common?

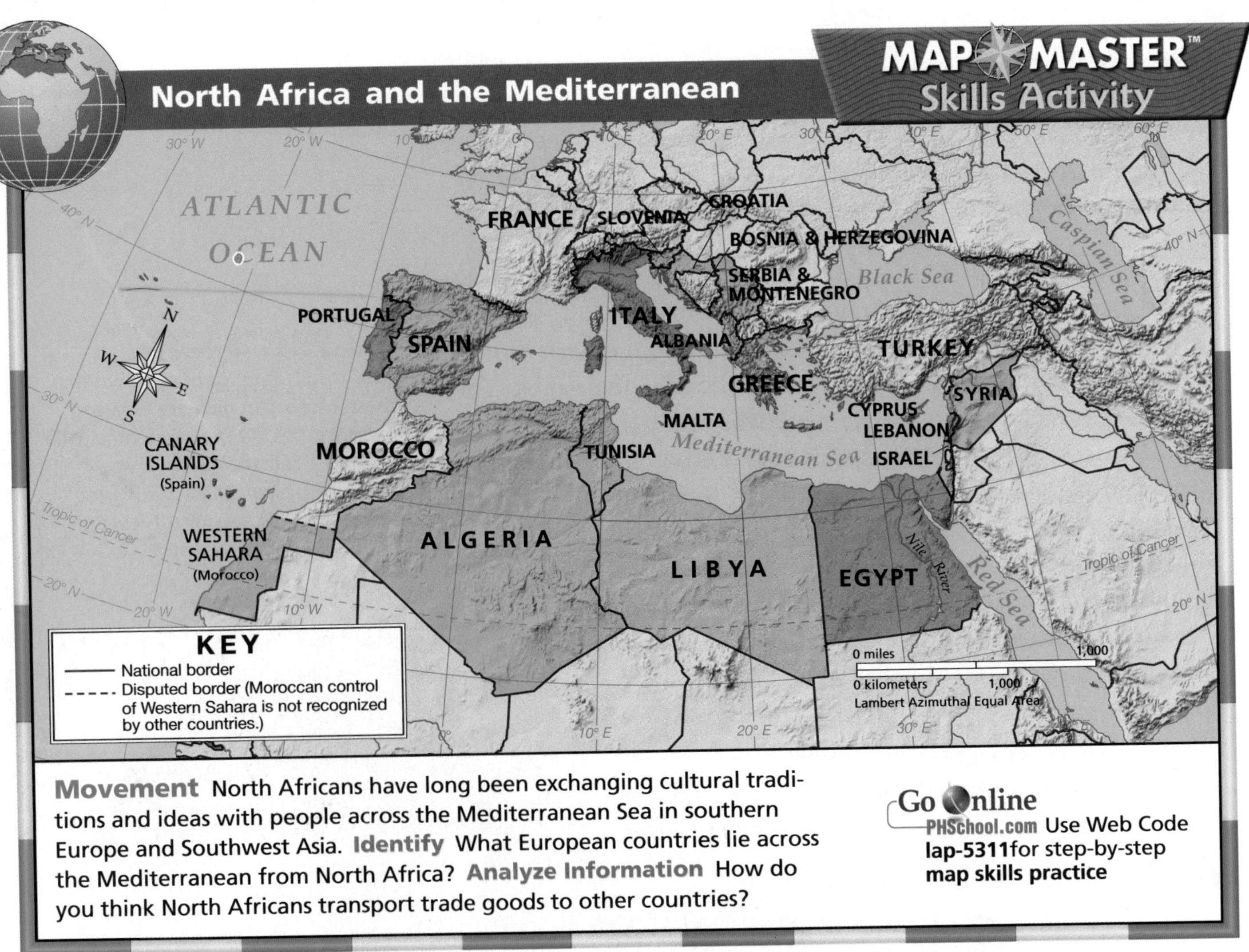

Movement North Africans have long been exchanging cultural traditions and ideas with people across the Mediterranean Sea in southern Europe and Southwest Asia. **Identify** What European countries lie across the Mediterranean from North Africa? **Analyze Information** How do you think North Africans transport trade goods to other countries?

Go Online PHSchool.com Use Web Code **lap-5311** for step-by-step map skills practice

Cultural Change in North Africa

Tunisian pottery

North Africa's mix of traditional and modern ways of life shows that culture does not stay the same forever. It changes all the time. Cultural changes often occur when people move from one place to another. As they travel, people share their customs and ideas with others. They also learn about new ideas and customs. The result is **cultural diffusion,** or the spread of customs and ideas to new places. *Diffusion* means "spreading out."

A Hub of Trade Study the map above. An important factor in the diffusion of culture in North Africa is location. Because of its location, North Africa has been a hub, or center, of trade for people from Europe, Asia, North Africa, and other parts of Africa. Thus, the peoples of these regions have come into contact with one another's cultures. Many customs and ideas have spread into and out of North Africa.

Conquering Empires The mixing of cultures in North Africa did not occur only through trade. It also occurred through conquest. North Africa was home to the ancient Egyptians, one of the world's oldest civilizations. Once the ancient Egyptians had developed trade links with ancient civilizations in both Europe and Southwest Asia, these civilizations competed with one another for power. The ancient Egyptians both conquered and were conquered by other empires. Through these conquests, more cultural diffusion occurred.

In Algeria, women in traditional Muslim clothes walk alongside women and men in Western dress.

Western and Muslim Cultures One of the more recent influences on North Africa is Western culture, meaning the cultures of Europe and North America. Some Muslims are concerned that their countries are becoming too Westernized. More people are wearing Western clothes, buying Western products, seeing films produced by the West, and adopting Western ideas. Some Muslims fear that these influences will lead to the loss of Muslim values and traditions. They want to preserve their way of life. All over Africa, people face the challenge of how to preserve the traditions they value as their countries change.

✓ Reading Check **With what regions have North Africans traditionally traded?**

Section 1 Assessment

Key Terms
Review the key terms at the beginning of this section. Use each term in a sentence that explains its meaning.

Target Reading Skill
Other than religion, what is an element of culture that most North Africans have in common?

Comprehension and Critical Thinking

1. **(a) Name** What are some elements of culture?
(b) Draw Conclusions How do you think cultural beliefs shape the way people behave?
2. **(a) Recall** What are the beliefs of the followers of Islam?
(b) Analyze Information How has Islam influenced the cultures of North Africa?
3. **(a) Locate** Describe North Africa's location.
(b) Cause and Effect How has North Africa's location contributed to cultural diffusion?
(c) Analyze Information Do you think that adding new elements to a culture has to lead to the loss of old ones?

Writing Activity
What is your culture? What traditions in your culture do you think are the most important ones to preserve? Write an essay describing these customs and explaining why you value them.

Writing Tip To help you get started, write a list of traditions and customs you practice throughout the year.

Section 2 The Cultures of West Africa

Prepare to Read

Objectives

In this section you will

1. Learn about West Africa's ethnic diversity.
2. Find out about the importance of family ties in West African culture.
3. Examine the West African tradition of storytelling.

Taking Notes

As you read, look for details about the cultures of West Africa. Copy the flowchart below, and use it to record your findings.

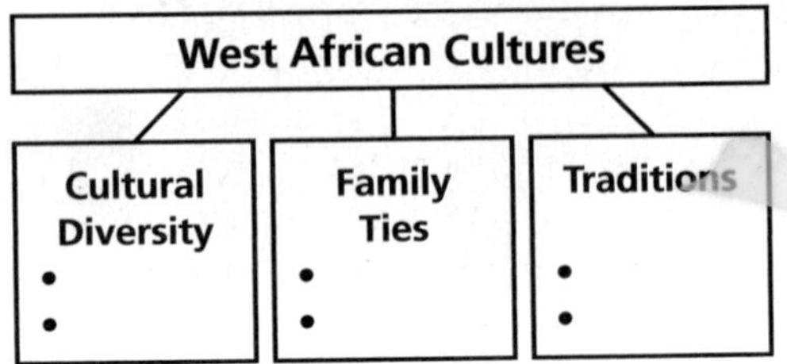

Target Reading Skill

Identify Contrasts Identifying contrasts between two groups or situations can help you see what is unique about each one. As you read this section, contrast the cultures in West Africa with the cultures in the United States. List the differences that relate to language and to family life.

Key Terms

- **cultural diversity** (KUL chur ul duh VUR suh tee) *n.* a wide variety of cultures
- **kinship** (KIN ship) *n.* a family relationship
- **nuclear family** (NOO klee ur FAM uh lee) *n.* the part of a family that includes parents and children
- **extended family** (ek STEN did FAM uh lee) *n.* the part of a family that includes parents, children, and other relatives
- **lineage** (LIN ee ij) *n.* a group of families descended from a common ancestor
- **clan** (klan) *n.* a group of lineages

Mauritanian students in school

In Mauritania (mawr uh TAY nee uh), North Africa meets West Africa. There, the Sahara merges into the tree-dotted grasslands of the savanna. But geography is not the only part of Mauritanian life that reveals major contrasts. Culture does, too. If you were to attend school in one of the small villages in southern Mauritania, you could see this firsthand. You would hear teachers speaking in French, even though they probably also know the country's official language, Arabic. Outside the classroom, students would speak the local language of their ethnic group, which might differ from town to town.

Cultural Diversity of West Africa

Being able to speak more than one language is useful in West Africa, which is home to hundreds of ethnic groups. The region is famous for its **cultural diversity,** or wide variety of cultures. Unlike the ethnic groups of North Africa, those of West Africa are not united by a single religion or a common language.

Many Languages in One Place
If you were shopping at this market in West Africa, you might hear a number of languages being spoken. **Draw Conclusions** *How do you think people communicate in situations like this?*

A Region of Many Languages Think about your community. Imagine that the people who live nearby speak a different language. How could you communicate with them? Suppose you want to shop in a store, eat in a restaurant, or attend a sports event taking place in the next town. It might seem like visiting another country.

This situation is exactly what many West Africans experience. The hundreds of ethnic groups in West Africa speak different languages. Sometimes groups in neighboring villages speak different languages. In order to communicate, most West Africans speak more than one language. Some speak four or five languages. This practice helps unify countries with many ethnic groups. People use these various languages when they travel or conduct business. They often use French, English, Portuguese, or a local language called Hausa to communicate among various ethnic groups.

Rural and Urban Workers The ethnic groups in West Africa differ in more than just the languages they speak. Like North Africans, West Africans make a living in various ways. Many West Africans live in rural areas. A typical village consists of a group of homes surrounded by farmland. The villagers grow food for themselves as well as cash crops to sell. In the Sahara and the dry Sahel just south of it, many people herd cattle, goats, sheep, or camels. Along the coast, most West Africans make a living by fishing. Some West Africans live in large cities where they may work in hospitals, hotels, or office buildings.

✓ Reading Check **How does cultural diversity affect the people of West Africa?**

West African Families

Like North Africans, West Africans see themselves as members of a number of groups. Just as you belong to a family, one or more ethnic groups, and a country, so do West Africans.

Target Skill **Identify Contrasts** A nuclear family and an extended family are similar. Contrast them to understand the important differences between them.

Kinship and Customs One of the strongest bonds that West Africans have is the bond of **kinship,** or family relationship. The first level of kinship is the **nuclear family,** which consists of parents and their children. The next level is the **extended family,** a group consisting of the nuclear family plus other relatives. It may include grandparents, aunts, uncles, and cousins. Often, members of a West African extended family all live together. They also work together and make decisions together. Family members care for the elderly, the sick, and the less well-off. They also watch over the children of other families in the village and willingly help neighbors.

Larger Kinship Groups In many rural areas, kinship reaches beyond extended families to larger groups. One such group is a **lineage,** or a group of families that can trace their descent back to a common ancestor. Some people also recognize larger kinship groups called clans. A **clan** is a group of lineages. As with a lineage, the people in a clan can all trace their roots back to a common ancestor. Members of a clan may be more distantly related to one another than members of a lineage because the group of members is larger in a clan.

West African Family Ties
Members of an extended family in Nigeria gather in front of their home (bottom). A woman in Ivory Coast cares for her granddaughter (below). **Identify Effects** *What effects do you think the strong kinship ties of West Africa have on communities?*

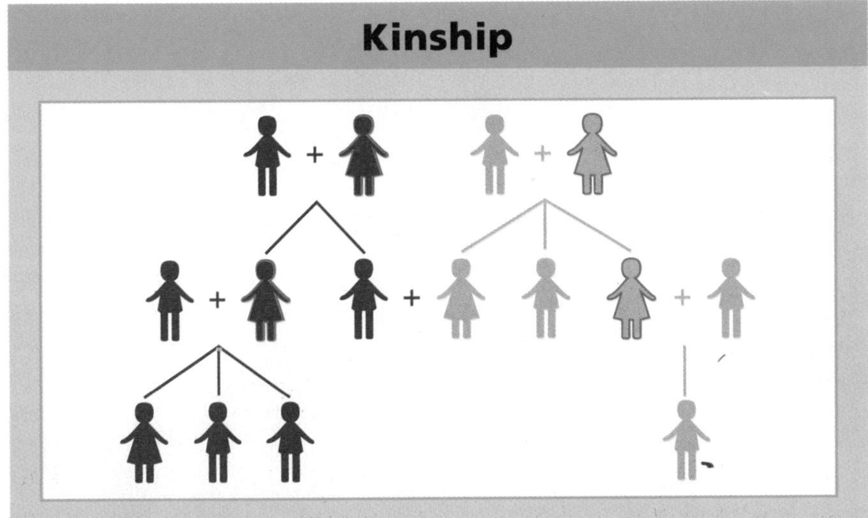

Diagram Skills

The diagram shows the extended family of the married couple at the center. The husband's lineage is in purple, and the wife's is in orange. In a matrilineal society, this family would trace descent through the women who are outlined in red.
Identify How many nuclear families exist in the extended lineage?
Synthesize What is the relationship of the woman at the top of the purple lineage to the three siblings at the bottom of it?

Tracing Lineage Different traditions govern the ways West African groups trace their ancestry. Some groups are matrilineal (mat ruh LIN ee ul), meaning that they trace their descent through female ancestors. In matrilineal societies, a person's father is not considered part of the person's lineage. Within the lineage, children consider their mother's brother their closest adult male relative. Their father is a member of another lineage. Most groups, however, are patrilineal (pat ruh LIN ee ul)—they trace their descent through the male side of the family.

Changes in Family Life Although traditional family ties are still strong in West Africa, family life is changing. More and more people are moving from rural villages to urban areas. This trend, known as urbanization, is occurring not only in Africa but throughout the world.

Many young men are looking for work to support themselves and their families. They travel long distances to West Africa's cities to find jobs. The women often stay in the rural homes. They raise the children and farm the land. The men come home from time to time to visit their families and to share what they have earned.

Families live close together in West African villages such as this one in Mali.

✓ Reading Check **What responsibilities do extended family members have toward one another?**

Master of Storytelling
Boys from an Ivory Coast village listen intently as a griot tells them a legend about their ethnic group's history. **Synthesize** *How does oral storytelling help preserve a culture's history?*

Keeping Traditions Alive

Cultural changes, such as urbanization, affect different families in different ways. As they adapt to these changes, most West Africans try to maintain strong family ties. They pass their history, values, and traditions on to the young.

Storytelling Traditions One important way in which West African traditions are being preserved is through the art of vivid and exciting storytelling. Traditional West African stories are spoken aloud rather than written down. A storyteller called a griot (GREE oh) passes a group's oral traditions on from one generation to another.

Stories of tricksters, animal fables, proverbs, riddles, and songs are all part of West Africa's oral tradition. The details in the stories tell about the histories of ethnic groups and kinships. At the same time, they teach children cultural values. An African proverb reflects the value that West Africans place on handing down traditions from generation to generation: "The young can't teach traditions to the old."

Discovery
CHANNEL
SCHOOL
Video
Learn about the importance of woven cloth in Africa.

African musicians perform around the world, from Massachusetts (left) to Ivory Coast (right).

Cultural Influence The traditions of West Africa have greatly influenced other cultures, especially American culture. Many of the enslaved Africans who were brought to the United States came from West Africa. They brought with them the only things they could: their ideas, stories, dances, music, and customs. The trickster tales of Br'er Rabbit, as well as blues and jazz music, have their roots in West Africa.

Today, West African culture—its stories, music, dances, art, cooking, and clothing—is popular in many countries outside of Africa. Griot guitarists and other musicians from West Africa have international followings. In recent years, four Africans have won the Nobel Prize for literature. One of them is West African—the Nigerian writer Wole Soyinka (WOH lay shaw YING kuh).

✓ Reading Check **What does a griot do?**

Section 2 Assessment

Key Terms

Review the key terms at the beginning of this section. Use each term in a sentence that explains its meaning.

Target Reading Skill

Identify one contrast between the way West Africans use language and the way Americans do.

Comprehension and Critical Thinking

1. (a) Recall In what ways is West Africa culturally diverse?

(b) Identify Effects How does cultural diversity create communication challenges for West Africans?

2. (a) Describe What kinds of kinship ties are found in West African societies?

(b) Draw Conclusions How do you think living together with members of one's extended family helps build a sense of community?

3. (a) Explain What purpose does storytelling serve in West African culture?

(b) Analyze What is the meaning of the proverb "The young can't teach traditions to the old"?

Writing Activity

Suppose you live with your extended family in a small village in West Africa. Make a list of the advantages and disadvantages of your way of life. Indicate which are most important to you.

For: An activity on the cultures of West Africa
Visit: PHSchool.com
Web Code: lad-5302

Comparing and Contrasting

Nathan and Antonio went to the mall to buy CDs. When Antonio saw the CD Nathan had chosen, he commented, "I like that CD. But I think the band's new CD is better. They use more drums on the new CD."

Nathan argued. "I disagree. I like the way the band sounded on the old CD. They had two singers, and the two voices together sounded better than this one singer's voice alone." The girl working at the register smiled. She couldn't hear any differences in the CDs. She thought they were both great.

When you look for differences between two or more items, you *contrast* them. To *compare,* you do one of two things: you look for similarities between two or more items, or you look for similarities *and* differences between two or more items. If you are asked to compare, ask if you should find similarities only, or similarities and differences.

Learn the Skill

Follow these steps to learn how to compare and contrast.

1. **Identify a topic and purpose.** What do you want to compare or contrast, and why? Some purposes for comparing and contrasting are to make a choice, to understand a topic, or to discover patterns.

2. **Select some categories for comparison and contrast.** For example, if you wanted to choose between two bikes, your categories might be color, cost, and types of tires.

3. **Make notes—or a chart—about the categories you are comparing or contrasting.** Some categories call for a yes or no answer. Other categories, such as color or cost, require that you note specific details.

4. **Notice the similarities and differences.** Are the details the same or different for each item?

5. **Draw conclusions.** Write a few sentences explaining whether the items are more similar or more different.

Practice the Skill

Use the steps below, plus your own knowledge, to compare and contrast the two scenes from Africa that are shown in the photographs on this page. Use what you find to determine a pattern in the photographs.

1. What is your topic? What is the purpose?
2. Study the photographs. Then write down at least three categories for comparison and contrast.
3. For each category, take notes on what the photographs show.
4. Now study your notes to see what is similar and what is different about the two photographs.
5. Write a conclusion that explains whether the scenes in the photographs are mostly similar or mostly different. Include a description of one pattern you see in the photographs. Can you describe a third photograph that would fit the pattern?

Chimpanzees in Tanzania

Giraffes in Kenya

Apply the Skill

Reread Sections 1 and 2 of this chapter. Use the steps you learned in this skill to compare and contrast the cultures of North Africa and West Africa.

Section 3

The Cultures of East Africa

Prepare to Read

Objectives

In this section you will

1. Find out how geography has affected the development of East African cultures.
2. Learn how and why ideas about land ownership are changing in East Africa.

Taking Notes

As you read, find details about the cultures of East Africa. Copy the concept web below, and use it to record your findings.

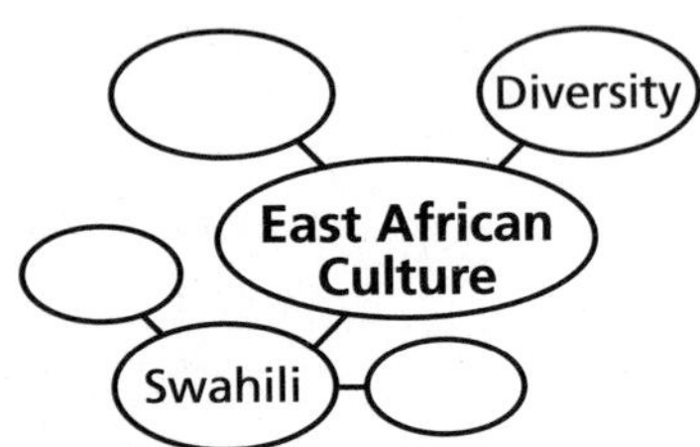

Target Reading Skill

Use Signal Words
Signal words point out relationships among ideas or events. Certain words or phrases, such as *like* and *as with*, can signal a comparison or a contrast. As you read this section, notice the comparisons between East Africa and other parts of Africa.

Key Terms

- **Swahili** (swah HEE lee) *n.* an ethnic group in East Africa that resulted from the mixing of African and Arab ways more than 1,000 years ago; also a language
- **heritage** (HEHR uh tij) *n.* the values, traditions, and customs handed down from one's ancestors

A woman in Lamu gets her hand decorated with henna.

In the neighborhood square, old friends often sit together playing dominoes. A man on a donkey may wander past amidst the occasional roar of motorcycles. Down the street, there is a store that sells spices next to a shop that offers fax services and Internet connections. Nearby, behind shuttered windows that filter the hot sun, women take turns making intricate designs on one another's hands using a natural dye called henna. In former East African city-states such as Lamu (LAH moo), in Kenya, and Zanzibar (ZAN zuh bahr), in Tanzania, such traditional and modern ways are interwoven.

Geography and Cultural Diversity

Like West Africa, East Africa is a region of great cultural diversity. In some parts of the region, such as Lamu and Zanzibar, the diversity reveals itself in the contrast between old and new ways. In other parts, it is reflected in the diversity of languages spoken or religions practiced.

Indian Ocean Connections Much of the cultural diversity of East Africa comes from contact among people from many cultures. Like other Africans, the people of East Africa have often been exposed to other cultures through trade. Turn to the political map of Africa on page 351 of the Regional Overview. Notice how much of East Africa's long coastline borders the Indian Ocean. This ocean provides a trade and travel route for East Africans as well as for the people living across the ocean to the east. These people include Arabs, Indians, and other Asians, even those from countries as far away from Africa as China and Malaysia.

Swahili Culture The connection across the Indian Ocean dates back to early times. Nearly 2,000 years ago, Arab traders began to settle in the coastal villages of East Africa. Members of various African cultures took on elements of Arab culture from the newcomers. The Arabs took on elements of African culture as well. The **Swahili** are an ethnic group that resulted from this mixing of African and Arab ways.

Most people who live in Lamu or Zanzibar are Swahili. A professor in Zanzibar described the history of the Swahili to a reporter in this way:

> **"We have always been middlemen—between the land and the sea, the producers and the buyers, the African and the Arabian. That is not a concern; it is our strength. We will survive. Swahili culture may not be quite the same tomorrow as today, but then nothing living is."**
>
> —*Professor Abdul Sheriff*

Swahili Arts and Crafts
Swahili craftsmen are known for carving front doors with detailed decoration on their frames. This one is in Zanzibar, Tanzania. **Analyze Images** *Why do you think people would choose a front door as a place to show their craft?*

One important strength of the Swahili people is their ability to adapt to other cultures. To adapt is to adjust to new things or circumstances. At the same time, the Swahilis try to preserve their **heritage,** or the values, traditions, and customs handed down from their ancestors.

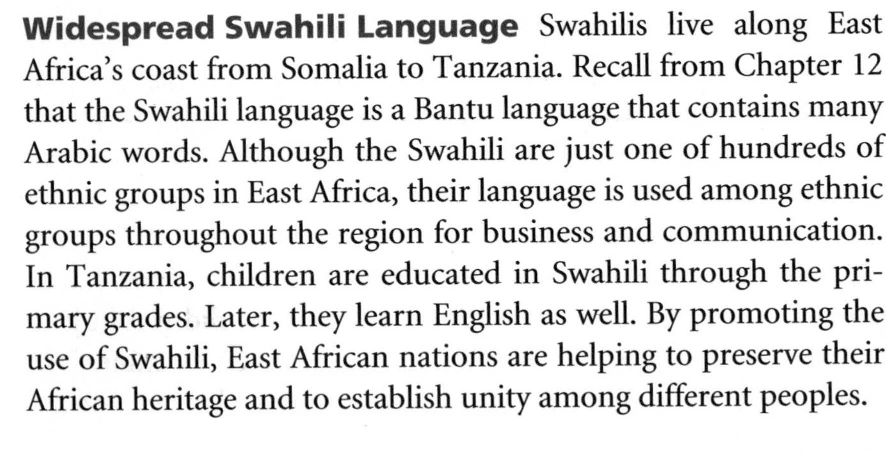

Widespread Swahili Language Swahilis live along East Africa's coast from Somalia to Tanzania. Recall from Chapter 12 that the Swahili language is a Bantu language that contains many Arabic words. Although the Swahili are just one of hundreds of ethnic groups in East Africa, their language is used among ethnic groups throughout the region for business and communication. In Tanzania, children are educated in Swahili through the primary grades. Later, they learn English as well. By promoting the use of Swahili, East African nations are helping to preserve their African heritage and to establish unity among different peoples.

Target Skill **Signal Words** What signal words are used to compare the number of languages spoken in East Africa and West Africa?

Other Languages As is true of West Africa, East Africa is home to many ethnic groups who speak different languages. It is not unusual for people in the region to know three languages or more. For example, in Ethiopia more than 80 languages are spoken, and in Kenya about 40 are spoken. About 1,000 languages can be heard in Sudan alone. The variety of languages spoken in the region is largely due to the long history of migrations of ethnic groups from other parts of the continent. For example, the Bantu migration that you read about earlier brought many Bantu-speaking peoples from West Africa to East Africa.

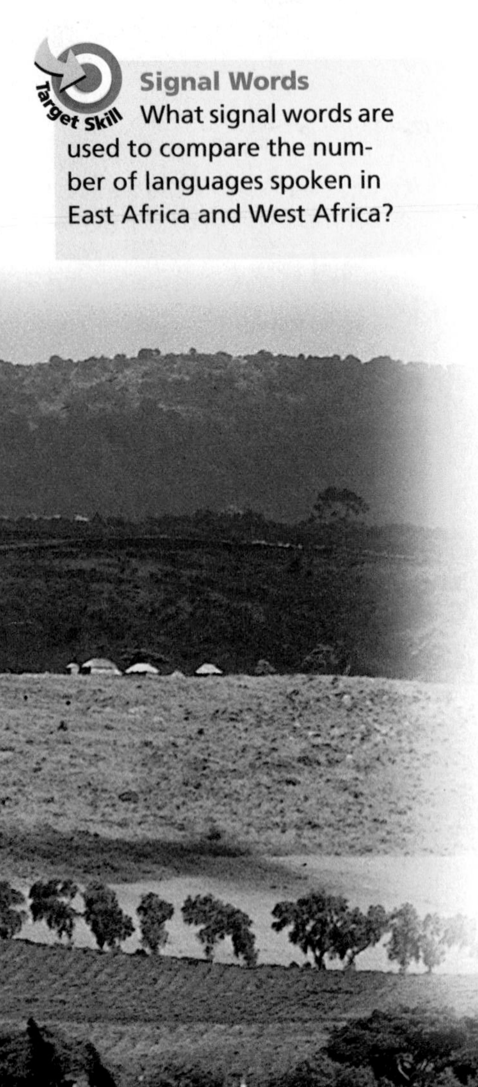

Religion As with languages, religious beliefs in East Africa reflect the cultural diversity of the region. Both Islam and Christianity have large followings there. Islam was introduced to East Africa by Arab traders. Christianity spread into Ethiopia in the A.D. 300s after being introduced to North Africa when the area was a part of the Roman Empire. During the 1800s, Europeans pushed into Africa and spread Christianity even farther. In addition, traditional religions are still practiced in East Africa.

✓ Reading Check **What religions are practiced by East Africans?**

Changing Ideas About Land

In East Africa, as in the rest of Africa, most people live in rural areas, where they farm and tend livestock. The ways in which they work the land and view land ownership are part of the culture of East Africans.

Before Land Was Owned Before Europeans took over parts of Africa in the 1800s, individual Africans did not buy or sell land. The very idea of owning land did not exist. Families had the right to farm plots of land, but the size and location of the plots might change over time.

Traditionally in Africa, extended families farmed the land to produce food for the whole group. Men cleared the land and broke up the soil. Women then planted the seeds, tended the fields, and harvested the crops. Meanwhile, the men herded livestock or traded goods.

The Rise and Fall of Plantations The practice of owning land privately was introduced into much of Africa by European settlers. In parts of East Africa, the British set up plantations. When many African countries became independent, their governments broke up the colonial plantations and sold the land to individual Africans.

Some land in East Africa is still available to buy. But much of it is poor farmland in areas where few people live. In fertile areas such as the Ethiopian Highlands and the Great Rift Valley, most of the land good for farming is already taken. Many people live in these fertile areas. In densely populated countries such as Rwanda (roo AHN duh) and Burundi (boo ROON dee), conflicts have developed over land.

The Legacy of Land
Agriculture is part of life all over East Africa. Farmers work fields of a large plantation (bottom). An Ethiopian farmer tends his fields (inset).
Synthesize Information *Why has farmland caused conflicts in some East African countries?*

Julius Nyerere, Tanzania's first president

Where Is Home? Traditionally, Africans feel a strong bond to the land where they grew up. Like the rest of Africa, East Africa is becoming increasingly urban. Yet even people who spend most of their time in a city often do not call it home. If asked where home is, an East African will usually name the village of his or her family or clan. Most people consider their life in the city temporary. They expect to return to their villages at some point.

Tanzania's former president Julius Nyerere (JOOL yus nyuh REHR uh) is one example. After he stepped down as president in 1985, Nyerere moved back to his home village. Although he was far from Dar es Salaam (DAHR es suh LAHM), one of Tanzania's two capital cities, Nyerere continued to be involved in world affairs. Until his death in 1999, he spent his mornings working in the fields, where he grew corn and millet on his farm.

In an interview in 1996, Nyerere said: "In a sense I am a very rural person. I grew up here, and [working in] Dar es Salaam was a duty. I did my duty and after retiring in 1985, I came back here and said, 'Ah, it's good to be back.' " Many other East Africans feel the same. They do their duty by earning money in the city, but they never forget their rural roots.

✓ Reading Check **How did East Africans farm before Europeans arrived?**

Section 3 Assessment

Key Terms

Review the key terms at the beginning of this section. Use each term in a sentence that explains its meaning.

Target Reading Skill

Make a list of all the signal words you found as you read this section. Describe the comparison that each signal word indicates.

Comprehension and Critical Thinking

1. (a) Locate Where in East Africa do the Swahilis live?

(b) Summarize How did East Africa become a region with great diversity of language and religion?

(c) Make Inferences What is the importance of the Swahili language in East Africa?

2. (a) Recall When was private land ownership introduced to East Africa?

(b) Summarize How have ideas about land ownership changed over time in East Africa?

(c) Identify Point of View How did traditional East African ideas about land differ from those of Europeans who took over parts of Africa?

Writing Activity

Write a description of the place that you consider home. Tell what home means to you and explain why. How does your meaning of home compare to Julius Nyerere's feelings about his homeland?

Writing Tip Before you begin, think of important details about your home that you can use in your description. Use vivid language to make your description come to life.

Section 4 The Cultures of Southern and Central Africa

Prepare to Read

Objectives

In this section you will

1. Learn about the cultural diversity of Southern Africa.
2. Examine different ways of life in Central Africa and learn about the diverse cultures of the region.

Taking Notes

As you read, look for details about the cultures of Southern and Central Africa. Copy the table below, and use it to record your findings.

Southern Africa	Central Africa
• • •	• • •

Target Reading Skill

Compare and Contrast Comparing and contrasting can help you sort out and analyze information. When you compare, you examine the similarities between things. When you contrast, you look at the differences.

As you read this section, compare and contrast the cultures of Southern and Central Africa. Look for similarities and differences in ethnic groups and in economic conditions.

Key Terms

- **migrant worker** (MY grunt WUR kur) *n.* a laborer who travels away from where he or she lives to find work
- **compound** (KAHM pownd) *n.* a fenced-in group of homes

Soccer is a popular sport all around the world. It is no surprise, then, that it is a favorite sport of people in the country of South Africa. But the fact that the sport is played there reveals more than just that South Africans love fun and recreation. It is proof of the changing political times in South Africa.

Soccer came to South Africa from Europe. As you will read in Chapter 17, Europeans settled in the region from the mid-1600s through the 1800s. After the country gained independence in 1910, the white minority of the population took charge of the government. As part of their rule, the white population denied other members of society certain basic rights. For example, black South Africans were not allowed to play on many of the nation's sports teams.

In 1994, the South African government was restructured, and equal rights were extended to all. Today, when black and white soccer players run onto the field, all South Africans have reason to cheer.

A member of South Africa's national soccer team

Diversity in Southern Africa

Like the rest of Africa, Southern Africa has a great deal of cultural diversity. Most of the people of Southern Africa are black Africans. They belong to a variety of ethnic groups, many of which speak separate languages. In addition, there are certain ethnic groups that have greater numbers of members in Southern Africa than in other parts of Africa—for example, people of European descent.

European Influence Southern Africa attracted Europeans for a variety of reasons. The Portuguese arrived in Mozambique in the 1500s and soon began transporting slaves out of Africa. In the 1600s, Dutch and British settlers moved to the Cape of Good Hope at the southern tip of Africa. They grew wheat and herded cattle. Many of the Dutch eventually spread to the north to places such as Malawi, where they started up a mining industry and enlisted local people as laborers. The British also moved north, to Zimbabwe and Zambia.

European Ethnic Groups Southern Africa is home to three main groups of people with European ancestry. One group is descended from the British settlers. These Africans speak English. Another group is Afrikaners (af rih KAHN urz), who are descendants of the Dutch settlers. They speak Afrikaans (af rih KAHNZ), a language related to Dutch. The third group, descended from the Portuguese settlers, speaks Portuguese.

Urbanization The cultural diversity of Southern Africa extends beyond ethnic differences. It is also represented by the contrast between rural and urban lifestyles. For hundreds of years, people in the region lived in villages or small cities. European settlers started a process of urbanization in Southern Africa. The region now includes a number of cities inhabited by more than 1 million people. The largest are Cape Town, Durban, and Johannesburg in South Africa and Harare in Zimbabwe.

Effects of Urbanization
Even though it sits nestled between ocean and mountains, Cape Town has grown to be one of South Africa's largest cities. Its population is about 3 million people. **Infer** *How do you think the presence of numerous large cities changes the culture of a region?*

Industry in South Africa South Africa is the richest, most urban, and most industrialized country in Africa. During the 1900s, South African industries created a great demand for labor. Hundreds of thousands of people came from nearby countries in Southern Africa to work on South African mines. They formed a large force of **migrant workers,** or laborers who travel away from where they live to find work. These migrant workers had to live together in **compounds,** or fenced-in groups of homes. They were far from their families, clans, and ethnic groups. They worked long hours in dangerous conditions for low wages.

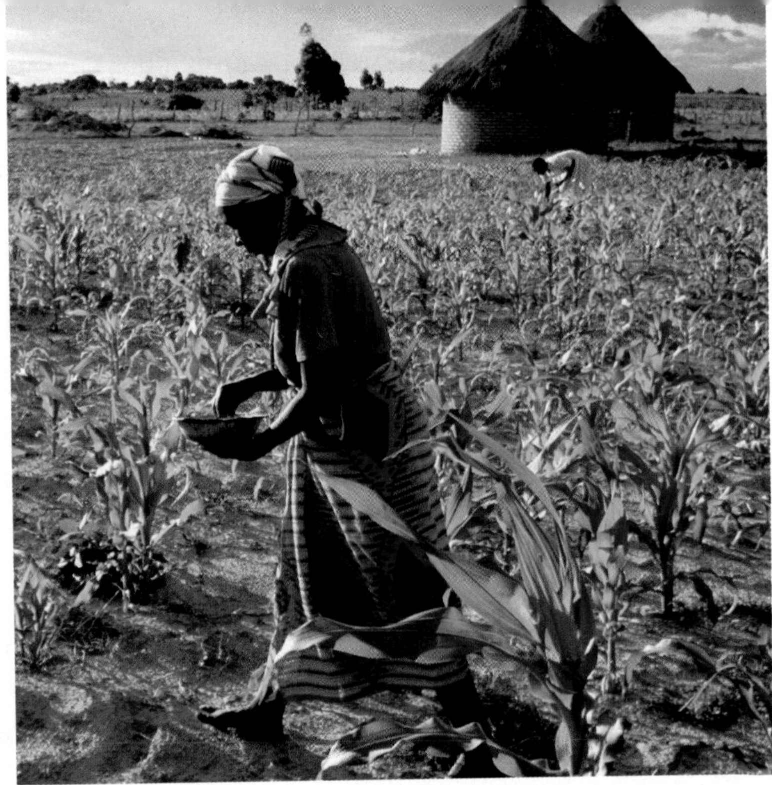

A woman in Zimbabwe spreads fertilizer on corn plants.

New Roles for Women The workers who migrated to South Africa for work were mostly men. While they were gone, the women had to take on the men's responsibilities. Traditionally, women had raised the children and farmed the land. Men had cared for the animals, dealt with local matters, and headed the households. Once the men were gone for a year or two at a time, the women began to make the household and community decisions. For most women, this change was a challenge. For example, many of the women had no training for the new tasks. But the change was also rewarding for many women because they gained new rights, responsibilities, and skills.

✓ Reading Check **Name two cities in Southern Africa that have a population of more than one million people.**

Life in Central Africa

Like the people of Southern Africa and the rest of Africa, Central Africans went through many cultural changes in the 1900s. But many people in the region still follow old traditions as well.

Economics and Culture In some ways, Central Africa's cultural diversity is a result of sharp economic contrasts that exist in the region. On the Atlantic coast, the countries of Angola, Congo, Gabon, Cameroon, and Equatorial Guinea have large oil reserves. The cities in these coastal areas tend to benefit most from the oil wealth. People living near the coast also gain more exposure to cultures outside of Africa, allowing for the exchange of traditions and customs.

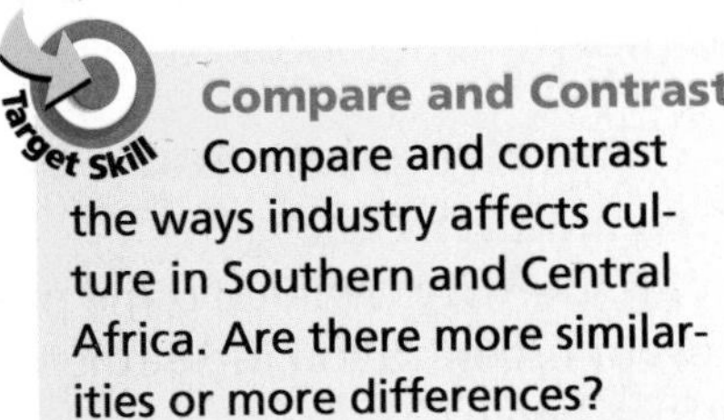

Compare and Contrast Compare and contrast the ways industry affects culture in Southern and Central Africa. Are there more similarities or more differences?

Links to Art

Mbuti Art The lives of the Mbuti (em BOO tee) are very different from the lives of most people in Central Africa. They are hunter-gatherers who live in the rain forests of Congo. The Mbuti live off the land the way their ancestors have for more than 3,000 years.

For example, they make some of their cloth out of tree bark. Men pound the bark with mallets until it is almost as soft as velvet. Then women draw shapes and patterns on the cloth. Many art galleries in the United States and Europe collect Mbuti bark-cloth drawings for their shapes and patterns.

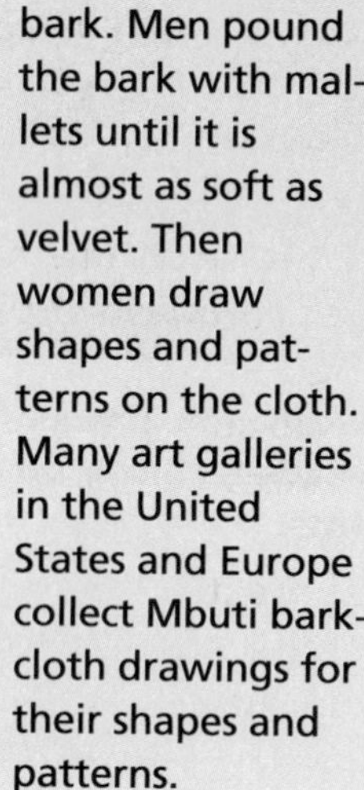

In contrast, living conditions get poorer as you move in from the coast to the interior areas of Angola, Congo, the Democratic Republic of the Congo, and the Central African Republic. There, village societies are organized by kinship groups, and land is owned by clans. In less-populated rural areas, individual families live and work on their own land.

Diverse Ways of Life Like the rest of the continent, Central Africa contains great cultural diversity. The Democratic Republic of the Congo alone has about 200 ethnic groups.

Millions of people live in crowded shantytowns or cinder-block apartments in Kinshasa, the largest city in the Democratic Republic of the Congo. They walk or take buses or trucks to work in factories, offices, and hotels. Millions of others live in rural areas. Some Central African people are Roman Catholic or Protestant. Others practice religions that blend Christian and traditional African beliefs. Still others are Muslim.

What one writer said about North Africa applies to Central and Southern Africa as well. To define the real North African, he said, "you have to define which one you mean: the rich or the poor, the Berber women of the mountains or the college girls on motorbikes. . . ." Old, new, and mixtures of the two live on in all regions of Africa.

✓ Reading Check **What are some examples of cultural diversity in Central Africa?**

Section 4 Assessment

Key Terms

Review the key terms at the beginning of this section. Use each term in a sentence that explains its meaning.

Target Reading Skill

Name two similarities between Southern Africa and Central Africa. Name two differences.

Comprehension and Critical Thinking

1. **(a) Identify** When did the process of urbanization in Southern Africa begin?
(b) Explain Why did people from all over Southern Africa migrate to South Africa?
(c) Identify Causes How were the lives of many Southern African women affected by South Africa even though the women never moved there?

2. **(a) Recall** What industry has brought wealth to some of the countries on Central Africa's Atlantic coast?
(b) Contrast How do the economics and culture of Central Africa's Atlantic coast differ from the economics and culture of its interior areas?

Writing Activity

Write a short report summarizing the ways in which economics have affected culture in Southern Africa and Central Africa. Point out any similarities or differences.

For: An activity on the region of Southern Africa
Visit: PHSchool.com
Web Code: lad-5304

Review and Assessment

◆ Chapter Summary

Section 1: The Cultures of North Africa

- Culture has many elements, such as food, language, and beliefs.
- Islam has greatly influenced life in North Africa.
- Because of North Africa's location, the people of the region have been exposed to the cultures of its trading partners, including Europe, Asia, and other parts of Africa.

Morocco

Section 2: The Cultures of West Africa

- West Africa has great ethnic diversity. Most West Africans speak several languages.
- West Africans are bound by strong kinship ties.
- West Africans have kept their cultural values alive by passing them on to younger generations.

Section 3: The Cultures of East Africa

- East Africa's location has contributed to the region's cultural diversity.
- Ideas about land use and ownership have changed over time, but even urban East Africans still feel a bond to their rural villages.

Section 4: The Cultures of Southern and Central Africa

- Southern Africa's diverse culture includes people with three types of European ancestry—Dutch, British, and Portuguese.
- South Africa has had strong economic and cultural influences on Southern Africa.
- Central Africa has great cultural diversity and economic contrasts.

Zimbabwe

◆ Key Terms

Match the definitions in Column I with the key terms in Column II. There are more terms than definitions.

Column I

1. the spread of customs and ideas from one culture to another
2. a group of families descended from a common ancestor
3. the values, traditions, and customs handed down from one's ancestors
4. the part of a family that includes parents and children only
5. an ethnic group in East Africa
6. a laborer who travels away from where he or she lives to find work

Column II

- **A** Quran
- **B** culture
- **C** cultural diffusion
- **D** cultural diversity
- **E** nuclear family
- **F** extended family
- **G** lineage
- **H** heritage
- **I** Swahili
- **J** migrant worker

Review and Assessment (continued)

Comprehension and Critical Thinking

7. **(a) Recall** What is culture?
   (b) Describe What are some elements of North Africa's culture?
8. **(a) Identify** What is the role of kinship in West African cultures?
   (b) Explain How is urbanization changing traditional family life in West Africa?
9. **(a) Locate** Describe East Africa's location.
   (b) Analyze Explain how location has affected East African cultures.
   (c) Summarize How does the Swahili language help unite the people of East Africa?
10. **(a) Recall** What were the traditional African ideas about owning and using land before European rule in the 1800s?
    (b) Make Generalizations How do East Africans view land use and land ownership today?
11. **(a) Recall** In what economic activities did Europeans in Southern Africa take part?
    (b) Identify Causes What economic activity in South Africa caused many Southern Africans to migrate to that country?
    (c) Make Inferences Is the life of a migrant worker an easy one?
12. **(a) Note** Describe the cultures of Central Africa.
    (b) Compare In what ways are the cultures of Central Africa like those in other parts of Africa?

Skills Practice

Comparing and Contrasting In the Skills for Life activity in this chapter, you learned how to compare and contrast. You learned how to note similarities and differences and then draw a conclusion based on your findings.

Review the steps you followed to learn this skill. Then reread the part of Section 1 called Cultural Change in North Africa and the part of Section 3 called Geography and Cultural Diversity. List the similarities and differences between the cultures of these two regions. Draw a conclusion about these cultures based on your findings.

Writing Activity: Language Arts

Suppose an exchange student from an African country has come to stay at your home for six weeks. You and your family are sharing your first dinner with this visitor. Write a dialogue in which you ask your visitor about African culture and the visitor asks you similar questions about your culture. Use what you have learned in this chapter to write your visitor's answers to questions.

MAP MASTER™ Skills Activity

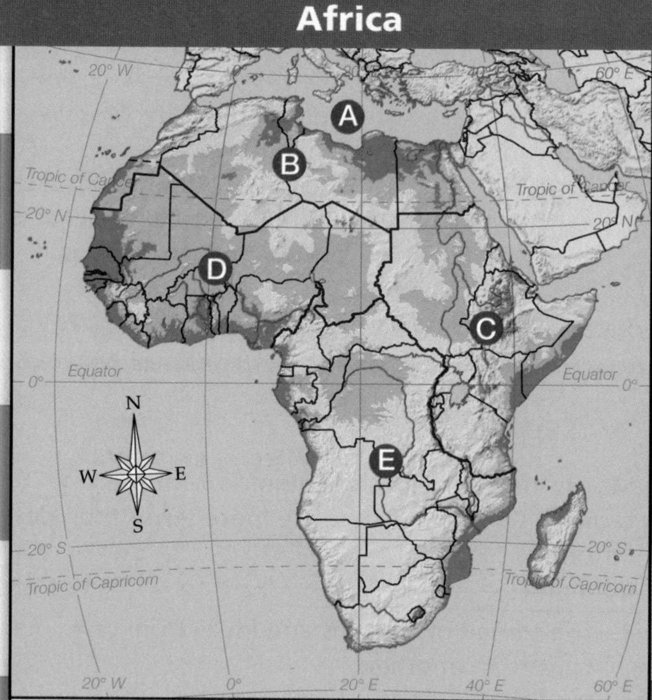

Place Location For each place listed, write the letter from the map that shows its location.

1. Mediterranean Sea
2. North Africa
3. West Africa
4. East Africa
5. Southern and Central Africa

Go Online PHSchool.com Use Web Code **lap-5320** for an **interactive map.**

Standardized Test Prep

Test-Taking Tips

Some questions on standardized tests ask you to analyze a graphic organizer. Study the concept web below. Then follow the tips to answer the sample question.

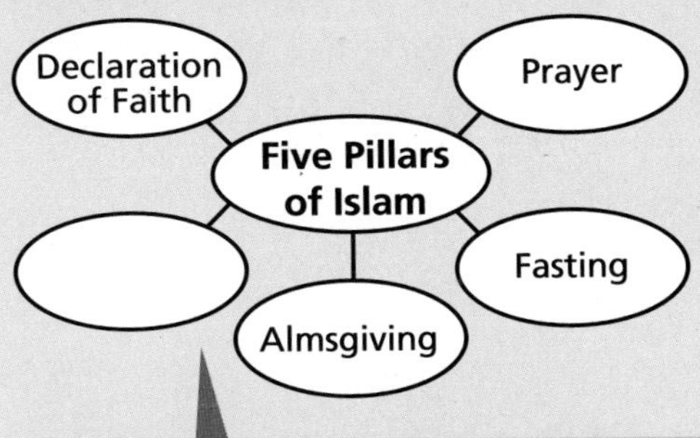

TIP When you study a concept web, notice the kind of information that goes in each oval. The main idea is in the center oval, and the supporting details are in the outer ovals.

Pick the letter that best answers the question.

What is the fifth Pillar of Islam that belongs on this concept web?

A The Quran
B Pilgrimage
C Duties of a Muslim
D The influence of Islam

TIP Use logic, or good reasoning, to be sure you choose an answer that makes sense.

Think It Through The center of the web says "Five Pillars of Islam"—meaning duties required by the religion—and each of the outer ovals shows one duty. What other pillar, or duty, belongs in an outer oval? You can rule out C and D because both are general ideas rather than specific duties. That leaves A and B. Even if you're not sure of the answer, you can see that the other outer ovals involve actions. Because pilgrimage involves an action, you can guess that B is the correct answer.

Practice Questions

Use the tips above and other tips in this book to help you answer the following questions.

1. Which of the following statements is true?
   A Cultural diffusion only occurs on coasts.
   B In general, Africa has little cultural diversity.
   C Cultural changes often occur during travel.
   D Cultural diffusion and cultural diversity are the same thing.

2. Which of the following best explains the meaning of the proverb "The young can't teach traditions to the old"?
   A Traditions do not interest young people.
   B Only adults know customs and traditions.
   C Young people are not the best teachers.
   D Adults must pass traditions on to young people.

3. A cultural group that lives in Southern Africa is the
   A Swahili. **B** Afrikaners.
   C Berbers. **D** Tuareg.

Use the Venn diagram below to answer Question 4. Choose the letter of the best answer.

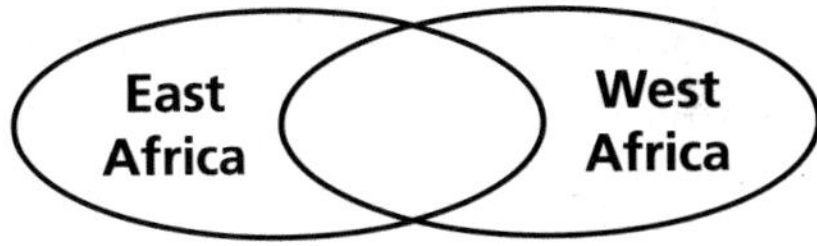

4. Which of the following could be listed in the part of the diagram where *East Africa* and *West Africa* intersect?
   A Cultures affected by coastal trade
   B Indian Ocean location
   C Br'er Rabbit tales
   D Swahili culture

Use Web Code **laa-5300** for **Chapter 13 self-test.**

Chapter

14 North Africa

Chapter Preview

This chapter will introduce you to some of the countries of North Africa.

Country Databank

The Country Databank provides data and descriptions of each of the countries in the region: Algeria, Egypt, Libya, Morocco, and Tunisia.

Section 1

Egypt
A Nation on the Nile

Section 2

Algeria
Varied Geography, Varied History

Target Reading Skill

Cause and Effect In this chapter you will focus on understanding causes and effects. Identifying causes and effects and recognizing signal words for causes and effects will help you learn as you read.

▶ Some North Africans live in the Sahara in oasis towns, such as Ghardaia, Algeria, shown here.

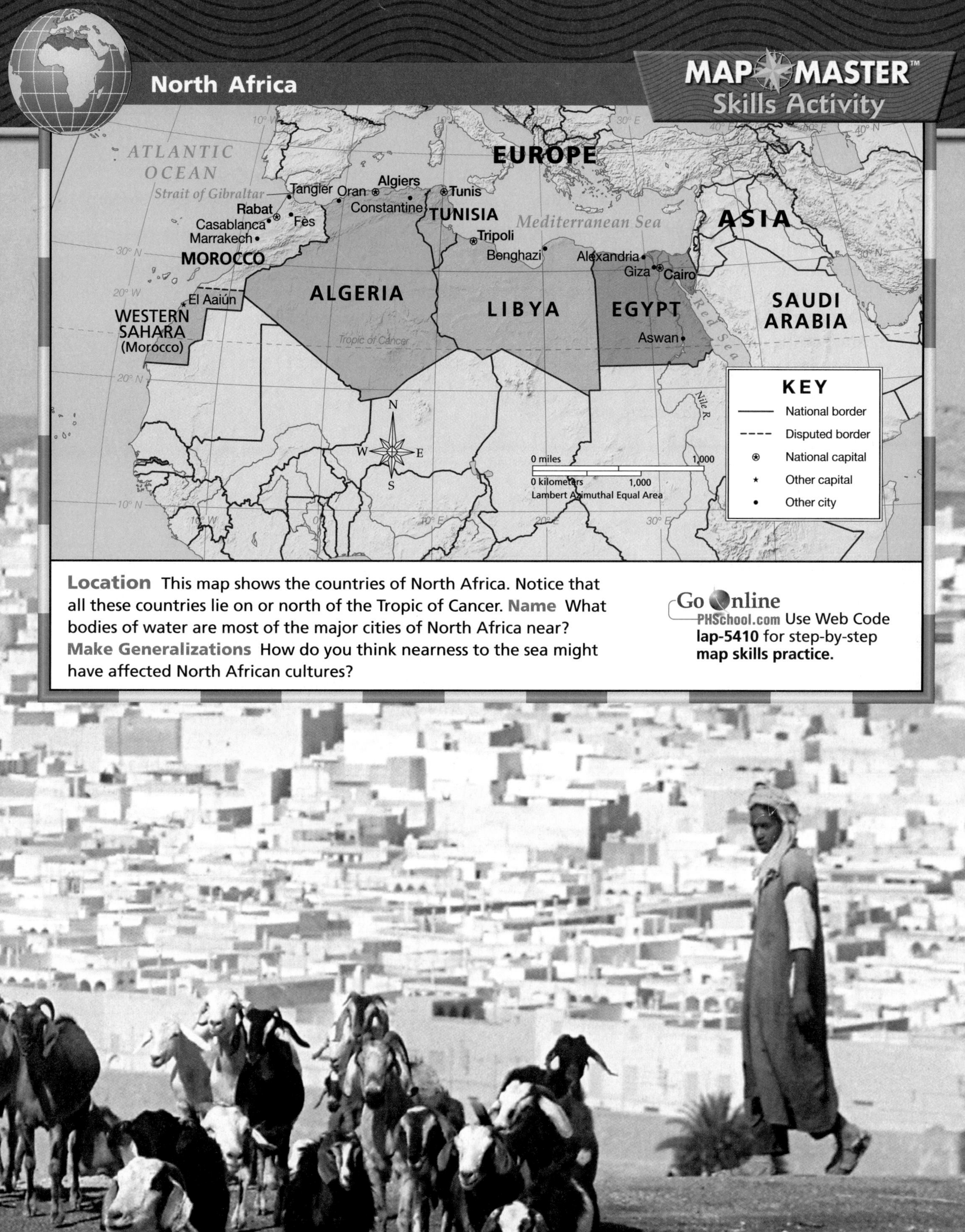

Location This map shows the countries of North Africa. Notice that all these countries lie on or north of the Tropic of Cancer. **Name** What bodies of water are most of the major cities of North Africa near? **Make Generalizations** How do you think nearness to the sea might have affected North African cultures?

Go Online
PHSchool.com Use Web Code **lap-5410** for step-by-step **map skills practice.**

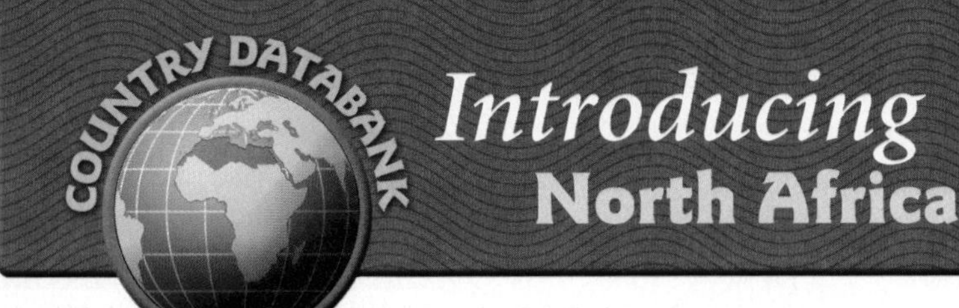

Introducing North Africa

Guide for Reading

This section provides an introduction to the five countries that make up the region of North Africa.

- Look at the map on the previous page and then read the paragraphs below to learn about each nation.
- Analyze the data to compare the countries.
- What are the characteristics that most of the countries share?
- What are some key differences among the countries?

Viewing the Video Overview

View the World Studies Video Overview to learn more about each of the countries. As you watch, answer these questions:

- What are some common features of the region?
- How does the availability of water influence where the people of North Africa live?

Discovery
CHANNEL
SCHOOL
Video
Explore the geography of North Africa.

Algeria

Capital	Algiers
Land Area	919,590 sq mi; 2,381,740 sq km
Population	32.3 million
Ethnic Group(s)	Arab, Berber, white
Religion(s)	Muslim, Christian, Jewish
Government	republic
Currency	Algerian dinar
Leading Exports	petroleum, natural gas, petroleum products
Language(s)	Arabiç (official), Tamazight (official), Kabyle, Shawia, Tamashek, French

Algeria (al JIHR ee uh) is Africa's second-largest country. It is bordered on the west by Mauritania and Morocco, on the north by the Mediterranean Sea, on the east by Tunisia and Libya, and on the south by Niger and Mali. Algeria has long acted as a bridge between Europe and other African lands to the south. Much of Algeria is covered by the Sahara. Most Algerians live in the north, where summers are hot and dry and winters are warm and wet. Following independence from France in 1962, Algeria made improvements in education and literacy. Since the 1990s, Algeria has struggled with economic troubles and civil war.

Algerian girl preparing food

Egypt

Capital	Cairo
Land Area	384,343 sq mi; 995,450 sq km
Population	70.7 million
Ethnic Group(s)	Eastern Hamitic, Nubian, white
Religion(s)	Muslim, Christian
Government	republic
Currency	Egyptian pound
Leading Exports	crude oil and petroleum products, cotton, textiles, metal products, chemicals
Language(s)	Arabic (official), French, English, Berber

Egypt (EE jipt) is bordered on the west by Libya, on the north by the Mediterranean Sea, Israel, and the Gaza Strip, on the east by the Red Sea, and on the south by Sudan. Most of the people live in the fertile valley and delta regions of the Nile River. The rest of Egypt is hot desert. Egypt is famous for the ancient civilization that developed there along the Nile. The ancient Egyptians built pyramids and monuments that today draw tourists and scholars from around the world. Egypt's capital, Cairo, is the largest city in Africa.

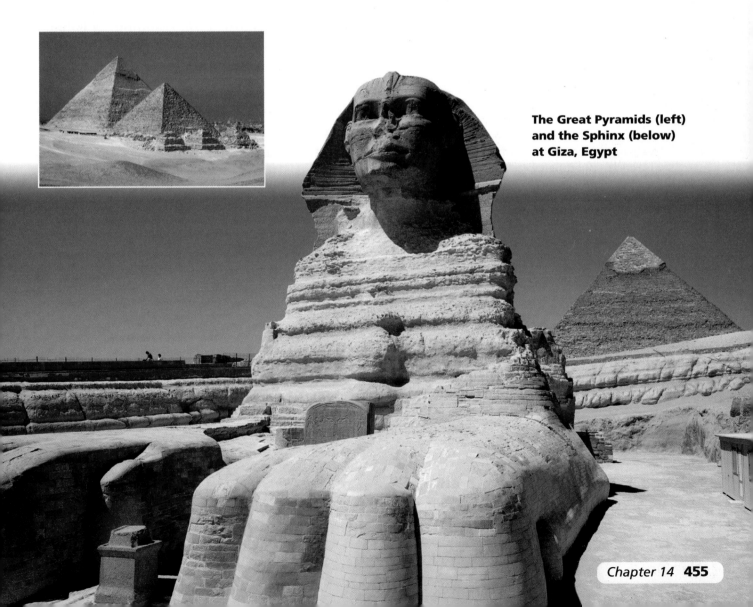

The Great Pyramids (left) and the Sphinx (below) at Giza, Egypt

Introducing North Africa (continued)

Libya

Capital	Tripoli
Land Area	679,358 sq mi; 1,759,540 sq km
Population	5.4 million
Ethnic Group(s)	Arab, Berber, white, Southwest Asian, South Asian
Religion(s)	Muslim
Government	local councils in theory; military dictatorship in practice
Currency	Libyan dinar
Leading Exports	crude oil, refined petroleum products
Language(s)	Arabic (official), Tuareg

Libya (LIB ee uh) is bordered on the west by Algeria and Tunisia, on the north by the Mediterranean Sea, on the east by Egypt and Sudan, and on the south by Chad and Niger. Each year, an average of four inches (10 centimeters) of rain falls in Libya. The country has no rivers that flow year-round. Instead, it relies on groundwater from desert oases and man-made wells. Most Libyans live in urban areas. Large oil and natural gas reserves are important to Libya's economy. Libya gained independence from Italy in 1951. Revolution followed in 1969, leading to the establishment of a Muslim government.

Morocco

Capital	Rabat
Land Area	172,316 sq mi; 446,300 sq km
Population	31.2 million
Ethnic Group(s)	Arab, Berber
Religion(s)	Muslim, Christian, Jewish
Government	constitutional monarchy
Currency	Moroccan dirham
Leading Exports	phosphates and fertilizers, food and beverages, minerals
Language(s)	Arabic (official), Tamazight, French, Spanish

Morocco (muh RAH koh) is a mountainous country in which earthquakes are common. It is bordered on the west by the Atlantic Ocean, on the north by the Strait of Gibraltar and the Mediterranean Sea, on the east by Algeria, and on the south by Western Sahara. In 1956, Morocco gained independence from France. A year later, Morocco claimed the Spanish colony of Western Sahara as its territory. Today, Morocco occupies Western Sahara, but most countries do not recognize the region as Morocco's possession. Morocco's largest city, Casablanca, lies in the west, along the Atlantic.

Moroccan pottery

Tunisia

Capital	Tunis
Land Area	59,984 sq mi; 155,360 sq km
Population	9.8 million
Ethnic Group(s)	Arab, Berber, white
Religion(s)	Muslim, Christian, Jewish
Government	republic
Currency	Tunisian dinar
Leading Exports	textiles, mechanical goods, phosphates and chemicals, agricultural products, hydrocarbons
Language(s)	Arabic (official), French

SOURCES: DK World Desk Reference Online; CIA World Factbook Online, 2002; *The World Almanac,* 2003

The famed ancient port city of Carthage was founded on the Gulf of Tunis, in the land of present-day Tunisia (too NEE zhuh). In A.D. 698, Carthage fell to the Arabs, who then established Tunis. Tunisia is North Africa's smallest country. It is wedged between Algeria on the west and Libya on the east. It is bordered on the north and east by the Mediterranean Sea. Tunisia is one of the Arab world's most liberal countries, where women make up about one third of the workforce. The importance of education is stressed in Tunisia. Since 1995, enrollment in colleges has doubled.

Berber drummers in Tunisia

Assessment

Comprehension and Critical Thinking

1. Compare and Contrast Compare and contrast the physical characteristics of the countries that make up North Africa.

2. Draw Conclusions What are some characteristics that most of the countries share?

3. Analyze Information What are some key differences among the countries?

4. Categorize What kinds of products are the major exports of North Africa?

5. Infer What part of North Africa's history can you infer from reading the list of languages that are spoken in each country?

6. Make a Bar Graph Create a bar graph showing the population of the countries in the region.

Keeping Current

Access the **DK World Desk Reference Online** at **PHSchool.com** for up-to-date information about all five countries in this chapter.

Web Code: **lae-5400**

Section 1

Egypt

A Nation on the Nile

Prepare to Read

Objectives

In this section you will

1. Find out how Islam influences Egyptian culture.
2. Learn about daily life in Egypt.

Taking Notes

As you read this section, look for details about life in Egypt. Copy the table below, and use it to record your findings.

Islam in Egypt	• •
Everyday Life in Egypt	• •

Target Reading Skill

Identify Causes and Effects Determining causes and effects can help you understand the relationships among situations or events. A cause makes something happen. An effect is what happens. As you read this section, note the effects Islam and the Nile River have had on life in Egypt.

Key Terms

- **Cairo** (KY roh) *n.* the capital of Egypt and the most populous city in Africa
- **Sharia** (shah REE ah) *n.* Islamic law, based on the words and deeds of Muhammad and on comments written by Muslim scholars and lawmakers
- **bazaar** (buh ZAHR) *n.* a traditional open-air market with shops or rows of stalls
- **fellaheen** (fel uh HEEN) *n.* peasants or agricultural workers in Egypt and other Arab countries

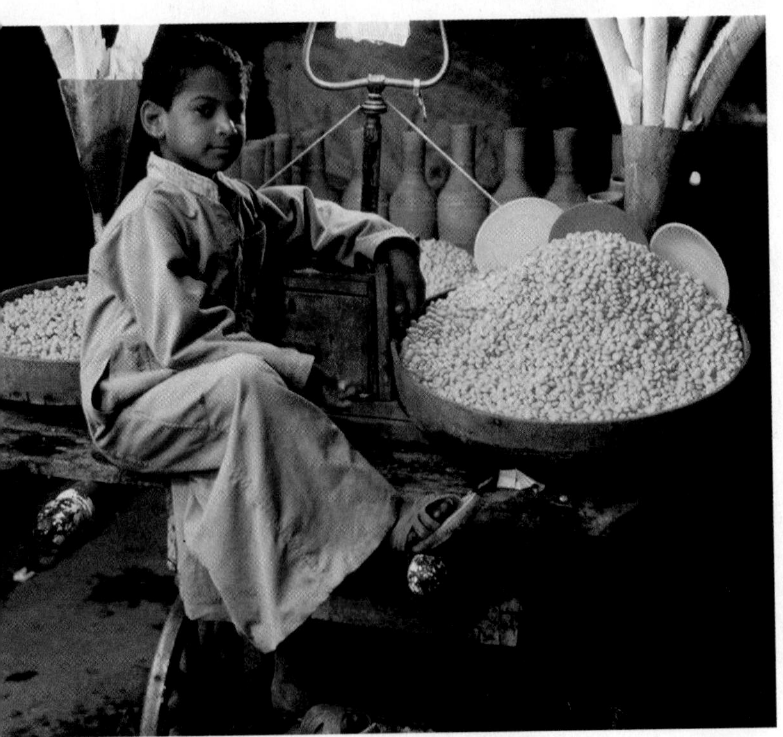

Egyptian boy at Ramadan evening meal

For one month of the year, the restaurants in **Cairo,** Egypt's capital, stand empty at noon. Egyptian teenagers try not to think about foods such as pita bread or sweet dates. Only certain people, such as the very young or those who are sick, eat regular meals. It is the Muslim holy month of Ramadan (ram uh DAHN). During this month, followers of Islam fast from dawn to dusk. To fast is to go without food for a period of time. During Ramadan, Muslims eat only after the sun has set.

But Muslims do more than fast during the month of Ramadan. They also focus on prayer and obedience to God. They try to avoid thinking unkind thoughts. And they help the poor and other people who are less fortunate than themselves.

Islam in Egypt

Egypt is located in North Africa. It lies across the Red Sea from Saudi Arabia, where Muhammad, the founder of Islam, was born. As you have read, Islam spread from Arabia across North Africa. Today, most North Africans are Muslim. This is true in Egypt, where Islam is the religion that most people practice. However, a minority of Egypt's population is Christian. Most Egyptian Christians are members of the Coptic Church, which is one of the oldest branches of Christianity in the world. Coptic Christianity existed in Egypt for a few hundred years before Islam did.

Islamic Practices Recall from Chapter 13 that the Quran is the sacred book of Islam. One of the Quran's requirements is that Muslims pray five times each day. Many Egyptians pray in mosques. While they pray, they face southeast so that they pray in the direction of the Muslim holy city of Mecca, in Saudi Arabia. Egyptians also often send their children to mosques to receive religious training. There, young students learn to read and memorize the Quran.

Islam and the Law The Quran is one of the main sources of **Sharia** (shah REE ah), or Islamic law. Sharia is based on the words and deeds of Muhammad, as well as on comments written by Muslim scholars and lawmakers. Muslims in North Africa and Southwest Asia try to renew their faith by living each day according to Sharia.

Most Muslims in Egypt agree that, in general, the laws of their country should be based on the laws of Islam. In 1980, the Egyptian government adopted a new constitutional amendment. This amendment identified Sharia as the main source of the laws of Egypt. Still, not all of Egypt's laws are based on Sharia. In recent years, some Egyptians have argued that all of Egypt's laws should match Islamic law exactly. On this issue, however, many Egyptian Muslims disagree.

✓ **Reading Check** **Why do Egyptian Muslims face southeast when they pray each day?**

Links to Math

Muslim Mathematicians
Beginning around A.D. 800, Muslims throughout the Arab world began developing and using important mathematical concepts. Much of the work done by these Muslim mathematicians has formed the basis of mathematics as it exists today. A number of Muslim mathematicians came from North Africa. For example, Abu Kamil (born A.D. 850) and Ibn Yusun (born A.D. 950) were Egyptian, while Ibn al-Banna (born A.D. 1256) is thought to have been Moroccan.

Muslim men praying in a mosque in Cairo

COUNTRY PROFILE — Focus on Geography

Egypt

The most important body of water in Egypt is the Nile River, which flows from the mountains of East Africa north to the Mediterranean Sea. Nearly all of Egypt's people live on the 4 percent of the land that is closest to the Nile's shores. Irrigation with Nile water allows agriculture to thrive, and one third of Egypt's workforce is employed in agriculture. Each month, however, thousands of Egyptians leave crowded farm communities to begin new lives in the cities. Study the map and charts to learn more about Egypt's changing society.

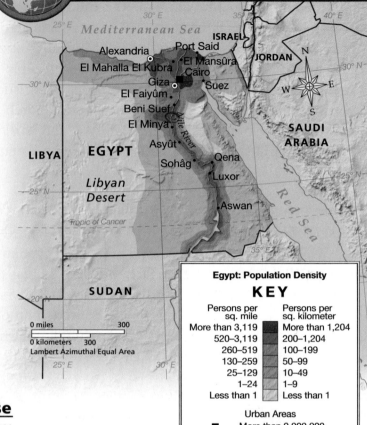

Mediterranean Sea
ISRAEL
JORDAN
SAUDI ARABIA
LIBYA
EGYPT
SUDAN
Libyan Desert
Red Sea
Nile River
Tropic of Cancer
Alexandria
Port Said
El Mansûra
El Mahalla El Kubra
Cairo
Giza
Suez
El Faiyûm
Beni Suef
El Minya
Asyût
Sohâg
Qena
Luxor
Aswan
25° E
30° E
35° E
40° E
30° N
25° N
20° N
N
S
E
W
0 miles 300
0 kilometers 300
Lambert Azimuthal Equal Area

Egypt: Population Density

KEY

Persons per sq. mile	Persons per sq. kilometer
More than 3,119	More than 1,204
520–3,119	200–1,204
260–519	100–199
130–259	50–99
25–129	10–49
1–24	1–9
Less than 1	Less than 1

Urban Areas

- ■ More than 9,999,999
- □ 5,000,000–9,999,999
- ⊙ 1,000,000–4,999,999
- ● 500,000–999,999
- • Less than 500,000
- — National border

Urban and Rural Population

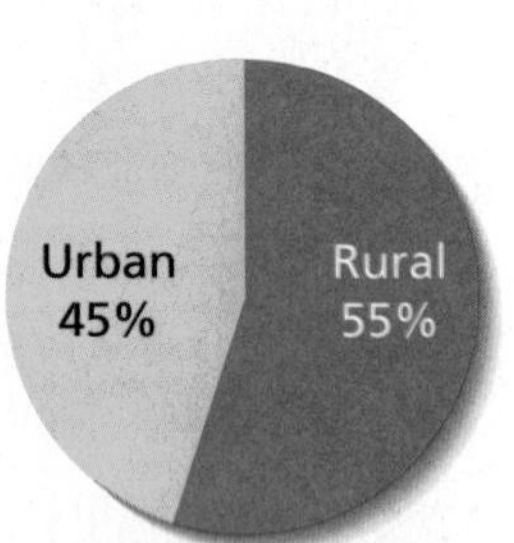

SOURCE: *DK World Desk Reference*

Land Use

3%
0.5%
96.5%

- Arable land
- Permanent crops
- Other

SOURCE: CIA World Factbook Online, 2003

The Nile River

Map and Chart Skills

1. **Locate** In what part of Egypt are most of the major cities located?
2. **Explain** How does Egypt's geography affect where in the country people live?
3. **Predict** What changes could Egyptians make that would allow them to live in areas where currently few people live?

Use Web Code **lae-5401** for **DK World Desk Reference Online.**

Daily Life in Egypt

As you can see from the circle graph in the Country Profile on page 460, Egypt's population is fairly evenly divided between people who live in cities and people who live in villages. City dwellers and villagers live very different lives. One thing they have in common, however, is their dependence on the life-giving waters of the Nile River.

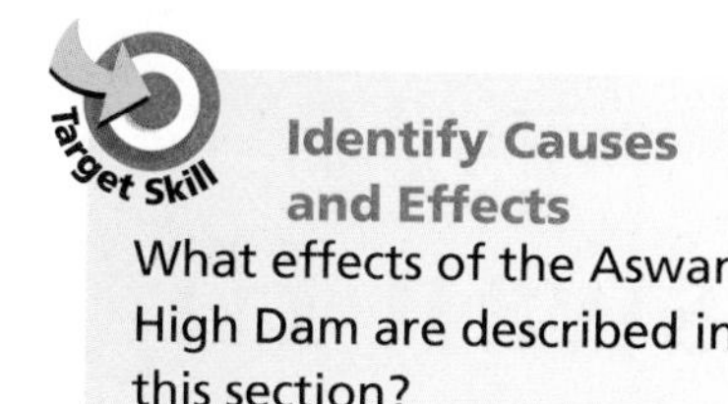

Identify Causes and Effects
What effects of the Aswan High Dam are described in this section?

Egypt's Water Source Look at the map of Egypt on page 460 in the Country Profile. You can see that Egypt is most densely populated along the Nile River and in the Nile Delta region. Now turn to page 462 and read about the Aswan High Dam. With the help of this dam, the Nile River allows Egypt's crops to be irrigated year-round. The river supplies water to people in the cities and in rural areas.

But farming practices and population pressures threaten Egypt's water supply. The Aswan High Dam blocks the Nile's rich silt from reaching farmland downstream. Without the silt, the Nile Delta has been shrinking. Farmers have to use more fertilizer to grow their crops. The fertilizers they use, along with waste that comes from urban areas, threaten the safety of Egypt's water supply.

City Life Nearly half of all Egyptians live in cities. Cairo, the nation's capital and largest city, is also the largest city in Africa. It is home to more than 10 million Egyptians. Some parts of Cairo are more than 1,000 years old. Other parts are very modern. Most people live in apartment buildings with electric fans or air conditioning. However, they frequently shop in traditional open-air markets called **bazaars.**

Many people move to the cities from rural areas. They hope to find a better education and jobs. As a result, Cairo is very crowded. There are traffic jams and housing shortages. Some people live in tents that they have set up on boats on the Nile. Others live in homes they have built in the huge cemeteries on the outskirts of Cairo. Overcrowding in Egypt's cities has even affected agriculture. Some farmland has been lost because people have built on it instead of farming on it.

Outdoor Markets
At a bazaar in Cairo, people buy goods from vendors who set up stands beneath umbrellas along the streets. **Contrast** *How do you think open-air markets are different from indoor shopping centers?*

Aswan High Dam

The Aswan High Dam is one of the modern world's greatest engineering projects. A force of 30,000 workers labored for ten years to build the dam out of layers of rock, clay, and cement. The dam serves three major purposes: it controls flooding, it provides electricity, and it supplies water for crops and drinking year-round. The dam produces nearly half of Egypt's electricity and all of its drinking water.

A View From Above
Located on the Nile River near Aswan, Egypt, the dam created the world's third-largest reservoir–Lake Nasser. The lake is 310 miles (500 kilometers) long.

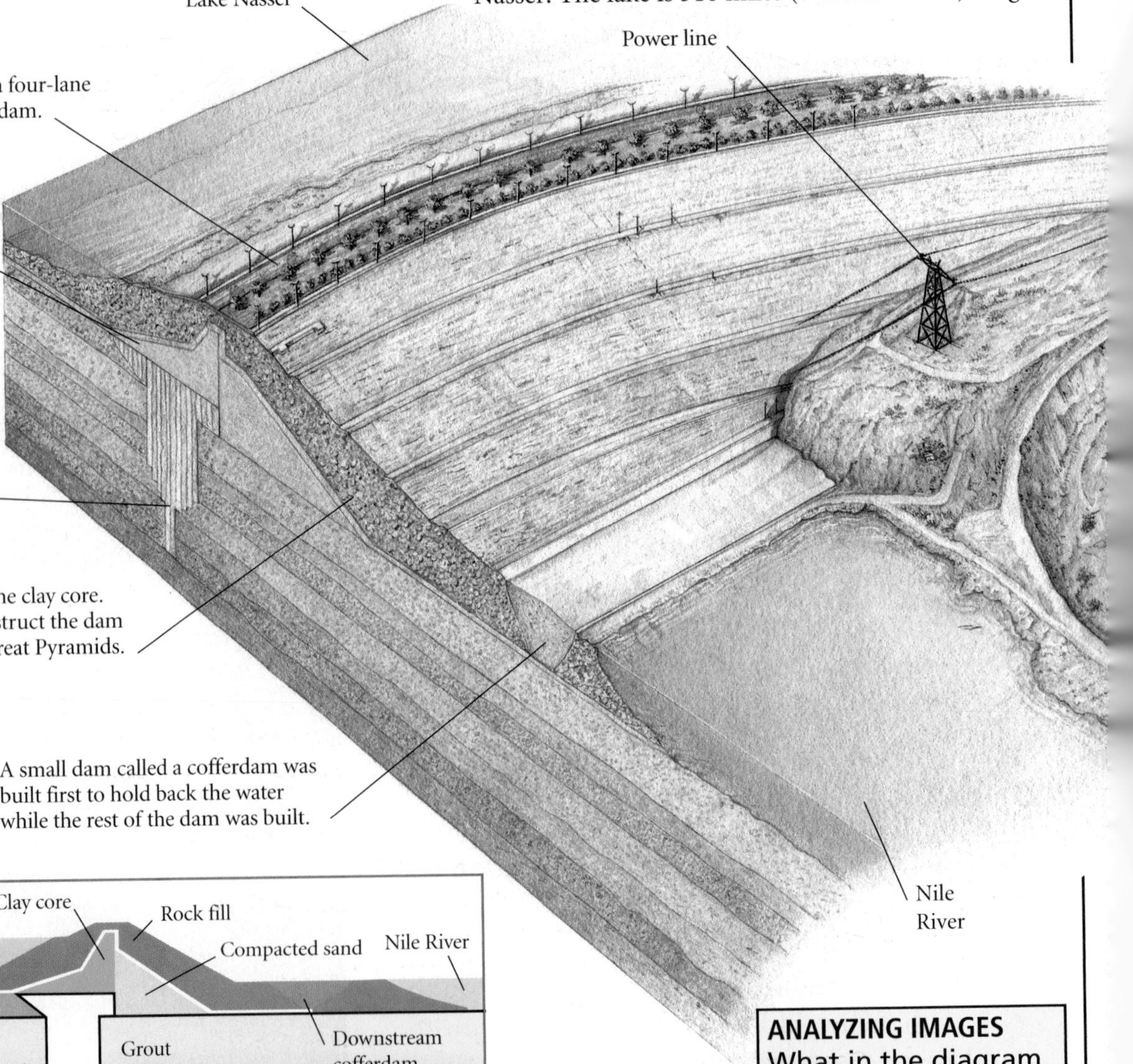

Lake Nasser

Power line

Vehicles can travel on a four-lane road on the top of the dam.

The core of the dam is made of solid clay.

A concrete barrier called a grout curtain runs the width of the dam. It keeps water from leaking out of the dam.

Layers of rock cover the clay core. The rock used to construct the dam could have built 17 Great Pyramids.

A small dam called a cofferdam was built first to hold back the water while the rest of the dam was built.

Nile River

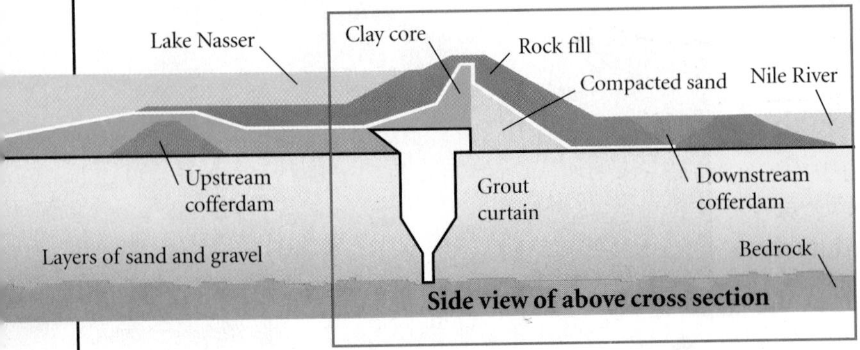

Lake Nasser

Clay core

Rock fill

Compacted sand

Nile River

Upstream cofferdam

Grout curtain

Downstream cofferdam

Layers of sand and gravel

Bedrock

Side view of above cross section

ANALYZING IMAGES
What in the diagram shows that power is being generated?

Rural Life Most of the people in Egypt's rural areas live in villages along the banks of the Nile River or in the Nile Delta region. In Egyptian villages, most of the people make their living by farming. Egypt's rural farmers are called **fellaheen** (fel uh HEEN). Most of the fellaheen do not own the land they farm. Good farmland is scarce because the riverbanks are so narrow. Some fellaheen farm small rented plots of land. Others work in the fields of rich landowners.

Discovery Channel SCHOOL Video
Learn about farming along the Nile in Egypt.

Many of the fellaheen live in homes built of mud bricks or of stones. Most of these homes are small. They may have from one to three rooms and a courtyard, which the family often shares with its animals. The roofs of the houses are typically flat. Therefore, the fellaheen can use their roofs as places to store food and firewood, to spread dates or other fruits out to dry, and to dry their laundry after washing it.

Fellaheen working near the Great Pyramids at Giza

✓ Reading Check **What land do the fellaheen farm?**

Section 1 Assessment

Key Terms
Review the key terms at the beginning of this section. Use each term in a sentence that explains its meaning.

Target Reading Skill
Many Egyptians are Muslim. What are two effects that Islam has had on life in Egypt?

Comprehension and Critical Thinking
1. (a) Recall Describe Egypt's location.
(b) Identify Cause and Effect How did location affect the spread of Islam into North Africa?
(c) Draw Conclusions In what ways does Islam influence Egyptian culture?
2. (a) Identify Where do most people in Egypt live?
(b) Compare How do the lives of city dwellers compare with the lives of villagers in Egypt?
(c) Analyze What is the importance of the Nile River to the people of Egypt?

Writing Activity
Write a letter from the point of view of a rural Egyptian visiting Cairo for the first time. You may want to include observations of things that a rural person would find unfamiliar or familiar.

For: An activity on Egypt
Visit: PHSchool.com
Web Code: lad-5401

Distinguishing Fact and Opinion

When Aretha got to class, she looked at the chalkboard. Every day, Mr. Copeland began class by writing a discussion topic on the board. On this day, he had written,

Life in Egyptian cities is better than life in rural Egypt.

Aretha wondered how someone decided this and raised her hand. "That statement doesn't tell the whole story! Whose life is it referring to? Are they wealthy or poor? And when did they live?"

Mr. Copeland smiled. "Exactly, Aretha! The statement cannot be proved. It's somebody's opinion."

Distinguishing between fact and opinion is something you need to do almost every day. Doing it helps you reach your own decisions about what you read, see, or hear.

Learn the Skill

To distinguish fact and opinion, use the following steps.

1. **Look for facts by asking what can be proved true or false.** A fact usually tells who, what, when, where, or how much.

2. **Ask how you could check whether each fact is true.** Could you do your own test, such as measuring or counting, or could you find information in a reliable source, such as an encyclopedia?

3. **Look for opinions by identifying personal beliefs or value judgments.** An opinion cannot be proved true *or* false. Look for words that signal personal feelings, such as *I think*. Look for words that judge, such as *better* and *worse* or *should* and *ought to*.

4. **Ask whether each opinion is supported by facts or good reasons.** A well-supported opinion can help you make up your own mind—as long as you recognize it as an opinion and not a fact.

Practice the Skill

Read the letter below from an American student who is traveling in Egypt with her father. Then use the following steps to analyze the letter for facts and opinions.

1. Identify the facts given about the writer's father.
2. Explain how each fact could be proved true or false.
3. Identify statements within the letter that express opinions. Explain whether each opinion signals a personal feeling or a judgment.
4. Which opinion in the letter do you think has the best factual support?

Dear Brenda,

I'm sure my dad will help you with your report on ancient Egypt. He has spent years researching the Valley of Kings, where many ancient Egyptian tombs have been found. Scientists like my dad have learned a lot about ancient Egypt because it had a system of writing, called hieroglyphics. Nobody knows more about hieroglyphics than my dad!

If you could visit while we are here, I know my dad would take you into places that most tourists don't get to see. You would be amazed to see the magnificent tombs. Grave robbers stole many of the mummies and much of the furniture from the tombs. The tomb paintings, which are still there, are unbelievably beautiful. Dad says that the bright colors have faded over time. But I still love looking at them and thinking of how those people lived. You would enjoy it, too, since you like ancient history so much. Please think about coming!

Your friend,
Dominique

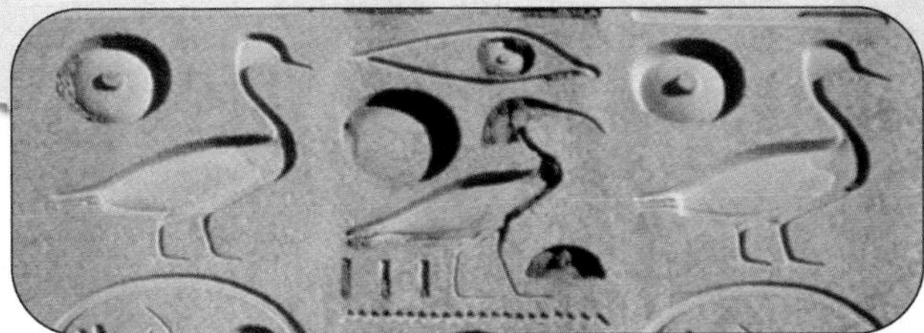

Egyptian hieroglyphs

Apply the Skill

Find the editorial page of a daily newspaper. Read through the editorials and select one that interests you. List several facts and several opinions from the editorial. Can the facts be proved? Are the opinions well supported? Explain what you find.

Section 2

Algeria

Varied Geography, Varied History

Prepare to Read

Objectives

In this section you will

1. Learn about the history and people of Algeria.
2. Find out about life in Algeria's different geographic regions.
3. Examine life in Algeria today.

Taking Notes

As you read, find details about Algeria's past and present. Copy the outline below, and use it to record your findings.

I. Algeria's history and people
  A. Algeria's past
    1.
    2.
  B.
II.

Target Reading Skill

Use Signal Words Signal words point out the relationships among ideas or events. To help identify the causes and the effects described in this section, look for words like *because, influence,* or *for that reason* that signal a cause or an effect.

Key Terms

- **souq** (sook) *n.* an open-air marketplace in an Arab city
- **casbah** (KAHZ bah) *n.* an old, crowded section of a North African city
- **terrace** (TEHR us) *n.* a flat platform of earth cut into the side of a slope, used for growing crops in steep places

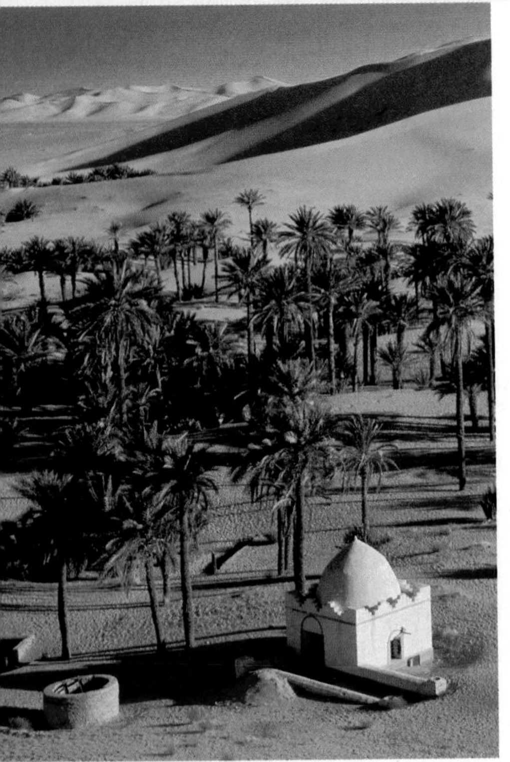

An Algerian desert home

The Sahara covers all of Algeria south of the Atlas Mountains, which cross the northern portion of Algeria from east to west. Water is in short supply in Algeria's desert lands. For that reason, fewer than 3 percent of Algeria's people live there. Because so much of Algeria is desert, more than 90 percent of Algerians live near the coast, where the weather is milder than in the Sahara.

Algeria's Mediterranean coast, its mountains, and its great desert lands are all part of the country's rich history. Algerians live in modern cities, in rural areas, and in the harsh desert. Geography, history, and culture all influence the way people live in Algeria today.

Algeria's History and People

Algeria has had a long and eventful history. Its Mediterranean location provided easy access to the markets of Europe. Algeria has also participated in trade with other parts of Africa for hundreds of years. Because of its location and resources, Algeria has been a treasure both to its people and to foreign invaders.

Early Foreign Occupations Parts of Algeria have long been occupied by outside groups. The earliest known invaders were the Phoenicians (fuh NISH unz), who were sea traders from the region of present-day Lebanon. The Phoenicians were attracted to Algeria's coast as early as two to three thousand years ago. With help from the Berbers, a North African ethnic group, the Phoenicians set up a trading post on the site of Algiers (al JEERZ). Today, Algiers is the capital of Algeria.

In the A.D. 100s, the Romans invaded Algeria. Berber farmers paid Roman taxes in grain and rented their land from Roman nobles. In the A.D. 600s, Arabs began to spread across North Africa. The Arabs conquered North Africa gradually, over hundreds of years. As a result, the Berber way of life began to change. For example, peace came to the region only after most Berbers accepted the religion of Islam.

Target Skill

Use Signal Words What word or phrase in the paragraph at the left signals a cause or an effect? Which does it signal?

Recent Occupations At different times, Algeria's valuable port cities have been commanded by the Spanish, by local pirates, and by the Ottoman Turks. In 1830, the French captured Algiers. The capture resulted in a long period of French colonial rule. Algeria gained independence from France in 1962.

Algeria's People Today, about 75 percent of Algeria's population is Arab, about 24 percent is Berber, and most of the rest is of European descent. Arabs and Berbers alike are Muslim, but many Berbers have combined Islam with their own traditional religious beliefs.

Arabic, several Berber languages, and French are the country's main languages. Many Algerians speak more than one of these languages. Arabic and Tamazight (TAHM uh zyt), a Berber language, are the country's two official languages.

✓ Reading Check **What foreign influences have been felt in Algeria?**

City on the Sea
The city of Algiers sits on hills overlooking a bay in the Mediterranean Sea. It has long served as one of Algeria's main ports.
Draw Conclusion *Why do you think the Phoenicians chose the site of Algiers for a trading post?*

COUNTRY PROFILE

Focus on Geography

Algeria

Both the climate and the physical geography of Algeria vary from place to place. The climate is very different in the south, where the Sahara lies, and along the Mediterranean coast of the north. The Sahara covers most of Algeria's land, but the desert climate is too harsh for most uses. There are no major rivers in Algeria, so the Mediterranean Sea is the only major source of water. Algeria's population is concentrated in the north, in a narrow band of cities and farmland. Study the map and charts to learn more about Algeria's geography.

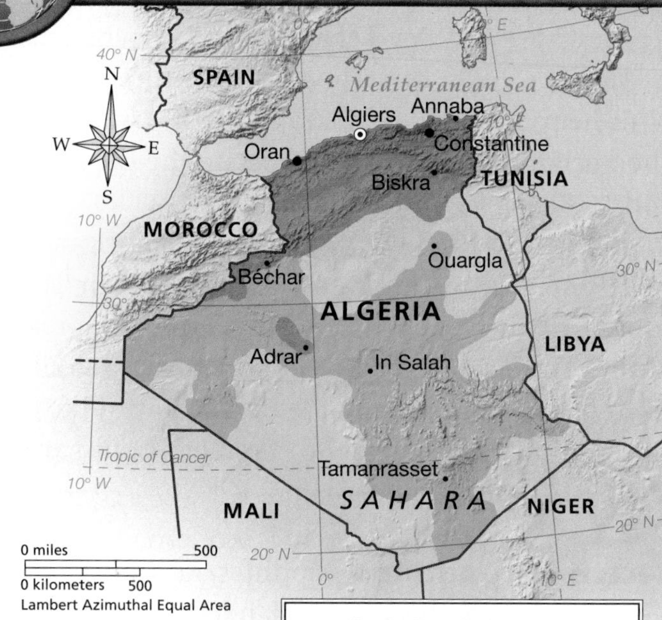

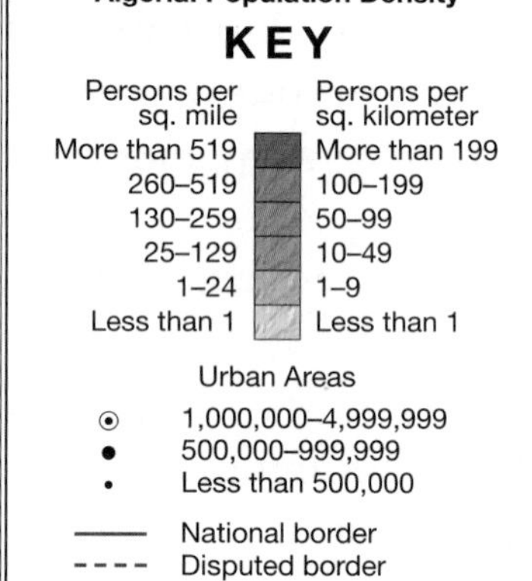

Type of Land

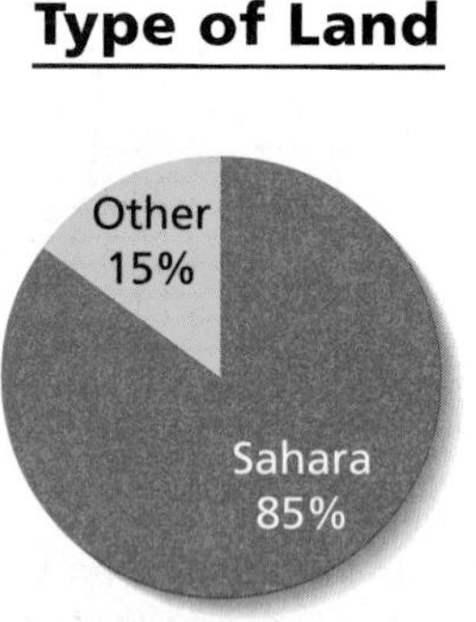

SOURCE: Atlapedia Online

Land Use

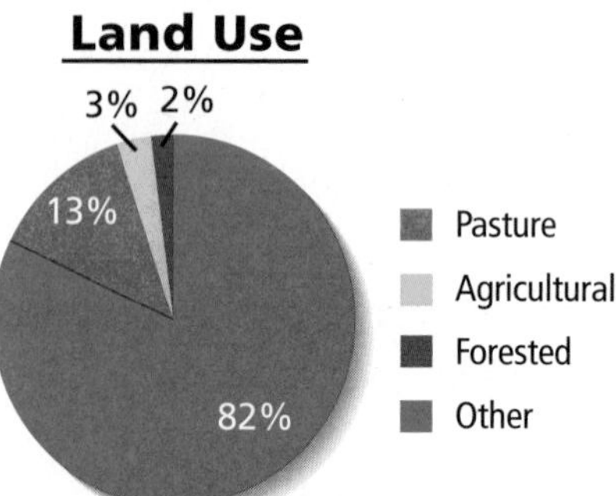

SOURCE: Atlapedia Online

Weather Chart

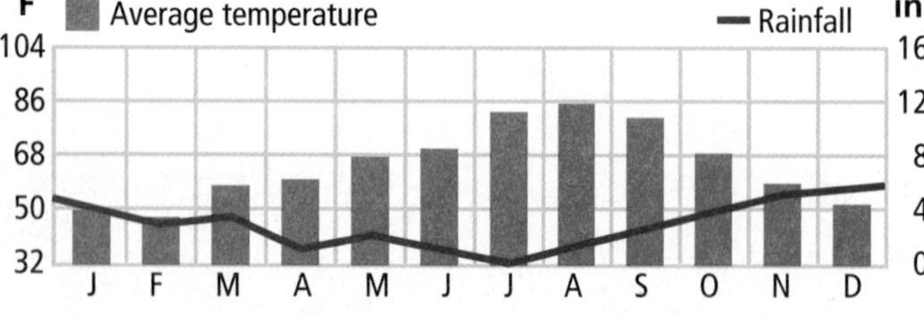

SOURCE: *DK World Desk Reference*

Map and Chart Skills

1. **Identify** In which three months does Algeria receive the greatest amount of rainfall?
2. **Draw Conclusions** Why do you think such a small percent of Algeria's land is used for agriculture?
3. **Synthesize Information** Why do most Algerians live near the Mediterranean Sea?

Use Web Code **lae-5402** for **DK World Desk Reference Online.**

Algeria's Geography

Most Algerians live in the country's coastal region, called the Tell. Algeria's best farmland is located in this region, as are most of its cities. More than half of Algeria's people live in cities.

Urban Living Many of the Algerians who live in cities are Arab, while some of them are Berber. At the heart of the cities are mosques and open-air marketplaces called **souqs** (sooks). In these souqs, merchants sell food, traditional crafts, and a variety of other goods from their stalls. Older parts of the cities are called **casbahs** (KAHZ bahz). The houses and stores in the casbahs are close together. Children play outside on the narrow, winding streets. Newer parts of the cities are modern, with wide streets and tall buildings made of steel and glass.

Rural Areas Most Berbers and many Arabs live in the countryside. Although the farmland tends to be of poor quality, about one third of Algerians are farmers. Algeria's farmers grow wheat and barley and raise livestock. In the mountains, they build **terraces,** or flat platforms of earth cut into a slope, one above another, for their crops. The terraces increase the amount of farmland and prevent the soil from washing away in the rain.

Finding Land to Farm
Much work goes into building terraces for farming, but the benefits are enormous in areas that are hilly or mountainous. Here, Algerian farmers work the fields below a terraced hillside. **Compare** *How do you think farming on flat land is different from farming on terraced hillsides?*

Traditionally, Algerians live with their extended families. In both urban and rural areas, homes feature several rooms with high walls surrounding an inner courtyard. Family members gather in the courtyard, which might have a garden or fountain.

Desert Dwellers Algeria is more than 80 percent desert. Among the small number of Algerians living in the desert, most settle in oasis towns, where water is available. There, people grow dates or citrus fruits.

Some people who live in the desert work for companies that produce oil and natural gas, Algeria's two main resources. Other desert dwellers are nomads, herding camels and other livestock suited to the climate. Like people in many parts of the world, these nomadic Algerians adapt to their climate by resting during the hottest hours of the day. By being resourceful, Berber and Arab nomads are able to survive the harsh desert conditions.

Discovery
CHANNEL
SCHOOL
Video
Learn how people farm in a desert oasis.

✓ Reading Check **How do Algerian desert dwellers make a living?**

An Algerian family

Algeria Today

Throughout the long periods of outside rule, native Algerians preserved many of their traditions. For example, while French was Algeria's official language, many people kept Arabic and Berber languages alive in their homes. Today, Algerians continue to express their customs and traditions.

Modern Home Life In both urban and rural areas, Algerians continue to value family. Many Algerians live with their extended families. However, young couples in urban areas are having fewer children than people did in previous generations. Urban Algerians also tend to live in smaller family groups.

Educating Algeria's Youth While under French rule, few non-European children received a good formal education. Since gaining independence, the Algerian government has worked hard to improve education for its children and young people. Most instruction is in Arabic. Children from ages 6 to 15 are required by law to attend school. Attendance is high in city schools but is lower in rural areas. New universities have been built to educate Algeria's young people. Some students attend colleges in other countries.

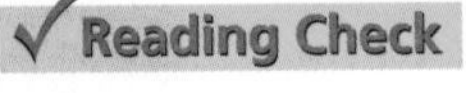
✓ Reading Check **Which language is used in most Algerian classrooms today?**

Section 2 Assessment

Key Terms
Review the key terms at the beginning of this section. Use each term in a sentence that explains its meaning.

Target Reading Skill
Review the section Algeria's History and People on pages 466 and 467. Find the words that signal causes or effects related to the foreign occupation of Algeria.

Comprehension and Critical Thinking
1. **(a) Name** What foreign groups have played a role in the history of Algeria?
(b) Explain What roles did Arabs and Berbers play in the history of Algeria?
2. **(a) Identify** In which geographic area do most Algerians live?
(b) Compare and Contrast Compare life for Algerians living in urban, rural, and desert areas. How are their lives similar? How are they different?
3. **(a) Recall** Describe education in Algeria today.
(b) Draw Conclusions What do you think is the importance of the language that is spoken in schools?

Writing Activity
Write an interview that you could conduct with someone living in Algeria today. Think of five questions you would like to ask this person. Try to ask questions that cover a number of different topics.

Writing Tip Try to avoid questions that could be answered with a *yes* or a *no*. Questions that begin with words such as *why* or *how* often lead to more interesting answers.

Chapter 14 Review and Assessment

◆ Chapter Summary

Section 1: Egypt

- Islam influences many parts of daily life in Egypt, including daily practices and the country's laws.
- Most of Egypt's population is centered along the Nile River, the country's main source of water in both urban and rural areas.

Cairo, Egypt

Section 2: Algeria

- At times over thousands of years, a variety of foreign groups have occupied Algeria.
- Most Algerians live in modern cities or in rural areas. A small number of Algerians, however, live in the desert.
- Family and education are both valued by Algerians today.

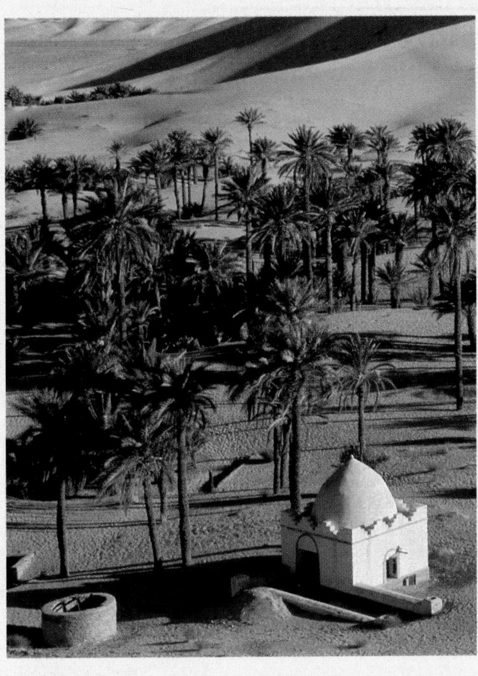

Algerian desert

◆ Key Terms

Each of the statements below contains a key term from the chapter. If the statement is true, write *true*. If it is false, change the highlighted term to make the statement true.

1. A traditional Egyptian open-air market is called a casbah.
2. Egypt's rural farmers are called fellaheen.
3. Souqs are platforms cut into the side of a slope.
4. Islamic law is called Cairo.
5. In Algeria, open-air markets may be called terraces.
6. The old section of Algiers is called the bazaar.
7. Sharia is the capital of Egypt.

Review and Assessment (continued)

◆ Comprehension and Critical Thinking

8. **(a) Recall** What are some common Islamic religious practices in Egypt?
   (b) Analyze Information What is the importance of Sharia to Muslims in Egypt?
9. **(a) Identify** What is the main source of Egypt's water supply?
   (b) Conclude How does the Aswan High Dam affect Egypt's water supply?
10. **(a) Describe** What is life like in Cairo?
    (b) Make Generalizations Why do so many Egyptians move from rural areas to cities such as Cairo?
    (c) Identify Effects What are some of the effects of overcrowding in Cairo?
11. **(a) Recall** Describe the geography of Algeria.
    (b) Explain How have people adapted to the geography and climate of Algeria?
    (c) Summarize What has been the importance of Algeria's coastal location throughout its history?
12. **(a) Identify** What languages are spoken in Algeria today?
    (b) Apply Information How do these languages reflect the history of Algeria?
13. **(a) Explain** How has the traditional view of family changed for urban Algerians?
    (b) Predict Do you think rural Algerians will change their view of family in a similar way? Explain why or why not.

◆ Skills Practice

Distinguishing Fact and Opinion In the Skills for Life activity in this chapter, you learned how to distinguish fact from opinion.

Review the steps you followed to learn this skill. Next, read a magazine article. List several facts and several opinions that are given in the article. Write down a way that each fact you listed can be proved. Then explain whether facts or reasons are given to support each opinion.

◆ Writing Activity: Science

Do research to learn about how people have used science to help them live in desert climates. Find out about nomadic living as well as life in an oasis town. Write a report describing your findings.

MAP MASTER™ Skills Activity

North Africa

Place Location For each place listed below, write the letter from the map that shows its location.

1. Cairo
2. Algeria
3. Mediterranean Sea
4. Egypt
5. Sahara

Go Online
PHSchool.com Use Web Code **lap-5420** for an **interactive map.**

Standardized Test Prep

Test-Taking Tips

Some questions on standardized tests ask you to identify main ideas. Read the paragraph below. Then follow the tips to answer the sample question.

A Berber household can include grandparents, parents, sons, daughters, and cousins. Family members all share one courtyard. Each married couple within the family has a house that opens onto the courtyard. All the windows of the house face the courtyard. The head of each family is a member of the village assembly that makes village laws.

TIP Some paragraphs have a topic sentence that states the main idea. Every sentence in the paragraph supports this idea.

Pick the letter that best answers the question.

TIP The best way to be sure you have picked the right answer is to read all four answer choices before deciding on one.

Which topic sentence is missing from this passage?

A The Berbers and the Arabs are Algeria's two main ethnic groups.

B An extended Berber family includes more than just a mother, a father, and children.

C Most Berbers from Algeria live in villages.

D Family is central to every part of Berber village life.

Think It Through By reading the paragraph, you will find that every sentence tells about Berber life. You can rule out A because the paragraph is not about Arabs. You can rule out C because the paragraph is not mainly about villages. That leaves B and D. B is about Berber families, but it could be a detail sentence in the paragraph; not all the sentences are about family members. The correct answer is D.

Practice Questions

Use the tips above and other tips in this book to help you answer the following questions. Read the paragraph below to answer Question 1. Choose the letter of the best answer.

Some desert dwellers work for companies that produce oil and natural gas. Others are nomads who herd camels and other livestock that are suited to the hot, dry climate. Like people in many parts of the world, these Algerians adapt to their climate by resting during the hottest hours of the day.

1. Which topic sentence is missing from the paragraph above?
   A Oil and natural gas are Algeria's two most important natural resources.
   B Algerians have found ways to work and survive in the desert.
   C It is difficult to live in the desert.
   D Agriculture and fuel industries thrive in the desert.

2. In Egypt, most people live
   A in Cairo.
   B in Alexandria.
   C in the valley and delta regions of the Nile.
   D in the Nile delta region.

3. Which of the following statements is true?
   A In Algeria, all Arabs and Berbers are Muslims.
   B In Algeria, Arabs and a small percentage of Berbers are Muslims.
   C In Egypt, most people are Coptic Christians.
   D In Egypt, almost half of the people are Coptic Christians.

Use Web Code **laa-5400** for **Chapter 14 self-test.**

Chapter

15 West Africa

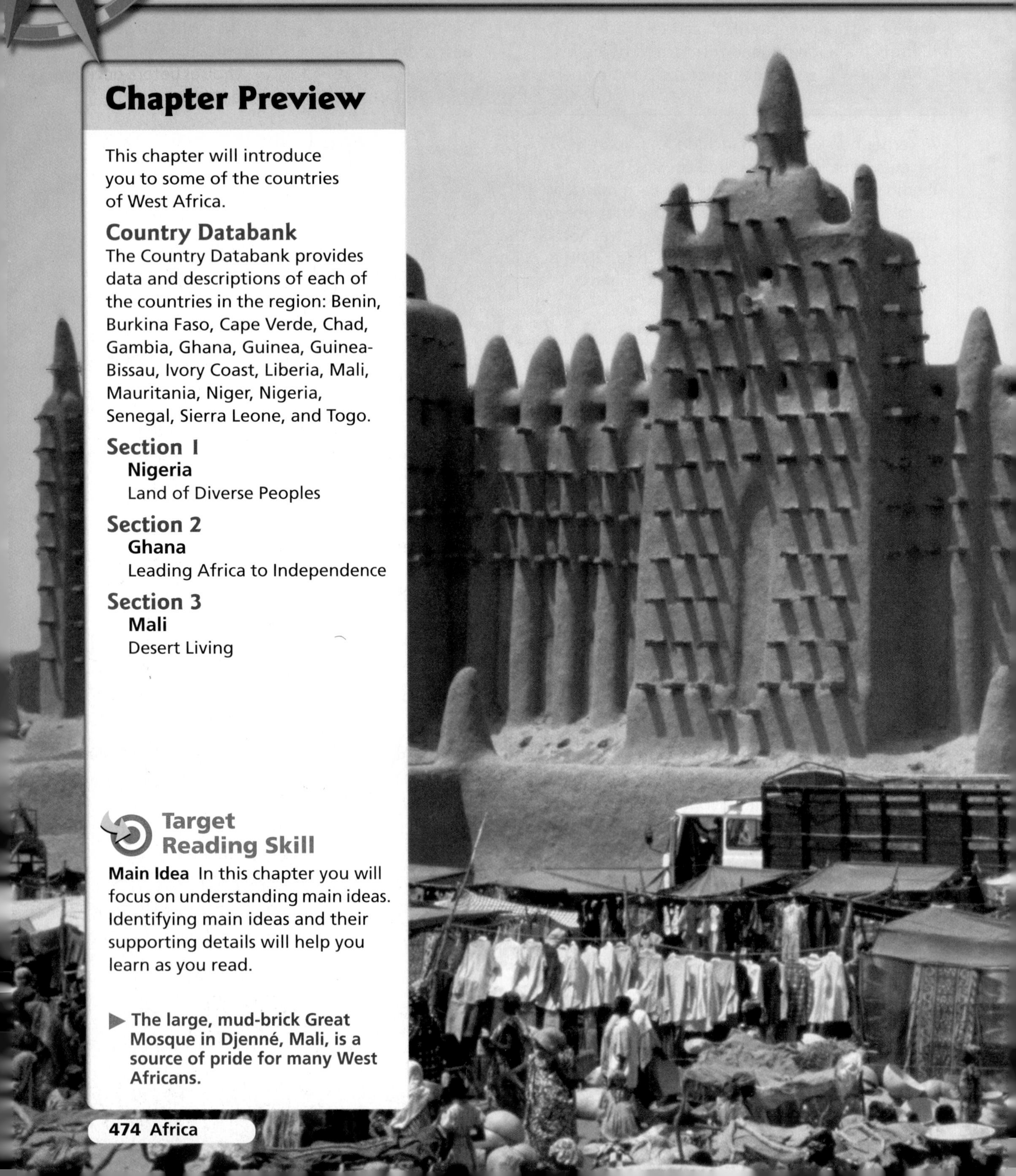

Chapter Preview

This chapter will introduce you to some of the countries of West Africa.

Country Databank

The Country Databank provides data and descriptions of each of the countries in the region: Benin, Burkina Faso, Cape Verde, Chad, Gambia, Ghana, Guinea, Guinea-Bissau, Ivory Coast, Liberia, Mali, Mauritania, Niger, Nigeria, Senegal, Sierra Leone, and Togo.

Target Reading Skill

Main Idea In this chapter you will focus on understanding main ideas. Identifying main ideas and their supporting details will help you learn as you read.

▶ **The large, mud-brick Great Mosque in Djenné, Mali, is a source of pride for many West Africans.**

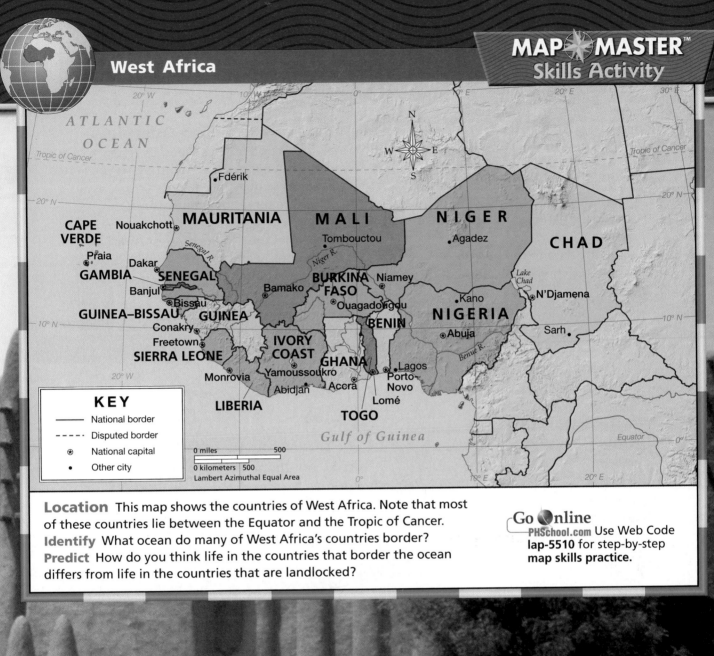

West Africa

MAP MASTER™ Skills Activity

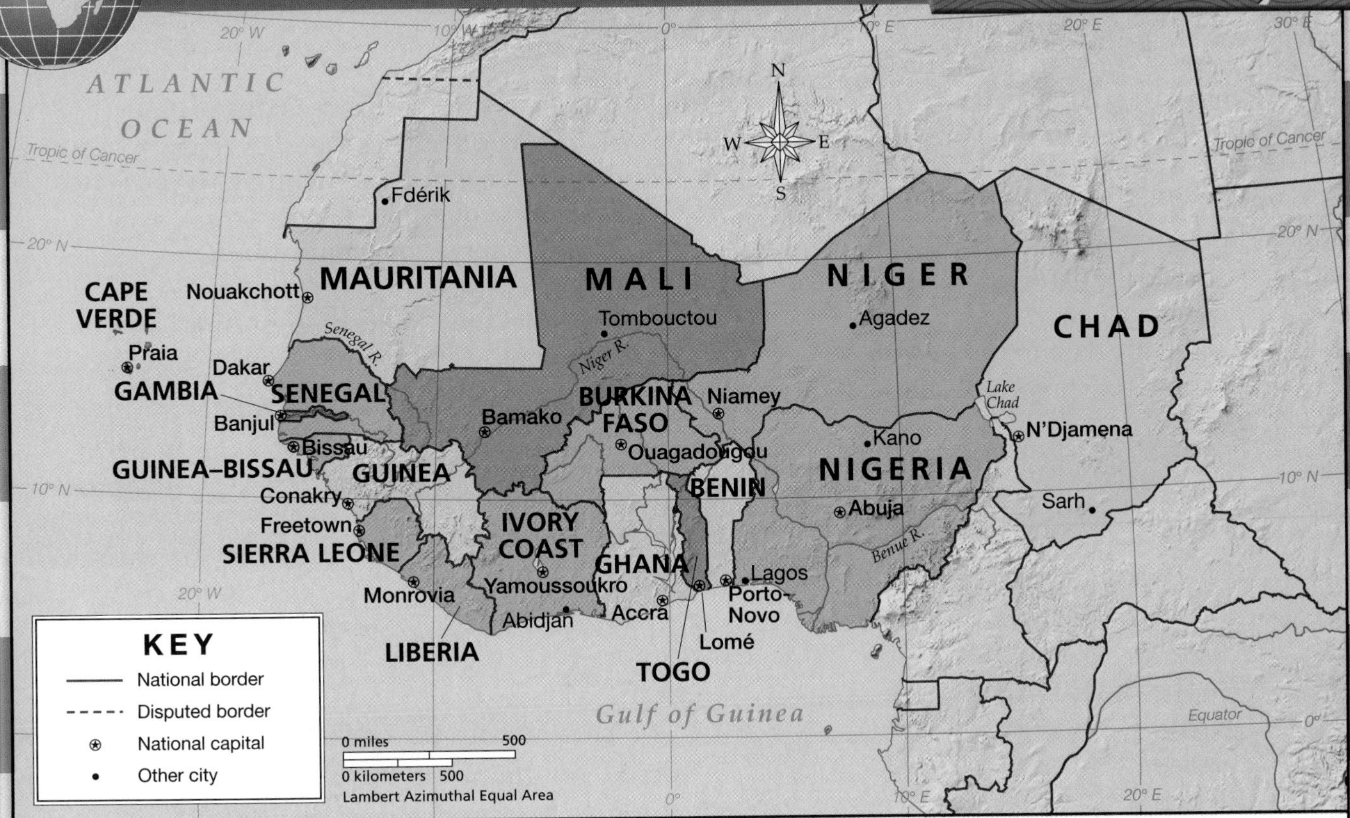

ATLANTIC OCEAN

Tropic of Cancer

Fdérik

CAPE VERDE
Praia
Nouakchott
MAURITANIA
MALI
NIGER
CHAD
Tombouctou
Agadez
Senegal R.
Niger R.
Dakar
GAMBIA
SENEGAL
Banjul
Bissau
GUINEA-BISSAU
GUINEA
Conakry
Freetown
SIERRA LEONE
Monrovia
LIBERIA
Bamako
BURKINA FASO
Ouagadougou
Niamey
Lake Chad
N'Djamena
Kano
NIGERIA
Abuja
Benue R.
BENIN
IVORY COAST
Yamoussoukro
Abidjan
GHANA
Accra
TOGO
Lomé
Lagos
Porto-Novo
Sarh
Gulf of Guinea
Equator

KEY

National border
Disputed border
National capital
Other city

0 miles 500
0 kilometers 500
Lambert Azimuthal Equal Area

Location This map shows the countries of West Africa. Note that most of these countries lie between the Equator and the Tropic of Cancer.
Identify What ocean do many of West Africa's countries border?
Predict How do you think life in the countries that border the ocean differs from life in the countries that are landlocked?

Go Online
PHSchool.com Use Web Code **lap-5510** for step-by-step **map skills practice.**

Introducing West Africa

Guide for Reading

This section provides an introduction to the 17 countries that make up the region of West Africa.

- Look at the map on the previous page and then read the paragraphs below to learn about each nation.
- Analyze the data to compare the countries.
- What are the characteristics that most of the countries share?
- What are some key differences among the countries?

Viewing the Video Overview

View the World Studies Video Overview to learn more about each of the countries. As you watch, answer these questions:

- What are some common features of the region?
- How does the climate of West Africa affect the people living there?
- What natural resources are important to the countries of West Africa?

Discovery
CHANNEL
SCHOOL
Video
Explore the geography of West Africa.

Benin

Capital	Porto-Novo
Land Area	42,710 sq mi; 110,620 sq km
Population	6.9 million
Ethnic Group(s)	42 ethnic groups, including Fon, Adja, Yoruba, Bariba
Religion(s)	traditional beliefs, Muslim, Christian
Government	republic
Currency	CFA franc
Leading Exports	cotton, crude oil, palm products, cocoa
Language(s)	French (official), Fon, Bariba, Yoruba, Adja, Houeda, Somba

The narrow country of Benin (beh NEEN) is bordered on the west by Togo, on the north by Burkina Faso and Niger, on the east by Nigeria, and on the south by the Atlantic Ocean. Seasons are rainy or dry. More than two thirds of Benin's people live in the south. Most live in or near either Porto-Novo, the capital, or Cotonou, the center of business. Present-day Benin was formed by the French in the late 1800s. Since it gained independence in 1960, it has been on a shaky path to democracy and stability. In 1990, Benin successfully opened politics to multiple parties.

Near Porto-Novo, Benin

Burkina Faso

Capital Ouagadougou
Land Area 105,714 sq mi; 273,800 sq km
Population 12.6 million
Ethnic Group(s) Mossi, Gurunsi, Senufo, Lobi, Bobo, Mande, Fulani
Religion(s) traditional beliefs, Muslim, Christian
Government parliamentary republic
Currency CFA franc
Leading Exports cotton, animal products, gold
Language(s) French (official), Mossi, Fulani, Tuareg, Dyula, Songhai

Burkina Faso (bur KEE nuh FAH soh) is bordered on the west and north by Mali, on the east by Niger and Benin, and on the south by Togo, Ghana, and Ivory Coast. The hot, dry north receives plentiful sunshine. The south is tropical, with more rainfall and a greater range of temperatures. Ninety percent of the population is rural—a higher percentage than in any other West African country. A French colony beginning in the 1890s, it gained independence as Upper Volta in 1960. Its name changed to Burkina Faso in 1984.

Cape Verde

Capital Praia
Land Area 1,557 sq mi; 4,033 sq km
Population 408,760
Ethnic Group(s) Creole, black, white
Religion(s) Roman Catholic, Protestant
Government republic
Currency Cape Verde escudo
Leading Exports fuel, shoes, garments, fish, hides
Language(s) Portuguese (official), Portuguese Creole

West Africa's smallest nation, Cape Verde (kayp vurd), lies in the Atlantic Ocean, west of Senegal. It consists of ten islands and five islets. One of them, Fogo Island, is home to an active volcano that last erupted in 1995. Throughout its history, periods with little rainfall have brought hardship on the nation. Cape Verde has been inhabited since 1462, when its first settlers arrived from Portugal. They brought enslaved Africans as well. In 1975, Cape Verde gained independence. Today, about half of Cape Verdeans live on the island of São Tiago.

Chad

Capital N'Djamena
Land Area 486,177 sq mi; 1,259,200 sq km
Population 9 million
Ethnic Group(s) 200 distinct groups, including Arab, Sara
Religion(s) Muslim, Christian, traditional beliefs
Government republic
Currency CFA franc
Leading Exports cotton, cattle, gum arabic
Language(s) Arabic (official), French (official), Sara, Maba

Chad (chad) is Africa's fifth-largest country. It is bordered on the west by Cameroon, Nigeria, and Niger; on the north by Libya; on the east by Sudan; and on the south by the Central African Republic. Its northern lands are covered by the Sahara and are spotted with extinct volcanoes. In the south, the Sahel gets slightly more rain. Lake Chad, in the west, was historically a stop for traders crossing the Sahara. The French controlled the region from 1900 to 1960, when it became independent. Chad has since faced civil wars and military takeovers of the government.

Introducing West Africa

Gambia

Capital	Banjul
Land Area	3,861 sq mi; 10,000 sq km
Population	1.5 million
Ethnic Group(s)	Mandinka, Fulani, Wolof, Jola, Serahuli
Religion(s)	Muslim, Christian, traditional beliefs
Government	republic
Currency	dalasi
Leading Exports	peanuts and peanut products, fish, cotton lint, palm kernels
Language(s)	English (official), Mandinka, Fulani, Wolof, Jola, Sonike

At 295 miles (475 kilometers) in length and 15 to 30 miles (24 to 48 kilometers) in width, Gambia (GAM bee uh) is a narrow country. It is surrounded by Senegal except on the west, where it borders the Atlantic Ocean. The Gambia River flows the entire length of the country. Gambia's economy depends on peanuts as a cash crop. Great Britain ruled Gambia from the early 1600s until 1965. In the early years after independence, Gambia's smooth transition from colonial rule to stable democracy stood as a model for other African nations. Beginning in 1989, however, a series of government takeovers shook the country.

Ghana

Capital	Accra
Land Area	89,166 sq mi; 230,940 sq km
Population	20.2 million
Ethnic Group(s)	Akan, Moshi-Dagomba, Ewe, Ga, Gurma, Yoruba, white
Religion(s)	Christian, traditional beliefs, Muslim
Government	constitutional democracy
Currency	cedi
Leading Exports	gold, cocoa, timber, tuna, bauxite, aluminum, manganese ore, diamonds
Language(s)	English (official), Twi, Fanti, Ewe, Ga, Adangbe, Gurma, Dagomba (Dagbani)

Ghana (GAH nuh) is bordered on the west by Ivory Coast, on the north by Burkina Faso, on the east by Togo, and on the south by the Atlantic Ocean. Ghana is rich in natural resources. It was originally referred to as the Gold Coast because of its abundant supply of gold. In addition, Ghana is viewed as a leader in African politics. The country became independent in 1957, making it the first African nation to achieve independence from the British as well as the first nation in modern Africa to be governed by black leaders.

Gold ornaments from Ghana

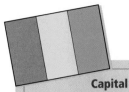

Guinea

Capital Conakry
Land Area 94,925 sq mi; 245,857 sq km
Population 7.8 million
Ethnic Group(s) Peuhl, Malinke, Soussou
Religion(s) Muslim, Christian, traditional beliefs
Government republic
Currency Guinea franc
Leading Exports bauxite, alumina, fish, diamonds, coffee, gold, agricultural products
Language(s) French (official), Fulani, Malinke, Soussou

Guinea (GIH nee) is neighbored by Guinea-Bissau, Senegal, Mali, Ivory Coast, Sierra Leone, and Liberia. The western border of the country runs along the Atlantic Ocean. Three major rivers—the Gambia, the Senegal, and the Niger—all have their sources in Guinea. The country is rich in natural resources. At least one third of the world's supply of bauxite comes from Guinea, which is the world's second-largest producer of the mineral, after Australia. Farming is also a dominant industry in Guinea, where many people produce cash crops as well as crops to support their families.

Guinea-Bissau

Capital Bissau
Land Area 10,811 sq mi; 28,000 sq km
Population 1.4 million
Ethnic Group(s) Balanta, Fula, Manjaca, Mandinga, Papel, white, mixed white and black
Religion(s) traditional beliefs, Muslim, Christian
Government republic
Currency CFA franc
Leading Exports cashew nuts, shrimp, peanuts, palm kernels, sawn lumber
Language(s) Portuguese (official), Portuguese Creole, Balante, Fulani, Malinke

The mainland of Guinea-Bissau (GIH nee bih SOW) is bordered by the Atlantic Ocean on the west, Senegal on the north, and Guinea on the east and south. The country also includes a group of islands off its Atlantic coast. Guinea-Bissau's economy revolves mostly around farming, with rice being its main product. About two thirds of the country's population is rural. The majority of people are of African descent. The remainder are of European or other foreign ancestry. About half of Guinea-Bissau's people practice traditional religions. Most of the other half practice Islam, and a small number practice Christianity.

Ivory Coast

Capital Yamoussoukro
Land Area 122,780 sq mi; 318,000 sq km
Population 16.8 million
Ethnic Group(s) Akan, Voltaiques (Gur), Northern Mandes, Krous, Southern Mandes
Religion(s) Muslim, Christian, traditional beliefs
Government republic
Currency CFA franc
Leading Exports cocoa, coffee, timber, petroleum, cotton, bananas, pineapples, palm oil, cotton, fish
Language(s) French (official), Akan, Kru, Voltaic

Ivory Coast (EYE vur ee kohst) is one of the largest countries on West Africa's coast. It is bordered on the west by Liberia and Guinea, on the north by Mali and Burkina Faso, on the east by Ghana, and on the south by the Gulf of Guinea. Mountains cover most of its western edge. Ivory Coast has one of the stronger economies in West Africa. Cocoa and coffee are major agricultural products. In fact, Ivory Coast produces more cocoa than any other country in the world. Since 1950, the country has become more and more urban. The country's population has also grown at a rapid rate.

Introducing West Africa

Spot-nosed monkey in Liberia

Liberia

Capital	Monrovia
Land Area	37,189 sq mi; 96,320 sq km
Population	3.3 million
Ethnic Group(s)	Kpelle, Bassa, Gio, Kru, Grebo, Mano, Krahn, Gola, Gbandi, Loma, Kissi, Vai, Dei, Bella, Mandingo, Mende, Americo-Liberians, Congo People
Religion(s)	traditional beliefs, Christian, Muslim
Government	republic
Currency	Liberian dollar
Leading Exports	rubber, timber, iron, diamonds, cocoa, coffee
Language(s)	English (official), Kpelle, Vai, Kru Bassa, Grebo, Kissi, Gola, Loma

Liberia (ly BIHR ee uh) never experienced European rule. It was Africa's first republic, founded in 1847 by freed slaves from the United States. It is bordered on the northwest by Sierra Leone, on the north by Guinea, on the east by Ivory Coast, and on the south and west by the Atlantic Ocean. Liberia is part of the West African Shield, a rock formation that is about 3 million years old. It also has rain forests in which animals such as monkeys, hippopotami, crocodiles, and lizards live. Today, 95 percent of Liberians are of African descent. The rest are mostly Americo-Liberians, descendants of the country's American-born founders.

Mali

Capital	Bamako
Land Area	471,042 sq mi; 1,220,000 sq km
Population	11.3 million
Ethnic Group(s)	Mande, Peul, Voltaic, Songhai, Tuareg, Moor
Religion(s)	Muslim, traditional beliefs, Christian
Government	republic
Currency	CFA franc
Leading Exports	cotton, gold, livestock
Language(s)	French (official), Bambara, Fulani, Senufo, Soninke

Mali (MAH lee) is one of West Africa's few landlocked countries. It is bordered on the west by Senegal and Mauritania, on the north by Algeria, on the east by Niger and Burkina Faso, and on the south by Ivory Coast and Guinea. The northern third of Mali is covered by the Sahara. To the south lies the Sahel, where cattle graze widely. The Senegal and Niger rivers flow through Mali. The country is named after an ancient empire that flourished in neighboring Niger.

Cattle herders in Mali

Mauritania

Capital	Nouakchott
Land Area	397,837 sq mi; 1,030,400 sq km
Population	2.8 million
Ethnic Group(s)	Maur, black, mixed
Religion(s)	Muslim
Government	republic
Currency	ouguiya
Leading Exports	iron ore, fish, fish products, gold
Language(s)	Arabic (official), Hassaniyah Arabic, Wolof, French

Mauritania (mawr uh TAY nee uh) is bordered on the west by the Atlantic Ocean, on the north by Western Morocco and Algeria, on the east and south by Mali, and on the south by Senegal. About two thirds of the country is covered by the Sahara. Many nomads once lived in the desert, but frequent droughts prevented many of them from staying there. For that reason, the population of the city of Nouakchott (nwahk SHAHT) has grown to around one million people.

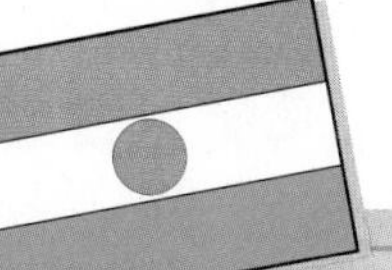

Niger

Capital	Niamey
Land Area	489,073 sq mi; 1,226,700 sq km
Population	11.3 million
Ethnic Group(s)	Hausa, Djerma, Songhai, Fula, Tuareg, Beri Beri, Arab, Toubou, Gourmantche
Religion(s)	Muslim, traditional beliefs, Christian
Government	republic
Currency	CFA franc
Leading Exports	uranium ore, livestock products, cowpeas, onions
Language(s)	French (official), Hausa, Djerma, Fulani, Tuareg, Teda

Niger (NY jur) is bordered on the west by Burkina Faso and Mali, on the north by Algeria and Libya, on the east by Chad, and on the south by Nigeria and Benin. Much of the country is arid Sahara or Sahel, although there are savannas in the south. Niger has often faced drought. Also, the country has faced long-term conflict between the northern and southern ethnic groups. Although politically stable after gaining independence in 1960, Niger has struggled to establish democracy. In 1990, seeking fairer treatment, the Tuareg people of the north rebelled against the government. The signing of a peace treaty in 1995 resolved the conflict.

Nigeria

Capital	Abuja
Land Area	351,648 sq mi; 910,768 sq km
Population	129.9 million
Ethnic Group(s)	250 distinct groups, including Hausa, Fulani, Yoruba, Igbo, Ijaw, Kanuri, Ibibio, Tiv
Religion(s)	Muslim, Christian, traditional beliefs
Government	republic
Currency	naira
Leading Exports	petroleum and petroleum products, cocoa, rubber
Language(s)	English (official), Hausa, Yoruba, Igbo

Nigeria (ny JIHR ee uh) has the largest population of any African country. It is bordered on the west by Benin, on the north by Niger, on the east by Chad and Cameroon, and on the south by the Atlantic Ocean. Members of at least 250 ethnic groups live in Nigeria. The country is one of the world's largest oil producers. It is also one of Africa's leaders in education. About 98 percent of Nigerian children attend elementary school, and the country is home to more than 50 colleges and universities. Still, corrupt government, ethnic conflict, and religious conflict have all troubled modern Nigeria.

Introducing West Africa

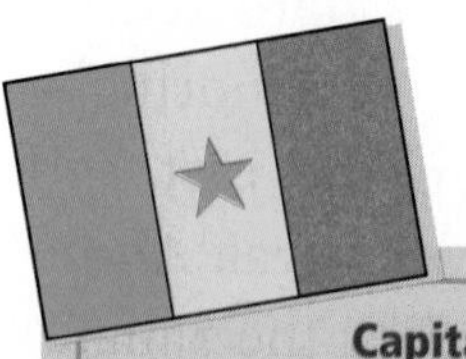

Senegal

Capital	Dakar
Land Area	74,131 sq mi; 192,000 sq km
Population	10.6 million
Ethnic Group(s)	Wolof, Pular, Serer, Jola, Mandinka, Soninke, white, Southwest Asian
Religion(s)	Muslim, Christian, traditional beliefs
Government	republic
Currency	CFA franc
Leading Exports	fish, peanuts, petroleum products, phosphates, cotton
Language(s)	French (official), Wolof, Fulani, Serer, Diola, Malinke, Soninke, Arabic

Senegal (SEN ih gawl) is bordered on the west by the Atlantic Ocean, on the north by Mauritania, on the east by Mali, and on the south by Guinea and Guinea-Bissau. Its capital, Dakar, is located on the westernmost reach of the African continent and is an important port for West Africa. Senegal was colonized by the French, and it became independent in 1960. The first president of the country, Léopold Senghor, is known as one of the great African poets.

Léopold Senghor

Sierra Leone

Capital	Freetown
Land Area	27,652 sq mi; 71,620 sq km
Population	5.6 million
Ethnic Group(s)	20 distinct groups, including Temne, Mende, Creole
Religion(s)	Muslim, traditional beliefs, Christian
Government	constitutional democracy
Currency	leone
Leading Exports	diamonds, rutile, cocoa, coffee, fish
Language(s)	English (official), Mende, Temne, Krio

Sierra Leone (see EHR uh lee OHN) is bordered on the west by the Atlantic Ocean, on the north and east by Guinea, and on the south by Liberia. Its capital city, Freetown, lies beside a huge natural harbor surrounded by low mountains. In 1787, the British established Sierra Leone as a place for freed African slaves to live. It later became a British colony and then gained independence in 1961. Since the 1990s, the country has suffered through intense civil wars. The people of Sierra Leone are known for the carved wooden masks they wear during performances, as well as for their carved ivory figures.

Carved wooden mask from Sierra Leone

Togo

Capital	Lomé
Land Area	20,998 sq mi; 54,385 sq km
Population	5.2 million
Ethnic Group(s)	37 distinct groups, including Ewe, Mina, Kabre, white, Southwest Asian
Religion(s)	traditional beliefs, Christian, Muslim
Government	republic
Currency	CFA franc
Leading Exports	cotton, phosphates, coffee, cocoa
Language(s)	French (official), Ewe, Kabye, Gurma

Togo (TOH goh) is bordered on the west by Ghana, on the north by Burkina Faso, on the east by Benin, and on the south by the Atlantic Ocean. The small country includes coastal lands, mountains, rivers, and plateaus. Many trees cover the southern plateaus, including baobab (BAY oh bab) trees, which are famous for their huge trunks. Togo is one of the world's largest producers of the mineral phosphate. Politically, one party has dominated since 1967. In the 1990s, however, the country made the formation of other political parties legal.

Baobab tree

SOURCES: DK World Desk Reference Online; CIA World Factbook Online, 2002; *The World Almanac*, 2003

Keeping Current

Access the **DK World Desk Reference Online** at **PHSchool.com** for up-to-date information about all 17 countries in this chapter.

Web Code: **lae-5500**

Assessment

Comprehension and Critical Thinking

1. Compare and Contrast Compare and contrast the histories of these countries.

2. Summarize What are some characteristics that most of the countries share?

3. Analyze Information What are some key differences among the countries?

4. Categorize What kinds of products are the major exports of this region?

5. Predict How might the region be affected by the presence of a great number of ethnic groups?

6. Make a Circle Graph Create a circle graph showing the forms of government held by the countries of West Africa and the percentage each form represents.

Section 1

Nigeria

Land of Diverse Peoples

Prepare to Read

Objectives

In this section you will

1. Learn to identify Nigeria's three main ethnic groups.
2. Understand the major events in Nigeria's history.
3. Find out about the conflicts Nigeria faced on its path to democracy.

Taking Notes

As you read this section, look for details about Nigeria's three main ethnic groups. Copy the chart below, and use it to record your findings.

Nigeria's Ethnic Groups		
Hausa-Fulani	Yoruba	Igbo
• •	• •	• •

Target Reading Skill

Identify Main Ideas It is impossible to remember every detail that you read. Therefore, good readers identify the main idea in every paragraph or section.

The main idea is the most important point in the section. For example, on page 489, the main idea of the paragraph under the heading Oil is stated here: "Another notable source of tension in Nigeria is the country's wealth of oil resources." All the other information in the paragraph supports this main idea.

Key Terms

- **multiethnic** (mul tee ETH nik) *adj.* having many ethnic groups living within a society
- **Hausa-Fulani** (HOW suh foo LAH nee) *n.* Nigeria's largest ethnic group
- **Yoruba** (YOH roo buh) *n.* Nigeria's second-largest ethnic group
- **Igbo** (IG boh) *n.* Nigeria's third-largest ethnic group

Nigerian youth

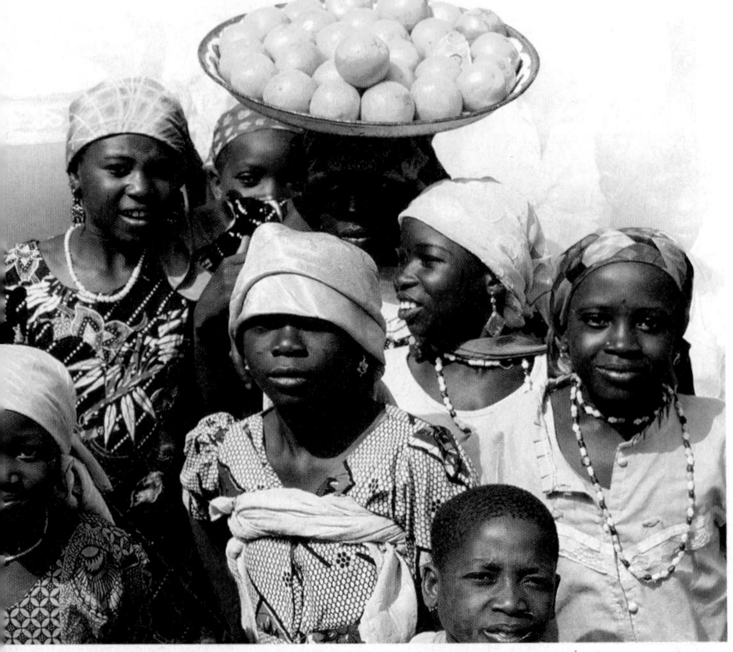

If you were planning to travel to Spain, you might learn Spanish. If you were planning to travel to Greece, you might try to learn Greek. But if you were traveling to Nigeria, would you study Nigerian? No, you would not even try to, because there is no such language. In fact, out of the more than 1,000 languages spoken in Africa, at least 200 are spoken in Nigeria alone.

If you find it hard to believe that so many languages can be heard in just one country, picture this: Nigeria is a little larger than the states of California, Oregon, and Washington combined. That means Nigeria could fit inside the United States about 11 times. But Nigeria has nearly half the population of the whole United States. At about 130 million people, Nigeria's population is the largest in Africa.

Ethnic Groups of Nigeria

Nigeria is **multiethnic,** which means that many ethnic groups live within its borders. In fact, it is home to more than 250 ethnic groups—most of whom speak different languages. English is the official language of Nigeria. However, the languages of Nigeria's major ethnic groups dominate the country.

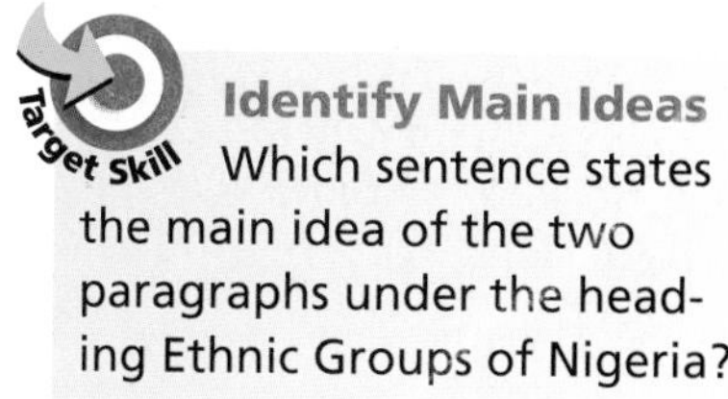

Identify Main Ideas Which sentence states the main idea of the two paragraphs under the heading Ethnic Groups of Nigeria?

These ethnic groups have inhabited Nigeria for many centuries. As you can see on the map in the Country Profile on page 487, the people of each group tend to live in certain parts of the country. Most members of Nigeria's largest ethnic group, the **Hausa-Fulani** (HOW suh foo LAH nee), live in the northwest. Nigeria's second-largest ethnic group, the **Yoruba** (YOH roo buh), make their home in the southwest. And the **Igbo** (IG boh), Nigeria's third-largest ethnic group, live mainly in the southeast. In addition, many smaller ethnic groups live in central Nigeria, and others are scattered throughout the country.

The Hausa-Fulani In the early 1800s, the Fulani entered northern Nigeria and conquered the Hausa there. The Fulani then ruled over the Hausa. But instead of imposing their own culture, many of the Fulani adopted the Hausa's language and practices. Over time, many Hausa and Fulani have intermarried, and the two groups have come to be known as the Hausa-Fulani.

The majority of Hausa-Fulani live in the countryside. Some herd cattle, while others farm crops such as peanuts and a grain called sorghum (SAWR gum). Still others produce crafts that are traded in markets. Trade has been an important part of the Hausa economy for hundreds of years—since long before the Fulani arrived. The Hausa built trading cities in northern Nigeria, each of which was enclosed by walls and housed a central market. Today, some of these cities, such as Kano, still thrive as centers of commerce.

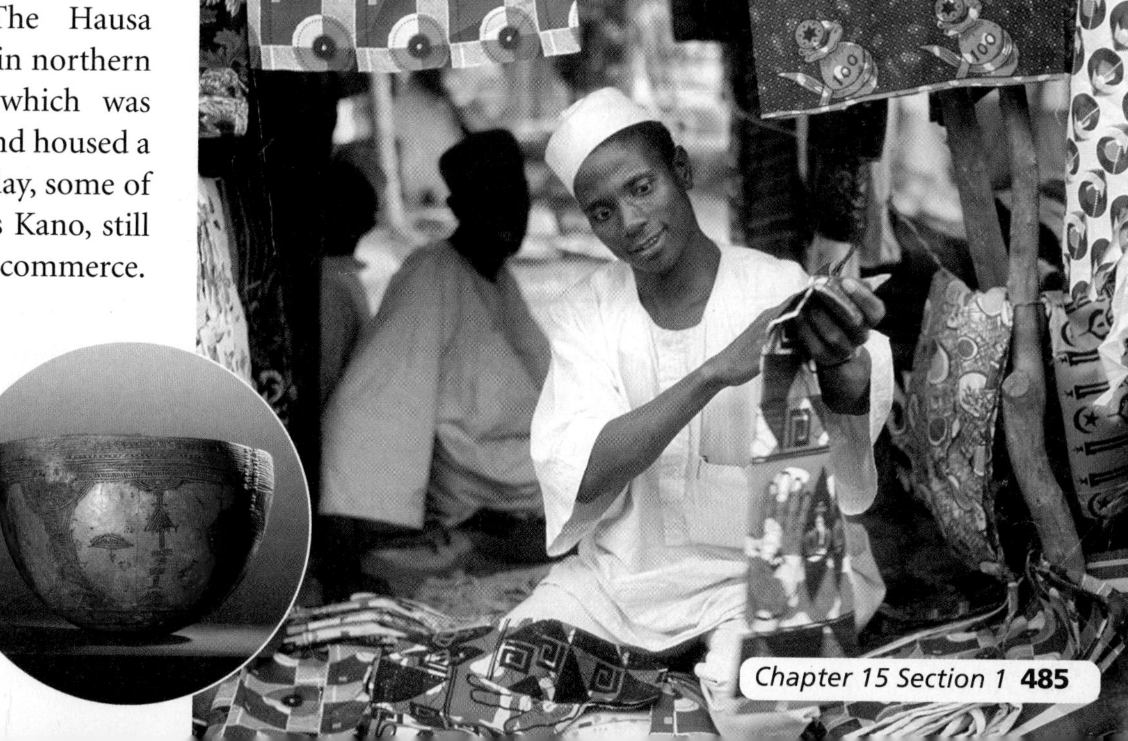

Trading City Still Thrives
Kano has been a center of trade for more than 1,000 years. Today, people from around the world visit Kano's Kurmi Market. Vendors sell everything from fabrics (below right) to carved calabash bowls (below left). **Draw Conclusions** *Why do you think trading centers such as Kano have been able to last so long?*

A Yoruba farming family

Links to
Language Arts

Wole Soyinka Wole Soyinka (WOH lay shaw YING kuh) is a Yoruba man who is known as one of Africa's most talented writers. In 1986, he won the Nobel Prize in Literature—the world's most celebrated prize for writing. Soyinka has written numerous plays, novels, poems, and autobiographical and nonfiction works. In his works, Soyinka often comments on Nigerian society in both serious and humorous ways. He also includes Yoruba folklore and traditions in his writing.

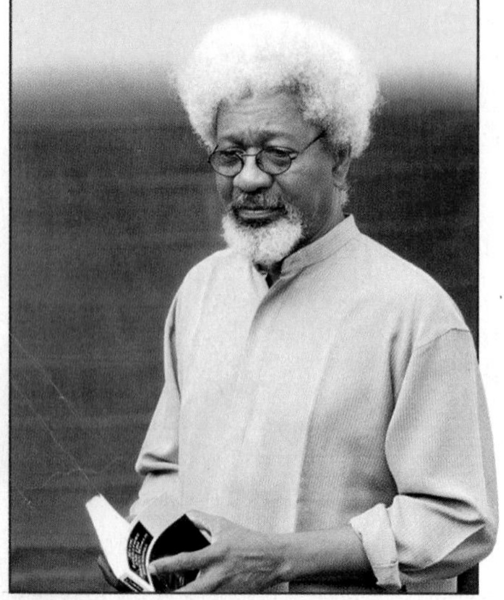

The Yoruba Historically, the Yoruba have been the most urban of Nigeria's major ethnic groups. The Yoruba tradition of building cities began around 1100 and continued for hundreds of years. Each Yoruba city was ruled by a king and was densely populated, including traders and many skilled artisans. Currently, the majority of residents of one of Africa's largest cities, Lagos, are Yoruba. The city was founded in the 1400s and served as the capital of Nigeria from 1960 to 1991.

Today, many Yoruba also live outside cities. Often they are farmers, traders, or craftspeople. The farmers tend to grow cash crops such as cacao. They also grow food for their own families. Yoruba families live in large compounds made up of several houses built around a shared yard. A Yoruba community has many of these compounds.

The Igbo The Igbo have traditionally been rural. They have not built large cities but rather live in small farming villages. The people in a village work closely together. Each village is ruled democratically by a council of elders that the people select. Council members work together to solve problems.

Today, many Igbo also live in cities. Throughout much of the past century, they have served as members of Nigeria's local and federal governments. As you will read, Nigeria became an independent country in 1960, and its first president, Benjamin Nnamdi Azikiwe (NUM dee ah ZEE kway), was Igbo.

✓ Reading Check **Which of Nigeria's ethnic groups is known as the most urban?**

COUNTRY PROFILE Focus on Culture

Nigeria

Nigeria is Africa's most heavily populated country and one of its most diverse. The country is rich in culture, but the differences can result in clashes. With more than 250 ethnic groups, tensions between the different groups have been hard to avoid. In addition, Muslim communities in the north and Christian communities in the south often face conflict today. Many northern states have adopted Islamic law. At the same time, Christian churches have drawn millions of new members. Study the map and charts to learn more about Nigeria's diverse population.

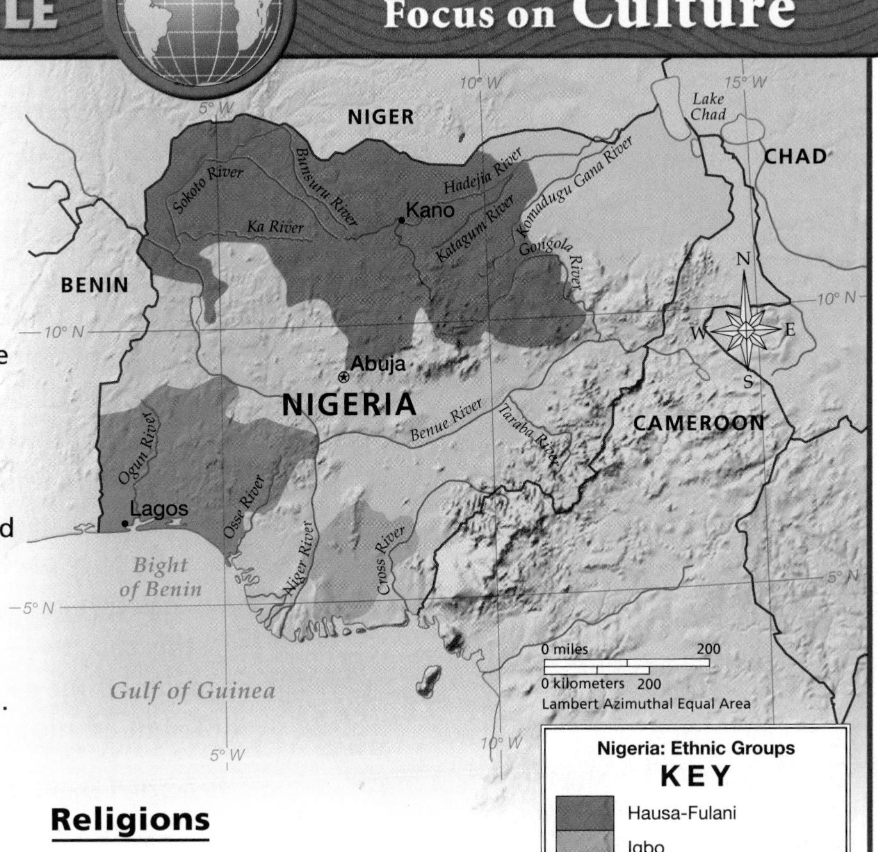

Ethnic Groups

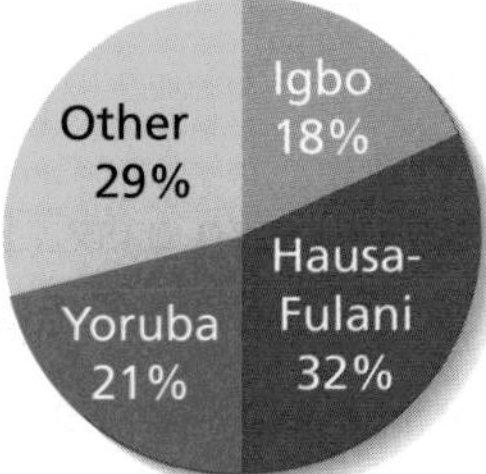

SOURCE: *DK World Desk Reference*

Religions

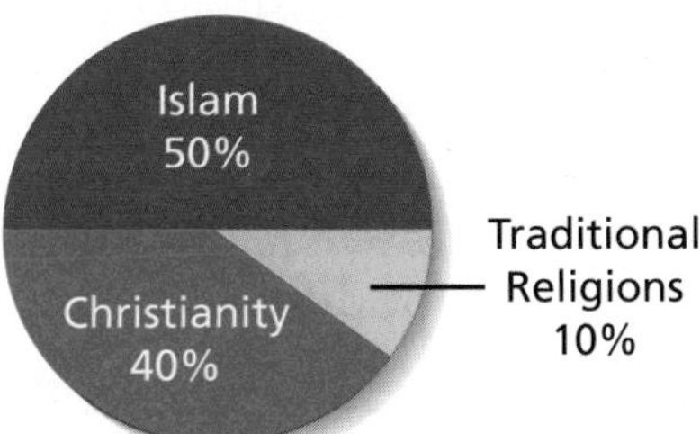

SOURCE: *DK World Desk Reference*

Tall, carved drums like these are made by Igbo people in Nigeria.

Map and Chart Skills

1. **Identify** What are two factors that make Nigeria a diverse country?
2. **Infer** Using the information given in the paragraph and the map above, which of Nigeria's largest ethnic groups can you infer is Muslim?
3. **Evaluate** Southern Nigeria has large oil reserves. How could this oil wealth play a role in the country's tensions?

Use Web Code **lae-5501** for **DK World Desk Reference Online.**

Nigeria's History

For thousands of years, the region of present-day Nigeria was ruled by many different African peoples who formed their own governments. In the late 1400s, however, Portugal began trading for slaves in West Africa. Soon, Great Britain and the Netherlands began trading in the region as well. By 1914, Great Britain had taken over Nigeria's government.

In 1960, Nigeria became an independent nation, with Lagos as its capital. Ethnic groups that had always lived separately had to learn to live and work together as one nation. In 1991, to help unify the country, Nigeria's government moved its capital from Lagos, in the south, to the city of Abuja (uh BOO juh). The new capital has two advantages. It is located in the middle of the country, relatively close to each of the three major ethnic groups. In addition, members of many different ethnic groups live in Abuja.

✓ Reading Check **What city became Nigeria's new capital in 1991?**

Lagos, Nigeria

The Path to Democracy

Unifying Nigeria's many ethnic groups has not been easy. These groups live in different areas, speak different languages, practice different religions, and sometimes have access to different amounts of economic resources. Only a few years after independence, conflicts began to arise. In 1966, a military group took over the government. The next year, civil war broke out as the Igbo tried to separate from Nigeria and form their own country. In 1970, after thousands had been killed or injured, the Igbo surrendered. The fighting ended, and Nigeria remained united. However, tensions remained high, and military control of the country continued for years.

Religion A key source of the tension in Nigeria is the religious diversity among the various ethnic groups. Most of the Hausa-Fulani practice Islam, while some Yoruba practice Islam and others practice Christianity. The Igbo are primarily Christian. Some members of these groups, as well as members of hundreds of others, also practice traditional African religions. Such religious diversity makes Nigeria rich in culture, but it also challenges national unity.

Discovery
CHANNEL
SCHOOL
Video
Learn about the impact of oil production on village life.

Oil Another notable source of tension in Nigeria is the country's wealth of oil resources. Nigeria's economy, which is one of the strongest in Africa, revolves around oil. Ninety-five percent of the income Nigeria earns from its exports to other countries comes from oil. However, while the government and the oil companies earn large profits from oil, the people who live on the oil-rich land do not. That is because most of the oil companies are foreign and use foreign workers. Many Nigerians want to gain a share of the work or income generated by the oil industry.

Democracy for Nigeria Since Nigeria gained its independence in 1960, many Nigerians have struggled to create a democratic government free of military rule. Finally, Nigeria's military leaders gave up their power. On May 29, 1999, an election was held for the first time in more than 15 years. Olusegun Obasanjo (oh loo SEG oon oh bah SAHN joh) was elected president of Nigeria. He was re-elected in 2003.

√ Reading Check **Which different religions do people in Nigeria practice?**

Oil workers in Port Harcourt, Nigeria

Section 1 Assessment

Key Terms

Review the key terms at the beginning of this section. Use each term in a sentence that explains its meaning.

Target Reading Skill

State three main ideas from Section 1. Tell whether each is the main idea of a paragraph or of a section under a red heading.

Comprehension and Critical Thinking

1. **(a) Recall** What are the three largest ethnic groups in Nigeria, and in which region does each group live?
(b) Evaluate Information Identify one feature that is unique to each of Nigeria's three major ethnic groups.
2. **(a) Locate** In what part of Nigeria is the country's capital, Abuja, located?
(b) Identify Causes Why did Nigeria's government think it was necessary to move the country's capital to Abuja?
3. **(a) Name** Which ethnic group tried to separate itself from Nigeria in 1967?
(b) Synthesize Information How is being a multiethnic country both good and bad for Nigeria?
(c) Predict What can Nigerians do in the future to resolve the conflicts in their country?

Writing Activity

Suppose that you are a Nigerian newspaper editor. Write an editorial supporting a movement for all Nigerians to use one common language. Be sure to say whether you think the common language should be English or another language, and explain why you think so.

For: An activity on Nigeria
Visit: PHSchool.com
Web Code: lad-5501

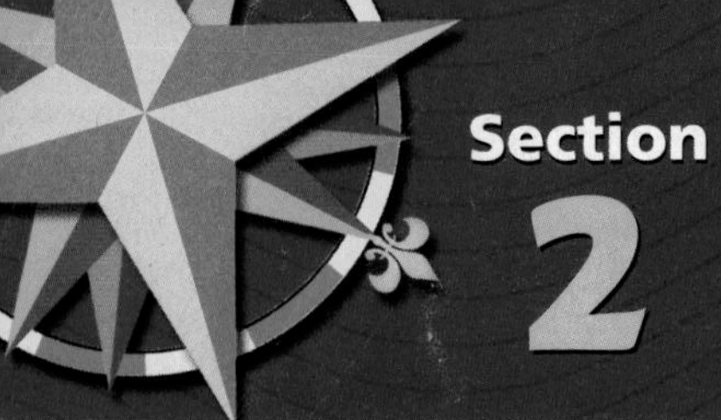

Section 2

Ghana

Leading Africa to Independence

Prepare to Read

Objectives

In this section you will

1. Learn about the years of British colonial rule in the area that is now called Ghana.
2. Find out about the beliefs that helped move Ghana toward independence.
3. Discover how Ghana changed after achieving independence.

Taking Notes

As you read this section, look for details about events in the history of Ghana's government. Copy the timeline below, and use it to record your findings.

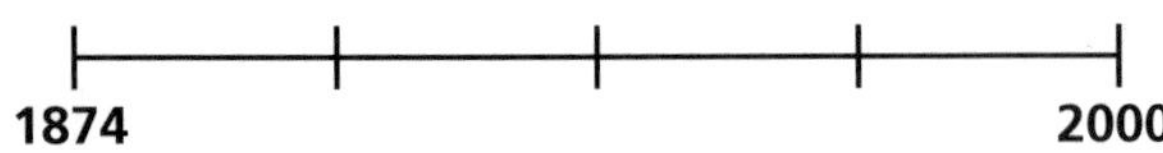

Target Reading Skill

Identify Implied Main Ideas Identifying main ideas can help you remember the most important ideas in your text. Sometimes the main ideas are not stated directly. In those cases, you must add up all the details in a paragraph or section, and then state the main idea yourself.

Key Terms

- **Kwame Nkrumah** (KWAH mee un KROO muh) *n.* founder of Ghana's independence movement and Ghana's first president
- **sovereignty** (SAHV run tee) *n.* political control
- **coup d'état** (koo day TAH) *n.* the sudden overthrow of a government by force

Kwame Nkrumah

In 1935, a 26-year-old student traveled by ship from Ghana to the United States. At that time, Ghana was called the Gold Coast because of its abundant supply of gold. The region had been ruled by Great Britain for more than 60 years. The student's visit to the United States was a turning point in his life. He was well aware that the people of his country did not have true freedom or equality. When he saw the Statue of Liberty for the first time, he felt determined to bring freedom to both his country and his whole continent. As he looked at the statue, he thought to himself, "I shall never rest until I have carried your message to Africa." The student's name was **Kwame Nkrumah**, and in 1957, he would become the leader who steered Ghana to independence.

Links Across Time

Asante Legacy The Asante did not submit to colonial rule without a struggle. In 1900, Yaa Asantewa (YAH ah uh sahn TEE wah), the Asante king's mother (at the right), led a war against the British. Even with more powerful weapons, the British took four months to defeat the queen mother's troops. After the war, the British began to treat the Asante more respectfully. Asante children still sing a song about "Yaa Asantewa, the warrior woman who carries a gun and a sword of state into battle."

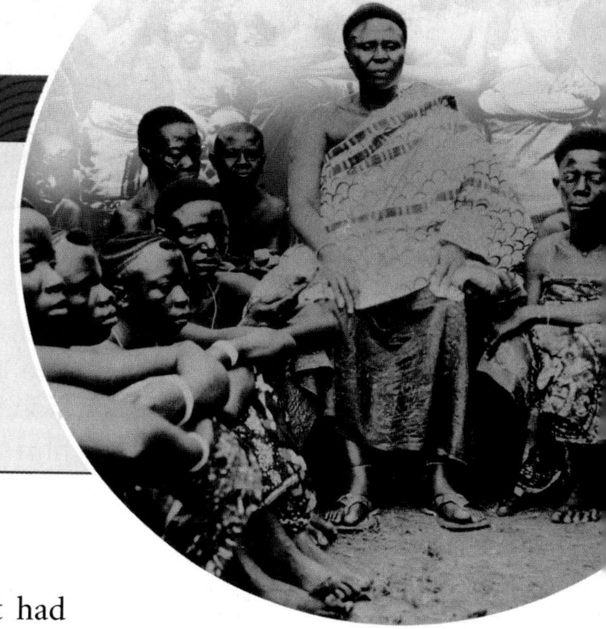

The Colonial Years

For hundreds of years, many Africans in the Gold Coast had wanted their people to be free to rule themselves. While the Europeans were trading gold and slaves on the Gold Coast, some members of a large local ethnic group called the Akan (AH kahn) formed the Asante (uh SAHN tee) kingdom. This kingdom became very rich from trade. It controlled parts of the northern savanna and the coastal south. The Asante used their wealth and power to try stopping the European takeover of their kingdom. Despite these efforts, in 1874 Great Britain succeeded in colonizing the Gold Coast. Great Britain then ruled the colony through chiefs it appointed or who already held authority.

Effects of British Control When the British colonized the Gold Coast, their main interest was controlling the colony's economy. They encouraged farmers to grow cacao beans, from which they produced cocoa. The British then sent the cocoa to factories in Britain where it was made into chocolate. The British also exported timber and gold.

The export of raw materials led to problems that became common throughout colonial Africa. For example, people began growing fewer food crops for themselves and more cash crops such as cacao, which brought in more money. Soon, Gold Coast Africans could no longer supply enough food for their own needs, so they had to import it.

A related problem was that processing cacao brought in more money than growing it did. Therefore, most of the profit was gained in Britain, not in the Gold Coast. Yet another concern was that people began spending more time farming and less time making traditional crafts. As a result, Gold Coast people began to depend on buying factory-made goods from the British.

A Symbol of Pride
Colorful kente (KEN tay) cloth was invented in Ghana in the 1100s as a cloth to be worn by royalty. Over time, it became common for all people in Ghana to wear kente. Many West Africans and African Americans wear kente today with great pride.
Analyze Information *Why would a piece of cloth serve well as a way to show pride in one's heritage?*

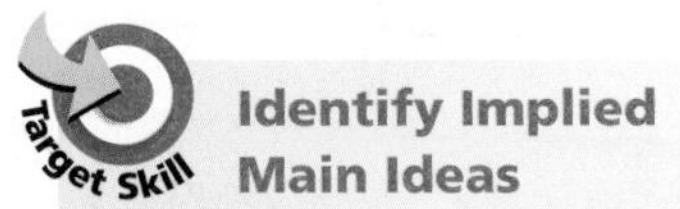

Identify Implied Main Ideas
In one sentence, state what all the details in the paragraph at the right express.

Mixing Old and New The British brought changes to some aspects of Gold Coast culture. For example, they built schools in the Gold Coast. Foreign missionaries ran the schools. Christianity began to replace traditional religions in many areas. Over the years, new ideas and ways of doing things came to traditional communities. Many people blended the new ways with the old African ways. For example, Kwame Nkrumah was born a Christian. But he also believed in parts of the traditional African religion. Nkrumah's respect for the old and the new ways helped him govern when Ghana became independent.

√ Reading Check **What goods did the British export from the Gold Coast?**

Moving Toward Independence

During the 1900s, Africans whose countries were under colonial rule organized to demand independence. The European countries, however, resisted giving up their colonies. Some Europeans claimed that the colonies were not ready to rule themselves. Nkrumah challenged this argument with a reminder that traditional African governments had ruled Africa's lands for thousands of years. The Akan, for example, had long governed democratically in the Gold Coast.

Traditional Government The Akan are the largest ethnic group in Ghana today. Historically, the Akan had governed democratically, allowing the people to choose their ruler. If the leader did not rule fairly, the people had the right to choose another ruler. Each new ruler received this warning about how to behave:

> **"Tell him that**
> **We do not wish greediness**
> **We do not wish that he should curse us**
> **We do not wish that his ears should be hard of hearing**
> **We do not wish that he should call people fools**
> **We do not wish that he should act on his own initiative [act alone] . . .**
> **We do not wish that it should ever be said 'I have no time. I have no time.'**
> **We do not wish personal abuse**
> **We do not wish personal violence."**
>
> *—Akan statement of political expectation*

A Symbolic Seat
Stools such as this one carry important symbolism for the Akan. When a new ruler takes office, the people say he has been "enstooled." They believe the stool the ruler sits on contains the soul of the nation. **Draw Conclusions** *Why do you think people would consider a seat an important symbol?*

Nkrumah Takes Action In 1947, after more than a decade of schooling in the United States and England, Nkrumah returned home. He found a region that was poor, despite an abundance of natural resources. Nkrumah believed that people should benefit from the wealth of their land. He traveled throughout the Gold Coast, convincing people to demand independence.

✓ Reading Check **What power did the Akan give their people over their ruler?**

COUNTRY PROFILE — Focus on Economics

Ghana

Ghana began its period of independence in the late 1950s with a wealth of natural resources. At the time, few people in Ghana had benefited from this wealth. As it has moved from a colony to an independent country with new priorities, Ghana has worked to change its economy. Mining has become much more important than farming. Ghana trades extensively with countries in Europe, North America, and Africa. Study the map and charts to learn more about the economy of Ghana.

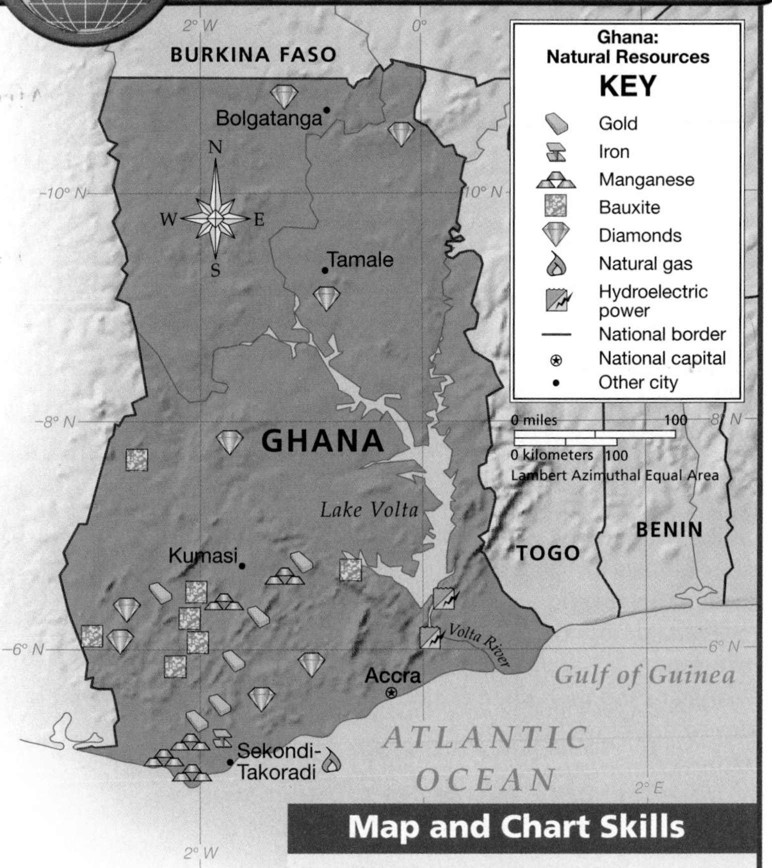

Export Destinations

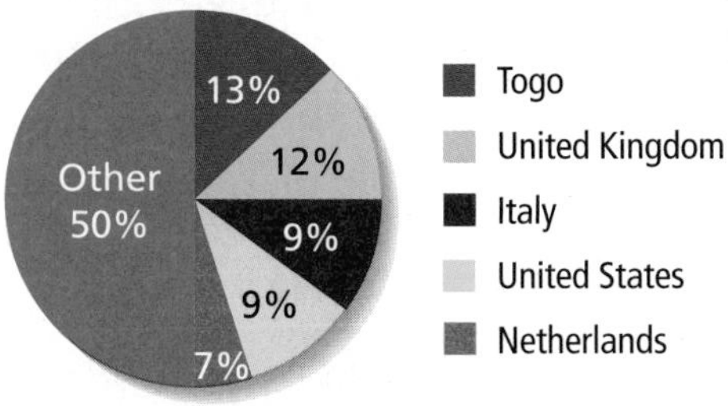

Togo 13%, United Kingdom 12%, Italy 9%, United States 9%, Netherlands 7%, Other 50%

SOURCE: *DK World Desk Reference*

Income From Mining, 2000

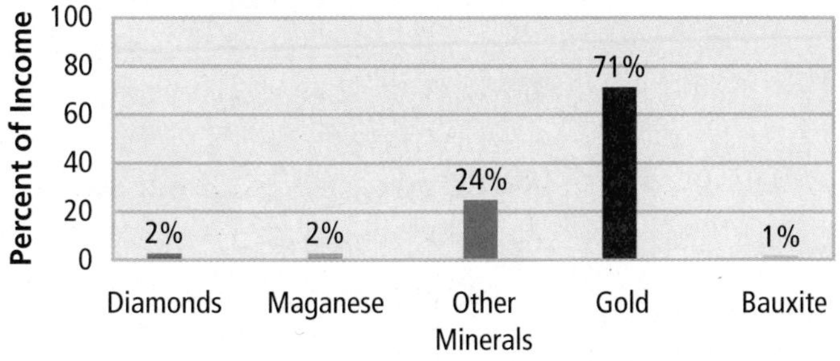

	Diamonds	Maganese	Other Minerals	Gold	Bauxite
Percent of Income	2%	2%	24%	71%	1%

SOURCE: United States Geological Survey

Ghana: Natural Resources

KEY: Gold; Iron; Manganese; Bauxite; Diamonds; Natural gas; Hydroelectric power; National border; National capital; Other city

BURKINA FASO, Bolgatanga, Tamale, GHANA, Lake Volta, Kumasi, TOGO, BENIN, Volta River, Accra, Sekondi-Takoradi, Gulf of Guinea, ATLANTIC OCEAN

0 miles 100; 0 kilometers 100; Lambert Azimuthal Equal Area

Map and Chart Skills

1. **Locate** Where is most of Ghana's gold located?
2. **Analyze** How much of Ghana's income comes from gold?
3. **Summarize** Explain whether Ghana sells most of its exports to one country or to a variety of countries.

Go Online PHSchool.com Use Web Code **lae-5502** for **DK World Desk Reference Online.**

Discovery CHANNEL SCHOOL Video
Learn about challenges facing Ghana's environment.

Independence Achieved

In 1957, some 22 years after making his pledge at the Statue of Liberty, Nkrumah gave a moving speech to his people. Great Britain, he said, had finally agreed to grant them **sovereignty** (SAHV run tee), or political control of their own country. Cheering, the people carried Nkrumah through the streets. Crowds sang victory songs to celebrate a dream come true.

Nkrumah became the leader and later the president of the new country. The government named the country Ghana after an African kingdom that flourished hundreds of years ago. Ghana was the first West African colony to gain independence. It was also the second country in all of Africa to become independent of European rule, after South Africa. The achievement of Ghana's independence would soon inspire many other Africans to push hard for—and achieve—freedom.

Nkrumah Overthrown Nine years after he had been carried through the streets a hero, Nkrumah was removed from office by a military **coup d'état** (koo day TAH), or takeover. Most Ghanaian (guh NAY un) citizens did not protest. In fact, many celebrated. Some even pulled down statues of Nkrumah.

How did a hero become an enemy? Nkrumah had formed great plans for Ghana. He borrowed huge amounts of money to make those plans happen quickly. For example, he spent millions of dollars on the construction of a conference center and a superhighway. In addition, he made an agreement with a United States company to build a dam on the Volta River. The dam would provide electricity and irrigation for people in rural areas. But when world prices of Ghana's chief export, cocoa, fell, Ghana could not pay back its loans. Many people blamed Nkrumah for the country's economic problems.

Nkrumah Toppled
Pulled down by angry citizens, the headless statue of Nkrumah lies on the ground in Accra, Ghana. After his overthrow, Nkrumah lived in Guinea and did not return to Ghana before his death. **Draw Inferences** *What do you think Ghanaians thought when they looked at the toppled statue of Nkrumah?*

A Hero Again Nkrumah's downfall did not end Ghana's problems. The country alternated between military and democratically elected governments. Few were successful. Over time, people began to think well again of Nkrumah. Many felt that he had done his best to help the country, especially by leading Ghana to independence. When he died in 1972, he was hailed as a national hero. Leaders around the world mourned his death.

Ghana's Government and Economy Today In 1981, Jerry Rawlings seized power, becoming Ghana's second long-term president. Rawlings, an Air Force pilot, had previously overthrown the government and ruled for a few months. As president from 1981 to 2000, Rawlings tried to reform the politics and economy of Ghana. He stressed the importance of Ghana's traditional values of hard work and sacrifice. Ghanaians supported Rawlings, and Ghana's economy began to grow.

Today, Ghana's economy continues to be dependent on the sale of cocoa. Even so, the economy has grown strong enough that Ghana has been able to build better roads and irrigation systems. The government under John Kufuor, who was democratically elected president in 2000, has continued implementing improvements in Ghana.

✓ Reading Check **How did Nkrumah lose his position as president?**

After Nkrumah's death, this mausoleum was built as a national monument in his honor.

Section 2 Assessment

Key Terms

Review the key terms at the beginning of this section. Use each term in a sentence that explains its meaning.

Target Reading Skill

State an implied main idea from Section 2 other than the one you identified on page 492.

Comprehension and Critical Thinking

1. (a) Explain How did the Gold Coast's economy change after the British began encouraging farmers to grow cacao beans?
(b) Summarize While the British ruled the Gold Coast, did traditional ways stay the same, disappear, or blend with the new?

2. (a) Recall When arguing for independence, how did Kwame Nkrumah respond to the European claim that the African colonies were not ready to rule themselves?
(b) Identify Causes Why did the economic conditions of the Gold Coast under colonial rule lead Africans there to believe they should rule themselves?

3. (a) Note Compared to other African colonies, when did Ghana gain independence?
(b) Identify Cause and Effect What caused people's attitudes toward Nkrumah to change before and after his death?

Writing Activity

Work with a partner to write about one or two changes you would like to see happen in your country or community. Consider obstacles to making these changes. Then write a plan that explains each change, how you would make it, and how you would overcome any obstacles.

For: An activity on Ghana
Visit: PHSchool.com
Web Code: lad-5502

Decision Making

Julia's neighbor, Mrs. Gonzalez, owns a dog that Julia loves to play with. One day Mrs. Gonzalez offered to pay Julia for walking the dog every morning and afternoon. That sounded to Julia like a fun way to earn some money. But she was already considering joining the swim team. Walking the dog twice a day as well as going to swim practice seemed like too many commitments. Julia realized she would have to decide between the two—but how?

Playing with Buster in the backyard

Some decisions are easy to make because one choice clearly has more to offer than the other. On the other hand, many decisions are difficult to make because all the choices have both positive and negative outcomes. Making good decisions means considering all the options before you decide.

Learn the Skill

Use these steps to make a good decision.

1. **Identify the issue.** Write a question explaining what needs to be decided.
2. **List the alternatives.** When you make a decision, you are choosing between at least two alternatives, or choices.
3. **For each alternative, list the likely outcomes, both positive and negative.** Every decision has outcomes, or effects. Use a decision-making grid like the one on page 497 to list the possible outcomes.
4. **Put a check mark (✓) next to the most important outcomes.** Marking the outcomes that matter most to you can help you reach your decision.
5. **Choose the option that seems best.** Write your decision in a sentence.

My Decision-Making Grid

Decision: Should I take the dog-walking job or join the swim team?

Alternatives	Likely Positive Outcomes	Likely Negative Outcomes
Take the dog-walking job.	Earn money. Get to play with a dog. Help my neighbor.	Don't have time for other activities. Don't get to spend time with friends.
Join the swim team.	Get exercise. Have fun. Meet new people.	Don't have time for other activities. Don't get to spend time with animals.

Practice the Skill

Suppose you win a contest at school and receive money as a prize. There is a certain item you have wanted to buy, and now you can afford it. But in three months your class is taking a field trip, and you know you will need to have some money for the trip. Follow the steps below to decide what to do with your prize money.

1. What is the decision you will make? Write down a question explaining what needs to be decided.
2. List the alternatives that you have to choose from. Are there two alternatives, or more?
3. Create a decision-making grid like the one above. Fill in the likely outcomes.
4. Put a check mark next to the outcomes that are most important to you.
5. Decide which alternative seems best to you. Write down an explanation of your reasoning.

Apply the Skill

Think of an important decision that you might have to make in the near future. It might have to do with school, friends, family, or something else. Create a decision-making grid to analyze the alternatives and outcomes. Then state your decision and your reasons for making it.

Section 3

Mali

Desert Living

Prepare to Read

Objectives

In this section you will

1. Discover how Mali's environment affects its economy.
2. Find out how desert can spread across the land.
3. Learn about the importance of preserving Mali's environment.

Taking Notes

As you read this section, look for details about the role of the Sahel in the life of the people of Mali. Copy the diagram below, and use it to record your findings.

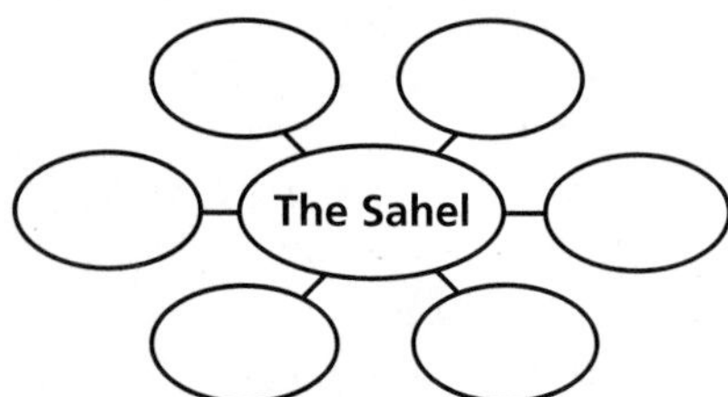

Target Reading Skill

Identify Supporting Details The main idea of a paragraph or section is supported by details that give further information about it. These details may explain the main idea by giving examples or reasons. As you read, note the details that support each main idea in the text.

Key Terms

- **desertification** (dih zurt uh fih KAY shun) *n.* the process by which fertile land becomes too dry or damaged to support life
- **overgrazing** (oh vur GRAYZ ing) *n.* allowing too much grazing by large herds of animals

Tombouctou, Mali

These days in Tombouctou (tohm book TOO), Mali, sand piles up against buildings. It coats the fur of camels. It gives a yellowish tint to everything in sight. Inside a hotel, a fine layer of red sand coats the lobby. Only a few of the rooms are taken. The manager is waiting for the river to rise, hoping it will bring customers.

But each year, as the climate slowly changes, the river rises a little later. "Ten years ago the first boat arrived on July 1," says Tombouctou politician Moulaye Haidara (moo LAH ee HY dah rah). "Five years ago it was July 15. Now, we're lucky if it's here by early August. In another five years, who knows?"

Mali's Environment

Tombouctou is located in the partly dry lands of the Sahel. As you can see on the map in the Country Profile on page 501, the Sahel lies between the Sahara and the savanna. The Sahara stretches over much of West Africa, and it is expanding all the time. In Mali, the Sahara covers about one third of the land. Few Malians inhabit the Sahara. Some live in the Sahel, while others live in the savanna, the one area of the country that receives abundant rainfall.

Resources of the Sahel The Sahel extends across Africa from Mauritania in the west to Ethiopia in the east. People have lived in the Sahel for thousands of years. They have long used its resources to earn their living. Malians in the Sahel herd animals and raise food crops to feed their families. Many earn extra money by raising cash crops as well. The rainy season, which lasts from May to August, is an ideal time for farming. During the rest of the year, farming is still possible in the Sahel thanks to water sources that exist year-round, such as the Niger River.

A Crossroads Location In the past, the Sahel's location as a crossroads between the Sahara and the savanna helped its economy flourish. For example, the city of Tombouctou was once a convenient stopping point for many camel caravans traveling between North Africa and the savanna. From the 1300s through the 1500s, Tombouctou thrived as one of Africa's wealthy centers of trade.

Today, people still live in Tombouctou, but they no longer practice trade on a large scale. Once European ships began trading along Africa's coast, trade through the Sahel decreased. Transporting goods by ship was faster and easier than sending them by camel. However, Tombouctou is still a crossroads for people traveling through the area.

✓ Reading Check **Which months are the best for farming in the Sahel?**

Table Skills

The table shows some of the groups of people who pass through Tombouctou and the ways they typically make a living. Below, a trader's camels carry salt to Tombouctou. **Identify** Which groups are traders? **Analyze Information** Based on the way they earn their living, what reasons do you think these groups have for passing through Tombouctou?

Activity in Tombouctou

Ethnic Group	Activities
Bambara	Farmers, traders
Berbers	Nomads
Fulani	Cattle herders
Mandingo	Farmers, traders
Songhai	Traders, gardeners
Tuareg	Nomads

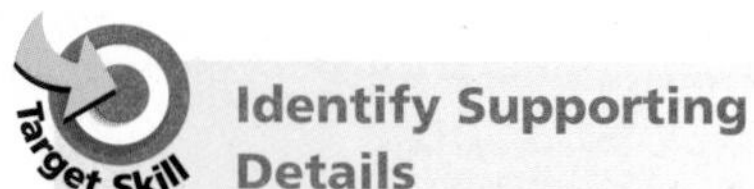

Identify Supporting Details

The main idea under the red heading The Desert Spreads is that desertification is threatening the ways people in Mali make a living. Which details in the paragraphs at the right tell about this problem?

The Desert Spreads

Mali has little industry. Most people make their living through trading, farming, or herding. However, these types of work are being threatened by **desertification,** the change of fertile land into land that is too dry or damaged to support life. In Mali and other countries of the Sahel, the desert is spreading south. Even the wetter lands in southwest Mali are at risk of becoming desert. But how does fertile land turn into desert? Scientists have identified two causes of desertification that may be at work in Mali.

Overgrazing One cause of desertification is **overgrazing,** or allowing too much grazing by large herds of animals. When animals graze, they often eat the roots of plants, which hold the soil in place. With the roots gone, the fierce winds of the Sahara erode the soil. The soil then blows into the air, creating yellow dust clouds. This loose soil is one reason that Tombouctou is slowly being covered in sand—the desert is taking over the land.

Drought Another cause of desertification is drought, which you will recall is a long period of little or no rain. Droughts can turn land into desert. Over the last 30 years, the Sahel has received much less rain than it did before. Some scientists argue that a few years of good rainfall could stop desertification.

✓ Reading Check **What does desertification do to fertile land?**

Diagram Skills

Overgrazing in the Sahara is the result of too much grazing by animals such as sheep, goats, camels, and cattle. **Identify** How does the soil become loosened when animals graze? **Predict** Do you think there are ways in which the people of the Sahara could avoid overgrazing their animals?

Overgrazing

The roots of a plant hold the soil in place.

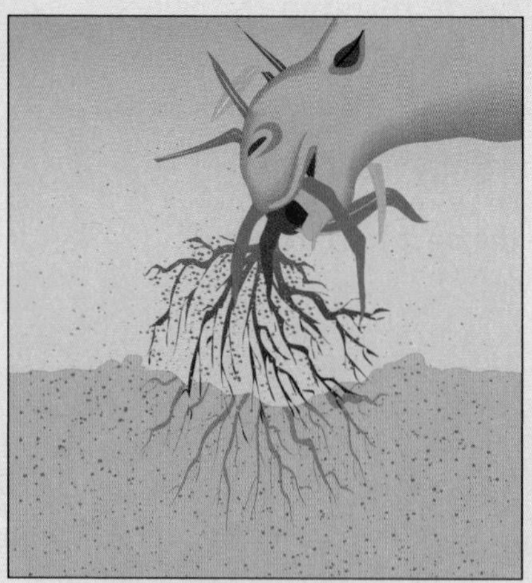

As a camel eats the plant and pulls up the roots, the soil is loosened.

Wind lifts the loosened soil from the ground and into the air.

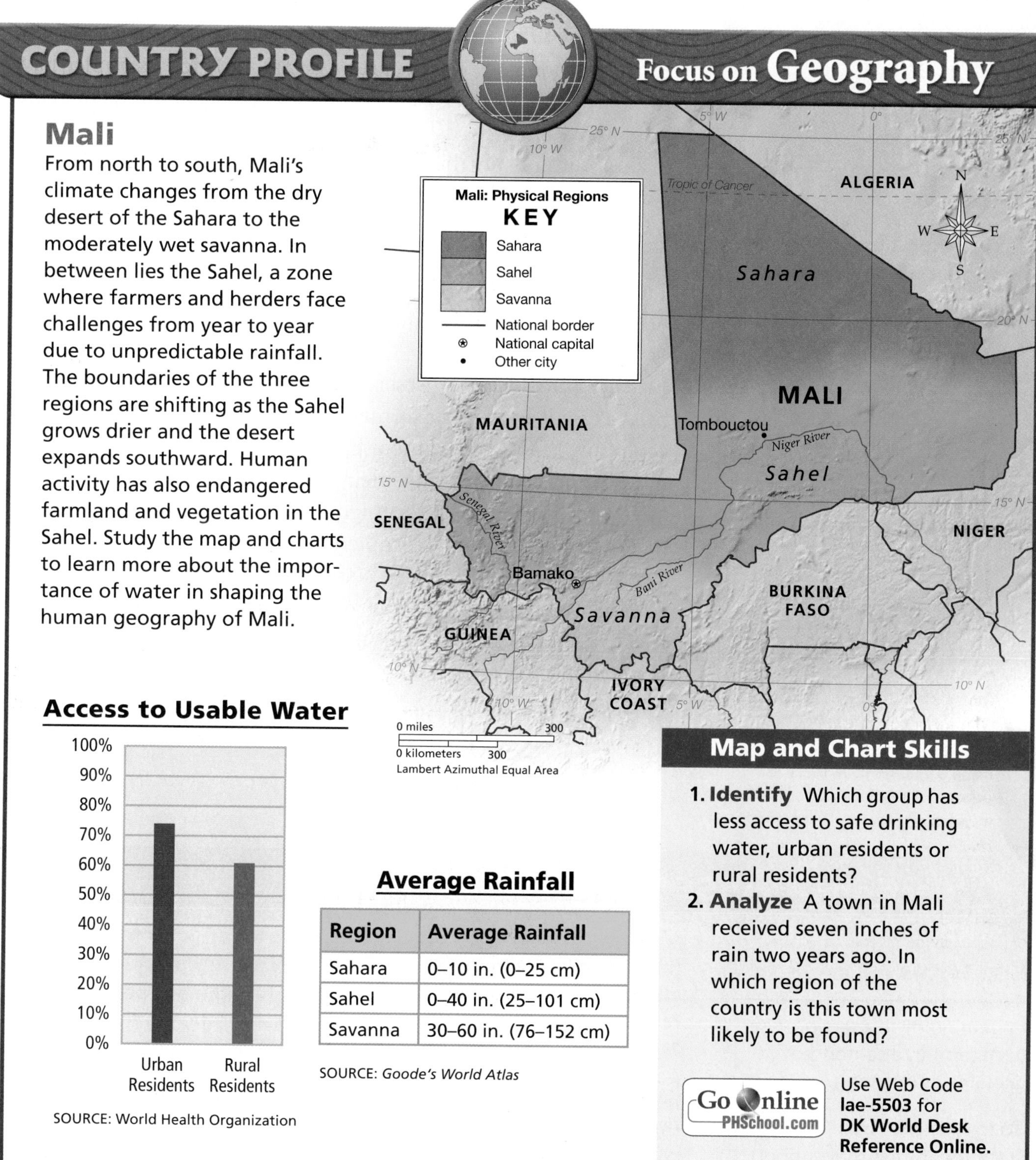

Mali

From north to south, Mali's climate changes from the dry desert of the Sahara to the moderately wet savanna. In between lies the Sahel, a zone where farmers and herders face challenges from year to year due to unpredictable rainfall. The boundaries of the three regions are shifting as the Sahel grows drier and the desert expands southward. Human activity has also endangered farmland and vegetation in the Sahel. Study the map and charts to learn more about the importance of water in shaping the human geography of Mali.

Access to Usable Water

SOURCE: World Health Organization

Average Rainfall

Region	Average Rainfall
Sahara	0–10 in. (0–25 cm)
Sahel	0–40 in. (25–101 cm)
Savanna	30–60 in. (76–152 cm)

SOURCE: *Goode's World Atlas*

Map and Chart Skills

1. **Identify** Which group has less access to safe drinking water, urban residents or rural residents?
2. **Analyze** A town in Mali received seven inches of rain two years ago. In which region of the country is this town most likely to be found?

Go Online PHSchool.com Use Web Code **lae-5503** for **DK World Desk Reference Online.**

Preserving the Environment

Many people around the world are concerned about the future of the Sahel. The United Nations has created a committee to help prevent desertification. Before the problem of desertification can be resolved, however, people living in the Sahel must learn how to avoid practices that make the problem worse.

Like this woman, most Tuaregs wear blue from head to toe.

Discovery
CHANNEL
SCHOOL
Video
Learn about government changes to farming.

A Way of Life in Danger Many people who live in the Sahel are nomads. The Tuareg (TWAH reg), for example, have lived in the desert and in the Sahel for many hundreds of years. They move their herds of goats, sheep, and camels south in the dry season and north in the wet season. The desertification of countries like Mali is threatening the Tuareg way of life. Moreover, during the 1970s and 1980s, Mali experienced several major droughts. Facing water and food shortages, some of the nomadic Tuareg have settled on farms or moved to cities. Others have built camps outside Tombouctou.

Finding Solutions Desertification has hurt Mali's economy by making it harder for farmers to grow cash crops. To help the economy, Mali's government has encouraged businesses to come to Mali and people to start their own businesses. Also, to help the environment, Mali's government has been studying the problem of desertification and is implementing programs to combat it. With the help of the United Nations, the government is working to educate people about better ways to use land. The government is also sponsoring irrigation and farming projects that will offset the effects of desertification.

✓ Reading Check **Why did many Tuareg settle on farms, move to cities, or build camps?**

Section 3 Assessment

Key Terms

Review the key terms at the beginning of this section. Use each term in a sentence that explains its meaning.

Target Reading Skill

State the details that support the main idea of the paragraphs under the red heading Preserving the Environment.

Comprehension and Critical Thinking

1. (a) **Identify** Name two ways in which the environment of the Sahel makes farming in the region possible.
(b) **Compare** Compare the effects of the environment on farming and on trade.

2. (a) **Recall** What are two possible causes of desertification in Mali?
(b) **Draw Conclusions** How much control do humans have in preventing desertification?

3. (a) **Describe** How has Mali's government responded to the negative effects of desertification on the economy?
(b) **Predict** If the government's efforts succeed, do you think some of the Tuareg will be able to return to their nomadic way of life?

Writing Activity

Overgrazing is one possible cause of desertification in the Sahel. In North America, what common activities may present a threat to its environment? Do you think those activities should be discouraged? Write a persuasive essay explaining why or why not.

Writing Tip Be sure to use persuasive language in your essay. Include reasons and examples that clearly support your argument.

Chapter 15 Review and Assessment

Chapter Summary

Section 1: Nigeria

- Nigeria is home to more than 250 ethnic groups. The largest are the Hausa-Fulani, the Yoruba, and the Igbo.
- After thousands of years of self-rule, Nigeria became a British colony in 1914. It gained independence from Great Britain in 1960.
- During Nigeria's move toward democracy, Nigerians have faced conflicts over religion and over the wealth gained by the oil industry.

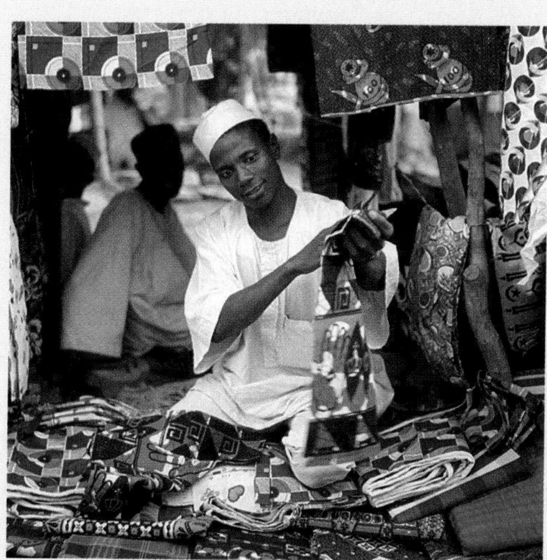

Kano, Nigeria

Section 2: Ghana

- In 1874, the British colonized the Gold Coast. They took control of the economy, built schools, and brought Christianity to the region.
- During the 1900s, Africans under colonial rule began organizing for independence. Kwame Nkrumah led the independence movement in the Gold Coast.
- In 1957, Ghana became the first West African country to become independent.

Section 3: Mali

Tuareg woman

- People in the Sahel have long relied on its resources and its location as a crossroads for trade.
- Desertification is occurring in Mali and other countries of the Sahel. Two possible causes are overgrazing and drought.
- Desertification threatens the ways of life of many people living in the Sahel. Mali's government is working to find solutions to this problem.

Key Terms

Match the definitions in Column I with the key terms in Column II.

Column I

1. Nigeria's second-largest ethnic group
2. having many ethnic groups living within a society
3. the process by which fertile land becomes too dry or damaged to support life
4. Ghana's first president
5. a sudden overthrow of a government by force
6. political control

Column II

A Kwame Nkrumah
B Yoruba
C sovereignty
D coup d'état
E desertification
F multiethnic

Chapter 15 Review and Assessment (continued)

◆ Comprehension and Critical Thinking

7. **(a) Name** List the three largest ethnic groups that live in Nigeria.
   (b) Explain What are two sources of conflict in Nigeria today?
   (c) Predict How might the new democratic government of Olusegun Obasanjo help resolve the country's conflicts?
8. **(a) Recall** During the colonial years, why did people in the Gold Coast have to start importing their food?
   (b) Synthesize Information When the British changed the structure of the Gold Coast's economy, how did the lifestyles of the people living there also change?
   (c) Infer According to Kwame Nkrumah's beliefs, did those lifestyle changes matter in the discussion of independence?
9. **(a) Explain** How did Tombouctou's location in the Sahel allow it to develop as a major trading center in the 1300s?
   (b) Summarize Did large-scale trading in Tombouctou end because of environmental change or because of social change? Explain.

◆ Skills Practice

Decision Making In the Skills for Life activity in this chapter, you learned how you can make good decisions.

Review the steps you followed to learn this skill. Then suppose that you have to make a choice between two after-school activities, such as writing for the school newspaper and acting in the school play. Create a decision-making grid. Put check marks next to the most important outcomes. Review the check marks and choose the option that seems best. Write a sentence stating your decision.

◆ Writing Activity: Geography

In the Sahel, overgrazing may be a cause of desertification. It might seem that a simple solution is to stop overgrazing. However, many people of the Sahel make their living from the animals that they graze. To prevent overgrazing, these people would have to change their ways of life. They would have to stop herding animals, herd fewer animals, or move elsewhere to herd their animals. Write a newspaper editorial explaining how you think this problem could be solved.

MAP MASTER™ Skills Activity

West Africa

Place Location For each place listed below, write the letter from the map that shows its location.

1. Nigeria
2. Ghana
3. Liberia
4. Tombouctou
5. Lagos
6. Abuja
7. Senegal
8. Mali

Go Online PHSchool.com Use Web Code **lap-5520** for an **interactive map.**

Standardized Test Prep

Test-Taking Tips

Some questions on standardized tests ask you to analyze an outline. Study the outline below. Then follow the tips to answer the sample question.

I. The Hausa-Fulani
  A. Cattle herders, farmers, craftspeople
  B. Built trading cities
II. The Yoruba
  A. Very urban
  B. Also many farmers, traders, craftspeople
III. ____________
  A. Rural farmers
  B. Governed by democratic councils

TIP Pay attention to the organization of the outline. Use that information to help you answer the question.

Pick the letter that best answers the question.

Which of the following major topics belongs next to III?

A The Nigerians
B Ethnic groups of Nigeria
C The Igbo
D Christians

TIP Use what you know about history, geography, or government to find the BEST answer.

Think It Through This outline is organized by major topics and details. The question asks you to find major topic III. Answer B is too general; it could be the subject of an entire outline. Answer D is not an ethnic group. That leaves A and C. You can use your knowledge of geography to help you. Nigerians are a general group—citizens of a country. The Hausa-Fulani and the Yoruba are specific groups—ethnic groups in Nigeria. The Igbo are also a Nigerian ethnic group, so the correct answer is C.

Practice Questions

Use the tips above and other tips in this book to help you answer the following questions. Use the outline below to answer Question 1. Choose the letter of the best answer.

I. Nkrumah overthrown
  A. Nkrumah removed from office by a coup d'état
  B. Nkrumah blamed for economic problems
II. ____________
  A. Continuing economic problems
  B. Improvement of public opinion about Nkrumah
III. Government and economy today

1. According to the outline, which of the following belongs next to II?
   A Independence achieved
   B A hero again
   C Traditional government
   D Mixing old and new

2. Which of the following was Nigeria's first capital after independence?
   A Kano
   B Abuja
   C Lagos
   D Tombouctou

3. How does Mali's savanna differ from the Sahel and the Sahara?
   A It gets less rain.
   B It has a more northern location.
   C It gets more rain.
   D It is inhabited by fewer people.

Use Web Code **laa-5500** for **Chapter 15 self-test.**

Chapter

16 East Africa

Chapter Preview

This chapter will introduce you to some of the countries that make up East Africa.

Country Databank

The Country Databank provides data and descriptions of each of the countries in the region: Burundi, Djibouti, Eritrea, Ethiopia, Kenya, Rwanda, Seychelles, Somalia, Sudan, Tanzania, and Uganda.

Section 1

Ethiopia
Religious Roots

Section 2

Tanzania
Determined to Succeed

Section 3

Kenya
Ties That Bind

Target Reading Skill

Context In this chapter you will focus on understanding context. Using context clues and recognizing nonliteral meanings will help you learn as you read.

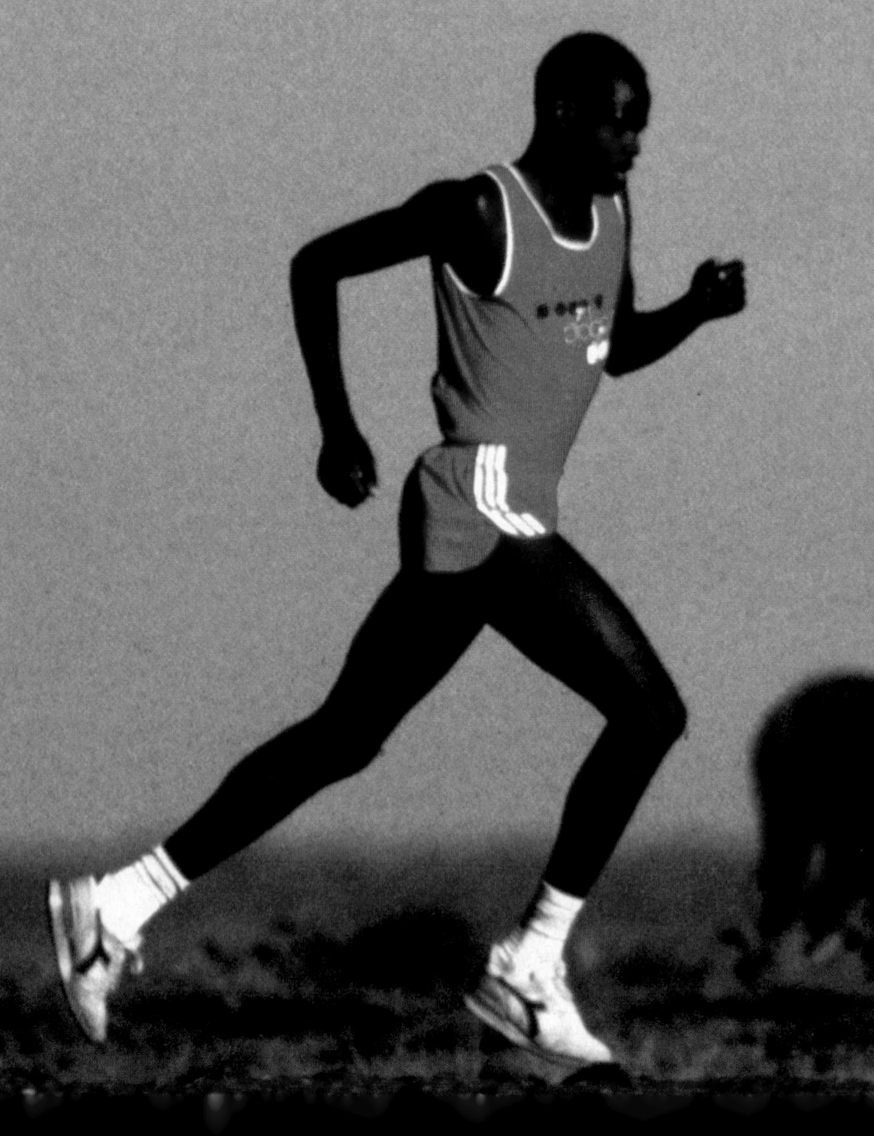

▶ **Many of the world's fastest runners are Kenyan. This man is training on the plains of Kenya.**

East Africa

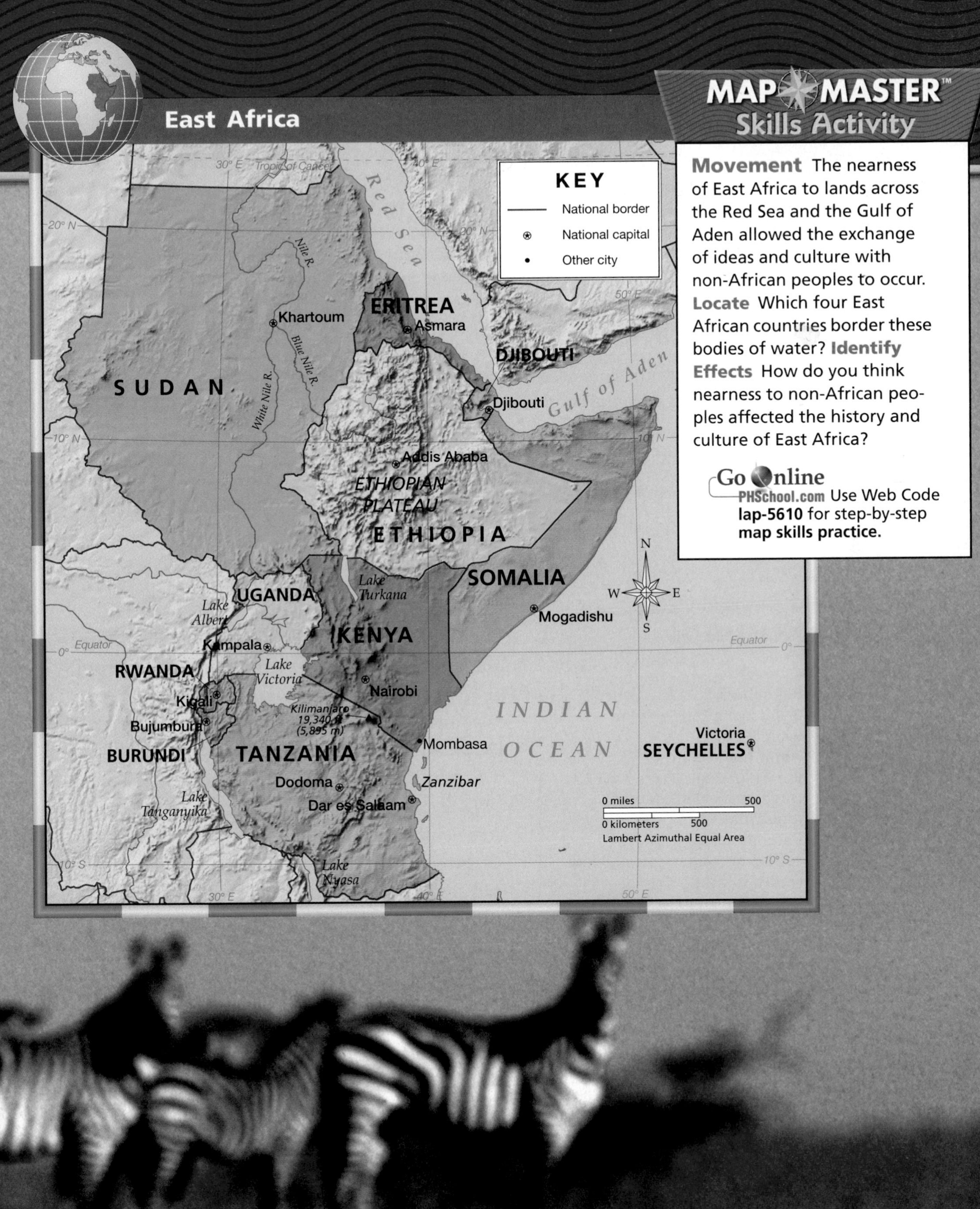

MAP MASTER™ Skills Activity

Movement The nearness of East Africa to lands across the Red Sea and the Gulf of Aden allowed the exchange of ideas and culture with non-African peoples to occur. **Locate** Which four East African countries border these bodies of water? **Identify Effects** How do you think nearness to non-African peoples affected the history and culture of East Africa?

Go Online PHSchool.com Use Web Code **lap-5610** for step-by-step **map skills practice.**

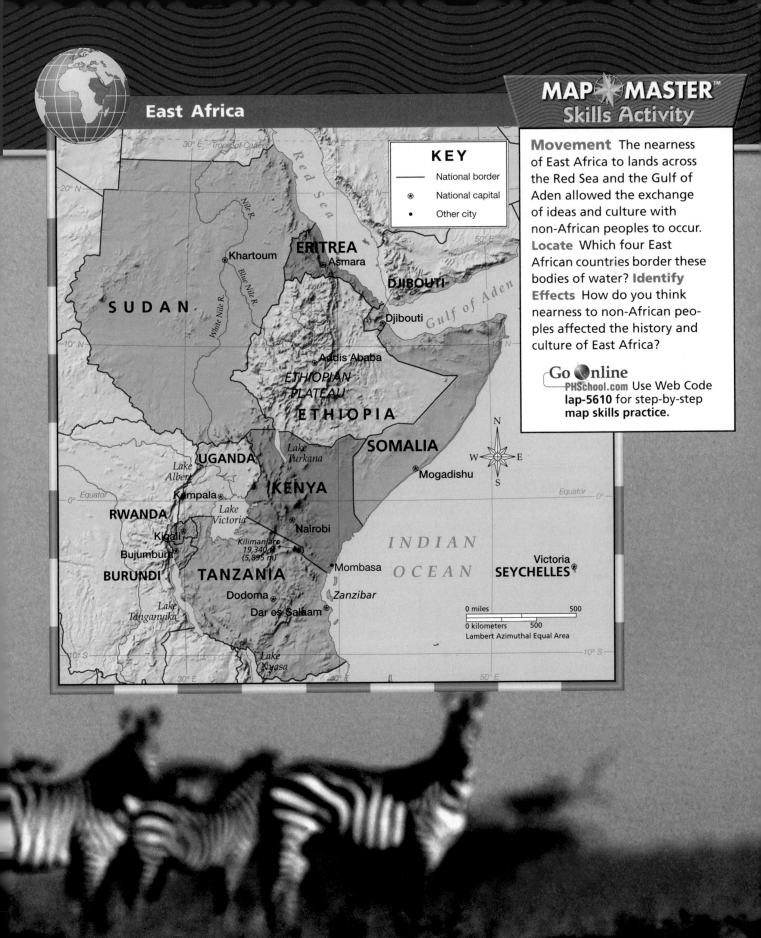

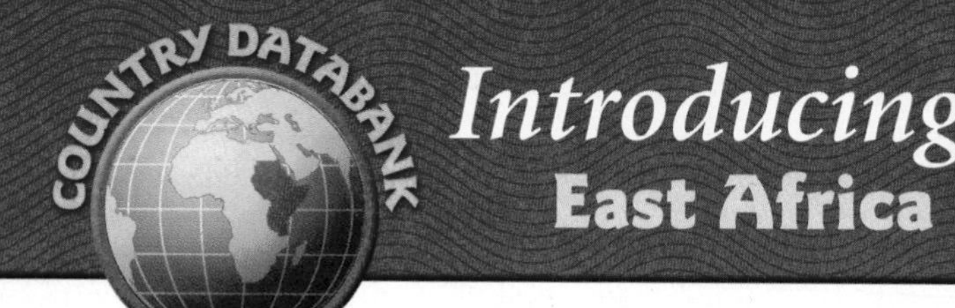

Introducing East Africa

Guide for Reading

This section provides an introduction to the eleven countries that make up the region of East Africa.

- Look at the map on the previous page and then read the paragraphs below to learn about each nation.
- Analyze the data to compare the countries.
- What are the characteristics that most of the countries share?
- What are some key differences among the countries?

Viewing the Video Overview

View the World Studies Video Overview to learn more about each of the countries. As you watch, answer these questions:

- What are some common features of the region?
- What are some of the geographic points of interest in East Africa?
- What accounts for the blend of cultures in this region?

Discovery
CHANNEL
SCHOOL
Video
Explore the geography of East Africa.

Burundi

Capital	Bujumbura
Land Area	9,903 sq mi; 25,650 sq km
Population	6.4 million
Ethnic Group(s)	Hutu, Tutsi, Twa
Religion(s)	Roman Catholic, Protestant, traditional beliefs, Muslim
Government	republic
Currency	Burundi franc
Leading Exports	coffee, tea, sugar, cotton, hides
Language(s)	French (official), Kirundi (official), Kiswahili

The small country of Burundi (boo ROON dee) is bordered on the west by the Democratic Republic of the Congo, on the north by Rwanda, and on the east and south by Tanzania. Beginning in the 1970s, the country faced fierce fighting between two ethnic groups, the Hutu and the Tutsi. In 2002, a new government signed a peace treaty to help end the conflict. However, the country remains unstable, with small conflicts continuing and the economy weakened from the many years of fighting.

Djibouti

Capital	Djibouti
Land Area	8,873 sq mi; 22,980 sq km
Population	472,810
Ethnic Group(s)	Issa, Afar, Somali, white, Arab, Ethiopian
Religion(s)	Muslim, Christian
Government	republic
Currency	Djibouti franc
Leading Exports	reexports, hides and skins, coffee (in transit)
Language(s)	Arabic (official), French (official), Somali, Afar

Djibouti (jih BOO tee) is bordered on the south by Somalia, on the south and west by Ethiopia, on the north by Eritrea and the Red Sea, and on the east by the Gulf of Aden. It was established in 1977, when it gained independence from France. Its capital, Djibouti, is an important port city for the country's economy. Otherwise, the economy is weak because the country has few natural resources. In the early 1990s, fighting broke out between the nation's two main ethnic groups. In 2001, a peace treaty ended the fighting.

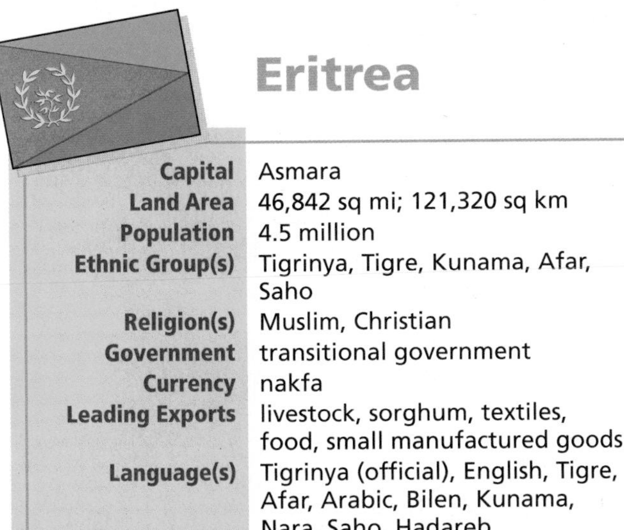

Eritrea

Capital	Asmara
Land Area	46,842 sq mi; 121,320 sq km
Population	4.5 million
Ethnic Group(s)	Tigrinya, Tigre, Kunama, Afar, Saho
Religion(s)	Muslim, Christian
Government	transitional government
Currency	nakfa
Leading Exports	livestock, sorghum, textiles, food, small manufactured goods
Language(s)	Tigrinya (official), English, Tigre, Afar, Arabic, Bilen, Kunama, Nara, Saho, Hadareb

Eritrea (ehr uh TREE uh) is bordered on the west and north by Sudan, on the north and east by the Red Sea, and on the south by Djibouti and Ethiopia. After being ruled by the Italians and then the British during the 1800s and early 1900s, Eritrea became independent in 1952. Ten years later, Ethiopia claimed Eritrea as its territory. After thirty years of fighting, Eritrea regained its independence in 1993. Eritrea's economy is weak from many years of war. However, the country's rich mineral resources offer hope for economic improvement.

An Eritrean girl

Ethiopia

Capital	Addis Ababa
Land Area	432,310 sq mi; 1,119,683 sq km
Population	67.7 million
Ethnic Group(s)	Oromo, Amhara, Tigre, Sidamo, Shankella, Somali, Afar, Gurage
Religion(s)	Muslim, Christian, traditional beliefs
Government	federal republic
Currency	Ethiopian birr
Leading Exports	coffee, qat, gold, leather products, oilseeds
Language(s)	Amharic (official), Tigrinya, Galla, Sidamo, Somali, English, Arabic

Ethiopia (ee thee OH pea uh) is bordered on the west by Sudan, on the north by Eritrea and Djibouti, on the east and south by Somalia, and on the south by Kenya. It is one of the oldest countries in the world. Unlike most African countries, it was never colonized by a European power—at each European attempt, the Ethiopians proved victorious. In the 1990s, Ethiopia became a federal republic with a constitution and free elections. In the past 50 years, the country has experienced war and severe famine, or lack of food. Establishing a stable economy has therefore been difficult.

Introducing East Africa

Cheetahs in a Kenyan national park

Kenya

Capital	Nairobi
Land Area	219,787 sq mi; 569,250 sq km
Population	31.3 million
Ethnic Group(s)	Kikuyu, Luhya, Luo, Kalenjin, Kamba, Kisii, Meru
Religion(s)	Protestant, Roman Catholic, traditional beliefs, Muslim
Government	republic
Currency	Kenya shilling
Leading Exports	tea, horticultural products, coffee, petroleum products, fish, cement
Language(s)	Kiswahili (official), English (official), Kikuyu, Luo, Kamba

Located along the Equator, Kenya (KEN yuh) is bordered on the west by Lake Victoria and Uganda, on the north by Sudan and Ethiopia, on the east by Somalia and the Indian Ocean, and on the south by Tanzania. The Great Rift Valley runs through the western half of the country. Kenya is home to the Kenyan Highlands, one of the most successful farming regions in Africa. The country is also a major center of business and trade in East Africa. In addition, many rare animals and numerous national parks have made tourism a strong industry in Kenya.

Rwanda

Capital	Kigali
Land Area	9,632 sq mi; 24,948 sq km
Population	7.4 million
Ethnic Group(s)	Hutu, Tutsi, Twa
Religion(s)	Christian, Muslim, traditional beliefs
Government	republic
Currency	Rwanda franc
Leading Exports	coffee, tea, hides, tin ore
Language(s)	French (official), English (official), Kinyarwanda (official), Kiswahili

Located just south of the Equator, Rwanda (roo AHN duh) is bordered on the west by the Democratic Republic of the Congo, on the north by Uganda, on the east by Tanzania, and on the south by Burundi. It is the most densely populated country in Africa. As in its neighbor Burundi, fierce civil war erupted in the early 1990s between the Tutsi and the Hutu. As a result, about 2 million Hutus migrated to neighboring countries. After the war's end, many of them returned to Rwanda. The country's economy is slowly improving.

Seychelles

Capital	Victoria
Land Area	176 sq mi; 455 sq km
Population	80,098
Ethnic Group(s)	white, black, South Asian, East Asian, Arab
Religion(s)	Christian
Government	republic
Currency	Seychelles rupee
Leading Exports	canned tuna, cinnamon bark, copra, petroleum products (reexports)
Language(s)	Seselwa (French Creole) (official), English, French

The 115 islands of Seychelles (say SHEL) are located in the Indian Ocean, northwest of Madagascar. The islands are known for their natural beauty and unique plants and animals. They are home to the coco de mer (KOH koh duh mehr), a plant that produces a coconut-like fruit that is one of the largest fruits in the world. In addition, some of the last giant tortoises in the world live there. In 1976, Seychelles gained its independence from the United Kingdom, and in 1993 it became a democracy. Tuna fishing and tourism are the leading economic activities of these islands.

Fishing near Seychelles (left); a giant tortoise (below)

Somalia

Capital	Mogadishu
Land Area	242,215 sq mi; 627,337 sq km
Population	7.8 million
Ethnic Group(s)	Somali, Bantu, Arab
Religion(s)	Muslim
Government	transitional government
Currency	Somali shilling
Leading Exports	livestock, bananas, hides, fish, charcoal, scrap metal
Language(s)	Somali (official), Arabic (official), English, Italian

Somalia (soh MAH lee uh) occupies the Horn of Africa, the easternmost point of the continent. It is bordered on the west by Kenya, Ethiopia, and Djibouti; on the north by the Gulf of Aden; and on the east by the Indian Ocean. Much of Somalia is semiarid desert. There is some fertile land along the coast and in the south near the capital, Mogadishu (moh gah DEE shoo). Most Somalis are farmers or nomadic herders. In recent years, Somalia has faced many severe problems, such as civil war, the collapse of its government, and famine.

Introducing East Africa

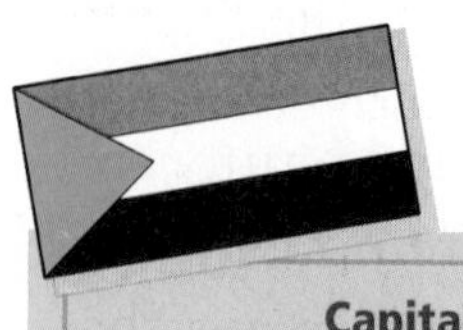

Sudan

Capital	Khartoum
Land Area	917,374 sq mi; 2,376,000 sq km
Population	37.1 million
Ethnic Group(s)	black, Arab, Beja
Religion(s)	Muslim, traditional beliefs, Christian
Government	authoritarian regime
Currency	Sudanese pound or dinar
Leading Exports	oil and petroleum products, cotton, sesame, livestock, groundnuts, gum arabic, sugar
Language(s)	Arabic (official), Dinka, Nuer, Nubian, Beja, Zande, Bari, Fur, Shilluk, Lotuko

In land area, Sudan (soo DAN) is the largest country in Africa. It is bordered on the west by the Central African Republic, Chad, and Libya; on the north by Egypt; on the east by the Red Sea, Eritrea, and Ethiopia; and on the south by Kenya, Uganda, and the Democratic Republic of the Congo. Both the Blue Nile and White Nile rivers flow through Sudan. Nearly 50 years of civil war have led to millions of deaths, migrations out of the country, and economic problems.

An ancient pyramid at Meroë, in present-day Sudan

Tanzania

Capital	Dar es Salaam and Dodoma
Land Area	342,099 sq mi; 886,037 sq km
Population	37.2 million
Ethnic Group(s)	Bantu, Asian, white, Arab
Religion(s)	Muslim, traditional beliefs, Christian
Government	republic
Currency	Tanzanian shilling
Leading Exports	gold, coffee, cashew nuts, manufactured goods, cotton
Language(s)	English (official), Kiswahili (official), Sukuma, Chagga, Nyamwezi, Hehe, Makonde, Yao, Sandawe

Tanzania (tan zuh NEE uh) is bordered on the west by Zambia, the Democratic Republic of the Congo, Burundi, and Rwanda; on the north by Uganda and Kenya; on the east by the Indian Ocean; and on the south by Mozambique and Malawi. It is home to Mount Kilimanjaro, Africa's tallest mountain. The Great Rift Valley forms the country's southwestern border. In 1964 the newly independent regions of Tanganyika and Zanzibar joined to become Tanzania. It is one of the world's poorest nations, but today Tanzania's manufacturing and mining industries are helping the economy boom.

Uganda

Capital	Kampala
Land Area	77,108 sq mi; 199,710 sq km
Population	24.7 million
Ethnic Group(s)	18 distinct groups, including Baganda, Ankole, Basoga, Iteso, Bakiga, Langi, Rwanda, Bagisu
Religion(s)	Roman Catholic, Protestant, traditional beliefs, Hindu, Muslim
Government	republic
Currency	New Uganda shilling
Leading Exports	coffee, fish and fish products, tea, gold, cotton, flowers, horticultural products
Language(s)	English (official), Luganda, Nkole, Chiga, Lango, Acholi, Teso, Lugbara

SOURCES: DK World Desk Reference Online; CIA World Factbook Online, 2002; *The World Almanac*, 2003

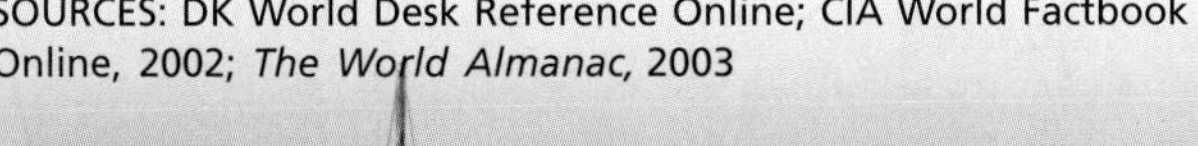

Uganda (yoo GAN duh) is bordered on the west by the Democratic Republic of the Congo, on the north by Sudan, on the east by Kenya, and on the south by Tanzania, Lake Victoria, and Rwanda. Uganda gained independence from Britain in 1962. It has since faced difficult political challenges. During the 1970s and 1980s, civil war led to hundreds of thousands of deaths as well as destruction of the country's economy. In 1986, peace was restored. Since the 1990s, Uganda has been celebrated for its return to economic success. The country has many natural resources, including copper and cobalt, as well as fertile soil and plentiful rain.

Lake Victoria

Assessment

Comprehension and Critical Thinking

1. **Draw Conclusions** What are some characteristics that most East African countries share?
2. **Analyze Information** What are some key differences among the countries?
3. **Compare** Compare the land areas and populations of Burundi and Sudan.
4. **Categorize** What kinds of products are the major exports of this region?
5. **Summarize** Which languages are spoken in more than one country in this region?
6. **Make a Bar Graph** Create a bar graph showing the land area, in square miles, of each of the countries in this region.

Keeping Current

Access the **DK World Desk Reference Online** at **PHSchool.com** for up-to-date information about all eleven countries in this chapter.

Web Code: **lae-5600**

Section 1

Ethiopia

Religious Roots

Prepare to Read

Objectives

In this section you will

1. Learn about the two major religions practiced in Ethiopia.
2. Understand the contrasts in the daily lives of rural and urban Ethiopians.

Taking Notes

As you read this section, look for details about religion and daily life in Ethiopia. Copy the table below, and use it to record your findings.

Culture of Ethiopia	
Religion	**Daily Life**
•	•
•	•

Target Reading Skill

Use Context Clues When you come across an unfamiliar word, you can sometimes figure out its meaning from clues in the context. The context refers to the surrounding words and sentences. As you read, look at the context for the word *isolated* in the last paragraph on page 515. Use the sentence that follows it as a clue. What do you think *isolated* means?

Key Terms

- **monastery** (MAHN uh stehr ee) *n.* a place where people, especially men known as monks, live a religious life
- **Geez** (gee EZ) *n.* an ancient Ethiopian language that was once used to write literature and religious texts but is no longer spoken

As a young boy, Iyasus Mo'a (ee YAH soos MOH uh) learned to read and write. Around the year 1241, he traveled from his home in Wag to Tigray (tee GRAY), both in northern Ethiopia. He walked a distance that today would take three days to drive.

Did he plan to enter a university in Tigray? No—at that time there were no universities in Ethiopia. Iyasus entered a Christian monastery. A **monastery** is a place where people, especially men known as monks, live a religious life. As a monk, Iyasus studied hard for many years and eventually also became a famous teacher. His students built monasteries and schools all over the region.

The monastery of Debre Damo, where Iyasus Mo'a became a monk in the 1200s

Christianity in Ethiopia Today An Ethiopian man takes part in a Christian celebration, wearing colorful silk clothing and carrying an elaborate gold cross. **Analyze Images** *What details in the picture provide clues that this man is involved in an important ceremony?*

Major Religions of Ethiopia

Iyasus Mo'a lived in ancient Ethiopia. He studied a language called Geez (gee EZ). **Geez is one of the world's oldest languages.** Much of Ethiopia's history was preserved by monks like Iyasus, who copied books in Geez by hand.

The religion Iyasus studied—Christianity—had spread to Ethiopia along trade routes. Ethiopia was a center of trade. Look at the physical map of Africa on page 352 of the Regional Overview. Find the Nile River and the Red Sea. The main source of the Nile River is in Ethiopia's highlands. Ethiopia once included present-day Eritrea as well. These lands border the Red Sea. As people traded goods along the Nile River and the Red Sea, they also learned about one another's religions.

Establishment of Christianity in Ethiopia Alexandria, a city in Egypt, was one of the first centers of Christianity. By the year A.D. 350, missionaries from Alexandria had brought Christianity to Ethiopia. Over time, Christians in Egypt and Ethiopia came to differ with Christians in Rome and Constantinople about certain beliefs. In A.D. 451, Egyptian Christians separated from the rest of the Christian Church. They formed an Egyptian branch of Christianity called the Coptic Christian Church. Coptic Christianity slowly spread from Egypt to Ethiopia.

Over time, Ethiopian Christians became isolated from Christians in other parts of the world. Ethiopia's mountains made it difficult for people who lived in the interior to travel to other areas. Some people did travel along the Nile River and the Red Sea. However, Ethiopian Christians were cut off from these travel routes in the A.D. 600s, when Muslim Arabs arrived in the region.

Links to Language Arts

Written Language Ethiopians began writing in Geez as early as the year A.D. 400. They used Geez to write literature and religious texts such as the one shown below. Ethiopia and Egypt were the only ancient African countries to develop their own writing systems. Many Islamic kingdoms of the time did produce written documents for religious and government purposes. However, these texts were written in Arabic, which was developed in Arabia.

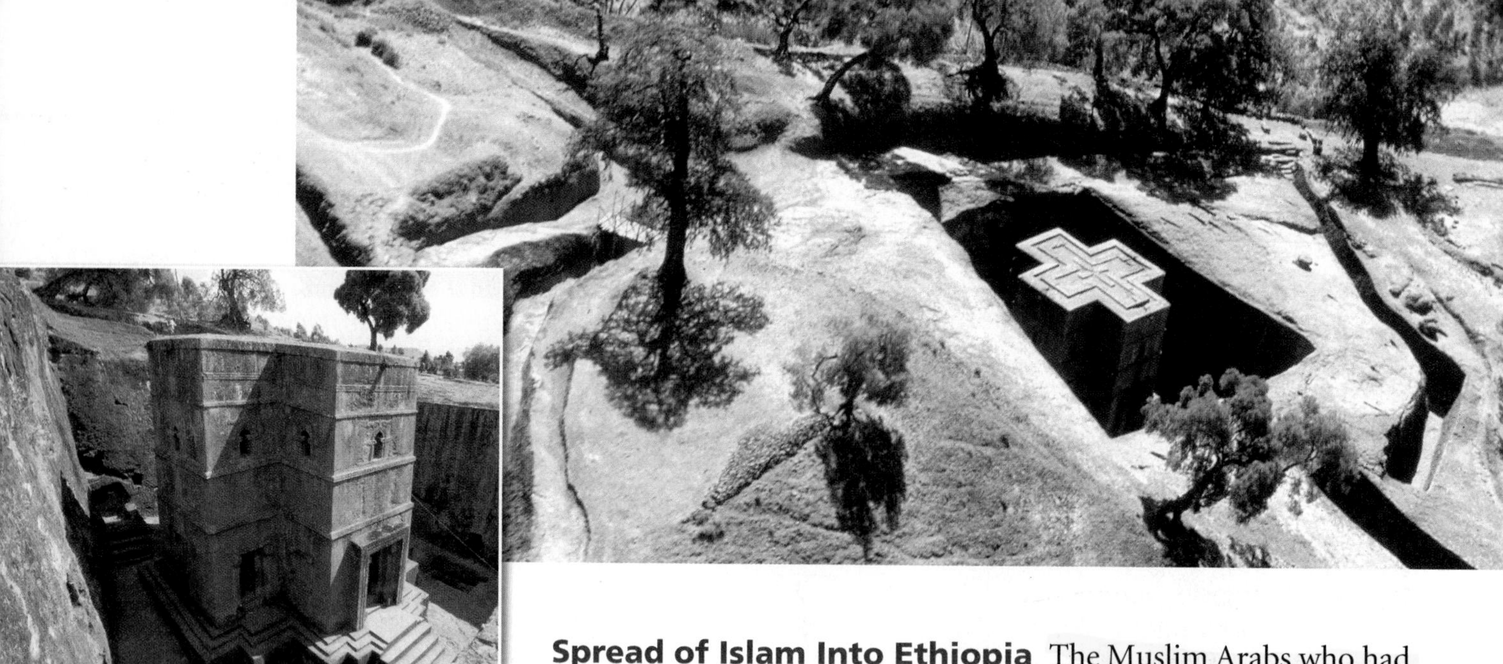

Underground Churches
Here you see St. George's Church of Lalibela from a side view (above left) and an overhead view (above right). The church was built in the shape of a cross. **Compare** *Compare the effects of looking at the church from the side and from above.*

Spread of Islam Into Ethiopia The Muslim Arabs who had begun to settle across North Africa did not attempt to take over Ethiopia. But they did move into nearby areas. Over time, Arab traders built cities along the trade routes of the Red Sea coast. Eventually, Muslim Arabs came to control trade in the entire region. And, in time, some Ethiopians adopted the Muslim faith.

A Unique Form of Christianity As Muslim Arabs took control of Ethiopia's coastal regions, Ethiopian Christians began moving farther inland. Finally, Christian Ethiopia became surrounded by Muslim-controlled areas. As a result, Christians in Ethiopia had very little contact with Christians elsewhere. The Ethiopian Christian Church developed into a unique form of Christianity with its own traditions and language, Geez.

Also unique to Ethiopian Christianity are the churches of a town called Lalibela (lah lee BAY lah). Once called Roha, it was the capital of Christian Ethiopia for about 300 years. It was renamed for its most famous ruler, Lalibela, who reigned during the late 1100s and early 1200s. The ruler Lalibela sponsored the construction of eleven churches unlike any others—they were built below the ground and cut out of solid rock. Many Christians today travel to Lalibela to visit the churches and celebrate their faith.

Target Skill **Use Context Clues** If you do not know what *reigned* means, consider the word's context. You know that Lalibela reigned for a few decades. You also know that he was the ruler of Roha. You could conclude that *reigned* means "was the ruler of."

Christian-Muslim Interaction Throughout most of Ethiopia's history, Christians and Muslims have coexisted peacefully. However, they have sometimes fought over religious issues. For example, they went to war with each other in the 1500s. Today, about 35 percent of Ethiopians are Christians and about 45 percent are Muslims. Most other Ethiopians practice traditional African religions, although a small number practice Judaism.

✓ **Reading Check** **How did Christianity first come to Ethiopia?**

COUNTRY PROFILE — Focus on Culture

Ethiopia

People have lived in Ethiopia longer than in most other countries on Earth. And for most of its history, the nation has ruled itself. Except for a short period of time before World War II, Ethiopia was never colonized by a European country.

Today, as for thousands of years, Ethiopian cultures have been centered mainly in the country's highlands. Many ethnic groups exist, but a few are much larger than the rest. Members of each ethnic group tend to live near one another. Study the map and charts to learn more about Ethiopia's people today.

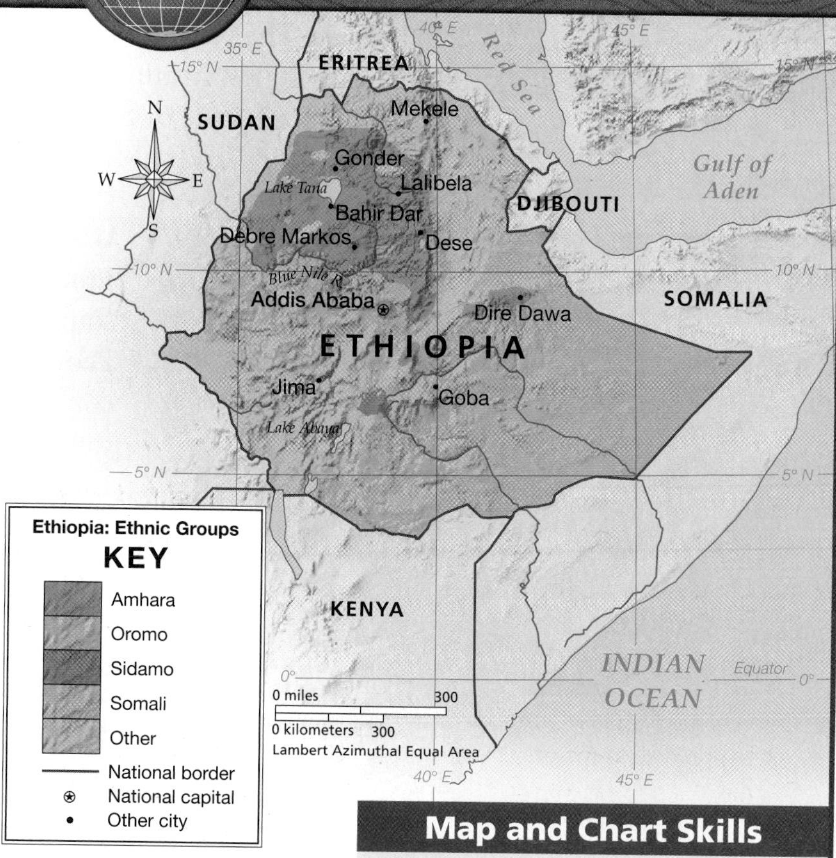

Population by Age

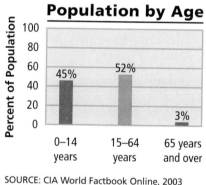

Age	Percent of Population
0–14 years	45%
15–64 years	52%
65 years and over	3%

SOURCE: CIA World Factbook Online, 2003

Ethnic Groups

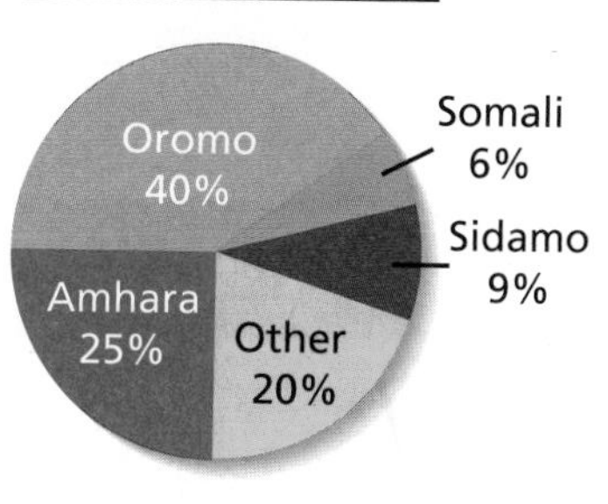

SOURCE: *DK World Desk Reference*

Map and Chart Skills

1. **Name** What is the largest ethnic group in Ethiopia?
2. **Identify** What percentage of Ethiopia's population is under 14 years of age?
3. **Analyze** What does this percentage tell you about Ethiopian society?

Use Web Code **lae-5601** for **DK World Desk Reference Online.**

Contrasts in Daily Life

Today, most Ethiopians, regardless of their religious background, live in rural areas. In fact, only about 10 percent of the population lives in cities. How do rural and urban life in Ethiopia differ? A look at the town of Lalibela reveals many clues about rural life in Ethiopia. The capital city of Addis Ababa (ad is AB uh buh), on the other hand, represents the urban life that some Ethiopians know.

Discovery
CHANNEL
SCHOOL
Video
Learn about life in an Ethiopian village.

Rural Ethiopia Public services such as electricity and running water are rare in rural Ethiopia. For example, no one in the town of Lalibela has electricity, and more people own donkeys than cars. The people who live in the areas surrounding Lalibela make a living by farming. In some rural areas, people make a living by herding cattle or by fishing. Some families specialize in jobs such as woodworking and beekeeping.

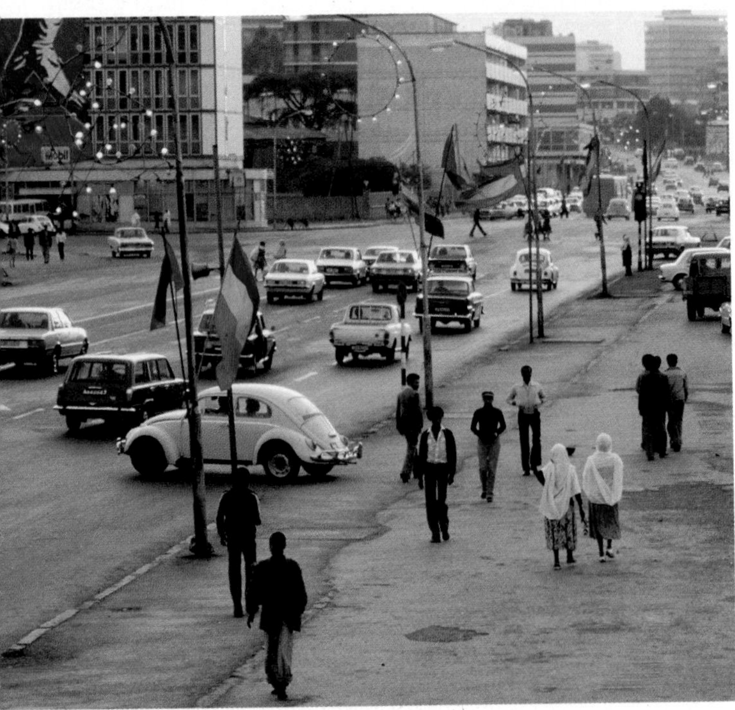
A street in Addis Ababa

Urban Ethiopia Addis Ababa, the capital of Ethiopia, lies about 200 miles (322 kilometers) south of Lalibela, in the center of the country. People in Addis Ababa have access to all the conveniences of city life—for example, running water, electricity, and modern hospitals. The city also has a university and a museum, as well as palaces built by ancient emperors. And Addis Ababa is a center of business and trade, with a population of almost 3 million that continues to grow. The city also houses the headquarters of several international organizations that work for the economic, political, and social well-being of Africa.

✓ Reading Check **Do most Ethiopians live in rural or in urban settings?**

Section 1 Assessment

Key Terms

Review the key terms at the beginning of this section. Use each term in a sentence that explains its meaning.

Target Reading Skill

Find the word *coexisted* in the last paragraph on page 516. Use context to figure out its meaning. What do you think it means? What clues helped you arrive at its meaning?

Comprehension and Critical Thinking

1. (a) Recall When did Christianity first come to Ethiopia?
(b) Summarize What led to the unique nature of the Christianity practiced in Ethiopia?
(c) Predict What do you think helps Christians and Muslims exist peacefully in Ethiopia today?

2. (a) Identify In what ways do rural Ethiopians make a living?
(b) Contrast How is life in Ethiopia's rural areas different from life in Addis Ababa?

Writing Activity

Write a paragraph encouraging travelers to visit the historic churches of Lalibela, Ethiopia. In it, explain how the Ethiopian Christian Church has been affected by the country's history.

For: An activity on Ethiopia
Visit: PHSchool.com
Web Code: lad-5601

Section 2

Tanzania

Determined to Succeed

Prepare to Read

Objectives

In this section you will

1. Find out about early reforms that the government of Tanzania made after independence.
2. Learn about continued social, economic, and political progress and reforms that have been made in Tanzania.

Taking Notes

As you read this section, look for details about social, economic, and political reforms in Tanzania. Copy the chart below, and use it to record your findings.

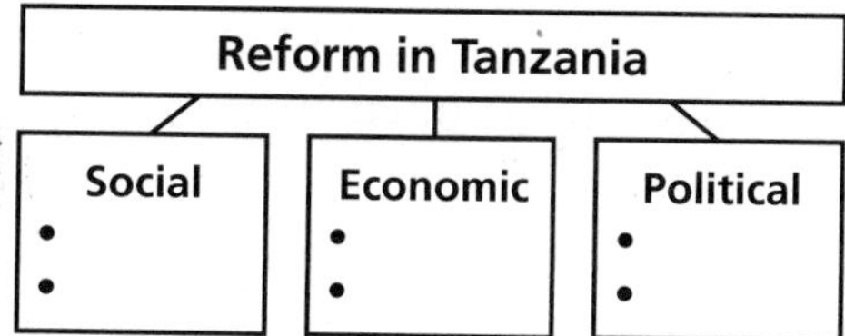

Target Reading Skill

Use Context Clues You can sometimes clarify the meaning of a word or phrase by using context—the surrounding words, phrases, and sentences. Sometimes the context will give a clear definition or explanation of the word. For example, each word highlighted in blue in this book is followed by a definition. As you read, look for other words that are accompanied by definitions or explanations.

Key Terms

- **lingua franca** (LING gwuh FRANG kuh) *n.* a language used for communication among people who speak different first languages
- **privatization** (pry vuh tih ZAY shun) *n.* the sale of government-owned industries to private companies
- **multiparty system** (MUL tee PAHR tee SIS tum) *n.* a political system in which two or more parties compete in elections

In October 1995, Dar es Salaam (DAHR es suh LAHM), Tanzania, looked ready for a celebration. Flags hung from buildings. People sang in the streets. Was it a holiday? Had a sports team become champions? No—an election was about to start. It would be the first election in more than 30 years to include more than one political party. Finally, voters would have a real choice among candidates with differing views. Tanzanians felt joyful, but they did not know what the future would hold. Other reforms their country had gone through had met with different levels of success.

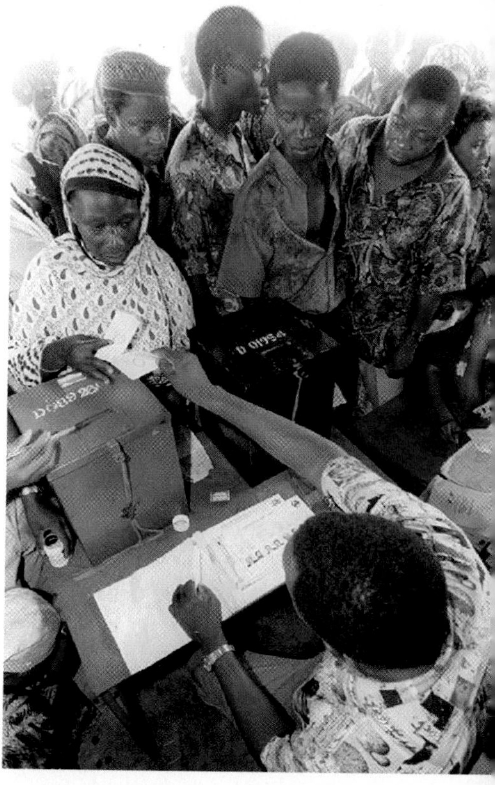

Tanzanians cast their votes.

Early Reforms After Independence

Tanzania lies on the Indian Ocean. This location has made it an important center of trade. During the last 2,000 years, this part of East Africa was first ruled mostly by Arabs, who settled there, and later by Germans and the British, who did not. The British named the mainland area that it ruled Tanganyika (tan guh NYEE kuh). Tanganyika became independent in 1961. In 1964, it joined with the island state of Zanzibar to form Tanzania.

Citizen Heroes

Amri Abedi

Amri Abedi was Tanzania's Minister of Justice, the mayor of Dar es Salaam, and the leader of a regional government—all at the same time. He took on so many jobs at once because when Tanzania became independent, it did not have enough educated citizens to run the government. Many of the people who did work in government had to work at more than one job to keep the government running smoothly.

Challenges for the New Nation When Tanzania became independent, most of its people were poor. Few were literate. According to Tanzania's then president, Julius Nyerere, the new republic had serious problems:

> **"We had 12 medical doctors in a population of 9 million. About 45 percent of children of schoolgoing age were going to school, and 85 percent of the adult population was illiterate."**
>
> —*Julius Nyerere*

A problem Nyerere wanted to avoid was tension among Tanzania's 120 ethnic groups. In many other African nations, ethnic groups fought against one another after independence. To ensure that ethnic conflicts would not occur in Tanzania, Nyerere adopted unusual social policies. Although some of these policies met with approval both at home and abroad, others were sharply criticized. Even today, debate continues over whether or not Nyerere made good choices for Tanzania.

A National Language One of Nyerere's social policies had to do with language. Various languages are spoken in East African homes, but many people also speak Swahili. As you read in Chapter 12, Swahili is one of Africa's most widely spoken languages. In East Africa, Swahili is a lingua franca (LING gwuh FRANG kuh). A **lingua franca** is a language used for communication among people who speak different first languages. To help unite all of Tanzania's ethnic groups, Nyerere made Swahili the national language.

A One-Party System Nyerere also established a new political system. He feared that political parties in Tanzania would be based on ethnic groups. If so, competition among parties could lead to competition or hatred among ethnic groups. This had happened in other newly independent African nations. Therefore, Nyerere established a one-party system. Elections still involved several candidates, but they were all members of the same party. Critics complained that having just one party encouraged corruption in the government.

Target Skill

Use Context Clues If you do not know what a one-party system is, look at the context. In the paragraph at the right, the phrase is followed by an explanation. Use this explanation to write a sentence describing a one-party system in your own words.

Economic Changes Next, Nyerere turned to the economy. He told Tanzanians that independence meant *uhuru na kazi* (oo HOO roo nah KAH zee)—"freedom and work." By this he meant that only hard work could end poverty. Nyerere said that Tanzania should be self-reliant. He did not want the country to depend on other nations for economic support.

Links Across
The World

Kwanzaa In the 1960s, many African Americans began celebrating family, community, and their African heritage with a holiday called Kwanzaa (KWAHN zah). Kwanzaa is based on several traditional African harvest festivals. Its name comes from a Swahili phrase that means "first fruits." The holiday celebrates a set of seven values that also have Swahili names. One of these values is ujamaa. Each night of the week-long holiday, families like the one shown here gather to light a candle and discuss one of the values.

To promote self-reliance, Nyerere established a program of *ujamaa* (oo JAH mah), which is Swahili for "togetherness" or "being a family." Tanzania's economy is based on farming. Nyerere called for all farmers to live in ujamaa villages, where they could work together and share resources. He believed this would help boost farm production. It would also make it easier for the government to provide clean water, education, and other services in an organized way.

✓ Reading Check **What language is the lingua franca of Tanzania?**

Progress and Continued Reform

By the time Nyerere stepped down as president in 1985, Tanzania had changed greatly. The country had a national language and very little ethnic conflict. Education and literacy had improved greatly. Proud of his success, Nyerere commented,

> **"When I stepped down, 91 percent of the adult population was literate, 100 percent of the children of school-going age were going to school. . . . We did not have enough engineers, but we had thousands . . . trained by ourselves. We did not have enough doctors, but we had . . . thousands trained by ourselves. That is what we were able to do . . . in a short period of independence."**
>
> —*Julius Nyerere*

However, Tanzania was still one of the poorest countries in the world. The ujamaa program had failed, and the economy was suffering. Many farm families had refused to move to the new villages. Crop production had decreased throughout the nation.

COUNTRY PROFILE

Focus on Economics

Tanzania

Like many African nations, Tanzania grows cash crops for export to other countries. The price of these cash crops on the world market greatly influences whether Tanzania's economy improves or declines. When the world price of coffee dropped from about $1.00 per pound in 1996 to less than $.40 per pound in 2003, many Tanzanians suffered. At the same time, the world price of tea rose, helping other Tanzanian farmers. Study the map and charts to learn more about the economy of Tanzania.

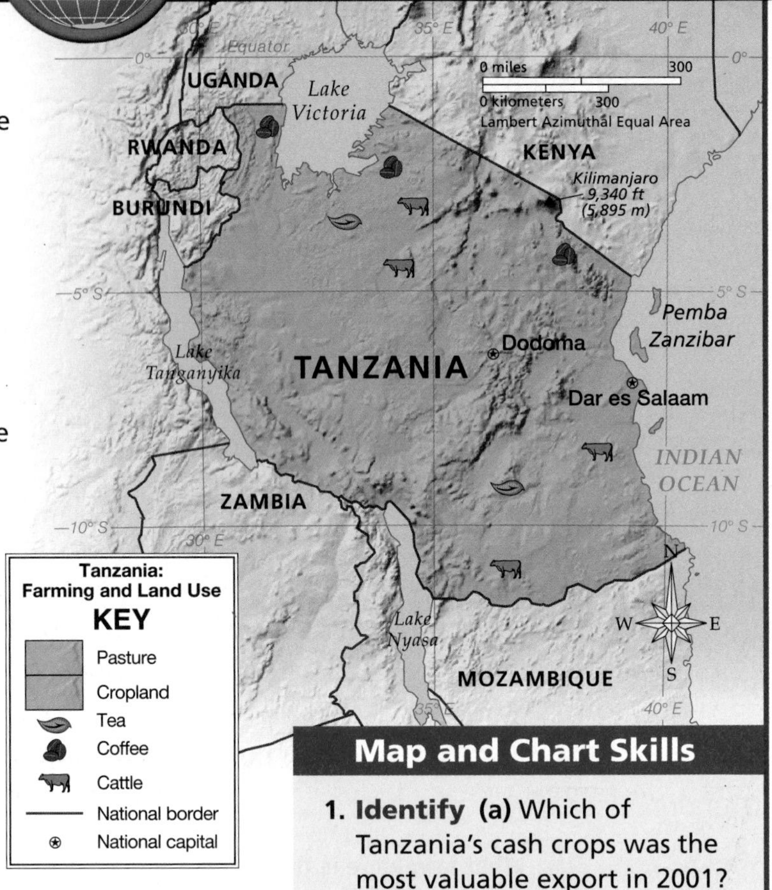

Economic Activity

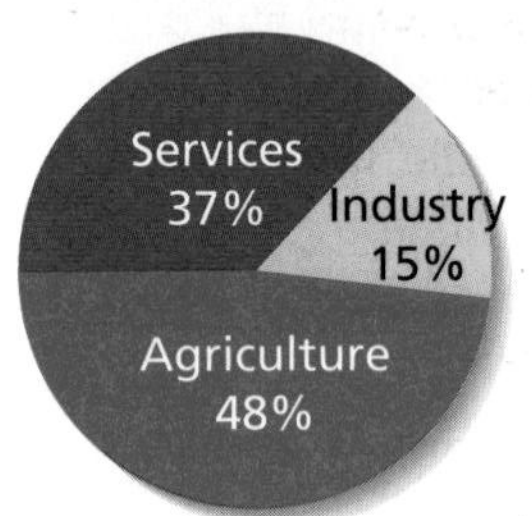

SOURCE: CIA World Factbook Online, 2003

Major Cash Crops, 2001

Crop	Exports (billions of Tanzanian shillings*)
Cashews	50.9
Coffee	49.6
Cotton seeds	29.2
Sisal	5.9
Tobacco	32.3

* $1 = approximately 1,000 Tanzanian shillings
SOURCE: Tanzanian Ministry of Agriculture and Food Security

Map and Chart Skills

1. **Identify** **(a)** Which of Tanzania's cash crops was the most valuable export in 2001? **(b)** Which was least valuable?
2. **Draw Conclusions** You can see that agriculture makes up nearly half of Tanzania's economy. Name one advantage and one disadvantage of basing an economy on selling cash crops to other countries.

Use Web Code **lae-5602** for **DK World Desk Reference Online.**

Discover how people make a living on Lake Victoria.

A New Era in Economics After Nyerere retired, Ali Hassan Mwinyi (AH lee hah SAHN um WEEN yee) was elected president. His government replaced some of Nyerere's unsuccessful programs. For example, the government ended Nyerere's failing ujamaa program. The government then encouraged farmers to use new farming methods and types of seeds in order to produce more cash crops. It also asked foreign countries for more help, and a number of them have since loaned money to Tanzania.

The government also decided to try privatization. **Privatization** is the sale of government-owned industries to private companies. Private companies, including some that are foreign-owned, now manage Tanzania's telephone and airline industries. The result of the new economic policies is that Tanzania's economy is improving more quickly and more smoothly than the economies of most other African nations.

Cashews: A New Cash Crop
Cashew nuts are one of the cash crops that Tanzanian farmers now produce for export to other countries. Coffee and cotton are also major export items.
Summarize *How can producing cash crops for export help improve a country's economy?*

Attempts at Political Reform Tanzania's new government also changed the election system. In 1992, the government began to allow new political parties to form. When a country has two or more political parties, it has a **multiparty system.** Tanzania's first elections under the multiparty system were held in October 1995.

But the 1995 and 2000 elections raised some issues that divided people. For example, in both elections, Nyerere's party won the most votes, so power remained with that party. Also, another party suggested that the island of Zanzibar should no longer be part of Tanzania. That would cause exactly the type of social split that Nyerere worried about. Whether Tanzania can achieve the same progress in politics as it has with its economy is still to be seen.

✓ **Reading Check** **What political change occurred in 1992?**

Section 2 Assessment

Key Terms
Review the key terms at the beginning of this section. Use each term in a sentence that explains its meaning.

Target Reading Skill
Find the word *self-reliant* on page 520. From its context, what do you think it means?

Comprehension and Critical Thinking
1. **(a) Explain** Why did Julius Nyerere decide to establish a one-party political system in Tanzania?
(b) Analyze Information In what ways can having a national language help prevent ethnic conflict in a country?
(c) Draw Conclusions If people had not had to move away from their homes, do you think the ujamaa program would have succeeded? Explain.
2. **(a) Identify** What improvements were made in Tanzania during Nyerere's presidency?
(b) Contrast Contrast the views Nyerere had on foreign involvement in Tanzania with the views that later government leaders had.

Writing Activity
How does Nyerere's slogan *uhuru na kazi,* or "freedom and work," apply to the kind of independence that you develop as you grow up? Write a paragraph explaining your response to this question.

For: An activity on the Ngorongoro Crater
Visit: PHSchool.com
Web Code: lad-5602

Writing a Summary

Early each morning, the President of the United States listens to a news briefing prepared just for him. His staff members put the briefing together by reading and listening to news from dozens of newspapers, radio stations, and television networks. They then select the most important stories and write a summary of each one.

Writing a summary of any kind of information involves identifying the main ideas and weaving them together based on what they have in common. Knowing how to write a summary will help you take tests, write essays, and understand what you read.

Learn the Skill

Use these steps to summarize information.

1. **Find and state the main idea of each paragraph or section you want to summarize.** You can often find a main idea in the topic sentence of a paragraph.

2. **Identify what the main ideas have in common.** Look for the ways the ideas are presented—for example, in chronological order, as causes and effects, as comparisons, or as a progression of ideas from simple to complex. Doing this will help you identify the overall focus of the information.

3. **Write a summary paragraph that begins with a topic sentence.** The summary should draw together the main ideas into a broad description of the information. The main ideas will be the supporting details of your topic sentence.

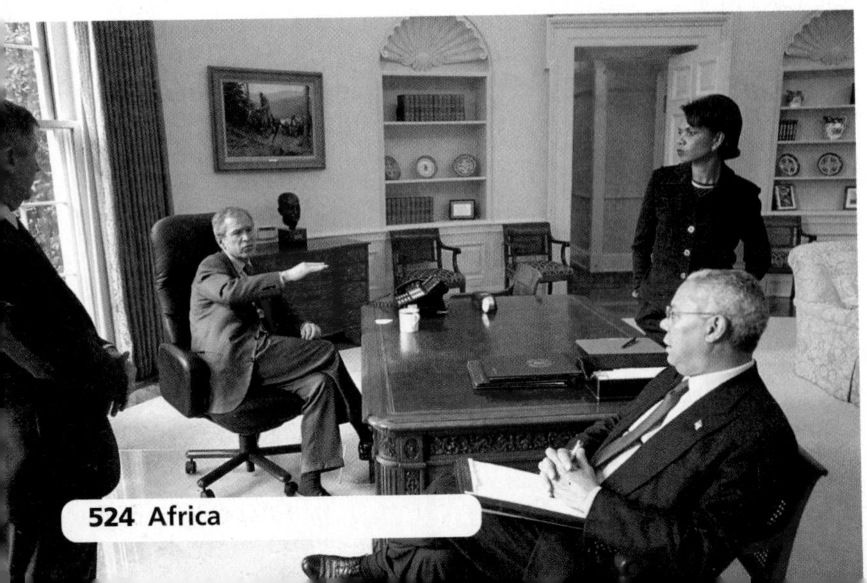

U.S. President George W. Bush discusses the day's events with his staff.

Practice the Skill

Read the section titled Major Religions of Ethiopia on pages 515–516. Then follow the steps below to summarize what you read.

1. Read the heading and subheadings in the section. These titles give you a general idea of the content. You can see that both Christianity and Islam are practiced in Ethiopia. Now read each paragraph and list its main idea.

2. The main ideas in this passage are in chronological order. They cover these dates: 350, 451, the 600s, the 1500s, and today. In what other ways are the main ideas related? What overall idea holds these paragraphs together?

3. You might use this topic sentence for your summary: *Ethiopia's location as a crossroads of trade and ideas has shaped its unique religious history.* Use this topic sentence, or write your own, and then complete the summary paragraph by adding explanations and details. The details will come from the main ideas on your list.

Ethiopian places of worship: the Church of St. Mary of Zion (above) and the Nagash mosque (below)

Apply the Skill

Read the section titled Early Reforms After Independence on pages 519–520. Use the steps in this skill to summarize the information.

Section 3 Kenya
Ties That Bind

Prepare to Read

Objectives
In this section you will
1. Learn about the peoples of Kenya.
2. Discover what life is like in rural Kenya.
3. Find out what life is like in urban Kenya.

Taking Notes
As you read this section, look for details about daily life in rural and urban Kenya. Copy the chart below, and use it to record your findings.

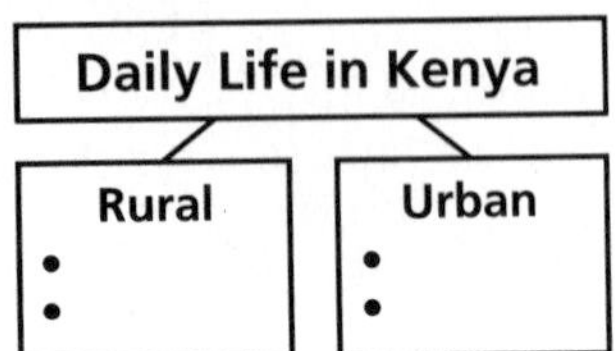

Target Reading Skill
Interpret Nonliteral Meanings Literal language is language that means exactly what it says. Nonliteral language uses images or comparisons to communicate an idea.

In this section you will read about "ties that bind" Kenyans together. When you see these words, ask yourself: Are Kenyans really tied together by something physical, or do the words have another meaning?

Key Terms
- **Kikuyu** (kee KOO yoo) *n.* the largest ethnic group in Kenya
- **Maasai** (mah SY) *n.* a seminomadic ethnic group in Kenya
- **seminomadic** (seh mee noh MAD ik) *adj.* combining nomadic wandering and farming in settlements
- **harambee** (hah RAHM bay) *n.* a social policy started by Jomo Kenyatta and meaning "let's pull together" in Swahili

"Where is your shamba?" is a question that two Kenyans usually ask each other when they first meet. A shamba is a small farm owned and run by a Kenyan family. Even Kenyans who move to the city think of the land where they were born as home. They return to it throughout their lives. Land is very important to Kenyans.

A Maasai family in Kenya standing in front of their land

Peoples of Kenya

Kenya's highest mountain, Mount Kenya, lies just south of the Equator. Southwest of Mount Kenya is a region of highlands that receives plenty of rain, so the land is good for farming. Most of Kenya's people are farmers. Many of them live in shambas dotting the countryside of the highlands. Others live along Kenya's coast, a warmer area that also has good farmland.

Kenya's Shared Culture Although some Kenyans are of European, Asian, or Arab descent, most come from families that have always lived in Africa. Kenya has plenty of cultural diversity—including more than 40 ethnic groups. Each ethnic group has distinct cultural features. But many groups have features in common, too. For example, some groups speak the same language as one another, and most Kenyans are either Christian or Muslim. Language and religion are some of the ties that bind the peoples of Kenya together.

Many Kenyans also share common values. Most Kenyans value their families as much as they value the land. Some families have six or more children. Members of extended families can be very close, often considering their cousins to be like brothers and sisters.

Kenya's Ethnic Groups The **Kikuyu** (kee KOO yoo) are Kenya's largest ethnic group. Many Kikuyu live in shambas in the highlands near Mount Kenya. They build round homes with mud walls and thatched roofs. The Kikuyu grow food and cash crops such as coffee and sisal, a fiber used to make rope. The **Maasai** (mah SY) are another ethnic group in Kenya, who traditionally make a living by farming and herding. The Maasai are **seminomadic,** which means they sometimes wander as nomads and sometimes live in settlements where they farm.

Ethnic Groups of Kenya
These women are Samburu people who, like the Maasai, are seminomadic herders. The women wear traditional Samburu dress—brightly patterned cloths and jewelry made of many colorful beads. **Evaluate** *Why do you think many peoples around the world dress traditionally?*

✓ Reading Check **How many ethnic groups live in Kenya?**

Life in Rural Kenya

As elsewhere in Africa, the majority of Kenya's farmers are women. They grow fruits and vegetables and herd livestock. Men also farm, but they usually raise cash crops, such as coffee and tea.

The way of life of many Kenyans is changing. As the population increases, many men and some women are moving to the cities to find work. Most women and children, however, stay in rural areas. Women are the primary caretakers of children, and it is expensive for women with children to move to a city. Many find it easier to support their families by farming.

Discovery
CHANNEL
SCHOOL
Video
Learn how growing beans has helped Kenya's economy.

Kenyans Working Together Kenya gained independence from the British in 1963. The first president, Jomo Kenyatta (JOH moh ken YAH tuh), began a social policy he called **harambee** (hah RAHM bay), which in Swahili means "let's pull together." Kenyatta encouraged harambee in many forms, including politics, farming, and education. For example, he had the government pay for a part of each child's education. In response, many villagers worked together to build and support their schools.

COUNTRY PROFILE — Focus on Geography

Kenya

Most Kenyans live in the countryside. The majority of the country's agricultural products are grown in the highlands region, where rainfall is sufficient for farming. An increasing number of Kenyans have moved to major cities. Nairobi, the largest business center in East Africa, is home both to very wealthy families and to people who live in slums. Study the map and charts to learn more about Kenya's land and people.

ETHIOPIA
SOMALIA
KENYA
Kisumu
Nairobi
Lake Victoria
TANZANIA
INDIAN OCEAN
Mombasa
Equator
5° N
0°
5° S
35° E
40° E

Kenya: Yearly Precipitation

KEY

Inches	Millimeters
More than 59	More than 1,499
40–59	1,000–1,499
20–39	500–999
10–19	250–499

National border
National capital
Other city

0 miles 250
0 kilometers 250
Lambert Azimuthal Equal Area

Major Agricultural Products, 2004

Product	Amount (metric tons)
Corn	2,700,000
Cassava	950,000
Plantains	370,000
Potatoes	500,000
Sugar cane	5,100,000
Sweet potatoes	535,000

SOURCE: *Britannica Book of the Year 2004*

Urban and Rural Population, 1950–2000

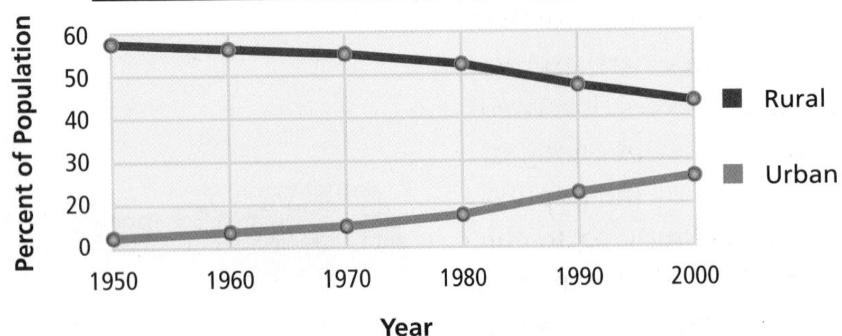

SOURCE: United Nations Food and Agriculture Organization

Map and Chart Skills

1. **Identify** What products did Kenya produce millions of metric tons of in the year 2004?
2. **Infer** In what region do you think Kenyans farm the least?
3. **Synthesize** Study the population graph. How do you think the trend shown has affected Kenya's agriculture?

Go Online PHSchool.com Use Web Code **lae-5603** for **DK World Desk Reference Online.**

Women's Self-Help Groups One of the best examples of how harambee is successful in Kenya is the rise of women's self-help groups in rural areas. Women in rural areas all over Kenya have formed these groups to solve problems in their communities. For example, many women felt it was not easy to farm, chop firewood, haul water, and take care of children all in one day. One woman commented, "My children were educated through the sweat of my brow."

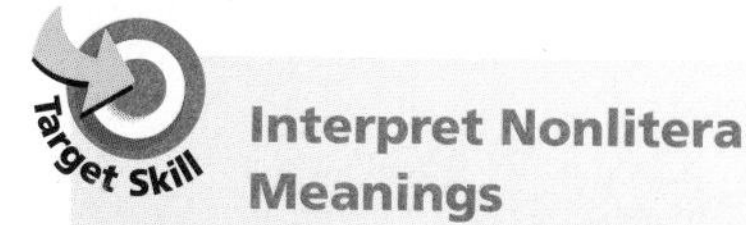

Interpret Nonliteral Meanings
What does the woman mean by saying that her children were educated through the sweat of her brow? Did she use the sweat to teach the children or to pay for their schooling? Restate what she means in your own words.

These self-help groups do a great variety of work. Some women's groups grow cash crops in addition to the crops they grow for their families to eat. Then they sell the cash crops and save the money as a group. The women meet to decide what to do with the money they have saved. In the mountain village of Mitero, Kikuyu women's groups have built a nursery school and installed water pipes for the community. They also loan money to women who want to start small businesses. Sometimes they give money to women who need to buy such necessities as a cow or a water tank. They also save money individually and use it to educate their children.

✓ Reading Check **What is the purpose of women's self-help groups in Kenya?**

Life in Urban Kenya

Kenya's capital, Nairobi (ny ROH bee), is an important business center and one of the largest cities in East Africa. Today it is considered Africa's main center of industry and manufacturing. Much of East Africa's banking and trade is centered there as well.

These Kikuyu women have formed a savings and loan club to support local businesses.

Working in the City Because Nairobi is a thriving city, many Kenyans move there looking for jobs. Every day, people arrive in Nairobi by train, bus, or *matatu* (muh TAH too)—minibus. Nairobi's population grew from one million in 1985 to more than two million in 2000. Many of Nairobi's newcomers walk to their jobs from the outskirts of the city. They may walk as far as ten miles each way because they cannot afford the cost of taking the bus to work.

When men move to Nairobi without their families, they often feel homesick for their loved ones in rural villages. Meanwhile, the women who remain in the villages must do much more work. Many people in Kenya have responded to this situation in the spirit of harambee—by working together.

Nairobi, Kenya

City Life Men who move to the city also work together. Many are saving money to buy land in the countryside. Men in Nairobi from the same ethnic group often welcome one another, share rooms, and help one another. Take Moses Mpoke (MOH zuz um POH kay) as an example. Mpoke is a Maasai. He owns land that is too dry for farming or grazing, but he could not move his livestock to find better grazing. After finishing high school, Mpoke moved to Nairobi to work.

Living in the city, Mpoke could have forgotten about his Maasai roots. But every weekend, he returns to his village to see his family and friends. When a visitor in his village asked Mpoke which is the real Moses Mpoke, the one in the city or the one in the village, he answered,

> **"This is the real Moses Mpoke, but the other is also me. In the week, I can live in the city and be comfortable. At weekends, I can live here [in my village] and be comfortable. The city has not stopped me from being a Maasai."**
>
> *—Moses Mpoke*

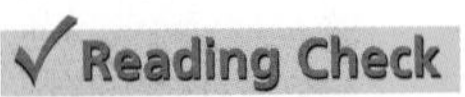

✓ Reading Check **How do Kenyans living in the city support one another?**

Section 3 Assessment

Key Terms

Review the key terms at the beginning of this section. Use each term in a sentence that explains its meaning.

Target Reading Skill

Find the phrase "in shambas dotting the countryside" on page 527. Explain in your own words what this means.

Comprehension and Critical Thinking

1. (a) Recall In what way do most Kenyans make their living?

(b) Compare What other traits do Kenya's different ethnic groups have in common?

2. (a) Explain Why do most Kenyan women stay in rural villages rather than move to the city?

(b) Summarize How have Kenya's government and Kenya's village women used harambee to help benefit village families?

3. (a) Describe What do many Kenyans who live in the city plan to do with the money they earn?

(b) Analyze Information What different hardships do men and women in Kenya face if the men decide to work in Nairobi?

Writing Activity

Consider the concept of harambee. It means that people work together for a common good. Write an account of how you have seen or would like to see harambee in your community or school.

Writing Tip Start your account with an explanation of what harambee is, so that readers can easily understand how your example fits into the concept.

Chapter 16 Review and Assessment

◆ Chapter Summary

Ethiopia

Section 1: Ethiopia

- Ethiopia has two major religions—Christianity and Islam. At times Ethiopian Christians and Muslims have fought each other, but today they live together peacefully.
- Most Ethiopians live in rural areas. Their daily lives are very different from those of Ethiopians in urban areas.

Section 2: Tanzania

- After independence, Tanzania's president Julius Nyerere established Swahili as the country's lingua franca, created a one-party political system, and encouraged farmers to live in ujamaa villages.
- Since Nyerere retired in 1985, Tanzania's government has encouraged privatization and other economic reforms as well as a multiparty political system.

Section 3: Kenya

- Kenyans come from 40 ethnic groups that are distinct but also share some values and characteristics. Many Kenyans are farmers.
- Most Kenyan farmers are women. To help solve community problems, many Kenyan women have formed various self-help groups.
- Many Kenyan men have had to move to the city to find work, but they often return to their villages on weekends or when they retire.

Kenya

◆ Key Terms

Each of the statements below contains a key term from the chapter. If it is true, write *true*. If it is false, change the highlighted term to make the statement true.

1. The Swahili word that means "let's pull together" is **harambee.**
2. **Kikuyu** is an ancient Ethiopian language.
3. A place where people live a religious life is a **multiparty system.**
4. People who speak different languages often communicate by speaking a **lingua franca.**
5. A country with two or more political parties has a **monastery.**

Review and Assessment (continued)

◆ Comprehension and Critical Thinking

6. (a) **Describe** How did Christianity and Islam spread into Ethiopia?
   (b) **Identify Effects** How did the spread of Islam cause Ethiopian Christians to become more isolated?
7. (a) **Identify** What public services are lacking in Ethiopia's rural areas?
   (b) **Make Generalizations** Do you think the prosperity of Addis Ababa could spread into rural Ethiopia? If it did, how would life change in rural areas?
8. (a) **Explain** Why did Julius Nyerere establish a lingua franca for Tanzania?
   (b) **Identify** What changes did Julius Nyerere make to Tanzania's economic and political systems?
   (c) **Contrast** What are some advantages of a one-party political system? Of a multiparty system?
9. (a) **Recall** Has Tanzania had greater success in economics or in politics?
   (b) **Analyze Information** Why has establishing a multiparty political system in Tanzania been a challenge?
10. (a) **Recall** What are some ties that bind the people of Kenya together?
    (b) **Summarize** How have rural Kenyans worked together to improve their lives?
    (c) **Identify Effects** The movement of men from Kenya's countryside to Nairobi can cause some hardship. How can it also help improve village life?

◆ Skills Practice

Writing a Summary In the Skills for Life activity in this chapter, you learned how to write a summary.

Review the steps you followed to learn this skill. Then reread the part of Section 3 titled Life in Rural Kenya. Find the main idea of each paragraph. Then identify what the main ideas have in common, and write a summary paragraph.

◆ Writing Activity: Language Arts

Think about the community you live in. Is it growing or becoming smaller? Think of reasons why your community may have developed in the way that it has. What are some positive changes that have occurred? What are some negative ones? Use your answers to write a newspaper editorial explaining your opinion on whether your community is developing in a way that benefits its citizens.

MAP MASTER™ Skills Activity

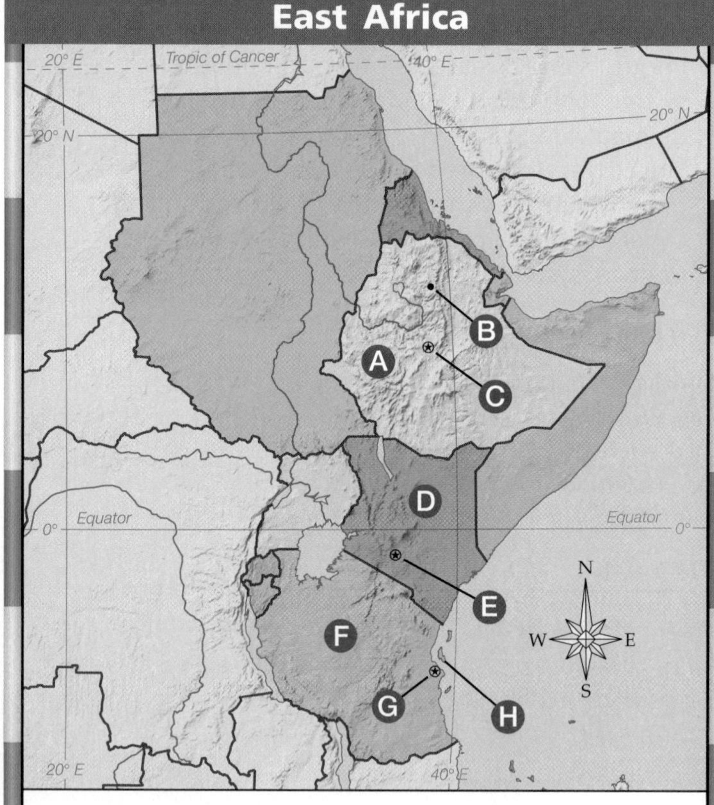

Place Location For each place listed, write the letter from the map that shows its location.

1. Ethiopia
2. Nairobi
3. Tanzania
4. Dar es Salaam
5. Zanzibar
6. Kenya
7. Addis Ababa
8. Lalibela

Go Online PHSchool.com Use Web Code **lap-5620** for an **interactive map.**

Standardized Test Prep

Test-Taking Tips

Some questions on standardized tests ask you to analyze a reading selection. Read the passage below. Then follow the tips to answer the sample question.

> Julius Nyerere became the first president of Tanzania in 1964. He made Swahili the national language to help unite his country's many ethnic groups. He encouraged farmers to live together in organized villages and to share resources. Many more schools were built, and literacy improved dramatically after independence. Many more Tanzanians were trained to be engineers, doctors, and teachers.

TIP Look for topics that are shared by all the sentences in the passage.

Pick the letter that best answers the question.

Which kind of resources in Tanzania does this passage describe?

- **A** natural resources
- **B** human resources
- **C** capital resources
- **D** entrepreneurial resources

TIP Before you read the paragraph, preview the question. Think about it as you read.

Think It Through The question asks what kind of resources the paragraph describes. Skim over each sentence of the paragraph. Each one mentions something about the people of Tanzania. You can eliminate answer A, natural resources, because those are materials found in the environment. You may not know the words *capital* or *entrepreneurial* in C and D, but you probably know that *human* has to do with people. The correct answer is B.

Practice Questions

Use the tips above and other tips in this book to help you answer the following questions. Use the passage below to answer Question 1. Choose the letter of the best answer.

> Lalibela is a town in Ethiopia. People travel there to visit a group of churches for which Lalibela is famous. The people who live there, however, do not have electricity. Most of them do not own cars. Most of them earn a living by farming.

1. Which is a detail that is described in this passage?
   - **A** The people who live in Lalibela love the churches there.
   - **B** The tourists who visit Lalibela cannot bring cars.
   - **C** Most of the people who live in Lalibela are farmers.
   - **D** Most of Lalibela's visitors are farmers.

2. Which of the following was NOT true of Tanzania's ujamaa program?
   - **A** The program's goal was to boost farm production.
   - **B** People had to work together to make the program successful.
   - **C** The government had to help out with the program.
   - **D** All farm families in Tanzania agreed to take part.

3. Which is the word for a family farm in Kenya?
   - **A** Maasai
   - **B** shamba
   - **C** harambee
   - **D** Kikuyu

Use Web Code **laa-5600** for **Chapter 16 self-test.**

A Promise to the Sun

By Tololwa M. Mollel

Prepare to Read

Background Information

Not all stories were written down when they were first told. Myths like the one you are about to read were originally told aloud. They were part of an oral tradition that people passed down from generation to generation.

These myths are meant to entertain the listener. They are also meant to explain something to the listener. Usually, they explain why aspects of the world are as they are. Myths often provide a moral lesson to the listener as well.

This story was written by Tololwa M. Mollel in the style of Maasai myths heard in his youth in Tanzania. Mollel is a well-known storyteller and author.

Objectives

In this section you will

1. Explore the natural world from a point of view that may not be familiar to you.
2. Learn how a storyteller can use animals and natural forces as characters to make a story more meaningful.

savannah alternate spelling of *savanna*
maize (mayz) *n.* corn
shrivel (SHRIH vul) *v.* to wrinkle as moisture is lost
wilt (wilt) *v.* to droop
withered (WITH urd) *adj.* shriveled and shrunken from drying out

Long ago, when the world was new, a severe drought hit the land of the birds. The savannah turned brown, and streams dried up. Maize plants died, and banana trees shriveled in the sun, their broad leaves wilting away. Even the nearby forest grew withered and pale.

The birds held a meeting and decided to send someone in search of rain. They drew lots to choose who would go on the journey. And they told the Bat, their distant cousin who was visiting, that she must draw, too. "You might not be a bird," they said, "but for now you're one of us." Everyone took a lot, and as luck would have it, the task fell to the Bat.

Over the trees and the mountains flew the Bat, to the Moon. There she cried, "Earth has no rain, Earth has no food, Earth asks for rain!"

A full moon rises over the Kenyan landscape.

The Moon smiled. “I can’t bring rain. My task is to wash and oil the night’s face. But you can try the Stars.”

On flew the Bat, until she found the Stars at play. “Away with you!” they snapped, angry at being interrupted. “If you want rain, go to the Clouds!”

The Clouds were asleep but awoke at the sound of the Bat arriving. “We can bring rain,” they yawned, “but the Winds must first blow us together, to hang over the Earth in one big lump.”

At the approach of the Bat, the Winds howled to a stop.

“We’ll blow the Clouds together,” they said, “but not before the Sun has brought up steam to the sky.”

As the Bat flew toward the Sun, a sudden scream shook the sky:

“Stop where you are, foolish Bat, before I burn off your little wings!”

The Bat shrank back in terror, and the Sun smothered its fire in rolls of clouds. Quickly the Bat said, “Earth has no rain, Earth has no food, Earth asks for rain!”

Clouds fill the East African sky.

“I’ll help you,” replied the Sun, “in return for a favor. After the rain falls, choose for me the greenest patch on the forest top, and build me a nest there. Then no longer will I have to journey to the horizon at the end of each day but will rest for the night in the cool and quiet of the forest.”

horizon (huh RY zun) *n.* the place where Earth and sky appear to meet

The Bat quickly replied, “I’m only a Bat and don’t know how to build nests, but the birds will happily make you one. Nothing will be easier—there are so many of them. They will do it right after the harvest, I promise—all in a day!”

And down the sky’s sunlit paths the Bat flew, excited to bring the good news to the birds.

The birds readily promised to build the nest.

“The very day after the harvest,” said the Sparrow.

“All in a day,” said the Owl.

“A beautiful nest it’ll be,” said the Canary.

“With all the colors of the rainbow,” said the Peacock.

So the Sun burnt down upon the earth, steam rose, Winds blew, and Clouds gathered. Then rain fell. The savannah bloomed, and streams flowed. Green and thick and tall, the forest grew until it touched the sky. Crops flourished and ripened—maize, bananas, cassava, millet, and peanuts—and the birds harvested. The morning after the harvest, the Bat reminded the birds about the nest. Suddenly the birds were in no mood for work. All they cared about was the harvest celebrations, which were to start that night and last several days.

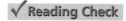

What promise does the Bat make to the Sun?

"I have to adorn myself," said the Peacock.

"I have to practice my flute," said the Canary.

"I have to heat up my drums," said the Owl.

"I have to help prepare the feast," said the Sparrow.

"Wait until after the celebrations," they said. "We'll do it then." But their hearts were not in it, and the Bat knew they would never build the nest.

What was she to do? A promise is a promise, she believed, yet she didn't know anything about making a nest. Even if she did, how could she, all on her own, hope to make one big enough for the sun?

The Sun set, and the Moon rose. The celebrations began. The drums throbbed, the flutes wailed, and the dancers pounded the earth with their feet.

throb (thrahb) *v.* to beat

Alone with her thoughts and tired, the Bat fell fast asleep.

She awoke in a panic. The Moon had vanished, the Stars faded. Soon the Sun would rise!

Slowly, the Sun peered out over the horizon in search of the nest.

Certain the Sun was looking for her, the Bat scrambled behind a banana leaf. The Sun moved up in the sky. One of its rays glared over the leaf. With a cry of fear, the Bat fled to the forest.

But even there, she was not long at peace. There was a gust of wind, and the forest opened for a moment overhead. The Bat looked up anxiously. Peeking down at her was the Sun.

She let out a shriek and flew away.

shriek (shreek) *n.* a sharp, shrill sound

As she flew, a cave came into view below. She dived down and quickly darted in.

There, silent and out of reach, she hid from the glare of the Sun.

She hid from the shame of a broken promise, a shame the birds did not feel.

Outside, the celebrations went on. The Owl's drums roared furiously. The Canary's flute pierced the air. And the Sparrow cheered the Peacock's wild dancing.

The Sun inched down toward the horizon. It lingered over the forest and cast one more glance at the treetops, hoping for a miracle. Then, disappointed, it began to set. The birds carried on unconcerned, the sounds of their festivities reaching into the cave.

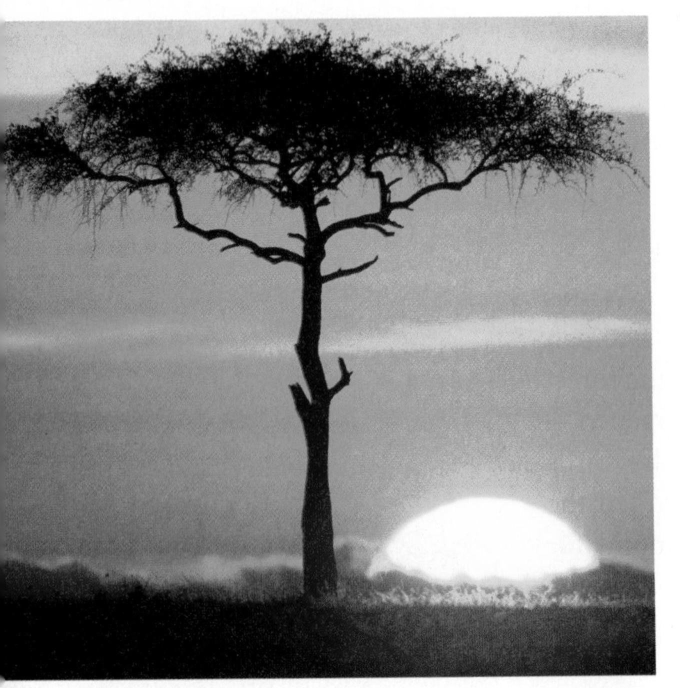

Sunrise in Kenya

But the Bat did not stir from her hiding place that night. Nor the next day. For many days and nights she huddled in the cave. Then gradually she got up enough courage to venture out—but never in daylight! Only after sunset with Earth in the embrace of night.

venture (VEN chur) *v.* to move forward in the face of danger
embrace (em BRAYS) *n.* hug

Days and months and years went by, but the birds didn't build the nest. The Sun never gave up wishing, though. Every day as it set, it would linger to cast one last, hopeful glance at the forest top. Then, slowly, very slowly, it would sink away below the horizon.

Year after year the Sun continued to drag up steam, so the Winds would blow, the Clouds gather, and rain fall. It continues to do so today, hoping that the birds will one day keep their promise and build a nest among the treetops.

As for the Bat, . . . she made a home in the cave, and there she lives to this day. Whenever it rains, though, she listens eagerly. From the dark silence of her perch, the sound of the down-pour, ripening the crops and renewing the forest, is to her a magical song she wishes she could be out dancing to.

And as she listens, the trees outside sway and bow toward the cave. It is their thank-you salute to the hero who helped turn the forests green and thick and tall as the sky.

About the Selection

A Promise to the Sun is a children's book written by Tololwa M. Mollel and published in 1992.

✓ Reading Check

How does the Bat's life change as a result of what happens in the story?

About the Author

Tololwa M. Mollel (b. 1952) is an Arusha-Maasai born in northern Tanzania. He was educated and has taught writing and theater in Tanzania and Canada. Mollel has written more than 15 children's books. He has based his books on African folklore, including traditional Maasai tales and themes from his childhood.

Review and Assessment

Thinking About the Selection

1. (a) Recall What favor did the Sun ask of the Bat?
(b) Explain Why did the Bat not keep her promise?
(c) Analyze What aspects of how a bat lives are explained by this story? What other natural events are explained by this story?

2. (a) Respond Why do you think that the birds did not feel as ashamed as the Bat did?
(b) Analyze What moral lesson does the story teach about making and keeping promises?

Writing Activity

Write a Myth Using this story as a model, write your own myth. You might want to write a myth in which the Bat makes peace with the Sun, or one in which another animal makes a promise to the Moon.

Chapter 17

Central and Southern Africa

Chapter Preview

This chapter will introduce you to some of the countries of Central and Southern Africa.

Country Databank

The Country Databank provides data and descriptions of each of the countries in the region: Angola, Botswana, Cameroon, Central African Republic, Comoros, Democratic Republic of the Congo, Equatorial Guinea, Gabon, Lesotho, Madagascar, Malawi, Mauritius, Mozambique, Namibia, Republic of the Congo, São Tomé and Príncipe, South Africa, Swaziland, Zambia, and Zimbabwe.

Section 1

Democratic Republic of the Congo
A Wealth of Possibilities

Section 2

South Africa
Struggle for Equality

Target Reading Skill

Sequence In this chapter you will focus on understanding sequence. Identifying sequence and recognizing sequence signal words will help you learn as you read.

▶ **Cape Town, South Africa, is an important port and center of industry in Southern Africa.**

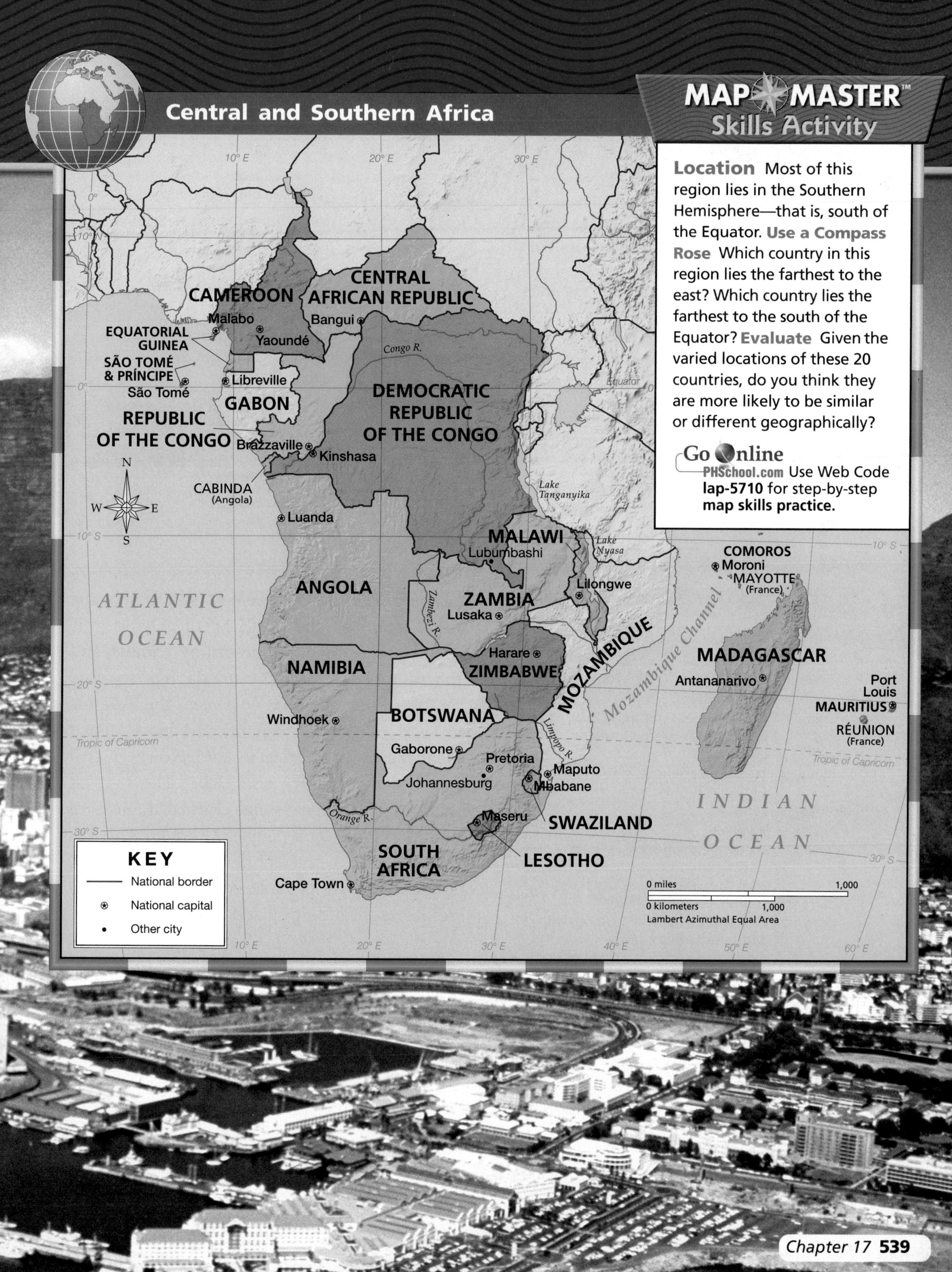

MAP MASTER™ Skills Activity

Location Most of this region lies in the Southern Hemisphere—that is, south of the Equator. **Use a Compass Rose** Which country in this region lies the farthest to the east? Which country lies the farthest to the south of the Equator? **Evaluate** Given the varied locations of these 20 countries, do you think they are more likely to be similar or different geographically?

Go Online PHSchool.com Use Web Code **lap-5710** for step-by-step **map skills practice.**

Introducing Central and Southern Africa

Guide for Reading

This section provides an introduction to the 20 countries that make up the region of Central and Southern Africa.

- Look at the map on the previous page and then read the paragraphs below to learn about each nation.
- Analyze the data to compare the countries.
- What are the characteristics that most of the countries share?
- What are some key differences among the countries?

Viewing the Video Overview

View the World Studies Video Overview to learn more about each of the countries. As you watch, answer these questions:

- What are some common features of the region?
- What obstacles do children in the Democratic Republic of the Congo face to get an education?

Discovery CHANNEL SCHOOL Video
Explore the geography of Central and Southern Africa.

Angola

Capital	Luanda
Land Area	481,551 sq mi; 1,246,700 sq km
Population	10.6 million
Ethnic Group(s)	Ovimbundu, Kimbundu, Bankongo, mixed white and black, white
Religion(s)	traditional beliefs, Roman Catholic, Protestant
Government	republic
Currency	kwanza
Leading Exports	crude oil, diamonds, refined petroleum products, gas, coffee, sisal, fish and fish products, timber, cotton
Language(s)	Portuguese (official), Umbundu, Kimbundu, Kikongo

Angola (ang GOH luh) is bordered on the west by the Atlantic Ocean, on the north by the Democratic Republic of the Congo, on the east by Zambia, and on the south by Namibia. Cabinda is a separate region of Angola that lies between the Atlantic Ocean and the Congo republics. Angola gained independence from Portugal in 1975. However, civil war gripped the country until 2002. The war left many thousands homeless and claimed the lives of an estimated 1.5 million people. Although Angola's economy has been severely damaged by the war, economic recovery is possible. Angola is rich in natural resources, including oil and diamonds.

Thatched-roof houses in Angola

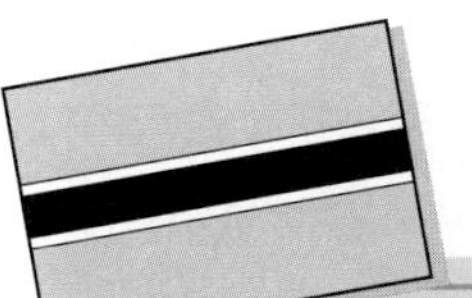

Botswana

Capital	Gaborone
Land Area	226,011 sq mi; 585,370 sq km
Population	1.6 million
Ethnic Group(s)	Tswana, Kalanga, Basarwa, Kgalagadi, white
Religion(s)	traditional beliefs, Christian
Government	parliamentary republic
Currency	pula
Leading Exports	diamonds, copper, nickel, soda ash, meat, textiles
Language(s)	English (official), Tswana, Shona, San, Khoikhoi, Ndebele

Botswana (baht SWAH nuh) is bordered on the west and north by Namibia, on the north and east by Zambia and Zimbabwe, and on the east and south by South Africa. When it was a British colony, Botswana was known as Bechuanaland (bech WAH nah land). After gaining independence in 1966, Botswana's government transformed the economy into one of the fastest-growing in the world. Diamond mining is Botswana's largest industry. AIDS poses a severe health threat to the country. Hundreds of thousands of people have the disease.

Cameroon

Capital	Yaoundé
Land Area	181,251 sq mi; 469,440 sq km
Population	16.1 million
Ethnic Group(s)	Cameroon Highlanders, Bantu, Kirdi, Fulani, Eastern Nigritic
Religion(s)	traditional beliefs, Christian, Muslim
Government	unitary republic
Currency	CFA franc
Leading Exports	crude oil and petroleum products, lumber, cacao beans, aluminum, coffee, cotton
Language(s)	French (official), English (official), Bamileke, Fang, Fulani

Cameroon (kam uh ROON) is bordered on the west by the Atlantic Ocean and Nigeria, on the north by Chad, on the east by the Central African Republic, and on the south by the Republic of the Congo, Gabon, and Equatorial Guinea. It has many forests and rivers and much good farmland. Present-day Cameroon was formed in 1961 by merging French Cameroon and a part of British Cameroon. The government has spent the last several decades improving farming conditions and building roads and railways. In terms of oil and agricultural resources, Cameroon is one of Africa's richest countries.

Central African Republic

Capital	Bangui
Land Area	240,534 sq mi; 622,984 sq km
Population	3.6 million
Ethnic Group(s)	Baya, Banda, Mandjia, Sara, Mbouri, M'Baka, Yakoma
Religion(s)	traditional beliefs, Protestant, Roman Catholic, Muslim
Government	republic
Currency	CFA franc
Leading Exports	diamonds, timber, cotton, coffee, tobacco
Language(s)	French (official), Sango, Banda, Gbaya

The Central African Republic (SEN trul AF rih kun rih PUB lik) is bordered on the west by Cameroon, on the north by Chad, on the north and east by Sudan, and on the south by the Democratic Republic of the Congo and the Republic of the Congo. It sits on a low plateau at the western end of the Sahel. Once a French colony called Ubangi-Shari (yoo BANG gee SHAH ree), the Central African Republic gained independence in 1960. After several government changes, the country became a democracy in 1993. In 2003, the government was overthrown. Elections for a new government were scheduled for late 2004.

Introducing Central and Southern Africa

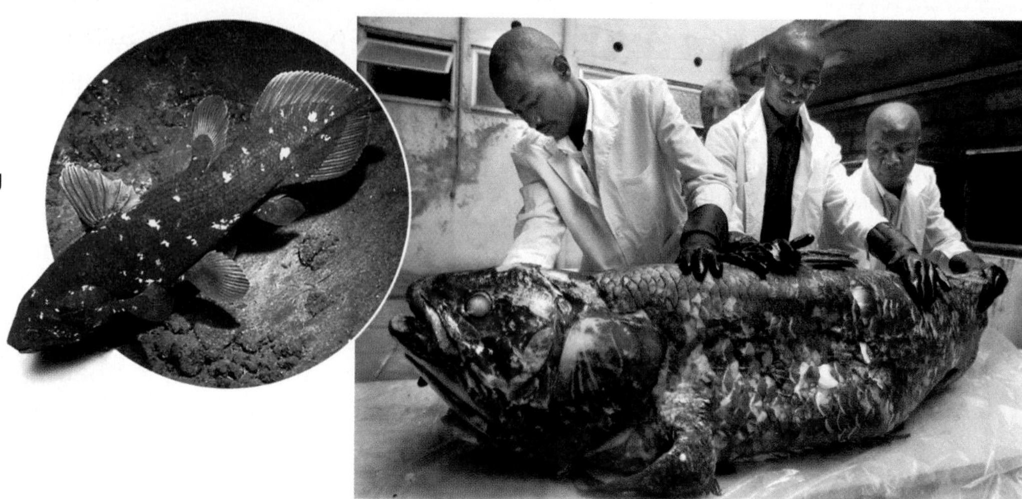

A live coelacanth (left); African scientists studying a dead coelacanth (right)

Comoros

Capital	Moroni
Land Area	838 sq mi; 2,170 sq km
Population	614,382
Ethnic Group(s)	Antalote, Cafre, Makoa, Oimatsaha, Sakalava
Religion(s)	Muslim, Roman Catholic
Government	independent republic
Currency	Comoros franc
Leading Exports	vanilla, ylang-ylang, cloves, perfume oil, copra
Language(s)	Arabic (official), French (official), Comoran (official)

Comoros (KAH muh rohz) is made up of three islands in the Indian Ocean, off the east coast of Mozambique. Numerous species of birds, animals, and fish live on and around the islands. The most famous of these is the coelacanth (SEE luh kanth), an extremely rare fish. Since gaining its independence from France in 1975, Comoros has experienced several major rebellions and civil wars. It is an extremely poor country. The population is growing rapidly, but the country has few natural resources or economic opportunities. Most of the people of Comoros are subsistence farmers.

Congo, Democratic Republic of the

Capital	Kinshasa
Land Area	875,520 sq mi; 2,267,600 sq km
Population	55.2 million
Ethnic Group(s)	more than 200 distinct ethnic groups, including Bantu, Hamitic
Religion(s)	Roman Catholic, Protestant, Muslim, traditional beliefs
Government	dictatorship
Currency	Congolese franc
Leading Exports	diamonds, copper, coffee, cobalt, crude oil
Language(s)	French (official), Kiswahili, Tshiluba, Kikongo, Lingala

The Democratic Republic of the Congo (dem uh KRAT ik rih PUB lik uv thuh KAHNG goh) lies on the Equator. It is bordered on the west by the Republic of the Congo; on the north by the Central African Republic and Sudan; on the east by Uganda, Rwanda, Burundi, and Tanzania; and on the south by Zambia. The rain forests of the Congo River basin cover much of the country. The country has suffered through years of civil war, which led to the deaths of about 3.5 million people. The nation has the potential for a strong economy, with many mineral resources, farmable land, and good soil.

Congo, Republic of the

Capital	Brazzaville
Land Area	131,853 sq mi; 341,500 sq km
Population	3.3 million
Ethnic Group(s)	Kongo, Sangha, M'Bochi, Take
Religion(s)	Christian, traditional beliefs, Muslim
Government	republic
Currency	CFA franc
Leading Exports	petroleum, lumber, plywood, sugar, cocoa, coffee, diamonds
Language(s)	French (official), Kongo, Teke, Lingala

The Republic of the Congo (rih PUB lik uv thuh KAHNG goh) lies on the Equator. It is bordered on the west by Gabon, on the north by Cameroon and the Central African Republic, on the east and south by the Democratic Republic of the Congo, and on the south by Angola. The Congo River forms the border with the Democratic Republic of the Congo. The Republic of the Congo gained independence from France in 1960. Since then, it has faced years of civil war. The nation has large supplies of oil and timber, and sales of oil have brought the country some wealth.

Equatorial Guinea

Capital	Malabo
Land Area	10,830 sq mi; 28,051 sq km
Population	498,144
Ethnic Group(s)	Bioko, Rio Muni
Religion(s)	Christian, traditional beliefs
Government	republic
Currency	CFA franc
Leading Exports	petroleum, timber, cocoa
Language(s)	Spanish (official), French (official), Fang, Bubi

Equatorial Guinea (ee kwuh TAWR ee ul GIH nee) lies just north of the Equator. It consists of five islands and a mainland area. The mainland is bordered on the west by the Atlantic Ocean, on the north by Cameroon, and on the east and south by Gabon. Many species of animals live on the mainland, including gorillas, leopards, antelopes, crocodiles, and snakes. After almost two hundred years as a Spanish colony, Equatorial Guinea gained independence in 1968. The economy is strong due to recently discovered oil reserves. Forestry, farming, and fishing are also important industries.

Gabon

Capital	Libreville
Land Area	99,489 sq mi; 257,667 sq km
Population	1.2 million
Ethnic Group(s)	Bantu, Fang, Bapounou, Nzebi, Obamba
Religion(s)	Christian, traditional beliefs, Muslim
Government	republic
Currency	CFA franc
Leading Exports	crude oil, timber, manganese, uranium
Language(s)	French (official), Fang, Punu, Sira, Nzebi, Mpongwe

Gabon (gah BOHN) is bordered on the west by the Atlantic Ocean, on the north by Equatorial Guinea and Cameroon, and on the east and south by the Republic of the Congo. The country gained its independence from France in 1960, and it became a democracy in 1990. Oil resources have made Gabon's economy very strong in comparison to the economies of other African countries. People live on only a small portion of Gabon's land. More than three quarters of the country is covered by rain forests that are inhabited by many kinds of animals and plants.

Introducing Central and Southern Africa

Lesotho

Capital	Maseru
Land Area	11,720 sq mi; 30,355 sq km
Population	2.2 million
Ethnic Group(s)	Sotho, white, Asian
Religion(s)	Christian, traditional beliefs
Government	parliamentary constitutional monarchy
Currency	loti
Leading Exports	manufactured goods, wool, mohair, food, live animals
Language(s)	English (off.), Sesotho (off.), Zulu

Lesotho (leh SOO too) is a tiny, mountainous country surrounded on all sides by South Africa. In 1966, the country became independent as a monarchy, or a government led by a king or a queen. Since that time, its government has been unstable. The country has been ruled by a king, by military leaders, and by elected leaders. Lesotho's economy depends heavily on South Africa. Many of Lesotho's men find work in the mines of South Africa. Despite widespread poverty, a large percentage of people in Lesotho are literate.

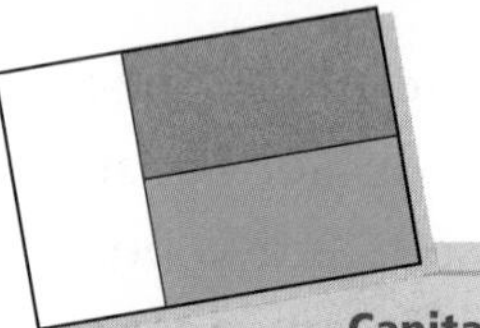

Madagascar

Capital	Antananarivo
Land Area	224,533 sq mi; 581,540 sq km
Population	16.5 million
Ethnic Group(s)	Malayo-Indonesian, Cotier, white, South Asian, Creole, Comoran
Religion(s)	traditional beliefs, Christian, Muslim
Government	republic
Currency	Malagasy franc
Leading Exports	coffee, vanilla, shellfish, sugar, cotton cloth, chromite
Language(s)	French (off.), Malagasy (off.)

Madagascar (mad uh GAS kur) is the world's fourth-largest island. It lies in the Indian Ocean, east of Mozambique. Before the French colonized Madagascar in 1886, it was an independent kingdom. The nation regained its independence in 1960 and became a democracy in the early 1990s. The nation's economy is based mainly on farming, fishing, and forestry. Madagascar is famous for plants and animals that cannot be found anywhere else on Earth. It is also well known for its spices, including vanilla. A larger percentage of people in Madagascar are literate than in most other African countries.

Malawi

Capital	Lilongwe
Land Area	36,324 sq mi; 94,080 sq km
Population	10.7 million
Ethnic Group(s)	Chewa, Nyanja, Tumbuka, Yao, Lomwe, Sena, Tonga, Ngongi, Ngonde, Asian, white
Religion(s)	Protestant, Roman Catholic, Muslim, traditional beliefs
Government	multiparty democracy
Currency	Malawi kwacha
Leading Exports	tobacco, tea, sugar, cotton, coffee, peanuts, wood products, apparel
Language(s)	English (official), Chichewa (official), Lomwe, Yao, Ngoni

Malawi (MAH lah wee) is bordered on the west, east, and south by Mozambique, on the west by Zambia, and on the north by Tanzania. The dominant geographical feature of this tiny country is Lake Nyasa (NYAH sah), Africa's third-largest body of water. In addition, Malawi lies alongside the Great Rift Valley. Malawi was called Nyasaland while under British rule. It became an independent nation in 1964. Malawi then became a democracy in the mid-1990s. The country's economy is mostly agricultural. Almost 90 percent of Malawians live in rural areas.

Mauritius

Capital	Port Louis
Land Area	784 sq mi; 2,030 sq km
Population	1.2 million
Ethnic Group(s)	Indo-Mauritian, Creole, Sino-Mauritian, Franco-Mauritian
Religion(s)	Hindu, Roman Catholic, Muslim, Protestant
Government	parliamentary democracy
Currency	Mauritian rupee
Leading Exports	iron ore, fish, fish products, gold
Language(s)	English (official), French Creole, Hindi, Urdu, Tamil, Chinese, French

Mauritius (maw RISH ee us) is made up of islands in the Indian Ocean east of Madagascar. The islands were colonized by Portugal in the 1500s. The country was claimed by the Dutch, the French, and the British before it gained independence in 1968. Since that time, it has turned a weak economy based on agriculture into a healthy economy based on manufacturing, banking, and tourism. Mauritius has a stable, democratic government. A majority of the people of Mauritius are descended from Indians who moved to the islands to work on sugar plantations in the 1800s.

Mozambique

Capital	Maputo
Land Area	302,737 sq mi; 784,090 sq km
Population	19.6 million
Ethnic Group(s)	Shangaan, Chokwe, Manyika, Sena, Makha, white, mixed white and black, South Asian
Religion(s)	traditional beliefs, Christian, Muslim
Government	republic
Currency	metical
Leading Exports	prawns, cashews, cotton, sugar, citrus, timber, electricity
Language(s)	Portuguese (official), Makua, Tsonga, Sena, Lomwe

Mozambique (moh zum BEEK) is bordered on the west by South Africa, Zimbabwe, Zambia, and Malawi; on the north by Tanzania; and on the east and south by the Atlantic Ocean. The Zambezi River divides the country into dry savanna in the south and fertile lands in the north. When it gained independence from Portugal in 1975, Mozambique was one of the world's poorest countries. It suffered through civil war from 1977 to 1992. Heavy flooding in 1999 and 2000 made the poor economy even worse. The people of Mozambique are relying on economic aid from other countries and new policies to improve their situation.

Namibia

Capital	Windhoek
Land Area	318,694 sq mi; 825,418 sq km
Population	1.8 million
Ethnic Group(s)	Ovambo, Kavango, Herero, Damara, Nama, Caprivian, Bushman, Baster, Tswana
Religion(s)	Christian, traditional beliefs
Government	republic
Currency	Namibian dollar
Leading Exports	diamonds, copper, gold, zinc, lead, uranium, cattle, fish
Language(s)	English (official), Ovambo, Kavango, Bergdama, German, Afrikaans

Namibia (nuh MIB ee uh) is bordered on the west by the Atlantic Ocean, on the north by Angola and Zambia, on the east by Botswana, and on the south by South Africa. Its land includes both the Namib and Kalahari deserts. Its economy is dependent on mining. Once a German colony, Namibia became part of South Africa after World War I. It became an independent country in 1990. Namibia still suffers from the effects of the system of racial inequality that South Africa imposed on it for decades. Its government and people are working to overcome these effects.

Introducing Central and Southern Africa

São Tomé and Príncipe

Capital	São Tomé
Land Area	386 sq mi; 1,001 sq km
Population	170,372
Ethnic Group(s)	mixed white and black, angolares, forros, servicais, tongas, white
Religion(s)	Christian
Government	republic
Currency	dobra
Leading Exports	cocoa, copra, coffee, palm oil
Language(s)	Portuguese (official), Portuguese Creole

São Tomé and Príncipe (sow toh MEE and PRIN suh pea) is made up of islands in the Gulf of Guinea, west of Gabon. The Portuguese discovered the uninhabited islands in the 1400s. They immediately built plantations and imported slaves to grow the islands' major resource, sugar cane. The islands began exporting coffee and cocoa in the 1800s. The nation gained independence in 1975. The first free elections were held in 1991. Although a poor country, São Tomé and Príncipe has very fertile land and is working to diversify its crops. It is also hoping to make use of oil reserves located in the Gulf of Guinea.

South Africa

Capital	Pretoria, Cape Town, Bloemfontein
Land Area	471,008 sq mi; 1,219,912 sq km
Population	43.6 million
Ethnic Group(s)	black, white, mixed white and black, South Asian
Religion(s)	Christian, traditional beliefs
Government	republic
Currency	rand
Leading Exports	gold, diamonds, platinum, other metals and minerals, machinery and equipment
Language(s)	Afrikaans, English, Ndebele, Pedi, Sotho, Swazi, Tsonga, Tswana, Venda, Xhosa, Zulu (all official)

South Africa (sowth AF rih kuh) occupies the southern tip of the African continent. With a wealth of natural resources, including gold and diamonds, it has the continent's strongest economy. Ruled by the Dutch in the 1800s and by the British in the 1900s, South Africa became independent in 1931. From that time until 1990, the country was known for apartheid, a harsh political system under which the races were separated from each other and discrimination against nonwhites was the law. After years of struggle, nonwhites won equality in 1994, when apartheid ended. The country then focused on healing the wounds of the past.

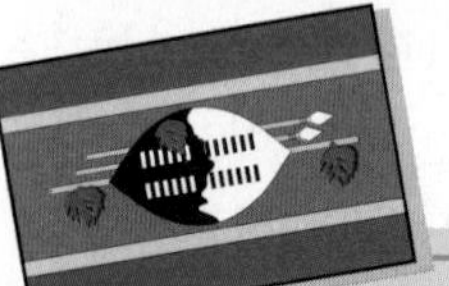

Swaziland

Capital	Mbabane
Land Area	6,642 sq mi; 17,203 sq km
Population	1.1 million
Ethnic Group(s)	black, white
Religion(s)	Christian, traditional beliefs, Muslim, Jewish
Government	monarchy
Currency	lilangeni
Leading Exports	soft drink concentrates, sugar, wood pulp, cotton yarn, fruit
Language(s)	English (official), siSwati (official), Zulu, Tsonga

Swaziland (SWAH zee land) is a small country that is surrounded by South Africa and Mozambique. More than 95 percent of the population belongs to the Swazi ethnic group. Swaziland gained independence from Great Britain in 1968. The country has a very diversified economy. Because it is landlocked, Swaziland depends mainly on South Africa to move goods in and out of the country. Swaziland is ruled by a king. However, many Swazis have been pressuring the government for democratic reforms, such as having a multiparty political system.

Zambia

Capital	Lusaka
Land Area	285,994 sq mi; 740,724 sq km
Population	10.1 million
Ethnic Group(s)	black, white
Religion(s)	Christian, Muslim, Hindu, traditional beliefs
Government	republic
Currency	Zambian kwacha
Leading Exports	copper, cobalt, electricity, tobacco, flowers, cotton
Language(s)	English (official), Bemba, Nyanja, Tonga, Kaonde, Lunda, Luvale, Lozi

Zambia (ZAM bee uh) is bordered on the west by Angola, on the north by the Democratic Republic of the Congo and Tanzania, on the east by Malawi and Mozambique, and on the south by Zimbabwe. Once a British colony called Northern Rhodesia, Zambia became independent in 1964. For decades, Zambia was under the rule of a single political party. In recent years, it has succeeded in establishing a multiparty democracy. Zambia's economy depends heavily on copper, which has made Zambia prosperous. However, falling copper prices have created serious economic problems.

Zimbabwe

Capital	Harare
Land Area	149,293 sq mi; 386,670 sq km
Population	11.3 million
Ethnic Group(s)	Shona, Ndebele, Asian, white
Religion(s)	Christian, traditional beliefs, Muslim
Government	parliamentary democracy
Currency	Zimbabwe dollar
Leading Exports	tobacco, gold, ferroalloys, textiles, clothing
Language(s)	English (official), Shona, Ndebele

Zimbabwe (zim BAHB way) is bordered on the west by Botswana and Zambia, on the north by Zambia, on the north and east by Mozambique, and on the south by South Africa. Once the British colony of Southern Rhodesia, Zimbabwe gained independence in 1980. Since then, the country has worked to overcome racial inequality and a troubled economy. Zimbabwe has many rivers and lakes that provide transportation, hydroelectric power, and irrigation. Along with Zambia, it is home to the world-famous Victoria Falls.

SOURCES: DK World Desk Reference Online; CIA World Factbook Online, 2002; *The World Almanac,* 2003

Assessment

Comprehension and Critical Thinking

1. Compare and Contrast Compare and contrast the economies of these countries.

2. Summarize What are some characteristics that most of the countries share?

3. Analyze Information What are some key differences among the countries?

4. Infer What can you infer about a country such as South Africa that has eleven official languages?

5. Predict How do you think life in the countries that have no borders on the ocean is different from life in the ones that do?

6. Make a Bar Graph Create a bar graph showing each language that is an official language in this region and how many countries speak that language.

Keeping Current

Access the **DK World Desk Reference Online** at **PHSchool.com** for up-to-date information about all 20 countries in this chapter.

Web Code: **lae-5700**

Section 1

Democratic Republic of the Congo A Wealth of Possibilities

Prepare to Read

Objectives

In this section you will

1. Discover the physical geography and important natural resources of the Democratic Republic of the Congo.
2. Learn about the country's economic and political challenges since independence.
3. Find out how different groups and leaders have reshaped the nation.

Taking Notes

Copy the outline below. As you read this section, look for details about the geography, natural resources, economics, and politics of the Democratic Republic of the Congo. Use the outline to record your findings.

I. Physical geography and resources
A. Geographic regions
1. ______________
2. ______________
B. Natural resources

Target Reading Skill

Understand Sequence A sequence is the order in which a series of events occurs. Noting the sequence of important events can help you understand and remember the events. You can track a sequence of events by simply listing the events in the order in which they happened. As you read this section, list the sequence of events in Congo's political history.

Key Terms

- **authoritarian government** (uh thawr uh TEHR ee un GUV urn munt) *n.* a nondemocratic form of government in which a single leader or a small group of leaders has all the power
- **nationalize** (NASH uh nuh lyz) *v.* to transfer ownership of something to a nation's government

An open-pit copper mine in Congo

Copper has been mined in the present-day Democratic Republic of the Congo since ancient times. In the early 1900s, demand for copper brought Europeans to the area. In 1930, a mining company found copper in an area called Kolwezi (kohl WAY zee). The company built a mine and hired miners and a host of other workers. Soon a small city of workers' houses arose. Meanwhile, miners started to dig down into the earth for the copper. They found it, too—right beneath their houses.

The Kolwezi area proved so rich in copper that, at first, miners found they barely had to scratch the surface to find the mineral. As time went on, however, the miners had to dig deeper. Soon they had dug a huge pit in the ground. They built terraces along the sloping walls of the pit. Then they mined each terrace, in a process called open-pit mining. Miners still dig for copper at the Kolwezi mine today.

Physical Geography and Resources

Since the 1930s, the Democratic Republic of the Congo has become one of the world's main sources of copper. Congo, as the country is often referred to, also has many other natural resources. These include gold, diamonds, forests, water, and wildlife. Congo's minerals and other resources have played an important role in the nation's history. (The country's neighbor, the Republic of the Congo, is also referred to as Congo. In this section, all references to Congo are to the Democratic Republic of the Congo.)

Geographic Regions The Democratic Republic of the Congo is Africa's third-largest country. It is equal in size to the area of the United States east of the Mississippi River. The country has four major geographic regions: the Congo basin, the northern uplands, the eastern highlands, and the southern uplands.

The Congo basin is covered by dense rain forest. Most Congolese (kahng guh LEEZ) live in the other three regions. The northern uplands, which run along the country's northern border, are covered in savanna. Grasslands and occasional thick forests spread across the eastern highlands. The southern uplands are high plains of grasslands and wooded areas. In each of these three regions, many people make a living as subsistence farmers.

Natural Resources About two thirds of Congo's people are farmers. However, mining produces most of the country's wealth. The Kolwezi and other huge copper deposits exist in the southern province of Katanga (kuh TAHNG guh). Congo is one of the top producers of diamonds in the world. It also has reserves of other valuable minerals such as gold. In addition, Congo has the potential to develop many hydroelectric plants. These are plants that use swiftly flowing river water to generate electricity.

Links to Science

From Water to Electricity At a hydroelectric plant, electricity is generated by flowing water. For that reason, these plants are usually built at the bottom of a dam. Water that collects behind the dam flows through turbines, which change the energy of the moving water into electricity. The water is not used up in the process—it continues to flow and can be used again for agriculture and other purposes. A large hydroelectric dam (below) sits on Inga Falls, along the Congo River.

Natural Resources in Congo's History Natural resources have dominated much of the history of the Democratic Republic of the Congo. For example, by the 1400s, the kingdoms of Kongo, Luba, and Lunda ruled much of the area. These kingdoms became powerful largely because they had fertile soil and plentiful rain and their people made iron tools that enabled them to farm more productively. Similarly, when the Portuguese arrived in the area in the 1480s, they came in search of a natural resource—gold.

Some 400 years later, during the scramble for Africa, King Leopold II of Belgium took control of present-day Congo. He ruled brutally, forcing Africans to harvest wild rubber without paying them. Belgium grew wealthy while Africans suffered, starved, and died, probably by the millions. Later, because of an international campaign to end Leopold's abuses, the Belgian government ruled less harshly. But it maintained its interest in Congo's resources, especially its copper and diamonds.

√ Reading Check **Which industry produces most of Congo's wealth?**

Economic and Political Challenges

In spite of its abundant natural resources, the Democratic Republic of the Congo has faced major economic and political challenges. During the 1900s, both the economy and the government of Congo faced a series of crises.

Congo Gains Independence As you have read, calls for independence echoed throughout the African continent during the mid-1900s. In 1960, the Democratic Republic of the Congo won its independence from Belgium. However, Congo's first years as an independent country proved to be difficult.

Belgium had done little to prepare Congo for self-rule. In addition, various groups fought one another for power. The foreign companies that controlled Congo's mines feared the unrest would hurt business. In 1965, these foreign companies helped a military leader, Joseph Mobutu (muh BOO too), take power. With a strong ruler in control, they thought their businesses would thrive.

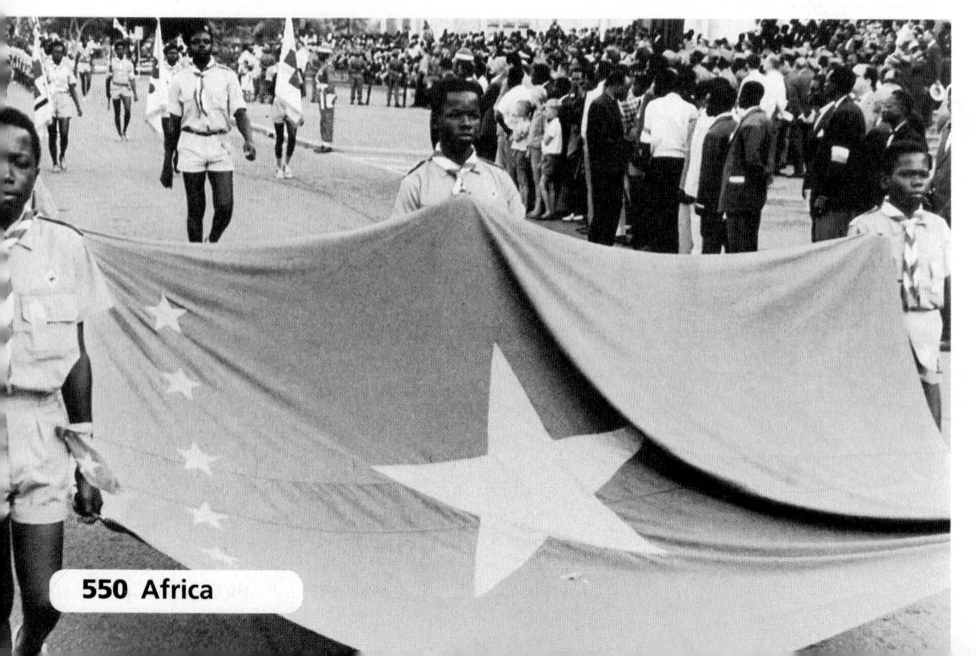

Celebrating Independence
At a celebration of the country's independence in 1960, boys carry the flag of the newly formed Democratic Republic of the Congo.
Predict *How do you think Congolese people felt when their country gained independence?*

Mobutu Makes Changes Mobutu tried to restore order in the country by setting up an **authoritarian government**—a nondemocratic form of government in which a single leader or small group of leaders has all the power. He also tried to cut ties with the colonial past. First, he renamed the country Zaire (zah IHR), a word that has traditional African roots. And he took on a new name for himself, Mobutu Sese Seko (muh BOO too SAY say SAY koh), which he considered more traditionally African. Then he nationalized foreign-owned industries. To **nationalize** is to transfer ownership to the government.

Target Skill **Understand Sequence** What important events led up to Mobutu's establishing an authoritarian government?

COUNTRY PROFILE Focus on Economics

Democratic Republic of the Congo

Congo's natural resources play a key role in its economy. The country's total earnings from exports in 2002 were around $1.2 billion. Minerals alone made up about 85 percent of those earnings, as they have in most recent years. Most of the economy's diversity comes from the variety of minerals produced. However, Congo does not use all of its natural resources. Thus, the country has potential for greater economic success. Study the map and charts to learn more about Congo's natural resources and economy.

Export Destinations

Destination	Percent of Total Exports
Belgium	64
Finland	4
Italy	3
India	3
Other	7
United States	19

SOURCE: *DK World Desk Reference*

Estimated Income From Mining, 2001

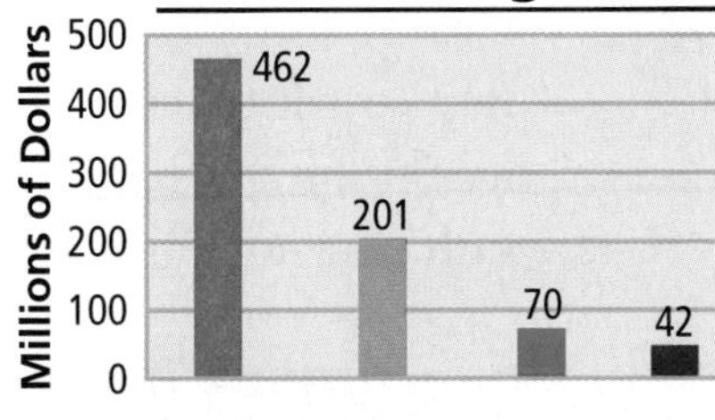

SOURCE: The Economist Intelligence Unit's *Country Profile 2003*

Map and Chart Skills

1. **Name** Which two countries buy most of Congo's exports?
2. **Identify** Which mineral earns the most income for Congo?
3. **Infer** How does the map support the idea that Congo has greater potential for using its natural resources?

Use Web Code **lae-5701** for **DK World Desk Reference Online.**

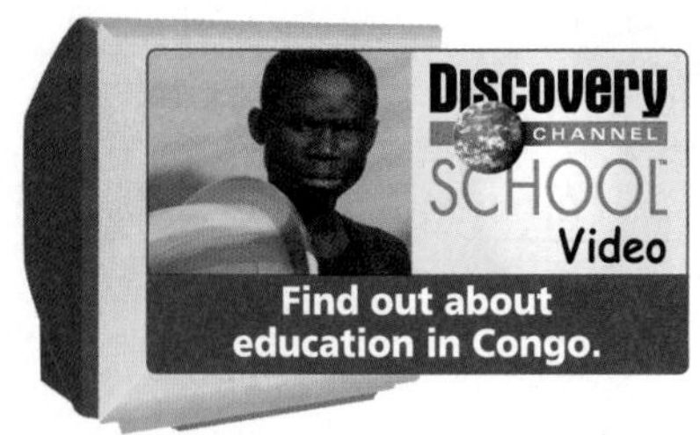

Discovery
CHANNEL
SCHOOL
Video
Find out about education in Congo.

Mobutu also borrowed money from foreign countries, such as the United States, for projects to improve Zaire's economy. But most of Mobutu's economic moves failed. Many government officials who ran the nationalized companies proved to be poor managers. Others stole their companies' profits. Mobutu and his supporters, too, kept much of Zaire's wealth for themselves.

Crisis In the mid-1970s, the world price of copper fell sharply. Suddenly Zaire was earning less and less from its major export. It could not pay back the money it had borrowed, and the economy quickly collapsed. Mobutu responded by cutting the amount of money spent by the government. The cutbacks caused hardship, especially for Zaire's poorest people. Fewer jobs were available, so many people could not earn a living. When political groups challenged Mobutu's policies, Mobutu crushed their efforts. He had many of his opponents imprisoned or killed.

✓ Reading Check **Why did Mobutu change the country's name?**

Reshaping the Nation

Throughout the 1980s, Mobutu ruled harshly, and Zaire's economy continually declined. Calls for reform came from inside and outside the country. In the early 1990s, Mobutu's grip on the country finally began to weaken.

Rebellion Against Government In 1996, a minor uprising began in eastern Zaire. A small ethnic group fought with the government's troops. The neighboring countries of Uganda, Rwanda, and Burundi supported the small group. With their help, the uprising turned into a rebellion against Mobutu's government. Zaire's army was unable to put down the rebellion.

Within months, the rebels gained control of much of eastern Zaire. By May 1997, the rebel army began closing in on the capital, Kinshasa. Alarmed, Mobutu fled to Morocco. He died there four months later. A leader of the rebel army, Laurent Kabila (law RAHN kuh BEEL uh), became the new president.

Showing Culture in Currency
The upper bill was printed while the name of the country was Zaire. The lower bill was printed after the name became the Democratic Republic of the Congo. **Analyze Images** *What aspects of the Congo are represented by the images on these bills?*

A New Government Takes Hold The rebel army soon controlled the whole country, which Kabila renamed the Democratic Republic of the Congo. Kabila vowed to establish a new constitution and hold national elections. But months went by without the promised reforms. Criticism quickly erupted. By early 1998, popular support for the new government was fading.

Rwandan President Paul Kagame (left) and Joseph Kabila sign peace agreements in 2002.

A Second Rebellion In August 1998, another armed rebellion began, this time against Kabila's government. Supported by Uganda and Rwanda, the new rebels threatened to overthrow the government. Angola, Namibia, and Zimbabwe backed Kabila's government. The civil war continued month after month.

Peace and Reform The war in Congo was the first war in post-independence Africa to involve several African nations. In July 1999, the heads of six of these countries met in Zambia to write a peace agreement. However, neither side fulfilled the agreement. Hostilities continued into 2001, when Kabila was killed. His son, Joseph Kabila, became president.

The younger Kabila began making significant reforms. He implemented programs to revive the economy. He replaced many corrupt government officials with well-trained officials. He also allowed the United Nations to send peacekeeping troops to Congo. By the end of 2002, many of the disagreements over the terms of peace had been settled. However, small conflicts did continue in the eastern part of the country. Congo has found that the path to peace is neither smooth nor easy.

✓ Reading Check **How was Congo's civil war unique for Africa?**

Section 1 Assessment

Key Terms
Review the key terms at the beginning of this section. Use each term in a sentence that explains its meaning.

Target Reading Skill
Place these events in the correct order: Joseph Kabila becomes president, a rebellion begins, a peace agreement is written.

Comprehension and Critical Thinking
1. (a) List What are some of Congo's natural resources?
(b) Analyze Information What role have these resources played in Congo's history?
2. (a) Describe What changes did Joseph Mobutu make in Congo?
(b) Evaluate What factors prevented Mobutu from bringing stability to Congo?
3. (a) Recall What caused Mobutu to flee the country?
(b) Summarize Once Laurent Kabila became president, how did the civil war in Congo change?
(c) Draw Conclusions In what ways has Joseph Kabila brought positive change to Congo?

Writing Activity
Suppose you are an editor for a newspaper. Write an editorial explaining the challenges Congo has faced and predicting how the country will overcome those challenges once peace returns to the nation.

Writing Tip Be sure to state the opinion you are explaining in your editorial. Then use details to support your opinion.

Analyzing Primary Sources

You have probably played the "telephone game." One person makes up a statement and whispers it to the next person. That person whispers it to the next person, and so on. As the statement is passed along, people do not always hear it correctly and it gets confused. By the end, it might not make any sense. If a sentence can get distorted in a matter of minutes, think what can happen to a sentence uttered by someone hundreds of years ago! That is one reason why primary sources are important.

Examples of primary sources

A primary source is information that comes directly from the person who wrote it, said it, or created it. Diaries, photographs, speeches, and recordings are all examples of primary sources. When information does not come directly from the person who created it, it is a secondary source. Newspapers, history books, and Web sites are examples of secondary sources.

Learn the Skill

Use the steps below to analyze a primary source.

1. **Identify who created the information, when it was created, and why.** Before you use any information, determine the source. Is it a primary source?

2. **Identify the main idea.** Make sure you understand what is being communicated, either in words or in visual form.

3. **Separate facts from opinions.** Facts can be proved or disproved. Opinions indicate personal feelings or judgments. A primary source might contain facts and opinions, and both can be valuable.

4. **Look for evidence of bias, or a one-sided view.** If a person's view is biased, it is influenced by certain factors, such as the person's family, culture, or location.

5. **Evaluate whether the source is reliable and whether it suits your purpose.** For factual evidence, you want a primary source that is believable and accurate. For an opinion, you want one that uses good reasoning.

Practice the Skill

Use the steps below to analyze the source in the box.

1. Read the background information and the quotation. Who is the speaker, and when did he speak these words? Is the quotation a primary source?
2. Write a sentence that summarizes Mandela's main point. What situation is he discussing?
3. Using the background information, identify as many facts and opinions as possible. Overall, is this quotation mostly fact or mostly opinion?
4. Do any parts of Mandela's statement show bias?
5. Would this source be of value if you were writing a history of South Africa? A biography of Nelson Mandela? Explain.

In 1994, democratic elections were held in South Africa for the first time. Never before had all South Africans been allowed to vote. After casting his vote, the man who would be elected president, Nelson Mandela, made this statement:

"This is for all South Africans an unforgettable occasion. It is the realization of hopes and dreams that we have cherished over decades. . . . We are starting a new era of hope, reconciliation [coming together] and nation building. We sincerely hope that by the mere casting of a vote the results will give hope to all South Africans and make all South Africans realize this is our country. We are one nation."

—Nelson Mandela, April 1994

Two women in Johannesburg, South Africa, proudly display the identification papers needed for voting in the historic 1994 election.

Apply the Skill

Read the quotation from the South African constitution on page 556. Follow the steps for analyzing a primary source and answer these questions:

1. What makes the quotation a primary source?
2. What is the main idea?
3. Is the information mostly fact or mostly opinion? Explain.
4. Is the information biased? Explain.
5. For what purpose might you use this source?

Section 2 South Africa
Struggle for Equality

Prepare to Read

Objectives

In this section you will

1. Understand how white rule in South Africa began.
2. Learn about the system of apartheid.
3. Find out how South Africans built a new nation after apartheid.

Taking Notes

As you read this section, look for details about South Africa before, during, and after apartheid. Copy the chart below, and use to it to record your findings.

South Africa		
Before Apartheid	During Apartheid	After Apartheid
• •	• •	• •

Target Reading Skill

Recognize Words That Signal Sequence Signal words point out relationships among ideas or events. To help keep the order of events clear as you read, look for words like *after, then,* and *in 1994* that signal the order in which events took place.

Key Terms

- **apartheid** (uh PAHR tayt) *n.* the legal system of South Africa in which the rights of nonwhites were greatly restricted
- **discriminate** (dih SKRIM ih nayt) *v.* to treat people differently, and often unfairly, based on race, religion, or sex
- **Nelson Mandela** (NEL sun man DEL uh) *n.* black leader of the African National Congress and South Africa's first president after apartheid ended

A choir celebrates the new constitution.

"We, the people of South Africa,
Recognize the injustices of our past;
Honour those who suffered for justice and freedom in our land;
Respect those who have worked to build and develop our country; and
Believe that South Africa belongs to all who live in it, united in our diversity."

—Preamble to the South African Constitution

So begins the constitution of South Africa. It was written in 1996, soon after nearly a century of harsh and unequal treatment of nonwhite South Africans had officially ended. The constitution's words were shaped by South Africans who came from many backgrounds and political parties. As a result, the 1996 constitution represents all South Africans in a new, democratic South Africa.

Beginning of White Rule

People have lived in present-day South Africa for thousands of years. In 1652, the first white Europeans arrived in the region and set up a colony. These Dutch settlers called themselves Boers (bohrz), the Dutch word for farmers. As you read in Chapter 13, the descendants of these settlers called themselves Afrikaners. They spoke a language related to Dutch, called Afrikaans.

British and French settlers arrived in South Africa by the late 1700s. For years, black South Africans fought the white settlers, who took their land. But by the late 1800s, the white settlers had forced the Africans off the best land.

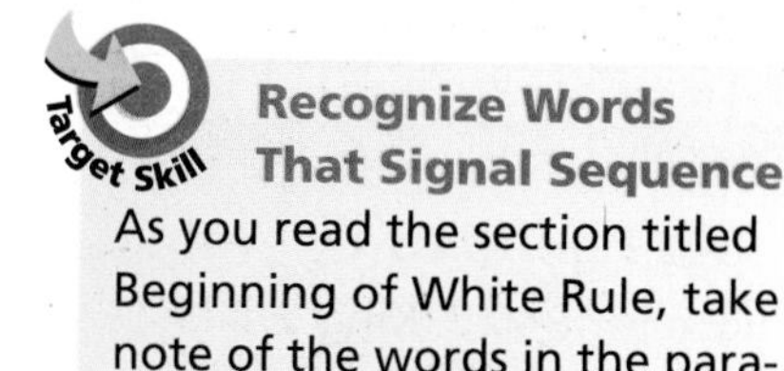

Recognize Words That Signal Sequence
As you read the section titled Beginning of White Rule, take note of the words in the paragraphs that signal sequence.

Cultures Clash The Afrikaners founded their own states. After diamonds and gold were discovered there, the British wanted control of the land. British prospectors, or people who explore for minerals, pushed Afrikaners off their farms.

The British and Afrikaners fought over the Afrikaner land from 1899 to 1902. The British proved victorious and took control of the Afrikaner states. In 1910, the British created the Union of South Africa by unifying all the land they controlled in the region.

Unequal Treatment The white-led government of the Union of South Africa passed several laws to keep land and wealth in white hands. For example, the government declared that blacks could live and own land in only 8 percent of the country. Blacks could work in white areas, but for very low wages. Other laws passed in the 1920s separated white and black workers. The best jobs and the highest wages were reserved for whites.

✓ Reading Check **When did the first white Europeans arrive in present-day South Africa?**

System of Apartheid

The British granted independence to South Africa in 1931. But in 1948, the Afrikaners took political control of the country from the English-speaking whites when the Afrikaner political party, the National Party, won the election.

New Laws Take Hold The new Afrikaner leaders named the system of treating whites and nonwhites by different rules **apartheid** (uh PAHR tayt). In Afrikaans, the word *apartheid* means "apartness." Apartheid laws made it legal to discriminate on the basis of race. To **discriminate** means to treat people differently, and often unfairly, based on race, religion, or sex.

Keeping People Apart
In this image from the apartheid era, a man sits on a bench designated for Europeans (white South Africans) only. **Analyze Images** *How does this image illustrate discrimination?*

Citizen Heroes

Stephen Biko

Born in 1946 in King William's Town, South Africa, Stephen Biko (BEE koh) studied to become a doctor. Instead, he became a South African hero as a leader of the struggle against apartheid. Biko taught that black South Africans could only become free of white rule if they viewed themselves as equal to whites. His ideas influenced thousands of students and adults throughout South Africa. The white-led government imprisoned Biko for his actions. He died in jail in 1977.

The laws separated South Africans into four groups—blacks, whites, coloreds, and Asians. Coloreds were people of mixed race. Asians were mainly people from India. Coloreds and Asians, who together made up 12 percent of the popuation, had a few rights. Blacks, who made up 75 percent of the population, had practically no rights at all.

Effects of Apartheid Apartheid affected every aspect of the lives of black South Africans. It forced thousands of them to move to ten poor, rural, all-black areas called homelands. These homelands had the driest and least fertile land in the country. There, blacks lived in poverty. Apartheid also strengthened existing laws that required all blacks to stay in homelands unless they could prove that whites would benefit from hiring them.

In addition, apartheid denied blacks citizenship rights, including the right to vote. The system kept blacks, coloreds, and Asians in low-paying jobs and put them in poor schools. It barred these groups from white restaurants, schools, and hospitals. In short, apartheid kept whites in control of the country.

Struggle to End Apartheid Many South Africans fought apartheid. Starting in the 1950s, blacks and some whites led peaceful protests against it. Over the following decades, South Africa's police met the protesters with deadly force many times. Thousands of men, women, and children were wounded, killed, or imprisoned. Protests, even peaceful ones, were banned. But the demonstrations continued. Many people were willing to risk everything for freedom.

In the 1970s, countries around the world joined the movement against apartheid. Many nations stopped trading with South Africa or lending it money. South Africa's athletes were banned from the Olympic Games. In 1990, these international pressures began to have an effect. F. W. de Klerk, an Afrikaner who was South Africa's president, led the government in abolishing the apartheid laws.

Legally ending apartheid was a major accomplishment. But much work lay ahead to make a reality of legal equality. In 1994, **Nelson Mandela** became South Africa's first black president and the leader who would fight to create a new, more equal system.

In 1993, Nelson Mandela (left) and F. W. de Klerk (right) together won the Nobel Peace Prize for helping end apartheid.

✓ Reading Check **What happened to South Africans who protested against apartheid?**

COUNTRY PROFILE Focus on Culture

South Africa

South Africa is home to more than 42 million people, and there is a great deal of diversity among them. Numerous black ethnic groups make up about 75 percent of the population. Of these groups, the Zulu and the Xhosa are the largest. The white population includes people of British, Dutch, German, French, and Portuguese descent. Other South Africans are of Indian or mixed descent. Study the map and charts to learn more about the people of South Africa.

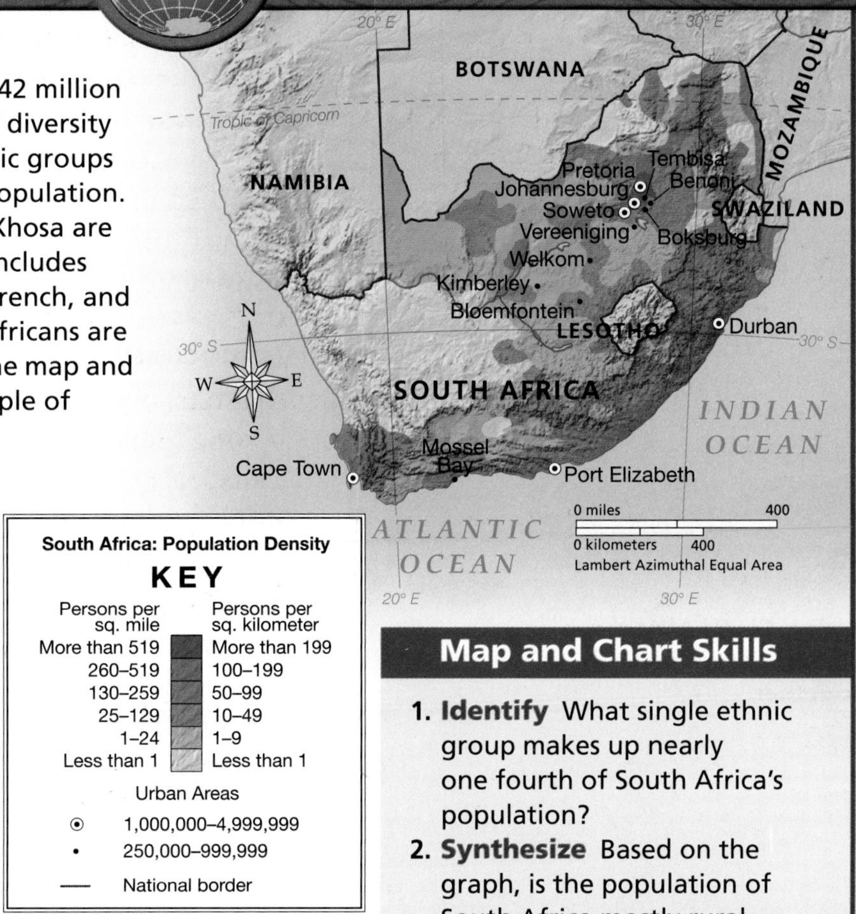

Urban and Rural Population

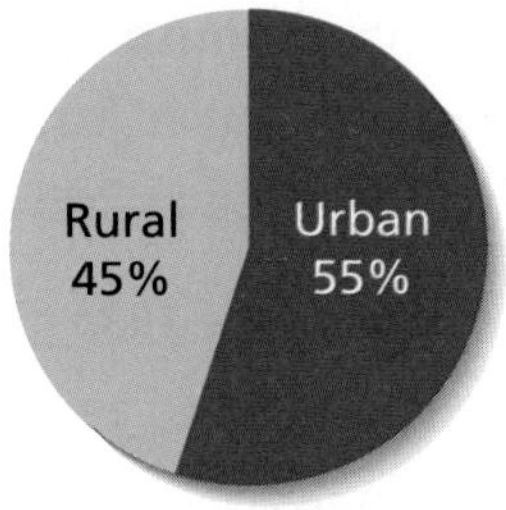

Rural 45%
Urban 55%

SOURCE: *DK World Desk Reference*

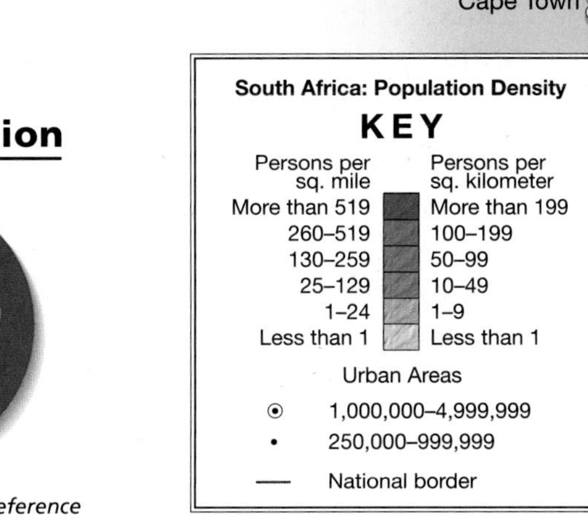

Ethnic Groups

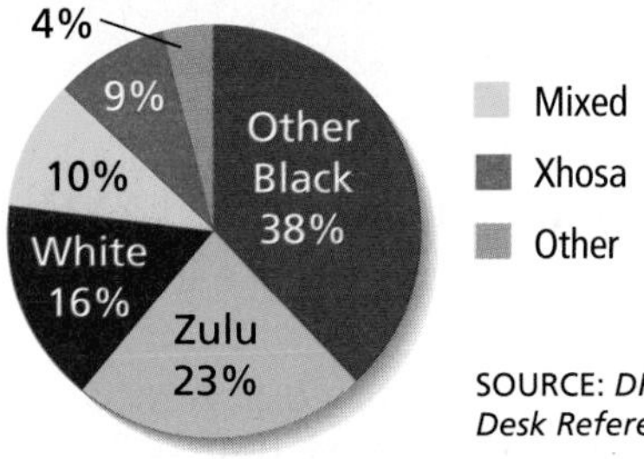

Other Black 38%
Zulu 23%
White 16%
10%
9%
4%

Mixed
Xhosa
Other

SOURCE: *DK World Desk Reference*

Map and Chart Skills

1. **Identify** What single ethnic group makes up nearly one fourth of South Africa's population?
2. **Synthesize** Based on the graph, is the population of South Africa mostly rural, mostly urban, or almost evenly divided between rural and urban? How does the information given on the map support this?

Use Web Code **lae-5702** for **DK World Desk Reference Online.**

Building a New Nation

Since the 1950s, Mandela had been a leader of the African National Congress (ANC), South Africa's first black-led political party. The ANC had long fought for full voting rights for all South Africans. In 1962, Mandela was sent to prison for life for fighting apartheid. After 28 years of public pressure, de Klerk freed Mandela in 1990. Mandela then became president of the ANC. In April 1994, for the first time, all South Africans were allowed to vote. Mandela and the ANC easily won the presidency.

Today, South Africans of all races attend school together.

New Challenges Blacks and some whites welcomed the end of apartheid. In some ways, however, South Africa has remained a divided society. For example, blacks and whites usually live in different neighborhoods, and whites control most of the country's biggest businesses. Still, new opportunities have been created for millions of blacks, and tensions have eased. Mandela's government proved it was committed to helping all citizens, regardless of race. In fact, the constitution that Mandela's government wrote in 1996 is considered a world model for human rights.

Democracy Continues In June 1999, South Africa held its second election in which all South Africans were free to vote. Mandela retired, and Thabo Mbeki (TAH boh em BEK ee), also a long-term leader of the ANC, became South Africa's next president. With the equality movement set into motion by Mandela, Mbeki has been able to focus on other important issues as well. He has put great energy into improving the economic situations of all South Africans. In addition, he has continued to strengthen South Africa's new, democratic government. Mbeki was reelected in 2004.

✓ Reading Check **What was unique about the 1994 election?**

Section 2 Assessment

Key Terms

Review the key terms at the beginning of this section. Use each term in a sentence that explains its meaning.

Target Reading Skill

Review the section titled Struggle to End Apartheid on page 558. Find the words that signal the sequence of events that helped end apartheid.

Comprehension and Critical Thinking

1. (a) **Name** Which groups of white Europeans settled in present-day South Africa?
(b) **Compare** How was the clash between white settlers and black South Africans similar to the clash between the white groups?

2. (a) **Describe** Describe the system of apartheid.
(b) **Draw Conclusions** What do you think it was about the system of apartheid that made the struggle to end it take so long?

3. (a) **Explain** How did apartheid finally end?
(b) **Analyze Information** Why do you think South Africans chose someone who was black as their first president after apartheid?

Writing Activity

Suppose you live in South Africa. Write a letter to a friend explaining your view of the changes that have taken place there. Include details about what has changed as well as how you think people have responded to the changes.

For: An activity on South Africa
Visit: PHSchool.com
Web Code: lad-5702

Chapter 17 Review and Assessment

◆ Chapter Summary

Section 1: Democratic Republic of the Congo

- The Democratic Republic of the Congo is rich in natural resources. These resources have helped shape the country's history.
- From the 1960s to the 1990s, Congo suffered under the authoritarian rule of Joseph Mobutu. It also suffered in the 1970s, when world prices of copper fell.
- During the 1990s, Congo faced civil wars that involved rebels in Congo. A number of neighboring countries also took part in the fighting.

Section 2: South Africa

- The Dutch, the British, and the French settled in South Africa. The British won control of the region and unified its lands as the Union of South Africa in 1910. It became independent in 1931.
- In 1948, the Afrikaners won political control of South Africa and legally established the system of apartheid. Many people who fought against this system were imprisoned, injured, or killed.
- Afrikaner president F. W. de Klerk legally ended apartheid in 1990. Nelson Mandela then became South Africa's first black president. He was followed in office by Thabo Mbeki.

Democratic Republic of the Congo

South Africa

◆ Key Terms

Match the definitions in Column I with the key terms in Column II.

Column I

1. the legal system of South Africa in which the rights of nonwhites were greatly restricted
2. black leader of the African National Congress and South Africa's first president after apartheid ended
3. a nondemocratic form of government in which a single leader or a small group of leaders has all the power
4. to treat people differently, and often unfairly, based on race, religion, or sex
5. to transfer ownership of something to a nation's government

Column II

A authoritarian government
B nationalize
C apartheid
D discriminate
E Nelson Mandela

Review and Assessment (continued)

◆ Comprehension and Critical Thinking

6. **(a) Recall** What important natural resources exist in the Democratic Republic of the Congo?
   (b) Draw Conclusions If mining produces most of Congo's wealth, why do you think so many Congolese are farmers, not miners?
7. **(a) Identify** What kind of government did Joseph Mobutu establish in Congo?
   (b) Draw Inferences How might this form of government have helped cause rebellion?
   (c) Analyze Information What caused the second rebellion in Congo?
8. **(a) Name** What name did Mobutu give his country? What name did Laurent Kabila give it?
   (b) Make Generalizations Why do you think a leader might want to change a country's name?
9. **(a) Recall** When did the system of apartheid in South Africa begin?
   (b) Summarize How did apartheid affect different groups of South Africans?
10. **(a) Define** What was an important form of protest that black South Africans used against apartheid?
    (b) Analyze Information How did the South African government respond to these protests?
11. **(a) Explain** How did the legal end to apartheid come about?
    (b) Draw Conclusions Why was it significant that South Africa's first president after apartheid was not white?
    (c) Predict Now that apartheid is over, do you think that South Africans will stop focusing on racial issues in politics? Explain.

◆ Skills Practice

Analyzing Primary Sources In the Skills for Life activity in this chapter, you learned how to analyze primary sources.

Review the steps you followed to learn this skill. Then reread the quotation from Tanzania's former president, Julius Nyerere, on page 521 of Chapter 16. Explain why the statement was made, what its main idea is, and which details are facts and which are opinions. Then explain whether you can identify any bias based on the background of the speaker.

◆ Writing Activity: History

Choose either South Africa or the Democratic Republic of the Congo. Write a list of five interview questions you would ask someone who has been elected president of the country. Be sure to consider what challenges the new president faces. Then exchange questions with a partner. Pretend that you are the president, and write answers to your partner's questions.

MAP MASTER™ Skills Activity

Central and Southern Africa

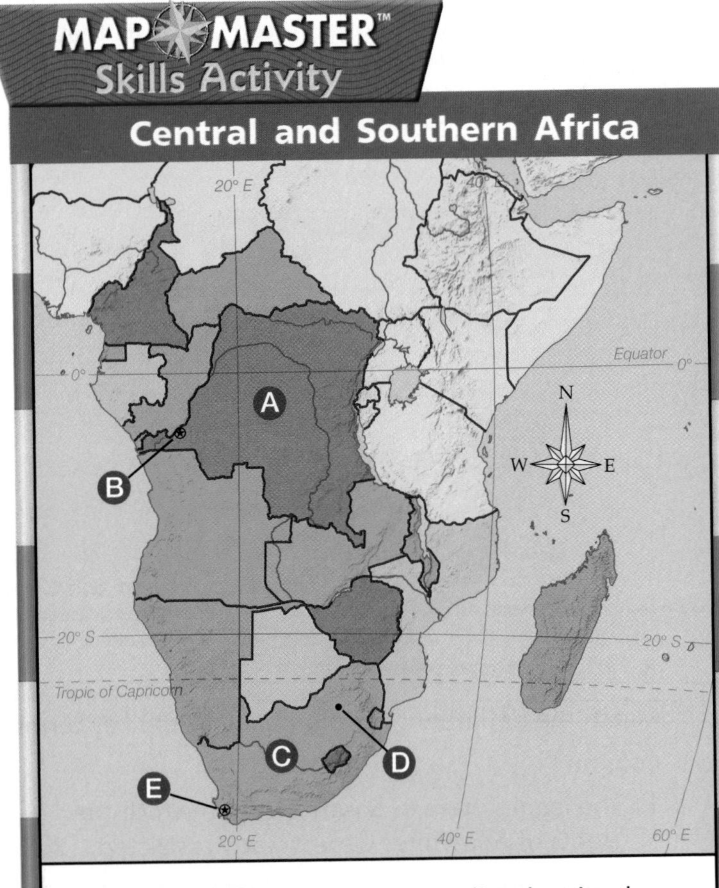

Place Location For each place listed, write the letter from the map that shows its location.

1. Cape Town
2. Johannesburg
3. Kinshasa
4. Democratic Republic of the Congo
5. South Africa

Go Online
PHSchool.com Use Web Code **lap-5720** for an **interactive map.**

Standardized Test Prep

Test-Taking Tips

Some questions on standardized tests ask you to identify a frame of reference. Read the passage below. Then follow the tips to answer the sample question.

> Apartheid separated South Africa into four groups: blacks, whites, coloreds, and Asians. In 1990, apartheid came to an end. In 1994, South Africa elected Nelson Mandela the nation's first black president. Someone hearing the news shouted, "What a happy day. At last my people will have some opportunities. I never believed this would happen in South Africa."

TIP Think about the author's purpose as you read. Is the author trying to give you information, convince you of something, or teach you how to do something?

Pick the letter that best answers the question.

Which onlooker probably made those comments?

A a white businessman who owned a large diamond mine

B a politician in a pro-Afrikaner party

C a black woman living in a rural homeland

D a white woman who left South Africa to protest apartheid

TIP Watch out for careless errors. Be sure you understand the question and consider each answer choice.

Think It Through Start with the author's purpose: to give you information about the end of apartheid. Then ask yourself: Who would be happy about the end of apartheid? You can rule out A and B because neither was denied opportunities under apartheid. That leaves C and D. A white woman who had left South Africa in protest would probably be happy about the end of apartheid but would not say it meant opportunities for *her* people. The correct answer is C.

Practice Questions

Use the passage below to answer Question 1. Choose the letter of the best answer. Use the tips above and other tips in this book to help you answer the following questions.

> "We need a new government. The one we have now does not rule fairly. It is no better than Mobutu's government. Our neighbors in Rwanda and Uganda agree with us. We must make a change."

1. Who would have been most likely to make this statement?

   A Laurent Kabila

   B Joseph Kabila

   C a member of the first rebellion that occurred in eastern Congo

   D a member of the second rebellion that occurred in eastern Congo

2. Which natural resource did NOT play a role in Congo's history?

   A diamonds

   B silver

   C gold

   D rubber

3. When did South Africa become independent?

   A 1910

   B 1931

   C 1948

   D 1990

Use Web Code **laa-5700** for **Chapter 17 self-test.**

Projects

Create your own projects to learn more about Africa. At the beginning of this book, you were introduced to the **Guiding Questions** for studying the chapters and special features. But you can also find answers to these questions by doing projects on your own or with a group. Use the questions to find topics you want to explore further. Then try the projects described on this page or create your own.

1. **Geography** What are the main physical features of Africa?
2. **History** How have historical events affected the cultures and nations of Africa?
3. **Culture** What features help define different African cultures?
4. **Government** What factors led to the development of different governments across Africa?
5. **Economics** What factors influence the ways in which Africans make a living?

Project
HOLD AN AFRICA CONFERENCE

Africa in the 2000s

As you read about Africa, organize a conference for the rest of your school about present-day life in Africa. Decide on several major topics for the conference, such as literature, arts, religion, and agriculture. Then form committees to plan the conference. One committee can plan an agenda, or list of events. Another can research the selected topics and give speeches at the conference. A publicity team can make posters to let students in other classes know about the conference. A press committee can write news reports about the speeches given at the conference.

Project
RESEARCH AFRICAN ART

African Masks

As you study Africa, find out about the tradition of mask-making in African countries. Look through books and magazines for information about different African mask-making traditions. Research the kinds of masks people make, the ways of making them, and the meanings that they have. Prepare a mini-museum display with pictures or sketches and detailed explanations of the masks and traditions you research. You may want to try making a mask of your own as well.

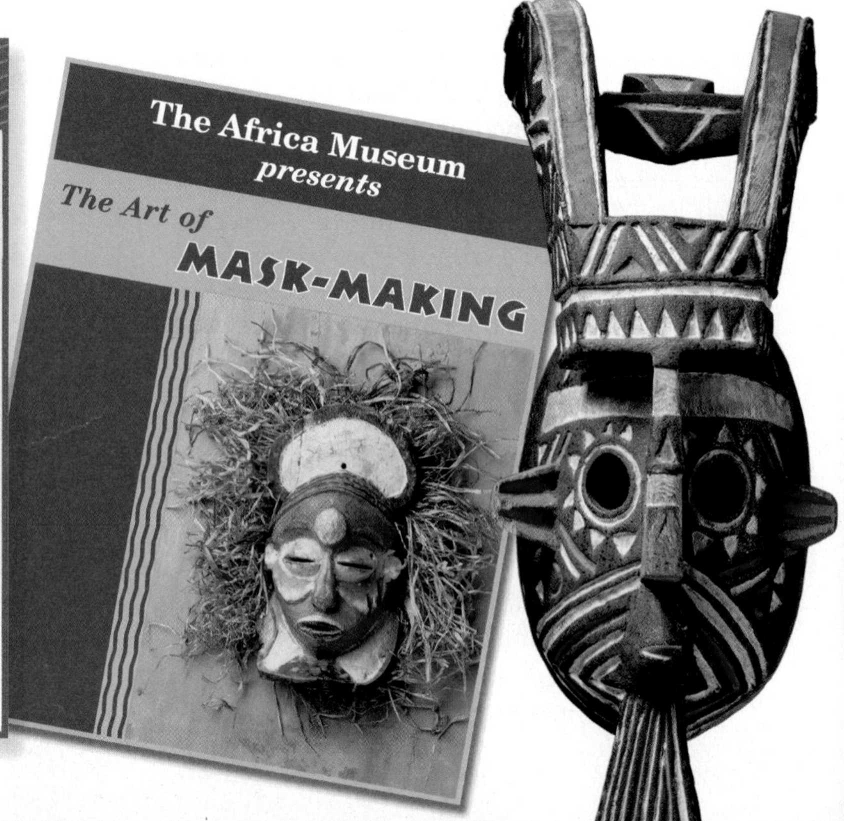

The Africa Museum
presents
The Art of
MASK-MAKING

How to Read Social Studies

 Target Reading Skills

The Target Reading Skills introduced on this page will help you understand the words and ideas in this book and in other social studies reading you do. Each chapter in the Asia and the Pacific section focuses on one of these reading skills. Good readers develop a bank of reading strategies, or skills. Then they draw on the particular strategies that will help them understand the text they are reading.

Chapter 18 Target Reading Skill

Reading Process When you use the reading process, you set a purpose for reading, predict what you are going to read, and ask questions about what you read.

Chapter 19 Target Reading Skill

Clarifying Meaning If you do not understand something right away, you can use several skills to clarify the meaning of words and ideas. In this chapter, you will practice rereading and reading ahead, paraphrasing, and summarizing.

Chapter 20 Target Reading Skill

Main Ideas In this chapter, you will practice these skills: identifying both stated and implied main ideas and identifying supporting details.

Chapter 21 Target Reading Skill

Context Using the context of an unfamiliar word can help you understand its meaning. Context includes the words, phrases, and sentences surrounding a word.

Chapter 22 Target Reading Skill

Word Analysis Word analysis means analyzing a word, or breaking the word into parts to help you recognize and pronounce it. In this chapter, you will analyze words to find roots, prefixes, and suffixes.

Chapter 23 Target Reading Skill

Sequence A sequence is the order in which a series of events occurs. In this chapter, you will practice understanding sequence and recognize words that signal sequence.

Chapter 24 Target Reading Skill

Comparison and Contrast Comparing means examining the similarities between things. Contrasting is looking at differences. In this chapter, you will practice these skills: comparing and contrasting, making comparisons, and identifying contrasts.

Chapter 25 Target Reading Skill

Cause and Effect Identifying cause and effect helps you understand relationships among situations or events. In this chapter, you will practice identifying causes and effects, understanding effects, recognizing multiple causes, and recognizing words that signal cause and effect.

Chapter 26 Target Reading Skill

Main Ideas Focusing on main ideas helps you remember the most important information in what you read. In this chapter, you will have another opportunity to practice identifying main ideas and supporting details.

ASIA AND THE PACIFIC

Asia and the Pacific is a huge region that covers more than one third of Earth's surface. Asia is the largest continent. It includes some of the world's largest and smallest countries. This region also includes the only continent that is also a country—Australia.

Guiding Questions

The text, photographs, maps, and charts in this book will help you discover answers to these Guiding Questions.

1. **Geography** What are the main physical features of Asia and the Pacific?
2. **History** How have ancient civilizations of Asia and the Pacific influenced the world today?
3. **Culture** What are the main characteristics of the cultures of Asia and the Pacific?
4. **Government** What types of government exist in Asia and the Pacific today?
5. **Economics** How do the people of this region make a living?

Project Preview

You can also discover answers to the Guiding Questions by working on projects. Two projects are listed on page 812 of this book.

Investigate Asia and the Pacific Islands

Asia is the largest continent in the world. The vast Pacific Ocean contains thousands of scattered islands and another continent—the country of Australia. The continent of Asia includes part of Russia. However, Russian Asia is not covered in these pages. Because most of Russia's people live in Europe, Russia is discussed with Europe.

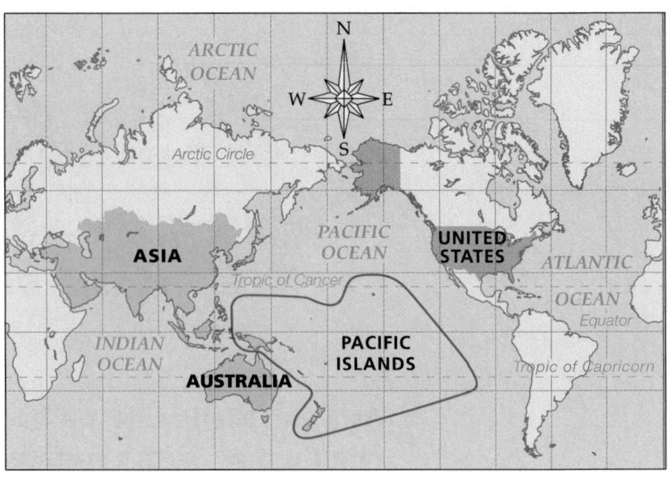

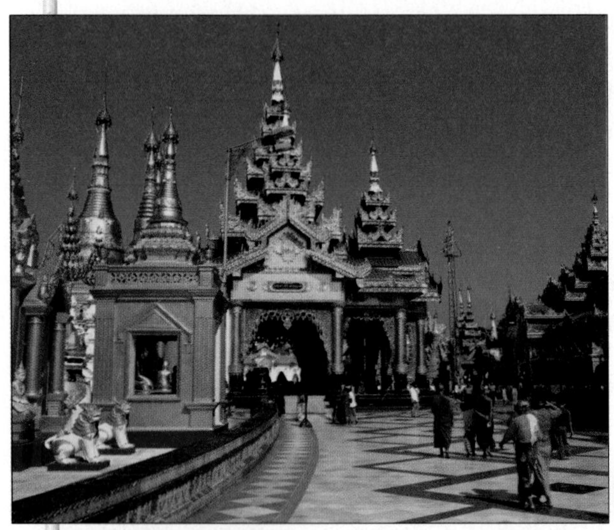

▲ **Myanmar, Asia**
Shwedagon Buddhist Temple, dating from about A.D. 1000.

LOCATION

1 Locate Asia and the Pacific Islands

In this book you will read about Asia, Australia, and the islands of the Pacific Ocean. This region is shaded green on the map above. What ocean lies between Asia and the United States? If you lived on the west coast of the United States, in which direction would you travel to reach Asia? If you lived on the most eastern tip of the Pacific islands, in which direction would you travel to reach the west coast of the United States?

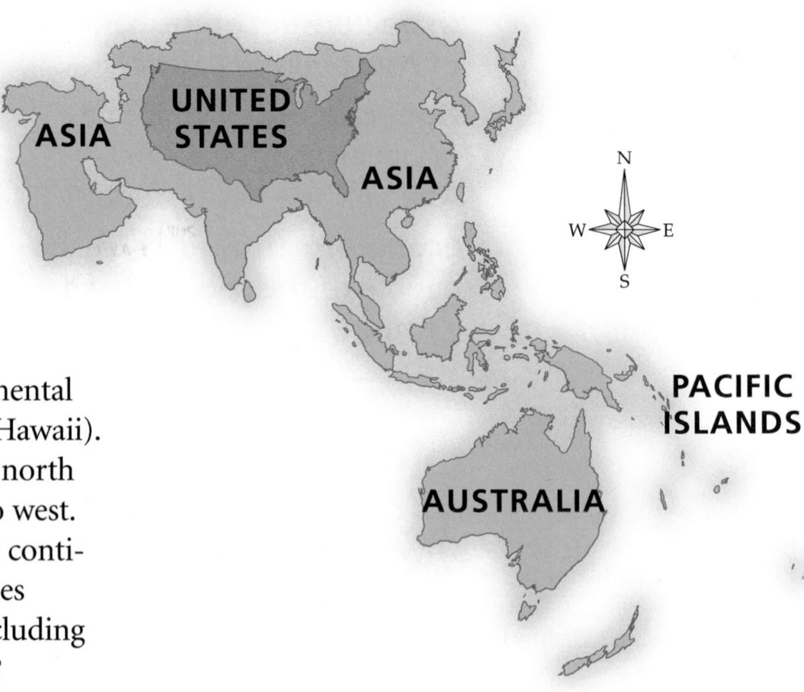

REGIONS

2 Estimate Asia's Size

Compare Asia's mainland to the continental United States (all states except Alaska and Hawaii). With a ruler, measure mainland Asia from north to south. Measure the distance from east to west. Now make the same measurements for the continental United States. About how many times longer and wider is mainland Asia (not including Russia) than the continental United States?

Political Asia

LOCATION

3 Investigate the Countries of Asia

Asia is the largest continent on the Earth. Which Asian country on the map below is the largest? Which country is the second largest? Asia has many countries that are located on islands. Name three of them. Iran is a large country in the western part of Asia. Name three countries that border Iran.

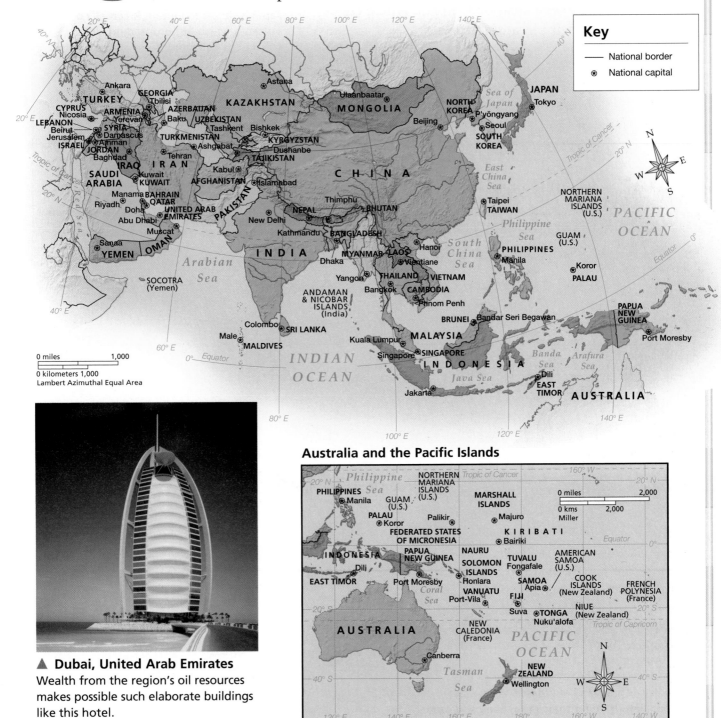

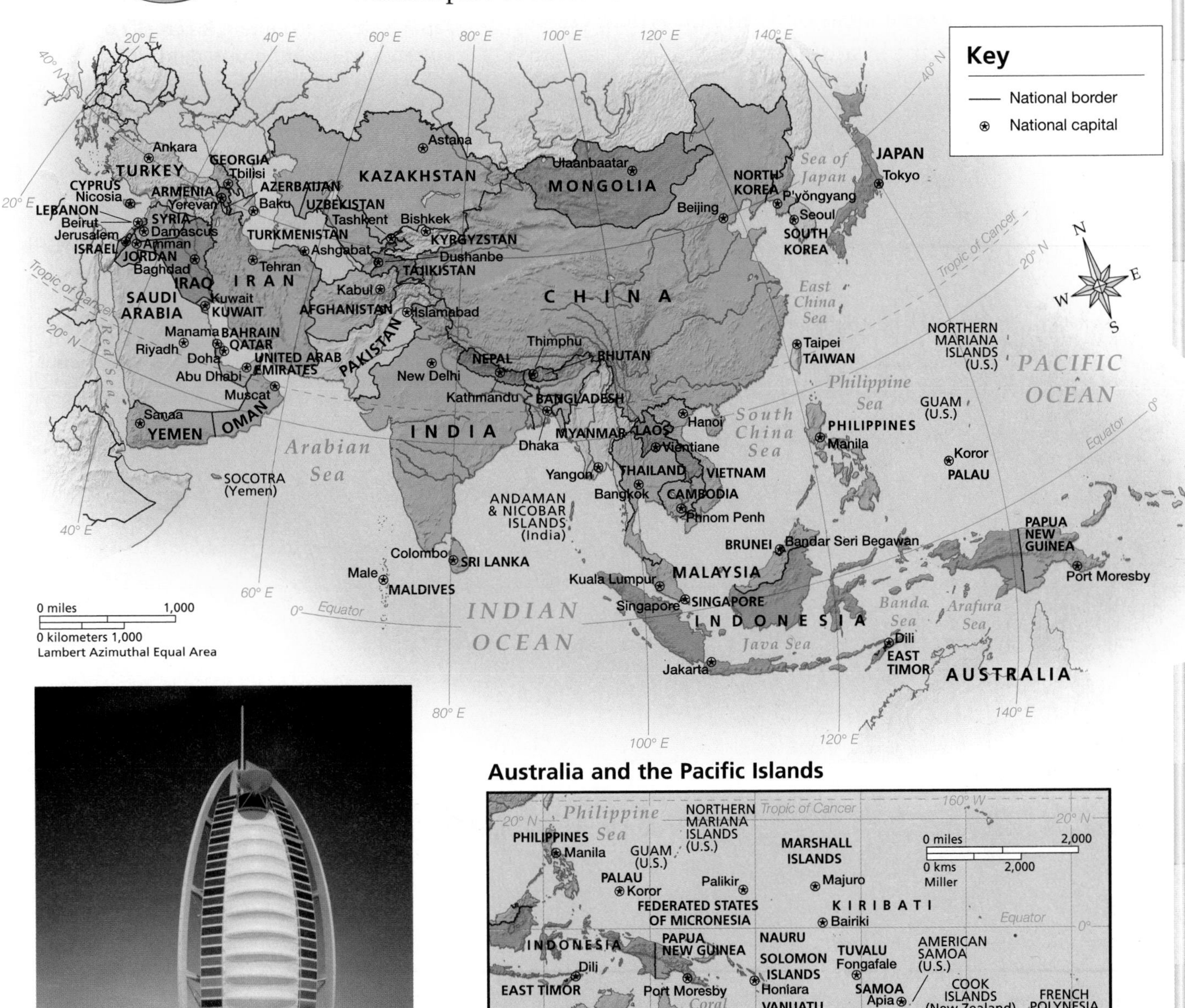

▲ **Dubai, United Arab Emirates**
Wealth from the region's oil resources makes possible such elaborate buildings like this hotel.

Australia and the Pacific Islands

Physical Asia

LOCATION

4 Examine the Physical Features of Asia

Asia is a continent of great physical contrasts, including towering mountains, high plateaus, and low-lying plains. Use the elevation key to identify the highest and lowest areas on the map. Where are they? Describe their physical features.

▲ **Mount Fuji, Japan**
Japan's tallest mountain is actually a volcano, which last erupted in 1707.

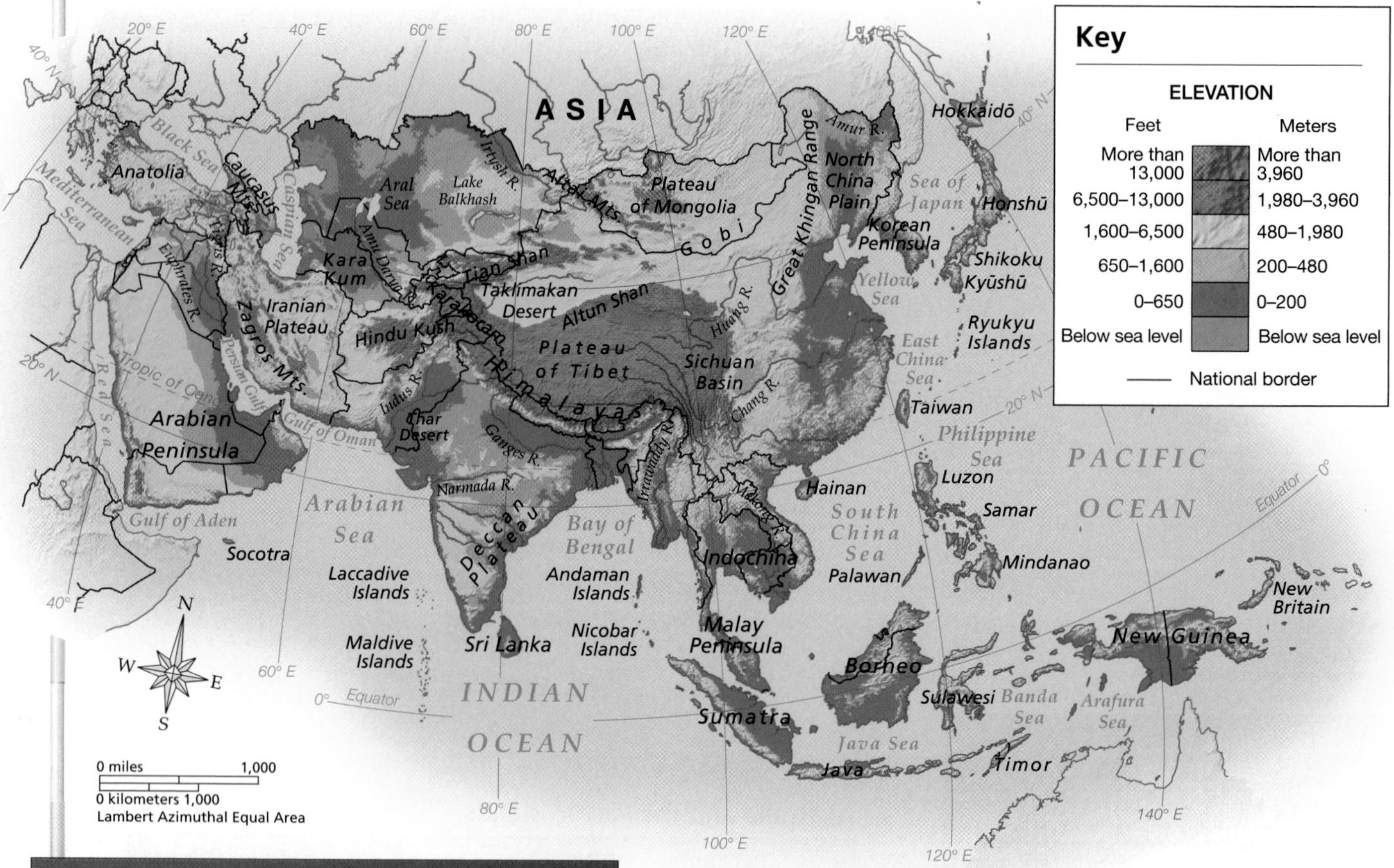

Key

ELEVATION

Feet	Meters
More than 13,000	More than 3,960
6,500–13,000	1,980–3,960
1,600–6,500	480–1,980
650–1,600	200–480
0–650	0–200
Below sea level	Below sea level

—— National border

0 miles 1,000
0 kilometers 1,000
Lambert Azimuthal Equal Area

▲ **Australian Outback**
The outback, in the dry, hot center of the country, is grassland and desert where few people live. Here ranchers raise sheep and cattle.

Australia and the Pacific Islands

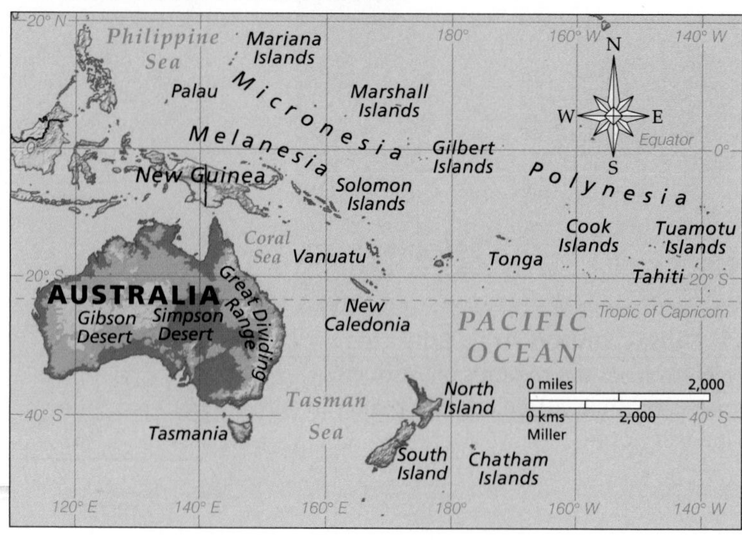

The Ring of Fire

Earth's crust is made up of plates that ride on top of molten earth called magma. The magma escapes in the form of lava when volcanoes erupt. Ninety percent of the world's active volcanoes circle the Pacific Ocean. Look at the map below. Why are these volcanoes described as a "Ring of Fire"?

▲ **Puu Oo Volcano, Hawaii**
The Puu Oo volcano spews molten lava as it erupts. The islands that we call Hawaii are the tops of volcanoes that rest on the ocean floor.

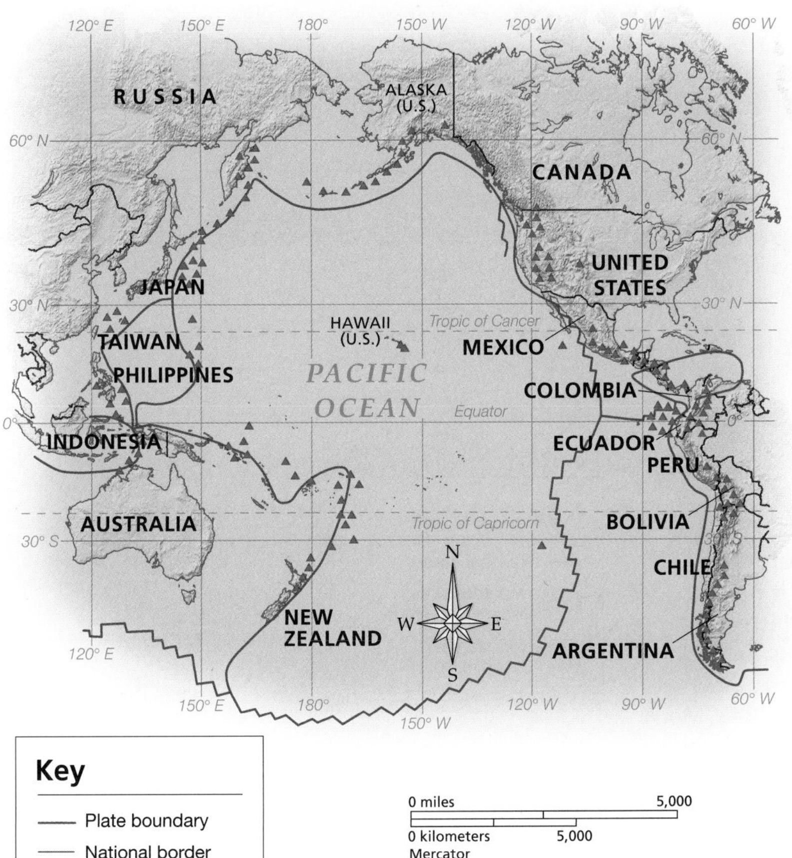

INTERACTION

5 Investigate The Ring of Fire

Where Earth's plates meet, plate boundaries are formed. With your finger, trace the plate boundaries on the map at left. Notice where the volcanoes are located in relation to the plate boundaries. Compare the location of volcanoes to the location of cities on the political map on page 569. Where might volcano eruptions cause the most damage to people?

PRACTICE YOUR GEOGRAPHY SKILLS

1. You begin your boat trip from Australia's north coast and travel west through Indonesia. After you pass Borneo and Java, you cross the Equator and enter a large body of water. What is its name?
2. Today you fly from the Himalayas along the 30° N parallel across the Indus River to the Zagros Mountains. What body of water are you near?
3. There are many volcanoes to the east of this island nation north of the East China Sea. What is the name of this country?

▲ **Boats Moored in Indonesia**

Focus on Countries in Asia

Now that you've investigated the geography of Asia and the Pacific, take a closer look at some of the countries that make up this vast region. The map shows the countries of Asia and the Pacific. The countries that you will study in depth in the second half of this book appear in yellow on the map.

Go Online PHSchool.com Use Web Code **lcp-6000** for the **interactive maps** on these pages.

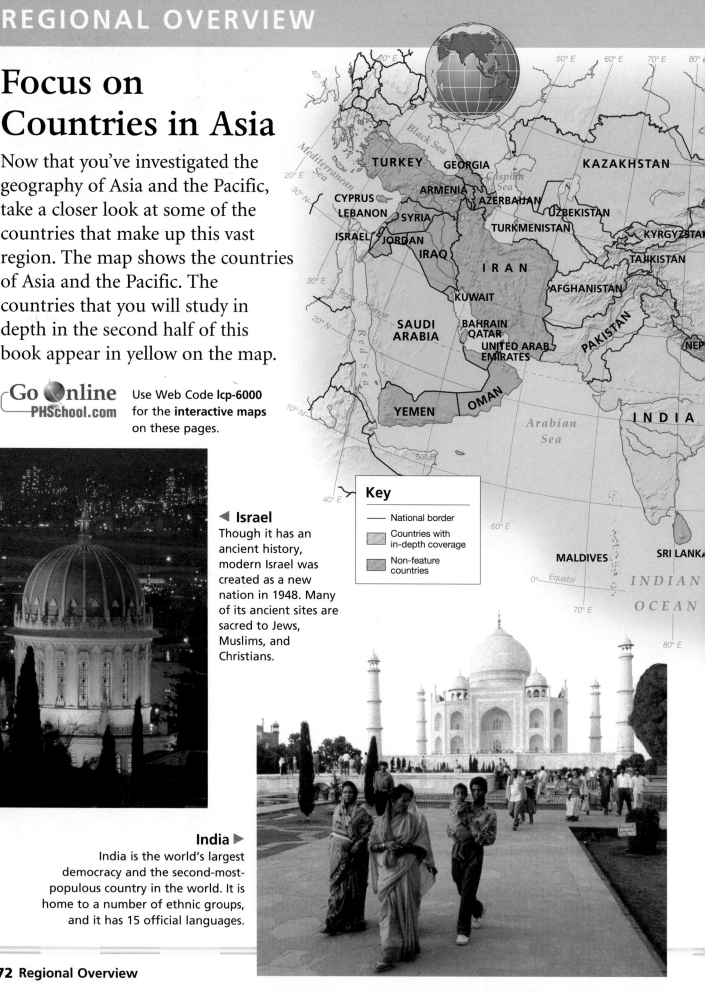

TURKEY
GEORGIA
KAZAKHSTAN
CYPRUS
LEBANON
ARMENIA
AZERBAIJAN
UZBEKISTAN
SYRIA
TURKMENISTAN
ISRAEL
JORDAN
KYRGYZSTAN
IRAQ
TAJIKISTAN
IRAN
AFGHANISTAN
KUWAIT
SAUDI ARABIA
BAHRAIN
QATAR
UNITED ARAB EMIRATES
PAKISTAN
NEPAL
YEMEN
OMAN
INDIA
MALDIVES
SRI LANKA
Black Sea
Mediterranean Sea
Caspian Sea
Red Sea
Arabian Sea
INDIAN OCEAN
Tropic of Cancer
Equator

Key
- National border
- Countries with in-depth coverage
- Non-feature countries

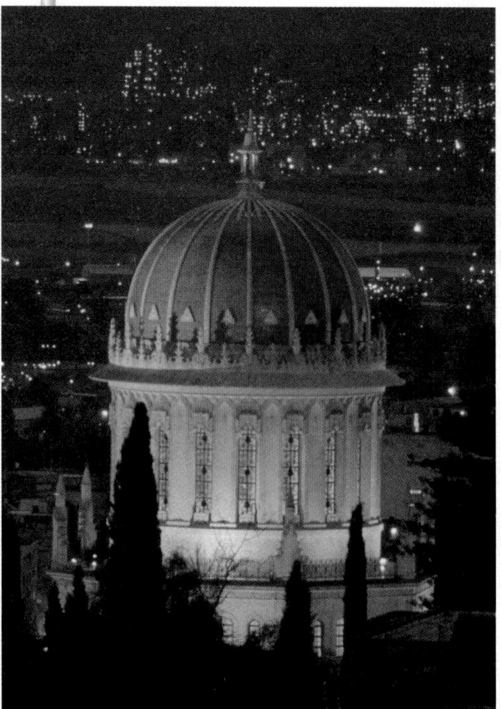

◀ **Israel**
Though it has an ancient history, modern Israel was created as a new nation in 1948. Many of its ancient sites are sacred to Jews, Muslims, and Christians.

India ▶
India is the world's largest democracy and the second-most-populous country in the world. It is home to a number of ethnic groups, and it has 15 official languages.

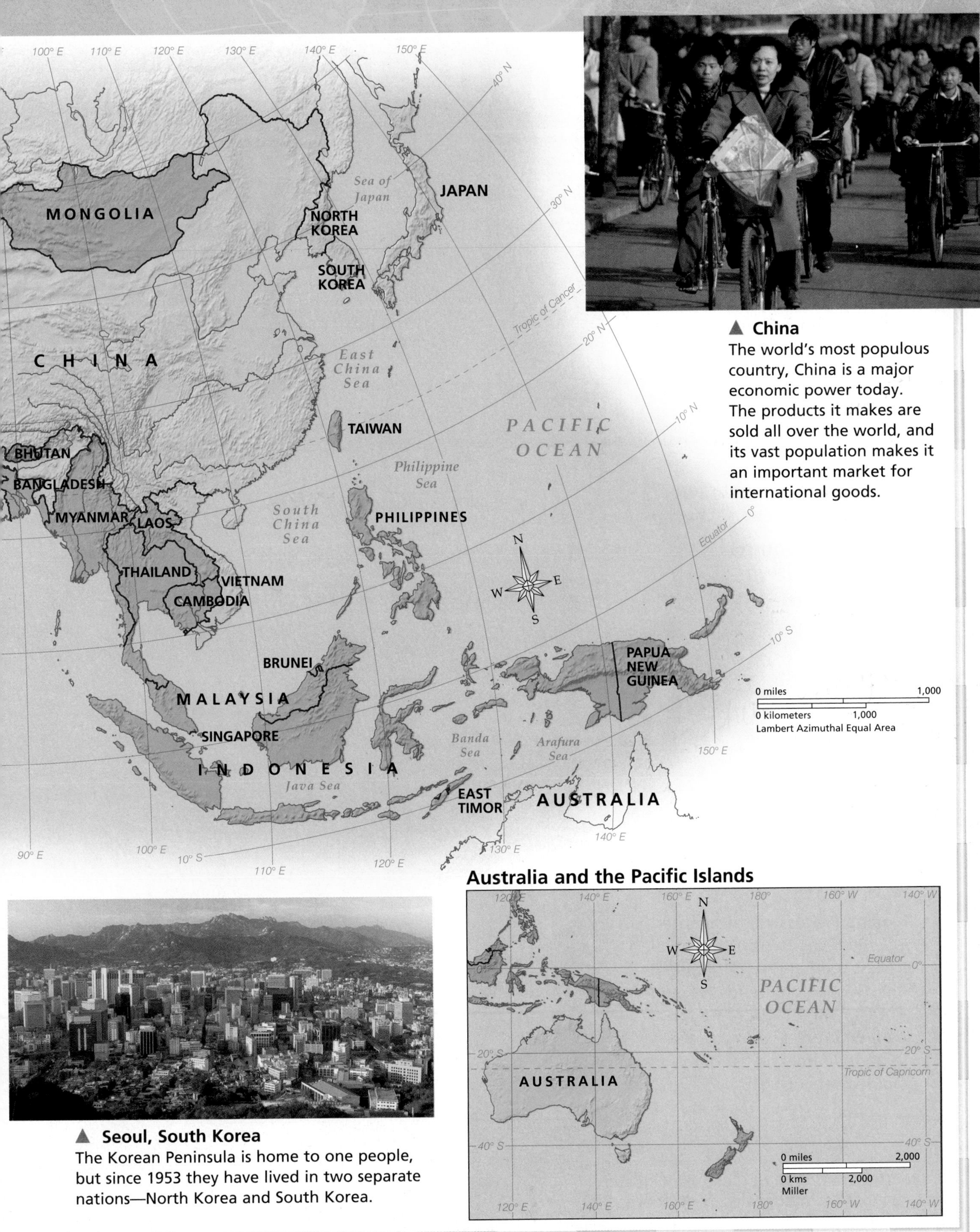

▲ **China**

The world's most populous country, China is a major economic power today. The products it makes are sold all over the world, and its vast population makes it an important market for international goods.

▲ **Seoul, South Korea**

The Korean Peninsula is home to one people, but since 1953 they have lived in two separate nations—North Korea and South Korea.

Chapter 18

East Asia: Physical Geography

Chapter Preview

This chapter will introduce you to the region of East Asia. This region includes China, Mongolia, North Korea, South Korea, Japan, and Taiwan.

Section 1
Land and Water

Section 2
Climate and Vegetation

Section 3
Natural Resources and Land Use

Target Reading Skill

Reading Process In this chapter you will focus on using the reading process to improve your reading skills. When you use the reading process, you set a purpose for reading, predict what you are going to learn, and ask questions about what you read.

▶ The Great Wall of China stretches across the mountains of northern China.

East Asia: Physical

MAP MASTER™ Skills Activity

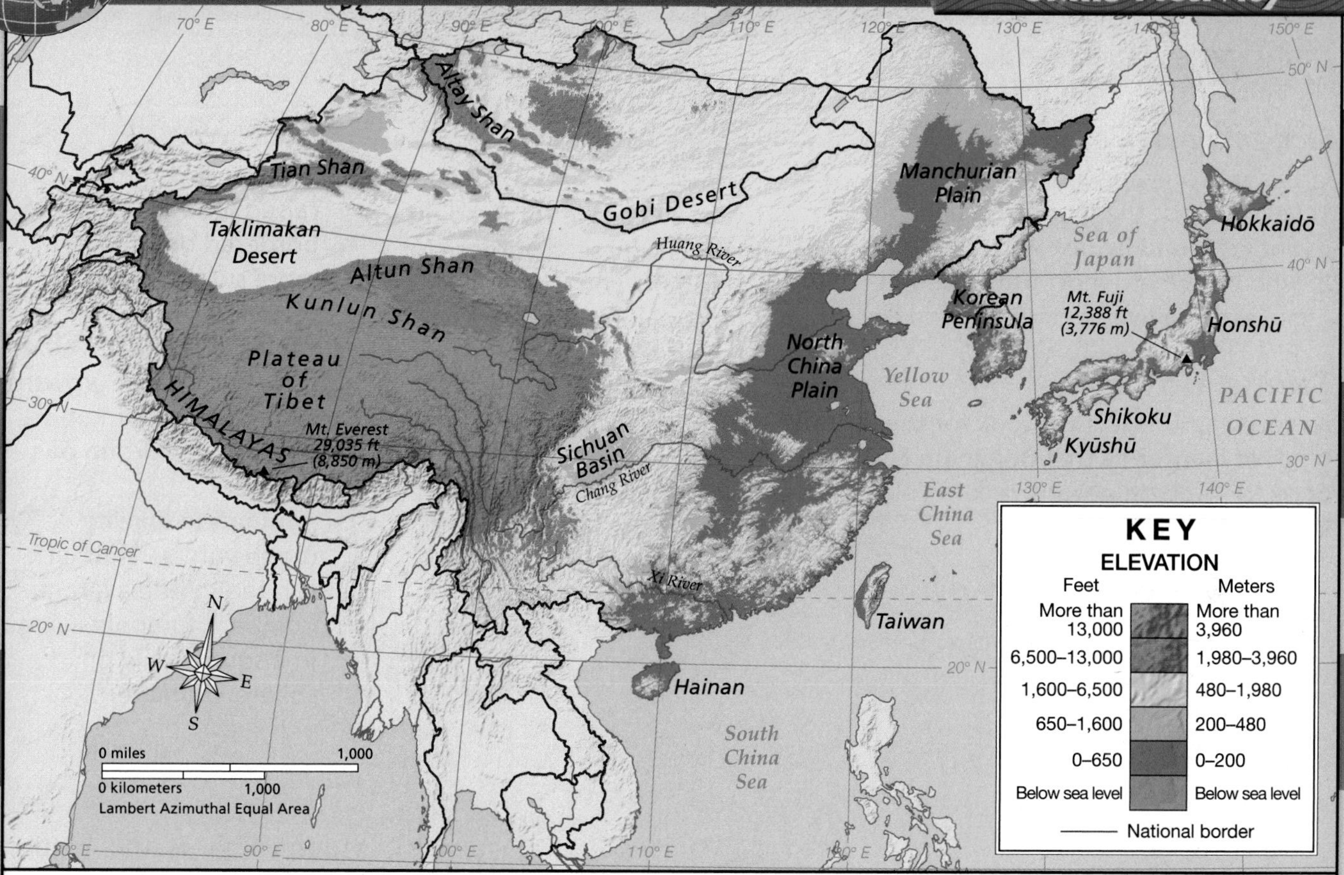

Place Notice that China is by far the largest country in East Asia.
Identify What area of high elevation lies north of the Himalayas?
Draw Conclusions How can you tell that China's greatest rivers, the Chang and the Huang, flow toward the east? Explain your answer.

Go Online PHSchool.com Use Web Code **lcp-6110** for step-by-step **map skills practice.**

Section 1 Land and Water

Prepare to Read

Objectives

In this section you will

1. Learn about the landforms and water bodies found in East Asia.
2. Find out where most of the people in East Asia live.

Taking Notes

As you read this section, look for the different types of landforms that dominate East Asia. Copy the web below and record your findings in it.

Target Reading Skill

Set a Purpose for Reading When you set a purpose for reading, you give yourself a focus. Before you read this section, look at the headings and pictures. Then set a purpose for reading. In this section, your purpose is to learn about the landforms and water bodies of East Asia.

Key Terms

- **plateau** (pla TOH) *n.* a raised area of level land bordered on one or more sides by steep slopes or cliffs
- **fertile** (FUR tul) *adj.* able to support plant growth
- **archipelago** (ahr kuh PEL uh goh) *n.* a group of islands
- **population density** (pahp yuh LAY shun DEN suh tee) *n.* the average number of people living in a square mile or square kilometer

At 12,388 feet (3,776 meters), Mount Fuji is the highest mountain in Japan. Each year, 150,000 to 200,000 people reach its summit. Visitors heading to the top can stay in mountain lodges and browse in souvenir shops that sell canisters of oxygen to make breathing easier at the high altitude.

A view of Mount Fuji, Japan

Landforms and Water Bodies

Mount Fuji is one of the many spectacular landforms that make up East Asia. A single nation, China, takes up most of East Asia's land. Mountains, highlands, and **plateaus,** or raised areas of level land bordered on one or more sides by steep slopes or cliffs, make up much of China's landscape. The other countries of this region are mountainous, like China. But only China and Mongolia also have wide plains and plateaus. Japan, Taiwan, North Korea, and South Korea have narrow plains that lie mainly along coasts and rivers.

The Himalayas Powerful natural forces created the rugged landscape of East Asia. About 50 million years ago, a huge piece of a continent collided with Asia. The collision caused Earth's surface to fold and buckle, forming the Himalayas and the Plateau of Tibet. The Himalayas are the highest mountains in the world. They include Mount Everest, the highest peak in the world. The Himalayas extend along the border of China and Nepal. The Plateau of Tibet is a huge highland area that lies north of the Himalaya mountains.

The Plateau of Tibet
The Plateau of Tibet is a vast, high area in China that includes the region of Tibet. These Tibetan women make their living by herding livestock. **Infer** *The Plateau of Tibet is called "the roof of the world." Why do you think this is so?*

Island Landscapes Natural forces also shaped the islands that make up Japan. Earthquakes forced some parts of the country to rise and others to sink. Erupting volcanoes piled up masses of lava and ash, forming new mountains. Japan's Mount Fuji is actually a volcano that has not erupted since 1707. Today, earthquakes and volcanoes are still changing the landscape in many parts of East Asia.

China: More Than One Billion People China is home to one of the oldest civilizations on Earth. With a population of more than one billion people, it also has more people than any other nation in the world.

Mountains and deserts make up more than two thirds of China's land. A desert is a dry region with little vegetation. The area of western and southwestern China has some of the highest mountains in the world. China's Gobi is the northernmost desert on Earth.

China's most important rivers, the Chang and the Huang, begin in Tibet and flow east. The Chang River is deep enough for cargo ships to sail on. More than 100 million people live along the banks of the Huang River. It runs through one of the most fertile regions of China, the North China Plain. **Fertile** soil is capable of supporting abundant plant growth. The North China Plain is covered with deposits of loess (LOH es), a brownish-yellow soil that is very fertile.

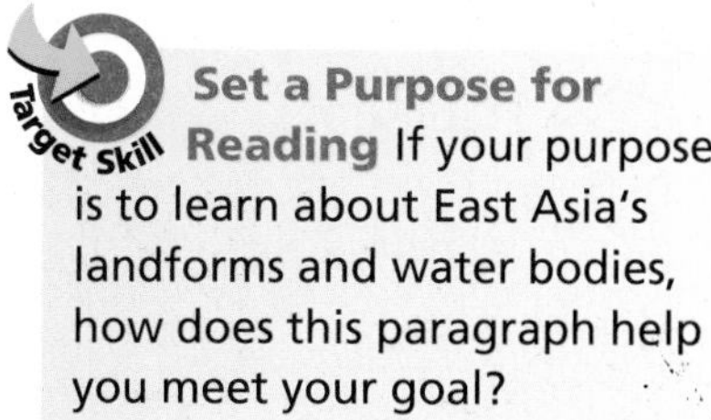

Set a Purpose for Reading If your purpose is to learn about East Asia's landforms and water bodies, how does this paragraph help you meet your goal?

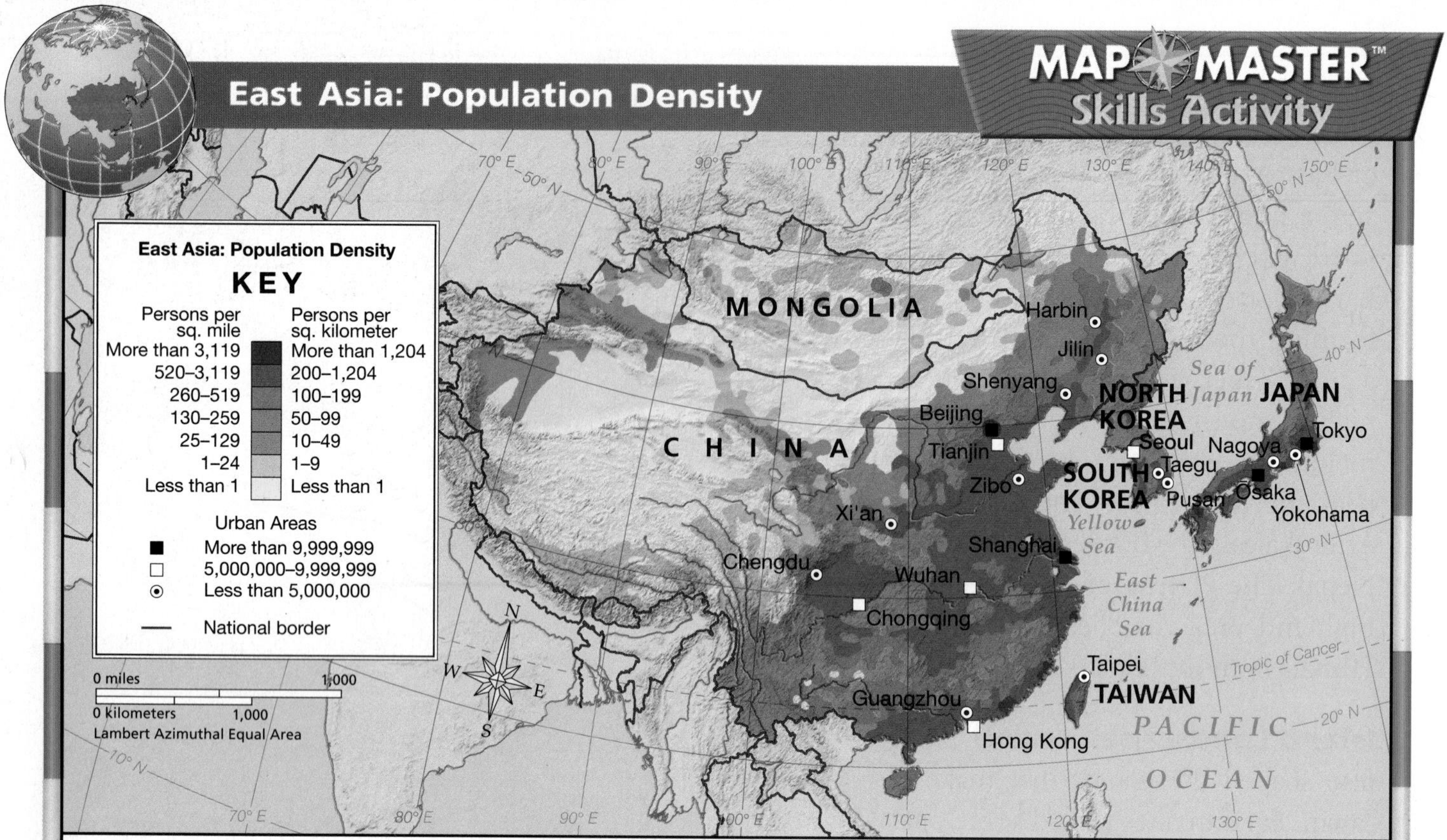

East Asia: Population Density

MAP MASTER™ Skills Activity

East Asia: Population Density

KEY

Persons per sq. mile	Persons per sq. kilometer
More than 3,119	More than 1,204
520–3,119	200–1,204
260–519	100–199
130–259	50–99
25–129	10–49
1–24	1–9
Less than 1	Less than 1

Urban Areas
- ■ More than 9,999,999
- □ 5,000,000–9,999,999
- ⊙ Less than 5,000,000
- — National border

0 miles 1,000
0 kilometers 1,000
Lambert Azimuthal Equal Area

MONGOLIA, CHINA, NORTH KOREA, SOUTH KOREA, JAPAN, TAIWAN, Harbin, Jilin, Shenyang, Beijing, Tianjin, Zibo, Xi'an, Chengdu, Wuhan, Chongqing, Shanghai, Guangzhou, Hong Kong, Taipei, Seoul, Taegu, Pusan, Nagoya, Osaka, Tokyo, Yokohama, Sea of Japan, Yellow Sea, East China Sea, PACIFIC OCEAN, Tropic of Cancer

Place A large number of China's people live in the eastern half of the country. **Use the Map Key** Which color represents the areas with the highest population density? **Compare** Find the North China Plain on the map on page 575. Is the population density of the North China Plain high or low?

Go Online PHSchool.com Use Web Code **lcp-6111 for step-by-step map skills practice.**

Learn about the key geographic features in East Asia.

Japan: An Island Country Japan is an **archipelago** (ahr kuh PEL uh goh), or group of islands, in the western Pacific Ocean. Japan has four main islands and more than 3,000 smaller ones. Every major Japanese city is located on the coast. As the map above shows, most of Japan's people live in coastal areas. Nearly 80 percent of the country is mountainous.

Japan's four main islands are Hokkaidō (hoh ky doh), Honshū (hahn shoo), Shikoku (shee koh koo), and Kyūshū (kyoo shoo). The largest and most populated of these is Honshū. Most of Japan's major cities, including its capital city of Tokyo, are located on Honshū.

The Koreas: Two Countries, One Peninsula The Korean Peninsula extends south into the Yellow Sea between China and Japan. A peninsula is a piece of land nearly surrounded by water. Since 1945, Korea has been divided into two separate countries, North Korea and South Korea.

✓ Reading Check **Which type of landform dominates Japan—mountains or plains?**

Population in East Asia

A crowded street in Seoul, the capital of South Korea

As you can see on the map on the previous page, the population of East Asia is spread unevenly across the land. Few people live in the deserts, plateaus, and mountains. Yet almost 1.5 billion people make their homes in East Asia. Most of the people live in the plains and coastal areas, where living and growing food are easier. These parts of East Asia have a very high **population density,** or average number of people living in a square mile (or square kilometer).

Look at the physical map of East Asia on page 575 and find the North China Plain. Now look at the population density map of East Asia on page 578. You can see that this area of China has a very high population density. That is because the land in the North China Plain is better suited for human settlement than the mountains and deserts of China. For example, the North China Plain is level and has fertile soil.

In East Asia, level ground must be shared by cities, farms, and industries. Almost half the population of Japan is crowded onto less than 3 percent of the country's land. In China, most of the population is located in the eastern half of the country, where the plains and coastal areas are located.

✓ Reading Check **Why does the North China Plain have such a high population density?**

Section 1 Assessment

Key Terms

Review the key terms at the beginning of this section. Use each term in a sentence that explains its meaning.

Target Reading Skill

How did having a purpose help you understand important ideas in this section?

Comprehension and Critical Thinking

1. (a) Recall What are the major landforms in East Asia?

(b) Locate In what part of China is the Plateau of Tibet?

(c) Contrast How are the landforms in eastern China different from the landforms in western China?

2. (a) Identify Name one type of landform in China where there is a high population density. You may refer to the maps in the section to answer.

(b) Draw Conclusions How does the physical geography of East Asia help explain why the eastern part of China is the most densely populated part of the country?

Writing Activity

Suppose that you are a travel agent helping a customer who wants to visit East Asia. Which landforms would you suggest that your customer visit? In which countries are these landforms located? Record your suggestions.

For: An activity on East Asia
Visit: PHSchool.com
Web Code: lcd-6101

Section 2 Climate and Vegetation

Prepare to Read

Objectives

In this section you will

1. Examine the major climate regions in East Asia.
2. Discover how climate affects people and vegetation in East Asia.

Taking Notes

As you read this section, look for details about how climate affects the people and vegetation in East Asia. Copy the table below and record your findings in it.

East Asia's Climates	
Effect on Vegetation	**Effect on People**
•	• Rice is the main food in southern China.

Target Reading Skill

Predict Making predictions about your text helps you set a purpose for reading and helps you remember what you read. Preview the section by looking at the headings, pictures, and maps. Then predict what the text might discuss about climate and vegetation in East Asia.

Key Terms

- **monsoon** (mahn SOON) *n.* a wind that changes direction with the change of season
- **typhoon** (ty FOON) *n.* a tropical storm that develops over the Pacific Ocean, with winds that reach speeds greater than 74 miles per hour
- **deciduous** (dee SIJ oo us) *adj.* falling off or shedding, as in leaves, seasonally or at a certain stage of development

You and your family are visiting Japan in the middle of February. All of you are trying to decide where to go for a long weekend. Your brother wants to go north to the island of Hokkaidō, where the skiing is perfect. Your parents, though, have had enough of winter. They would like to go to the island of Okinawa (oh kee nah wuh). The water there is warm enough for swimming. Which would you prefer—sun or snow?

East Asia's Climate Regions

Look at the climate map on the next page. It shows that East Asia has seven climate regions. Two of them—the tropical wet region and the subarctic region—cover a comparatively small part of the land. The five major climate regions are semiarid, arid, humid subtropical, humid continental, and highland.

Downhill skiing in Japan

East Asia: Climate Regions

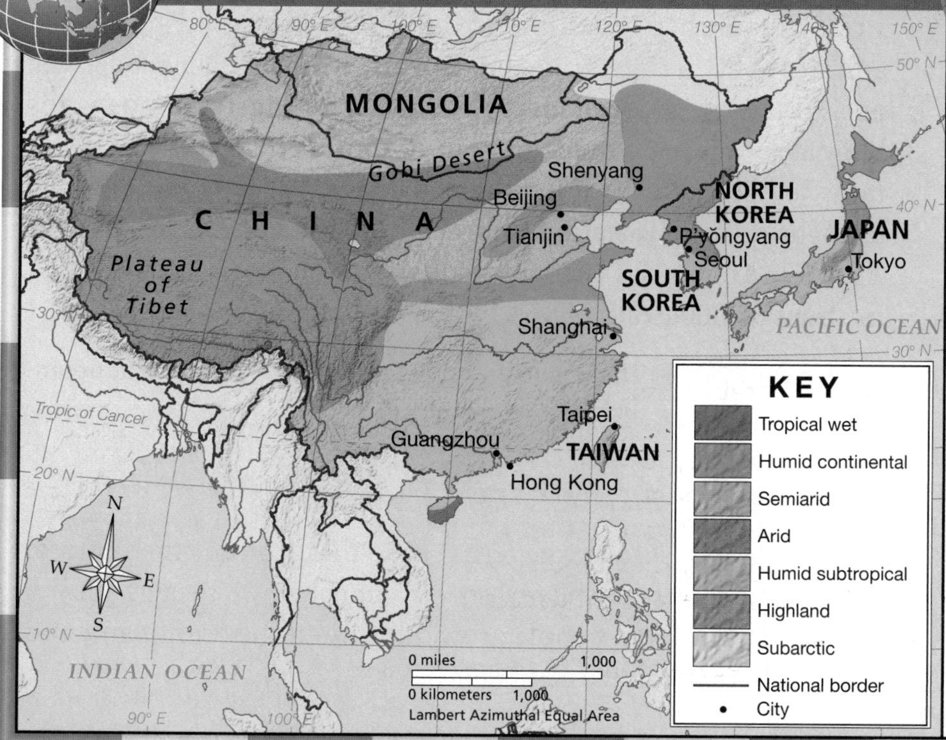

MAP MASTER™ Skills Activity

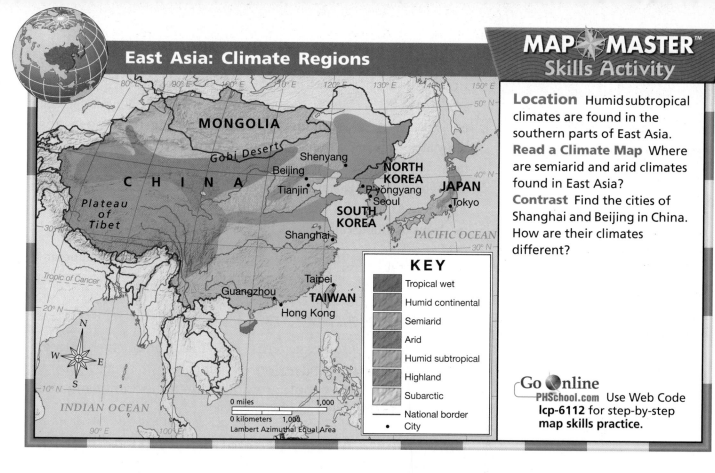

Location Humid subtropical climates are found in the southern parts of East Asia.

Read a Climate Map Where are semiarid and arid climates found in East Asia?

Contrast Find the cities of Shanghai and Beijing in China. How are their climates different?

Go Online PHSchool.com Use Web Code **lcp-6112** for step-by-step **map skills practice.**

KEY: Tropical wet; Humid continental; Semiarid; Arid; Humid subtropical; Highland; Subarctic; National border; • City

MONGOLIA, CHINA, NORTH KOREA, SOUTH KOREA, JAPAN, TAIWAN, Gobi Desert, Plateau of Tibet, Shenyang, Beijing, Tianjin, P'yongyang, Seoul, Tokyo, Shanghai, Taipei, Guangzhou, Hong Kong, PACIFIC OCEAN, INDIAN OCEAN, Tropic of Cancer

0 miles 1,000; 0 kilometers 1,000; Lambert Azimuthal Equal Area

A Variety of Climates A large part of eastern China has a humid subtropical climate—cool winters and hot summers with plenty of rain. To the north is a humid continental area of warm summers and cold winters. Because South Korea and Japan are almost completely surrounded by water, summers are a bit cooler and winters are a bit warmer than in other places at the same latitude.

In contrast, the northern interior of China is very dry, with arid and semiarid climate regions. There, temperatures can range from very hot to very cold. To the south, the Plateau of Tibet has a cool, dry, highland climate.

Monsoons Monsoons strongly affect the climates of East Asia. **Monsoons** are winds that change direction with the change of season. In summer, Pacific Ocean winds blow northwest toward the Asian continent. They bring rainfall that starts in June as a drizzle. The Japanese call this the "plum rain" because it begins just as the plums begin to ripen on the trees. The winds cause hot, humid weather and heavier rain in July.

In winter, the winds blow toward the east. The winds that begin in the interior of northern Asia are icy cold and very dry. In parts of China, the winds produce dust storms that can last for days. Where they cross warm ocean waters, these monsoons pick up moisture. Farther inland, they drop it as rain or snow.

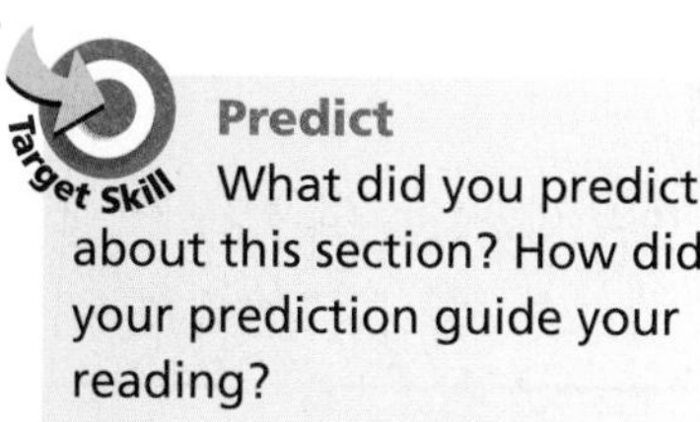

Target Skill **Predict** What did you predict about this section? How did your prediction guide your reading?

Links Across Time

Divine Winds Typhoons twice saved Japan from invaders. In 1274, Kublai Khan, a great leader of China's Mongol people, sent a fleet of warships to Japan. The Mongols got only as far as the island of Kyūshū. A typhoon frightened them back to China. When Kublai Khan tried again in 1281, a typhoon destroyed his huge fleet. The Japanese called this typhoon *kamikaze*, or "divine wind."

Typhoons East Asia has hurricanes like those that sometimes strike the southern coastline of the United States during August and September. These violent storms, which develop over the Pacific Ocean, are called **typhoons.** Whirling typhoon winds blow at speeds of 74 miles an hour or more. The winds and heavy rains they bring can cause major damage. Killer typhoons have brought great devastation and death to some countries in East Asia. For example, a typhoon that struck China in 1922 resulted in about 60,000 deaths.

✓ Reading Check **Name and describe two types of storms that occur in East Asia.**

The Influences of Climate

In East Asia, climate governs everything from the natural vegetation, which is shown on the map below, to agriculture. Climate affects what people grow, how often they can plant, and how easily they can harvest their fields.

How Climate Affects Vegetation in East Asia Much of the plant life in East Asia is strong enough to stand seasonal differences in temperature and rainfall. Bamboo, for example, grows remarkably quickly during the wet season in southern China and Japan. Yet it can also survive dry spells by storing food

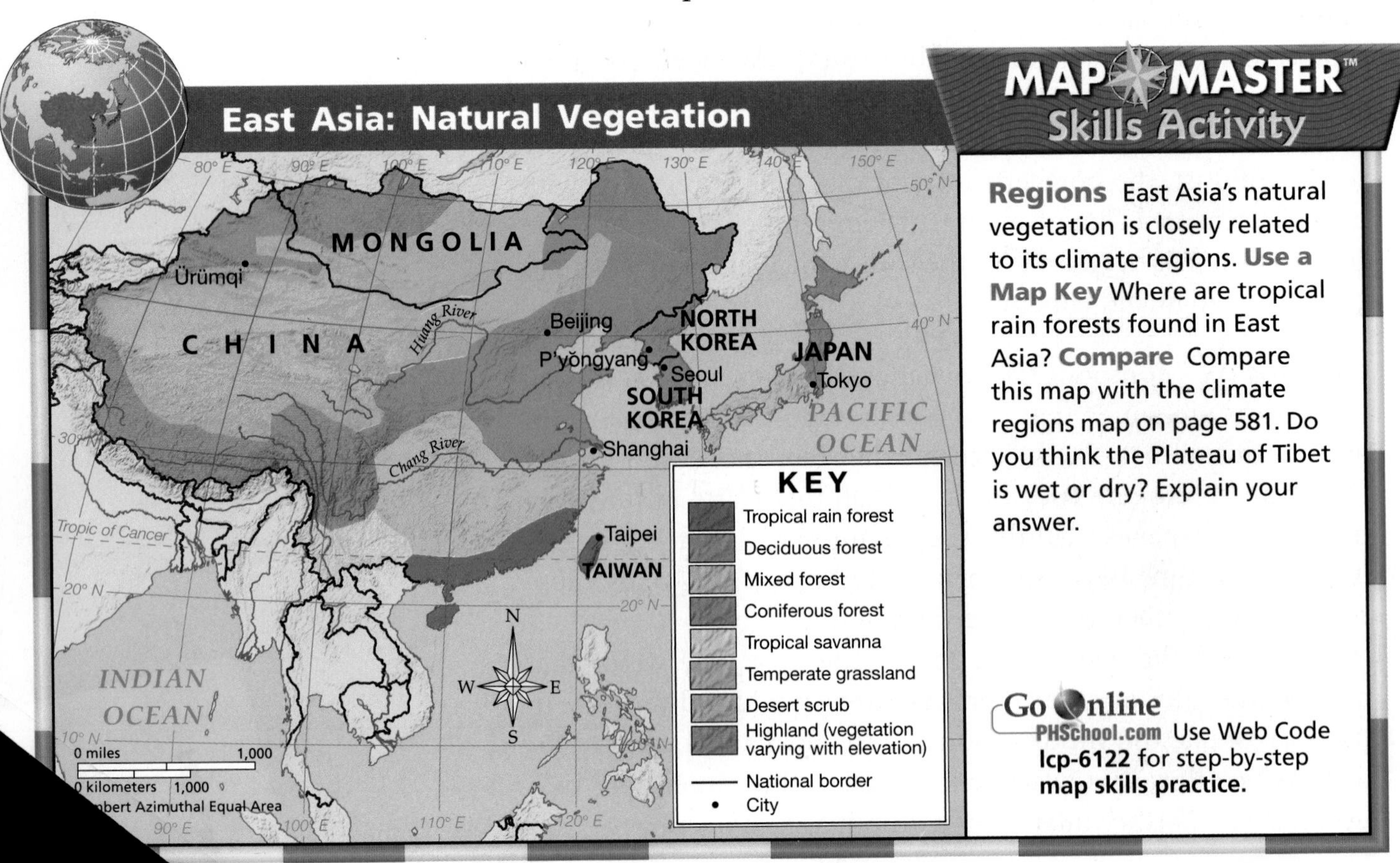

MAP MASTER™ Skills Activity

Regions East Asia's natural vegetation is closely related to its climate regions. **Use a Map Key** Where are tropical rain forests found in East Asia? **Compare** Compare this map with the climate regions map on page 581. Do you think the Plateau of Tibet is wet or dry? Explain your answer.

Go Online PHSchool.com Use Web Code **lcp-6122** for step-by-step **map skills practice.**

in its huge root system. Shrubs and many small flowering plants in the deserts of China spring up rapidly after summer rains. **Deciduous** (dih SIJ oo us), **or leaf-shedding,** trees change with the seasons. Maples, birches, and other trees turn the hillsides of Japan and the Koreas gold, orange, and red, once summer gives way to fall.

Brilliant Fall Colors in Japan
Most parts of Japan have spring, summer, fall, and winter. At this teahouse in the city of Nara, it is still warm enough to sit outdoors in October and November. **Analyze Images** *How can you tell the trees in the photo are deciduous trees?*

How Climate Affects People in East Asia

Climate greatly affects life in East Asia. The region around the Huang River in China is a good example. The Chinese word *Huang* means "yellow." The river gets its name from the brownish-yellow loess that is blown by the desert winds. The river picks up the loess and deposits it to the east on the North China Plain. The loess covers a huge 125,000-square-mile (324,000-square-kilometer) area around the river. This plain is one of the best farming areas in China.

The Huang River also floods. A system of dams helps control the waters. But the river can still overflow during the monsoons. Floods gave the Huang River its nickname, "China's Sorrow."

The diet of East Asians is also affected by climate. Because rice grows best in warm weather, it is the main crop—and food—of people in southern China. In the cooler north, wheat and other grains grow better than rice. This means that people in the north eat more flour products, such as noodles.

✓ Reading Check **How does bamboo survive during dry spells in southern China and Japan?**

Section 2 Assessment

Key Terms

Review the key terms at the beginning of this section. Use each term in a sentence that explains its meaning.

Target Reading Skill

What did you predict about this section? How did your prediction guide your reading?

Comprehension and Critical Thinking

1. (a) Recall What are the five major climate regions in East Asia?
(b) Summarize What kind of winters and summers are found in a humid subtropical climate?
2. (a) Identify Name three ways climate affects agriculture in East Asia.
(b) Generalize How does the climate affect what people eat in China?

Writing Activity

Write a letter to a friend who is planning a long trip to East Asia. Explain what climate conditions can occur in different areas. Include suggestions for clothing.

For: An activity on East Asia's climate
Visit: PHSchool.com
Web Code: lcd-6102

Using Reliable Information on the Internet

Your teacher has given you an assignment to write a report about the Gobi Desert in Mongolia and China. To research your report, you are asked to find articles, photos, and statistics about the Gobi Desert.

"Use a variety of good sources on the Internet," your teacher urges. "An encyclopedia article is a good start for basic facts. But if you search further, you might find stories from people who live there. You might also find photographs that will help you to describe the land in your own words."

You enter the word *Gobi* on an Internet search engine, and receive 123,000 "hits"—that is, Web sites that contain the word *Gobi*. How can you find reliable, useful information among all these sites?

Learn the Skill

To find information from Web sites you can trust, follow the steps below.

1. **Decide on your search terms.** Make a list of what you are looking for. For example, try *Gobi Desert* or *Gobi climate.*

2. **Notice the Web site's Internet address.** The address, or URL, will include a period followed by a three-letter abbreviation. Among the most common are ".com," ".edu," ".gov," and ".org." Just about anyone can set up a Web site with a .com (commercial) address. Schools and universities use a .edu (education) address. Nonprofit organizations such as museums use .org. Official government sites carry a .gov address.

3. **Try to identify the author and date of information on a Web site.** The author and date often appear on the Web page. But many sites are anonymous—they do not identify the author. Do not use information from anonymous sites. It may be out of date or it may be written by an author who has no particular expertise about the topic.

4. **Choose a reliable source, or use more than one source, if needed.** Encyclopedias are reliable. They are written by people who have knowledge about a wide range of subject areas and they present facts. Sources with .gov and .edu are generally reliable, as are newspapers, magazines, and television network news sites.

Practice the Skill

Use the steps in the skill to do some research on a computer.

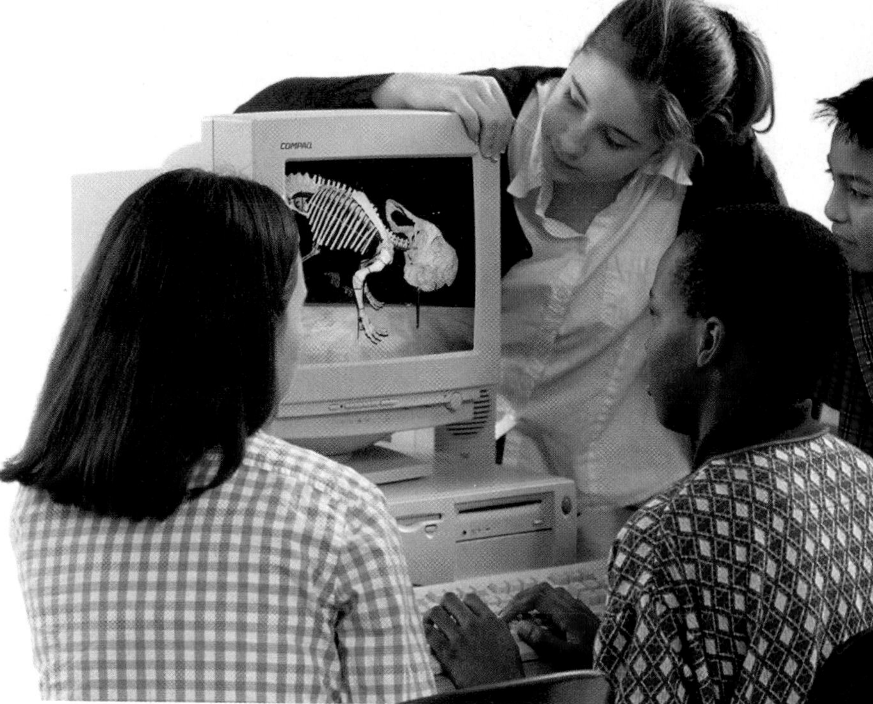

Reliable Web sites can help you research Gobi dinosaurs—or any school assignment.

1. If a search for *Gobi* gives you thousands of results, what additional search terms could you use to narrow the search?

2. Look for a site with a .gov address from the government of China or Mongolia. Or try a United States government Web site for statistics about the location and size of the Gobi. Why is it a good idea to go to an .edu address to research the Gobi?

3. Would it matter if an online map of the Gobi was created this year or 50 years ago? Would it matter if a graph of average rainfall in the Gobi was from this year or 50 years ago? Explain.

4. Say you read about a recent discovery of dinosaur bones in the Gobi. The news appears on an archaeology Web site, but the author and date are unidentified. Where would you find a reliable source of this news?

Apply the Skill

Suppose your neighbor writes a letter to the editor of the Internet edition of your local newspaper. In the letter, she writes, "The population in our community has doubled in the last year." Is this reliable information? Then you go to your local government's Web site and read this: "Town population doubles in just one year, according to government statistics." Is this information reliable? Name two Web sites you could go to in order to find the actual statistics. Explain why each is reliable.

Section 3 Natural Resources and Land Use

Prepare to Read

Objectives

In this section you will
1. Learn about East Asia's major natural resources.
2. Find out how the people of East Asia use land to produce food.

Taking Notes

Copy the table below. As you read, look for the headings that appear in large red type. Turn these headings into questions. Use the table to record your answers to these questions.

Natural Resources and Land Use in East Asia	
Questions	Answers

Target Reading Skill

Ask Questions Preview the headings, pictures, and maps to see what this section is about. Find the main headings in this section. (They appear in large red type.) Turn these headings into questions. Then read to answer your questions. Write your questions and answers in the Taking Notes table.

Key Terms

- **developing country** (dih VEL up ing KUN tree) *n.* a country that has low industrial production and little modern technology
- **developed country** (dih VEL upt KUN tree) *n.* a country with many industries and a well-developed economy
- **terrace** (TEHR us) *n.* a level area in a hillside
- **double-cropping** (DUB ul KRAHP ing) *v.* to grow two or more crops on the same land

Coal miners in China

When planning their economies, all countries ask these three basic questions: What will be produced? How will it be produced? For whom will it be produced? For the countries of East Asia, the answers to these questions depend largely on factors surrounding these two things: natural resources and land use.

Natural resources are materials found in nature. They include fertile land, minerals, water, and forests. Natural resources can be used to produce all sorts of goods, from cars to sweatshirts. Land use is linked to natural resources. To improve their economies, governments have to decide how to use the land and the natural resources they contain.

East Asia's Natural Resources

East Asia's lands and waters are filled with abundant natural resources. As the map on the next page shows, East Asia has natural resources that can be used to produce energy, such as coal, oil, and water for hydroelectric power. Other resources in East Asia are the raw materials for manufactured goods, such as electronic equipment. The water bodies and fertile land of East Asia are also important resources.

East Asia: Natural Resources

MAP MASTER™ Skills Activity

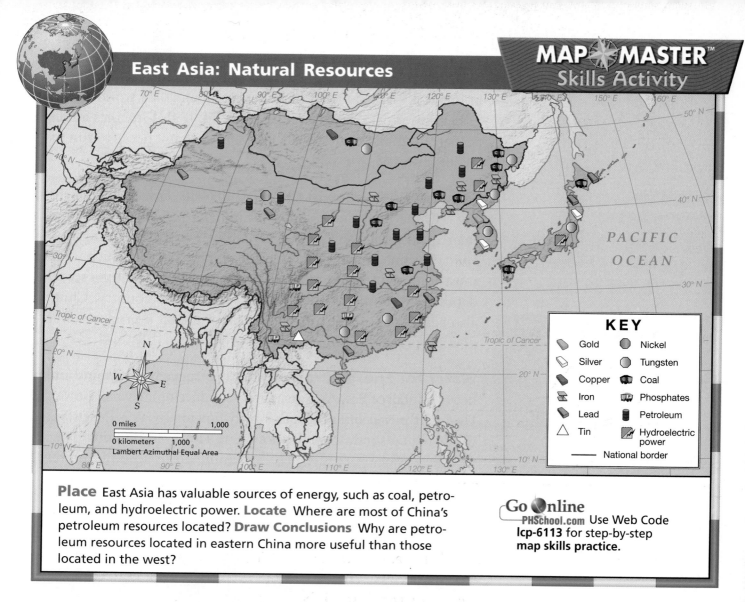

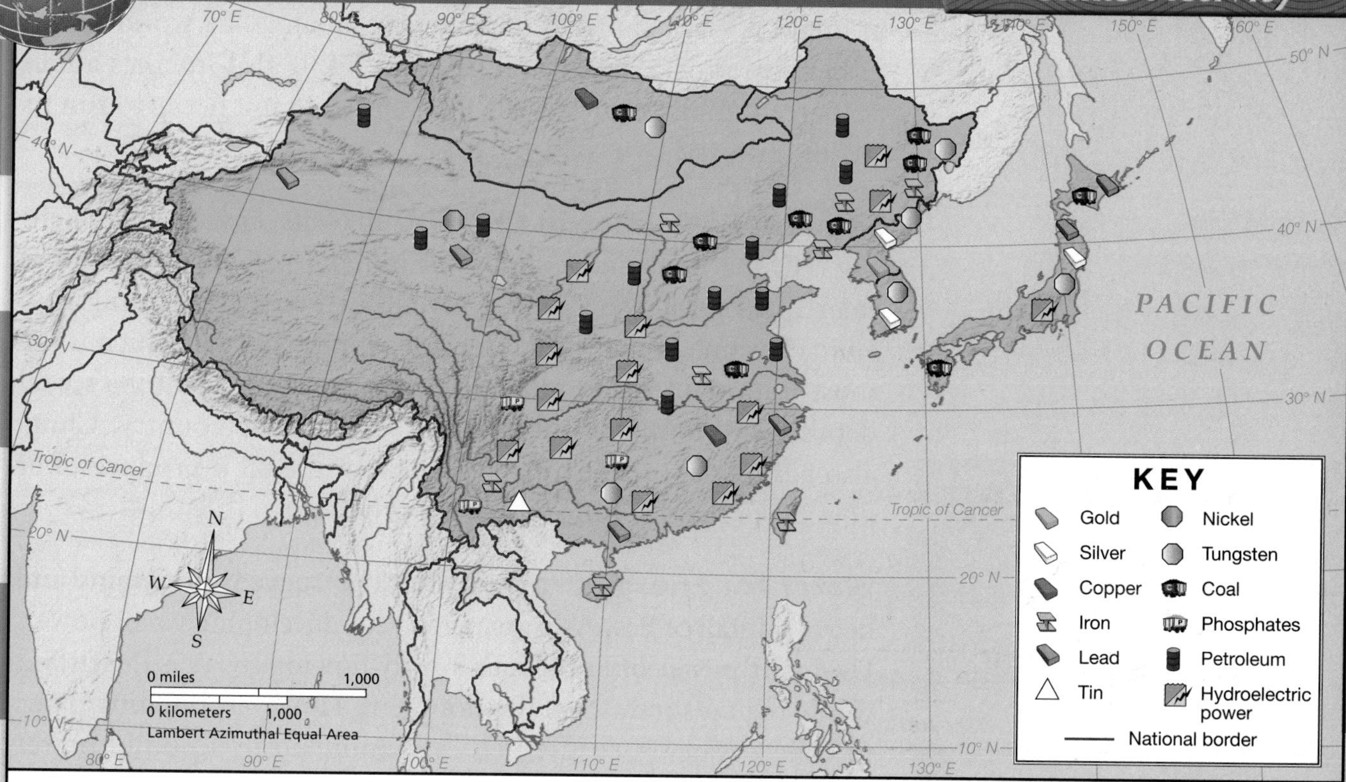

KEY
- Gold
- Silver
- Copper
- Iron
- Lead
- Tin
- Nickel
- Tungsten
- Coal
- Phosphates
- Petroleum
- Hydroelectric power
- National border

PACIFIC OCEAN

0 miles 1,000
0 kilometers 1,000
Lambert Azimuthal Equal Area

Place East Asia has valuable sources of energy, such as coal, petroleum, and hydroelectric power. **Locate** Where are most of China's petroleum resources located? **Draw Conclusions** Why are petroleum resources located in eastern China more useful than those located in the west?

Go Online PHSchool.com Use Web Code **lcp-6113** for step-by-step **map skills practice.**

Mineral Resources in the Two Koreas East Asia has plenty of mineral resources, but they are unevenly distributed. Some countries have more and other countries have less. The two Koreas, for example, have limited mineral resources. Coal and iron, which are used in manufacturing, are plentiful in North Korea. But there is little coal or iron in South Korea, where much more manufacturing takes place. The only minerals that are in large supply in the South are tungsten and graphite.

If South Korea could share North Korea's coal and iron, both countries would benefit. But the two do not share resources, since they are hostile toward each other. North Korea is a **developing country**—one that has low industrial production and little modern technology. South Korea is a **developed country**—one with many industries and a well-developed economy. Because of its limited resources, South Korea must import the iron, crude oil, and chemicals it needs for its industries. Nevertheless, it has become one of East Asia's richest economies. It exports, or sells, many manufactured goods to other nations.

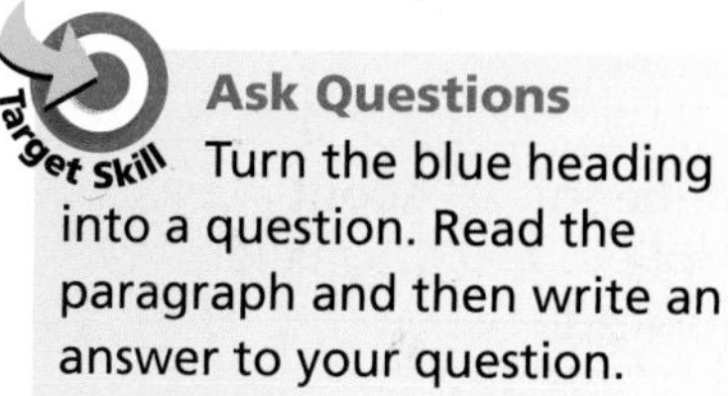

Ask Questions Turn the blue heading into a question. Read the paragraph and then write an answer to your question.

Mineral Resources in Japan Japan is a modern industrial society. Yet Japan—like South Korea—has few mineral resources. It imports vast quantities of minerals. Japan is the world's largest importer of coal, natural gas, and oil. It also imports about 95 percent of the iron ore, tin, and copper that it needs to run its major industries.

Mineral Resources in China Unlike its East Asian neighbors, China has a large supply of mineral resources. For more than 2,000 years, the Chinese have mined copper, tin, and iron. China has one of the world's largest supplies of coal, which is the most important of its mineral resources. Most of China's coal deposits are found in the northern part of the country. China also has oil deposits. China uses most of the oil it produces, but does export some crude oil and oil products.

Water for Energy Production The rugged mountains and heavy rainfall of East Asia are perfect for developing water power. Using the power of East Asia's swiftly flowing rivers is important to the region's industrial development. However, building dams to collect water is costly. It is even more costly to build power plants that produce hydroelectricity. Hydroelectricity is electricity produced by using the power of flowing water.

The Three Gorges Dam

Location	Chang River
Width	1.4 miles (2,309 meters)
Height	607 feet (185 meters)
Start date	1994
Expected completion date	2009
Number of construction workers	About 250,000
Purpose	Flood control, hydroelectricity
Number of people displaced	About 1.5 million

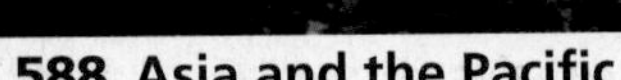

In 2002, China produced about 17 percent of its electricity from hydroelectric power. The Chinese government expects this figure to increase when China finishes building the Three Gorges Dam across the Chang River. The Three Gorges Dam will be one and a half miles wide and more than 600 feet high. China is building the dam not only to produce electricity but also to control the frequent floods on the Chang River.

Water for Aquaculture East Asia's ocean and inland waters have been an important source of food for the region's people. Aquaculture, or fish farming, has been practiced in Asia for centuries. During the 1980s and 1990s, however, aquaculture production in Asia greatly expanded. This was due, in part, to the fact that overfishing and pollution had decreased the supply of saltwater and freshwater fish. The increase was also due to advances in the practice of aquaculture. In East Asia, China is the leading aquaculture producer. Japan, South Korea, and Taiwan are also among the top aquaculture producers in the world. Aquaculture includes farm-raised fish, shrimp, oysters, mussels, clams, and seaweed.

✓ Reading Check **Based on what you have read, is Japan a developed country or a developing country?**

The World's Largest Dam
The bottom photo shows the Three Gorges Dam in China under construction. The top photo shows what the Three Gorges area looked like before construction began. The middle photo shows a model of the completed dam. China is building the dam to produce hydroelectricity. **Contrast** *Study the two small photos. How will the dam change the landscape of the Three Gorges area?*

A Japanese farmer displays his harvest of rice.

Using the Land to Produce Food

In order to feed its large population, East Asians need to farm every bit of available land. With so many mountains and plateaus, only a small percentage of the land can be cultivated. Only about 14 percent of China, 12 percent of Japan, and 14 percent of North Korea can be farmed. South Korea's 19 percent is about equal to the percentage of land farmed in the United States.

Terrace Farming In China, Japan, and parts of Korea, farmers cut horizontal steps called **terraces** into steep hillsides to gain a few precious yards of soil for crops. Farmers even use the land at the sides of roads and railway lines for planting.

Double-Cropping Where climate and soil allow, farmers practice **double-cropping,** growing two or more crops on the same land in the same season or at the same time. In China, farmers often plant one type of crop between the rows of another crop in order to grow more food. In some parts of southern China, farmers are even able to grow three crops in a year. In southern Japan, rice seeds are sowed in small fields. When the seedlings are about a foot high, they are replanted in a larger field after wheat has been harvested from it.

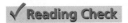

✓ Reading Check **What is the difference between terrace farming and double-cropping?**

Section 3 Assessment

Key Terms

Review the key terms at the beginning of this section. Use each term in a sentence that explains its meaning.

Target Reading Skill

What questions did you ask about this section?

Comprehension and Critical Thinking

1. **(a) Recall** Name three natural resources in East Asia that can be used to produce energy.
(b) Contrast Which country has a larger supply of mineral resources, China or Japan?
(c) Infer How could a country develop its economy without a large supply of mineral resources?

2. **(a) Recall** What two farming techniques do East Asian farmers use to make up for a shortage of farmland?
(b) Infer Why might East Asian farmers be interested in learning about faster-growing crops?

Writing Activity

Suppose you are a reporter for a television news program. Write a report that tells how the waters of East Asia are an important resource for its people. Include at least two ways water is used in East Asia.

For: An activity on East Asia
Visit: PHSchool.com
Web Code: lcd-6103

Chapter 18 Review and Assessment

◆ Chapter Summary

Section 1: Land and Water

- Mountains, plains, and plateaus are the main landforms in East Asia. The Chang and Huang rivers are major bodies of water.
- Most people in East Asia live in the plains and coastal areas.

China

Section 2: Climate and Vegetation

- East Asia's five major climate regions are semi-arid, arid, humid subtropical, humid continental, and highlands. Monsoons have a strong effect on the climate of East Asia.
- The climate of East Asia supports vegetation, such as bamboo, that is strong enough to stand seasonal differences in temperature and rainfall. Winds blow fertile soil, which is then carried by the Huang River to the North China Plain.

Japan

Section 3: Natural Resources and Land Use

- China has more mineral resources than its neighbors. Water in East Asia is used to produce hydroelectricity and to support aquaculture.
- East Asia's physical landscape leaves a small amount of land available for farming. Terraces and double-cropping are two ways East Asian farmers get the most food out of the land that is used for farming.

◆ Key Terms

Each of the statements below contains a key term from the chapter. If the statement is true, write *true*. If the statement is false, rewrite the statement to make it true.

1. A **plateau** is a dry region with little vegetation.
2. When soil is **fertile,** it is capable of supporting abundant plant growth.
3. **Population density** measures the average number of people living in a square mile or square kilometer.
4. A **monsoon** is a tropical storm that occurs over the Pacific Ocean.
5. **Deciduous** trees shed their leaves in the fall.
6. A **developed country** has a low level of industrial production.
7. A **developing country** has many industries and a well-developed economy.
8. When farmers use **double-cropping,** they build steps into hillsides to increase farmland.

Review and Assessment (continued)

◆ Comprehension and Critical Thinking

9. **(a) Recall** Which East Asian countries have mountains, wide plains, and plateaus?
(b) Locate Where are the Himalayas located?
10. **(a) Name** Name two major rivers in China.
(b) Recall Which of these rivers flows through the North China Plain?
(c) Identify Effect How does this river make the North China Plain a fertile region?
11. **(a) List** What are Japan's four main islands?
(b) Compare and Contrast How is the physical geography of Japan different from the physical geography of the Koreas?
12. **(a) Identify** Which parts of East Asia have a very high population density?
(b) Summarize Why does most of the population in China live in the eastern half of the country?
13. **(a) Explain** How does water affect the climates of the Koreas and Japan?
(b) Summarize What does the summer monsoon do in East Asia and in what direction does it blow?
14. **(a) Define** What three basic questions do countries ask when planning their economies?
(b) Summarize How do Japan and South Korea make up for their lack of mineral resources?
15. **(a) Locate** Where is the Three Gorges Dam?
(b) Predict How might the Three Gorges Dam affect energy production in China?
16. **(a) Explain** How have the farmers of East Asia made the best use of the land for farming?
(b) Apply Information Which farming method is linked to the physical landscape of East Asia?

◆ Skills Practice

Using Reliable Information on the Internet
Review the steps you followed to learn this skill. Then explain why an Internet encyclopedia is a reliable source.

◆ Writing Activity: Geography

Create a geographic dictionary of these items: plateau, plain, volcano, monsoon, mountain, peninsula. Arrange the list in alphabetical order. Write a definition, using your textbook to find a real-life example of each term. The example must be located in East Asia. Include the country where your example is located.

MAP MASTER™ Skills Activity

Place Location For each place listed below, write the letter from the map that shows its location.

1. Himalayas
2. North China Plain
3. Huang River
4. Plateau of Tibet
5. Chang River
6. Mount Fuji

Go Online PHSchool.com Use Web Code **ldp-6120** for an **interactive map.**

East Asia

70° E 80° E 90° E 100° E 110° E 120° E 130° E 140° E 150° E
50° N 40° N 30° N 20° N
A B C D E F
N S E W
Tropic of Cancer

Standardized Test Prep

Test-Taking Tips

Some questions on standardized tests ask you to identify the main topic of a reading passage. Study the passage below. Then follow the tips to answer the sample question.

> Desert winds blow silt into the Huang River. The Huang, or Yellow, River gets its name from this brownish-yellow loess. The river carries and deposits loess to the east. The loess covers 125,000 square miles (324,000 square kilometers) on the North China Plain. This great plain is one of China's best farming regions.

TIP Some paragraphs contain a topic sentence that states its main idea. All other sentences in the paragraph support this point.

Pick the letter of the statement that best answers the question.

Which is the best topic sentence for this paragraph?

A ~~Climate influences everything from natural vegetation to agriculture.~~

B ~~Loess is rich yellow-brown silt or clay.~~

C Climate affects life in the region around the Huang River.

D The Huang River is known as China's Sorrow because of its damaging floods.

TIP Rule out answer choices that don't make sense. Then pick the best answer from the remaining choices.

Think It Through You can rule out A because the statement is too general. It could be the topic for a paragraph on any region of the world. However, B is too specific; it could be another detail in the paragraph. Similarly, D is another detail, one that might be included in a different paragraph about flooding on the Huang. The correct answer is C.

Practice Questions

Use the passage below to answer Question 1. Use the tips above to help you.

> In summer, the monsoon blows northwest from the Pacific Ocean toward the Asian continent. The summer monsoon brings hot, humid weather and rainfall to East Asia. In winter, the monsoon blows toward the east. Where they cross warm ocean waters, such as the South China Sea, these monsoons pick up moisture. Later, they drop it as rain or snow.

1. Which is the best topic sentence for the above paragraph?

A People need rain to grow crops.

B Monsoons have a strong effect on climate in East Asia.

C The South China Sea is located off China's southern coast.

D The Pacific Ocean is the deepest ocean in the world.

Use the tips above and other tips in this book to help you answer the following questions.

2. Which country takes up most of East Asia's land?

A Japan
B Mongolia
C China
D South Korea

3. Most of the people in Japan live

A in coastal areas.

B in mountainous areas.

C on Japan's wide plains.

D on plateaus.

4. The Huang River runs through a fertile region of East Asia called

A Mongolia.

B Taiwan.

C the North China Plain.

D Tibet.

Use Web Code **lca-6100** for a **Chapter 18 self-test.**

Chapter 19

South, Southwest, and Central Asia: Physical Geography

Chapter Preview

In this chapter, you will examine the physical geography of South, Southwest, and Central Asia. This huge region includes many countries and a range of landforms.

Section 1
South Asia
Physical Geography

Section 2
Southwest Asia
Physical Geography

Section 3
Central Asia
Physical Geography

Target Reading Skill

Clarifying Meaning In this chapter, you will focus on understanding what you read by rereading and reading ahead, paraphrasing, and summarizing.

▶ **An American climbing team below the summit of Mount Everest, the world's tallest peak**

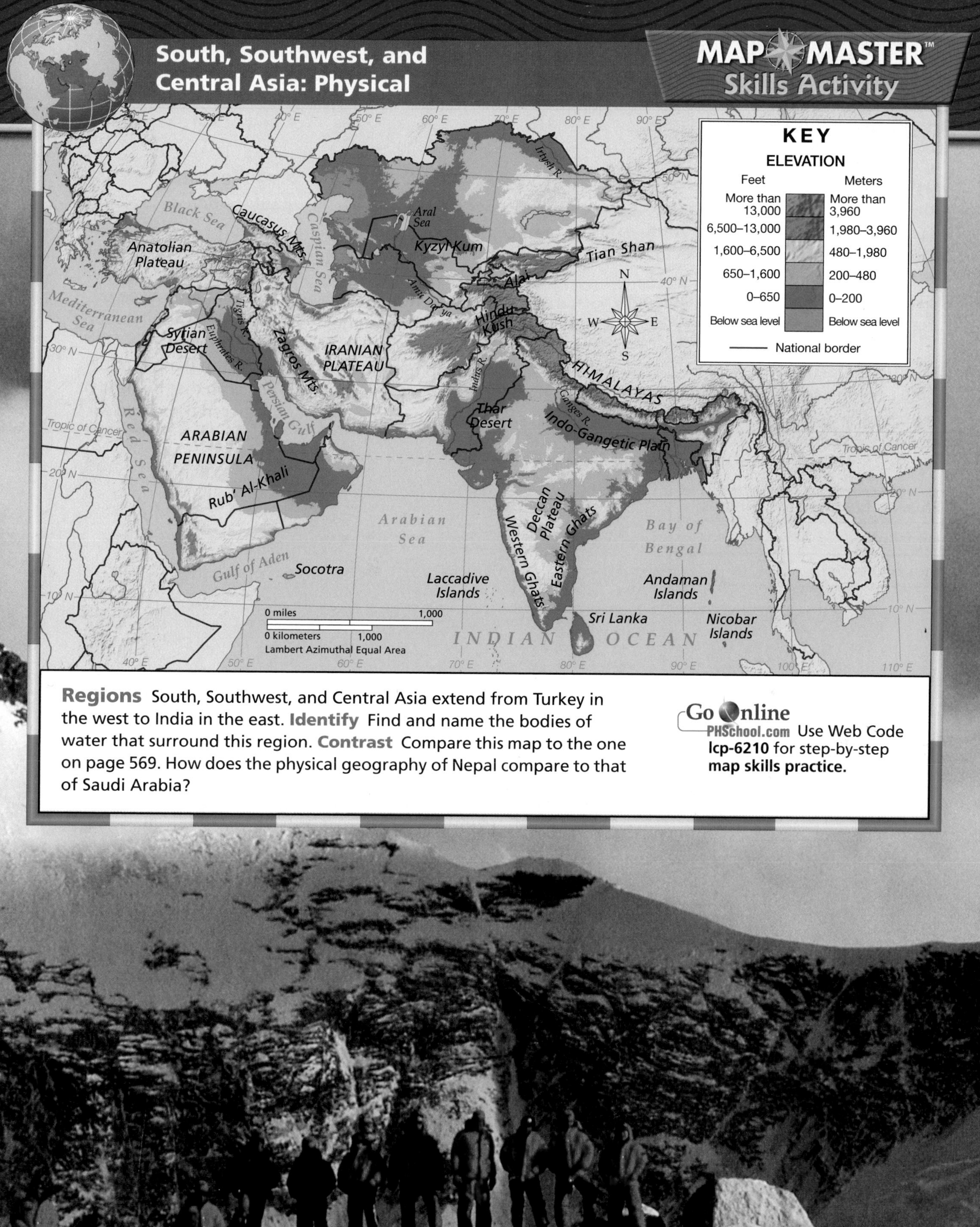

Regions South, Southwest, and Central Asia extend from Turkey in the west to India in the east. **Identify** Find and name the bodies of water that surround this region. **Contrast** Compare this map to the one on page 569. How does the physical geography of Nepal compare to that of Saudi Arabia?

Go Online PHSchool.com Use Web Code **lcp-6210** for step-by-step **map skills practice.**

Section 1

South Asia

Physical Geography

Prepare to Read

Objectives

In this section, you will

1. Learn about the landforms of South Asia.
2. Discover the most important factor that affects climate in South Asia.
3. Examine how people use the land and resources of South Asia.

Taking Notes

As you read this section, look for details about the physical features of South Asia. Copy the table below and record your findings in it.

Physical Features	Details
Himalayas	
Indus River	

Target Reading Skill

Rereading or Reading Ahead If you do not understand a certain passage, reread it to look for connections among the words and sentences. It might also help to read ahead, because a word or an idea may be explained further on.

Key Terms

- **subcontinent** (SUB kahn tih nunt) *n.* a large landmass that is a major part of a continent
- **alluvial** (uh LOO vee ul) *adj.* made of soil deposited by rivers
- **cash crop** (kash krahp) *n.* a crop that is raised or gathered to be sold for money on the local or world market

Mountain climbing in the Himalayas

Two hundred million years ago, the Indian subcontinent was attached to the east coast of Africa. A **subcontinent** is a large landmass that is a major part of a continent. Scientists believe that at that time, all of Earth's continents were joined. Starting about 200 million years ago, the Indian subcontinent broke apart from Africa and slid slowly toward Asia. About 50 million years ago, the Indian subcontinent collided with Asia. Northern India and southern Asia crumpled where they met, forming the mountains of the Himalayas. The Himalayas contain the tallest peaks in the world.

South Asia: Physical

KEY

ELEVATION

Feet	Meters
More than 13,000	More than 3,960
6,500–13,000	1,980–3,960
1,600–6,500	480–1,980
650–1,600	200–480
0–650	0–200

—— National border

0 miles 500
0 kilometers 500
Lambert Azimuthal Equal Area

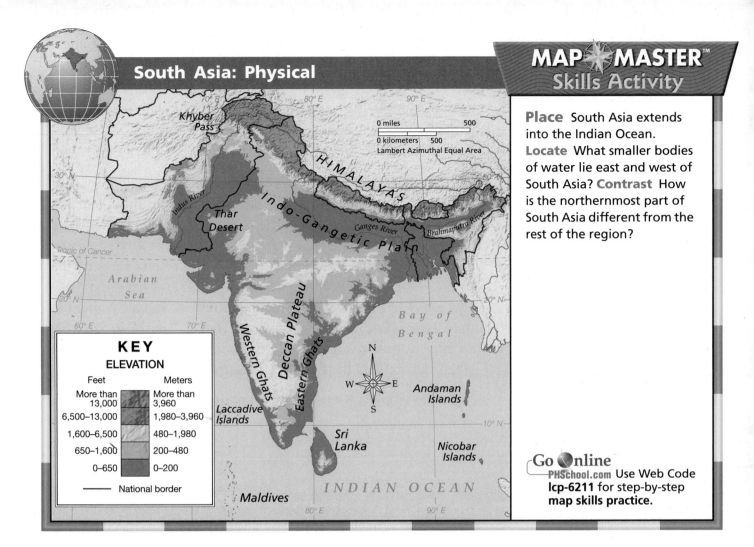

MAP MASTER™ Skills Activity

Place South Asia extends into the Indian Ocean. **Locate** What smaller bodies of water lie east and west of South Asia? **Contrast** How is the northernmost part of South Asia different from the rest of the region?

Go Online PHSchool.com Use Web Code **lcp-6211** for step-by-step **map skills practice.**

Major Landforms of South Asia

The largest nation in South Asia is India. It extends from the Himalayas down to the narrow tip of the Indian subcontinent in the south. Pakistan (PAK ih stan) and Afghanistan (af GAN ih stan) lie to the west of India. Along India's northern border, the kingdoms of Nepal (nuh PAWL) and Bhutan (BOO tahn) lie along the slopes of the Himalayas. To the east is Bangladesh (BAHNG luh DESH). The island nations of Sri Lanka (sree LAHNG kuh) and the Maldives (MAL dyvz) lie off the southern tip of India.

A Natural Barrier Find the Himalayas on the map above. Notice that they form a barrier between South Asia and the rest of Asia. This huge mountain range stretches some 1,550 miles (2,500 kilometers) from east to west. Mount Everest, the world's tallest mountain, is located in the Himalayas. Mount Everest rises to 29,035 feet (8,850 meters). That's about five and a half miles high! More than 100 mountains in the Himalayas soar above 24,000 feet (7,300 meters). The Himalayas present the greatest challenge in the world to mountain climbers.

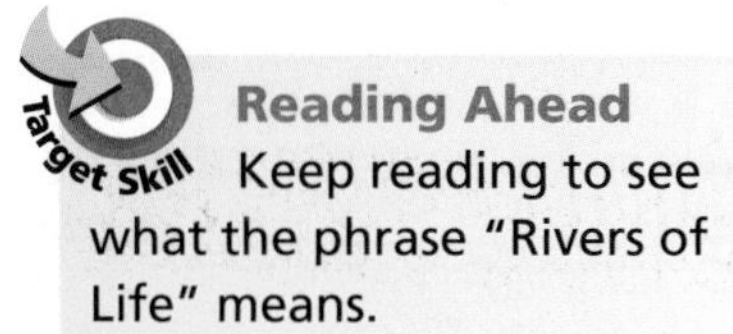

Reading Ahead Keep reading to see what the phrase "Rivers of Life" means.

Rivers of Life The two major rivers in South Asia—the Ganges and the Indus—begin in the Himalayas. The Ganges flows across northern India and empties into the Bay of Bengal. The Indus flows westward from the Himalayas into Pakistan. South Asia's rivers carry water and minerals to support farming. The plains around the rivers, therefore, are fertile and heavily populated.

Plains and Plateaus Huge plains cover the northern part of the Indian subcontinent. They stretch from the mouth of the Indus River to the mouth of the Ganges River. These plains are **alluvial,** which means they are made of soil deposited by rivers. Alluvial plains have rich, fertile soil. As a result, parts of the Indus, Ganges, and Brahmaputra (brah muh POO truh) river valleys are excellent areas for farming. South of India's plains lies the Deccan Plateau. The word *deccan* means "south" in Sanskrit, an ancient Indian language. Two mountain ranges, the Western Ghats (gawts) and the Eastern Ghats, frame the Deccan Plateau.

✓ **Reading Check** **Name the two major rivers in South Asia.**

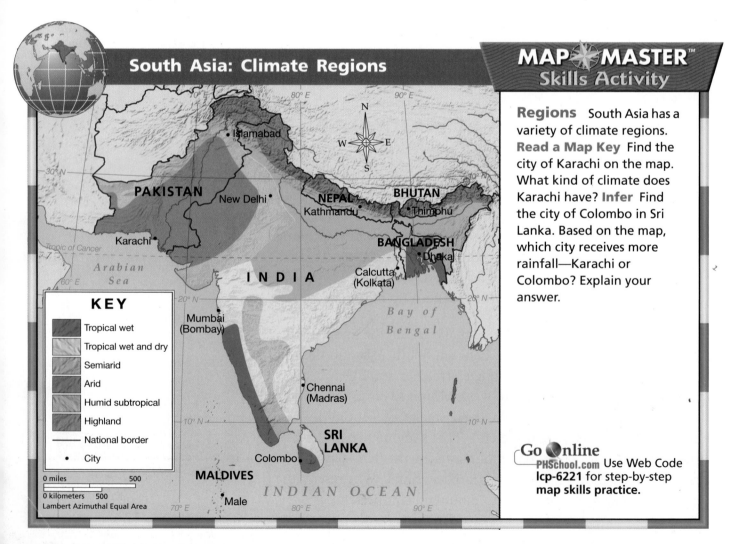

South Asia: Climate Regions

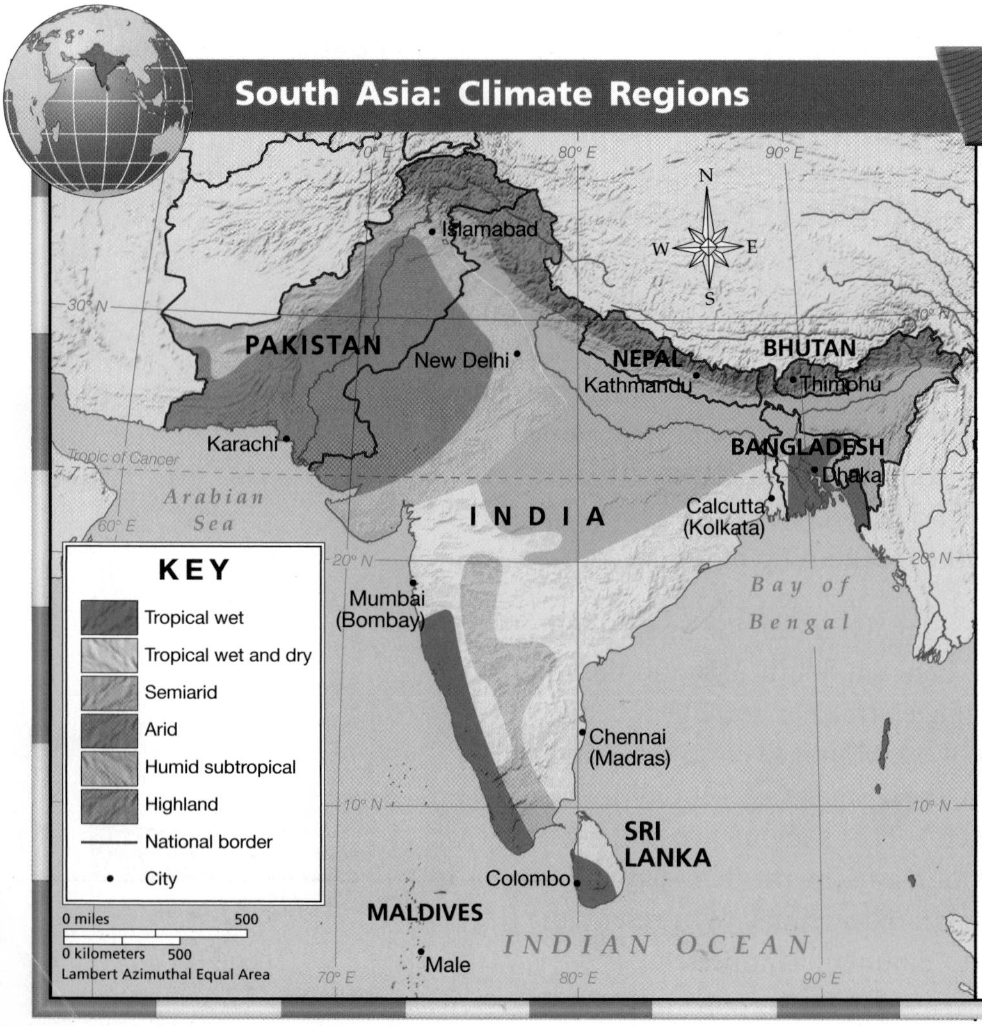

KEY

- Tropical wet
- Tropical wet and dry
- Semiarid
- Arid
- Humid subtropical
- Highland
- National border
- • City

0 miles 500
0 kilometers 500
Lambert Azimuthal Equal Area

PAKISTAN, Islamabad, Karachi, New Delhi, NEPAL, Kathmandu, BHUTAN, Thimphu, BANGLADESH, Dhaka, INDIA, Calcutta (Kolkata), Mumbai (Bombay), Chennai (Madras), SRI LANKA, Colombo, MALDIVES, Male, Arabian Sea, Bay of Bengal, INDIAN OCEAN, Tropic of Cancer

MAP MASTER™ Skills Activity

Regions South Asia has a variety of climate regions. **Read a Map Key** Find the city of Karachi on the map. What kind of climate does Karachi have? **Infer** Find the city of Colombo in Sri Lanka. Based on the map, which city receives more rainfall—Karachi or Colombo? Explain your answer.

Go Online PHSchool.com Use Web Code **lcp-6221 for step-by-step map skills practice.**

The Climates of South Asia

Monsoons are the single most important factor that affects the climate of South Asia. Monsoons are winds that change direction with the change of seasons. The summer monsoons blow across South Asia from the southwest. During the winter, the winds change direction and blow from the northeast.

The Summer Monsoons From June to early October, steady winds blow over the surface of the Arabian Sea and the Indian Ocean. The air picks up a great deal of moisture. Then, the air passes over the hot land along the western tip of India. As the moist air passes over the hot land, it rises and loses its moisture in the form of rain. The rains that fall along the coastline cool the land somewhat. When the next air mass blows in, it travels farther inland before losing its supply of moisture. In this way, the monsoon rains work their way inland until they finally reach the Himalayas.

The Winter Monsoons During the winter months, the monsoons change direction, and the winds blow from the frigid northeast. These winds move dry, cold air toward South Asia. The Himalayas block the cold air. The countries of South Asia enjoy dry winter weather, with temperatures averaging 70°F (21°C).

√ Reading Check **What are monsoons?**

Land Use in South Asia

About 70 percent of the population in South Asia live in rural areas. Most of these people are crowded into fertile river valleys. Here, they grow whatever crops the soil and climate of their particular region will allow.

Links to Science

India's Salt Lake During the hot months, the 90-square-mile (230-square-kilometer) Sambhar (SAM bar) Lake in northwestern India is dry. Oddly, during this time the lake bed looks as though it is covered in snow. The white blanket is not snow but a sheet of salt. This salt supply has been harvested as far back as the 1500s. It is still an important resource for the region today.

Tea Harvest in India
Tea is a major crop in India. Workers harvest fresh tea leaves by hand. The leaves are then processed and dried. Dried tea is sometimes packed in tea bags. **Infer** *How can you tell harvesting leaves is labor-intensive?*

The densely populated city of Dhaka is Bangladesh's capital.

Cash Crops Some countries of South Asia produce cash crops such as tea, cotton, coffee, and sugar cane. A **cash crop** is one that is raised or gathered to be sold for money on the local or world market. Growing cash crops often brings in a great deal of money, but it can also cause problems. The economy of a region can become dependent on world prices for the crops. When prices fall, the cash crops do not bring in enough money. When cash crops fail, farmers may not earn enough money.

Mineral Resources The earth beneath India holds a vast supply of mineral wealth. Iron ore and coal are plentiful. Other important minerals include copper, limestone, and bauxite—an ore that contains aluminum. India has only a small amount of oil. Because of this, India relies heavily on hydroelectricity and nuclear power plants.

Population and Land Use South Asia is one of the most densely populated regions in the world. Most of the people live in areas that have plenty of rainfall. These include coastal areas, as well as northeastern India and the country of Bangladesh. The population is lower in areas where it is more difficult for people to live.

✓ Reading Check **Where do most of the people in South Asia live?**

Section 1 Assessment

Key Terms
Review the key terms at the beginning of this section. Use each term in a sentence that explains its meaning.

Target Reading Skill
What words were you able to clarify by rereading?

Comprehension and Critical Thinking
1. (a) **Recall** Which landform forms a natural barrier between South Asia and the rest of Asia?
(b) **Connect** How do the Ganges and the Indus rivers relate to this landform?
2. (a) **Identify** From which direction does the summer monsoon blow across South Asia?
(b) **Contrast** How is the winter monsoon different from the summer monsoon in South Asia?
3. (a) **List** Give some examples of the cash crops raised in South Asia.
(b) **Summarize** Why may cash crops cause problems for the economies of South Asian countries?

Writing Activity
Write a two-paragraph description of a television show about the geography and resources of South Asia. In your description, include at least three locations in South Asia. Tell what your camera crew will film in each location.

For: An activity on South Asia
Visit: PHSchool.com
Web Code: lcd-6201

Section 2

Southwest Asia
Physical Geography

Prepare to Read

Objectives

In this section, you will

1. Learn about the major landforms of Southwest Asia.
2. Find out what the two most important resources in Southwest Asia are.
3. Examine how people use the land in Southwest Asia.

Taking Notes

As you read this section, look for details about Southwest Asia's major physical features, including climate. Copy the table below and record your findings in it.

Physical Features of Southwest Asia	Details
Desert	
Persian Gulf	
Arabian Peninsula	
Dry climate	

Target Reading Skill

Paraphrasing When you paraphrase, you state what you have read in your own words. Here is a paraphrase of the first paragraph under the red heading on page 607: "Land in Southwest Asia is used mainly for agriculture, nomadic herding, and producing oil. The region has a small percentage of arable land. Most farming takes place in the northern part of the region."

As you read this section, paraphrase the first paragraph after each red heading.

Key Terms

- **oasis** (oh AY sis) *n.* an area in a desert region where fresh water is usually available from an underground spring or well
- **petroleum** (puh TROH lee um) *n.* an oily liquid formed from the remains of ancient plants and animals; a fuel
- **nonrenewable resource** (nahn rih NOO uh bul REE sawrs) *n.* a natural resource that cannot be quickly replaced once it is used
- **standard of living** (STAN durd uv LIV ing) *n.* a measurement of a person's or a group's education, housing, health, and nutrition

The Rub' al-Khali (roob ahl KHAH lee), or "Empty Quarter," of the Arabian Peninsula is the largest all-sand desert in the world. Almost nothing lives in this flat, hot territory. Ten years may pass between rainfalls. The sand dunes do not stay in one place—they gradually move as they are blown by the wind.

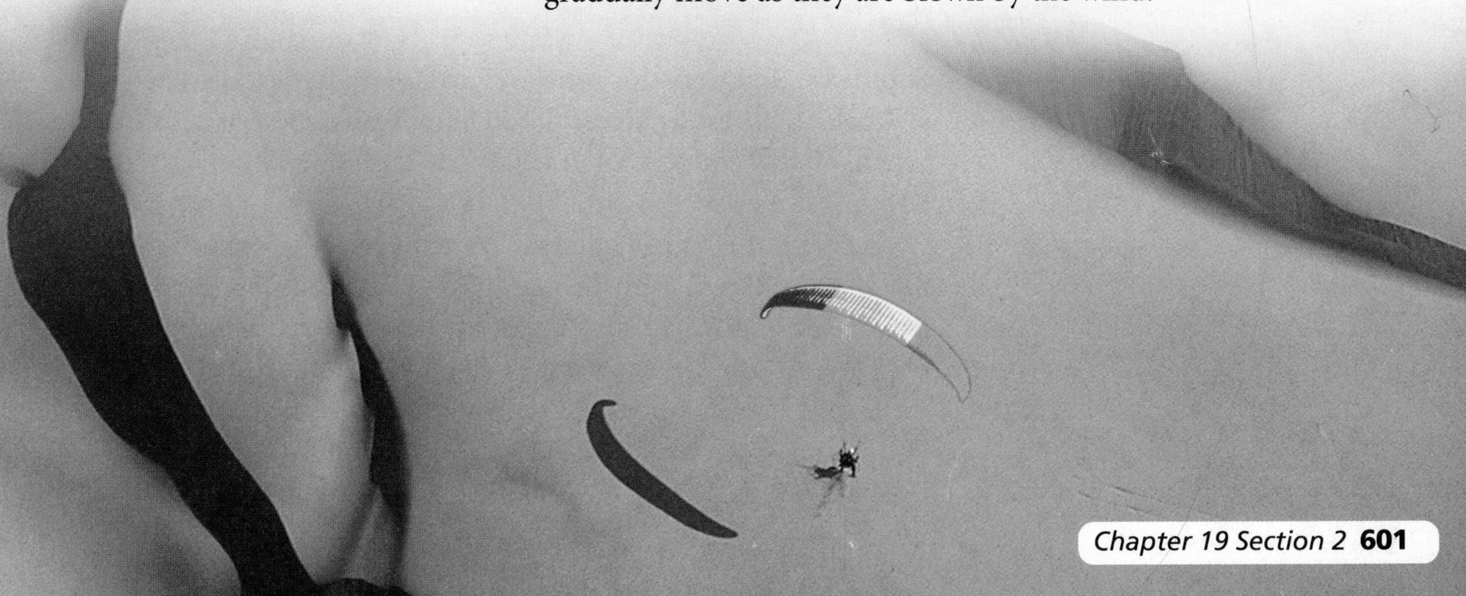

A parachutist lands in the Rub' al-Khali desert in Saudi Arabia.

Southwest Asia: Physical

MAP MASTER™ Skills Activity

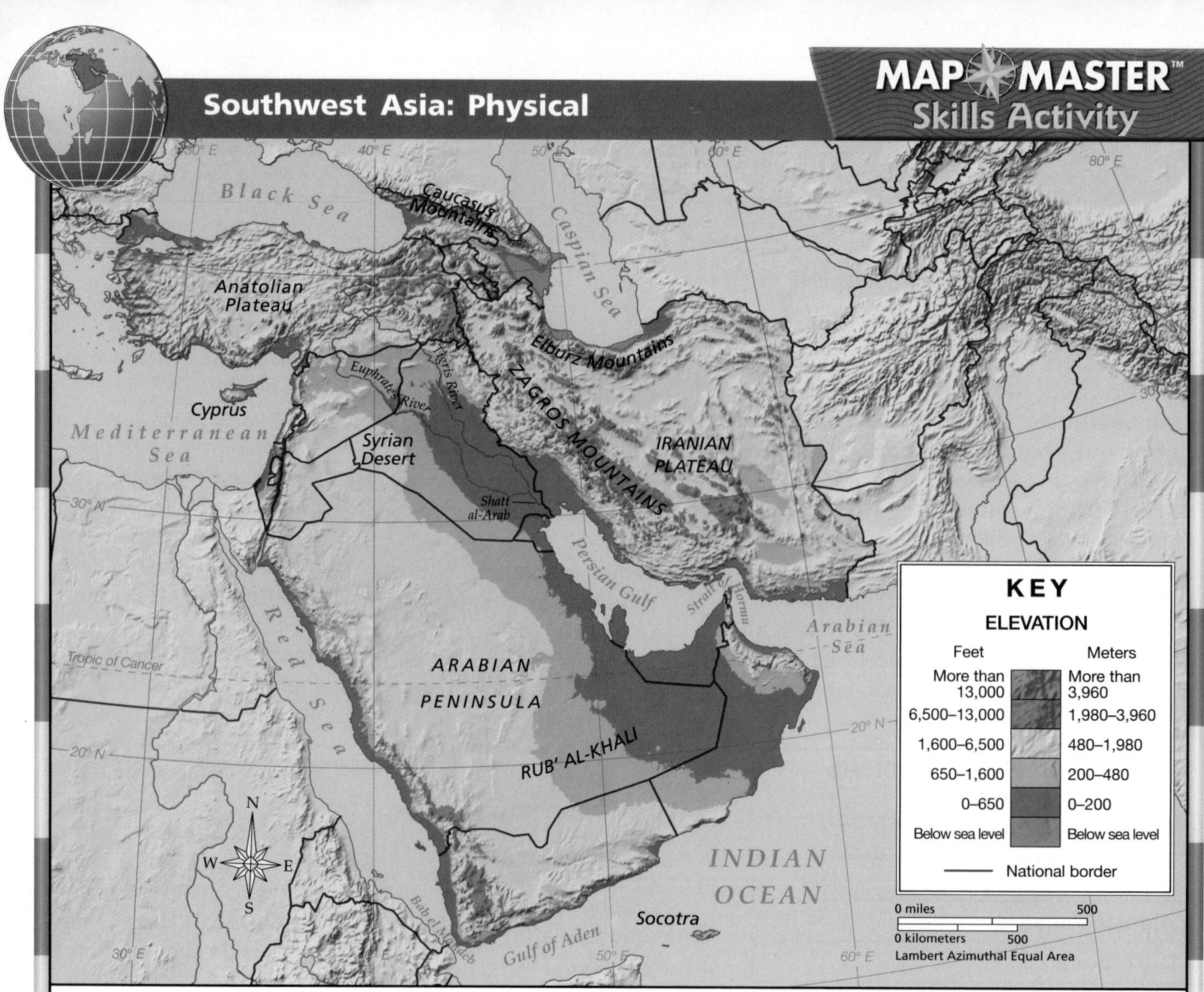

KEY

ELEVATION

Feet	Meters
More than 13,000	More than 3,960
6,500–13,000	1,980–3,960
1,600–6,500	480–1,980
650–1,600	200–480
0–650	0–200
Below sea level	Below sea level

— National border

0 miles 500
0 kilometers 500
Lambert Azimuthal Equal Area

Place Southwest Asia includes land between the Caucasus Mountains and the Gulf of Aden, including the Arabian Peninsula. **Read an Elevation Map** At what elevation is most of the land in Southwest Asia? Use the map key to find out. **Compare** Which body of water is larger—the Red Sea or the Persian Gulf?

Go Online PHSchool.com Use Web Code **lcp-6212** for step-by-step **map skills practice.**

A Dry Region Bordered by Water

Southwest Asia contains some of Earth's largest deserts. The Rub' al-Khali is almost as big as the state of Texas. Deserts also cover much of the country of Iran, Syria, and Iraq. Many parts of Southwest Asia receive little rain. Water is very valuable here.

Some of the region's deserts are covered with sand. In others, the land is strewn with pebbles, gravel, and boulders. Travelers passing through these dry areas are relieved when they find an oasis (oh AY sis). An **oasis** is a small area in a desert region where fresh water is usually available from an underground spring or well. Sometimes, an oasis can support a community of people. Farmers can grow crops. Nomadic shepherds can raise livestock.

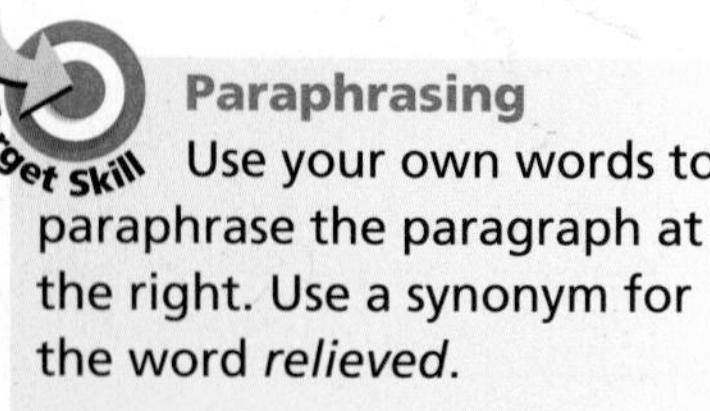

Paraphrasing Use your own words to paraphrase the paragraph at the right. Use a synonym for the word *relieved*.

Two Historic Rivers Few plants grow in most Southwest Asian deserts. Some of the most fertile soil in the world, however, lies along the Tigris (TY gris) and Euphrates (yoo FRAY teez) rivers. When these rivers flood, they deposit rich soil along their banks. The Tigris and the Euphrates rivers begin in Turkey and flow south through Iraq. They join to form the Shatt-al-Arab, which flows into the Persian Gulf. In ancient times, the land between these two rivers supported one of the world's first civilizations. The region was known as Mesopotamia. Here, people learned to raise plants and animals for food, relying on the rich soil provided by the rivers.

Mountains and Plateaus As you can see on the physical map of Southwest Asia, the Tigris and Euphrates rivers begin in the mountains of Turkey. Iran also has mountains. The Zagros Mountains extend along the western part of Iran. The Elburz Mountains extend along the northern coast of Iran. The mountains give way to large plateaus in both Turkey and Iran.

Seas and Gulfs Much of the land of Southwest Asia borders bodies of water that separate countries within the region. These bodies of water also separate Southwest Asia from other regions. The Red Sea separates Southwest Asia and Africa. The Mediterranean Sea forms Southwest Asia's western border. The Black Sea forms Turkey's northern border. The Caspian Sea forms part of the boundary between Southwest Asia and Central Asia. The Persian Gulf separates Iran from the Arabian Peninsula.

Iraq's capital, Baghdad, lies on both banks of the Tigris River. The small photo shows a mosque, or Islamic place of worship, in Istanbul, Turkey.

MAP MASTER™ Skills Activity

Southwest Asia: Climate Regions

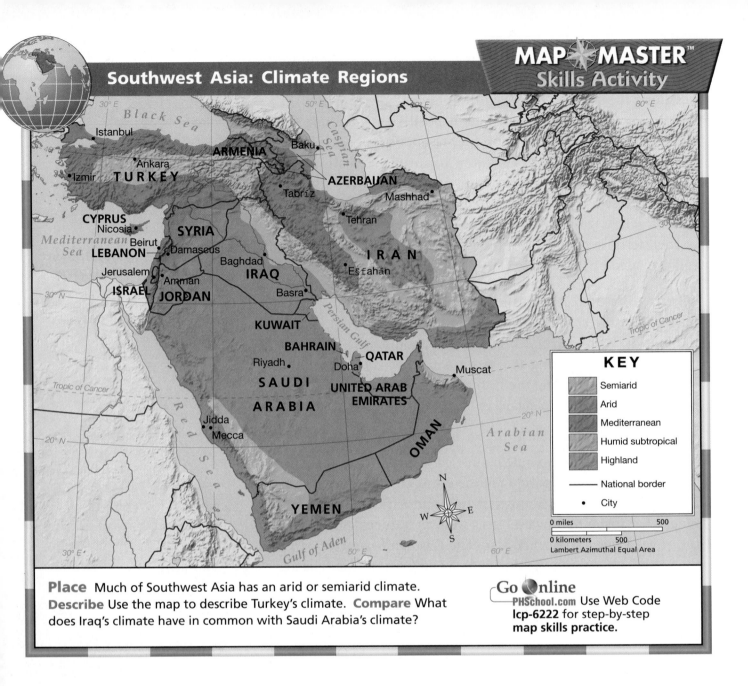

KEY

- Semiarid
- Arid
- Mediterranean
- Humid subtropical
- Highland
- National border
- City

0 miles 500
0 kilometers 500
Lambert Azimuthal Equal Area

Place Much of Southwest Asia has an arid or semiarid climate. **Describe** Use the map to describe Turkey's climate. **Compare** What does Iraq's climate have in common with Saudi Arabia's climate?

Go Online PHSchool.com Use Web Code **lcp-6222 for step-by-step map skills practice.**

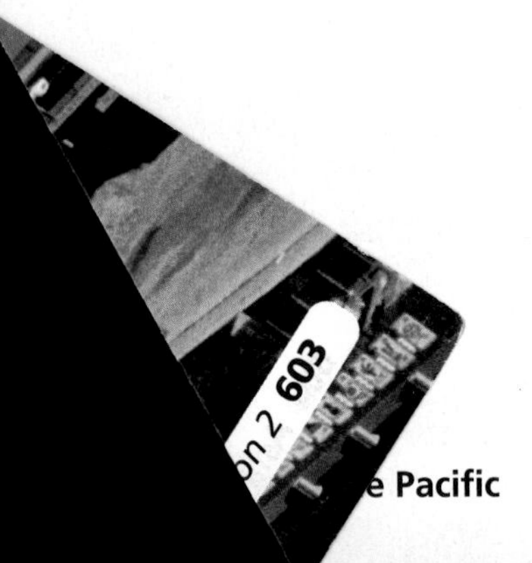

A Hot, Dry Climate Most of Southwest Asia has an arid or a semiarid climate. Much of the region receives less than 10 inches (25 centimeters) of rain each year. It is no wonder, then, that nearly two thirds of Southwest Asia is desert!

Because the desert air contains little moisture, few clouds form over the dry land. As a result, temperatures may reach as high as 125°F (52°C) during the day. At night, they may drop to as low as 40°F (4°C).

Some parts of Southwest Asia have a Mediterranean climate, with hot, dry summers and mild, rainy winters. The coasts of the Mediterranean, Black, and Caspian seas as well as the mountainous areas of the region have a Mediterranean climate.

✓ **Reading Check** **Which two countries in Southwest Asia have mountains?**

Southwest Asia's Major Natural Resources

The two most important natural resources in Southwest Asia are petroleum and water. **Petroleum** (puh TROH lee um) is an oily, flammable liquid formed from the remains of ancient plants and animals. It is found under Earth's surface. Petroleum deposits take millions of years to form. Petroleum is a **nonrenewable resource**—a natural resource that cannot be quickly replaced once it is used.

Petroleum is the source of gasoline and other fuels. People all over the world depend on petroleum to fuel cars and trucks, provide energy for industry, and heat homes. Petroleum is the natural resource that brings the most money into Southwest Asia. Water, however, is the resource that people there need most. Since much of Southwest Asia has a dry climate, the water in the region must be used carefully.

Petroleum Large deposits of petroleum, also called oil, can be found in only a few places on Earth. As a result, petroleum-rich countries play a key role in the world's economy. Southwest Asia is the largest oil-producing region in the world. Petroleum is Southwest Asia's greatest export.

Oil wealth allows many Southwest Asian countries to increase the standard of living of their people. **Standard of living** is a measurement of a person's or a group's education, housing, health, and nutrition. These countries have enough money to build schools and hospitals and to import goods from other countries. They can also import workers. Most of the people living in oil-rich Kuwait are citizens of other countries, including Pakistan, India, and Bangladesh.

Southwest Asia has more than half of the world's oil reserves. But some countries in the region have little or no oil. These countries tend to have a lower standard of living than their oil-rich neighbors. They do not have the income that petroleum brings.

Oil pipelines in Saudi Arabia

Water from the Sea of Galilee is carried to southern Israel by the National Water Carrier.

Water To grow crops in this dry region, people usually must irrigate their land. Saudi Arabia, for example, has no permanent rivers. It has wadis (WAH deez), or stream beds that may hold water when seasonal rains fall but are dry much of the year. People there irrigate their crops by pumping water from deep underground wells. In other parts of Southwest Asia, wells are not as necessary. People use water from rivers and streams to irrigate the dry areas of the country.

The nations of Southwest Asia have continued to build irrigation systems. But irrigation cannot solve the problem of water scarcity. Too much irrigation can use up the water that is available. In an area with little rainfall, water that is taken from a river is not soon replaced. When a river runs through more than one nation, each nation is affected by the others' irrigation systems.

✓ Reading Check **What benefits has petroleum brought to the countries of Southwest Asia?**

Southwest Asia: Natural Resources

MAP MASTER™ Skills Activity

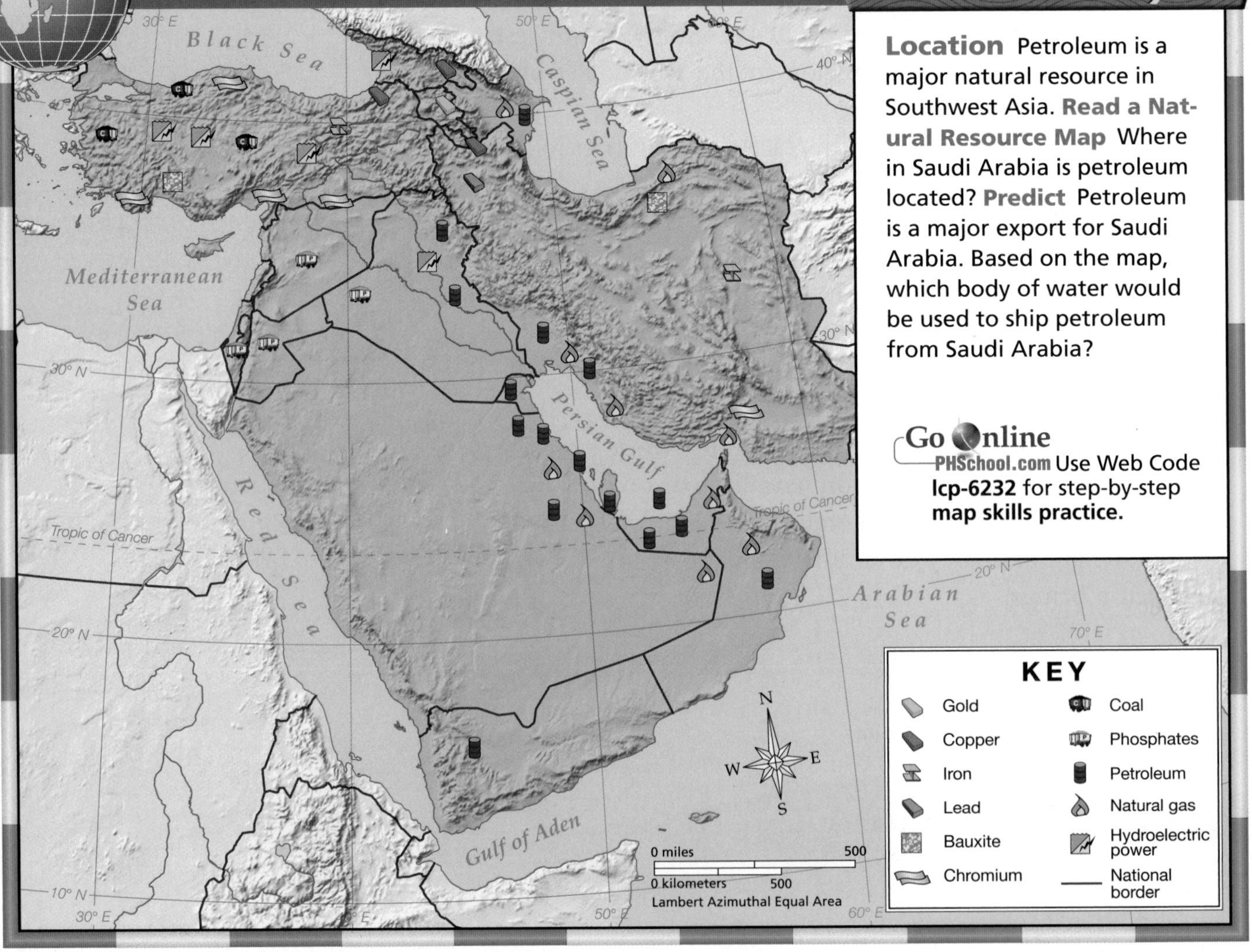

Location Petroleum is a major natural resource in Southwest Asia. **Read a Natural Resource Map** Where in Saudi Arabia is petroleum located? **Predict** Petroleum is a major export for Saudi Arabia. Based on the map, which body of water would be used to ship petroleum from Saudi Arabia?

Go Online
PHSchool.com Use Web Code **lcp-6232 for step-by-step map skills practice.**

Black Sea
Caspian Sea
Mediterranean Sea
Persian Gulf
Red Sea
Arabian Sea
Gulf of Aden
Tropic of Cancer
30° E
50° E
60° E
70° E
40° N
30° N
20° N
10° N

KEY
Gold
Copper
Iron
Lead
Bauxite
Chromium
Coal
Phosphates
Petroleum
Natural gas
Hydroelectric power
National border

0 miles 500
0 kilometers 500
Lambert Azimuthal Equal Area

Using the Land in Southwest Asia

People use the land in Southwest Asia in three major ways: for agriculture, for nomadic herding, and for producing oil. Because of the region's climate, only a small percentage of the region is made up of arable land. Most of this farmland is located in the northern part of the region, with commercial farming taking place along the coasts. There, the Mediterranean climate makes it possible for people to grow a wide variety of crops.

Various commercial farm products are raised in Israel and Turkey. In Israel, these include citrus fruits, cotton, peanuts, and sugar cane. Turkey's commercial farms produce such crops as wheat, barley, cotton, sugar beets, fruits, olives, and corn.

For centuries, Arabic-speaking nomadic herders known as Bedouins (BED oo inz) have lived in Southwest Asia's deserts herding camels, goats, and sheep. Instead of settling in one place, Bedouins moved over a large area of land, seeking grass and water for their animals. Today the Bedouin make up about 10 percent of the population of Southwest Asia. In recent times, settlement policies of countries in Southwest Asia have forced many Bedouins to settle in one place.

✓ Reading Check **What are some of Turkey's commercial farming crops?**

Links to Science

Dead Sea Alive With Minerals The Dead Sea, a lake between Israel and Jordan, is too salty to support fish or plant life. But it does help support Israel's economy. The sea is full of minerals. The Israelis take out potash—a mineral used for explosives and fertilizer—as well as table salt and a variety of other minerals for export.

Section 2 Assessment

Key Terms

Review the key terms at the beginning of this section. Use each term in a sentence that explains its meaning.

Target Reading Skill

Reread the first paragraph after the heading Two Historic Rivers on page 603. Then, using your own words, paraphrase the paragraph. Begin your paraphrase with the sentence, "Rich soil lies along the banks of the Tigris and Euphrates rivers."

Comprehension and Critical Thinking

1. **(a) Recall** What kind of land covers much of Southwest Asia?
(b) Identify Name one major desert, two seas, and one mountain range in Southwest Asia.
(c) Explain Give a location for the desert, the seas, and the mountain range in the previous question.

2. **(a) Identify** What are the two most important natural resources in Southwest Asia?
(b) Explain Why are irrigation systems important in Southwest Asia?

3. **(a) Recall** What are three major ways that people use the land in Southwest Asia?
(b) Summarize What are some commercial farm products of Southwest Asia?

Writing Activity

Write a paragraph that describes water from the point of view of a person living in the United States on the coast of the Atlantic Ocean. Then write another paragraph from the point of view of a person living in a desert region in Southwest Asia. Exchange your paragraphs with a partner. How are your paragraphs similar to or different from those of your partner?

For: An activity on Southwest Asia
Visit: PHSchool.com
Web Code: lcd-6202

Identifying Main Ideas

Keith was just starting his homework when his mother popped her head into the room.

"What assignment are you working on?" she asked.

"I'm reading an article on petroleum mining in Southwest Asia," Keith replied. "Did you know that more than half of Saudi Arabia's oil reserves are found in just eight oil fields, including the largest onshore oil field in the world?"

"That's a fascinating detail," Keith's mother said. "What's the main idea of the article?"

"That's the assignment," Keith answered. "We have to read the article and identify the main idea."

A main idea is the most important information in a paragraph or reading passage. A main idea is not the same as a topic. Knowing how to identify main ideas will make you a better reader and a better student.

Identifying main ideas is an essential study skill.

Learn the Skill

To identify the main idea in a paragraph, follow these steps:

1. **Identify the topic of the paragraph.** The topic of a paragraph tells what the paragraph is about. Look for a sentence that identifies the topic. It is called a "topic sentence," and it is often the first sentence of a paragraph. Also, it sometimes—but not always—states the main idea.

2. **Look for an idea that all the sentences in the paragraph have in common.** In a well-written paragraph, most of the sentences provide details that support or explain the main idea.

3. **State the main idea in your own words.** Write what you think is the main idea in your own words. Write a complete sentence. Avoid writing a sentence that is too broad or too specific. Remember that a main idea focuses on the most important information about the topic. Even if a detail is interesting, it may not be the most important information. A main idea should always be a complete sentence.

Practice the Skill

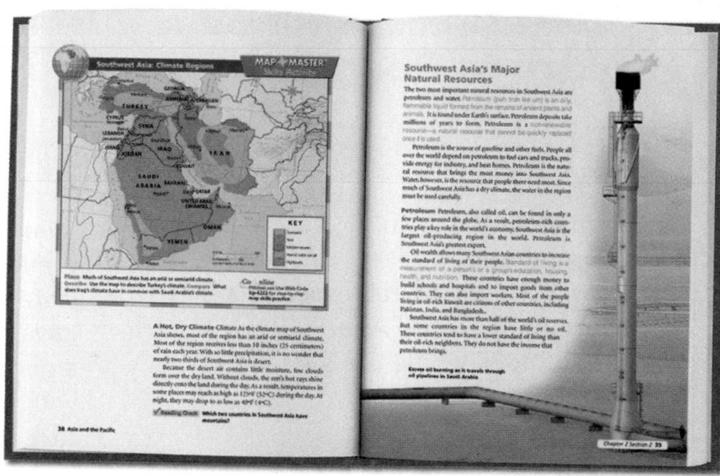

Now turn to page 605 and study the first paragraph under the heading Southwest Asia's Major Natural Resources. Use the steps on the previous page to find the main idea of the paragraph.

1. What is the topic of the paragraph? Remember that the topic of a paragraph is not necessarily the same as a main idea. For example, the topic of a paragraph is usually a subject, such as petroleum mining in Southwest Asia.
2. In a word or phrase, write down what you think each sentence is about. Then look at the words you've listed and find a common idea among them.
3. Look for the most important information about the topic. Write a complete sentence that states the most important information. Be sure your sentence focuses on the most important information. Why is the following statement too broad? *Southwest Asia has many natural resources.* Why is the following statement too specific? *Petroleum is found under Earth's surface.*

Apply the Skill

Read the following paragraph. Use the steps you learned to write a statement giving the main idea of this paragraph.

With about one fourth of the world's oil, Saudi Arabia is the leading country in the Organization of Petroleum Exporting Countries (OPEC). OPEC is an organization of countries with economies that rely on money from oil exports. As a group, OPEC decides how much oil its members will produce and at what price to sell it. Besides Saudi Arabia, members consist of Algeria, Indonesia, Iran, Iraq, Kuwait, Libya, Nigeria, Qatar, the United Arab Emirates, and Venezuela. OPEC produces about 40 percent of the world's crude oil.

Section 3
Central Asia
Physical Geography

Prepare to Read

Objectives
In this section, you will
1. Learn about the main physical features of Central Asia.
2. Discover which natural resources are important in Central Asia.
3. Find out how people use the land in Central Asia.

Taking Notes
As you read this section, look for details about the physical geography of Central Asia. Copy the diagram below and record your findings in it.

Land	Climate	Natural Resources
• •	• •	• •

Target Reading Skill
Summarizing When you summarize, you review and state the main points you have read. Summarizing is a good technique to help you better understand a text. A good summary identifies the main ideas, states them in the order in which they appear, and notes when one event causes another to happen. As you read, pause occasionally to summarize what you have read.

Key Term
- **steppe** (step) *n.* vast, mostly level, treeless plains that are covered in grasses

This rocket, carrying the *Mars Express,* was launched from Baikonur in 2003.

On the treeless plains of Central Asia sprawls the Baikonur (by kuh NOOR) Cosmodrome, the largest space-launch center in the world. Baikonur is the site of several historic spaceflights. In 1957, the first artificial satellite was launched from Baikonur. The first mission to put a human in space blasted off from Baikonur in 1961. In 2003, the *Mars Express,* a European mission to send a spacecraft to Mars, was launched from Baikonur.

Baikonur is located in Kazakhstan (kah zahk STAHN), the largest and northernmost country in Central Asia. To its south are Uzbekistan (ooz BEK ih stan), Kyrgyzstan (kihr gih STAN), Turkmenistan (turk MEN ih stan), and Tajikistan (tah jik ih STAN). Afghanistan forms the southern border of Central Asia. Except for Afghanistan, the countries of Central Asia were once part of the Soviet Union.

Central Asia's Main Physical Features

Central Asia's main physical features are highlands, deserts, and steppes. **Steppes** are vast, mostly level, treeless plains covered with grassland vegetation. Central Asia's mountains are in the southeastern part of the region. The Tian Shan and Pamir mountain ranges cover much of Kyrgyzstan and Tajikistan. The Tian Shan range also extends into China. The Pamir extend into Afghanistan, where they meet the Hindu Kush mountains.

To the west of these mountain ranges, the elevation drops and the land flattens. The Kara Kum desert covers much of the land in Turkmenistan. The Kyzyl Kum desert covers much of neighboring Uzbekistan. The Kirghiz Steppe is located in Kazakhstan.

Steppes in Central Asia

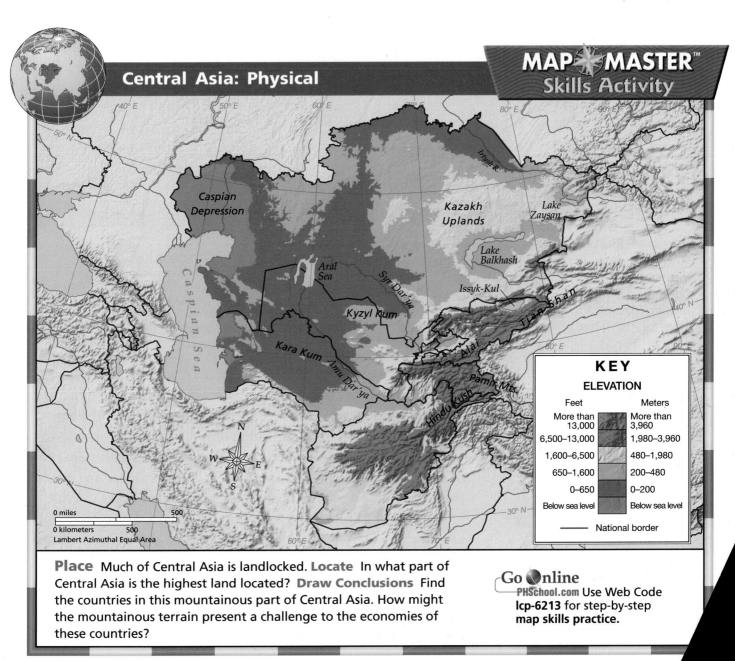

MAP MASTER™ Skills Activity

Central Asia: Physical

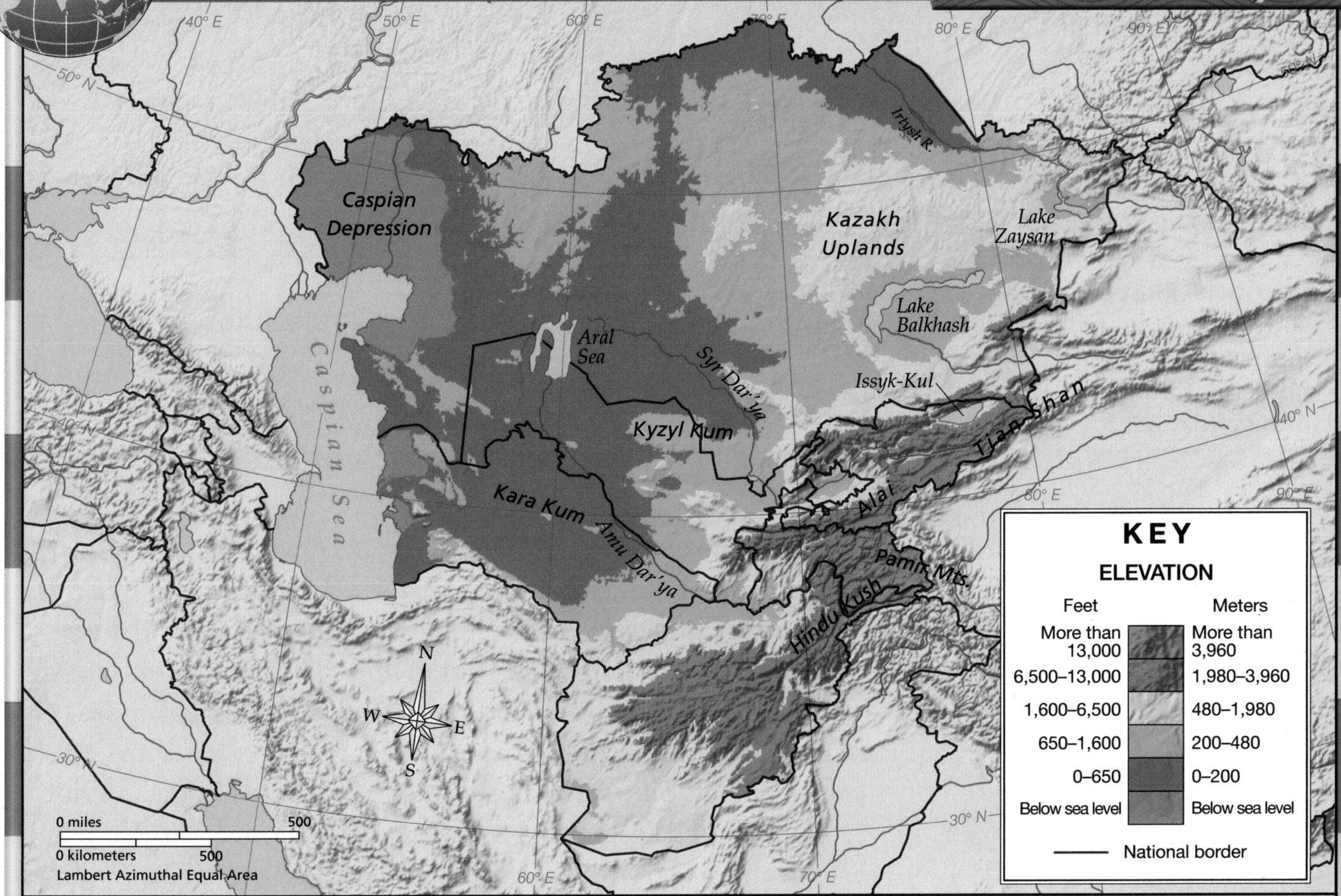

Caspian Depression
Kazakh Uplands
Lake Zaysan
Lake Balkhash
Aral Sea
Syr Dar'ya
Irtysh R.
Issyk-Kul
Tian Shan
Kyzyl Kum
Kara Kum
Amu Dar'ya
Alai
Pamir Mts.
Hindu Kush
Caspian Sea

KEY

ELEVATION

Feet	Meters
More than 13,000	More than 3,960
6,500–13,000	1,980–3,960
1,600–6,500	480–1,980
650–1,600	200–480
0–650	0–200
Below sea level	Below sea level

—— National border

0 miles 500
0 kilometers 500
Lambert Azimuthal Equal Area

Place Much of Central Asia is landlocked. **Locate** In what part of Central Asia is the highest land located? **Draw Conclusions** Find the countries in this mountainous part of Central Asia. How might the mountainous terrain present a challenge to the economies of these countries?

Go Online PHSchool.com Use Web Code **lcp-6213** for step-by-step **map skills practice.**

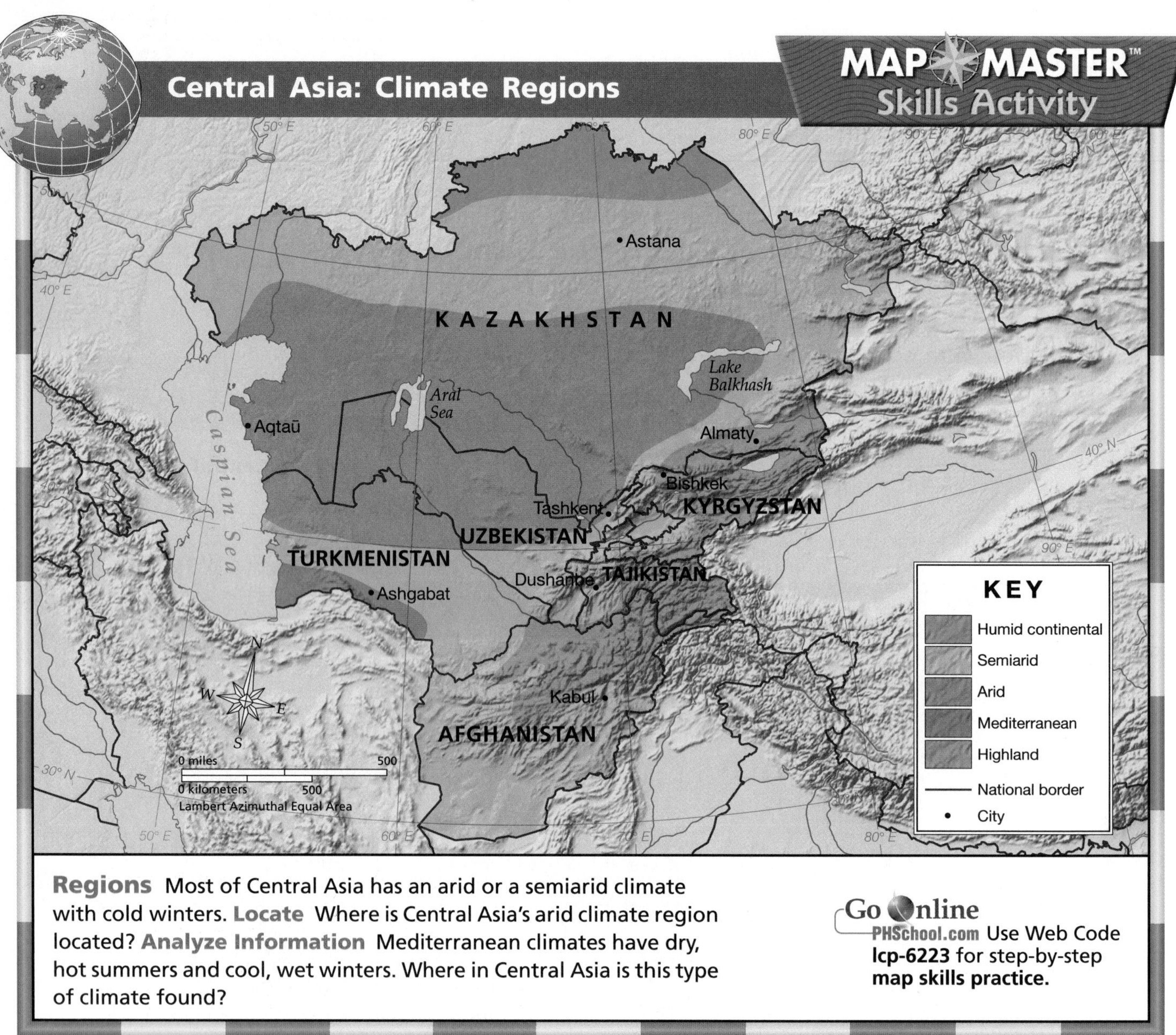

Regions Most of Central Asia has an arid or a semiarid climate with cold winters. **Locate** Where is Central Asia's arid climate region located? **Analyze Information** Mediterranean climates have dry, hot summers and cool, wet winters. Where in Central Asia is this type of climate found?

Go Online PHSchool.com Use Web Code **lcp-6223** for step-by-step **map skills practice.**

Most of Central Asia has a dry climate. A wide band of semiarid land surrounds the arid region that covers much of the interior. The arid areas receive less precipitation than the semiarid areas.

Two bodies of water stand out in the dry region of Central Asia. They are the Caspian Sea and the Aral Sea. The Caspian Sea, the largest lake in the world, is actually a salt lake. It has some of the world's largest oil reserves. The Aral Sea is located in the interior.

Also a salt lake, the Aral Sea was once the fourth-largest inland lake in the world. Now many boats there rest on dry land. In the 1960s, the former Soviet Union began to channel water from rivers that feed the sea to irrigate crops. As a result, the Aral Sea began to dry up.

Target Skill **Summarizing** Summarize the paragraph at the right. Be sure to include the reason why the [illegible] Sea is drying up.

Reading Check **What type of climate does most of Central Asia have?**

Natural Resources in Central Asia

As in Southwest Asia, petroleum is a major natural resource in Central Asia. Another major natural resource in the region is natural gas. Kazakhstan is one of three Central Asian countries that have large oil and gas reserves. The other two are Uzbekistan and Turkmenistan. Turkmenistan has the fifth-largest reserve of natural gas in the world. These countries are working to develop the oil and gas industry.

Central Asia has other valuable minerals in addition to petroleum and natural gas. Kazakhstan has rich deposits of coal, much of which it exports to Russia, Ukraine, and Kyrgyzstan. Kazakhstan is the largest exporter of coal to other former Soviet republics as well. Kyrgyzstan, Tajikistan, and Uzbekistan are important gold producers. Other major mineral resources in the region are copper, iron ore, lead, and uranium.

✓ Reading Check **What are two major natural resources in Central Asia?**

Drilling for oil in Kazakhstan

Central Asia: Natural Resources

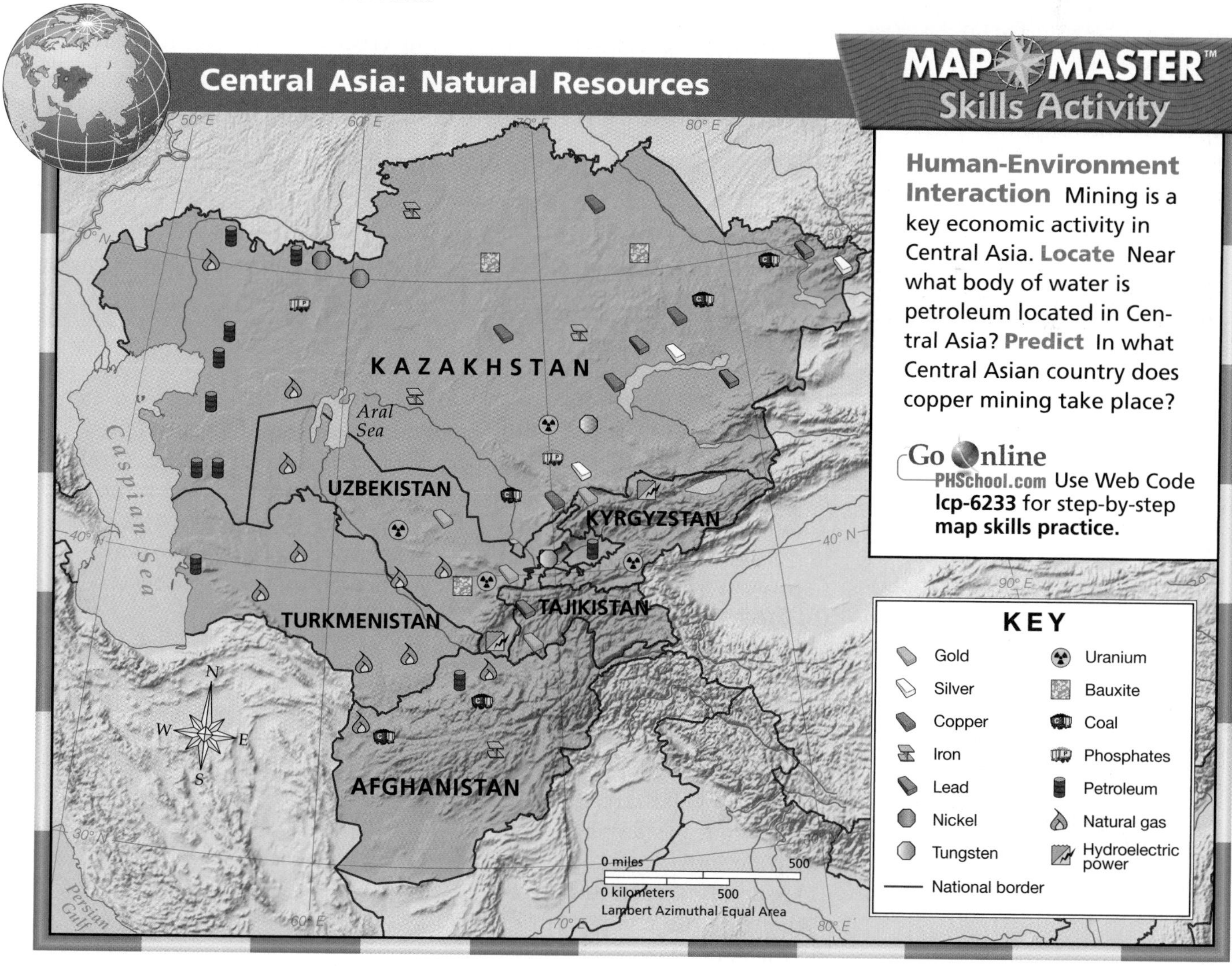

KAZAKHSTAN
UZBEKISTAN
KYRGYZSTAN
TAJIKISTAN
TURKMENISTAN
AFGHANISTAN
Aral Sea
Caspian Sea
Persian Gulf
50° E 60° E 70° E 80° E 90° E
30° N 40° N 50° N
0 miles 500
0 kilometers 500
Lambert Azimuthal Equal Area

KEY

Gold	Uranium
Silver	Bauxite
Copper	Coal
Iron	Phosphates
Lead	Petroleum
Nickel	Natural gas
Tungsten	Hydroelectric power
National border	

MAP MASTER™ Skills Activity

Human-Environment Interaction Mining is a key economic activity in Central Asia. **Locate** Near what body of water is petroleum located in Central Asia? **Predict** In what Central Asian country does copper mining take place?

Go Online PHSchool.com Use Web Code **lcp-6233 for step-by-step map skills practice.**

Abandoned boats lie rusting on land that was once the bottom of the Aral Sea.

Land Use in Central Asia

Most of the land in Central Asia is used for agriculture, especially livestock raising and commercial farming. People in Central Asia have raised sheep, horses, goats, and camels for thousands of years. Cotton is a major crop in Uzbekistan, Turkmenistan, and Tajikistan.

Agriculture in Central Asia depends on irrigation. In the 1960s, the Soviet Union started a huge irrigation project to bring water to Central Asia. The Soviet Union wanted to increase cotton production. Canals were built to carry fresh water from two rivers to irrigate the cotton fields. Between 1960 and 1980, cotton production in the Soviet Union more than tripled.

The irrigation projects turned Central Asia into a leading cotton producer. But they also caused major damage to the Aral Sea. The Amu Darya and Sry Darya rivers flow into the Aral Sea. Over the decades, heavy irrigation has taken great amounts of water from these two rivers. As a result, the Aral Sea is drying up. The land around the Aral Sea is affected, too. Huge quantities of pesticides were used on the cotton crops. These chemicals have polluted the soil. The destruction of the Aral Sea has been called one of the world's worst environmental disasters.

✓ Reading Check **How has irrigation affected the land in Central Asia?**

Section 3 Assessment

Key Terms

Review the key terms at the beginning of the section. Use each term in a sentence that explains its meaning.

Target Reading Skill

Write a summary of the first paragraph under the heading Natural Resources in Central Asia. Be sure to use your own words and include the main idea and details in the order in which they appeared.

Comprehension and Critical Thinking

1. (a) Recall What are Central Asia's three main physical features?

(b) Transfer Information If you were to draw a map of Central Asia, where would these main physical features be located?

2. (a) Identify What are two important natural resources in Central Asia?

(b) Draw Inferences With which Central Asian country might an American energy company want to work to develop natural gas resources? Explain why.

3. (a) Explain What major crop raised in Uzbekistan, Turkmenistan, and Tajikistan depends on irrigation?

(b) Identify Cause and Effect What were the effects of irrigation on the Aral Sea?

Writing Activity

As in many regions around the world, the economies of Central Asian countries depend on the availability of water. Write a paragraph suggesting ways in which your community can wisely conserve water.

For: An activity on Central Asia
Visit: PHSchool.com
Web Code: lcd-6203

Chapter 19 Review and Assessment

◆ Chapter Summary

Section 1: South Asia: Physical Geography

- The Himalayas are a major landform in South Asia. The region also includes the Ganges and Indus rivers, fertile plains, and a plateau framed by the Western Ghats and the Eastern Ghats.
- The climate of South Asia is greatly affected by the monsoons.
- South Asia is a densely populated and generally rural region. Most of the people work in agriculture, and most of the land is used for farming.

India

Israel

Section 2: Southwest Asia: Physical Geography

- Much of Southwest Asia is a peninsula. The region has a dry climate and contains some of Earth's largest deserts.
- Petroleum and water are Southwest Asia's most important and valuable natural resources.
- Land in Southwest Asia is used mainly for agriculture, for nomadic herding, and for producing oil.

Section 3: Central Asia: Physical Geography

- Highlands, deserts, steppes, and a generally dry climate are Central Asia's main physical features. Much of the region is located inland.
- Central Asia's most valuable natural resources are oil and natural gas.
- Most of the land in Central Asia is used for agriculture, especially livestock raising and commercial farming. Because the region is dry, agriculture in Central Asia depends on irrigation.

◆ Key Terms

Match the definitions in Column I with the key terms in Column II.

Column I

1. a large landmass that is a major part of a continent
2. a crop that is raised to be sold for money on the local or world market
3. an oily liquid used as a fuel
4. an area in a desert region where fresh water is usually found
5. a natural resource that cannot be quickly replaced once it is used up
6. a measurement of a person's or group's education, housing, health, and nutrition
7. a vast, mostly level, treeless plain

Column II

- **A** standard of living
- **B** oasis
- **C** steppe
- **D** petroleum
- **E** subcontinent
- **F** nonrenewable resource
- **G** cash crop

Review and Assessment (continued)

◆ Comprehension and Critical Thinking

8. **(a) Define** What are the two most important rivers in South Asia?
   (b) Identify Effects How do the rivers of South Asia affect farmland?
9. **(a) Recall** What percentage of the population in South Asia lives in rural areas?
   (b) Apply Information How does rainfall relate to population patterns in South Asia?
10. **(a) Locate** Where are the Tigris and Euphrates rivers located?
    (b) Analyze Information What are some of the factors that explain why one of the world's first civilizations grew in Mesopotamia rather than on the Arabian Peninsula?
11. **(a) Identify** What is Southwest Asia's greatest export?
    (b) Infer Southwest Asia has more than half of the world's oil reserves. Why might the United States have an interest in this region?
12. **(a) Name** Name one way that people use the land in Southwest Asia.
    (b) Predict Where would you expect to find a commercial farm in Southwest Asia—in Saudi Arabia or in Turkey? Give at least two reasons to support your answer.
13. **(a) List** What are three facts about the geography of Central Asia?
    (b) Summarize Why is the Aral Sea shrinking?

◆ Skills Practice

Identifying Main Ideas Review the steps you followed on page 608 to learn how to identify main ideas. Then re-read the first paragraph on page 613. Write a sentence that states the main idea.

◆ Writing Activity: Science

Suppose that you are a science reporter assigned to write about the Aral Sea. Do research to learn more about how the area around the Aral Sea has been affected by heavy irrigation. Write a brief article about the current situation.

MAP MASTER™ Skills Activity

South, Southwest, and Central Asia

Place Location For each place listed below, write the letter from the map that shows its location.

1. Rub' al-Khali
2. Mediterranean Sea
3. Euphrates River
4. Himalayas
5. Indian Ocean
6. Aral Sea

Go Online
PHSchool.com Use Web Code **lcp-6220** for step-by-step **map skills practice.**

A
B
C
D
E
F
30° N
15° N
Tropic of Cancer
30° E
45° E
60° E
75° E
90° E
105° E
120° E
N
S
E
W

Standardized Test Prep

Test-Taking Tips

Some questions on standardized tests ask you to analyze parts of a map. Study the map key below. Then follow the tips to answer the sample question.

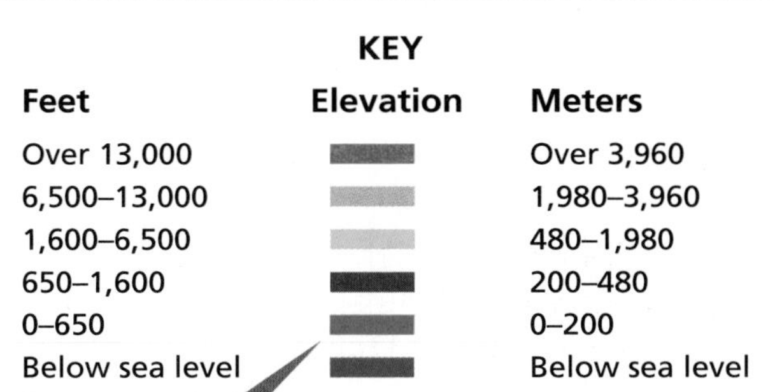

KEY

Feet	Elevation	Meters
Over 13,000		Over 3,960
6,500–13,000		1,980–3,960
1,600–6,500		480–1,980
650–1,600		200–480
0–650		0–200
Below sea level		Below sea level

TIP On a map key, the color column lines up with the data on the information column or columns. To find the required information, move from a given color to the data on the left or right.

Pick the letter that best answers the question.

On an elevation map, most of the area around the Ganges River is colored green. According to the key at the left, how many meters is the elevation in that area?

A below sea level
B 0–200
C 0–650
D 650–1,600

TIP Preview the question. Keep it in mind as you study the information on the map key.

Practice Questions

Use the tips above and other tips in this book to help you answer the following questions.

1. Scientists think that about 50 million years ago, the Indian subcontinent slowly collided with Asia to form
   A the island nation of Sri Lanka.
   B the Western Ghats.
   C the Himalayas.
   D Mesopotamia.

2. The alluvial plains in northern India make the area ideal for
   A mining.
   B farming.
   C aquaculture.
   D hydroelectricity.

3. South Asian countries have climates with warm, dry winters because
   A they are located along the Equator.
   B they are located in a desert region.
   C the Himalayas block cold air blown by the winter monsoon.
   D the Eastern Ghats block cold air blown by the winter monsoon.

Use the passage below to answer Question 4.

> In the winter, the people of eastern Kazakhstan wrap themselves in fur to brave the freezing temperatures. Snow covers the ground as far as the eye can see. Livestock must dig through the ice to feed on the tough grass underneath. But the straight roads of the countryside never need to be plowed. Engineers built the roads slightly higher than the surrounding land. The strong winds keep the roads free of snow.

4. This paragraph is missing a topic sentence. What is the best topic sentence for this paragraph?
   A Winters in eastern Kazakhstan are extremely cold and snowy.
   B Engineers in Kazakhstan are among the best in the world.
   C Some people in eastern Kazakhstan raise livestock for a living.
   D Summers in Kazakhstan are extremely hot.

Use Web Code **lca-6200** for **Chapter 19 self-test.**

Chapter 20

Southeast Asia and the Pacific Region: Physical Geography

Chapter Preview

In this chapter, you will learn about Southeast Asia and the Pacific Region—a region of the world that includes islands, peninsulas, and the world's smallest continent.

Section 1
Southeast Asia
Physical Geography

Section 2
Australia and New Zealand
Physical Geography

Section 3
The Pacific Islands
Physical Geography

Main Idea In this chapter, you will focus on identifying the main ideas in the sections and paragraphs you read. You will also focus on identifying the details that support each main idea.

▶ A lush rain forest in the Philippines

Southeast Asia and the Pacific Region: Physical

MAP MASTER™ Skills Activity

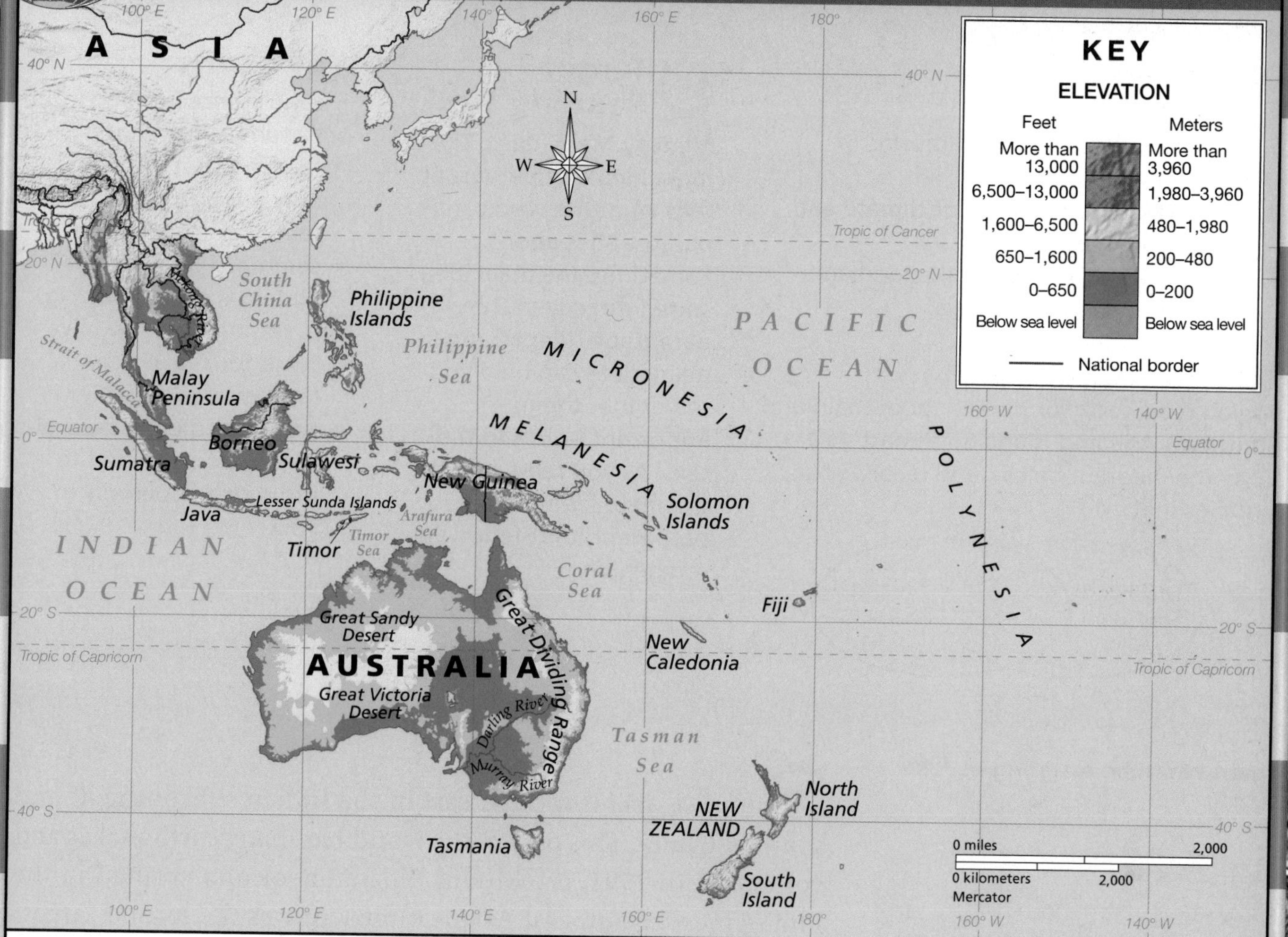

ASIA
South China Sea
Philippine Islands
Philippine Sea
MICRONESIA
MELANESIA
POLYNESIA
PACIFIC OCEAN
Strait of Malacca
Malay Peninsula
Borneo
Sumatra
Sulawesi
New Guinea
Java
Lesser Sunda Islands
Arafura Sea
Timor Sea
Timor
Solomon Islands
INDIAN OCEAN
Coral Sea
Fiji
New Caledonia
AUSTRALIA
Great Sandy Desert
Great Victoria Desert
Great Dividing Range
Darling River
Murray River
Tasman Sea
Tasmania
NEW ZEALAND
North Island
South Island
Tropic of Cancer
Tropic of Capricorn
Equator
100° E
120° E
140° E
160° E
180°
160° W
140° W
40° N
20° N
0°
20° S
40° S
N
S
E
W

KEY

ELEVATION

Feet	Meters
More than 13,000	More than 3,960
6,500–13,000	1,980–3,960
1,600–6,500	480–1,980
650–1,600	200–480
0–650	0–200
Below sea level	Below sea level

National border

0 miles 2,000
0 kilometers 2,000
Mercator

Place Much of Southeast Asia and the Pacific Region is located between the Tropic of Cancer and the Tropic of Capricorn. **Identify** Name the continents in Southeast Asia and the Pacific Region. **Draw Conclusions** What kind of climate would you expect most of these countries to have? Explain your answer.

Go Online PHSchool.com Use Web Code **lcp-6310** for step-by-step **map skills practice.**

Section 1

Southeast Asia

Physical Geography

Prepare to Read

Objectives

In this section, you will

1. Learn about the major landforms of Southeast Asia.
2. Find out about the kinds of climate and vegetation in Southeast Asia.
3. Examine how people use the land and resources of Southeast Asia.

Taking Notes

As you read, look for details about mainland Southeast Asia and island Southeast Asia. Copy the diagram below, and record your findings in it.

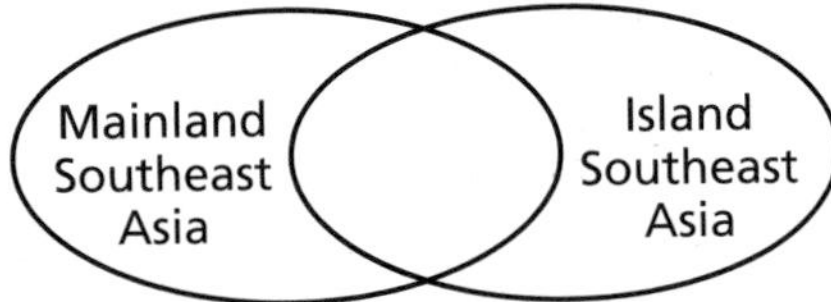

Target Reading Skill

Identify Main Ideas The main idea of a paragraph tells what the whole paragraph is about. Sometimes the main idea is stated directly in the paragraph. Identifying main ideas can help you remember the most important points in the text. As you read, identify the main idea of each paragraph that follows a red heading.

Key Terms

- **subsistence farming** (sub SIS tuns FAHR ming) *n.* farming that provides only enough food for a family or for a village
- **commercial farming** (kuh MUR shul FAHR ming) *n.* raising crops and livestock for sale on the local or world market
- **paddy** (PAD ee) *n.* a level field that is flooded to grow rice, especially in Asia

Mount Pinatubo erupting in 1991

Southeast Asia is located east of the Indian subcontinent and south of China. This part of the world has many earthquakes and volcanoes. In 1991, the Mount Pinatubo volcano erupted in the Philippines, a Southeast Asian country. It was the second-largest volcanic eruption of the twentieth century. About 58,000 people moved to safety, but about 800 people died. The eruption threw nearly 20 millions tons of gas and ash 21 miles (34 kilometers) into the atmosphere. The gas cloud spread around Earth. For two years, this gas cloud caused global temperatures to drop by about 1°F (0.5°C). Volcanoes are one physical feature of Southeast Asia. What are other major physical features of Southeast Asia? How do they affect land use in the region?

The Land of Southeast Asia

Southeast Asia is divided into mainland and island areas. The mainland is a peninsula that juts south from the main area of Asia. The islands extend east and west between the Indian and the Pacific oceans. Locate the mainland and the islands on the map on the next page.

Southeast Asia: Physical

MAP MASTER™ Skills Activity

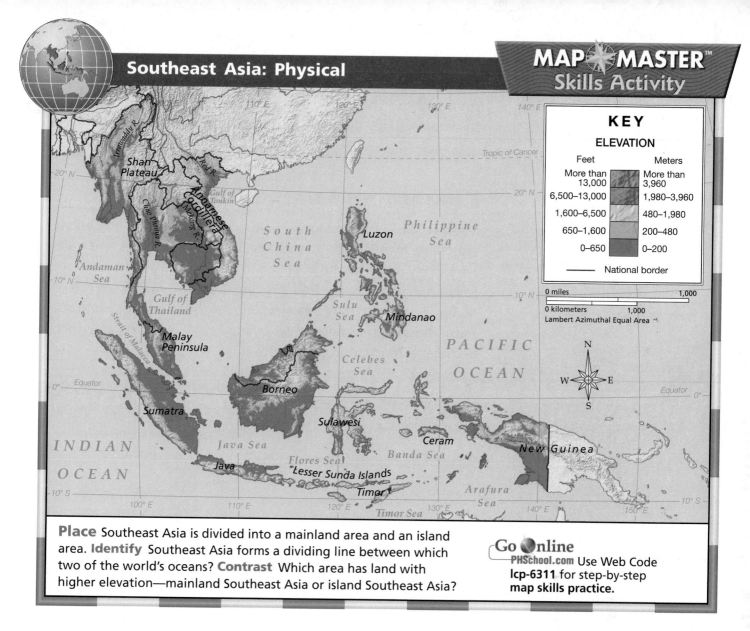

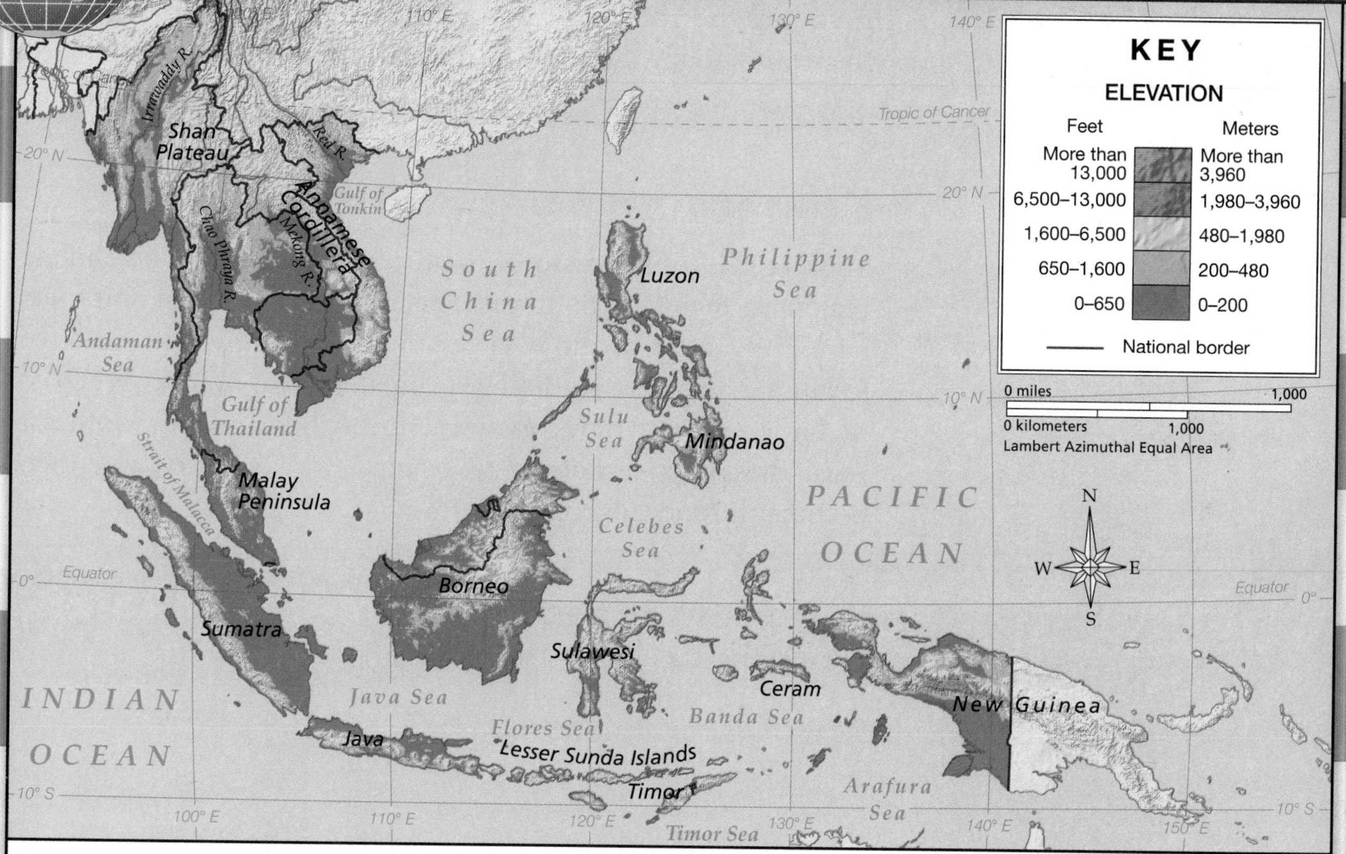

KEY

ELEVATION

Feet	Meters
More than 13,000	More than 3,960
6,500–13,000	1,980–3,960
1,600–6,500	480–1,980
650–1,600	200–480
0–650	0–200

National border

0 miles 1,000
0 kilometers 1,000
Lambert Azimuthal Equal Area

N S E W

Place Southeast Asia is divided into a mainland area and an island area. **Identify** Southeast Asia forms a dividing line between which two of the world's oceans? **Contrast** Which area has land with higher elevation—mainland Southeast Asia or island Southeast Asia?

Go Online PHSchool.com Use Web Code **lcp-6311** for step-by-step **map skills practice.**

Mainland Southeast Asia The nations of mainland Southeast Asia are Cambodia, Laos (LAH ohs), Malaysia (muh LAY zhuh), Myanmar (MYUN mahr), Thailand (TY land), and Vietnam. Note that Malaysia is part of mainland Southeast Asia as well as of island Southeast Asia. Much of this area is covered by forested mountains. Most people live in the narrow river valleys between mountain ranges.

Island Southeast Asia Five major nations make up island Southeast Asia: Singapore, Malaysia, Brunei (broo NY), Indonesia, and the Philippines. The largest of the island nations is Indonesia. Indonesia's biggest island is Sumatra. Singapore is a tiny nation, located at the tip of the Malay Peninsula. The country of Malaysia lies partly on the mainland and partly on the island of Borneo. The Philippines is a country made up of some 7,000 islands.

Tourists riding elephants through the forests of Thailand

The Ring of Fire The islands of Southeast Asia are part of the Ring of Fire. That is a region of volcanoes and earthquakes surrounding the Pacific Ocean. Most of the mountainous islands there are actually the peaks of underwater volcanoes.

✓ Reading Check **Name the largest nation in island Southeast Asia.**

Climate and Vegetation

Look at the climate map of Southeast Asia below. The climate regions in mainland Southeast Asia between Myanmar and Vietnam are similar to those in South Asia. On the west coast of Myanmar, there is a tropical wet climate, just as on the west coast of India. As you move eastward through mainland Southeast Asia, the climate changes to tropical wet and dry and then becomes humid subtropical.

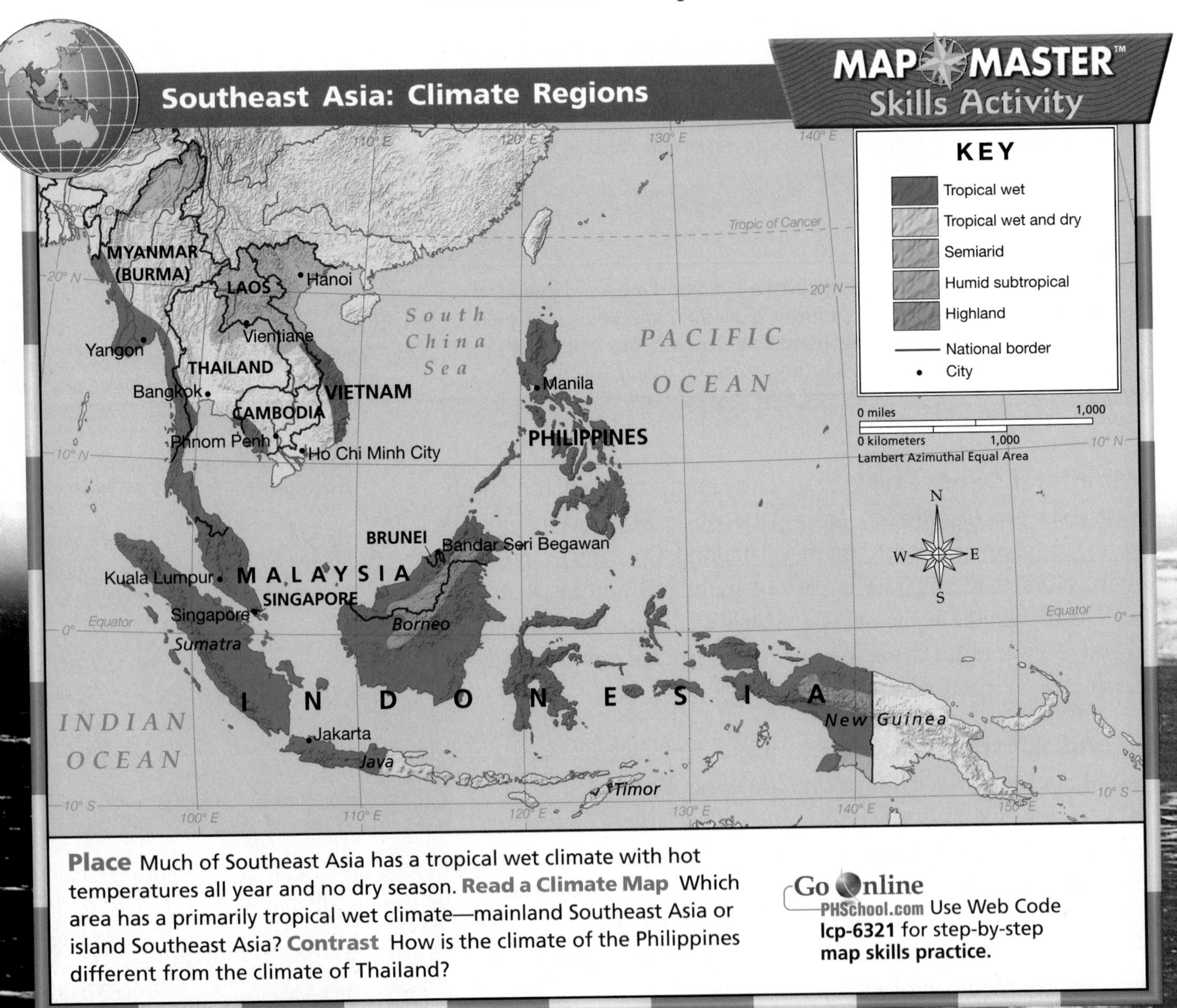

Place Much of Southeast Asia has a tropical wet climate with hot temperatures all year and no dry season. **Read a Climate Map** Which area has a primarily tropical wet climate—mainland Southeast Asia or island Southeast Asia? **Contrast** How is the climate of the Philippines different from the climate of Thailand?

Go Online
PHSchool.com Use Web Code **lcp-6321** for step-by-step **map skills practice.**

Multiple Monsoons However, when you get to the southeastern coast of Vietnam, the pattern changes. The climate is again tropical wet. It supports tropical rain forests—thick forests that receive at least 60 inches (152 centimeters) of rain a year. Why is this area so wet? The answer is that summer monsoons bring rains to this coast just as they do to the western coast.

In fact, there are two separate summer monsoons. An Indian Ocean monsoon blows from the southwest, and a Pacific Ocean monsoon blows from the southeast. Each brings heavy summer rain to the Southeast Asian coast that it hits. Also, during the Northern Hemisphere's winter, winds off the central Pacific Ocean blow from the northeast. This winter monsoon brings heavy rains to the southern Philippines and Indonesia. Because most of Indonesia is in the Southern Hemisphere, the heavy rain from December to March is a summer monsoon there.

Effects of a Tropical Wet Climate Most of island Southeast Asia has a tropical wet climate that supports tropical rain forests. Southeast Asia contains the second-largest tropical rain forest region in the world.

The rain forests of Southeast Asia are lush and thick with vegetation. However, there are disadvantages to living in the tropical climate of Southeast Asia—typhoons. When typhoons hit land, the high winds and heavy rain often lead to widespread property damage and loss of life.

✓ Reading Check **How does the northeast monsoon affect the southern Philippines and Indonesia?**

Monsoons in Southeast Asia
The photos below show the effect of monsoons in Cambodia. Monsoons bring rains that can sometimes flood streets. **Analyze Images** *How do people get around when monsoon flooding is severe?*

Using the Land and Resources of Southeast Asia

Growing Rice in Indonesia
In most of Southeast Asia, people grow rice by hand. Farmers use water buffalo to plow the fields. Rice seedlings are transplanted by hand to the fields, which have been flooded with water. **Analyze Images** *Which photo shows people transplanting rice seedlings to the fields?*

Many of the people in Southeast Asia make their living from the land. Some live in villages, where they build their own houses and grow their own food. Farming that provides only enough for a family or for a village is called **subsistence farming.** Many use the same building and farming methods that their ancestors relied upon thousands of years ago. Other people in Southeast Asia work on plantations—large farming operations designed to raise crops for profit, or cash crops. Plantation agriculture is a type of commercial farming. **Commercial farming** is the raising of crops and livestock for sale on the local or world market.

Farming Farming is a major economic activity in Southeast Asia, even though the region's cities and industries have been growing rapidly. In most Southeast Asian countries, more than 40 percent of the population work in agriculture. People farm—and live—in the river valleys of mountainous mainland Southeast Asia and on the lowland plains of island Southeast Asia. Crops include cash crops such as coffee, tea, and rubber. In Indonesia and Malaysia, rubber is grown on plantations and is a major export crop. Other major crops are soybeans, sugar cane, fruit, and, most important, rice.

The Importance of Rice Rice has been the chief crop in Southeast Asia for centuries. Rice needs a hot climate and plenty of water to grow. In fact, rice grows best when it is planted in the water. In Southeast Asia, farmers use the paddy system to grow rice. A **paddy** is a level field that is flooded to grow rice. Indonesia and Thailand are among the top rice-producing countries in the world. In Southeast Asia, rice is also an important part of the people's diet. It is a food crop as well as a cash crop.

Southeast Asia: Rain Forest Destruction

MAP MASTER™ Skills Activity

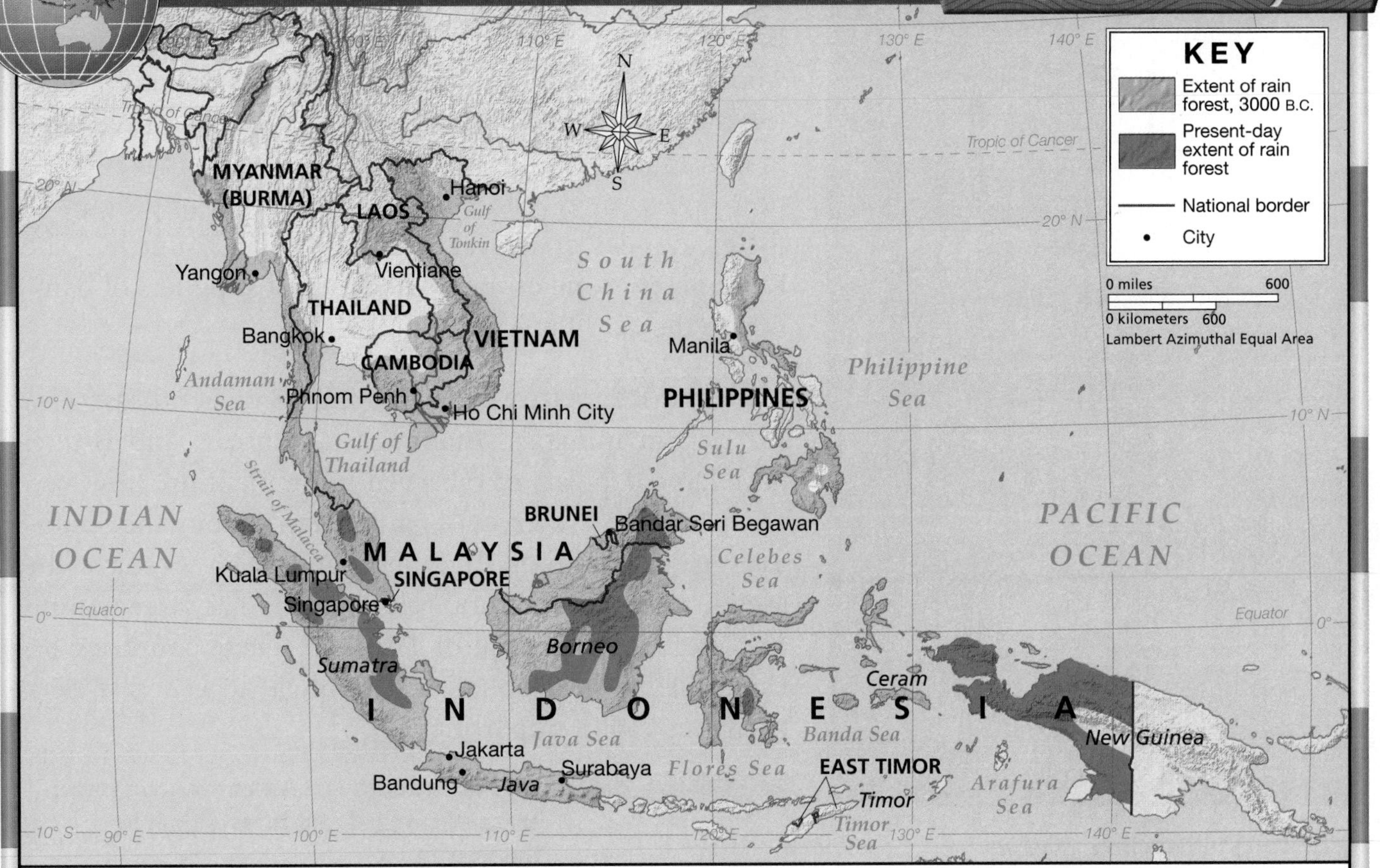

KEY

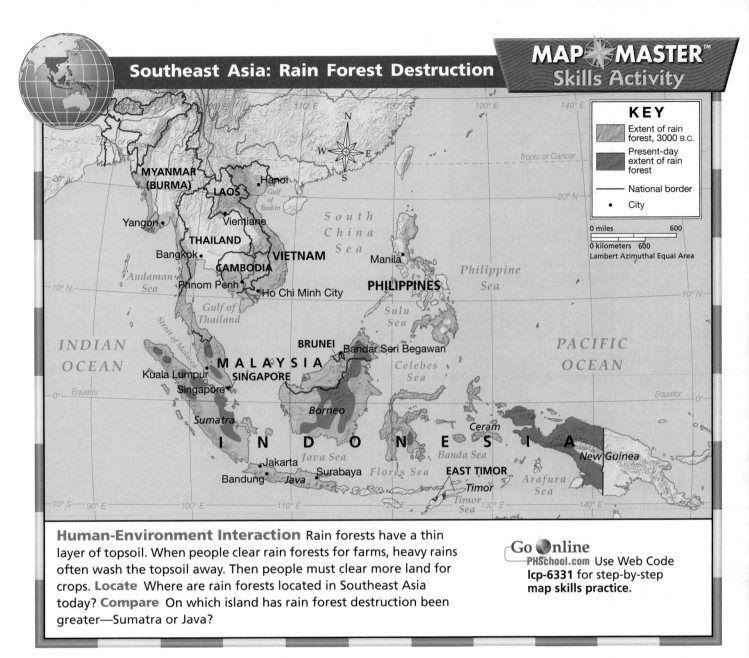

- Extent of rain forest, 3000 B.C.
- Present-day extent of rain forest
- National border
- City

0 miles 600
0 kilometers 600
Lambert Azimuthal Equal Area

Human-Environment Interaction Rain forests have a thin layer of topsoil. When people clear rain forests for farms, heavy rains often wash the topsoil away. Then people must clear more land for crops. **Locate** Where are rain forests located in Southeast Asia today? **Compare** On which island has rain forest destruction been greater—Sumatra or Java?

Go Online
PHSchool.com Use Web Code **lcp-6331** for step-by-step **map skills practice.**

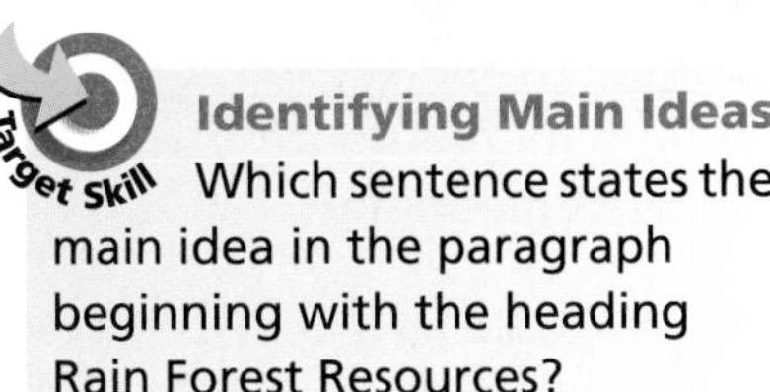

Identifying Main Ideas Which sentence states the main idea in the paragraph beginning with the heading Rain Forest Resources?

Rain Forest Resources Southeast Asia's tropical rain forests cover large areas in the region. Rain forests contain a great variety of plant and animal life. In Southeast Asia, rain forests are a source of lumber, medicines, and chemicals used in industry. Tropical rain forests once covered nearly all of Southeast Asia. Over the years, huge sections have been cut down to provide lumber and to create farmland. On the island of Java in Indonesia, more than 90 percent of the rain forest has been cleared.

One challenge for the nations of Southeast Asia is balancing the need for economic growth with the need for rain forests. Thailand has made some progress toward conserving its rain forests. In 1988, hundreds of people in Thailand were killed by huge mudslides. The mudslides occurred because trees that had held the soil on the hillsides had been cut down. In 1989, Thailand banned logging in natural forests.

Bamboo stems being used as scaffolding in Laos

Bamboo as a Resource One forest resource that Southeast Asian people have long used for shelter is bamboo. Bamboo is a type of fast-growing grass that produces a woody stem. Giant bamboo can grow to about 100 feet (30 meters) tall. Millions of people in Southeast Asia live in houses made of bamboo. It is also used to make irrigation pipes, ropes, and bridges. Bamboo is important to the economies of several Southeast Asian countries. The Philippines is one of the world's largest suppliers of bamboo to the world market.

Mineral Resources The countries of Southeast Asia are rich in minerals. Indonesia, Myanmar, and Brunei have large deposits of oil. Even more plentiful, however, are the region's reserves of natural gas. Among the Southeast Asian countries, Indonesia and Malaysia have the largest reserves of natural gas. Thailand has large natural gas reserves in the Gulf of Thailand. These countries are using their own supplies of natural gas to generate electricity instead of importing oil.

✓ Reading Check **Why does Southeast Asia now have fewer areas of tropical rain forests than in the past?**

Section 1 Assessment

Key Terms
Review the key terms at the beginning of this section. Use each term in a sentence that explains its meaning.

Target Reading Skill
Write the main idea of each paragraph that follows a red heading in this section.

Comprehension and Critical Thinking
1. (a) **Recall** What kind of landform makes up mainland Southeast Asia?
(b) **Compare and Contrast** How is mainland Southeast Asia similar to and different from island Southeast Asia?
2. (a) **Recall** What kind of climate does most of island Southeast Asia have?
(b) **Synthesize Information** Why does the southeastern coast of Vietnam have the same climate as most of island Southeast Asia?
3. (a) **List** Give some examples of cash crops raised in Southeast Asia.
(b) **Contrast** What is the difference between subsistence farming and commercial farming?
(c) **Draw Conclusions** How can rice be a product of both commercial and subsistence farming?

Writing Activity
Write a paragraph that explains why commercial logging and commercial farming have a destructive effect on tropical rain forests.

For: An activity about Southeast Asia's geography
Visit: PHSchool.com
Web Code: lcd-6301

Section 2 Australia and New Zealand: Physical Geography

Prepare to Read

Objectives

In this section, you will

1. Find out why Australia and New Zealand have unique physical environments.
2. Learn about Australia's physical geography.
3. Explore New Zealand's physical geography.

Taking Notes

As you read, look for details about the physical geography of Australia and New Zealand. Copy the table below, and record your findings in it.

Physical Geography	
Australia	New Zealand

Target Reading Skill

Identify Supporting Details The main idea of a paragraph is supported by details that give further information about it. These details may explain the main idea or give examples or reasons. Look at the first paragraph on page 628. The first sentence is the main idea. The rest of the sentences support this main idea. How do the details about marsupials support the main idea?

Key Terms

- **marsupial** (mahr SOO pea ul) *n.* an animal, such as a kangaroo, that carries its young in a body pouch
- **tectonic plate** (tek TAHN ik playt) *n.* a huge slab of rock that moves very slowly over a softer layer beneath the surface of Earth's crust
- **geyser** (GY zur) *n.* a hot spring that shoots a jet of water and steam into the air
- **fiord** (fyawrd) *n.* a long, narrow inlet or arm of the sea bordered by steep slopes created by glaciers

What bird is strange looking, has a long bill, does not fly, and only comes out at night to hunt? If you said a kiwi, you are right. The people of New Zealand are so proud of this unusual bird that they have made it their national symbol. The people even call themselves "Kiwis." The bird is one of many unique animals found in New Zealand and its neighbor to the west, Australia.

The kiwi has appeared on New Zealand stamps since 1898.

Unique Physical Environments

Australia lies between the Pacific Ocean and the Indian Ocean. New Zealand lies in the Pacific Ocean to the east of Australia. Both countries are in the Southern Hemisphere, south of the Equator. This means that their seasons are the opposite of those in the United States. They are far from other continents, which has made them unique.

Ayers Rock, known in the Aboriginal language as Uluru, is located in central Australia. Kangaroos are common in Australia.

Unique Plants and Animals New Zealand and Australia are so far from other continents that many of their animals and plants are found nowhere else on Earth. Only in New Zealand can you find kiwis and yellow-eyed penguins. Eighty-four percent of the plants in New Zealand's forests grow nowhere else. Australia has many unique creatures, such as the kangaroo and the koala. They are **marsupials** (mahr SOO pea ulz), or animals that carry their young in a body pouch. Marsupials *are* found elsewhere in the world. The opossum of North America, for instance, is a marsupial. But in Australia, almost all mammals are marsupials. This is not true anywhere else on Earth.

Moving Plates of Rock The uniqueness of New Zealand and Australia is the result of forces beneath Earth's surface. According to the theory of plate tectonics, the outer "skin," or crust of Earth, is broken into huge, moving slabs of rock called **tectonic plates.** These plates move independently, sometimes colliding and sometimes sliding against one another. Australia, New Zealand, and the Pacific islands are all part of the Indo-Australian plate. Once, it was part of a landmass that included Africa. Then, several hundred million years ago, the Indo-Australian plate broke away. Slowly—at a rate of an inch or two each year—it moved northeast toward Asia.

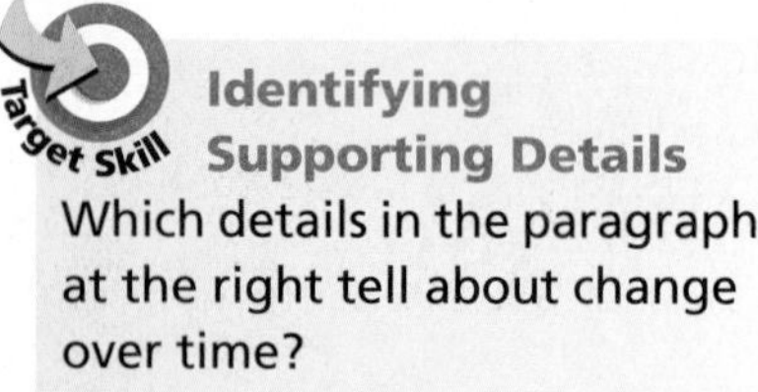

Target Skill **Identifying Supporting Details**
Which details in the paragraph at the right tell about change over time?

Movement and Change Over Time As the plates moved, Australia and the Pacific islands moved farther from Africa. Over the centuries, small changes have occurred naturally in the animals and plants of Australia and the islands. For instance, many birds have lost the ability to fly, even though they still have small wings. Because Australia and the islands are so isolated, these animals have not spread to other regions.

✓ Reading Check **In which hemisphere are Australia and New Zealand located?**

Australia's Physical Geography

Australia is Earth's smallest continent. It is about as large as the continental United States (the part of the United States located between Canada and Mexico, not including Alaska and Hawaii). Most Australians live along Australia's eastern and southeastern coasts. Australia's physical geography explains why.

Find the region along Australia's east coast on the map below. This region receives ample rain. Winds blowing westward across the Pacific Ocean pick up moisture. As the winds rise to cross the Great Dividing Range, the moisture falls as rain. These winds also help make the climate mild and pleasant. Most Australians live here, in cities. Australia's most important rivers, the Murray and the Darling, flow through the region. They flow across a vast plain that contains Australia's most fertile farmland.

✓ Reading Check **How does the physical geography of Australia explain where the people live?**

Australia and New Zealand: Physical

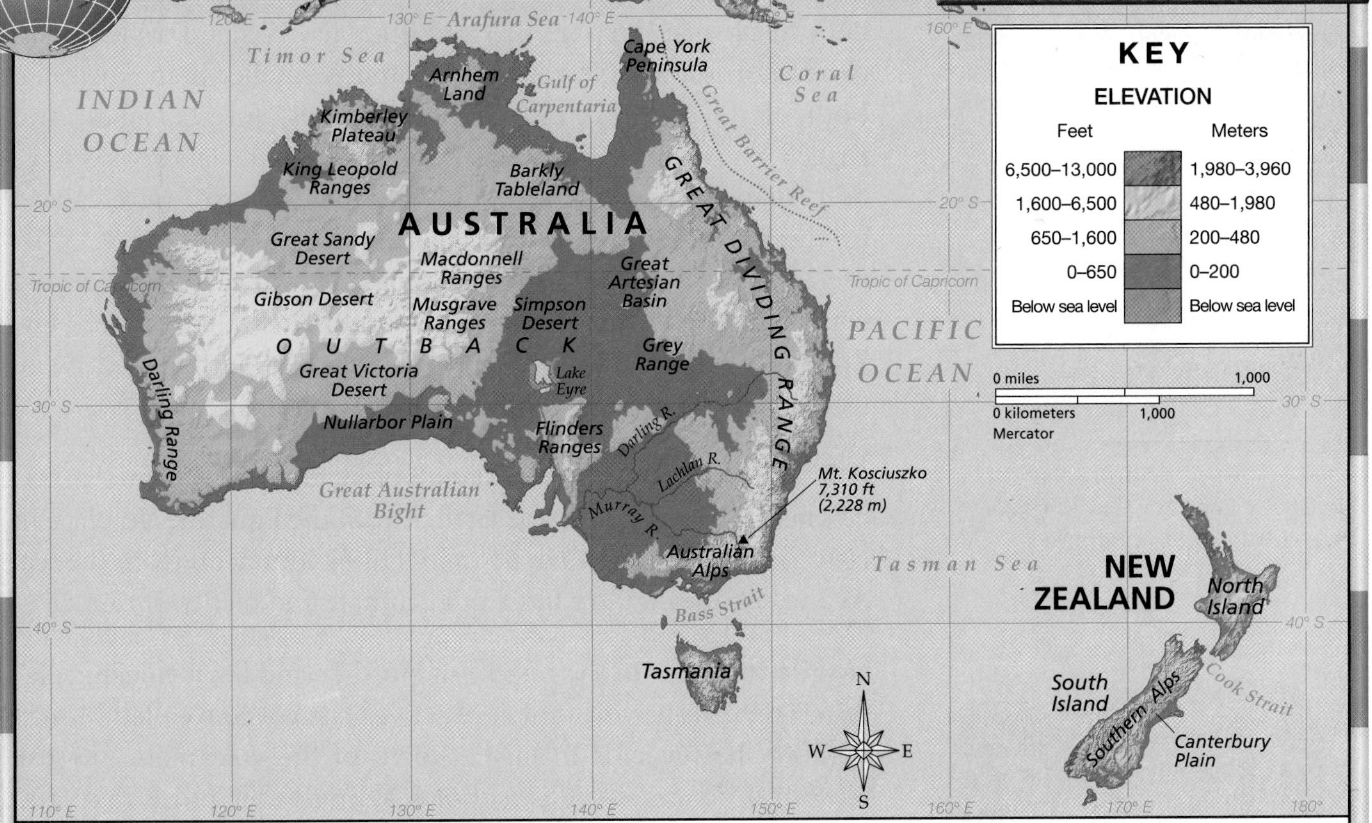

MAP MASTER™ Skills Activity

Place Apart from the Great Dividing Range, most of Australia is quite flat. **Locate** Where in Australia is the Great Dividing Range located? **Compare** Which of New Zealand's islands is more mountainous—North Island or South Island?

Go Online PHSchool.com Use Web Code **lcp-6312** for step-by-step **map skills practice.**

Mount Cook National Park
New Zealand's Mount Cook National Park, located in the Southern Alps, is popular with hikers and mountain climbers. **Infer** *Is this group of people out to climb a mountain or enjoy a day hike?*

New Zealand's Physical Geography

Look at the map on page 629 and find New Zealand. Made up of two major islands, New Zealand is much smaller than Australia. Both of its major islands have highlands, forests, lakes, and rugged, snowcapped mountains. New Zealand's landforms have been shaped by volcanoes. The volcanoes, in turn, were caused by the movement of tectonic plates. Where plates meet, often there are earthquakes and volcanoes. New Zealand is located where the Pacific plate meets the Indo-Australian plate. New Zealand's major islands, North Island and South Island, were formed by volcanoes when these plates collided.

A Mild Climate New Zealand's climate is cooler than Australia's because New Zealand is farther from the Equator. No place in New Zealand is more than 80 miles (129 kilometers) from the sea. As a result, the country has a mild climate and plenty of rainfall.

North Island In the middle of North Island lies a volcanic plateau. Three of the volcanoes are active. The volcano called Mount Egmont, however, is inactive. North of the volcanoes, **geysers (GY zurz), or hot springs,** shoot scalding water more than 100 feet (30.5 meters) into the air. New Zealanders use this energy to produce electricity. North Island is where New Zealand's capital city of Wellington is located. The country's largest city, Auckland, is also located on North Island.

Discovery
CHANNEL
SCHOOL
Video
Explore the land of Southeast Asia and the Pacific Region.

South Island South Island has a high mountain range called the Southern Alps. Mount Cook, the highest peak in the range, rises to 12,349 feet (3,764 meters). Glaciers cover the mountainsides. Below, crystal-clear lakes dot the landscape. **Fiords (fyawrds), or narrow inlets bordered by steep slopes,** slice the southwest coastline. Here, the mountains reach the sea. To the southeast lies a flat, fertile land called the Canterbury Plain. This is where farmers produce most of New Zealand's crops. Ranchers also raise sheep and cattle here.

Comparing Australia and New Zealand New Zealand is like Australia in several ways. In both countries, most of the population lives in cities along the coast. More than four out of five New Zealanders live in towns and cities. Both Australia and New Zealand have important natural resources such as coal, iron ore, and natural gas. The two countries also raise sheep and cattle and grow similar crops.

New Zealand is different from Australia in a number of ways, too. New Zealand is much smaller but has higher mountains than those in Australia. New Zealand has glaciers, while Australia does not. The two countries also have different climates.

√ Reading Check **Where do most people in New Zealand live—in urban areas or in rural areas?**

Links Across

The World

Steam Heat Geysers are found in three places in the world: the northwestern United States, Iceland, and New Zealand. In these places, movements of tectonic plates have created deep cracks in Earth's crust. Water seeps down into the cracks until it reaches very hot rocks. The heat raises the temperature of the water until it is so hot that it bursts upward in a shower of water and steam.

Section 2 Assessment

Key Terms

Review the key terms at the beginning of this section. Use each term in a sentence that explains its meaning.

Target Reading Skill

The main idea of the last paragraph in this section is that Australia and New Zealand are different in many ways. State the details that support this main idea.

Comprehension and Critical Thinking

1. (a) **Recall** Where do most of the people in Australia live?
(b) **Identify Cause and Effect** How have Australia's geography and climate affected where Australians live?
2. (a) **Recall** How were New Zealand's North Island and South Island formed?
(b) **Compare and Contrast** How is the physical geography of New Zealand different from that of Australia? How is it similar?
3. (a) **Explain** How are the population patterns similar in Australia and New Zealand?
(b) **Draw Conclusions** Why do most of the people in New Zealand live near the coasts?

Writing Activity

Write a list of adjectives that describe Australia. Then write a list of adjectives that describe New Zealand. Include at least three adjectives for each country. Using the information in this section, write a fact related to each adjective on your list.

For: An activity about Australia
Visit: PHSchool.com
Web Code: lcd-6302

Skills for Life

Identifying Cause and Effect

Have you ever tossed a stone into a pond and watched what happens? As soon as that stone hits the surface and sinks, circles of ripples, or waves, begin to move away from that spot in ever-widening circles. This is one case of cause and effect. Tossing the stone started the waves moving away from the spot where the stone landed. Understanding this relationship between cause and effect is useful in school and in daily life.

Learn the Skill

Being able to identify causes and effects helps you to understand what you read. To learn this skill, follow the steps below.

1. **Look for a cause-and-effect relationship.** Remember the pebble in the pond. As you read, ask yourself, "Why did this happen?" or "How did this happen?" Look for words such as *because, so,* and *as a result.* These words sometimes signal a cause-and-effect relationship.

2. **Identify the effect or effects.** Like the ripples that appear in a pond, an effect is what happens. A cause may have more than one effect. List the effect(s) you have identified.

3. **Identify the cause or causes.** A cause makes something happen. An effect may have more than one cause. List the cause(s) of the effect(s) you identified in Step 2.

4. **State the cause and effect.** A simple cause-and-effect statement might read, "A caused B." A is the cause, and B is the effect. A cause that produced three effects might be stated as, "A caused B, C, and D." A is the cause; its effects are B, C, and D.

A stone tossed into this pond caused the ripples to form. The stone is the cause, and the ripples are the effect.

Practice the Skill

To practice identifying a cause-and-effect relationship, read the paragraph below, using the steps on the previous page.

1. What words signal a possible cause-and-effect situation?
2. Identify the effect by filling in the blank in the following sentence: "Why do ________ happen?" The word you use to fill in the blank is the effect.
3. The effect you identified is triggered by two causes. What are the two causes?
4. State the cause-and-effect relationship in a sentence. Your sentence should give an answer to this question: What causes tsunamis?

Tsunamis (soo NAH mees) are powerful waves caused by earthquakes or volcanic eruptions that take place underwater. When an earthquake happens under the ocean floor or when an underwater volcano erupts, both of these actions cause circles of waves like the ones that form when you throw a stone into a pond. The result is a wave that is extremely forceful and fast. In deep water, tsunamis can move as fast as 500 to 600 miles (800 to 960 kilometers) per hour. As a tsunami approaches land, the speed slows down and the wave grows in height, sometimes as high as a ten-story building. The wave pushes inland, carrying boulders, boats, and buildings along until its energy is gone. In 1998, three huge tsunamis struck Papua New Guinea (PAP yoo uh noo GIH nee), a country located on an island north of Australia. More than 1,000 people were killed.

Apply the Skill

Read the passages titled Moving Plates of Rock and Movement and Change Over Time on page 628. Use the steps in the skill to identify one cause that explains why New Zealand and Australia are unique.

Section 3

The Pacific Islands

Physical Geography

Prepare to Read

Objectives

In this section, you will

1. Examine features of high islands and low islands.
2. Learn about the three main island groups.
3. Find out what kind of climate and vegetation the islands have.
4. Discover how land is used in the Pacific islands.

Taking Notes

As you read this section, look for details about the three major Pacific island groups. Copy the diagram below, and record your findings in it.

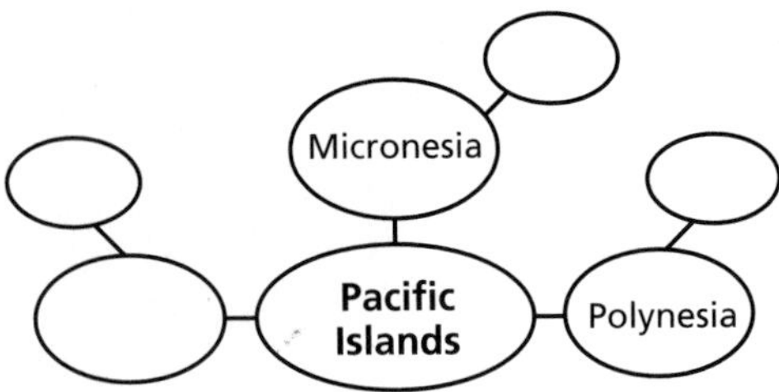

Target Reading Skill

Identify Main Ideas
Sometimes the main idea in a paragraph or reading passage is not stated directly. All the details add up to a main idea, but you must state the main idea yourself. As you read, look for main ideas that are not stated directly.

Key Terms

- **high island** (hy EYE lund) *n.* an island formed from the mountainous top of an ancient volcano
- **low island** (loh EYE lund) *n.* an island formed from coral reefs or atolls
- **atoll** (A tawl) *n.* a small coral island in the shape of a ring
- **coral** (KAWR ul) *n.* a rock-like material made up of the skeletons of tiny sea creatures, most plentiful in warm ocean water

Scuba diving in the Pacific islands

The Pacific Ocean, which covers nearly one third of Earth's surface, is dotted with thousands of islands. Some are barely large enough for a person to stand on. Others cover thousands of square miles. The Pacific islands include the second-largest island in the world. This is New Guinea. Half of this island is actually part of Indonesia. The other half is the independent country of Papua New Guinea (PAP yoo uh noo GIH nee). The Pacific islands also include the world's smallest independent island nation. This is the country of Nauru (NAH oo roo), which has a total land area of just 8 square miles (21 square kilometers).

Geographers divide these thousands of islands into three main groups. Melanesia (mel uh NEE zhuh) means "black islands." Micronesia (my kruh NEE zhuh) means "small islands." Polynesia (pahl uh NEE zhuh) means "many islands." Each of these groups covers a particular area, and any island that falls inside the boundaries of one of these areas belongs to that group.

High Islands and Low Islands

Geographers also divide the Pacific islands into high islands and low islands. **High islands** are mountainous and have been formed by volcanoes. The soil, which consists of volcanic ash, is very fertile. Because of their size and because people can grow crops there, high islands can support more people than low islands.

Low islands are made up of coral reefs or atolls. An **atoll** (A tawl) is a small coral island in the shape of a ring. The ring encloses a shallow pool of ocean water called a lagoon. Often, the lagoon has one or more openings to the sea. An atoll may rise only a few feet above the water. Low islands have this shape and low elevation because they are coral reefs. **Coral** is a rocklike material made up of the skeletons of tiny sea creatures. A reef develops until it nears the surface. Then sand and other debris accumulate on the reef's surface, raising the island above the level of the water.

Far fewer people live on low islands than on high islands. In part, this is because low islands are quite small. Also, low islands have poor, sandy soil and little fresh water, so it is difficult to raise crops. Most low islanders survive by fishing. They may also grow coconuts, yams, and a starchy root called taro.

A traditional house on a high island in Polynesia

√ Reading Check **On which type of island do most Pacific island people live?**

A Coral Atoll

A South Pacific Atoll

The diagram below shows how a coral atoll is formed. 1 It begins as a fringe of coral around a volcanic island. 2 The coral continues to build as the island is worn away. 3 Eventually, only a ring of coral remains. The aerial view of an atoll at the left shows the ring structure of the coral.

Melanesia, Micronesia, and Polynesia

The island group with the most people is Melanesia, which is north and east of Australia. Most of Melanesia's large islands are high islands. New Guinea, for example, has two ranges of high mountains. The western half of New Guinea is called Irian Jaya (IHR ee ahn JAH yuh). It is part of the country of Indonesia. The eastern half is Papua New Guinea, the largest and most populated Melanesian country. Some smaller Melanesian islands are Fiji, the Solomon Islands, and New Caledonia.

Made up largely of low islands, Micronesia covers an area of the Pacific as large as the continental United States. Most of the islands of Micronesia lie north of the Equator. Some of Micronesia's 2,000 islands are less than 1 square mile (2.6 square kilometers) in area. The largest is Guam, which is 209 square miles (541 square kilometers). Most of Micronesia's islands are divided into groups. The largest are the Caroline, Gilbert, Marshall, and Mariana islands. Guam is part of the Marianas.

Polynesia is the largest island group in the Pacific. It includes the fiftieth state of the United States, Hawaii. Polynesia consists of a great many high islands, such as Tahiti and Samoa. Dense rain forests cover their high volcanic mountains. Along the shores are palm-fringed, sandy beaches. The Tuamotus and Tonga are examples of Polynesia's few low islands and atolls.

✓ Reading Check **Which island group contains Hawaii?**

Living in the Pacific Islands
The bottom photo on the opposite page shows a traditional canoe in Fiji. Below left, fishers haul nets in the waters of Fiji. Below right, some people in Papua New Guinea farm for a living. The inset photo on the opposite page shows children playing volleyball in Vanuatu.

Climate and Vegetation of the Pacific Islands

The Pacific islands lie in the tropics. Temperatures are hot year-round. Daytime temperatures can reach as high as the 80s and mid-90s in degrees Fahrenheit (around 30°C). Nighttime temperatures average about 75°F (24°C). The ocean winds keep the temperatures from getting too high.

Some Pacific islands have wet and dry seasons. Most islands, however, receive heavy rainfall all year long. In Hawaii, for example, volcanic peaks such as Mauna Kea (MOW nuh KAY uh) receive 100 inches (250 centimeters) of rain each year. Usually the rain falls in brief, heavy downpours. Some low islands, however, receive only scattered rainfall.

Target Skill **Identify Main Ideas** In one sentence, state what the paragraph at the left is about.

Because of high temperatures, plentiful rainfall, and fertile soil, high islands such as Papua New Guinea and the Hawaiian Islands have rich vegetation. Tropical rain forests cover the hills. Savanna grasses grow in the lowlands. Low islands, on the other hand, have little vegetation. The poor soil supports only palm trees, grasses, and small shrubs.

√ Reading Check **Why do low islands have little vegetation?**

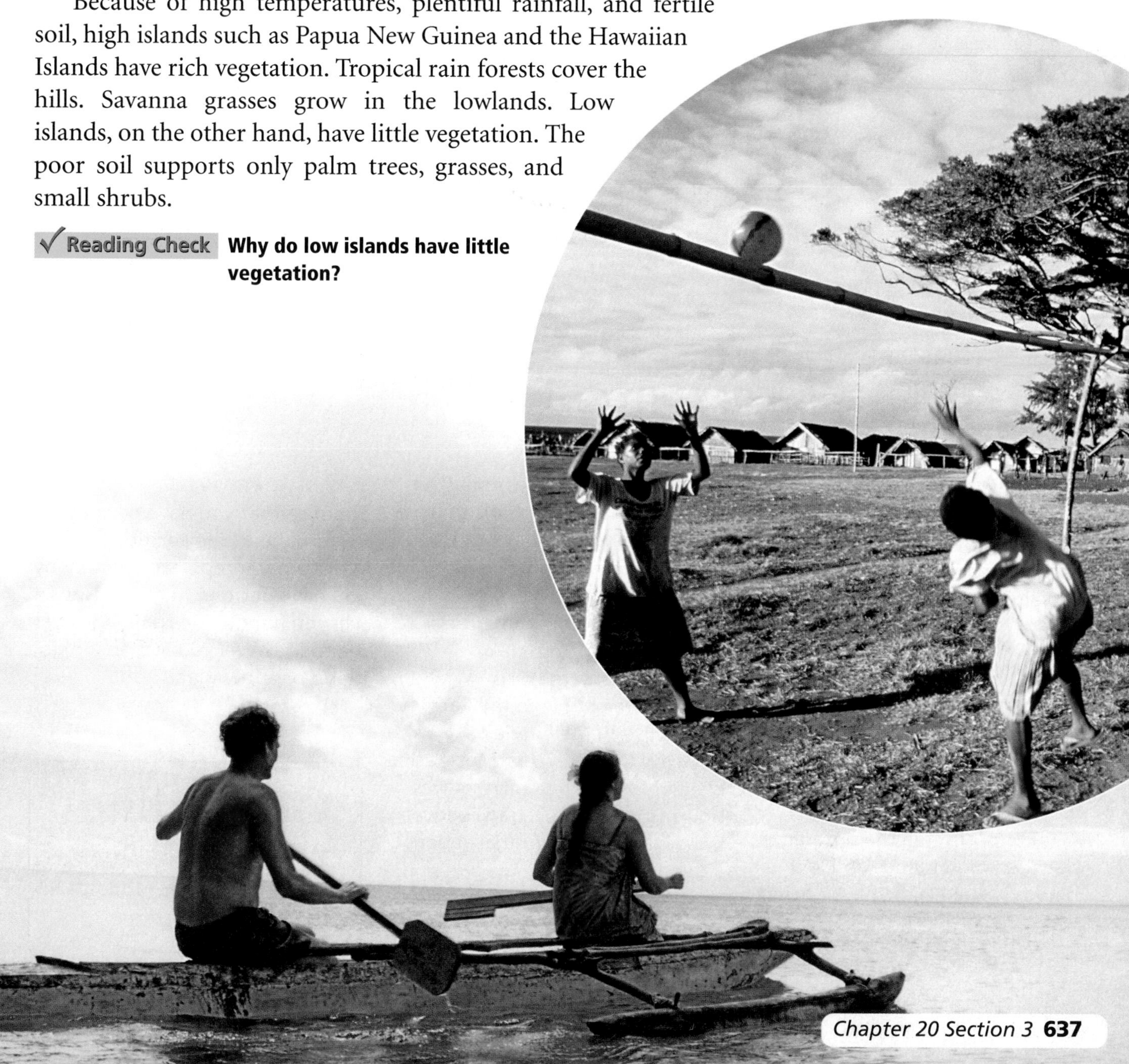

A worker harvests ripe coconuts in Fiji.

Natural Resources and Land Use

The Pacific island region has few natural resources. The coconut palm is its most important resource. It provides food, clothing, and shelter. Another important resource is fish.

Cash Crops Some Pacific island countries, such as the nation of Fiji, grow cash crops. Fiji is a nation of some 300 islands in Melanesia. The Fiji islands' fertile, volcanic soil and hot, wet climate are good for growing sugar cane. Sugar is a major export for Fiji. Another important cash crop for many Pacific island countries is copra. Copra, or dried coconut, is used in margarine, cooking oils, soaps, and cosmetics. The people in Fiji also work as subsistence farmers, growing their own food crops such as taro, yams, and sweet potatoes.

Tourism The Pacific islands' most valuable resource may be their natural beauty. Tourism provides a key source of income in the region. Many Pacific island nations are working to develop their tourist industries. The greatest number of visitors to the Pacific islands come from Australia. Nearly as many come from the United States.

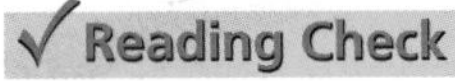

Give two examples of cash crops grown in the Pacific islands.

Section 3 Assessment

Key Terms

Review the key terms at the beginning of this section. Use each key term in a sentence that explains its meaning.

Target Reading Skill

Read the paragraph titled Tourism, above. Write a sentence that states the main idea.

Comprehension and Critical Thinking

1. (a) **Explain** Tell the difference between high islands and low islands in the Pacific.
(b) **Make Generalizations** The people on high islands often have a better standard of living than people on low islands. Explain why this might be so.

2. (a) **Recall** Name the three Pacific island groups.
(b) **Apply Information** Why do most of the people in the Pacific islands live in Melanesia?
(c) **Draw Conclusions** Most Pacific islands have few natural resources. How might this affect trade between these islands and industrial nations around the world?

Writing Activity

Suppose that you have decided to live on one of the Pacific islands. Write a paragraph explaining why you have decided to move. How will you handle the challenges of island life? Will you live on a high island or a low island?

For: An activity on the Pacific islands
Visit: PHSchool.com
Web Code: lcd-6303

Chapter 20 Review and Assessment

◆ Chapter Summary

Section 1: Southeast Asia Physical Geography

- Southeast Asia is divided into mainland and island areas. Mainland Southeast Asia is a peninsula. Island Southeast Asia is part of the Ring of Fire, a region of volcanoes and earthquakes.
- Most of Southeast Asia has a tropical wet climate.
- Farming is a major economic activity in Southeast Asia, although the region's cities and industries have been growing rapidly.
- Southeast Asian rain forests are a source of lumber, medicines, and materials used in industry. The region's remaining rain forests are in danger of destruction from commercial logging and farming.

Section 2: Australia and New Zealand Physical Geography

- Because Australia and New Zealand are far from other landmasses, many of their plants and animals are found nowhere else on Earth.
- Australia is the smallest continent. Most people live along its eastern and southern coasts.
- New Zealand is made up of two mountainous islands.

Australia

Cambodia

Section 3: The Pacific Islands Physical Geography

- The Pacific islands are divided into three main groups: Melanesia, Micronesia, and Polynesia.
- Within these groups, there are high islands and low islands.
- Because the Pacific islands lie in the tropics, temperatures are hot all year.
- The Pacific islands have few natural resources, but some island countries are able to grow cash crops such as sugar and copra, or dried coconut. Tourism is growing in importance in the region.

◆ Key Terms

Use each key term in a sentence that explains its meaning.

1. fiord
2. paddy
3. subsistence farming
4. commercial farming
5. marsupial
6. tectonic plate
7. geyser
8. high island
9. low island
10. coral

◆ Comprehension and Critical Thinking

11. (a) **List** Which countries make up mainland Southeast Asia?
    (b) **Explain** Why is Malaysia part of both mainland Southeast Asia and island Southeast Asia?
12. (a) **Explain** Why does Southeast Asia have more than one summer monsoon?
    (b) **Summarize** Describe the effects of summer monsoons in Southeast Asia.
13. (a) **Name** Which two Southeast Asian countries are among the world's leading rice producers?
    (b) **Analyze Information** Why would a subsistence farmer in Southeast Asia raise rice instead of rubber?
14. (a) **Name** What is one mountain range in Australia?
    (b) **Locate** Where is this mountain range located relative to Australia's east coast?
15. (a) **Recall** Describe the major features of New Zealand's geography.
    (b) **Compare and Contrast** How are Australia and New Zealand different from and similar to each other?
16. (a) **Identify** Where do most people in the Pacific islands live—on high islands or on low islands?
    (b) **Draw Conclusions** You have read about high islands and low islands. What conclusion can you reach about why more people live on one kind than another?

◆ Skills Practice

Identifying Cause and Effect Review the steps you followed to learn this skill. Then reread the first paragraph on page 620. Identify three effects of the eruption of Mount Pinatubo.

◆ Writing Activity: Math

Suppose that it is Monday at 12 noon where you live. Calculate what day and time it is in Bangkok, Thailand; in Jakarta, Indonesia; and in Sydney, Australia. You will need to use a world time zones map, which you can find in an atlas. Do research to learn more about time zones and the International Date Line. Then write a paragraph about the International Date Line.

MAP MASTER™ Skills Activity

Southeast Asia and the Pacific

Place Location For each place listed below, write the letter that shows its location on the map.

1. Malay Peninsula
2. South China Sea
3. Philippine Islands
4. Australia
5. New Guinea
6. Micronesia

Go Online PHSchool.com Use Web Code **lcp-6320** for an **interactive map.**

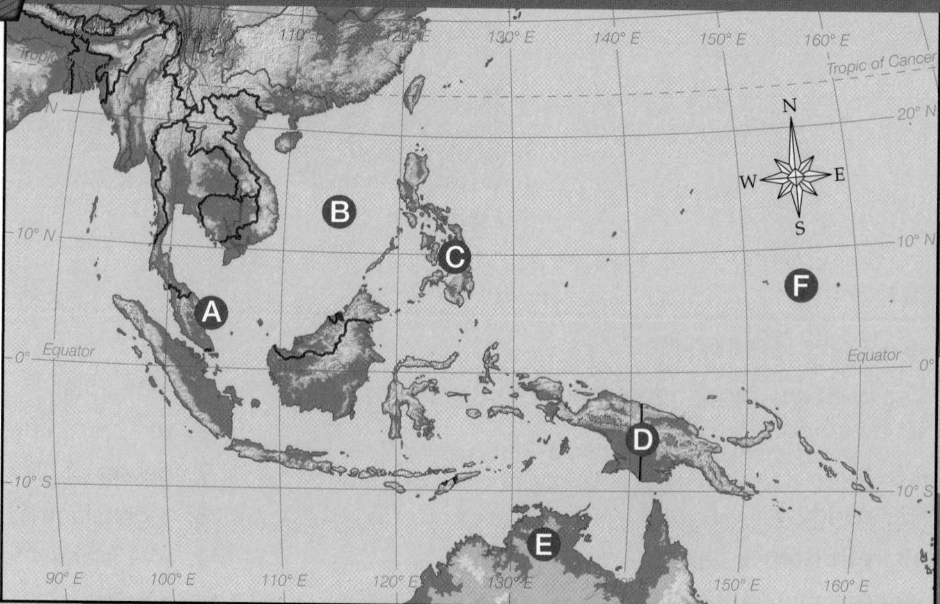

Standardized Test Prep

Test-Taking Tips

Some questions on standardized tests ask you to analyze graphic organizers. Study the Venn diagram below. Then follow the tips to answer the sample question.

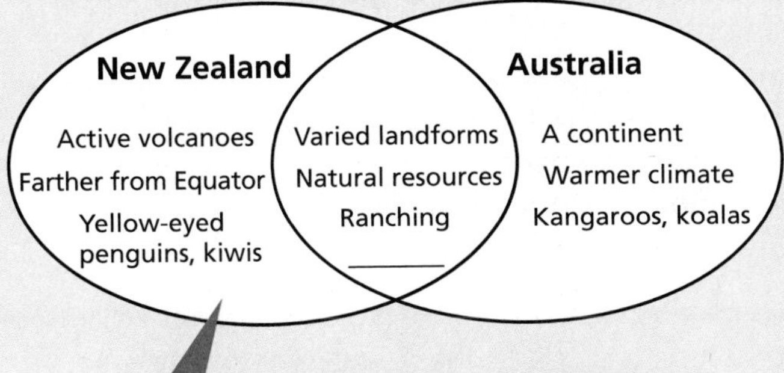

TIP A Venn diagram lists ways that two things are the same and different. This kind of chart is good for writing or note-taking.

Pick the letter that best answers the question.

Which of the following belongs in the blank in the overlapping space?

A compare and contrast

B population mostly in cities

C Great Dividing Range

D geysers

Think It Through The question asks you to choose another example for the overlapping space—in other words, ways that both countries are the same. You can rule out C and D because the Great Dividing Range is in Australia and geysers are only in New Zealand. You can eliminate A, because it describes the chart—not an example in the chart. The correct answer is B, because the population of both countries is mostly in cities.

Practice Questions

Use the tips above and other tips in this book to help you answer the following questions.

1. Thailand, Cambodia, and Vietnam are part of
   A island Southeast Asia.
   B Polynesia.
   C Micronesia.
   D mainland Southeast Asia.

2. Most Australians live along Australia's eastern and southeastern coasts. Based on this information, what conclusion can be drawn about the location of Australia's cities?
   A Most of Australia's cities are located in the interior of the continent.
   B Most of Australia's cities are located along Australia's eastern and southeastern coasts.
   C Most of Australia's cities are located along Australia's northern coast.
   D Most of Australia's cities are located along Australia's western coast.

3. New Zealand's North Island and South Island were formed by
   A volcanoes. **B** coral.
   C earthquakes. **D** geysers.

Use the Venn diagram below to answer Question 4.

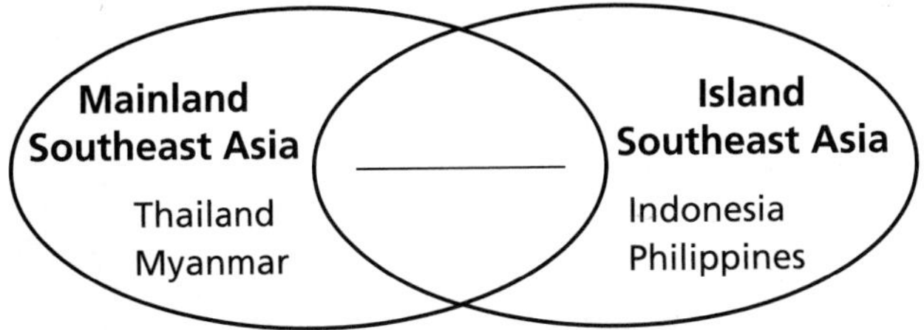

4. Which of the following belongs in the blank in the overlapping space?
   A Vietnam **B** Australia
   C Malaysia **D** Cambodia

Use Web Code **lca-6300** for **Chapter 20 self-test.**

Chapter 21

East Asia: Cultures and History

Chapter Preview

East Asian cultures are among the oldest in the world. In this chapter, you will learn about East Asian cultures and their long histories.

Section 1
Historic Traditions

Section 2
People and Cultures

Target Reading Skill

Context In this chapter, you will focus on using context to help you understand the meanings of unfamiliar words. Context includes the words, phrases, and sentences surrounding a particular word.

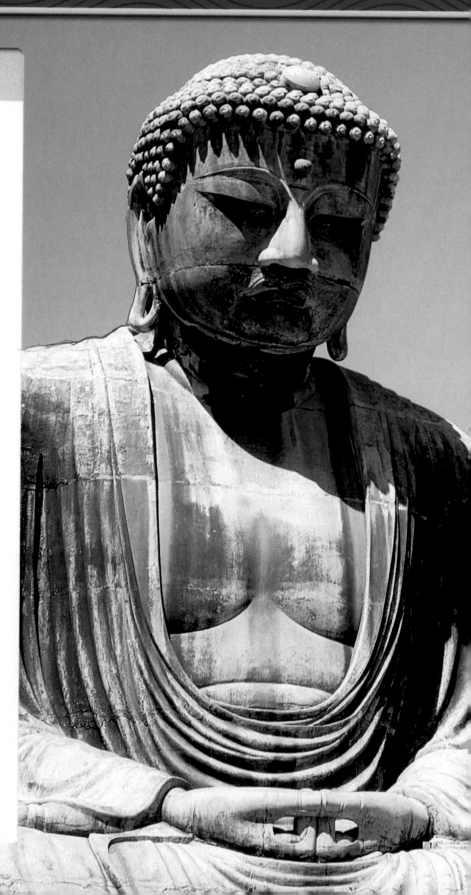

▶ **The Great Buddha of Kamakura is the second-largest statue of Buddha in Japan.**

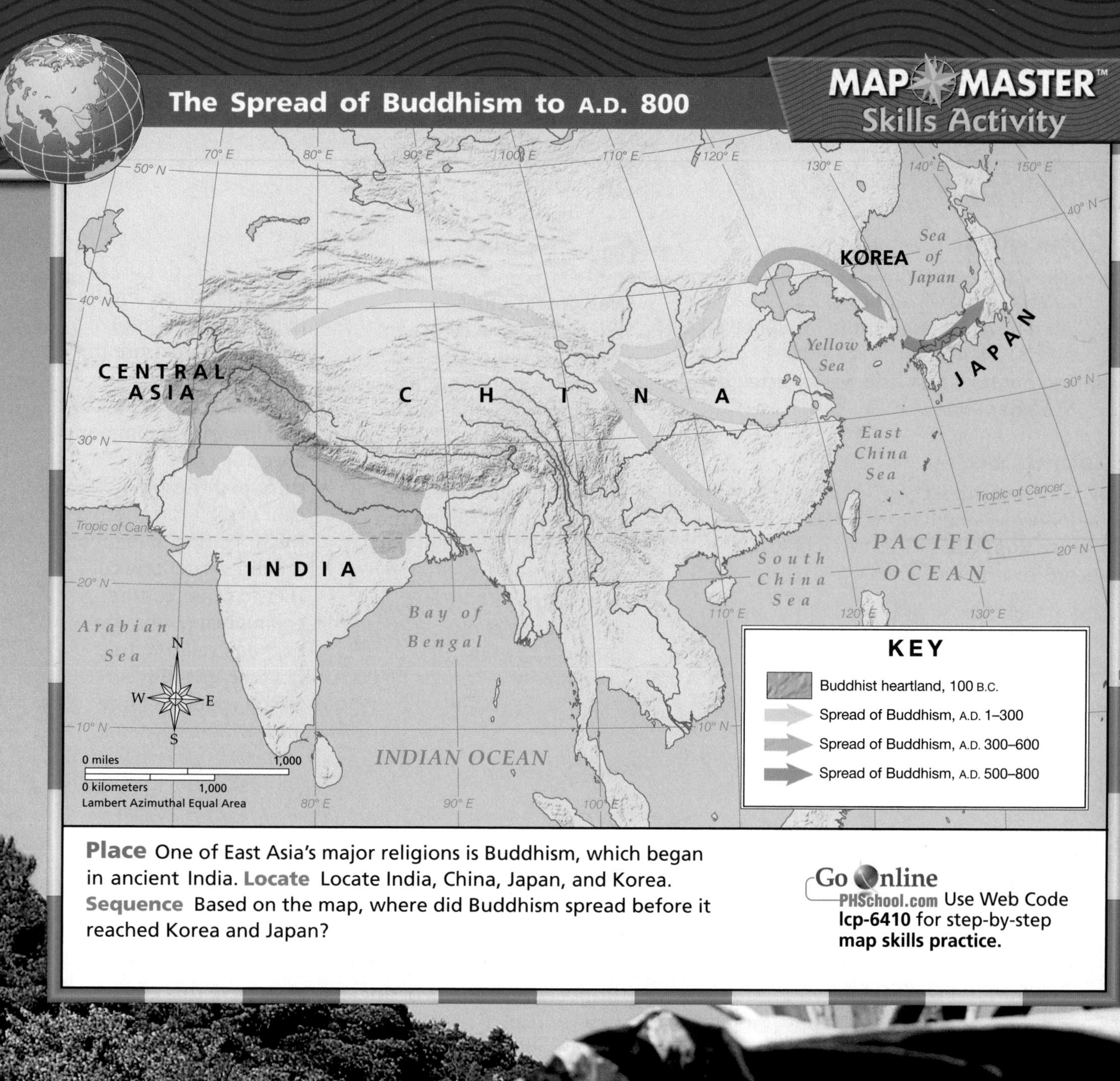

Place One of East Asia's major religions is Buddhism, which began in ancient India. **Locate** Locate India, China, Japan, and Korea. **Sequence** Based on the map, where did Buddhism spread before it reached Korea and Japan?

Go Online PHSchool.com Use Web Code **lcp-6410** for step-by-step **map skills practice.**

Section 1

Historic Traditions

Prepare to Read

Objectives

In this section you will

1. Learn about civilizations of East Asia.
2. Learn how Chinese culture influenced the rest of East Asia.
3. Find out how East Asia was affected by Western nations.

Taking Notes

As you read this section, look for details about major achievements throughout East Asia's history. Copy the concept web below, and record your findings in it.

Target Reading Skill

Use Context Clues

When you come across an unfamiliar word, you can sometimes figure out its meaning from clues in the context. The context refers to the surrounding words and sentences. Sometimes the context will define the word. In this example, the phrase in italics tells what an emperor is: "Ancient China was ruled by an emperor—*a male ruler of an empire.*"

Key Terms

- **emperor** (EM pur ur) *n.* a male ruler of an empire
- **dynasty** (DY nus tee) *n.* a series of rulers from the same family
- **clan** (klan) *n.* a group of families with a common ancestor
- **cultural diffusion** (KUL chur ul dih FYOO zhun) *n.* the spreading of ideas or practices from one culture to other cultures
- **communist** (KAHM yoo nist) *adj.* relating to a government that controls a country's large industries, businesses, and land

In this painting, Confucius is shown standing with his students.

More than two thousand years ago, one of the most important thinkers of ancient times gave this advice:

> **"Let the ruler be a ruler and the subject a subject.**
>
> **A youth, when at home, should act with respect to his parents, and, abroad, be respectful to his elders. He should be earnest and truthful. He should overflow in love to all, and cultivate the friendship of the good.**
>
> **When you have faults, do not fear to abandon them."**

These words are from the teachings of Confucius (kun FYOO shus), who lived in China about 500 B.C. He taught that all individuals have duties and responsibilities. If a person acts correctly, the result will be peace and harmony. Confucius's ideas helped to guide Chinese life for hundreds of years.

Civilizations of East Asia

Regions of Asia and Africa produced civilizations earlier than China's. A civilization has cities, a central government, workers who do specialized jobs, and social classes. Of the world's early civilizations, however, only China's has survived. This makes it the oldest continuous civilization in the world. Korea and Japan are not as old, but they, too, have long histories.

The Great Wall of China

China's Middle Kingdom For much of its history, China had little to do with the rest of the world. The Great Wall of China first started in the 600s B.C. as many small unconnected walls between warring states. Over time, it became a symbol of China's desire to keep the world at a distance. In fact, Chinese leaders had such pride that they named their country the Middle Kingdom. To them, it was the center of the universe.

Ancient Achievements The Chinese had reason to believe that their civilization was the greatest in the world. They invented paper, gunpowder, silk weaving, the magnetic compass, the printing press, and clockworks. Chinese engineers were experts at digging canals, building dams and bridges, and setting up irrigation systems. Chinese scientists made major discoveries in mathematics and medicine.

Dynasties in China Starting in ancient times, China was governed by an **emperor**—a male ruler of an empire. An empire is an area of many territories and people that are controlled by one government. A series of emperors from the same family is a **dynasty**. Chinese history is described in terms of dynasties. The chart below lists major dynasties of China.

Chart Skills

The chart below shows major dynasties of China. They ruled China from ancient times to A.D. 1911. **Identify** Which dynasty was the first to develop the Chinese calendar? **Sequence** Which was developed in China first—paper money or iron tools?

Major Dynasties of China

Major Dynasty	Major Achievements
Shang (c. 1766–c. 1122 B.C.)	Well-developed writing, first Chinese calendar, bronze casting.
Zhou (c. 1122–c. 256 B.C.)	Writing laws, iron tools and plows in use.
Qin (221 B.C.–206 B.C.)	First great Chinese Empire. Much of the Great Wall built.
Han (206 B.C.–A.D. 220)	Government based on Confucianism. Buddhism introduced.
Tang (A.D. 618–A.D. 907)	Sculpture and poetry flourish.
Song (A.D. 906–A.D. 1279)	Block printing and paper money developed. Gunpowder first used.
Ming (A.D. 1318–A.D. 1644)	Porcelain, the novel, and drama flourish.
Qing (A.D. 1644–A.D. 1911)	Increased trade with Europe. Last Chinese dynasty.

Korea and China Although Korea's original settlers came from north-central Asia, Korea's history is closely tied to China. Around 1200 B.C., during a time of troubles in China, some Chinese moved to the Korean Peninsula. Later, other Chinese settled in the southern part of the peninsula. In this way, Chinese people brought Chinese knowledge and customs to the Koreans.

As in China, dynasties ruled Korea. While China had many dynasties, Korea had only three. The first was the Shilla. The Shilla dynasty unified Korea as one country in A.D. 668.

Target Skill — Use Context Clues If you do not know what *unified* means, look in the surrounding words for a context clue. Here, the phrase following *unified* explains what the term means.

Years of Isolation in Japan For much of Japan's history, **clans,** or groups of families who claim a common ancestor, fought each other for land and power. Around A.D. 500, one clan, the Yamato (yah MAH toh), became powerful. Claiming descent from the sun goddess, Yamato leaders took the title of emperor. Many emperors sat on Japan's throne. For a long time they had little power. Instead, shoguns (SHOH gunz), or "emperor's generals," made the laws. Warrior nobles, the samurai (SAM uh ry), enforced these laws. Together, the shoguns and samurai ruled Japan for more than 700 years.

Japan was isolated from the outside world from about 1640 to 1853. Japanese leaders believed that isolation, or separation, was the best way to keep the country united. Japan finally was forced to trade with the West in the 1800s.

✓ Reading Check **Name at least four major achievements of the Chinese civilization.**

Timeline Skills

Japan has interacted with other countries and regions except for one period in its history. **Note** When did Japan close its borders to the rest of the world? **Analyze Information** Which European country introduced Christianity to Japan?

Events in Japanese History

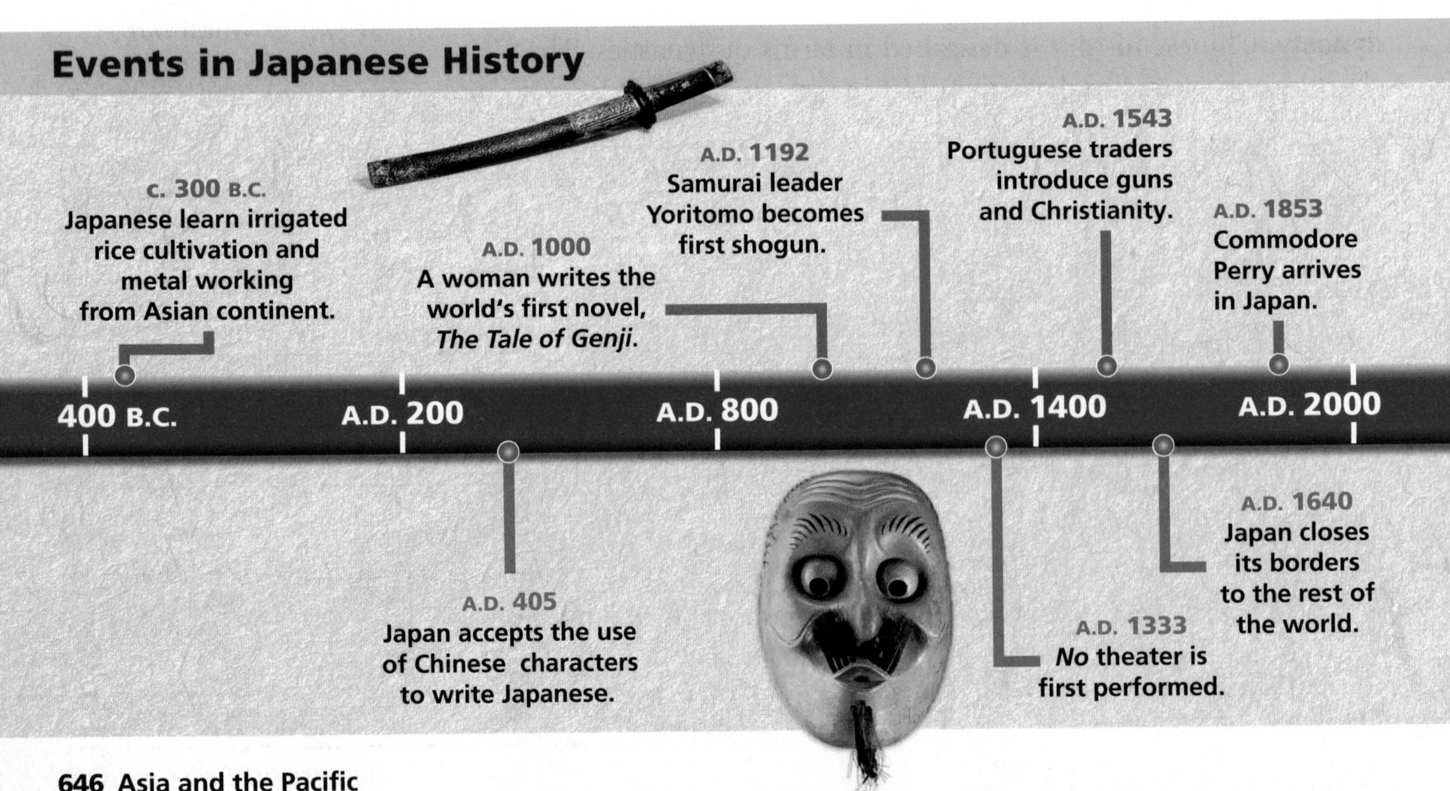

c. 300 B.C. Japanese learn irrigated rice cultivation and metal working from Asian continent.
A.D. 1000 A woman writes the world's first novel, *The Tale of Genji.*
A.D. 1192 Samurai leader Yoritomo becomes first shogun.
A.D. 1543 Portuguese traders introduce guns and Christianity.
A.D. 1853 Commodore Perry arrives in Japan.
400 B.C.
A.D. 200
A.D. 800
A.D. 1400
A.D. 2000
A.D. 405 Japan accepts the use of Chinese characters to write Japanese.
A.D. 1333 *No* theater is first performed.
A.D. 1640 Japan closes its borders to the rest of the world.

EYEWITNESS TECHNOLOGY

Paper Making

Civilization developed as people learned first to speak and to draw, and then to write. By the time of the Han dynasty in China, civilization included government, trade, record-keeping, and poetry. Paper was needed for all of these activities. Cai Lun, an official of the Han dynasty, is said to have invented this useful material.

Making paper pulp
People in Xishuangbanna, China, split open bamboo stems to extract pulp.

1 Fibers are gathered from bamboo, mulberry bark, cotton or linen cloth, grass, straw, or wood—and then chopped up, beaten, and soaked in water.

2 Workers pound the water-soaked fibers to a pulp.

3 A paper mold—a box with wooden sides and a fine wire screen—is dipped into a vat of pulp and slowly raised.

4 Workers then shake the mold until the water drains off and the wet fibers cover the screen with a thin web of pulp.

5 While still damp, the sheet of paper is peeled off the mold.

6 The paper sheets are pasted on a wall to dry. A fire might be lit to help the drying process.

Paper dyeing
Women lay out freshly dyed paper to dry in Bhaktapur, Nepal.

ANALYZING IMAGES
Why did it make sense to make paper near a source of water?

Links Across

The World

West Meets East The West has been greatly influenced by East Asia. In ancient Rome, wealthy people prized clothing made from Chinese silk. Silk production came to Europe from China. Eastern art influenced the design of Western architecture and furniture. Traders imported porcelain, pottery made from a fine white clay, from East Asia. Europeans and Americans called it "china." All these examples show cultural diffusion, or the spreading of ideas and practices from one culture to others.

The Spread of Cultures in East Asia

In ancient times, China was far ahead of the rest of the world in inventions and discoveries. Thus, it is not surprising that many Chinese discoveries spread to Korea and Japan. This process of **cultural diffusion,** or spreading of ideas from one culture to other cultures, happened early. The teachings of Confucius were among the first ideas to be passed along. The religion of Buddhism (BOOD iz um), which China had adopted from India, later spread to Korea and Japan. East Asian culture owes much to the early exchanges among China, Japan, and Korea. In each case, the countries changed what they borrowed until the element of culture became their own.

✓ Reading Check **Give an example of cultural diffusion between China and Korea.**

Westerners in East Asia

In the 1800s, Europeans and Americans began to produce great amounts of manufactured goods. East Asia seemed to be a good place to sell these products. Western trading ships began to sail to Asian ports.

The Opening of East Asia In 1853, U.S. Commodore Matthew Perry sailed with four warships to Japan. He forced Japan to grant trading rights to the United States. The opening up of China to Europe was different. The British, French, Germans, Portuguese, Russians, and Japanese gained control over parts of China. Other countries then feared losing the opportunity to share in China's riches. In 1899, the United States announced the policy that China should be open for trade with all nations equally. For a while, nations halted their efforts to divide up China.

New Forces in the 1900s Many Chinese blamed the emperor for the foreign powers in their country. In 1911, revolution broke out in China. The rule of emperors ended, and a republic was set up.

Meanwhile, Japan was becoming more powerful. Its leaders sought to control other Asian countries. One of their reasons was to make sure that Japan would have resources to fuel its growing industries. Japanese attacks on other Asian and Pacific lands led to the start of World War II in East Asia in 1941. In 1945, the United States and its allies defeated Japan.

Government in Japan
Japan's legislative branch is called the Diet. The Diet elects a prime minister, who heads the executive branch. Members of the Diet are shown in 2001 applauding the election of Junichiro Koizumi as prime minister. **Analyze Images** *Which man in the photo is Koizumi? Explain your answer.*

After World War II ended, civil war broke out in China between two groups, the Nationalists and the Communists. The Communists won the war in 1949 and made China a **communist** nation, one in which the government owns large industries, businesses, and most of the country's land.

After World War II, Korea was divided into two parts. Communists ruled North Korea. South Korea turned to Western nations for support. In 1950, North Korea invaded South Korea. The United States sent 480,000 troops to help South Korea. The Korean War lasted for three years, killing about 37,000 U.S. soldiers and more than 2 million Koreans. Neither side won. The battle line at the end of the war, in 1953, remains the border between the two Koreas today.

American veterans visiting a memorial in South Korea marking the 50th anniversary of the Korean War

√ Reading Check **How did Japan's actions lead to the start of World War II in East Asia?**

Section 1 Assessment

Key Terms

Review the key terms at the beginning of this section. Use each term in a sentence that explains its meaning.

Target Reading Skill

Find the phrase *foreign powers* on page 648. Use context clues to figure out its meaning. What clues helped you figure out its meaning?

Comprehension and Critical Thinking

1. **(a) List** Name at least four achievements of the Chinese civilization.
(b) Find Main Ideas How was the Chinese civilization ruled from ancient times to 1911?

2. **(a) Identify** Give one example of cultural diffusion in East Asia.
(b) Make Generalizations Cultural diffusion can take place when people move from one place to another. When they do, they take their culture with them. Based on what you have read in this section, what are some other ways in which cultural diffusion can happen?

3. **(a) Recall** Why did U.S. Commodore Matthew Perry sail to Japan in 1853?
(b) Compare and Contrast How was the opening up of China to Europe different from the opening up of Japan?

Writing Activity

Suppose that you are a European merchant traveling through China in the 1300s. Use the chart on page 645 to write three short diary entries about the inventions and achievements you find there.

For: An activity on East Asia's history
Visit: PHSchool.com
Web Code: lcd-6401

Reading Route Maps

Think of three inventions that had an important effect on human progress. What comes to mind: Farming? Books? Cars?

Did you think of *roads?*

The development of road networks has helped human civilization to grow and spread. Roads have been the lifelines of trade, communication, and human migration for thousands of years. Some of the world's oldest roads are in East Asia.

Learn the Skill

A map that shows roads is called a route map. Follow these steps to learn how to read a route map.

1. **Read the title of the map and become familiar with its features.** First, get a general idea of what region the map shows. Use the compass rose to figure out direction on the map.

2. **Study the key to understand its symbols.** Most modern road maps use colored lines to indicate various types of roads, from country roads to interstate highways. Other maps use colors to show land, sea, and air routes. The colors and what they represent are shown in the key. Notice what other symbols in the key represent, including cities.

3. **Trace routes on the map.** Gather information about the route by studying the features on the map. Use the scale of miles to calculate distances. Notice physical features and landmarks along the journey. Make note of any geographic barriers that would affect speed or comfort on the trip.

4. **Interpret the map.** Use information you gather from the map to draw conclusions about the route. On historical maps you can draw conclusions about why travelers and traders took certain routes and traveled at certain times of the year.

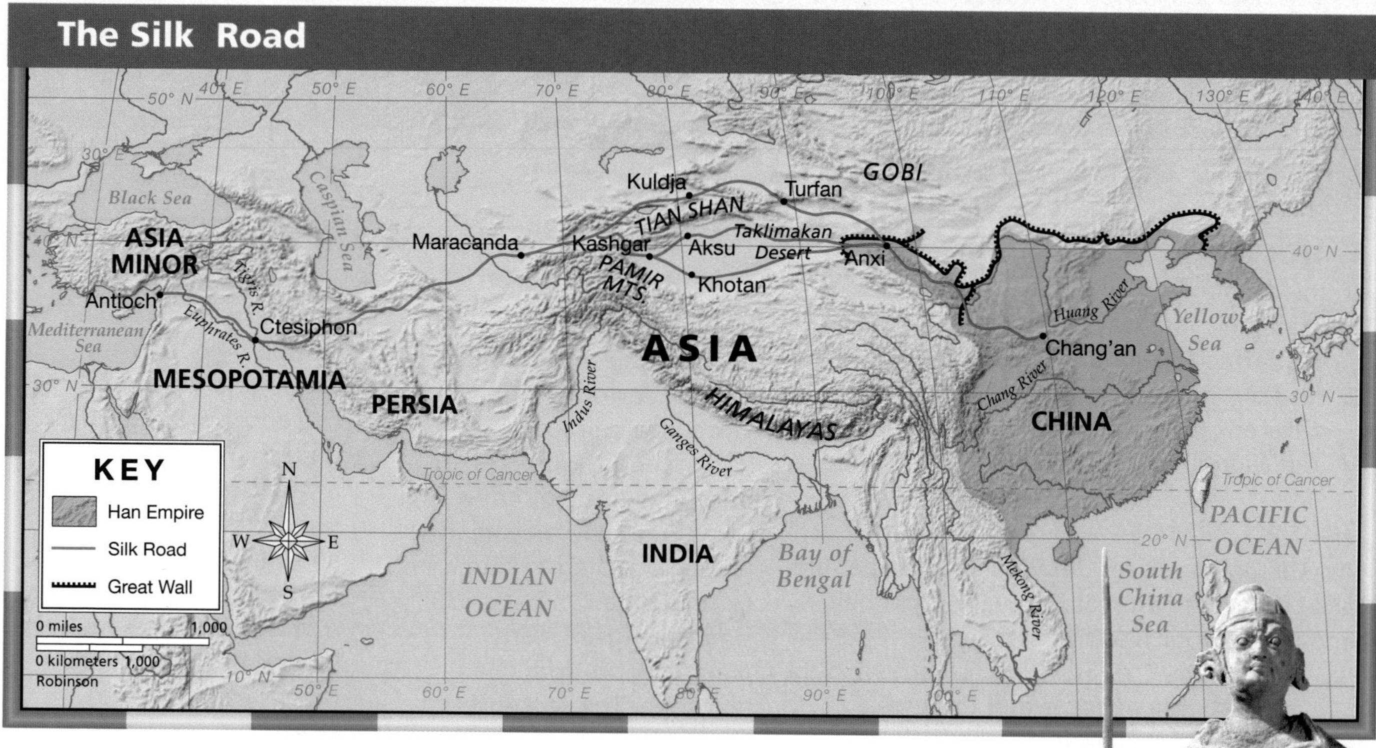

Practice the Skill

Study the map and follow the steps on the previous page to practice reading a route map.

1. Read the title of the map and study the map to observe its main features. What region does it show? What type of map is it—modern or historical, a standard road map, or some other kind? What is its purpose?

2. Look at the key on this map. What features does it identify?

3. With your finger, start at the city of Chang'an, in China, and trace the general paths of the Silk Road. Using the compass rose, determine the direction of the route. What continents or regions did the Silk Road cross? Where did it end? Did it include travel over mountains?

4. The Silk Road was created over time, as local and regional routes became connected to form one long route. Write a paragraph that describes the route and draws conclusions about how and why it took the particular path shown on the map.

Apply the Skill

Find a street map of your community. Use the steps in the Learn the Skill section to trace the route from your house to your school or to some other location you know, such as a park. Write a paragraph that draws conclusions about the route you found.

Section 2 People and Cultures

Prepare to Read

Objectives

In this section you will

1. Examine some ways in which East Asia's past affects its modern-day culture.
2. Find out how the people of China are different from the people of the Koreas and Japan.

Taking Notes

As you read, look for details about the people and culture of East Asia. Copy the chart below, and record your findings in it.

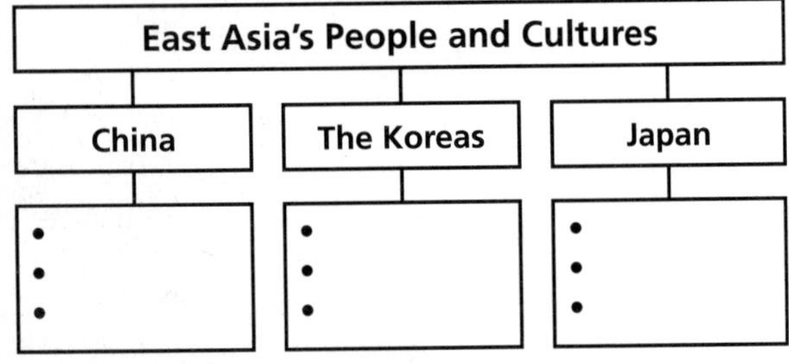

Target Reading Skill

Use Context Clues
Context, the words and phrases surrounding a word, can help you understand a word or phrase you do not know. Sometimes you may need to keep reading to find a context clue. On page 653, find the phrase *many marriages are still arranged.* The sentence that follows this phrase explains what an arranged marriage is.

Key Terms

- **commune** (KAHM yoon) *n.* a community in which people own land as a group and where they live and work together
- **dialect** (DY uh lekt) *n.* a variation of a language that is unique to a region or an area
- **nomad** (NOH mad) *n.* a person who has no settled home but who moves from place to place
- **homogeneous** (hoh moh JEE nee us) *adj.* identical or similar
- **ethnic group** (ETH nik groop) *n.* a group of people who share such characteristics as language, religion, and ancestry

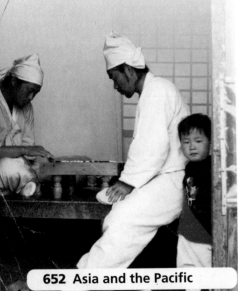

Two men play a game of Go in a small South Korean village.

The Chinese game weiqi (WAY chee) has ancient cultural roots. One player has 181 black stones standing for night. The other has 180 white stones standing for day. The goal is to surround and capture the opponent's stones. But to the Chinese, weiqi is more than a game. For centuries, Buddhists have used it to discipline the mind. Today, you can see people playing this ancient game throughout East Asia. Another name for this traditional Chinese game is Go.

Tradition and Change

In East Asia, tradition mixes with change in a thousand ways. Businesspeople in Western suits greet each other in the traditional way—with a bow. Ancient palaces stand among skyscrapers. Everywhere in Japan, China, and the Koreas, reminders of the past mingle with activities of the present.

Shanghai at Night
Shanghai, China, is a bustling city with skyscrapers and superhighways. The small photo shows Nanjing Road, one of the principal streets in Shanghai. **Analyze Images** *Do you think Shanghai is a large or a small city? Explain your answer.*

Communism Changes Chinese Farming When the Communists took power in 1949, they began to make major changes. The government ended the old system of land ownership. It created **communes,** communities in which land is held in common and where members live and work together.

Many Chinese farmers were bitter at losing their land. They were accustomed to living in family groups that worked together in small fields. The farmers resisted the communes. Food production fell, and China suffered terrible food shortages. Only when the government allowed some private ownership did food production grow.

Changes in Chinese Life Beginning in the 1970s, the Communists also tried to slow China's population growth by attacking the idea of large families. Chinese couples were supposed to wait until their late twenties to marry. They were not supposed to have more than one child per family. Chinese families with only one child could receive special privileges. For example, couples in urban areas could receive a payment of money. In rural areas, the reward could be more land.

Under communism, the position of women improved. One of the first laws the Communists passed allowed a woman to own property, choose her husband, and get a divorce. Today, however, men still hold most of the power, and many marriages are still arranged. That is, parents or other family members decide who will marry whom.

Japan's Capsule Hotels
In densely populated Japan, people have developed unique ways to use space. Capsule hotels are one such example. They are used mainly by businessmen who have missed the last train home. Each capsule usually has a bed, a television, a radio, and an alarm clock.
Analyze Images *What are most of the people in the photo doing?*

Old and New in China Old traditions in China are strongest in rural areas. Yet even in the cities, a visitor sees examples of the old China. In cities like Beijing, the capital of China, the streets are filled with three-wheeled cabs pedaled like tricycles. These pedicabs share the roads with buses, cars, and taxis. Tiny shops exist side by side with modern buildings.

Changes in the Koreas In both Koreas, daily life is influenced by long-standing traditions. The family is still important, although the average family is smaller today than before. In rural areas, grandparents, parents, aunts, and uncles may live in one household. In the cities, usually just parents and children live as one household.

As in China, modern ways are much more visible in Korean urban areas. Also, as is true all over the world, the role of women has changed. In the past, Korean women had few opportunities. Today, women can work and vote.

Target Skill **Use Context Clues** Use the last two sentences in this paragraph to help you define *traditional customs.* Check your definition by looking up *traditional* and *custom* in a dictionary.

A Blend of Old and New in Japan Japan is the most modern of the East Asian countries. The Japanese use more modern technology than the rest of East Asia. Nearly 80 percent of the population lives in urban areas. Once Japanese workers reach home, however, many still follow traditional customs. For example, they may change into kimonos, or robes. They may sit on mats at a low table to have dinner.

✓ **Reading Check** **Which is the most modern country in East Asia?**

East Asia's People

East Asia is a mix of cultures both old and new. Within each of the area's countries, however, the people tend to share a single culture.

Discovery Channel School Video
Learn about the history of China's merchant class.

China: The Han and Other Chinese Ethnic Groups About 19 of every 20 Chinese people trace their ancestry to the Han ethnic group. As you can see on the map below, the Han live mostly in the eastern half of China. Although they have a common written language, they speak different dialects from region to region. A **dialect** is a variation of a language that is unique to a region or area. The other Chinese come from 55 different minority groups. These groups live mainly in western and southern China. With so many different ethnic groups, China is one of the most ethnically diverse nations in the world.

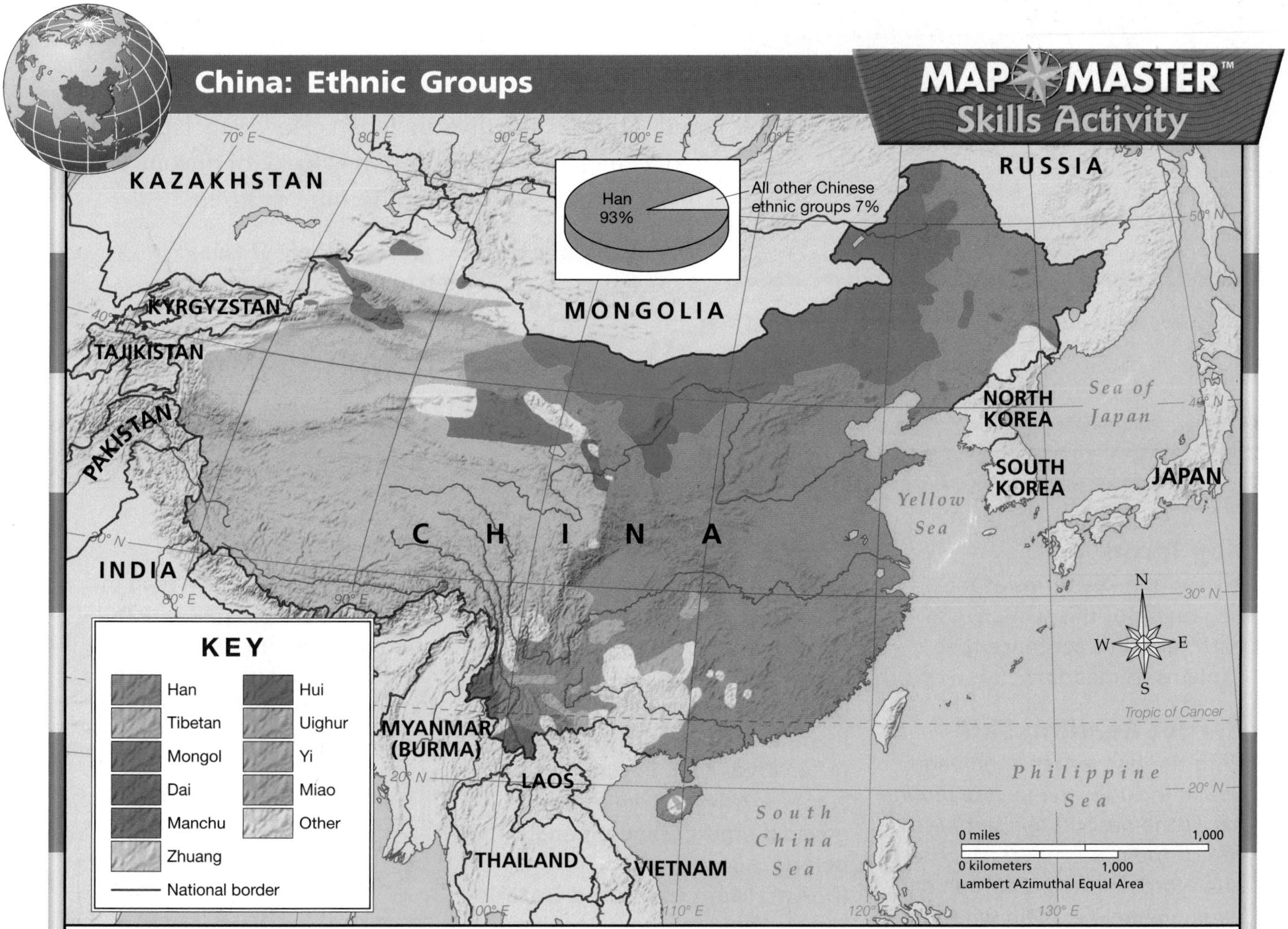

China: Ethnic Groups

MAP MASTER™ Skills Activity

Place Although China is an ethnically diverse country, 93 percent of the Chinese people are from the Han ethnic group. **Identify** In what part of China do Tibetans live? **Infer** In what country outside China would you expect Mongolians to live?

Go Online PHSchool.com Use Web Code **lcp-6412** for step-by-step **map skills practice.**

Shoppers in Seoul, South Korea

Korea and Japan: Few Minorities Historians believe that the ancient Korean language was brought to Korea by nomads from the north. **Nomads** are people who have no settled home but who move from place to place, usually on a seasonal basis. Over centuries, these groups lost their separate traditions. They formed one **homogeneous** (hoh moh JEE nee us) group, which means identical or similar. Today, even with the division of Korea into two countries, the population is quite homogeneous. There are few minority groups.

Because it is an island nation that isolated itself from the world for a long time, Japan has one of the most homogeneous populations on Earth. Nearly all of the people belong to the same **ethnic group**, a group of people who share such characteristics as language, religion, ancestry, and cultural traditions. Minority groups are few. Small numbers of Koreans and Chinese also live in Japan. However, Japan has strict rules on immigration. It is hard for anyone who is not Japanese by birth to become a citizen.

Reading Check **How are the people of China different from the people of the Koreas and Japan?**

Section 2 Assessment

Key Terms

Review the key terms at the beginning of this section. Use each term in a sentence that explains its meaning.

Target Reading Skill

Find the last sentence on page 652. It includes the phrase *reminders of the past mingle with activities of the present.* Which phrases and words in the paragraph on page 652 help explain what the phrase means?

Comprehension and Critical Thinking

1. (a) Recall In what two major ways did the Communists make changes in the Chinese way of life?
(b) Summarize How is modern life in East Asia more visible in urban areas than in rural areas?
2. (a) Identify To which ethnic group do most Chinese people belong?
(b) Find Main Ideas and Details Why is China said to be an ethnically diverse country?
(c) Summarize Why are the populations of the Koreas and Japan homogeneous?

Writing Activity

Based on what you have read in this section, write a paragraph describing how tradition and change exist together in East Asia. Include at least three supporting details for your topic sentence.

For: An activity on East Asia's culture
Visit: PHSchool.com
Web Code: lcd-6402

Chapter 21 Review and Assessment

◆ Chapter Summary

Section 1: Historic Traditions

- China has the oldest continuous civilization in the world. Starting in ancient times, a series of dynasties ruled China.
- Paper, gunpowder, silk weaving, and the magnetic compass are among China's many cultural and technical achievements.
- The Shilla people unified Korea as one country. A series of shoguns ruled Japan for more than 700 years.
- In the 1800s, western nations became interested in East Asia as a market to sell goods.

Japanese *No* mask

Section 2: People and Cultures

- China has been governed under a Communist system since 1949. The Communist party has made major changes in the Chinese way of life.
- Although China is becoming more modern, old traditions are still followed, especially in rural areas of the country.
- As in China, modern ways of life in the Koreas are more visible in urban areas. Japan is the most modern of the East Asian countries but also lives by its historic traditions.
- Most people in China belong to the Han ethnic group. Korea's history resulted in a homogeneous population. As in the Koreas, nearly all Japanese people belong to the same ethnic group.

Shanghai, China

◆ Key Terms

Each of the statements below contains a key term from the chapter. If the statement is true, write *true.* If it is false, rewrite the statement to make it true.

1. An emperor is the male ruler of an empire.
2. A clan is a series of rulers from the same family.
3. A dynasty is a group of families with a common ancestor.
4. Cultural diffusion is the spreading of ideas or practices from one culture to other cultures.
5. People with the same dialect use a variation of a language that is unique to their region or area.
6. A nomad is a community in which people own land as a group and where they live together and work together.
7. A homogeneous group includes people who are identical or similar.
8. An ethnic group shares such characteristics as language, religion, ancestry, and cultural traditions.

Chapter 21

Review and Assessment (continued)

◆ Comprehension and Critical Thinking

9. **(a) Explain** What is a civilization?
(b) Describe What are some achievements of the ancient Chinese civilization?
(c) Make Generalizations Give some examples of how ancient Chinese achievements still affect the world today.

10. **(a) Recall** To which ethnic group do most of the people in China belong?
(b) Summarize How does China's population differ from the populations of Japan and the Koreas in terms of ethnic diversity?

11. **(a) Define** What is a dynasty?
(b) Contrast How is China governed today, and how is that government different from China's government in ancient times?

12. **(a) Recall** About what percentage of people in Japan live in urban areas?
(b) Synthesize Information Give examples of how life in East Asia reflects past traditions and present traditions.
(c) Predict Why might past traditions be followed more in rural areas of East Asia than in urban areas?

13. **(a) Recall** When did the Communists come into power in China?
(b) Summarize What changes did the Communists make to the Chinese way of life?

◆ Skills Practice

Reading Route Maps In the Skills for Life activity in this chapter, you learned how to read route maps. Review the steps you followed to learn this skill. Then use the map on page 651 to name two rivers in Mesopotamia that the Silk Road crossed. If a traveler was heading west on the Silk Road, which river would he cross first?

◆ Writing Activity: History

As you have read in this chapter, paper was invented in ancient China, as were many other things. Choose one of the inventions named in this chapter, and do research in the library or on the Internet to learn more about it. Find out how it was made and used in ancient China. Also, find out how the invention spread to other parts of the world. Write a paragraph about what you have learned.

MAP MASTER™ Skills Activity

Place Location For each place listed below, write the letter from the map that shows its location.

1. Mongolia
2. China
3. Taiwan
4. North Korea
5. South Korea
6. Japan

Go Online PHSchool.com Use Web Code **lcp-6420** for an **interactive map.**

East Asia

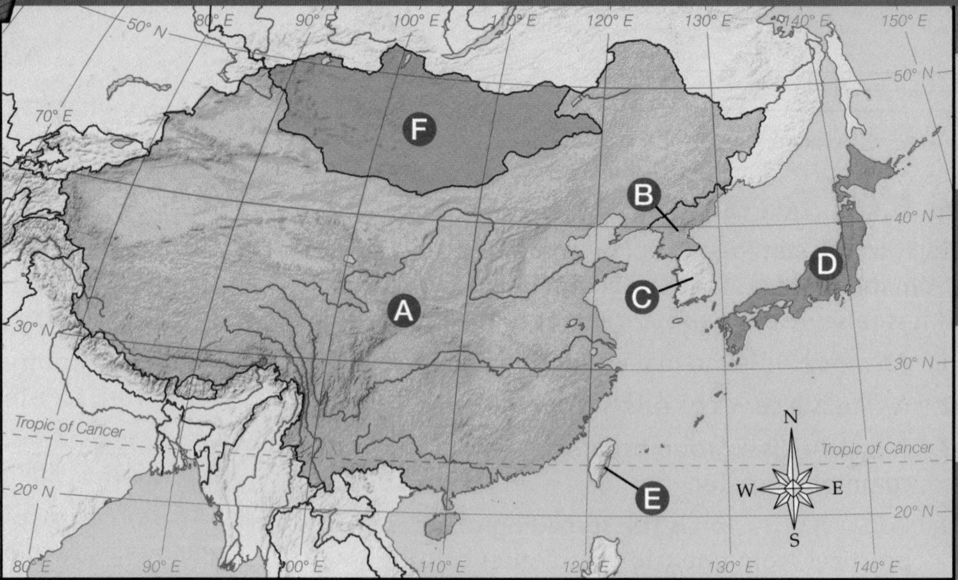

Standardized Test Prep

Test-Taking Tips

Some questions on standardized tests ask you to analyze timelines. Study the timeline below. Then follow the tips to answer the sample question.

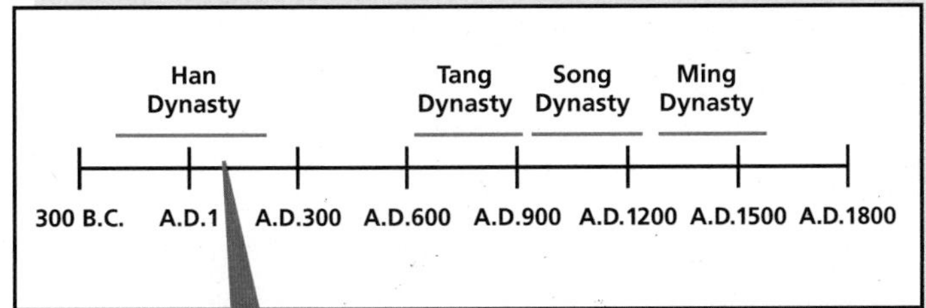

TIP To read a timeline, first figure out the timespan between dates (in this case it is 300 years). Then line up each event or dynasty with the nearest date or dates and estimate.

Pick the letter that best answers the question.

The world's oldest printed book was found in China. It was made around A.D. 868, during the

A Han dynasty.
B Tang dynasty.
C Song dynasty.
D Ming dynasty.

TIP Rewrite the sentence in your own words to make sure you understand what it is asking: *During which dynasty was the oldest book made?*

Think It Through The oldest book was made around A.D. 868. You can eliminate Han and Ming (A and D) because they are not near that date. Now look closely at the timeline: A.D. 868 is between A.D. 600 and A.D. 900. The Song Dynasty started *after* A.D. 900. So the correct answer is B, the Tang Dynasty.

Practice Questions

Use the tips above and other tips in this book to help you answer the following questions.

1. Based on the timeline above, the Tang dynasty lasted about
   A 100 years.
   B 200 years.
   C 300 years.
   D 400 years.

2. The religion of Buddhism, which China adopted from India, is an example of
   A cultural migration.
   B irrigation.
   C cultural diffusion.
   D Communist rule.

3. Which statement correctly describes Chinese culture?
   A Everyone in China belongs to the same ethnic group.
   B Chinese people speak different dialects from region to region.
   C Old traditions and ways of life are illegal in China.
   D There are two ethnic groups in China.

Use Web Code **lca-6400** for **Chapter 21 self-test.**

Chapter 22

South, Southwest, and Central Asia: Cultures and History

Chapter Preview

In this chapter, you will learn about the cultures and history of three regions in Asia: South Asia, Southwest Asia, and Central Asia.

Word Analysis In this chapter, you will focus on analyzing words. For example, you will learn to break unfamiliar words into parts to understand the words.

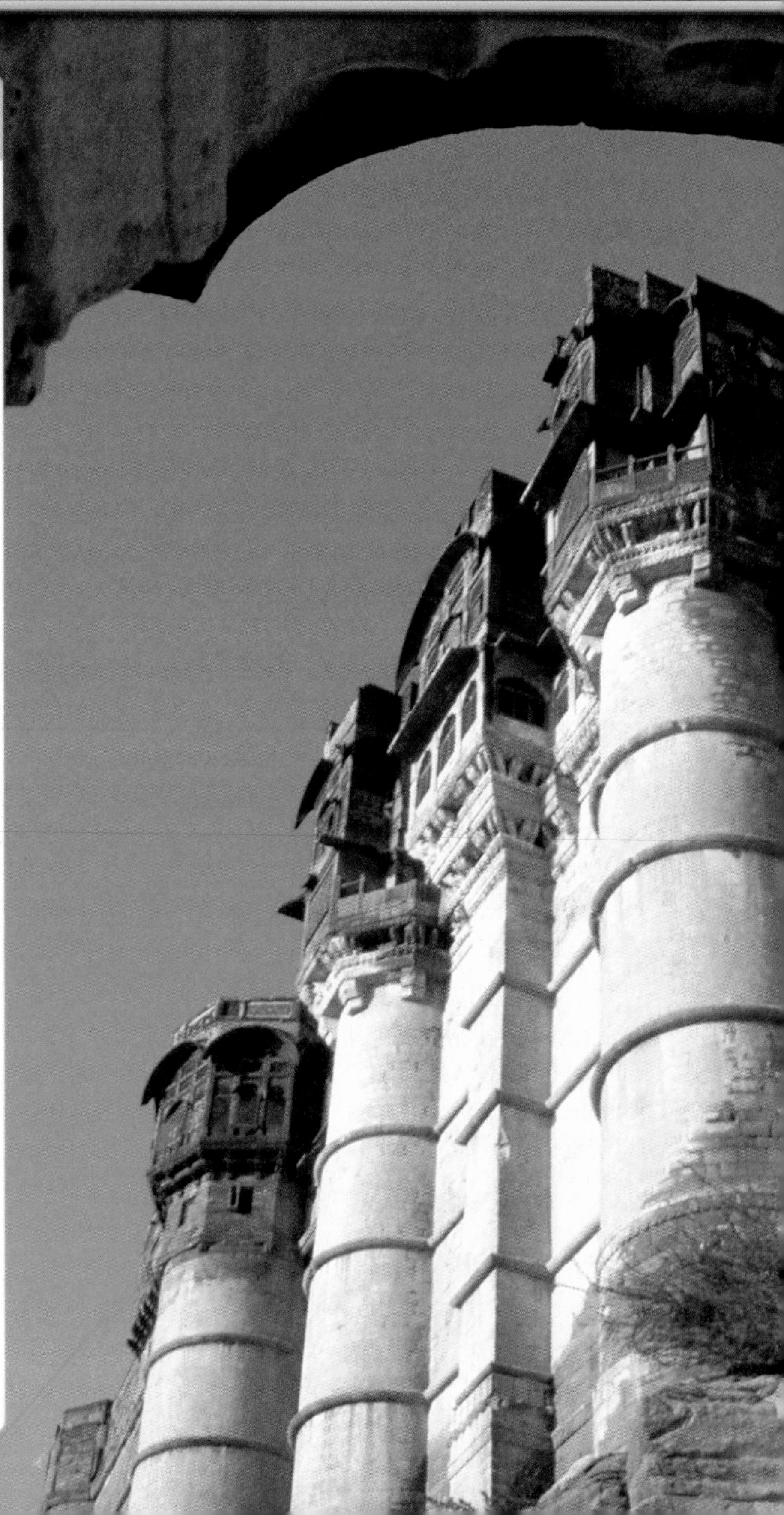

▶ **Amber Fort is one of the many forts and palaces of South Asia. It is located in India.**

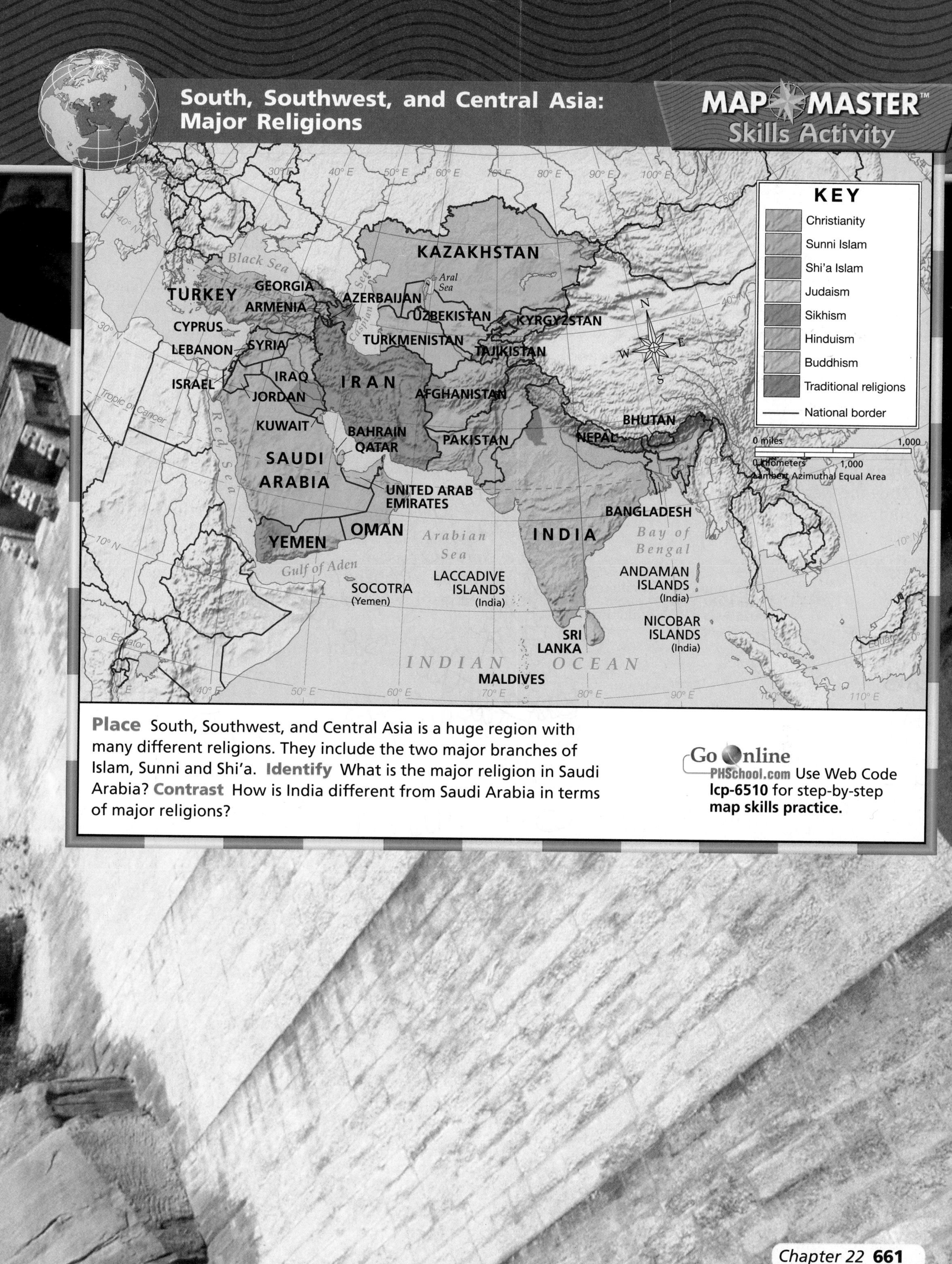

Place South, Southwest, and Central Asia is a huge region with many different religions. They include the two major branches of Islam, Sunni and Shi'a. **Identify** What is the major religion in Saudi Arabia? **Contrast** How is India different from Saudi Arabia in terms of major religions?

Go Online PHSchool.com Use Web Code **lcp-6510** for step-by-step **map skills practice.**

Section 1 South Asia
Cultures and History

Prepare to Read

Objectives

In this section, you will

1. Find out which religions became part of South Asian cultures.
2. Understand which empires shaped the history of South Asia.
3. Learn about the present-day religions and languages of South Asian cultures.

Taking Notes

As you read this section, look for main ideas about the history and cultures of South Asia. Copy the web below, and record your findings in it.

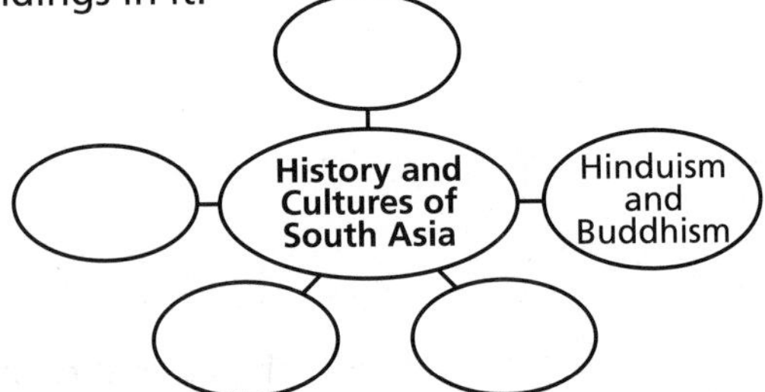

Target Reading Skill

Analyze Word Parts When you come across a word you do not know, break the word into parts to help you recognize it and pronounce it. This may help you find its root and prefix. A root is the part of the word that has meaning by itself. A prefix goes in front of the root and changes its meaning. In this section you will find the word *nonviolent*. Break it into a root and a prefix to learn its meaning.

Key Terms

- **caste** (kast) *n.* in the Hindu religion, a social group into which people are born and which they cannot change; each group with assigned jobs
- **colony** (KAHL uh nee) *n.* a territory ruled by another nation
- **boycott** (BOY kaht) *n.* a refusal to buy or use goods and services to show disapproval or bring about change
- **partition** (pahr TISH un) *n.* a division into parts or portions

In 1921, scientists digging near the Indus River came upon the ruins of an ancient city they called Mohenjo-Daro (moh HEN joh DAH roh). The city was amazingly well planned, with wide, straight streets and large buildings. It had a sewer system and a large walled fortress. Mohenjo-Daro was part of a civilization that developed about 4,500 years ago. The people who lived there were part of the Indus Valley civilization, one of the world's oldest civilizations.

Over the centuries, many other people moved into South Asia. All of them contributed to South Asian culture. South Asian culture, in turn, influenced cultures of other regions. Hinduism (HIN doo iz um) and Buddhism (BOO diz um), two religions that developed in South Asia, are practiced by hundreds of millions of people all over the world.

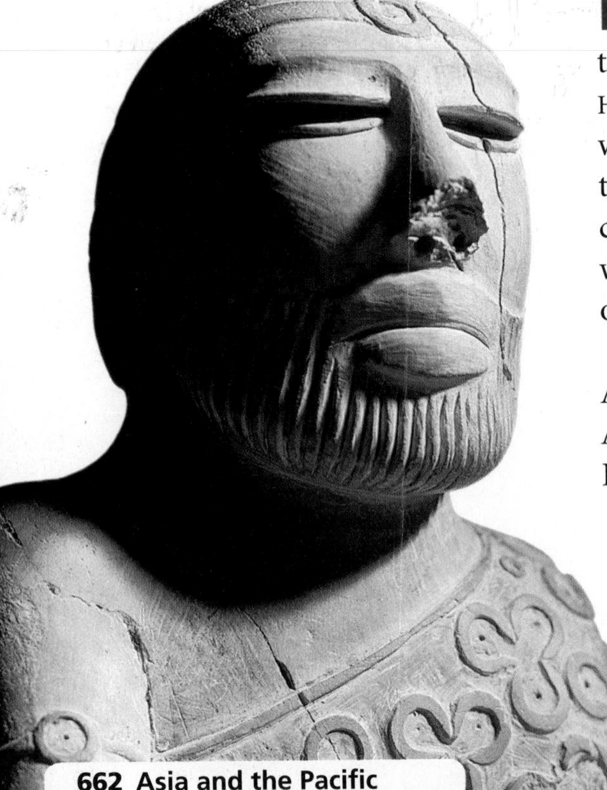

This ancient statue of a priest-king was unearthed at Mohenjo-Daro.

New Religions

The Indus Valley civilization flourished from about 2500 B.C. to about 1600 B.C. By 1500 B.C., however, the civilization was coming to an end. Scholars are uncertain why this happened.

About the same time that the Indus Valley civilization was weakening, newcomers came to the region, probably from Central Asia. They brought different languages and beliefs to the region. The newcomers merged with the people of the Indus Valley. A new culture combined the ancient languages and beliefs of the region with the language and religion of the newcomers. This mixed culture is known as Aryan culture. The people who practiced this culture are known as Aryans (AYR ee unz).

The Aryans ruled northern India for more than 1,000 years. They divided people into four classes—priests and the educated; rulers and warriors; farmers, artisans, and merchants; and laborers. Europeans later called the division the caste (kast) system. A **caste** is a social group into which people are born and which they cannot change.

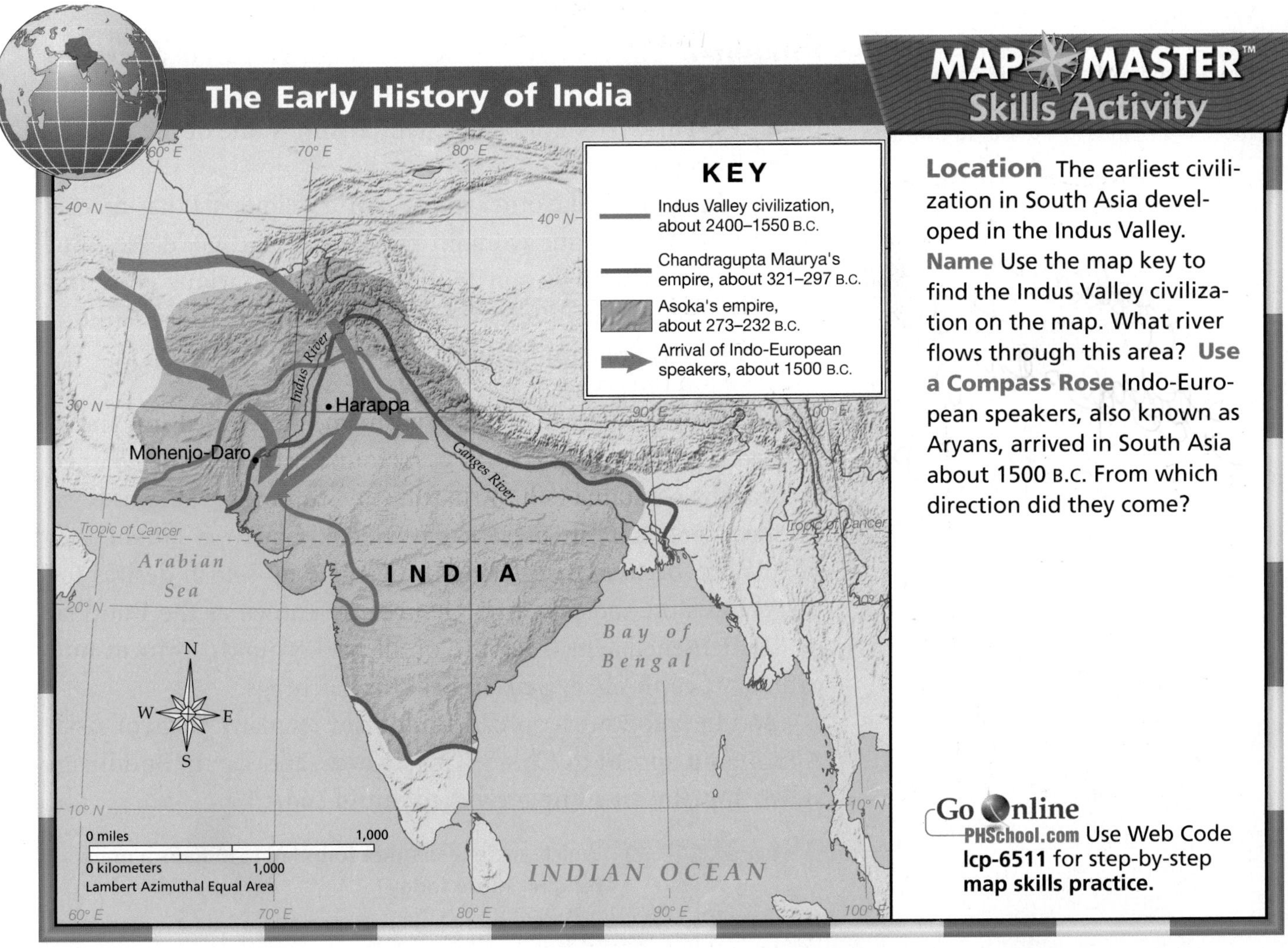

Location The earliest civilization in South Asia developed in the Indus Valley. **Name** Use the map key to find the Indus Valley civilization on the map. What river flows through this area? **Use a Compass Rose** Indo-European speakers, also known as Aryans, arrived in South Asia about 1500 B.C. From which direction did they come?

Go Online
PHSchool.com Use Web Code **lcp-6511** for step-by-step **map skills practice.**

Three Main Hindu Gods
One of the world's oldest religions, Hinduism dates back more than 3,000 years. Shown here are the three main gods in the Hindu trinity

1. Brahma is regarded as the creator of the universe. According to Hindu writings, Brahma originally had five heads. His fifth head was destroyed by Shiva because Brahma had offended him.
2. Vishnu is worshipped as the preserver of the universe.
3. Shiva appears in many different forms, including the destroyer of the universe.

Hinduism The caste system became a central part of a new system of belief that also emerged from Aryan religious ideas and practices. This system of beliefs, Hinduism, is one of the world's oldest living religions.

Hinduism is unlike other major world religions. It has no one single founder. Hindus worship many gods and goddesses, but they believe in a single spirit. To Hindus, the various gods and goddesses represent different parts of this spirit. Today, Hinduism is the main religion of India.

Buddhism Buddhism, like Hinduism, developed in India. According to Buddhist tradition, its founder was a prince named Siddhartha Gautama (sih DAHR tuh GOW tuh muh). He was born in about 560 B.C., in present-day Nepal. Gautama taught that people can be free of suffering if they give up selfish desires for power, wealth, and pleasure. He became known as the Buddha, or "Enlightened One." People of all backgrounds, princes and ordinary people alike, went to hear his teachings.

Buddha's followers spread Buddhism to many parts of Asia. Although it spread to China, Tibet, Korea, and Japan, Buddhism slowly but almost completely died out in India.

✓ Reading Check **Which ancient religion founded in India is a main religion there today?**

From Empires to Nations

Today, South Asia is a region of independent countries. Starting in ancient times, however, a series of empires rose and fell in the region. Before South Asian countries became independent in the 1900s, the region was under European control.

This lion sculpture originally stood at the top of one of Asoka's pillars.

The Maurya Empire Around 321 B.C., a leader named Chandragupta Maurya (chun druh GOOP tuh MOWR yuh) conquered many kingdoms. By the time of his death in 298 B.C., the Maurya Empire covered much of the Indian subcontinent.

Chandragupta's grandson, Asoka (uh SOH kuh), became emperor in 268 B.C. After one bloody battle, Asoka gave up war and violence. He changed his beliefs to Buddhism and vowed to rule peacefully. Asoka had stone pillars set up across India. Carved into the pillars were his laws and beliefs in fair and just government.

The Maurya Empire lost power not long after Asoka's death. By about 185 B.C. the empire collapsed as rival leaders fought for power.

The Gupta Empire About 500 years after the Mauryas, the Gupta Empire again united much of the Indian subcontinent. The Guptas ruled from A.D. 320 to about A.D. 550. Gupta emperors set up a strong central government that was supported by trade and farming.

Under Gupta rule, India enjoyed a period of great cultural achievement. Gupta mathematicians developed the system of writing numerals that we use today. These numerals are called "Arabic" numerals. Arabs carried them from India to Southwest Asia and Europe. People built splendid temples of stone decorated with carvings. Artists created wall paintings of Buddhist stories in temples built inside caves at Ajanta (uh JUN tuh) in western India.

Weak rulers and foreign invaders led to the fall of the Gupta Empire. The empire lasted until about A.D. 550.

The Mughal Empire In the A.D. 700s, people from the north began moving into northern India. They introduced the religion of Islam to the area. According to its followers, Islam is the set of beliefs revealed to the prophet Muhammad. He began teaching these beliefs around A.D. 610 in Southwest Asia. Islam eventually spread westward into North Africa and eastward into Central and South Asia.

Links to Math

Decimal Numbers By about A.D. 600, Indian astronomers were using the decimal system—a numbering system based on tens. Their system also had place values and a zero. This made it easy to add, subtract, multiply, and divide. Europeans were using Roman numerals at this time. They later switched to this decimal, or Hindu-Arabic, system, which is used worldwide today.

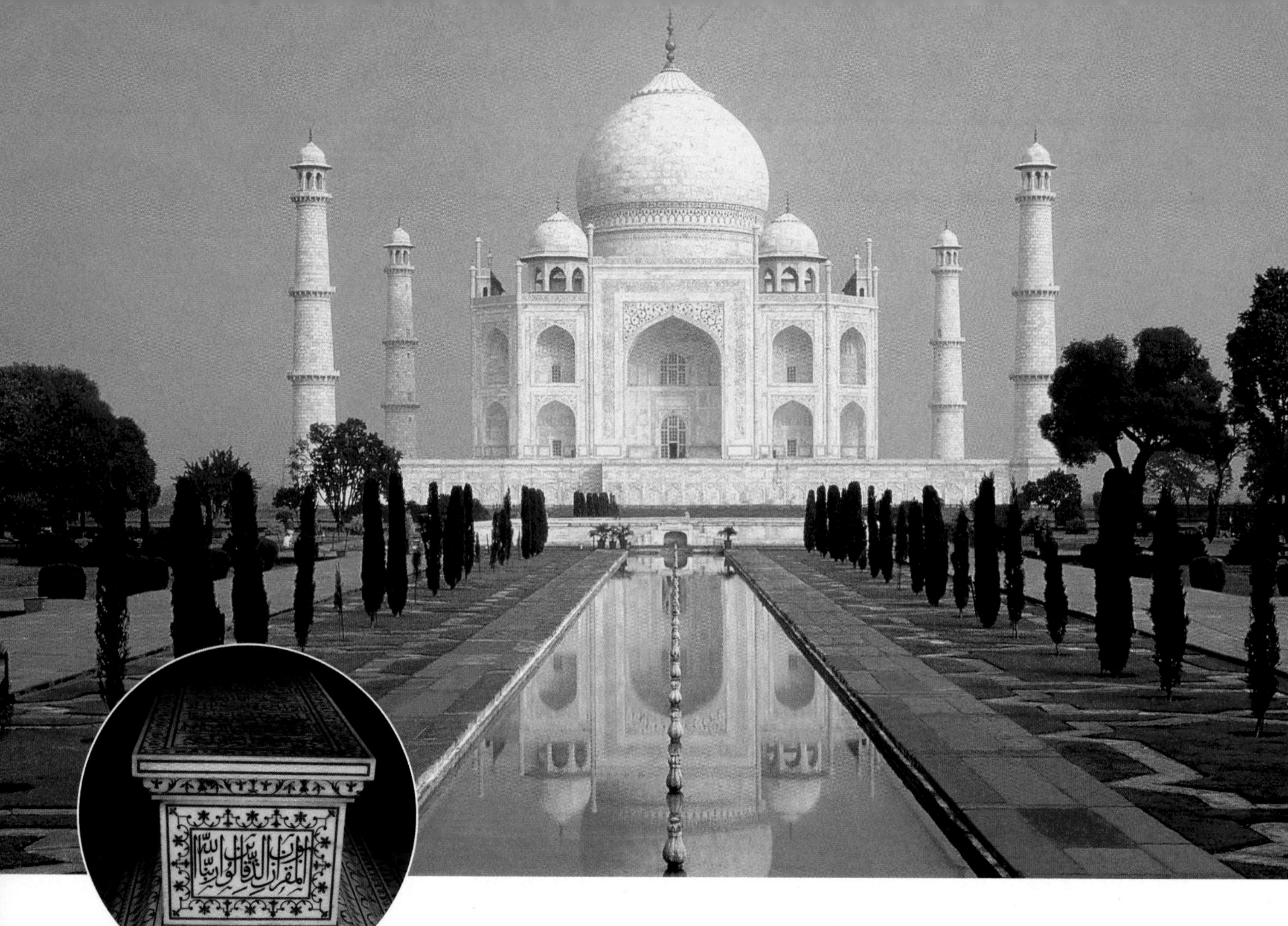

The Taj Mahal, India
The Taj Mahal is considered to be one of the world's most beautiful buildings. Emperor Shah Jahan had it built as a tomb for his wife. The small photo shows the actual tomb inside the marble structure. **Analyze Images** *How does the large photo show symmetry in the design of the Taj Mahal?*

Among these Muslims, or followers of Islam, who settled in India were the Mughals (MOO gulz). They arrived in the 1500s and established an empire. Akbar (AK bahr), who ruled the Mughal Empire from 1556 to 1605, allowed all people to worship freely, regardless of their religion. He also generously supported the arts and literature.

Akbar's grandson, Shah Jahan (shah juh HAHN), built many grand buildings. Perhaps the greatest is the Taj Mahal (tahzh muh HAHL), which still stands today. He had it built as a magnificent tomb for Mumtaz Mahal (mum TAHZ muh HAHL), his wife. The cost of this and other of Jahan's building projects was enormous. It drained the empire of money and, eventually, helped to cause the empire's collapse in the 1700s.

Target Skill

Analyze Word Parts Look for the word *subcontinent* in this paragraph. The prefix *sub-* means "under." Now define the word *subcontinent.*

The British in India By the late 1700s, much of the Indian subcontinent had come under British rule. Until 1858, a trading company known as the British East India Company controlled most of India. The British government ended the rule of the British East India Company in 1858. From that time until 1947, India was controlled by Britain as a colony of Britain's empire. A **colony** is a territory ruled by another nation.

Independence and Division In the early 1900s, a strong independence movement emerged in India. Its leader was Mohandas K. Gandhi (GAHN dee). Gandhi called for people to resist British rule. However, Gandhi stressed that they use nonviolent means. For example, he urged a boycott of British goods. A **boycott** means a refusal to buy or use goods and services to show disapproval or bring about change. Gandhi played a major part in forcing Britain to grant India its independence in 1947.

As independence approached, Muslims feared that their rights would not be protected in a land where Hindus were the majority. Fighting erupted as demands arose for a state where Muslims would be the majority. In 1947 this led to the **partition**, or division, of the subcontinent into two nations, Pakistan and India. Muslims would be the majority in Pakistan. Hindus would be the majority in India.

This partition did not stop the fighting. About one million people were killed. Gandhi himself was murdered by a Hindu who was angered at Gandhi's concern for Muslims.

Indian Independence leader Mohandas Gandhi

Conflict in South Asia Conflict between India and Pakistan continued throughout the 1900s. In 1971, Indian troops helped East Pakistan break away from Pakistan to form the nation of Bangladesh (BAHNG luh desh). Pakistan and India have fought over the question of which country controls Kashmir (KASH mihr), an area on the border of India and Pakistan. In 1998, both nations tested nuclear weapons. The continuing threat of conflict that might involve nuclear weapons in the region concerns the United States and other countries.

√ Reading Check **What are some contributions from the Maurya, Gupta, and Mughal empires?**

Republic Day in India
Every January 26, Indians celebrate Republic Day to mark the adoption of the Indian constitution on January 26, 1950.
Infer *Which national flag do you think is shown in the photo?*

Selling spices at an open-air market in India

South Asian Cultures Today

South Asia's long history continues to shape its cultures. Two major examples are religion and languages.

Many Religions Hinduism and Islam are the major religions of South Asia today. About 80 percent of the people in India are Hindus. Hinduism is also the major religion in Nepal. Islam is the main religion in Pakistan and Bangladesh. Other religions in South Asia include Christianity, Sikhism (SEEK iz um), and Jainism (JY niz um). Sikhism began as a religion that combined Hindu and Muslim beliefs. Followers of Jainism believe that violence toward or injury of any living thing is wrong.

Many Languages Many different languages are spoken in South Asia. The languages of South Asia generally belong to two families. Dravidian (druh VID ee un) languages are spoken in southern India. Indo-European languages are spoken in northern India and most of the rest of South Asia. The Aryans who came into South Asia in ancient times spoke Indo-European languages. One of the languages in this group is Hindi (HIN dee). About 30 percent of the people in India speak Hindi. Hindi is one of 15 languages recognized by the Indian government. English is also widely used as an official language in India.

✓ Reading Check **In which two South Asian countries is Hinduism the major religion?**

Section 1 Assessment

Key Terms

Review the key terms at the beginning of this section. Use each term in a sentence that explains its meaning.

Target Reading Skill

Find the word *uncertain* on page 663 in the first paragraph under the heading New Religions. The prefix *un-* means "not." What is the meaning of *uncertain*?

Comprehension and Critical Thinking

1. **(a) Recall** Which group of people developed the caste system?
(b) Sequence Which developed first, Hinduism or Buddhism?
2. **(a) Name** Which empire introduced Islam to South Asia?
(b) Identify Effect What major issues led to the partition of India in 1947?
3. **(a) Identify** What is the main religion in Pakistan?
(b) Make Generalizations How can the movement of people from one place to another affect language in a region?

Writing Activity

Suppose you are traveling throughout South Asia. Write a letter to your family in which you describe ways in which the history of the region is shown in its present-day culture.

Writing Tip Your letter should begin with a greeting and end with a closing and a signature. The body of the letter contains the information you want to communicate to your reader.

Section 2

Southwest Asia

Cultures and History

Prepare to Read

Objectives

In this section, you will

1. Find out that one of the world's earliest civilizations grew in Southwest Asia.
2. Understand that three of the world's great religions began in Southwest Asia.
3. Examine the different ethnic groups and religions of Southwest Asia.
4. Learn about the conflict between Arabs and Israelis in Southwest Asia.

Taking Notes

As you read this section, look for details about the three main religions that developed in Southwest Asia. Copy the chart below, and record your findings in it.

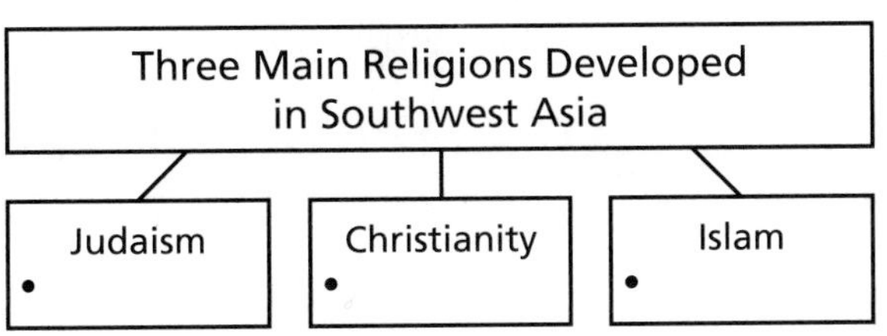

Target Reading Skill

Analyze Word Parts Breaking an unfamiliar word into parts can help you understand the word. Word parts include roots and suffixes. A root is the base of a word that has meaning by itself. A suffix comes at the end of a root word. Suffixes change the meanings of root words. In this section you will read the word *creation*. The suffix *-ion* makes the word a noun. If you know what *create* means, you can figure out the meaning of *creation*.

Key Terms

- **monotheism** (MAHN oh thee iz um) *n.* a belief that there is only one god
- **muezzin** (myoo EZ in) *n.* a person whose job is to call Muslims to pray
- **Holocaust** (HAHL uh kawst) *n.* the systematic killing of more than six million European Jews and others by Nazi Germany before and during World War II

In this ancient carving, Hammurabi receives his code of laws from the sun god.

Hammurabi's Code was written about 3,800 years ago in Southwest Asia. People have described its laws as demanding "an eye for an eye." But there was more to the code than that.

> **"If the robber is not caught, the man who has been robbed shall formally declare whatever he has lost . . . and the city and the mayor . . . shall replace whatever he has lost for him. . . . If a person is too lazy to make the dike of his field strong and there is a break in the dike and water destroys his own farmland, that person will make good the grain [tax] that is destroyed."**
>
> —*from Hammurabi's Code*

The law punished people severely for wrongdoings. But it also offered justice to people who had been hurt through no fault of their own.

Mesopotamia

Hammurabi ruled the city of Babylon from about 1800 B.C. to 1750 B.C. He united the region along the Tigris and Euphrates rivers. Located in present-day Iraq, this region was called Mesopotamia, which is derived from Greek words meaning "between the rivers." Mesopotamia was one of the world's earliest civilizations.

The people of Mesopotamia developed a system of writing. They also produced ideas about law that still affect people today. For example, they believed that all citizens must obey the same set of laws.

Explore the history of trade in Southwest Asia.

People had lived in Mesopotamia for thousands of years before Hammurabi united it. By 3500 B.C., the area became a center of farming and trade. The Tigris and Euphrates rivers flooded every year, leaving fertile soil along their banks. People dug irrigation ditches to bring water to fields that lay far from the river. Irrigation helped them to produce crop surpluses, or more than they needed for their own use.

✓ Reading Check **In what present-day country did Mesopotamia develop?**

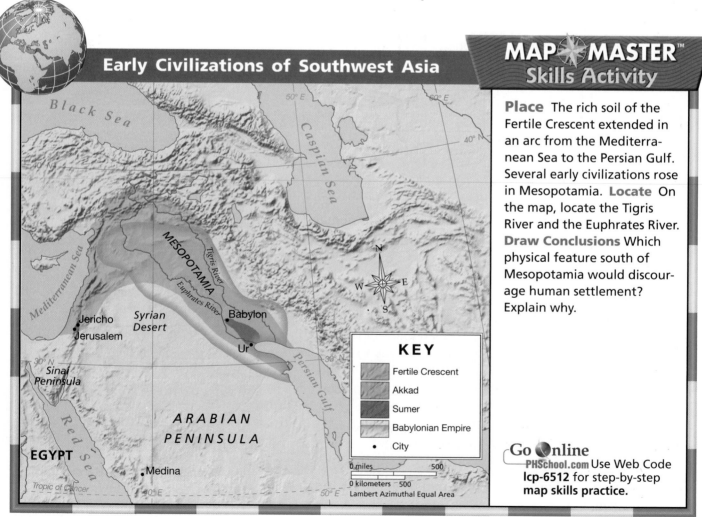

Early Civilizations of Southwest Asia

Black Sea
Caspian Sea
Mediterranean Sea
MESOPOTAMIA
Tigris River
Euphrates River
Babylon
Ur
Jericho
Jerusalem
Syrian Desert
Sinai Peninsula
Persian Gulf
Red Sea
EGYPT
ARABIAN PENINSULA
Medina
Tropic of Cancer
40° N
30° N
40° E
50° E
60° E

KEY
- Fertile Crescent
- Akkad
- Sumer
- Babylonian Empire
- • City

0 miles 500
0 kilometers 500
Lambert Azimuthal Equal Area

MAP MASTER™ Skills Activity

Place The rich soil of the Fertile Crescent extended in an arc from the Mediterranean Sea to the Persian Gulf. Several early civilizations rose in Mesopotamia. **Locate** On the map, locate the Tigris River and the Euphrates River. **Draw Conclusions** Which physical feature south of Mesopotamia would discourage human settlement? Explain why.

Go Online
PHSchool.com Use Web Code **lcp-6512** for step-by-step **map skills practice.**

Birthplace of Three Religions

Three of the world's greatest religions—Judaism, Christianity, and Islam—have their roots in Southwest Asia. About 2000 B.C., according to Hebrew religious writings, a man later known as Abraham founded the religion that would become known as Judaism. He lived in present-day Israel. Almost 2,000 years later, Jesus, the founder of Christianity, began preaching in present-day Israel. In about A.D. 600, Islam's founder and prophet, Muhammad, began teaching in present-day Saudi Arabia.

People who practice these three religions share a belief in monotheism. **Monotheism** is a belief in only one god. The followers of these religions also worship the same God—known as Allah in Islam.

Islam Of the three religions, Islam has by far the most followers in Southwest Asia today. They are called Muslims. The sights and sounds of Islam are everywhere in Southwest Asia. One sound is the call of the **muezzin** (myoo EZ in), a person whose job is to call Muslims to pray. Five times a day, Muslims stop what they are doing and pray. In large cities, the call to prayer is broadcast over loudspeakers. Throughout Southwest Asia, as well as other regions in the world, Muslims gather to worship in buildings called mosques. One of the most famous is the Dome of the Rock, shown in the photo on this page.

Jerusalem, A Holy City
Jerusalem is holy to Jews, Christians, and Muslims because events important to their religions took place there. The golden-domed building is the Dome of the Rock. It stands over the rock from which Muslims believe the prophet Muhammad rose into heaven. **Infer** *Why might Muslims from around the world want to visit Jerusalem?*

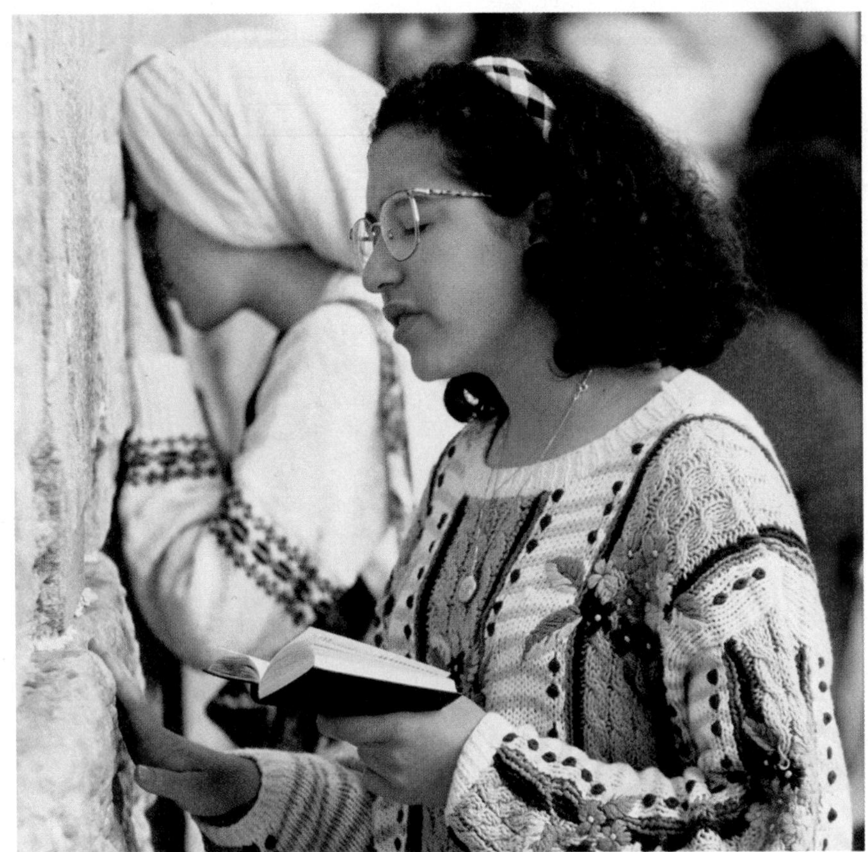

These women are praying at the Western Wall, held sacred by Jews as the remains of the Second Temple.

The New Testament of the Christian Bible describes Jesus as a good shepherd who lays down his life for his sheep.

Judaism At the heart of Judaism is the Torah (TOH ruh), five books that make up the Jews' most sacred text. According to the Torah, about 2000 B.C. Abraham, a Mesopotamian man, became convinced that there was one god, not many. He migrated to Canaan, where he became the ancestor of the Jewish people. Canaan was an area of land located along the eastern shore of the Mediterranean Sea. Hundreds of years later, it became known as Palestine. From ancient times, Jews saw Palestine as their homeland. The Torah also contains the Ten Commandments. They established religious duties toward God as well as rules for moral and ethical behavior.

Christianity Christianity first developed around A.D. 30. The religion is based on the teachings of Jesus, a Jew who traveled throughout Palestine. Christians later adopted the Torah as the first five books of the Old Testament of the Christian Bible. The first four books of the New Testament of the Christian Bible are the Gospels. They tell about the life and teachings of Jesus. According to the Gospels, Jesus taught that his followers would have eternal life. Like Islam and Judaism, Christianity began in Southwest Asia and spread throughout the world.

√ Reading Check **Why is Southwest Asia considered the birthplace of Judaism, Christianity, and Islam?**

Diverse Cultures in Southwest Asia

More than 3,000 years ago, the land of Southwest Asia was at the center of trading routes that extended across Europe, Africa, and Asia. Time after time, groups from within and outside the region conquered it. The movement of people across Southwest Asia gave the region a unique character. People of many different ethnic groups and religious beliefs settled there.

Arabic-speaking Arabs are the largest ethnic group in the region, and Islam is their main religion. But not all Southwest Asians are Arabs. Many Southwest Asians do not speak Arabic and many people, including Arabic-speaking Arabs, practice religions other than Islam.

A Mix of Ethnic Groups The people in Southwest Asia belong to a mix of ethnic groups. Today, Arabs are the main ethnic group in Saudi Arabia, Jordan, Syria, Iraq, Lebanon, and other countries on the Arabian Peninsula. Arabs also live in territories occupied by Israel. Non-Arab people live mainly in Israel, Turkey, and Iran. In Israel, about 80 percent of the population is Jewish. The remaining 20 percent is mostly Arab. In Turkey, about 80 percent of the population is Turkish. The rest of Turkey's population is Kurdish. Kurdish people also live in communities in Syria, Iraq, and Iran. In Iran, about 50 percent of the people are Persian. The rest belong to a number of different ethnic groups.

About half of Iran's population is Persian.

A Variety of Religions Except for Israel, the majority of the people in each country in Southwest Asia are Muslim. Even within the Islamic religion, however, there are differences. Muslims are divided into two main groups—Sunnis (SOO neez) and Shi'as (SHEE uz). Today, about 90 percent of Muslims are Sunni. Most of the Muslims in both Iran and Iraq, however, are Shi'as.

In Israel, about 80 percent of the people are Jewish. Muslims make up about 20 percent of the population. A small percentage of people in Israel are Christian. Christians also live in Syria, Turkey, Lebanon, and Iraq.

√ Reading Check **To which branch of Islam do most Muslims belong?**

Scenes of Hope
A Jewish boy and a Palestinian boy walk together in Israel (left). Jewish and Palestinian children from Israel play soccer at the first Children's Friendship Soccer Match, held in 2003 in Japan (right). **Infer** *Why might friendship help solve conflict?*

Southwest Asia: Recent History

Differences among various groups of people have led to conflict in Southwest Asia. As you have read, Judaism has ancient roots in Palestine. Over many years, a few Jews continued to live in Palestine. But most had been forced in ancient times to migrate to other parts of the world. In the late 1800s, Jews from around the world began to return to their homeland. This alarmed the Arabs who lived there. For hundreds of years, they had claimed Palestine as their homeland, too.

The Formation of Israel Before and during World War II, Nazi Germany killed more than six million Jews in Europe solely because they were Jewish. This became known as the **Holocaust**. After the war, many of those who had survived decided to migrate to Palestine. On May 14, 1948, Jews declared the formation of their own state, Israel. Their state was recognized by the United Nations.

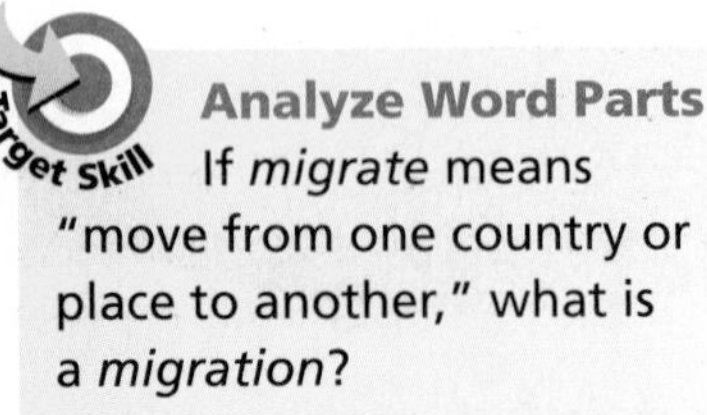

Analyze Word Parts
If *migrate* means "move from one country or place to another," what is a *migration*?

Arab-Israeli Conflict The day after the state of Israel was declared, the Arab nations of Egypt, Iraq, Jordan, Lebanon, and Syria invaded Israel. These nations supported the Palestinians. Israel drove away the Arab forces. Hundreds of thousands of Palestinians fled from Jewish territory. They lived as refugees in other Arab nations or in territories under Israeli rule. Even larger numbers of Jews were forced to leave Arab countries, and most resettled in Israel. Since 1948, Israel and the Arab nations that border it have fought a number of bloody wars.

Efforts Toward Peace In 1993, Israel and the Palestinian government—known as the Palestine Liberation Organization (PLO)—formally recognized each other. In 2000, fighting broke out between Israel and the Palestinians once again. In 2003, the United States, Israeli leaders, and the PLO agreed on a new peace plan. The plan called for Israel to agree to the creation of a Palestinian state and for the PLO to agree to Israel's right to exist in peace.

In Iraq, statues of Saddam Hussein were toppled after he was removed from power in 2003.

War With Iraq After Iraq's defeat in the 1991 Persian Gulf War, Iraqi leader Saddam Hussein (suh DAHM hoo SAYN) refused to cooperate with United Nations inspectors sent to ensure that Iraq destroyed its most dangerous weapons. In March 2003, U.S. forces attacked Iraq in an invasion supported by Great Britain and several other nations. Three weeks after the start of the war, Saddam fell from power and went into hiding. American officials began working with Iraqi leaders to set up a democratic system of government. In December 2003, U.S. troops captured Saddam.

√ Reading Check **Give one example of conflict in Southwest Asia.**

Section 2 Assessment

Key Terms

Review the key terms at the beginning of this section. Use each term in a sentence that explains its meaning.

Target Reading Skill

Define *irrigation*. The root word means "to supply with water by artificial methods." The suffix *–ion* means "act or process."

Comprehension and Critical Thinking

1. (a) Identify Tell where Mesopotamia is located.
(b) Summarize What are two achievements of the civilizations of Mesopotamia?

2. (a) List What three major religions grew in Southwest Asia?
(b) Contrast What do all three religions have in common?

3. (a) Name What is Southwest Asia's main ethnic group today?
(b) Analyze Information Give one example of ethnic or religious diversity in the region of Southwest Asia.

4. (a) Name What area do both Palestinians and Israelis claim as a homeland?
(b) Summarize What issue has caused conflict between the Palestinians and the Israelis?

Writing Activity

Write a paragraph that begins with this topic sentence: *Southwest Asia is a region with different ethnic groups and religious beliefs.* Include supporting details about at least three countries in the region.

Writing Tip Include at least two sentences about ethnic groups and at least two sentences about religions. Be sure to include supporting details.

Recognizing Bias

A baseball coach chooses his own son over other, better players, to play in a tournament game. The mayor hires her friends to fill important city jobs instead of seeking the most qualified people. The politician who wants to give business to family members says his son-in-law is the best builder to build a new school.

All these situations are examples of bias. Bias is an attitude that favors one way of feeling or acting over any other. Bias prevents someone from making a fair judgment based on facts and reason. Biased speech or writing often contains opinions stated as facts.

Learn the Skill

Knowing how to recognize bias is an important skill you will need in school and in life. To identify bias in what you read, follow the steps below.

1. **Look for opinions.** Opinions are beliefs that cannot be proved. Biased statements often appear to be facts but are actually opinions.
2. **Look for loaded words and phrases and exaggerations.** Loaded words and phrases cannot be proved. They are intended to produce a strong emotional response. To exaggerate means to enlarge a fact or statement beyond what is actual or true.
3. **Look for missing facts.** Biased speech often leaves out facts that do not support the author's bias.
4. **Determine whether the text presents only one point of view.** Writing that is biased presents only one point of view about an issue or a topic. The point of view may be positive or negative.
5. **Determine whether the text contains bias.** Review the text and draw a conclusion about it.

Traveling Through Turkey by Bus

A group of 150 American tourists spent a busy morning at a market in Istanbul, Turkey, arriving at 7 AM just as sellers opened for business.

The Americans were visiting Istanbul on a tour to study the cultures of Turkey. The tourists spent about an hour shopping at the market.

"We usually don't get such a large group so early in the morning," one shop owner commented.

The tourists arrived so early that some shop owners had not yet opened for business. In a narrow section of the market, four tourists bumped into a display and knocked it over. The visitors stopped to help the shop owner fix the display.

The next stop for the Americans' cultural tour will be Turkey's capital, Ankara. The group is traveling through Turkey by bus.

Greedy Tourists Mob Market

A crowd of greedy American tourists invaded a market in the city of Istanbul, Turkey, buying everything in sight.

In a burst of energy rarely seen from Americans who prefer to drive everywhere instead of walk, the bargain-hunters swarmed out of tour buses to examine the products on display. Shop owners were overwhelmed as the impatient Americans roamed through the market.

One group of tourists overturned tables in their quest for bargains.

Americans should use better manners when they shop in other countries instead of barging into stores and being rude.

The next stop for the mob of American tourists is Turkey's capital city, Ankara.

Practice the Skill

Read the two reports above. Then use the steps on the previous page to determine which report shows bias.

1. Opinions often contain words such as *I believe* and *should.* Which report contains an opinion?
2. Look for loaded words or phrases and exaggerations in the reports. How is the phrase "greedy American tourists" an example of a loaded phrase? Which report contains the phrase "buying everything in sight"? Is this a factual statement or an exaggeration?
3. Which report includes facts, such as the number of tourists and the time of day?
4. Which report presents a point of view about American tourists? Is the point of view negative or positive?
5. Based on your review, which report shows bias? State the bias in a complete sentence.

A market in Istanbul, Turkey

Apply the Skill

Find an article about Turkey in the news, either in a newspaper or a magazine. Use the steps shown here to decide whether the article contains bias. Explain your reasoning.

Section 3 Central Asia
Cultures and History

Prepare to Read

Objectives

In this section, you will

1. Learn that many cultures and peoples influenced Central Asia in ancient times.
2. Discover how Central Asian nations became independent and why they are a focus of world interest.

Taking Notes

As you read this section, look for details about the topics listed in the outline below. Copy and continue the outline and record your details in it.

I. Meeting Place of Empires
   A. Early history
      1. ____________
      2. ____________
   B. The Silk Road
      1. ____________
      2. ____________

Target Reading Skill

Recognize Word Origins A word's origin is where the word comes from. The word *government* contains the root word *govern*, which comes from the Latin word *gubernare*, meaning "to steer." The suffix *-ment* means "act or process." Knowing a word's origin can better help you understand the word's meaning. How is government related to the process of "steering" a country?

Key Term

- **collective farm** (kuh LEK tiv farhm) *n.* in a Communist country, a large farm formed from many private farms collected into a single unit controlled by the government

A growing film industry is one example of change in Central Asia.

American fighter planes prepare for takeoff at an airbase in Central Asia. They are part of a new U.S. military force in the region. American soldiers came to fight a war in Afghanistan in 2001. Now they are based in several Central Asian countries.

American troops are not the only foreign visitors in Central Asia these days. Russian soldiers are also there. Political leaders from various countries are making official visits. Investors and business leaders are arriving too. They are coming from the United States, Russia, China, France, Turkey, and other countries. All these foreign visitors reflect Central Asia's growing international importance. The new countries of Central Asia are becoming the focus of world attention.

Samarkand, Uzbekistan A Silk Road caravan is the subject of a sculpture near the Registan, an ancient square in Samarkand. Samarkand was a major city along the Silk Road, an ancient trade route crossing Central Asia that linked China and Europe. **Apply Information** *Based on what you know about Central Asia's location, how can you be certain the Silk Road was a land route?*

Meeting Place of Empires

Long ago, Central Asia was a meeting place for ancient cultures and peoples. Located between East Asia and Europe, Central Asia was a crossroads for trade caravans and conquering armies. Over time, dozens of ethnic groups settled there. Each group brought new ideas and ways of living.

The Silk Road More than 2,000 years ago, a trade route called the Silk Road linked China and Europe. The Silk Road brought Central Asia into contact with East Asia, Southwest Asia, and Europe. For hundreds of years, caravans brought Chinese silk and Asian spices to the West. They carried items such as glass, wool, gold, and silver to the East. Along with goods, the traders exchanged ideas and inventions. Cities like Samarkand (sam ur KAND), in present-day Uzbekistan (ooz BEK ih stan), grew up at oases along the route and became wealthy centers of trade and learning.

Invasion and Conquest The Silk Road generated wealth, but it also attracted invaders. Waves of conquerors fought to control Central Asia. Although some ruled for hundreds of years, each group was eventually replaced by new invaders.

Each conqueror left a mark on the region. For example, about A.D. 700, a Muslim empire spread across large stretches of Central Asia. The Muslims had the greatest impact on the culture of the region. Many of the people of Central Asia adopted Islam. Today, most people in this region are Muslims.

Links Across The World

Lands for Empires In the 1200s, much of Central Asia was part of the largest land empire the world has ever known. Genghis Khan (GEN gis kahn), a leader of the Mongols, united his nomadic people into a strong fighting force. He conquered much of China and then swept west over Central Asia. At his death in 1227, his empire extended from the Sea of Japan to the Caspian Sea.

Ashgabat's Sunday Market
Ashgabat is the capital and largest city of Turkmenistan. Its Sunday market attracts thousands of people. Here, a family displays the traditional dark red carpets of Turkmenistan. **Compare and Contrast** *How is shopping at an outdoor market similar to and different from the way most Americans shop?*

By the late 1200s, the rise of sea trade led to the decline of the Silk Road. Ships began carrying goods between China and the seaports of Europe. These sea routes were faster and easier than the overland routes across Asia. As a result, trade declined in Central Asia. This, however, did not stop foreign powers from trying to control the region.

Under Russian Rule In the 1800s, both Russia and Britain tried to expand their empires into Central Asia. Russia was more successful. One of the most important cities Russia captured was the city of Tashkent, Uzbekistan, in 1865.

Russia built railroads, factories, and large farms in Central Asia. Some Russians moved into the region, bringing new ways of life. But most people continued to live as they always had. They practiced Islam and lived as nomadic herders.

The Soviet Union In 1922, Russian Communists formed the Soviet Union. The Soviets extended Communist control over a vast area of Central Asia. They divided the region into five separate states, which they called republics. They also forced people to stop living as nomads and give up their traditional way of life. People had to work on **collective farms**, large farms controlled by the government. The Communist government formed collectives by taking over smaller private farms and livestock herds and combining them into larger units. Soviet collectives did not always produce enough food for people to eat. At least one million Central Asians starved to death during the 1930s.

While the Soviets built new industries, schools, and hospitals in Central Asia, they allowed people few freedoms. The Soviets outlawed the practice of religion and tried to stamp out Muslim culture. Many mosques—places of Islamic worship—were torn down in the mid-1900s.

The Afghan-Soviet War In 1979, the Soviets tried to extend their control over Central Asia by invading Afghanistan. Most people in Afghanistan opposed the Soviet occupation. Afghan forces fought the Soviets. Small groups of soldiers launched attacks against Soviet forces in control of Afghanistan. The Afghan fighters called themselves mujahedin (moo jah heh DEEN), or Islamic holy warriors.

In ten years of warfare, the Soviet army never managed to defeat the Afghan forces. In 1989, the Soviets finally gave up and withdrew their troops. The government they left behind later fell to the Afghan forces. War continued, however, as the Afghans fought each other for power. Eventually, a group known as the Taliban managed to take control of most of the country, but Afghanistan remained unstable.

✓ Reading Check **What impact did Soviet rule have on Central Asia?**

After Independence

The Soviet defeat in Afghanistan helped bring an end to Soviet power. In 1991, the Soviet Union broke up. The five Soviet republics of Central Asia became independent nations.

The New States After independence, each of these countries adopted a name that reflected its main ethnic group. The suffix *-stan* is a Persian term that means "place of, or land." So, for example, Kazakhstan means "place of the Kazakhs," or "Kazakh land." Together with Afghanistan, these countries are sometimes referred to as "the Stans."

The new countries are different in many ways. The largest country, Kazakhstan, is mostly flat and has important natural resources, such as oil and natural gas. The smallest country, Tajikistan, is mountainous and very poor. Nevertheless, the countries have many things in common, including Islamic culture. They also face many of the same challenges as they work to develop their economies.

A woman in Kyrgyzstan plays a traditional stringed instrument.

Children at their desks at a school in Kyrgyzstan

Recognize Word Origins
Find the word *governing* in the first sentence of this paragraph. Compare this word to the word *government*. What is the same? What is different?

Challenges and Opportunities Since independence, the new countries of Central Asia have learned to start governing themselves. Most are weighed down by weak economies. Many people do not have jobs. Health care and education are poor and hard to get.

However, all the countries of Central Asia now proudly celebrate their culture and Islam. Mosques that had fallen into ruin are being rebuilt. The people of Central Asia are teaching their children about their religion. Other benefits of independence include the right to use native languages in schools, literature, and the daily news media.

 **What does the suffix *-stan* mean in the names of the Central Asian countries?**

Section 3 Assessment

Key Terms
Review the key terms at the beginning of this section. Use each term in a sentence that explains its meaning.

Target Reading Skill
You read about the benefits of independence in Central Asia in this section. The Latin root word *bene* means "good or well." What do you think *benefit* means?

Comprehension and Critical Thinking
1. (a) Recall Where is Central Asia located?
(b) Identify Effects Describe one way that Soviet rule affected Central Asia.
2. (a) Explain How did the Central Asian republics under Soviet control gain their independence?
(b) Identify Central Issues How has Central Asia changed since becoming independent from the former Soviet Union?
(c) Make Generalizations Central Asian countries are now in charge of their own governments. You read that the root word of *governing* means "to steer." How is governing a country related to the idea of steering?

Writing Activity
The countries of Central Asia have many tasks to accomplish as they organize their nations. Using the information in this section, write a list of the challenges facing Central Asian countries. Write a brief explanation of why you think each challenge is an important one to tackle.

For: An activity about Central Asia
Visit: PHSchool.com
Web Code: lcd-6503

Chapter 22 Review and Assessment

◆ Chapter Summary

Section 1: South Asia Cultures and History

- Two ancient religions, Hinduism and Buddhism, developed in India. Hinduism is a major religion in South Asia today.
- During its long history, South Asia has been shaped by Indian empires and British rule.
- South Asia's religions and languages have been affected by the region's history.

Ancient Indian sculpture

Section 2: Southwest Asia Cultures and History

- One of the world's earliest civilizations grew in Southwest Asia.
- Three of the world's greatest religions have their roots in Southwest Asia.
- People of many different ethnic groups and religious beliefs settled in Southwest Asia.
- Differences among various people, especially over land claims, have led to conflict and struggle in Southwest Asia.

Section 3: Central Asia Cultures and History

- A crossroads between East Asia and Europe, Central Asia was influenced by many cultures and peoples in ancient times.
- After decades of Soviet rule, independent nations emerged in Central Asia and are working to govern themselves.

Samarkand, Uzbekistan

◆ Key Terms

Each of the statements below contains a key term from the chapter. If the statement is true, write *true*. If the statement is false, rewrite the statement to make it true.

1. According to Hinduism, a **caste** is a social group into which people are born and which they cannot change.
2. A **boycott** is a refusal to buy or use goods and services to show disapproval or bring about social or political change.
3. A **colony** is an independent nation that has its own government.
4. **Monotheism** is the belief that there is only one god.
5. A **muezzin** is a person whose job is to call Muslims to prayer.
6. More than six million Jews and others died in the **Holocaust.**
7. A **collective farm** is owned and operated by one farmer.

Review and Assessment (continued)

Comprehension and Critical Thinking

8. (a) **Identify** Identify Mohenjo-Daro.
   (b) **Sequence** When did Aryans first come to South Asia?
   (c) **Identify Effects** What new religion grew out of Aryan beliefs and practices?
9. (a) **Recall** Who is considered the founder of the religion Buddhism?
   (b) **Summarize** Describe the spread of Buddhism after its founder's death.
10. (a) **Identify** Who was Asoka?
   (b) **Identify Effects** How did Buddhist beliefs affect Asoka?
11. (a) **Name** Under which empire did India experience a period of great cultural achievement?
   (b) **Sequence** Which empire followed that one?
   (c) **Contrast** How were these two empires different in terms of religious beliefs?
12. (a) **Recall** Who played a major part in forcing Britain to grant independence to India?
   (b) **Analyze** Why was India's independence followed by heavy fighting between Hindu and Muslim groups?
13. (a) **Recall** What are the two main religions in South Asia today?
   (b) **Apply Information** What are other religions in South Asia?
14. (a) **Identify** Of the three religions founded in Southwest Asia, which has the most followers there today?
   (b) **Sequence** Of the three religions founded in Southwest Asia, which is the oldest?
15. (a) **Name** What is the largest ethnic group in Southwest Asia today?
   (b) **Synthesize Information** Give an example showing that Southwest Asia is a region of many different ethnic groups and religious beliefs.

Skills Practice

Recognizing Bias Review the steps you followed on page 676 to learn this skill. Then write a sentence that explains what bias is.

Writing Activity: Language Arts

The English language includes contributions from the Arabic language. Use a dictionary to research and learn about the history of these words: *admiral, algebra, cipher, cotton, sherbet,* and *zenith*. Write a paragraph on what you learned about the Arabic and English languages.

MAP MASTER™ Skills Activity

South, Southwest, and Central Asia

Place Location For each place listed below, write the letter from the map that shows its location.

1. Iraq
2. Israel
3. Kazakhstan
4. Indus River
5. Afghanistan
6. Bangladesh

Go Online PHSchool.com Use Web Code lcp-6520 for an interactive map.

Standardized Test Prep

Test-Taking Tips

Some questions on standardized tests ask you to analyze a reading selection. Read the passage below. Then follow the tips to answer the sample question.

> The Silk Road was an important trade route across Central Asia that linked China and Europe more than 2,000 years ago. Caravans carried Chinese silk to the west. They also brought glass, wool, gold, and silver eastward. Merchants traded more than just goods. They also exchanged ideas and inventions. Many ancient cities along the Silk Road, including Samarkand, became wealthy centers of trade and learning.

Pick the letter that best answers the question.

One city that sprang up in Central Asia along the Silk Road was

A China.
B Europe.
C Mohenjo-Daro.
D Samarkand.

TIP Use what you know about geography and history to find the BEST answer choice.

Think It Through Reread the question: The answer must be a city in Central Asia. You can rule out A and B as they are not cities. That leaves C and D. In Section 1, you read that Mohenjo-Daro is an ancient city in South Asia. In Section 2, you read that Samarkand is in Central Asia. The correct answer is D.

Practice Questions

Use the reading selection below to answer Question 1.

> The discovery and production of oil in the Arabian Peninsula brought dramatic changes to Riyadh, Saudi Arabia's capital. Once a small country town, Riyadh is now a modern city with wide highways and skyscrapers of steel and glass. It boasts luxury hotels, large hospitals, and one of the biggest airports in the world. By 2003, Riyadh was one of the world's fastest-growing cities.

1. What conclusion can be made from this reading selection?
   A Riyadh benefited from a worldwide increase in air travel.
   B Riyadh is a fast-growing city because it has luxury hotels.
   C Wealth from Arabian oil production has transformed Riyadh.
   D Riyadh was the smallest town in Saudi Arabia.

Use the tips above and other tips in this book to help you answer the following questions.

2. Which of the following events in South Asia happened last?
   A Asoka ruled the Maurya Empire in India.
   B Aryans came to South Asia probably from Central Asia.
   C India became a colony in the British Empire.
   D During the Gupta Empire, mathematicians developed Arabic numerals.

3. People who practice Judaism, Christianity, and Islam share a belief in
   A the caste system.
   B monotheism.
   C many gods.
   D Buddha.

Use Web Code **lca-6500** for a **Chapter 22 self-test.**

Chapter 23

Southeast Asia and the Pacific Region: Cultures and History

Chapter Preview

In this chapter, you will learn about the cultures and history of Southeast Asia and Australia, New Zealand, and the Pacific islands.

Section 1
Southeast Asia
Cultures and History

Section 2
The Pacific Region
Cultures and History

Target Reading Skill

Sequence In this chapter, you will focus on understanding the order in which a series of events occurs. This is called sequence.

▶ **Women sell prepared food and fruits and vegetables at a floating market in Thailand.**

Southeast Asia and the Pacific Region: Major Religions

MAP MASTER™ Skills Activity

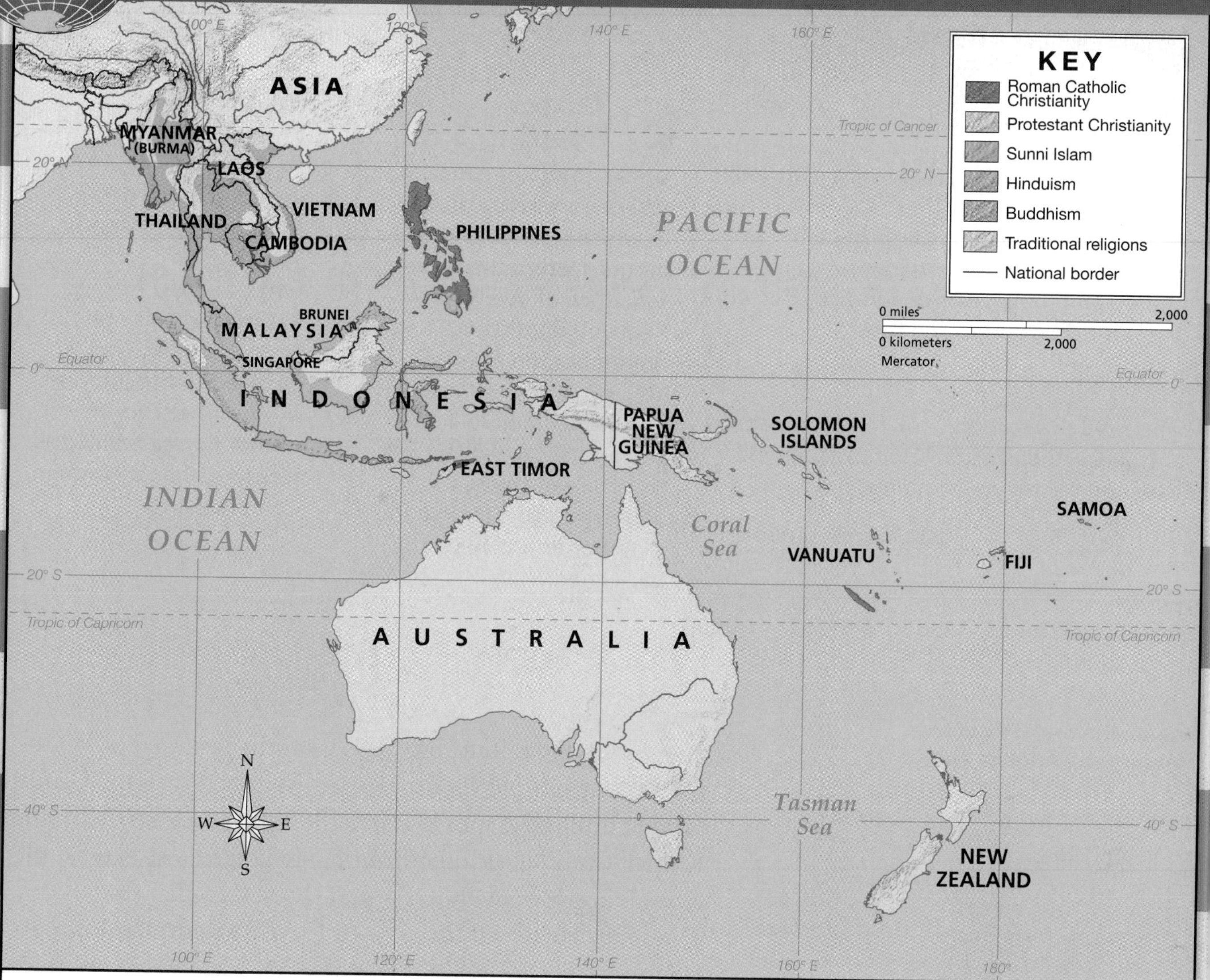

KEY
- Roman Catholic Christianity
- Protestant Christianity
- Sunni Islam
- Hinduism
- Buddhism
- Traditional religions
- National border

Place Southeast Asia and the Pacific Region have a mix of religions that reflect the region's diverse history. **Identify** What is the major religion in most of the Philippines? **Infer** The Philippines was a colony held by Spain between the late 1500s and 1898. What do you think is the major religion of Spain?

Go Online PHSchool.com Use Web Code **lcp-6610** for step-by-step **map skills practice.**

Section 1

Southeast Asia

Cultures and History

Prepare to Read

Objectives

In this section you will

1. Find out why Southeast Asia is a culturally diverse region.
2. Learn how colonial powers affected Southeast Asia.
3. Understand how years of conflict affected Vietnam, Cambodia, and Laos.

Taking Notes

As you read this section, look for details about events in Southeast Asia. Copy the timeline below, and record your findings on it.

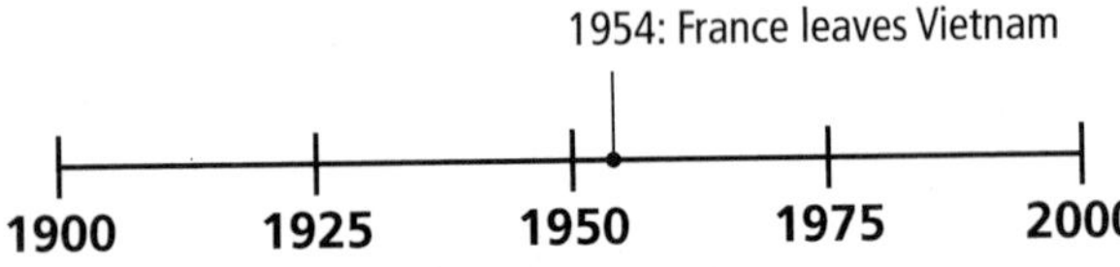

Target Reading Skill

Understand Sequence A sequence is the order in which a series of events occurs. Noting the sequence of events can help you understand and remember the events. You can track events by making a timeline, like the one shown at the left. As you read this section, add events to the timeline in the order in which they happened.

Key Terms

- **Khmer Empire** (kuh MEHR EM pyr) *n.* an empire that included much of present-day Cambodia, Thailand, Malaysia, and part of Laos
- **nationalist** (NASH uh nul ist) *n.* a person who is devoted to the interests of his or her country
- **Khmer Rouge** (kuh MEHR roozh) *n.* the Cambodian Communist party

One of the majestic stone buildings at Angkor Wat

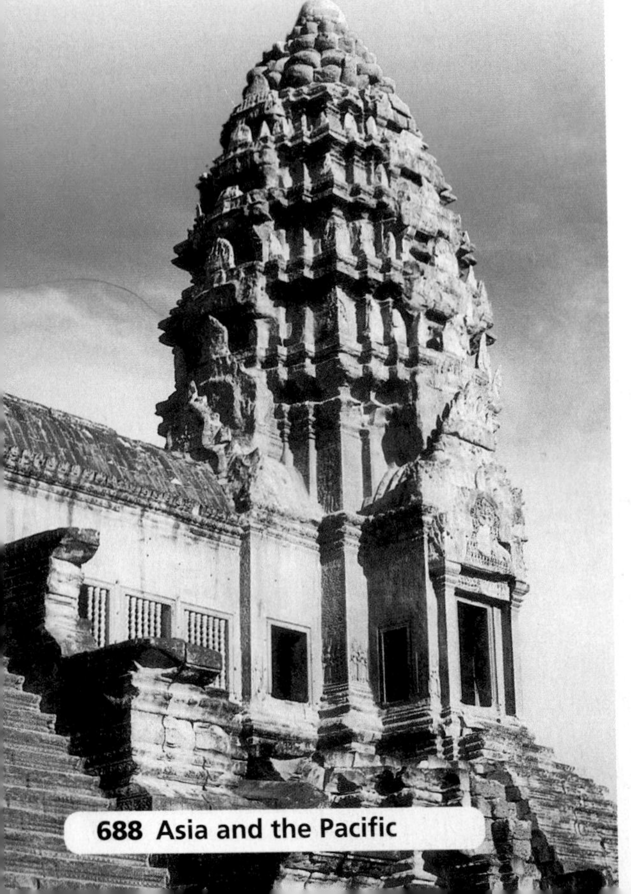

Deep in the rain forests of Cambodia lies Angkor Wat—the largest temple in the world. Angkor Wat is a Hindu temple built of stone. It was built in the A.D. 1100s by the Khmer (kuh MEHR) civilization. At its greatest extent, the **Khmer Empire** included much of present-day Cambodia, Thailand, Malaysia, and part of Laos. The empire was at its height from about A.D. 800 to 1434. The Khmer Empire was one of many kingdoms in Southeast Asia.

A Region of Diversity

The peoples of Southeast Asia developed their own cultures before outside influences shaped the region. Southeast Asia's mountains kept groups of people apart from one another. As a result, each group developed its own way of life.

When outside influences came to Southeast Asia, many of them came from India and China. Southeast Asia is located between India and China. Because of this location, the cultures of Southeast Asia were strongly affected by India and China.

The Impact of India and China India affected Southeast Asian cultures mainly through trade. Nearly 2,000 years ago, Indian traders sailed across the Indian Ocean to Southeast Asia. Indians introduced the religion of Hinduism to the region. Later, around A.D. 200, Indians brought Buddhism to Southeast Asia.

Long after Hinduism and Buddhism spread throughout the region, Indians brought Islam to Southeast Asia. Muslim traders from northern India, then under Muslim rule, carried Islam to Indonesia and the Philippines.

China's effect on Southeast Asia was felt primarily in Vietnam. In 111 B.C., the Chinese conquered Vietnam. They ruled the country for more than 1,000 years. During that time, the Vietnamese began using Chinese ways of farming. They also began using the ideas of Confucius, the ancient Chinese philosopher, to run their government.

Discovery
CHANNEL
SCHOOL
Video
Learn about
festivals in Thailand.

Major Religions of Southeast Asia Today, there are Hindus in Indonesia and Malaysia. Buddhists and Muslims, however, eventually outnumbered Hindus in the region. Buddhism is the main religion in Myanmar, Thailand, Laos, Vietnam, and Cambodia today. Islam is the religion of the majority of the people in Malaysia and Indonesia. In fact, Indonesia has the largest Muslim population in the world. Singapore has a mix of religions that include Muslims, Buddhists, Hindus, and Christians.

European missionaries brought Christianity to Southeast Asia in the 1500s. Today, most of the people in the Philippines are Christian. There are small groups of Christians in Malaysia and Indonesia, too.

✓ **Reading Check** **What are the major religions of Southeast Asia?**

Buddhism in Southeast Asia
According to Buddhist tradition, Buddhism was founded in India in the 500s B.C. by Siddhartha Gautama, known as the Buddha. This gigantic sculpture of the Buddha is in Laos.
Apply Information *Name another Southeast Asian country where Buddhism is the main religion.*

Colonial Rule in Southeast Asia

Europeans brought more than Christianity to Southeast Asia. Traders from Europe arrived in the region in the 1500s. They hoped to gain control of the rich trade in silks, iron, silver, pearls, and spices. At first, Portugal, the Netherlands, and other European nations built trading posts there. From these small posts, Europeans expanded their power. By the 1800s, European nations had gained control of most of Southeast Asia.

As the map below shows, by 1914 Thailand was the only country in Southeast Asia that was not under colonial rule. Thailand was known as Siam until 1939. Spain ruled the Philippines for about 350 years. In 1898, however, the United States defeated Spain in the Spanish-American War. Control of the Philippines passed to the United States.

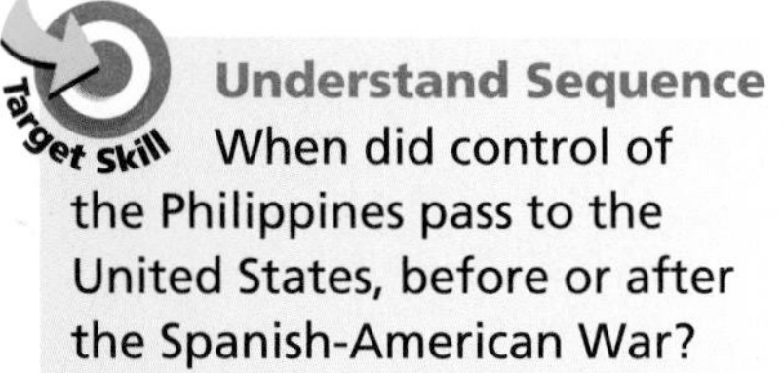

Target Skill — Understand Sequence When did control of the Philippines pass to the United States, before or after the Spanish-American War?

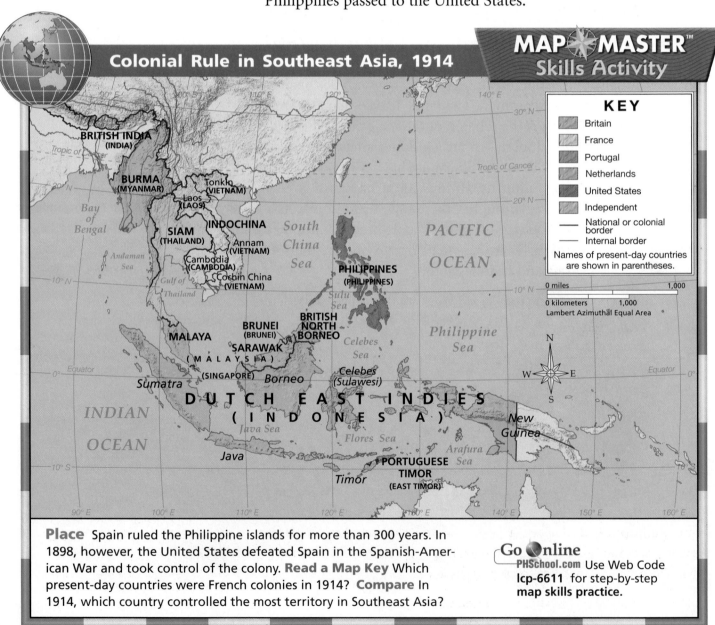

MAP MASTER™ Skills Activity

Colonial Rule in Southeast Asia, 1914

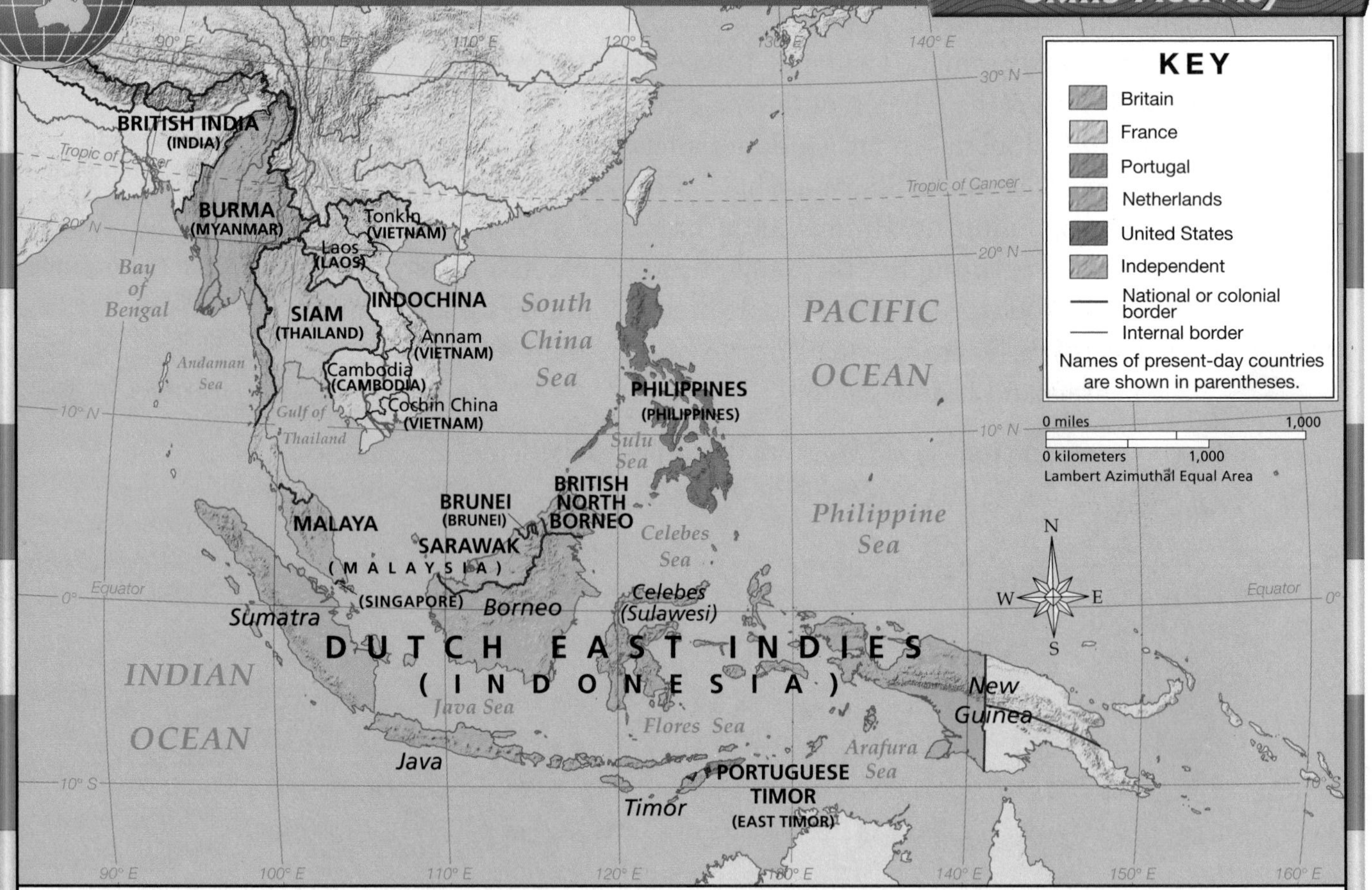

KEY
- Britain
- France
- Portugal
- Netherlands
- United States
- Independent
- National or colonial border
- Internal border

Names of present-day countries are shown in parentheses.

Lambert Azimuthal Equal Area

Place Spain ruled the Philippine islands for more than 300 years. In 1898, however, the United States defeated Spain in the Spanish-American War and took control of the colony. **Read a Map Key** Which present-day countries were French colonies in 1914? **Compare** In 1914, which country controlled the most territory in Southeast Asia?

Go Online PHSchool.com Use Web Code **lcp-6611 for step-by-step map skills practice.**

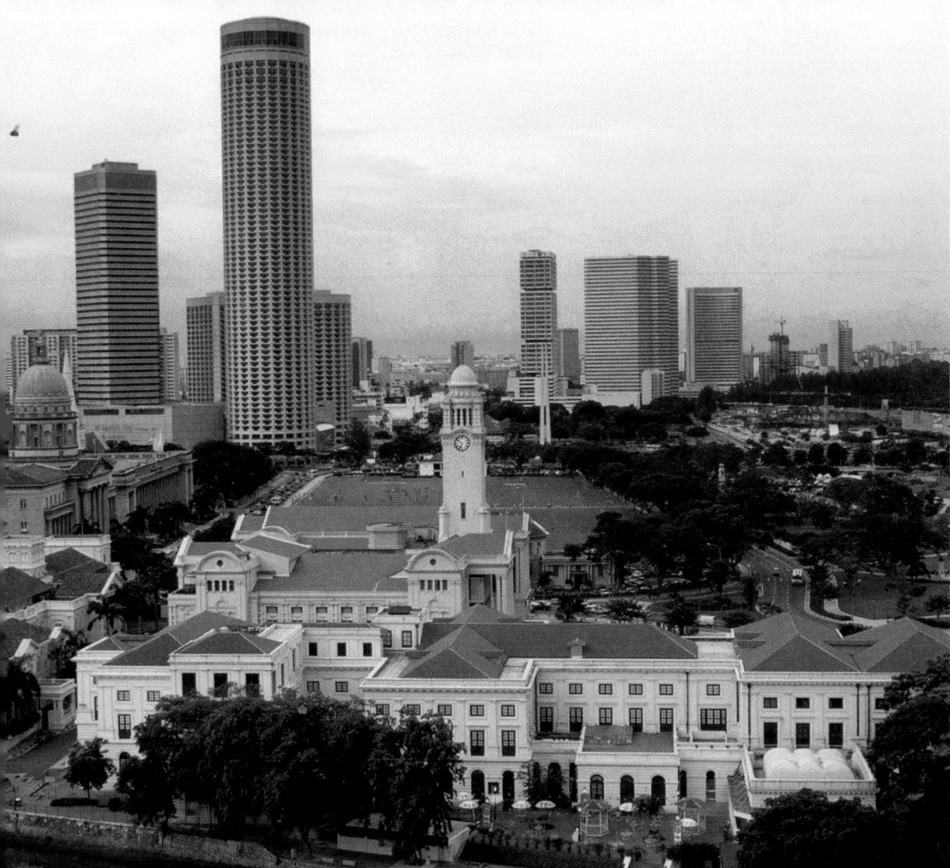

Singapore has a mix of building styles, from British colonial architecture to modern skyscrapers.

Effects of Colonial Rule Colonial rulers built a network of roads, bridges, ports, and railroads in Southeast Asia. Good transportation was essential for the economic success of the colonies. This new network made moving people and goods across the region much easier. The colonial powers also built schools, which helped to produce skilled workers for colonial industries. Education gave some Southeast Asians the skills to become teachers, doctors, government workers, and more.

The Road to Independence By the early 1900s, nationalists were organizing independence movements throughout the countries of Southeast Asia. A **nationalist** is someone who is devoted to the interests of his or her country. But, by the time World War II broke out in 1939, the Japanese had begun to move into Southeast Asia. During the war, the Japanese invaded mainland Southeast Asia and drove out the European colonial powers.

After the Japanese were defeated in World War II, Western nations hoped to regain power in Southeast Asia. But Southeast Asians had other hopes. They wanted independence.

Southeast Asian countries did gain independence. Some, like the Philippines and Burma (now called Myanmar), won their freedom peacefully. Others, including Laos, Cambodia, Vietnam, Malaysia, and Indonesia, had to fight for it.

✓ Reading Check **How did the United States gain control of the Philippines?**

Citizen Heroes

Aung San Suu Kyi

The country of Myanmar has had a military government since 1962. The key leader in Myanmar's fight for democracy was a woman named Aung San Suu Kyi (awn san soo chee). The government tried to stop her efforts. Suu Kyi was placed under house arrest from 1989 to 1995. In 1991, Suu Kyi won the Nobel Peace Prize for her work to bring democracy and human rights to Myanmar through peaceful means. In spite of the government's efforts to stop her, she stayed in Myanmar and continued to work for freedom and democracy.

Vendors display their fruit on bicycles in Hanoi, Vietnam.

Vietnam, Cambodia, and Laos

The road to independence was especially violent in Laos, Cambodia, and Vietnam. These countries were formerly controlled by France. Together, they were known as French Indochina. After World War II ended in 1945, France tried to take back Indochina from Japan. Nationalist forces in Vietnam fought back against the French. In 1954, they forced France to give up power and leave.

The Vietnam War The Vietnamese forces that defeated France declared Vietnam's independence. They wanted Vietnam to be a Communist country. This concerned leaders in the United States. Since the end of World War II, the United States had worked to prevent communism from spreading. Its main rival, the Soviet Union, had worked to expand communism by bringing other countries under its control.

In 1954, Vietnam was divided into two parts. The government of North Vietnam was Communist. The government of South Vietnam was non-Communist. Communist leaders in North Vietnam used force in an effort to unite the country under Communist rule. Helped by the United States, South Vietnam fought back.

At first, the United States sent military advisers and supplies to South Vietnam. Later, it sent hundreds of thousands of American soldiers to Vietnam. After years of fighting, the United States began to withdraw its forces. In 1975, North Vietnam took over South Vietnam and reunited the country under a Communist government.

Cambodia and Laos Cambodia and Laos had gained independence from France in 1953. Pulled into the conflict over Vietnam, both countries went through years of violence as Communists and non-Communists struggled for power. During the war, the United States bombed Cambodia and Laos to destroy Communist North Vietnamese forces there.

In 1975, the Cambodian Communist party called the **Khmer Rouge** (kuh MEHR roozh) took over the government of Cambodia. Opposed to modern technology and Western ways of life, the Khmer Rouge moved the entire urban population to rural areas and forced them to work in the fields. Over the next four years, the Khmer Rouge killed more than a million Cambodians. Even after the Khmer Rouge leader, Pol Pot, was driven out in 1979, fighting continued among different groups trying to gain control of the government. Elections in 1998 brought in a government that worked to make Cambodia more stable.

Cambodian children reading in school

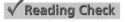

√ Reading Check **Which country did the United States support with troops during the Vietnam War?**

Section 1 Assessment

Key Terms

Review the key terms at the beginning of this section. Use each term in a sentence that explains its meaning.

Target Reading Skill

List these events in the order in which they occurred: Vietnam comes under Communist rule; Nationalists organize independence movements throughout Southeast Asia; elections are held in Cambodia.

Comprehension and Critical Thinking

1. (a) Recall Between which two large Asian countries is Southeast Asia located?
(b) Summarize How did this location affect the development of Southeast Asia's cultures?
(c) Apply Information Give one example showing that Southeast Asia has diverse religions.

2. (a) Explain Why did Europeans begin traveling to Southeast Asia in the 1500s?
(b) Identify Effects What were some positive and negative effects of colonial rule in Southeast Asia?

3. (a) Identify What present-day countries made up French Indochina?
(b) Sequence What happened in Vietnam in 1954?
(c) Identify Point of View Why was the United States concerned about Vietnam in 1954?

Writing Activity

Complete this sentence: *Southeast Asian cultures have been shaped by*_____. Use your completed sentence as a topic sentence for a paragraph about Southeast Asian cultures. Use the information in this section to write your paragraph.

Writing Tip To complete the topic sentence, review this section. Choose two or three features that have shaped Southeast Asian cultures. Be sure to include supporting details for your topic sentence.

Drawing Conclusions

Ena walked into class wearing a bright red silk dress. Her anklet of tiny bells chimed each time she moved. Smiling, she took some objects out of a large box.

Maria watched as Ena put up a beautiful picture of the full moon. Next, Ena placed a small, handmade boat on the table. Then she put a small dish of rice next to it.

Maria looked at the calendar. The date was April 13. Tonight there would be a full moon.

Maria smiled. "Ena is going to tell us about the Cambodian New Year." "How do you know?" Paul asked. Maria laughed. "Yesterday we read about how Cambodians celebrate the New Year," she reminded Paul. "In April when the moon is full, they send boats down the river and make offerings to relatives. Look at what Ena has in her display." Maria had noticed some important details and drew the correct conclusion.

Drawing conclusions means adding clues, or evidence, that you read or see, to what you already know. A conclusion is a judgment.

Learn the Skill

Follow the steps below to learn how to draw a reliable conclusion.

1. **Identify what you know is true.** Use these facts as clues. Maria identified the following facts as clues:

   a. Ena was dressed up and wore an anklet of tiny bells.

   b. Ena displayed a picture of a full moon along with a boat and a bowl of rice.

2. **Add these facts to what you already know.** Maria had heard about the Cambodian New Year. She knew how Cambodians celebrated this special holiday.

3. **Add two or more clues to what you already know to draw a reasoned conclusion.** Maria put together the two clues she saw with what she already knew to reach the conclusion that Ena was going to tell about the Cambodian New Year.

Practice the Skill

Read the passage titled The Vietnam War, on page 692. Then use the steps on the previous page to draw conclusions about why the United States withdrew its troops from Vietnam in 1973.

1. Answer these questions in order to find facts: How did Vietnam become independent after World War II? What country was the main rival of the United States after the end of World War II? Why did the United States send soldiers to Vietnam?

2. Use the facts to build on what you already know. For example, you know that the Vietnamese were successful in driving the French out of their country. If Vietnam had that kind of military success with the French, maybe they could defeat the United States forces, too.

3. Add the clues you have discovered to what you already know. What conclusion can you draw about why the United States withdrew its troops from Vietnam in 1973?

Women dressed in silk clothing attend a New Year's celebration in Hanoi, Vietnam.

Apply the Skill

Turn to page 691 and reread the passage titled Effects of Colonial Rule. Then use the steps in this skill to draw a conclusion about why Southeast Asians fought for independence from their colonial rulers.

Section 2

The Pacific Region

Cultures and History

Prepare to Read

Objectives

In this section you will

1. Find out how people settled Australia and New Zealand.
2. Learn which groups shaped the cultures of Australia and New Zealand.
3. Understand how Pacific island nations have been affected by other cultures.

Taking Notes

As you read this section, look for details about the cultures and history of Australia, New Zealand, and the Pacific islands. Copy and complete the outline below.

I. Settlement
- **A. The Maori of New Zealand**
- **B. Aborigines in Australia**
- **C. The Arrival of the British**

II. The Cultures of Australia and New Zealand

Target Reading Skill

Recognize Signal Words Signal words point out relationships among ideas or events. To help keep the order of events clear, look for words like *first, before, later, next,* and *recently*. These words help show the order in which events took place. Signal words sometimes, but not always, come at the beginning of a sentence.

Key Terms

- **Maori** (MAH oh ree) *n.* a native of New Zealand whose ancestors first traveled from Asia to Polynesia, and later to New Zealand
- **Aborigine** (ab uh RIJ uh nee) *n.* a member of the earliest people of Australia, who probably came from Asia
- **penal colony** (PEEN ul KAHL uh nee) *n.* a place where people convicted of crimes are sent
- **station** (STAY shun) *n.* in Australia, a large ranch for raising livestock

Stone statues on Easter Island

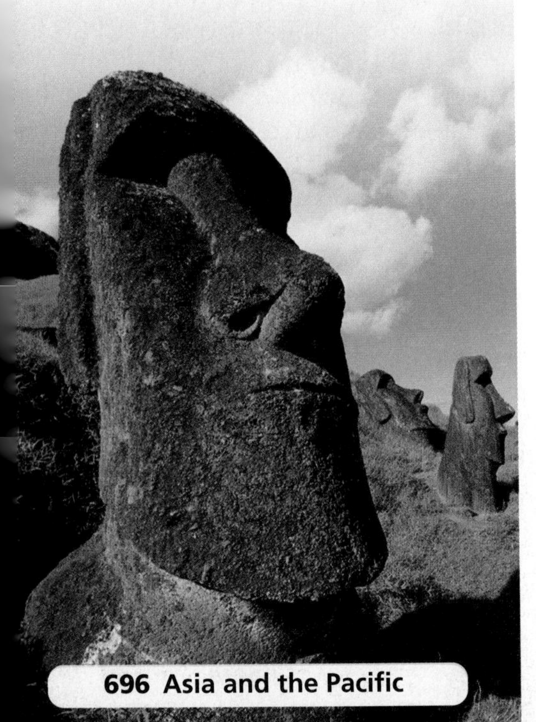

Hundreds of giant stone statues dot the landscape of Easter Island, a tiny island in the South Pacific. Made of volcanic rock, the statues are from 10 to 40 feet (3 to 12 meters) high. Some weigh more than 50 tons (45 metric tons). A European who saw them in 1722 was amazed:

> **"The stone images . . . caused us to be struck with astonishment because we could not comprehend how it was possible that these people, who are devoid of heavy thick timber for making any machines . . . had been able to erect such images."**
>
> *—Dutch explorer Jacob Roggeveen, 1722*

Settlement

Easter Island's statues still impress people. Easter Island is part of the island group of Polynesia. The island belongs to Chile, a country in South America. Scientists have wondered how people first came to this faraway island, as well as to the other parts of the Pacific region.

The Maori of New Zealand The earliest people in New Zealand were the Maori (MAH oh ree). **Maori** are natives of New Zealand. Their ancestors first traveled from Asia to Polynesia. Then, about 1,000 years ago, the Maori traveled across the ocean to New Zealand. According to Maori legend, seven groups set out in long canoes to find a new homeland. A storm tossed their boats ashore on New Zealand. The Maori quickly adapted to their new home. They settled in villages, making a living as hunters and farmers. But the Maori also prized fighting and conquering their enemies. They often fought other groups of Maori over the possession of land. The Maori used storytelling to pass on their beliefs and tales of their adventures.

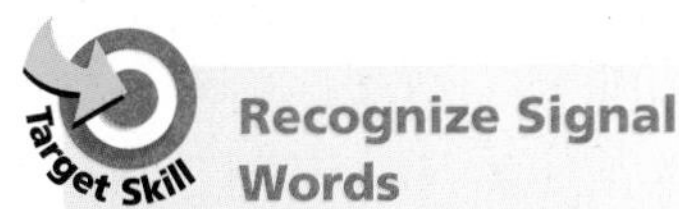

Recognize Signal Words
In the paragraph at the left, which words signal, or tell you, when and how the Maori came to New Zealand?

Aborigines in Australia Many scientists think that the earliest settlers in Australia, the **Aborigines** (ab uh RIJ uh neez), came from Asia more than 40,000 years ago. For thousands of years, they hunted and gathered food along the coasts and river valleys.

During this time, the Aboriginal population in Australia flourished. People lived in small family groups that moved from place to place in search of food and water. All had strong religious beliefs about nature and the land.

The Arrival of the British In 1788, the British founded the first colony in Australia as a penal colony. A **penal colony** is a remote place where people convicted of crimes are sent. Soon, other colonists settled in Australia. Some worked for the prison facilities. Others went to find new land. Then, in 1851, gold was discovered. The population soared. Not long after, Britain stopped sending convicts to Australia. In 1901, Australia gained its independence.

The British settled New Zealand at about the same time as Australia. In 1840, the British took control of New Zealand. The colony, with its fine harbors and fertile soil, attracted many British settlers. New Zealand gained independence in 1947.

✓ Reading Check **How did people settle Australia and New Zealand?**

Links to Art

Maori Canoes The Maori showed their standing in society by the works of art they owned. For instance, a person might own elaborately carved and painted war canoes. Some were as long as 100 feet (30 meters). Human figures were carved along the hull and into the prow, which is the front part of the boat. The figures often had eyes made of mother-of-pearl. Canoes were painted red and decorated with feather streamers. Today these canoes are important artifacts preserved in museums.

The Cultures of Australia and New Zealand

Today, most Australians and New Zealanders are descendants of British settlers. They share British culture, holidays, and customs. Most Australians and New Zealanders enjoy a high standard of living. Employment in farming, mining, manufacturing, and service industries have made the nations prosperous.

Aborigines Since the arrival of Europeans, the Aborigines have suffered great hardships. In the colonial period, settlers forced these native peoples off their lands. Tens of thousands died of European diseases. Others were forced to work on sheep and cattle **stations,** which in Australia are extremely large ranches. The settlers forced Aborigines to adopt European ways. As a result, the Aborigines began to lose their own customs and traditions. More tragically, starting in the 1800s and continuing into the 1960s, Aboriginal children were taken from their families, often by force, to live with non-Aborigines. Today, Aborigines make up less than 1 percent of the country's population.

European and Asian Immigrants People other than the British also settled in Australia. During the gold rush of the 1850s, many people came, including Chinese. Chinese people continue to settle in Australia today. About 2.6 percent of Australia's population is Chinese.

Australians All
About 92 percent of Australians are Caucasian, 7 percent are Asian, and less than 1 percent are Aborigine. Australia's Aborigine heritage was honored at the 2000 Olympic Games when track athlete Kathy Freeman, an Aborigine, lit the Olympic torch. **Summarize** *How were Aborigines affected by the arrival of Europeans?*

Farmers planting vegetables in Tasmania, an island south of Australia

After World War II, many Europeans migrated to Australia. They came from Ireland, Italy, Yugoslavia, Greece, and Germany. In the 1970s, people fleeing the war in Vietnam settled in Australia. Today, people from all over the world continue to arrive.

The Maori Way of Life When New Zealand became a British colony, Britain promised to protect Maori land. Settlers, however, broke that promise. For many years, the settlers and the Maori clashed violently. The settlers defeated the Maori in 1872. After their defeat, the Maori were forced to adopt English ways. Maori culture seemed in danger of being destroyed. Slowly, however, Maori leaders gained more power. Laws now allow the Maori to practice their customs and ceremonies.

Today about 15 percent of New Zealand's population is Maori. Most Maori now live in urban areas. Many speak both Maori and English. Thanks to their artists, writers, and singers, Maori culture is an important part of New Zealand life.

Other Peoples of New Zealand After World War II, many Europeans migrated to New Zealand. People from Polynesia have settled there as well. Today, more Polynesians live in New Zealand's largest city, Auckland, than in any other city in the world. Although most New Zealanders are of European background, the Asian population has grown rapidly.

√ Reading Check **What is the main ethnic group in Australia and New Zealand today?**

Girls from the Cook Islands, in Polynesia, wearing flower garlands, or *leis*.

The Cultures of the Pacific Islands

Scientists believe that the first people to inhabit the Pacific islands came from Southeast Asia more than 30,000 years ago.

A Variety of Cultures Because of the distances between islands, groups could not easily communicate with one another. Therefore, each group developed its own language, customs, and religious beliefs. However, the island people did have many things in common. Their ocean environment shaped their lives. It fed them and was their main means of transportation and trade. Most built their lives around their small villages.

From Colonies to Independence In the 1800s, Western nations began to take an interest in the Pacific islands. Britain, France, and Germany set up trading posts and naval bases on many islands. By 1900, the United States, Britain, France, and Germany had claimed nearly every island in the region.

After World War II, most Pacific islands gained independence, and life began to improve. By then, traditional island cultures had blended with cultures from Europe, America, and other countries. Most governments were democratic. Most churches were Christian. Many Pacific islanders read and spoke English.

✓ Reading Check **What were Pacific island cultures like after World War II?**

Section 2 Assessment

Key Terms

Review the key terms at the beginning of this section. Use each term in a sentence that explains its meaning.

Target Reading Skill

Reread the paragraph on page 697 with the heading The Arrival of the British. Find the words that signal time related to the settlement of Australia.

Comprehension and Critical Thinking

1. (a) Apply Information From where do scientists believe the native peoples of Australia came?
(b) Compare In what ways are the histories of the Aborigines and the Maori similar?
2. (a) Recall From which country are most of the people in Australia and New Zealand descended?
(b) Identify Effects How did the settlement of Australia and New Zealand affect native peoples there?
3. (a) Recall From where do scientists believe the first people to live in the Pacific islands came?
(b) Draw Conclusions Why might people who live on an island be able to preserve their culture for a long period without change?

Writing Activity

Write 10 brief entries for a timeline that shows events in the history and cultures of Australia, New Zealand, and the nearby Pacific islands.

Writing Tip Use complete sentences for your timeline entries. This will help make the sequencing of events easier to follow.

Chapter 23 Review and Assessment

◆ Chapter Summary

Section 1: Southeast Asia Cultures and History

- The people of Southeast Asia developed cultures that later blended with influences from India, China, and Europe.
- By the 1800s, European nations had gained control of most of Southeast Asia.
- After World War II ended in 1945, Southeast Asian countries gained independence.
- After Vietnam became independent, it was divided into Communist North Vietnam and non-Communist South Vietnam. In the Vietnam War, the two sides fought for control of the country for nearly 30 years.
- The United States supported South Vietnam during the Vietnam War. Hundreds of thousands of American soldiers fought in Vietnam. Fighting spread to Cambodia and Laos.
- The Vietnam War ended in 1975 when North Vietnam took over South Vietnam and united the country under a Communist government.

Buddha sculpture, Laos

The Cook Islands, Polynesia

Section 2: The Pacific Region Cultures and History

- Aborigines first settled Australia, and the Maori first settled New Zealand.
- In 1788, the British set up their first colony in Australia. Australia was a British colony until it became independent in 1901.
- Britain took control of New Zealand in 1840. New Zealand became independent in 1947.
- Most Australians and New Zealanders are descended from the British and share British culture, holidays, and customs.
- Australia's population now includes Aborigines, Asians, and people with European backgrounds. New Zealand's population includes Maori, Asians, and Polynesians.

◆ Key Terms

Match the definitions in Column I with the key terms in Column II.

Column I

1. a remote place where people convicted of crimes are sent
2. a member of the earliest people of Australia
3. a person who is devoted to the interests of his or her country
4. in Australia, a large ranch for raising livestock
5. a member of the native people of New Zealand

Column II

A nationalist
B Aborigine
C Maori
D penal colony
E station

Review and Assessment (continued)

◆ Comprehension and Critical Thinking

6. **(a) Identify** Identify the Khmer Empire.
   (b) Identify Cause How did Hinduism and Buddhism come to Southeast Asia?
7. **(a) List** What are three religions in Southeast Asia today?
   (b) Apply Information Name three countries in Southeast Asia in which Buddhism is the main religion today.
8. **(a) Identify** Identify French Indochina.
   (b) Identify Causes Why did the French leave Vietnam in 1954?
   (c) Summarize Describe the conflict in Vietnam, including U.S. involvement.
9. **(a) Explain** How did Aborigines live before the British came to Australia?
   (b) Summarize Describe life for the Maori today.
10. **(a) Recall** What happened in Australia in 1788?
    (b) Draw Conclusions How does the history of Australia and New Zealand help explain why their cultures reflect a British heritage?
11. **(a) Name** On what island group do historians believe the people of the Pacific islands first settled?
    (b) Make Generalizations Describe Pacific island cultures after World War II.

◆ Skills Practice

Drawing Conclusions Review the steps you followed on page 694 to learn this skill. Then reread Links to Art on page 697 and draw a conclusion about the level of skill needed to make a Maori canoe.

◆ Writing Activity: Math

Population density is the average number of people living in a square mile or square kilometer. To calculate a country's population density, divide the total population by the total land area. Use an almanac or encyclopedia to find the land areas in square miles and populations for Australia, Thailand, and Vietnam. Be sure to find whole numbers. Calculate the population density of each country to the nearest whole number. Create a table that shows your data. Then write a short paragraph about your findings.

MAP MASTER™ Skills Activity

Place Location For each place listed below, write the letter from the map that shows its location.

1. Thailand
2. Vietnam
3. Indonesia
4. Australia
5. New Zealand
6. The Philippines

Go Online PHSchool.com Use Web Code **lcp-6620** for an **interactive map.**

Southeast Asia and the Pacific Region

Standardized Test Prep

Test-Taking Tips

Some questions on standardized tests ask you to find cause and effect. Read the passage below. Then follow the tips to answer the sample question at the right.

> In the 1100s, the Khmer Empire extended across much territory. It included lands that are now Cambodia and much of Laos, Thailand, and Vietnam. There were many other kingdoms in Southeast Asia at that time. Because of geography, however, the others were small. The mountains of Southeast Asia isolated people, who had little contact with anybody outside their own valley. Each group developed its unique way of life. The region became rich in cultures.

TIP In a cause-and-effect relationship, the effect is what happens and the cause is what makes it happen.

Pick the letter that best answers the question.

Southeast Asia was rich in cultures because—

A the Khmer Empire extended across much territory.

B mountains isolated groups of people in their own valleys.

C there were many other kingdoms in Southeast Asia in the 1100s.

D the Khmer Empire forced different groups to pull together.

TIP Look for words, such as *because, so,* and *as a result* that point to a cause-and-effect relationship.

Think It Through The fourth sentence in the passage says that "because of geography" many Southeast Asian kingdoms were small. You can eliminate A and D because the Khmer Empire did not produce these small kingdoms. C simply restates the idea that the area is rich in cultures. The correct answer is B.

Practice Questions

Use the passage below to answer Question 1.

> Beginning in the early 1900s, Australia's population grew steadily. Until the end of World War II in 1945, most of Australia's immigrants came from Great Britain. After the war ended, large numbers of immigrants came from other countries in Europe. In recent years, many immigrants have come from East Asia and Southeast Asia because of Australia's nearby location, and because of Australia's high standard of living.

1. Many immigrants recently have come to Australia from Asian countries because
   A they were not welcome in other countries.
   B Australia has a high standard of living.
   C they could afford to travel to Australia.
   D many immigrants from Great Britain were making Asian countries too crowded.

2. During the Vietnam War, fighting spread to
   A Malaysia.
   B Australia.
   C the Philippines.
   D Cambodia.

3. The first colony in Australia was set up by
   A Great Britain.
   B the United States.
   C China.
   D France.

Use Web Code **lca-6600** for a **Chapter 23 self-test.**

Literature

The Clay Marble

By Minfong Ho

Prepare to Read

Background Information

Think of someone you admire. What special gift or quality does that person have? Some people have the ability to show us a new way of looking at things.

In 1980, civil war in Cambodia forced thousands of Cambodians to leave their homes and move to refugee camps near the border of Thailand and Cambodia. Among these refugees were many children. There was very little food, and living conditions were poor. *The Clay Marble* tells the story of twelve-year-old Dara, who lives in one such camp. Dara's friend Jantu, another girl in the camp, makes toys out of little scraps and trinkets she finds at the camp.

Objectives

In this selection, you will

1. Discover how Jantu deals with the challenge of living in a refugee camp.
2. Find out how the author uses point of view to tell a story.

It amazed me, the way she shaped things out of nothing. A knobby branch, in her deft hands, would be whittled into a whirling top. She would weave strips of a banana leaf into plump goldfish or angular frogs. A torn plastic bag and a scrap from some newspaper would be cut and fashioned into a graceful kite with a long tail. A couple of old tin cans and a stick would be transformed into a toy truck.

One of the many refugee camps along the Thai-Cambodian border. The last refugee camp closed in 1999.

Whenever Jantu started making something, she would withdraw into her own private world and ignore everything around her. Leaving me to mind her baby brother, she would hunch over her project, her fierce scowl keeping at bay anybody who might come too close or become too noisy. But if I was quiet and kept my distance, she didn't seem to mind my watching her.

And so I would stand a little to one side, holding the baby on my hip, as Jantu's quick fingers shaped, twisted, smoothed, rolled whatever material she happened to be working with into new toys.

"How do you do it?" I asked her one day, after she had casually woven me a delicate bracelet of wild vines.

"Well, you take five vines of about the same length—elephant creeper vines like this work well—and you start braiding them, see. Like this . . ."

"No, I don't mean just this bracelet," I said. "I mean the goldfish, too, and the kites and toy trucks and . . ."

"But they're all different," Jantu said. "You make them different ways."

"But how do you know what to make? Is there some . . . some kind of magic in your hands, maybe?"

Jantu looked puzzled. "I don't know," she said, turning her hands over and examining them with vague interest. They looked like ordinary hands, the fingernails grimy, the palms slightly calloused. "I don't see anything there," she said. "Nothing that looks like magic." She shrugged and dismissed the subject.

Yet the more I watched her, the more convinced I became that Jantu's hands were gifted with some special powers, some magic. How else could anyone explain how she made that wonderful mobile, of two delicate dolls husking rice?

Even from the start, I knew it was going to be something special. For three days Jantu had kept me busy scrounging up a collection of old cloth and string. Then, as I sat cross-legged watching her, she fashioned two straw dolls in sarongs and straw hats and, with dabs of sticky rice, glued their feet onto a smooth branch. Carefully she tied strings connecting the dolls' wrists and waists, so that when one doll bent down, the other one straightened up. Each doll held a long thin club, with which, in turn, one would pound at a tiny mortar as the other doll lifted up its club in readiness. Jantu held up the mobile and showed me how a mere breath of wind would set the two dolls in motion.

sarong (suh RAWNG) *n.* a loose garment made of a long strip of cloth wrapped around the body

mortar (MAWRT ur) *n.* a dish in which seed or grain is pounded or ground

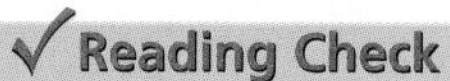

What materials does Jantu use to make the dolls?

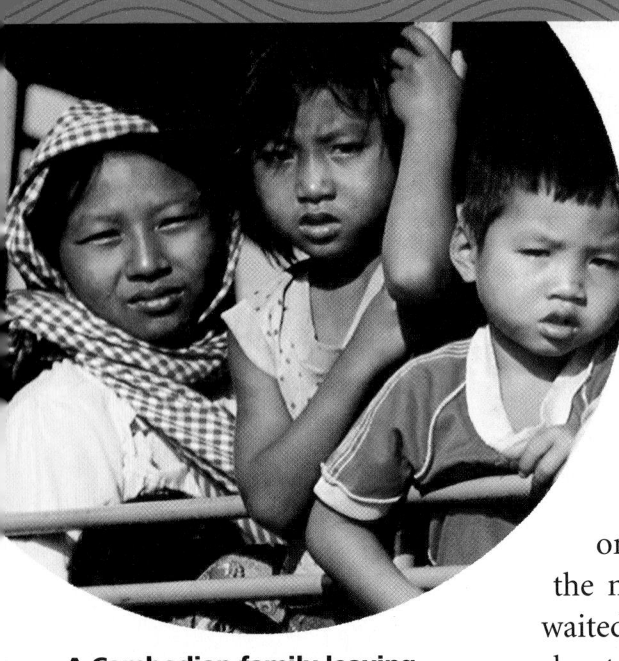

A Cambodian family leaving their refugee camp to return home

Pound and lift, up and down, the two dolls took turns crushing the rice with exactly the same jerky rhythm that real village women pounded it to get the brown husks off. There were even some real grains in the miniature mortar set between the two dolls. It was the cleverest thing I had ever seen.

Children crowded around Jantu, pressing in from all sides to watch her work it. "Let me hold it," I begged, standing next to Jantu. "I helped you find the stuff for the dolls."

Jantu nodded. Breathlessly I held it carefully and blew on it. It worked! One of the dolls bent down and pounded the mortar with its club. The other doll straightened up and waited its turn. I was still engrossed with it when someone shouted a warning: "Watch out, Chnay's coming!"

Even in my short stay at the camp, I'd heard of Chnay. He liked to break things, and he was a bully. An orphan, Chnay made his way to the Border alone. Too young to be recruited into the resistance army, Chnay roamed the fields by himself, scrounging for food and sleeping wherever he liked.

Chnay sauntered up and shoved his way through to us. "What've you got there?" he demanded.

"Nothing," I said, trying to hide the toy behind me.

Laughing, Chnay snatched it away from me. One of the dolls was ripped loose and dropped to the ground.

As I bent over to retrieve it, Chnay pushed me aside. "Leave it," he said. "That's for kids. Look what I have." He thrust his arm out. It was crawling with big red ants, the fierce kind that really sting when they bite. "I'm letting them bite me. See?" he bragged. Already small fierce welts were swelling up on his arm, as some ants kept biting him.

"That's dumb!" I exclaimed. Dodging behind him, I tried to snatch the mobile back from him.

Chnay flung the toy to the ground, scattering straw and red ants into the air.

I grabbed on to his hand, but he was taller than I, and much stronger. He shoved me aside and stomped on the dolls until they were nothing but a pile of crushed sticks and rags. Then, kicking aside a boy who stood in his way, Chnay strode off, angrily brushing red ants off his arm.

I squatted down beside the bits of dolls and tried to fit them together, but it was no use. The delicate mobile was beyond repair. I could feel my eyes smarting with angry tears. "I should've held on to it more tightly," I said bitterly. "I shouldn't have let him grab it away from me."

recruit (rih KROOT) *v.* to persuade someone to join
resistance army (rih ZIS tuns AHR mee) *n.* an army of people resisting, or opposing, the group holding political power in a country
saunter (SAWN tur) *v.* to walk in an idle or a casual manner

retrieve (rih TREEV) *v.* to get something back again

Jantu knelt next to me and took the fragments of the dolls out of my hands. "Never mind," she said quietly, putting them aside. "We can always start something new."

"But it took you so long to make it," I said.

Idly Jantu scooped up a lump of mud from a puddle by her feet and began to knead it in her hands. "Sure, but the fun is in the making," she said.

She looked down at the lump of mud in her hands with sudden interest. "Have you ever noticed how nice the soil around here is?" she asked. "Almost like clay." She smoothed the ball with quick fingers, then rolled it between her palms.

When she opened her palm and held it out to me, there was a small brown ball of mud cupped in it. "For you," she announced.

I looked at it. Compared to the delicate rice-pounding mobile, this was not very interesting at all. "I don't want it," I said. "It's just a mud ball."

"No, it's not. It's a marble," Jantu said. Her eyes sparkling, she blew on it. "There! Now it's a magic marble."

I took it and held it. Round and cool, it had a nice solid feel to it. I glanced at Jantu. She was smiling. Slowly I smiled back at her.

Maybe, I thought, maybe she did put some magic in the marble. After all, why else would I feel better, just holding it?

About the Selection

This reading selection is from a chapter in *The Clay Marble*, a novel for young readers written by Minfong Ho and published in 1991.

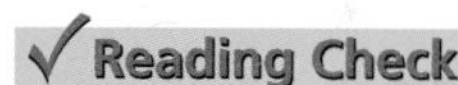

What happens to Jantu's dolls?

About the Author

Minfong Ho (b. 1951) was born in Rangoon, Myanmar (Burma). She grew up in Singapore and Thailand and studied at Cornell University in New York. In 1980, Ho worked as a volunteer in a refugee camp on the Cambodian-Thai border. Her experiences helped her write *The Clay Marble*. She is the author of numerous children's fiction books about life in Southeast Asia.

Review and Assessment

Thinking About the Selection

1. (a) Respond How did you feel about Chnay while reading this selection?
(b) Infer How do you think Jantu felt about what Chnay did to the dolls?

2. (a) Recall How would Jantu act when she started to make something?
(b) Analyze For Jantu, what is important, making toys or the toys themselves? Give evidence for your answer.

3. (a) Recall What does Jantu do with the lump of mud she scoops up?
(b) Contrast How is Dara's opinion of the lump of mud different from Jantu's opinion?
(c) Conclude What symbolic meaning might the clay marble have?

Writing Activity

Write an Essay Choose a person who has been important in your life. Write an essay that tells who the person is and what special qualities he or she has. Tell why these qualities are important to you. Include an introduction and a conclusion in your essay.

Chapter

24 East Asia

Chapter Preview

This chapter focuses on key countries in East Asia: China, Japan, North Korea, and South Korea.

Country Databank

The Country Databank provides data and descriptions of each of the countries of East Asia: China, Japan, North Korea, South Korea, Taiwan, and Mongolia.

Section 1

China
Transforming Itself

Section 2

Japan
Tradition and Change

Section 3

The Koreas
A Divided Land

Target Reading Skill

Comparison and Contrast In this chapter, you will focus on using comparison and contrast to help you analyze information.

▶ **Dressed in traditional clothing, a Korean man plays a stringed instrument called a komungo.**

MAP MASTER™ Skills Activity

East Asia: Political

Regions The region of East Asia is dominated by China. It is the largest country in East Asia and the second-largest in land area in the world.

Identify East Asia has two countries that are islands. What are their names?

Contrast How is Japan different from Taiwan in terms of land area?

Go Online PHSchool.com Use Web Code **lcp-6710** for step-by-step **map skills practice.**

Introducing East Asia

Guide for Reading

This section provides an introduction to the countries that make up the region of East Asia.

- Look at the map on the previous page and then read the paragraphs below to learn about each nation.
- Analyze the data to compare the countries.
- What are the characteristics that most of the countries share?
- What are some key differences among the countries?

Viewing the Video Overview

View the World Studies Video Overview to learn more about each of the countries. As you watch, answer this question:

- How does the land use in China compare to land use in Japan?

Discovery CHANNEL SCHOOL Video
Learn about the key geographic features in East Asia.

China

Capital	Beijing
Land Area	3,600,927 sq mi; 9,326,410 sq km
Population	1.29 billion
Ethnic Group(s)	Han, Zhaung, Uygur, Hui, Tibetan, Miao, Manchu, Mongol, Buyi, Korean
Religion(s)	traditional beliefs, Buddhist, Muslim, Christian
Government	Communist state
Currency	yuan
Leading Exports	machinery and equipment, textiles and clothing, footwear, toys and sporting goods, mineral fuels
Language(s)	Mandarin (official), Wu, Cantonese, Hsiang, Min, Hakka, Kan

With more than one billion people, China (CHY nuh) is the most populous country in the world. China ranks as the second-largest country in the world in land area and is the largest country in East Asia. The history and culture of China date back about 3,500 years. Since 1949, the country has been governed under a Communist system. In recent years, China has worked to build its economy. Exporting goods to countries around the world has played a major part in helping China's economy grow.

Beijing, China

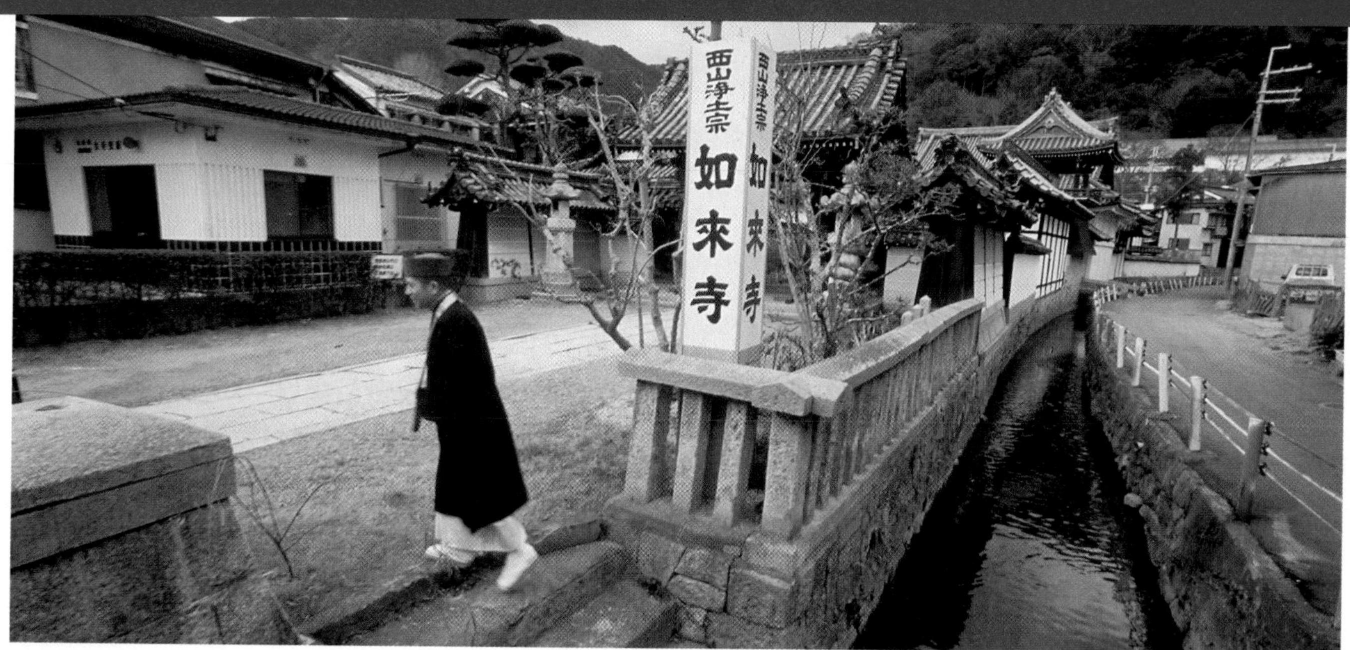

A priest outside a temple in Japan

Japan

Capital	Tokyo
Land Area	144,689 sq mi; 374,744 sq km
Population	127 million
Ethnic Group(s)	Japanese, Korean, Chinese, Brazilian, Southwest Asian
Religion(s)	traditional beliefs, Buddhist, Christian
Government	constitutional monarchy
Currency	yen
Leading Exports	motor vehicles, semiconductors, office machinery, chemicals
Language(s)	Japanese (official), Korean, Chinese

Japan (juh PAN) is an island country located east of North Korea and South Korea. Japan's four main islands and thousands of small islands lie between the Sea of Japan and the Pacific Ocean. Most of Japan's land is rugged and mountainous. Japan succeeded in building a strong economy in the decades after World War II. Although its economy has declined in recent years, Japan still has one of the largest economies in the world. Japan is among the world's leading producers of motor vehicles and electronic equipment.

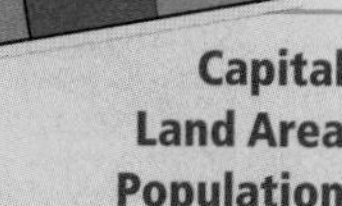

Mongolia

Capital	Ulaanbaatar
Land Area	600,540 sq mi; 1,555,400 sq km
Population	2.6 million
Ethnic Group(s)	Mongol, Turkic, Tungusic, Chinese, Russian
Religion(s)	Buddhist, Muslim, traditional beliefs, Christian
Government	parliamentary
Currency	tugrik
Leading Exports	copper, livestock, animal products, cashmere, wool, hides, fluorspar, other nonferrous metals
Language(s)	Khalka Mongolian, Kazakh, Chinese, Russian

Mongolia (mahn GOH lee uh) is a landlocked country bordered by Russia to the north and China to the south. Mongolia has very little land suitable for growing crops. Most of the labor force works in raising and herding livestock. Industry in Mongolia takes place chiefly in the capital city of Ulaanbaatar and consists primarily of livestock products, such as dairy products, meats, and woolen textiles. Mongolia is rich in mineral resources as well. The mining of copper, gold, coal, and other minerals contributes to Mongolia's economy.

Introducing East Asia

North Korea

Capital	Pyongyang
Land Area	46,490 sq mi; 120,410 sq km
Population	22.3 million
Ethnic Group(s)	Korean, Chinese, Japanese
Religion(s)	Buddhist, traditional beliefs, Christian
Government	authoritarian socialist
Currency	North Korean won
Leading Exports	minerals, metallurgical products, manufactured goods (including armaments), agricultural and fishery products
Language(s)	Korean (official), Chinese

North Korea (nawrth kuh REE uh) is located on the northern part of the Korean Peninsula. Before World War II ended in 1945, Korea was one country. From 1910 to 1945, Korea was controlled by Japan. When Japan was defeated in World War II, Korea was divided into two parts. The northern part was occupied by the Soviet Union and the southern part was occupied by the United States. In 1948, North Korea and South Korea were established as separate nations. Since then, North Korea has been governed under a communist system. The government supports a huge military and an extensive weapons program, including weapons of mass destruction.

South Korea

Capital	Seoul
Land Area	37,911 sq mi; 98,190 sq km
Population	48.3 million
Ethnic Group(s)	Korean, Chinese
Religion(s)	Christian, Buddhist, traditional beliefs
Government	republic
Currency	South Korean won
Leading Exports	electronic products, machinery and equipment, motor vehicles, steel, ships, textiles, clothing, footwear, fish
Language(s)	Korean (official), Chinese

The nation of South Korea (sowth kuh REE uh) was established in 1948. South Korea is located on the southern half of the Korean Peninsula. South Korea went through many years of political unrest under a number of different rulers. The country's first democratic elections were held in 1987. Since the 1960s, South Korea has achieved remarkable economic growth. Despite an economic slowdown in the late 1990s, South Korea's economy continued to grow in 2002. Its major industries include car production, electronics, shipbuilding, steel, textiles, and footwear. Political relations between South Korea and North Korea have been strained since the Korean War in the 1950s.

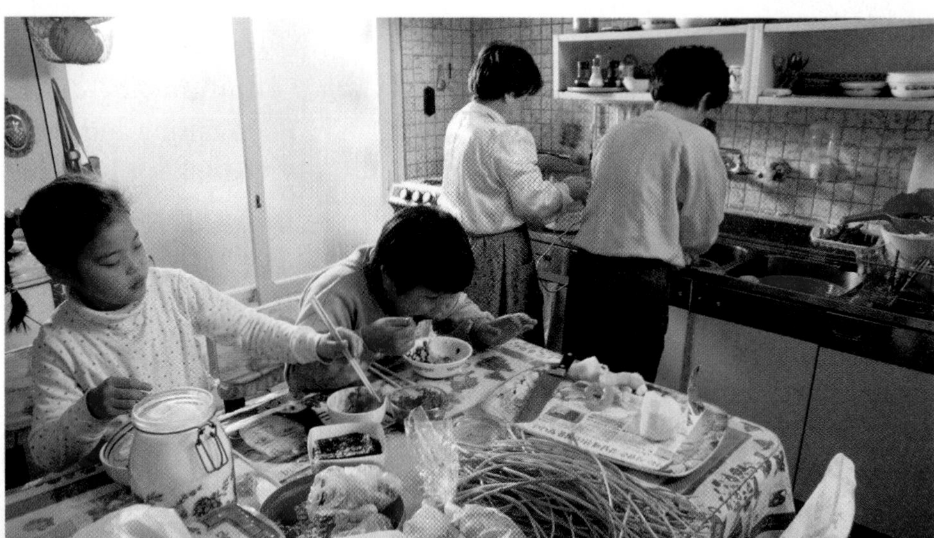

Children eating dinner in South Korea

Taiwan

Capital	Taipei
Land Area	12,456 sq mi; 32,260 sq km
Population	22.5 million
Ethnic Group(s)	Taiwanese, Chinese, aborigine
Religion(s)	Buddhist, traditional beliefs, Christian
Government	multiparty democracy
Currency	Taiwan dollar
Leading Exports	machinery and electrical equipment, metals, textiles, plastics, chemicals
Language(s)	Mandarin Chinese (official), Amoy Chinese, Hakka Chinese

SOURCES: DK World Desk Reference Online; CIA World Factbook Online, 2002; *World Almanac*, 2003

Taiwan (ty wahn) is an island country located off the southeastern coast of China. The formation of Taiwan as a nation was the result of a power struggle between two political parties in China. One party, the Chinese Communists, gained control of China in 1949. The other party, the Nationalists, fled to Taiwan and set up a government there. During the 1950s and 1960s, Taiwan built a strong economy based on manufacturing industries. Manufacturing is still important in Taiwan today, but growing service industries, such as banking, bring in more money to the nation's economy.

An aerial view of Taipei, Taiwan

Assessment

Comprehension and Critical Thinking

1. **Compare** Compare the physical size and the population size of China to the other countries in East Asia.
2. **Draw Conclusions** What are the characteristics that most of the countries share?
3. **Contrast** What are some key differences among the countries?
4. **Categorize** What kinds of products are the leading exports of this region?
5. **Infer** What can you infer about a country if many of its exports are made in factories?
6. **Make a Bar Graph** Create a bar graph showing the population of the countries in this region.

Keeping Current

Access the **DK World Desk Reference Online** at **PHSchool.com** for up-to-date information about all six countries in this chapter.

Web Code: **lce-6700**

Section 1 China
Transforming Itself

Prepare to Read

Objectives
In this section, you will
1. Find out how China controlled its economy from 1949 to 1980.
2. Learn about the growth of Taiwan since 1949.
3. Discover how China's government operated after the death of Mao Zedong.
4. Examine aspects of life in China today.

Taking Notes
As you read this section, look for details about how China was governed under the Communist party. Copy the diagram below, and record your findings in it. Write the similarities in the space where the ovals overlap. Write the differences in the space where the ovals do not overlap.

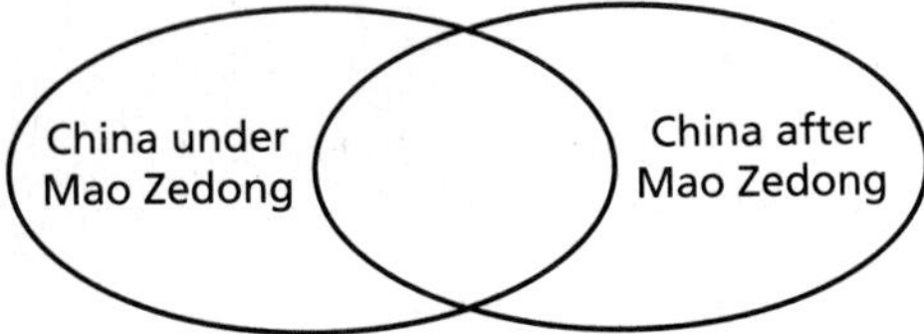

Target Reading Skill
Compare and Contrast
Comparing and contrasting can help you analyze information. When you compare, you look at the similarities between things. When you contrast, you look at the differences. As you read this section, look for similarities and differences in how China was governed under the Communist party. Write the information in your Taking Notes table.

Key Terms
- **radical** (RAD ih kul) *adj.* extreme
- **Red Guards** (red gahrdz) *n.* groups of students who carried out Mao Zedong's policies during the Cultural Revolution
- **free enterprise system** (free ENT ur pryz SIS tum) *n.* an economic system in which people can choose their own jobs, start private businesses, own property, and make a profit
- **gross domestic product** (grohs duh MES tik PRAHD ukt) *n.* the total value of all goods and services produced in an economy

Bicycles remain a major form of transportation in China.

In 1985, the total number of cars, buses, and trucks in all of China was about 320,000. Most people in cities rode bicycles or walked to get around. In 2001, the number of cars, buses, and trucks had grown to 18 million. During that time, China had experienced tremendous economic growth.

Changes continue as China works to build its economy. In the past, China's Communist government tightly controlled the economy. Today, however, China is in the process of moving toward an economy with fewer government controls.

China's Economy, 1949–1980

In 1949, the Chinese Communist party set up a new government with leader Mao Zedong (mow dzuh doong) in charge. Under Mao, the government took over China's economy. Factories, businesses, and farmland came under the government's control.

China Under Mao
Mao launched the Great Leap Forward in order to improve China's economy. The small photo above shows a poster promoting the program. Mao declared the Cultural Revolution in 1966. In the large photo, Red Guards read a book of Mao's writings. **Summarize** *How did the Great Leap Forward affect China's economy?*

The Great Leap Forward In 1958, Mao began a **radical, or extreme,** program called the "Great Leap Forward." Its goal was to increase output from farms and factories. The program turned out to be a giant step backward. The Communists rushed to increase production by forcing people to work on large communes. But they ignored the need for experience and planning. For example, they ordered a huge increase in steel production. Thousands of untrained workers built backyard furnaces for making steel and other products. Much of the steel they produced was of poor quality and useless.

The focus on industry took farmers away from farming. At the same time, poor weather destroyed crops, resulting in a severe food shortage. Between 1959 and 1961, an estimated 30 million people died from starvation.

The Cultural Revolution In 1966, Mao introduced another radical policy called the Cultural Revolution. His aim was to create a completely new society with no ties to the past. He began by closing schools and urging students to rebel against their teachers and their families. The students formed bands of radicals called **Red Guards.** These bands destroyed some of China's most beautiful ancient buildings. They beat and imprisoned many Chinese artists, professors, and doctors. Anyone they considered to be against Mao's policies was attacked.

When the Red Guards raged out of control and began to threaten Mao's government, they were imprisoned, too. The Cultural Revolution kept China in turmoil until its conclusion in 1976. Years of chaos left China in disorder, with hundreds of thousands of its citizens dead. The focus on political revolution disrupted China's economic growth.

✓ Reading Check **What was the purpose of China's Great Leap Forward?**

Links Across Time

China's Government
China's government is a dictatorship. In a dictatorship, the power to govern is held by one person. By contrast, a democracy is a form of government in which the power to govern rests with the people. A dictatorship has complete power over the people. It may also have control of nearly everything people do. Examples of dictatorships in the past include those in the former Soviet Union and Germany. Shown below is Mao Zedong, leader of China's government from 1949 to 1976.

Taiwan Since 1949

After their defeat by the Communists in 1949, the Nationalists fled to Taiwan, an island 100 miles (161 kilometers) off mainland China's southeast coast. They formed a new government and called their country the Republic of China.

The Nationalists followed the free enterprise system. Under the **free enterprise system,** people can choose their own jobs, start private businesses, own property, and make profits. Even in the 1950s, Taiwan's free enterprise economy was one of Asia's strongest. The Chinese on Taiwan started programs that increased farm output and brought in more money. This money helped Taiwan build new ports and railroads.

Taiwan also had the support of foreign countries. Both Taiwan and China claimed to be the "real" China. The Communists on mainland China claimed the right to rule Taiwan. The Nationalists on Taiwan claimed the right to rule the rest of China. At first, the United States and other Western countries supported Taiwan. Taiwan sold computers and other electronic products to the rest of the world. Taiwan's economy grew dramatically.

√ Reading Check **What kind of economic system does Taiwan have?**

Changes in China

Meanwhile, many Western countries refused to trade with China. At the same time, some of Mao's policies hurt the country. During the 1970s, the Communists realized that they needed new policies in order to improve China's economy and its relations with the rest of the world.

First, China began repairing relations with the West. In 1971, China was allowed to join the United Nations. In 1972, Richard Nixon became the first American president to visit China. This historic trip opened up trade between the two nations.

China launched the world's first magnetic levitation, or maglev, passenger train system. Powerful magnets work to lift and propel the train.

COUNTRY PROFILE

Focus on Economics

China

China has a large and complex economy. As the land use map at the right shows, much of China's land is devoted to farming to feed its large population. Most of this land is used for subsistence farming, or growing food mainly for the farm family rather than for sale. Now look at the graphs below. China's exports, or sales to other countries, are greater than its imports, or purchases from other countries. These exports have helped China's economy to grow. However, agriculture remains the main source of jobs in China.

China: Land Use

KEY

- Commercial farming (without rice)
- Commercial farming (with rice)
- Subsistence farming (without rice)
- Subsistence farming (with rice)
- Nomadic herding
- Forestry
- Manufacturing and trade
- Little or no activity
- National border

Foreign Trade

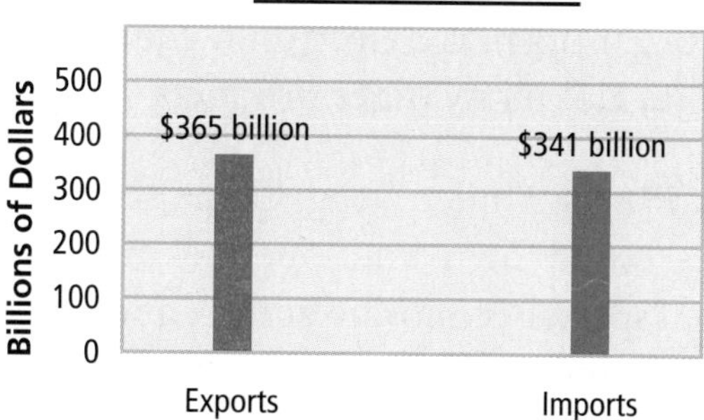

SOURCE: World Trade Organization, 2002

Labor Force by Sector

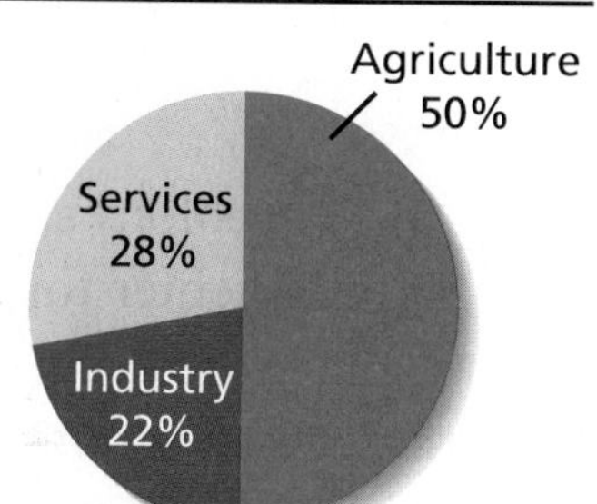

SOURCE: *CIA World Factbook*, 2003

Exports by Sector

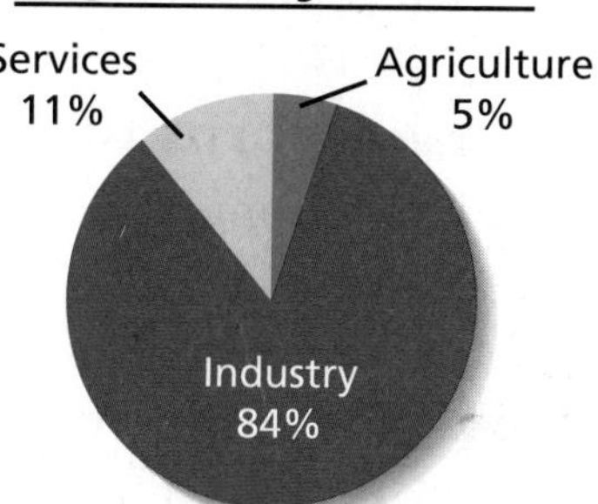

SOURCE: World Trade Organization, 2002

Map and Chart Skills

1. **Identify** Which economic sector in China uses the most land and employs the most people?
2. **Contrast** Which economic sector accounts for most of China's exports?
3. **Infer** Are China's farm products sold mainly inside or outside of China?

Use Web Code **Ice-6711** for **DK World Desk Reference Online.**

The New China
Sun Dong An Plaza in Beijing, China, includes seven floors of stores, a food court, a multiscreen movie complex, and parking for about 500 cars and about 3,500 bicycles. **Compare and Contrast** *How is Sun Dong An Plaza similar to and different from an American shopping mall?*

New Leaders After Mao died in 1976, moderate leaders gained power in China. By 1981, Deng Xiaoping (dung show ping) was leader of China. Deng carried out a program called the Four Modernizations. This program focused on improvements in farming, industry, science, and defense. During the next 20 years, China gradually allowed some free enterprise. Privately owned Chinese factories began to make electronic equipment, clothes, computer parts, toys, and many other products.

New Economic Plans Under Deng, China set up areas where foreign companies could own and operate businesses. These areas included five "special economic zones" and 14 cities along China's coast. They helped bring in money to China's economy. The Chinese Communist party also allowed some Chinese citizens to run private businesses. By the end of the 1990s, private businesses were producing about 75 percent of China's gross domestic product. **Gross domestic product** is the total value of all goods and services produced in an economy.

Hong Kong Returns to China In 1997, China took back control of Hong Kong, which had been a British colony since the late 1800s. Hong Kong had long been a major center for trade, banking, and shipping. China agreed to allow the economy of Hong Kong to operate without changes for the next 50 years. China also agreed that during this period Hong Kong could largely govern itself.

✓ Reading Check **What happened to Hong Kong in 1997?**

China Today

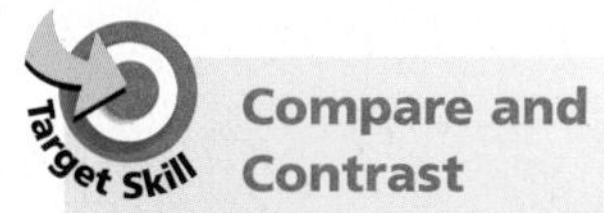
Target Skill

Compare and Contrast How was China different after Mao Zedong died?

Today, China is a major economic power. It has formed good relations with many nations. Yet the government has often been criticized for the way it treats its people. China has one political party, which is the Chinese Communist party. Under China's government, its citizens do not have political freedom.

The Chinese government has used violence against people who have called for a democratic government. In 1989, tens of thousands of people gathered in Tiananmen Square in Beijing, China's capital, to demand greater political freedoms. When the people refused to leave, the government sent in tanks and troops. Thousands of people were killed or wounded.

Many nations question how they should relate to a country with such a poor human rights record. Still, most of them continue to remain trade partners with China. China's population makes it a huge market for goods, and China manufactures many items for other countries. In 2003, Hu Jintao became China's president and leader of the Chinese Communist party. Experts on China expected Hu to keep developing an economy with fewer government controls. With the Chinese Communist party firmly in control, however, the country's political system was not expected to change.

Discovery
CHANNEL
SCHOOL
Video
Learn about desertification in China.

✓ **Reading Check** **How did China's government respond to the democracy movement in 1989?**

Section 1 Assessment

Key Terms

Review the key terms at the beginning of this section. Use each term in a sentence that explains its meaning.

Target Reading Skill

Explain one way China's government was the same and one way it was different after Mao's death?

Comprehension and Critical Thinking

1. (a) Identify Who took control of China in 1949?

(b) Summarize Why did the Chinese government launch the Great Leap Forward?

2. (a) Define What is the Republic of China?

(b) Contrast How is Taiwan different from China?

3. (a) Identify Identify Deng Xiaoping.

(b) Find the Main Idea What economic changes took place under Deng's leadership?

(c) Explain Why has the Chinese government been criticized for the way it treats its people?

Writing Activity

Write a paragraph comparing and contrasting China before and after Mao Zedong's death. Include a description of how China's economy has changed during this time.

Writing Tip Compare and contrast the Great Leap Forward with the Four Modernizations program. How were these programs alike? How were they different?

Section 2

Japan

Tradition and Change

Prepare to Read

Objectives

In this section, you will

1. Learn about the growth of Japan's economy.
2. Find out about successes and challenges in Japan's economy.
3. Examine aspects of life in Japan.

Taking Notes

As you read this section, look for ways in which tradition and change have helped Japan develop its economy. Copy the web diagram below, and record your findings in it.

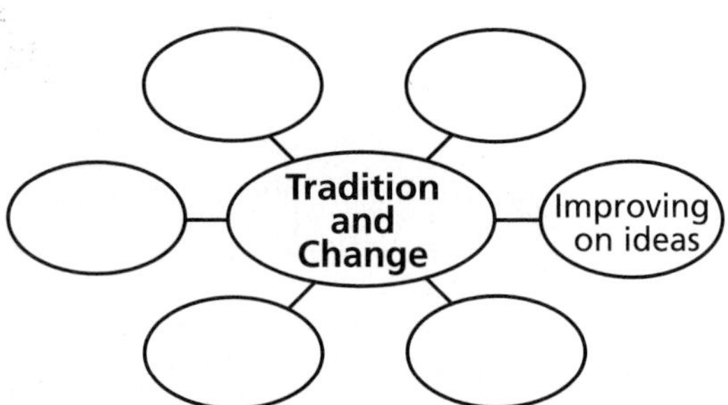

Target Reading Skill

Make Comparisons When you make comparisons, you note how things are alike. As you read this section, compare tradition and change in terms of how they have helped Japan build its economy. Write your information in the Taking Notes web diagram.

Key Terms

- **subsidy** (SUB suh dee) *n.* money given by a government to assist a private company
- **recession** (rih SESH un) *n.* a period during which an economy and the businesses that support it shrink, or make less money
- **birthrate** (BURTH rayt) *n.* the number of live births each year per 1,000 people
- **labor** (LAY bur) *n.* the work people do for which they are paid

A robot demonstration in Japan

In the 1990s, employees of Japanese companies would gather to sing the company song. One song included the words, "Let's put our strength and minds together . . . grow, industry, grow, grow, grow!" A Japanese car company handed out a weekly newsletter that included pep talks to help its employees work more efficiently. Another Japanese car company held an Idea Expo each year. Employees competed in designing unique vehicles. The event reminded workers that each new product is the result of a company-wide team effort.

Harmony and teamwork are important in the Japanese way of life. Tradition and change are also important. Present-day Japan is a modern, urban country where traditional ways blend with the new.

Building a Developed Economy

Once Japan finally opened its ports to other countries in the 1800s, it welcomed new ideas and inventions from the West. For years, the Japanese worked to build major industries. By the 1920s, Japan had become an important manufacturing country.

Japan's Economy After World War II After World War II ended in 1945, however, Japan was in ruins. The United States helped to rebuild Japan's industries. In addition, the Japanese government helped industries by giving them subsidies. A **subsidy** is money given by a government to assist a private company. This allowed companies to build large factories and sell more goods, which boosted the country's economy.

High-Technology Industries Since the 1960s, Japan has produced some of the world's most modern industrial robots. By the 1970s, the Japanese were making more watches and cameras than the Swiss and the Germans. By the 1980s, Japan made and sold a large share of the world's cars, electronic goods, skiing gear, and bicycles. Japan also produced huge amounts of steel, ships, televisions, and CDs.

In addition, Japanese companies improved existing products. For example, the videocassette recorder (VCR) was invented in the United States. But production costs for making VCRs in the United States were thought to be too high. A Japanese company bought the invention. Japan today is a leading maker of VCRs.

Japanese companies also had new ideas of their own. You are probably familiar with portable stereos and small, hand-held electronic games. These products were invented by the Japanese. In 1983, a European company and a Japanese company introduced the first compact disc. Working with European and American companies, Japanese companies also developed the digital video disc (DVD).

✓ Reading Check **What are some high-technology products made in Japan?**

Japan's Robotics Industry
Below, a Japanese robotics designer watches as a humanoid robot steps over a barrier. Increased robot use may be one solution for Japan's labor shortage. **Analyze** *What characteristics does this robot have that would make it suitable as a replacement for a human worker?*

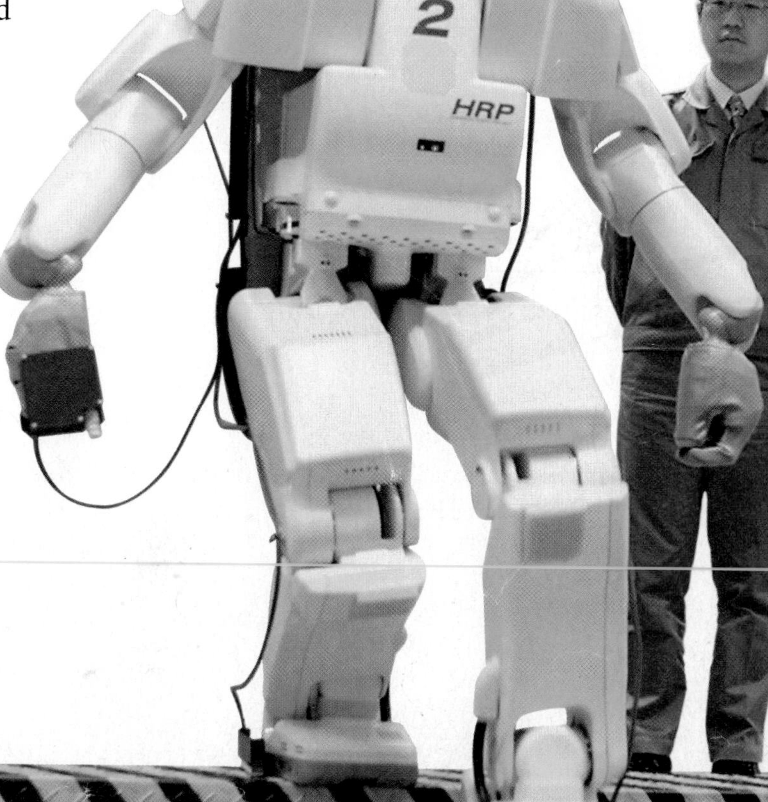

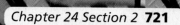

Successes and Challenges

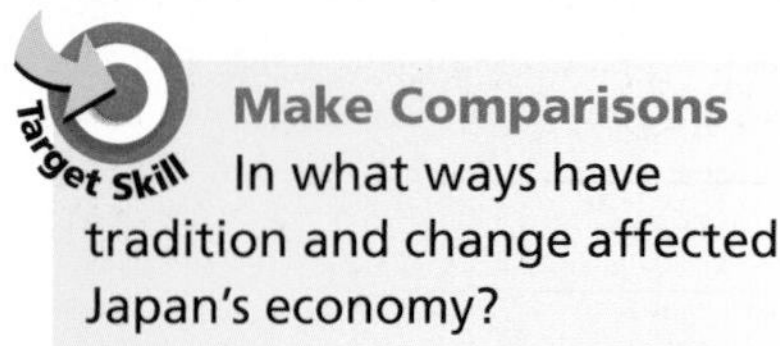

Make Comparisons In what ways have tradition and change affected Japan's economy?

By the 1980s, Japan had one of the world's largest and strongest economies. Japan's economy depended on exporting its products to the rest of the world. Americans and Europeans eagerly bought Japanese products—particularly cars, television sets, and electronics. Yet Japanese people did not buy many goods from America and Europe.

Other countries grew angry because even though they bought many Japanese products, the Japanese did not buy theirs. This led to poor trade relations between Japan and other countries. On top of that, in the early 1990s, the Japanese economy suffered a severe recession. A **recession** is a period of time when an economy and the businesses that support it shrink, or make less money. To overcome the recession, some companies began laying off their employees. Unemployment in Japan rose.

Japan still has one of the largest economies in the world, even though its economy continued to decline into 2003. Manufacturing remains an important part of Japan's economy. Today, however, more people work in Japan's service industries than in manufacturing. Service industries include jobs in banking, communications, sales, hotels, and restaurants. More of the country's wealth comes from service industries as well.

✓ Reading Check **How was Japan affected by the recession in the 1990s?**

Inspecting a turbine in Yokohama, Japan (large photo); a Japanese-made electronic book reader (small photo)

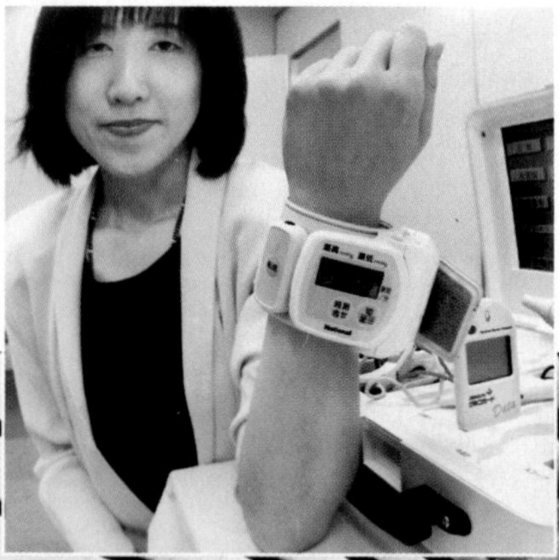

Japan

Japan is one of the world's most densely populated countries. Japan is about the same size as the states of California or Montana. But it has almost half as many people as the entire United States. The bar graph below the map shows that Japan has about the same population density as Massachusetts. Massachusetts is one of the most densely populated U.S. states. Yet, as you can see on the map, forests and farmland cover most of Japan. How is this possible? Japan preserves large areas of forest and farmland because most of its people are crowded into the small part of the country that is urban. Compare the circle graphs below showing land use in Massachusetts and Japan. Even though Japan has nearly the same overall density as Massachusetts, it devotes much less of its space to urban development. This is mainly because its cities are compact, with little of the sprawling suburban development that we know in the United States.

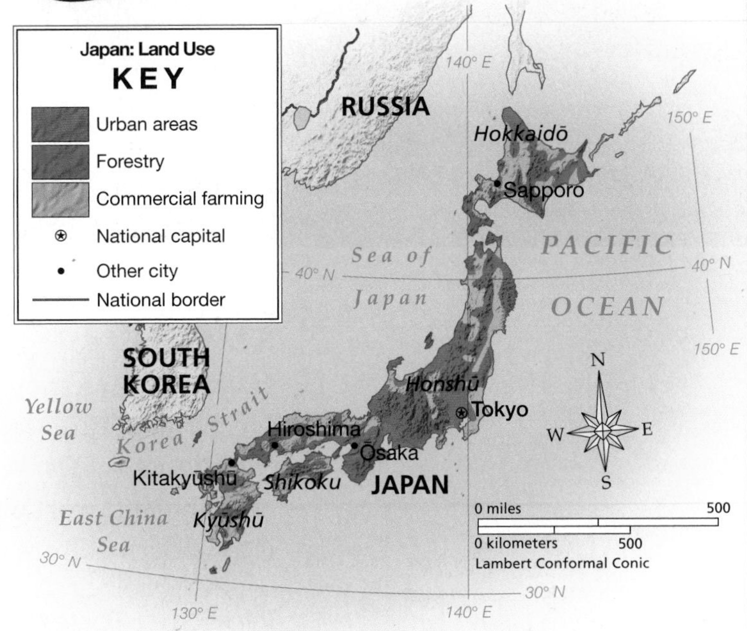

Population Density Comparison

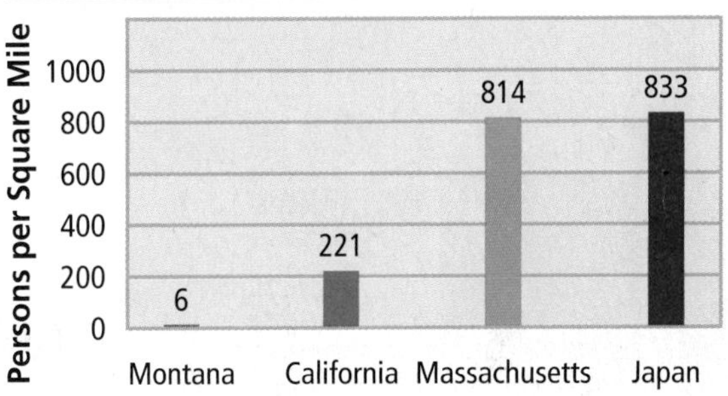

SOURCE: *The World Almanac*, 2003

Land Use

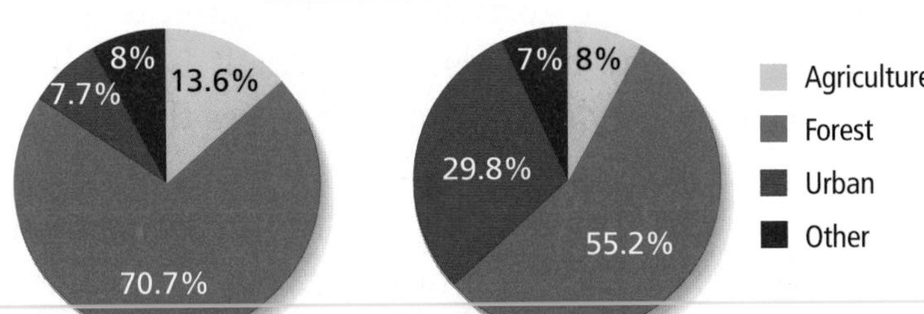

Japan

SOURCE: Japan National Land Agency, 1995

Massachusetts

SOURCE: U.S. Natural Resources Conservation Service, 1997

Map and Chart Skills

1. **Identify** What percentages of Japan's land are devoted to agriculture and forest?
2. **Compare** Does Japan devote more or less land to agriculture and forest than Massachusetts?
3. **Synthesize** What explains this difference?

Use Web Code **lce-6712** for **DK World Desk Reference Online.**

Life in Japan

Harmony, ceremony, and order have long been important in Japanese culture. Japanese people have generally followed these traditional values. While the past is honored, however, new ways of living and working have been introduced in Japan. The result is a modern culture with features that are unique to the country.

Discovery
CHANNEL
SCHOOL
Video
Learn about the ways of the samurai in Japan.

Working Together Working together as a group has long been a tradition in Japan. One way Japanese manufacturing companies have worked together is by forming *keiretsu* (kay ret soo). This is a Japanese term that describes a group of companies that join together to work toward one another's success. Some keiretsu included the companies that make goods, the companies that provide the raw materials for those goods, and the companies that sell the goods. The Japanese car industry has followed this model. Although still part of the country's economy, keiretsu have been joined by a growing number of small businesses.

Changing Roles The role of marriage is another example of tradition and change in Japan. Marriage has been the most acceptable social position for a Japanese man or woman. Today, however, more and more Japanese men and women are choosing not to marry or to delay marriage. One result is that Japan's birthrate is low. A country's **birthrate** measures the number of live births each year per 1,000 people.

The role of Japanese women in the work force has changed, too. Before World War II, few women in Japan worked outside the home. Today, there are more Japanese women working full time or part time than women who stay at home full time.

Although about half of Japan's work force is made up of women, men hold most of the management positions. In 2003, women headed just 5 percent of the companies in Japan. This compared with more than 40 percent of U.S. companies being headed by women.

Japanese Students
Like American schoolchildren, these Japanese students enjoy clowning for the camera. Most public school students in Japan wear uniforms. **Analyze** *What purpose do you think school uniforms serve?*

Facing the Future As Japan heads into the future, its challenge is to find a way of maintaining its wealth. One of the resources a country needs to produce goods and services is labor. **Labor** is the work people do for which they are paid. Japan does not have a growing labor force of young workers. In the United States and Europe, a steady supply of immigrants helps keep the labor force growing. In the past, Japan has limited immigration.

Japan's low birthrate affects the labor force. Fewer and fewer workers have to support an aging population no longer working. This makes the cost of producing goods and services higher in Japan than in countries with growing populations.

✓ Reading Check **Why is the cost of producing goods and services higher in Japan than in other Asian countries?**

Section 2 Assessment

Key Terms
Review the key terms at the beginning of this section. Use each term in a sentence that explains its meaning.

Target Reading Skill
What are two ways in which tradition and change have helped Japan build its economy?

Comprehension and Critical Thinking
1. (a) Recall Describe what Japan's economy was like by the 1920s.
(b) Summarize Tell how Japan's economy grew from the 1960s to the 1980s.
2. (a) Identify What happened that disturbed Japan's economy in the early 1990s?
(b) Identify Effects How did this affect Japan?
3. (a) Explain What tradition helps explain why Japanese companies formed *keiretsu?*
(b) Identify What is one resource a country needs to produce goods and services?
(c) Draw Conclusions How would a low birthrate affect a country's labor force?

Writing Activity
Japan has an aging population. Based on the information in this section, brainstorm a list of what Japan can do to increase its labor force. Write your list and add a short description of each idea.

For: An activity on Japan
Visit: PHSchool.com
Web Code: lcd-6702

Synthesizing Information

James and his family were going to host a Japanese exchange student for the summer. The student, Hiro, would be arriving in three weeks.

James decided to send information about his town to Hiro. First, he got a map that showed the mountains and lakes in the area. Then, James took photos of his favorite places in town. James added photos of his friends at school and playing soccer. His mother gave him a brochure that told about the area. Finally, James made a video showing his family, his apartment, and even his cat.

Soon, James had a mountain of information. He showed it to his dad.

"You've done a great job," his dad said. "But maybe you should synthesize some of this information. After all, Hiro may not have time to digest all of these things."

When you synthesize information, you combine information from several different sources. You find the main ideas and weave them into a conclusion. Synthesizing information is a very important skill in school and in life.

Learn the Skill

Follow these steps to synthesize information.

1. **Identify the main idea in each piece of information.** Main ideas are big, important ideas that are supported by details. You may want to write the main ideas down. The main idea for James is to tell about his town.

2. **Find details that support your main ideas.** Details will give you more information about your main ideas. One detail that James chose to share was that some children in his town like to play soccer.

3. **Look for connections between the pieces of information.** These connections might be similarities, differences, causes, effects, or examples. Jot down these connections.

4. **Draw conclusions based on the connections you found.** What broad, general statements can you make that tie your main ideas together?

Japan's Modern Economy

Main Ideas	Supporting Details	Connections
1. By the 1980s Japan had one of the world's largest and strongest economies.	• Japan loaned large amounts of money to other countries. • Japan exported its products to the rest of the world.	• Japan imported few goods.
2. In the early 1990s Japan suffered a severe recession.		

Practice the Skill

Use the steps on the previous page to synthesize information about Japan's modern economy. Reread the text on page 722 under the heading Successes and Challenges. Then make a table like the partially completed one above.

1. Study the information about Japan's economy from the 1980s to the present. Add one or two main ideas to the two ideas on the table above.
2. Now find details that support each main idea and add them to the chart. The details already listed add more information about Japan's strong economy in the 1980s.
3. Are the pieces of information connected in some way? Consider cause and effect. The connection already included is a possible cause for the decline in Japan's economy. Add other connections to the chart.
4. Draw some conclusions from the connections you find. See whether you can use these conclusions to answer the question, "Why did Japan's economy decline in the early 1990s?"

The Tokyo Stock Exchange is part of Japan's economy. This stock trader is using a hand signal to show he wants to sell stocks.

Apply the Skill

Use the steps on the previous page to synthesize information about how life has changed in modern Japan. Select information from the text and photos in the section Life in Japan on page 724. Focus on a single aspect of Japanese life, such as family life or work life.

Section 3

The Koreas

A Divided Land

Prepare to Read

Objectives

In this section, you will

1. Understand why North Korea has been slow to develop.
2. Find out how South Korea became an economic success.

Taking Notes

As you read this section, look for differences between North Korea and South Korea. Copy the table below, and record your findings in it.

North Korea	South Korea
•	• High economic growth

Target Reading Skill

Identify Contrasts When you identify contrasts, you examine differences. North Korea and South Korea are very different. As you read, look for differences between these two countries. Write them down in the Taking Notes table.

Key Terms

- **demilitarized zone** (dee MIL uh tuh ryzd zohn) *n.* an area in which no weapons are allowed
- **truce** (troos) *n.* a cease-fire agreement
- **diversify** (duh VUR suh fy) *v.* to add variety to
- **famine** (FAM in) *n.* a huge food shortage

North Korea and South Korea have a border unlike any other in the world. On a map, the border looks like a simple line. In reality, the border runs through the middle of what former President Bill Clinton called "the scariest place on Earth."

The border runs through the DMZ or **demilitarized zone** (dee MIL uh tuh ryzd zohn), an area in which no weapons are allowed. The DMZ is about 2.5 miles (4 kilometers) wide and about 151 miles (248 kilometers) long. Barbed wire, land mines, watchtowers, and thousands of weapons line both sides.

Children in South Korea

On North Korea's side, an estimated one million troops patrol the border. South Korea has about 600,000 troops. Why does the DMZ exist? In 1953, a **truce,** or cease-fire agreement, ended the Korean War. But no peace treaty was signed. Since then, the world's most heavily armed border has divided the two countries.

More than the DMZ divides the Koreas. The two countries have very different economies and governments as well.

A section of the DMZ that divides North Korea and South Korea

North Korea: Economic Challenges

North Korea (the Democratic People's Republic of Korea) is a communist country under a dictatorship. The government runs the economy. The country has kept itself closed to much of the world. This has kept out new technology and fresh ideas. Yet North Korea is rich in mineral resources. Until the end of World War II, it was the industrial center of the Korean Peninsula.

Today, North Korea cannot compete with South Korea. It still manufactures poor-quality goods in government-owned factories. Little has been done to **diversify,** or add variety to, the economy. Overall, North Korea's economy is in poor shape.

Farming methods, too, are outdated in North Korea. Many farmers burn hillsides to prepare for planting crops. After a few years of this, the good soil may be washed away by rain. Then the fields can no longer be farmed. In 1995, North Koreans faced **famine,** or a huge food shortage, and starvation. North Korean officials estimated that about 220,000 people died from famine between 1995 and 1998. For the first time, North Korea asked noncommunist countries for aid.

√ Reading Check **How did famine affect North Korea?**

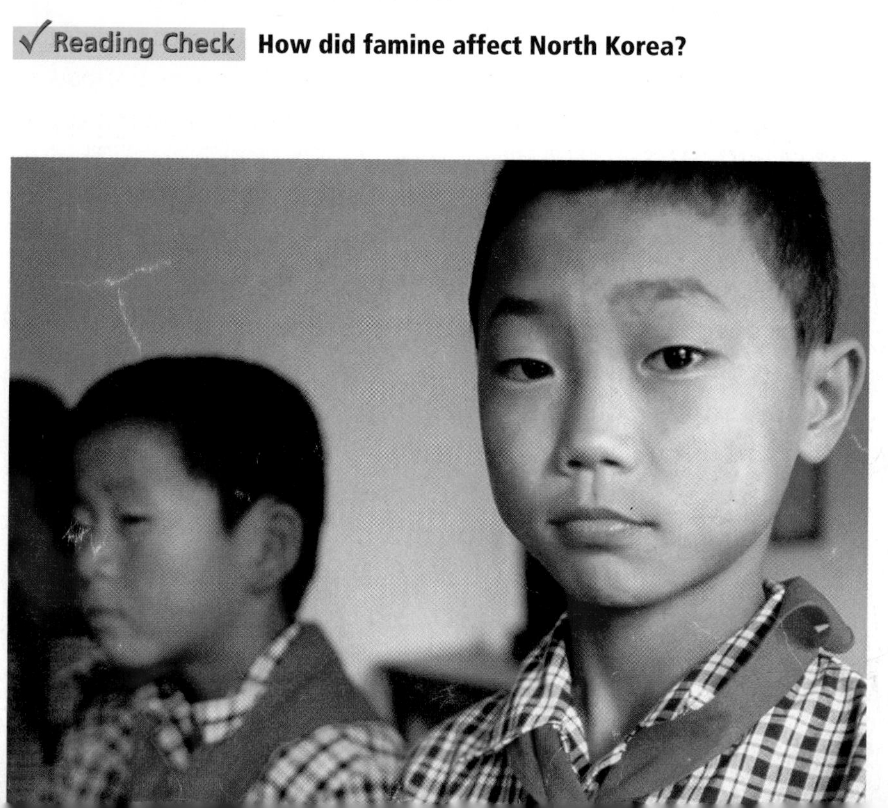

Children in North Korea

Soccer is a popular sport in South Korea.

South Korea: Economic Growth

In the mid-1950s, South Korea (the Republic of Korea) had agricultural resources but few industries. Fifty years later, South Korea has become a leading economic power.

South Korea is a democracy with an economy based on free enterprise. After World War II, South Korea's factories focused on making cloth and processed foods. Later, South Korea developed heavy industry. Today, South Korea is among the world's leading shipbuilders. It has a growing electronics industry that exports radios, televisions, and computers. South Korea is a leading producer of the silicon chips used in computers. South Korea also has large refineries, or factories that process oil. The oil products are used to make plastics, rubber, and other goods.

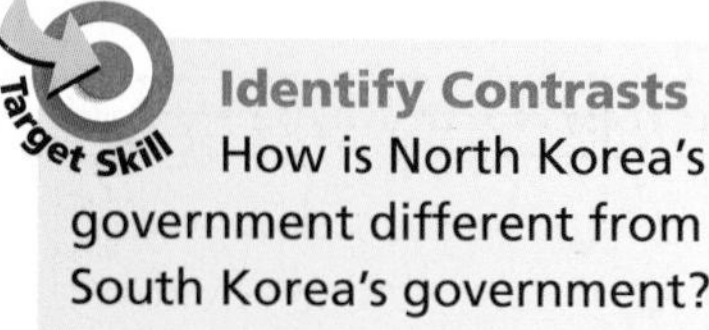

Target Skill **Identify Contrasts** How is North Korea's government different from South Korea's government?

The government of South Korea has focused on the growth of industry. But it has also helped farmers. Some programs helped increase crop production. Other programs improved housing, roads, and water supplies and brought electricity to rural areas.

Despite its successes, South Korea faces a number of challenges. Like Japan, it lacks many natural resources. It must import large amounts of raw materials to keep industry running. Major imports are oil, iron, steel, and chemicals.

√ Reading Check **What are some products made in South Korea?**

Years of Tension

Many Koreans hope that one day North Korea and South Korea will once again be one country. But relations between the two Koreas have remained tense since the end of the Korean War. North Korean and South Korean troops have had numerous violent clashes. Better relations seemed possible in 2000. The leaders of the two countries met in Pyongyang, the capital of North Korea, and agreed to work toward peace and cooperation.

COUNTRY PROFILE — Focus on Economics

The Koreas

The Koreas have very different economies. The map at right shows that North Korea is rich in natural resources. However, its communist system has hurt its economy. The graph below shows that South Korea's gross domestic product, or economic output, has soared, while North Korea's has failed to grow.

Manufacturing electronics in South Korea

The Koreas: Natural Resources

KEY

- Gold
- Silver
- Copper
- Iron
- Lead
- Tungsten
- Coal
- Graphite
- Hydroelectric power
- Manufacturing
- National capital
- National border

0 miles 250
0 kilometers 250
Lambert Conformal Conic

CHINA · NORTH KOREA · SOUTH KOREA · P'yŏngyang · Seoul · Sea of Japan · Yellow Sea · Korea Strait · Cheju-Do

Gross Domestic Product, 1982–2002

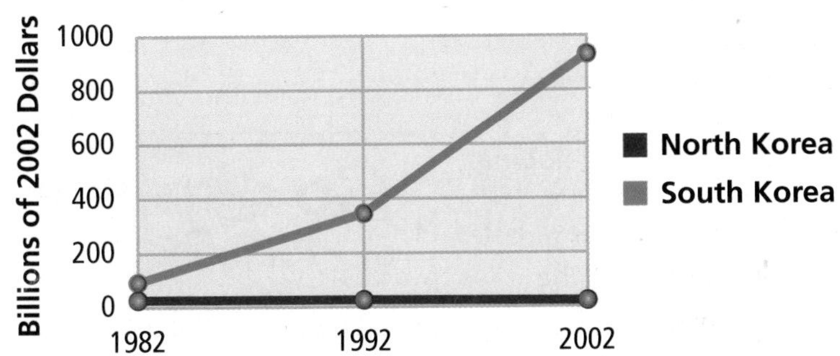

SOURCE: *Encyclopaedia Britannica Book of the Year; The World Almanac*

Map and Chart Skills

1. **List** Using the map, name at least three natural resources that are found in North Korea but not South Korea.
2. **Contrast** Based on your reading and the graph at the left, discuss the differences between the economies of North and South Korea.

Use Web Code **lce-6713** for **DK World Desk Reference Online.**

Links to Science

Nature in the DMZ The land inside the DMZ has been untouched by human settlement for more than 50 years. As a result, the DMZ has become a peaceful haven for wildlife. Living in the DMZ are several rare and endangered species. They include eagles, cranes, and bears. Some people believe there are tigers in the DMZ. If North Korea and South Korea ever sign a peace agreement, some people want to preserve the DMZ as a peace park. Other people want to use the land to develop Korea's economy.

In 2002, North Korea's government made a shocking announcement. Even though it had previously agreed not to, North Korea said it had been developing nuclear weapons. The news damaged hopes for peace between the two countries and caused great worldwide concern, especially in South Korea, Japan, China, and Russia. The United States, South Korea, and Japan called for North Korea to give up its nuclear weapons program. The United States also said it was working with the countries of the region to find a peaceful solution to the problem.

In 2002, President George W. Bush visited the DMZ on his first trip to South Korea. He said,

> **"When satellites take pictures of the Korean peninsula at night, the South is awash in light. The North is almost completely dark. . . . We want all the Koreans to live in the light. My vision is clear: I see a peninsula that is one day united in commerce and cooperation, instead of divided by barbed wire and fear."**
>
> *—President George W. Bush*

✓ Reading Check **What happened when North Korea announced it was developing nuclear weapons?**

Section 3 Assessment

Key Terms

Review the key terms at the beginning of this section. Use each term in a sentence that explains its meaning.

Target Reading Skill

Using your Taking Notes chart, explain ways in which North Korea and South Korea are different.

Comprehension and Critical Thinking

1. (a) Identify What kind of government and economy does South Korea have?
(b) Identify Causes What are some reasons for South Korea's economic success?

2. (a) Identify What kind of government does North Korea have?
(b) Analyze Why has North Korea's economy lagged behind South Korea's?

3. (a) Explain What event seemed to point to better relations between North Korea and South Korea?
(b) Identify Effects What was the effect of North Korea's announcing that it was developing nuclear weapons?
(c) Draw Inferences What did President Bush mean when he said the United States wanted all Koreans to "live in the light"?

Writing Activity

When North Korea and South Korea were divided, families were divided, too. Based on what you have read about the Koreas, write a paragraph that states your viewpoint on the issue of reunifying the two countries.

For: An activity on the Koreas
Visit: PHSchool.com
Web Code: lcd-6703

Chapter 24

Review and Assessment

◆ Chapter Summary

Section 1: China

- China tried two economic programs from 1949 to 1980, including the Great Leap Forward and the Cultural Revolution.
- Under a free enterprise system, Taiwan developed a successful economy.
- After the death of Chinese leader Mao Zedong, China followed a different path that included many changes to develop the economy.
- China today is a major economic power with a government that has fewer controls over the economy, but that does not allow political freedom for its citizens.

Section 2: Japan

- Japan worked hard to build a successful, highly developed economy.
- Although its economy declined in the 1990s, Japan still has one of the largest economies in the world.
- Japan has a modern culture that combines traditional Japanese values with new ways of working and living.
- One of Japan's challenges for the future is finding a way of maintaining its wealth, despite an aging population and a low birthrate.

China

Section 3: The Koreas

- South Korea has a democratic government with an economy based on free enterprise.
- North Korea has a communist government that controls the economy.

Japan

◆ Key Terms

Match the definitions in Column I with the key terms in Column II.

Column I

1. an economic system in which people can choose their own jobs, start private businesses, own property, and make a profit
2. extreme
3. a huge food shortage
4. to add variety to
5. the number of live births in a nation each year per 1,000 people

Column II

A radical
B free enterprise system
C birthrate
D diversify
E famine

Chapter 24 Review and Assessment (continued)

◆ Comprehension and Critical Thinking

6. (a) **Identify** What was the purpose of the Cultural Revolution?
   (b) **Compare and Contrast** How was the Cultural Revolution similar to and different from the Great Leap Forward?
7. (a) **Define** Where and what is Taiwan?
   (b) **Identify Point of View** How does the government of Taiwan view China?
8. (a) **Explain** What was the Four Modernizations program of the 1990s?
   (b) **Identify Effects** Describe one change in China's economy under this program.
9. (a) **Note** Give examples of some of the high-technology products made in Japan.
10. (a) **Summarize** How was the formation of keiretsu an example of the Japanese tradition of working together?
11. (a) **Define** What is labor?
    (b) **Summarize** What is one reason that Japan has a declining labor force?
12. (a) **Describe** What was North Korea like before the end of World War II?
    (b) **Contrast** How is North Korea's government and economy different from South Korea's?
13. (a) **List** Name four products that are made in South Korea.
    (b) **Compare** Why is South Korea similar to Japan in terms of what the country must do to keep industry running?

◆ Skills Practice

Synthesizing Information Review the steps you learned in the Skills for Life lesson in this chapter. Then review the text and pictures in Section 1. Synthesize the information and draw a conclusion about how China has changed since 1949.

◆ Writing Activity: Language Arts

Written Chinese is based on characters, rather than on an alphabet. Each Chinese character represents a word or an idea. The complete Chinese writing system has more than 40,000 characters. Use an encyclopedia to look up information about the Chinese language and the Chinese writing system. Write a brief report that describes Chinese writing.

MAP MASTER™ Skills Activity

Place Location For each place listed below, write the letter from the map that shows its location.

1. China
2. Japan
3. Taiwan
4. South Korea
5. North Korea
6. Beijing

Go Online PHSchool.com Use Web Code lcp-6720 for an **interactive map.**

East Asia

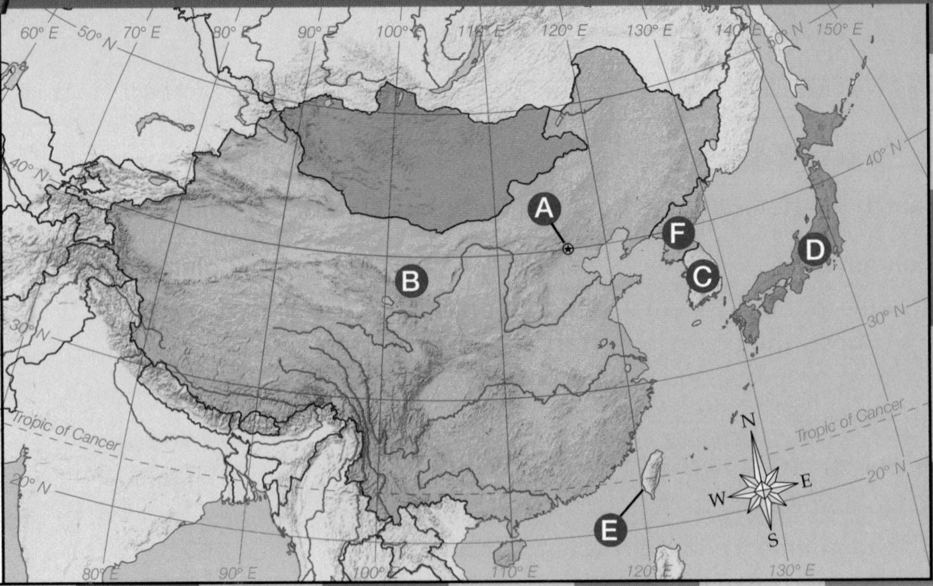

60° E 70° E 80° E 90° E 100° E 110° E 120° E 130° E 140° E 150° E
50° N 40° N 30° N 20° N
Tropic of Cancer
A B C D E F
N S E W

Standardized Test Prep

Test-Taking Tips

Some questions on standardized tests ask you to analyze graphic organizers. Study the concept web below. Then follow the tips to answer the sample question at the right.

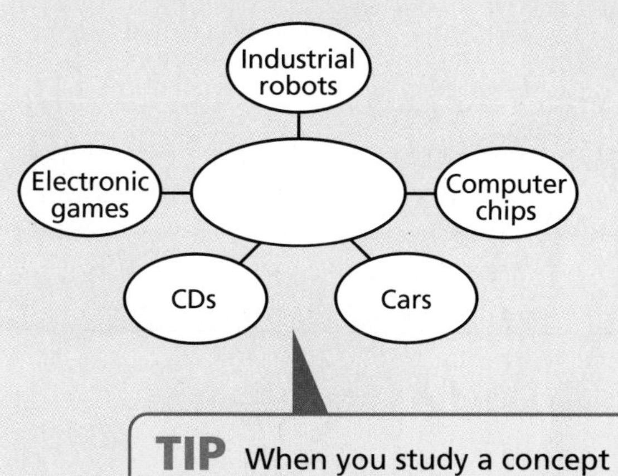

TIP When you study a concept web, think about what kind of information belongs in each part.

Pick the letter that best answers the question.

Which title should go in the center of the web?

- **A** Skiing Gear
- **B** Exports
- **C** Japanese Exports
- **D** Japanese Imports

TIP Read all four answer choices. Then choose the BEST answer from the remaining choices.

Think It Through The question asks you to choose a title for the center of the web—in other words, an idea that covers the information in all of the outer circles. You can rule out A because it is too specific: skiing gear belongs in an outer circle. However, B is too general. Although it is correct, there is probably a better answer. That leaves C or D. Look over the items in the outer circles. Are they goods that Japan sells to the rest of the world (exports) or buys from other countries (imports)? Look for at least one product on the web that you are sure is an export or import. (For instance, do you know any Americans who own a Japanese car?) The correct answer is C.

Practice Questions

Use the tips above and other tips in this book to help you answer the following questions.

1. How are the governments of China and North Korea similar?
   - **A** They are both ruled by kings.
   - **B** They both have communist governments.
   - **C** They both follow the free enterprise system.
   - **D** They both have democratic governments.
2. In Japan, you could expect to find
   - **A** special economic zones.
   - **B** a high birthrate.
   - **C** a growing labor force.
   - **D** an economy based on manufacturing goods for export.
3. In 1997, Hong Kong was returned to
   - **A** Taiwan.
   - **B** China.
   - **C** Japan.
   - **D** South Korea.

Use the concept web below to answer Question 4.

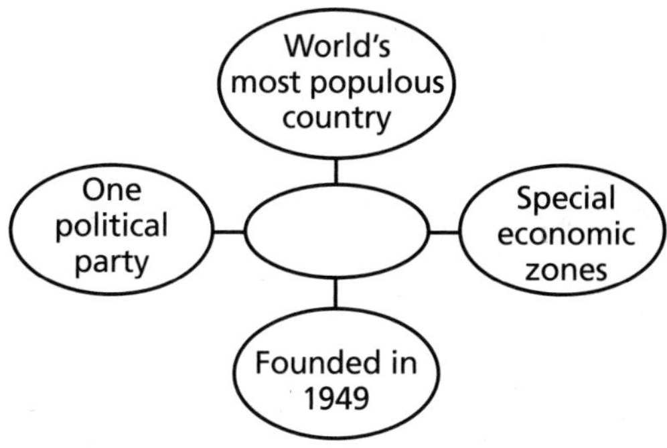

4. Which title should go in the center of the web?
   - **A** Japan
   - **B** North Korea
   - **C** China
   - **D** Taiwan

Use Web Code **lca-6700** for **Chapter 24 self-test.**

Chapter

25 South, Southwest, and Central Asia

Chapter Preview

This chapter focuses on four key countries in South Asia and Southwest Asia: India, Pakistan, Israel, and Saudi Arabia. The chapter also focuses on the countries of the Stans, in Central Asia.

Country Databank

The Country Databank provides data and descriptions of each of the countries of South Asia, Southwest Asia, and Central Asia.

Target Reading Skill

Cause and Effect In this chapter, you will practice understanding causes and effects.

▶ **A man docking a small boat in Jordan**

South, Southwest, and Central Asia: Political

MAP MASTER™ Skills Activity

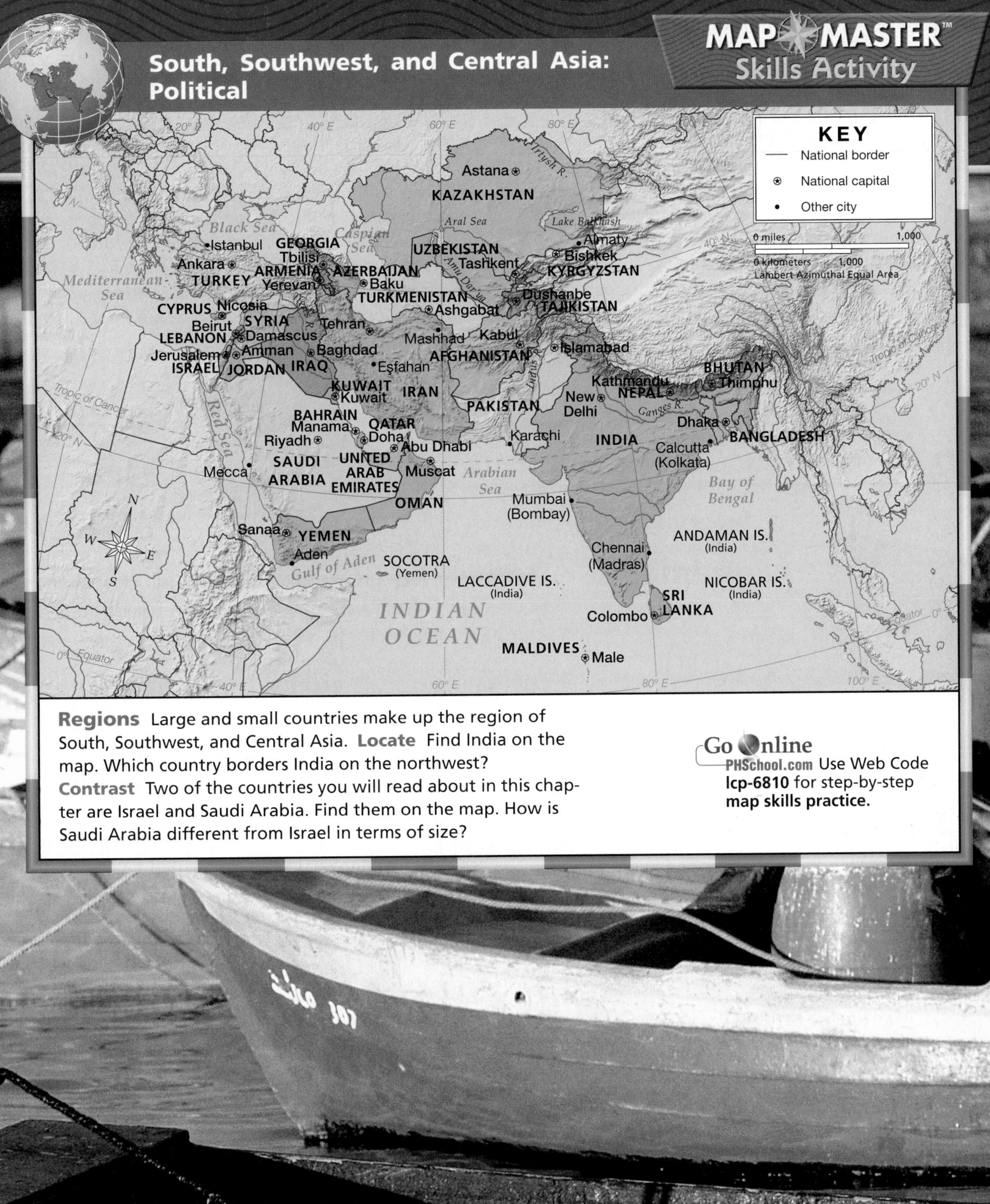

Regions Large and small countries make up the region of South, Southwest, and Central Asia. **Locate** Find India on the map. Which country borders India on the northwest?

Contrast Two of the countries you will read about in this chapter are Israel and Saudi Arabia. Find them on the map. How is Saudi Arabia different from Israel in terms of size?

Go Online
PHSchool.com Use Web Code **lcp-6810** for step-by-step **map skills practice.**

Introducing South, Southwest, and Central Asia

Guide for Reading

This section provides an introduction to the countries that make up the region of South, Southwest, and Central Asia.

- Look at the map on the previous page and then read the paragraphs below to learn about each nation.
- Analyze the data to compare the countries.
- What are the characteristics that most of the countries share?
- What are some key differences among the countries?

Viewing the Video Overview

View the World Studies Video Overview to learn more about each of the countries. As you watch, answer this question:

- South, Southwest, and Central Asia encompass many geographic extremes. What are some of them?

Discovery
CHANNEL
SCHOOL
Video
Explore the land of South, Southwest, and Central Asia.

Afghanistan

Capital	Kabul
Land Area	250,000 sq mi; 647,500 sq km
Population	27.8 million
Ethnic Group(s)	Pashtun, Tajik, Hazara, Uzbek, Aimaks, Baloch, Turkmen
Religion(s)	Muslim
Government	transitional
Currency	new afghani
Leading Exports	fruits and nuts, handwoven carpets, wool, cotton, hides and pelts, precious and semi-precious gems
Language(s)	Pashtu (official), Dari (official), Tajik, Farsi, Uzbek, Turkmen

Afghanistan (af GAN ih stan) is a landlocked country in Central Asia. Conflict and war have troubled this extremely poor country. A ten-year war between the Soviet Union and Afghanistan left the country in ruins when Soviet forces finally withdrew in 1989. A group known as the Taliban came to power in 1996. The Taliban governed Afghanistan under a very strict interpretation of Islamic law. In 2001, U.S.-led forces drove the Taliban from power. In 2002, Hamid Karzai was elected president. The government he headed faced enormous challenges in bringing peace and stability to the country.

A girl reading out loud in an Afghanistan classroom

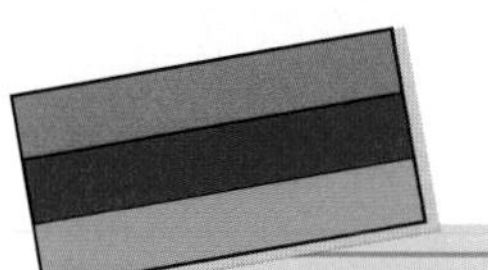

Armenia

Capital	Yerevan
Land Area	10,965 sq mi; 29,400 sq km
Population	3.3 million
Ethnic Group(s)	Armenian, Azeri, Russian, Kurd
Religion(s)	Christian, traditional beliefs
Government	republic
Currency	dram
Leading Exports	diamonds, scrap metal, machinery and equipment, copper ore
Language(s)	Armenian (official), Russian

Located in Southwest Asia east of Turkey, Armenia (ahr MEE nee uh) is a small, landlocked country with an ancient history. Ancient Armenia was the first country in the world to officially adopt Christianity as its religion. The Ottoman Empire conquered Armenia in the 1500s. During World War I, Armenians suffered greatly under Ottoman rule. An estimated 600,000 to 1.5 million Armenians died in what historians called the first genocide in the 1900s. Between 1920 and 1991, Armenia was part of the Soviet Union. Armenia declared its independence from the Soviet Union in 1991.

Azerbaijan

Capital	Baku
Land Area	33,243 sq mi; 86,100 sq km
Population	7.8 million
Ethnic Group(s)	Azeri, Dagestani, Russian, Armenian
Religion(s)	Muslim, Christian
Government	republic
Currency	manat
Leading Exports	oil and gas, machinery, cotton, foodstuffs
Language(s)	Azerbaijani (official), Russian

Azerbaijan (ahz ur by JAHN) is a small country in Southwest Asia located on the west coast of the Caspian Sea. Once part of the Soviet Union, Azerbaijan was the first Soviet republic to declare its independence. Within Azerbaijan is a region called Nagorno-Karabakh (nah GAWR noh kahr ah BAHK). Armenians living in this region wish to become part of Armenia. Between 1988 and 1994, Azerbaijan and Armenia fought a war over which country would control Nagorno-Karabakh. The issue remains a concern today. Azerbaijan has plentiful petroleum and natural gas resources.

Bahrain

Capital	Manama
Land Area	257 sq mi; 665 sq km
Population	656,397
Ethnic Group(s)	Bahraini, Arab, Asian
Religion(s)	Muslim
Government	constitutional hereditary monarchy
Currency	Bahraini dinar
Leading Exports	petroleum and petroleum products, aluminum, textiles
Language(s)	Arabic (official)

Bahrain (bah RAYN) is a tiny island country located in the Persian Gulf east of Saudi Arabia. Bahrain has used its petroleum resources to develop its economy. Aware that it is running out of oil, Bahrain has turned to petroleum processing and refining and has established itself as an international banking center. Unemployment and shrinking oil reserves are major economic problems in Bahrain.

Introducing South, Southwest, and Central Asia

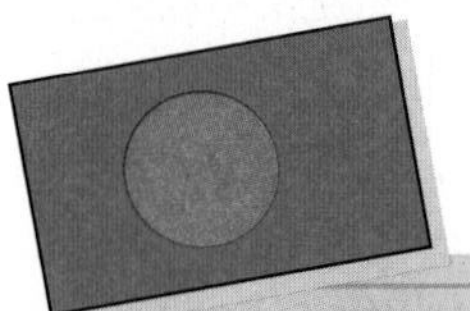

Bangladesh

Capital	Dhaka
Land Area	51,705 sq mi; 133,910 sq km
Population	133.4 million
Ethnic Group(s)	Bengali
Religion(s)	Muslim, Hindu
Government	parliamentary democracy
Currency	taka
Leading Exports	clothing, jute and jute goods, leather, frozen fish and seafood
Language(s)	Bengali (official), Urdu, Chakma, Marma (Magh), Garo, Khasi, Santhali, Tripuri, Mro

Bangladesh (BAHNG luh desh) is located in South Asia. Most of Bangladesh lies on a plain formed by the soil deposited by three powerful rivers that empty into the Bay of Bengal. Most of the country is close to sea level and has a tropical wet climate with heavy rainfall. Low elevation and heavy rainfall contribute to floods that sometimes cause major damage. In 1998, the worst flooding in Bangladesh's history left nearly two thirds of the country underwater. Agriculture is an important part of Bangladesh's economy, and serious flooding can ruin the crops.

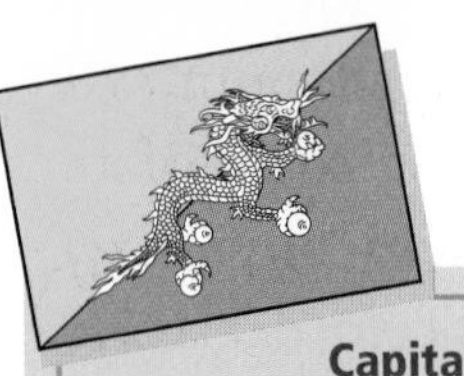

Bhutan

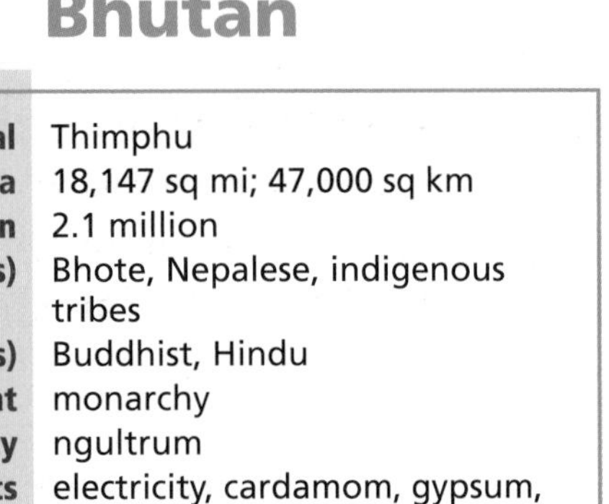

Capital	Thimphu
Land Area	18,147 sq mi; 47,000 sq km
Population	2.1 million
Ethnic Group(s)	Bhote, Nepalese, indigenous tribes
Religion(s)	Buddhist, Hindu
Government	monarchy
Currency	ngultrum
Leading Exports	electricity, cardamom, gypsum, timber, handicrafts, cement, fruit, precious stones, spices
Language(s)	Dzongkha (official), Nepali, Assamese

Bhutan (BOO tahn) is a small, landlocked country in South Asia located between India and China. Mountains cover most of Bhutan. These are the Himalayas, the highest mountains in the world. Bhutan's economy is based on agriculture and forestry. Although about 3 percent of Bhutan's land is suitable for growing crops, about 90 percent of the labor force works in farming. Most of the people live in small rural villages. Tourism is an important economic activity in Bhutan. To protect the environment and preserve Bhutan's mostly Buddhist culture, the government limits the number of people who visit Bhutan each year.

Cyprus

Capital	Nicosia
Land Area	3,568 sq mi; 9,240 sq km
Population	767,314
Ethnic Group(s)	Greek, Turkish
Religion(s)	Christian, Muslim
Government	republic
Currency	Cypriot pound and Turkish lira
Leading Exports	citrus, potatoes, grapes, cement, clothing and shoes, textiles
Language(s)	Greek (official), Turkish (official)

Cyprus (SY prus) is an island country located south of Turkey in the Mediterranean Sea. The majority of the people in Cyprus are Greek. About 12 percent of the population is Turkish. In 1974, Turkey invaded Cyprus and won control over a northern region of the island. Today, Greek Cypriots live in the southern two thirds of the island while the Turkish Cypriots occupy the northern third. In 1983, the Turkish region declared independence as a separate nation, which was recognized only by Turkey. The Greek Cypriot region has a prosperous economy.

Georgia

Capital	Tbilisi
Land Area	26,911 sq mi; 69,700 sq km
Population	5 million
Ethnic Group(s)	Georgian, Armenian, Russian, Azeri, Ossetian, Greek, Abkhaz
Religion(s)	Christian, Muslim
Government	republic
Currency	lari
Leading Exports	scrap metal, machinery, tea, chemicals, citrus fruits, other agricultural products
Language(s)	Georgian (official), Abkhazian (official), Russian

Georgia (JAWR juh) emerged as an independent nation in 1991 during the collapse of the Soviet Union. Georgia is located in Southwest Asia between Turkey and Russia. Mountains cover much of the country. Since independence, differences among Georgia's many ethnic groups have led to violence and civil war. Farming is a major economic activity. Georgia is rich in minerals, including copper. An oil pipeline extending from Azerbaijan across Georgia to Turkey is expected to strengthen the economy.

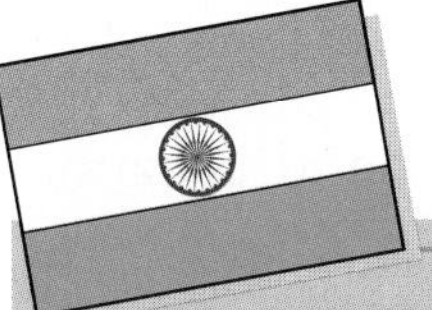

India

Capital	New Delhi
Land Area	1,147,949 sq mi; 2,973,190 sq km
Population	1.05 billion
Ethnic Group(s)	Indo-Aryan, Dravidian, Mongoloid
Religion(s)	Hindu, Muslim, Christian, Buddhist, traditional beliefs
Government	federal republic
Currency	Indian rupee
Leading Exports	textile goods, gems and jewelry, engineering goods, chemicals
Language(s)	Hindi (official), English (official), Urdu, Bengali, Marathi, Telugu, Tamil, Bihari, Gujarati, Kanarese

India (IN dee uh) is the largest country in South Asia and the second-most-populated country in the world. Only China has a larger population than India. India's history dates back to ancient times, with one of the world's earliest civilizations developing in the Indus Valley. A former British colony, India today consists of 28 states governed under a democratic system. A wide range of activities support India's economy. These include farming and modern industries such as textiles, steel, and computer software.

Iran

Capital	Tehran
Land Area	631,660 sq mi; 1,636,000 sq km
Population	66.6 million
Ethnic Group(s)	Persian, Azari, Gilaki and Mazandariani, Kurd, Arab, Lur, Baloch, Turkmen
Religion(s)	Muslim, Jewish, Christian
Government	theocratic republic
Currency	Iranian rial
Leading Exports	petroleum, carpets, fruits and nuts, iron and steel, chemicals
Language(s)	Farsi (official), Azerbaijani, Gilak, Mazanderani, Kurdish, Baluchi, Arabic, Turkmen

Known as Persia until 1935, Iran (ih RAN) became a republic governed under Islamic law in 1979. Islam is the official religion and nearly 100 percent of Iranians are Muslim. About half of the population belongs to the Persian ethnic group. Petroleum is the most important of Iran's natural resources. Iran's economy depends on the oil industry. In 1979, the people of Iran revolted against the country's shah, or ruler. In 1980, Iraq invaded Iran, beginning an eight-year war fought over territory claimed by both countries.

Introducing South, Southwest, and Central Asia

Iraq

Capital	Baghdad
Land Area	166,858 sq mi; 432,162 sq km
Population	24.7 million
Ethnic Group(s)	Arab, Kurd, Turkoman, Assyrian
Religion(s)	Muslim, Christian
Government	republic
Currency	Iraqi dinar
Leading Exports	crude oil
Language(s)	Arabic (official), Kurdish, Turkic languages, Armenian, Assyrian

Iraq (ih RAHK) became the focus of world attention in 1990 when Iraqi troops invaded Kuwait, a small, oil-rich country southeast of Iraq. Led by the United States, a group of 32 countries launched the Persian Gulf War, defeating Iraq and freeing Kuwait. After the war, the United Nations required Iraq to give up its chemical and nuclear weapons programs. Iraq's refusal to do so over a 12-year period led to a U.S.-led invasion of Iraq in 2003. The war against Iraq brought about the removal of Iraq's government under dictator Saddam Hussein.

Israel

Capital	Jerusalem
Land Area	7,849 sq mi; 20,330 sq km
Population	6 million
Ethnic Group(s)	Jewish, Arab
Religion(s)	Jewish, Muslim, Christian
Government	parliamentary democracy
Currency	shekel
Leading Exports	machinery and equipment, cut diamonds, software, agricultural products, chemicals, textiles and clothing
Language(s)	Hebrew (official), Arabic (official), Yiddish, German, Russian, Polish, Romanian, Persian

Israel (IZ ree ul) lies between Egypt and Lebanon and borders the Mediterranean Sea. After World War II, the United Nations created Israel, a country made of Arab and Jewish states. Arab nations in Southwest Asia opposed the formation of Israel and fought a series of wars in which the Israelis were victorious. Israel extended its borders and placed restrictions on Israeli Arabs. However, violence between Jews and Arabs continued. Peace talks have been conducted many times in the last several decades, but have been hampered by Palestinian terrorist attacks and aggressive Israeli military counter-terrorism operations.

Jordan

Capital	Amman
Land Area	35,510 sq mi; 91,971 sq km
Population	5.3 million
Ethnic Group(s)	Arab, Circassian, Armenian
Religion(s)	Muslim, Christian
Government	constitutional monarchy
Currency	Jordanian dinar
Leading Exports	phosphate, fertilizers, potash, agricultural products, manufactured goods, pharmaceuticals
Language(s)	Arabic (official)

Jordan (JAWRD un) is a Southwest Asian country located northwest of Saudi Arabia. After gaining its independence from the British in 1946, the country was ruled for more than forty years by King Hussein. King Hussein successfully led his country through many important reforms, including the establishment of parliamentary elections and a peace treaty with Israel. After his death in 1999, King Hussein's son, Abdullah, took the throne and continued working to bring economic reforms. Jordan's economy is based on the export of phosphate, tourism, and shipping. Phosphate is used to make fertilizer.

Kazakhstan

Capital	Astana
Land Area	1,030,810 sq mi; 2,669,800 sq km
Population	16.7 million
Ethnic Group(s)	Kazakh, Russian, Ukrainian, Uzbek, Uighur
Religion(s)	Muslim, Christian
Government	republic
Currency	tenge
Leading Exports	oil and oil products, ferrous metals, machinery, chemicals, grain, wool, meat, coal
Language(s)	Kazakh (official), Russian, Uighur, Korean, German

Kazakhstan (kah zahk STAHN) is a former Soviet republic, located northwest of China, that struggles to find its national identity. The native people of the area are descendants of Turkic and Mongol tribes who for years did not think of themselves as a nation. Russia conquered these peoples in the 1700s. During the mid-1900s, many Soviet citizens came to cultivate the country's northern pastures as part of a governmental agricultural project. After the country gained independence in 1991, some of these native Russians left. Today, the country is moving quickly to establish a market economy as well as a national identity.

Kuwait

Capital	Kuwait City
Land Area	6,880 sq mi; 17,820 sq km
Population	2.1 million
Ethnic Group(s)	Arab, South Asian
Religion(s)	Muslim, Christian, Hindu, traditional beliefs
Government	nominal constitutional monarchy
Currency	Kuwaiti dinar
Leading Exports	oil and refined products, fertilizers
Language(s)	Arabic (official), English

Kuwait (koo WAYT) is a small country on the Persian Gulf. Its neighbors are Iran, Iraq, and Saudi Arabia. Mainly desert, the country has large oil and gas reserves. Ninety-five percent of its export earnings are from oil. In 1990, Kuwait was invaded by neighboring Iraq. The United States and other countries came to Kuwait's defense in a conflict known as the Persian Gulf War. After the war ended in 1991, Kuwait spent billions on repairs to its oil infrastructure and built a wall on its Iraqi border.

Kuwaitis celebrating the end of the Persian Gulf War

Introducing South, Southwest, and Central Asia

Kyrgyzstan

Capital	Bishkek
Land Area	73,861 sq mi; 191,300 sq km
Population	4.8 million
Ethnic Group(s)	Kyrgyz, Russian, Uzbek, Tatar, Ukrainian
Religion(s)	Muslim, Christian
Government	republic
Currency	som
Leading Exports	cotton, wool, meat, tobacco, gold, mercury, uranium, hydropower, machinery, shoes
Language(s)	Kyrgyz (official), Russian (official)

Kyrgyzstan (kihr gih STAN) is a mountainous Central Asian country located west of China. In the late 1800s, Kyrgyzstan was annexed by Russia. It gained its independence from the Soviet Union more than one hundred years later. Currently, Kyrgyzstan's rural population is growing faster than its urban population. The country is agriculturally self-sufficient, which gives it an economic advantage. Kyrgyzstan is focused on many of the same issues that face other nations in the region. These include improving its economy and making democratic reforms.

Lebanon

Capital	Beirut
Land Area	3,950 sq mi; 10,230 sq km
Population	3.7 million
Ethnic Group(s)	Arab, Armenian
Religion(s)	Muslim, Christian
Government	republic
Currency	Lebanese pound
Leading Exports	foodstuffs, textiles, chemicals, metal products, electrical products, jewelry, paper products
Language(s)	Arabic (official), French, Armenian, Assyrian

Lebanon (LEB uh nahn) is a Southwest Asian nation on the Mediterranean Sea, bordered by Israel and Syria. Although it only became a nation in modern times, it has some of the world's most ancient human settlements. The country has a Muslim majority and a large minority of Christians. Lebanon has suffered from a 16-year civil war and an invasion by Israel in 1981. It faces many challenges as it tries to rebuild. Lebanon has one of the highest literacy rates in the region and is a vibrant economic and cultural center.

Maldives

Capital	Malé
Land Area	116 sq mi; 300 sq km
Population	320,165
Ethnic Group(s)	South Indian, Sinhalese, Arab
Religion(s)	Muslim
Government	republic
Currency	rufiyaa
Leading Exports	fish, clothing
Language(s)	Dhivehi (Maldivian)

Maldives (MAL dyvz) is a group of about 1,300 islands in the Indian Ocean southwest of India. Today, only about 200 of these small coral islands are inhabited. Located at the center of Arab trade routes, the islands were a stopping place for Arab traders who brought Islam with them. For much of their history, the Maldives were ruled by Muslim sultans, but the islands became a British protectorate in 1887. The country gained independence from the British in 1965. A major economic goal for the Maldives is the growth of a tourist trade.

Nepal

Capital	Kathmandu
Land Area	52,818 sq mi; 136,800 sq km
Population	25.9 million
Ethnic Group(s)	Brahman, Chetri, Newar, Gurung, Magar, Tamang, Rai, Limpu, Sherpa, Tharu
Religion(s)	Hindu, Buddhist, Muslim
Government	parliamentary democracy and constitutional monarchy
Currency	Nepalese rupee
Leading Exports	carpets, clothing, leather goods, jute goods, grain
Language(s)	Nepali (official), Maithilli, Bhojpuri

Nepal (nuh PAWL) is a country with a recent history of troubled leadership. Though a kingdom traditionally ruled by a series of royal families, in 1990 Nepal formed a multiparty government with a modern constitution. This began a period of political turmoil, including the killing of most of the royal family, a dissolved parliament, and the postponement of elections. The current king is working to resolve differences and hold elections once again. One of the poorest nations in the world, Nepal's economy depends on agriculture and the tourists who come to see the Himalayas that dominate the country's physical geography.

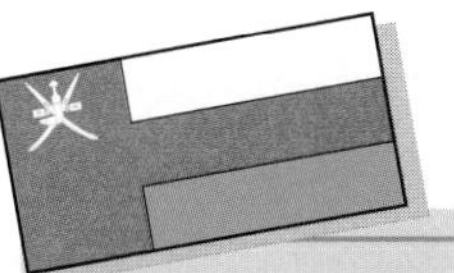

Oman

Capital	Muscat
Land Area	82,030 sq mi; 212,460 sq km
Population	2.7 million
Ethnic Group(s)	Arab, Baluchi, South Asian, African
Religion(s)	Muslim, Hindu
Government	monarchy
Currency	Omani rial
Leading Exports	petroleum, reexports, fish, metals, textiles
Language(s)	Arabic (official), Baluchi

Oman (oh MAHN) shares a western border with Yemen, the United Arab Emirates, and Saudi Arabia. To the east, it is bordered by the Arabian Sea, the Gulf of Oman, and the Persian Gulf. The nation is ruled by a monarch. Although the country is the least developed of the Persian Gulf nations, the current sultan's efforts to modernize have increased Oman's standing in the international community. Oil exports have brought some prosperity to Oman. The country also has a large fishing industry.

Pakistan

Capital	Islamabad
Land Area	300,664 sq mi; 778,720 sq km
Population	147.7 million
Ethnic Group(s)	Punjabi, Sindhi, Pashtun (Pathan), Baloch, Muhajir
Religion(s)	Muslim, Christian, Hindu
Government	federal republic
Currency	Pakistani rupee
Leading Exports	textiles (clothing, cotton cloth, and yarn), rice, other agricultural products
Language(s)	Urdu (official), Punjabi, Sindhi, Pashtu, Baluchi, Brahui

Pakistan (PAK ih stan) is a nation with a history of conflict among its many religious and ethnic groups. Pakistan is located on the shores of the Arabian Sea with India to the east, Iran and Afghanistan to the west, and China to the north. Pakistan was created in 1947, when tensions between Muslims and Hindus caused the British to divide British India into Muslim Pakistan and mostly-Hindu India. In 1971, East Pakistan became the separate country of Bangladesh. Tensions with India have continued since Pakistan was created. At the end of the 1900s, Pakistan began testing nuclear weapons.

Introducing South, Southwest, and Central Asia

Qatar

Capital	Doha
Land Area	4,416 sq mi; 11,437 sq km
Population	793,341
Ethnic Group(s)	Arab, South Asian
Religion(s)	Muslim
Government	traditional monarchy
Currency	Qatari riyal
Leading Exports	petroleum products, fertilizers, steel
Language(s)	Arabic (official)

Qatar (kah TAHR) is an oil-rich monarchy on the northeastern tip of the Arabian Peninsula. The country is a small peninsula in the Persian Gulf. A single family has ruled Qatar since the mid-1800s. With plentiful oil and natural gas resources, Qatar is one of the wealthiest nations in Southwest Asia and provides free health care and education to its citizens. It has a large immigrant population, made up of people from northern Africa, the Indian subcontinent, and Iran, who come to Qatar to work in the oil industry.

Saudi Arabia

Capital	Riyadh and Jiddah
Land Area	756,981 sq mi; 1,960,582 sq km
Population	23.5 million
Ethnic Group(s)	Arab, mixed black and Asian
Religion(s)	Muslim
Government	monarchy
Currency	Saudi riyal
Leading Exports	petroleum and petroleum products
Language(s)	Arabic (official)

Saudi Arabia (SAW dee uh RAY bee uh) is an oil-rich nation bordering the Red Sea and the Persian Gulf north of Yemen. Medina and Mecca, two of Islam's holiest cities, are located in Saudi Arabia. This large country is more than 95 percent desert, but oil discovered there in the 1930s quickly brought it into a position of economic power. In 1990, Saudi Arabia received 400,000 Kuwaiti refugees following Iraq's invasion of Kuwait. It played a key role as a launching point for the United States-led military effort to free Kuwait from Iraqi occupation. Today, the royal family of Saudi Arabia faces the issues of a growing population and a petroleum-dominated economy.

Sri Lanka

Capital	Colombo
Land Area	24,996 sq mi; 64,740 sq km
Population	19.6 million
Ethnic Group(s)	Sinhalese, Tamil, Moor, Burgher, Malay, Vedda
Religion(s)	Buddhist, Hindu, Christian, Muslim
Government	republic
Currency	Sri Lankan rupee
Leading Exports	textiles and clothing, tea, diamonds, coconut products, petroleum products
Language(s)	Sinhala (official), Tamil (official), English (official), Sinhalese-Tamil

Sri Lanka (sree LAHNG kuh) is made up of a large island and several small coral islands in the Indian Ocean off the coast of India. This small nation was controlled by other countries until 1948, when it finally gained its independence. Independence did not, however, bring stability to the country. Civil war between the majority Sinhalese group, made up of Buddhists, and the minority Tamil group, made up mainly of Hindus and Muslims, has raged for more than 20 years. A land of great physical and cultural diversity, Sri Lanka is the world's largest exporter of tea.

A lace shop at an outdoor market in Syria

Syria

Capital	Damascus
Land Area	71,062 sq mi; 184,050 sq km
Population	17.2 million
Ethnic Group(s)	Arab, Kurd, Armenian
Religion(s)	Muslim, Christian
Government	republic under military regime
Currency	Syrian pound
Leading Exports	crude oil, textiles, fruits and vegetables, raw cotton
Language(s)	Arabic (official), French, Kurdish, Armenian, Circassian, Turkic languages, Assyrian, Aramaic

Syria (SIHR ee uh) is a Southwest Asian country on the shores of the Mediterranean Sea, between Lebanon and Turkey. After World War I, the French controlled Syria until its independence in 1946. Since that time, Syria has been governed by a series of military leaders. The country opposes its neighbor, Israel, to whom it lost an area known as the Golan Heights in 1967 during the Arab-Israeli War. Though Syria has large oil supplies, much of its income from oil is spent on military defense.

Tajikistan

Capital	Dushanbe
Land Area	55,096 sq mi; 142,700 sq km
Population	6.7 million
Ethnic Group(s)	Tajik, Uzbek, Russian
Religion(s)	Muslim
Government	republic
Currency	somoni
Leading Exports	aluminum, electricity, cotton, fruits, vegetable oil, textiles
Language(s)	Tajiki (official), Russian

Tajikistan (tah jik ih STAN) is a struggling former Soviet republic located in Central Asia. After gaining independence from the Soviet Union in 1991, the nation went through a five-year civil war and three changes in government. The country has 14 percent of the world's uranium reserves, but has not successfully developed this resource. Tajikistan faces many challenges, including an unstable economy, poor health care, and continuing conflict among ethnic groups.

Introducing South, Southwest, and Central Asia

Turkey

Capital	Ankara
Land Area	297,590 sq mi; 770,760 sq km
Population	67.3 million
Ethnic Group(s)	Turkish, Kurd
Religion(s)	Muslim
Government	republican parliamentary democracy
Currency	Turkish lira
Leading Exports	clothing, foodstuffs, textiles, metal manufactured goods, trasport equipment
Language(s)	Turkish (official), Kurdish, Arabic, Circassian, Armenian, Greek, Georgian, Ladino

Turkey (TUR kee) is a primarily Muslim country that straddles two continents—Asia and Europe. Its location on the Black Sea and Mediterranean Sea has always made it a crossroads of trade and culture. Turkey has a strong economy and has great influence in the region. However, a major fault line leaves many Turkish cities vulnerable to earthquakes. The country's two main ethnic groups, Turks and Kurds, are in conflict. Many Kurds seek to form their own state.

Turkmenistan

Capital	Ashgabat
Land Area	188,455 sq mi; 488,100 sq km
Population	4.7 million
Ethnic Group(s)	Turkmen, Uzbek, Russian, Kazakh
Religion(s)	Muslim, Christian
Government	republic
Currency	manat
Leading Exports	gas, oil, cotton fiber, textiles
Language(s)	Turkmen (official), Uzbek, Russian

Turkmenistan (turk MEN ih stan) is a former Soviet republic which borders the Caspian Sea between Kazakhstan and Iran. Turkmenistan is mostly desert. Only 2 percent of the total land area is suitable for agriculture. The country gained its independence in 1991 and formed a democracy, but the president exercises complete control over the government. Culturally, Turkmenistan is dominated by Sunni Muslims. It has abundant natural gas reserves and is currently working to improve its ability to extract and transport this valuable resource.

United Arab Emirates

Capital	Abu Dhabi
Land Area	32,000 sq mi; 82,880 sq km
Population	2.4 million
Ethnic Group(s)	Arab, South Asian
Religion(s)	Muslim
Government	federation
Currency	UAE dirham
Leading Exports	crude oil, natural gas, reexports, dried fish, dates
Language(s)	Arabic (official), Farsi, Indian and Pakistani languages, English

The United Arab Emirates (yoo NYT id AR ub EM ur uts) was created when seven Southwest Asian states united as a single nation. The United Arab Emirates (UAE) is bordered by the Gulf of Oman and the Persian Gulf between Saudi Arabia and Oman. The UAE is mostly desert. With few water resources, the country relies on an extensive irrigation system. The UAE is rich in oil and natural gas resources. It has a strong economy and good health care and education. It has taken on an important role in the affairs of the region.

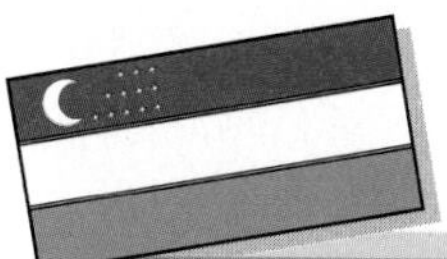

Uzbekistan

Capital	Tashkent
Land Area	164,247 sq mi; 425,400 sq km
Population	25.5 million
Ethnic Group(s)	Uzbek, Russian, Tajik, Kazakh, Karakalpak, Tatar
Religion(s)	Muslim, Christian
Government	republic
Currency	som
Leading Exports	cotton, gold, energy products, mineral fertilizers, ferrous metals, textiles, food products, automobiles
Language(s)	Arabic (official)

Uzbekistan (ooz bek ih STAN) is a former Soviet republic in Central Asia north of Afghanistan. Conquered by Russia in the late 1800s, it came under Communist control in 1924. Heavy growing of cotton and grain by the Soviet Union depleted its water supplies and polluted the land in many areas. Since it gained its independence in 1991, Uzbekistan has looked to develop its extensive mineral and oil resources. However, the country's economy still depends on agriculture. Uzbekistan is one of the largest exporters of cotton in the world.

Yemen

Capital	Sana
Land Area	203,849 sq mi; 527,970 sq km
Population	18.7 million
Ethnic Group(s)	Arab, mixed black and Arab, South Asian
Religion(s)	Muslim
Government	republic
Currency	Yemeni rial
Leading Exports	crude oil, coffee, dried and salted fish
Language(s)	Arabic

Yemen (YEM un) is located at the southern tip of the Arabian Peninsula. Bordered by Saudi Arabia and Oman, it occupies a fertile strip along the Red Sea. Yemen's recent history is one of conflict, including years of civil war that led to the country being divided in half. In 1990, the country was reunited, but still remains politically unstable. Yemen has large oil, gas, and mineral reserves. Agriculture continues to support most of the population.

SOURCES: DK World Desk Reference Online; CIA World Factbook Online, 2002; *World Almanac*, 2003

Assessment

Comprehension and Critical Thinking

1. **Identify** What is the most common ethnic group in the region?
2. **Apply Information** What is the language in countries that include this ethnic group?
3. **Draw Conclusions** What are the characteristics that most of the countries share?
4. **Contrast** What are some key differences among the countries?
5. **Summarize** In which region is petroleum a leading export, South Asia or Southwest Asia?
6. **Make a Bar Graph** Create a bar graph showing the population of the four most populous countries in this region.

Keeping Current

Access the **DK World Desk Reference Online** at **PHSchool.com** for up-to-date information about the countries in this chapter.

Web Code: **lce-6800**

Section 1

India

In the Midst of Change

Prepare to Read

Objectives

In this section you will

1. Learn about key features of India's population.
2. Examine the state of India's economy.
3. Understand major challenges facing India.

Taking Notes

As you read this section, look for ways in which India's growing population has an effect on its development. Copy the chart below, and record your findings in it.

CAUSE	EFFECTS
• India's population is growing.	•

Target Reading Skill

Identify Causes and Effects Identifying causes and effects helps you understand how events and situations are related. A cause makes something happen. An effect is what happens as a result. As you read this section, think of India's growing population as a cause. What are the effects of this cause on India's development?

Key Terms

- **textiles** (TEKS tylz) *n.* cloth made by weaving or by knitting
- **malnutrition** (mal noo TRISH un) *n.* poor nutrition caused by a lack of food or an unbalanced diet
- **life expectancy** (lyf ek SPEK tun see) *n.* the average number of years a person is expected to live
- **literacy rate** (LIT ur uh see rayt) *n.* the percentage of a population age 15 and over that can read and write

Students at a private school for boys in Rajasthan, India

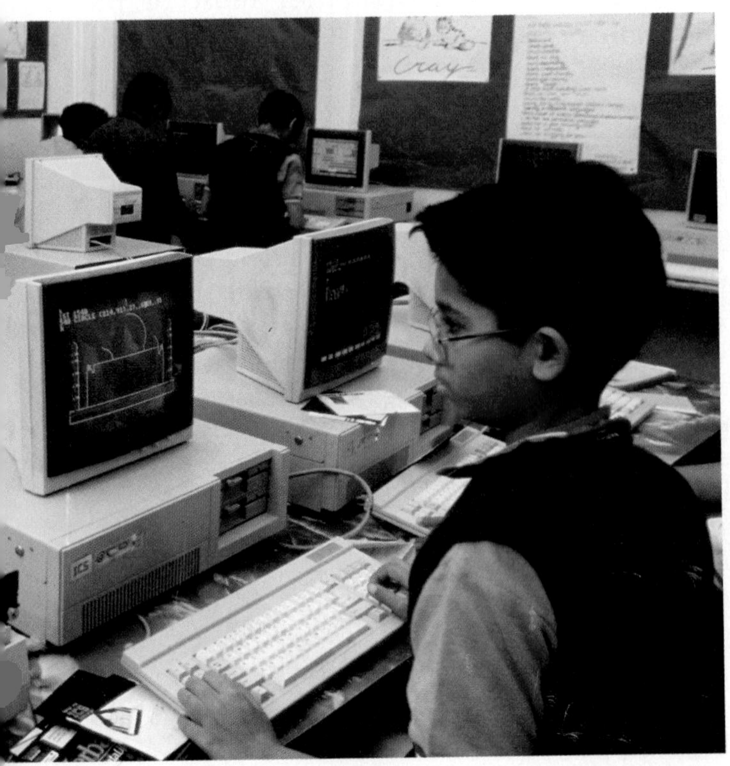

In Chapter 7, you read that the gross domestic product (GDP) is the total value of all the goods and services produced in an economy. India's gross domestic product is $2.6 trillion. This makes India's GDP the fourth highest in the world. Yet the standard of living in India is very low compared with many other countries, even though India's GDP is higher. This is because India's $2.6 trillion is shared by more than one billion people. If you divided that $2.6 trillion by India's population, each person would have about $2,500. By comparison, Germany's GDP is about $2 trillion. But Germany has a much lower population than India has. If you divided Germany's $2 trillion by its population, each person would have about $24,000.

India's large population presents many challenges to the country. At the same time, India's people are an important resource in the drive to develop the country.

India's Middle Class
Although about one fourth of India's population is poor, India has a growing middle class that earns enough money to spend on consumer goods from pizza to cars. The growth of India's middle class is one result of its growing economy. **Analyze Images** *Do you think this photo shows an urban area or a rural area? Explain your answer.*

Key Features of India's Population

India is the second-most-populated country in the world. Only China's population is bigger. India's population is changing in ways that affect the country's development.

A Growing Population India has a population of more than one billion people. This large population is growing. India has one of the world's highest population growth rates. By 2050, India is expected to be the world's most populated country.

Growing Urban Areas About 72 percent of India's population lives in rural areas. But with such a large population, that means nearly 300 million people were living in urban areas in 2000. By 2030, the urban population of India is expected to reach more than 600 million. Using 2002 population figures, that equals the combined total populations of the United States, Brazil, and Russia.

An Expanding Middle Class About one fourth of India's people lives in poverty. They earn just enough money to buy the food they need to survive. In recent years, however, India's middle class has been growing. People in the middle class are neither very rich nor very poor. They earn enough money to buy goods and services that improve their lives. By some estimates, India's middle class is one of the largest in the world.

√ Reading Check **What are some key features of India's population?**

Discovery
CHANNEL
SCHOOL
Video
Learn about the effects of India's caste system.

A worker checks electronic circuit boards in Bangalore (large photo); other workers assemble watches (small photo).

A Growing Economy

India has the second-fastest-growing economy in Asia. Only China's economy is growing faster. A democratic government supports India's economy. In the early 1990s, the government made changes to speed economic progress. For example, the government made it easier for foreign companies to do business in India. India's middle class helps the economy, too. The middle class provides a huge market for goods and services produced and sold in India. As the middle class grows, the number of poor people in India is expected to decrease.

Expanding industries in India are also helping the country's economy. One of India's major industries is computer software programming. India has large numbers of highly educated and skilled workers in the computer software industry. India's computer software has become a major export. Products such as electrical appliances are being manufactured in greater numbers. India also has a thriving film industry. More movies are produced in India than in any other country.

India imports more than it exports, but the country can produce all its own food. India exports **textiles,** or cloth, making cotton and silk clothing that are sold worldwide. Gemstones and jewelry are another major export. The United States buys the largest share of India's exports.

√ Reading Check **What are some major industries in India?**

COUNTRY PROFILE Focus on Culture

India

India has great cultural diversity, or variety. Most Indians are Hindus. As you can see on the map, however, Muslims, followers of Islam, are a majority in one of India's states. But there are Muslims in every other state in India. Millions of Indians practice Christianity, Sikhism, and other religions. Indians also speak hundreds of different languages. Hindi has more speakers than any other language in India. However, many other languages have millions of speakers, and most Indians speak a language other than Hindi.

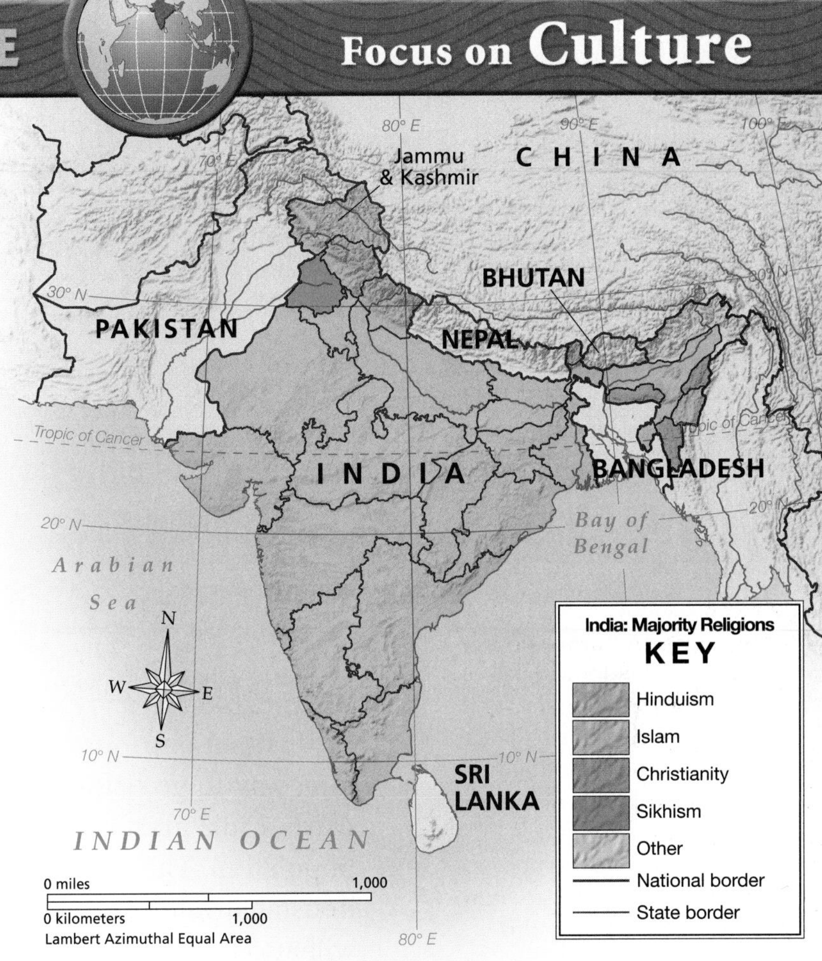

Religions

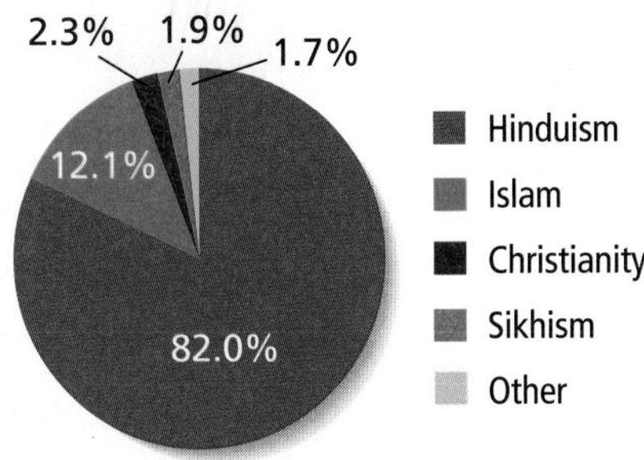

SOURCE: Census of India, 1991

Where Muslims Live

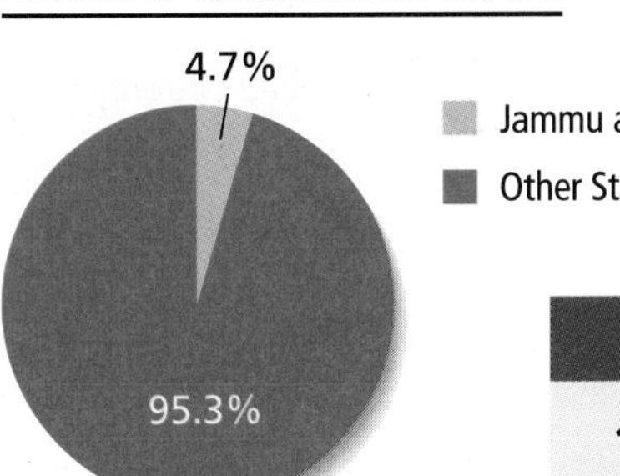

SOURCE: Census of India, 1991

Languages

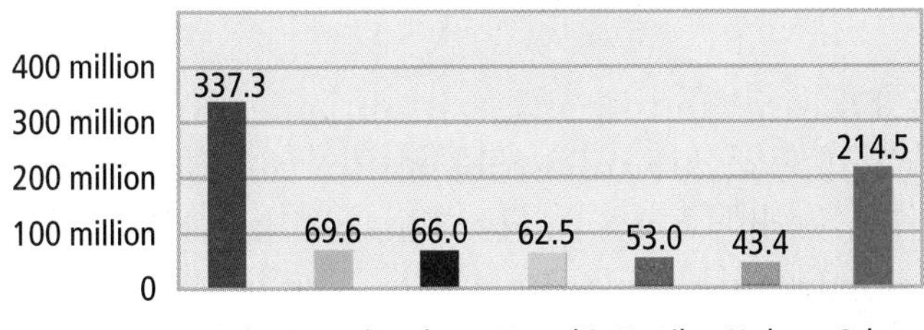

SOURCE: Census of India, 1991

Map and Chart Skills

1. **Locate** Which is the only state on the map with a Muslim majority?
2. **Note** Based on the graphs, what percentage of India's Muslims live in that state?
3. **Infer** Would you expect states with a Hindu majority to have many people belonging to other religions?

Use Web Code **lce-6801** for **DK World Desk Reference Online.**

Wind Power and Camel Power
India is a world leader in wind energy production. In many rural villages, however, people still use traditional methods to obtain power. At the right, a camel turns a wheel that pumps water.
Identify Effects *India's monsoons bring strong winds to much of the country. How does this affect the potential to create electricity from wind power?*

Progress and Challenges

With about one fourth of its people living in poverty, India has a long way to go before all of its people enjoy higher living standards. India must meet the challenge of taking care of its growing population. The millions of people born each year will need jobs, housing, health care, and education. Food, water, and electricity will also be in higher demand. Another challenge facing India is its relations with its neighbor Pakistan.

Tensions Between India and Pakistan Kashmir is an area of land on the northern borders of India and Pakistan. Since becoming independent in 1947, India and Pakistan have both claimed Kashmir as part of their territory. The disagreement over Kashmir has led to fighting between the two countries. Tensions grew worse after India tested nuclear weapons in 1998. Pakistan responded by holding its own nuclear weapons tests. Fighting broke out again in Kashmir in 2003, followed by more weapons tests by both countries. Although both countries agreed to begin talks to peacefully settle the dispute over Kashmir, violence continues to trouble the region.

Identify Causes and Effects
What effects can a growing population have on the need for jobs, education, and housing?

Health Care Disease and **malnutrition,** or poor nutrition caused by a lack of food, are still problems for millions of Indian people. Yet progress has been made. The country has not suffered from major famine since the 1940s. The government has taken steps to improve health care. More government-paid doctors work in rural areas. The government has also launched programs that protect people from certain diseases.

As a result of these efforts, people in India are living longer. The average life expectancy in India has increased from 53 years in 1981 to 63 years in 2003. **Life expectancy** is the average number of years a person is expected to live. It is an important measure of how well a country is caring for its citizens.

People in India, like these young students, benefit from being educated.

Education Another way that is used to measure how well a country is taking care of its people is the literacy rate. A country's **literacy rate** shows the percentage of the population age 15 and over that can read and write. India's literacy rate is far lower than the literacy rate in the United States, but it is rapidly rising. In 1991, just over 50 percent of India's population were literate. In 2001, the literacy rate had risen to about 65 percent. Thanks to ongoing efforts to improve education, India's literacy rate is continuing to rise.

√ Reading Check **How has India improved health care and education for its people?**

Section 1 Assessment

Key Terms

Review the key terms at the beginning of this section. Use each term in a sentence that explains its meaning.

Target Reading Skill

Using your Taking Notes chart, identify three effects of India's growing population.

Comprehension and Critical Thinking

1. (a) Recall What is the population of India?
(b) Find Main Ideas Why is India expected to be the world's most populated country by 2050?
(c) Identify Effects One effect of rapid urban growth is increased pollution. What might be some other effects of India's rapid urban growth?

2. (a) Note How does India's middle class help the country's economy?
(b) Identify Causes What are some other factors that are helping India's economy?

3. (a) Explain How have changes in health care increased life expectancy in India?
(b) Predict Give some reasons that a nation would want its citizens to read and write.

Writing Activity

Write an entry in your journal describing some of the challenges India must meet to take care of its growing population. Be sure to consider such factors as food and health care. Which of these challenges do you think is most important? Give one or two reasons for your answer.

For: An activity on India
Visit: PHSchool.com
Web Code: lcd-6801

Section 2

Pakistan

An Economy Based on Agriculture

Prepare to Read

Objectives

In this section you will

1. Find out that Pakistan's economy is based on agriculture.
2. Learn about Pakistan's industries.

Taking Notes

As you read this section, look for ways in which Pakistan's water supply has affected its economy. Copy the chart below, and record your findings in it.

CAUSE	EFFECTS
• Water is in short supply in Pakistan.	•

Target Reading Skill

Understand Effects A cause makes something happen. An effect is what happens as the result of a specific cause. Sometimes one cause may produce several effects. As you read this section, note the effects of Pakistan's water supply on its economy. Write the effects in the Taking Notes chart.

Key Terms

- **drought** (drowt) *n.* a long period of dry weather
- **Green Revolution** (green rev uh LOO shun) *n.* a worldwide effort to increase food production in developing countries
- **self-sufficient** (self suh FISH unt) *adj.* able to supply one's own needs without any outside assistance
- **tributary** (TRIB yoo tehr ee) *n.* a river that flows into a larger river

Tarbela Dam on the Indus River provides water for irrigation.

Rainfall is scarce throughout much of Pakistan. What water the country gets is a precious resource. Pakistan's water supply includes three main sources: the Indus River, monsoon rains, and slow-melting glaciers. To make the most of its water supply, Pakistan built the world's largest irrigation system. Without rainfall, however, the gigantic system of dams, canals, ditches, and reservoirs cannot deliver the water needed for Pakistan's farms.

In 2001, Pakistan was in the middle of an extreme **drought**—a long period of dry weather. The government was so concerned over the lack of water that it considered melting part of the glaciers in northern Pakistan. One idea was to spray on charcoal, which would raise the temperature of the ice. Later that year, however, the government decided to give up the plan due to environmental concerns.

An Agricultural Nation

Pakistan's economy is based mostly on agriculture. That is why water is so important there. About half of Pakistan's labor force works in agriculture.

Farming Most of Pakistan's farming takes place in the Indus River basin, where the irrigation system is located. Cotton, wheat, sugar cane, and rice are grown there. Pakistan is among the world's top ten cotton producers. Farmers in Pakistan grow so much rice that the country exports it to other countries.

Wheat is the major food crop in Pakistan. The green revolution has helped Pakistan's farmers grow more wheat. Starting in the 1940s, **the Green Revolution** was a worldwide effort to increase food production in developing countries, including Pakistan and India. The program introduced modern farming methods and special varieties of wheat, rice, and corn that yielded more grain. The year 2000 was the first year in recent history that Pakistan did not have to import wheat. Instead, the country had enough wheat to export its extra to Afghanistan. Becoming self-sufficient in wheat production and having enough to export are major goals in Pakistan. Being **self-sufficient** means Pakistan can supply its own goods without outside assistance.

Wheat Harvest in Pakistan
Although most of Pakistan's wheat is used for food within the country, Pakistan succeeded in exporting wheat for the first time in 2000. **Analyze Images** *How does the lack of modern farm machinery indicate that this wheat was raised by a subsistence farmer?*

Discovery
CHANNEL
SCHOOL
Video
Learn about Pakistan's efforts to improve education.

Target Skill **Understand Effects** In this section, look for details about what happens in Pakistan because of the limited water supply. What are the effects of Pakistan's limited water supply?

Managing the Water Supply Pakistan's farmers use thousands of canals and ditches to move water from the Indus River and its tributaries to their fields. A **tributary** is a river that flows into a larger river. In this way, farmers maintain a steady flow of water, even during droughts. As more land is irrigated, more acres are farmed. This increases the amount of crops.

Irrigation solves many farming problems, but it creates others. For example, river water contains small amounts of salts. When water evaporates, the salts are left behind. Over time, salts build up in the soil, causing plant growth to slow. Pakistani scientists are trying to find a way to treat the salt-damaged soil. They are also working to develop a type of wheat that can grow in salty soil.

Pakistanis have another water problem, one that is the opposite of drought. During the monsoon season, damaging floods can occur. One solution is the large dams built by the government. The dams catch and hold monsoon rains. The waters are then released, as needed, into irrigation canals.

Links Across The World

Cricket One of the most popular sports in Pakistan is cricket. Played with a bat and a ball, cricket is a team sport widely played in Great Britain and in former colonies of the British Empire. Cricket is also popular in India, Bangladesh, Sri Lanka, Australia, and New Zealand. Like Pakistan, these countries were once British territories. In 1992, Pakistan's international cricket team won the Cricket World Cup.

✓ Reading Check **How has irrigation helped Pakistan develop an economy based on agriculture?**

Industry in Pakistan

In addition to helping farmers, dams such as the Tarbela—on the Indus River in northern Pakistan—speed industrial growth. Dams capture the energy of rushing water to create hydroelectricity. In Pakistan, hydroelectric power plants produce electricity to run textile mills and other factories. Most industry is located near the sources of hydroelectric power, on the plains of the Indus River.

Making steel at a small factory near Lahore, Pakistan

COUNTRY PROFILE

Focus on Culture

Pakistan

As the map and graphs show, Pakistan has several different ethnic groups, whose members speak several different languages. However, Islam is very much the dominant religion. Islam is the majority religion for every major ethnic group in Pakistan. Only very small minorities practice religions other than Islam.

A Pashtun woman in Pakistan

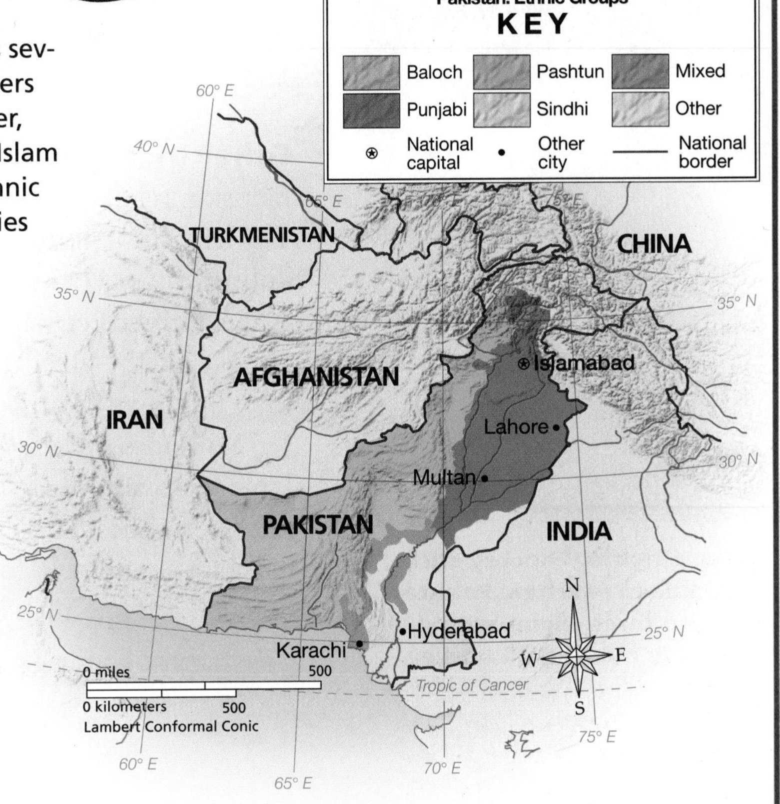

Religions

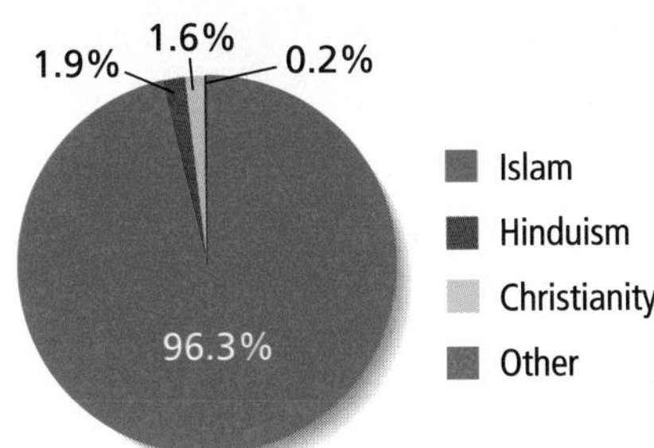

Languages

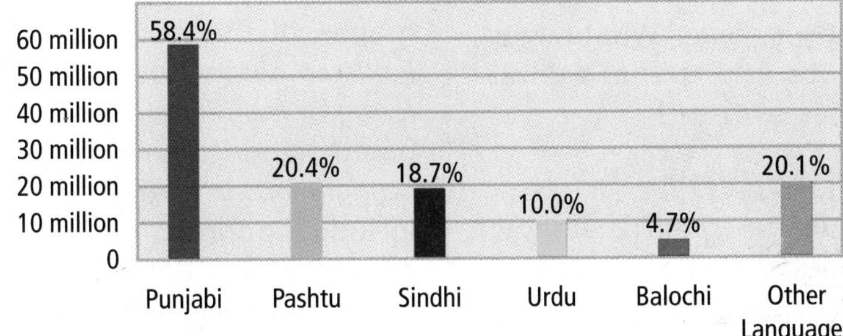

SOURCE: Pakistan Statistics Division, 1998

Map and Chart Skills

1. **Locate** Based on the map, which two languages are spoken across the largest areas of Pakistan?
2. **Identify** Based on the graph, which of these languages has the most speakers?
3. **Synthesize** What might explain why one language has so many more speakers, even though both are spoken across areas of similar size?

Use Web Code **Ice-6802** for **DK World Desk Reference Online.**

Top-quality field hockey sticks are made in Pakistan. Pakistan has won three Olympic gold medals in men's field hockey.

Industry Based on Agriculture Pakistan began its growth in industry by building on what its people knew best: agriculture. Today, Pakistan's economy depends largely on its textile industry. More than 60 percent of the country's exports come from the textile industry. Pakistan's textile products include yarn, cloth, and garments made from cotton grown by the country's farmers.

Other Industries in Pakistan Although most industries in Pakistan relate to farming, the nation has other industries as well. The chemical industry produces paint, soap, dye, and insect-killing sprays. Pakistan uses one of its natural resources, limestone, to make cement. Several steel mills allow Pakistan to make almost all the steel it needs. Producing steel can be less costly than buying it from other countries.

Millions of Pakistanis work in small workshops instead of in large factories. Workshops produce field hockey sticks, furniture, knives, saddles, and carpets. Pakistan is famous for its beautiful carpets. Some sell for as much as $25,000 in Pakistan—and $50,000 in New York or London.

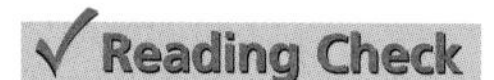

Give an example of an industry in Pakistan based on agriculture.

Section 2 Assessment

Key Terms

Review the key terms at the beginning of this section. Use each term in a sentence that explains its meaning.

Target Reading Skill

Describe two or more effects of Pakistan's water supply on the economy. Use the information in your Taking Notes chart.

Comprehension and Critical Thinking

1. (a) Recall Where does most of the farming in Pakistan take place?

(b) Summarize How did the green revolution help Pakistan's farmers grow more wheat?

(c) Identify Effects What is one negative effect of heavy irrigation in Pakistan?

2. (a) Explain How does Pakistan's textile industry help the country's economy?

(b) Identify Causes What factor explains why Pakistan has a developed textile industry?

Writing Activity

Write a brief paragraph that shows your understanding of how the people of Pakistan have responded to conditions in their physical environment. Be sure to include ways Pakistan has developed an economy based mainly on agriculture even though it has a dry climate.

Writing Tip Begin your paragraph with this topic sentence: *Pakistan has met the challenge of building an economy based on agriculture by developing a vast irrigation system.* Include supporting details about Pakistan's climate, the Indus River, Pakistan's irrigation system, and farming.

Section 3

Israel

Economics and Cultures

Prepare to Read

Objectives

In this section you will

1. Discover how Israel's economy has grown and changed over the years.
2. Learn about the different peoples living in Israel.

Taking Notes

As you read this section, look for the major ideas about the economy and cultures of Israel. Copy the diagram below, and record your findings in it.

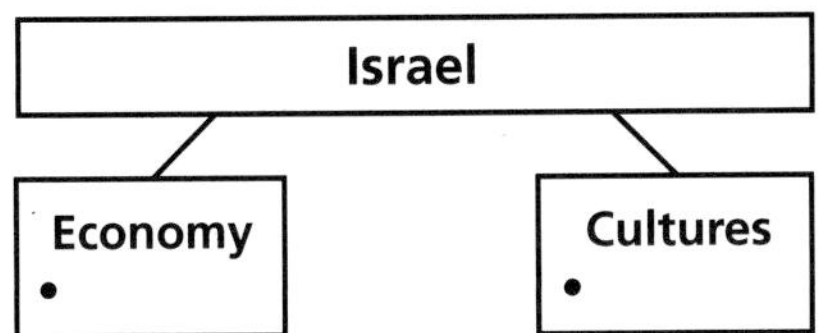

Target Reading Skill

Recognize Multiple Causes Sometimes multiple causes make one effect happen. As you read, look for three causes that have contributed to Israel's success in agriculture.

Key Terms

- **irrigation** (ihr uh GAY shun) *n.* the watering of crops using canals and other artificial waterways
- **kibbutz** (kih BOOTS) *n.* a cooperative settlement
- **West Bank** (west bank) *n.* a disputed region on the western bank of the Jordan River
- **Gaza Strip** (GAHZ uh strip) *n.* a disputed region on the Mediterranean coast

It is spring in the country of Israel. The khamsin (kam SEEN) has come. The khamsin is a wind—a hot wind—that blows into the country from the south. *Khamsin* means "wind of 50 days."

For many days, the hot khamsin will blow over a harsh landscape. The southern half of Israel is the unforgiving Negev Desert, an arid land of plains and mountains. As the wind continues north, it raises waves on a huge salt-water lake with little life. The lake is called the Dead Sea. The shore of the Dead Sea is the lowest spot on Earth. Rocky highlands lie north of the lake.

Israel is a rugged land, as harsh as the khamsin is hot. Yet the peoples of Israel have turned this dry and rocky place into a country with a modern economy and vibrant cultures.

Harvesting hay on a kibbutz in Galilee, Israel

Israel's Economy

Fresh water and land suitable for farming are in especially short supply in Israel. Historically, people in the region made their living by herding animals across the desert, not by farming.

Agriculture The people of Israel have managed to make farms in their desert. They grow fruits, vegetables, cotton, and other crops. How can they farm in a land with little water?

As in Pakistan, the answer is irrigation. **Irrigation** is the watering of crops using canals and other artificial waterways. Water from the Sea of Galilee, a freshwater lake in northern Israel, is pumped through a vast network of canals and pipelines. Other technological achievements have contributed to Israel's success in agriculture. During the 1950s, the Israelis drained Lake Hula, in northern Israel, and nearby swamps. This created an additional 12,000 acres of farmland.

Another factor in the success of Israeli agriculture has been cooperation among farm workers. Most of them live in small farming villages called *moshavim* (moh shah VEEM). The workers cooperate by combining their money to buy equipment and sharing information about new methods of farming. They also pool their crops to get a better price.

Manufacturing Today, about one in four Israelis work in manufacturing. Major Israeli industries include textiles, processed foods, fertilizers, and plastics. Many companies manufacture goods for the Israeli military. But most Israeli industry is in high technology. Israeli electronic and scientific equipment is respected around the world.

This woman is making electronic cash registers at a factory in Dimona, a town in the Negev Desert.

Kibbutzim Some manufacturing is done on cooperative settlements called kibbutzim. People who live on a **kibbutz** (kih BOOTS) cooperate in all parts of life. They eat together, work together, and share profits equally. Originally, most kibbutzim were farming communities. Today, modern farming machinery has replaced the need for many farm workers. As a result, many kibbutzim have turned to manufacturing.

COUNTRY PROFILE Focus on Government

Israel

Israel controls two types of land. The orange area on the map is Israel within its pre-1967 borders. This is the territory that the United States and other countries consider part of Israel. Its people are mostly Israeli Jews. Since 1967, Israel has controlled the lands known as the occupied territories, whose people are mostly non-Israeli Arabs. Including the occupied territories, Israel controls an area slightly larger than New Jersey, one of the smallest and most crowded U.S. states. Yet the population under Israeli control is larger than New Jersey's. Partly because there is so little land, there are sharp conflicts between Israelis and Arabs over control of this land.

Israel and the Occupied Territories: Population

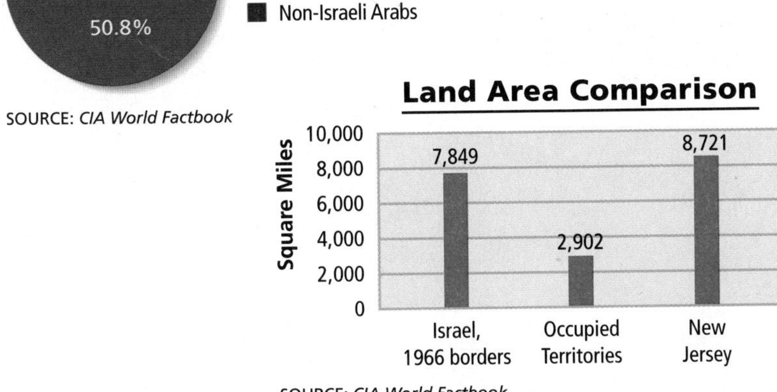

Map and Chart Skills

1. **Identify** Of the three areas under Israeli control, which is largest?
2. **Contrast** Which of these areas is the smallest?
3. **Synthesize** What percentage of the people under Israeli control are Arabs?

Use Web Code Ice-6803 for DK World Desk Reference Online.

Discovery
CHANNEL
SCHOOL
Video
Explore the city of Jerusalem in Israel.

Service Industries Today, service industries are the most important part of the Israeli economy. Service industries are industries that provide services instead of manufactured goods.

One type of service industry is trade. Israel borders the Mediterranean Sea. Its chief port city is Haifa, which has a deep-water harbor, excellent for docking ships. Many Israeli exports leave through Haifa. Many imports arrive there as well. Israel must import much of what it needs, since it has few natural resources. Imports include oil for energy and grain for food.

✓ Reading Check **What industry is the most important part of the Israeli economy?**

The People of Israel

Israel is home to about 6.5 million people. More than 90 percent of them live in cities. Israel's largest cities are Jerusalem, the manufacturing center of Tel Aviv, and the coastal city of Haifa.

Jews Today, about 80 percent of the people of Israel consider themselves to be Jews. Yet there is great diversity among Israeli Jews. When Israel was founded in 1948, most of the Jewish people who moved to Israel came from Europe and North America. They helped shape the culture and government of their new country. Because these people came from modern, developed countries, Israel became a modern, developed country, too.

Later, groups of Jews came from Middle Eastern countries. Beginning in the mid-1970s, tens of thousands of Ethiopian Jews from Africa have emigrated to Israel. More recently, many Jewish immigrants have come from Russia—nearly a million in the 1990s. Overall, nearly 3 million people have settled in Israel since the country was founded.

Children and teachers create crafts at a kibbutz daycare school in Israel.

Religious Diversity Most people in Israel practice Judaism. A small percentage of the country's population is Christian or follows other religions. The single largest religion after Judaism, however, is Islam. About 15 percent of Israel's population is Muslim.

Palestinian Arabs Most Muslims in Israel are Palestinian Arabs. Israel was founded in 1948 on land that was known as Palestine. Both Jews and Palestinian Arabs have long claimed Palestine as their homeland. In a series of wars with its Arab neighbors, Israel won portions of Egypt, Jordan, and Syria. Arabs called these areas the "occupied territories." Today, the occupied territories include the West Bank, the Gaza Strip, and the Golan Heights. The **West Bank** is an area on the west bank, or edge, of the Jordan River. The **Gaza Strip** is a small area of land along the Mediterranean Sea.

For decades, relations between the Palestinians and the Israelis have been marked by violence despite efforts on both sides to achieve peace. Several issues have divided the two groups. For example, many Palestinians whose families fled after the Arab-Israeli wars wanted to return to the land where their families had lived. Israelis have opposed the return of large numbers of Palestinians. Many Israelis insisted that a peace agreement protect Israeli settlements in the occupied territories. Palestinians, however, have opposed this idea.

A Palestinian open-air market in Jerusalem, Israel

✓ Reading Check **What is the single largest religion in Israel after Judaism?**

Section 3 Assessment

Key Terms

Review the key terms at the beginning of this section. Use each term in a sentence that explains its meaning.

Target Reading Skill

What are three causes of Israel's success in agriculture?

Comprehension and Critical Thinking

1. (a) Explain How can Israeli farmers grow crops in a desert?

(b) Main Idea What type of industry is most important to the Israeli economy?

(c) Synthesize Information Why do you think high technology has become an important part of the Israeli economy?

2. (a) Recall About what percentage of Israel's population is Muslim?

(b) Identify the Main Idea Give an example of the diversity among Israeli Jews.

Writing Activity

Would you enjoy living on a kibbutz? Write a paragraph that explains why or why not.

Writing Tip Give specific reasons for your explanation. Your first sentence should answer the basic question—whether or not you would like to live on a kibbutz. The following sentences should give specific reasons for your answer.

Section 4 Saudi Arabia
Oil and Islam

Prepare to Read

Objectives
In this section you will
1. Learn how oil has affected Saudi Arabia's development and economy.
2. Discover how Islam affects everyday life in Saudi Arabia.
3. Understand the main features of Saudi Arabia's government.

Taking Notes
As you read this section, look for ways in which oil and Islam have shaped Saudi Arabia. Copy the table below, and record your findings in it.

Oil	Islam
•	•
•	•

Target Reading Skill
Understand Effects
Sometimes one cause may produce several effects. As you read, note two effects of oil wealth on the development of Saudi Arabia. Write them in your Taking Notes chart.

Key Terms
- **hajj** (haj) *n.* a pilgrimage or journey to Mecca undertaken by Muslims during the month of the hajj
- **Quran** (koo RAHN) *n.* the holy book of Islam
- **monarchy** (MAHN ur kee) *n.* a state or a nation in which power is held by a monarch—a king, a queen, or an emperor

Kingdom Tower in Riyadh

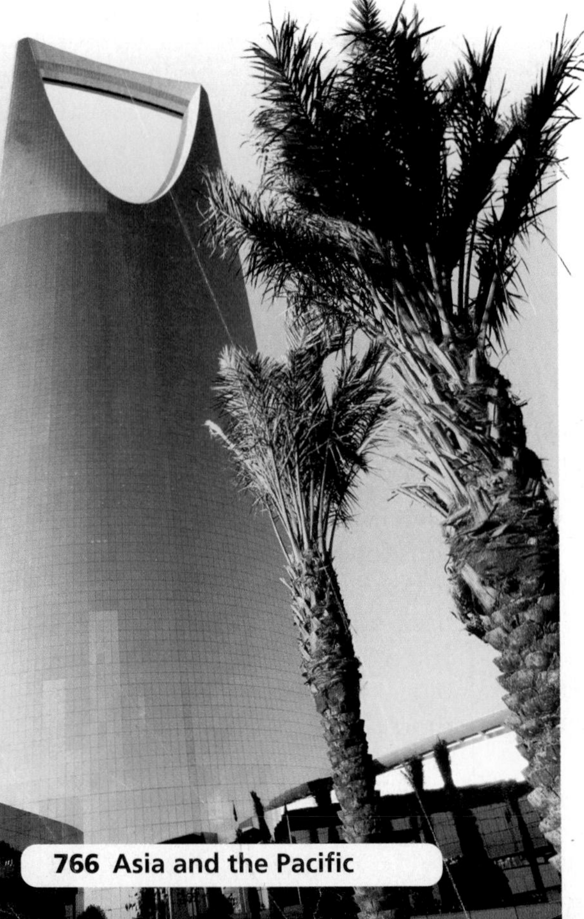

For more than a thousand years, Muslims from all over the world have been making pilgrimages to Mecca, Saudi Arabia. By going to Mecca, they honor the memory of Abraham, who is said to have built the first house of worship there. The pilgrimage to Mecca is called the **hajj** (haj). Muslims must make the hajj at least once in their lifetime. The hajj used to be long, hard, and dangerous. Muslims traveled across mountains and deserts by foot, horse, or camel to reach Mecca. Today, many pilgrims travel there by airplane. Roads link Mecca with other Saudi Arabian cities. Modern hotels line the streets of Mecca. Mecca is the birthplace of Islam's founder, Muhammad, and considered the holiest city in Islam.

Oil Wealth and Saudi Arabia

In 1900, Mecca was a very poor town. Saudi Arabia was one of the poorest countries in the world. Many of its people made a living by herding livestock. Like most of the countries of Southwest Asia, Saudi Arabia is mostly desert.

An Economy Based on Oil But in the 1930s, everything changed. People discovered oil in Southwest Asia. Oil reserves changed the fortunes of Saudi Arabia and several other countries in the region. It made them rich. When night falls in Riyadh (ree YAHD), Saudi Arabia's capital, the skyline begins to glow. The lights of the many apartment and office buildings flicker on. Large buildings line the city streets. When oil prices are high, buildings go up at a rapid pace. Money pours in, allowing communities like Riyadh to modernize. But when oil prices are down, the economy of the entire country is affected. Many large building projects grind to a stop.

Saudi Arabia has the most important oil economy in the world. Under its deserts lie more than 260 billion barrels of oil. Saudi Arabia has about one fourth of the world's oil. No other country on Earth exports more petroleum.

Target Skill **Understand Effects** How does the blue heading signal information on the effects of oil on Saudi Arabia's economy?

Changes From Oil Wealth Projects paid for with oil money have changed the lives of all Saudi Arabians. Beginning in the late 1960s, the Saudi Arabian government spent billions of dollars from oil sales to modernize the country. The Saudis built modern highways, airports, seaports, and a telephone system. Villages that had always depended on oil lamps were hooked up to electric power grids.

The nation's oil wealth made it possible to build a large school system. Saudi Arabia built thousands of schools. The country has eight major universities. In 1900, many Saudi Arabians could not read or write. But today, Saudi students are becoming doctors, scientists, and teachers.

√ Reading Check **About how much of the world's oil is in Saudi Arabia?**

Saudi and American men working at the Saudi American Bank in Riyadh

COUNTRY PROFILE

Focus on Economics

Saudi Arabia

Saudi Arabia has the world's largest known oil reserves. Its economy is heavily dependent on oil. As you can see on the map, much of Saudi Arabia's land area has little or no activity other than oil production. The rest of the land supports a thin population of nomadic herders. One result of Saudi Arabia's heavy dependence on oil is that its gross domestic product per capita, or the average value of goods and services per person, has not increased much over the years. This is because oil prices have been fairly steady in recent years. Although Saudi Arabia has increased oil production, its population has increased, too, so production per person has not changed much.

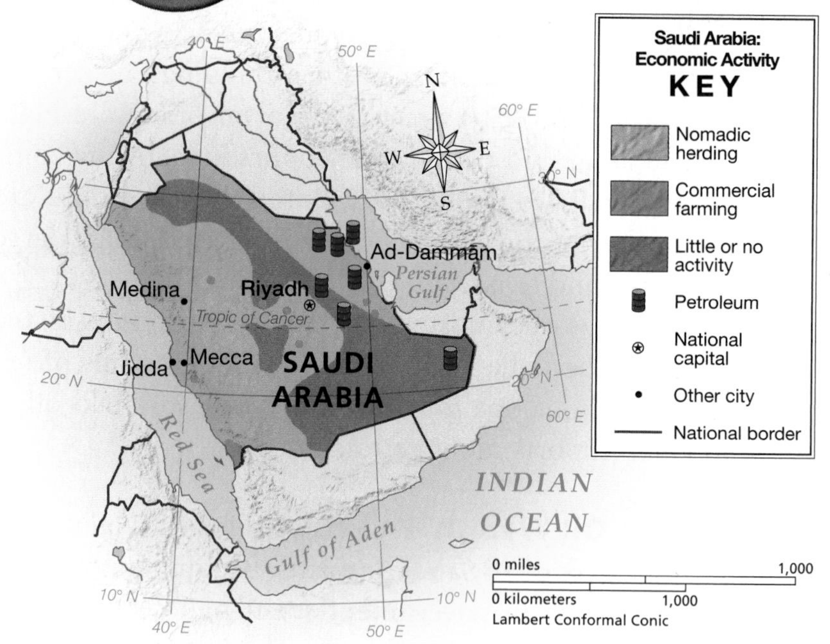

Exports

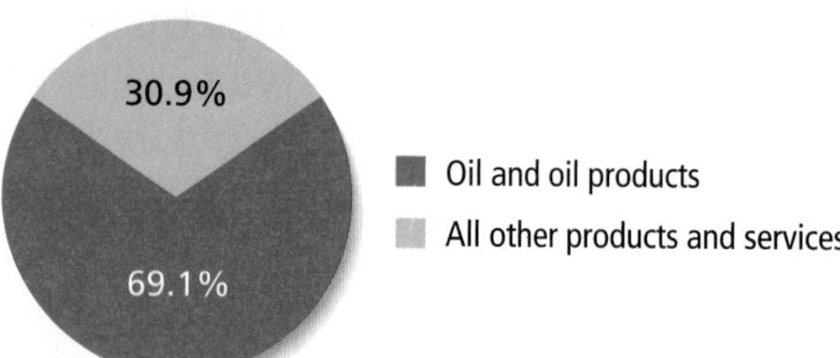

SOURCE: World Bank, 2002

Gross Domestic Product Per Capita, 1986–2002

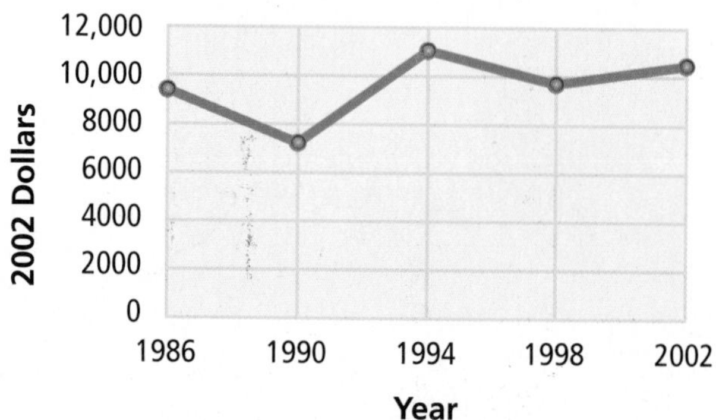

SOURCE: *The World Almanac;* United Nations Statistics Division

Map and Chart Skills

1. **Identify** What percentage of Saudi Arabia's exports is made up of oil and oil products?
2. **Infer** How does the map help to explain Saudi Arabia's dependence on oil?
3. **Predict** How would Saudi Arabia's economy be affected if oil prices dropped sharply? If oil prices jumped?

Use Web Code **Ice-6804** for **DK World Desk Reference Online.**

Everyday Life in Saudi Arabia

Using their oil wealth, Saudis have imported computers, cellular phones, and televisions. But before a new product is used, the nation's religious leaders study it. They decide whether each import may be used by Muslims. Only imports that they believe do not undermine Muslim values may be used in daily life. In Saudi Arabia, Islam regulates most people's lives.

Islamic Traditions For example, cities like Riyadh have department stores, hotels, and universities. But they have no movie theaters or night clubs. The Wahhabi (wah HAH bee) branch of Islam, which most Saudi Arabians follow, forbids such entertainment.

Alcohol and pork are illegal in Saudi Arabia. All shops close five times a day when Muslims pray. Saudi Arabians use Western inventions to improve their lives, but they make sure these inventions do not interfere with Islamic traditions.

The Role of Women Many laws and traditions in Saudi Arabia deal with the role of women. Women are protected in certain ways. They are also forbidden to do certain things.

For example, when Saudi women go out in public, they must cover themselves with a full-length black cloak. This is one of the rules of the country. Another rule is that women may not drive cars.

When Saudi Arabia built new schools, women became better educated. Many women now take advantage of increased opportunities for higher education. Despite the changes, women and men usually remain separate. Boys and girls go to different schools. At the university level, women study separately from men. Female students watch male teachers over a video system.

Saudi Arabian Women
According to Islamic law, Saudi Arabian women appearing in public must wear a long, black cloak, a scarf, and a veil covering the face, (bottom photo). The small photo shows a female Saudi doctor examining a male patient.

Drilling for Oil

The modern world depends on oil. Oil affects people every day, in almost every way. It fuels cars, heats homes, and is used to create electricity. Oil is located deep within Earth's surface, on land and under the oceans. The rotary drill, shown here, is often used to extract oil from land. It works like a giant screwdriver. As the drill turns round and round, it forces itself deeper through the ground.

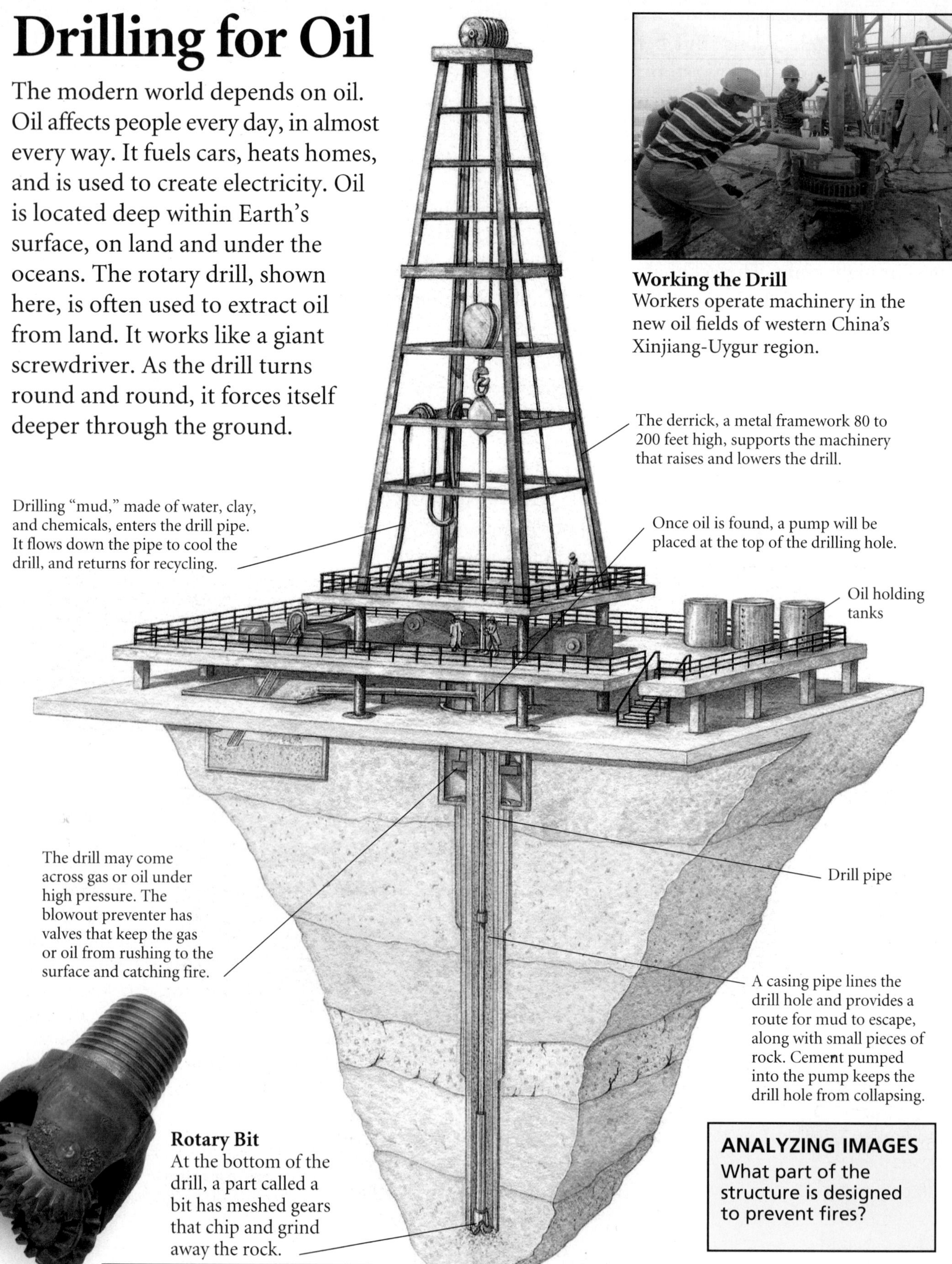
The derrick, a metal framework 80 to 200 feet high, supports the machinery that raises and lowers the drill.
Drilling "mud," made of water, clay, and chemicals, enters the drill pipe. It flows down the pipe to cool the drill, and returns for recycling.
Once oil is found, a pump will be placed at the top of the drilling hole.
Oil holding tanks
The drill may come across gas or oil under high pressure. The blowout preventer has valves that keep the gas or oil from rushing to the surface and catching fire.
Drill pipe
A casing pipe lines the drill hole and provides a route for mud to escape, along with small pieces of rock. Cement pumped into the pump keeps the drill hole from collapsing.

Working the Drill
Workers operate machinery in the new oil fields of western China's Xinjiang-Uygur region.

Rotary Bit
At the bottom of the drill, a part called a bit has meshed gears that chip and grind away the rock.

ANALYZING IMAGES
What part of the structure is designed to prevent fires?

The Influence of the Quran Most of the rules governing daily life in Saudi Arabia come from the **Quran,** the holy book of Islam. The word *Quran* means "the recitation" or "the reading." It consists of 114 chapters said to have been revealed by God to Muhammad. Muslims view the Quran as a guide for living. It provides guidelines on all aspects of life and religion.

√ Reading Check **How is Islam a part of daily life in Saudi Arabia?**

The Government of Saudi Arabia

Islam guides more than daily life in Saudi Arabia. Saudi Arabia's government is based on the Quran and Islamic law. The country is an absolute monarchy ruled under Islamic law. A **monarchy** is a state or a nation in which power is held by a monarch. A monarch is a king, a queen, or an emperor.

The king serves as head of the Council of Ministers, which acts as the executive and legislative branches of the government. The king decides who will serve on the Council of Ministers. Traditionally, the Council includes the Crown Prince and members of the royal family. Political parties and elections are not allowed in Saudi Arabia.

√ Reading Check **What kind of government does Saudi Arabia have?**

Links to Science

Circles of Wheat In Saudi Arabia, some parts of the desert have what is called "sweet" sand. This sand is not too salty, so plants can grow in it. In a place with sweet sand, wells are dug and fields are planted. Often, the fields are circular, with the well at the center. A long pipe with sprinklers swings around the well, irrigating the field. Wheat, alfalfa, and even pumpkins are grown in such areas.

Learn what brings millions of Muslims to Mecca each year.

Section 4 Assessment

Key Terms

Review the key terms at the beginning of this section. Use each term in a sentence that explains its meaning.

Target Reading Skill

What are two ways that oil wealth has affected the development of Saudi Arabia?

Comprehension and Critical Thinking

1. (a) Recall On what natural resource is Saudi Arabia's economy based?
(b) Apply Information How did wealth from oil change Saudi Arabia?
(c) Generalize How has the Saudi Arabian government used oil wealth to improve the lives of its citizens?

2. (a) Explain Give two examples of the ways Islam affects daily life in Saudi Arabia.
(b) Identify Point of View How do Muslims view the Quran?

3. (a) Describe Describe Saudi Arabia's system of government.
(b) Evaluate Information Why do you think political parties are not permitted in Saudi Arabia?

Writing Activity

Economists estimate that Saudi Arabia has enough oil to last for about 90 years of production at its present rate. In recent years, the Saudi Arabian government has used oil wealth to develop industries outside of petroleum. These include the iron and steel industries, construction, and chemicals. Write a paragraph that explains why Saudi Arabia might want to diversify its economy.

Writing Tip As you work on your paragraph, keep in mind that petroleum is a nonrenewable resource.

Interpreting Bar Graphs

Look at the picture below. The man is pushing a standard-size oil barrel that holds 42 gallons. The barrel is about the size of a large trash can.

Imagine 20 of these barrels standing together in a corner of your classroom. Would they fill up your classroom? If you stacked them, how many could fit into the room? You could probably squeeze in a few hundred.

If just a few hundred barrels of oil would fill your classroom, imagine how much space 8 million barrels would fill! You probably can't even picture that many barrels. Yet it is important for people to visualize huge numbers like these because they often represent facts we need to understand.

A bar graph is a useful tool for thinking about and comparing large numbers. It is a simple, easy-to-read way of showing a large amount of information.

Learn the Skill

Review the following steps to help you understand how to read bar graphs.

1. **Read the title to see what the bar graph is about.** The title identifies the topic of the bar graph.
2. **Read the labels to find out what each axis represents.** An axis is a line at the side or bottom of a graph. The horizontal axis is called the *x*-axis. Here you will find the categories of your data. The vertical axis is called the *y*-axis. The *y*-axis shows value or quantity.
3. **Look at the data to see if you can find similarities, differences, increases, or decreases.** What information does the horizontal axis show? What information does the vertical axis show?
4. **Make one or more general statements about what the graph shows.** You will have to compare and analyze the data in the bar graph in order to draw a conclusion or make a prediction about the topic of the bar graph.

Practice the Skill

Use the steps you have just learned to read the bar graph on the right.

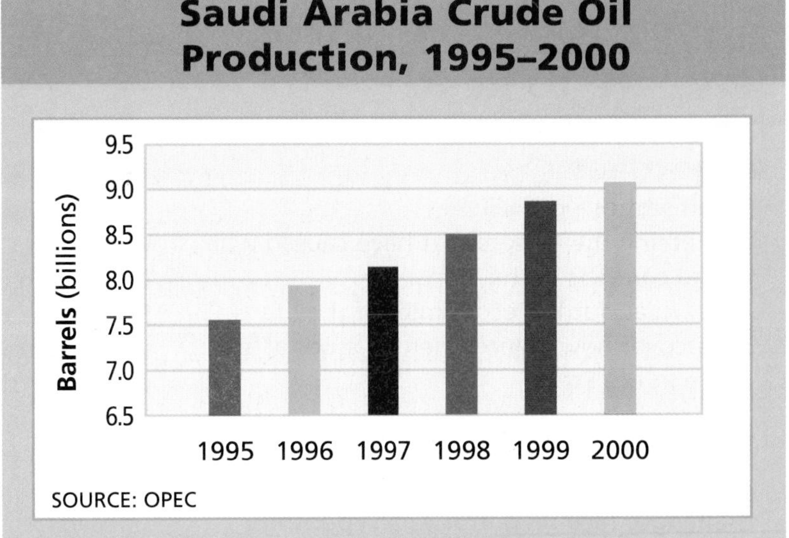

1. Jot down the subject of the bar graph. What does the bar graph show?
2. Look at the labels. What does the x-axis represent? What does the y-axis represent?
3. Now compare the data. What information can you read from the x-axis and the y-axis? Use it to answer the following questions: About how much oil did Saudi Arabia produce in 1995? In 2000? In what year did Saudi Arabia produce 8.5 billion barrels of oil?
4. Analyze the data to make a prediction. From 1999 to 2000, Saudi Arabia increased its crude oil production by about 3 billion barrels per year. Based on this rate of increase, how much crude oil would you expect Saudi Arabia to produce in 2001?

Apply the Skill

Follow the steps in this skill lesson to read the bar graph below. What is the bar graph about? What does the x-axis represent? The y-axis? Which country has the greatest reserves?

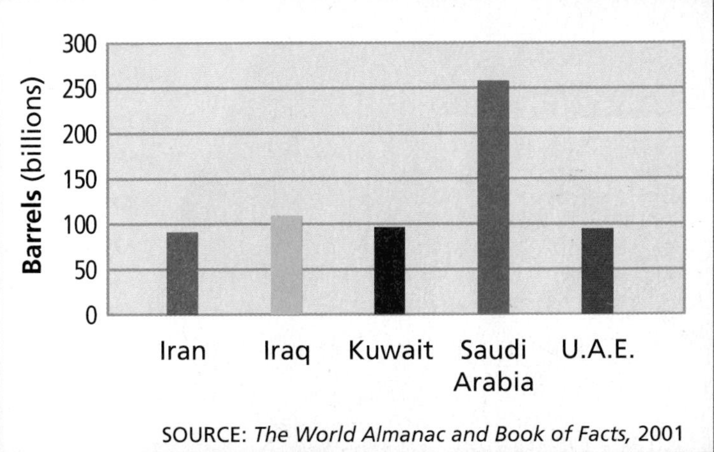

Section 5 The Stans
A Diverse Region

Prepare to Read

Objectives
In this section you will
1. Examine the factors that have caused war and conflicts in the Stans.
2. Learn about the economies of the Stans.
3. Discover how environmental issues affect life in the Stans.

Taking Notes
As you read, look for details about the challenges facing Central Asian countries. Copy the chart below, and record your findings in it.

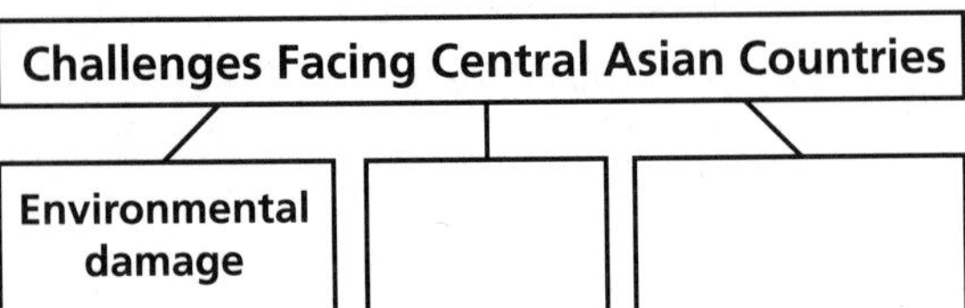

Target Reading Skill
Recognize Cause-and-Effect Signal Words
Sometimes certain words, such as *because*, *affect*, or *as a result*, signal a cause or an effect. In this section, look for these words to better understand conditions in Central Asia.

Key Terms
- **refugee** (ref yoo JEE) *n.* a person who flees war or other disasters
- **dictatorship** (DIK tay tur ship) *n.* a form of government in which power is held by a leader who has absolute authority
- **landlocked** (LAND lahkt) *adj.* having no direct access to the sea

Sharbat Gula holds the magazine that made her picture famous.

Sharbat Gula was a child when she first experienced the hardships of war. The Soviet Union invaded Afghanistan in 1979. Her village was destroyed in the fighting. Her parents were killed. She fled to neighboring Pakistan, where she lived in a camp for **refugees,** people who flee war or other disasters.

In 1985, a photographer named Steve McCurry took a picture of Sharbat at a refugee camp in Pakistan. The picture became famous. People around the world became more aware of the war and suffering in Afghanistan.

Seventeen years later, McCurry went back to the region to find Sharbat. He managed to trace her to a small village in Afghanistan. She was married and had children. She said she hoped that her children would have more opportunities than she had. She hoped they would get an education. Many people in Central Asia share Sharbat's hope for a better life. In addition to Afghanistan, this region includes Kazakhstan, Uzbekistan, Tajikistan, Turkmenistan, and Kyrgyzstan.

An Afghan Classroom
This picture of a girl's school in Kabul was taken when schools reopened after the fall of the Taliban government. The Taliban shut down most schools when it took over in 1996. **Analyze** *Why was the reopening of schools in Afghanistan seen as a return to a stable life?*

Warfare and Unrest in Afghanistan

The war that caused Sharbat to flee Afghanistan lasted for ten years, until the Soviet troops withdrew in 1989. But that wasn't the end of the fighting in Afghanistan.

Conflict in Afghanistan A group of militant Islamic people called the Taliban gained power in Afghanistan in 1996. The Taliban established very strict Islamic rule. It limited freedoms and executed or severely punished those who violated their laws. Under the Taliban, girls were not allowed to attend school, and women were barred from working outside the home. Television, music, and the Internet were banned.

The Taliban had the support of radical Muslims from other countries. One of these supporters was Osama bin Laden, a wealthy Saudi Arabian who moved to Afghanistan. In 1996, the Taliban placed bin Laden under its protection.

A Campaign Against Terrorism Bin Laden was the leader of al-Qaeda, a terrorist group. He was the leading suspect in the terrorist attacks of September 11, 2001 that destroyed the World Trade Center in New York City, damaged the Pentagon in Washington, D.C., and killed nearly 3,000 people. Because the Taliban refused to hand bin Laden over to the United States, American troops invaded Afghanistan in October 2001. Aided by Afghan rebels opposed to the Taliban, the United States quickly overthrew the Taliban government. Since late 2001, a new, democratic government has tried to bring peace and stability to Afghanistan.

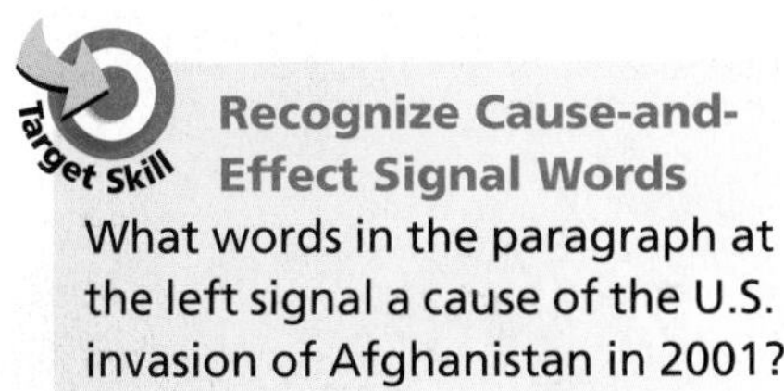

Recognize Cause-and-Effect Signal Words
What words in the paragraph at the left signal a cause of the U.S. invasion of Afghanistan in 2001?

✓ Reading Check **What happened in Afghanistan after the terrorist attacks on September 11, 2001?**

Citizen Heroes

Professors and Students in Herat, Afghanistan

Herat, a city in western Afghanistan, has for centuries been a center of Afghan culture and learning. Its literary heritage is especially rich, upheld by a Literary Circle founded in 1920. When the Taliban took control of Herat in 1995, they made it a crime to educate girls and women. Professors from the university and members of the Literary Circle risked their lives to help young women continue to study. Because women were allowed to sew, the Literary Circle held study sessions disguised as sewing classes. Instead of sewing, the women would study literature. Thousands of women and girls were secretly taught in Herat during Taliban rule.

Conflicts in Other Central Asian Countries

Afghanistan was not the only Central Asian country to experience conflict. Tensions among rival leaders, clans, and ethnic groups also affected other countries in the region.

Ethnic Disputes Central Asia is a mixture of various ethnic groups and cultures. For many years, strong Soviet rule kept ethnic and clan tensions under control. As Soviet rule came to an end, however, these tensions increased. In some countries, competing groups came into conflict. In Kazakhstan, for example, disputes arose between Kazakhs and Russians over issues of political and economic power under the new government.

Political Conflicts The situation in Tajikistan was worse. There, conflicts between rival groups erupted in violence. A bloody civil war raged through much of the 1990s and left the country in ruins. In Uzbekistan, conflict broke out in the Ferghana Valley. This fertile region, which borders Tajikistan and Kyrgyzstan, came under attack from radical Muslim groups. They wanted to overthrow the government of Uzbekistan and found an Islamic state.

Uzbekistan's government fought back against its opponents. It jailed critics of the government and outlawed radical groups. Other governments in the region also cracked down on opponents. They curbed political freedoms and violated human rights. Since independence, several countries of Central Asia have turned toward **dictatorship**—a form of government in which authority is held by an all-powerful ruler.

Children in Kyrgyzstan outside a yurt, a portable dwelling used by nomads in Central Asia

Help for Central Asia The United States and other Western countries expressed concern about the rise of dictators in the region. They called on the Stans to create democratic governments. The United States also took steps to help the region. It provided training, equipment, and money—$594 million in 2002—to build democracy and to improve economies. One program, for example, trained judges in Kyrgyzstan and Tajikistan.

✓ **Reading Check** **What conflicts have disrupted life in the Stans?**

COUNTRY PROFILE Focus on History

The Stans

The Stans' ethnic and religious makeup reflects their history. Over the centuries, waves of invaders have swept across the Stans. People speaking Iranian languages came thousands of years ago. They adopted Islam more than 1,000 years ago. Iranian speakers today include the Tajiks, the Pashtuns, and the Hazaras. About a thousand years ago, invaders brought Turkic languages, such as Uzbek and Kazakh. Finally, during the 1800s, Russians conquered the region. The Russians brought a new religion, Orthodox Christianity. Still, most of the region's people practice Islam.

Religions

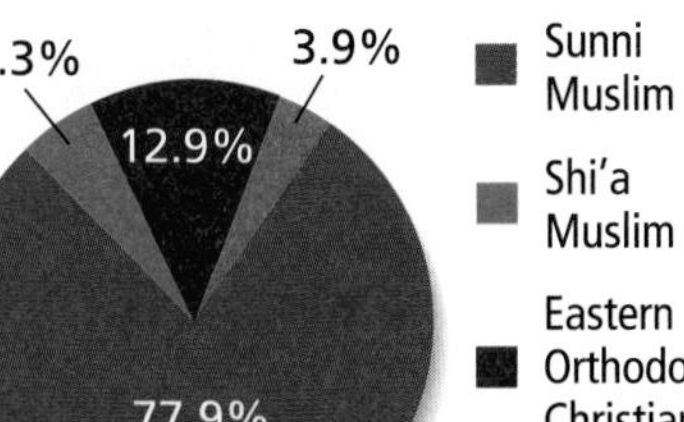

SOURCE: *CIA World Factbook;* Ethnologue

Ethnic Makeup

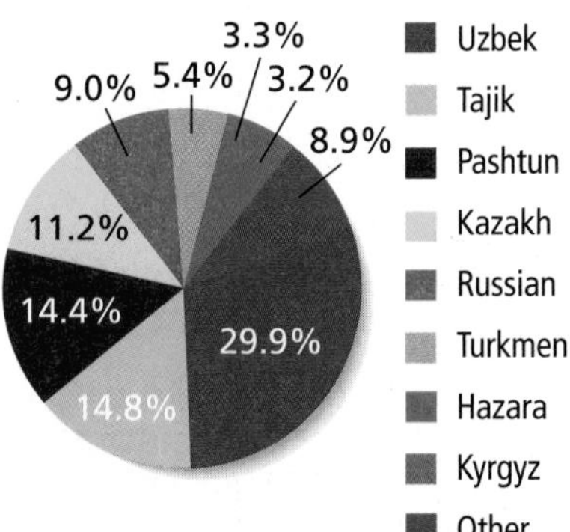

SOURCE: *CIA World Factbook;* Ethnologue

Map and Chart Skills

1. **Name** What is the largest ethnic group in the Stans?
2. **Recall** What kind of language does this group speak?
3. **Synthesize** Based on the region's history, which ethnic group probably includes most of the region's Orthodox Christians?

Use Web Code **lce-6805** for **DK World Desk Reference Online.**

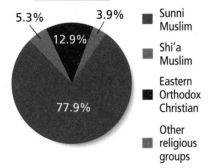

Economic Conditions in Central Asia

The Stans are generally poor countries. Agriculture is the main economic activity, although manufacturing, mining, and energy production are increasingly important. The growth of industry may offer better economic prospects in the future.

Agriculture Farming is the mainstay of Central Asian economies. During the Soviet era, large cotton farms produced huge amounts of cotton for export. Cotton farming is still important in the region—especially around the Ferghana Valley—but other types of farming have also increased. Production of grains, fruits, vegetables, and livestock has grown in recent years.

Some farms in Central Asia are large, like the cotton farms of Uzbekistan, but most are small. For most small farmers, life is a struggle. It is difficult to grow enough food or earn enough money to provide a decent living.

Sharbat Gula's life is typical for people who live in the country. Her village lies in the hills of eastern Afghanistan. Villagers plant small plots of corn, wheat, and rice on terraces built into the hillsides. They may also have a few walnut trees and maybe a sheep or two. To make money, Sharbat's husband works at a bakery in a nearby city. He makes less than one dollar a day. That's barely enough for Sharbat's family to buy the things they need to survive.

Chart Skills

The Stans are generally poor countries with developing economies. **Compare** What is one economic activity all the countries in the Stans have in common?

Economies of Central Asian Countries

Country	Economic Activities
Afghanistan	Farming and livestock raising. Small-scale production of textiles, furniture, cement.
Kazakhstan	Farming, oil and coal mining, steel production, textiles.
Kyrgyzstan	Farming and livestock raising. Cotton, tobacco, wool and meat.
Tajikistan	Mainly farming, mostly cotton. One large aluminum plant.
Turkmenistan	Major cotton-producing country. Production of natural gas, oil, and textiles.
Uzbekistan	Major cotton exporter. Large producer of gold and oil.

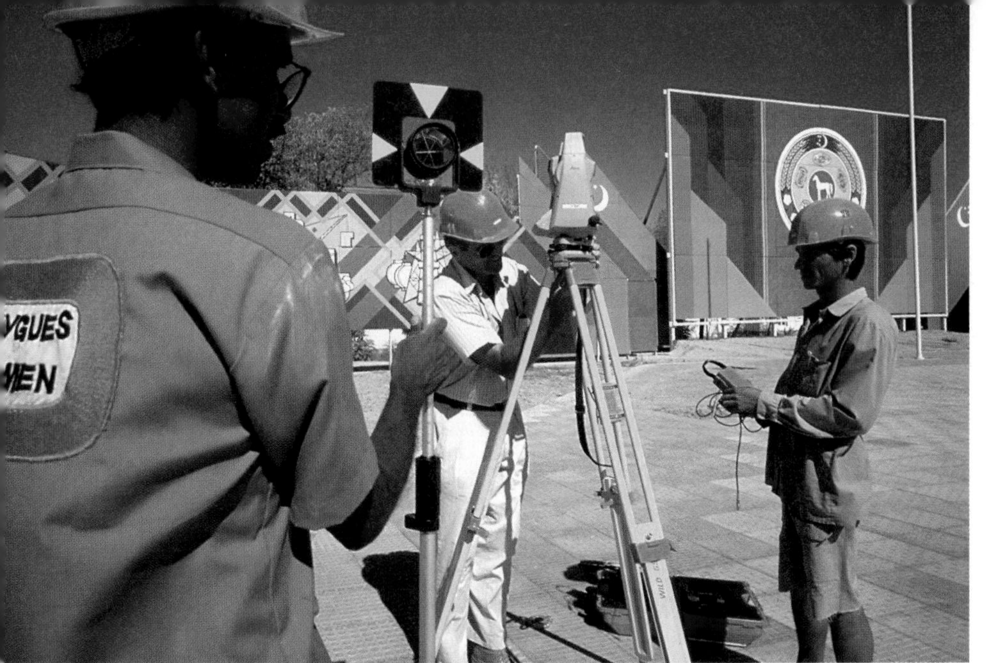

Working on a construction site in Turkmenistan

Industry Not all Central Asians live in rural areas, however. Many live in growing cities, like Almaty, Kazakhstan, and Tashkent, Uzbekistan. Many residents live in apartments and work in offices or factories. Many of the industries in the Stans date back to the Soviet era. They are generally old and unproductive. Gradually, however, some factories and mines are being modernized. Much of the focus is on the development of Central Asia's energy and mineral resources.

Several of the Stans are rich in oil, natural gas, and minerals such as coal, gold, iron ore, and uranium. Kazakhstan has major oil reserves, while Turkmenistan is rich in natural gas. Foreign oil and gas companies are exploring ways to develop and export these resources. One problem is that these countries are **landlocked,** with no direct access to the sea. Plans are underway to build pipelines to carry oil and gas out of the region.

√ Reading Check **What are the main features of Central Asian economies?**

Environmental Issues

The new countries of Central Asia face the challenging task of restoring and protecting the environment. In the past, the Soviet Union caused great environmental damage in the region.

One major environmental challenge involves nuclear fallout. For years, the Soviet Union conducted nuclear tests in northern Kazakhstan. Nuclear explosions left the region with severe radiation pollution. Radiation has caused serious health problems, including cancer and birth defects. This pollution will take years, even decades, to clean up.

Links to Art

Saving Art Central Asia has a rich artistic tradition. Many works of art have been destroyed, however, as a result of war and other conflicts. In Kabul, Afghanistan, for example, the Taliban destroyed priceless art in the National Museum. They also destroyed two giant Buddha statues at Bamiyan. Efforts are now underway to restore or save the remaining art treasures. Foreign countries and international agencies, such as the United Nations, are working with the Afghan government to preserve the country's artistic heritage. An ancient bronze sculpture from the National Museum in Kabul is shown below.

The natural beauty of the Stans is an important asset for the future. Shown here are the Tian Shan mountains in Kyrgyzstan.

As you read in Chapter 19, another major challenge is the drying of the Aral Sea. For years, the Soviets diverted water from rivers feeding the sea to irrigate cotton fields. As a result, the sea is now drying up.

Still, vast areas of Central Asia remain undeveloped and undamaged. These environmentally healthy lands are a key resource for Central Asia. If the Stans can preserve their environment, it will be an important asset for their future.

Discovery
CHANNEL
SCHOOL
Video
Learn why the Aral Sea is shrinking.

√ Reading Check **How have environmental problems affected the Stans?**

Section 5 Assessment

Key Terms

Review the key terms at the beginning of this section. Use each term in a sentence that explains its meaning.

Target Reading Skill

Review the text about environmental issues. Find the words that signal effects on Central Asia's environment.

Comprehension and Critical Thinking

1. (a) **Explain** How did the Taliban come to power in Afghanistan?
(b) **Summarize** Why did the United States invade Afghanistan in 2001?

2. (a) **Recall** Name a Central Asian country other than Afghanistan that has experienced recent conflicts.
(b) **Make Generalizations** In general, how has the United States helped Central Asian countries?

3. (a) **Identify** What is the main economic activity in Central Asian countries?
(b) **Apply Information** How might mineral resources help Central Asian countries develop their economies?

4. (a) **Recall** How has nuclear testing affected Kazakhstan?
(b) **Identify Causes** What caused the Aral Sea to shrink?

Writing Activity

Suppose that you are a news reporter covering Central Asia. Write a brief news report about economic conditions and challenges in Central Asia.

For: An activity on the Stans
Visit: PHSchool.com
Web Code: lcd-6805

Chapter 25 Review and Assessment

◆ Chapter Summary

Section 1: India

- India is the second-most-populated country in the world. India also has a rapidly growing population.
- India has a large middle class that provides a huge market for goods and services.
- Despite India's fast-growing economy, about one fourth of the population lives in poverty.

India

Section 2: Pakistan

- Pakistan has been working hard to improve its economy.
- Pakistan's economy is based largely on agriculture.
- Pakistan's textile industry is an important part of the economy. Other industries include making chemicals and steel.

Israel

Section 3: Israel

- Service industries are the most important part of Israel's well-developed economy.
- About 80 percent of the people of Israel are Jewish. About 15 percent are Palestinian Arabs living in the West Bank and the Gaza Strip.

Section 4: Saudi Arabia

- Oil production is the main economic activity in Saudi Arabia. No other country in the world exports more petroleum.
- Saudi Arabia has used its wealth from oil to make the country more modern.
- Islam guides daily life in Saudi Arabia. Islam is also the basis for Saudi Arabia's government and laws.

Section 5: The Stans

- The countries of Central Asia face many challenges in creating peaceful, prosperous, and stable nations.
- Agriculture is the main economic activity in the countries of Central Asia. Manufacturing, mining, and energy production are becoming important.

◆ Key Terms

Each of the statements below contains a key term from the chapter. If the statement is true, write *true*. If it is false, rewrite the statement to make it true.

1. Life expectancy measures the percentage of the population age 15 or over that can read and write.
2. Poor nutrition caused by a lack of food or an unbalanced diet is called malnutrition.
3. Drought, a long period of dry weather, is a major problem in Pakistan.
4. Irrigation is a worldwide effort to increase food production in developing countries.
5. Today, many Muslims make the hajj by airplane.
6. A refugee is a person who flees war or other disasters.

Chapter 25 Review and Assessment (continued)

◆ Comprehension and Critical Thinking

7. (a) **Recall** What is the population of India?
   (b) **Summarize** Why is India expected to have the world's largest population by 2050?
8. (a) **Explain** How does India's middle class help the nation's economy?
   (b) **Identify Effects** What is one effect of India's efforts to improve health care?
9. (a) **Explain** Why is water shortage a major problem for Pakistan?
   (b) **Draw Inferences** Why might a manufacturing company in Pakistan be located on the plains of the Indus River?
   (c) **Make Generalizations** Why would education be considered important in making a nation more prosperous?
10. (a) **Identify** Give one example of how technology has helped Israel succeed in agriculture.
    (b) **Summarize** How do the manufacturing and service industries improve Israel's economy?
11. (a) **Identify** What natural resource has helped Saudi Arabia build its economy and modernize the country?
    (b) **Identify Effects** How has oil wealth affected the lives of Saudi Arabians?
12. (a) **Describe** What kind of government does Saudi Arabia have?
    (b) **Analyze** What is the connection between Islam and the government of Saudi Arabia?
13. (a) **Name** Which Central Asian country was controlled by the Taliban?
    (b) **Summarize** What factors have caused wars and conflicts in the Stans?

◆ Skills Practice

Interpreting Bar Graphs Name one Southwest Asian country that is not shown on the graph on the bottom of page 773. How would you find out whether it had any oil reserves?

◆ Writing Activity: Math

Use the Country Databank on pages 738–749 to look up the population of five countries discussed in this chapter. Make a bar graph that shows each country's population. Be sure to label the horizontal axis and the vertical axis of the graph. Include a title for your graph.

MAP MASTER™ Skills Activity

South, Southwest, and Central Asia

Place Location For each place listed below, write the letter from the map that shows its location.

1. Israel
2. India
3. Pakistan
4. Kazakhstan
5. Saudi Arabia
6. Aral Sea

Go Online
PHSchool.com Use Web Code **lcp-6820** for an **interactive map.**

Standardized Test Prep

Test-Taking Tips

Some questions on standardized tests ask you to analyze a reading selection. Read the passage below. Then follow the tips to answer the sample question at the right.

> The Negev Desert takes up two thirds of Israel's land. Only three or four inches of rain fall there each year. Yet Israeli farmers grow fruits and vegetables on the desert. They also plant trees there to prevent erosion. For water, Israeli farmers use an irrigation system that is controlled by computer. Plastic tubes carry underground water straight to the crops. This water is salty, so Israelis developed plants that can soak up the water but not the salt.

TIP Think about the author's purpose as you read. Is the author trying to give information, convince you about something, or explain how something works?

Pick the letter that best answers the question.

This paragraph answers which question?

A What is the Negev Desert in Israel like?

B What are Israeli farms like?

C How has Israel reclaimed the Negev Desert for farmland?

D How can an irrigation system bring water to desert land?

Think It Through Start with the author's purpose: to give you information about Israeli farms in the Negev Desert. What question is the passage answering about Israeli farms on the Negev Desert? You can eliminate D because it is not related specifically to Israeli farms. You can rule out A because it does not address the question of farms at all. That leaves B and C. Both ask questions about Israeli farms, but B does not include the Negev Desert. The correct answer is C.

Practice Questions

Use the tips above and other tips in this book to help you answer the following questions.

Use the passage below to answer Question 1.

> Landlocked Kazakhstan is the largest of the five former Soviet republics in Central Asia. It is about four times the size of Texas. Kazakhstan's most important natural resource is oil. In 2003, the country's oil reserves were estimated to be between 9 and 17.6 million barrels.

1. What information best supports the prediction that Kazakhstan could be a major oil exporter?

   A Kazakhstan is the largest of the former Soviet republics in Central Asia.

   B Kazakhstan is larger than Texas.

   C Kazakhstan's oil reserves are estimated to be as great as 17.6 million barrels.

   D Kazakhstan is landlocked.

2. What is one effect of India's efforts to improve health care?

   A India's literacy rate is increasing.

   B India's life expectancy is increasing.

   C Malnutrition is increasing.

   D India's film industry is growing.

Use Web Code **lca-6800** for **Chapter 25 self-test.**

Chapter

26 Southeast Asia and the Pacific Region

Chapter Preview

This chapter focuses on Vietnam, a country in mainland Southeast Asia, and on Australia, the only country that is also a continent.

Country Databank

The Country Databank provides data and descriptions of each of the countries of Southeast Asia and the Pacific Region.

Section 1

Vietnam
A Nation Rebuilds

Section 2

Australia
A Pacific Rim Country

Target Reading Skill

Main Idea In this chapter you will focus on identifying main ideas and supporting details.

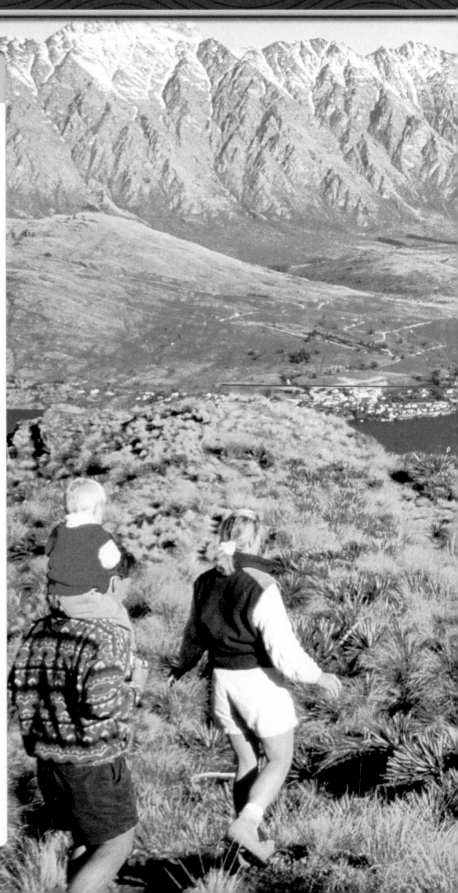

▶ **Hiking in the mountains of New Zealand**

MAP MASTER™ Skills Activity

Southeast Asia and the Pacific Region: Political

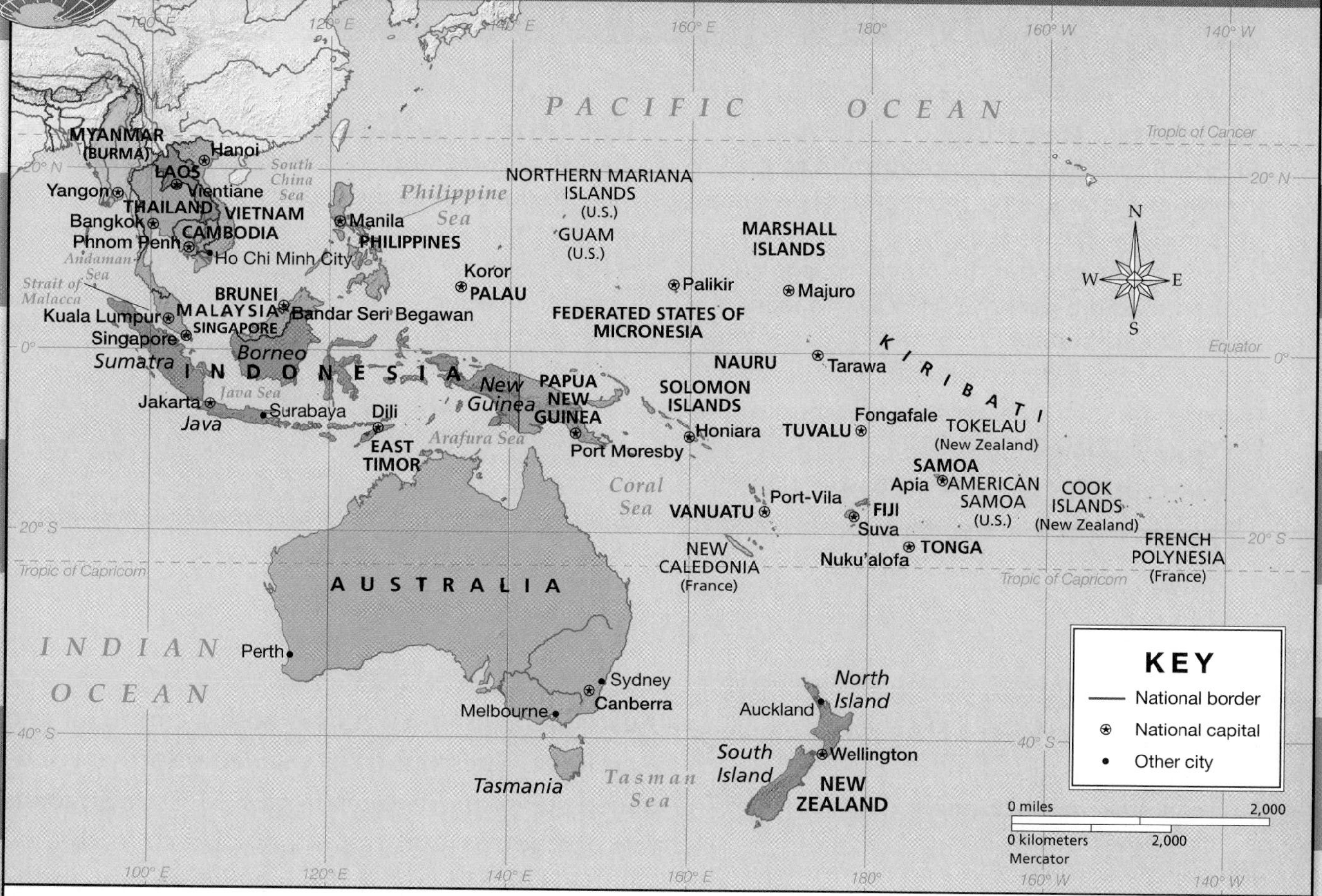

PACIFIC OCEAN
INDIAN OCEAN
MYANMAR (BURMA)
Hanoi
LAOS
Vientiane
Yangon
THAILAND
VIETNAM
Bangkok
Phnom Penh
CAMBODIA
Ho Chi Minh City
South China Sea
Andaman Sea
Strait of Malacca
Manila
PHILIPPINES
Philippine Sea
NORTHERN MARIANA ISLANDS (U.S.)
GUAM (U.S.)
MARSHALL ISLANDS
Koror
PALAU
Palikir
Majuro
BRUNEI
MALAYSIA
Bandar Seri Begawan
Kuala Lumpur
SINGAPORE
Singapore
FEDERATED STATES OF MICRONESIA
Borneo
Sumatra
INDONESIA
NAURU
Tarawa
KIRIBATI
New Guinea
PAPUA NEW GUINEA
SOLOMON ISLANDS
Jakarta
Java Sea
Java
Surabaya
Dili
EAST TIMOR
Arafura Sea
Port Moresby
Honiara
TUVALU
Fongafale
TOKELAU (New Zealand)
SAMOA
Apia
AMERICAN SAMOA (U.S.)
COOK ISLANDS (New Zealand)
Coral Sea
VANUATU
Port-Vila
FIJI
Suva
TONGA
Nuku'alofa
NEW CALEDONIA (France)
FRENCH POLYNESIA (France)
AUSTRALIA
Perth
Sydney
Canberra
Melbourne
Tasmania
Tasman Sea
Auckland
North Island
South Island
Wellington
NEW ZEALAND
Tropic of Cancer
Equator
Tropic of Capricorn
100° E
120° E
140° E
160° E
180°
160° W
140° W
20° N
0°
20° S
40° S
N
S
E
W

KEY
- National border
- National capital
- Other city

0 miles 2,000
0 kilometers 2,000
Mercator

Regions Much of Southeast Asia and the Pacific Region is located between the Tropic of Cancer and the Tropic of Capricorn.
Identify Which countries have land south of the Tropic of Capricorn?
Contrast What climate would you expect most of these countries to have? Explain your answer.

Go Online
PHSchool.com Use Web Code **lcp-6910** for step-by-step **map skills practice.**

Introducing Southeast Asia and the Pacific Region

Guide for Reading

This section provides an introduction to the countries that make up the region of Southeast Asia and the Pacific Region.

- Look at the map on the previous page and then read the paragraphs below to learn about each nation.
- Analyze the data to compare the countries.
- What are the characteristics that most of the countries share?
- What are some key differences among the countries?

Viewing the Video Overview

View the World Studies Video Overview to learn more about each of the countries. As you watch, answer this question:

- How do the countries in Southeast Asia and the Pacific depend on their diverse natural resources to support their people?

Explore the land of Southeast Asia and the Pacific Region.

Australia

Capital	Canberra
Land Area	2,941,283 sq mi; 7,617,930 sq km
Population	19.6 million
Ethnic Group(s)	white, Asian, Aboriginal
Religion(s)	Protestant, Roman Catholic, traditional beliefs
Government	democratic, federal-state system recognizing the British monarch as sovereign
Currency	Australian dollar
Leading Exports	coal, gold, meat, wool, aluminum, iron ore, wheat, machinery and transport equipment
Language(s)	English (official), Italian, Cantonese, Greek, Arabic, Vietnamese, Aboriginal languages

Australia (aw STRAYL yuh) is both a continent and a country. The country is divided into five continental states and two territories. Most Australians live on the coast, as the interior is extremely dry. All the state capitals, including Sydney, are on the coast. The national capital, Canberra, is located inland. Australia is a country of great physical diversity, from deserts to snow-capped mountains. It also has the Great Barrier Reef, the largest coral reef in the world. Tourism is Australia's main industry, although it also has important farming and mining industries.

Wool is a leading Australian export.

Brunei

Capital	Bandar Seri Begawan
Land Area	2,035 sq mi; 5,270 sq km
Population	350,898
Ethnic Group(s)	Malay, East Asian, indigenous tribes
Religion(s)	Muslim, Buddhist, Christian, traditional beliefs
Government	constitutional sultanate
Currency	Brunei dollar
Leading Exports	crude oil, natural gas, refined products
Language(s)	Malay (official), English, Chinese

Brunei (broo NY) is a largely Muslim country in Southeast Asia. The same family, the Sultanate of Brunei, has been in power for more than six hundred years. At one point between the 1400s and 1600s, the nation controlled parts of Borneo and the Philippines. Later, the country experienced problems related to royal succession, colonization, and piracy. In the late 1800s, Brunei came under British rule for almost one hundred years, until it gained its independence in 1984. The nation is rich in oil and natural gas and has a relatively strong economy.

Cambodia

Capital	Phnom Penh
Land Area	68,154 sq mi; 176,520 sq km
Population	12.8 million
Ethnic Group(s)	Khmer, Vietnamese
Religion(s)	Buddhist
Government	multiparty democracy under a constitutional monarchy
Currency	riel
Leading Exports	timber, rubber, rice, fish
Language(s)	Khmer (official), French, Chinese, Vietnamese, Cham

Cambodia (kam BOH dee uh) is located on the Gulf of Thailand in Southeast Asia. It is bordered by Thailand, Vietnam, and Laos. Communist Khmer Rouge forces took over Cambodia in 1975. More than a million people died or were executed when the Khmer Rouge ordered the evacuation of all cities and towns. After decades of violent political conflict, a national election in 1998 brought renewed political stability to Cambodia. Today, with massive international donations, Cambodia struggles to maintain a stable government and establish a working economy.

East Timor

Capital	Dili
Land Area	5,794 sq mi; 15,007 sq km
Population	952,618
Ethnic Group(s)	Austronesian (Malayo-Polynesian), Papuan, East Asian
Religion(s)	Roman Catholic, Muslim, Protestant, Hindu, Buddhist, traditional beliefs
Government	republic
Currency	U.S. dollar
Leading Exports	coffee, sandalwood, marble
Language(s)	Tetum (Portuguese-Austronesian) (official), Bahasa Indonesia, Portuguese

East Timor (eest TEE mawr) is located in Southeast Asia, northwest of Australia. East Timor includes the eastern half and the Oecussi region of the island of Timor as well as two smaller islands. Once a Portuguese colony, East Timor declared its independence in 1975. Nine days after declaring independence, however, it was invaded and occupied by Indonesia. In 1999, the United Nations supervised an election in which the people of East Timor voted for independence from Indonesia. Though Indonesian militias protested with violence, East Timor was internationally recognized as an independent democratic nation in May 2002.

Introducing Southeast Asia and the Pacific Region

Federated States of Micronesia

Capital	Palikir
Land Area	271 sq mi; 702 sq km
Population	135,869
Ethnic Group(s)	Micronesian, Polynesian
Religion(s)	Roman Catholic, Protestant
Government	constitutional government
Currency	U.S. dollar
Leading Exports	fish, clothing, bananas, black pepper
Language(s)	English (official), Trukese, Pohnpeian, Mortlockese, Losrean

The Federated States of Micronesia (FED ur ayt id stayts uv my kruh NEE zhuh) is an island group in the North Pacific Ocean. It consists of all the Caroline Islands except Palau. Once under United States control, the Federated States of Micronesia (FSM) became independent in 1986. The United States still provides the country with financial aid and military protection. The FSM is working to overcome long-term concerns such as high unemployment, overfishing, and dependence on United States aid. Most Micronesians live without running water or electricity.

Fiji

Capital	Suva
Land Area	7,054 sq mi; 18,270 sq km
Population	856,346
Ethnic Group(s)	Fijian, South Asian, white, other Pacific Islander, East Asian
Religion(s)	Hindu, Protestant, Roman Catholic, Muslim
Government	republic
Currency	Fiji dollar
Leading Exports	sugar, clothing, gold, timber, fish, molasses, coconut oil
Language(s)	English (official), Fijian, Hindi, Urdu, Tamil, Telugu

Fiji (FEE jee) is an island group in the South Pacific Ocean. Fiji consists of two main islands and hundreds of smaller islands. After nearly one hundred years as a British colony, Fiji became an independent democracy in 1970. Fiji has a history of ethnic conflict between native Fijians and those of Indian ancestry. This conflict has caused great political instability over the past few decades and has weakened Fiji's economy.

Indonesia

Capital	Jakarta
Land Area	705,188 sq mi; 1,826,440 sq km
Population	231.3 million
Ethnic Group(s)	Javanese, Sundanese, Madurese, coastal Malay
Religion(s)	Muslim, Protestant, Roman Catholic, Hindu, Buddhist
Government	republic
Currency	rupiah
Leading Exports	oil and gas, electrical appliances
Language(s)	Bahasa Indonesia (official), Javanese, Sundanese, Madurese, Dutch

Indonesia (in duh NEE zhuh) is an island nation located between the Indian and Pacific Oceans. It is Southeast Asia's largest and most populous country, and the world's largest archipelago. It is also the world's most populous Muslim nation. Once known as the Dutch East Indies, Indonesia achieved independence from the Netherlands in 1949. It currently suffers from violent political and religious conflicts, widespread poverty, and government corruption. However, it has large energy and mineral resources, and its economy is strengthening.

Kiribati

Capital	Bairiki (Tarawa Atoll)
Land Area	313 sq mi; 811 sq km
Population	96,335
Ethnic Group(s)	Micronesian, Polynesian
Religion(s)	Roman Catholic, Protestant, Muslim, traditional beliefs
Government	republic
Currency	Australian dollar
Leading Exports	copra, coconuts, seaweed, fish
Language(s)	English (official), Micronesian dialect

Kiribati (kihr uh BAS) is a group of 33 coral atolls in the Pacific Ocean. It lies on the Equator about halfway between Hawaii and Australia. Once called the Gilbert Islands, part of a British colony, Kiribati became independent in 1979. Great Britain had mined the islands for their phosphate deposits for decades. Although the phosphate ran out in 1980, Kiribati succeeded in winning some payment from Britain for what it had taken. With very few natural resources, Kiribati has a limited economy. However, it grows enough food to support its citizens without imports.

Laos

Capital	Vientiane
Land Area	89,112 sq mi; 230,800 sq km
Population	5.8 million
Ethnic Group(s)	Lao Loum, Lao Theung, Lao Soung, Vietnamese, East Asian
Religion(s)	Buddhist, traditional beliefs
Government	communist state
Currency	new kip
Leading Exports	wood products, clothing, electricity, coffee, tin
Language(s)	Lao (official), Mon-Khmer, Yao, Vietnamese, Chinese, French

Laos (LAH ohs) is a landlocked Communist country in Southeast Asia bordered by Vietnam, Cambodia, Thailand, Myanmar, and China. After six hundred years as a monarchy, Laos became a communist nation in 1975. The country has many mineral resources and produces large amounts of coffee and timber. Still, it is one of the world's least developed countries and depends on foreign aid. Laotians are mostly Buddhists. The majority of the population lives in rural areas and works in farming.

Malaysia

Capital	Kuala Lumpur and Putrajaya
Land Area	126,853 sq mi; 328,550 sq km
Population	22.7 million
Ethnic Group(s)	Malay, East Asian, indigenous tribes, South Asian
Religion(s)	Muslim, Buddhist, traditional beliefs, Hindu, Christian
Government	constitutional monarchy
Currency	ringgit
Leading Exports	electronic equipment, petroleum and liquefied natural gas, wood
Language(s)	Bahasa Malaysia (official), Malay, Chinese, Tamil, English

Malaysia (muh LAY zhuh) consists of a peninsula and the northern third of the island of Borneo in the South China Sea. It shares borders with Thailand, Indonesia, Singapore, and Brunei. The country, made up of parts of former British colonies, was formed in 1963. Although Malaysia is considered a developing country, its economy was one of the fastest growing in the world from 1987 to 1997. The Asian financial crash of 1997 slowed but did not stop this growth. Malaysia exports large amounts of oil, natural gas, and palm oil.

Introducing Southeast Asia and the Pacific Region

Marshall Islands

Capital	Majuro
Land Area	70 sq mi; 181.3 sq km
Population	73,360
Ethnic Group(s)	Micronesian
Religion(s)	Christian
Government	constitutional government in free association with the United States
Currency	U.S. dollar
Leading Exports	copra (dried coconut), coconut oil, handicrafts
Language(s)	English (official), Marshallese (official), Japanese, German

The Marshall Islands (MAHR shul EYE lundz) is a group of 34 islands in the North Pacific Ocean. Once under United States control, the Marshall Islands became independent in 1986. The island nation maintains ties to the United States and heavily depends on it for economic support. The money the United States provides the islands makes up almost two thirds of its total income. The Marshall Islands faces ongoing problems of few natural resources, high unemployment, and poverty.

Myanmar

Capital	Rangoon
Land Area	253,953 sq mi; 657,740 sq km
Population	42.2 million
Ethnic Group(s)	Burman, Shan, Karen, Rakhine, East Asian, South Asian, Mon
Religion(s)	Buddhist, Christian, Muslim, traditional beliefs
Government	military regime
Currency	kyat
Leading Exports	clothing, food, wood products, precious stones
Language(s)	Burmese (Myanmar) (official), Karen, Shan, Chin, Kachin, Mon, Palaung, Wa

Myanmar (MYUN mahr), also known as Burma, is a Southeast Asian nation bordered by Thailand, China, India, the Andaman Sea, and the Bay of Bengal. There are mountains in the north, but the fertile Irrawaddy basin dominates the rest of the country. Myanmar is rich in natural resources, and its economy is mainly agricultural. Once a British colony, Myanmar gained its independence in 1948. Since that time, it has had a history of ethnic conflict and political instability. Today, its government is run by the military.

Nauru

Capital	Yaren District
Land Area	8 sq mi; 21 sq km
Population	12,329
Ethnic Group(s)	Nauruan, Pacific Islanders, East Asian, white
Religion(s)	Protestant, Roman Catholic
Government	republic
Currency	Australian dollar
Leading Exports	phosphate
Language(s)	Nauruan (official), Kiribati, Chinese, Tuvaluan, English

Nauru (nah OO roo) is an island in the South Pacific Ocean. The world's smallest independent republic, Nauru was once a German and then a British colony. It gained its independence in 1968. For decades, the United Kingdom, New Zealand, and Australia mined Nauru for its phosphate. The income from phosphate, Nauru's only export, has made its people very wealthy. However, mining activities caused great environmental damage. With phosphate mining expected to run out, Nauru faces the great challenge of keeping its economy from collapsing.

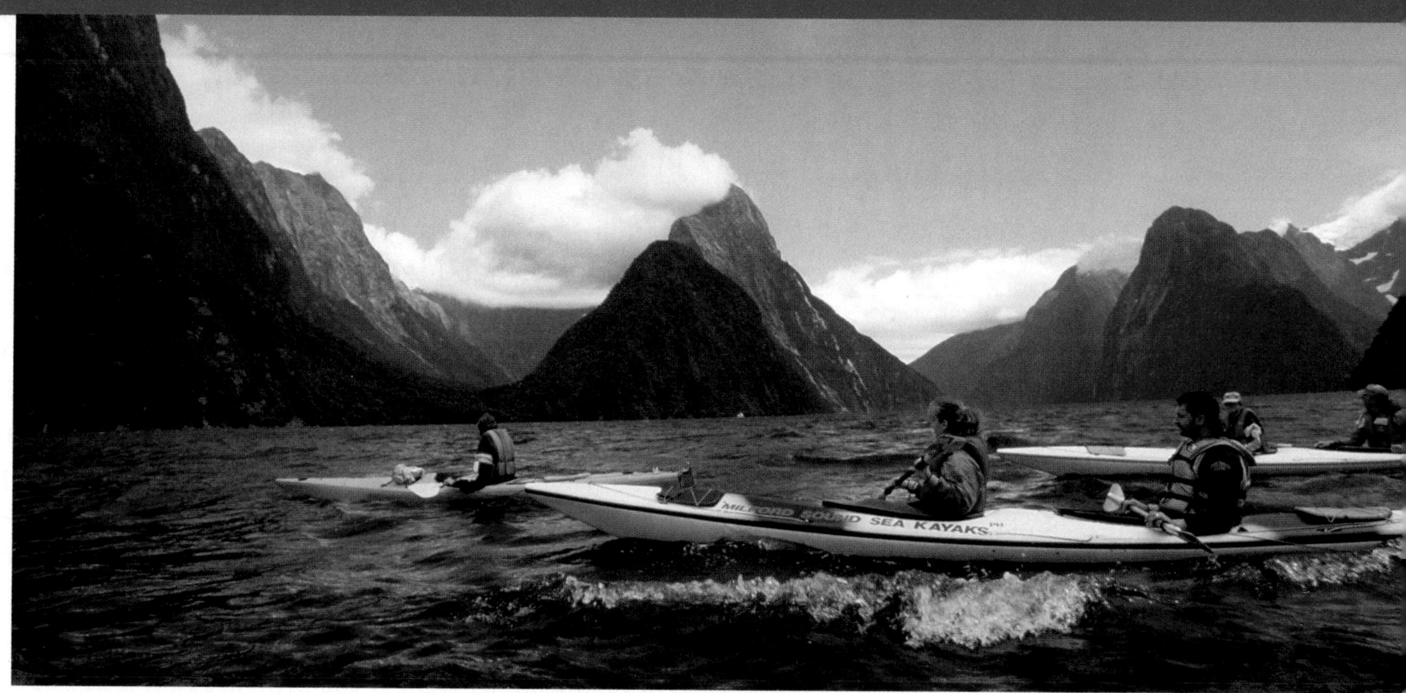

Sea kayaks in Milford Sound in Fiordland National Park, New Zealand

New Zealand

Capital	Wellington
Land Area	103,737 sq mi; 268,680 sq km
Population	3.8 million
Ethnic Group(s)	white, Maori, Pacific Islander, Asian
Religion(s)	Protestant, Roman Catholic
Government	parliamentary democracy
Currency	New Zealand dollar
Leading Exports	dairy products, meat, wood and wood products, fish, machinery
Language(s)	English (official), Maori (official)

New Zealand (noo ZEE lund) is made up of two large islands and a number of smaller islands in the South Pacific Ocean. It lies about 1,000 miles southeast of Australia. Settled by the Polynesian Maori in about A.D. 800, New Zealand became a British colony during the 1800s and an independent nation in 1907. New Zealand's economy is based on agricultural exports—particularly butter and wool—as well as manufacturing. New Zealand has some of the world's most varied scenery, and tourism is an important industry.

Palau

Capital	Koror
Land Area	177 sq mi; 458 sq km
Population	19,409
Ethnic Group(s)	Palauan, Asian, white
Religion(s)	Christian, traditional beliefs
Government	constitutional government in free association with the United States
Currency	U.S. dollar
Leading Exports	shellfish, tuna, copra, clothing
Language(s)	Palauan (official), English (official), Japanese, Angaur, Tobi, Sonsorolese

Palau (pah LOW) is an archipelago made up of several hundred islands in the North Pacific Ocean southeast of the Philippines. Palau, once governed by the United States and the United Nations, became independent in 1994. It is now a constitutional democracy but maintains close ties to the United States and relies on it for financial aid. Its economy is developing and is primarily agricultural, with a growing tourism industry.

Introducing Southeast Asia and the Pacific Region

Papua New Guinea

Capital Port Moresby
Land Area 174,849 sq mi; 452,860 sq km
Population 5.2 million
Ethnic Group(s) Melanesian, Papuan, Negrito, Micronesian, Polynesian
Religion(s) Protestant, Roman Catholic, traditional beliefs
Government constitutional monarchy with parliamentary democracy
Currency kina
Leading Exports oil, gold, copper ore, logs, palm oil, coffee, cocoa, crayfish, prawns
Language(s) English (official), Pidgin English, Papuan, Motu, around 750 native languages

Papua New Guinea (pap YOO uh noo GIH nee) is a group of islands—including the eastern half of the island of New Guinea—located between the Coral Sea and the South Pacific Ocean. Papua New Guinea became independent from Australia in 1975. Since then, its political situation has been somewhat unstable due to conflicts between many political parties. Papua New Guinea's people are extraordinarily diverse, with around 750 different languages spoken there. Its economy is mainly agricultural, though it has significant mineral and oil resources as well. A gas pipeline between Papua New Guinea and Australia is expected to bring in almost $220 million per year.

Philippines

Capital Manila
Land Area 115,123 sq mi; 298,170 sq km
Population 84.5 million
Ethnic Group(s) Malay, East Asian
Religion(s) Roman Catholic, Protestant, Muslim, Buddhist
Government republic
Currency Philippine peso
Leading Exports electronic equipment, machinery and transport equipment
Language(s) English (official), Filipino (official), Tagalog, Cebuano, Hiligaynon, Samaran, Ilocano, Bikol

The Philippines (FIL uh peenz) is an island nation in the western Pacific Ocean, between the Philippine Sea and the South China Sea. It consists of more than 7,000 islands, about 1,000 of which are inhabited. The Philippines became independent from the United States in 1946. Since that time, it has suffered a troubled political history, including dictatorships. The Philippines has more than 100 ethnic groups and is the only Christian nation in Southeast Asia. It has large mineral deposits that have not been fully developed.

Samoa

Capital Apia
Land Area 1,133 sq mi; 2,934 sq km
Population 178,631
Ethnic Group(s) Samoan, mixed white and Polynesian, white
Religion(s) Protestant, Roman Catholic
Government constitutional monarchy
Currency tala
Leading Exports fish, coconut oil and cream, copra
Language(s) Samoan (official), English (official)

Samoa (suh MOH uh) is a group of nine volcanic islands located in the South Pacific Ocean. Only four of the nine islands are inhabited, and more than 70 percent of the population lives on one island. Samoa became independent from New Zealand in 1962, when it established a democratic government. Samoa is one of the world's least developed countries and is dependent on foreign aid. However, its expanding manufacturing and tourism industries and increasing agricultural exports are helping its economy to grow.

Singapore

Capital	Singapore
Land Area	264 sq mi; 683 sq km
Population	4.5 million
Ethnic Group(s)	East Asian, Malay, South Asian
Religion(s)	Buddhist, Muslim, Christian, Hindu, traditional beliefs
Government	parliamentary republic
Currency	Singapore dollar
Leading Exports	machinery and equipment (including electronics), consumer goods, chemicals, mineral fuels
Language(s)	Malay (official), English (official), Mandarin (official), Tamil (official)

Singapore (SING uh pawr) is a group of islands located in Southeast Asia between Malaysia and Indonesia. Singapore was established as a British trading colony in 1819. It became independent in 1965. Singapore is currently one of the most important trading ports in Asia and one of the world's most prosperous countries. Ethnic Chinese make up about 80 percent of its population.

Solomon Islands

Capital	Honiara
Land Area	10,633 sq mi; 27,540 sq km
Population	494,786
Ethnic Group(s)	Melanesian, Polynesian, Micronesian, white, East Asian
Religion(s)	Protestant, Roman Catholic, traditional beliefs
Government	parliamentary democracy
Currency	Solomon Islands dollar
Leading Exports	timber, fish, copra, palm oil, cocoa
Language(s)	English (official), Pidgin English, Melanesian Pidgin

The Solomon Islands (SAHL uh mun EYE lundz) is a group of islands in the South Pacific Ocean east of Papua New Guinea. The Solomons are an archipelago of several hundred islands spread over 250,000 square miles. Most are coral reefs, and the majority of the population lives on the six largest islands. The Solomon Islands have been settled for thousands of years. In 1978, the island nation achieved independence from the United Kingdom. However, ethnic conflict and a high crime rate have caused instability and weakened the economy in recent years.

Thailand

Capital	Bangkok
Land Area	197,594 sq mi; 511,770 sq km
Population	62.5 million
Ethnic Group(s)	Thai, East Asian
Religion(s)	Buddhist, Muslim, Christian, Hindu
Government	constitutional monarchy
Currency	baht
Leading Exports	computers, transistors, seafood, clothing, rice
Language(s)	Thai (official), Chinese, Malay, Khmer, Karen, Miao

Thailand (TY land) is located in Southeast Asia, between the Andaman Sea and the Gulf of Thailand. It is bordered by Laos, Cambodia, Myanmar, and Malaysia. Thailand's central plain is fertile and densely populated. The country has enjoyed rapid economic growth in recent decades. However, this growth has used up many of its natural resources and strained its water supplies. Thailand, once called Siam, is the only Southeast Asian country that has never been taken over by a European power. It is now a constitutional monarchy.

Introducing Southeast Asia and the Pacific Region

Tonga

Capital	Nuku'alofa
Land Area	277 sq mi; 718 sq km
Population	106,137
Ethnic Group(s)	Polynesian, white
Religion(s)	Christian
Government	hereditary constitutional monarchy
Currency	pa'anga (Tongan dollar)
Leading Exports	squash, fish, vanilla beans, root crops
Language(s)	Tongan (official), English (official)

Tonga (TAHNG guh) is an archipelago of 170 islands located in the South Pacific Ocean northeast of New Zealand. Tonga's economy is based on agriculture and tourism but depends heavily on foreign aid. The country also imports much of its food. Tonga remains the only monarchy in the Pacific region and its king controls the nation's politics, despite calls in recent years for greater democracy.

Tuvalu

Capital	Fongafale
Land Area	10 sq mi; 26 sq km
Population	10,800
Ethnic Group(s)	Polynesian, Micronesian
Religion(s)	Protestant, traditional beliefs
Government	constitutional monarchy with a parliamentary democracy
Currency	Australian dollar and Tuvaluan dollar
Leading Exports	copra, fish
Language(s)	English (official), Tuvaluan, Kiribati

Tuvalu (too vuh LOO) is a tiny island group located in the South Pacific Ocean. It lies about halfway between Hawaii and Australia, or about 650 miles north of Fiji. Tuvalu has a total land area of about 10 square miles (26 square kilometers). Tuvalu was part of a British colony until its independence in 1978. Tuvalu's economy is based mainly on subsistence farming and fishing. However, the tiny nation also gets about $50 million per year from leasing out its Internet domain name ".tv."

Vanuatu

Capital	Port-Vila
Land Area	4,710 sq mi; 12,200 sq km
Population	196,178
Ethnic Group(s)	Melanesian, white, Southeast Asian, East Asian, Pacific Islander
Religion(s)	Protestant, Roman Catholic, traditional beliefs
Government	parliamentary republic
Currency	vatu
Leading Exports	copra, kava, beef, cocoa, timber, coffee
Language(s)	Bislama (official), English (official), French (official)

Vanuatu (van wah TOO) is a small island nation located in the South Pacific Ocean. It lies about three quarters of the way from Hawaii to Australia, or about 500 miles west of Fiji. Vanuatu is an archipelago of 80 volcanic islands spread over about 4 50 miles. However, only about 12 of the islands are of any size. Vanuatu was once called the New Hebrides. The islands were settled in the 1800s and ruled jointly by Great Britain and France from 1906. In 1980, Vanuatu became an independent republic. The economy is based primarily on agriculture and fishing.

Vietnam

Capital	Hanoi
Land Area	125,621 sq mi; 325,360 sq km
Population	81.1 million
Ethnic Group(s)	Vietnamese, East Asian, Hmong, Thai, Khmer, Cham
Religion(s)	Buddhist, Christian, traditional beliefs, Muslim
Government	communist state
Currency	dông
Leading Exports	crude oil, marine products, rice, coffee, rubber, tea, clothing, shoes
Language(s)	Vietnamese (official), Chinese, Thai, Khmer, Muong, Nung, Miao, Yao, Jarai

SOURCES: DK World Desk Reference Online; CIA World Factbook Online, 2002; *World Almanac,* 2003

Vietnam (vee et NAHM) is located along the eastern coast of the Indochinese peninsula in the South China Sea. France occupied Vietnam during the late 1800s. France continued to rule until 1954, when Communist forces under leader Ho Chi Minh defeated the French and took over the northern part of the country. The United States then helped South Vietnam resist Communist rule by fighting the North Vietnamese in the Vietnam War. The United States withdrew its military forces in 1973, and all of Vietnam was united under Communist rule. Still recovering from years of war, the government has allowed some private enterprise to strengthen its weak economy.

A woman weaves in a village in Vietnam. Most people in Vietnam live in rural areas.

Assessment

Comprehension and Critical Thinking

1. Name Name two Southeast Asian countries that are island nations.

2. Draw Conclusions What are the characteristics that most of the countries share?

3. Contrast What are some key differences among the countries?

4. Categorize Which countries in the region have monarchies?

5. Contrast How are the governments of Laos and Vietnam different from those of the other countries in the region?

6. Make a Bar Graph Create a bar graph showing the land area of the five most populous countries in this region.

Keeping Current

Access the **DK World Desk Reference Online** at **PHSchool.com** for up-to-date information about all the countries in this chapter.

Go Online
PHSchool.com
Web Code: lce-6900

Section 1 Vietnam
A Nation Rebuilds

Prepare to Read

Objectives

In this section you will

1. Find out how Vietnam was divided by conflicts and war.
2. Learn how Vietnam has rebuilt its economy.

Taking Notes

As you read this section, look for details about how Vietnam has developed since the Vietnam War. Copy the diagram below and record your findings in it.

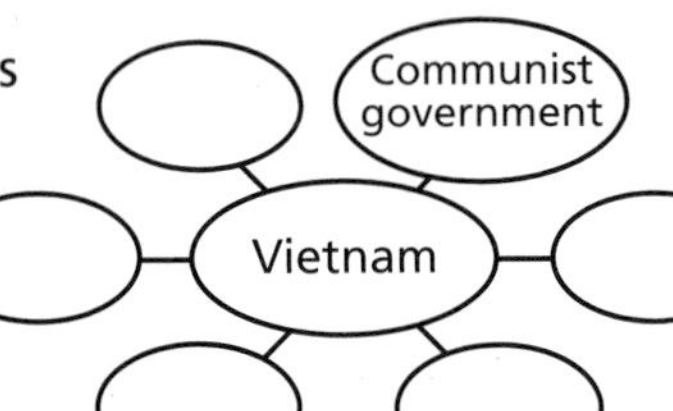

Target Reading Skill

Identify Main Idea The main idea of a paragraph tells what the whole paragraph is about. On page 800, the main idea of the paragraph with the heading Rebirth in Ho Chi Minh City is "Vietnam's greatest successes have been in rebuilding its cities." As you read this section, identify the main idea of each paragraph that follows a blue heading.

Key Terms

- **civil war** (SIV ul wawr) *n.* a war between political parties or regions within the same country
- **domino theory** (DAHM uh noh THEE uh ree) *n.* a belief that if one country fell to communism, neighboring nations would also fall, like a row of dominoes

New industries in Vietnam

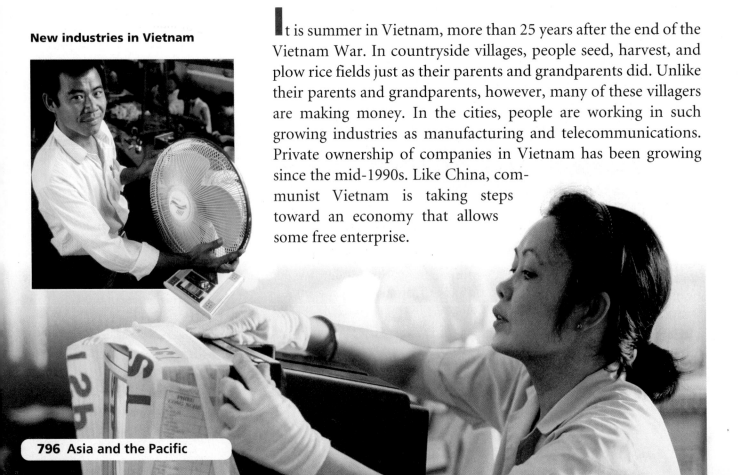

It is summer in Vietnam, more than 25 years after the end of the Vietnam War. In countryside villages, people seed, harvest, and plow rice fields just as their parents and grandparents did. Unlike their parents and grandparents, however, many of these villagers are making money. In the cities, people are working in such growing industries as manufacturing and telecommunications. Private ownership of companies in Vietnam has been growing since the mid-1990s. Like China, communist Vietnam is taking steps toward an economy that allows some free enterprise.

Decades of Conflict and War

The people of Vietnam have survived a long period of conflict. First, an alliance of Communists and Nationalists in Vietnam fought against France from 1946 to 1954. Second, a civil war followed. A **civil war** is a war between political parties or regions within the same country. During the Vietnam War, North Vietnam fought South Vietnam and its ally, the United States.

Presidential Palace in Hanoi
The Presidential Palace is used as offices for Vietnam's government. The palace was built by the French and used as headquarters for the French government until 1954. Note the flag of Vietnam is displayed.
Analyze Images *How are change and continuity shown in this photo?*

Vietnam Divided After the French defeat in 1954, a treaty divided Vietnam into northern and southern parts. Communists controlled the northern half. A non-communist government supported by the United States ruled South Vietnam. The treaty said that, eventually, an election would be held to reunite the country under one government.

These elections were never held, largely because the United States and Ngo Dinh Diem (en GOH din dee EM), the leader of South Vietnam, feared that the Communists might win. At that time, U.S. leaders believed in the **domino theory**. They thought that a Communist victory would cause other countries in Southeast Asia to fall to communism, like a row of dominoes.

Meanwhile, the Communists were trying to take over the south by force. In 1959, they launched a war to achieve this goal. They were led by Communist leader Ho Chi Minh (hoh chee min). Ho Chi Minh's forces were called the Viet Cong.

U.S. troops taking part in a mission in South Vietnam in 1967

American Involvement in the Vietnam War Communist leader Ho Chi Minh wanted to unite Vietnam under northern rule. Operating from the north, he aided Communist forces in the south. As the Communists threatened South Vietnam, the United States took an active role. At first, the United States sent thousands of military advisors to help the South Vietnamese. Later, hundreds of thousands of American troops arrived. Through the 1960s, the United States sent more troops to Vietnam. By 1968, there were more than 500,000 U.S. troops in Vietnam.

By the early 1970s, Vietnam had been at war for more than 30 years. The fighting spread to neighboring Laos and Cambodia as well. North Vietnam sent supplies along the Ho Chi Minh Trail through Laos and Cambodia to its troops in South Vietnam. In 1970, the United States bombed the Ho Chi Minh Trail and then invaded Cambodia. In 1971, South Vietnamese troops attacked North Vietnamese bases in Laos.

As the fighting continued, American casualties increased. Millions of people in the United States were calling for an end to the war. In 1973, the United States finally ended its part in the war when the last American combat soldiers left South Vietnam. More than 3 million Americans had served in the Vietnam War. More than 58,000 American troops died in the war, and another 150,000 were seriously wounded.

✓ Reading Check **Why did North Vietnam launch a war against South Vietnam?**

Links to Art

Water Puppets In Vietnam, a type of puppet theater uses a pond for a stage. Water puppet shows started centuries ago. In these shows, a puppeteer guides wooden figures so that they appear to wade through the water. The puppets are attached to rods and strings hidden underwater. Audiences sit at the water's edge. Stage settings of trees and clouds are also placed on the pond.

COUNTRY PROFILE Focus on **Culture**

Vietnam

Most people in Vietnam are ethnic Vietnamese, but Vietnam has more than 90 ethnic minorities. Ethnic Vietnamese live mainly in the lowlands of the north, the south, and a thin coastal strip. Fertile soils in the lowlands support a dense population, as you can see on the map. The largest minority, the ethnic Chinese, live mainly in lowland cities. Other minorities inhabit the rugged highlands, where farming is difficult and population densities are low.

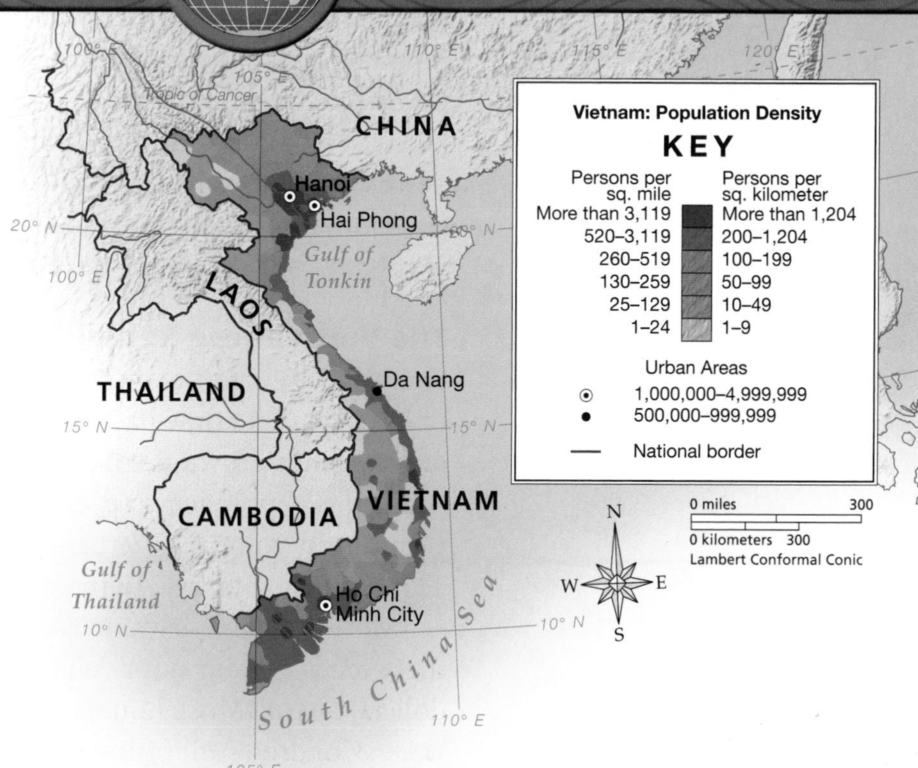

Ethnic Groups

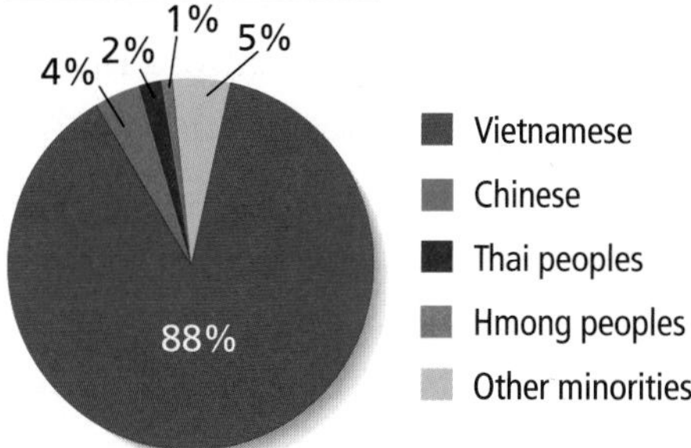

SOURCE: *DK World Desk Reference;* Ethnologue

Peoples of Vietnam

Ethnic Group	Where They Live
Vietnamese	Coastal strip, lowlands, major cities
Chinese	Major cities, northern lowlands
Thai peoples	Northern highlands
Hmong peoples	Northern highlands
Other minorities	Northern and central highlands, border regions

SOURCE: Ethnologue

Map and Chart Skills

1. **Identify** What percentage of Vietnam's people are ethnically Vietnamese or Chinese?
2. **Describe** These groups live in the fertile lowlands, with more than 259 persons per square mile. Do these lowlands cover more than 50 percent of Vietnam's area?
3. **Analyze** How can you explain the difference between these percentages?

Use Web Code **lce-6901** for **DK World Desk Reference Online.**

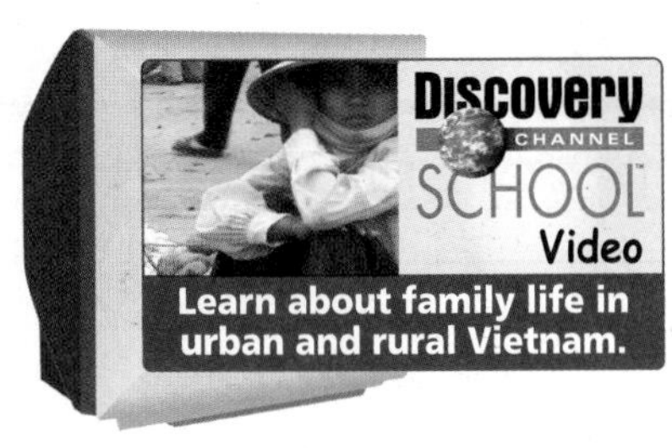
Discovery
CHANNEL
SCHOOL
Video
Learn about family life in urban and rural Vietnam.

After the Vietnam War

After the United States pulled out its troops, North Vietnam conquered South Vietnam in 1975. In 1976, the country was reunited under a communist government. Vietnam had been devastated by the war. More than a million Vietnamese had been killed or wounded. Homes, farms, factories, and forests had been destroyed. Bombs had torn cities apart. Fields were covered with land mines, or hidden explosives. The Vietnamese people were worn out. Still ahead was the huge effort of rebuilding.

The Vietnamese Rebuild In the years after the war, the communist government in Vietnam strictly controlled the lives of its citizens. As time passed, however, it was clear that the economy was not growing. Like the Chinese, the Vietnamese had to adapt their approach to economic growth. Although it is still a communist country, Vietnam now allows some free enterprise. This has helped many Vietnamese improve their lives.

Most Vietnamese live in rural areas. In spite of some progress, these areas remain poor. Whole families live on a few hundred dollars a year. Most houses have no indoor toilets or running water. Children suffer from a lack of healthy food. Vietnam is still among the poorest nations in Asia.

Contruction projects reflect the spirit of change in Vietnam. Here, workers lay a foundation for a new building in Ho Chi Minh City.

Rebirth in Ho Chi Minh City Vietnam's greatest success has been in rebuilding its cities. Hanoi in the north is the capital. The city of Saigon (sy GAHN), in the south, was renamed Ho Chi Minh City after the Communist leader. It is the most prosperous city in Vietnam and is the center of trade. Americans who visit Ho Chi Minh City today find some of the same things they would find at home, such as American-style ice cream and cable news networks on television.

Some Vietnamese who live in the city enjoy greater prosperity. They buy designer clothing and watches, stereo systems, video recorders, and jewelry. Many of these people run restaurants or hotels, buy and sell land or buildings, or own factories, all of which help stimulate Vietnam's economy.

A girl from the Hmong ethnic group (left) and a city shopper (inset) show rural and urban life in Vietnam.

Economic Recovery Vietnam enjoyed high economic growth during most of the 1990s. In 1986, Vietnam's government began an economic recovery program aimed chiefly at attracting foreign investors. As a result, Vietnam became one of the fastest-growing economies in the world. From 1990 to 1997, the economy grew each year by an average of about 8 percent. Agricultural output doubled, turning Vietnam from a country once dependent on food imports to the world's second-largest exporter of rice. Although economic growth slowed in the late 1990s, Vietnam continued its efforts to improve the economy.

Target Skill **Identify Main Ideas** Which sentence states the main idea in the paragraph on this page?

√ Reading Check **Which city in Vietnam is the most prosperous and the nation's center of trade?**

Section 1 Assessment

Key Terms

Review the key terms at the beginning of this section. Use each term in a sentence that explains its meaning.

Target Reading Skill

Write the main idea of each paragraph that follows a blue heading in this section.

Comprehension and Critical Thinking

1. (a) Recall When did the United States withdraw from the Vietnam War?

(b) Summarize What conflicts have divided Vietnam since the end of World War II?

2. (a) Describe Describe conditions in Vietnam when the Vietnam War ended.

(b) Make Generalizations What successes has Vietnam had in rebuilding its economy?

(c) Identify Point of View Why do you think Saigon was renamed Ho Chi Minh City after the Vietnam War?

Writing Activity

Write a summary that describes Vietnam since the Vietnam War. Use this title for your summary: Vietnam: A Country, Not a War. Focus on the country's economic development.

Writing Tip Be sure to look closely at the pictures and the Country Profile in this section to help you as you write your description.

Using a Flowchart

Rice is one of the most important crops in Vietnam. It is grown on almost 75 percent of all cultivated land. Most Vietnamese farmers live in the lowland and delta area. This area's wetlands and heavy rains make it perfect for growing rice.

Most Southeast Asian farmers grow rice the same way that their ancestors did thousands of years ago. They build shallow fields called paddies. They flood the paddies with water. They plant rice in seedling beds. Farmers transplant the rice seedlings in the paddies by hand. They also harvest the rice by hand.

You've just read a description of how rice is grown. But sometimes it is easier to figure out how something works by following the steps in a flowchart.

Traditional Rice Farming

Farmers build a rice paddy.

↓

The paddy is flooded with water.

↓

Farmers use water buffalo to plow and smooth out the paddy.

↓

Farmers prepare seedling beds alongside the paddy and plant rice seed in seedling beds.

↓

After seedlings are 4 to 6 inches tall, farmers transplant them into the paddy.

↓

Farmers weed, fertilize, and add water regularly to the paddy.

↓

When the rice turns from green to gold, it is harvested.

A flowchart shows the sequence of steps used to complete an activity. It shows the steps in the order they happen. Sometimes the steps are illustrated. A flowchart usually uses arrows to show how steps follow one another.

Learn the Skill

Here are the steps you will need to follow when you read a flowchart.

1. **Read the title.** Read the title first to find out what the flowchart is about. The title of the flowchart at the left is Traditional Rice Farming.
2. **Find the arrows.** The arrows will tell you the order in which you should read the chart. Find the beginning and start there.
3. **Read the flowchart carefully.** If there are illustrations, study them, but be sure to read the text next to them. Think about how one step leads to the next step. What are the connections? If there are no illustrations, try imagining each step to help you understand the sequence.

Practice the Skill

Use the steps and the flowchart on the previous page to practice reading a flowchart.

1. Read the title of the flowchart first. Explain what the flowchart will tell you.
2. Find the beginning of the chart. Identify the first step of the chart. Start there and follow the arrows through each step.
3. Now read the flowchart carefully. Your reading of the flowchart should help you understand the steps in traditional rice farming. Now answer these questions: What is the first step in traditional rice farming? What happens after the paddy is flooded with water? Where do the farmers prepare seedling beds? How tall are the rice seedlings when the farmers transplant them into the paddy? How do the farmers know when it is time to harvest the rice?

Traditional Rice Processing

Thresh, or beat, the rice plants to separate the rice husks from the plant.

↓

Dry the rice husks.

↓

Thresh the rice husks to remove the rice grains from the husks.

↓

Thresh the rice again to separate the husks from rice grains.

↓

Store the rice in a dry place.

Apply the Skill

Use the steps in this skill to read the flowchart above. What is the chart about? How are the rice husks separated from the plant? Why is the rice threshed three times?

Section 2 Australia
A Pacific Rim Country

Prepare to Read

Objectives
In this section you will
1. Learn about the major economic activities in Australia.
2. Find out how Aboriginal people in Australia are working to improve their lives.

Taking Notes
Copy the diagram. As you read, record details about Australia's economy.

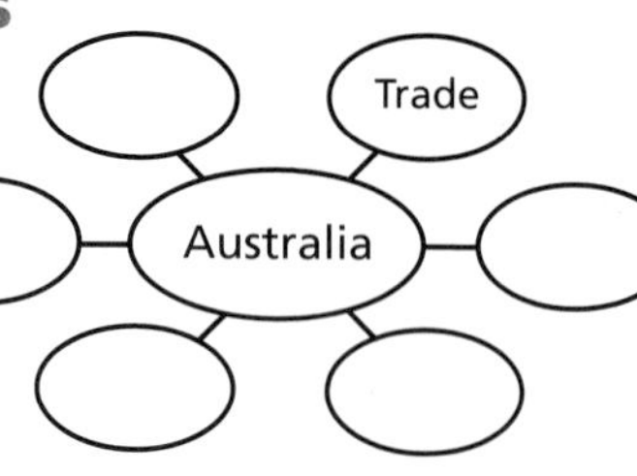

Target Reading Skill
Identify Supporting Details On page 806, look at the paragraph with the heading Ranching. The first sentence is the main idea. The rest of the sentences support the main idea. What details in this paragraph explain the part ranching plays in Australia's economy?

Key Terms
- **outback** (OWT bak) *n.* the dry land consisting of plains and plateaus that makes up much of central and western Australia
- **artesian well** (ahr TEE zhun wel) *n.* a well from which water flows under natural pressure without pumping

Michael Chang owns a successful trading company in Sydney, Australia's largest city. From his office in a modern glass skyscraper, he sometimes watches Sydney's busy harbor. What interests him most are the large cargo ships.

John Koeyers and his family own a huge cattle ranch in northwest Australia. He uses helicopters and trucks to round up the herds on his ranch. The Koeyers sell most of their cattle to companies in Asian nations.

Charlie Walkabout is director of Anangu Tours. Anangu Tours is owned and run by Aboriginal people. The company has won awards for its tours of Uluru, also known as Ayers Rock.

Sydney, Australia, has a beautiful and busy harbor.

Economic Activities

Michael Chang, the Koeyers, and Charlie Walkabout are all Australians. The meaning of *Australian* has changed since Australia achieved independence. It is no longer "British." It now reflects the diversity of Australia's people. Today, Australia has close ties with other nations of the Pacific Rim. These nations border the Pacific Ocean. They include Japan, South Korea, China, and Taiwan. The United States is another major Pacific Rim nation. It is one of Australia's key trading partners. Australia's economy depends on trade with Pacific Rim countries.

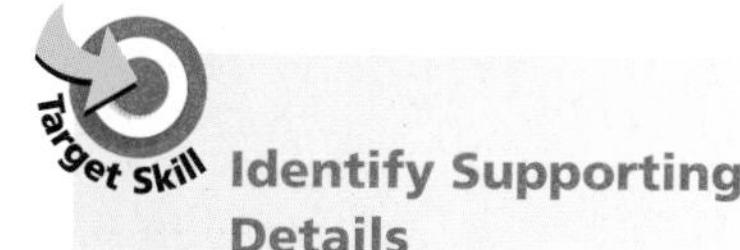

Identify Supporting Details
What details in this paragraph explain the meaning of the "Pacific Rim"?

Trade Michael Chang's trading company is just one of hundreds of companies that do business with Pacific Rim countries. He sends various products to many countries in Asia. Rancher John Koeyers is involved in trade, too. Large cargo ships transport his cattle to South Korea and Taiwan. Other cargo ships carry products such as Australian wool and meat to foreign markets. Cargo ships also carry Australia's minerals to Japan.

Farming It seems strange that farm products are an important export for Australia, because only about 7 percent of Australia's land is good for farming. Most of this land is in southeastern Australia and along the east coast. The country's few rivers are in those areas. Farmers use the river water to irrigate their crops. Australian farmers raise barley, oats, and sugar cane. However, their most valuable crop is wheat. Australia is one of the world's leading wheat growers and exporters.

Ranching Ranching is another major part of Australia's economy. Australian sheep and cattle provide lamb, mutton, and beef for export. Australia is the world's leading wool producer. Most cattle and sheep are raised on large ranches called stations. Some of the largest stations are in the outback. The **outback** is the name Australians use for the dry land that makes up much of the central and western part of the country. Few people live on its plains and plateaus.

COUNTRY PROFILE — Focus on Geography

Australia

Australia is a large but thinly populated country. It covers about the same area as the United States, not including Alaska and Hawaii. But it has only about 20 million people, a smaller population than Texas. As the graph shows, most of its people live in urban areas. Australia's largest urban areas lie along its southeast coast. On the map, they are the areas labeled "manufacturing and trade." They cover only a very small part of the country. Much of the country consists of huge ranches and farms—labeled "livestock raising" and "commercial farming" on the map—and large deserts—labeled "limited economic activity." There are also forests in the southeast and aboriginal land, used for hunting and gathering, mainly in the north.

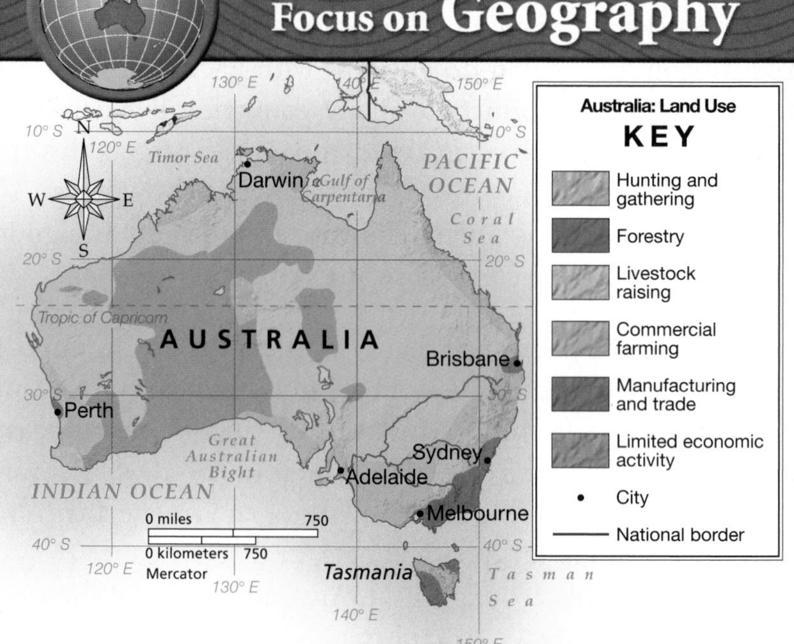

Urban and Rural Population

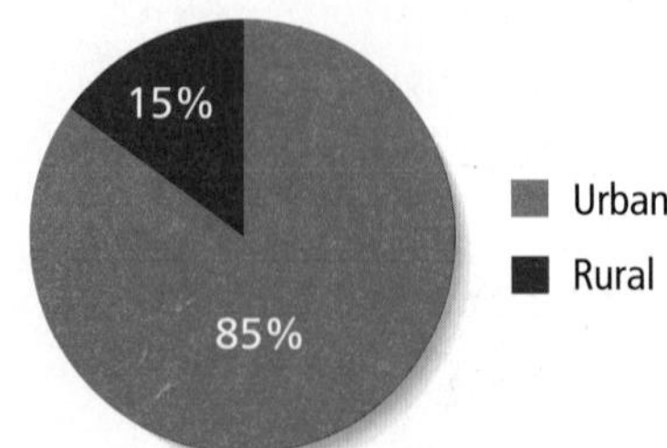

SOURCE: *DK World Desk Reference*

Map and Chart Skills

1. **Recall** Where do most Australians live?
2. **Infer** About how many people live in Australia's rural areas?
3. **Compare** How does Australia's population density compare with that of the United States?

Use Web Code **lce-6902** for **DK World Desk Reference Online.**

British Heritage in Australia The majority of Australians have a British ancestry. Australia's British heritage is shown in Australia's national flag, which includes the flag of the United Kingdom. Australia's flag also includes the Southern Cross, a constellation visible in the Southern Hemisphere. **Conclude** *Why is the Southern Cross an appropriate symbol for Australia?*

For example, the Koeyers' ranch is in a hot, dry area in northwest Australia. It covers 1 million acres (404,686 hectares) and has about 7,000 head of cattle. Another outback station, near Alice Springs in the center of Australia, is even larger. It covers nearly 12,000 square miles (31,080 square kilometers)—larger than the state of Maryland. Even with this much land, sometimes the cattle can barely find enough grass for grazing. Fresh water also is scarce. Rain falls rarely, and the region has only a few small streams. To supply water for their cattle, ranchers use underground **artesian wells.** These are wells from which water flows under natural pressure without pumping.

✓ Reading Check **How does ranching help Australia's economy?**

Aborigines: Improving Lives

The people of Anangu Tours are proud of the awards they have won for their tours of Uluru. Aboriginal guides conduct the tours in their own language and an interpreter translates the words into English. Aboriginal people in Australia are working hard to preserve their culture. They are having a growing role in the economic life of the country.

Aboriginal leaders have worked to improve the lives of their people. Their schools now teach Aboriginal languages. Aborigines again celebrate important events with ancestral songs and dances. Artists have strengthened Aboriginal culture by creating traditional rock paintings and tree bark paintings.

Discovery
CHANNEL
SCHOOL
Video
Learn about the different regions of Australia.

Aboriginal leaders have helped their people in another important way, too. They have influenced the government of Australia. The government has begun to return Aboriginal land to them. The government has also built schools and hospitals on their land. It has begun to protect some of their sacred places as well.

Aborigines have gained more rights. But their main goal is to regain their ancestral lands. Though Australia's courts have helped, many ranchers and farmers now live on those lands. These people strongly oppose giving the land back. This issue may take many years to resolve.

✓ Reading Check **What is a main goal for Aboriginal people in Australia?**

Australian Aboriginal cave paintings date back thousands of years and are among the world's earliest art.

Section 2 Assessment

Key Terms

Review the key terms at the beginning of this section. Use each term in a sentence that explains its meaning.

Target Reading Skill

Find the text on ranching on page 806. What details support the information about ranching in Australia?

Comprehension and Critical Thinking

1. (a) Explain What is the Pacific Rim?

(b) Apply Information Based on what you know about Australia's location, explain why Australia's economy depends on trade with Pacific Rim countries.

2. (a) Recall Give two examples showing how Aboriginal people are working to improve their lives.

(b) Compare As the United States grew, Native Americans were forced from their homelands and moved to reservations. For years, Native Americans have been fighting to regain their original homelands. How does this compare with the history and struggle of the Aborigines?

Writing Activity

Use the information in this section and in the Country Profile on page 786 to write an article about Australia for a news magazine. The article should describe the main types of work people do in Australia.

For: An activity about Australia
Visit: PHSchool.com
Web Code: lcd-6902

Review and Assessment

◆ Chapter Summary

Section 1: Vietnam

- After decades of conflict and war, Vietnam is now a communist country that allows some free enterprise.
- Although still among the poorest countries in the world, Vietnam has made great strides in rebuilding its economy.
- Vietnam has become a leading exporter of rice.

Vietnamese water puppets

Section 2: Australia

- Australia is a Pacific Rim country with an economy based on trade.
- Farming and ranching are key parts of Australia's economy.
- Aboriginal people in Australia are working to preserve their culture and have a role in the economic life of the country.

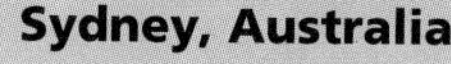
Sydney, Australia

◆ Key Terms

Match the definitions in Column I with the key terms in Column II.

Column I

1. a well from which water flows under natural pressure without pumping
2. a war between political parties or regions within the same country
3. a belief that if one country fell to communism, neighboring nations would also fall, like a row of dominoes
4. the dry land that makes up much of central and western Australia

Column II

A civil war
B outback
C artesian well
D domino theory

Chapter 

Review and Assessment (continued)

◆ Comprehension and Critical Thinking

5. **(a) Recall** Who was Vietnam in conflict with from 1946 to 1954?
(b) Explain What were the Viet Cong?
(c) Summarize Describe the involvement of the United States in the Vietnam War.

6. **(a) Recall** Why did the United States end its involvement in the Vietnam War?
(b) Identify Effects What was one result of the Vietnam War?

7. **(a) Note** Where do most people in Vietnam live?
(b) Contrast How are rural areas in Vietnam different from Ho Chi Minh City?

8. **(a) Name** What is the capital of Vietnam?
(b) Locate In what part of Vietnam is Hanoi located?
(c) Apply Information Why was Saigon renamed Ho Chi Minh City?

9. **(a) Recall** On what kinds of products does Australia depend for a prosperous foreign trade?
(b) Infer Why do few people make their home in Australia's outback?

10. **(a) Note** What are important goals for Australia's Aboriginal people?
(b) Conclude How is Anangu Tours helping to preserve Aboriginal culture?

◆ Skills Practice

Using a Flowchart In the Skills for Life activity in this chapter, you learned how to read a flowchart. Review the steps you learned to use this skill. Then use the flowchart on page 802 to tell what happens after farmers transplant rice seedlings into the rice paddy.

◆ Writing Activity: Language Arts

Storytelling is an important part of Aboriginal culture. Do library research to find and read an Aboriginal folk tale from Australia. Write a report that summarizes the folk tale.

MAP MASTER™ Skills Activity

Place Location For each place listed below, write the letter from the map that shows its location.

1. Pacific Ocean
2. Australia
3. Vietnam
4. Philippines
5. Sydney
6. New Zealand

Go Online PHSchool.com Use Web Code **lcp-6920** for an **interactive map.**

Southeast Asia and the Pacific Region

A
B
C
D
E
F
Tropic of Cancer
Equator
Tropic of Capricorn
20° N
0°
20° S
40° S
100° E
120° E
140° E
160° E
180°
160° W
N
S
E
W

Standardized Test Prep

Test-Taking Tips

Some questions on standardized tests ask you to analyze point of view. Read the passage below. Then, follow the tips to answer the sample question.

> In 1973, the United States ended its part in the Vietnam War. American military advisers and troops were sent home. As American helicopters flew off from the capital, someone watching them said, "I had better hurry to the American embassy. Maybe one of my American friends there can help me escape from Vietnam and go to America."

Pick the letter that best answers the question.

Which onlooker might have made that statement?

A a North Vietnamese soldier who had been fighting for years

B an American soldier who got separated from his company

C a South Vietnamese woman who had worked for the Americans

D a protestor who had been supporting North Vietnam during the war

TIP Be sure you understand the question. Who said the words that begin, "I had better hurry to the American embassy . . ."?

Think It Through You can eliminate A and D because neither person would have friends at the American embassy. You can eliminate B because an American soldier would not have a reason to escape from Vietnam. The correct answer is C.

Practice Questions

Use the tips above and other tips in this book to help you answer the following questions.

1. What did the United States fear would happen if it did NOT help South Vietnam fight against North Vietnam?
   - **A** The French would take control.
   - **B** North Vietnam would invade China.
   - **C** Communists would take over South Vietnam.
   - **D** The United States would lose control of North Vietnam.

2. The Vietnam War finally ended in 1975 when
   - **A** North Vietnam surrendered.
   - **B** U.S. forces invaded Cambodia.
   - **C** North Vietnam gained control over all of South Vietnam.
   - **D** the United States signed a peace treaty with North Vietnam.

3. Some of Australia's trading partners in the Pacific Rim include the United States, China, Taiwan, and
   - **A** India.
   - **B** Italy.
   - **C** Egypt.
   - **D** Japan.

Use Web Code **lca-6900** for **Chapter 26 self-test.**

Projects

Create your own projects to learn more about Asia and the Pacific. At the beginning of this book, you were introduced to the **Guiding Questions** for studying the chapters and special features. But you can also find answers to these questions by doing projects on your own or with a group. Use the questions to find topics you want to explore further. Then try the projects described on this page or create your own.

1. **Geography** What are the main physical features of Asia and the Pacific?
2. **History** How have ancient civilizations of Asia and the Pacific influenced the world today?
3. **Culture** What are the main characteristics of the cultures of Asia and the Pacific?
4. **Government** What types of government exist in Asia and the Pacific today?
5. **Economics** How do the people of this region make a living?

Project

RESEARCH EXPORTS AND TRADE

Asia and the Pacific Trade Fair

With your class, plan a trade fair for the countries of Asia and the Pacific. As you read this book, choose a country to research. Find out about its major products, factories, and trading partners. Set up a booth to show and tell visitors about trade in your country. Bring books about the country and make posters, pamphlets, and charts for your booth.

Project

CREATE A MAP AND POSTER DISPLAY

Agriculture in Asia and the Pacific

Draw a large map of Asia and the Pacific and hang it in your classroom. As you read about different kinds of farm products, mark them on the appropriate location on your map. Choose ten farm products and design a small poster for each one. On each poster, write the farm product and a country in Asia and the Pacific where this product comes from. Find or draw a picture for each poster.

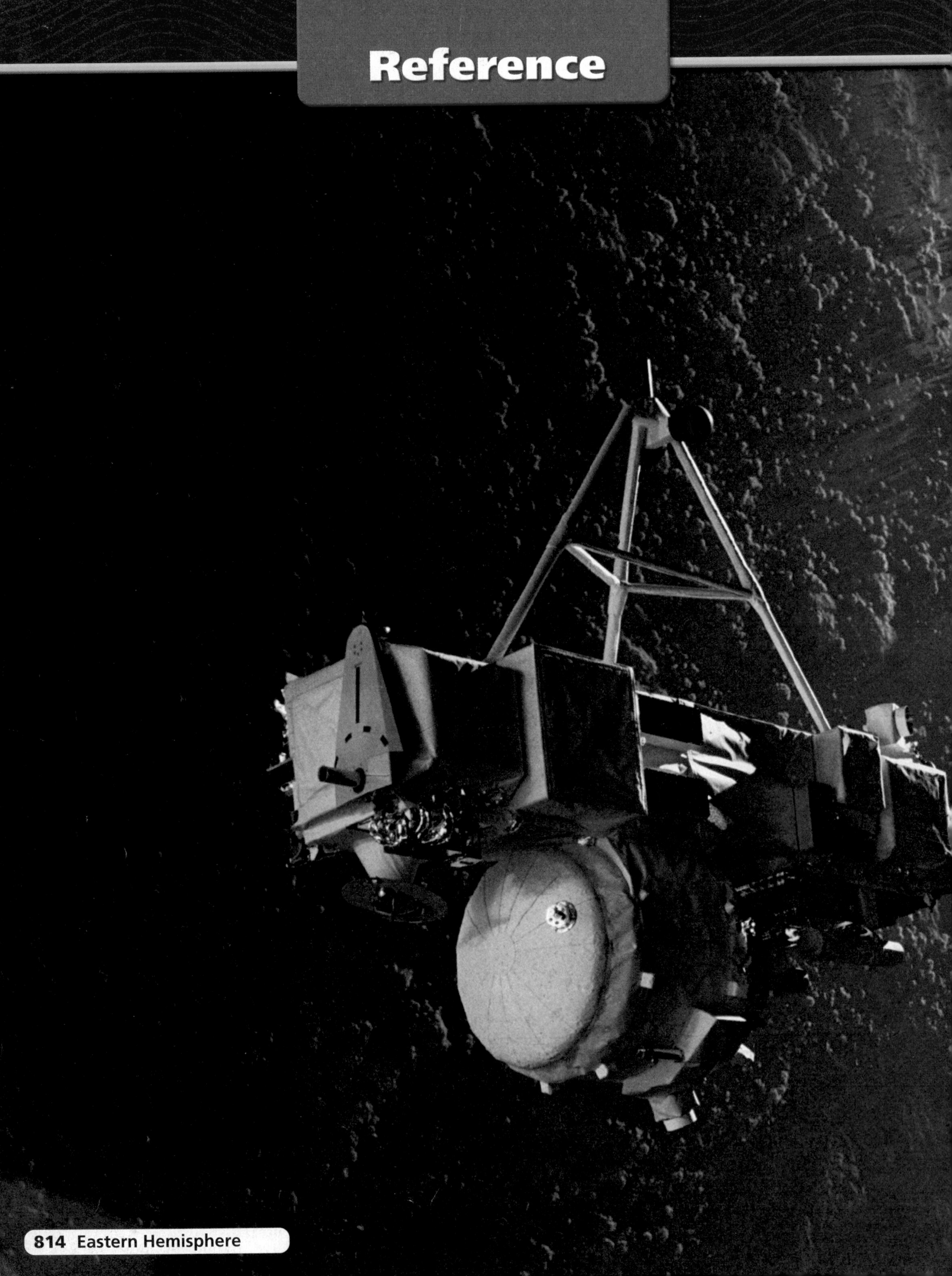

Table of Contents

Atlas

The World: Political

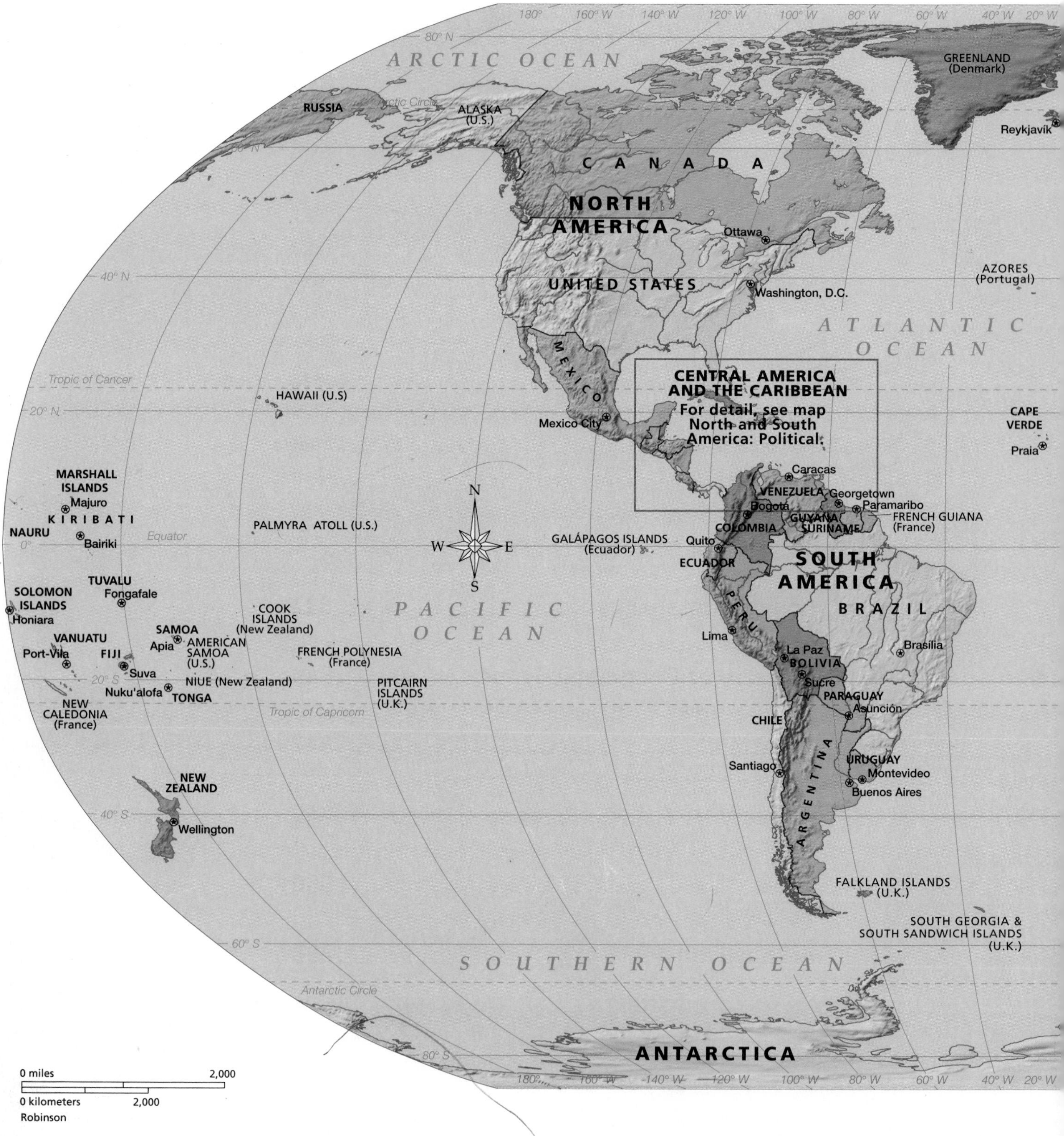

ARCTIC OCEAN
RUSSIA
ALASKA (U.S.)
GREENLAND (Denmark)
Reykjavík
CANADA
NORTH AMERICA
Ottawa
UNITED STATES
Washington, D.C.
AZORES (Portugal)
ATLANTIC OCEAN
MEXICO
Mexico City
CENTRAL AMERICA AND THE CARIBBEAN
For detail, see map North and South America: Political.
HAWAII (U.S)
Tropic of Cancer
CAPE VERDE
Praia
Caracas
VENEZUELA
Georgetown
Paramaribo
FRENCH GUIANA (France)
Bogotá
GUYANA
SURINAME
COLOMBIA
Quito
ECUADOR
GALÁPAGOS ISLANDS (Ecuador)
SOUTH AMERICA
BRAZIL
PERU
Lima
Brasília
La Paz
BOLIVIA
Sucre
PARAGUAY
Asunción
CHILE
Santiago
ARGENTINA
URUGUAY
Montevideo
Buenos Aires
FALKLAND ISLANDS (U.K.)
SOUTH GEORGIA & SOUTH SANDWICH ISLANDS (U.K.)
MARSHALL ISLANDS
Majuro
KIRIBATI
NAURU
Bairiki
Equator
PALMYRA ATOLL (U.S.)
TUVALU
Fongafale
SOLOMON ISLANDS
Honiara
VANUATU
Port-Vila
FIJI
Suva
SAMOA
Apia
AMERICAN SAMOA (U.S.)
COOK ISLANDS (New Zealand)
PACIFIC OCEAN
FRENCH POLYNESIA (France)
NIUE (New Zealand)
Nuku'alofa
TONGA
PITCAIRN ISLANDS (U.K.)
NEW CALEDONIA (France)
Tropic of Capricorn
NEW ZEALAND
Wellington
SOUTHERN OCEAN
Antarctic Circle
ANTARCTICA

0 miles 2,000
0 kilometers 2,000
Robinson

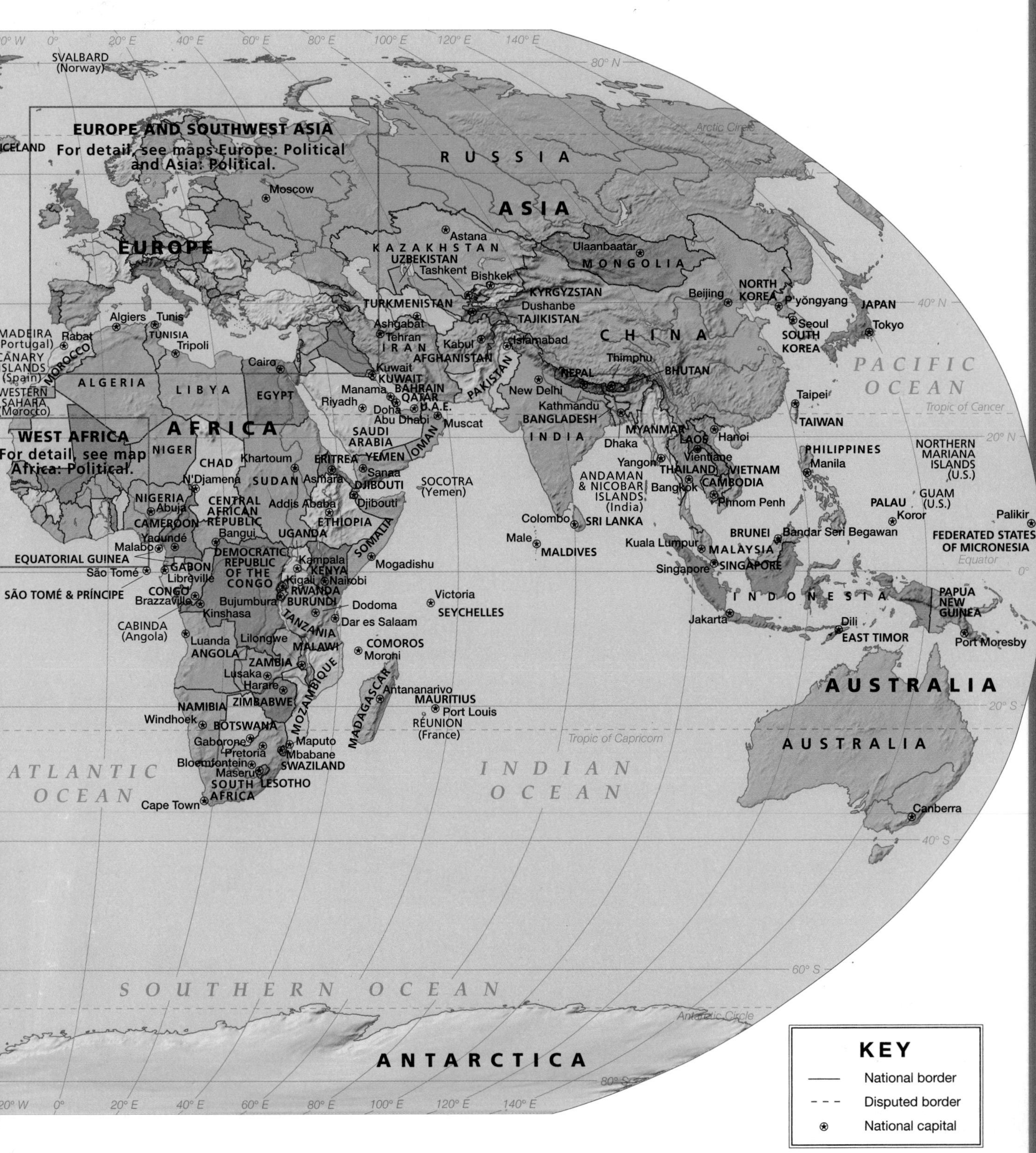

20° W
0°
20° E
40° E
60° E
80° E
100° E
120° E
140° E
80° N
SVALBARD (Norway)
EUROPE AND SOUTHWEST ASIA
For detail, see maps Europe: Political and Asia: Political.
ICELAND
Arctic Circle
RUSSIA
Moscow
ASIA
EUROPE
Astana
KAZAKHSTAN
UZBEKISTAN
Tashkent
Bishkek
Ulaanbaatar
MONGOLIA
KYRGYZSTAN
Dushanbe
TAJIKISTAN
TURKMENISTAN
Ashgabat
Tehran
IRAN
Kabul
AFGHANISTAN
Islamabad
PAKISTAN
Beijing
NORTH KOREA
P'yŏngyang
JAPAN
Tokyo
Seoul
SOUTH KOREA
40° N
CHINA
Thimphu
BHUTAN
NEPAL
New Delhi
Kathmandu
BANGLADESH
Dhaka
INDIA
MYANMAR
Yangon
LAOS
Vientiane
Hanoi
THAILAND
Bangkok
VIETNAM
CAMBODIA
Phnom Penh
Taipei
TAIWAN
PACIFIC OCEAN
Tropic of Cancer
20° N
PHILIPPINES
Manila
NORTHERN MARIANA ISLANDS (U.S.)
GUAM (U.S.)
PALAU
Koror
Palikir
FEDERATED STATES OF MICRONESIA
Equator
0°
MADEIRA (Portugal)
Rabat
MOROCCO
CANARY ISLANDS (Spain)
WESTERN SAHARA (Morocco)
Algiers
Tunis
TUNISIA
Tripoli
ALGERIA
LIBYA
Cairo
EGYPT
Kuwait
KUWAIT
Manama
BAHRAIN
QATAR
Riyadh
Doha
U.A.E.
Abu Dhabi
Muscat
OMAN
SAUDI ARABIA
YEMEN
Sanaa
ERITREA
Asmara
DJIBOUTI
Djibouti
SOCOTRA (Yemen)
AFRICA
WEST AFRICA
For detail, see map Africa: Political.
NIGER
CHAD
Khartoum
SUDAN
N'Djamena
NIGERIA
Abuja
CAMEROON
Yaoundé
CENTRAL AFRICAN REPUBLIC
Bangui
Addis Ababa
ETHIOPIA
UGANDA
SOMALIA
Mogadishu
Malabo
EQUATORIAL GUINEA
São Tomé
SÃO TOMÉ & PRÍNCIPE
GABON
Libreville
CONGO
Brazzaville
DEMOCRATIC REPUBLIC OF THE CONGO
Kinshasa
Kampala
KENYA
Nairobi
Kigali
RWANDA
BURUNDI
Bujumbura
Dodoma
TANZANIA
Dar es Salaam
Victoria
SEYCHELLES
CABINDA (Angola)
Luanda
ANGOLA
Lilongwe
MALAWI
COMOROS
Moroni
ZAMBIA
Lusaka
Harare
ZIMBABWE
MOZAMBIQUE
MADAGASCAR
Antananarivo
MAURITIUS
Port Louis
RÉUNION (France)
NAMIBIA
Windhoek
BOTSWANA
Gaborone
Pretoria
Maputo
Mbabane
SWAZILAND
Bloemfontein
Maseru
LESOTHO
SOUTH AFRICA
Cape Town
Colombo
SRI LANKA
Male
MALDIVES
ANDAMAN & NICOBAR ISLANDS (India)
Kuala Lumpur
MALAYSIA
Singapore
SINGAPORE
BRUNEI
Bandar Seri Begawan
INDONESIA
Jakarta
Dili
EAST TIMOR
PAPUA NEW GUINEA
Port Moresby
AUSTRALIA
AUSTRALIA
20° S
Tropic of Capricorn
ATLANTIC OCEAN
INDIAN OCEAN
Canberra
40° S
60° S
SOUTHERN OCEAN
Antarctic Circle
ANTARCTICA
80° S
KEY
National border
Disputed border
National capital

The World: Physical

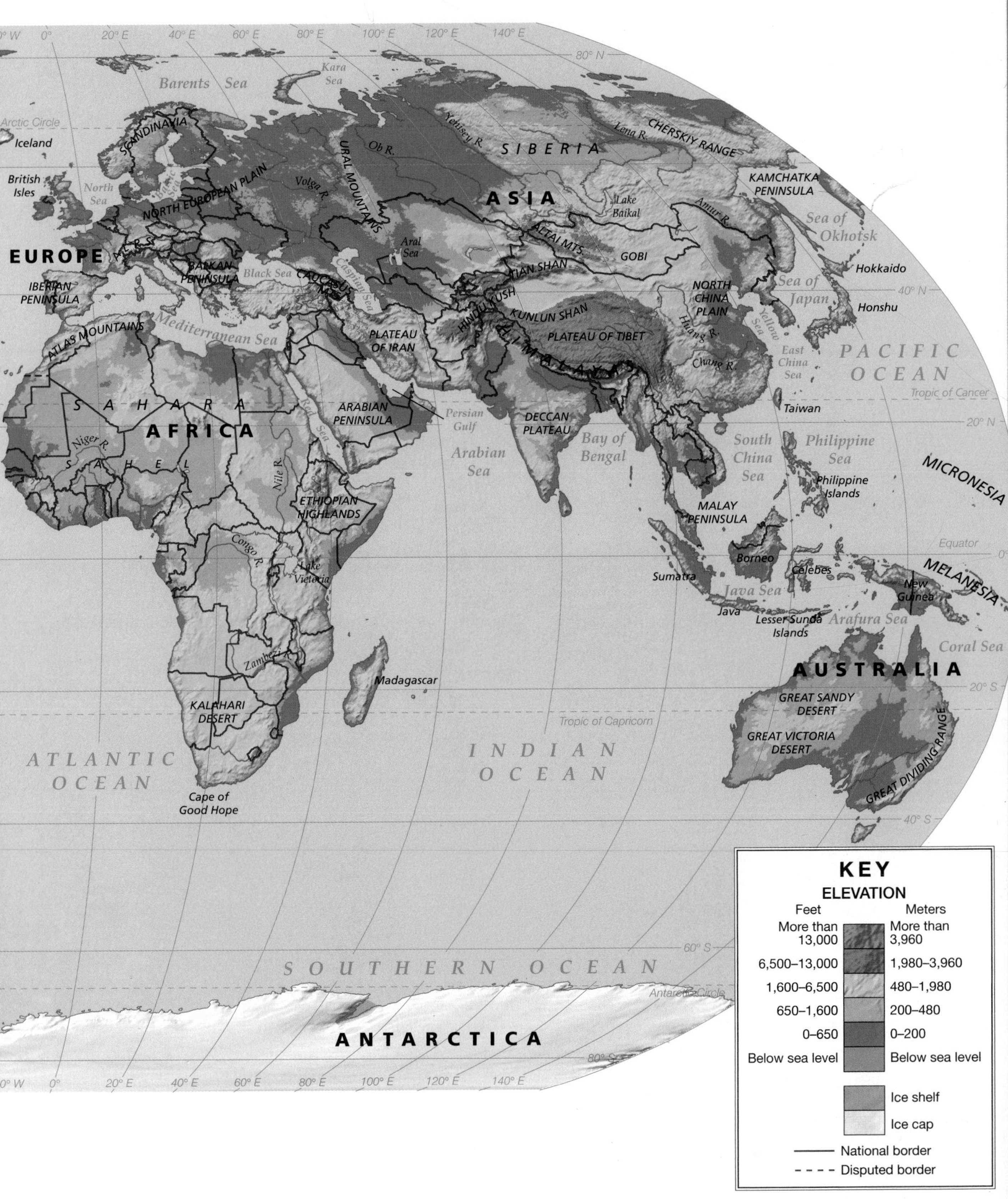

EUROPE
ASIA
AFRICA
AUSTRALIA
ANTARCTICA
SIBERIA
Iceland
British Isles
SCANDINAVIA
NORTH EUROPEAN PLAIN
URAL MOUNTAINS
IBERIAN PENINSULA
BALKAN PENINSULA
CAUCASUS MTS.
ALPS
ATLAS MOUNTAINS
SAHARA
SAHEL
ETHIOPIAN HIGHLANDS
KALAHARI DESERT
Cape of Good Hope
Madagascar
ARABIAN PENINSULA
PLATEAU OF IRAN
DECCAN PLATEAU
HINDU KUSH
KUNLUN SHAN
PLATEAU OF TIBET
HIMALAYAS
TIAN SHAN
ALTAI MTS.
GOBI
NORTH CHINA PLAIN
CHERSKIY RANGE
KAMCHATKA PENINSULA
Hokkaido
Honshu
Taiwan
Philippine Islands
MALAY PENINSULA
Sumatra
Borneo
Celebes
Java
Lesser Sunda Islands
New Guinea
MICRONESIA
MELANESIA
GREAT SANDY DESERT
GREAT VICTORIA DESERT
GREAT DIVIDING RANGE
Barents Sea
Kara Sea
North Sea
Baltic Sea
Black Sea
Caspian Sea
Aral Sea
Mediterranean Sea
Red Sea
Persian Gulf
Arabian Sea
Bay of Bengal
South China Sea
Philippine Sea
East China Sea
Yellow Sea
Sea of Japan
Sea of Okhotsk
Java Sea
Arafura Sea
Coral Sea
Lake Baikal
Lake Victoria
Ob R.
Yenisey R.
Lena R.
Amur R.
Volga R.
Huang R.
Chang R.
Niger R.
Nile R.
Congo R.
Zambezi R.
PACIFIC OCEAN
INDIAN OCEAN
ATLANTIC OCEAN
SOUTHERN OCEAN
Arctic Circle
Tropic of Cancer
Equator
Tropic of Capricorn
Antarctic Circle
80° N
40° N
20° N
0°
20° S
40° S
60° S
80° S
20° W
0°
20° E
40° E
60° E
80° E
100° E
120° E
140° E
KEY
ELEVATION
Feet
Meters
More than 13,000
More than 3,960
6,500–13,000
1,980–3,960
1,600–6,500
480–1,980
650–1,600
200–480
0–650
0–200
Below sea level
Below sea level
Ice shelf
Ice cap
National border
Disputed border

North and South America: Political
ASIA
ARCTIC OCEAN
EUROPE
Bering Strait
Beaufort Sea
Bering Sea
ALASKA (U.S.)
GREENLAND (Denmark)
Baffin Bay
Great Bear Lake
Great Slave Lake
Hudson Bay
Labrador Sea
CANADA
Lake Winnipeg
Great Lakes
Ottawa
UNITED STATES
New York City
Washington, D.C.
Ohio R.
Mississippi R.
Los Angeles
ATLANTIC OCEAN
Rio Grande
Gulf of Mexico
MEXICO
Mexico City
PACIFIC OCEAN
DOMINICAN REPUBLIC
BAHAMAS
PUERTO RICO (U.S.)
VIRGIN ISLANDS (U.S.)
ST. KITTS & NEVIS
ANTIGUA & BARBUDA
GUADELOUPE (France)
DOMINICA
MARTINIQUE (France)
ST. LUCIA
BARBADOS
ST. VINCENT & THE GRENADINES
GRENADA
TRINIDAD & TOBAGO
Havana
Nassau
CUBA
HAITI
JAMAICA
Kingston
Santo Domingo
Port-au-Prince
Belmopan
BELIZE
HONDURAS
GUATEMALA
Guatemala
Tegucigalpa
San Salvador
NICARAGUA
EL SALVADOR
Managua
San José
COSTA RICA
Panama
PANAMA
Caribbean Sea
Caracas
Georgetown
VENEZUELA
GUYANA
Paramaribo
Cayenne
SURINAME
FRENCH GUIANA (France)
Bogotá
COLOMBIA
GALÁPAGOS ISLANDS (Ecuador)
Quito
ECUADOR
Equator
Amazon R.
PERU
BRAZIL
São Francisco R.
Lima
Brasília
La Paz
BOLIVIA
Lake Titicaca
Sucre
Paraná R.
PARAGUAY
Rio de Janeiro
São Paulo
Tropic of Cancer
Tropic of Capricorn
Arctic Circle
CHILE
Asunción
URUGUAY
Santiago
Buenos Aires
ARGENTINA
Montevideo
Río de la Plata
ATLANTIC OCEAN
FALKLAND ISLANDS (U.K.)
Tierra del Fuego
Cape Horn
KEY
National border
National capital
Other city
0 miles 2,000
0 kilometers 2,000
Lambert Azimuthal Equal Area
N S E W

North and South America: Physical

ASIA
ARCTIC OCEAN
Bering Strait
Beaufort Sea
Mt. McKinley 20,320 ft (6,194 m)
Bering Sea
Aleutian Islands
Alaska Range
Gulf of Alaska
Mackenzie R.
Great Bear Lake
Great Slave Lake
Greenland
Baffin Bay
Davis Strait
Baffin Island
Labrador Sea
Hudson Bay
EUROPE
ROCKY MOUNTAINS
GREAT PLAINS
CANADIAN SHIELD
Lake Winnipeg
Newfoundland
Great Lakes
Missouri R.
Colorado R.
Ohio R.
Appalachian Mts.
Mississippi R.
ATLANTIC OCEAN
Rio Grande
Baja California
Sierra Madre Occidental
Sierra Madre Oriental
Gulf of Mexico
Gulf of California
Tropic of Cancer
Yucatán Peninsula
Cuba
Hispaniola
Lesser Antilles
Greater Antilles
Caribbean Sea
PACIFIC OCEAN
Isthmus of Panama
Orinoco R.
Guiana Highlands
Equator
Galápagos Islands
Amazon R.
AMAZON BASIN
ANDES
São Francisco R.
Brazilian Highlands
Lake Titicaca
Gran Chaco
Paraguay R.
Paraná R.
Tropic of Capricorn
Aconcagua 22,834 ft (6,960 m)
Pampas
Río de la Plata
Patagonia
ATLANTIC OCEAN
Falkland Islands
Tierra del Fuego
Cape Horn
Arctic Circle
N
W
E
S
KEY
ELEVATION
Feet
Meters
More than 13,000
More than 3,960
6,500–13,000
1,980–3,960
1,600–6,500
480–1,980
650–1,600
200–480
0–650
0–200
Ice cap
National border
0 miles
2,000
0 kilometers
2,000
Lambert Azimuthal Equal Area
180°
160° W
140° W
120° W
100° W
80° W
60° W
40° W
20° W
0°
60° N
40° N
20° N
0°
20° S
40° S

United States: Political

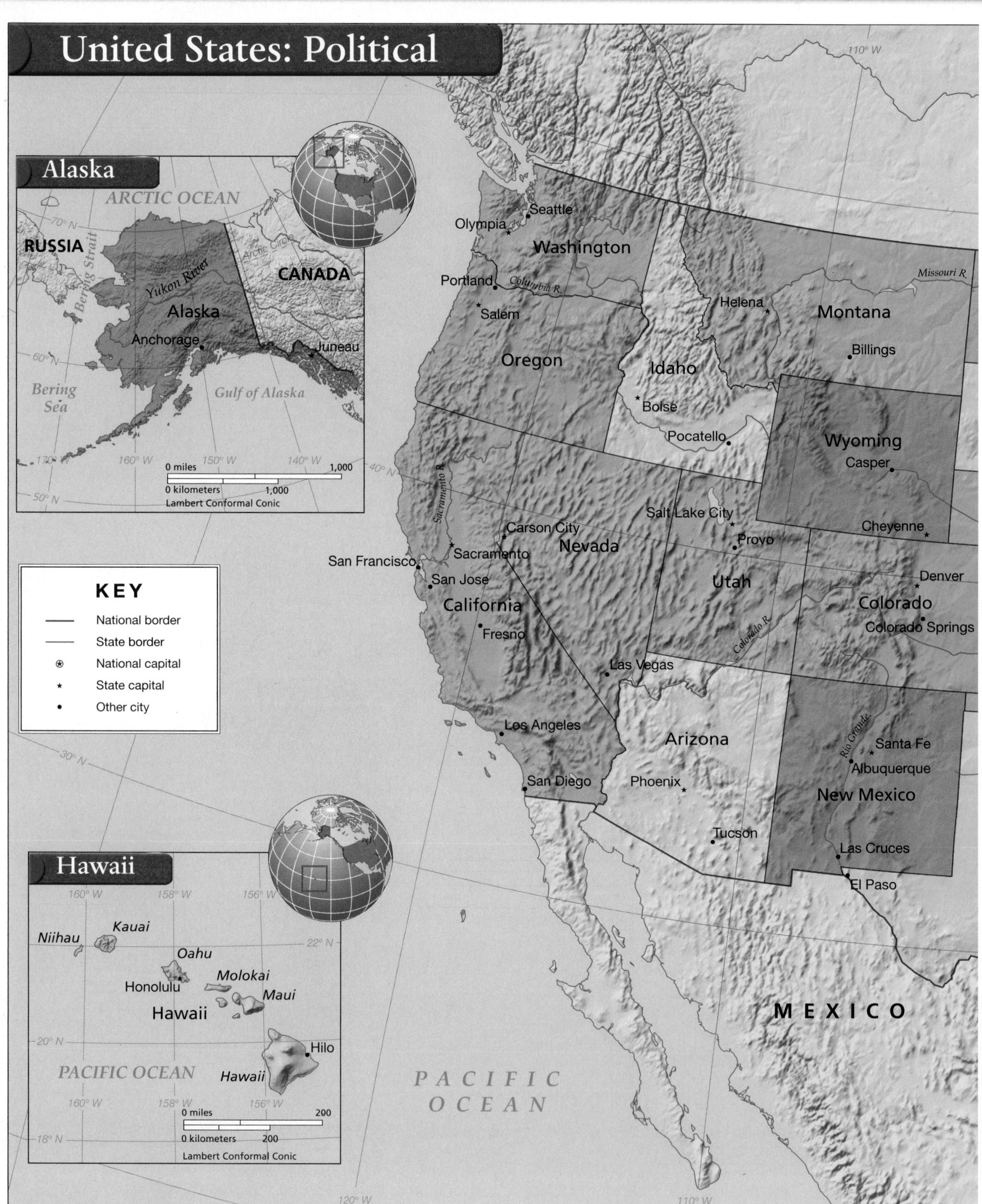

Alaska
ARCTIC OCEAN
RUSSIA
Bering Strait
Arctic Circle
CANADA
Yukon River
Alaska
Anchorage
Juneau
Bering Sea
Gulf of Alaska
0 miles 1,000
0 kilometers 1,000
Lambert Conformal Conic
KEY
National border
State border
National capital
State capital
Other city
Hawaii
Niihau
Kauai
Oahu
Honolulu
Molokai
Maui
Hawaii
Hilo
PACIFIC OCEAN
Hawaii
0 miles 200
0 kilometers 200
Lambert Conformal Conic
Seattle
Olympia
Washington
Portland
Columbia R.
Salem
Oregon
Helena
Montana
Missouri R.
Billings
Idaho
Boise
Pocatello
Wyoming
Casper
Cheyenne
Sacramento R.
Carson City
Sacramento
Nevada
Salt Lake City
Provo
Utah
San Francisco
San Jose
California
Fresno
Denver
Colorado
Colorado Springs
Colorado R.
Las Vegas
Los Angeles
Arizona
San Diego
Phoenix
Rio Grande
Santa Fe
Albuquerque
New Mexico
Tucson
Las Cruces
El Paso
MEXICO
PACIFIC OCEAN

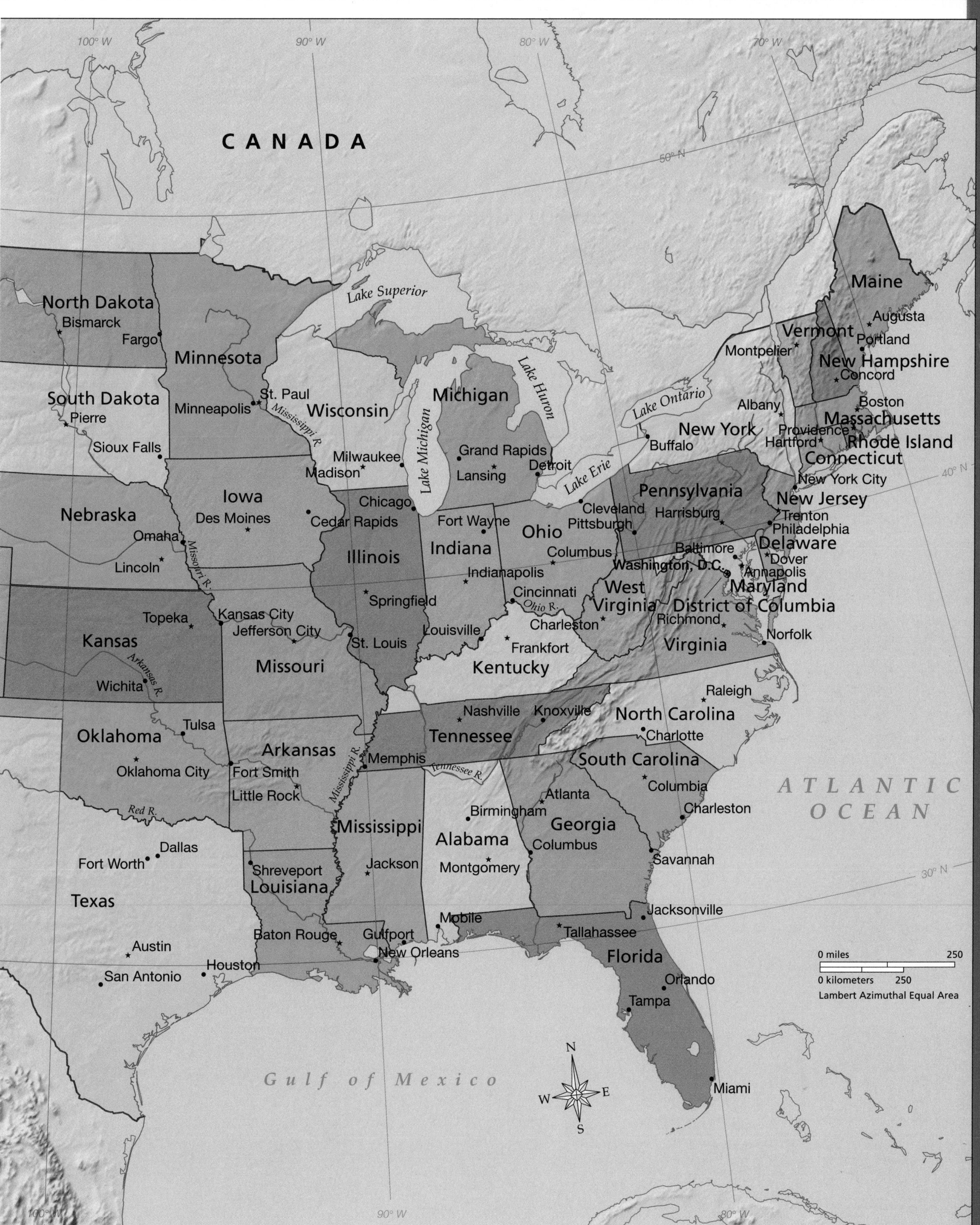
CANADA
Lake Superior
Lake Michigan
Lake Huron
Lake Ontario
Lake Erie
North Dakota
Bismarck
Fargo
Minnesota
South Dakota
Pierre
Sioux Falls
St. Paul
Minneapolis
Mississippi R.
Wisconsin
Milwaukee
Madison
Michigan
Grand Rapids
Lansing
Detroit
Maine
Augusta
Portland
Vermont
Montpelier
New Hampshire
Concord
Albany
Boston
Massachusetts
New York
Buffalo
Providence
Hartford
Rhode Island
Connecticut
New York City
New Jersey
Trenton
Philadelphia
Pennsylvania
Harrisburg
Pittsburgh
Cleveland
Nebraska
Omaha
Lincoln
Iowa
Des Moines
Cedar Rapids
Chicago
Illinois
Springfield
Indiana
Fort Wayne
Indianapolis
Ohio
Columbus
Cincinnati
Ohio R.
Missouri R.
Delaware
Dover
Baltimore
Washington, D.C.
Annapolis
Maryland
District of Columbia
West Virginia
Charleston
Richmond
Virginia
Norfolk
Kansas
Topeka
Wichita
Arkansas R.
Kansas City
Jefferson City
Missouri
St. Louis
Louisville
Frankfort
Kentucky
Nashville
Knoxville
Tennessee
North Carolina
Raleigh
Charlotte
Oklahoma
Tulsa
Oklahoma City
Fort Smith
Arkansas
Little Rock
Memphis
Tennessee R.
Mississippi R.
Red R.
South Carolina
Columbia
Charleston
Atlanta
Birmingham
Georgia
Columbus
Alabama
Montgomery
Mississippi
Jackson
Savannah
ATLANTIC OCEAN
Dallas
Fort Worth
Texas
Shreveport
Louisiana
Baton Rouge
Gulfport
Mobile
New Orleans
Tallahassee
Jacksonville
Florida
Orlando
Tampa
Miami
Austin
San Antonio
Houston
Gulf of Mexico
N
E
S
W
0 miles 250
0 kilometers 250
Lambert Azimuthal Equal Area
100° W
90° W
80° W
70° W
50° N
40° N
30° N

Europe: Political

Europe: Physical

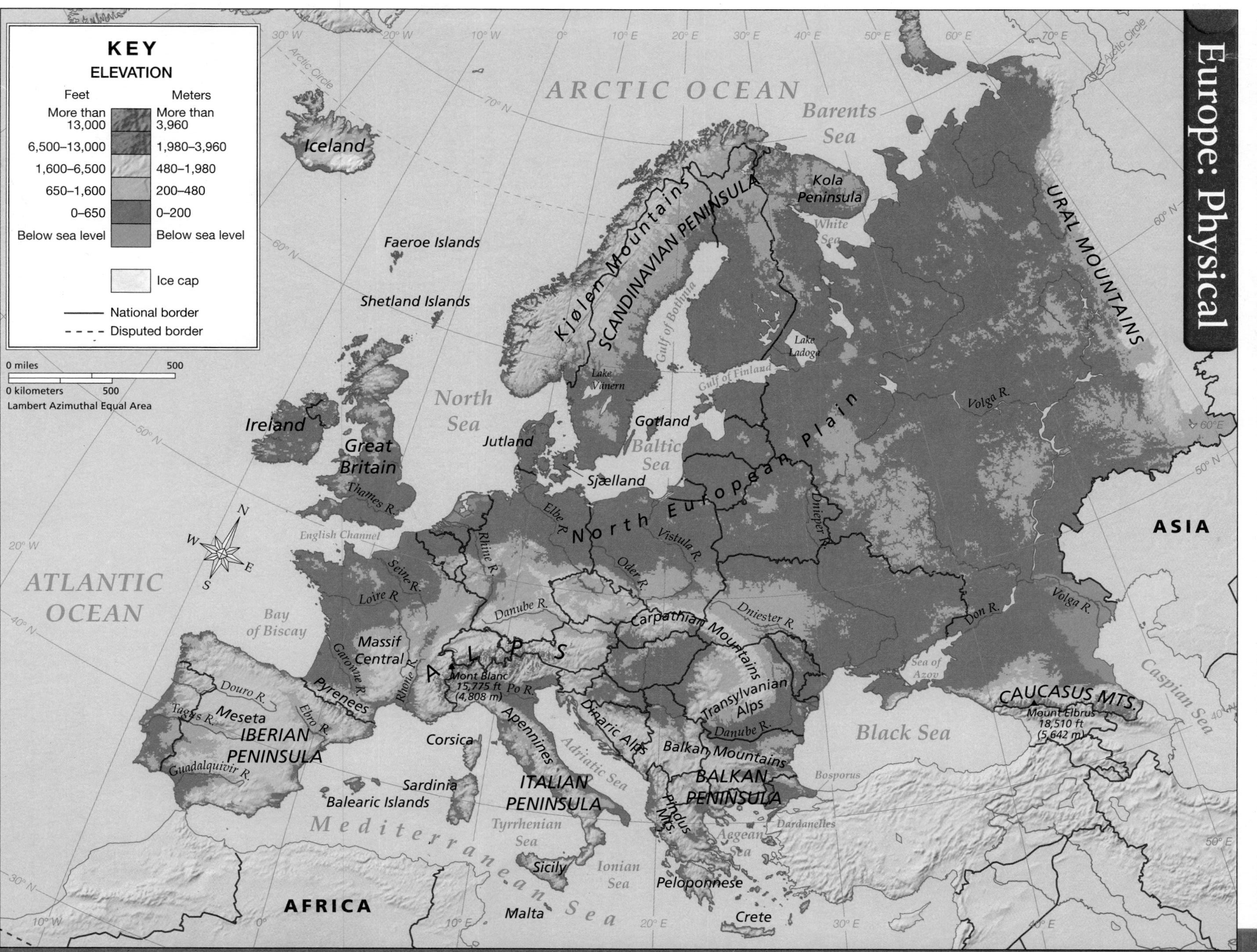

KEY
ELEVATION
Feet
Meters
More than 13,000
More than 3,960
6,500–13,000
1,980–3,960
1,600–6,500
480–1,980
650–1,600
200–480
0–650
0–200
Below sea level
Below sea level
Ice cap
National border
Disputed border
0 miles
500
0 kilometers
500
Lambert Azimuthal Equal Area
ARCTIC OCEAN
ATLANTIC OCEAN
ASIA
AFRICA
URAL MOUNTAINS
Barents Sea
White Sea
Kola Peninsula
Lake Ladoga
Volga R.
Don R.
Sea of Azov
Black Sea
Caspian Sea
CAUCASUS MTS.
Mount Elbrus 18,510 ft (5,642 m)
Bosporus
Dardanelles
Dnieper R.
Dniester R.
North European Plain
Gulf of Finland
Gulf of Bothnia
SCANDINAVIAN PENINSULA
Kjølen Mountains
Lake Vänern
Gotland
Baltic Sea
Sjælland
Jutland
North Sea
Vistula R.
Oder R.
Elbe R.
Rhine R.
Danube R.
Carpathian Mountains
Transylvanian Alps
Balkan Mountains
BALKAN PENINSULA
Aegean Sea
Crete
Pindus Mts.
Peloponnese
Dinaric Alps
Adriatic Sea
Ionian Sea
ALPS
Mont Blanc 15,775 ft (4,808 m)
Po R.
Apennines
ITALIAN PENINSULA
Tyrrhenian Sea
Sicily
Malta
Corsica
Sardinia
Mediterranean Sea
Rhone R.
Seine R.
Loire R.
Massif Central
Garonne R.
Pyrenees
Ebro R.
IBERIAN PENINSULA
Meseta
Douro R.
Tagus R.
Guadalquivir R.
Balearic Islands
Bay of Biscay
English Channel
Thames R.
Great Britain
Ireland
Iceland
Faeroe Islands
Shetland Islands
Arctic Circle

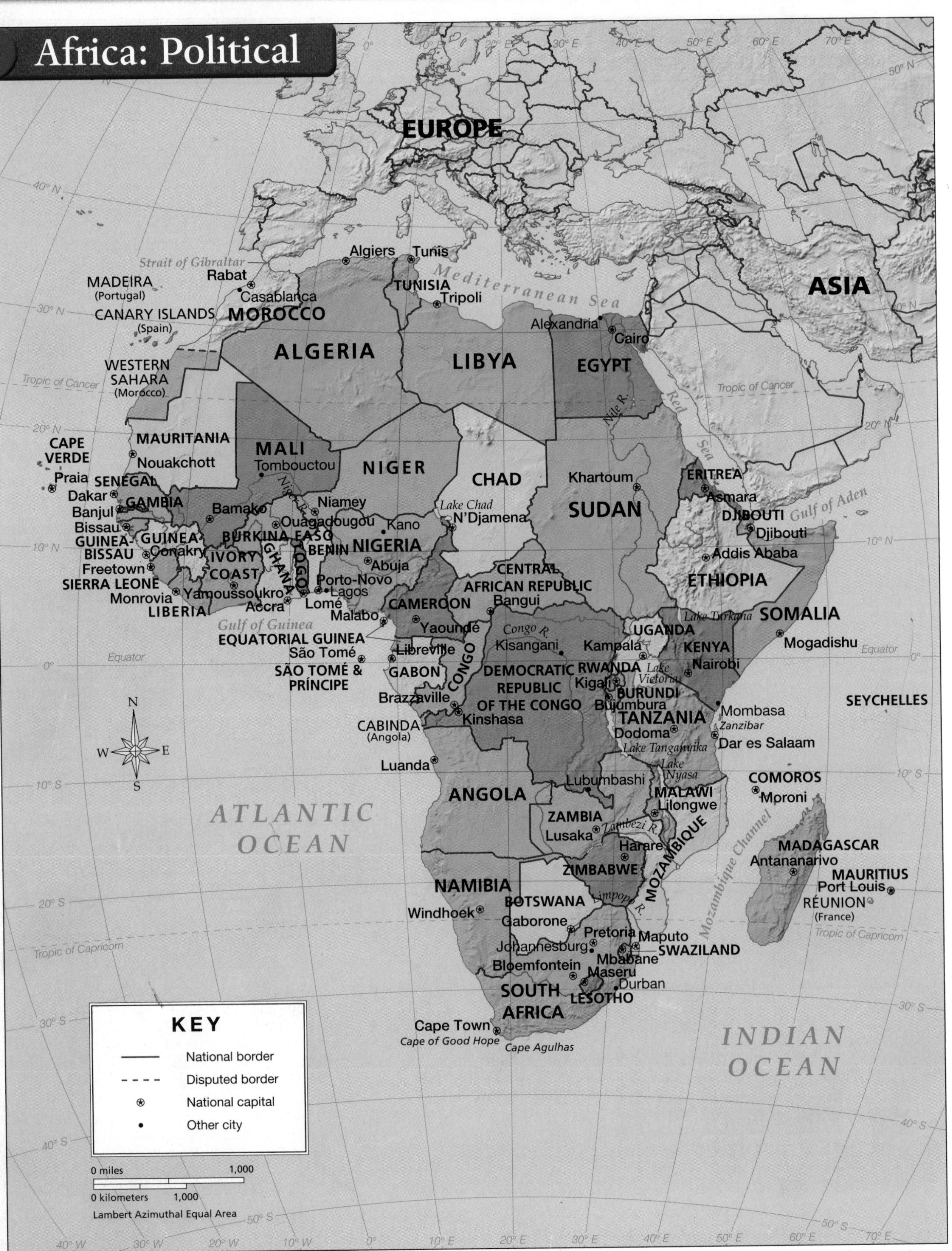

Africa: Political
EUROPE
ASIA
Strait of Gibraltar
Mediterranean Sea
MADEIRA (Portugal)
CANARY ISLANDS (Spain)
WESTERN SAHARA (Morocco)
Rabat
Casablanca
MOROCCO
Algiers
Tunis
TUNISIA
Tripoli
ALGERIA
LIBYA
Alexandria
Cairo
EGYPT
Nile R.
Red Sea
Tropic of Cancer
MAURITANIA
Nouakchott
CAPE VERDE
Praia
SENEGAL
Dakar
GAMBIA
Banjul
Bissau
GUINEA-BISSAU
GUINEA
Conakry
Freetown
SIERRA LEONE
Monrovia
LIBERIA
MALI
Tombouctou
Bamako
Niger R.
NIGER
Niamey
BURKINA FASO
Ouagadougou
IVORY COAST
Yamoussoukro
GHANA
Accra
TOGO
Lomé
BENIN
Porto-Novo
Lagos
NIGERIA
Abuja
Kano
CHAD
Lake Chad
N'Djamena
SUDAN
Khartoum
ERITREA
Asmara
DJIBOUTI
Djibouti
Gulf of Aden
Addis Ababa
ETHIOPIA
SOMALIA
Mogadishu
Lake Turkana
CENTRAL AFRICAN REPUBLIC
Bangui
CAMEROON
Yaoundé
Malabo
Gulf of Guinea
EQUATORIAL GUINEA
São Tomé
SÃO TOMÉ & PRÍNCIPE
Libreville
GABON
CONGO
Brazzaville
Kinshasa
CABINDA (Angola)
Congo R.
Kisangani
DEMOCRATIC REPUBLIC OF THE CONGO
UGANDA
Kampala
KENYA
Nairobi
RWANDA
Kigali
Lake Victoria
BURUNDI
Bujumbura
TANZANIA
Dodoma
Lake Tanganyika
Mombasa
Zanzibar
Dar es Salaam
SEYCHELLES
Equator
Luanda
ANGOLA
Lubumbashi
Lake Nyasa
MALAWI
Lilongwe
COMOROS
Moroni
ZAMBIA
Lusaka
Zambezi R.
Harare
ZIMBABWE
MOZAMBIQUE
Mozambique Channel
MADAGASCAR
Antananarivo
MAURITIUS
Port Louis
RÉUNION (France)
NAMIBIA
Windhoek
BOTSWANA
Gaborone
Limpopo R.
Pretoria
Johannesburg
Maputo
Mbabane
SWAZILAND
Bloemfontein
Maseru
Durban
SOUTH AFRICA
LESOTHO
Cape Town
Cape of Good Hope
Cape Agulhas
Tropic of Capricorn
ATLANTIC OCEAN
INDIAN OCEAN
N
W
E
S
KEY
National border
Disputed border
National capital
Other city
0 miles 1,000
0 kilometers 1,000
Lambert Azimuthal Equal Area

Africa: Physical

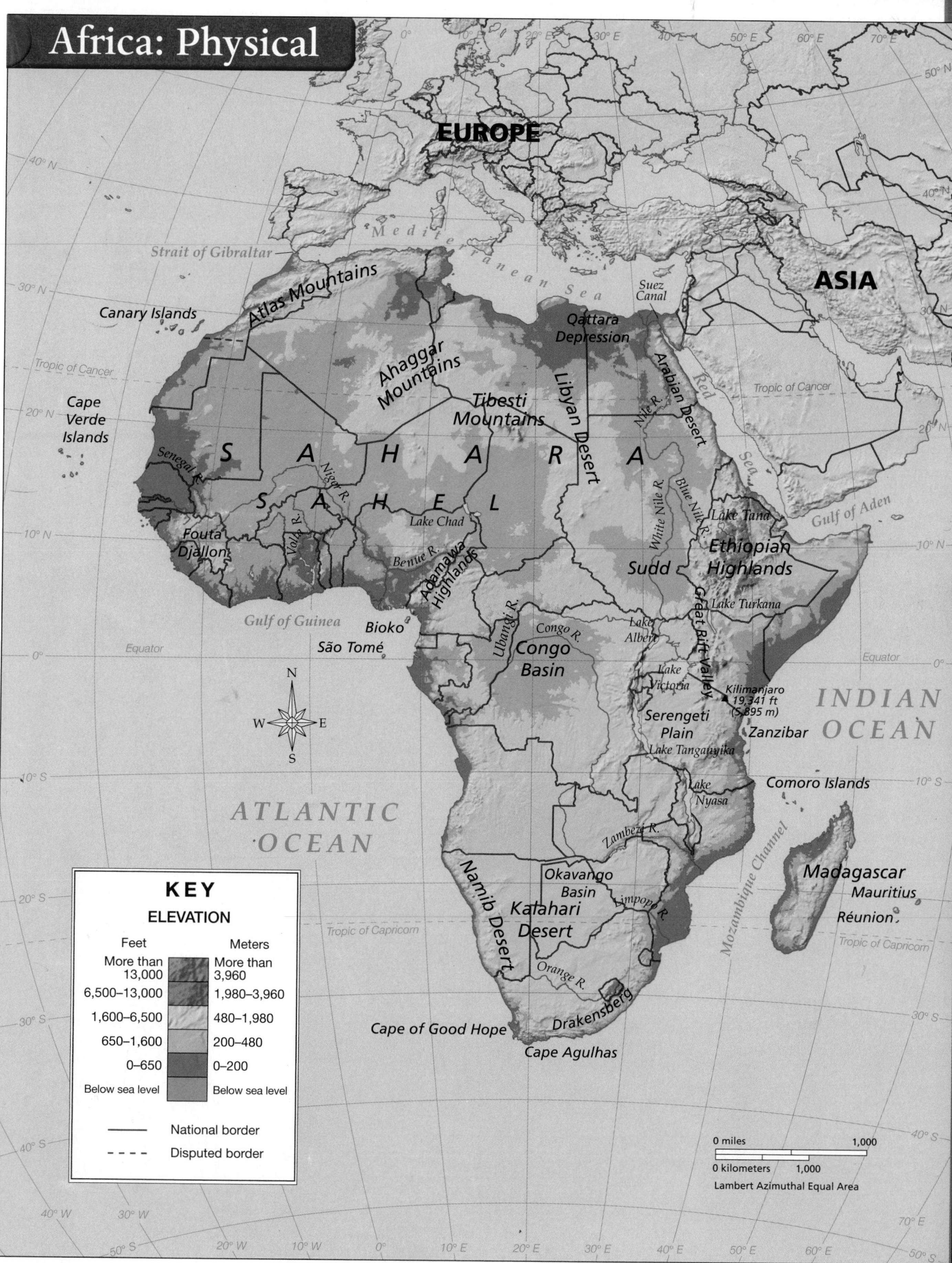

Asia: Political

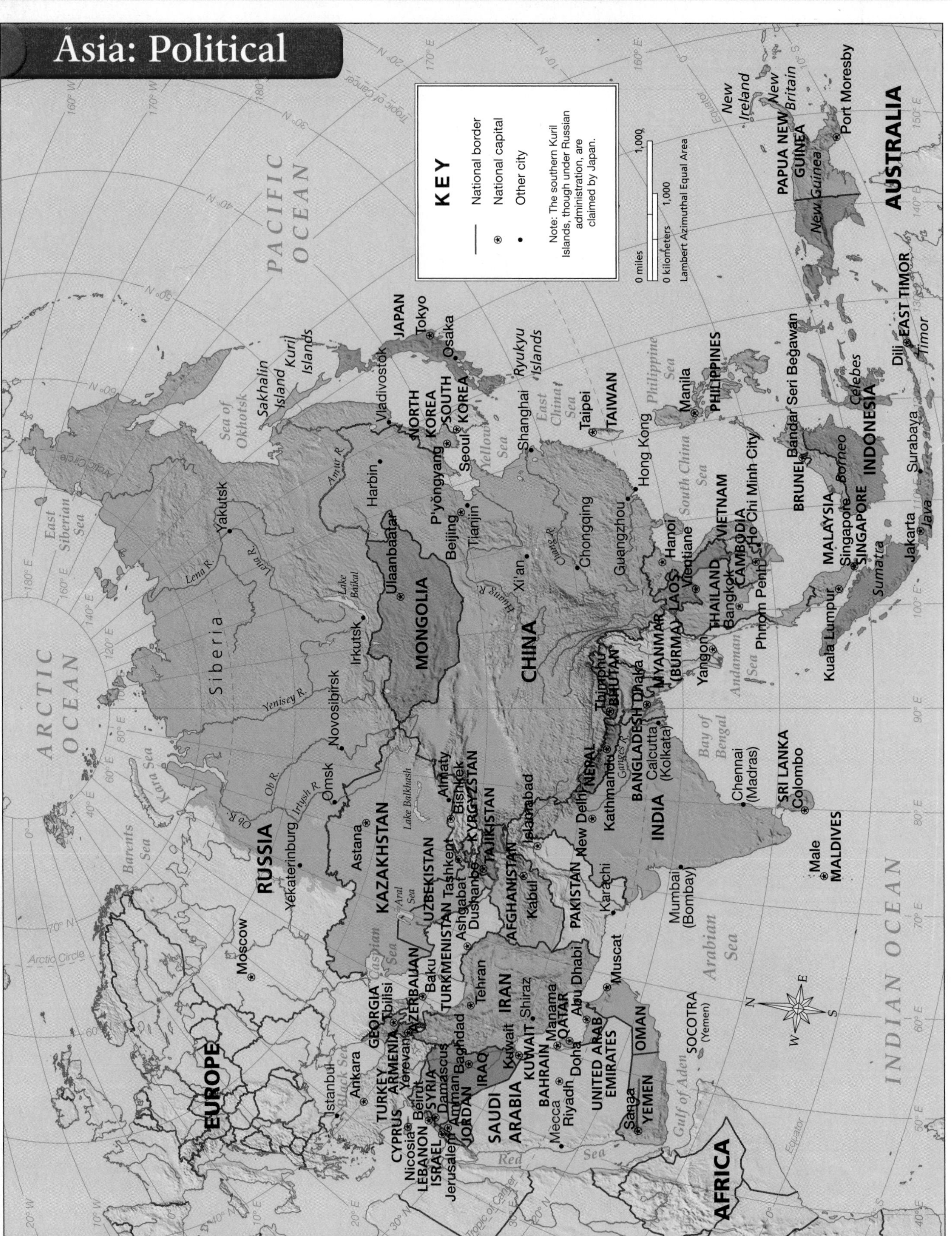

KEY
National border
National capital
Other city
Note: The southern Kuril Islands, though under Russian administration, are claimed by Japan.
0 miles 1,000
0 kilometers 1,000
Lambert Azimuthal Equal Area
ARCTIC OCEAN
PACIFIC OCEAN
INDIAN OCEAN
EUROPE
AFRICA
AUSTRALIA
RUSSIA
Siberia
Moscow
Yekaterinburg
Omsk
Novosibirsk
Irkutsk
Yakutsk
Vladivostok
Barents Sea
Kara Sea
East Siberian Sea
Sea of Okhotsk
Sakhalin Island
Kuril Islands
Ob R.
Irtysh R.
Yenisey R.
Lena R.
Amur R.
Lake Baikal
Arctic Circle
Tropic of Cancer
Equator
KAZAKHSTAN
Astana
Almaty
Lake Balkhash
Aral Sea
Caspian Sea
UZBEKISTAN
Tashkent
TURKMENISTAN
Ashgabat
KYRGYZSTAN
Bishkek
TAJIKISTAN
Dushanbe
AFGHANISTAN
Kabul
PAKISTAN
Islamabad
Karachi
INDIA
New Delhi
Mumbai (Bombay)
Calcutta (Kolkata)
Chennai (Madras)
Ganges R.
NEPAL
Kathmandu
BHUTAN
Thimphu
BANGLADESH
Dhaka
SRI LANKA
Colombo
MALDIVES
Male
Arabian Sea
Bay of Bengal
Andaman Sea
MONGOLIA
Ulaanbaatar
CHINA
Beijing
Tianjin
Harbin
Xi'an
Chongqing
Guangzhou
Shanghai
Hong Kong
Huang R.
Chang R.
NORTH KOREA
P'yŏngyang
SOUTH KOREA
Seoul
JAPAN
Tokyo
Osaka
Yellow Sea
East China Sea
Ryukyu Islands
TAIWAN
Taipei
PHILIPPINES
Manila
Philippine Sea
South China Sea
MYANMAR (BURMA)
Yangon
THAILAND
Bangkok
LAOS
Vientiane
VIETNAM
Hanoi
Ho Chi Minh City
CAMBODIA
Phnom Penh
MALAYSIA
Kuala Lumpur
SINGAPORE
Singapore
BRUNEI
Bandar Seri Begawan
INDONESIA
Jakarta
Surabaya
Sumatra
Java
Borneo
Celebes
EAST TIMOR
Dili
Timor
New Guinea
PAPUA NEW GUINEA
Port Moresby
New Britain
New Ireland
TURKEY
Ankara
Istanbul
Black Sea
CYPRUS
Nicosia
LEBANON
Beirut
SYRIA
Damascus
ISRAEL
Jerusalem
JORDAN
Amman
IRAQ
Baghdad
GEORGIA
Tbilisi
ARMENIA
Yerevan
AZERBAIJAN
Baku
IRAN
Tehran
Shiraz
KUWAIT
Kuwait
BAHRAIN
Manama
QATAR
Doha
UNITED ARAB EMIRATES
Abu Dhabi
OMAN
Muscat
SAUDI ARABIA
Riyadh
Mecca
YEMEN
Sanaa
SOCOTRA (Yemen)
Gulf of Aden
Red Sea
N
S
E
W

Asia: Physical

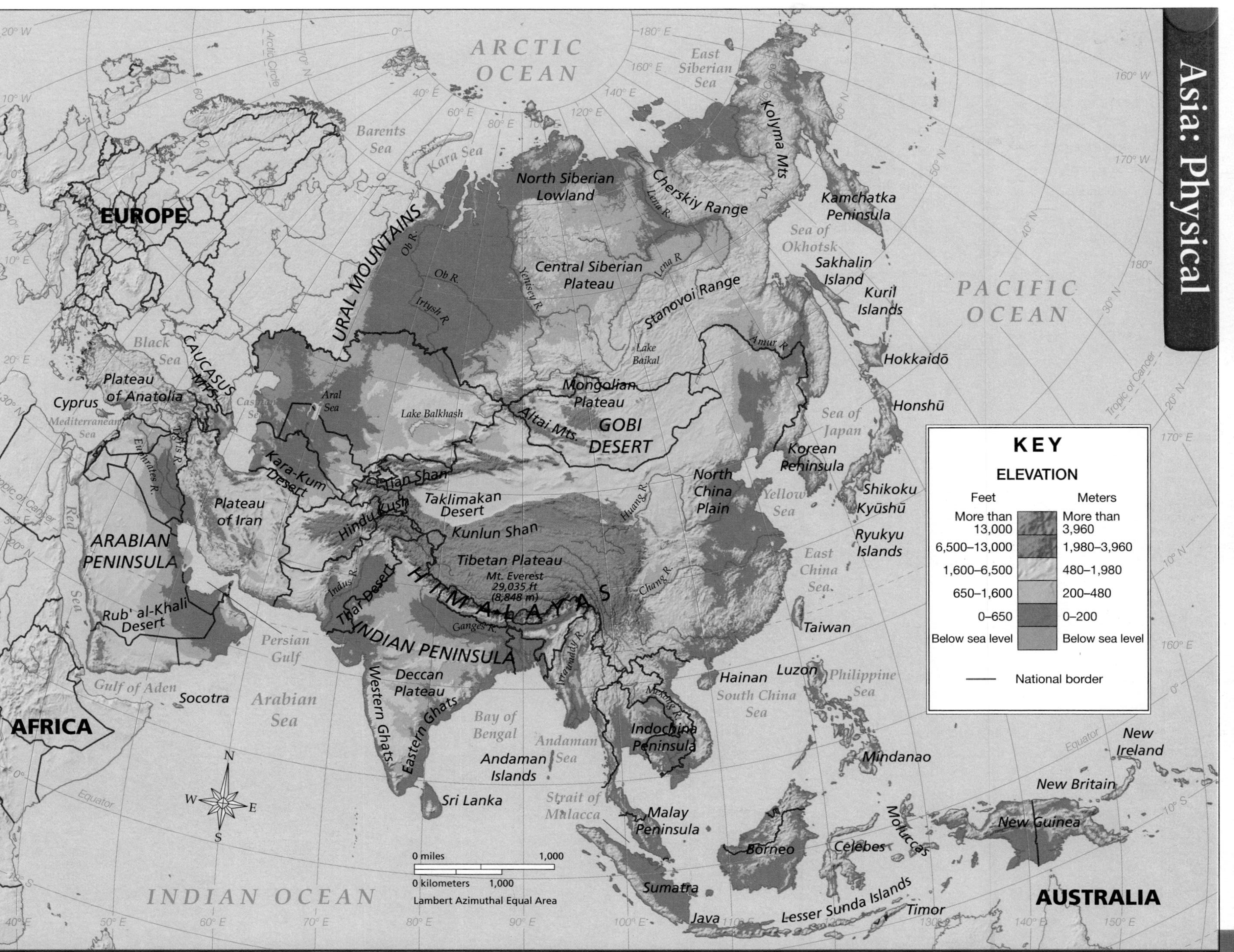

KEY
ELEVATION
Feet
Meters
More than 13,000
More than 3,960
6,500–13,000
1,980–3,960
1,600–6,500
480–1,980
650–1,600
200–480
0–650
0–200
Below sea level
Below sea level
National border
ARCTIC OCEAN
PACIFIC OCEAN
INDIAN OCEAN
EUROPE
AFRICA
AUSTRALIA
Barents Sea
Kara Sea
East Siberian Sea
Sea of Okhotsk
Sea of Japan
Yellow Sea
East China Sea.
Philippine Sea
South China Sea
Andaman Sea
Bay of Bengal
Arabian Sea
Persian Gulf
Gulf of Aden
Red Sea
Mediterranean Sea
Black Sea
Caspian Sea
Aral Sea
Lake Balkhash
Lake Baikal
Strait of Malacca
URAL MOUNTAINS
CAUCASUS MTS.
Kolyma Mts
Cherskiy Range
Stanovoi Range
Altai Mts.
Tian Shan
Hindu Kush
Kunlun Shan
HIMALAYAS
Western Ghats
Eastern Ghats
North Siberian Lowland
Central Siberian Plateau
Mongolian Plateau
GOBI DESERT
Taklimakan Desert
Tibetan Plateau
Mt. Everest 29,035 ft (8,848 m)
North China Plain
Kara-Kum Desert
Plateau of Iran
Plateau of Anatolia
ARABIAN PENINSULA
Rub' al-Khali Desert
INDIAN PENINSULA
Deccan Plateau
Thar Desert
Indochina Peninsula
Malay Peninsula
Korean Peninsula
Kamchatka Peninsula
Sakhalin Island
Kuril Islands
Hokkaidō
Honshū
Shikoku
Kyūshū
Ryukyu Islands
Taiwan
Hainan
Luzon
Mindanao
Borneo
Celebes
Moluccas
Sumatra
Java
Lesser Sunda Islands
Timor
New Guinea
New Britain
New Ireland
Andaman Islands
Sri Lanka
Socotra
Cyprus
Ob R.
Irtysh R.
Yenisey R.
Lena R.
Amur R.
Huang R.
Chang R.
Mekong R.
Irrawaddy R.
Ganges R.
Indus R.
Tigris R.
Euphrates R.
Arctic Circle
Tropic of Cancer
Equator
0 miles 1,000
0 kilometers 1,000
Lambert Azimuthal Equal Area
N
S
E
W

Oceania

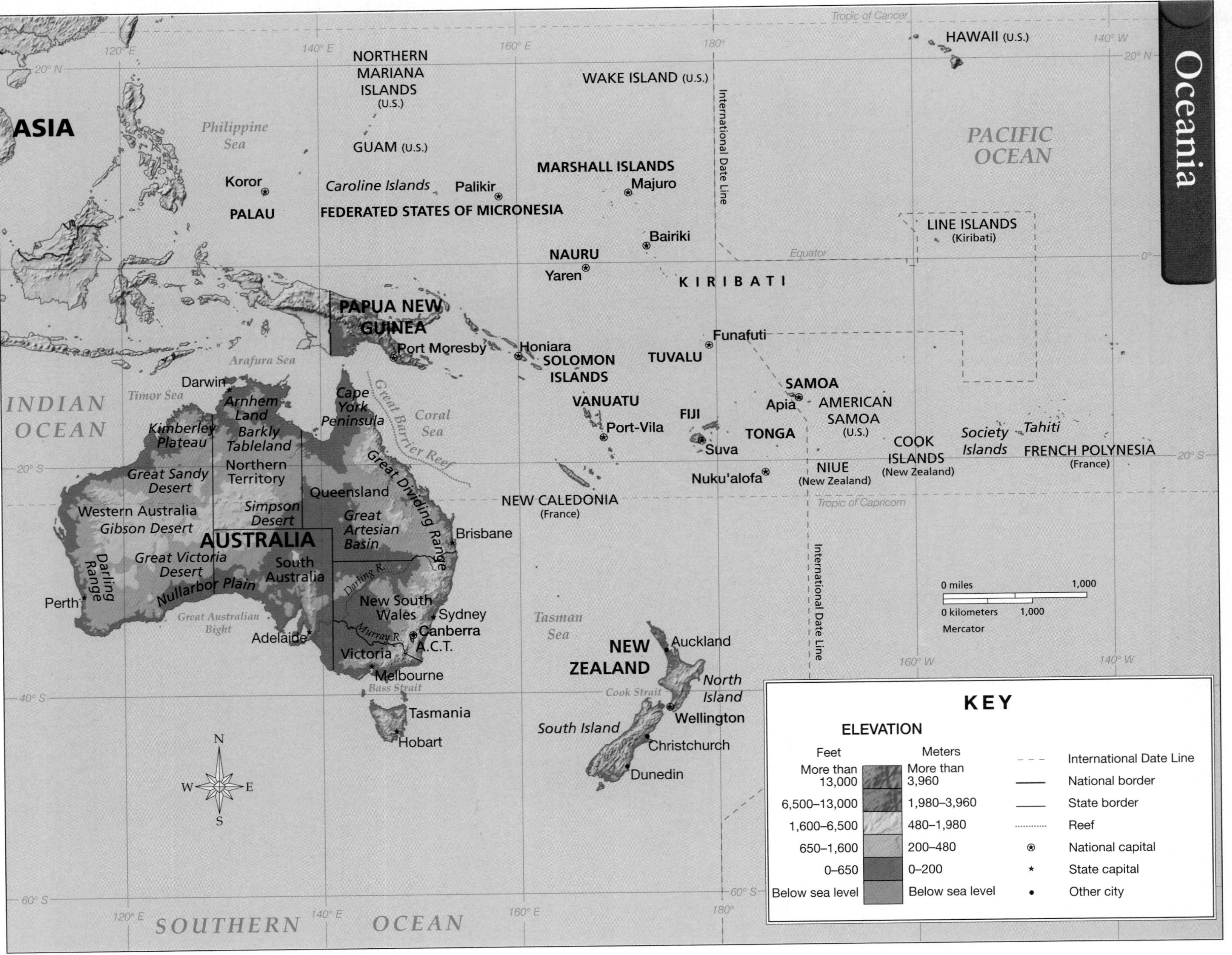

ASIA
INDIAN OCEAN
SOUTHERN OCEAN
PACIFIC OCEAN
Philippine Sea
Timor Sea
Arafura Sea
Coral Sea
Tasman Sea
Great Australian Bight
Bass Strait
Cook Strait
Great Barrier Reef
HAWAII (U.S.)
NORTHERN MARIANA ISLANDS (U.S.)
GUAM (U.S.)
WAKE ISLAND (U.S.)
MARSHALL ISLANDS
Majuro
Koror
PALAU
Caroline Islands
Palikir
FEDERATED STATES OF MICRONESIA
NAURU
Yaren
Bairiki
K I R I B A T I
LINE ISLANDS (Kiribati)
PAPUA NEW GUINEA
Port Moresby
Honiara
SOLOMON ISLANDS
TUVALU
Funafuti
VANUATU
Port-Vila
FIJI
Suva
SAMOA
Apia
AMERICAN SAMOA (U.S.)
TONGA
Nuku'alofa
NIUE (New Zealand)
COOK ISLANDS (New Zealand)
Society Islands
Tahiti
FRENCH POLYNESIA (France)
NEW CALEDONIA (France)
International Date Line
Equator
Tropic of Cancer
Tropic of Capricorn
AUSTRALIA
Darwin
Arnhem Land
Kimberley Plateau
Barkly Tableland
Northern Territory
Cape York Peninsula
Queensland
Great Dividing Range
Great Artesian Basin
Brisbane
Great Sandy Desert
Western Australia
Gibson Desert
Simpson Desert
Great Victoria Desert
South Australia
Nullarbor Plain
Darling Range
Perth
Adelaide
Darling R.
Murray R.
New South Wales
Sydney
Canberra
A.C.T.
Victoria
Melbourne
Tasmania
Hobart
NEW ZEALAND
Auckland
North Island
Wellington
South Island
Christchurch
Dunedin
20° N
0°
20° S
40° S
60° S
120° E
140° E
160° E
180°
160° W
140° W
N
S
E
W
0 miles 1,000
0 kilometers 1,000
Mercator
KEY
ELEVATION
Feet
Meters
More than 13,000
More than 3,960
6,500–13,000
1,980–3,960
1,600–6,500
480–1,980
650–1,600
200–480
0–650
0–200
Below sea level
Below sea level
International Date Line
National border
State border
Reef
National capital
State capital
Other city

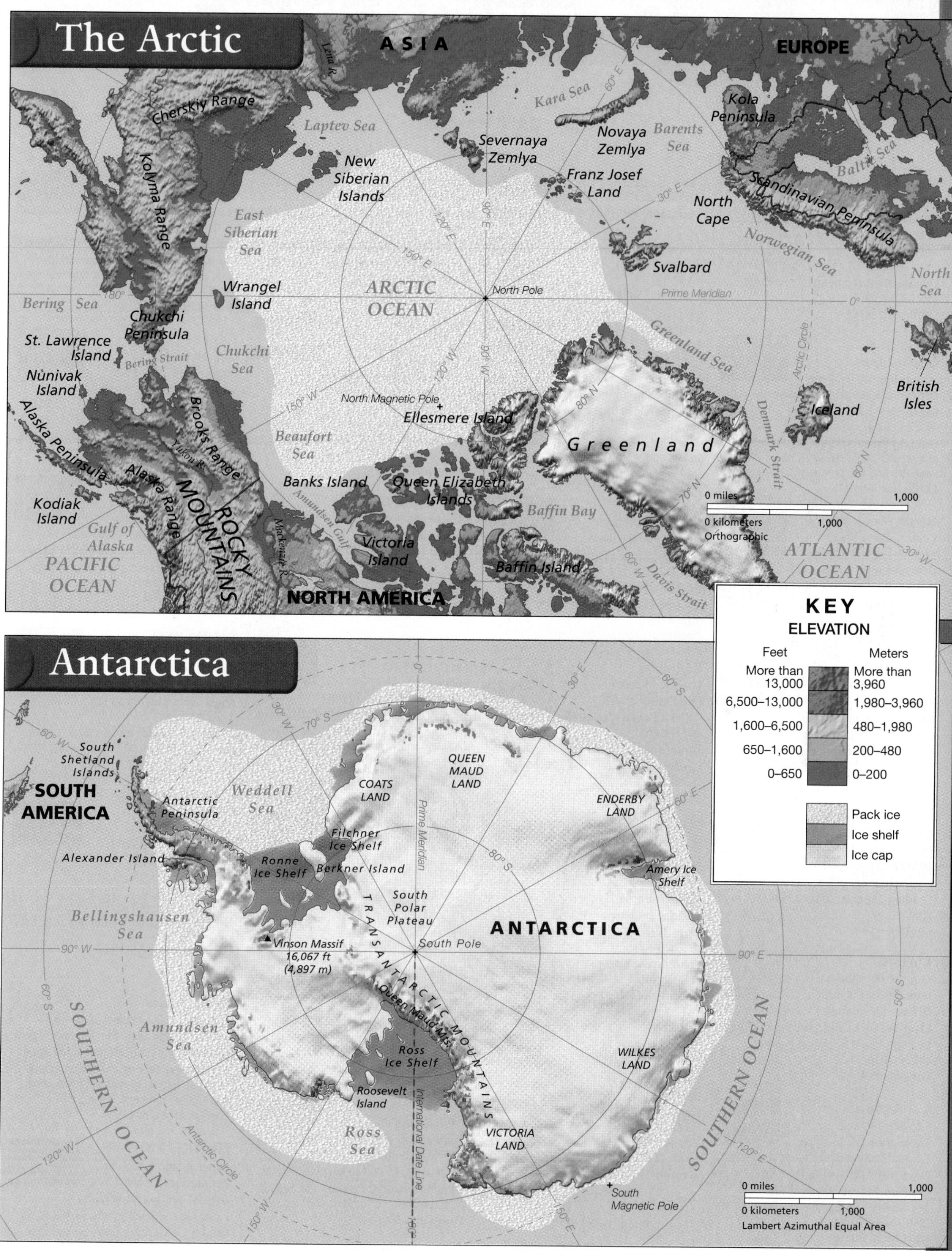
The Arctic
ASIA
EUROPE
Lena R.
Cherskiy Range
Kolyma Range
Laptev Sea
Kara Sea
Novaya Zemlya
Barents Sea
Kola Peninsula
Baltic Sea
Severnaya Zemlya
New Siberian Islands
Franz Josef Land
North Cape
Scandinavian Peninsula
East Siberian Sea
Norwegian Sea
Svalbard
North Sea
Wrangel Island
ARCTIC OCEAN
North Pole
Bering Sea
Prime Meridian
Chukchi Peninsula
Greenland Sea
St. Lawrence Island
Bering Strait
Chukchi Sea
Arctic Circle
Nunivak Island
British Isles
North Magnetic Pole
Iceland
Alaska Peninsula
Brooks Range
Ellesmere Island
Yukon R.
Beaufort Sea
Greenland
Denmark Strait
Alaska Range
ROCKY MOUNTAINS
Banks Island
Queen Elizabeth Islands
Kodiak Island
Amundsen Gulf
Baffin Bay
Gulf of Alaska
Mackenzie R.
Victoria Island
ATLANTIC OCEAN
PACIFIC OCEAN
Baffin Island
Davis Strait
NORTH AMERICA
0 miles 1,000
0 kilometers 1,000
Orthographic
KEY
ELEVATION
Feet
Meters
More than 13,000
More than 3,960
6,500–13,000
1,980–3,960
1,600–6,500
480–1,980
650–1,600
200–480
0–650
0–200
Pack ice
Ice shelf
Ice cap
Antarctica
South Shetland Islands
SOUTH AMERICA
Weddell Sea
COATS LAND
QUEEN MAUD LAND
ENDERBY LAND
Antarctic Peninsula
Filchner Ice Shelf
Alexander Island
Ronne Ice Shelf
Berkner Island
Amery Ice Shelf
South Polar Plateau
Bellingshausen Sea
ANTARCTICA
Vinson Massif 16,067 ft (4,897 m)
South Pole
TRANSANTARCTIC MOUNTAINS
Queen Maud Mts.
Amundsen Sea
Ross Ice Shelf
WILKES LAND
SOUTHERN OCEAN
Roosevelt Island
International Date Line
Ross Sea
VICTORIA LAND
Antarctic Circle
South Magnetic Pole
0 miles 1,000
0 kilometers 1,000
Lambert Azimuthal Equal Area

Country Databank

Africa

Algeria
Capital: Algiers
Population: 32.3 million
Official Languages: Arabic and Tamazight
Land Area: 2,381,740 sq km; 919,590 sq mi
Leading Exports: petroleum, natural gas, petroleum products
Continent: Africa

Angola
Capital: Luanda
Population: 10.6 million
Official Language: Portuguese
Land Area: 1,246,700 sq km; 481,551 sq mi
Leading Exports: crude oil, diamonds, refined petroleum products, gas, coffee, sisal, fish and fish products, timber, cotton
Continent: Africa

Benin
Capital: Porto-Novo
Population: 6.9 million
Official Language: French
Land Area: 110,620 sq km; 42,710 sq mi
Leading Exports: cotton, crude oil, palm products, cocoa
Continent: Africa

Botswana
Capital: Gaborone
Population: 1.6 million
Official Language: English
Land Area: 585,370 sq km; 226,011 sq mi
Leading Exports: diamonds, copper, nickel, soda ash, meat, textiles
Continent: Africa

Burkina Faso
Capital: Ouagadougou
Population: 12.6 million
Official Language: French
Land Area: 273,800 sq km; 105,714 sq mi
Leading Exports: cotton, animal products, gold
Continent: Africa

Burundi
Capital: Bujumbura
Population: 6.4 million
Official Languages: Kirundi and French
Land Area: 25,650 sq km; 9,903 sq mi
Leading Exports: coffee, tea, sugar, cotton, hides
Continent: Africa

Cameroon
Capital: Yaoundé
Population: 16.1 million
Official Languages: English and French
Land Area: 469,440 sq km; 181,251 sqmi
Leading Exports: crude oil and petroleum products, lumber, cocoa, aluminum, coffee, cotton
Continent: Africa

Cape Verde
Capital: Praia
Population: 408,760
Official Language: Portuguese
Land Area: 4,033 sq km; 1,557 sq mi
Leading Exports: fuel, shoes, garments, fish, hides
Location: Atlantic Ocean

Central African Republic
Capital: Bangui
Population: 3.6 million
Official Language: French
Land Area: 622,984 sq km; 240,534 sq mi
Leading Exports: diamonds, timber, cotton, coffee, tobacco
Continent: Africa

Chad
Capital: N'Djamena
Population: 9 million
Official Languages: Arabic and French
Land Area: 1,259,200 sq km; 486,177 sq mi
Leading Exports: cotton, cattle, gum arabic
Continent: Africa

Comoros
Capital: Moroni
Population: 614,382
Official Languages: Arabic, Comoran, and French
Land Area: 2,170 sq km; 838 sq mi
Leading Exports: vanilla, ylang-ylang, cloves, perfume oil, copra
Location: Indian Ocean

Congo, Democratic Republic of the
Capital: Kinshasa
Population: 55.2 million
Official Language: French
Land Area: 2,267,600 sq km; 875,520 sq mi
Leading Exports: diamonds, copper, coffee, cobalt, crude oil
Continent: Africa

Congo, Republic of the
Capital: Brazzaville
Population: 3.3 million
Official Language: French
Land Area: 341,500 sq km; 131,853 sq mi
Leading Exports: petroleum, lumber, sugar, cocoa, coffee, diamonds
Continent: Africa

Djibouti
Capital: Djibouti
Population: 472,810
Official Languages: Arabic and French
Land Area: 22,980 sq km; 8,873 sq mi
Leading Exports: reexports, hides and skins, coffee (in transit)
Continent: Africa

Egypt
Capital: Cairo
Population: 70.7 million
Official Language: Arabic
Land Area: 995,450 sq km; 384,343 sq mi
Leading Exports: crude oil and petroleum products, cotton, textiles, metal products, chemicals
Continent: Africa

Equatorial Guinea
Capital: Malabo
Population: 498,144
Official Languages: Spanish and French
Land Area: 28,050 sq km; 10,830 sq mi
Leading Exports: petroleum, timber, cocoa
Continent: Africa

Eritrea
Capital: Asmara
Population: 4.5 million
Official Language: Tigrinya
Land Area: 121,320 sq km; 46,842 sq mi
Leading Exports: livestock, sorghum, textiles, food, small manufactured goods
Continent: Africa

Ethiopia
Capital: Addis Ababa
Population: 67.7 million
Official Language: Amharic
Land Area: 1,119,683 sq km; 432,310 sq mi
Leading Exports: coffee, qat, gold, leather products, oilseeds
Continent: Africa

Gabon
Capital: Libreville
Population: 1.2 million
Official Language: French
Land Area: 257,667 sq km; 99,489 sq mi
Leading Exports: crude oil, timber, manganese, uranium
Continent: Africa

Gambia
Capital: Banjul
Population: 1.5 million
Official Language: English
Land Area: 10,000 sq km; 3,861 sq mi
Leading Exports: peanuts and peanut products, fish, cotton lint, palm kernels
Continent: Africa

Ghana
Capital: Accra
Population: 20.2 million
Official Language: English
Land Area: 230,940 sq km; 89,166 sq mi
Leading Exports: gold, cocoa, timber, tuna, bauxite, aluminum, manganese ore, diamonds
Continent: Africa

Guinea
Capital: Conakry
Population: 7.8 million
Official Language: French
Land Area: 245,857 sq km; 94,925 sq mi
Leading Exports: bauxite, alumina, gold, diamonds, coffee, fish, agricultural products
Continent: Africa

Guinea-Bissau
Capital: Bissau
Population: 1.4 million
Official Language: Portuguese
Land Area: 28,000 sq km; 10,811 sq mi
Leading Exports: cashew nuts, shrimp, peanuts, palm kernels, lumber
Continent: Africa

Ivory Coast
Capital: Yamoussoukro
Population: 16.8 million
Official Language: French
Land Area: 318,000 sq km; 122,780 sq mi
Leading Exports: cocoa, coffee, timber, petroleum, cotton, bananas, pineapples, palm oil, cotton, fish
Continent: Africa

Kenya
Capital: Nairobi
Population: 31.3 million
Official Languages: Swahili and English
Land Area: 569,250 sq km; 219,787 sq mi
Leading Exports: tea, horticultural products, coffee, petroleum products, fish, cement
Continent: Africa

Lesotho
Capital: Maseru
Population: 2.2 million
Official Languages: Sesotho and English
Land Area: 30,355 sq km; 11,720 sq mi
Leading Exports: manufactured goods (clothing, footwear, road vehicles), wool and mohair, food and live animals
Continent: Africa

Liberia
Capital: Monrovia
Population: 3.3 million
Official Language: English
Land Area: 96,320 sq km; 37,189 sq mi
Leading Exports: rubber, timber, iron, diamonds, cocoa, coffee
Continent: Africa

Libya
Capital: Tripoli
Population: 5.4 million
Official Language: Arabic
Land Area: 1,759,540 sq km; 679,358 sq mi
Leading Exports: crude oil, refined petroleum products
Continent: Africa

Madagascar
Capital: Antananarivo
Population: 16.5 million
Official Languages: French and Malagasy
Land Area: 581,540 sq km; 224,533 sq mi
Leading Exports: coffee, vanilla, shellfish, sugar, cotton cloth, chromite, petroleum products
Location: Indian Ocean

Malawi
Capital: Lilongwe
Population: 10.7 million
Official Languages: English and Chichewa
Land Area: 94,080 sq km; 36,324 sq mi
Leading Exports: tobacco, tea, sugar, cotton, coffee, peanuts, wood products, apparel
Continent: Africa

Mali
Capital: Bamako
Population: 11.3 million
Official Language: French
Land Area: 1,220,000 sq km; 471,042 sq mi
Leading Exports: cotton, gold, livestock
Continent: Africa

Mauritania
Capital: Nouakchott
Population: 2.8 million
Official Language: Arabic
Land Area: 1,030,400 sq km; 397,837 sq mi
Leading Exports: iron ore, fish and fish products, gold
Continent: Africa

Mauritius
Capital: Port Louis
Population: 1.2 million
Official Language: English
Land Area: 2,030 sq km; 784 sq mi
Leading Exports: clothing and textiles, sugar, cut flowers, molasses
Location: Indian Ocean

Morocco
Capital: Rabat
Population: 31.2 million
Official Language: Arabic
Land Area: 446,300 sq km; 172,316 sq mi
Leading Exports: phosphates and fertilizers, food and beverages, minerals
Continent: Africa

Mozambique
Capital: Maputo
Population: 19.6 million
Official Language: Portuguese
Land Area: 784,090 sq km; 302,737 sq mi
Leading Exports: prawns, cashews, cotton, sugar, citrus, timber, bulk electricity
Continent: Africa

Namibia
Capital: Windhoek
Population: 1.8 million
Official Language: English
Land Area: 825,418 sq km; 318,694 sq mi
Leading Exports: diamonds, copper, gold, zinc, lead, uranium, cattle, processed fish, karakul skins
Continent: Africa

Niger
Capital: Niamey
Population: 11.3 million
Official Language: French
Land Area: 1,226,700 sq km; 489,073 sq mi
Leading Exports: uranium ore, livestock products, cowpeas, onions
Continent: Africa

Nigeria
Capital: Abuja
Population: 129.9 million
Official Language: English
Land Area: 910,768 sq km; 351,648 sq mi
Leading Exports: petroleum and petroleum products, cocoa, rubber
Continent: Africa

Rwanda
Capital: Kigali
Population: 7.4 million
Official Languages: Kinyarwanda, French, and English
Land Area: 24,948 sq km; 9,632 sq mi
Leading Exports: coffee, tea, hides, tin ore
Continent: Africa

São Tomé and Príncipe
Capital: São Tomé
Population: 170,372
Official Language: Portuguese
Land Area: 1,001 sq km; 386 sq mi
Leading Exports: cocoa, copra, coffee, palm oil
Location: Atlantic Ocean

Senegal
Capital: Dakar
Population: 10.6 million
Official Language: French
Land Area: 192,000 sq km; 74,131 sq mi
Leading Exports: fish, groundnuts (peanuts), petroleum products, phosphates, cotton
Continent: Africa

Seychelles
Capital: Victoria
Population: 80,098
Official Languages: English and French
Land Area: 455 sq km; 176 sq mi
Leading Exports: canned tuna, cinnamon bark, copra, petroleum products (reexports)
Location: Indian Ocean

Sierra Leone
Capital: Freetown
Population: 5.6 million
Official Language: English
Land Area: 71,620 sq km; 27,652 sq mi
Leading Exports: diamonds, rutile, cocoa, coffee, fish
Continent: Africa

Somalia
Capital: Mogadishu
Population: 7.8 million
Official Languages: Somali and Arabic
Land Area: 627,337 sq km; 242,215 sq mi
Leading Exports: livestock, bananas, hides, fish, charcoal, scrap metal
Continent: Africa

South Africa
Capital: Cape Town, Pretoria, and Bloemfontein
Population: 43.6 million
Official Languages: Eleven official languages: Afrikaans, English, Ndebele, Pedi, Sotho, Swazi, Tsonga, Tswana, Venda, Xhosa, and Zulu
Land Area: 1,219,912 sq km; 471,008 sq mi
Leading Exports: gold, diamonds, platinum, other metals and minerals, machinery and equipment
Continent: Africa

Sudan
Capital: Khartoum
Population: 37.1 million
Official Language: Arabic
Land Area: 2,376,000 sq km; 917,374 sq mi
Leading Exports: oil and petroleum products, cotton, sesame, livestock, groundnuts, gum arabic, sugar
Continent: Africa

Swaziland
Capital: Mbabane
Population: 1.1 million
Official Languages: English and siSwati
Land Area: 17,20 sq km; 6,642 sq mi
Leading Exports: soft drink concentrates, sugar, wood pulp, cotton yarn, refrigerators, citrus and canned fruit
Continent: Africa

Tanzania
Capital: Dar es Salaam and Dodoma
Population: 37.2 million
Official Languages: Swahili and English
Land Area: 886,037 sq km; 342,099 sq mi
Leading Exports: gold, coffee, cashew nuts, manufactured goods, cotton
Continent: Africa

Togo
Capital: Lomé
Population: 5.2 million
Official Language: French
Land Area: 54,385 sq km; 20,998 sq mi
Leading Exports: cotton, phosphates, coffee, cocoa
Continent: Africa

Tunisia
Capital: Tunis
Population: 9.8 million
Official Language: Arabic
Land Area: 155,360 sq km; 59,984 sq mi
Leading Exports: textiles, mechanical goods, phosphates and chemicals, agricultural products, hydrocarbons
Continent: Africa

Uganda
Capital: Kampala
Population: 24.7 million
Official Language: English
Land Area: 199,710 sq km; 77,108 sq mi
Leading Exports: coffee, fish and fish products, tea, gold, cotton, flowers, horticultural products
Continent: Africa

Zambia
Capital: Lusaka
Population: 10.1 million
Official Language: English
Land Area: 740,724 sq km; 285,994 sq mi
Leading Exports: copper, cobalt, electricity, tobacco, flowers, cotton
Continent: Africa

Zimbabwe
Capital: Harare
Population: 11.3 million
Official Language: English
Land Area: 386,670 sq km; 149,293 sq mi
Leading Exports: tobacco, gold, iron alloys, textiles and clothing
Continent: Africa

Asia and the Pacific

Afghanistan
Capital: Kabul
Population: 27.8 million
Official Languages: Pashtu and Dari
Land Area: 647,500 sq km; 250,000 sq mi
Leading Exports: agricultural products, hand-woven carpets, wool, cotton, hides and pelts, precious and semiprecious gems
Continent: Asia

Armenia
Capital: Yerevan
Population: 3.3 million
Official Language: Armenian
Land Area: 29,400 sq km; 10,965 sq mi
Leading Exports: diamonds, scrap metal, machinery and equipment, brandy, copper ore
Continent: Asia

Australia
Capital: Canberra
Population: 19.6 million
Official Language: English
Land Area: 7,617,930 sq km; 2,941,283 sq mi
Leading Exports: coal, gold, meat, wool, alumina, iron ore, wheat, machinery and transport equipment
Continent: Australia

Azerbaijan
Capital: Baku
Population: 7.8 million
Official Language: Azerbaijani
Land Area: 86,100 sq km; 33,243 sq mi
Leading Exports: oil and gas, machinery, cotton, foodstuffs
Continent: Asia

Bahrain
Capital: Manama
Population: 656,397
Official Language: Arabic
Land Area: 665 sq km; 257 sq mi
Leading Exports: petroleum and petroleum products, aluminum, textiles
Continent: Asia

Bangladesh
Capital: Dhaka
Population: 133.4 million
Official Language: Bengali
Land Area: 133,910 sq km; 51,705 sq mi
Leading Exports: garments, jute and jute goods, leather, frozen fish and seafood
Continent: Asia

Bhutan
Capital: Thimphu
Population: 2.1 million
Official Language: Dzongkha
Land Area: 47,000 sq km; 18,147 sq mi
Leading Exports: electricity, cardamom, gypsum, timber, handicrafts, cement, fruit, precious stones, spices
Continent: Asia

Brunei
Capital: Bandar Seri Begawan
Population: 350,898
Official Language: Malay
Land Area: 5,270 sq km; 2,035 sq mi
Leading Exports: crude oil, natural gas, refined products
Continent: Asia

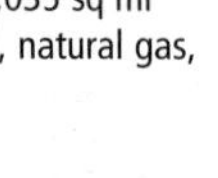

Cambodia
Capital: Phnom Penh
Population: 12.8 million
Official Language: Khmer
Land Area: 176,520 sq km; 68,154 sq mi
Leading Exports: timber, garments, rubber, rice, fish
Continent: Asia

China
Capital: Beijing
Population: 1.29 billion
Official Languages: Mandarin and Chinese
Land Area: 9,326,410 sq km; 3,600,927 sq mi
Leading Exports: machinery and equipment, textiles and clothing, footwear, toys and sports goods, mineral fuels
Continent: Asia

Cyprus
Capital: Nicosia
Population: 767,314
Official Languages: Greek and Turkish
Land Area: 9,240 sq km; 3,568 sq mi
Leading Exports: citrus, potatoes, grapes, wine, cement, clothing and shoes
Location: Mediterranean Sea

East Timor
Capital: Dili
Population: 952,618
Official Languages: Tetum and Portuguese
Land Area: 15,007 sq km; 5,794 sq mi
Leading Exports: coffee, sandalwood, marble
Continent: Asia

Fiji
Capital: Suva
Population: 856,346
Official Language: English
Land Area: 18,270 sq km; 7,054 sq mi
Leading Exports: sugar, garments, gold, timber, fish, molasses, coconut oil
Location: Pacific Ocean

Georgia
Capital: Tbilisi
Population: 5 million
Official Languages: Georgian and Abkhazian
Land Area: 69,700 sq km; 26,911 sq mi
Leading Exports: scrap metal, machinery, chemicals, fuel reexports, citrus fruits, tea, wine, other agricultural products
Continent: Asia

India
Capital: New Delhi
Population: 1.05 billion
Official Languages: Hindi and English
Land Area: 2,973,190 sq km; 1,147,949 sq mi
Leading Exports: textile goods, gems and jewelry, engineering goods, chemicals, leather manufactured goods
Continent: Asia

Indonesia
Capital: Jakarta
Population: 231.3 million
Official Language: Bahasa Indonesia
Land Area: 1,826,440 sq km; 705,188 sq mi
Leading Exports: oil and gas, electrical appliances, plywood, textiles, rubber
Continent: Asia

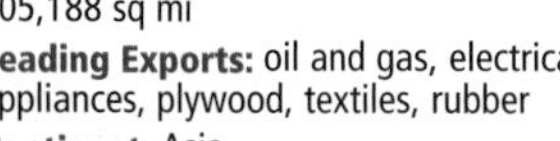

Iran
Capital: Tehran
Population: 66.6 million
Official Language: Farsi
Land Area: 1,636,000 sq km; 631,660 sq mi
Leading Exports: petroleum, carpets, fruits and nuts, iron and steel, chemicals
Continent: Asia

Iraq
Capital: Baghdad
Population: 24.7 million
Official Language: Arabic
Land Area: 432,162 sq km; 166,858 sq mi
Leading Exports: crude oil
Continent: Asia

Israel
Capital: Jerusalem
Population: 6.0 million
Official Languages: Hebrew, Arabic
Land Area: 20,330 sq km; 7,849 sq mi
Leading Exports: machinery and equipment, software, cut diamonds, agricultural products, chemicals, textiles and apparel
Continent: Asia

Japan
Capital: Tokyo
Population: 127 million
Official Language: Japanese
Land Area: 374,744 sq km; 144,689 sq mi
Leading Exports: motor vehicles, semiconductors, office machinery, chemicals
Continent: Asia

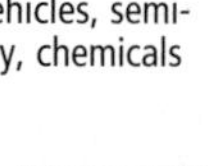

Jordan
Capital: Amman
Population: 5.3 million
Official Language: Arabic
Land Area: 91,971 sq km; 35,510 sq mi
Leading Exports: phosphates, fertilizers, potash, agricultural products, manufactured goods, pharmaceuticals
Continent: Asia

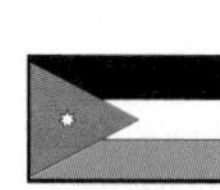

Kazakhstan
Capital: Astana
Population: 16.7 million
Official Language: Kazakh
Land Area: 2,669,800 sq km; 1,030,810 sq mi
Leading Exports: oil and oil products, ferrous metals, machinery, chemicals, grain, wool, meat, coal
Continent: Asia

Kiribati
Capital: Bairiki (Tarawa Atoll)
Population: 96,335
Official Language: English
Land Area: 811 sq km; 313 sq mi
Leading Exports: copra, coconuts, seaweed, fish
Location: Pacific Ocean

Korea, North
Capital: Pyongyang
Population: 22.3 million
Official Language: Korean
Land Area: 120,410 sq km; 46,490 sq mi
Leading Exports: minerals, metallurgical products, manufactured goods (including armaments), agricultural and fishery products
Continent: Asia

Korea, South
Capital: Seoul
Population: 48.3 million
Official Language: Korean
Land Area: 98,190 sq km; 37,911 sq mi
Leading Exports: electronic products, machinery and equipment, motor vehicles, steel, ships, textiles, clothing, footwear, fish
Continent: Asia

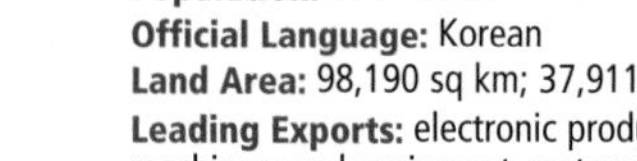
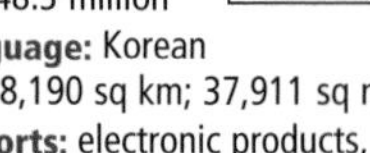
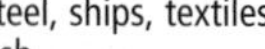
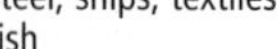

Kuwait
Capital: Kuwait City
Population: 2.1 million
Official Language: Arabic
Land Area: 17,820 sq km; 6,880 sq mi
Leading Exports: oil and refined products, fertilizers
Continent: Asia

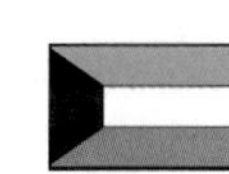

Kyrgyzstan
Capital: Bishkek
Population: 4.8 million
Official Languages: Kyrgyz and Russian
Land Area: 191,300 sq km; 73,861sq mi
Leading Exports: cotton, wool, meat, tobacco, gold, mercury, uranium, hydropower, machinery, shoes
Continent: Asia

Laos
Capital: Vientiane
Population: 5.8 million
Official Language: Lao
Land Area: 230,800 sq km; 89,112 sq mi
Leading Exports: wood products, garments, electricity, coffee, tin
Continent: Asia

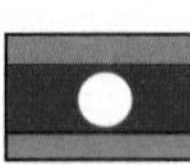
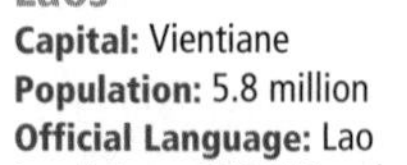

Lebanon
Capital: Beirut
Population: 3.7 million
Official Language: Arabic
Land Area: 10,230 sq km; 3,950 sq mi
Leading Exports: foodstuffs and tobacco, textile, chemicals, precious stones, metal and metal products, electrical equipment and products, jewelry, paper and paper products
Continent: Asia

Malaysia
Capital: Kuala Lumpur and Putrajaya
Population: 22.7 million
Official Language: Bahasa Malaysia
Land Area: 328,550 sq km; 126,853 sq mi
Leading Exports: electronic equipment, petroleum and liquefied natural gas, wood and wood products, palm oil, rubber, textiles, chemicals
Continent: Asia

Maldives
Capital: Malé
Population: 320,165
Official Language: Dhivehi (Maldivian)
Land Area: 300 sq km; 116 sq mi
Leading Exports: fish, clothing
Location: Indian Ocean

Marshall Islands
Capital: Majuro
Population: 73,360
Official Languages: Marshallese and English
Land Area: 181.3 sq km; 70 sq mi
Leading Exports: copra cake, coconut oil, handicrafts
Location: Pacific Ocean

Micronesia, Federated States of
Capital: Palikir (Pohnpei Island)
Population: 135,869
Official Language: English
Land Area: 702 sq km; 271 sq mi
Leading Exports: fish, garments, bananas, black pepper
Location: Pacific Ocean

Mongolia
Capital: Ulaanbaatar
Population: 2.6 million
Official Language: Khalkha Mongolian
Land Area: 1,555,400 sq km; 600,540 sq mi
Leading Exports: copper, livestock, animal products, cashmere, wool, hides, fluorspar, other nonferrous metals
Continent: Asia

Myanmar (Burma)
Capital: Rangoon (Yangon)
Population: 42.2 million
Official Language: Burmese (Myanmar)
Land Area: 657,740 sq km; 253,953 sq mi
Leading Exports: apparel, foodstuffs, wood products, precious stones
Continent: Asia

Nauru
Capital: Yaren District
Population: 12,329
Official Language: Nauruan
Land Area: 21 sq km; 8 sq mi
Leading Exports: phosphates
Location: Pacific Ocean

Nepal
Capital: Kathmandu
Population: 25.9 million
Official Language: Nepali
Land Area: 136,800 sq km; 52,818 sq mi
Leading Exports: carpets, clothing, leather goods, jute goods, grain
Continent: Asia

New Zealand
Capital: Wellington
Population: 3.8 million
Official Languages: English and Maori
Land Area: 268,680 sq km; 103,737 sq mi
Leading Exports: dairy products, meat, wood and wood products, fish, machinery
Location: Pacific Ocean

Oman
Capital: Muscat
Population: 2.7 million
Official Language: Arabic
Land Area: 212,460 sq km; 82,030 sq mi
Leading Exports: petroleum, reexports, fish, metals, textiles
Continent: Asia

Pakistan
Capital: Islamabad
Population: 147.7 million
Official Languages: Urdu and English
Land Area: 778,720 sq km; 300,664 sq mi
Leading Exports: textiles (garments, cotton cloth, and yarn), rice, other agricultural products
Continent: Asia

Palau
Capital: Koror
Population: 19,409
Official Languages: English and Palauan
Land Area: 458 sq km; 177 sq mi
Leading Exports: shellfish, tuna, copra, garments
Location: Pacific Ocean

Papua New Guinea
Capital: Port Moresby
Population: 5.2 million
Official Language: English
Land Area: 452,860 sq km; 174,849 sq mi
Leading Exports: oil, gold, copper ore, logs, palm oil, coffee, cocoa, crayfish, prawns
Location: Pacific Ocean

Philippines
Capital: Manila
Population: 84.5 million
Official Languages: Filipino and English
Land Area: 298,170 sq km; 115,123 sq mi
Leading Exports: electronic equipment, machinery and transport equipment, garments, coconut products
Continent: Asia

Qatar
Capital: Doha
Population: 793,341
Official Language: Arabic
Land Area: 11,437 sq km; 4,416 sq mi
Leading Exports: petroleum products, fertilizers, steel
Continent: Asia

Samoa
Capital: Apia
Population: 178,631
Official Languages: Samoan and English
Land Area: 2,934 sq km; 1,133 sq mi
Leading Exports: fish, coconut oil cream, copra, taro, garments, beer
Location: Pacific Ocean

Saudi Arabia
Capital: Riyadh and Jiddah
Population: 23.5 million
Official Language: Arabic
Land Area: 1,960,582 sq km; 756,981 sq mi
Leading Exports: petroleum and petroleum products
Continent: Asia

Singapore
Capital: Singapore
Population: 4.5 million
Official Languages: Malay, English, Mandarin, Chinese, and Tamil
Land Area: 683 sq km; 264 sq mi
Leading Exports: machinery and equipment (including electronics), consumer goods, chemicals, mineral fuels
Continent: Asia

Solomon Islands
Capital: Honiara
Population: 494,786
Official Language: English
Land Area: 27,540 sq km; 10,633 sq mi
Leading Exports: timber, fish, copra, palm oil, cocoa
Location: Pacific Ocean

Sri Lanka
Capital: Colombo
Population: 19.6 million
Official Language: Sinhala, Tamil, and English
Land Area: 64,740 sq km; 24,996 sq mi
Leading Exports: textiles and apparel, tea, diamonds, coconut products, petroleum products
Continent: Asia

Syria

Capital: Damascus
Population: 17.2 million
Official Language: Arabic
Land Area: 184,050 sq km; 71,062 sq mi
Leading Exports: crude oil, textiles, fruits and vegetables, raw cotton
Continent: Asia

Taiwan
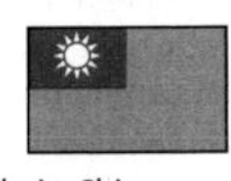
Capital: Taipei
Population: 22.5 million
Official Language: Mandarin Chinese
Land Area: 32,260 sq km; 12,456 sq mi
Leading Exports: machinery and electrical equipment, metals, textiles, plastics, chemicals
Continent: Asia

Tajikistan
Capital: Dushanbe
Population: 6.7 million
Official Language: Tajik
Land Area: 142,700 sq km; 55,096 sq mi
Leading Exports: aluminum, electricity, cotton, fruits, vegetables, oil, textiles
Continent: Asia

Thailand
Capital: Bangkok
Population: 62.5 million
Official Language: Thai
Land Area: 511,770 sq km; 197,564 sq mi
Leading Exports: computers, transistors, seafood, clothing, rice
Continent: Asia

Tonga
Capital: Nuku'alofa
Population: 106,137
Official Languages: Tongan and English
Land Area: 718 sq km; 277 sq mi
Leading Exports: squash, fish, vanilla beans, root crops
Location: Pacific Ocean

Turkey

Capital: Ankara
Population: 67.3 million
Official Language: Turkish
Land Area: 770,760 sq km; 297,590 sq mi
Leading Exports: apparel, foodstuffs, textiles, metal manufactured goods, transport equipment
Continent: Asia

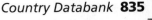

Turkmenistan
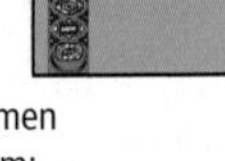
Capital: Ashgabat
Population: 4.7 million
Official Language: Turkmen
Land Area: 488,100 sq km; 188,455 sq mi
Leading Exports: gas, oil, cotton fiber, textiles
Continent: Asia

Asia and the Pacific (continued)

Tuvalu

Capital: Fongafale
Population: 10,800
Official Language: English
Land Area: 26 sq km; 10 sq mi
Leading Exports: copra, fish
Location: Pacific Ocean

United Arab Emirates

Capital: Abu Dhabi
Population: 2.4 million
Official Language: Arabic
Land Area: 82,880 sq km; 32,000 sq mi
Leading Exports: crude oil, natural gas, reexports, dried fish, dates
Continent: Asia

Uzbekistan

Capital: Tashkent
Population: 25.5 million
Official Language: Uzbek
Land Area: 425,400 sq km; 164,247 sq mi
Leading Exports: cotton, gold, energy products, mineral fertilizers, ferrous metals, textiles, food products, automobiles
Continent: Asia

Vanuatu

Capital: Port-Vila
Population: 196,178
Official Languages: English, French, and Bislama
Land Area: 12,200 sq km; 4,710 sq mi
Leading Exports: copra, kava, beef, cocoa, timber, coffee
Location: Pacific Ocean

Vietnam

Capital: Hanoi
Population: 81.1 million
Official Language: Vietnamese
Land Area: 325,320 sq km; 125,621 sq mi
Leading Exports: crude oil, marine products, rice, coffee, rubber, tea, garments, shoes
Continent: Asia

Yemen

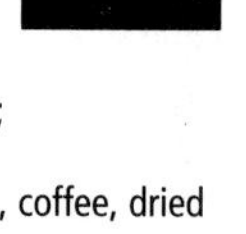

Capital: Sanaa
Population: 18.7 million
Official Language: Arabic
Land Area: 527,970 sq km; 203,849 sq mi
Leading Exports: crude oil, coffee, dried and salted fish
Continent: Asia

Europe and Russia

Albania

Capital: Tiranë
Population: 3.5 million
Official Language: Albanian
Land Area: 27,398 sq km; 10,578 sq mi
Leading Exports: textiles and footwear, asphalt, metals and metallic ores, crude oil, vegetables, fruits, tobacco
Continent: Europe

Andorra

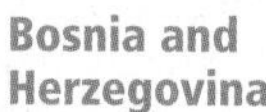

Capital: Andorra la Vella
Population: 68,403
Official Language: Catalan
Land Area: 468 sq km; 181 sq mi
Leading Exports: tobacco products, furniture
Continent: Europe

Austria

Capital: Vienna
Population: 8.2 million
Official Language: German
Land Area: 82,738 sq km; 31,945 sq mi
Leading Exports: machinery and equipment, motor vehicles and parts, paper and paperboard, metal goods, chemicals, iron and steel, textiles, foodstuffs
Continent: Europe

Belarus

Capital: Minsk
Population: 10.3 million
Official Languages: Belarussian and Russian
Land Area: 207,600 sq km; 80,154 sq mi
Leading Exports: machinery and equipment, mineral products, chemicals, textiles, food stuffs, metals
Continent: Europe

Belgium

Capital: Brussels
Population: 10.3 million
Official Languages: Dutch and French
Land Area: 30,230 sq km; 11,172 sq mi
Leading Exports: machinery and equipment, chemicals, metals and metal products
Continent: Europe

Bosnia and Herzegovina

Capital: Sarajevo
Population: 4.0 million
Official Language: Serbo-Croat
Land Area: 51,129 sq km; 19,741 sq mi
Leading Exports: miscellaneous manufactured goods, crude materials
Continent: Europe

Bulgaria

Capital: Sofía
Population: 7.6 million
Official Language: Bulgarian
Land Area: 110,550 sq km; 42,683 sq mi
Leading Exports: clothing, footwear, iron and steel, machinery and equipment, fuels
Continent: Europe

Croatia

Capital: Zagreb
Population: 4.4 million
Official Language: Croatian
Land Area: 56,414 km; 21,781 sq mi
Leading Exports: transport equipment, textiles, chemicals, foodstuffs, fuels
Continent: Europe

Czech Republic

Capital: Prague
Population: 10.3 million
Official Language: Czech
Land Area: 78,276 sq km; 29,836 sq mi
Leading Exports: machinery and transport equipment, intermediate manufactured goods, chemicals, raw materials and fuel
Continent: Europe

Denmark

Capital: Copenhagen
Population: 5.4 million
Official Language: Danish
Land Area: 42,394 sq km; 16,368 sq mi
Leading Exports: machinery and instruments, meat and meat products, dairy products, fish, chemicals, furniture, ships, windmills
Continent: Europe

Estonia

Capital: Tallinn
Population: 1.4 million
Official Language: Estonian
Land Area: 43,211 sq km; 16,684 sq mi
Leading Exports: machinery and equipment, wood products, textiles, food products, metals, chemical products
Continent: Europe

Finland

Capital: Helsinki
Population: 5.2 million
Official Languages: Finnish and Swedish
Land Area: 305,470 sq km; 117,942 sq mi
Leading Exports: machinery and equipment, chemicals, metals, timber, paper, pulp
Continent: Europe

France

Capital: Paris
Population: 59.8 million
Official Language: French
Land Area: 545,630 sq km; 310,668 sq mi
Leading Exports: machinery and transportation equipment, aircraft, plastics, chemicals, pharmaceutical products, iron and steel, beverages
Continent: Europe

Germany

Capital: Berlin
Population: 83 million
Official Language: German
Land Area: 349,223 sq km; 134,835 sq mi
Leading Exports: machinery, vehicles, chemicals, metals and manufactured goods, foodstuffs, textiles
Continent: Europe

Greece

Capital: Athens
Population: 10.6 million
Official Language: Greek
Land Area: 130,800 sq km; 50,502 sq mi
Leading Exports: food and beverages, manufactured goods, petroleum products, chemicals, textiles
Continent: Europe

Hungary

Capital: Budapest
Population: 10.1 million
Official Language: Hungarian
Land Area: 92,340 sq km; 35,652 sq mi
Leading Exports: machinery and equipment, other manufactured goods, food products, raw materials, fuels and electricity
Continent: Europe

Iceland
Capital: Reykjavík
Population: 279,384
Official Language: Icelandic
Land Area: 100,250 sq km; 38,707 sq mi
Leading Exports: fish and fish products, animal products, aluminum, diatomite, ferrosilicon
Location: Atlantic Ocean

Ireland
Capital: Dublin
Population: 3.9 million
Official Languages: Irish Gaelic and English
Land Area: 68,890 sq km; 26,598 sq mi
Leading Exports: machinery and equipment, computers, chemicals, pharmaceuticals, live animals, animal products
Continent: Europe

Italy
Capital: Rome
Population: 57.7 million
Official Language: Italian
Land Area: 294,020 sq km; 113,521 sq mi
Leading Exports: fruits, vegetables, grapes, potatoes, sugar beets, soybeans, grain, olives, beef, diary products, fish
Continent: Europe

Latvia
Capital: Riga
Population: 2.4 million
Official Language: Latvian
Land Area: 63,589 sq km; 24,552 sq mi
Leading Exports: wood and wood products, machinery and equipment, metals, textiles, foodstuffs
Continent: Europe

Liechtenstein
Capital: Vaduz
Population: 32,842
Official Language: German
Land Area: 160 sq km; 62 sq mi
Leading Exports: small specialty machinery, dental products, stamps, hardware, pottery
Continent: Europe

Lithuania
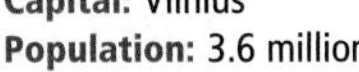

Capital: Vilnius
Population: 3.6 million
Official Language: Lithuanian
Land Area: 65,200 sq km; 25,174 sq mi
Leading Exports: mineral products, textiles and clothing, machinery and equipment, chemicals, wood and wood products, foodstuffs
Continent: Europe

Luxembourg
Capital: Luxembourg
Population: 448,569
Official Languages: Luxembourgish, French, and German
Land Area: 2,586 sq km; 998 sq mi
Leading Exports: machinery and equipment, steel products, chemicals, rubber products, glass
Continent: Europe

Macedonia, The Former Yugoslav Republic of
Capital: Skopje
Population: 2.1 million
Official Languages: Macedonian and Albanian
Land Area: 24,856 sq km; 9,597 sq mi
Leading Exports: food, beverages, tobacco, miscellaneous manufactured goods, iron and steel
Continent: Europe

Malta
Capital: Valletta
Population: 397,499
Official Languages: Maltese and English
Land Area: 316 sq km; 122 sq mi
Leading Exports: machinery and transport equipment, manufactured goods
Location: Mediterranean Sea

Moldova
Capital: Chişinău
Population: 4.4 million
Official Language: Moldovan
Land Area: 33,371 sq km; 12,885 sq mi
Leading Exports: foodstuffs, textiles and footwear, machinery
Continent: Europe

Monaco
Capital: Monaco
Population: 31,987
Official Language: French
Land Area: 1.95 sq km; 0.75 sq mi
Leading Exports: no information available
Continent: Europe

Netherlands
Capital: Amsterdam and The Hague
Population: 16.1 million
Official Language: Dutch
Land Area: 33,883 sq km; 13,082 sq mi
Leading Exports: machinery and equipment, chemicals, fuels, foodstuffs
Continent: Europe

Norway
Capital: Oslo
Population: 4.5 million
Official Language: Norwegian
Land Area: 307,860 sq km; 118,865 sq mi
Leading Exports: petroleum and petroleum products, machinery and equipment, metals, chemicals, ships, fish
Continent: Europe

Poland
Capital: Warsaw
Population: 38.6 million
Official Language: Polish
Land Area: 304,465 sq km; 117,554 sq mi
Leading Exports: machinery and transport equipment, intermediate manufactured goods, miscellaneous manufactured goods, food and live animals
Continent: Europe

Portugal
Capital: Lisbon
Population: 10.1 million
Official Language: Portuguese
Land Area: 91,951 sq km; 35,502 sq mi
Leading Exports: clothing and footwear, machinery, chemicals, cork and paper products, hides
Continent: Europe

Romania
Capital: Bucharest
Population: 22.3 million
Official Language: Romanian
Land Area: 230,340 sq km; 88,934 sq mi
Leading Exports: textiles and footwear, metals and metal products, machinery and equipment, minerals and fuels
Continent: Europe

Russia
Capital: Moscow
Population: 145 million
Official Language: Russian
Land Area: 16,995,800 sq km; 6,592,100 sq mi
Leading Exports: petroleum and petroleum products, natural gas, wood and wood products, metals, chemicals, and a wide variety of civilian and military manufactured goods
Continents: Europe and Asia

San Marino
Capital: San Marino
Population: 27,730
Official Language: Italian
Land Area: 61 sq km; 24 sq mi
Leading Exports: building stone, lime, wood, chestnuts, wheat, wine, baked goods, hides, ceramics
Continent: Europe

Serbia and Montenegro
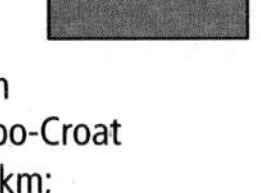

Capital: Belgrade
Population: 10.7 million
Official Language: Serbo-Croat
Land Area: 102,136 sq km; 39,435 sq mi
Leading Exports: manufactured goods, food and live animals, raw materials
Continent: Europe

Slovakia
Capital: Bratislava
Population: 5.4 million
Official Language: Slovak
Land Area: 48,800 sq km; 18,842 sq mi
Leading Exports: machinery and transport equipment, intermediate manufactured goods, miscellaneous manufactured goods, chemicals
Continent: Europe

Slovenia
Capital: Ljubljana
Population: 1.9 million
Official Language: Slovene
Land Area: 20,151 sq km; 7,780 sq mi
Leading Exports: manufactured goods, machinery and transport equipment, chemicals, food
Continent: Europe

Spain
Capital: Madrid
Population: 40.1 million
Official Languages: Spanish, Galician, Basque, and Catalan
Land Area: 499,542 sq km; 192,873 sq mi
Leading Exports: machinery, motor vehicles, foodstuffs, other consumer goods
Continent: Europe

Sweden
Capital: Stockholm
Population: 8.9 million
Official Language: Swedish
Land Area: 410,934 sq km; 158,662 sq mi
Leading Exports: machinery, motor vehicles, paper products, pulp and wood, iron and steel products, chemicals
Continent: Europe

Europe and Russia (continued)

Switzerland
Capital: Bern
Population: 7.3 million
Official Languages: German, French, and Italian
Land Area: 39,770 sq km; 15,355 sq mi
Leading Exports: machinery, chemicals, metals, watches, agricultural products
Continent: Europe

Ukraine
Capital: Kiev
Population: 48.4 million
Official Language: Ukrainian
Land Area: 603,700 sq km; 233,090 sq mi
Leading Exports: ferrous and nonferrous metals, fuel and petroleum products, machinery and transport equipment, food products
Continent: Europe

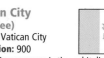

United Kingdom
Capital: London
Population: 59.8 million
Official Languages: English and Welsh
Land Area: 241,590 sq km; 93,278 sq mi
Leading Exports: manufactured goods, fuels, chemicals, food, beverages, tobacco
Continent: Europe

Vatican City (Holy See)

Capital: Vatican City
Population: 900
Official Languages: Latin and Italian
Land Area: 0.44 sq km; 0.17 sq mi
Leading Exports: no information available
Continent: Europe

Latin America

Antigua and Barbuda
Capital: Saint John's
Population: 67,448
Official Language: English
Land Area: 442 sq km; 171 sq mi
Leading Exports: petroleum products, manufactured goods, machinery and transport equipment, food and live animals
Location: Caribbean Sea

Argentina
Capital: Buenos Aires
Population: 37.8 million
Official Language: Spanish
Land Area: 2,736,690 sq km; 1,056,636 sq mi
Leading Exports: edible oils, fuels and energy, cereals, feed, motor vehicles
Continent: South America

Bahamas
Capital: Nassau
Population: 300,529
Official Language: English
Land Area: 10,070 sq km; 3,888 sq mi
Leading Exports: fish and crawfish, rum, salt, chemicals, fruit and vegetables
Location: Caribbean Sea

Barbados
Capital: Bridgetown
Population: 276,607
Official Language: English
Land Area: 431 sq km; 166 sq mi
Leading Exports: sugar and molasses, rum, other foods and beverages, chemicals, electrical components, clothing
Location: Caribbean Sea

Belize
Capital: Belmopan
Population: 262,999
Official Language: English
Land Area: 22,806 sq km; 8,805 sq mi
Leading Exports: sugar, bananas, citrus, clothing, fish products, molasses, wood
Continent: North America

Bolivia
Capital: La Paz and Sucre
Population: 8.5 million
Official Languages: Spanish, Quechua, and Aymara
Land Area: 1,084,390 sq km; 418,683 sq mi
Leading Exports: soybeans, natural gas, zinc, gold, wood
Continent: South America

Brazil
Capital: Brasília
Population: 176 million
Official Language: Portuguese
Land Area: 8,456,510 sq km; 3,265,059 sq mi
Leading Exports: manufactured goods, iron ore, soybeans, footwear, coffee, autos
Continent: South America

Chile
Capital: Santiago
Population: 15.5 million
Official Language: Spanish
Land Area: 748,800 sq km; 289,112 sq mi
Leading Exports: copper, fish, fruits, paper and pulp, chemicals
Continent: South America

Colombia
Capital: Bogotá
Population: 41 million
Official Language: Spanish
Land Area: 1,038,700 sq km; 401,042 sq mi
Leading Exports: petroleum, coffee, coal, apparel, bananas, cut flowers
Continent: South America

Costa Rica
Capital: San José
Population: 3.8 million
Official Language: Spanish
Land Area: 51,660 sq km; 19,560 sq mi
Leading Exports: coffee, bananas, sugar, pineapples, textiles, electronic components, medical equipment
Continent: North America

Cuba
Capital: Havana
Population: 11.2 million
Official Language: Spanish
Land Area: 110,860 sq km; 42,803 sq mi
Leading Exports: sugar, nickel, tobacco, fish, medical products, citrus, coffee
Location: Caribbean Sea

Dominica
Capital: Roseau
Population: 73,000
Official Language: English
Land Area: 754 sq km; 291 sq mi
Leading Exports: bananas, soap, bay oil, vegetables, grapefruit, oranges
Location: Caribbean Sea

Dominican Republic
Capital: Santo Domingo
Population: 8.7 million
Official Language: Spanish
Land Area: 48,380 sq km; 18,679 sq mi
Leading Exports: ferronickel, sugar, gold, silver, coffee, cocoa, tobacco, meats, consumer goods
Location: Caribbean Sea

Ecuador
Capital: Quito
Population: 13.5 million
Official Language: Spanish
Land Area: 276,840 sq km; 106,888 sq mi
Leading Exports: petroleum, bananas, shrimp, coffee, cocoa, cut flowers, fish
Continent: South America

El Salvador
Capital: San Salvador
Population: 6.4 million
Official Language: Spanish
Land Area: 20,720 sq km; 8,000 sq mi
Leading Exports: offshore assembly exports, coffee, sugar, shrimp, textiles, chemicals, electricity
Continent: North America

Grenada
Capital: Saint George's
Population: 89,211
Official Language: English
Land Area: 344 sq km; 133 sq mi
Leading Exports: bananas, cocoa, nutmeg, fruit and vegetables, clothing, mace
Location: Caribbean Sea

Guatemala
Capital: Guatemala City
Population: 13.3 million
Official Language: Spanish
Land Area: 108,430 sq km; 41,865 sq mi
Leading Exports: coffee, sugar, bananas, fruits and vegetables, cardamom, meat, apparel, petroleum, electricity
Continent: North America

Guyana
Capital: Georgetown
Population: 698,209
Official Language: English
Land Area: 196,850 sq km; 76,004 sq mi
Leading Exports: sugar, gold, bauxite/alumina, rice, shrimp, molasses, rum, timber
Continent: South America

Haiti
Capital: Port-au-Prince
Population: 7.1 million
Official Languages: French and French Creole
Land Area: 27,560 sq km; 10,641 sq mi
Leading Exports: manufactured goods, coffee, oils, cocoa
Location: Caribbean Sea

Honduras
Capital: Tegucigalpa
Population: 6.6 million
Official Language: Spanish
Land Area: 111,890 sq km; 43,201 sq mi
Leading Exports: coffee, bananas, shrimp, lobster, meat, zinc, lumber
Continent: North America

Jamaica

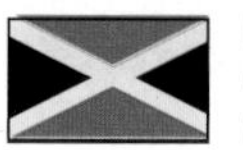

Capital: Kingston
Population: 2.7 million
Official Language: English
Land Area: 10,831 sq km; 4,182 sq mi
Leading Exports: alumina, bauxite, sugar, bananas, rum
Location: Caribbean Sea

Mexico

Capital: Mexico City
Population: 103.4 million
Official Language: Spanish
Land Area: 1,923,040 sq km; 742,486 sq mi
Leading Exports: manufactured goods, oil and oil products, silver, fruits, vegetables, coffee, cotton
Continent: North America

Nicaragua

Capital: Managua
Population: 5 million
Official Language: Spanish
Land Area: 120,254 sq km; 46,430 sq mi
Leading Exports: coffee, shrimp and lobster, cotton, tobacco, beef, sugar, bananas, gold
Continent: North America

Panama

Capital: Panama City
Population: 2.9 million
Official Language: Spanish
Land Area: 75,990 sq km; 29,340 sq mi
Leading Exports: bananas, shrimp, sugar, coffee, clothing
Continent: North America

Paraguay

Capital: Asunción
Population: 5.9 million
Official Language: Spanish
Land Area: 397,300 sq km; 153,398 sq mi
Leading Exports: electricity, soybeans, feed, cotton, meat, edible oils
Continent: South America

Peru

Capital: Lima
Population: 28 million
Official Languages: Spanish and Quechua
Land Area: 1,280,000 sq km; 494,208 sq mi
Leading Exports: fish and fish products, gold, copper, zinc, crude petroleum and byproducts, lead, coffee, sugar, cotton
Continent: South America

Saint Kitts and Nevis

Capital: Basseterre
Population: 38,736
Official Language: English
Land Area: 261 sq km; 101 sq mi
Leading Exports: machinery, food, electronics, beverages, tobacco
Location: Caribbean Sea

Saint Lucia

Capital: Castries
Population: 160,145
Official Language: English
Land Area: 606 sq km; 234 sq mi
Leading Exports: bananas, clothing, cocoa, vegetables, fruits, coconut oil
Location: Caribbean Sea

Saint Vincent and the Grenadines

Capital: Kingstown
Population: 116,394
Official Language: English
Land Area: 389 sq km; 150 sq mi
Leading Exports: bananas, eddoes and dasheen, arrowroot starch, tennis racquets
Location: Caribbean Sea

Suriname

Capital: Paramaribo
Population: 436,494
Official Language: Dutch
Land Area: 161,470 sq km; 62,344 sq mi
Leading Exports: alumina, crude oil, lumber, shrimp and fish, rice, bananas
Continent: South America

Trinidad and Tobago

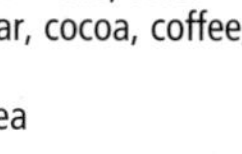

Capital: Port-of-Spain
Population: 1.2 million
Official Language: English
Land Area: 5,128 sq km; 1,980 sq mi
Leading Exports: petroleum and petroleum products, chemicals, steel products, fertilizer, sugar, cocoa, coffee, citrus, flowers
Location: Caribbean Sea

Uruguay

Capital: Montevideo
Population: 3.4 million
Official Language: Spanish
Land Area: 173,620 sq km; 67,100 sq mi
Leading Exports: meat, rice, leather products, wool, vehicles, dairy products
Continent: South America

Venezuela

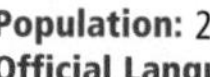

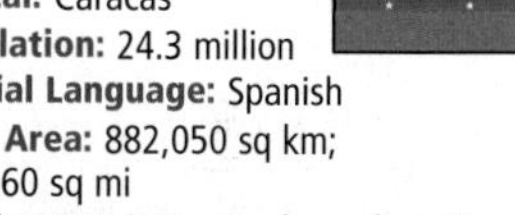

Capital: Caracas
Population: 24.3 million
Official Language: Spanish
Land Area: 882,050 sq km; 340,560 sq mi
Leading Exports: petroleum, bauxite and aluminum, steel, chemicals, agricultural products, basic manufactured goods
Continent: South America

United States and Canada

Canada

Capital: Ottawa
Population: 31.9 million
Official Languages: English and French
Land Area: 9,220,970 sq km; 3,560,217 sq mi
Leading Exports: motor vehicles and parts, industrial machinery, aircraft, telecommunications equipment, chemicals, plastics, fertilizers, wood pulp, timber, crude petroleum, natural gas, electricity, aluminum
Continent: North America

United States

Capital: Washington, D.C.
Population: 281.4 million
Official Language: English
Land Area: 9,158,960 sq km; 3,536,274 sq mi
Leading Exports: capital goods, automobiles, industrial supplies and raw materials, consumer goods, agricultural products
Continent: North America

SOURCE: CIA World Factbook Online, 2002

Glossary of Geographic Terms

basin
an area that is lower than surrounding land areas; some basins are filled with water

bay
a body of water that is partly surrounded by land and that is connected to a larger body of water

butte
a small, high, flat-topped landform with cliff-like sides

▲ butte

canyon
a deep, narrow valley with steep sides; often with a stream flowing through it

cataract
a large waterfall or steep rapids

◀ cataract

delta
a plain at the mouth of a river, often triangular in shape, formed where sediment is deposited by flowing water

flood plain
a broad plain on either side of a river, formed where sediment settles during floods

glacier
a huge, slow-moving mass of snow and ice

hill
an area that rises above surrounding land and has a rounded top; lower and usually less steep than a mountain

island
an area of land completely surrounded by water

isthmus
a narrow strip of land that connects two larger areas of land

mesa
a high, flat-topped landform with cliff-like sides; larger than a butte

mountain
a landform that rises steeply at least 2,000 feet (610 meters) above surrounding land; usually wide at the bottom and rising to a narrow peak or ridge

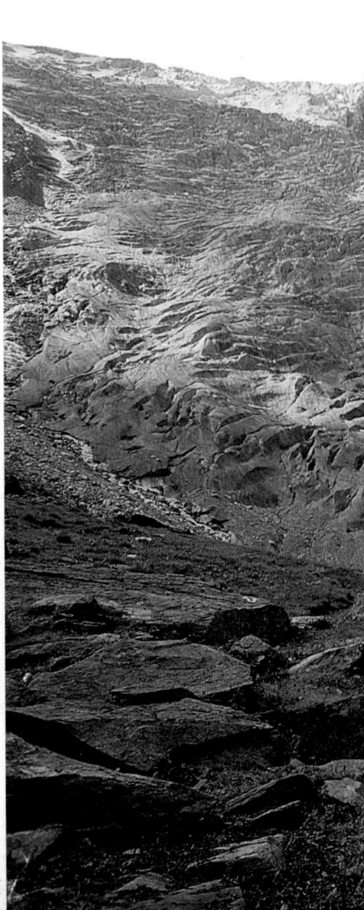

▶ glacier

delta

mountain pass
a gap between mountains

peninsula
an area of land almost completely surrounded by water but connected to the mainland

plain
a large area of flat or gently rolling land

plateau
a large, flat area that rises above the surrounding land; at least one side has a steep slope

river mouth
the point where a river enters a lake or sea

strait
a narrow stretch of water that connects two larger bodies of water

tributary
a river or stream that flows into a larger river

valley
a low stretch of land between mountains or hills; land that is drained by a river

volcano
an opening in Earth's surface through which molten rock, ashes, and gases escape from the interior

volcano

Gazetteer

A

Abuja (9°12′ N, 7°11′ E) the capital of Nigeria, p. 488

Addis Ababa (9°2′ N, 38° 42′ E) the capital of Ethiopia, p. 518

Africa (10° N, 22° E) the world's second-largest continent, surrounded by the Mediterranean Sea, the Atlantic Ocean, the Indian Ocean, and the Red Sea, p. 15

Aksum an ancient city in northern Ethiopia that was a powerful kingdom and trade center from about A.D. 200 to A.D. 600, p. 391

Algeria (28° N, 3° E) a country in North Africa, officially the Democratic and Popular Republic of Algeria, p. 466

Algiers (36°47′ N, 3°3′ E) the capital of Algeria, p. 467

Alice Springs (23°42′ S, 133°53′ E) a town in Northern Territory, Australia, p. 807

Almaty (43°15′ N, 76°57′ E) the largest city of Kazakhstan, a country in Central Asia, p. 779

Alpine Mountain System (46° N, 10° E) a range of mountains that extends through south-central Europe; Europe's highest mountain system, p. 151

Angkor Wat (13°26′ N, 103°52′ E) an archaeological site in present-day Angkor, in northwest Cambodia; the world's largest religious temple complex, p. 688

Antarctic Circle (66°30′ S) a line of latitude around Earth near the South Pole, p. 32

Antarctica (87° S, 60° E) the continent that contains the South Pole; almost completely covered by an ice sheet, p. 35

Antofagasta (23°39′ S, 70°24′ W) a coastal city in Chile, p. 43

Appalachian Mountains (41° N, 77° W) a mountan system in eastern North America, p. 39

Aral Sea (45° N, 60° E) an inland saltwater sea in Kazakhstan and Uzbekistan, p. 612

Arctic a region located around the North Pole, p. 31

Arctic Circle (66°30′ N) a line of latitude around Earth near the North Pole, p. 30

Asia (50° N, 100° E) the world's largest continent, the main part of the Eurasian landmass, surrounded by the Arctic Ocean, the Pacific Ocean, the Indian Ocean, the Mediterranean Sea, and Europe, p. 54

Athens (37°58′ N, 23°43′ E) the capital city of modern Greece; the world's most powerful cultural center in the 400s B.C., p. 177

Auckland (36°52′ S, 174°46′ E) the largest city in New Zealand, located on North Island, p. 630

Australia (25° S, 135° E) a continent in the Southern Hemisphere, the world's smallest continent; also a country including the continent and Tasmania, p. 68

B

Balkan Peninsula (44° N, 23° E) a region in southeastern Europe, also known as the Balkans, p. 321

Bangladesh (24° N, 90° E) a coastal country in South Asia, officially the People's Republic of Bangladesh, p. 66

Benin an ancient African kingdom in the forest region of West Africa, p. 397

Berlin (52°31′ N, 13°24′ E) the capital city of Germany; once divided into East Berlin and West Berlin, p. 292

Bosnia and Herzegovina (44° N, 18° E) a country in Eastern Europe, p. 324

Brazil (10° S, 55° W) the largest country in South Amercia, p. 71

Brunei (5° N, 115° E) a country in Southeast Asia, located on the island of Borneo, p. 82

C

Cairo (30°3′ N, 31°15′ E) the capital of Egypt and the most populous city in Africa, p. 458

Canada (60° N, 95° W) a large country in North America, p. 63

Canterbury Plain (44° S, 172° E) the lowland area of east-central South Island, New Zealand, p. 631

Cape of Good Hope (34°18′ S, 18°26′ E) the cape at the southern end of the Cape Peninsula in South Africa, p. 400

Cape Town (33°48′ S, 18°28′ E) one of the capitals and largest cities in South Africa, p. 446

Carthage an ancient city-state established in present-day Tunisia by the Phoenicians, which maintained control over Mediterranean trade from the late 500s B.C. through the 200s B.C., p. 394

Central America (11° N, 80° W) the part of Latin America south of Mexico and north of South America. It includes the seven republics of Guatemala, Honduras, El Salvador, Nicaragua, Costa Rica, Panama, and Belize, p. 103

Central Africa countries in the central and southern regions of Africa, p. 359

Central Asia a region in Asia including Kazakhstan, Kyrgystan, Tajikistan, Turkmenistan, Uzbekistan, and other countries, p. 610

Central Uplands a region of mountains and plateaus in the center of Southern Europe, p. 151

Chang River (32° N, 121° E) the longest river in Asia, flowing through China to the East China Sea, p. 577

Chernobyl (51°16′ N, 30°14′ E) the city in northern Ukraine where a nuclear power station accident occurred in 1986, p. 332

China (35° N, 105° E) a large country in East Asia, officially the People's Republic of China, p. 20

Congo, Democratic Republic of the (4° S, 25° E) a country in Central Africa, formerly called Zaire, p. 548

Congo River (6°4′ S, 12°24′ E) a river in Central Africa that flows into the Atlantic Ocean, p. 361

Cuba (22° N, 80° W) the largest island country in the Caribbean Sea, p. 68

Czechoslovakia a former Central European country that contained the present-day countries of the Czech Republic and Slovakia, p. 233

D

Danube River (45° N, 30° E) a river that flows 1,770 miles (2,850 kilometers) from Germany to the Black Sea, p. 153

Dar es Salaam (6°48′ S, 39°17′ E) one of two capitals of Tanzania, p. 444

Denmark (56° N, 10° E) a country in Northern Europe, p. 118

E

East Africa countries in the eastern region of Africa, p. 359

East Asia a region of Asia including China, Japan, Mongolia, North Korea, South Korea, and Taiwan, p. 575

Eastern Ghats (14° N, 79° E) a mountain range forming the eastern edge of the Deccan Plateau in India, p. 598

Egypt (27° N, 30° E) a country in North Africa, officially the Arab Republic of Egypt, p. 60

Equator (0°) a line of latitude that circles Earth at the center of the tropics, midway between the North and South poles, along which days and nights are always equal in length, p. 11

Ethiopia (9° N, 39° E) a country in East Africa, p. 514

Euphrates River (31° N, 46° E) a river that flows south from Turkey through Syria and Iraq. The ancient civilizations of Babylon and Ur were situated near its banks. p. 603

Eurasia the world's largest landmass; contains the continents of Europe and Asia, p. 149

Europe (50° N, 28° E) the world's second-smallest continent; a peninsula of the Eurasian landmass bordered by the Arctic Ocean, the Atlantic Ocean, the Mediterranean Sea, and Asia, p. 43

F

Florida (28° N, 8° W) a state in the southeastern United States that is largely a peninsula, p. 12

France (46° N, 2° E) a country in Western Europe, p. 268

G

Ganges River (23° N, 90° E) a river in India and Bangladesh flowing from the Himalaya Mountains to the Bay of Bengal; considered by Hindus to be the most holy river in India, p. 598

Genoa (44°25′ N, 8°57′ E) a seaport city of Italy, p. 104

Georgia (33° N, 83° W) a state in the southeastern United States, p. 12

Germany (51° N, 10° E) a country in Western Europe, p. 97

Ghana (8° N, 1° W) a country in West Africa, officially the Republic of Ghana, p. 490; an early African empire located in parts of present-day Mauritania and Mali, p. 395

Great Dividing Range (25° S, 147° E) a series of plateaus and mountain ranges in eastern Australia, p. 629

Great Plains (42° N, 100° W) a semiarid plain located in North America, stretching from the Rio Grande at the U.S.-Mexico border in the south to the Mackenzie River Delta in the north, and from the Canadian Shield in the east to the Rocky Mountains in the west, p. 128

Great Rift Valley the major branch of the East African Rift System, p. 360

Great Wall of China (41° N, 117° E) a fortification wall which, with all its extensions, stretches 4,000 miles (6,400 kilometers) through China; constructed from about 600 B.C. to A.D. 1600, p. 645

Great Zimbabwe an ancient city-state in southeastern Zimbabwe that was a powerful trade center from about A.D. 1100 to 1500, p. 393

Greece (39° N, 22° E) a country in southeastern Europe, p. 93

Greenland (70° N, 40° W) a self-governing island in the northern Atlantic Ocean; a possession of Denmark; Earth's largest island, p. 18

Greenwich (51°28′ N, 0°) a borough of London, England, and location of the Royal Greenwich Observatory, whose site serves as the basis for longitude and for setting standard time, p. 12

Gulf Stream a warm ocean current in the North Atlantic; flowing northeastward off the North American coast, p. 43

H

Himalayas (28° N, 84° E) the Central Asian mountain range extending along the India-Tibet border, through Pakistan, Nepal, and Bhutan, and containing the world's highest peaks, p. 577

Hindu Kush (36° N, 72° E) a mountain range in Central Asia, p. 611

Ho Chi Minh City (10°45′ N, 106°40′ E) the largest city in Vietnam, named for a former President of North Vietnam; formerly Saigon, p. 797

Huang River (38° N, 118° E) the second-longest river in China, flowing across northern China to the Yellow Sea; also known as the Yellow River, p. 577

I

India (20° N, 77° E) a large country occupying most of the Indian subcontinent in South Asia, p. 40

Indonesia (5° S, 120° E) a country in Southeast Asia consisting of many islands, p. 93

Indus River (24° N, 68° E) a river rising in Tibet and flowing through India and Pakistan into the Arabian Sea, p. 598

Iran (32° N, 53° W) a country in Southwest Asia, p. 82

Iraq (33° N, 44° E) a country in Southwest Asia, officially the Republic of Iraq, p. 602

Italy (43° N, 13° E) a boot-shaped country in Southern Europe, p. 104

J

Jakarta (6°10′ S, 106°48′ E) the capital and largest city of Indonesia, p. 71

Japan (36° N, 138° E) an island country in the Pacific Ocean off the east coast of Asia, consisting of four main islands, p. 63

Java (7° S, 110° E) the fourth-largest island in the Republic of Indonesia, an archipelago in the Indian and Pacific oceans, p. 625

K

Kalahari Desert a desert in Southern Africa, p. 359

Kashmir (34° N, 76° E) a disputed territory in northwest India, parts of which have been claimed by India, Pakistan, and China since 1947, p. 667

Kazakhstan (48° N, 68° E) the largest country in Central Asia, officially the Republic of Kazakhstan, p. 610

Kenya (1° N, 38° E) a country in East Africa, officially the Republic of Kenya, p. 526

Kilwa an Islamic city-state, located on an island off the coast of present-day Tanzania, that was powerful during the late A.D. 900s, p. 393

Kuwait (29° N, 48° E) a country in Southwest Asia, officially the Republic of Kuwait, p. 743

L

Lagos (6°27′ N, 3°24′ E) a city and main port of Nigeria, p. 488

Lalibela (12°2′ N, 39°02′ E) a town in Ethiopia that is famous for its stone churches carved in the 1100s, p. 516

Libya (27° N, 17° E) a country in North Africa, p. 82

London (51°30′ N, 0°10′ W) the capital and largest city of the United Kingdom, p. 22

M

Macedonia (42° N, 22° E) a country in Eastern Europe, p. 325

Malaysia (3° N, 113° E) a country in Southeast Asia, p. 103

Mali (17° N, 4° E) a country in West Africa, officially the Republic of Mali, p. 498; an ancient African empire located in present-day Mali, p. 396

Mecca (21°27′ N, 39°49′ E) a city in western Saudi Arabia; bithplace of the prophet Muhammad and most holy city for Islamic people, p. 766

Mediterranean Sea (35° N, 20° E) the large sea that separates Europe and Africa, p. 603

Melanesia (13° S, 164° E) the most populous of the three groups of Pacific islands; includes Fiji, Papua New Guinea, and others, p. 634

Mesopotamia a historic region in western Asia between the Tigris and Euphrates rivers; one of the cradles of civilization, p. 603

Mexico (23° N, 102° W) a country in North America, south of the United States, p. 67

Miami (25°46′ N, 80°11 W) a city on the southeast coast of Florida, p. 12

Micronesia (11° N, 159° E) one of the three groups of Pacific islands; includes Guam, the Marshall Islands, and others, p. 634

Middle Kingdom the name given to China by its Chinese leaders, p. 645

Milky Way a galaxy consisting of several billions of stars, including the sun, p. 28

Moscow (55°45′ N, 37°35′ E) the capital city of modern Russia; the home of the tsars, p. 201

Mount Everest (27°59′ N, 86°56′ E) the highest point on Earth, located in the Himalayas on the border between Nepal and China, p. 54

Mount Fuji (35°22′ N, 138°44′ E) the highest mountain in Japan; a dormant volcano and sacred symbol of Japan, p. 576

Mount Kenya (0°9′ S, 37°19′ E) a volcanic mountain in central Kenya, p. 527

Mount Kilimanjaro (3°04′ S, 37°22′ E) the tallest mountain in Africa, located in Tanzania, p. 359

Myanmar (22° N, 98° E) a country in Southeast Asia, also known as Burma, p. 82

N

Nairobi (1°17′ S, 36°49′ E) the capital of Kenya, p. 529

Namib Desert a desert extending along the Atlantic Coast of Southern Africa, p. 359

Negev Desert (30° N, 35° E) a triangular, arid region in southwest Israel, touching the Gulf of Aqaba, p. 761

Nepal (28° N, 83° E) a country in South Asia, p. 54

Netherlands, the (52° N, 6° E) a country in Northern Europe, p. 148

New York (43° N, 75° W) a state in the northeastern United States, p. 132

New York City (40°43′ N, 74°1′ W) a large city and port at the mouth of the Hudson River in the state of New York; the largest city in the United States, p. 84

New Zealand (41° S, 174° E) an island country in the Pacific Ocean, p. 122

Niger River (5°33′ N, 6°33′ E) a river in West Africa that flows from Guinea into the Gulf of Guinea, p. 361

Nigeria (10° N, 8° E) a country in West Africa, officially the Federal Republic of Nigeria, p. 484

Nile River (30°10′ N, 31°6′ E) the longest river in the world, flowing through northeastern Africa into the Mediterranean Sea, p. 361

Nile Valley the fertile land located on both sides of the Nile River in northeastern Africa; site of one of the earliest civilizations, p. 63

North Africa the countries of northern Africa, p. 359

North America (45° N, 100° W) the world's third-largest continent, consisting of Canada, the United States, Mexico, Central America, and many islands, p. 17

North Atlantic Current a warm ocean current in the North Atlantic, flowing northeastward toward Europe, p. 43

North China Plain a large, fertile plain in northeastern China, p. 577

North European Plain a plain extending from Russia to France; contains Europe and Russia's most productive farmland and largest cities, p. 151

North Island (39° S, 176° E) the smaller and more northern of the two islands that make up New Zealand, p. 630

North Korea (40° N, 127° E) a country in East Asia, officially the Democratic People's Republic of Korea, p. 82

North Pole (90° N) the northernmost end of Earth's axis, located in the Arctic Ocean, p. 11

North Sea (56° N, 3° E) an arm of the Atlantic Ocean located between Great Britain and the European mainland, p. 164

Northwestern Highlands a mountainous, forested region in Northern Europe, p. 151

Norway (62° N, 10° E) a country in Northern Europe, p. 118

Nubia an ancient region in North Africa, p. 387

P

Palestine (32° N, 35° E) a historical region at the east end of the Mediterranean Sea, now divided between Israel and Jordan, p. 672

Pamir (38° N, 73° E) a mountain range in Central Asia, p. 611

Pangaea according to scientific theory, a single landmass that broke apart to form today's separate continents; thought to have existed about 180 million years ago, p. 38

Papua New Guinea (6° S, 150° E) an island country in the southwest Pacific; the eastern half of New Guinea, officially the Independent State of Papua New Guinea, p. 634

Paris (48°52′ N, 2°20′ E) the capital city of France, p. 268

Peru Current a cold-water current of the southeast Pacific Ocean; flows northward between 40° S and 4° S, p. 43

Philippines (13° N, 122° E) an island country in Southeast Asia, officially the Republic of the Philippines, p. 67

Poland (52° N, 19° E) a country in Eastern Europe, p. 312

Polynesia (4° S, 156° W) largest of the three groups of Pacific islands; includes New Zealand, Hawaii, Easter, and Tahiti islands, p. 634

R

Rhine River (52° N, 6° E) a river that flows about 865 miles (1,391 kilometers) from Switzerland to the Netherlands, p. 153

Ring of Fire a circle of volcanic mountains that surrounds the Pacific Ocean, including those on the islands of Japan and Indonesia, in the Cascades of North America, and in the Andes of South America, p. 33

Riyadh (24°38′ N, 46°43′ E) the capital of Saudi Arabia, p. 767

Rocky Mountains (48° N, 116° W) the major mountain range in western North America, extending from central New Mexico to northeastern British Columbia, p. 12

Rome (41°54′ N, 12°29′ E) the capital of modern Italy; one of the world's greatest ancient civilizations and empires, p. 81

Rotterdam (51°55′ N, 4°28′ E) a seaport city in the Netherlands, p. 131

Rub' al-Khali (20° N, 51° E) the largest all-sand desert in the world, located on the Arabian peninsula; the "Empty Quarter," p. 601

Ruhr (51° N, 7° E) an industrial region in Germany; also a river there, p. 166

Russia (60° N, 80° E) a country stretching across eastern Europe and northern Asia, the largest country in the world, p. 3

S

Sahara the largest tropical desert in the world, covering almost all of North Africa, p. 53

Sahel the region in West and Central Africa that forms an intermediate climate zone between the dry Sahara to the north and the humid savannas to the south, p. 369

St. Louis (38°37′ N, 90°11′ W) a major city in Missouri, on the Mississippi River, p. 45

St. Petersburg (59°55′ N, 30°15′ E) a city and important cultural center in Russia, p. 243

Samarkand (39°40′ N, 67°15′ E) a city in Uzbekistan, p. 679

San Francisco (37°46′ N, 122°25′ W) a coastal city in California, p. 45

São Paulo (23°32′ S, 46°37′ W) the largest city in Brazil, p. 48

Sarajevo (43°52′ N, 18°25′ E) the capital city of Bosnia and Herzegovina, p. 319

Saudi Arabia (25° N, 45° E) a country in Southwest Asia, p. 101

Scandinavia a historical region of Northern Europe that included Norway, Finland, Sweden, Denmark, and Iceland, p. 161

Seoul (37°33′ N, 125°58′ E) the capital of South Korea, p. 579

Serbia and Montenegro (44° N, 21° E) a country in Eastern Europe, p. 326

Siberia (65° N, 110° E) a resource-rich region of northeastern Russia; contains the West Siberian Plain, the Central Siberian Plateau, and the East Siberian Uplands, p. 151

Silesia (51° N, 17° E) a coal-rich region where Poland, the Czech Republic, and Germany meet, p. 167

Silk Road a 4,000-mile-long ancient trade route linking China to the Mediterranean area in the west, p. 651

Slovenia (46° N, 15° E) a country in Eastern Europe, p. 323

Songhai an ancient African empire located in present-day Mali, Niger, and Nigeria, p. 396

South Africa (30° S, 26° E) a country in Southern Africa, officially the Republic of South Africa, p. 70

South America (15° S, 60° W) the world's fourth-largest continent, bounded by the Caribbean Sea, the Atlantic Ocean, and the Pacific Ocean, and linked to North America by the Isthmus of Panama, p. 17

South Asia a region of Asia that includes Afghanistan, Bangladesh, Bhutan, India, Maldives, Nepal, Pakistan, and Sri Lanka, p. 597

South Island (43° S, 171° E) the larger and more southern of the two islands composing New Zealand, p. 630

South Korea (37° N, 128° E) a country in East Asia, p. 67

South Pole (90° S) the southernmost end of Earth's axis, located in Antarctica, p. 12

Southeast Asia a region of Asia including Brunei, Cambodia, Indonesia, Laos, Malaysia, Myanmar (Burma), Philippines, Singapore, Thailand, Timor, and Vietnam, p. 620

Southern Africa countries in the southern regions of Africa, p. 359

Southwest Asia a region of Asia including Iran, Iraq, Israel, Jordan, Kuwait, Lebanon, Saudi Arabia, Syria, Turkey, and others, p. 602

Soviet Union a former communist country that included present-day Russia and several other Eastern European countries, p. 209

Sweden (62° N, 15° E) a country in Northern Europe, p. 276

Switzerland (47° N, 121° E) a country in central Europe, p. 78

Sydney (33°52′ S, 151°13′ E) the capital of New South Wales, on the southeastern coast of Australia, and the largest city in Australia, p. 804

T

Taiwan (23° N, 121° E) a large island country off the southeast coast of mainland China, formerly Formosa; since 1949, the Nationalist Republic of China, p. 713

Tanzania (6° S, 35° E) a country in East Africa, officially the United Republic of Tanzania, p. 519

Thailand (15° N, 100° E) a country in Southeast Asia, officially the Kingdom of Thailand, p. 793

Tigris River (31° N, 47° E) a river that flows through Turkey, Iraq, and Iran to the Persian Gulf. The ancient civilizations of Nineveh and Ur were situated near its banks. p. 603

Tokyo (35°42′ N, 139°46′ E) the capital and largest city of Japan, also the largest city in the world, p. 63

Tombouctou (16°46′ N, 3°1′ E) a city in Mali near the Niger River; in the past an important center of Islamic education and a stop along trans-Saharan trade routes (also spelled *Timbuktu*), p. 498

Tropic of Cancer (23°30′ N) the northern boundary of the tropics, or the band of Earth that receives the most direct light and heat energy from the sun. Such a region lies on both sides of the Equator. p. 30

Tropic of Capricorn (23°30′ S) the southern boundary of the tropics. *See Tropic of Cancer,* p. 31

U

Ukraine (49° N, 32° E) a country in Eastern Europe, p. 327

United Kingdom (54° N, 2° E) a nation in Northern Europe that includes Great Britain and Northern Ireland, p. 260

United States (38° N, 97° W) a large country in North America, p. 12

Ural Mountains (60° N, 60° E) a mountain range in northern Eurasia that forms the border between Europe and Asia, p. 149

V

Vatican City (41°54′ N, 12°27′ E) a city-state completely surrounded by Rome, Italy; the seat of the Roman Catholic Church, p. 81

Vietnam (16° N, 108° E) a country in Southeast Asia, officially the Socialist Republic of Vietnam, p. 67

Volga River (46° N, 48° E) Europe's longest river, flowing 2,291 miles (3,687 kilometers) through western Russia to the Caspian Sea, p. 153

W

West Africa countries in the western region of Africa, p. 359

Western Ghats (14° N, 75° E) a mountain range forming the western edge of the Deccan Plateau in India, p. 598

Y

Yugoslavia a former Eastern European country that contained the present-day countries of Serbia and Montenegro, Bosnia and Herzegovina, Croatia, Slovenia, and Macedonia, p. 219

Z

Zambezi River a river in Central and Southern Africa that flows into the Indian Ocean, p. 361

Glossary

A

Aborigine (ab uh RIJ uh nee) *n.* a member of the earliest people of Australia, who probably came from Asia, p. 697

absolute location (AB suh loot loh KAY shun) *n.* the exact position of a place on Earth, p. 12

absolute monarchy (AB suh loot MAHN ur kee) *n.* a system of complete control by a king or a queen who inherits the throne by birth, p. 82

acculturation (uh kul chur AY shun) *n.* the process of accepting new ideas from one culture and fitting them into another culture, p. 106

aerial photograph (EHR ee ul FOHT uh graf) *n.* a photographic image of Earth's surface taken from the air, p. 17

agriculture (AG rih kul chur) *n.* farming, including growing crops and raising livestock, p. 94

alliance (uh LY uns) *n.* a formal agreement to pursue common interests, formed between governments, often for military purposes, p. 196

alluvial soil (uh LOO vee ul soyl) *n.* soil deposited by water; fertile topsoil left by rivers after a flood, p. 598

apartheid (uh PAHR tayt) *n.* the former legal system of South Africa in which the rights of nonwhites were greatly restricted, p. 557

archipelago (ahr kuh PEL uh goh) *n.* a group of islands, p. 578

arid (A rid) *adj.* dry, p. 44

artesian well (ahr TEE zhun wel) *n.* a well from which water flows under natural pressure without pumping, p. 807

atmosphere (AT muh sfeer) *n.* a layer of gases surrounding a planet, p. 35

atoll (A tawl) *n.* a small coral island in the shape of a ring, p. 635

authoritarian government (uh thawr uh TEHR ee un GUV urn munt) *n.* a nondemocratic form of government in which a single leader or small group of leaders has all the power, p. 551

axis (AK sis) *n.* an imaginary line around which a planet turns. Earth's axis runs through its center from the North Pole to the South Pole. p. 29

B

barometer (buh RAHM uh tur) *n.* an instrument for forecasting changes in the weather; anything that indicates a change, p. 89

basilica (buh SIL ih kuh) *n.* a Roman Catholic church that has a special high status because of its age or history, p. 284

bazaar (buh ZAHR) *n.* a traditional open-air market with shops or rows of stalls, p. 461

biodiversity (by oh duh VUR suh tee) *n.* a large variety of living things in a region, p. 129

birthrate (BURTH rayt) *n.* the number of live births each year per 1,000 people, p. 64

blizzard (BLIZ urd) *n.* a heavy snowstorm with strong winds, p. 47

boycott (BOY kaht) *n.* a refusal to buy or use certain products or services, p. 410

C

Cairo (KY roh) *n.* the capital of Egypt and the most populous city in Africa, p. 458

canopy (KAN uh pea) *n.* the dense mass of leaves and branches forming the top layer of a forest, p. 52

Cape of Good Hope (kayp uv good hohp) *n.* a former province of the Republic of South Africa; the point of land at the southern end of the Cape Peninsula, South Africa, p. 400

capitalism (KAP ut ul iz um) *n.* an economic system in which private individuals or private groups of people own most businesses, p. 75

cardinal directions (KAHR duh nul duh REK shunz) *n.* north, east, south, and west, p. 11

casbah (KAHZ bah) *n.* an old, crowded section of a North African city, p. 469

cash crop (kash krahp) *n.* a crop grown mostly for sale rather than for the needs of a farmer's family, p. 376

caste (kast) *n.* in the Hindu religion, a social group into which people are born and which they cannot change. Each group has assigned jobs. p. 663

chernozem (CHEHR nuh zem) *n.* rich, black soil, productive for farming, p. 329

city-state (SIH tee stayt) *n.* a city with its own government that was both a city and an independent state, p. 81

civil engineering (SIV ul en juh NIHR ing) *n.* the technology for building structures that alter the landscape, such as dams, roads, and bridges, p. 131

civil war (SIV ul wawr) *n.* a war between political parties or regions within the same country, p. 797

civilization (sih vuh luh ZAY shun) *n.* a society that has cities, a central government, and social classes and that usually has writing, art, and architecture, p. 94

clan (klan) *n.* a group of families with a common ancestor, p. 434

climate (KLY mut) *n.* the average weather of a place over many years, p. 40

collective farm (kuh LEK tiv fahrm) *n.* in a Communist country, a large farm formed from many private farms collected into a single unit and controlled by the government, p. 330

colonization (kahl uh nih ZAY shun) *n.* the movement of settlers and their culture to a new country, p. 125

colonize (KAHL uh nyz) *v.* to settle in an area and take control of its government, p. 404

colony (KAHL uh nee) *n.* a territory ruled by another nation, p. 188

commercial farmer (kuh MUR shul FAHR mur) *n.* a farmer who grows most of his or her food for sale rather than for the needs of his or her family, p. 76

commercial farming (kuh MUR shul FAHR ming) *n.* the raising of crops and livestock for sale on the local or world market, p. 415

commune (KAHM yoon) *n.* a community in which people own land as a group and in which they live and work together, p. 653

communism (KAHM yoo niz um) *n.* an economic system in which the central government owns farms, factories, and offices, p.75

communist (KAHM yoo nist) *adj.* relating to a government that controls a country's large industries, businesses, and land, p. 649

compass rose (KUM pus rohz) *n.* a diagram of a compass showing direction on a map, p. 21

compound (KAHM pownd) *n.* a fenced-in group of homes, p. 447

conformal map (kun FAWR mul map) *n.* a flat map of the entire planet Earth, which shows correct shapes but not true distances or sizes; also known as a Mercator projection after geographer Gerardus Mercator, p. 18

coniferous tree (koh NIF ur us tree) *n.* a tree that produces cones that carry seeds, p. 52

constitution (kahn stuh TOO shun) *n.* a set of laws that defines and limits a government's power, p. 83

constitutional monarchy (kahn stuh TOO shun ul MAHN ur kee) *n.* a government in which the power of the king or the queen is limited by law, p. 83

consumer (kun SOOM ur) *n.* a person who buys and uses goods and services, p. 74

copse (kahps) *n.* a thicket of small trees or shrubs, p. 89

coral (KAWR ul) *n.* a rocklike material made up of the skeletons of tiny sea creatures, most plentiful in warm ocean water, p. 635

core (kawr) *n.* the ball of hot metal at the center of Earth, p. 34

coup d'état (koo day TAH) *n.* the sudden overthrow of a government by force, p. 494

crust (krust) *n.* the thin layer of rocks and minerals that surrounds Earth's mantle, p. 34

cultural diffusion (KUL chur ul dih FYOO zhun) *n.* the movement of customs and ideas from one culture to other cultures, p. 106

cultural diversity (KUL chur ul duh VUR suh tee) *n.* a wide variety of cultures, p. 432

cultural landscape (KUL chur ul LAND skayp) *n.* the parts of a people's environment that they have shaped and that reflect their culture, p. 93

cultural trait (KUL chur ul trayt) *n.* a skill, custom, idea, or way of doing things that forms part of a culture, p. 92

culture (KUL chur) *n.* the way of life of a people, including their language, beliefs, customs, and practices, p. 92

D

death rate (deth rayt) *n.* the number of deaths each year per 1,000 people, p. 64

deciduous tree (dee SIJ oo us tree) *n.* a tree that loses its leaves in the fall, p. 52

deforestation (dee fawr uh STAY shun) *n.* a loss of forest cover in a region, p. 129

degrees (dih GREEZ) *n.* units that measure angles or temperature, p. 11

demilitarized zone (dee MIL uh tuh ryzd zohn) *n.* an area in which no weapons are allowed, p. 728

democracy (dih MAHK ruh see) *n.* a government in which citizens govern themselves, p. 177

demography (dih MAH gruh fee) *n.* the scientific study of population change and population distribution, p. 60

dependency (dee PEN dun see) *n.* a region that belongs to another state, p. 81

desert (DEZ urt) *n.* a dry region with little vegetation, p. 52

desert scrub (DEZ urt skrub) *n.* desert vegetation that needs little water, p. 52

desertification (dih zurt uh fih KAY shun) *n.* the process by which fertile land becomes too dry or damaged to support life, p. 500

developed nation (dih VEL upt NAY shun) *n.* a nation with many industries and advanced technology, p. 76

developing nation (dih VEL up ing NAY shun) *n.* a nation with few industries and simple technology, p. 76

dialect (DY uh lekt) *n.* a variation of a language that is unique to a region or area, p. 231

dictator (DIK tay tur) *n.* a ruler with complete power over a country, p. 82

dictatorship (DIK tay tur ship) *n.* a form of government in which the power is held by a leader who has absolute authority, p. 776

direct democracy (duh REKT dih MAHK ruh see) *n.* a form of government in which all adults take part in decisions, p. 82

discriminate (dih SKRIM ih nayt) *v.* to treat people differently, and often unfairly, based on race, religion, or sex, p. 557

distortion (dih STAWR shun) *n.* loss of accuracy. Every map projection causes some distortion of shape or size. p. 17

diversify (duh VUR suh fy) *v.* to add variety; to expand a country's economy by increasing the variety of goods produced, p. 378

domesticate (duh MES tih kayt) *v.* to adapt wild plants or animals and breed them for human use, p. 386

domino theory (DAHM uh noh THEE uh ree) *n.* a belief that if one country fell to communism, neighboring nations would also fall, like a row of dominoes, p. 797

double-cropping (DUB ul KRAHP ing) *v.* to grow two or more crops on the same land in the same season or at the same time, p. 590

drought (drowt) *n.* a long period of dry weather, p. 367

dynasty (DY nus tee) *n.* a series of rulers from the same family, p. 645

E

economic sanctions (ek uh NAHM ik SANGK shunz) *n.* actions to limit trade with nations that have violated international laws, p. 326

economy (ih KAHN uh mee) *n.* a system for producing, distributing, consuming, and owning goods, services, and wealth, p. 74

elevation (el uh VAY shun) *n.* the height of land above sea level, p. 359

embargo (em BAHR goh) *n.* a ban on trade, p. 323

emperor (EM pur ur) *n.* a male ruler of an empire, p. 645

empire (EM pyr) *n.* a state containing several countries, p. 81

energy (EN ur jee) *n.* usable heat or power; capacity for doing work, p. 115

entrepreneur (ahn truh pruh NOOR) *n.* a person who develops original ideas in order to start new businesses, p. 316

environment (en VY run munt) *n.* natural surroundings, p. 120

equal-area map (EEK wul EHR ee uh map) *n.* a map showing landmasses with the correct sizes, but with altered shapes, p. 19

Equator (ee KWAYT ur) *n.* the line of latitude around the middle of the globe, p. 11

Equiano, Olaudah (ek wee AHN oh, oh LOW duh) *n.* an antislavery activist who wrote an account of his enslavement, p. 402

equinox (EE kwih nahks) *n.* one of two days in the year when the sun is directly over the Equator and the day is almost exactly as long as the night; known as spring and fall equinoxes, p. 30

erosion (ee ROH zhun) *n.* a process in which water, ice, or wind removes pieces of rock, p. 39

ethics (ETH iks) *n.* the standards or code of moral behavior distinguishing between right and wrong, p. 101

ethnic group (ETH nik groop) *n.* a group of people who share the same ancestors, culture, language, or religion, p. 231

euro (YUR oh) *n.* the official currency of the European Union, p. 209

extended family (ek STEN did FAM uh lee) *n.* a family that includes several generations, p. 97

F

famine (FAM in) *n.* a huge food shortage, p. 729

fault (fawlt) *n.* a crack in Earth's crust, p. 37

fellaheen (fel uh HEEN) *n.* peasants or agricultural workers in Egypt and other countries of the Arab world, p. 463

fertile (FUR tul) *adj.* able to support plant growth, p. 577

feudalism (FYOOD ul iz um) *n.* a system in which land was owned by kings or lords but held by vassals in return for their loyalty, p. 181

fiord (fyawrd) *n.* a long, narrow inlet or arm of the sea bordered by steep cliffs created by glaciers, p. 631

foreign minister (FAWR in MIN is tur) *n.* a government official who is in charge of a nation's foreign affairs, p. 211

fossil fuel (FAHS ul FYOO ul) *n.* a fuel formed over millions of years from animal and plant remains, including coal, petroleum, and natural gas, p. 117

free enterprise system (free ENT ur pryz SIS tum) *n.* an economic system in which people can choose their own jobs, start private businesses, own property, and make a profit, p. 716

G

Gaza Strip (GAHZ uh strip) *n.* a disputed region on the Mediterranean coast, p. 765

Geez (gee EZ) *n.* an ancient Ethiopian language that was once used to write literature and religious texts but is no longer spoken, p. 515

geographic information systems (jee uh GRAF ik in fur MAY shun SIS tumz) *n.* computer-based systems that store and use information linked to geographic locations, p. 17

geography (jee AHG ruh fee) *n.* the study of Earth, p. 10

geyser (GY zur) *n.* a hot spring that shoots a jet of water and steam into the air, p. 630

globe (glohb) *n.* a model of Earth with the same round shape as Earth itself, p. 16

goods (gudz) *n.* physical products, p. 75

government (GUV urn munt) *n.* a system that sets up and enforces laws and institutions in a region, p. 80

Green Revolution (green rev uh LOO shun) *n.* the increased use of chemicals and machinery in agriculture since the 1950s that has greatly increased the world's food supply. It has also created environmental challenges. p. 65

gross domestic product (grohs duh MES tik PRAHD ukt) *n.* the total value of all goods and services produced in an economy, p. 718

H

hajj (haj) *n.* a pilgrimage or journey to Mecca undertaken by Muslims during the month of the hajj, p. 766

harambee (hah RAHM bay) *n.* a social policy started by Jomo Kenyatta and meaning "let's pull together" in Swahili, p. 528

Hausa-Fulani (HOW suh foo LAH nee) *n.* Nigeria's largest ethnic group, p. 485

hemisphere (HEM ih sfeer) *n.* one half of Earth, p. 11

hemlock (HEM lahk) *n.* an evergreen tree with drooping branches and short, flat needles, p. 89

heritage (HEHR uh tij) *n.* the customs and practices passed from one generation to the next, p. 239

high island (hy EYE lund) *n.* an island formed from the mountainous tops of ancient volcanoes, p. 635

high latitudes (hy LAT uh toodz) *n.* the areas north of the Arctic Circle and south of the Antarctic Circle, p. 32

hill (hil) *n.* a landform with a rounded top that rises above the surrounding land but that is lower and less steep than a mountain, p. 35

Holocaust (HAHL uh kawst) *n.* the killing of millions of Jews and others by the Nazis in World War II, p. 295

homogeneous (hoh moh JEE nee us) *adj.* to be the same or similar, p. 656

human-environment interaction (HYOO mun en VY run munt in tur AK shun) *n.* how people affect the environment and the physical characteristics of their surroundings and how the environment affects them, p. 13

humid continental climate (HYOO mid kahn tuh NENT ul KLY mut) *n.* a climate with moderate to hot summers but very cold winters, supporting grasslands and forests, p. 51

hurricane (HUR ih kayn) *n.* a violent tropical storm, or cyclone, that forms over the Atlantic Ocean, p. 47

hybrid (HY brid) *n.* a plant that is created by cross breeding different types of the same plant, p. 417

hydroelectric power (hy droh ee LEK trik POW ur) *n.* the power produced by water-driven turbines, p. 166

I

Igbo (IG boh) *n.* Nigeria's third-largest ethnic group, p. 485

immigrant (IM uh grunt) *n.* a person who moves to a new country in order to settle there, p. 67

imperialism (im PIHR ee ul iz um) *n.* the political and economic control of one country by another, p. 195

Industrial Revolution (in DUS tree ul rev uh LOO shun) *n.* the life-changing period in the 1800s when the production of goods shifted from hand work to machines in factories, p. 191

industrialization (in dus tree ul ih ZAY shun) *n.* the development of manufacturing in an economy, p. 125

inflation (in FLAY shun) *n.* an increase in the general level of prices, p. 338

institution (in stuh TOO shun) *n.* a custom or organization with social, educational, or religious purposes, p. 95

interdependent (in tur dee PEN dunt) *adj.* dependent on one another, p. 79

international (in tur NASH uh nul) *adj.* involving more than one nation, p. 84

investor (in VES tur) *n.* someone who spends money on improving a business in the hope of making more money if the business succeeds, p. 337

irrigation (ihr uh GAY shun) *n.* the watering of crops using canals and other artificial waterways, p. 94

K

key (kee) *n.* the section of a map that explains the symbols and shading on the map, p. 21

Khmer Empire (kuh MEHR EM pyr) *n.* an empire that included much of present-day Cambodia, Thailand, and Malaysia, and part of Laos, p. 688

Khmer Rouge (kuh MEHR roozh) *n.* a Communist party that took over the government of Cambodia in 1975, p. 693

kibbutz (kih BOOTS) *n.* a cooperative settlement in Israel, p. 763

Kikuyu (kee KOO yoo) *n.* the largest ethnic group in Kenya, p. 527

kinship (KIN ship) *n.* a family relationship, p. 434

L

labor (LAY bur) *n.* the work people do, for which they are paid, p. 725

land reform (land ree FAWRM) *n.* the process of dividing large properties into smaller ones, p. 288

landform (LAND fawrm) *n.* a shape or type of land, p. 35

landlocked (LAND lahkt) *adj.* having no direct access to the sea, p. 779

landmass (LAND mas) *n.* a large area of land, p. 19

latitude (LAT uh tood) *n.* the distance north or south of the Equator, measured in units called degrees, p. 11

lichen (LY kun) *n.* a plant that is a combination of a fungus and an algae and that grows and spreads over rocks and tree trunks, p. 39

life expectancy (lyf ek SPEK tun see) *n.* the average number of years a person is expected to live, p. 65

lineage (LIN ee ij) *n.* a group of families descended from a common ancestor, p. 434

lingua franca (LING gwuh FRANG kuh) *n.* a language used for communication among people who speak different first languages, p. 520

literacy rate (LIT ur uh see rayt) *n.* the percentage of a population age 15 and older that can read and write, p. 755

literate (LIT ur it) *adj.* able to read and write, p. 418

loess (LOH es) *n.* a type of rich, dustlike soil, p. 165

longitude (LAHN juh tood) *n.* the distance east or west of the Prime Meridian, measured in degrees, p. 11

low island (loh EYE lund) *n.* an island formed from coral reefs or atolls, p. 635

low latitudes (loh LAT uh toodz) *n.* the area between the Tropic of Cancer and the Tropic of Capricorn, p. 32

M

Maasai (mah SY) *n.* a seminomadic ethnic group in Kenya, p. 527

magma (MAG muh) *n.* soft, hot, molten rock, p. 36

malnutrition (mal noo TRISH un) *n.* poor nutrition caused by a lack of food or an unbalanced diet, p. 754

Mandela, Nelson (man DEL uh, NEL sun) *n.* black leader of the African National Congress and South Africa's first president after apartheid ended, p. 558

mantle (MAN tul) *n.* the thick, rocky layer around Earth's core, p. 34

manufacturing (man yoo FAK chur ing) *n.* the process of turning raw materials into finished products, p. 123

Maori (MAH oh ree) *n.* a native of New Zealand whose ancestors first traveled from Asia to Polynesia, and later to New Zealand, p. 697

marine west coast climate (muh REEN west kohst KLY mut) *n.* moderate climate occurring in areas cooled by ocean currents, supporting forests more often than grasses, p. 51

marsupial (mahr SOO pea ul) *n.* an animal that carries its young in a body pouch, such as a kangaroo, p. 628

Mediterranean climate (med uh tuh RAY nee un KLY mut) *n.* moderate climate that receives most of its rain in winter and has hot and dry summers, supporting plants with leathery leaves that hold water, p. 51

meridian (muh RID ee un) *n.* a line of longitude, p. 12

Middle Ages (MID ul AY juz) *n.* the time between ancient and modern times, about A.D. 500–1500, p. 176

middle latitudes (MID ul LAT uh toodz) *n.* the areas between the high and low latitudes, p. 32

migrant worker (MY grunt WUR kur) *n.* a laborer who travels away from where he or she lives to find work, p. 447

migration (my GRAY shun) *n.* the movement of people from one country or region to another in order to make a new home, p. 67

mineral (MIN ur ul) *n.* a natural resource that is obtained by mining, such as gold, iron, or copper, p. 114

monarch (MAHN urk) *n.* the ruler of a kingdom or an empire, such as a king or a queen, p. 186

monarchy (MAHN ur kee) *n.* a state or a nation in which power is held by a monarch—a king, a queen, or an emperor, p. 771

monastery (MAHN uh stehr ee) *n.* a place where people, especially men known as monks, live a religious life, p. 514

monotheism (MAHN oh thee iz um) *n.* a belief that there is only one god, p. 671

monsoon (mahn SOON) *n.* a wind that changes direction with the change of season, occurring especially in southern Asia and Africa, p. 581

mountain (MOWN tun) *n.* a steep landform that usually rises more than 2,000 feet (610 meters) above sea level or the surrounding flatlands, p. 35

muezzin (myoo EZ in) *n.* a person whose job is to call Muslims to pray, p. 671

multiethnic (mul tee ETH nik) *adj.* having many ethnic groups living within a society, p. 485

multiparty system (MUL tee pahr tee SIS tum) *n.* a political system in which two or more parties compete in elections, p. 523

N

national debt (NASH uh nul det) *n.* the amount of money a government owes, p. 280

nationalism (NASH uh nul iz um) *n.* pride in one's country, p. 406

nationalist (NASH uh nul ist) *n.* a person who is devoted to the interests of his or her country, p. 691

nationalize (NASH uh nuh lyz) *v.* to transfer ownership of something to a nation's government, p. 551

nation-state (NAY shun stayt) *n.* a state that is independent of other states, p. 81

natural resource (NACH ur ul REE sawrs) *n.* a material found in nature, such as minerals, soil, and vegetation, p. 114

navigable (NAV ih guh bul) *adj.* wide and deep enough for ships to travel through, p. 153

Nkrumah, Kwame (un KROO muh, KWAH mee) *n.* founder of Ghana's independence movement and Ghana's first president, p. 490

nomad (NOH mad) *n.* a person who has no settled home but moves from place to place, p. 370

nonrenewable resource (nahn rih NOO uh bul REE sawrs) *n.* a natural resource that cannot be replaced once it is used, p. 116

nuclear family (NOO klee ur FAM uh lee) *n.* a mother, a father, and their children, p. 97

O

oasis (oh AY sis) *n.* an area in a desert where fresh water is usually available from a spring or well, p. 367

ocean current (OH shun KUR unt) *n.* a moving stream of water in the ocean created by uneven heating of Earth's surface, p. 43

oligarchy (AHL ih gahr kee) *n.* a government controlled by a small group of people, p. 82

orbit (AWR bit) *n.* the path one body makes as it circles around another, p. 28

outback (OWT bak) *n.* the dry land consisting of plains and plateaus that makes up much of central and western Australia, p. 806

overgrazing (oh vur GRAYZ ing) *n.* allowing too much grazing by large herds of animals, p. 500

P

paddy (PAD ee) *n.* a level field that is flooded to grow rice, especially in Asia, p. 624

Pan-Africanism (pan AF rih kun iz um) *n.* the belief that all Africans should work together for their rights and freedoms, p. 407

parallel (PA ruh lel) *n.* in geography, a line of latitude, p. 12

Parliament (PAHR luh munt) *n.* the lawmaking body of the United Kingdom, p. 264

partition (pahr TISH un) *n.* a division into parts or portions, p. 667

penal colony (PEEN ul KAHL uh nee) *n.* a place where people convicted of crimes are sent, p. 697

permafrost (PUR muh frawst) *n.* a permanently frozen layer of ground below the top layer of soil, p. 161

petroleum (puh TROH lee um) *n.* an oily liquid formed from the remains of ancient plants and animals; used as a fuel, p. 116

philosophy (fih LAHS uh fee) *n.* a system of ideas and beliefs, p. 269

pilgrimage (PIL gruh mij) *n.* a religious journey, p. 396

plain (playn) *n.* a large area of flat or gently rolling land, p. 35

plantation (plan TAY shun) *n.* a large farm where cash crops are grown, p. 401

plate (playt) *n.* in geography, a huge section of Earth's crust, p. 36

plateau (pla TOH) *n.* a large, raised area of mostly level land bordered on one or more sides by steep slopes or cliffs, p. 35

polar climate (POH lur KLY mut) *n.* a climate of the high latitudes that is cold all year and has short summers, p. 51

pollution (puh LOO shun) *n.* waste, usually made by people, which makes a place's air, water, or soil less clean, p. 132

population (pahp yuh LAY shun) *n.* total number of people in an area, p. 60

population density (pahp yuh LAY shun DEN suh tee) *n.* the average number of people living in a square mile or square kilometer, p. 62

population distribution (pahp yuh LAY shun dis trih BYOO shun) *n.* the way the population is spread out over an area, p. 60

precipitation (pree sip uh TAY shun) *n.* water that falls to the ground as rain, sleet, hail, or snow, p. 40

Prime Meridian (prym muh RID ee un) *n.* the meridian that runs through Greenwich, England; 0° longitude, p. 11

privatization (pry vuh tih ZAY shun) *n.* selling government-owned industries to private companies, p. 523

producer (pruh DOOS ur) *n.* a person who makes products that are used by other people, p. 74

projection (proh JEK shun) *n.* the method of mapping Earth on a flat surface, p. 18

propaganda (prahp uh GAN duh) *n.* the spread of ideas designed to support a cause, p. 242

push-pull theory (push pul THEE uh ree) *n.* a theory of migration claiming that difficulties "push" people to leave their old homes, while a hope for better living conditions "pulls" them to a new country or region, p. 68

Q

Quran (koo RAHN) *n.* the holy book of Islam; also spelled Koran, p. 428

R

radical (RAD ih kul) *adj.* extreme, p. 715

rain shadow (rayn SHAD oh) *n.* the area on the dry, sheltered side of a mountain, which receives little rainfall, p. 157

raw materials (raw muh TIHR ee ulz) *n.* natural resources that must be processed to be useful, p. 114

recession (rih SESH un) *n.* a period during which an economy and the businesses that support it shrink, or make less money, p. 722

Red Guards (red gahrdz) *n.* groups of students who carried out Mao Zedong's policies during the Cultural Revolution, p. 715

refugee (ref yoo JEE) *n.* a person who leaves his or her homeland for personal safety or to escape persecution, p. 774

region (REE jun) *n.* an area with a unifying characteristic such as climate, land, population, or history, p. 12

relative location (REL uh tiv loh KAY shun) *n.* the location of a place described in relation to places near it, p. 12

Renaissance (REN uh sahns) *n.* a period of European history that was characterized by the rebirth of interest in learning and art, p. 184

renewable resource (rih NOO uh bul REE sawrs) *n.* a natural resource that can be replaced, p. 115

representative (rep ruh ZEN tuh tiv) *n.* a person who represents, or stands for, a group of people, p. 264

representative democracy (rep ruh ZEN tuh tiv dih MAHK ruh see) *n.* a government run by representatives that the people choose, p. 83

reunification (ree yoo nih fih KAY shun) *n.* the process of becoming unified again, p. 297

revolution (rev uh LOO shun) *n.* a circular journey, p. 28; a far-reaching change, such as the overthrow of an existing government, with another government taking its place, p. 188

revolutionary (rev uh LOO shuh neh ree) *adj.* relating to or causing the overthrow of a government or other great change, p. 204

rift (rift) *n.* a deep crack in Earth's surface, p. 360

rotation (roh TAY shun) *n.* a complete turn, p. 29

rural (ROOR ul) *adj.* having to do with the countryside, p. 71

S

sanitation (san uh TAY shun) *n.* disposal of sewage and waste, p. 65

satellite image (SAT uh lyt IM ij) *n.* an image of Earth's surface taken from a satellite in orbit, p. 17

savanna (suh VAN uh) *n.* a region of tall grasses with scattered trees, p. 52

scale (skayl) *n.* relative size, p. 16

secede (sih SEED) *v.* to leave a group, especially a political group or a nation, p. 323

self-sufficient (self suh FISH unt) *n.* able to supply one's own needs without outside assistance, p. 757

semiarid climate (sem ee A rid KLY mut) *n.* a hot, dry climate with little rain, supporting only shrubs and grasses, p. 51

seminomadic (seh mee noh MAD ik) *adj.* combining nomadic wandering and farming in settlements, p. 527

services (SUR vih siz) *n.* work done for other people that does not produce goods, p. 123

Sharia (shah REE ah) *n.* Islamic law, based on the words and deeds of Muhammad and on comments written by Muslim scholars and lawmakers, p. 459

shrine (shryn) *n.* a holy place, p. 313

single market (SING ul MAHR ket) *n.* system in which goods, services, and capital move freely with no barrier; used to describe the European Union, p. 210

social class (SOH shul klas) *n.* a grouping of people based on rank or status, p. 97

social structure (SOH shul STRUK chur) *n.* a pattern of organized relationships among groups of people within a society, p. 96

society (suh SY uh tee) *n.* a group of people sharing a culture and social structure, p. 96

solstice (SAHL stis) *n.* one of two days in the year when the sun is directly overhead at its farthest point from the Equator. Summer solstice, in the hemisphere where the sun is overhead, is the longest day and the shortest night of the year. Winter solstice, on the same day in the opposite hemisphere, is the shortest day and the longest night of the year. p. 30

souq (sook) *n.* an open-air marketplace in an Arab city, p. 469

sovereignty (SAHV run tee) *n.* political control, p. 494

standard of living (STAN durd uv LIV ing) *n.* the level at which a person or nation lives, as measured by the availability of food, clothing, shelter, and so forth, p. 605

state (stayt) *n.* a region that shares a government, p. 80

station (STAY shun) *n.* in Australia, a large ranch for raising livestock, p. 698

steppe (step) *n.* vast, mostly level treeless plains that are covered in grass, p. 611

subarctic climate (sub AHRK tik KLY mut) *n.* a continental dry climate with cool summers and cold winters, p. 51

subcontinent (SUB kahn tih nunt) *n.* a large landmass that is a major part of a continent, p. 596

subsidy (SUB suh dee) *n.* money given by a government to assist a private company, p. 721

subsistence farming (sub SIS tuns FAHR ming) *n.* farming that provides only enough food for a family or a village, p. 77

Swahili (swah HEE lee) *n.* an ethnic group of Africans who have mixed African and Arab ancestry and who live along the coast of East Africa; also a Bantu language, p. 441

T

technology (tek NAHL uh jee) *n.* any way of putting knowledge to practical use, p. 76

tectonic plate (tek TAHN ik playt) *n.* a huge slab of rock that moves very slowly over a softer layer beneath the surface of Earth, p. 628

temperature (TEM pur uh chur) *n.* the hotness or coldness of air or some other substance, p. 40

terrace (TEHR us) *n.* a horizontal ridge made in a hillside to create farmland, save water, or lessen erosion, p. 469

textile (TEKS tyl) *n.* a cloth product, p. 192

Tombouctou (tohm book TOO) *n.* city in Mali near the Niger River; also spelled *Timbuktu*, p. 396

tornado (tawr NAY doh) *n.* a storm in the form of a swirling funnel of wind, moving as fast as 200 miles (320 kilometers) per hour, p. 47

treaty (TREE tee) *n.* an agreement in writing made between two or more countries, p. 84

tributary (TRIB yoo tehr ee) *n.* a river or stream that flows into a larger river, p. 153

tropical cyclone (TRAWP ih kul SY klohn) *n.* an intense wind and rain storm that forms over oceans in the tropics, p. 47

truce (troos) *n.* a cease-fire agreement, p. 729

tsar (zahr) *n.* emperor of Russia, p. 202

tundra (TUN druh) *n.* a cold, dry region covered with snow for more than half the year, p. 51

typhoon (ty FOON) *n.* a tropical storm in which winds reach speeds greater than 74 miles (118 kilometers) an hour and that occurs over the Pacific Ocean, p. 582

U

urban (UR bun) *adj.* located in cities and nearby towns, p. 71

urbanization (ur bun ih ZAY shun) *n.* the movement of people to cities, p. 70

V

vegetation (vej uh TAY shun) *n.* plants that grow in a region, p. 50

vertical climate (VUR tih kul KLY mut) *n.* the overall weather patterns of a region, as influenced by elevation; the higher the elevation, the colder the climate, p. 54

W

weather (WETH ur) *n.* the condition of the air and sky from day to day, p. 40

weathering (WETH ur ing) *n.* a process that breaks rocks down into tiny pieces, p. 39

welfare state (WEL fair stayt) *n.* a country in which many services and benefits are paid for by the government, p. 277

West Bank (west bank) *n.* a disputed region on the western bank of the Jordan River, p. 765

westernization (wes tur nuh ZAY shun) *n.* the adoption of Western culture, p. 200

Y

Yoruba (YOH roo buh) *n.* Nigeria's second-largest ethnic group, p. 485

Index

The *m*, *g*, or *p* following some page numbers refers to maps (*m*), charts, tables, graphs, timelines or diagrams (*g*), or pictures (*p*).

A

C

D

E

F

G

H

I

J

K

M

N

O

P

Q

R

S

T

U

V

X

Y

Z

Acknowledgments

Cover Design

Pronk&Associates

Staff Credits

The people who made up *World Studies ©05* team—representing design services, editorial, editorial services, educational technology, marketing, market research, photo research and art development, production services, project office, publishing processes, and rights & permissions—are listed below. Bold type denotes core team members.

Greg Abrom, Ernie Albanese, Rob Aleman, Susan Andariese, **Rachel Avenia-Prol,** Leann Davis Alspaugh, Penny Baker, Barbara Bertell, **Peter Brooks,** Rui Camarinha, John Carle, **Lisa Del Gatto,** Paul Delsignore, Kathy Dempsey, Anne Drowns, Deborah Dukeshire, Marlies Dwyer, **Frederick Fellows,** Paula C. Foye, Lara Fox, Julia Gecha, **Mary Hanisco,** Salena Hastings, Lance Hatch, Kerri Hoar, **Beth Hyslip,** Katharine Ingram, Nancy Jones, John Kingston, Deborah Levheim, Constance J. McCarty, **Kathleen Mercandetti,** Art Mkrtchyan, Ken Myett, **Mark O'Malley,** Jen Paley, Ray Parenteau, **Gabriela Pérez Fiato,** Linda Punskovsky, Kirsten Richert, **Lynn Robbins,** Nancy Rogier, Bruce Rolff, Robin Samper, Mildred Schulte, Siri Schwartzman, **Malti Sharma,** Lisa Smith-Ruvalcaba, Roberta Warshaw, Sarah Yezzi

Additional Credits

Jonathan Ambar, Tom Benfatti, Lisa D. Ferrari, Paul Foster, Florrie Gadson, Phil Gagler, Ella Hanna, Jeffrey LaFountain, Karen Mancinelli, Michael McLaughlin, Lesley Pierson, Debi Taffet

DK The DK Designs team who contributed to ***World Studies © 05*** were as follows: Hilary Bird, Samantha Borland, Marian Broderick, Richard Czapnik, Nigel Duffield, Heather Dunleavy, Cynthia Frazer, James A. Hall, Lucy Heaver, Rose Horridge, Paul Jackson, Heather Jones, Ian Midson, Marie Ortu, Marie Osborn, Leyla Ostovar, Ralph Pitchford, Ilana Sallick, Pamela Shiels, Andrew Szudek, Amber Tokeley.

DK Maps

Maps and globes were created by **DK Cartography.** The team consisted of Tony Chambers, Damien Demaj, Julia Lunn, Ed Merritt, David Roberts, Ann Stephenson, Gail Townsley, Iorwerth Watkins.

Illustrations

Kenneth Batelman: **177, 223, 372, 438;** Richard Bonson/DK Images: **416, 647;** Richard Draper/DK Images: **462;** Chris Orr/DK Images: **241, 769;** DK Images: **31, 34, 36, 41, 43, 194, 769 bl;** DK Images/Still Pictures: **769 t;** Trevor Johnston: **189;** Kevin Jones Associates: **140;** Jen Paley: **148, 155, 157, 162, 164, 169, 176, 183, 186, 191, 193, 200, 208, 222, 229, 237, 238, 247, 260, 262, 268, 269, 272, 276, 278, 280, 283, 285, 291, 292, 294, 312, 314, 316, 319, 320, 327, 328, 336, 339, 345, 358, 364, 367, 374, 384, 390, 398, 400, 401, 405, 413, 414, 426, 428, 432, 435, 439, 440, 451, 458, 460, 465, 466, 468;** Jun Park: **500, 635;** Pronk&Associates: **484, 485, 490, 493, 497, 498, 499, 501, 517, 519, 522, 526, 528, 548, 551, 556, 559**

Photos

Cover Photos

tl, Romana Huq/First Light Associated Photographers; **tm,** Mary Louise MacDonald/Masterfile Corporation; **tr,** Charles Cecil/Cecil Images; **b,** Elinor Donohoe/Getty Images Inc.

Title Page

Elinor Donohoe/Getty Images Inc.

Table of Contents

iv–v b, K Yamashita/Mon Tresor/Panoramic Images; **v t,** Galen Rowell/Corbis; **vi t,** Demetrio Carrasco/Dorling Kindersley; **vi b,** Bob Krist/Corbis; **vii t,** Wolfgang Kaehler/Corbis; **vii b,** AP Photo/Boris Grdanoski; **viii t,** The British Library/Topham-HIP/Image Works; **viii b,** Hicks/Premium/Panoramic Images; **ix t,** SuperStock, Inc.; **ix b,** Robert Frerck/Odyssey Productions, Inc.; **x t,** Robert Everts/Getty Images Inc.; **x–xi b,** Dave Starrlet/Artbase, Inc.; **xi t,** Dave Bartruff/Danita Delimont; **xii t,** Karen Su/Getty Images, Inc.; **xii–xiii b,** Macduff Everton/Getty Images, Inc.; **xiii t,** Camermann International; **xiv t,** Reuters/Corbis; **xiv b,** Alison Wright/Corbis; **xv t,** AP/Wide World Photos; **xv b,** Dallas & John Heaton/Corbis; **xvi,** Staffan Widstrand/Corbis; **xviii,** Christie's Images; **xix,** Bettmann/Corbis; **xx both,** Discovery Channel School; **xxii all,** The British Museum; **xxiv–xxv,** Wolfgang Kaehler/Corbis

Learning With Technology

xxvi, Discovery Channel School

Reading and Writing Handbook

RW, Michael Newman/PhotoEdit; **RW1,** Walter Hodges/Getty Images, Inc.; **RW2,** Digital Vision/Getty Images, Inc.; **RW3,** Will Hart/PhotoEdit; **RW5,** Jose Luis Pelaez, Inc./Corbis

MapMaster Skills Handbook

M, James Hall/DK Images; **M1,** Mertin Harvey/Gallo Images/Corbis; **M2–3 m,** NASA; **M2–3,** (globes) Planetary Visions: **M5 br,** Barnabas Kindersley/DK Images; **M6 tr,** Mike Dunning/DK Images; **M10 b,** Bernard and Catherine Desjeux/Corbis; **M11,** Hutchinson Library; **M12 b,** Pa Photos; **M13 r,** Panos Pictures; **M14 l,** Macduff Everton/Corbis; **M14 t,** MSCF/NASA; **M15 b,** Ariadne Van Zandbergen/Lonely Planet Images; **M16 l,** Bill Stormont/Corbis; **M16 b,** Pablo Corral/Corbis; **M17 t,** Stone Les/Sygma/Corbis; **M17 b,** W. Perry Conway/Corbis

Guiding Questions

1, Christine Osborne/World Religions Photo Library

World Overview

2 l, 2 t, DK Images; **3 l,** Daniel Laine/Corbis; **3 tr,** DK Images; **3 br,** Sipa/Rex Features; **4 bl,** Layne Kennedy/Corbis; **4 tr,** DK Images; **5 t,** Royalty Free Images/Corbis; **6 t,** Roger Ressmeyer/Corbis; **7 br,** Amet Jean Pierre/Sygma/Corbis; **7 tr,** DK Images

Chapter One

8–9, Johnson Space Center/NASA; **10,** Steve Gorton/DK Images; **13,** M. Balan/DK Images; **14,** Will & Deni McIntyre/Corbis; **15 b,** Richard Powers/Corbis; **15 t,** DK Images; **16,** Peter Wilson/DK Images; **17,** MSFC/NASA; **23,** Johnson Space Center/NASA

Chapter Two

26–27, George H. Huey/Corbis; **28,** Daniel Pyne/DK Images; **30 bl,** Alan Briere/DK Images; **30–31,** sun, DK Images; globes, Planetary Visions; **31 tr,** Barnabas Kindersley/DK Images; **33,** Brenda Tharp/Corbis; **35,** C. M. Leask/Eye Ubiquitous; **36 bl,** James Balog/Getty Images; **37 tr,** James A. Sugar/Corbis; **39,** Alan Hills/DK Images; **40,** Galen Rowell/Corbis; **41 tr,** Hutchison Library; **43 tr,** Royalty Free Images/Corbis; **44 b,** Demetrio Carrasco/DK Images; **45 bl,** Chris Stowers/DK Images; **46 m,** DK Images; **46 bl,** NASA; **46 tr,** N.H.P.A.; **46 mr,** Lelan Statom, meteorologist; Mark Martin, photojournalist/network operations manager, WTVF-Newschannel 5 Network, Nashville, Tenn.; **47,** Claude Charlier/Corbis; **48 t,** Michael S. Yamashita/Corbis; **50,** Liu Liqun/Corbis; **51 br,** Terry W. Eggers/Corbis; **51 tr,** Denver Museum of Nature and Science; **52,** Alan Watson/DK Images; **53 t,** Photowood Inc./Corbis; **53 bl,** Neil Lukas; **53 br,** Stephen Hayward/DK Images; **54,** Galen Rowell/Corbis; **55,** George H. Huey/Corbis

Chapter Three

58–59, Keren Su/Corbis; **60,** James Strachan/Getty Images; **61 t,** Royalty Free Images/Corbis; **62 bl,** Wolfgang Kaehler/Corbis; **63 br,** Peter Wilson/DK Images; **64 t,** Howard Davies/Corbis; **65 b,** Patricia Aithie/Ffotograff; **66,** Dirk R. Frans/Hutchison Library; **67,** Bettmann Corbis; **68,** Dave King/DK Images; **69 bl,** Bettmann/Corbis; **70 bl,** Hulton-Deutsch Collection/Corbis; **70 br,** Paul Almasy/Corbis; **71,** Stephanie Maze/Corbis; **72,** Bill Ross/Corbis; **74,** Rob Reichenfeld/DK Images; **75 t,** Corbis; **76,** Philip Blenkinsop/DK Images; **77 b,** Tom Wagner/Corbis; **78 l,** Mark E. Gibson/Corbis; **78 b,** Annebicque Bernard/Sygma/Corbis; **78 r,** Mary Ann McDonald/Corbis; **79,** Peter Blakely/SABA/Corbis;

80, Patrick Durand/Sygma/Corbis; **81,** Franz-Marc Frei/Corbis; **82,** Tom Haskell/Sygma/Corbis; **83 t,** Pa Photos; **83 b,** Ron Sachs/Rex Features; **84,** Joseph Sohm/Chromosohm Inc./Corbis; **85,** Keren Su/Corbis; **88,** Peter Finger/Corbis

Chapter Four

90–91, Bryan Colton/Assignments Photographers/Corbis; **92,** Royalty Free Images/Corbis; **93 b,** Dennis Degnan/Corbis; **94 tl,** Geoff Brightling/DK Images; **94 b,** Richard Leeney/DK Images; **94 ml,** Museum of English Rural Life; **95,** Kim Sayer/DK Images; **96,** DK Images; **97,** Rob Lewine/Corbis; **98 t,** Richard T. Nowitz/Corbis; **98 b,** Barnabas Kindersley/DK Images; **99 b,** Demetrio Carrasco/DK Images; **100 t,** Barnabas Kindersley/DK Images; **100 b,** Peter Wilson/DK Images; **101,** B.P.S. Walia/DK Images; **102,** Foodpix/Getty Images; **103 l,** Christine Osborne/World Religions Photo Library; **104,** DK Images; **105 b,** Dallas and John Heaton/Corbis; **105 t,** Royalty Free Images/Corbis; **106,** DK Images; **107 mr,** Tom Wagner/Corbis; **107 tr,** Sony/Newscast; **108,** Penny Tweedy/Panos Pictures; **109,** Bryan Colton/Assignments Photographers/Corbis

Chapter Five

112–113, M. L. Sinibaldi/Corbis; **114,** Liba Taylor/Corbis; **116 t, 116–117,** Chinch Gryniewitz/Ecoscene/Corbis; **117 t,** Royalty Free Images/Corbis; **118,** Corbis; **119,** Bob Krist/Corbis; **120,** Holt Studios International; **121 t,** Bob Rowan; Progressive Image/Corbis; **121 b,** Hutchison Library; **122 l,** Paul A. Souders/Corbis; **122 r,** DK Images; **123 l,** James L. Amos/Corbis; **123 mr,** DK Images; **124,** David Noble/Pictures Colour Library; **125,** Oliver Strewe/Getty Images; **126,** Dennis O'Clair/Getty Images; **127,** DK Images; **128,** Paul A. Souders/Corbis; **129 t,** Wayne Lawler; Ecoscene/Corbis; **129 b,** Martin Wyness/Still Pictures; **130 t,** Benjamin Rondel/Corbis; **130 b,** DK Images; **131,** Frans Lemmens/Getty Images; **132,** Syracuse Newspapers/David Lassman/The Image Works/Topfoto; **133,** M. L. Sinibaldi/Corbis

Guiding Questions

139, Wally McNamee/Corbis

Regional Overview

140, ABC Press-Hofstee/Sygma/Corbis; **141,** Royalty-Free/Corbis; **142,** Roger Antrobus/Corbis; **143 t,** Anders Ryman/Corbis; **143 b,** DK Images; **144 t,** DK Images; **144 b,** Raymond Gehman/Corbis; **145 t,** Jose Fuste Raga/Corbis; **145 b,** Uwe Schmid/Corbis

Chapter Six

146–147, Derek Croucher/Corbis; **148,** Wolfgang Kaehler/Corbis; **149 t,** The Fringe/Index Stock Imagery, Inc.; **149 b,** Konrad Wothe/Minden Pictures; **151 t,** Discovery Channel School; **151 b,** Ray Juno/Corbis; **152,** Natalie Fobes/Getty Images, Inc.; **153,** Zefa Visual Media-Germany/Index Stock Imagery, Inc.; **154,** Gregor Schmid/Corbis; **155 t,** Angela Maynard/Life File/Getty Images, Inc.; **155 b,** Dean Conger/Corbis; **156,** William Manning/Corbis; **158 t,** Dean Conger/Corbis; **158 b,** Mary Rhodes/Animals Animals/Earth Scenes; **161,** Wolfgang Kaehler/Corbis; **162,** Bob Krist/Corbis; **164,** Arnulf Husmo/Getty Images, Inc.; **165,** Paul Thompson/Eye Ubiquitous/Corbis; **166,** Dr. Eric Chalker/Index Stock Imagery, Inc.; **167 t,** Ed Kashi/Corbis; **167 b,** Chris Niedenthal/Time Life Pictures/Getty Images Inc.; **168,** Dave G. Houser/Corbis; **169 l,** Breck P. Kent/Animals Animals/Earth Scenes; **169 m,** Mark Schneider/Visuals Unlimited; **169 r,** Michael St. Maur Sheil/Corbis; **170,** Sovfoto/Eastfoto; **171 t,** Mary Rhodes/Animals Animals/Earth Scenes; **171 b,** Ed Kashi/Corbis

Chapter Seven

174–175, John Elk III/Lonely Planet Images; **176,** AFP Photo/John Mottern/Corbis; **178,** Scala/Art Resource, NY; **179 t,** ML Sinibaldi/Corbis; **179 b,** Alinari/Art Resource, NY; **180 l,** McRae Books, Srl; **180 r,** Erich Lessing/Art Resource, NY; **181 t,** HIP/Scala/Art Resource, NY; **181 b,** R. G. Ojeda/Réunion des Musées/Art Resource, NY; **182 t,** Adam Woolfit/Corbis; **182 b,** Owen Franken/Corbis; **183,** Bettmann/Corbis; **184 t,** John Heseltine/Corbis; **184 b,** Bridgeman Art Library; **185 tl,** Musée du Louvre/Philippe Sebert/Dorling Kindersley; **185 tr,** The Granger Collection, New York; **185 bl,** Bettmann/Corbis; **185 br,** James L. Amos/Corbis; **186,** Historical Picture Archive/Corbis; **187 t,** Archivo Iconografico, S.A./Corbis; **187 b,** Art Resource; **188 l,** The Granger Collection; **188 r,** Picture History; **190 t,** Bettmann/Corbis; **190 b,** Sheila Terry/Photo Researchers, Inc.; **191,** Corbis; **192 l,** Dorling Kindersley Media Library; **192 r,** The Granger Collection, New York; **193 l,** Art Resource, NY; **193 m,** Bettmann/Corbis; **193 r,** Scala/Art Resource, NY; **194 t,** Science & Society Picture Library; **196 t,** The Granger Collection, NY; **196 b,** Museum of the City of New York; **197,** AP/Wide World Photos; **198,** Giraudon/Art Resource, NY; **199 t,** Roger Wood/Corbis; **199 b,** Christi Graham and Nick Nichols/Dorling Kindersley; **200,** Archivo Iconografico, S.A./Corbis; **202 t,** Discovery Channel School; **202 b,** Christie's Images/Corbis; **203,** Bettmann/Corbis; **204 t,** Hulton-Deutsch Collection/Corbis; **204 b,** Bettmann/Corbis; **205 t,** Yevgeny Khaldei/Getty Images, Inc.; **205 b,** U.S. Army; **206 t,** Corbis; **206 b,** PhotoDisc/Getty Images, Inc.; **207,** AFP/Corbis; **208 t,** Time Life Pictures/Getty Images, Inc.; **208 b,** Culver Pictures, Inc.; **210 t,** Thomas Dannenberg/Masterfile Corporation; **210 b,** AP/Wide World Photos; **211,** M. Taner/Masterfile Corporation; **212,** AP/Wide World Photos/Lawrence Jackson; **213,** Thomas Dannenberg/Masterfile Corporation

Literature

217, Giraudon/Art Resource, NY; **218,** Scala/Art Resource, NY

Chapter Eight

220–221, Holton Collection/SuperStock, Inc.; **222,** Georgina Bowater/Corbis; **224,** Powerstock/Index Stock Imagery, Inc.; **225 t,** Howard Davies/Corbis; **225 b,** Terry Why/Index Stock Imagery, Inc.; **226 t,** SuperStock International; **226 b,** Sion Touhig/Getty Images, Inc.; **227 t,** Discovery Channel School; **227 bl,** Sean Gallup/Getty Images, Inc.; **227 br,** Julio Etchart/The Image Works; **228,** H. Mollenhauer/Masterfile Corporation; **229,** William Miller/University of Texas at Austin; **230,** Chin Allana/Corbis Sygma; **231 l,** AP Photo/Boris Grdanoski; **231 r,** Taner/Masterfile Corporation; **233 t,** Reuters NewMedia Inc./Corbis; **233 b,** Peter Turnle/Corbis; **234,** Anthony Cassidy/Getty Images, Inc.; **235,** Archivo Iconografico, S.A./Corbis; **236,** David Turnley/Corbis; **237,** Richard Haynes; **238,** David Sutherland/Getty Images, Inc.; **239 l,** A. Kuznetsov/Trip Photographic; **239 r,** Dean Conger/Corbis; **240,** James Hill/Getty Images, Inc.; **241 t,** Bettmann/Corbis; **241 b,** RIA, Novosti; **242 t,** Laski Diffusion/East News/Liaison/Getty Images Inc.; **242 bl,** Topham/The Image Works; **242 bm,** Bettmann/Corbis; **242 br,** Swim Ink/Corbis; **243 l,** Scala/Art Resource, NY; **243 m,** Liaison/Getty Images, Inc.; **243 r,** Archivo Iconografico, S.A./Corbis; **244,** Gideon Mendel/Corbis; **245 t,** Sion Touhig/Getty Images, Inc.; **245 b,** Laski Diffusion/East News/Liaison/Getty Images Inc.

Chapter Nine

248–249, Simeone Huber/Getty Images, Inc.; **250 t,** Discovery Channel School; **250 b,** Ric Ergenbright/Corbis; **251,** Willy Thiria/Corbis; **252,** Staffan Widstrand/Corbis; **255,** Swim Ink/Corbis; **256,** Staffan Widstrand/Corbis; **258,** Chris Trotman/Corbis; **260,** TravelPix/Getty Images, Inc.; **261,** Robert Estall/Corbis; **263,** Bridgeman Art Library; **264 t,** Royal Collection Enterprises Ltd.; **264 b,** AP Photo/John Stillwell, Pool; **265 t,** The British Library/Topham-HIP/Image Works; **265 m,** AP/Wide World Photos/Donald McLeod-POOL; **265 b,** Peter Macdiarmid/Reuters NewMedia/Corbis; **266 t,** Topham/The Image Works; **266 b,** Discovery Channel School; **266 m,** Rykoff Collection/Corbis; **267,** Annie Griffiths Belt/Corbis; **268,** Nogues Alain/Corbis Sygma; **269 t,** Stapleton Collection/Corbis; **269 tm,** Elisabeth Louise Vigee-Lebrun/Galleria degli Uffizi, Florence, Italy/Bridgeman Art Library; **269 bm,** National Gallery Collection; by kind permission of the Trustees of the National Gallery, London/Corbis; **269 b,** Christie's Images/Corbis; **270,** K. Yamashita/Mon Tresor/Panoramic Images; **271 t,** Snark/Art Resource, NY; **271 b,** Discovery Channel School; **273 l,** Philippe Desmazes/AFP/Getty Images, Inc.; **273 r,** Stuart Cohen/The Image Works; **274,** EPA/Alfred France Out/AP/Wide World Photos; **275,** C. Garroni Parisi/Das Fotoarchiv/Peter Arnold, Inc.; **276,** Björn Andrén Bilder; **277 t,** Steve Raymer/Corbis; **277 b,**

Blaine Harrington; **279 t,** Discovery Channel School; **279 b,** AP/Wide World Photos/Toni Sica; **281,** SuperStock, Inc.; **282,** Macduff Everton/Corbis; **283,** John Miller/Robert Harding World Imagery; **284,** Owen Franken/Corbis; **286 t,** Discovery Channel School; **286 b,** Hulton Archive Photos/Getty Images Inc.; **287 t,** Allsport UK/Getty Images, Inc.; **287 b,** Mimmo Jodice/Corbis; **288,** Shaun Egan/Getty Images, Inc.; **289,** Burstein Collection/Corbis; **290,** Stephen Studd/Getty Images, Inc.; **292,** AP/Wide World Photos; **293,** Hulton-Deutsch Collection/Corbis; **294,** Collection of Stuart S. Corning, Jr. Photo © Rob Huntley/Lightstream; **295 t,** Sovfoto/Eastfoto; **295 b,** Bettmann/Corbis; **296,** David Brauchli/Corbis; **297 t,** Bettmann/Corbis; **297 b,** Discovery Channel School; **298,** Ken Straiton/Corbis; **299,** Burstein Collection/Corbis

Chapter Ten

302–303, Jonathan Blair/Corbis; **304,** Discovery Channel School; **306,** Niall Benvie/Corbis; **308,** Barry Lewis/Corbis; **309 t,** Topham Picturepoint/Image Works; **309 b,** Dave King/Dorling Kindersley; **310,** Tim Thompson/Corbis; **312,** Hideo Haga/The Image Works; **313 t,** AP/Wide World Photos/Rudi Blaha; **313 b,** Raymond Gehman/Corbis; **315 t,** Discovery Channel School; **315 b,** Peter Turnley/Corbis; **317 t,** Raymond Gehman/Corbis; **317 b,** Hicks/Premium/Panoramic Images; **318,** Raymond Gehman/Corbis; **319 t,** David Cannon/Allsport/Getty Images, Inc.; **319 b,** AP/Wide World Photos/Rikard Larma; **321 t,** Jonathan Blair/Corbis; **321 b,** Jim McDonald/Corbis; **323,** Jules Frazier/Getty Images, Inc.; **324 t,** Discovery Channel School; **324 b,** Ron Haviv/VII Photo; **325,** AP/Wide World Photos/EPA/Georgi Licovski; **326,** Janez Skok/Corbis; **327,** Novosti/Sovfoto; **329 t,** Mary Evans Picture Library; **329 m,** TASS/Sovfoto; **329 b,** Robert Capa/Magnum Photo Library; **330–331 b,** TASS/Sovfoto; **331 t,** Ed Kashi/Corbis; **332 t,** Discovery Channel School; **332 b,** Yann Arthus-Bertrand/Corbis; **333,** Sean Sprague/Peter Arnold, Inc.; **334,** Raymond Gehman/Corbis; **335,** Paul Almasy/Corbis; **336,** Peter Turnley/Corbis; **337 t,** Discovery Channel School; **337 m,** TASS/Sovfoto; **337 b,** Demetrio Carrasco/Getty Images, Inc.; **338,** TASS/Sovfoto; **340,** Alain Le Garsmeur/Getty Images, Inc.; **341 t,** B&C Alexander/AgPix; **341 b,** Reuters NewMedia Inc./Corbis; **342,** Marc Garanger/Corbis; **343,** Hideo Haga/The Image Works

Projects

346 t, Andy Crawford/Dorling Kindersley; **346 b,** Wally McNamee/Corbis

Guiding Questions

349 t, Christie's Images/SuperStock, Inc.; **349 b,** Heini Schneebeli/Bridgeman Art Library

Regional Overview

350 l, G. Hind/Still Pictures; **351 t,** Liba Taylor/Corbis; **352 t,** Chris Lisle/Corbis; **352 b,** Patrick Ward/Corbis; **353 t,** Sharna Balfour/Gallo Images; **353 b,** David Ball/Corbis; **354 ml,** Liba Taylor/Corbis; **354 b,** Leanne Logan/Lonely Planet Images; **355 t,** Geert Cole/Lonely Planet Images; **355 mr,** Harlmut Schwarzbach/Still Pictures; **355 br,** Gallo Images/Corbis

Chapter Eleven

356–357, Tim Davis/Corbis; **358,** Richard Cummins/Corbis; **359 t,** Discovery Channel School; **359 b,** Martin Rogers/Getty Images, Inc.; **360–361,** Jason Lauré/Lauré Communications; **362,** Roger Wood/Corbis; **363,** SuperStock, Inc.; **364,** Jason Edwards/Lonely Planet Images; **366 t,** Hal Beral/Corbis; **366–367 b,** Panoramic Images; **368–369 b,** SuperStock, Inc.; **369 t,** F. Lemmens/Masterfile Corporation; **370,** Lorne Resnick/Getty Images, Inc.; **371,** Robert Patrick/Corbis Sygma; **373,** Ariadne Van Zandbergen/Lonely Planet Images; **374,** Victor Englebert/Victor Englebert Photography; **374 inset,** Dave King/Dorling Kindersley; **376,** Jason Lauré/Lauré Communications; **377 t,** AFP/Corbis; **377 b,** Tim Boyle/Getty Images, Inc.; **378,** Eric Miller/iAfrika Photos; **379,** Martin Rogers/Getty Images, Inc.

Chapter Twelve

82–383, J. D. Dallet/AGE Fotostock; **384,** Juan Carlos Munoz/AGE Fotostock; **t,** Lauros/Giraudon/The Bridgeman Art Library; **385 m,** John Reader/Photo Researchers, Inc.; **385 b,** Robert Sisson/National Geographic Image Collection; **386,** Martin Harvey/Gallo Images/Corbis; **387 t,** Erich Lessing/Art Resource, NY; **387 b,** The Art Archive/Egyptian Museum Turin/Dagli Orti; **389,** David Turnley/Corbis; **390 all,** The British Museum; **392 t,** Anthony Bannister/Gallo Images/Corbis; **392 b,** Corbis; **393,** David Reed/Corbis; **394 both,** Pictor International/Agency ImageState/Alamy; **396 t,** The Granger Collection, New York; **396 b,** Saudi Arabia-Ramadan/AFP/Corbis; **397,** Christie's Images/SuperStock, Inc.; **398,** Yann Arthus-Bertrand/Corbis; **399,** Dorling Kindersley/The Science Museum London; **400 l,** Ingrid Roddis/Lonely Planet Images; **400 r,** The Granger Collection, New York; **401 t,** The Granger Collection, New York; **401 b,** Discovery Channel School; **402 t,** The Granger Collection, New York; **402 b,** Wilberforce Museum, Hull/Dorling Kindersley; **404 t,** The Art Archive/Private Collection; **404 b,** The British Library, London, UK/Topham-HIP/The Image Works; **405,** Chris Steele-Perkins/Magnum Photos; **406 both,** Peter Turnley/Corbis; **407,** Corbis; **409 l,** Hulton-Deutsch Collection/Corbis; **409 r,** M. & E. Bernheim/Woodfin Camp & Associates; **410 t,** Joao Silva/New York Times Pictures; **410–411 b,** Peter Turnley/Corbis; **413,** One Mile Up, Inc./Fotosearch Stock Photography; **414,** Michael S. Lewis/Corbis; **415 t,** A. Ramey/Woodfin Camp & Associates; **415 b,** Charles O. Cecil/Words & Pictures/PictureQuest; **416 t,** Michael S. Lewis/Corbis; **417 t,** Yann Arthus-Bertrand/Corbis; **417 b,** Sandro Vannini/Corbis; **418,** Willem de Lange/PictureNET Africa; **419,** Liba Taylor/Corbis; **420,** Wolfgang Kaehler Photography; **421 l,** Christie's Images/SuperStock, Inc.; **421 r,** Peter Turnley/Corbis

Chapter Thirteen

424–425, Kennan Ward/Corbis; **426,** Getty Images, Inc.; **427,** Glen Allison/Getty Images, Inc.; **428,** Francois Perri/Cosmos/Woodfin Camp & Associates; **429,** Jim Erickson/Corbis; **430,** Jon Arnold Images/Alamy; **431,** Francois Perri/Cosmos/Woodfin Camp & Associates; **432,** Jason Lauré/Lauré Communications; **433,** M. & E. Bernheim/Woodfin Camp & Associates; **434 t,** Craig Pershouse/Lonely Planet Images; **434 b,** Robert Frerck/Odyssey Productions, Inc.; **435,** Yann Arthus-Bertrand/Corbis; **436 t,** M. & E. Bernheim/Woodfin Camp & Associates; **436 b,** Discovery Channel School; **437 l,** Courtesy of Balla Tounkara; **437 r,** Bob Burch/Index Stock Imagery/PictureQuest; **439 l,** Gunter Ziesler/Peter Arnold, Inc.; **439 r,** Rich Kirchner/NHPA; **440,** Ariadne Van Zandbergen/Lonely Planet Images; **441,** Yadid Levy/AGE Fotostock; **442–443 b,** Wolfgang Kaehler Photography; **443 t,** Peter Marlow/Magnum Photos; **444,** Sipa Press; **445,** Popperfoto/Alamy Images; **446,** Chris Harvey/Stone Allstock/Getty Images Inc.; **447,** Ian Murphy/Getty Images, Inc.; **448,** Christie's Images, Inc.; **449 l,** Jim Erickson/Corbis; **449 r,** Ian Murphy/Getty Images

Chapter Fourteen

452–453, Photolibrary.com; **454 t,** Discovery Channel School; **454 b,** Claudia Wiens/Peter Arnold, Inc.; **455 t,** F. J. Jackson/Alamy Images; **455 b,** Paul Hardy/Corbis; **456,** Damien Simonis/Lonely Planet Images; **457,** Patrick Ward/Corbis; **458,** Harry Gruyaert/Magnum Photos; **459,** Stock Image/SuperStock, Inc.; **460,** Nik Wheeler/Corbis; **461,** Nik Wheeler; **462,** Lloyd Cluff/Corbis; **463 t,** Discovery Channel School; **463 b,** Mark Henley/Panos Pictures; **464,** David Young-Wolff/PhotoEdit; **465,** Carmen Redondo/Corbis; **466,** Robert Everts/Getty Images Inc.; **467,** Francoise Perri/Woodfin Camp & Associates; **469 t,** Abbas/Magnum Photos; **469 b,** Discovery Channel School; **470,** Tiziana and Gianni Baldizzone/Corbis; **471 l,** Harry Gruyaert/Magnum Photos; **471 r,** Robert Everts/Getty Images Inc.

Chapter Fifteen

474–475, Yann Arthus-Bertrand/Corbis; **476 b,** Art Directors/Jane Sweeney; **478 bl,** Ancient Art&Architecture/DanitaDelimont.com; **478 br,** Robert Burch/Bruce Coleman Inc.; **480 tr,** Robert Burch; **480 b,** AP/Wide-World Photos; **482 mr,** AFP/Corbis; **482 b,** Beryl Goldberg; **483 tr,** Luis Marden/National Geographic/Getty Images, Inc.; **484 bl,** Sally Mayman/Getty Images, Inc.; **485 br,** Paul Almasy/Corbis; **485 bl,** Werner Forman/Art Resource NY; **486 bl,** McPherson Colin/Corbis/Sygma; **486 tr,** Betty Press/Panos Pictures; **487 b,** Hamill Gallery of African Art, Boston MA; **488 tl,** Bruno Barbey/Magnum Photos; **489 tr,** Campbell William/Corbis/Sygma; **490–491,** Dave Starrett/Artbase Inc.; **490 bl,** Bettman/Corbis; **491 tr,** Hulton-Deutsch Collection/Corbis; **492 bl,** Hamill Gallery of

African , Boston MA; **494 b,** AP/Wide World Photos; **495 tr,** Robert Burch; **496 ml,** agestate/firstlight.ca; **497 mr,** Jonathan Nourok/PhotoEdit Inc.; **497 br,** Davtarrett/Artbase Inc.; **498–499,** Ali Atay/Atlas; **498 bl,** Wolfgang Kaehler/rbis; **502 tl,** Art Directors/Mary Jelliffe; **503 ml,** Paul Almasy/Corbis; **503 mr,**t Directors/Mary Jelliffe

Chaptexteen

506–50 Robert Bourgoing; **509 tr,** Sheila McKinnon/Mira.com; **510 t,** EdwardRoderick, Edward/MaXx Images; **511 m,** © 2003 Norbert Wu/wwobertwu.com; **511 mr,** Wolfgang Kaehler Photography; **512 tr,** AFP/Cos; **513 m,** Art Directors/Fiona Good; **514 b,** Robert Patrick/rbis/Sygma; **515 br,** M. & E. Bernheim/Woodfin Camp & Associates; **515 tl,** Le Bartruff/Danita Delimont; **516 tr,** Dave Bartruff/Danita Delimont; **516 tl,** KMuller/Woodfin Camp & Associates; **518 ml,** Robert Caputo/Aurora Photos; **9 br,** Reuters; **521 t,** Kwame Zikomo/SuperStock; **523 tr,** Howard Davies/Cbis; **524 bl,** Eric Draper/White House/Getty Images, Inc.; **525 tr,** Art DirectoAndrew Gasson; **525 br,** David Pluth/Fotografx; **526 b,** Robert Burch; **527 tr,** chele Burgess/MaXx Images; **529 mr,** Betty Press/Woodfin Camp & Associat **530 tl,** DigtalVision/Artbase Inc.; **531 tr,** Dave Bartruff/Danita Delimo **531 m,** Robert Burch; **534 br,** Paul Souders/Getty Images, Inc.; **535 tr,** hotodiscRed/Artbase Inc.; **536 bl,** Jeremy Woodhouse/Masterfile Corporon; **537,** Tololwa M. Mollel

Chapteeventeen

538–53 Eric Nathan/Alamy Images; **540 b,** Volkmar Wentzel/Getty Images, Inc.; **54tr,** AFP/Corbis; **542 tl,** Max-Planck-Institut Seewiesen; **548,** Jason Lauré/Lré Communications; **549 b,** Patrick Roberts/Corbis/Sygma; **550 bl,** Bettma/Corbis; **552 bl,** Artbase Inc.; **553 tr,** Reuters/Corbis; **554 tl,** Photodc/Artbase Inc.; **554 ml,** Photodisc/Artbase Inc.; **554 bl,** Photod/Artbase Inc.; **555 m,** Paula Bronstein/Impact Visuals; **556 bl,** Charles O'Rearorbis; **557 br,** TimeLifePictures/Getty Images, Inc.; **558 br,** AP/WidWorld Photos; **560 tl,** Owen Franken/Corbis; **561 ml,** Artbase Inc.; **561 mr**AP/WideWorld Photos

Project

564, Hni Schneebeli/Bridgeman Art Library

Guidin Questions

567, AP/Corbis

Regionl Overview

568 l, avid Ball/Corbis; **569 bl,** Massimo Listri/Corbis; **570 t,** José Fuste Raga/Crbis; **570 bl,** Paul A. Souders/Corbis; **571 t,** James A. Sugar/Corbis; **571 b,** avid Samuel Robbins/Corbis; **572 l,** Richard T. Nowitz/Corbis; **572 br,** JeremyHorner/Corbis; **573 tr,** Damien Simonis/Lonely Planet Images; **573 bl,** Boheman Nomad Picturemakers/Corbis

Chaptr Eighteen

574–575, Boden-Ledingham/Masterfile; **576 bl,** Dallas&John Heaton/Corbis; **577 tr,** Keren Su/Getty Images; **578 bl,** Michael S. Yamashita/Corbis; **579 tr,** Catherine Karnow/Corbis; **580 b,** Scott Markewitz/Getty Images; **582 ml,** Private Collection/Ancient Art and Architecture Collection Ltd/Bridgeman Art Library; **583 tr,** Heatons/Firstlight.ca; **585 tr,** Mug Shots/Corbis; **585 tr(inset),** Kevin Schafer/Corbis; **586 bl,** AFP/Corbis; **588–589 b,** Liu Liqun/Corbis; **589 tr,** Keren Su/Corbis; **589 br,** Keren Su/Corbis; **590 tl,** B.S.P.I./Corbis; **591 ml,** Keren Su/Getty Images; **591 mr,** Scott Markewitz/Getty Images

Chapter Nineteen

594–595, Galen Rowell/Corbis; **596 b,** Alan Kearney/Getty Images; **599 b,** Will Curtis/Getty Images; **599 lr,** Eisenhut&Mayer/Foodpix; **599 mr,** Artbase Inc.; **600 tl,** R. Ian Lloyd/Masterfile; **601 b,** George Steinmetz; **603 b,** George Gerster/Photo Researchers Inc.; **603 mr,** H. Spichtinger/zefa; **605 r,** George Steinmetz; **606 tl,** Israel Talby; **607 tr,** Hugh Sitton/Getty Images; **608 bl,** Myrleen Ferguson/Photoedit Inc.; **609 tr,** Business Essentials/Artbase Inc.; **609 br,** Donovan Resse/Getty Images; **609 tr (inset),** George Steinmetz; **610 bl,** TASS/Sovfoto/Sergei Kazak; **611 tr,** James Strachan/Getty Images; **613 tr,** Reuters/Corbis; **614 tl,** TASS-S-54679/Sovfoto/Eastfoto; **615 ml,** James Strachan/Getty Images; **615 tr,** Israel Talby

Chapter Twenty

618–619, Paul A. Souders/Corbis; **620 bl,** Photodisc/ArtBase Inc.; **621 br,** Dorling Kindersley/DK Images; **622–623 bg,** ACE; **623 (inset),** AFP/Corbis; **624 ml,** Martin Puddy/Getty Images; **624 b,** R. Ian Lloyd/Masterfile; **626 tl,** Frank Siteman/Maxximages.com; **627 br,** Tui De Roy/Auscape; **627 mr,** Artbase Inc.; **628 ml,** Jeremy Woodhouse/Masterfile; **628 t,** Tim Flach/Getty Images; **630 t,** Mike Langford/Auscape; **631 tr,** John Lamb/Getty Images; **632 b,** William Gottlieb/Corbis; **633 bg,** The Bridgeman Art Library/Getty Images; **634 bl,** G.Bell/Zefa/Masterfile; **635 bm,** Yann Arthurs-Bertrand/Corbis; **635 tr,** Trip/Ask Images; **636 br,** Photography.com.au; **636 bl,** Photography.com.au; **636–637 bg,** Macduff Everton/Getty Images; **637 mr,** James Strachan/Getty Images; **638 tl,** Trip/M.Jelliffe; **639 tr,** AFP/Corbis; **639 bm,** Jeremy Woodhouse/Masterfile; **639 bm,** Tim Flach/Getty Images

Chapter Twenty-One

642–643, John Dakers-Eye Ubiquitous/Corbis; **644 bl,** Bridgeman Art Library; **645 tr,** Carl & Ann Purcell/Corbis; **646 b,** © Lee Boltin/Boltin Picture Library; **647 t,** DK Images/Wolfgang Kaehler/Corbis; **647 b,** Macduff Everton/Corbis; **648 bl,** Haruyoshi Yamaguchi/Corbis/Sygma; **649 tr,** AFP/Getty Images; **650 l,** Michael S. Yamashita/Corbis; **651 mr,** Werner Forman/Art Resource, NY; **652 bl,** SETBOUN/Corbis; **653 t,** Daryl Benson/Masterfile; **653 mr,** Dale Wilson/Masterfile; **654 t,** Paul Chesley/Getty Images; **656 tl,** James A. Sugar/Corbis; © Lee Boltin/Boltin Picture Library; **657 mr,** Dale Wilson/Masterfile

Chapter Twenty-Two

660–661, Bob Krist/Corbis; **662 bl,** Archivo Iconografico S.A./Corbis; **664 tl,** Michael Freeman/Corbis; **664 tm,** Burstein collection/Corbis; **664 tr,** Burstein collection/Corbis; **665 tr,** Camermann International; **666 t,** Miles Ertman/Masterfile; **666 inset,** Archivo Iconografico S.A./Corbis; **667 tl,** Hulton Deutsch Collection/Corbis; **667 b,** Kapoor Baldev/Corbis; **668 tl,** Frans Lemmens/ZEFA/Masterfile; **669 br,** Gianni Dagli Orti/Corbis; **671 t,** Shai Ginott/Corbis; **672 tr,** Paul Chesley/Getty Images; **672 l,** Scala/Art Resource; **673 r,** Peter Turnley/Corbis; **674 tl,** Ricki Rosen/Corbis; **674 tr,** Reuters/Corbis; **675 tr,** Christophe Calais/Ivisual/Corbis; **676 l,** Ed Brock/Corbis; **677 r,** David W. Hamilton/Getty Images; **678 bl,** Dean Conger/Corbis; **679 t,** Daniel Sheehan/The Image Works; **679 br,** The Bridgeman Art Library/Getty Images; **680 t,** David Samuel Robbins/Corbis; **681 br,** David Samuel Robbins/Corbis; **682 tr,** Nevada Weir/Corbis; **683 tl,** Camermann International; **683 mr,** Daniel Sheehan/The Image Works

Chapter Twenty-Three

686–687, David Noton/Masterfile; **688 bl,** DK Images; **689 b,** Manfred Gottschalk/agefotostock/firstlight.ca; **691 tl,** Miles Ertman/Masterfile; **692 t,** Paul Chesley/Getty Images; **693 tr,** Howard Davies/Corbis; **694 bl,** Chad Elhers/Getty Images; **694 inset,** Foodphotography/MaxXimages.com; **695 b,** Leonard de Selva/Corbis; **696 bl,** Kevin Schafer/Getty Images; **697 b,** Graeme Matthews/PhotoNewZealand.com; **698 br,** Reuters/Corbis; **698 bl,** Rob Walls; **699 t,** R. Ian Lloyd/Masterfile; **700 tl,** Nicolas DaVore/Getty Images; **701 bl,** Manfred Gottschalk/agefotostock/firstlight.ca; **701 tr,** Nicolas DaVore/Getty Images; **704 b,** Time-Life Pictures/Getty Images; **706 tl,** Jason Bleibtreu/Corbis/Sygma

Chapter Twenty-Four

708–709, John Elk/Getty Images; **710 b,** Grant Faint/Getty Images; **711 t,** Don Stevenson/MaxXImages.com; **712 b,** Nathan Benn/Corbis; **713 m,** Bill Lai/IndexStock/MaxX Images; **714 bl,** Chris Shinn/Getty Images; **715 t,** Bettmann/Corbis; **715 mr,** Collection: Stefan Landsberger; **716 ml,** Bettmann/

ters/Corbis; **718 t,** Walter Bibikow/Getty Images; **718 inset,** etty Images; **720 bl,** APWideWorld; **721 br,** Reuters/Corbis; **722** s; **722 b,** Alan Levinson/Getty Images; **724–725 t,** Ettagale Communications; **726 ml,** Bob Daemmrich/StockBoston; **727 mr,** Story/Corbis; **728 b,** Janet Wishnetsky/Corbis; **729 b,** Jeremy Corbis; **730 t,** APWideWorld; **731 ml,** DigitalVision/Artbase Inc.; **732 ml,** /Artbase Inc.; **733 tr,** Chris Shinn/Getty Images; **734 mr,** Reuters/Corbis

apter Twenty-Five

736–737, Annie Griffiths Belt/Corbis; **738 r,** AFP/Corbis; **743 b,** Peter Turnley/Corbis; **747 t,** Alison Wright/Corbis; **750 bl,** Anna Clopet/Corbis; **751 t,** Kapoor Baldev/Corbis; **752 t,** Derimais Lionel/Corbis/Sygma; **752 (inset),** David H. Wells/Corbis; **754 tl,** Michael S. Yamashita/Corbis; **754 tr,** Sheldon Collins/Corbis; **755 tr,** David Katzenstein/Corbis; **756 bl,** Christine Osborne/Corbis; **757 t,** Jonathan Blair/Corbis; **757 (inset),** Jonathan Blair/Corbis; **758 br,** AFP/Corbis; **759 ml,** Antoine Serra/Corbis; **760 tl,** AFP/Corbis; **761 br,** Richard T. Nowitz/Corbis; **762 b,** Ricki Rosen/Saba/Corbis; **764 b,** Zev Radovan/PhotoEdit Inc.; **765 tr,** Izzet Keribar/Coral Planet; **766 bl,** James Sparshatt/Corbis; **767 b,** John Moore/The Image Works; **769 (inset),** Jacques Langeuin/Corbis/Sygma; **769 b,** David Turnley/Corbis; **770 t,** DK Images/Still Pictures; **770 bl,** DK Images; **772 l,** Caroline Penn/Corbis; **773 b,** R. Ian Lloyd; **774 bl,** Steve McCurry/Magnum Photos Inc.; **775 t,** AFP/Corbis; **776 b,** Janet Wishnetsky/Corbis; **778 bl,** Zylberman Lauren/Corbis/Sygma; **779 br,** Volker Thewalt; **779 tl,** Zylberman Lauren/Corbis/Sygma; **780 tr,** James Strachan/Getty Images

Chapter Twenty-Six

784–785, Philip&Karen Smith/Getty Images; **786 b,** J. Raga/Zefa/Masterfile; **791 t,** Paul A. Souders/Corbis; **795 m,** Alyx Kellington/MaxXimages.com; **796 ml,** Owen Franken/Corbis; **796 b,** Steve Raymer/Corbis; **797 t,** R. Ian Lloyd/Masterfile; **798 bl,** Dallas&John Heaton/Corbis; **798 tr,** Bettman/Corbis; **800 bl,** Tim Page/Corbis; **801 tl,** Charles Coates/Impact Photos; **801 tr,** AP WideWorld; **803 b,** BohemianNomadPicturemakers/Corbis; **804–805 b,** Ray Juno/Corbis; **807 t,** Corbis/Artbase Inc.; **808 mr,** John Van Hasselt/Corbis; **809 mc,** Ray Juno/Corbis; **809 tr,** Dallas&John Heaton/Corbis

Projects

812 b, Robert Essel NYC/Corbis; **812 mr,** AFP/Corbis

Reference

814–815, Johnson Space Center/NASA

Glossary of Geographic Terms

840 t, A & L Sinibaldi/Getty Images, Inc; **840 b,** John Beatty/Getty Images, Inc; **840–841 b,** Spencer Swanger/Tom Stack & Associates; **841 t,** Hans Strand/Getty Images, Inc.; **841 m,** Paul Chelsey/Getty Images, Inc.

Text

Chapter Three

88–89, Excerpt from *My Side of the Mountain* by Jean Craighead George. Copyright © 1959 by Jean Craighead George.

Chapter Seven

216, Excerpt from *Pearl in the Egg: A Tale of the Thirteenth Century* by Dorothy van Woerkom. Copyright © 1980 by Dorothy van Woerkom.

Chapter Eleven

369, Excerpt from "Where Hospitality Is an Oasis," by Christine Negroni, *The New York Times,* January 19, 2003. **374,** From *Cocoa Comes to Mampong,* by D. Anang. Copyright © 1949. Reprinted with the permission of Methodist Book Dep.

Chapter Thirteen

441, Excerpt from "Swahili Coast: East Africa's Ancient Crossroads," by Robert Caputo, *National Geographic,* October 2001. **444,** From "African States in Still Sowing Seeds for Future," by James C. McKinley, Jr., *The New York Times.*

Chapter Fifteen

492, From *Ghana in Transition,* by David E. Apter. Copyright © 1955, 1963, and 1972 by Princeton University Press.

Chapter Sixteen

520–521, From "Three Leaders," by Andrew Meldrum, *Africa Report,* September–October 1994. Copyright © 1994 by *Africa Report.* **530,** From "Back to No Man's Land," by George Monbiot, *Geographical Magazine,* July 1994. Copyright © 1994 by *Geographical Magazine.* **534,** From *A Promise to the Sun* by Tololwa M. Mollel. Text Copyright © 1991 by Tololwa M. Mollel. By permission of Little, Brown, and Company.

Chapter Seventeen

555, Excerpt from "Nelson Mandela's Statement After Voting in South Africa's First Democratic Election, Inanda, Kwazulu Natal, 27 April 1994," by Nelson Mandela, the African National Congress. **556,** Excerpt from "Preamble: Constitution of the Republic of South Africa by the Constitutional Assembly," Policy and Law Online News.

Chapter Twenty-Three

704, Excerpt from *The Clay Marble,* by Minfong Ho. Copyright © 1991, by Minfong Ho.

Note: Every effort has been made to locate the copyright owner of material used in this textbook. Omissions brought to our attention will be corrected in subsequent editions.